12—

Traditional Chinese Stories

TRADITIONAL CHINESE STORIES

Themes and Variations

EDITED BY Y. W. MA AND JOSEPH S. M. LAU

1986
CHENG & TSUI COMPANY
BOSTON   WORCESTER

Copyright © 1986 by Y. W. Ma and Joseph S. M. Lau

Originally published by Columbia University Press, 1978

CHENG & TSUI COMPANY, INC.

25 West Street, Boston, MA 02111
421 Main Street, Worcester, MA 01608

Library of Congress Cataloging in Publication Data:

Y. W. Ma and Joseph S. M. Lau
Traditional Chinese Stories: Themes and Variations
(C & T Asian Literature Series)
I. Y. W. Ma and Joseph S. M. Lau   II. Title   III. Series
86-71550

ISBN 0-88727-071-9

Printed in the United States of America

*The Editors join in dedicating this book to
Professor C. T. Hsia, who has
given a new meaning to the study of
Chinese fiction*

PREFACE

This anthology represents the fulfillment of a long-held wish on the part of the Editors to make available a one-volume collection of traditional Chinese stories that would demonstrate the vitality and variety of this genre in its various stages of development. Hence the present title: *Traditional Chinese Stories: Themes and Variations.* Though currently there are several collections of traditional Chinese stories on the market, to the best knowledge of the Editors, not one of them covers as extensive a period as the present volume. In a sense, this collection is itself an illustrative history of Chinese story from the earliest times to the early Republican era, even though the contents are arranged thematically rather than chronologically. In view of the fact that there are as yet no comparable Chinese story anthologies available, the Editors are planning to bring out a Chinese edition of the present volume in the near future.

Besides being comprehensive, the stories included here are also meant to be representative. In making the selections, the Editors based their judgment not only on the intrinsic merit of a story as a story, but also on the importance of a given story in the total context of the evolution of Chinese fiction. This explains the inclusion of a few stories which, unless examined in relation to their larger historical context, would read more like a fable (e.g., "The Chung-shan Wolf"), an anecdote ("Liu Ling"), or a religious sermon ("The Great Maudgalyayana Rescues His Mother from Hell") than a story proper in the modern sense of the word. Historically, these are no less a legitimate part of Chinese fiction than the well-known *San-yen* collections.

Readers will note that the principle of transla-tion observed throughout this volume has been that of faithfulness to the original. Unlike some of our predecessors who have seen fit to delete all the descriptive poems in the preambles of the *San-yen* stories, we have retained them *in toto,* however unwieldy they proved to be for translation and however unnecessary they would seem in relation to the general structure of the story. Similarly, we felt no qualms about keeping those "spicy" passages which, in Herbert A. Giles's days, would have offended "ears polite."

Except for two cases noted at the end of this Preface, all the translated stories were commissioned especially for this anthology even though some of the stories are easily available in existing translations. In some cases the problem of copyright prevented the Editors from adopting the excellent works of our predecessors; in other cases we wished to give our readers a contemporary version of the original in modern English.

Every translation has gone through the hands of the Editors, with Y. W. Ma doing the first reading and Joseph S. M. Lau doing the second. Most of the footnotes have been supplied by the Editors. Needless to say, should any error remain, be it factual or technical, the fault is to be shared by the Editors.

The project was first started by Y. W. Ma in the summer of 1974 with a circular sent out to some fifty fiction specialists requesting reaction and recommendations. The response was most heartening. Joseph Lau, who happened to be contemplating a similar venture at that time, immediately gave up his own and became a partner of Y. W. Ma. Valuable comments and suggestions from other colleagues have been taken into consideration and, whenever feasible, incorporated into the present format. We would like to take this opportunity to thank the long list of noted scholars who have corresponded with us.

This book would not have become a reality without institutional and individual support. First of all, we would like to thank all our translators, who have generously given of their time and labor. To the University of Hawaii and the University of Wisconsin, we acknowledge with gratitude the financial assistance which has helped us defray most of the editorial expenses. Y. W. Ma wishes to express his debt to the University of Hawaii for two intramural research grants (1974–1976), including the award of two Research Assistantships to Lorraine Lieu (1974–1975) and Robert L. Miller (1975–1976). Joseph S. M. Lau is grateful to the American Council of Learned Societies for a grant relieving him of teaching responsibilities for the academic year 1975–1976. He also would like to thank the Graduate School of the University of Wisconsin for awarding him a Project Assistantship as well as a summer grant for 1975.

Lynette Nakagawara and Darlene Sugi deserve special thanks for having produced a clean typescript from a bundle of manuscripts invariably marked with truly multicolored editorial revisions.

But for the untiring service of Shirley Hishinuma, Secretary of the Department of East Asian Literature at Hawaii, this project would have been much delayed. Through the various stages of the preparation of this anthology, she has served as the indispensable bridge of communications between Hawaii and Wisconsin, between the Editors and the translators. We would like to extend to her our sincere appreciation and gratitude for her uncomplaining heroism.

To Karen Mitchell of Columbia University Press, the Editors wish to express more than a perfunctory note of thanks for her superb editorial work. Her expertise has proved most helpful in rearranging some of the almost untranslatable poems into their present more intelligible forms.

Two of the translations used in this anthology have previously been published elsewhere: James R. Hightower, "The Story of Ying-ying" in his article "Yüan Chen and 'The Story of Ying-ying,'" *Harvard Journal of Asiatic Studies,* 33 (1973), 90–123; C. T. Hsia and Susan Arnold Zonana, "The Case of the Dead Infant," in *Renditions,* 2 (Spring 1974), 53–64. For permission to reprint them here (with a few minor changes) the Editors wish to thank their translators. Thanks are also due to Dr. Glen W. Baxter and Mr. George Kao, respectively Publication Director of the Harvard-Yenching Institute and Editor of *Renditions.*

Finally, we would like to express our gratitude to Ho Hwai-shouh, who graciously allowed us to use his painting "Homage to the Past" as the basis for the jacket of this book; to Pi-twan H. Wang, doctoral candidate and Project Assistant in the Department of East Asian Languages and Literature at the University of Wisconsin, for reading the proofs and for making valuable suggestions toward improving the quality of the translations; and to Jane Parish Yang for checking the page proofs.

Y. W. MA
JOSEPH S. M. LAU

CONTENTS

CONTENTS

CONTENTS

xi

CONTENTS

EXPLANATIONS

ROMANIZATION SYSTEM AND THE
TRANSLATION OF SPECIAL TERMS

(1) Chinese characters are romanized according to the Wade-Giles system as seen in R. H. Mathews, *Chinese-English Dictionary*, rev. ed. (Cambridge, Mass.: Harvard University Press, 1963), with the following modifications. To avoid mispronunciation, *i* as a syllable in personal names and placenames is changed to *yi; i* is still used in bibliographical titles to make it easier for the reader to identify them in library catalogs. Names of well-known persons with long established romanized forms of their own, such as Confucius, are given in their familiar spellings; names of all the provinces in the Ch'ing period and in modern times (such as Kansu, Hopei, Szechwan), well-known cities (e.g., Hangchow, Shanghai, Yangchow), and major rivers (e.g., Yellow River, Yangtze) are spelled according to either the old Post Office system or their established forms.

(2) *Li*, the Chinese unit of measuring distance, is given in its romanized form instead of either translating it as "mile" or converting it into the exact distance in the English system of linear measurement. One *li* is approximately one-third of a mile.

(3) As in the case of *li*, the unit of area *mou*, which equals slightly less than one-sixth of an acre, is given in the romanized form.

(4) *Ch'ih*, the Chinese unit of short linear measurement, is rendered as "foot." The difference between the Chinese *ch'ih* and the English foot is quite minimal, though the exact length of the Chinese *ch'ih* varied from time to time.

(5) In the traditional Chinese way of counting age, a newborn baby is regarded as one year old, and it is two years old after the next New Year according to the lunar calendar (usually in late January or early February). The ages of the characters in the stories are given as they appear in the original texts.

(6) Our way of handling the temple titles (*miaohao*) of the sovereigns and their reign titles (*nienhao*) needs to be explained. A Chinese ruler is generally not known to posterity by his own name: he is referred to in history according to the title that was given to him posthumously when his ancestral tablet was established in the imperial clan temple. Han Kao-tsu (the founder of Western Han Dynasty) and Sung Hui-tsung (the penultimate ruler of the Northern Sung Dynasty), for example, are such temple titles. Common as this practice is in Chinese, however, keeping these titles in their romanized forms would certainly create unavoidable confusion of identity in translations. For one thing, the designations of many of the major dynasties, such as Chou, Ch'in, Han, Wei, Wu, T'ang, and Chin (the Jurchen dynasty), happen to be among the common surnames in China. While Han Kao-tsu is undoubtedly the founder of the Han Dynasty, in romanization he could also be a Mr. Han with Kao-tsu as his given name—unless the whole nomenclature is to be distinguished by Chinese characters. Furthermore, none of the dynasty founders chose his own surname for the designation of his dynasty; the surname of the Han founder was Liu, that of T'ang was Li, and that of Sung was Chao. Even for the emperors of those dynasties whose titles are not the same as some surnames (e.g., Ming and Ch'ing), this kind of confusion could still exist. The fact that there are many homonyms in the Chinese language only makes the confusion all the more serious. Therefore, a temple title such as Sung Hui-tsung is consistently translated in this anthology as Emperor Hui-tsung of the Sung (or Northern Sung) Dynasty, and so on. Some earlier emperors (mostly pre-T'ang) have their temple titles in the variant form of *-ti* (emperor) instead of *-tsung* (ancestor). One such case is Han Wu-ti; this is rendered as Emperor Wu of the Han Dynasty, without the "-ti" suffix. As seen in the case of the Han founder, the first emperor of a dynasty is sometimes known as *-tsu* (founder); most of the dynasty founders since the T'ang were given this designation. A title such as Han Kao-tsu is translated as Emperor Kao-tsu of the Han Dynasty. The titles of pre-Han rulers are usually given as *-wang* (king); a title like that of the last sovereign of the Western Chou Dynasty, Chou Yu-wang, is thus rendered as King Yu of the Chou Dynasty.

Most of the pre-Ming emperors used more than one reign title to mark the years when they were on the throne; Empress Wu of the brief Chou Dynasty (684–705) had altogether eighteen reign periods, some lasting for just a few months. Despite the confusion of the short reign periods, this system has long been used to chronologize events in traditional China. When a reign period is first mentioned in a story, it is rendered in this anthology as "the So-and-so (in transcription) reign period" with the corresponding years in Western calendar given in brackets; if a certain year of the reign period is mentioned, only that particular year in Western equivalence is provided (see also no. 7 in the following section "Footnotes and Other Explanatory Materials"). If the same reign period appears again in the story, the rendering is sometimes simplified as "the So-and-so reign."

Since nearly all of the Ming and Ch'ing emperors used just one reign title throughout the years when they were in power, they are some-

times referred to by the titles of their reign periods. Therefore Emperor Shen-tsung of the Ming Dynasty, whose only reign title is Wan-li, is also known as the Wan-li Emperor (*Wan-li ti*). Readers may be familiar with the famous early Ch'ing emperor Sheng-tsu (r. 1662–1722), who is much better known, particularly in the West, as the K'ang-hsi Emperor after the title of his single reign period.

(7) Scholar-bureaucrats in traditional China usually had more than one name—having four or five names was not uncommon. The original given name, mainly for official or legal purposes, was not as commonly used as the others. Of the other names, *tzu*, which we consistently render as "styled" names in the anthology, was often the one to be used in addressing someone in conversation and in correspondence; to do so implied intimacy and respect. Almost as a rule, people of the same generation would address one another by styles. Even the styles of some modern Chinese leaders found their way into English. For example, Sun Wen, the founder of the Republic of China, is much better known in the West by his style Yat-sen. Today, some Chinese, particularly scholars, still use styled names.

(8) Chinese married women were (some still are) known by their maiden family names followed by a *shih*, although they might also be known as Mrs. So-and-so. Thus "Wang-shih" refers to a married woman whose original family name is Wang. "Wang-shih" cannot be rendered as Madam Wang or Mrs. Wang. Having more than one wife, for wealthy men, was common in traditional China. *Shih* applied to both the first wife and the concubines, although only the first wife was considered the legal spouse of the man with all the concomitant privileges. All the children of the man, including those by the concubines, would address only the first wife as their mother. If she wished, the first wife might treat the concubines as her maids. After the death of the first wife, the man could promote one of his

concubines to his legal spouse or he could re-marry and his new wife would take that position; such is the case in the story "Magistrate T'eng and the Case of Inheritance."

(9) In order not to burden the readers with a multitude of minor placenames in romanization, the names of local places (such as bridges, tem-ples, streets), if translatable, are rendered accord-ing to their meanings. One term needs to be ex-plained here. Ch'ang-an, the capital of T'ang China, was rather evenly divided into one hundred and ten *li* (not counting the palace com-plex at the northern side of the city). *Li,* as an in-tracity division with streets and lanes in it, is con-sistently translated as "quarter" in all the T'ang tales concerning Ch'ang-an.

(10) The translation of Buddhist terms is based mainly on W. E. Soothill and Lewis Hodous, *A Dictionary of Chinese Buddhist Terms, with Sanskrit and English Equivalents, a Chinese Index and a Sanskrit-Pali Index* (London: Kegan Paul, Trench, Truber, 1937). The Editors have also consulted the multivolume encyclopedic dictionary compiled by Mochizuki Shinkō, *Bukkyō dai jiten* (The Grand Buddhist Dictionary) (Tokyo: Sekai seiten kankō kyōkai, 1932–1966), 10 vols. The handy volume *A Dictionary of Buddhism,* introduced by T. O. Ling (New York: Charles Scribner's Sons, 1972), has also been useful; this dictionary is taken from *A Dictionary of Comparative Religion,* edited by S. G. F. Brandon (London: Weidenfeld and Nicolson, 1970). We have anglicized proper names and those few terms left in the Sanskrit, omitting the customary diacritical marks.

(11) The translation of institutional titles has presented a number of problems, for if the func-tions of the offices and their places in the overall government structure are not understood, literal translation of these terms is bound to be mislead-ing. Furthermore, the titles and their capacities changed from one dynasty to another. Since we believe that the meanings of these titles should be self-explanatory in accurate translations, we have,

in most cases, chosen not to add notes to describe these terms. A host of technical research tools has been consulted in the procedure of translation. The basic reference is Huang Pen-chi, *Li-tai chih-kuan piao* (Tables of Official Posts in the Various Dynasties) (Peking: Chung-hua shu-chü, 1965). For each major dynasty appearing in the selected stories, the following reference works have been used:

Han Rafe de Crespigny, ed., *Official Titles of the Former Han Dynasty as Translated and Transcribed by H. H. Dubs* (Canberra: Aus-tralian National University Press, 1967).

T'ang Eugene Feifel S. V. D., *Po Chü-i as a Cen-sor: His Memorials Presented to Emperor Hsien-tsung during the Years 808–810* (The Hague: Mouton, 1961), pp. 25–33.

Colin Mackerras, *The Uighur Empire (744–840) According to the T'ang Dynastic Histories* (Canberra: Australian National University Press, 1968), pp. 194–96.

Robert des Rotours, *Traité des examens, traduit de la Nouvelle Histoire des T'ang (Chap. XLIV, XLV)* (Paris: Ernest Leroux, 1932).

Robert des Rotours, *Traité des fonction-naires et traité de l'armée, traduit de la Nou-velle Histoire des T'ang (Chap. XLVI–L)* (Leyden: E. J. Brill, 1948), 2 vols.

Bernard S. Solomon, tr., *The Veritable Record of the T'ang Emperor Shun-tsung (February 28, 805–August 1, 805): Han Yü's Shun-tsung shih-lu* (Cambridge, Mass.: Harvard University Press, 1955).

Sung Chang Fu-jui, *Les fonctionnaries des Song: Index des titres* (Paris: Mouton, 1962).

E. A. Kracke, Jr., *Translation of Sung Civil Service Titles* (Paris: École Practique des Hautes Études, 1957).

Ming Charles O. Hucker, "Governmental Or-ganization of the Ming Dynasty," *Har-vard Journal of Asiatic Studies,* 21 (1958), 1–66. Reprint in *Studies of Government In-stitutions in Chinese History,* edited by John

L. Bishop (Cambridge, Mass.: Harvard University Press, 1968), pp. 59–124.

Charles O. Hucker, "An Index to the Terms and Titles in 'Government Organization of the Ming Dynasty,'" *Harvard Journal of Asiatic Studies*, 23 (1960–1961), 127–51. Reprint in *Studies of Government Institutions in Chinese History*, pp. 127–51.

Ch'ing H. S. Brunnert and V. V. Hagelstrom, *Present Day Political Organization of China*, revised by N. Th. Kolessoff, translated from the Russian by A. Beltchenko and E. E. Moran (Shanghai: Kelly and Walsh, 1912).

William F. Mayers, *The Chinese Government: A Manual of Chinese Titles, Categorically Arranged and Explained*, 3d ed., rev. by G. M. H. Playfair (Shanghai: Kelly and Walsh, 1897).

E-tu Zen Sun, *Ch'ing Administrative Terms: A Translation of the Terminology of the Six Boards with Explanatory Notes* (Cambridge, Mass.: Harvard University Press, 1961).

(12) Although the problem of handling the terms related to the civil service examination system is less complicated than that of the institutional titles, the examinations themselves were by no means uniform throughout the long period from the T'ang Dynasty to the end of the Ch'ing era. Fortunately, only a few basic terms appear in the selected stories. The examinations (or selections without actual examinations), *mutatis mutandis*, were conducted at the three different levels of the county (or prefecture), the province, and the national capital. The successful candidates of the county or prefectural level were known as *hsiu-ts'ai* (also known as *sheng-yüan* in the Ch'ing period). *Hsiu-ts'ai* examinations were conducted in the T'ang period (see the beginning of the story "The Courtesan Li Wa"). In Sung times, this term was used to refer to those unsuccessful in civil service examinations. In the Ming and Ch'ing dynasties, *hsiu-ts'ai* referred to the students of the government schools at the local level; no

examinations were involved. During the T'ang and Sung periods, *chü-jen* meant the candidates taking part in the metropolitan examinations. In Ming and Ch'ing times, *chü-jen* referred to the successful candidates of provincial examinations. From T'ang through Ch'ing, those who passed the metropolitan examinations were known as *chin-shih*, which was a badge of social distinction and a stepping-stone to official career. By virtue of a palace examination, the best successful *chin-shih* of a certain metropolitan examination would be determined; he was known as *chuang-yüan*. To help pay government bills, the practice of selling academic titles (usually those of the lower ranks) became more and more popular in the Ming and particularly in the Ch'ing period (see the story "The Shansi Merchant"). In Ch'ing times, special selections held as an act of imperial favor enabled some *hsiu-ts'ai* to attain the rank of *kung-sheng* (senior *hsiu-ts'ai*). They were eligible for official posts after a further examination. The best reference for the examination system throughout the ages is Teng Ssu-yü, *Chung-kuo k'ao-shih chih-tu shih* (A History of the Chinese Examination System) (Taipei: Hsüeh-sheng shu-chü, 1966; originally published in 1936). For the Ch'ing system, which is more complicated than that of any previous dynasty, see T'ung-tsu Ch'ü, *Local Government in China under the Ch'ing* (Cambridge, Mass.: Harvard University Press, 1962). There is a handy summary of the Ch'ing system at the end of the English translation of the novel *The Scholars* (*Ju-lin wai-shih*) by Yang Hsien-yi and Gladys Yang (Peking: Foreign Languages Press, 1957; Grosset and Dunlap reprint, 1972).

FOOTNOTES AND OTHER EXPLANATORY MATERIALS

(1) Footnotes are arranged on the basis of first occurrence. To locate footnotes that have appeared in earlier pages, please use the Index to Footnotes at the end of the book.

(2) Footnotes are in the main confined to names of persons, placenames, allusions, titles of works, unique textual problems, and special terms. Places within a city are generally not explained. For allusions that can be expressed and understood in English, no notes have been used.

(3) The research tools consulted most frequently are: Shu Hsin-ch'eng, et al., *Tz'u-hai* (A Sea of Terms) (Shanghai: Chung-hua shu-chü, 1936–1937); Morohashi Tetuji, *Dai Kan-Wa jiten* (The Grand Chinese-Japanese Dictionary) (Tokyo: Daishükan, 1955–1960), 13 vols.; Tsang Li-ho, et al., *Chung-kuo ku-chin ti-ming ta tz'u-tien* (A Dictionary of Past and Present Chinese Placenames) (Shanghai: Shang-wu yin-shu kuan, 1931), and a number of atlases, such as *Chung-kuo fen-sheng ti-t'u* (Provincial Maps of China) (Hong Kong: Ta-chung shu-chü, n.d.). Other useful references are E. T. C. Werner, *A Dictionary of Chinese Mythology* (Shanghai: Kelly and Walsh, 1932) and William F. Mayers, *A Chinese Reader's Manual* (Shanghai: American Presbyterian Mission Press, 1874). Hope Wright's *Alphabetical List of Geographical Names in Sung China* (Paris: École Practique des Hautes Études, 1956) has been helpful for Sung geographical terms. These are supplemented by more specific dictionaries, such as Lu Tan-an, *Hsiao-shuo tz'u-yü hui-shih* (Collected Explanations of Phrases Found in Chinese Fiction) (Peking: Chung-hua shu-chü, 1962), the Buddhist dictionaries mentioned above, and previous translations with good explanatory notes, such as Uchida Sennosuke, *Tōdai denki* (T'ang Tales) (Tokyo: Meiji shoin, 1971) and André Lévy, *L'antre aux fantômes des collines de l'ouest* (Paris: Gallimand, 1972). Learned publications on problems related in the stories have also been consulted; for example, Jen Yu-tsai's *T'ang Te-tsung Feng-t'ien ting-nan chi ch'i shih-liao chih yen-chiu* (On the Incident of the T'ang Emperor Te-tsung's Taking Shelter in the Feng-t'ien Area and the Sources on This Incident) (Taipei: Chung-kuo hsüeh-shu chu-tso chiang-chu wei-yüan-hui, 1970) has been used in understanding the rebellion described in the story "Wu-shuang the Peerless," and Paul Pelliot's *Histoire ancienne du Tibet* (Paris: Librairie d'Amérique et d'Orient, 1961) is the major source in explaining the Tibetan invasion mentioned in "The World Inside a Pillow."

(4) The dates of birth and death of eminent figures, along with their biographical data, depend on a number of special references besides the basic tools given above. Among the frequently consulted are: Chiang Liang-fu, *Li-tai jen-wu nien-li pei-chuan tsung-piao* (A Table of the Dates and Places of Birth, Dates of Death, with Epitaphs and other Biographical Materials Listed, of the Personalities of the Various Dynasties), rev. ed. (Peking: Chung-hua shu-chü, 1959); Wang Pao-hsien, *Li-tai ming-jen nien-p'u tsung-mu* (A Comprehensive Catalog of Yearly-Arranged Biographies) (Taichung: Tung-hai ta-hsüeh t'u-shu kuan, 1965); Mai Chung-kuei, *Sung Yüan li-hsüeh chia chu-shu sheng-tsu nien-piao* (A Table of the Dates of Birth and Death of Sung and Yüan Philosophers and Their Works) (Hong Kong: Hsin-ya yen-chiu so, 1968); Weng T'ung-wen, *Répertoire des dates des hommes célèbres des Song* (Paris: Mouton, 1962); Wang Te-yi, Ch'ang Pi-te, et al., *Sung-jen chuan-chi tzu-liao so-yin* (Index to Biographical Materials of Sung Figures) (Taipei: Ting-wen shu-chü, 1974–1976), 6 vols.; Cheng Ch'ien, "Sung-jen sheng-tsu k'ao shih-li" (Examples of the Problems Concerning the Dates of Birth and Death of Sung Figures), *Yu-shih hsüeh-chih*, 6:1 (Jan. 1967), 1–50; 6:2 (July 1967), 1–52; and the continuation in *Yu-shih hsüeh-chih*, 7:4 (Dec. 1968), 1–48; and a list of errata in *Yu-shih hsüeh-chih*, 10:3 (Sept. 1972), 1–12; Kuo-li Chung-yang t'u-shu kuan, comp., *Ming-jen chuan-chi tzu-liao so-yin* (Index to Biographical Materials of Ming Figures) (Taipei: Kuo-li Chung-yang t'u-shu kuan, 1965), 2 vols.; Ch'en Nai-chien, *Ch'ing-tai pei-chuan wen t'ung-chien* (Index to Ch'ing Epitaphical Writings) (Peking: Chung-hua shu-chü, 1959); Arthur Hummel, ed., *Eminent Chinese of the Ch'ing Period (1644–1912)* (Washington, D.C.: Government Printing Office, 1943–1944), 2 vols.

(5) The dates of the dynasties and the reign periods are set according to Wan Kuo-ting, et al., *Chung-kuo li-shih chi-nien piao* (Chronological Tables of Chinese History) (Hong Kong: Shang-wu yin-shu kuan, 1958) and Liu Shih-hsin, *Shih-erh ch'ao-tai ti-wang nien-piao* (Chronological Tables of the Rulers of the Twelve Major Dynastic Periods) (Hong Kong: Yung-she t'ang shu-wu, 1968).

(6) The term "watch" has not been included in the footnotes because of its different intervals according to seasonal changes; the summer night is shorter than the winter night. The night, whether in the winter or in the summer, is divided into five watches, with each equivalent to about two hours. The third watch marks midnight, and the end of the fifth watch is close to daybreak.

(7) One type of explanatory material that is not given as footnotes but incorporated in the translation (marked by brackets) is the duration of a given reign period of a certain emperor and the conversion of a Chinese date into the Western correspondence. This arrangement is intended to have the time setting of the story clearly spelled out, even though some other stories may carry the same dates or reign periods.

(8) There are two other kinds of explanatory material incorporated in the translation. One is minor information needed to clarify a small point; this kind of explanation is usually not significant enough to warrant a separate note and is thus given in brackets in the translation. The other kind involves the inclusion of additional words not in the original text. These words are added in brackets either for the sake of English usage or to spell out a meaning latent in the original.

ORGANIZATION OF THE ANTHOLOGY

This anthology offers three kinds of framework within which traditional Chinese stories can be read: formal, thematic, and chronological. The formal aspects of the selections are discussed in a section on "The Five Forms of the Traditional Chinese Story." The selections themselves are arranged in thematic groups. The "Chronological Order" puts the selections in their historical perspective. The "Biobibliographical Notes" provide data on authors (also on the editors and compilers) and on recommended editions as well as on collections from which the stories have been selected. Thus the reader should have little difficulty in rearranging the selections if he desires to read them in historical sequence or within individual forms. Even if the reader wishes to proceed according to the collections from which the stories have been selected, it is possible to do so by means of information provided in the "Biobibliographical Notes." In other words, the Editors have done their best to accommodate the individual needs of the reader, no matter from what angle he chooses to examine the stories.

THEMATIC ARRANGEMENT OF THE SELECTIONS

Nearly all modern anthologies of traditional Chinese stories, whether in the original or in English, Japanese, or French translations, are arranged either chronologically or generically (sometimes both). Some draw upon only one or two sources. To publish another anthology edited in either of these ways would amount to no more than a ritualistic repetition. It is hoped that this volume, by adopting a thematic approach, will be useful not only to readers of Chinese fiction but also to students of comparative literature.

There are various ways to handle an arrangement by themes. If we were to follow the conventional method of some English short-story anthologies, we would have used such a mixture of headings as "the scapegoat," "the cautionary tale," "tragic vision," "the parable," "satire," "irony," "the success story," "friendship," "individual world," "allegory," "fantasy," "symbolic reality," "the misfit," "the detective story," etc. This arrangement would have given rise to frequent overlapping, since there would be various methods by which to classify the selections.

In order to avoid this pitfall, themes in all the stories here are viewed with respect to a single, fixed element—the character, be it human or supernatural. No story, however simple, can do without this element. It is also the least complicated of all the elements commonly shared by stories of various lengths and degrees of complexity. Yet even with this fixed bearing, a certain amount of overlapping remains unavoidable. The truth is that while a chronological arrangement can be made foolproof, a thematic arrangement is bound to be controversial. We have found no story which is thematically so well defined that it could not have been included with some justification in another category. For example, "Eternal Prisoner under the Thunder Peak Pagoda" could have been placed in "The Dedicated Lover" section, instead of in "The Superhuman Maiden" section. Both "The Case of the Dead Infant" and "The Couple Bound in Life and Death" could have been included in "The *Femme Fatale*" section, instead of, respectively, in "The Ingrate" and "The Dedicated Lover" sections. The same is certainly true of "The Boot That Reveals the Culprit," which could have gone in "The Trickster" section instead of "The Detective." Thus the eighteen sections of themes should in no case be considered final. A new group, for example, could be created by putting together "The Boot That Reveals the Culprit" and "The Case of the Dead Infant" as a section of stories on "The Lonely Woman." Perhaps the above can be summarized in one reasonable caveat: the classification used here has essentially been made for the sake of convenience, as well as for a point of departure.

The introductory observations preceding each section are intended to be as concise as possible. Their main purpose is to explain the substance of a given character and the reason for including him or her under a certain theme. It should also be noted that we have refrained from either revealing too much information about the stories and or imposing upon the reader our own reading of the story. Within sections the stories are arranged chronologically. This makes it possible to examine the variations, if any, of a certain prototype historically in the hands of different authors and storytellers. Formal considerations have played a part in the making of each section. With the exception of the section on "The Dream Adventurer," all the sections include at least two stories in different forms and from different periods. The sections formed by the use of these guidelines vary greatly in size and the stories vary greatly in quality. This is due to the availability of materials (e.g., the number of recorded and extant *pien-wen* tales leaves very little choice), the quality of a particular type of story ("The Henpecked Judge Who Loses a Governorship" represents a compromise choice from among the generally poor stories toward the end of the *hua-pen* tradition), and the differing popularity of themes (love themes certainly generate more good stories).

The following chart will further illustrate the possibility of other thematic arrangements:

A. Selfless Friend—Knight-Errant—Self-Proclaimed Hero—Ingrate
   (A. 1 Knight-Errant—Self-Proclaimed Hero)
   (A. 2 Selfless Friend—Ingrate)
   (A. 3 Ingrate—Heartless Lover)
B. Heartless Lover—Dedicated Lover—Reunited Couple—*Femme Fatale*
   (B. 1 Heartless Lover—Dedicated Lover)
   (B. 2 Dedicated Lover—Reunited Couple)
   (B. 3 Heartless Lover—Dedicated Lover—Reunited Couple—*Femme Fatale*—Superhuman Maiden—Ghost Wife)
C. Superhuman Maiden—Ghost Wife
D. Almost Fortunate Man—Faithless Seeker
E. Dream Adventurer—Archetypal Questing Man

F. Judge—Detective—Master Thief—Trickster
   (F. 1 Judge—Detective)
   (F. 2 Master Thief—Trickster)

All the stories in this volume can be rearranged, if one wants to, according to the six categories (from A to F) listed in the above chart. Each of these six categories comprises stories with some thematic affinities. For example, the most observable unifying element found in category A is the concept of *yi* (commonly translated as "righteousness"). Within certain categories, some further sectional combinations are still possible, such as we have suggested in categories A, B, and F.

FIVE FORMS OF TRADITIONAL CHINESE STORIES

A Chinese story can be as short as one paragraph (e.g., "Hsün Chü-po Visits His Friend") or as long as a novelette ("The Oil Peddler Courts the Courtesan"). This variety in length is matched by the variety in style and content. For a reader making his first contact with Chinese stories, what strikes him most is probably the meticulousness with which the storyteller describes details. For example, what happens to the major character after the denouement greatly interests the storyteller, so much so that even the lives of his offspring are often related. In a sense, the average story in the *pien-wen, hua-pen,* or *kung-an* forms is really a short novel in its comprehensiveness.

The Chinese have for centuries used the term *hsiao-shuo* for fiction (the original meaning was "roadside gossip" or "smalltalk") to designate forms of writing held in low regard. Thanks to the pioneering efforts in the 1920s of such scholars as Hu Shih (1891–1962) and Lu Hsün (pseudonym of Chou Shu-jen, 1881–1936), the *hsiao-shuo* has since become almost as respectable a genre as classical poetry. Along with this popularity, however, there have been serious controversies regarding the definition of *hsiao-shuo.* Some literary historians, for instance, trace the origin of

Chinese fiction to the list of works labeled *hsiao-shuo* in the *Han-shu* (The History of the Western Han Dynasty), completed shortly after A.D. 92. Judging from fragments of these works that have survived, these writings can hardly be called fiction in the modern sense of the word. Nor, in our opinion, can passages from early historical works be regarded as fiction, properly speaking. No matter how lively the portraits of historical figures through the use of direct speech, they are nevertheless historical figures meant to be the eyewitnesses of history. Indeed, unless one draws a line between fiction and history, it might even be possible to find some of the earliest examples of Chinese story in the markings on oracle bones. It would be a great irony if the ingenuity of a historian in recording fact should be read as fiction. It is for this reason that we have included only one selection from the *Shih-chi* (The Historical Records) in this anthology. In doing this, we have no other intention than to demonstrate to the reader the extent to which Chinese fiction is indebted to Ssu-ma Ch'ien for the art of portraying characters as well as creating dramatic situations.

The chronological scope of this anthology is determined by our position in regard to the nature of fiction. Since we subscribe to the view that a work of fiction is a work of the creative imagination rather than historical fact, we do not find it necessary to go beyond the second century A.D. for our earliest examples because in our view writings before that period were intended as history. From "Scholar T'an" in the *Lieh-i chuan* (Records of Marvels) to "The Broken Hairpin" (1916), this anthology covers altogether seventeen hundred years. Three years after the publication of the latter story the May Fourth Movement began, ushering in a new era of Chinese literature with a different direction and a different sensibility. What follows below is a brief description of five forms of the *hsiao-shuo* genre which developed in China prior to the appearance of Lu Hsün's "The Diary of a Madman" (1918), generally regarded as the first modern Chinese story. These forms are the *pi-chi, ch'uan-ch'i, pien-wen, hua-pen,* and *kung-an* (see "Biobibliographical Notes" for the Chinese characters).

Pi-chi

The *pi-chi,* or jottings, is the most enduring of the five forms. Other forms (such as the *pien-wen* and the *hua-pen*) are limited to a certain period, but the *pi-chi* remained popular up to the end of the nineteenth century. Our selections of *pi-chi,* however, are largely culled from Six Dynasties collections, because other types of fiction had not yet been developed during this period. Two convenient labels have been traditionally used by literary historians to classify these writings: *chih-kuai* (tales of the supernatural), of which "Scholar T'an" is one example, and *chih-jen* (tales of human beings), to which the story of "Liu Ling" belongs.

True to its name, a *pi-chi* sketch is an experience in verbal economy: its main purpose is merely to give a brief account of a supposed happening. Aside from the distinction according to the periods in which they were written, *pi-chi* stories are sometimes not so easily distinguishable from *ch'uan-ch'i* (tales of the marvelous), the next form of story to be discussed. *Pi-chi* and *ch'uan-ch'i* have traditionally been handled in a similar manner and they are sometimes included in the same story collections. Moreover, both *pi-chi* and *ch'uan-ch'i* are written in the classical language (*wen-yen*). Some criteria are obviously needed by which to distinguish post–Six Dynasties *pi-chi* from *ch'uan-ch'i* tales.

The distinction we propose to make between a *pi-chi* and a *ch'uan-ch'i* tale is the means by which each form handles given elements in the story. In a typical *pi-chi* the brevity of the form imposes a mandatory limitation on the number of characters, on the development of characters, and on the selection of details. A *pi-chi* usually can accommodate no more than one episode; when the action nears the climax (if there is one), it is also

close to the end. A sense of "comprehensiveness," the hallmark of many *ch'uan-ch'i* stories, is seldom found in the *pi-chi*. With this in mind, we consider the following selections, chronologically arranged, to belong in the *pi-chi* group:

"Scholar T'an"
"Han P'ing and His Wife"
"Hsün Chü-po Visits His Friend"
"Liu Ling"
"Prince Tan of Yen"
"Hou Po"
"The Wit of the Master Thief"
"Nieh Yi-tao the Magistrate"
"The Shansi Merchant"

Ch'uan-ch'i

With the exception of *pien-wen* tales, stories written by T'ang writers are generally regarded as *ch'uan-ch'i*. These T'ang stories have been divided into four major thematic groups by modern scholars—love stories, historical stories, knight-errantry, and the supernatural. No classification, of course, can claim to be final. For our purposes, however, even such a conventional categorization will suffice to demonstrate that the T'ang stories have a much broader variety of subjects to offer than their *pi-chi* predecessors.

Some of the most easily identifiable features of T'ang *ch'uan-ch'i* stories can be listed: (1) the liberal use of incidental poems; (2) the occurrence of the national capital in the setting; (3) the presence of didactic commentaries which conclude the stories; and (4) the use of a narrator who is also a witness to the event. These features, however, no longer appear regularly in *ch'uan-ch'i* tales after the T'ang. For their painstaking attention to details and conscious effort at characterization, T'ang *ch'uan-ch'i* have been most instrumental in the development of realism in Chinese fiction during later periods.

It can be argued that any full-length story written in the classical language after the Sung is a continuation of the *ch'uan-ch'i* tradition. Thus, not only are many of the stories in the early Ch'ing collection, *Liao-chai chih-i* (Tales of the Unusual from the Leisure Studio), considered to be *ch'uan-ch'i,* but even "The Broken Hairpin," in spite of its date (1916), can be considered the last flowering of this popular tradition. Altogether, twenty-six of the selections in this anthology belong to this category (again, the arrangement is chronological):

"Miss Jen"
"The World Inside a Pillow"
"The Legendary Marriage at Tung-t'ing"
"The Courtesan Li Wa"
"The Story of Ying-ying"
"Feng Yen"
"Scholar Ts'ui"
"Tu Tzu-ch'un"
"Scholar Chang"
"Wu-shuang the Peerless"
"In Search of a Heart"
"The Tragedy of Pu Fei-yen"
"The Poetess Yü Hsüan-chi"
"The Fake Knight-Errant"
"Empress Chao Fei-yen"
"The Golden Phoenix Hairpin"
"The Chung-shan Wolf"
"The Strong Kid of the Ch'in-huai Region"
"The Taoist Priest of the Lao Mountains"
"Nieh Hsiao-ch'ien"
"The Lady Knight-Errant"
"Red Jade"
"The Monk's Magic"
"The Leper Girl"
"The Broken Hairpin"

Pien-wen

The term *pien-wen* refers to a unique group of stories (and some ballads) which, until they were discovered at a Tun-huang temple in 1900, had remained in obscurity for at least nine hundred years. Among the multitude of Tun-huang manuscripts are some eighty stories and ballads of a special generic form which can be readily observed in our selection. Since some of these manuscripts carry the term *pien-wen,* and since no other similar samples have been found elsewhere, this group of stories has henceforth been known as *Tun-huang pien-wen.*

Pien-wen probably means "popularized text." The genesis of this type of literature is generally attributed to the desire of Buddhist monks in T'ang times (or even as early as the Six Dynasties) to make their religious sermons more accessible to the less sophisticated public by way of "popularization." The result is that the essence of difficult sutras is embodied in a fictional form. With only a few exceptions (such as stories about historical events or contemporary topics), most of the extant *pien-wen* have a religious orientation. A typical *pien-wen* is made up of alternating prose and verse passages. The prose sections are meant for narration and the verse sections for chanting. (There is, however, a small number of texts composed entirely of either prose or verse.) Though it is widely believed that the *pien-wen* form has exercised considerable influence on the later development of oral literature and on the performing arts, its exact influence has yet to be determined.

"The Great Maudgalyayana Rescues His Mother from Hell" is the only *pien-wen* story selected for this anthology.

Hua-pen

According to Lu Hsün, the *hua-pen* are the prompt-books used by professional storytellers in Sung times. Recently, however, most specialists no longer subscribe to this view, and instead regard *hua-pen* as merely another term for "story." Whatever its true historical meaning, *hua-pen* is used in this volume to classify the form of stories included in such Ming works as *Ku-chin hsiao-shuo.* Here are some of the most salient features of *hua-pen* stories: (1) use of the vernacular larded with the stock expressions of professional storytellers; (2) liberal admixture of colloquialisms and archaisms; (3) frequent inclusion of rhymed passages, idioms, or poems for narrative or descriptive purposes;

(4) routine preamble before the feature story. In addition to these formal properties, what is perhaps most noteworthy in a *hua-pen* story is its great compulsion to be "comprehensive" in its coverage of details, a tradition inherited from the T'ang *ch'uan-ch'i* and pushed one step further.

One reason why we do not interpret *hua-pen* as prompt-books is that acceptance of Lu Hsün's theory would necessitate reading all vernacular stories which use Ming setting as imitations (*ni hua-pen*) of Sung stories. If the term is understood to simply mean "story," such a distinction is no longer necessary. Unless further discoveries of earlier works should be made in the future, it is safe to assume that the *hua-pen* tradition stretched from the middle of the Northern Sung period to the interregnum between the Ming and the Ch'ing. No more vernacular stories were produced in the Ch'ing period, and no major earlier collections were still in circulation.

To use a single term to cover the extensive period from the Northern Sung through the Ming is not to ignore the enormous changes the *hua-pen* underwent. For instance, toward the end of the Ming Dynasty, one notes the general decrease in the use of colloquialisms, rhymed passages, and incidental poems. The sequence of poems intended as a preamble, such as is found in "Artisan Ts'ui and His Ghost Wife" and in "A Mangy Taoist Exorcises Ghosts," is a feature uncommon in later *hua-pen*. While the preamble in earlier works is rather flexible in form, it becomes a more formalized and independent unit with the passage of time. The prelude in "The Sham Commander Reclaims His Beauty" has not one but two separate stories. "A Taste of Immortality" (title supplied by the Editors) is originally a preamble to a much longer story. Ironically, what was perhaps intended as a stylistic refinement in the later stories has proven to be more of a liability than an asset; the vividness, spontaneity, and primitive vitality which so distinguished earlier stories were "polished" away. In their place we find an intrusion of

didacticism. Worse still, toward the end of Ming times, the book markets were flooded with all sorts of *hua-pen* hastily pieced together to meet popular demand. If reasons must be offered to explain the disappearance of the *hua-pen* tradition after the Ming, certainly one of the most important of them would be the deterioration of quality through mass production. "The Henpecked Judge Who Loses a Governorship" is included here as an example of the *hua-pen* in decline.

The twenty-two *hua-pen* titles in this volume are, in chronological order:

"Yang Wen, the Road-Blocking Tiger"
"Sung the Fourth Raises Hell with Tightwad Chang"
"Artisan Ts'ui and His Ghost Wife"
"A Mangy Taoist Exorcises Ghosts"
"Eternal Prisoner under the Thunder Peak Pagoda"
"The Boot That Reveals the Culprit"
"The Jest That Leads to Disaster"
"Han Wu-niang Sells Her Charms at the New Bridge Market"
"The Pearl Shirt Reencountered"
"Wu Pao-an Ransoms His Friend"
"Magistrate T'eng and the Case of Inheritance"
"Loach Fan's Double Mirror"
"The Sung Founder Escorts Ching-niang One Thousand *Li*"
"Tu Shih-niang Sinks the Jewel Box in Anger"
"The Case of the Dead Infant"
"The Oil Peddler Courts the Courtesan"
"The Couple Bound in Life and Death"
"Old Servant Hsü"
"The Swindler Alchemists"
"A Taste of Immortality"
"The Sham Commander Reclaims His Beauty"
"The Henpecked Judge Who Loses a Governorship"

Kung-an

Kung-an literally means a legal case or the court desk used by a judge. Unlike the four forms described above, *kung-an* fiction is distinguished not only by form but also by content, and it can be either a story or a novel. The *kung-an* tradition dates at least as far back as the middle of the Northern Sung period and still continues today (witness the revival of Lord Pao stories in Taiwan and Hong Kong). If we limit ourselves to the period from the middle Northern Sung to the early Ch'ing, we may define *kung-an* as a short piece of fictional writing which involves the committing of a crime and its subsequent legal handling. Such a story may be in the form of a *pi-chi*, a *ch'uan-ch'i,* or a *hua-pen.* Therefore, a story like "Magistrate T'eng and the Case of Inheritance" is both a *hua-pen* and a *kung-an* story. Thus the stories we list as *kung-an* stories have also been included in the listings for the other forms of fiction.

During the Wan-li reign period (1573–1620) of the Ming Dynasty, a large number of a special kind of *kung-an* collections appeared. These are crime stories in which the actions of a clever judge are the center of attention. The titles of these collections invariably include *kung-an* as a label. The average length of one of these stories is comparable to that of a typical *ch'uan-ch'i.* However, the language is demonstrably different, usually crude and cumbersome. Compared with a typical *hua-pen,* it lacks two characteristic features: the descriptive rhymed passages and the preamble. A conservative definition of the term *kung-an* would state that only the stories in these Ming collections, such as our two Lord Pao stories (asterisked), can be regarded as *kung-an.* However, since our criteria for selection have been guided by both content and form, our understanding of the term is rather liberal and all the following titles, including those not from the Ming, are regarded as *kung-an:*

"Sung the Fourth Raises Hell with Tightwad Chang"
"Nieh Yi-tao the Magistrate"
"The Boot That Reveals the Culprit"
"The Jest That Leads to Disaster"
"The Jade-Faced Cat"*
"Lion Cub Lane"*
"Magistrate T'eng and the Case of Inheritance"
"The Case of the Dead Infant"
"Yen-chih"

CHRONOLOGY OF CHINESE HISTORY: MAJOR DYNASTIES AND PERIODS

For the sake of completeness, all the major dynasties and periods are listed here, even though a number of them do not appear in the selected stories.

Hsia	ca. 2100–ca. 1600 B.C.
Shang (Yin)	ca. 1600–ca. 1028 B.C.
Chou	ca. 1027–256 B.C.
Western Chou	ca. 1027–771 B.C.
Eastern Chou	770–256 B.C.
Spring and Autumn	722–468 B.C.
Warring States	403–221 B.C.
Ch'in	221–207 B.C.
Western (Former) Han	206 B.C.–8 A.D.
Hsin	9–25
Eastern (Later) Han	25–220
Three Kingdoms	220–265
Wei (North China)	220–263
Shu (Szechwan)	221–263
Wu* (Yangtze Valley)	222–280
Chin	265–420
Western Chin	265–317
Eastern Chin*	317–420

Southern and Northern Dynasties   420–589

		Sixteen Kingdoms (North China)	304–439
Southern Dynasties (South China)		Northern Dynasties (North China)	
		Northern Wei	386–534
Former (Liu) Sung*	420–479		
Southern Ch'i*	479–502		
Southern Liang*	502–557		
		Eastern Wei	534–550
		Western Wei	535–557
		Northern Ch'i	550–577
		Northern Chou	557–581
Southern Ch'en*	557–589		
Sui	581–618		
T'ang	618–684, 705–907		
Chou	684–705		

*These six are collectively known as the Six Dynasties because they all had their capitals established at Chien-k'ang (modern Nanking). They do not, however, constitute a continuous chronological line.

CHRONOLOGY OF CHINESE HISTORY: MAJOR DYNASTIES AND PERIODS

Five Dynasties and Ten Kingdoms	902–979	Northern Sung	960–1126
Five Dynasties:		Southern Sung	1127–1279
Later Liang	907–923	Hsi-hsia (Tanguts)	1038–1227
Later T'ang	923–936	Chin (Jurchen)	1115–1234
Later Chin	936–946	Yüan (Mongol)	1260–1368
Later Han	947–950	Ming	1368–1644
Later Chou	951–960	Southern Ming	1644–1648
Ten Kingdoms	902–979	Ch'ing (Manchu)	1644–1911
Liao (Khitan)	916–1125	Republic of China	1912–
Sung	960–1279	People's Republic of China	1949–

THE SELFLESS FRIEND

Of the three stories grouped in this section, the first one, "Hsün Chü-po Visits His Friend," needs little explanation, if only because counterparts of Hsün Chü-po are not wanting in Western literature. But unless one stretches the common assumptions of friendship as defined by Aristotle in *Nicomachean Ethics,* one will be at a loss to translate the meaning of Wu Pao-an's sacrifice (in "Wu Pao-an Ransoms His Friend") for a friend he has never met. Even in a literature with such a long tradition of cherished friendship as the Chinese, Wu Pao-an is unique as an impassioned illustration of the saying, "A man will gladly lay down his life for one who appreciates him, just as a woman will make herself beautiful for one who delights in her person." In "Old Servant Hsü," Hsü's devotion to his widowed mistress and her sons typifies the traditional Chinese relationship between master and servant, or ruler and subject. Strictly speaking, of course, his selfless service to his mistress is more a demonstration of personal loyalty than an indication of friendship in the usual sense of the word.

HSÜN CHÜ-PO VISITS HIS FRIEND

From *Shih-shuo hsin-yü*

TRANSLATED BY JOHN KWAN-TERRY

Hsün Chü-po[1] traveled a great distance to see his friend, who was stricken ill. It happened that at this time the prefecture came under attack by the Tartars.

"Death will soon claim me," his friend said to Chü-po. "Please leave while you may!"

"I've come a long way to see you," Chü-po replied, "and you ask me to leave? Is this proper conduct for Hsün Chü-po, to cast aside the principle of righteousness and run away, leaving his friend behind?"

Then the Tartars came, and they said to Chü-po, "Our great armies are here and the people have fled the land. What manner of man are you that dare to linger?"

"My friend lies ill, and I cannot endure the thought of leaving him," Chü-po answered. "Spare his life and take mine in its stead!"

At this, the Tartars marveled. "Indeed, we are iniquitous men who have come to the land of the righteous." So they gathered their troops and departed, and the prefecture was saved from destruction.

[1] He was a native of Ying-ch'uan (central and southern portion of the present Honan Province) and lived in the period of Emperor Huan (r. 147–167) of the Eastern Han Dynasty.

WU PAO-AN RANSOMS HIS FRIEND

From *Ku-chin hsiao-shuo*

TRANSLATED BY JOHN KWAN-TERRY

To the ancients, friendship was a bond of the heart;
To men of the present day, it is but a social act.
Friendship of the heart survives life and death;
Will superficial friendship share hardships and sorrows?
Today, the traffic is thick with men and horses;
Day and night are an endless round of receiving and
*   escorting;*
The host will lead his wife and children out to honor his guests,
*   and*
Amid wine and toasting, friends become sworn brothers.
But when it comes to the smallest difference in profit, they will
*   become enemies;*
How then will they behave when calamity falls?
Consider Yang and Tso of yesteryear,[1] friends unto death,
Honored among men in our chronicles even now.

This *tz'u* poem,[2] entitled "Contracting True Friendship," deplores the treacherousness of men in these days, and the difficulty of establishing true friendships. When wine cups are passed around, we are just like brothers. But as soon as a flea of a problem besets us that involves the slightest hint of profit and loss, we do not care for one another's company anymore. How true is the saying: "Easily a thousand brothers will share your wine and meat, but when misfortune calls, hardly one of them will be left." There are even those who are dear brothers in the morning but who have already become enemies in the evening. No sooner have they put down their wine cups and crossed the threshold than they face one another with arrows drawn. That is why T'ao Yüan-ming decided not to cultivate friendships,[3] Chi Shu-yeh desired to break off all relationships,[4] and Liu Hsiao-piao[5] left behind an essay on "Terminating Friendships." They all recalled with pain the ways of the world and put down their thoughts in resentment.

The two friends in this story you're about to

---

[1] Yang Chiao-ai and Tso Po-t'ao were two loyal friends of the Spring and Autumn period. They were totally devoted to each other.

[2] *Tz'u* is a genre of poetry which came into existence in T'ang times and became the major form of poetry in the following Five Dynasties and Sung periods. Composed of lines of irregular length (as against the linear regularity of *shih* poetry), a *tz'u* poem is governed by the pattern of a musical tune, which in turn has its own prescribed tonal structure and rhyme scheme. There were as many as six hundred musical tunes, but the music for almost all the tunes has been lost. Only the verbal patterns and the titles of those tunes still exist.

[3] Yüan-ming was the style of the great Six Dynasties poet T'ao Ch'ien (365–427). In his celebrated rhyme-prose "The Return," he expressed his desire to sever all friendships.

[4] In a well-known letter, Chi K'ang (styled Shu-yeh, 223–262) severed his friendship with Shan T'ao (205–283) because the latter repeatedly attempted to recommend the former to the officialdom against his wish.

[5] Hsiao-piao was the style of Liu Chün (462–521).

4

hear had never seen each other. But because they were united by a sense of loyalty, when adversity befell them, through life and death they went to each other's aid. Of such stuff is a friendship of the heart made. Truly:

Observe when Kung Yü dusted his cap to go,[6]
Or Ching K'o polished his sword for the mission.[7]

It is said that during the K'ai-yüan reign period [713–741][8] of the T'ang Dynasty, the prime minister and Duke Tai-kuo, Kuo Chen, styled Yüan-chen,[9] was from Wu-yang[10] in the Ho-pei Circuit.[11] He had a nephew by the name of Kuo Chung-hsiang. This young man was accomplished in both the military and the civil arts, but because of his tendency to fight for the weak and the wronged, and his habit of flouting conventions, nobody saw fit to advance him in his career. His father, seeing that he had grown in years and had not yet accomplished anything, wrote a letter [to Yüan-chen] and instructed him [to take the letter] to the capital and pay his respects to his uncle, who might be prevailed upon to give him a start in his career.

Once Yüan-chen advised his nephew, "Even if the man of worth has not distinguished himself in the examinations, or obtained high rank or supreme position, he can still do as Pan Ch'ao[12] and Fu Chieh-tzu[13] did—prove his worth in a foreign land and thereby gain riches and honor. But relying solely on family connections as a stepping-stone, one cannot expect to distinguish himself." In deference, Chung-hsiang expressed assent.

Meanwhile, reports from the border had arrived in the capital, bringing the news that the cave-dwelling barbarians in the south were up in arms. What had happened was that in the days following her seizure of power, Empress Wu Tse-t'ien[14] had obtained her subjects' loyalty through a policy of bribery and subornation. As a result, the tribes of the Nine Ravines and Eighteen Caves[15] were given a modest bounty every year, and a big one every three years. But when Emperor Hsüan-tsung ascended the throne, he abolished this practice, in consequence of which the barbarian rabble at once rose up in revolt and invaded many prefectures and counties, causing great havoc wherever they went.

The emperor thereupon appointed Li Meng governor-general of Yao-chou[16] and ordered him to advance his troops to the attack and suppress the rebellion. Li Meng received the imperial de-

---

[6] "To dust the cap" means to have oneself prepared for a career in the officialdom. Kung Yü (fl. 48 B.C.) entered the officialdom with his close friend Wang Chi; their friendship was such that it was said that Kung dusted his cap in preparation for his own appointment as soon as Wang became an official. From this it can be inferred that good friends take actions simultaneously.

[7] Ching K'o was a knight-errant toward the end of the Warring States period. He took on an impossible mission for the sake of friendship. See "Prince Tan of Yen" in this volume.

[8] The second of the three reign periods of Emperor Hsüan-tsung (r. 712–756) of the T'ang Dynasty.

[9] Kuo Chen (656–713) was known for his military ventures against the Tibetans, Turks, and other central Asians. His short-lived prime minister (711–712) ended in disgrace and banishment. Since this story is largely based on facts, the time setting of the story corresponds with his prime ministry.

[10] Wu-yang (a name used in the preceding Sui Dynasty) was actually known as Wei-chou in the T'ang period. The location is to the east of Ta-ming County at the southwestern border of the present Hopei Province.

[11] The Ho-pei Circuit covered the present Hopei Province and the land to the north of the Yellow River in the provinces of Shantung and Honan.

[12] Pan Ch-ao (32–92) was an outstanding general of the Eastern Han period who secured the Chinese control of the Tarim basin (in modern Sinkiang Province).

[13] Fu Chieh-tzu was a celebrated commander under Emperor Chao (r. 86–74 B.C.) of the Western Han Dynasty. He was responsible for placing the Tarim basin under Chinese control and bringing security to this part of the Silk Road, essential for transcontinental communications between China and the West. In this respect, he was Pan Ch'ao's precursor.

[14] Empress Wu Tse-t'ien (r. 684–705) deposed her own son, Emperor Chung-tsung (r. 684; restoration 705–710), and established the Chou Dynasty, which interrupted T'ang rule for two decades. Thus she became the first female sovereign in the history of China.

[15] Referring to the various aboriginal tribes who lived in what is now southwestern China, particularly those in the present Yunnan Province.

[16] Other than what is given in the story, little is known of Li Meng. Yao-chou is in the north of modern Yunnan Province.

cree, and before setting out on his mission paid a special visit to the prime minister to take his leave and obtain instructions. Kuo Yüan-chen reminded him, "Seven times Chu-ko, Duke Wu of old, captured Meng Huo, each time conquering him with wit and not force.[17] If your campaign is conducted with resourcefulness, you can be sure of success. My nephew, Kuo Chung-hsiang, is a man of some talent. I am sending him with you on this mission, so that when you have destroyed the rebels and returned with honor, thanks to you he may gain some recognition."

Then he called Chung-hsiang to come forward and be presented to Li Meng. Li observed Chung-hsiang's distinguished bearing. Besides, he was the prime minister's nephew; the prime minister himself had entrusted him to his care, so how would he dare refuse? So he promptly installed Chung-hsiang in his troops as an aide-de-camp. Chung-hsiang bade his uncle farewell and set out with Li Meng.

They reached the Chien-nan Circuit.[18] Thereabouts lived a man who came from the same district as Chung-hsiang. His surname was Wu, his personal name Pao-an, and his style was Yung-ku. At that time, he was a sheriff in Fang-yi County in the prefecture of Sui-chou in Tung-ch'uan.[19] Although he had never seen Chung-hsiang before, he had always known that he was a man of righteousness with a high degree of public spirit, always ready to render assistance to others. Wu therefore composed a letter which he sent to Chung-hsiang by special messenger. Chung-hsiang opened the letter and read:

I, Wu Pao-an, am an unworthy man. It is my great fortune to have been born in the same district as yourself. Although I have neglected to pay my respects to you, I have long held your name in the utmost admiration and esteem. With a man of your ability to assist General Li in this campaign against the petty bandits, victory will be a matter of hours. For many years, I have labored at my studies with unflinching diligence; but the only office I hold is sheriff in this desolate place beyond the Chien Mountains,[20] with my native district farther than dreams can reach. In addition, my term of service is coming to an end, and it is not at all certain when I shall receive my next appointment. I fear that I am not among the limited few selected by the Ministry of Personnel. I have heard that you, sir, have the spirit of the ancients and are always quick to respond to the distress of others. Able-bodied men are needed now when our great armies are on the march. If, in consideration of the fact that we both came from the same native place, you deign to use even a man of such meager talents as myself, so that I may render my service under you in the lowliest capacity, your boundless generosity will leave me forever in your debt.

Chung-hsiang reflected on what he had read and sighed. "I've never seen this man before in my life, and yet he asks for my help in an hour of need; clearly he must be someone who understands me. A man of character who does not go to the aid of a trusting friend will never live down

[17] Chu-ko Liang (181–234), Duke Wu-hsiang, was the celebrated adviser to Liu Pei (161–223), founder of the kingdom of Shu of the Three Kingdoms period. The legendary loyalty of Chu-ko and his exceptional intelligence are constantly celebrated in Chinese popular literature, especially in the historical novel *San-kuo chih yen-i* (Romance of the Three Kingdoms). Meng Huo was the chieftain of the aborigines living in the western part of modern Yunnan. After the death of Liu Pei, Chu-ko Liang decided to assist Liu's son in fulfilling his father's goal of reunifying China. Because Chu-ko wanted to make sure that the aborigines to the southwest of Shu would not take advantage of the military vacuum, he led repeated expeditions to bring Meng Huo to heel before undertaking any military campaigns against the kingdom of Wei in the north or the kingdom of Wu in the south. Seven times he captured Meng and each time released him unconditionally, until at long last Meng was totally convinced of the superiority of the Shu armies and swore not to cause any more trouble.
[18] The Chien-nan Circuit covered the land from the southeastern part of modern Kansu Province to the northeastern part of Yunnan, including most of the fertile land in the Szechwan basin.

[19] Tung-ch'uan is approximately equal to the eastern part of the present Szechwan Province. The location of the Sui-chou Prefecture in T'ang times is at the modern town of Sui-ning, close to the center of the Szechwan basin.
[20] Big Chien Mountain and Small Chien Mountain in northern Szechwan. Chien-nan (see footnote 18) refers to the land to the south of this area.

his sense of shame." He therefore spoke highly of Wu Pao-an's abilities to Li Meng, and begged that he be used in some capacity in the army. The governor-general listened to Chung-hsiang, and then ordered that a dispatch be sent to Sui-chou to summon Wu Pao-an to serve as a clerk.

No sooner had the orders been given to the messenger than reports reached Li Meng that the barbarians were becoming more violent and daring and were advancing into the interior. The governor-general then issued the order to march that very night. When his troops arrived at Yao-chou, they found the barbarian forces madly plundering and seizing people. Completely unprepared for an attack, the barbarians were taken by surprise and fled in all directions in the utmost confusion. Their ranks disintegrated, and great numbers were killed, so that the rout was total. With a great show of valor, Li led his army on relentlessly in pursuit of the enemy for fully fifty *li*. As darkness approached, Li's forces pitched camp.

It was then that Kuo Chung-hsiang ventured to advise the governor-general: "No one is as rapacious or unruly as the barbarians. Now that they have been defeated and have fled, your name will surely inspire awe. This is the time to return to our base, and then send men out to spread word of your mighty deeds. We should make it possible for the barbarians to surrender, but we must not advance so far into their territories that we might be trapped by their cunning tricks."

But Li Meng thundered back, "The barbarians have lost their wits! If we don't strike now and clear out all their hideouts, when shall we have another chance? Not a word more. Just watch me crush these scum!"

The next day, they broke camp and continued the march. After a few days, they reached the territory of the Black Barbarians.[21] They found themselves enclosed in fold upon fold of moun-

tains, and wrapped in a dense blanket of trees and grass; they could not tell where the road ahead lay. Li Meng began to feel a grave apprehension, so he ordered a temporary retreat to a level plain where they could set up camp and at the same time find some natives who could give them directions.

Then suddenly from every direction in the mountains and valleys an uproar of drums and gongs broke out. Barbarian soldiers were swarming down the mountains and covering the whole countryside. Their chief was Meng Hsi-nu-lo.[22] In his hands he brandished a wooden crossbow and poisoned arrows, and not one of his shots missed the mark. He led the chieftains of the various tribes in racing through forests and over ranges without effort, moving as easily as birds fly or animals run. The T'ang forces were decimated by the ambush; and being unfamiliar with the terrain, what resistance could they have put up? Governor-General Li was an able and valiant fighter, but what could a hero do under the circumstances? He looked around and, seeing that few of his troops were left from the massacre, said with a sigh, "I'm to blame for not listening to Kuo Chung-hsiang, and now I have to suffer shame from these beasts." So saying, he drew from his boot a dagger and cut his throat. By this time, the entire army had been wiped out. It was recorded in verse in later times:

Ma Yüan's bronze pillars stood as monuments for all ages;[23]
Chu-ko's flag-towers subdued the Nine Ravines.

[21] In T'ang times, the Na-khi (*na* = black, *khi* = man) tribe of the Wu-man (literally Black Barbarians) lived in the northeastern part of modern Yunnan.

[22] Here is a case of anachronism. Meng (the surname) Hsi-nu-lo (618–674), the chieftain of the Na-khi tribe of Meng-she, was the founder of the Nan-chao Kingdom. This tribe expanded their territory from their base in the south of modern Yunnan and eventually brought all the land in that province under their control. Meng Hsi-nu-lo ruled from 653 to 674, four to five decades before the Wu Pao-an event. The Nan-chao Kingdom lasted until 902.

[23] The celebrated Han general Ma Yüan (14 B.C.–49 A.D.) led a three-year expedition to Chiao-chih (Tonkin in modern North Vietnam) in 42–44. After the success of the military action, he set up bronze pillars at the border to commemorate the event.

How did it happen that all the troops of T'ang were lost?
Hapless the fate of their general named Li.

Another poem censured General Li for not heeding the words of Kuo Chung-hsiang, thus bringing disaster on himself:

It was not that the general's luck had turned;
An army advanced into grave danger, cut off from help.
If only he had heeded the warning to retreat,
What barbarians would have dared look back again?

Kuo Chung-hsiang was among those taken prisoner. Observing his noble carriage, Hsi-nu-lo questioned him, and on discovering that he was the nephew of Kuo Yüan-chen, gave him to Wu-lo, the chieftain of his cave. These southern barbarians had never harbored great ambition; they were only greedy for the material goods of China. Chinese captured as prisoners would be shared among the chieftains of the caves: those chieftains whose merit was greater would receive more prisoners, and those who had achieved less would be given fewer prisoners. As the prisoners were divided in this way, no distinction was made between the men of worth and those who were stupid and vulgar. All were treated alike as slaves, to run errands for the barbarians, to cut grass and chop wood, to feed the horses and tend the sheep. If there were many prisoners, the owners would trade them among themselves. Nine out of ten of the Chinese brought here would prefer to die. But the barbarians guarded them and they had no way to seek death. Truly, for them life was a ceaseless round of miseries. As a result of this battle, a great number of Chinese were taken prisoner. Many among them were men of rank, and when the barbarians had interrogated them one by one and found out who they were, they were allowed to write to their relatives in China to ask for ransom. In this way, the barbarians could make a sizable profit. Would there be anyone among those captured, do you think, who would not long to return to his native land? Thus, as soon as they knew what the barbarians wanted, all of them, whether of poor family or rich, lost no time in sending off messages to their homes. If a man's family had absolutely no way to pay the ransom, then that was the end of it. But if there were means, even if it meant going around borrowing to dredge up a small sum here and a small sum there, what family would not do it willingly to make up the ransom? The barbarian chiefs were greedy and heartless brutes, so that no matter how poor and alone in the world you might be, they would extort thirty rolls of high-quality silk before they would let you go. For a man of higher rank, there was no telling how much they would exact. Thus, when Wu-lo heard that Kuo Chung-hsiang was the nephew of the incumbent prime minister, he set a high price on him, demanding one thousand rolls of silk.

At this, Kuo Chung-hsiang thought to himself, "If they ask for one thousand rolls of silk, only my uncle can help meet this demand. But the way is far, over mountains and passes. How am I to get a letter to him?" Suddenly he got an idea: "Wu Pao-an is a friend who understands me. Although we had never met, I spared no efforts in recommending him to Governor-General Li just because of the few lines he wrote me, and secured for him the post of clerk. Surely he will cherish that gesture of concern I have shown him. It is fortunate that he set out late and so is saved from this calamity. By now, he must have reached Yao-chou. If I can send him an appeal and get him to deliver a letter to Ch'ang-an,[24] won't that solve my problem?" Thereupon, he wrote a letter addressed to Pao-an in which he described at length the hardships he was suffering and the amount of ransom that Wu-lo was demanding:

Pao-an, if you do not forsake me and convey the message to my uncle, then I might be ransomed soon and live again. Otherwise, while living I'll remain a slave, and when dead, a captive ghost in these barbarian wastes. Can you bear the thought of this?

[24] The site of Ch'ang-an, the capital of the T'ang Dynasty, is near the modern city of Sian in Shensi Province.

8

At the end of the letter he added some lines of verse:

Willingly [like me] Chi-tzu became a slave in a foreign land,[25]
And Su Wu suffered hardships in bygone years.[26]
I know that your spirit is generous, and your heart will feel my
    grief;
Like the ancients, you will leave your own affairs to relieve the
    ills of others.

After Chung-hsiang finished his letter, it happened that an officer who had been in charge of supplies in Yao-chou was ransomed and released. Chung-hsiang therefore grasped this opportunity and entrusted the letter to him. With envy, he saw others leaving. He was struck with an uncontrollable grief, and tears began streaming down his face like rain in spite of himself. Truly:

With his eyes, he followed the other birds as they soared away;
But whither could he fly, his body bound by a cage?

For the time being, let us say no more of what happened to Kuo Chung-hsiang among the barbarians. Let us describe what Wu Pao-an did as soon as he received the letter of appointment from Governor-General Li. He realized that he had been recommended by Kuo Chung-hsiang; so leaving behind him in Sui-chou his wife, Chang-shih, and his newborn child who was not yet a year old, he hastened to Yao-chou to assume his post, accompanied by a servant. There he heard the news of Li's death and was filled with consternation. But he did not know the whereabouts of Chung-hsiang, or whether he was dead or alive, so he stayed on to find out. Just then, the supply

[25] Chi-tzu was the uncle of King Chou (?–1027 B.C.), the last ruler of the Shang Dynasty. When the notoriously cruel emperor turned a deaf ear to the advice of Chi-tzu, the latter feigned madness, became a slave, and fled to Korea.
[26] Su Wu (140–60 B.C.), a commander of the Western Han Dynasty, was captured by the Huns after his armies were defeated in an expedition. As a captive Su endured all sorts of hardship, lived on snow, and was later transferred to what is now Lake Baikal in Siberia to tend sheep. Nineteen years later he was permitted to return to China when the relationship between the Chinese and the Huns had improved as a result of state marriages.

officer who had been released by the barbarians returned, carrying with him the letter from Chung-hsiang. Wu Pao-an was overcome with grief as he opened the letter. He immediately wrote a reply assuring Chung-hsiang that the ransom would be collected and left it with the supply officer, asking him to forward it to the barbarians at the first opportunity to put Chung-hsiang's heart at ease. After that, he hurriedly gathered his belongings and set out for Ch'ang-an. From Yao-chou to Ch'ang-an is some three thousand *li*, and the district of eastern Szechwan lies along the route. Pao-an, however, did not call at his home but headed straight for the capital, where he requested an audience with Prime Minister Kuo Yüan-chen. But something had happened that no one could have known: Yüan-chen had passed away a month ago, and all the members of his family had left to escort the coffin back to his native place.

All his hopes dashed, Wu Pao-an felt completely defeated. He had used up all his funds, and now there was nothing he could do but sell his horses and servants to meet his daily expenses. He then turned around and made his way back to Sui-chou. On seeing his wife and child, he burst into tears. Chang-shih asked him the cause of this, whereupon Pao-an recounted to her how Kuo Chung-hsiang had been taken prisoner in the south. "Now I must go there and ransom him, but I don't have the means. How can my heart be at rest if he is stranded in that distant wilderness, hoping against hope?" He finished, and began weeping again.

Chang-shih tried to console him, saying, "As they always say, 'Even the most able housewife cannot make gruel without rice.' Now that there is no way to accomplish what your heart desires, maybe you have to give it up as a matter beyond your control."

Pao-an shook his head. "It was but a chance letter that Kuo received from me," he said, "and yet he showed me the greatest consideration and rec-

9

ommended me for a high post. Now he is hanging between life and death and has placed his life in my hands; how can I bear the thought of forsaking him in his hour of need? If I cannot assure Kuo's return, I swear that I will not live on alone."

Thereupon he disposed of all the family possessions, but the sum came to only two hundred rolls of silk. So he left his wife and child, and went on his way to buy and sell. Anxious that letters might arrive from the barbarians, he did not wander far, but plied his trade in Yao-chou and nearby. From dawn to dusk he moved about, rushing here and hurrying there, paying little heed to the tattered garments on his back or the coarse fare that was his food. Not a cent, not a grain of corn would he throw away, but would scrimp and save to buy more silk. When he had one roll, he set his heart on ten; when he had ten, he set his heart on a hundred. As soon as he had collected a hundred rolls, he would deposit them in the treasury in Yao-chou. Waking or sleeping, his thoughts were full of Kuo Chung-hsiang, so that there was no room in his memory even for his wife and child. In this way, he spent fully ten years on the road, but had accumulated only seven hundred rolls of silk, still short of the required thousand. Truly:

Thousands of li from home he labored for meager gain,
Sustained by that bond of feeling between true friends.
Ten years had passed, but he was still in the barbarians' debt;
How long before the day he could see his dear friend?

Let us follow another thread of the story and describe the sad, lonely life that Chang-shih, Wu Pao-an's wife, and their little child led in Sui-chou. In the beginning, there were still people who would assist them in small ways out of regard for Wu Pao-an's former standing as a sheriff. But when no news came from Wu Pao-an as the years went by, people stopped paying attention to them. As the family had no savings to rely on, when more than ten years had passed, they could not find enough to eat or to wear. Finding it impossi-

ble to maintain the bare necessities of life, Chang-shih gathered up her few worn-out household goods and sold them to obtain some money for traveling expenses. Then she took her eleven-year-old child with her and, asking her way, she set out for Yao-chou to look for her husband. They covered no more than forty *li* a day, resting at night and traveling by day. Thus when they reached Jung-chou,[27] funds were exhausted, and she did not know what to do. She thought of continuing her journey by begging, but she had never done this before and she was too ashamed to do it now. Pondering on her miserable state, she thought to herself that it would be better if she were dead. But when she looked at her eleven-year-old child, she couldn't bear the thought of leaving him. Turning her mind this way and that and staring into the deepening twilight, she sat down at the foot of the Wu-meng Mountains[28] and loudly burst into tears.

Her lamentations caught the attention of an official who was passing by just then. This official, Yang An-chü, was the new governor-general of Yao-chou, on his way to fill Li Meng's post. He was traveling by the way of the express route from Ch'ang-an to his place of appointment when, passing the foot of the Wu-meng Mountains, he heard heartrending sounds of weeping and noticed that they came from a woman. He therefore stopped the carriage and asked her to come forward so that he might find out what was wrong. Leading her eleven-year-old child by the hand, Chang-shih went over to him and said, weeping, "I am the wife of Wu Pao-an, the sheriff of Fang-yi County in the Sui-chou Prefecture, and this child is my son. My husband's friend, Kuo Chung-hsiang, was taken prisoner by the barbarians. Bent on securing one thousand rolls

[27] The modern city of Yi-pin at the southern part of the Szechwan basin.
[28] This mountain range stretches from the northeastern part of Yunnan into the western part of Kweichow.

10

of silk to pay his ransom, my husband deserted us, and has long been living in Yao-chou. We haven't heard from him for ten years. Destitute, and with no one to turn to, I have set out in person to look for him. But now all my money is gone and road is long; that is why I am weeping so bitterly."

An-chü wondered in silence and sighed to himself. "Here truly is a man of honor. I regret that I never have had an opportunity to be his friend!" Then he said to Chang-shih, "Lady, please don't worry. A lowly and unworthy official, I have been appointed governor-general of Yao-chou. As soon as I reach there, I shall dispatch men to look for your husband. As for your traveling expenses, they will be my responsibility. Please go to the courier station ahead, where lodging will be arranged for you."

Chang-shih stopped her weeping and bowed in gratitude. Even so, her heart was filled with apprehension. But the governor-general had sped off in his carriage like the wind.

Chang-shih and her son, one supporting the other, made their way step by step to the courier station. Governor-General Yang had already instructed the officer in charge to take care of them. After finding out who they were, he provided them with a room and food. At the fifth watch the next morning, the governor-general resumed his journey before them. Acting on orders from the governor-general, the officer in charge gave them ten thousand in cash for traveling expenses, had a carriage prepared for them, and arranged for some of his men to escort them to Yao-chou, where they would be lodged at the courier station in P'u-p'eng. Chang-shih's heart overflowed with gratitude. Verily:

The good shall receive assistance from the good;
The wicked shall meet their end at the hands of the wicked.

The story continues, and we learn that as soon as Yang An-chü reached Yao-chou, he sent men out in every direction to trace the whereabouts of Wu Pao-an. They located him in a matter of days. An-chü invited him to his tribunal and came down the steps to receive him personally. Taking Pao-an by the hand, he led him to the reception hall, proffering words of kindness and concern all the while. He then said to Pao-an, "I've often heard how the ancients contracted friendships that endured beyond life. Now I finally see a living example in your person. Your wife and child have come a long distance to see you. They're now lodged at the courier station. I humbly request that you go there now and have a happy reunion after these ten years of separation. As for the rolls of silk that you still need, please leave them to me."

"What your humble servant is doing for his friend is only his duty," Pao-an replied. "How dare I then presume, sir, to burden you with it?"

"It is because I admire your generous spirit that I wish to help you fulfill your desire."

Pao-an bowed in gratitude and said, "Sir, since you deign to favor me with this kindness, I dare not persist in declining. I still lack one third of the number I need. If I can obtain this sum now, I can go immediately to the barbarians in person and ransom my friend. And after that, it still would not be too late to see my wife and child."

At that time, An-chü was still new in his office. Thus he had to borrow four hundred rolls of government silk from the treasury, which he gave to Pao-an together with a fully outfitted horse. Pao-an was overjoyed. After accepting the four hundred rolls of silk, which with the seven hundred he had made a total of one thousand one hundred, he rode straight to the borders of the land of the southern barbarians. There he found a sinicized barbarian to carry a message for him to the barbarian camp. To this man he gave the extra hundred rolls of silk to be used for expenses. All he wanted was Chung-hsiang's return, and he would not ask for more. Truly:

11

Even at this hour, to be able to see him again
Is worth more than all the gold in Yüeh-yang.[29]

Let us now describe how, in Wu-lo's keeping, K'uo Chung-hsiang was at first well treated, with no lack of food or drink, because it was expected that he would bring a heavy ransom. But after more than a year had passed and no one had come from China to negotiate, Wu-lo was displeased. He decreased Chung-hsiang's rations, giving him only one meal a day, and sent him to tend the war elephants. Unable to endure the hard life and racked with longing for home, Kuo stole away and headed toward the north one day when Wu-lo was out hunting. But the barbarian territory was criss-crossed with steep, treacherous mountain paths, so that after Chung-hsiang had run for a day and a night, the soles of his feet were torn and bleeding. In the end he was caught and taken back by a band of barbarian herdsmen who had pursued him with the speed of the wind. Wu-lo, raging with fury, resold him as a slave to Hsin-ting, the chief of a southern cave which was some two hundred *li* from Wu-lo's territory.

This Hsin-ting was a most ferocious and cruel taskmaster. If a man's work displeased him in the slightest way, he would have him flogged a hundred strokes of the whip until his back was blue and swollen; and this happened more than once. Chung-hsiang could not stand the pain or the misery any longer, so when the opportunity presented itself, he tried to escape again. But, unfamiliar with the terrain, he wandered around in the mountains and was once more captured, this time by the barbarians from his cave, who took him to Hsin-ting. Hsin-ting would have none of him and sold him to a cave further south. Thus Chung-hsiang was taken farther and farther away.

The master of this cave was known as the Wild Bodhisattva, and was even more of a terror. When he learned that Kuo Chung-hsiang had repeatedly tried to escape, he took two wooden boards, each three or four inches thick and measuring five or six feet long, had Chung-hsiang stand with one foot on each board, and drove iron nails right through the tops of his feet into the boards. During the day, Chung-hsiang had to move about with his feet nailed to the boards in this manner, and at night he was thrown into a hole in the ground, the opening of which was firmly covered with thick, heavy boards. The barbarians of the cave would then sleep on the boards to keep guard over him, so that, caged in this way, he could not even make the smallest effort to turn his body. Often, too, the places on his feet where the nails had gone in discharged blood and pus. Indeed, it was like suffering the tortures of hell. There is a poem that bears witness:

Sold to the southern barbarians, farther and farther south he
moved,
Buried in a pit, clamped in nails and boards, in agony
unendurable.
For ten years, no message reached him from the Central
Plain;[30]
In dreams he beheld his dear friend, but could not speak a
word.

Let us now retrace our steps and describe how the barbarian to whom Wu Pao-pan had entrusted his message came to see Wu-lo and informed him of the offer to ransom Kuo Chung-hsiang. When Wu-lo realized he could now have the whole thousand rolls of silk, he was overjoyed. He sent messengers to the cave in the south to buy back Kuo Chung-hsiang. The chief, Hsin-ting, directed them to the cave of the Wild Bodhisattva. After paying the purchase price, they took a pair of pincers and pulled out the nails implanted in Kuo Chung-hsiang's feet. The nails had been in the flesh for a long time, so that when

[29] Lü Tung-pin (fl. 841), one of the Eight Immortals in Chinese mythology, changed the stone at the Yüeh-yang Tower into gold. The famous Yüeh-yang Tower, situated at the west of Yüeh-yang County in northeastern Hunan Province, was built by the T'ang poet Chang Yüeh (667–730).

[30] The land along the lower course of the Yellow River.

the pus had congealed they became like a natural part of the feet. Thus, when they were pulled out now, the pain was much harder to bear than when they had first been driven in. Blood splattered the floor and Chung-hsiang immediately passed out. When he regained consciousness after a long time, he could hardly move an inch. So he was put in a leather sack and two of the barbarians carried it on a pole between them. In this manner, he was brought to the tent of Wu-lo. Wu-lo did not care in the least whether Chung-hsiang was alive or dead. As soon as he had received the rolls of silk, he handed him over to the barbarian who had been acting as an intermediary, so that he might deliver him to Wu Pao-an.

When Chung-hsiang was brought to him, Pao-an beheld him as though he were his own flesh and blood. Only now did these two friends meet face to face. As soon as they lay eyes on each other, even before they could utter a word, they fell on each other's shoulders and wept, each not sure whether this was all a dream. It goes without saying that Chung-hsiang was overwhelmed with gratitude to Pao-an. On his part, Pao-an was filled with grief to see how drawn and exhausted Chung-hsiang looked—like some strange creature that was neither man nor ghost—and that he could not move his two feet at all. Pao-an therefore gave him his horse to ride while he followed on foot behind, and together they entered Yao-chou and made their way to the residence of Governor-General Yang.

As it happened, Yang An-chü had served under Kuo Yüan-chen as an adviser, so that although he and Chung-hsiang had never crossed each other's paths, they had had some connection through their families. Moreover, Yang was a true and upright gentleman, not one who would change his attitude according to the situation of the moment. Once he saw Chung-hsiang, he was overcome with joy. He offered Kuo a bath, gave him new clothes, and ordered the army physician to tend to the wounds in his feet. Pampered with so much care

and rest and nutritious food and drink, in less than a month Chung-hsiang regained his former health.

We shall now describe how Pao-an went to the courier station in P'u-p'eng to see his wife and child only after his return from the barbarians. When they had first separated, the child was still an infant, but now he was already eleven years old. Time had indeed sped swiftly, and Wu Pao-an was [both] saddened [and pleased] by this family reunion after so many years of absence. Yang An-chü held Wu Pao-an in high esteem because of his loyal spirit and honorable conduct. He always spoke in praise of him before people, and he wrote letters to high officials in Ch'ang-an relating to them how Pao-an had put the ransom of his friend before the well-being of even his own family. Then he lavished on him valuable gifts and generous provisions and sent him off to the capital to wait for an official appointment. All the officials in the district of Yao-chou, witnessing these demonstrations of warm regard for Pao-an from the governor-general, followed suit and sent substantial presents in their turn. Chung-hsiang remained with the governor-general to serve as his aide-de-camp. Pao-an collected all the presents that had been given to him and gave half of them to Chung-hsiang for his own use. Chung-hsiang repeatedly declined this offer, but Pao-an turned a deaf ear, so in the end, there was nothing he could do but accept the half share. After expressing his gratitude to the governor-general, Pao-an set out with his wife and young son for Ch'ang-an. Chung-hsiang accompanied him beyond the borders of Yao-chou, and there, with expressions of anguish and sorrow, they parted. Leaving his family behind in Sui-chou, Pao-an set out alone to the capital. There, his official rank was raised to that of assistant in P'eng-shan County in the prefecture of Mei-chou.[31] Pao-an was happy that, since Mei-chou was still in western Shu,[32] his ap-

[31] The text has Mei-chou misprinted as Chia-chou.
[32] Shu is approximately the present Szechwan Province.

pointment would make it easier for him to fetch his family.

Let us now pick up the story of Kuo Chung-hsiang. Having been with the barbarians for such a long time, Chung-hsiang was well familiar with the dance and music of the barbarians. Among the women of the barbarians, there were many who were very beautiful, yet they were valued below the men. During his three years in office, Chung-hsiang repeatedly sent men to the barbarians' caves to buy young and beautiful girls. Altogether he bought ten such beauties, whom he then personally taught how to sing and dance, how to dress and adorn themselves. Then, in order to repay Yang An-chü for his many kindnesses to him, Chung-hsiang presented the girls to the governor-general as a special gift so that his needs might be attended to. But An-chü said with a smile, "I esteem your high virtue, and therefore found personal satisfaction in helping to bring about the fulfillment of a noble action. If you speak of repayment, will you not be treating me like a merchant?"

"Sir, it is only through your goodness and kindness that I am now enjoying a new lease on life," Chung-hsiang replied. "I therefore bought these barbarian girls to offer to you as a small gesture of my gratitude. If you persist in declining this gift, then I shall not be able to rest easy even in death."

Prevailed upon by his earnestness, An-chü at last said, "I have a young daughter whom I love dearly. At your insistence, I will accept just one of these girls to keep my daughter company. As for the others, please forgive me for not complying with your request."

Then Chung-hsiang presented the remaining nine girls to the nine senior military officers whom Yang most trusted, in order that his gesture might spread word of the virtues of his noble patron.

At this time, the central court was reviewing the military achievements of the late Duke Tai-kuo [Kuo Yüan-chen] and resolved that the nation had use for the services of his sons and nephews. Yang An-chü therefore composed a memorandum to the emperor:

> The late Prime Minister Kuo Chen had a nephew by the name of Chung-hisang who, while serving under General Li Meng, foresaw the outcome of the barbarians' maneuver, and forewarned him of it. During his subsequent captivity in the barbarian caves, circumstances made manifest his inflexible virtue. Ten years elapsed before he was able to return to his homeland. For three years now, he has been selfless in his services as adviser to your servant. [Your servant begs that] the services of the deceased be recorded and the merits of the living be recognized.

In consequence of this petition, Kuo Chung-hsiang was granted the post of executive inspector of the Wei-chou Prefecture.[33] At home his father and his wife had received news that Chung-hsiang was missing in action in barbarian territory, and when they heard nothing further of him through the years, they had presumed him dead long since. Thus, when suddenly they received a letter from him, informing them that he would be coming to join them and take them to his place of appointment in Wei-chou, all the members of the family, young and old alike, were beside themselves with joy.

Chung-hsiang held office in Wei-chou for two years, during which time the fame of his name spread far and wide. He was then promoted to be the comptroller of revenue in the Tai-chou Prefecture.[34] Three years later, his father fell ill and died, whereupon Chung-hsiang escorted the coffin back to his native place in the Ho-pei Circuit.

Then one day, when the funeral was over, Chung-hsiang sighed and said to himself, "I was ransomed by the sole effort of my friend Wu, and it is because of this that I can now enjoy the remaining years of my life. While my father was

[33] Ling-ch'iu County in modern Shansi Province.
[34] Tai County in Shansi Province.

alive, my duty was to support and serve him, and I've had no opportunity to repay that debt of kindness. Now that my father has passed away and the mourning rites are over, I can no longer forget my benefactor." He therefore made inquiries, and upon learning that Wu Pao-an had not returned from his place of office, he went in person to P'eng-shan County in Mei-chou to look for him.

It turned out, in a way no one would have expected, that on completing his term of office, Pao-an had been too poor to journey to the capital to await reappointment, and had resigned himself to making a living at P'eng-shan. Six years previously, both he and his wife had fallen ill during an epidemic and died. Their bodies had been wrapped in straw mats and buried in the waste ground at the back of the Yellow Dragon Temple. Their son, Wu T'ien-yu, had been taught since childhood by his mother to read and write. He was supporting himself by tutoring youngsters in the area.

When Chung-hsiang heard this, he was overwhelmed with grief, and sobbed without restraint. He then had some mourning clothes made of coarse sackcloth, and with a belt of white hemp girt about his waist and a staff in his hand, he made his way to the Yellow Dragon Temple. As he stood before the graves, he mourned for Pao-an with tears and loud lamentations. Then with full ceremony, he offered sacrifices and poured libations. When the rites were finished, he sought out Wu T'ien-yu. On seeing his friend's son, he took off his own robes and put them on him, addressing him as his younger brother, and invited him to discuss plans to take his parents' remains to their native place for reburial. Then, after composing a prayer to inform Pao-an's spirit of their intentions, he had the graves opened and found there two dried skeletons, which were all that remained. Chung-hsiang cried bitterly and could not be consoled; among the onlookers, not one could hold back his tears.

Chung-hsiang had prepared two silk bags to contain the bones of Pao-an and his wife. Afraid that the bones might get mixed up, thereby making it difficult to arrange them in their proper order for reburial, he marked the position on each piece with ink. He put the bones in the bags, placed them together in a bamboo basket, and then put the basket on his back and started walking. But Wu T'ien-yu remonstrated, saying that since they were the bones of his own father and mother, it was he who should be carrying them, and he reached for the basket. But what could induce Chung-hsiang to relinquish it? Still weeping, he said, "Yung-ku labored for ten years for my sake. Carrying his bones for a little while is the least gesture I can make to show my gratitude."

Chung-hsiang wept every step of the way. Every time they stopped at an inn, he would put the basket in the seat of honor and scatter rice and wine before it as an offering before he and T'ien-yu had their meal. At night, in the same way, he would make sure that the basket was in a safe and suitable place before he dared go to bed himself. They covered the journey from Mei-chou to Wei-chün,[35] a distance of several thousand *li*, entirely on foot. Although the wounds on Chung-hsiang's feet where the nails had been driven through into the boards had healed, the blood vessels had in fact been damaged, so that after several days of continuous walking, his feet became black and swollen and sent out shocks of pain. He could see that soon he would not be able to move another step, but he had made up his mind not to let anyone help him with the load; so he had to force himself to endure the pain and struggle on. There is a poem that says:

Too late to repay his friend, he honors him in death;
Day and night on foot he hurries, a load of bones on his back.

[35] Wei-chün is the other name for Wei-chou (see footnote 10). At the beginning of the story the author used an old name for the native place of Kuo and Wu, but here he shifts to the current name without giving any explanation. This inconsis-

Straining his gaze toward P'ing-yang,[36] thousands of li *away,*
He silently wonders, how long to reach the native place?

Chung-hsiang thought about his condition and about the long road before him and did not know what to do. That evening, they stopped at an inn to spend the night. Chung-hsiang set out wine and rice before the basket and, with tears in his eyes, made repeated prostrations before it, pleading earnestly in prayer: "May the spirits of Wu Pao-an and his wife manifest their divine power. May they intervene and rid Chung-hsiang's feet of pain and trouble so that he can walk with ease again and reach Wu-yang at an early date to perform the burial." Wu T'ien-yu joined in the supplication at his side, and made repeated prostrations himself. When Chung-hsiang got up the next morning, he could feel that his feet had become light and strong again; and all the way to Wu-yang, they gave him no more pain. This must have been the work of Heaven intervening to help a good man, and not just the work of Wu Pao-an's spirit.

Now when Chung-hsiang returned to his own home, he asked Wu T'ien-yu to live with him. He swept clean the front hall and erected ancestral tablets to Wu Pao-an and his wife. Then he went and bought burial garments and two sets of coffins, and prepared everything for the reburial. He put on mourning clothes and, together with Wu T'ien-yu, he observed mourning and received other mourners by the graves. Meanwhile, he had employed workmen to build the tomb; every detail of the burial arrangements was the same as when he had buried his father. In addition, he set up a stone tablet on which was recorded at length how Pao-an put his friend's ransom before the well-being of his own family. In this way, Pao-an's goodness would be made fully manifest to every

passerby who stopped to read the tablet. For three years, Chung-hsiang observed mourning, dwelling with Wu T'ien-yu in a hut by the graveside. During this time, he instructed T'ien-yu in the Confucian classics, so that he would become well-versed in scholarship and would thus be in a position to begin a career as an official.

At the end of the three-year period, Chung-hsiang was called upon to return to Ch'ang-an to fill an official post. He thought about Wu T'ien-yu, how he had no family now and had not yet taken a wife. So he selected from among the nieces in his family a woman of high moral character and arranged a betrothal for him. He also apportioned to him the eastern courtyard and chambers of the house, where he was to wed his bride and live. Then Chung-hsiang divided his family fortune into two equal portions and gave one to T'ien-yu. Indeed:

Years past, he left his wife and child to help a friend;
Today, his orphan is showered with favors in return.
Truly, give but a melon and you find the debt repaid;
A good man never betrays another good man's grace.

Chung-hsiang went to the capital after the mourning period. There he received an appointment as the chief administrator of the Lan-chou Prefecture,[37] in addition to the honorific title of Court High Official-at-Large.[38] But the memory of Pao-an was ever in Chung-hsiang's mind, so one day he submitted a memorandum to the throne, which read, in brief, as follows:

Your servant has heard that where there is virtue, it should be encouraged, and that this is held as an edict of the land; where there is kindness, it should be repaid, and this, too, is held as a man's duty. Your servant was formerly in the service of the late Li Meng, the governor-general of Yao-chou, when he led the campaign against the barbarians and secured a resounding victory at the first encounter. Your ser-

---

tency on the storyteller's part perhaps results from textual corruption.

[36] Since there was no such place in T'ang times and the context suggests that the place referred to is the native place of Kuo and Wu, "P'ing-yang" is likely a misprint for Wu-yang.

[37] In the northwestern part of modern Shansi Province.

[38] A loose translation of *Chao-san-ta-fu*. This title did not carry any specific duties.

vant then spoke against pursuing the enemies into their territories, and advised that the utmost restraint in this respect should be exercised. But our commander paid no heed, and in consequence, our army was totally routed.

Born of one of China's old and honorable families, your servant yet lived to become a captive in the remote barbarian wastes. To feed their greed, the barbarians demanded silk from the prisoners in exchange for their freedom. They said that since your servant was the nephew of the prime minister, they would exact one thousand rolls. But thousands of *li* lay between me and my family, and there was no means of getting my letter across the distance. For ten years, I was tortured, my body torn and battered, my bitter tears never ceasing. Although I had the resolve to tend [sheep, as Su Wu did, bearing the hardship,] I might have had to wait indefinitely for someone to shoot down the goose.[39]

But Wu Pao-an, the sheriff of Fang-yi County in the Sui-chou Prefecture, happened to arrive in Yao-chou at this time. He came from the same home district as your servant, and although we had never met, we respected each other as men of honor. For this reason, he undertook to secure my ransom. He planned and labored in a hundred ways, he cast his family aside for many years, his face became pale and emaciated, his wife and child suffered in cold and hunger. He snatched me from the grip of death, and set me on a new path to life. But before I had repaid this great debt of human kindness, he died without warning.

Your servant has now been favored with office and rank, but T'ien-yu, the son of Pao-an, has only coarse rice for food and patched garments to wear. Your unworthy servant feels the shame of it. Moreover, T'ien-yu is in the prime of life and steeped in scholarship, fully ready for office. I therefore beg that I be permitted to yield my present post to T'ien-yu. In this way, the country's concern for encouraging goodness and my duty to repay kindness will both be

[39] See footnote 26. After the relationship between the Chinese and the Huns had improved, the Chinese government used the pretext that the emperor had shot down a goose carrying a message from Su Wu to bring the Huns to acknowledge that Su was still alive. The Chinese demanded his release, and the Huns acceded to their request.

fulfilled. If your servant is thus allowed to retire from service, he will have no regrets for the rest of his declining years. This statement I submit with reverence, risking death that I may speak without reserve.

It was the twelfth year of the T'ien-pao reign period [753]. After the memorandum was submitted, it was conveyed to the Ministry of Rites for careful deliberation. This event occasioned considerable interest among the officials of the court. It was observed that although Pao-an was the first to perform the deed of kindness, it was just as unusual for Chung-hsiang to demonstrate such integrity and generosity. Indeed, he had no need to feel shame before his deceased friend. The Ministry of Rites therefore prepared a reply to the memorandum in which they lavished praise on Kuo Chung-hsiang's conduct and recommended that an exception be made in his case and his request granted, as an example to the populace. Thus Wu T'ien-yu was to be appointed sheriff of Lan-ku County, while Chung-hsiang was to remain in his original post. Since Lan-ku adjoined Lan-chou—a situation arranged by the officials of the Ministry of Rites as a measure of their sympathy—the two men were able to meet as often as possible.

After the emperor had endorsed the recommendations, Chung-hsiang received the notice of appointment on Wu T'ien-yu's behalf, gave thanks for the imperial favor, and left the capital. He returned to Wu-yang and turned over the letter of appointment to T'ien-yu. Then they prepared sacrifices and libations and offered them in worship before the graves of both families as they saluted and took leave of the deceased. Afterward, they selected an auspicious day and, taking their families with them, set off together for the Western Capital[40] to take up their posts.

This was a major event of those days, and the news of it spread far and wide. Everyone mar-

[40] In T'ang times, the name Western Capital referred to different places at different times. In the period involved here, it should mean the city of Ch'ang-an.

17

veled that not even the ancient records of friendship between Kuan and Pao[41] or Yang and Tso could compare with the attachment Wu and Kuo had for each other. Later, Kuo Chung-hsiang in Lan-chou and Wu T'ien-yu in Lan-ku both achieved fame as administrators, and were promoted to posts elsewhere. In order to commemorate the event, the people of Lan-chou built the

Shrine of Mutual Loyalty, where sacrifices were made to Wu Pao-an and Kuo Chung-hsiang. Here, from all over the region, people would come to offer prayers whenever they had a contract to make or an oath to swear, and to this day they have not stopped burning incense in worship. This is recorded in a poem:

Holding hands daily does not prove affection;
Only in calamity will one know who is true.
Witness the deeds of loyalty of Kuo and Wu,
Who had not even met like the common run of "friends."

---

[41] Kuan Chung and Pao Shu-ya of the Spring and Autumn period were another model pair of devoted friends.

18

OLD SERVANT HSÜ

From *Hsing-shih heng-yen*

TRANSLATED BY SUSAN ARNOLD ZONANA AND THE EDITORS

When even a dog or a horse is attached to its owner,
How much more must a human being love his master!
When one serves as an attendant for even one day, his body
*   belongs to his master.*
Master and servant share feelings like a father and son.
Their relationship is like prince and subject.
It is not right for the master to mistreat his servant.
The servant who cheats his master injures propriety.
The faithful servant makes a model citizen.
His loyalty does not change whether his master is rich or poor.
His spirit will live on in history.

During the reign of Emperor Hsüan-tsung [r. 712–756] of the T'ang Dynasty, there was an official by the name of Hsiao Ying-shih,[1] styled Mou-t'ing, and he was a native of Lan-ling.[2] From his youth he had been intelligent and fond of learning. He had extensive knowledge of Confucianism, Buddhism, Taoism, and the nine schools of learning.[3] He was well versed in a whole range of different disciplines. From astronomy to geography, there was nothing he did not understand, nothing he did not know. Truly he carried a great collection of books in his mind; from his brush came phrases as lofty as those of ancient times. When he was just nineteen he passed the highest imperial examinations with flying colors, and his reputation as a knowledgeable and talented man spread throughout the land.

In his household there was a servant named Tu Liang, who had waited on him in his study from the time Hsiao was very young. Whatever Tu Liang was ordered to do, he did without second thoughts, even in the face of danger. Not half a coin did he save for himself.

When he attended Hsiao Ying-shih at his studies, he did not wait for orders but anticipated his master's needs, and brought out fruits, delicacies, and drink to serve. He would sometimes prepare a pot of tea to help his master clear his thoughts, or warm a cup of wine to relieve his fatigue. He waited upon him straight through the night until morning, and never dozed. If he saw that Hsiao had reached a point in his studies where he was well satisfied, he, too, felt completely happy as he stood at his side.

This Hsiao Ying-shih was fine and admirable in every way, except that he had two faults. "What

---

[1] The following story about the T'ang scholar-official Hsiao Ying-shih (717–768) does not have much factual basis. After he offended the prime minister Li Lin-fu (?–752) and suffered other political setbacks, Hsiao still held a number of middle-level official posts. In these capacities, he was always enthusiastic in promoting the well-being of younger scholars.

[2] Modern Yi County in southern Shantung Province, close to the border with Kiangsu Province.

[3] The nine major schools of learning before the Han period are, in their traditional order, those of the Confucians, Taoists, diviners, legalists, logicians, Mohists, political advisers, miscellaneous writers, and agriculturists.

were those two faults?" you might ask. The first was that he was conceited and insolent because of his ability, and he treated others with disdain. No sooner had he stepped into the ranks of official-dom than he promptly offended the prime minis-ter. If the prime minister had been a broad-minded fellow, he might not have minded too much. But it happened that the one he insulted was the dreaded Li Lin-fu,[4] who was most jealous of anyone more gifted than he. He was nick-named Li the Cat, and who knows how many high officials had been ruined at his hands? He was re-ally a cold-blooded executioner. Now that Hsiao had provoked him, how could anyone expect Li to pass off the offense lightly? He hatched a little scheme and Hsiao lost everything, almost includ-ing his life. Fortunately, Hsiao's mentor came to his rescue, so he was able to return to his own home after being removed from office.

The second thing was that Hsiao had a fiery quick temper. At a trifling offense, his temper would flare up, his two eyes flaming like fireballs. If a servant had made the slightest of errors, Hsiao would beat him. His method of beating was also different from that of others. How was it dif-ferent? When others punish the servants of the house, they certainly take into consideration the degree of the wrongdoing. They then demand a flogging board and instruct someone else to do the beating accordingly. In determining whether the servants deserve ten or twenty lashes, they are making a distinction among degrees of punish-ment.

But Hsiao Ying-shih paid no attention to the nature of the offense at all. If his temper was in the slightest provoked, he would shout and curse again and again. He would not even bother to use a board or ask anyone else to do the beating but would personally grab the victim and throw him to the ground. Choosing any household utensil at

hand, he would flog his servant to his heart's con-tent. While he was at it, he would listen to no one's pleas to stop, but would continue the beat-ing until the victim gasped for breath. If he still was not satisfied, he would even go so far as to bite him a few times before he stopped. Hsiao's servants were terrorized by his severity, and they all left for different places, so that in time, only one servant, Tu Liang, remained.

Now Hsiao Ying-shih, when left with just this one domestic, should have become more lenient about things, and then all would have been well. But he was by nature temperamental, addicted to fits of temper, and had a free-roaming fist. He did not change his behavior in the least, but just con-tinued to act as before. In the past, when he had many servants with him, he could only beat one at a time. Now that there was only Tu Liang left, he began to beat him all the more frequently.

As for Tu Liang, when faced with this kind of unreasonable master, he should have followed his fellow servants' example, and that would have been the end of it. But he was determined not to retreat a step, and was willing to endure Hsiao's abuses. Often he was beaten until his skin opened, his flesh split, and blood poured from his head. But still he had not a moment's regret, and did not utter one word of complaint. When a beating came to an end, he would simply readjust his clothing and bear the pain, then stand by his mas-ter's side as before to supply his needs.

"Storyteller, if what you said is true, a servant such as Tu Liang is not only one in a thousand: he is certainly peerless in the whole world. This Hsiao Ying-shih was not as unenlightened as a black lantern or a stuffed-up bamboo tube. He was in fact a genius who had been highly success-ful in examinations, had served at the central court, and had thoroughly studied the classics. Could such a person fail to distinguish right from wrong? Could he have beaten people so savagely without the least thought of compassion or repen-tance?"

Honored readers, there is something you don't

---

[4] The calculating and ambitious Li Lin-fu was execrated in history as responsible for bringing the disasters which befell China in the second half of the reign of the T'ang emperor Hsüan-tsung.

know. Truly, as the common saying goes, "Mountains and rivers are easy to alter; a man's disposition is difficult to change." From the beginning Hsiao Ying-shih had always been fond of Tu's mild deference. After a beating he would feel deeply remorseful, and think, "This servant has followed me for so many years, and he has never done anything atrocious. Why did I beat him so cruelly? From now on I definitely must stop." But when his temper flared again, before you know it his fists and feet would recklessly rain blows on Tu's body.

This cannot be blamed on Hsiao's quick temper alone. Whenever Tu heard a shout, he acted just like a ghost that has seen Chung K'uei,[5] and knelt down on the ground. Since Hsiao had a fondness for beating people, and since Tu assumed such a posture of subjugation before him, Hsiao could not help but gratify him with a few strokes.

Tu Liang had a distant cousin named Tu Ming who happened to live next door to Hsiao's residence. Seeing his cousin frequently beaten in this way, Tu Ming could not restrain his anger, and urged Tu Liang, "Those who work as servants all come from poor families. Just because they are poor, they offer their labor to others in exchange for a living. Then, too, they naturally hope that the master they serve will one day become prosperous, so that they might enjoy some reflected glory. Under their master's protection, they might start a small family enterprise from scratch and live happily for the latter half of their lives.

"But brother, what do you expect to gain by following this wretch? From morning to night you work yourself to death to serve him and all you get is beating and humiliation. What good is there in following such an unappreciative person?

"You see, no one in his household could put up with him. They all ran away! Why don't you do the same thing and seek another position? Many

---

[5] Chung K'uei is the slayer of devils in Chinese mythology. Unlike the usual pattern of evolution, the myth about him as a devil-slayer originated not from events about a historical person but from a dream of the T'ang emperor Hsüan-tsung.

who are not half as good as you have already found good places in the households of important officials. They eat well, dress well—not to mention the extra money they occasionally make!

"Who wouldn't go out of his way to curry favor when one of these walks through the gates of the tribunal? Over there someone calls out, 'Uncle So-and-So, may I bother you with a small matter?' Before he can answer, someone over here calls out also, 'Uncle So-and-So, I've a problem on which I would appreciate your help.' Really, they're so much sought after that they simply don't have time to attend to all the requests.

"Brother, with your intelligence, your knowledge, and your thoughtfulness for others, you'd be a most welcome addition to the service of any high and influential person.

"Although that wretch of yours is a *chin-shih,* he offended Prime Minister Li right at the start of his career and completely ruined himself. So now he sits at home! It will indeed be a miracle if he ever gets an official position. What is it in him that makes you stick to him?"

"Do you think I don't know all this?" Tu Liang replied. "If I felt the way you do, I'd have left him years ago without your telling me to. But as the old saying goes, 'A good subject chooses his master and then serves him; a good bird chooses its tree and then roosts there.' Although servants are lower class, we must select a good employer. The only thing that is the matter with my master is that he has a quick temper. Other than this, I doubt that I could find someone comparable to him in other qualities."

Tu Ming said, "Throughout the whole country there are countless officials, statesmen, imperial relatives, powerful families; in what way are they not comparable to this poor scholar-official of yours?"

"They have only two things, rank and wealth," Tu Liang said.

"Well, what else do you want?" said Tu Ming.

"Rank is an empty show and wealth stinks," said Tu Liang. "Of what value are they? How can they be compared to the great talent and broad learning of my master, who can pick up a brush and instantly write ten thousand words as lofty as clouds and as colorful as flowers, without needing a draft? I simply love this one thing in him. This is the only reason I'm unwilling to leave him."

When Tu Ming heard his cousin reveal that he loved his master's talent and learning, he unwittingly broke into laughter and said, "Now let me ask you, brother, since you love this talent and learning of his, when you suffer from hunger, will they feed you? When you are cold, will they keep you warm?"

"You're joking," said Tu Liang. "The talent and learning are his; how could they relieve my hunger and cold?"

Tu Ming pressed his point further. "Since they can neither relieve your hunger nor protect you from cold, what good is it to love him so? Now the people who have rank are only too happy to chase after influence and ally themselves with the most powerful. No one cares much about talent and learning. You and I are only servants. Who can blame us if we care only about our most basic needs, like food and clothing, and a little money to keep? But you're so impractical that not only do you love his 'talent and learning,' but you also willingly submit yourself to his abuses. You're really a fool!"

Tu Liang laughed and said, "I didn't bring any money with me when I was born and I don't expect to make any. I will just go on as before."

"It seems that he hasn't beaten you enough," said Tu Ming. "That's why you still want to go back and get more."

"I appreciate your concern and your sympathy," said Tu Liang. "It's only that my master has such marvelous talent and learning that even though he may beat me to death, I'm still willing to serve him."

Consequently, Tu Liang did not listen to his cousin's advice, and continued to serve Hsiao

Ying-shih as before. He paid no attention to whether he might be struck with a fist today or receive a blow with a cudgel tomorrow. In only a few years the beatings gradually gave Tu Liang pain over his entire body. He became a consumptive and began to spit blood. At first he still forced himself to answer to the needs of his master, but later he couldn't take any more maltreatment and was more or less confined to bed. Finally, he was no longer able to leave his bed.

When Hsiao saw him spitting blood, he realized that the beating had caused it. He felt deep regret in his heart, and hoped that Tu might still recover. He asked a doctor to attend to him and personally served him the medicines. Tu lingered on for a couple of months and then passed away.

While Hsiao was making preparations for Tu's funeral, his mind was filled with the many good qualities of his late servant, and tears rolled from his eyes.

Hsiao was accustomed to Tu's usual service; and his loss was felt all the more keenly when he realized how inconvenient things were without his old servant around. He tried to look for a replacement everywhere, but who would want to serve a master with such a bad reputation? Even if someone did come, he certainly would not measure up to Hsiao's expectations. At times, when Hsiao was deep in his reading, he would forget that Tu Liang was no longer by his side. He would raise his head to look for him, and then, when he didn't see him, close his book and weep.

Later on, when Hsiao learned that Tu Liang had not listened to the advice of Tu Ming, he suddenly felt short of breath and tears coursed down his cheeks. He called out loudly, "Tu Liang! I've spent a lifetime in studying, but I've never met a man who could appreciate my talent, and I've spent my whole life in poverty. Who would have thought that you were my only true friend? I have eyes but cannot see. I've done a great injustice to you; that is my crime!"

Before he had finished speaking, blood spurted

from his mouth. From this time on he also became consumptive. He burned all his books and kept calling Tu's name. After several months of illness, he died. In his will he directed that Tu Liang be moved and buried in the same place with him. There is a poem that bears witness:

Amid those who rush to take bribes and seek power,
How many men have you ever seen who admire great talent?
If those in power could act like Tu Liang,
How could misplaced talents dwell in the wilderness?

"Storyteller, this Tu Liang loved talent and was attached to his master; he certainly was one of the rare men of all times. It seems, however, that he did have an obstinate streak, and was not completely admirable. If you have another unique story, let's have it now."

Honored readers, sit tight—don't be impatient. This little episode I've just told you is simply the preamble. I haven't yet reached the main story.

My main story is also about a servant, who was even more remarkable than Tu Liang. Through his own effort he established a huge family business to support his master's widow and her orphaned children. He arranged for the marriages of the widow's three daughters and found wives for her two young sons. When he died, he was found to possess not even half a coin of his own. His name has been handed down through history.

Before I tell this story, allow me to put in a word of advice to those who are servants: to make a good name for yourself, study the ways of our hero and follow his example of serving his master wholeheartedly. Don't ever be ungrateful, for ingratitude is a most ugly word.

You may wonder in what dynasty and in what area this story took place. Actually, it took place in the present dynasty, during the reign of the Chia-ching Emperor,[6] at the Brocade Sand Village several *li* outside Ch'un-an County in the Yen-chou Prefecture in Chekiang Province.

In that village there was a farmstead with a family named Hsü, consisting of three brothers. The oldest of them was Hsü Yen, the second Hsü Chao. Each of them had one son. The third brother was named Hsü Che. He had married a girl of the Yen family (Yen-shih), who had given birth to two boys and three girls.

The deceased father of the three brothers had willed that his sons should live together and share the farm work. The brothers had acquired one ox and one horse. There was also an old servant named A-chi[7] who was already past fifty; he and his wife had one son who was in his teens.

This A-chi had been born and raised in the village. When A-chi's parents passed away, he had no money for funeral preparations. For this reason he sold himself to the Hsü family. He was a faithful, attentive, and careful person. He rose at dawn and retired late, and was very hard working.

As Hsü Yen's father had benefited greatly from A-chi, he treated him with unusual kindness. But when Hsü Yen's generation took over the management of the family, they treated him lightly because they saw that he was so advanced in years. Moreover, A-chi was not a tactful person. Whenever the Hsü brothers did something wrong, A-chi would faithfully remonstrate with them.

Hsü Che was more considerate than his two brothers, so occasionally he would listen to A-chi's advice. Hsü Yen and Hsü Chao, however, were very conceited. Offended by A-chi's interventions, they shouted at him and sometimes even gave him a few solid fists.

A-chi's wife admonished him, "When a man reaches your age, it's time to just mind your own business. This is the world of the younger generation. Times have changed and so have customs. Let them go their own way. Why do you stick

---

[6] Chia-ching is the title of the only reign period of Emperor Shih-tsung (r. 1522–1566) of the Ming Dynasty.

[7] The surname of A-chi, though not mentioned here, is understood to be Hsü, as it was the custom in traditional China for servants sold to a family to adopt the family name of their master.

your finger in their affairs and invite this kind of humiliation?"

"As the old master has treated me kindly, I feel obliged to say what I think is right," replied A-chi.

"You've done your duty," said his wife, "so no one can blame you anymore."

From then on A-chi took his wife's advice and kept his mouth shut. Since he was no longer intervened in the brothers' affairs, he also saved himself further humiliation and disgrace. The saying of the ancients is fitting:

If one shuts his mouth and hides his tongue,
He can live in peace everywhere.

Suddenly one day Hsü Che contracted typhoid fever, and died within several days. Yen-shih and her children wept their hearts out. She had to attend the funeral arrangements and perform sacrifices to the dead.

A couple of months later Hsü Yen consulted with Hsü Chao: "You and I have only one son each, but our third brother had two sons and three daughters. His part of the household is equivalent to both of ours. Even when he was alive and shared the farm work, it was a bad deal for us. How much more so now that he is dead!

"Night and day we toil and suffer hardship to earn a living only to feed his brood of freeloaders. Right now this is still a small matter, but when our children have grown up and married, we would have to take care of his children's marriage, too. Wouldn't we then have to divide the estate into four more parts?

"I want to divide everything immediately into three shares and cast aside this dead weight. From then on, whether they starve or not, it wouldn't be our responsibility. The only thing I'm concerned about is that father stated clearly in his will that we must not divide the property. If we now disobey his words, people will gossip. What should we do then?"

If Hsü Chao had not been a heartless man, he would have stopped his brother from harboring such thoughts. However, since he himself had been of the same mind for a long time, what his brother had said became a welcome suggestion. So he answered, "Although father did leave a will, it's merely the words of a dead man, and certainly not an imperial decree which cannot be disobeyed. Besides, what outsider would dare to interfere in our family's business?"

Hsü Yen concurred with his idea, and in no time they had secretly divided all the lands and property at the expense of their nieces and nephews, who were given what was left over by their uncles.

"Now how about the ox and the horse?" asked Hsü Yen.

Hsü Chao thought it over for some time, and then said, "No problem. That A-chi and his wife are already old and soon they wouldn't be of any use at all. While they are alive, they're surely just three hangers-on, not to mention the fact that we even have to pay for their coffins when they die. So let's use A-chi as a part of the property and send him over to third brother's widow. Could you think of a better way to relieve ourselves of this burden?"

Having agreed upon their plan, the next day they prepared a feast and asked several relatives and neighbors to come over. They also invited Yen-shih and their two nephews. These two children, Fu-erh and Shou-erh, were seven and five. They came straight to the front of the hall following their mother. Even she did not know why they had been summoned. She only saw Hsü Yen stand up and say, "Honored relatives, we have an announcement to make:

"Our late father had few assets to bequeath to us in the first place. Largely due to the efforts of us brothers, the family has now acquired some small property. It was indeed our father's hope that we brothers should take care of one another until old age, and then hand down the property to our children to divide it among themselves.

"Unfortunately, our third brother died recently, and our sister-in-law does not know the ins and outs of our family property. Furthermore, the way with family fortunes is hard to predict. Should we be lucky enough to make a lot of money and divide it evenly among our nephews, all will be well. But if by any chance we lost our capital, then people would suspect that we must have manipulated the family property so that our sister-in-law and her orphans would lose. This would then be interpreted as betraying our flesh and blood.

"Therefore, we two brothers, after some deliberation, have decided that the best thing to do is to divide the property into three shares, so that each can make the best use of the capital. This will save later quarrels. Since you're all our relatives, we have invited you especially to come and give us your advice."

Then Hsü Yen reached into his sleeve and produced three documents of division, and he said, "We've divided everything equally. All we need trouble you to do is place your personal seals on them."

When Yen-shih heard him say that the estate was to be divided, tears gushed from her eyes. "Uncles," she said, weeping, "I am a widow and the children are small. We're like footless crabs! How can I support my family? It was in father's will that we should not divide the property. I still think it's best for you two to manage the household and support my children until they are grown. Then we'll accept whatever you give us and I shall raise no objection to whatever decision you make."

"Sister," said Hsü Chao, "there has never been an unending feast. Even a union of a thousand years is bound to have its day of separation. Father has passed away and we don't have to rely on his words anymore. Yesterday first brother wanted to allot the horse and ox to you. I thought, since your children are still young, who would take care of these animals? Therefore I suggested that A-chi be given to be your help and support.

"Although A-chi is old, his muscles are still strong. He is even better than the young men in farm work. His wife spins thread, so that she wouldn't be a burden to you either. Given a couple of years, their son will also be able to work in the fields. You don't need to worry."

When Yen-shih heard the brothers talking this way, she knew quite well that the division was already an accomplished fact. When she realized that they had cut her off and that she had no way to argue with them, she wept unceasingly.

The relatives and neighbors examined the documents of division, and although they discovered that the division was not equitable, none wanted to interfere. Who would want to offend the two brothers by pointing out their unfairness? They all placed their signatures on the documents, and advised Yen-shih to accept it as such. Then they joined the banquet. Truly:

The argument for the three documents of division seems
*   logical;*
When in the division of property men and animals are
*   considered equal, the argument sounds*
*   even more natural.*
But as the old man is thought to be less useful
*   than the ox and horse,*
The orphans and widow weep silently to the west wind.

Let us resume our story with A-chi. Very early that morning he had been sent to buy this and that, to invite Chang and invite Li. He had no knowledge of what was going on. He happened to be in the South Village to see a certain relative, and when he returned the matter of property division had already been settled.

As he was approaching the front door, he was confronted by his wife. She was afraid that when he became aware of the situation, he would go over and let loose a string of words. She dragged him over to one side and told him, "Today the first master has divided the family property. Don't you go over there meddling again! You'll be only inviting trouble if you do."

When A-chi heard this, he started and said, "The old master's will instructed that they must not divide the property. How can they push the orphans and the widow aside when the third master has just passed away? How could they make a living? If I don't say it, who will be willing to speak out for them?"

No sooner had he finished speaking than he began to move. His wife stopped him again and said, "Even an honest official cannot pass judgment on family affairs. Many relatives and neighbors have come to bear witness to the occasion and not one of them has said a word. Who are you but a servant? You're certainly not a clan elder! What could you do?"

A-chi said, "What you say is true, and I'll keep my mouth shut if the division they've made is fair. But if they've played any dirty tricks, I'll certainly speak out, come what may." After a little pause, he again asked, "Do you know which household we've been given to?"

"Frankly, I don't know," she replied.

A-chi went to the front of the hall, where he saw everyone drinking. Since they were on the point of getting high, it wouldn't have been good for him to burst in and ask questions, so he stood at the side.

A next-door neighbor happened to raise his head and saw him, and said, "Old Hsü, today you've been given to the third branch. She's a widow. You must do your best to help her."

A-chi replied casually, "I'm an old man and can't work anymore." As he was saying this, he secretly thought to himself, "So, that's it. They wouldn't have given me to the third branch if they still had some respect for my usefulness. What a way to kick me out! But I swear I'll vindicate myself and I'll build a big business for the widow and orphans. See if they will still look down on me then!"

Consequently, he did not inquire further about the allotments, but turned and went directly to the doorway of Yeh-shih's room, from which he heard weeping. A-chi stopped to listen.

"Heaven," wept Yen-shih, "I thought that we would support each other until old age. Who could have thought that after only half the way you would leave me and the children behind, helpless? I had hoped to rely on your older brothers to support the children until they were grown. Who could have known that before your bones had turned cold, they would make the divisions? Tell me, with no one to turn to, how am I to manage this family?"

She went on, "Even in the division of property, they know what they're doing, but I've been kept in the dark, leaving everything to their mercy. How could I know whether it's fair or not? But I have become aware of their basic cruelty through just one thing. The ox can plow the fields, the horse can be hired out to others, and they took them all away, leaving me only A-chi and his wife, who will have to look to me for support."

When A-chi heard this, he suddenly pulled up the door screen and shouted, "Third mistress, do you mean to say that I'm nothing but an extra burden on your household, that I'm not as good as an ox or a horse?"

His sudden barging in and shouting had greatly startled Yen-shih. She restrained her tears and asked, "Then what do you have to say?"

A-chi replied, "Although it is true that the ox can help with the farm and the horse can be rented out for a profit, still you have to pay someone to feed and take care of them. Now consider me, your old servant. My vitality and strength have not yet declined even though I am old. I can still walk; I can still bear hardship.

"As for doing business, although I've never done it, I do know something about it. If you can raise some capital in a short time and let me go out to do business, the interest on that investment after a few trips in one year can be many times better than the ox and the horse.

26

"As for my wife, who is good at spinning, she, too, can help out a bit with the expenses for firewood, water, and such.

"As for your allotted property, whether it is good or bad doesn't matter. Just rent it out to others and collect a few piculs of grain as payment.

"As for you and your children, please also make some plans for earning a living so that you don't have to draw money from your assets. If you manage your household this way while I do business for you outside, there is no reason why you can't come up with something in a few years. Why should you worry?"

Yen-shih began to see that what he said had some truth in it, so she said, "If you would make such an effort for me, I couldn't be happier. My only worry is that since you're already advanced in years, you may not be able to bear such hardships."

A-chi said, "Although I am old, my health is still good, and I don't say this just to please you. I rise early and retire late. For this, I don't think the younger generation can keep up with me. Anyway, there's no need for you to worry."

"What business do you plan to do?" asked Yen-shih.

"The rule in trading," said A-chi, "is that if the capital is large, then do it in a great way; if the capital is small, do it on a small scale. I must go out first and then decide according to the situation. What I can say now is that I'll do whatever is profitable. It's not something I can decide here at home."

"Reasonable," said Yen-shih. "Let me think it over."

A-chi also asked to see the document of division. He marked off one by one the household items allotted in the document and moved them off to one side. Then he went to the front of the hall to wait on the house guests. The crowd of relatives and neighbors continued their feasting until late at night before they finally left.

The next day Hsü Yen immediately summoned a workman to divide the house into two parts, and he told Yen-shih to use a separate door for her family to come and go.

On the one hand, Yen-shih was busily engaged in reorganizing her household. On the other hand, she took out her clothing and ornaments and quietly instructed A-chi to sell them. They were exchanged for a total of twelve taels of silver, which Yen-shih handed over to A-chi, saying, "This small amount of money is all I have. The fate of the family depends on it. Now here it is. I don't expect great profits; I shall be satisfied with just a small return. Exercise your best judgment in all transactions; and when you are on the road, you must also be very careful. We can't afford to come off badly or we will be laughed at by the older brothers."

As she was talking, she broke into tears. A-chi said, "Please rest assured, your old servant is quite knowledgeable in this. I won't fail you."

Yen-shih asked further, "When will you start?"

"Now that I have the capital," replied A-chi, "I'll leave tomorrow morning."

"Don't you want to select an auspicious day?"

"I'm setting out to seek a livelihood, so it is already an auspicious day. What need is there for another one?" Thereupon he took the silver and hid it in his belt.

He went to his room and said to his wife, "I'm leaving tomorrow morning to do some business. Could you take my old clothes and put them right here?"

The fact is, A-chi had discussed his plan only with his mistress, so even his wife had been kept in the dark. Greatly taken by surprise by his sudden move, she asked, "Where are you going? What sort of business are you going to do?"

A-chi then told her the story. She said, "Ai-ya! Where do you get such ideas! Old as you are, you've never been engaged in business matters before. Just by what means and schemes did you manage to get this capital? The money of a widow

27

and her orphans is their very life and blood. If anything goes wrong, not only will they become a laughingstock, but they will also be deprived of their lifelong savings, not to mention the regret you will suffer for the rest of your life. Take my advice and return the money to the mistress immediately. Instead, we'll rise early and go to bed late, work on the farm as before, only harder. That way, we may live in peace."

A-chi said, "What do you know, wife? You're talking nonsense. How do you know that I'm no good in business? How do you know I'll spoil the whole thing before I even start?"

And so without paying any more attention to his wife, he went to prepare his clothes and bedding himself. He had no bag in which to keep them, so he had to make a bundle. He also made a waist bag and prepared some dry provisions. He then went to market to buy an umbrella and a pair of hempen sandals.

With everything ready, next morning he went first to Hsü Yen and Hsü Chao and said, "I'm going to take a trip today to do some business. There will be no one at home to take care of the family. Although the families have separated, I still hope that you two gentlemen will kindly look after the widow and the orphans."

When the two Hsü brothers heard this, they could not help laughing secretly, and they replied, "That's something you don't have to worry about. Just remember when you've made some money to bring us some presents when you return."

"Of course," A-chi said; then he turned around and went home. There he ate and bid farewell to his mistress. He put on his hempen sandals, placed the bundle and the umbrella on his back, and again reminded his wife to be constantly watchful. As he was about to go out the gate, Yen-shih repeatedly urged him to take care. A-chi nodded in assent, and with a firm tread, he set out.

Meanwhile the Hsü brothers waited until A-chi had left, then laughed and said, "It's so ridiculous that third sister-in-law doesn't have any common sense. Instead of consulting us about business matters, she listened to the words of that old slave and entrusted her money to him. Since he has never done any business before, how can he have any experience? No doubt about it, he's swindled the widow and orphans, just for the sake of having a good time himself. So our sister-in-law's capital has already gone down the drain."

Hsü Chao said, "Before the family was separated, she didn't bring the money out to use. Now that we've just divided, she gave the money to A-chi to do business with. What's more, since our third sister-in-law didn't come to our family with very much of a dowry, the money she gave A-chi must have been siphoned off by our third brother when father was alive."

"In any case, our third sister-in-law has bypassed us to do business. But if we stop her, then people will say we're just jealous. So we'll just wait until A-chi returns with every penny lost; then we'll have a good laugh at her." Truly:

Observe the melee from the clouds above.
Who wins, who loses in the end?
The strength of the horse can be tested only by the length of its
*   journey.*
Man's heart will be revealed only through the passage of time.

While traveling, A-chi thought constantly, "What trade would be best to try?" Then suddenly an idea dawned on him: "I've heard that it is profitable to deal in lacquer; besides, the place is close by. Why not give it a try?"

Having made up his mind, he went straight to the Ch'ing-yün Mountain,[8] a place where lacquer had traditionally been produced and where sales were conducted through agents. A-chi stopped at a wholesale house. There were many customers lining up for their turns.

[8] This mountain has yet to be located. Judging from the fact that A-chi's trading activity was basically limited to Chekiang and the neighboring provinces of Kiangsu and Fukien, it is possible that this mountain is within the same area.

A-chi thought, "How can I afford the time and money to wait my turn?"

He came up with a plan. Making an excuse, he dragged the wholesaler to a village tavern, where he treated him to a few cups of wine, and said, "I'm a small dealer with little capital. I can't afford the time to wait for days. Since we both come from the same place, I hope you will do me a favor and put me on the priority list. The next time I come around, I'll treat you to a great feast."

It happened that this wholesaler had a real thirst for wine. Having received A-chi's favor, he felt obliged to accommodate him and grant his request.

That evening, the wholesaler went to each villager's house to collect the amount of lacquer requested and stored it in the containers. Afraid that the traders would protest should they discover this, he deposited the lacquer at a neighbor's, and the next day he rose at the fifth watch and sent A-chi on his way.

A-chi was delighted that he had such a good start in business. He instructed the porters to carry the goods out to the mouth of the Hsin-an River.[9] Then he had a second thought: "As Hangchow[10] is not far from here, I don't think I can get a good price for it there." Subsequently he hired a boat and went straight to Soochow.[11]

It just happened that there was a shortage of lacquer in Soochow. When the people saw his cargo arrive, it was received like precious jewels. In less than three days it was sold out. All the transactions were done in cash and nothing was done on credit. Subtracting his expenses, he cleared more than a hundred percent profit. After giving thanks to Heaven and Earth, he quickly gathered his things together and continued on his trip. But then he thought, "I must return by boat, and yet I have no cargo. Carrying this money with me is a heavy responsibility. Why don't I carry along some other type of goods and make some more profit?"

After making some inquiries, he learned that a great quantity of rice had arrived at Feng-ch'iao,[12] and the price had forthwith fallen quite a bit. "I'll bet I would make a few taels if I took in some rice," he said to himself.

He bought more than sixty piculs of rice and went straight to Hangchow to sell it. It was then the middle of the seventh month, and there had been no rain in Hangchow for a month. The rice sprouts had all dried up and been ruined, so the price of rice had soared.

Since each picul in A-chi's load was a little more than the standard weight, he made a further profit of more than ten taels of silver. He said to himself, "It's indeed fortunate that my business ventures have all been successful. I think it must be due to the good luck of my mistress."

Just then another idea came to his mind: "While I'm here, why don't I go ask about the price of lacquer? Since it's not far from Soochow, I could even save some traveling expenses."

After some careful inquiries, he found out that the price here was even much higher than in Soochow. You may ask, why? Those who traded in lacquer all assumed that since Hangchow was close by, the price would be low. Since all the traders left for faraway places, there was always a shortage in Hangchow. As the common saying

[9] Originating in southern Anhwei Province, the Hsin-an River cuts eastward through Chekiang Province, with its name changed a few times in different sections, until it reaches Hangchow under the name of the Ch'ien-t'ang River before it flows into the sea. From its source to Chien-te in central Chekiang, it is generally known as the Hsin-an River.
[10] Situated at the mouth of the Ch'ien-t'ang River, Hangchow, including the West Lake area to the west of the city, has for almost a thousand years been a center of art, literature, scholarship, and Buddhism. As the capital of the Southern Sung Dynasty, it became synonymous with the fabulous material culture the period was famous for. After the Sung period, it has remained to the present day a place celebrated for its incomparable scenic beauty.
[11] Situated in Southwestern Kiangsu Province, close to the border with Chekiang Province and some fifty miles to the west of Shanghai, Soochow is a city celebrated for its scenic beauty, cultural heritage, textile products, and handicrafts.

[12] In northeastern Chekiang.

goes, "Goods have no true value; that which is scarce is expensive." Because of this, the price of lacquer in Hangchow is higher than in other areas. When A-chi learned of this, he was overjoyed and immediately departed for Ch'ing-yün Mountain in the middle of the night.

He had prepared in advance some gifts for the wholesaler, and as before he treated him to a few cups of wine. When the wholesaler received these favors, his face broke into broad smiles. He repeated his former actions and quietly sent A-chi first on his way.

In less than two or three days after his arrival in Hangchow, the lacquer was sold out. When he figured the profit against the capital, it was several taels more, though it was less than the profit he had made on the first trip. He said to himself, "Next time I might as well go to a more distant place."

He settled his accounts with the middleman, gathered his things together, and started his journey. But then he thought, "I've been away from home for quite some time now; the mistress must certainly be anxious. I should go back to give her a report so that she won't have to worry on my account."

But he changed his mind again: "There's always a delay of two days in collecting the lacquer; why not go first to the mountain, take the money, and tell the wholesaler to get things ready ahead of time. After that I'll return home; isn't that more convenient both ways?"

Having made up his mind, he went to the mountain, handed over the money to the middleman, and returned home. Truly:

His first trade in lacquer yields a twofold profit.
His first venture reaps good results.

Meanwhile, Yen-shih had lived in suspense from morning until night since A-chi left. Her constant cause for worry was that A-chi might have lost her capital. Furthermore, she picked up rumors spread by the two brothers behind her back, and she was plagued with even more misgivings.

One day as she was just sitting in the house in silent melancholy, she suddenly saw her two boys enter and call out in a befuddled manner, "A-chi has come back."

When Yen-shih heard this, she ran anxiously out to meet him. There was A-chi, already standing before her. His wife, too, was following behind him. A-chi came forward and bowed deeply. The sight of A-chi made her heart flutter, for she was fearful that what he was going to say would shatter her hopes.

"What business did you do? Have you made some profit?" she asked.

A-chi folded his hands over his heart, and replied calmly, "First, I'm grateful to Heaven and Earth for their protection. Second, thanks to your blessings for my good fortune. I dealt in the lacquer business, and I've made a five- to sixfold profit. It was like this and that; this way and that way. I was afraid that you'd worry about me, so I've returned just to give you a report."

Yen-shih was exhilarated when she heard this, and she asked, "Where's the money now?"

"I didn't bring it back but left it with my wholesaler to collect some lacquer," said A-chi. "Tomorrow morning I'll leave again."

The whole family was in a blissful mood. A-chi rested one night, and at dawn the next day he set out again. After saying good-bye to Yen-shih, he returned to the Ch'ing-yün Mountain.

Now let us speak of the Hsü brothers, who had been to a party at a neighbor's that evening, and were dead drunk. Because of this, they knew nothing of A-chi's return. The next day they went over together and asked, "We heard that A-chi has returned from his venture in business. How much money has he made?"

Yen-shih replied, "I'm happy to tell you, uncles, that he has traded in the lacquer business, and has made a five- to sixfold profit."

Hsü Yen said, "Such good luck! If he keeps up like that, before long, you'll be a rich woman."

"Please don't make fun of us," said Yen-shih. "If we can manage to avoid hunger and cold, I'll be more than satisfied."

Hsü Chao asked, "Where is he now? How long has he been gone? Why didn't he come to see me? Such impertinence!"

"He left at dawn this morning," Yen-shih replied.

"Why did he leave so quickly?" said Hsü Chao.

"How about the money?" Hsü Yen asked. "Have you had a look at it?"

"He said that he had left it with his wholesaler to buy goods," said Yen-shih. "He didn't carry it back home."

At this Hsü Yen guffawed. "I thought that the capital and profit had already been placed in your hands. Now what he said is merely empty words. He has indeed filled your eyes and left your stomach hungry. Although he has made quite a clamoring in your ear, you still don't know where the money is, where the profit is. You just accepted what he said as truth. Since he's a broker, his left hand doesn't trust his right hand; how could he return home and leave the money with an outsider? As I see it, most probably he has squandered the capital, and used these lies to deceive you."

"Sister," said Hsü Chao, also taking his turn, "actually, we're not supposed to meddle in your family's problems. But after all, you're a woman and are not well informed about the affairs of the outside world. Since you had the money, you should have consulted the two of us, and we would have advised you to buy a few *mou* of land. That would have been a good long-range plan. That A-chi, what business does he know? And yet, you left us in the dark and gave him the money to fool around with. I think the capital was either part of your dowry or third brother's personal savings. Since it wasn't anything stolen, how can you treat it so lightly?"

As the two brothers took turns attacking her servant, not only did she have no way to contradict them, but she herself gradually became suspicious of A-chi's intentions. The result was that her daylong happiness shrank to various kinds of sorrow and anxiety. But we shall say no more of this for the moment.

Meanwhile, A-chi had returned to the Ch'ing-yün Mountain with great speed. The trader had everything prepared; the goods were marked off and handed over.

This time A-chi did not sell the lacquer in Soochow or Hangchow, but he headed straight for the Hsing-hua area,[13] where the profit was even better. When he had sold his goods, he learned that the price of rice there was one tael for three piculs, and that the measurements used were larger than the standard ones. He recalled that Hangchow was suffering from a shortage at present, and that he had earned a profit on his previous trip there. Now if he bought rice in the producing area, very likely he could double his profit.

Thus, he loaded up a large cart with rice and set off for Hangchow. He sold the rice at exactly one tael and two pennies per picul. The excess from the oversize measurements alone was enough to pay for his transportation expenses.

Among the lacquer traders on the mountain, he was now regarded as a big customer, and whenever he came, the wholesaler was full of compliments. Partly owing to Yen-shih's destined good fortune, and partly owing to A-chi's shrewdness in his business dealings, he realized great profits from whatever commodities he traded in. As he made several good deals in succession, he accumulated more than two thousand taels.

Seeing that it was getting close to the end of the year, he reminded himself, "I'm carrying too much money for one old man. It's too much of a

[13] A prefecture of the Ming and Ch'ing dynasties on the eastern seaboard of central Fukien Province.

31

gamble. If I should make a slip, all the earnings would be lost. As it's getting close to the end of the year, those at home must be expecting me. I think it is best for me to go home and look into the possibility of buying some lands to serve as our base. After that I can take what remains and go out again to try my luck."

At this time he had all equipment necessary for taking a business trip. All he needed to do was to wrap the taels tightly one by one and conceal them in a waist pouch. By boat and on hired horses, he traveled by night and rested by day because he didn't want to take any risks. He reached home in a few days and immediately carried the luggage in.

When his wife saw that her husband had returned, she reported to Yen-shih, who received the news with both happiness and dread. She was happy because A-chi had returned, but she was afraid because she did not know how had he fared in business. Because the Hsü brothers had mocked her previously, she was now even more worried than before.

Taking three steps in two, she ran to the outer hall, where she gazed at the pile of luggage A-chi had brought in. She recognized that this did not resemble the effects of one who has failed in business and her heart calmed down a bit. However, she still could not help asking, "How did this latest business fare? Did you bring home the money?"

A-chi came forward, bowed, and said, "Don't worry, mistress. I'll report to you all the details." He moved all the luggage into Yen-shih's room, took out the silver taels which he had wrapped one by one, and handed them over to Yen-shih.

At the sight of so much money, Yen-shih was overcome with joy. At once she opened the chests and the baskets to store the money. A-chi then related to her all his business ventures. Because Yen-shih was afraid to stir up trouble, she did not mention a word of what Hsü Yen had said to her that day. Instead, she praised A-chi over and over. "We owe everything to you. Please go and rest." She also reminded him, "If the uncles come to make inquiries, you mustn't tell them the true story."

"I understand," A-chi said.

As he was talking, there was a knock on the door outside. It turned out to be none other than the Hsü brothers, who had heard that A-chi had returned. They had come to hear the news.

A-chi stepped forward and made two deep bows.

Hsü Yen said, "I heard that you had a stroke of good fortune in your early business ventures. Have you made as much profit as last time in this trip?"

A-chi said, "Thanks for your concern. After I've deducted the capital and traveling expenses, I've made a profit of some forty or fifty taels."

Hsü Chao said, "Ai-ya, the last time you said you had a five- to sixfold profit. This time, how come you've been away again for so long and come back with less?"

"Don't mind the profit, great or little," Hsü Yen said. "I'd just like to know whether he has brought the money back this time!"

"I have already handed it over to the mistress," A-chi said.

Then the two men turned around and left without saying anything.

After A-chi had consulted Yen-shih about the purchase of some lands, he quietly engaged someone to look for good prospects. In general, a wealthy man produces a spendthrift. There was a powerful family named Yen in this Brocade Sand Village. They were extremely wealthy and had acres and acres of land. They had only one son by the name of Shih-pao, which connotes, "the property can be kept for generations." However, this Yen Shih-pao had no specialty except gambling. This gambler of a son had so outraged the father that he finally died of despair. Because Yen Shih-pao was such a spendthrift, the villagers had replaced his name with a homonym meaning "Spend-It-All." Together with a band of good-for-nothings, Spend-It-All devoted his life to all pursuits of pleasure day and night, finally using up the family cash and valuables. Then he began to sell the family lands. He said that since this selling of odds and ends did not produce the sums needed, he would gladly throw out a thousand *mou* for sale if someone could offer him more than three thousand taels in cash in one payment.

Although there were wealthy people in the village, they could not raise so much money at one time. Thus he had no offers. As time went by, with the end of the year approaching, Spend-It-All felt more pressed for money. He was willing to take half the price with a farmhouse as a bonus.

By chance A-chi got word of this and immediately sent a broker to obtain details about the property. Afraid that someone else might buy it first, he made an agreement to complete the transaction the next day.

When Spend-It-All heard that there was a buyer, he was delighted. Usually he would not spend even a minute at home, but this day he did not take a step out of the door. He was waiting for the broker to take him to A-chi.

Meanwhile, A-chi had a feeling that Spend-It-All was some sort of a gourmet. With this in mind, the first thing he did early in the morning was to have the cook prepare some extra delicacies and fine wine for him. Then he said to Yen-shih, "The transaction today is no small matter. Mistress, you're a woman, and the two masters are too young. I'm only a servant who can't speak on your behalf while negotiating with him. It would be more proper to invite the uncles next door to come serve as witnesses."

"Go over and invite them, then," said Yen-shih.

A-chi went immediately to Hsü Yen's doorway; the brothers were talking just inside the door. A-chi said, "Today the mistress is buying a few *mou* of land. She asked me especially to come and invite you gentlemen to oversee the transaction for her."

Although the two assented verbally, in their hearts they were quite unhappy that Yen-shih had not entrusted them with doing it for her in the first place.

Hsü Yen said, "Since she wanted to buy some land, why didn't she ask you and me instead of A-chi? She didn't even care to tell us until the deal is about to close. I wonder where they found small pieces of land to buy in this village?"

Hsü Chao said, "Just be patient. The suspense will soon be over."

The two men sat and waited at the entrance until almost noon, when they saw Spend-It-All, accompanied by several brokers and two servants carrying a card case, come smiling, clapping his hands, and tapping his feet all along the way. All entered the door on the other side of the partition.

When the Hsü Yen brothers saw this they were really startled. "Wow! How strange! I heard that Spend-It-All wanted to sell a thousand *mou* of land at a fixed price of more than three thousand taels. I don't believe third sister-in-law has so much money! Is it possible that Spend-It-All has changed his mind and is willing to sell it piecemeal?" They were overwhelmed with suspense. Then they followed the group into the house. After they had exchanged greetings, the guests and the hosts were seated separately.

A-chi came forward and said, "Master Yen, we already discussed and settled the price of the land yesterday. We'll stick to the agreement, and will not reduce the offer. On your part, Master Yen, you'll please also keep your own word to avoid any possible complications."

Spend-It-All protested, "When a man of honor has given his word in doing business, even a team of four horses cannot retrieve it. If I've made any change, call me any name you want."

A-chi said, "If such is the case, we'll draw up the deed and then weigh the silver."

The paper, ink, brush, and ink-slab were all ready and had only to be brought over. Spend-It-All took up the brush and settled the deal by writing a contractual agreement. Then he said, "To save you from worry, I'll first draw up a draft contract, how would that be?"

"That would be fine," said A-chi.

The Hsü brothers saw on the contract that it really was for a thousand *mou* of land and a farmhouse at the selling price of one thousand five hundred taels. Stunned, the two men stared at each other, their tongues hanging out—for a long time they were not able to draw them back in. Both secretly thought, "A-chi certainly has made money in business, but it couldn't be this much! Could it be that he's been a robber, or dug up a hidden treasure? It's really beyond me."

After the brokers had finished signing the papers, A-chi handed the document over to Yen-shih. He had already borrowed a scale, which he set on the table. Together with Yen-shih, he took out the silver to weigh; it was all pure silver.

Fire blazed in the eyes of Hsü Yen and Hsü Chao, and smoke rushed out from their throats. Would that they could push everyone aside, take it all, and go!

After a while the weighing was finished, and a feast was set on the table. They drank until late at night before they dispersed.

The next day A-chi said to Yen-shih, "That farmhouse is extremely big; why not move over there to live? It would be easier for us to take care of storing the harvested rice."

Aware that the Hsü brothers were jealous, Yen-shih herself was only too eager to stay away from them. She went along with A-chi's suggestion, and selected the sixth day of the first month of the year to move to the new house.

A-chi also employed a tutor for the instruction of the two young masters, Hsü K'uan, the elder, and Hsü Hung, the younger.

The household was now completely put in order. Seeing Yen-shih purchase a thousand *mou* of land, the villagers all spread rumors that she had discovered some hidden treasure, and that she had a fabulous amount of silver. Even the night stool, as the rumor had it, was made of silver. Who would not come to curry favor with her?

After helping Yen-shih settle the family, A-chi went out to do business as before. This time he dealt not only in lacquer but in whatever he heard was profitable. What the family had gathered in rice and grain they used to increase their capital in business.

Ten years later the property of the family had multiplied many times. All of Spend-It-All's lands and houses eventually fell into Yen-shih's hands. Their courtyard was bustling with visitors. They had herds of oxen and horses. Servants, hired farmhands, and such numbered a hundred. What a picture of prosperity! Truly:

Starting from nothing, riches and honor
Are gained through a willingness to toil.
I ask you to behold the lazy, idle ones;
Their faces carry the aspect of hunger and cold.

Later Yen-shih's three daughters were all married into neighboring wealthy families. Hsü K'uan and Hsü Hung, too, each took a wife. A-chi managed all the bethrothal gifts for the brides and bridegrooms; Yen-shih didn't have to move a little finger for all these arrangements.

A-chi also learned that with their extensive property, they would have to pay heavy taxes. He purchased for Hsü K'uan and his brother the title of students of imperial academies and thus exempted them from certain land taxes.

Yen-shih saw to it that A-chi's son took a wife. Realizing that A-chi was in his failing years, she kept him at home to manage affairs and did not permit him to leave home. She also allotted horses for his carriage.

From when he first went into business, A-chi had never himself eaten anything fancy, had never had a fine suit of clothes made for himself. He would first ask Yen-shih's permission before he would use a small piece of silk. Moreover, he was a stickler for the social proprieties. Should he see one of the clansmen, no matter whether the fellow was young or old, A-chi would naturally stand up. If he met clansmen when he was riding, he would get down and move out of the way to the side of the road; he would not proceed until they had passed him. Because of this, there was not one relative or neighbor who did not respect A-chi. Even Yen-shih and her children treated him like a venerable elder.

As for Hsü Yen and Hsü Chao, although they also had earned some landed property, it was still as far from Yen-shih's property as heaven is from earth. They always openly showed their jealousy. A-chi was aware of their sentiments, and advised Yen-shih to give each of them a hundred taels in cash. He also had a new grave mound erected to bury Hsü Che's father and mother together.

The old servant lived in good health until he was eighty years old, when he fell sick. Yen-shih wanted to call in a doctor to attend to him, but he said, "When a man gets to be eighty, death is a natural ending. Why waste money?" He stood firm on this and refused to take any medicine.

Yen-shih and her children took turns waiting at his bedside, at the same time preparing the funeral clothing and the coffin.

A-chi lay in bed for several days, and gradually his condition worsened. Then he asked Yen-shih and her children to come into the house and sit down, and he said, "I've now used up my strength, and I shall leave this world without regrets. However, there's one thing in which I may have overstepped my bounds, and for which I must ask your forgiveness."

With tears falling, Yen-shih said, "What we've got today we owe to you. Whatever instructions you may want to give us, we'll carry them out."

A-chi took out from beside his pillow two documents and handed them over to Yen-shih. He said, "The two young masters have already grown up; later on they're bound to press for a division

of the property. If they should then argue about their shares, the intimate relationship between brothers would be destroyed. Because of this, long ago I took all the lands, houses, property, and such things and divided them into equal parts. Today I hand them over to the two young masters, so that each one will control his possessions."

He further enjoined them, "It's not easy to find an honest man from among the servants. Watch over your interests yourself; don't entrust them to others so easily."

Restraining their tears, Yen-shih and her children received his parting words. A-chi's wife and his son both stood before his bed weeping, and he also had a few words for them. Suddenly he said, "There's one thing I feel uneasy about. I have not said good-bye face to face with the two uncles. Could you go and invite them over?"

Yen-shih immediately sent a servant with this special request. Hsü Yen and Hsü Chao said, "In good times he wouldn't even lift a finger to help us. He thinks of us only when he is about to die. What impertinence! No, we won't go!"

There was nothing the servant could do but turn back. So Hsü Hung himself had to hurry over to invite them. The two men did not want to offend their nephew and so they reluctantly followed him. The old man could no longer speak. He just looked at them a couple of times, nodded his head, and passed away.

That his own wife, son, and daughter-in-law were all thrown into deep mourning for him needs no mentioning here. Even Yen-shih and her children all broke into wails of grief. All the domestic help in the household, old and young, male and female, shed tears while recalling A-chi's many kindnesses and virtues. Only Hsü Yen and Hsü Chao, on the contrary, looked pleased.

Pitiable that the old man:

Toiled like a silkworm spinning its cocoon;
When the cocoon becomes silk, the silkworm dies.

35

He also resembled the bee gathering pollen to make honey,
Whose sweetness in the end is only to be harvested by people.

Yen-shih and her children wept for some time, and then went out to prepare for the funeral. When Hsü Yen and Hsü Chao saw that both the coffin and the clothing were of excellent quality, they dragged Hsü K'uan and his brother to one side and said, "He was just a servant of the family; an ordinary funeral would be quite enough. Why waste so much money to give him such a pompous burial? Even your grandfather and father did not have such impressive arrangements."

Hsü K'uan said, "My family's fortune was all of his making. We would feel guilty if we did not give him a proper funeral."

Hsü Chao said smilingly, "You're a grown-up man now, but you are still an innocent. It was your family's destiny to have this good luck; how could it be attributed to his ability? One more thing: since he was in business for so many years, he must have cut a big slice for his private hoard, which you don't even know about. And now you're using your own money for his purpose!"

Hsü Hung said, "You shouldn't speak ill of him this way! I've observed him daily and discovered that he honestly handed over to my mother even the smallest change. I certainly don't think he has any private hoard."

"The hoard he made must be hidden somewhere," Hsü Chao said. "Do you think he would be foolish enough to let you see it? If you don't believe me, let's search that house now. I believe at the very least he has a thousand in silver."

"Even if this is the case, it's his earnings," said Hsü K'uan. "How can we take what's legally his?"

"Even if you don't want to take it," said Hsü Yen, "there's no harm in taking a look to prove my point."

The words of the uncles gave the two brothers some cause for misgiving. As a result, without informing Yen-shih, they all went to A-chi's house,

made up an excuse to send all the servants away, closed the door, opened the chests and the baskets, and searched everything. Not a penny was found, nothing but a few old clothes.

Hsü Chao said, "He must have hidden it in his son's house. Let's go there."

They discovered a parcel with not more than two taels of silver in it. Within the parcel was an account. Hsu K'uan read it carefully. The money was actually the remainder of the three taels of silver that Yen-shih had given A-chi's son at the time of his marriage.

Hsü Hung said, "Didn't I say that he has no private hoard? See what we've done? if we don't hurry and put things back in order and if someone should run into us at this moment, what would they think?"

Having lost face, Hsü Yen and Hsü Chao went straight home without taking leave of Yen-shih. When Hsü K'uan reported this to his mother, she was all the more saddened. She had the whole family put on mourning, and gave order for mourning ceremonies to begin. In a great way they made their final tribute to A-chi.

After the forty-nine days of mourning, A-chi was buried beside the new grave mound. Everything for the burial ceremony was conducted most generously.

As Hsü K'uan and his brother recalled how loyal, diligent, and frugal A-chi had been in his lifetime, and that he had no savings to his name, they could no longer bear to treat his wife and children as servants. After the burial sacrifices were finished, they bestowed on her some property and silver totaling over a thousand taels, so that she could live her life independently.

The people of the neighborhood all filed a joint petition to the authorities, requesting that A-chi be granted posthumous recognition. After the local authorities had made an investigation, they sent a report to their superiors, who in turn drew up a memorandum for the emperor's attention.

The emperor graciously issued a decree that an honorary arch be erected as a testimonial to A-chi's loyalty.

From then on the descendants of this branch of the Hsü family were prolific, and the wealthiest in Ch'un-an. A-chi's descendants were also quite prosperous. Indeed:

Advanced in years, muscles failing, and placed on the same footing with horses and oxen,
With a thousand in cash he bought an estate which surpassed all others.
With a clear conscience he carried out his trust to care for the orphans.
Those servants who have no sense of righteousness should be ashamed.

THE KNIGHT-ERRANT

The figure of the righteous man-at-arms as a champion of justice (*hsia*) is one of the perennial favorites celebrated in traditional Chinese literature. Lacking an equivalent in English, we have used "knight-errant" as a matter of convenience for *hsia* and its variants. It goes without saying that the Chinese knight-errant referred to here is the product of a culture very different from that of medieval Europe.

The Chinese knight-errant is usually seen as a man of extraordinary martial skill (his outward appearance often belies his inward strength) and spiritual discipline. Subscribing to what seems to us to be a very narrow and personal code of honor, he would often offer his services in the name of justice and benevolence to anyone who happens to cater to his fancy. The adventure of Chao K'uang-yin (in "The Sung Founder Escorts Ching-niang One Thousand *Li*") fits this description well. From a woman's point of view, however, one wonders if Chao is the savior or the murderer in this story.

A Chinese knight-errant may offer his service to someone not so much for the defense of justice as for the sake of returning the favors he has received from the one who appreciates him. Ching K'o (in "Prince Tan of Yen") risks his life to assassinate the king of Ch'in nominally for a national cause, but he is actually performing the act of reciprocation expected of him after being so lavishly treated by Prince Tan. The rather strange behavior of Officer Ku in "Wu-shuang the Peerless" cannot be properly understood without reference to the principle of *pao* (reciprocation) in traditional Chinese society.

39

THE BIOGRAPHY OF YÜ JANG

From *Shih-chi*

TRANSLATED BY WILLIAM H. NIENHAUSER, JR.

Yü Jang was a man of the state of Chin.[1] For-merly he had served the heads of the Fan and Chung-hang clans, but found no means of gain-ing recognition. He left them and served the earl of Chih, who truly honored and favored him. When the earl made war on Lord Hsiang of Chao, Lord Hsiang conspired with the states of Han and Wei[2] to annihilate the earl. After elimi-nating him, they divided his lands into three parts. Lord Hsiang felt such great enmity for the earl of Chih that he lacquered the latter's skull and made it into a drinking cup.

Yü Jang fled to the mountains and said with a sigh: "For a man to die for one who understood him is like a woman making herself pretty for one who loves her. Since the earl of Chih understood me, I should sacrifice my life to avenge him. If I can repay him in this way, my soul need not be ashamed." Then changing his name and taking on the guise of a criminal,[3] he entered the palace as a criminal sentenced to hard labor so that he could work at repairing the privy. With a dagger hidden under his clothes, he hoped to stab Lord Hsiang.

When Lord Hsiang went to the privy, he be-came suspicious and questioned the criminal working there. Yü Jang was found to be conceal-ing a weapon.

"I wanted to avenge the earl of Chih," Yü de-clared.

The lord's attendants wanted to execute him, but Lord Hsiang said, "He's a righteous man. Out of respect I can only avoid him. The earl of Chih died with no heir, and yet this subordinate of his wanted to avenge him. He is truly one of the world's worthy men." Finally, he had Yü released.

After a short time, Yü Jang smeared his body with lacquer to make it appear leprous, swallowed charcoal to make his voice harsh, made his out-ward appearance unrecognizable, and came beg-ging in the marketplace. Even his wife failed to

[1] Chin was one of the major states toward the end of the Spring and Autumn period; its territory covered the land be-tween the southern part of the present Shansi Province and the southern part of Hopei Province.

[2] Chao, Han, and Wei were three of the seven major states in the Warring States period. Chao encompassed the southern part of the present Hopei Province, the eastern part of Shansi Province, and the land to the north of the Yellow River in Honan Province. Han included the eastern part of Shensi Province and the northwestern part of Honan. Wei spanned the northern part of modern Honan and the southwestern part of Shansi Province. These lands were built primarily on the former territory of Chin.

[3] Or, perhaps, mutilating himself to gain the appearance of a criminal (various mutilations such as tatooing or amputation were used as punishments then).

recognize him. He met a friend who did know him and said, "Aren't you Yü Jang?"

"Yes, I am."

In tears, his friend said, "With your talents, if you offered your service to Lord Hsiang, you'd surely be admitted as a close aide. Once you're so accepted, you could do what you've been desiring. Wouldn't that be a lot easier? Would this not be a simpler way to avenge yourself on Lord Hsiang than causing hurt to your person and making yourself suffer?"

"If I were to present myself as his servant," Yü Jang replied, "and yet seek to kill him, I'd be harboring two minds in serving one lord. What I am doing now calls for great sacrifice. But the very reason I'm doing it is to bring shame to those later subordinates who serve their lords with two minds." Then he left.

Some time later, soon after Lord Hsiang left his residence, Yü Jang hid under a bridge over which Lord Hsiang was to pass. When the lord reached the bridge, his horse shied, and he said, "Yü Jang must be here!" He sent men to investigate and, indeed, it was Yü Jang. Thereupon Lord Hsiang reprimanded him: "Did you not formerly serve the houses of Fan and Chung-hang? The earl of Chih destroyed them, and yet you sought no revenge but offered your service to him. Now that the earl is dead, why in this instance alone do you feel such a pressing need for revenge?"

"When I served Fan and Chung-hang, they both treated me like a common fellow, and I therefore repaid them as an ordinary fellow might. But the earl treated me like a man of national eminence, and I thus must requite him as a man of national eminence should."

Lord Hsiang sighed deeply and in tears said, "Alas for you, Yü Jang! What you did for the earl of Chih won you a great name. I pardoned you once and that was the limit of what I could do for you. You should have known it, for now I cannot release you again." He then ordered his soldiers to surround Yü Jang.

"I've heard that an enlightened sovereign does not conceal the merits of a man," Yü Jang said, "and a loyal servant has the duty to die for his name. Formerly, my lord, you pardoned me and there was no one in the empire who did not praise your magnanimity. For what I've done today, I'll certainly suffer death, but I beseech you to let me strike at your robes as a gesture of revenge so that I can thereby die without regret. I don't dare to hope for your consent, but am merely taking the liberty of disclosing what is in my heart."

Then Lord Hsiang, feeling that there was nothing more righteous to do, ordered a servant to take his robes to Yü Jang. Yü Jang drew his sword, leaped three times,[4] and struck them, calling out, "Now I will be able to face the earl of Chih down below!" Then he fell on his sword and died. On that day all those men of a kindred spirit in Chao shed tears for him.

[4] Leaping was a ritual means for expressing extreme grief.

PRINCE TAN OF YEN

From *Yen Tan-tzu*

TRANSLATED BY PETER RUSHTON AND THE EDITORS

Prince Tan of Yen was ill-treated by the king of Ch'in when he was held as a goodwill hostage there.[1] Troubled by this, the prince wanted to return home. The king ignored his request, and said sarcastically, "If you can make the crows' heads turn white and horses grow horns, then you may leave." Prince Tan gazed up to heaven and sighed, whereupon the crows' heads did indeed turn white and the horses grew horns.

The king, much against his will, was obliged to let the prince go. He built a booby-trapped bridge in the hope of ensnaring the prince, but the latter crossed the bridge safely as the trap failed to work. At night when he reached a border pass, the gate was closed. He imitated a cock crowing and the neighborhood cocks soon followed suit; thus the prince was able to make his escape.[2]

His resentment of Ch'in was deep-seated and he longed for revenge. He did all he could to support brave knights. In a letter to his mentor Ch'ü Wu, the prince wrote:

Tan, so unworthy, was born in a rustic country and brought up in a barren land. I have never had an opportunity to receive the refined instructions of a learned and noble man, or the principles of an enlightened person. However, there is something which I humbly wish to lay before you, and it would be fortunate indeed if you, my teacher, would condescend to look into the matter. I have heard that what causes a man's shame is to be disgraced and yet live in this world. What shames a worthy maid is to have her chastity violated. For these reasons there have been those who would stand having their throats cut and those who would not flee from the boiling cauldron. Could it be that they relished death and abhorred life? It is because in their hearts they valued something else more. Recently the king of Ch'in has violated the heavenly ordained human relationships, and he acts like a tiger or wolf. Of all the feudal lords, he was the most ill-mannered in his treatment of me. Each time I think of this I am mortified to my very marrow. Yet I am fully aware that the state of Yen is no match for Ch'in, and that we do not have the strength to oppose them in the long run. Therefore I intend to gather the country's brave knights and all the heroes within the four seas; I am prepared to offer what we have in this country and empty the national treasury to support them. With lavish gifts and sweet words we can

[1] Yen and Ch'in were among the last few contending states of the Warring States period that still survived after the collapse of the Eastern Chou Dynasty, the nominal central authority, in the year 256 B.C. The territory of Yen was roughly equal to the modern provinces of Hopei and Liaoning. Ch'in was the largest and westernmost of all the states, with all the Chinese territory to the west of Ch'ang-an County in modern Shensi. In point of fact, Prince Tan left Ch'in in 232 B.C.

[2] The reason was that the gatekeeper, on hearing the crowing, thought that it was already dawn and opened the gate.

purchase the good will of Ch'in. If Ch'in covets our presents and believes our words, then a single sword will do the job of an army of a million. In a moment's time my endless shame will be removed. Otherwise while I am alive I will have no courage to face the world and when I die I will harbor resentment down in the Nine Springs.[3] The heads of the other states will surely point to this and laugh. Worse still, no one can tell who will possess the land north of the Yi River.[4] This undoubtedly will be the shame of you and the other officials of this state as well. I respectfully send this letter in the hope that you will give it due consideration.

Ch'ü Wu in his letter of response said:

I have heard that "He who makes hasty decisions will fail in his action, and he who is bent on vengeance injures his nature." At present, Your Highness wishes to rid yourself of your anger and shame and remove your deep-rooted resentment. This is truly something your servant should not evade, though it may mean that his body will be pulverized and his head smashed to pieces. I understand that the wise do not hope for good luck in attaining their merit, and the clear-headed do not act on impulse alone in order to indulge the desires of their hearts. Only when the plan cannot fail does one proceed; only when one's security is guaranteed does one act. In this way one can initiate an action without making a faulty start and can execute it without danger of stumbling. In spite of Your Highness's high regard for individual valor and faith in individual effort to achieve your goal, I cannot but beg to conclude that this is simply rashness on your part. I propose that we form an alliance with Ch'u, unite our strength with Chao, and join with Han and Wei.[5] Only then can we hope to confront Ch'in, for then Ch'in can be destroyed. Though it would seem that Han and Wei are on intimate terms with Ch'in, this is

only an appearance. If you were to raise an expeditionary force, then Ch'u would come in response, and Han and Wei would surely follow. It is apparent just how great a force this would be. If Your Highness follows my strategy, your insult will be avenged, and as for your humble servant, my worries will be resolved as well. Your Highness, please give my proposal careful consideration.

The prince was not happy to receive this letter. He summoned Ch'ü Wu to pursue the matter further with him. Ch'ü Wu said, "I believe that if Your Highness follows my advice, all the lands north of the Yi River will never have cause to worry about Ch'in, and all the neighboring states will seek us out for assistance."

"But this dallying will not do; I don't have the patience to wait," the prince replied.

"I've given due consideration to this matter," Ch'ü Wu responded. "In our policy toward Ch'in, it is better to proceed deliberately than hastily. If we join with Ch'u and Chao, and ally with Han and Wei, the strategy may take some time; but it will surely be accomplished. This is what I consider most practical."

In the midst of this, the prince lay down in his bed and did not listen. Ch'ü Wu then said, "As I'm not able to plan for Your Highness, I wish to arrange for T'ien Kuang, a man of profound and farsighted strategies, to have an audience with you."

To this the prince respectfully assented.

When T'ien Kuang called upon the prince, the prince, out of respect, received him next to the stairway and then bowed. Once they were seated, Prince Tan said, "[I feel honored that] my teacher did not consider Yen so barbarous a country and me so unworthy a person that he could not condescend to come to this lowly land. Yen is a poor state in the northern reaches near the barbarian territories, and yet you felt no shame in coming here, giving me the chance to wait on you and to look upon your jade countenance. This is made possible only through the protection of our

[3] The Chinese version of Hades (same as the Yellow Springs).
[4] The Yi River marked the southern boundary of the state of Yen.
[5] Ch'u was the southernmost of all the states. Between it and Yen were the three states of Han, Wei, and Chao. Uniting all these states would have formed an alliance effectively confining Ch'in to the extreme west.

country by the divine spirits of my ancestors, who brought you here."

"Ever since my adolescence," T'ien Kuang replied, "I've admired your lofty conduct and your good name. What instructions has the prince for me?"

The prince advanced on his knees and with tears flowing said, "I was once held as a hostage in the state of Ch'in and was treated badly. Day and night this afflicts my mind, and it is my desire to take revenge on Ch'in. But if we compare the populations of the two states, Ch'in is definitely bigger; if we calculate the relative strength of the two, Yen again is the weaker. I'd like to talk of alliances, but with my mind set on revenge I cannot. I regularly eat without tasting and spend the nights tossing in restlessness. Even if Yen were to perish on the same day as Ch'in, I'd feel as happy as if I were resurrected from my own ashes. I wish you could come up with a workable plan for me."

"This is a grave matter of state. Please permit me to think it over," T'ien Kuang replied.

Thereupon T'ien Kuang was housed in the finest quarters, and the prince had him catered to three times a day. He was ever solicitous of T'ien's well-being.

Three months passed, and the prince thought it odd that T'ien Kuang had not brought up the matter with him again. Thus he called upon T'ien Kuang and, after dismissing the servants, asked, "Sir, since you stooped to take pity on me and promised to offer me your good plan, I've been anxious to hear from you. It has now been three months. Do you have something in mind?"

"Even if you hadn't come," T'ien Kuang replied, "I'd have put myself to the task. But I've heard that a good steed in its prime can gallop a thousand *li* at a stretch with ease, and yet when it becomes a jaded nag it cannot even saunter. By the time Your Highness heard of me, I had already become an old man. Even if I had some good plans to offer you, you might not find them

feasible. Similarly, even if I had wanted to offer you the strength of my arms, you might find it too feeble. I've observed the men around you but I couldn't find anyone up to the task. Hsia Fu is a man whose daring is in his blood; when aroused his face turns red. Sung Yi's boldness is in his veins; when angered his face turns blue. Wu Yang's courage lies in his bones; when stirred his countenance grows pale. I know of one Ching K'o, a man of divine valor. When he is provoked, his visage remains unchanged, and he has wide learning and a strong memory. He is a man of heroic character and sturdy build. He doesn't seize upon triviality, but longs to accomplish great deeds. He once made his home in the state of Wei. More than ten worthy nobles escaped trouble because of his help. All the others are mediocrities and are not suitable for the task. If Your Highness wants to insure the success of your plan, you must enlist the service of this man."

The prince left his mat, bowed twice, and said, "If through your connection I can strike up a friendship with Ching, then the state of Yen will surely endure forever. This, however, cannot be achieved without your help."

T'ien Kuang then started off [for Wei], with the prince himself accompanying him to the door. Taking T'ien Kuang's hand, he advised, "This is an affair of state. Please be discreet about it."

"Certainly," T'ien Kuang said, smiling.

T'ien Kuang proceeded to call upon Ching K'o saying, "Please forgive my presumptuousness, but I have mentioned your name to the prince. The crown prince of Yen is truly a hero. He has a great admiration for you. I hope that you would not doubt my word on this."

To this Ching K'o responded, "I only have a lowly ambition, but I've said that if a man appreciates me I'll devote myself to him without regard for my person. Yet for someone with a different temperament, I'd not pluck out a hair. Now since you advise me to associate myself with the prince, I shall respectfully follow your wish."

45

Then T'ien Kuang said to Ching K'o, "Now I've heard that a man should leave no room for doubt about his trustworthiness. When the prince was seeing me off he said, 'This is an affair of state. Please be discreet about it.' This means that he doesn't trust me. To be distrusted and still live in this world is my shame." Facing Ching K'o, he bit his tongue to commit suicide. Ching K'o then proceeded to Yen.

On his arrival in Yen, Ching was drawn in a chariot driven by the prince himself. The prince vacated the seat on the left, and Ching held on to the chariot strap without yielding that seat to the prince.[6] After they were seated and the retinue filled the hall, Ching K'o said, "T'ien Kuang praised Your Highness's compassionate manner, and spoke of your uncommon abilities and lofty behavior which reaches to heaven, of your great renown which fills mens' ears. So when I left Wei for Yen, I regarded neither the difficulties toilsome nor the distance wearisome. Your Highness has treated me with the favor of an old friend and received me with the respect of a new guest. That I did not return such deferential gestures is due to my trusting one who understands me."

"I trust that Mr. T'ien is in good health," the prince then said.

"When Kuang was about to see me off," Ching K'o replied, "he said that Your Highness had cautioned him about a matter of state. He was ashamed of not being trusted in such an affair. Right in front of me, he bit his tongue and died."

At this the prince was aghast and grew pale. Sobbing and whimpering he moaned, "I did not warn him because I distrusted him. Now he has killed himself and I am undone before the world." For a long while he was lost in despondency.

One day the prince invited Ching K'o to a feast. When the wine had taken its toll, the prince rose to propose a toast. But Hsia Fu came forward and declared, "I've heard that if one is not praised in his native place, then no one should discuss his aspiration; if a horse cannot pull a cart, then no one can decide about its quality. Recently Ching K'o has come from afar. What counsel has he for the crown prince?"

This was intended to provoke Ching K'o, who replied, "A man of universal ambition may not necessarily be popular in his native place. As for a horse recognized as a thousand-*li* mount, why hitch it to a cart? In times past when Lü Wang was still a butcher and a fisherman, he was among those of the lowest stature; he met up with King Wen to become the counselor of the Chou reign. If a superb horse is hitched to a salt cart, it cannot be better than a cart horse; but if it comes across a Po-lo,[7] it can stride a thousand *li*. Must the excellence of a man be viewed in relation to his native place and the fitness of a horse be judged by its hauling power?"

Hsia Fu persisted and again asked Ching K'o what instructions he had for the prince. Ching replied, "I shall lead Yen in the manner of Duke Shao of Chou,[8] emulating his influence. My highest hope is to add a fourth to the Three Emperors or at least to add a sixth to the Five Princes.[9] How do you feel about this?"

All those present approved, and throughout the banquet hall no one could outwit him. The prince was delighted, thinking that having attained the service of Ching K'o he need no longer be worried about Ch'in.

On another day the prince and Ching K'o went

---

[6] The prince asked Ching K'o to take the seat of honor and Ching took it without showing any sign of modesty. This indicates that Ching was an arrogant person.

[7] Po-lo (with the double surname Sun-fu), of the Spring and Autumn period, was well known for his ability to identify superb horses at first sight.

[8] Duke Shao of Chou was the youngest brother of King Wu of the Chou Dynasty (r. 1027–1025 B.C.). He was once enfeoffed in Yen and, according to legend, his good government won the hearts of the people.

[9] The Three Emperors were the founders of the Hsia, Shang, and Chou dynasties. The Five Princes were five well-known heads of state in the Spring and Autumn period: Duke Huan of the state of Ch'i, Duke Wen of the state of Chin, Duke Hsiang of the state of Sung, Duke Mu of the state of Ch'in, and Duke Chuang of the state of Ch'u.

to the Eastern Palace, where they stood by a pond and gazed upon the view. Ching took up pieces of broken tile and threw them at the frogs. The prince ordered a man to present Ching with a plate of gold nuggets, which he threw at the frogs. When he had thrown them all and was offered another plate he said, "It is not that I want to save your gold that I stop, but my arm has grown sore."

On another occasion, the two of them were riding out on some superb horses, and Ching K'o said, "I've heard that the liver of such steeds makes good dishes." At this the prince had one of the horses killed and presented the liver to Ching K'o.

Some time later, General Fan of Ch'in, having committed an offense in that state and become the object of its urgent pursuit, came to Prince Tan for refuge. The prince entertained him on a terrace in Hua-yang.[10] During the party the prince brought out a beauty skilled on the lute. Ching K'o remarked, "Fair are the hands of the lute player." The prince offered her to Ching who said, "I only admire her hands." The prince then had her hands cut off, and on a jade plate offered them to Ching K'o.

The prince often ate at the same table and slept in the same bed as Ching K'o. Once Ching placidly told the prince, "I've been here in your service for three years and Your Highness has treated me most generously. There was the gold I threw at the frogs, the liver of the superb steeds, the beauty's lovely hands presented to me on a jade plate. Even a common man treated in this manner would be exceedingly happy and willing to be employed for tasks fit for a dog or a horse. Now I've constantly served at the side of the noble man, and I've heard that with the code of a hero death may be weightier than the T'ai Mountains[11] or lighter than swansdown. The difference only lies in the purpose one serves. Now, Your High-

ness, may I ask your instructions as to the end I am to serve?"

The prince straightened his garments and replied with great seriousness, "I once journeyed to Ch'in, but their treatment of me was improper. I'm ashamed to live under the same sky with them. Since you've not thought too badly of me in condescending to come to my small state, I want to entrust this matter to you, if only I can find the right words to speak my mind."

"Of the powerful states in the world today none is stronger than Ch'in," Ching K'o replied. "Your strength is not such that you can overawe the feudal lords, and they are not willing to come to your service. If Your Highness were to lead your masses to confront Ch'in, it would be like using sheep to seize a wolf, or wolves to pursue a tiger."

"I've long pondered these troubles but I've not been able to come up with any definite plan," said the prince.

"Fan Yü-ch'i has committed an offense in Ch'in, and Ch'in ardently seeks his capture," Ching K'o replied. "There is also the land of Tu-k'ang,[12] which Ch'in covets. If I were to obtain the head of Fan Yü-ch'i and a map of Tu-k'ang, then this matter could be accomplished."

"If this affair could be executed," the prince said, "I would gladly offer the state of Yen. But General Fan came to me in dire straits. I cannot bring myself to betray him."

Ching K'o was silent, making no response to what the prince had said.

So the matter rested for five months. Fearing that Ching K'o might change his mind, the prince called on him and asked, "Ch'in has recently destroyed the state of Chao and its troops are fast approaching Yen. The situation has become critical. Though I wish to follow your plan, how can it be done? I wish to send Wu Yang to make a trial first. What do you think of this?"

Ching replied in a fury, "Who is the fellow

---

[10] Shang County in modern Shensi Province.
[11] A famous mountain range (also known as the Eastern Mountains); in Shantung Province.

[12] A piece of fertile land around the modern Cho County in Hopei.

Your Highness intends to send on a mission of no return? A mere boy! The reason I haven't left is that I'm waiting for my partner."

Thereupon Ching secretly went to see Fan Yü-ch'i and said, "I've heard that you committed an offense in Ch'in and that your father, mother, wife, and children were all burned to death. I also understand that there's a reward of a fief of ten thousand households and a thousand catties of gold for your capture. I'm sorry for your sake. There is, however, one way to remove your disgrace and also absolve the shame of Yen. I wonder if you would be interested?"

"I've brooded over this constantly. Day and night I restrain my tears, but I don't know how to solve my dilemma. May I have the good fortune to receive your instructions? I long to hear your command."

"I want your head, which will be offered to Ch'in along with a map of the Tu-k'ang territory. The king of Ch'in will surely be pleased, and he will certainly receive me. Then with my left hand I shall seize his sleeve and with my right thrust a dagger into his breast. I shall punish him for the offense of ill-treating Yen, and denounce him to avenge you. The shame of the insult to Yen will be erased, and your accumulated anger will be removed."

Fan Yü-ch'i rose, grasped his own wrist, and clutched his sword saying, "This is what I've always wanted day and night, and today I know what I should do." He then cut his own throat. His head hung down his back, his eyes still open.

When the prince heard of this, he rode over immediately. He fell prostrate over Fan Yü-ch'i's corpse and wept, unable to overcome his grief. Soon realizing that there nothing else to be done, he had Fan Yü-ch'i's head packed in a box along with a map of Tu-k'ang to be presented to Ch'in. Wu Yang was chosen as Ching K'o's assistant.

Ching K'o set out for Ch'in without selecting an auspicious day. The prince and those who knew of the plan all wore white mourning garb and

caps, and accompanied them to a spot above the waters of the Yi River. Ching K'o rose, offered a toast and sang:

The wind is howling;
Cold is the water of River Yi.
The stout heroes once departed,
Never to return.

Kao Chien-li[13] plucked the lute and Sung Yi accompanied him in singing. Their roaring sound roused the assembly to such emotional heights that their hair stood up against their caps. The mournful tune brought all of those present to tears. The two men mounted the chariot and departed without looking back. Hsia Fu came before their chariot when they passed by and slit his throat to send the two men on their way.

In passing through Yang-chai,[14] Ching K'o purchased some meat. There was a dispute over its weight. Wu Yang wished to strike the butcher who was rude to Ching K'o, but Ching prevented him.

Traveling west, they entered Ch'in and reached the capital of Hsien-yang.[15] Through the central court registrar Meng, the communiqué they brought from Yen was read:

> Prince Tan of Yen, awed by the might of the Great King, today offers the head of Fan Yü-ch'i and a map of the territory of Tu-k'ang, desiring to be your vassal in the northern border.

The king of Ch'in was delighted. He received the envoys from Yen in the presence of the various officials and several hundred armed soldiers. Ching K'o carried the head of Fan Yü-ch'i, and Wu Yang, the map. Bells and drums sounded, and the assembly cheered: "Long live the King!"

Wu Yang was greatly frightened at this; he had difficulty even moving his feet and his face turned

[13] A close friend of Ching K'o.
[14] Yü County in the present Honan Province.
[15] Wei-ch'eng in the present Shensi Province.

ashen. The king thought this odd. Ching K'o glanced back at Wu Yang, stepped forward and apologized: "This man is a lowly barbarian of the north. He has never before seen the countenance of the Son of Heaven. I wish Your Majesty would forgive him so that we may be able to fulfill our mission in your presence."

"Take the map and bring it forward," the king said to Ching K'o.

The king opened the map. When it had been completely unrolled the dagger appeared. Ching K'o with his left hand grabbed the king's sleeve, and in his right hand the dagger stood poised before the king's breast. Then he upbraided him, "You've long harried Yen. You cruelly covet all the land within the four seas. There is no way to satisfy your greed. Though General Fan Yü-ch'i was without fault, you exterminated his entire family. I carry out the revenge of the entire land upon you. Now that the mother of the king of Yen is sick, we are obliged to finish our job as soon as possible.[16] If you follow my orders you will live; if not then you will die."

"As this is the case," the king said, "I must follow your directions, but I entreat you to permit me to hear some lute music before I die."

---

[16] This sentence is ambiguous and does not make much sense. Here is possibly a case of textual corruption. This sentence may also be interpreted as followed: The king of Yen is without fault and time was pressing upon us to finish the job.

A song girl was called out to play the lute. The song went:

An unlined garment of fine silk gauze
If pulled will tear.
A folding screen eight feet long
Can be leaped over.
The sword with the windlass-shaped pommel
If first pushed back can then be drawn.

Ching K'o did not understand the meaning of the song,[17] but the king, following the song, first pushed back the scabbard and then drew his sword. He wrenched back from his sleeve and jumped over the screen to flee. Ching K'o took up the dagger and threw it at the king. It cut an ear and struck a bronze pillar, striking sparks. The king then turned back and cut off Ching's hands. Ching leaned against a pillar and laughed. Squatting, he denounced the king: "I thought this matter could be handled easily, but you, knave, were able to fool me. I only regret having failed in avenging Yen and accomplishing my deed!"[18]

---

[17] Perhaps because of unfamiliarity with the local speech.

[18] Apparently the text is incomplete, with some episodes missing toward the end of the story. According to the biography of Ching K'o in the *Shih-chi* (The Historical Records), the king of Ch'in was so furious at the assassination plot, which occurred in 227 B.C., that he sent his troops to overrun the state of Yen. Prince Tan was eventually executed by the order of his own father (the king of Yen) in a futile endeavor to stop the advancing Ch'in armies. This was followed by a moving but unsuccessful attempt by Kao Chien-li on the life of the king of Ch'in.

49

FENG YEN

From T'ai-p'ing kuang-chi

TRANSLATED BY WILLIAM H. NIENHAUSER, JR.

Feng Yen was a hero from Wei.[1] His ancestors were not particularly distinguished. While young he was a wild one given to ball games and cock-fights. Once in some marketplace a fight broke out over a question of money. Yen was drawn there and in assisting the wronged party hit and killed someone. Thus he took cover in the countryside. As the official search for him heightened, he fled to Hua,[2] where he grew close to the young men of the Hua garrison, joining them in their usual amusements.

At that time his lordship Prime Minister Chia Tan[3] was in Hua and, recognizing Yen's talents, kept him in his headquarters [for his own service]. When Yen was out for a stroll of the neighborhood one day, he saw a woman in a doorway watching him even as she veiled herself with her sleeve. Her appearance was so seductive that her intentions were not to be missed. So Yen took her as a lover. Her husband, Chang Ying, however, was the garrison commander of Hua. When Ying heard of the affair, he beat his wife repeatedly. For this her family and friends all hated and resented him.

Once when Ying had gone to drink with friends, Yen, seizing the opportunity, lay again in his bedchamber, shutting the door. On Ying's return, his wife opened the door to let him in, at the same time concealing Yen behind her skirt. Yen then, crouching low, tiptoed to cover; and as he was turning around to hide behind the door, his kerchief fell to the pillow near Ying's sword. Ying was drunk and had fallen asleep. Yen pointed to his kerchief, asking the woman to get it, but she handed him the sword instead. Yen looked at her for a long time, then slit her throat, put on his kerchief, and left.

The following morning when Ying got up and saw that his wife had been murdered, he was amazed. Just as he was about to go and surrender himself, his neighbors, thinking that Ying had actually killed her, bound him and went to inform the wife's parents. The relatives all came and one said, "You have been beating our daughter regularly out of jealousy and then accused her falsely

---

[1] Approximately equal to the northern part of the present Honan Province and the southwestern part of Shansi Province.

[2] The prefecture of Hua (Hua-chou) in the T'ang period was in modern Honan Province.

[3] Here is a case of identifying a person by a high position he is known for, even though the incident in question took place at an earlier time in his career. Chia Tan (730–805) was the prefect of Hua-chou from 786 to mid-793 (along with other concurrent positions); then he served as one of the prime ministers from mid-793 to the end of his life. The time setting of this story is thus during his prefectship at Hua-chou.

of indiscretions. Now you've even killed her with no justification! How could it have been someone else who killed her? If that were the case, why would you still be alive?"

They held Ying and gave him more than a hundred strokes with the bamboo, so that he could no longer speak. The officials placed him under arrest for murder. Since the truth was nowhere to be found, he was forced to suffer such injustice. Several dozen constables from the bureau of justice, armed with poles, took Ying to the marketplace. More than a thousand onlookers surrounded the area. Suddenly, a man pushed through the crowd and called out, "Hold! Don't sentence an innocent man to death! I stole his wife and I killed her. You should imprison me."

The constables took hold of the man who made the confession—it turned out to be Yen! The judge took him before Lord Chia and stated the charges in detail. Chia in turn relayed the details of the case to the emperor, offering his resignation in exchange for Yen's life. The emperor felt this to be just and sent down a proclamation granting amnesty to all those who had received the death penalty in the city of Hua.

In eulogy let it be said: "I [the storyteller] esteem the words of the Grand Historian[4] and also am fond of relating events in which justice and righteousness are upheld. Those things which my associates had experienced or witnessed, they often told me. During the Yüan-ho period [806–820][5] Auxiliary Secretary Liu Yüan-t'ing[6] related this account of Feng Yen to me, thus making it possible for it to be recorded and handed down. Alas! An immoral and treacherous mind is worse than flood or fire and certainly to be dreaded! but Yen's killing of an unjust person, his exonerating an innocent man—these are truly the ways of the heroes of old!"

---

[4] Ssu-ma Ch'ien (145–86 B.C.?). For a biographical description of this remarkable historian, see the entry for *Shih-chi* in the Biobibliographical Notes at the end of this anthology.

[5] The only reign period of Emperor Hsien-tsung of the T'ang Dynasty.

[6] Liu Yüan-t'ing was an envoy best known for his negotiations with the Tibetans in the early 820s.

WU-SHUANG THE PEERLESS

From *T'ai-p'ing kuang-chi*

TRANSLATED BY DALE JOHNSON

Wang Hsien-k'o was the nephew of Liu Chen, a minister at the central court during the Chien-chung reign [780–783].[1] Hsien-k'o's father died while he was still a youngster, so he and his mother went to live with her brother, Uncle Liu Chen. Liu's daughter, Wu-shuang [The Peerless], was a few years younger than Hsien-k'o. As children they were such intimate playmates that Liu Chen's wife often teased Hsien-k'o, calling him "our son-in-law."

For several years Liu Chen took care of his widowed elder sister in this way, and gave special attention to Hsien-k'o's upbringing. One day his sister, Mrs. Wang, fell ill. When her condition got worse, she summoned Liu Chen to her side to make a request of him: "I have only one son, and you know how much I love him. My worry is that I may not be able to see him married. Wu-shuang is so pretty and intelligent, and I'm deeply fond of her. In the future, please don't marry her into another family. I entrust Hsien-k'o's welfare to your care. If you promise me, I can close my eyes without regret."

"Please put your mind at ease and you will get well," Liu Chen consoled her. "Don't trouble yourself about such matters."

His sister, however, did not recover. Hsien-k'o took his mother's body back home to Hsiang-Teng[2] to be buried. When the mourning period had ended, he pondered: "I am orphaned and alone in the world. I should marry and continue the family line. Wu-shuang is grown up. I don't think my uncle would break his promise just because he is a high and respected official." Thereupon he packed his belongings and went to the capital.

At this time Liu Chen was the tax commissioner in the Department of State Affairs. He lived in a large and imposing mansion, where men of high station thronged the gates. He received Hsien-k'o and housed him in the family school with the other young men of the Liu clan. The relationship between uncle and nephew was as cordial as ever, but the subject of marriage was never mentioned.

On one occasion Hsien-k'o peeped at Wu-shuang through a crack in the window and beheld her graceful bearing and radiant beauty, equal to

---

[1] The first of the three reign periods of the T'ang emperor Te-tsung (r. 780–805).

[2] The collective name for both Hsiang-yang and the neighboring Teng-ch'eng in the present Hupeh Province.

that of the gods and immortals. Deeply worried that the wedding plans would go awry, in desperation he sold his possessions and raised several million in cash, which he spent lavishly on the attendants and domestic servants of his aunt and uncle to win their favor. To the same end, he also entertained them at parties and banquets, which gained him access to the inner apartments. All his cousins, with whom he lived, treated him with considerable respect.

On the occasion of his aunt's birthday, he presented her with rare and exotic gifts, and hair ornaments carved out of rhinoceros horn and jade, which pleased her immensely. Ten days later, he sent an old crone to broach to his aunt the subject of matrimony.

"It is what I'd like to see accomplished myself," she replied, "and I will discuss it with my husband."

Several evenings later, a maid came to report, "Mistress spoke to the master about your engagement, but the master said 'I never really agreed to it.' Judging by his manner, I'm afraid their opinions are not the same."

When Hsien-k'o heard this, he grew so despondent that he passed a sleepless night. But he was as attentive to Liu Chen as ever, lest his uncle reject him.

One day Liu set off for the court before dawn. But just at sunrise, he came galloping back unexpectedly, bathed in sweat and short of breath, and commanded, "Bolt the main gates! Bolt the main gates!" The household was alarmed and startled by this strange turn of events. "The soldiers at Ching-yüan have revolted," he explained after he could catch his breath. "Yao Ling-yen[3] and his troops have occupied the Immaculacy Palace. The Son of Heaven has fled through the north gate of the palace complex, and all the officials at court

have fled to the provisional capital. I've returned here only because of my wife and daughter."

He sent for Hsien-k'o right away, and said to him, "I urgently need your help. Help me take care of my household and I'll give Wu-shuang to you in marriage." Hsien-k'o was thrilled to hear this command, and bowed in grateful assent.

Liu Chen had some twenty carts packed with gold, silver, silk, and brocade, and instructed Hsien-k'o, "Change your clothing and conduct these goods through the Longview Gate. Find a secluded inn and take lodging there. I'll escort your aunt and Wu-shuang out of the city through the Cathay Gate and take a roundabout route to join you."

Hsien-k'o followed these instructions, but at sundown he was still awaiting their arrival at an inn outside the city. The city gates had been secured and bolted since noon. He had his sight fixed toward the south until he could no longer bear the strain. Taking a torch, he mounted his piebald horse and rode round the walls to the Cathay Gate, but found it also bolted. A band of men bearing white staffs, sitting and standing about, were guarding the gate. Dismounting, Hsien-k'o inquired politely, "What has caused the commotion within the city?" Shortly after which he added, "Who has passed through the gates today?"

"Marshal Chu has ascended the throne,"[4] volunteered a guard, "and this afternoon a man of high station with heavy baggage, accompanied by several women, attempted to pass through this gate, but he was recognized as Tax Commissioner Liu of the Department of State Affairs by some people in the street, so the officer in charge didn't dare let him pass. Toward evening, mounted troops came in pursuit and he was taken to the north." Upon this Hsien-k'o could no longer contain his tears, but he could do no more than return to the inn and wait.

[3] Yao Ling-yen, the regional commander of Ch'ing-yüan (in modern Kansu Province), revolted in 783. He overran the capital and supported Chu Tz'u as the emperor.

[4] Marshal Chu is the Chu Tz'u referred to in footnote 3.

Near the end of the third watch the city gates suddenly opened, and torchlights lit up the sky like dawn. Wielding swords and other weapons, soldiers rode out shouting, "Kill anyone who tries to escape the city!" They searched the areas outside the walls for fleeing court officials. Hsien-k'o abandoned his baggage wagons and fled in terror. He returned to Hsiang-yang, where he lived in a village for three years.

Later, upon learning that the rebellion had been quelled, that the capital was restored to order, and that there was peace throughout the realm, he went to the capital to seek news of his uncle. Reaching a street at the southern part of the New Prosperity Quarter, he had reined in his horse, wondering what to do next, when a man abruptly appeared and bowed before him. A closer look revealed him to be a former servant, Sai-hung. Sai-hung was born in the Wang family, but Liu Chen had sought his service frequently and, finding him helpful, had eventually taken him into his own household as a servant. As they clasped hands and wept, Hsien-k'o asked, "Are my aunt and uncle safe?"

"They're both at the residence in the Success Quarter," replied Sai-hung.

"I'll go there at once," declared Hsien-k'o, overjoyed.

But Sai-hung stopped him, saying, "I've gained my freedom and I'm now living in a small house where I sell silks for a living. It's already nightfall. Please spend the night in my quarters. In the morning we can go together to see them." Thereupon he conducted Hsien-k'o to his house, where wine and meat were laid out in abundance. Later that night Sai-hung made a full report: "Your uncle and his wife have been executed for serving the rebel government; Wu-shuang has been taken into the royal quarters as a servant."

Hearing this news, Hsien-k'o cried out with such anguish that all the neighbors were moved to pity. "Wide though the world is," he said to Sai-hung, "I see no friend or relative, nor do I know where to go." Then he added, "Are there any of the former family servants left?"

"There is only Wu-shuang's former maid, Ts'ai-p'in," replied Sai-hung. "She is now serving in the household of General Wang Sui-chung, captain of the Imperial Guards."

"There is no chance that I will ever see Wu-shuang again," said Hsien-k'o, "but if I could see Ts'ai-p'in, I could die content."

Thereupon he presented his visiting card and paid his respects to Sui-chung, observing the protocol due an uncle of his own clan. He related the entire story from beginning to end and expressed a desire to redeem Ts'ai-p'in with a large cash settlement. Sui-chung was deeply moved by this manifestation of trust and granted his request. Hsien-k'o rented a house and set up housekeeping with Sai-hung and Ts'ai-p'in.

Sai-hung urged him continually, "Master, now that you have attained your majority, you should seek an official post. To live in despair and unhappiness like this is no way to spend your remaining years." Touched by his words, Hsien-k'o approached Sui-chung and asked him to exercise his influence to secure him a post. Sui-chung introduced him to Li Ch'i-yün, mayor of the capital. Ch'i-yün, taking into account Hsien-k'o's former status, named him magistrate of Fu-p'ing County,[5] and concurrently placed him in charge of the Ch'ang-lo courier station.

Several months later, an announcement arrived that thirty palace ladies, escorted by palace envoys, were en route to the imperial mausoleum to clean and put the place in order. They were traveling in ten curtained carriages and were to spend the night at the Ch'ang-lo courier station. Hsien-k'o said to Sai-hung, "I've heard that most of the women selected to serve in the royal quarters are ladies of high-born families. It is possible that Wu-shuang is among this group. Will you take a look for me?"

[5] This place is still known today as Fu-p'ing (in Shensi Province).

"There are thousands of palace ladies," replied Sai-hung. "How could Wu-shuang possibly be among them?"

"Take a look, anyway," said Hsien-k'o. "The course of human events is difficult to predict."

Thereupon, Sai-hung, disguised as a courier-station attendant, was sent to brew tea outside the curtains that enclosed the ladies' chambers. Hsien-k'o paid him three thousand in cash and instructed him, "Attend strictly to your tea utensils, and don't shirk your duties even for a second. If you learn anything, report it at once."

"Very well, very well," muttered Sai-hung, and left.

The palace ladies were all behind the curtains, inaccessible to view. He could hear nothing more than the usual babble and chatter of the evening, but as the night wore on the commotion gradually subsided. Sai-hung was hunched over the fire, scouring his teacups, fighting the urge to doze, when suddenly he heard a voice behind the curtain calling him: "Sai-hung! Sai-hung! How did you know I was here? Is your master in good health?" Then the words dissolved into sobbing.

"My master is in charge of this courier station," said Sai-hung. "He suspected that you might be here tonight and sent me to convey his greetings."

"I can't speak further," she said. "Tomorrow, after I have gone, take the letter which you will find under the purple bedding in the northeast chamber to your master." With these words, she withdrew. Then, suddenly, from behind the curtain came the sound of a great commotion.

"She has fainted!" someone said. A palace officer rushed out for a tonic to revive her, and Sai-hung learned that it was for Wu-shuang. He reported these events at once to Hsien-k'o who, in great excitement, asked, "Is there any way I can see her?"

"The Wei Bridge just happens to be under repair," Sai-hung informed him. "You may disguise yourself as an officer in charge of the repair work and stand near the spot where the carriage will pass as it crosses the bridge. If she recognizes you, she'll pull up the curtain for you."

Hsien-k'o did as Sai-hung told him, and as the third carriage passed by, the curtain parted and it was Wu-shuang indeed. It was a sight which filled Hsien-k'o with as much grief as did his longing for her.

In the meantime, Sai-hung found the letter under the bedding in the apartment Wu-shuang had occupied and delivered it to Hsien-k'o. There on five sheets of flowered notepaper, in Wu-shuang's own hand, was her sad and tragic story in full detail, which he read with bitter tears in his eyes. He thought he had lost Wu-shuang for good when he came upon a postscript:

> I have heard several times that there is a man of chivalrous spirit in the Fu-p'ing County, an officer named Ku. Can you seek his help?

Hsien-k'o submitted his resignation to the prefecture, requesting that he be relieved of duties at the courier station, but he retained his post as magistrate of Fu-p'ing County. He instigated a search for the whereabouts of Officer Ku and learned that he was living in a cottage in the country. Hsien-k'o went there to pay a visit and was received by Ku. Thereafter, he took care to insure that Ku was provided with whatever he needed. He sent him elegant silks and precious stones in such quantities that it would be difficult to record them all. But for the space of a year he never mentioned what he was really after.

Upon serving out his term of office, Hsien-k'o retired there in the district. One day Ku appeared unannounced and said, "I am a man who lives by his muscles, but am now getting on in years, and good for nothing. But you've been very kind to me, and I feel that there must be something you'd like me to do for you. Since I am a man who knows what gratitude means and fully appreciate your generosity to me, I am ready to put my life in your hands to do a service in return."

Hsien-k'o knelt weeping on the ground and related the whole story. Ku raised his gaze toward the heavens, and tapping his head with his hands several times said, "This is not an easy task, nor is it a thing that can be fulfilled in a morning or a night, but I'll try do my best for you."

"I only hope to see her again in this life," Hsien-k'o said, bowing. "How dare I impose a time limit?"

He heard no further news for half a year.

One day there was a rap at the gate. Hsien-k'o opened it to discover a letter from Ku, which read:

My messenger has returned from the Mao Mountain.[6] Please come at once.

Hsien-k'o galloped off to see Ku, but the old man uttered not a word. Hsien-k'o asked about the messenger. "He has already been disposed of," said Ku. "Will you have some tea?" Later, as the night deepened, Ku asked, "Is there a woman in your household who knows Wu-shuang?" Hsien-k'o mentioned Ts'ai-p'in, and had her summoned immediately. Ku looked her over carefully, then smiled and said, "Leave her with me for a few days. You may go home now."

Several days later, news spread that a high official had passed through the place and that a palace lady of the imperial mausoleum had been executed. Hsien-k'o, filled with a strange premonition, instructed Sai-hung to find out who had been executed. He reported that it had been Wu-shuang. Sobbing, Hsien-k'o said with a sigh, "I had my hopes pinned on Ku. Now she is dead! What more can I say?" As he was speaking, tears coursed down his face uncontrollably.

Very late the same night he heard a frantic rapping at the gate, and opened it to find Ku carrying a bamboo litter. "This is Wu-shuang," he said. "To all appearances she is dead, but her heart is slightly warm. She'll revive the day after

[6] This mountain, in Kiangsu Province, is the principal peak of the Mao Mountain range and is a divine spot of the Taoist religion.

tomorrow, and you can nurse her along with the aid of this tonic. Make sure that no one learns of it."

Hsien-k'o carried her in his arms into the house and kept a lonely vigil over her. At dawn her body began to warm, but when she saw Hsien-k'o she uttered one cry and fainted again. He tried to revive her throughout the rest of the day, but she did not regain consciousness until evening.

"I would like to borrow Sai-hung to dig a pit for me behind the house," said Ku to Hsien-k'o. When the pit was sufficiently deep, he drew his sword and severed Sai-hung's head, which tumbled into the pit. Hsien-k'o was terrified.

"Don't be alarmed," said Ku. "I'm not about to repay your kindness in full. Recently I learned of a Taoist priest on the Mao Mountain who possessed a miraculous drug. It causes anyone who takes it to suffer an instant death, but three days afterward the person revives. I sent a messenger to obtain some and managed to get one pill. Yesterday I asked Ts'ai-p'in to disguise herself as a palace officer and order Wu-shuang to end her life with this pill on account of her former connections with the rebel government. Then I went to the mausoleum and passed myself off as a blood relative so as to ransom her body with one hundred rolls of silk. All couriers who assisted me on the road were bribed generously to insure that nothing would leak out. The messenger from the Mao Mountain and the litter bearers were all put to death outside the city. For you, I'll also cut my own throat. Don't stay here any longer. Outside the gate are ten men, five horses, and two hundred rolls of silk. At the fifth watch take Wu-shuang and flee. Change your names and cover your traces to avoid ensuing disaster." Saying this Ku raised his sword, and before Hsien-k'o could restrain him his head tumbled to the ground. Hsien-k'o covered the bodies of Ku and Sai-hung and buried them.

Leaving before dawn, they eventually traveled through western Shu and the Yangtze gorges until they reached Chu-kung,[7] where they took temporary lodgings. When the news of danger in the capital had subsided, Hsien-k'o collected his household and returned to Hsiang-Teng, where he lived in his country residence. There, with Wu-shuang, he lived to a ripe old age and raised a houseful of children.

Alas! Many indeed are the separations and re-unions that occur in human life, but seldom have I heard of a comparable case. I would go so far as to say that this is unique in history. Wu-shuang lost her freedom in a political upheaval, yet Hsien-k'o's determination to rescue her was undaunted even at the risk of his life. But their re-union would not have materialized without the unusual assistance of Ku, which resulted in the loss of more than ten innocent lives. Once forced to flee for their very lives, they were eventually able to return to their native place, where they lived fifty years as husband and wife. Is this not a remarkable tale indeed!

[7] Modern Chiang-ling County in Hupeh Province, the site of the second capital of the state of Ch'u of the Warring States period.

THE SUNG FOUNDER ESCORTS CHING-NIANG ONE THOUSAND *LI*

From *Ching-shih t'ung-yen*

TRANSLATED BY LORRAINE S. Y. LIEU AND THE EDITORS

Rabbits run and birds fly, but faster and more swift is time;
A hundred years of worldly affairs always seem so ephemeral.
Dynasties of riches and honors are like a midnight dream;
Generations of emperors last as long as a chess game.
Yü[1] *established the nine provinces and T'ang*[2] *took over the*
*   reign;*
Ch'in[3] *swallowed the six states and Han*[4] *ascended the throne.*
There are not many days even in a hundred years' time;
In vain one tries day and night to make up for lost pleasures.

During the last years of the Sung Dynasty, there lived in the Stone Chamber Mountain[5] of the Ho-tung Circuit[6] a hermit who did not reveal his own name to others but called himself "The Old Man of Stone." Those who knew him said that he was a heroic man of great talent. During the invasion of

the barbarians, he went to the army to present his strategies, but they were not accepted. He then organized his own voluntary army and managed to recover several prefectures. Later, however, when he saw that the situation was deteriorating by the day, he realized that the game was over. Henceforth he changed his identity and went into the mountain to live in seclusion. He took "Mountain" as his surname, supported himself by farming, and refused to talk about career prospects. He would, however, talk endlessly about the rise and fall of the various dynasties when he was engaged with someone in such a discussion.

Once two scholars from a nearby mountain, one young and one old, strolled by the Stone Chamber and ran into the hermit. Their conversation turned to the founding of the three dynasties—Han, T'ang, and Sung.

"In what respect is the Sung Dynasty superior to the Han and T'ang?" the hermit asked.

"In placing civilian causes over military strength," replied one of the scholars.

"No high minister was executed during the dynasty," answered the other.

The hermit laughed heartily and said, "What you two gentlemen have said is not quite right.

---

[1] Yü founded the Hsia Dynasty in ca. 2100 B.C. He was well known for his work in solving the problems of chronic flooding that once plagued northern China. He was also remembered for dividing the country into nine provinces, thus establishing the first model of administrative division in Chinese history.

[2] T'ang founded the Shang Dynasty in ca. 1600 B.C.

[3] Here Ch'in refers to the state of Ch'in which annexed all the other states toward the end of the Warring States period and unified China in 221 B.C.

[4] Han refers to the Western Han Dynasty.

[5] A fictitious placename.

[6] The Ho-tung Circuit in Sung times covered the present Shansi Province plus the northern tip of Shensi Province.

Han frequently engaged in conquering its neighboring states, and though the Confucian scholars took exception to its excessive military exploits, the barbarians were terrified and called it the "Mighty Han." Later, Emperor Wu of the kingdom of Wei[7] still had to depend upon its lingering glory to suppress the Huns. In early T'ang, the militia system greatly strengthened the country. Even though the central government was later weakened by the insubordination of regional powers, the administration was still able to rule by striking a balance of power among them. As for the Sung Dynasty, after the peace pact with the Tartars at Ch'an-yüan,[8] it gave up its military adventures almost completely. Later, it made a practice of paying off enemies for the sake of peace. As a result, Chin and Yüan rose up one after the other and finally conquered the country. So this is the disadvantage of promoting civilian causes at the expense of military strength! As for not executing high officials, this is of course an act of kindness. On the other hand, as the crimes of the evil ministers were not punished, the principle of justice was compromised, resulting in more violations of the law by opportunists who had no consequences to fear even if they were caught. It can be said in conclusion that the Sung Dynasty was destroyed at the hands of the evil ministers. Even though in the end T'o-chou's[9] head was sent to

the court of the barbarians in a box, and Ssu-tao[10] was assassinated by menials as a form of appeasement, it was already too late. How could Sung be considered superior to Han and T'ang?"

"Then in what way was Sung superior?" the two scholars asked.

"Though it was not equal to Han and T'ang in other respects," the hermit replied, "Sung was superior in that its emperors were not preoccupied with women and sex."

"How is that so?" the two of them wondered.

"The Han founder doted on Consort Ch'i; Emperor T'ai-tsung of the T'ang [r. 627–649] had an incestuous relationship with his sister-in-law; Empress Lü[11] and Empress Wu[12] nearly toppled the country; Fei-yen[13] and T'ai-chen[14] both brought shame to the royal palace. But even though there were pleasure-seeking Sung emperors, none was guilty of licentiousness. That was why the empresses Kao, Ts'ao, Hsiang, and

[7] Emperor Wu was the posthumous title given to Ts'ao Ts'ao (155–220) by his son, Ts'ao P'ei (r. 220–226) after the founding of the kingdom of Wei, one of the contending powers of the Three Kingdoms period.

[8] The peace treaty of 1004 so overwhelmingly favored the kingdom of Liao, founded by the Khitan (a proto-Mongol people) to the north of China, that it amounted to an open admission of the military weakness of the Sung government. The location of Ch'an-yüan is to the southwest of the present Pu-yang County in Hopei Province.

[9] Han T'o-chou (1151–1202) was the arrogant and egoistical prime minister who served under Emperor Ning-tsung (r. 1195–1224) of the Southern Sung Dynasty. As a means of broadening his own power base, Han advocated military actions against the Jurchen (a proto-Manchu people), who had established the Chin Dynasty in North China seven decades earlier. After the campaigns failed, the Sung government executed Han and sent his head to the Chin court in a box.

[10] Chia Ssu-tao (?–1275) was a prime minister toward the end of the Southern Sung, notorious for his corruption and incompetence. He was accused of taking no action against the invading Mongols. Once out of the emperor's favor and disgraced, he was banished and was killed by his opponents on his way to Kao-chou (in modern Kwangtung Province).

[11] Lü Chih, the empress of Emperor Kao-tsu (r. 206–195 B.C.), the Han founder, was notorious for her cruelty and ambition. She was not only responsible for the brutal death of Consort Ch'i, the favorite of the emperor, but also dominated the central court and mistreated the relatives of the emperor.

[12] Wu Chao (better known as Wu Tse-t'ien) was the empress of Emperor Kao-tsung (r. 650–683) of the T'ang Dynasty. Soon after the death of Kao-tsung, she deposed her own son, Emperor Chung-tsung, established the Chou Dynasty, and ruled for almost two decades (684–705) as the first female sovereign in Chinese history. She passed the throne back to her son in old age.

[13] Chao Fei-yen was the empress of Emperor Ch'eng (r. 32–29 B.C.) of the Western Han Dynasty. See "Empress Chao Fei-yen" in this anthology.

[14] Yang T'ai-chen, better known as Yang Kuei-fei or Consort Yang, was the favorite of Emperor Hsüan-tsung of the T'ang Dynasty. The emperor's infatuation with her has frequently been cited as the cause for Hsüan-tsung's inattention to state affairs. She was also held responsible for bringing her incompetent relatives into key government posts as well as inciting An Lu-shan to muster power to start a rebellion. (See the beginning of "Han Wu-niang Sells Her Charms at the New Bridge Market" in this anthology.)

Meng were held up as paragons of feminine virtues.[15] Both Han and T'ang are way behind Sung in this respect."

Fully convinced, the two scholars left. Indeed:

If you want to know the universal truths of history,
You must ask someone of wisdom and insight.

I've just mentioned that the Sung emperors did not have a weakness for women, and this was due to the good example set by Emperor T'ai-tsu. After he became emperor, he went to court early, stopped the usual banquets, and visited his harem only occasionally. He was already an iron-willed hero, straight and forthright, even before he came to power. Listen to this story, "Escorting Ching-niang One Thousand *Li*," and you'll understand. Indeed:

When this story is told, his righteousness echoes through a
  thousand ages;
When it is mentioned, his valor soars into the highest heaven.
He is the true ruler of the eight hundred commanderies,[16]
Showing his courage and gallantry with a cudgel.

But first let me use a quatrain to describe the chaos during the Five Dynasties period:

The houses of Chu, Li, Shih, Liu, and Kao,
Respectively of the dynasties Liang, T'ang, Chin, Han, and
  Chou,
Fifteen emperors in all,
Brought chaos for fifty years.[17]

---

[15] The commendable behavior of emperors was considered to be partly due to the good influence of their wives. These four empresses of the Northern Sung period all served as empress dowagers, ruling the country for their sons. In chronological order, the sequence should be different, with Ts'ao as the empress of Emperor Jen-tsung (r. 1023–1063), Kao the empress of Ying-tsung (r. 1064–1067), Hsiang the empress of the Shen-tsung (r. 1068–1085), and Meng the empress of Che-tsung (r. 1086–1100).

[16] Commanderies were districts of military jurisdiction.

[17] The Five Dynasties period is a confusing era to deal with because so many small states existed simultaneously, with the five "major" dynasties passing from one to another, while each of the five dynasties only lasted for a short period of time. Besides, as a form of wish-fulfillment most of these regimes deliberately chose for their dynastic labels the names of the previous "regular" dynasties, such as Han, Chou, and T'ang, and they also repeated among themselves in making their choices.

These five dynasties were all regional powers, and they never brought the country to unity. During that time, the country was divided and people had no fixed leader. Even though Later Chou marked the end of the Five Dynasties, there were still five kingdoms and three districts. Which were the five kingdoms?[18]

Kuo Wei of Chou,[19]
Liu Ch'ung of Northern Han,[20]
Li Ching of Southern T'ang,[21]
Meng Ch'ang of Shu,[22]
Liu Sheng of Southern Han.[23]

Which were the three districts?[24]

Their chronology is as follows: Liang (907–923), T'ang (923–936), Chin (936–946), Han (947–950), and Chou (951–960). To distinguish them from the previous regular dynasties of the same names, these five dynasties are known to posterity as Later Liang, Later T'ang, etc. They are considered as representing the legitimate line of central governments.

[18] This is certainly an ambiguity. The texts reads as if all the five kingdoms and three districts existed simultaneously with the Later Chou. But actually Chou is here counted as one of the five kingdoms. Generally, however, the entire period between the T'ang and Sung dynasties is collectively known as the period of the Five Dynasties and the Ten Kingdoms. With exceptions of Chou and Hu-nan (see footnote 27), the regimes given in the two following lists are among the "Ten Kingdoms."

[19] Kuo Wei, or Emperor T'ai-tsu (r. 951–953), was the founder of the Later Chou.

[20] Liu Ch'ung (personal name usually given as Min), or Emperor Shih-tsu (r. 951–954), was the founder of the kingdom of Northern Han, which lasted from 951 to 979.

[21] Li Ching, or Emperor Chung-chu (r. 943–961), was the second emperor of the kingdom of Southern T'ang, which lasted from 937 to 975.

[22] Shu here refers to the kingdom of Later Shu (934–965). There was another, slightly earlier Shu, known to posterity as the Former Shu, which lasted from 903 to 925. Meng Ch'ang, or Emperor Hou-chu (r. 935–965), was the second and the last emperor of the Later Shu.

[23] Liu Sheng, or Emperor Chung-tsung (r. 943–957), was the fourth emperor of the kingdom of Southern Han, which lasted from 909 to 971. Here the storyteller must have done some research, as all of the four emperors from Li Ch'ung to Liu Sheng were in fact in power when Kuo Wei ran his Later Chou Dynasty.

[24] The accuracy of the previous list is no longer maintained in this second list. The "Ten Kingdoms" are treated equally by historians as national entities without discrimination. Factual errors also abound in this second list.

Ch'ien Tso of Wu-yüeh,[25]
Kao Pao-jung of Ching-nan,[26]
Chou Hsing-feng of Hu-nan.[27]

Though these five states and three districts existed, Chou finally established itself as the legitimate dynasty, succeeding the Liang, T'ang, Chin, and Han dynasties.

The Sung founder, Chao K'uang-yin,[28] once served under Chou as the commander of the palace guards. Later, with the coup at Ch'en-ch'iao,[29] he replaced Chou and became the emperor. He then united the country and named the dynasty "Great Sung."

Before he came to power, everyone used to call him "Master Chao" or "Young Chao" because his father, Chao Hung-yin,[30] was the district defense commandant of Yüeh-chou[31] under Han. Chao K'uang-yin had a face as red as blood, his eyes looked like two morning stars, and he had the strength to battle ten thousand men and an ex-

pansiveness of spirit that could swallow up the four seas. He was especially fond of making friends with the heroes of the world; and being a chivalrous man, he did not hesitate to draw his sword, and offered his help to right a wrong whenever he saw one. He was indeed the master of busybodies and the leader of troublemakers.

To begin with, Chao disrupted the royal theater and caused a disturbance at the royal garden at Pien-ching;[32] this offended the last emperor of Han,[33] and he had to flee to far-off places. When he arrived at Hu-ch'iao[34] in the Kuan-hsi area,[35] he killed Tung Ta and got the famous horse Red Unicorn.[36] He then eliminated Sung Hu at Huang-chou;[37] beat Li Tzu-ying to death with three blows of his cudgel at Shuo-chou;[38] and exterminated the entire family of Li-Han-ch'ao, the prince of Lu-chou.[39]

When he came to the T'ai-yüan area,[40] he met his uncle Chao Ching-ch'ing, who was at that time a Taoist priest at the Clear Oil Monastery. Ching-ch'ing invited him to stay there, but unfortunately K'uang-yin fell sick and was confined to bed for three months. After he had recovered, Ching-ch'ing kept him company day and night, urging him to rest and forbidding him to wander about the place.

One day, Ching-ch'ing had to go out to attend to some business. He reminded K'uang-yin, "My nephew, please be patient and rest. You mustn't walk about, since you're just beginning to recover."

How could K'uang-yin possibly sit still after Ching-ch'ing had left? He thought, "So I won't go

[25] The kingdom of Wu-yüeh lasted from 902 to 978. Ch'ien Tso, or Prince Chung-hsien, was the third ruler and he ruled the regime from 942 to 947. That means he was not in power at the same time as Kuo Wei.

[26] The kingdom of Ching-nan (sometimes known as Nan-p'ing) lasted from 913 to 963. Kao Pao-jung, or Prince Chen-yi, was the third ruler of the regime and he ruled from 949 to 960. He was the only ruler mentioned in the second list who was actually in power at the same time as Kuo Wei.

[27] A blatant falsification of history. None of the fifteen regimes between the T'ang and the Sung dynasties was known as Hu-nan. Chou was not one of the ruling houses of that period and, of course, none of the rulers of this period was known as Chou Hsing-feng. There was, however, a Chou Hsing-feng in the Five Dynasties period, but he served as a regional commander under the Later Chou.

[28] Chao K'uang-yin was born in 927. He ascended the throne in 960.

[29] A courier station to the northeast of K'ai-feng in the present Honan Province.

[30] The first word of the given name, *hung* "flood", is incorrect. It should be *hung* "vast". This might be a case of taboo, as the word *hung* "flood" forms the first part of the first reign title of the Ming Dynasty. This indicates that this story was written in the Ming period because writers in traditional China were generally required to avoid using the words in the given names of the emperors of the current dynasty.

[31] Modern Yüeh-chou County on the east shore of the Tung-t'ing Lake.

[32] K'ai-feng in modern Honan Province.

[33] This refers to Emperor Yin (r. 948–950) of the Later Han.

[34] A fictitious place.

[35] Kuan-hsi refers to the area to the west of the Han-ku Pass at the border between the modern provinces of Shansi and Honan.

[36] This and the following supposedly chivalrous acts by Chao are apparently the storyteller's flattering fabrications.

[37] In eastern part of modern Hupeh Province.

[38] In northern Shansi Province.

[39] Lu-chou in southeastern Shansi.

[40] In central Shansi.

outside, but surely there's no harm in taking a stroll within the monastery."

He left his room and walked around the monastery, going from one hall to another. He first went to the Hall of the Taoist Trinity, strolling through its two corridors with their seventy-two statues; then after he had viewed the Temple of the Eastern Mountains, he turned to the Hall of Serenity. He uttered a sigh in admiration of what he saw:

A golden furnace houses a flame of a thousand years;
A jade lamp keeps its light for ten thousand ages.

After he had passed the Panoramic Mansion and the Jade Emperor Chamber, he found himself surrounded by a number of majestic and spacious buildings. Chao could not help but applaud the spectacle of such magnificence. The Clear Oil Monastery was indeed an endless wonder which he could never get tired of touring. When he turned to the quiet area around the Hall of the Netherworld, he saw a small hall just opposite the Temple of Descendants. Above its doorway was written "Hall of Evil Subjugation" and its doors were tightly shut. Chao looked it over for a while and was just about to turn around when he heard a woman sobbing. Chao cocked his ears and listened: the sound was coming from within the hall.

"How strange!" thought Chao. "This is a residence for priests. Why is a woman hidden here? There must be something shady going on here. I must go and ask for a novice for the key to the doors. I can't feel at ease until I know what's going on inside." He returned to his room and asked a novice for the key.

"Master himself keeps the key," said the novice. "There is something of utmost importance there, and entrance of unauthorized persons is prohibited."

"No wonder 'One can never take anything or any man for granted,' " thought Chao. "So my uncle isn't a good man after all. Now I see why he told me so many times to sit still and not wander around—so that he could carry on this business!

What kind of behavior is that for a priest? I'm going to smash open that door and see what he says."

But as he was about to move, Ching-ch'ing came in sight. Chao approached him in a rage and, without even addressing him as "uncle," he exploded: "What a fine priest you are to have done a thing like this!"

Taken by surprise, Ching-ch'ing said, "I haven't done anything!"

"Who is locked up inside the Hall of Evil Subjugation?" demanded Chao.

Realizing what his nephew was referring to, Ching-ch'ing said, waving his hands, "My nephew, don't meddle in other people's business."

Enraged, K'uang-yin bellowed like thunder, "A priest is supposed to have renounced the world; he's supposed to be chaste and incorruptible. Why is there a woman locked up inside the hall, crying and weeping? There must be an illicit affair going on. Check your own conscience! If you can explain everything clearly, we may still talk it over. Don't you dare fool me, we aren't of the same kind!"

Seeing that K'uang-yin spoke so sharply and severely, Ching-ch'ing said, "My nephew, you've wrongly accused me."

"Whether or not I've wrongly accused you is a small matter, but tell me first—is there a woman inside the hall?"

"Yes," admitted Ching-ch'ing.

"Where did she come from?" persisted K'uang-yin.

Ching-ch'ing knew that his nephew had a very bad temper; nevertheless he still wanted to withhold the truth from him. Evasively, he said, "There *is* a woman, but she has nothing to do with the priests in this monastery."

"You're the head of the monastery; even if it's not your doing, surely you should know who has placed her here."

"Nephew, please calm down. This woman was put in our custody about a month ago by two no-

torious bandits. I don't know where they kidnapped her from. All they demand is that we
keep a close watch over her. If anything goes
wrong, we'll be wiped out. Since you haven't fully
recovered, I didn't mention it to you."

"Where are the bandits now?"

"They're off somewhere else for the time
being."

Unconvinced, K'uang-yin said, "Don't give me
this nonsense! Go and unlock the doors and call
the girl out. I want to question her myself." When
he had finished speaking, he took his iron cudgel
and charged forward.

Ching-ch'ing knew how explosive his temper
could be and that standing in his way would do no
good, so he took the key, hurried after him to the
hall, and unlocked the doors. When the girl heard
the sound of the lock turning, she thought that
the bandits had returned and cried even louder.
As soon as the doors were opened, Chao strode inside without letting his uncle precede him. The
woman had hidden herself behind the statue, all
curled up in fright. As K'uang-yin approached
her, he put down the cudgel and took a good look
at her. She was indeed quite beautiful:

Her brows were like ranges of spring mountains;
Her eyes were like pools of autumn waters.
Filled with sadness and despair,
She was just like Hsi-tzu in agony.[41]
On the verge of tears and sobs,
She was just like Consort Yang when her hair was sheared.[42]
The sound of her zither gone mute,
She was just like Consort Ming before crossing the border.[43]

---

[41] Hsi-tzu (fl. 480 B.C.), or Hsi-shih, was one of the most
famous beauties in the history of China, and she was thought
to be at her most charming when she was in pain. Hsi-tzu is
remembered for her role in helping the state of Yüeh to destroy the rival state of Wu.

[42] Consort Yang (see footnote 14) once sheared her hair to
express her devotion to Emperor Hsüan-tsung. It meant that
everything she owned belonged to the emperor; even her hair,
one of the few things she received from her parents at birth,
was not beyond sacrifice.

[43] Consort Ming was better known as Wang Chao-chün. In
spite of her beauty, she did not have the opportunity of meet-

Had she composed songs for the Tartar reed pipe,
She would outshine Ts'ai Yen who was forced to stay with the
barbarians.[44]
Heaven had endowed her with a tantalizing beauty,
Which is more than a painting can capture.

"Young lady, I'm not one of those lewd fellows," K'uang-yin assured her. "Don't be afraid.
Tell me where your home is and who kidnapped
and brought you here. If there is any injustice, I'll
help you."

The woman then wiped away her tears with her
sleeves and bowed deeply to K'uang-yin, who returned her courtesy.

"Sir, what is your name?" she asked first.

"This is Master Chao from Pien-ching," Ching-
ch'ing answered for him.

"Sir, please listen to my case—" she said, but she
had hardly begun before the tears trickled down
her cheeks.

It turned out that her surname was also Chao,
and her given name was Ching-niang. She lived in
the Little Prosperity Village in the Hsieh-liang
County of P'u-chou,[45] and she had just turned
seventeen. She had accompanied her father to
Yang-ch'ü County[46] to burn incense at the Northern Mountains[47] in fulfillment of a vow. On the
way, they met two bandits, Chang Kuang-erh,

---

ing the emperor (Emperor Yüan [r. 48–33 B.C.] of the Western
Han Dynasty) after serving in the palace for quite a few years
because she refused to bribe the influential palace painter,
Mao Yen-shou. One night she played the zither to express her
loneliness and the music attracted the attention of the emperor. But it was already too late. Mao, for fear of being punished, fled to the Huns and persuaded the chieftain to demand
Wang Chao-chün as a condition of peace. The emperor had
no alternative but to send Chao-chün to the Huns for a political marriage.

[44] Ts'ai Yen, better known as Ts'ai Wen-chi, the daughter of
the late Han scholar Ts'ai Yung (113–192), was kidnapped by
the Huns. She was later ransomed by Ts'ao Ts'ao.

[45] P'u-chou is situated at the southwestern tip of Shansi.
From T'ai-yüan to P'u-chou is about two hundred miles.

[46] To the northeast of T'ai-yüan.

[47] This is another name for the Heng (Eternal) Mountains,
a mountain range stretching from Shansi to Hopei. See also
footnote 53.

nicknamed Flying All Over, and Chou Chin, nick-named Rolling All Along. When they saw how beautiful Ching-niang was, they spared her fa-ther's life and abducted her to the Temple of the Mountain God. Chang and Chou argued over who should marry her and neither would give way. They discussed the matter for several days and, fearing that this would damage their brotherhood, they put Ching-niang in the custody of the Clear Oil Monastery, instructing the Taoists to feed and guard her with care. Then they went elsewhere to look for another beautiful girl so that the two bandits could be married on the same day. Chang and Chou had been gone for a month and had not yet returned. The Taoists were afraid of them and had to take care of Ching-niang as instructed.

After Ching-niang had told her story, K'uang-yin said to his uncle, "I behaved very rudely just then and nearly offended you, uncle. Ching-niang is a woman of good family unfortunately captured by bandits; who will rescue her if I don't?" He then said to Ching-niang, "Young lady, don't worry. Let me take care of everything. I guaran-tee that you'll be able to return to your home and see your parents again."

"Thank you for your kindness in rescuing me from danger," said Ching-niang. "But unfortu-nately my home is more than a thousand *li* away; how can a single girl like me make such a perilous journey?"

"Certainly I wouldn't want to leave you in the lurch like this," said K'uang-yin, "Whatever the length of the journey, I'll escort you home per-sonally."

Ching-niang bowed and thanked him. "If I could be so fortunate, you would indeed be my second parent."

"My nephew, you mustn't do that," Ching-ch'ing said. "These bandits are horrible and pow-erful people: even the authorities dare not offend them. Now that you've rescued this young lady, it'll certainly be very hard for me to deny respon-sibility. If they come back to ask me for her, what shall I say? This will certainly implicate me!"

"If one is brave," K'uang-yin said, laughing, "one can go anywhere under heaven; but if one is timid, one cannot move a single inch. I have never failed to do the righteous thing and do not feel threatened even before ten thousand men. Those bandits might be fierce, but how can they com-pare with the prince of Lu-chou? They, too, have ears, and must have heard of my name. Since you Taoists are afraid of trouble, I'll leave my marks here so that you can answer the bandits."

No sooner had he finished than he twirled his iron cudgel and, thrusting his body forward, struck hard on the dark red window frame. With a "Crack," the lattice shattered and fell. With an-other stroke, he crushed the four window frames completely out of shape. Ching-niang, trembling with fear, had hidden herself in a far-off corner, while Ching-ch'ing turned ashen and called out repeatedly, "What sin!"

"If the bandits return, just tell them that I've broken into the hall and taken her away by force," K'uang-yin said. [As the saying goes], " 'Every in-justice has its oppressor, and every debt has its creditor.' If they want to look for me, tell them to head for P'u-chou."

"P'u-chou is a thousand *li* away, with all those bandits on the way," Ching-ch'ing said. "It would be difficult even for you to travel alone, not to mention having to take care of this lady. You should think it over carefully."

"At the end of the Han Dynasty, during the time of the Three Kingdoms," K'uang-yin said, laughing, "Kuan Yün-ch'ang [48] singlehandedly saw his two sisters-in-law on a thousand-*li* journey to safety. He went through five passes and killed

[48] Kuan Yü (160–219), styled Yün-ch'ang, was one of the two sworn brothers of Liu Pei, the founder of the kingdom of Shu of the Three Kingdoms period. Kuan was regarded as the symbol of loyalty, brotherhood, and martial strength, and his heroic deeds had been greatly enhanced in history and in fic-tion. In the Ch'ing period, he was deified as God Kuan, the god of war.

64

six generals, going all the way to Ku-ch'eng[49] to join Lord Liu.[50] This kind of action befits a hero. If I can't even rescue one lady, what kind of man am I? If my enemies and I are destined to meet on the way, I shall surely kill them all."

"Even so," Ching-ch'ing said, "I still have one more thing to remind you of: in ancient times, men and women didn't share the same mat when they sat, and they didn't share the same bowl when they ate. Even though your intention to see the lady home is good and honorable, yet how could others understand? When they see a young man and a young woman traveling together, they're bound to be suspicious. Not only would such gossip compromise your kind intention, but your good name will also be blemished."

"Uncle," K'uang-yin said, laughing, "please don't blame me for saying this: you Taoists do love to put on airs, and your actions often don't match with your real intentions. We knights-errant listen only to our consciences; we never worry about what others would say."

When Ching-ch'ing saw that his nephew's mind was already set, he asked, "When do you plan to leave?"

"Tomorrow morning."

"I'm afraid that you haven't fully recovered."

"That doesn't matter."

Ching-ch'ing instructed a novice to prepare some wine to bid them farewell. During the feast, K'uang-yin said to Ching-niang, "Lady, my uncle has just mentioned that our traveling together might cause suspicion and gossip, so I'd like to take advantage of this occasion to pledge brotherhood with you. My surname is Chao and so is yours. Five hundred years ago our ancestors were actually one family. Hence, let us address each other as brother and sister."

"Sir, you're a person of high stature," said Ching-niang. "How would I dare presume?"

"This is really a good idea, if you two are to

travel together," Ching-ch'ing said. Accordingly, he told a novice to take out a prayer mat.

Ching-niang asked her benefactor to sit down and intoned, "Please accept this kowtow from your sister."

K'uang-yin stood aside and returned the bow. Then Ching-niang bowed to Ching-ch'ing, calling him "uncle." During the dinner, Ching-ch'ing related many of his nephew's heroic deeds, and Ching-niang was overjoyed. The feast lasted until after the first watch that night. Ching-ch'ing let Ching-niang sleep in his bedroom and slept with K'uang-yin in an outer chamber.

When the cock crowed at the fifth watch, Ching-ch'ing got up to eat breakfast and have some dried beef and provisions prepared for their trip. K'uang-yin saddled the Red Unicorn, bound the baggage securely, and reminded Ching-niang, "Sister, you must dress like a peasant. If you wear heavy makeup and flashy clothes, you might invite trouble."

After breakfast, K'uang-yin disguised himself as a traveler, and Ching-niang dressed as a peasant girl, with the usual snowcap pulled down over her brows. The two of them said good-bye to Ching-ch'ing. Seeing them to the door, Ching-ch'ing suddenly thought of something: "Nephew, I'm afraid you can't leave today. There is still something I want to discuss with you."

What was Ching-ch'ing referring to? Truly:

The magpie soars high only with feathers;
A tiger without fangs and claws cannot go on the hunt.

"Two persons cannot ride on one horse. The lady has tiny bound feet; how could she keep up with you on foot? Wouldn't that slow down the journey? Why not take some time to hire a carriage for her," said Ching-ch'ing.

"I've considered this matter for some time; a carriage would only add to my burden. I'll let sister ride this horse, and I'm willing to walk the thousand *li* on foot without regrets," answered K'uang-yin.

---

[49] The event is entirely fictitious.
[50] Liu Pei.

65

"I'm already imposing on you to take such a long journey," said Ching-niang. "I only regret that I'm not a man and don't know how to ride. But under no circumstances would I take your horse."

"You're a girl and need some means of transportation. My feet aren't small; they're just right for walking," insisted K'uang-yin.

Ching-niang refused persistently, but K'uang-yin would not agree. Finally, she had to mount the horse. K'uang-yin strapped on his sword, took his iron cudgel, then bowed and bade his uncle farewell.

"Be careful on the way, nephew," said Ching-ch'ing. "I'm afraid you might meet those two bandits. You must be extra careful! Make it a thorough job when you do kill them, so that we won't be involved."

"No problem," K'uang-yin assured him. Then he gave the horse a slap and shouted, "Go." The horse sped off while Chao followed behind with big strides.

They ate and drank on the way when they were hungry and thirsty, taking lodging only at night and setting off at dawn. In a few days' time, they had reached Chieh-hsiu County in Fen-chou.[51] The Red Unicorn was a horse of great endurance and ability with a speed as fast as wind and lightning. The journey from the Clear Oil Monastery to Fen-chou was less than three hundred li, and the horse could have made it within half a day, but since Chao was on foot and Ching-niang, being a woman, was unaccustomed to riding a horse, he held the reins taut and the horse walked along at an easy pace. Furthermore, there were many bandits along the way, making it necessary to start off late and retire early. Hence they only made slightly more than a hundred li each day.

One day they arrived at a place called Yellow Thatch Hamlet at the foot of a small hill. There had been a village, but because of the chaos of the times, the people had all run away, and only a tiny

inn remained. Since it was growing dark and before them was nothing but the wilderness, Chao said to Ching-niang, "Let's rest here for the night and we'll start off again early tomorrow morning."

"As you wish," agreed Ching-niang.

The innkeeper took their baggage while Ching-niang dismounted and took off her snowcap. As he caught a glimpse of her, the innkeeper's tongue hung out and he couldn't draw it back. He thought to himself, "How could there be such a beauty!" He led the horse to the back of the house and tied it, while Chao asked Ching-niang to go inside and rest.

When the innkeeper came back, he stared stupidly at Ching-niang. "What's on your mind, innkeeper?" Chao asked.

"What relation is this young lady to you?"

"She's my sister."

"Sir, not that I'm one to talk, but you really shouldn't have brought such a beautiful girl on such a long journey."

"Why?"

"Some fifteen li from here is the Chieh Mountain, where the land is barren and deserted. Only bandits frequent it, and if they happened to find out about her, not only would you have to give her to them as their leader's bride for nothing, you would also have to send along some luck money."

Enraged, Chao thundered, "You impudent rascal! How dare you scare your guests with lies." He punched the innkeeper in the face. The latter spat blood and dashed out. Then the innkeeper's wife was heard complaining in the kitchen.

"Brother," said Ching-niang, "you've been too cross with him."

"He shouldn't have taken the liberty of saying what he did. He doesn't look like a decent sort, that's why I gave him some warning [by punching him] first."

"Since we are lodging here, we must not offend him."

"What's there to be afraid of?"

---

[51] To the southwest of T'ai-yüan.

Ching-niang went to the kitchen to see the wife of the innkeeper and comforted her for a long time before the latter finally calmed down and started a fire to prepare dinner.

When Ching-niang returned to the room, there was still light inside and the lamp had not been lit. As Chao was sitting and talking with Ching-niang, he saw a man come over and stand by the doorway, craning his neck to look inside the room.

"Who dares to spy on us!" Chao shouted.

"I've come to chat with the innkeeper," said the man. "It has nothing to do with you, sir." Then he went to the kitchen and talked with the innkeeper's wife in a low voice for a while before leaving.

When he saw all this, Chao's suspicions were aroused. By the time the lamp was lit, the innkeeper had not yet returned, and the woman brought dinner to their room. After the meal, Chao first told Ching-niang to close the door and go to sleep. Then, saying that he had to go to the bathroom, he took a look around the house, carrying both his sword and his cudgel.

At about the second watch, he heard the Red Unicorn neighing and kicking in the shed at the back of the house. It was near the end of tenth month, and the moon was just rising. Chao tiptoed forward and saw that the horse had kicked a man to the ground. When the man saw him coming, he struggled frantically to his feet and ran. Knowing that he was a horse thief, Chao chased after him, and before he realized it, he had already run quite a distance.

When he got to the Swift Stream Bridge, he lost sight of the man. All he saw was a small hut by the bridge with a light inside. As Chao suspected that the man was hiding inside, he ventured in. He saw an old man with a white beard sitting properly in the middle of the earthen bed, reading a scripture. What was he like?

Mist-like eyes,
Frost-like beard,
Eyebrows like willow catkins in the wind,
Face the color of peach blossoms.
If he isn't the star Venus in heaven,
He must be the god of the mountain.

When the old man saw Chao come in, he quickly got up and bowed. Chao returned the courtesy and asked, "What scripture are you reading, sir?"

"The *Scripture of Heavenly Redemption*," replied the old man.

"What use is there in reading it?"

"Seeing the world falling apart, I hope that the Son of Heaven will soon emerge to restore order and deliver the people from their misery."

Chao was delighted when he heard this, for it matched his own thoughts. He asked further, "There's quite a number of bandits around this area; do you know their whereabouts?"

"Sir, are you not the one accompanying a young lady on horseback, and the two of you are presently lodging at the Yellow Thatch Hamlet at the foot of the hill?"

"That's right."

"It's fortunate that you met me, for you've almost run into danger."

Chao asked for an explanation. The old man invited him to take the seat of honor and, after taking a seat to the side himself, he spoke with great ease: "Two bandits have recently come to the Chieh Mountain. They've gathered a group of cohorts, and together they've plundered and caused disturbances throughout the Fen-Lu area.[52] One of them is Chang Kuang-erh, nicknamed Flying All Over, and the other is Chou Chin, nicknamed Rolling All Along. Half a month ago, they abducted a woman from somewhere. Unable to settle a dispute as to who should marry her, they put her up at some other place and decided to wait until they found another beauty and then get married together. All the inns along this road were told by the bandits that if they should chance to see a beauty, and if they reported to the bandit chiefs immediately, they would be hand-

[52] Fen-chou and Lu-chou mentioned above.

67

somely rewarded. When you arrived this evening, the innkeeper notified Chou Chin right away, and Wildfire Yao Wang was sent to investigate. He reported, 'Not only is the woman beautiful, but she is also riding a fine horse. There is only one man with her, so there's nothing to fear.' They have one man called Swiftfoot Ch'en Ming who can cover three hundred *li* in one day. He was sent to steal the horse first while the rest of them made camp in the Red Pine Forest further down the road. They're waiting for you to pass by at the fifth watch to attack you. You must take precautions."

"So that's it! How do you come to know all this, sir?"

"I've lived here for a long time, and I'm aware of everything that goes on. But when you meet the bandits, please don't mention me."

Chao thanked him for his advice; then he took his cudgel, got up, and went back the same way. The door of the inn was half open, so he slipped inside.

Let us go back to the innkeeper. He had come home in order to help Ch'en Ming steal the horse and was talking with his wife in the room while she warmed some wine for him. At the sight of Chao coming through the door, he immediately slipped behind the lamp. Chao thought of a plan, and told Ching-ning to ask for some wine. When the innkeeper's wife took an empty jar and went to the wine cask behind the door to ladle wine, Chao struck her from behind with his cudgel, taking her by surprise, and she fell to the ground, dropping the wine jar. When he heard his wife calling out in pain, the innkeeper grabbed his sword and hurried into the room, where Chao was waiting leisurely for his victim to appear. Chao's hand rose, his cudgel struck, and the innkeeper fell. Another two strokes and both of them were dead. Ching-niang was shocked but it was too late for her to stop him. She asked Chao why he had to kill them, and Chao related to her what the old man had said. Ching-niang was so fright-

ened that her face turned ashen. "If the journey is so perilous, what should we do?"

"No matter what happens, I'll be around," Chao assured her. "Don't worry."

He bolted the main door and went to warm some wine in the kitchen. After drinking himself half drunk, he fed the horse, plugged the openings of the horse bells so that they wouldn't make noise, and then tied the baggage on securely. He dragged the two bodies to the woodpile inside the kitchen and set fire to it, and to both the front and the back doors. When he saw that the flames were burning high, he helped Ching-niang mount the horse and they set off.

By then it was almost dawn. They passed by the Swift Stream Bridge, hoping to find the old man and get directions, but the house where he had read the scripture had already disappeared. All they saw was a tiny temple with earthen walls about three feet high. Inside the temple, a statue of the local deity sat to one side. Chao then realized that it was this deity who had appeared before him and instructed him the previous night. He thought to himself, "He called me 'sir' and dared not take the main seat in my presence, so I must be someone extraordinary. If I rise to power someday, I will certainly give him a title."

Chao hurried the Red Unicorn on, and after traveling for a short distance they came to a forest with foliage not unlike flaming clouds. Chao called out, "Slow down, sister. I think that's the Red Pine Forest—" Before he had finished, a man with an iron pitchfork emerged from the bushes and thrust the pitchfork at Chao. Chao blocked the attack easily with his iron cudgel. The man retreated as he fought, hoping to draw Chao into the forest. Enraged, Chao raised his cudgel with both hands, cried out loudly, and struck off half the man's skull. The man turned out to be none other than Wildfire Yao Wang. Chao told Ching-niang to hold the horse for the moment: "I'm going ahead into the forest to finish off those bandits. Then we'll start off again."

"Please be careful, brother," Ching-niang pleaded.

Chao strode ahead. Truly:

The sacred emperor is assisted by a hundred spirits;
A mighty general is surrounded by his majestic air.

Inside the Red Pine Forest, Rolling All Along Chou Chin had made camp with forty or fifty followers. When he heard sounds of footsteps outside the forest, he thought that Yao Wang, who had been scouting, was reporting back. With a long spear in his hand, he emerged from the bushes and ran right into Chao. Chao knew that he was one of the bandit chiefs and, without saying a word, lifted his cudgel and struck down. Chou Chin fought back with his spear. It was only after the two had exchanged around twenty blows that the followers inside the forest realized that Chou Chin had encountered the enemy. They beat the gong and rushed forward together, surrounding the two of them.

"Why don't you come on forward, all of you!" challenged Chao. With his cudgel swinging, he seemed to be surrounded by a golden dragon and wrapped in a jade python. Those who met his cudgel were flung about like autumn leaves in the wind, and those who went near him dropped everywhere like fallen flowers. He sent them flying in all directions. Chou Chin became afraid and his movements slowed down accordingly. Chao struck him down with one blow. Shouting in confusion, the bandits all ran off.

When Chao walked back, Ching-niang was nowhere to be seen. He searched frantically all around, but Ching-niang had already been carried off by several bandits to the other side of the Red Pine Forest. Chao hurried after them and shouted, "Bandits! Where do you think you're going?"

When the bandits saw Chao coming after them, they abandoned Ching-niang and scattered in all directions. "You must have been frightened, sister!" said Chao.

"Two of those men recognized me because they had followed the bandit chiefs to the Clear Oil Monastery," said Ching-niang. "They said then, 'Chief Chou is fighting with that traveler, but I don't think he's a match for our chief. We'll take you over to Chief Chang first.'"

"I've already killed that scoundrel Chou Chin. But I wonder where Chang Kuang-erh is?"

"Let's hope that you won't run into him," said Ching-niang.

Chao hurried the horse along, and after traveling for about forty *li* they arrived at a small town. Chao, feeling hungry, held the rein so that he could help Ching-niang dismount and enter the restaurant. The several waiters they saw were all busy preparing meals, and none of them would wait on the passing guests. Chao was suspicious, but since he was with Ching-niang, he did not want to stir up trouble, so he simply [left again and] led the horse past the restaurant. Along the way they saw nothing but closed doors. Even the door of a tiny house at the other end of the town was shut tight. Chao was confused, and when he knocked, no one answered. He walked around the house, tied the horse to a tree, and tapped softly on the back door. An old woman opened the door and peeked out, looking rather frightened. Chao immediately stepped into the house and bowed to the old woman, saying, "Madam, please don't be afraid. I'm only a traveler passing through with a female relative. We'd like to have a meal, and we'll leave as soon as possible."

Looking frightened, the old woman hushed Chao into silence. When Ching-niang had also came in, she closed the door.

"The restaurant over there is busy preparing for a banquet. What officials are you expecting?" asked Chao.

The old woman waved her hands and said, "Sir, please mind your own business."

"What is so serious about this business?" asked Chao. "Can you possibly explain to me, a traveler from afar?"

69

"The chief Flying All Over will pass by here today," replied the old woman. "This village has collected money to prepare a banquet for them so they'll leave us in peace. My son is also helping out there at the restaurant."

When Chao heard that, he thought, "That's it! I might as well take this chance to finish them off once and for all, and save the Clear Oil Monastery from further trouble." So he said, "Madam, this is my sister. We're on our way to make a promised offering at the Southern Mountains.[53] I'm afraid she might be frightened if we run into the bandits, so could I trouble you to let her stay here for a while? We'll leave after the chief has passed through and I'll certainly pay you well."

"What a fine lady," said the old woman. "It'll be no trouble for you two to hide here, but you mustn't cause trouble."

"Being a man, I can take care of myself. I'm going outside just to see what's happening."

"Be careful," cautioned the old woman. "I have some pancakes here and I can boil some water for you, but cooking a meal would be inconvenient."

Chao took his cudgel and left as before through the back door. He was going to mount the horse to meet the bandits when he suddenly thought, "I said that I'd walk the thousand *li* when I was at the Clear Oil Monastery. I wouldn't be a real man if I went on horseback out of fear of the bandits." He ran back up the street with large strides. He thought of a plan and went into the restaurant, calling out in a swaggering manner, "The chief will be here shortly. I'm his advance man. Have you got the food ready?"

"It's all ready," replied the people inside the restaurant.

"Set a table so I can eat first," said Chao.

As they were long accustomed to being bullied by the bandits, who would dare to question his identity? Moreover, they hoped that he would put

in a good word for them with the bandit chief. Thus, large portions of fish and meat along with warmed wine and hot rice were served. Chao ate heartily. When he was almost full, there was a commotion outside and someone announced, "The chief is here. Set up the incense table quickly."

Without hurrying at all, Chao took his iron cudgel and went outside. He saw that the townspeople, carrying around two dozen spears, swords, and staffs, were leading the way. When they reached the door of the restaurant, they all knelt down. Flying All Over Chang Kuang-erh rode in on a tall horse, with Swiftfoot Ch'en Ming following close behind him holding a whip in his hand. Behind them was a band of some forty to fifty bandits and about ten carriages. Since both [Chang Kuang-erh and Chou Chin] were bandit chiefs, do you know why Chang was so much more imposing? Actually, the bandits had no fixed rules to their movements; [either could have been the one to set up the ambush,] and when they heard that there was only one traveler, they had not taken him seriously. That was why Chou Chin had underestimated his enemy. This Chang Kuang-erh had gone on separately and was robbing in another area when Swiftfoot Ch'en Ming reported, "Second chief has already captured a beautiful woman and asks you to meet him at the Chieh Mountain." So Chang gathered his band and came, passing villages and towns in splendor and majesty.

Chao hid himself behind the north wall and kept a close watch. When the horse came close enough, he yelled, "Bandit, here is my cudgel!" and soared up from the crowd to zoom down like an eagle descending from midair. Faster done than said, Chang's horse shied and leaped forward. Chao's cudgel came down hard and broke one of its front legs. It fell down in pain, but Chang Kuang-erh had already released his hold and jumped down from the horse. Ch'en Ming, who was behind Chang, attacked with his cudgel,

[53] This is another name for the Heng (Eternal) Mountains in modern Honan Province. Here the text is incorrect (see footnote 47).

but Chao easily struck him down with a single blow. Brandishing a sword in each hand, Chang charged at Chao, but Chao leaped into an open space to fight with him. After they had exchanged more than ten blows, Chang slashed down with his sword, but Chao's cudgel hit him on his fingers. The sword fell from Chang's right hand, and he felt helpless with only one left in his left hand, so he turned tail and ran.

"That's why they call you Flying All Over, eh," shouted Chao. "See if you can fly up there [to heaven] today." He took a quick step forward and struck down on the back of Chang's head, smashing it beyond recognition. How sad it is that the two powerful bandits should die on the same day. It was truly:

The three souls "flying all over,"
The seven spirits "rolling all along."[54]

The rest of the bandits were all about to run away when Chao shouted, "I am Master Chao of Pien-ching. My feud is only with bandits Chang Kuang-erh and Chou Chin. Since they're both dead, I wouldn't hold anything against you."

The bandits threw down their weapons and prostrated themselves on the ground, saying, "We've never seen a hero like you, and we're willing to serve you as our chief."

Chao laughed heartily and said, "I don't even care for official ranks; how could I degrade myself by becoming a bandit?" When Chao saw that Ch'en Ming was among them, he called out, "Were you the one who came to steal my horse last night?"

Ch'en Ming kowtowed and admitted his guilt.

"Come with me," Chao told them, "and I'll treat you all to a meal."

The men went with him into the restaurant and Chao instructed the owner, "Today, I've elimin-

ated two menaces from your area. These are good people. Let them eat the food which you've prepared and I'll take care of them afterward. But save Chang Kuang-erh's table for me; I've some use for it." The owner of course had to obey.

When everyone had eaten, Chao asked Ch'en Ming, "I've heard that you can walk three hundred *li* in a day. With your ability, why did you get involved with the bandits? I've a job for you right now. Are you willing to take it?"

"General, ask me to do anything," said Ch'in Ming. "I won't refuse even if it means going through fire and water."

"When I was at Pien-ching, I made a lot of trouble in the royal garden and disrupted the royal theater. That was why I fled here. Could I trouble you to go to Pien-ching and find out what's happening there? Meet me in half a month's time at the place of Abbot Chao at the Clear Oil Monastery in T'ai-yüan. Be there without fail."

Chao then borrowed a brush and ink-slab, wrote his uncle Chao Ching-ch'ing a letter, and gave it to Ch'en Ming. He then brought out the bandits' carriages and loot and divided them into three portions. One portion he distributed among the inhabitants of the town as compensation for the past disturbances of the bandits. He also told the townspeople to take the bandits' corpses and weapons to the authorities and claim rewards. Another portion he divided among the bandits for food and clothing so that they could return to their homes and start new lives. He divided the third portion in half and gave both halves to Ch'en Ming, one for traveling expenses and the other to be sent to the Clear Oil Monastery to pay for repairing the windows and doors of the Hall of Evil Subjugation. When Chao had finished the distribution, everyone was satisfied and grateful to him.

Chao told the owner of the restaurant to bring the table of food originally reserved for Chang Kuang-erh to the old woman's house. The woman's son also came to meet Chao and Ching-

[54] Both "three souls" and "seven spirits" are Taoist terms. Of the three souls of a man, one goes up to heaven, another goes down to earth, while the third stays by the corpse. All the seven spirits of the body are of evil nature.

niang. When Chao related to the old woman how he had eliminated the bandits, everyone was overjoyed. Chao said to Ching-niang, "Throughout this journey, I've never acted as a host. Today, [as the saying goes], may I 'borrow someone else's flower to present to the Buddha,' and drink with you to allay your fright?" That Ching-niang was grateful goes without saying.

That night, Chao took out ten taels in cash from his bag to give to the old woman, and he and Ching-niang spent the night in her house.

Ching-niang's mind was now occupied with Chao's kindness to her. "In the past," she thought, "even a mere courtesan like Red Duster had the courage to choose her own hero.[55] For one thing, I owe him more than I can hope to repay for his kindness to me. But even from the standpoint of looking for a husband, where else can I find a comparable person?" She thought of offering herself but was too embarassed to speak up. "But," she went on thinking, "if I don't speak my mind, how would a straightforward man like him know about my tender feelings toward him?" These thoughts turned over and over in her mind and she was sleepless the whole night long. It was dawn before she knew it and the cock was already crowing.

Chao rose, saddled the horse, and was ready to leave. Ching-niang felt depressed; then an idea suddenly occurred to her. Along the way, she pretended that she was suffering from a terrible stomachache and asked to relieve herself several times. Whenever she mounted and dismounted, she asked Chao to help her, during which she pressed herself against him, clinging to his neck and shoulder in a most seductive way. When they

took lodging, she complained about the cold, then about the heat, asking him to remove a quilt this time and to add a blanket another time. How could a man resist her soft fragrance and warmth? But being a straightforward and honorable man, Chao failed to understand the real meaning of Ching-niang's complaints. All he did was to double his efforts to take good care of her.

They traveled for a few more days and came to the Ch'ü-wo area, only some three hundred *li* from P'u-chou.[56] That night, they stayed in a deserted village. Ching-niang thought to herself, "Now that we're nearly home, if I let my shyness keep me from speaking, I'll miss my chance; and once we're home, everything will be over, and then it'll be too late for regrets." After dark, not a sound was heard around them, and the dim lamp flickered. Ching-niang had not yet gone to sleep; she was weeping and sighing before the lamp.

"Why are you so unhappy, sister?" asked Chao.

"I've something to tell you from the bottom of my heart," she replied. "But I'm afraid that it would be impudent of me. Please don't be offended."

"Nothing should be offensive between brother and sister. Feel free to tell me everything."

"I'm a sheltered and pampered girl and I've never even ventured beyond my own home. Unfortunately, in my journey with my father to make an offering, I fell into the hands of bandits and was locked up in the Clear Oil Monastery. It was only a matter of luck that the bandits left and my life was prolonged for several days; otherwise I would not have met you. Had the bandits tried to assault me, I'd have died rather than be compromised. Now that you've rescued me and escorted me a thousand *li* on foot, and killed my enemies so that they can't pose any more threat to me, you've put me in your debt, beyond repayment. So, if you don't find me too ugly, I'm willing to serve you as your wife in the hope that I can

---

[55] This refers to a legend of how a maid serving Yang Su (?–606), a high official toward the end of the Sui Dynasty, eloped with a young man whom she rightly recognized to be on his way to becoming an eminent figure. Later the young man, Li Ching (571–649), assisted the T'ang founder in establishing the new dynasty. A fictional account of Red Duster can be found in the T'ang tale "The Curly-Bearded Stranger ("Ch'iu-jan k'o chuan"), available in *T'ai-p'ing kuang-chi* 193.

[56] The proportion of the distance is about right. The journey should have been two-thirds over when they reached Ch'ü-wo.

repay part of my debt. But I don't know whether you'll allow me to do so or not."

"Sister, you're wrong," Chao said, laughing heartily. "We met by chance, and I rescued you simply because I took pity on your plight, not because I lusted for your beauty. Furthermore, we share the same surname and should not be married. Since we've vowed to be brother and sister, we'll be violating proper human relationships if you become my wife. Like Liu Hsia-hui,[57] I don't feel the least tempted even with a beauty sitting on my lap. On your part, don't follow the wanton and dissolute example of Wu Meng-tzu.[58] Stop talking so foolishly or we'll be made a laughingstock."

Ching-niang was filled with shame, and for a long time she was left speechless. Then she spoke again: "My benefactor, please forgive my impudence in speaking again. I'm not a wanton. It's just that you're the one who has saved my life, and I have nothing to give you but myself. If I'm not good enough to be your wife, at least allow me to serve you as a maid so that I may die content."

Chao was enraged. "I'm an upright man. I've never done anything evil or improper in all my life. Why do you take me for a petty man who expects a reward for a small favor or someone who serves his personal interest in the name of public service? If you don't abandon these evil thoughts, I'll leave right away and mind my own business. Don't blame me for leaving you in the lurch then!" Chao looked and sounded very stern indeed.

Ching-niang bowed deeply and said, "Now I understand your real character. You're even more upright than Liu Hsia-hui or the man from the state of Lu.[59] I'm only a woman, and my under-

standing is limited by my experiences. I do hope you'll forgive me."

Chao then calmed down and said, "Sister, it's not that I'm a man without feelings. It was out of my sense of righteousness that I decided to escort you on foot through this thousand-*li* journey. Now if I had any evil designs on you, I wouldn't be any different from those two bandits. My original sincerity would become deceit and I would become the laughingstock of all the heroes."

"Your advice is wise. If I can't repay your immense kindness in this life, I shall certainly do so after my death."

The two of them talked until dawn. Truly:

The fallen flower wishes to follow the flowing stream;
Yet the flowing stream is callous toward the fallen flower.

From this time on, Ching-niang respected Chao even more, and his compassion for her grew. Nothing special happened as they approached P'u-chou. Even though Ching-niang lived in the Little Prosperity Village, she did not know the way there, and Chao had to ask for directions. When Ching-niang saw the landscape of her native place from horseback, she was deeply moved.

On the other hand, ever since Squire Chao of the Little Prosperity Village had lost Ching-niang, the old couple had thought about her and wept every day for more than two months. When a tenant came to report that Ching-niang had returned on horseback, followed by a red-faced man holding a cudgel, the squire said, "Oh no! The bandit has come to demand her dowry!"

"It can't be just one bandit," Ching-niang's mother said. "Tell our son Chao Wen to go and have a look."

"How can you retrieve your meat from the tiger's mouth? Sister had been abducted by the bandits; why should they send her back? It must be someone that looks like her. It couldn't be her—"

But before he had finished, Ching-niang had already entered the main hall. When her parents

---

[57] Liu Hsia-hui of the Spring and Autumn period was well known for his alleged indifference toward women.

[58] The wife of Duke Chao (r. 541–509 B.C.) of the state of Lu of the Spring and Autumn period.

[59] According to legend, a man of the state of Lu refused to let a widow enter his house one rainy night.

saw their daughter, they all embraced one another and wept. When they had finally stopped crying, they asked Ching-niang how she had managed to return. Ching-niang briefly related how the bandits had locked her up in the Clear Oil Monastery, and how she was fortunate enough to meet K'uang-yin, who upon seeing this injustice, rescued her, vowed to be her brother, then escorted her a thousand *li* on foot and finally slew the two bandits on the way. "Now my benefactor is here; we must show him proper respect."

Squire Chao hurried out of the hall to meet K'uang-yin. Bowing, he thanked him: "If it weren't for your bravery, my daughter would certainly have remained in the hands of the bandits, and we would never have seen one another again." He told Ching-niang and her mother to thank K'uang-yin and also called his son Chao Wen out to thank their benefactor.

The tenants slaughtered a pig and prepared a feast in honor of K'uang-yin. Chao Wen secretly said to his father, " 'A good deed never goes beyond one's front door, but a bad one travels a thousand *li*.' Sister was abducted by the bandits, and this alone is already a misfortune for the family. Now she has returned with that red-faced man. As the saying goes, 'Who will get up early if not for one's own profit?' She must have had relations with that man; otherwise, why would he escort her a thousand *li* home? After sister has gone through so many traumatic experiences, who would want to marry her? Why not ask this man to be your son-in-law? It'll be like killing two birds with one stone, and it'll also keep others from gossiping."

Squire Chao was an old man who hardly had an idea of his own. When he heard what his son had said, he told Ching-niang's mother to ask her: "You and this young man Chao have traveled one thousand *li* together, so you must have given yourself to him. Now your brother has told your father to ask him to marry you. What do you think about this?"

"Master Chao is upright and selfless," replied Ching-niang. "He and I have vowed to be brother and sister, as close as if we were of the same parents. He's never uttered an improper word. I hope you and father will let him stay here for half a month or so, just to show our gratitude. Please don't mention this matter again."

Ching-niang's mother related what she had said to the squire, but he didn't think much of it. Shortly, the feast was prepared and Squire Chao asked K'uang-yin to take the seat of honor, while the old couple themselves sat across from him. Chao Wen and Ching-niang sat respectively on his left and right. After several rounds of wine, Squire Chao spoke up: "I've something to say. My entire family is grateful to you for saving my daughter's life, but we've nothing with which to repay you. Fortunately, my daughter is not yet betrothed. May I then offer her as your wife? I hope you won't refuse."

When Chao heard this, his temper flared. "You dotard!" he shouted, "I came here out of righteousness, but you've insulted me with such words. If I coveted her beauty, we'd have been married on the way. Why should I bother to escort her a thousand *li*? Since you can't even discern good from bad, all my efforts are wasted on you!"

After this, he overturned the table and charged directly for the door. The old Chao couple trembled with fear; and Chao Wen, seeing how ferocious K'uang-yin was, dared not venture forward either. But Ching-niang was greatly troubled and went forward to hold onto Chao's sleeve, pleading, "Please don't be angry. For my sake."

Chao turned a deaf ear to her. Jerking away from her, he ran to untie the Red Unicorn from the willow tree, jumped into the saddle, and galloped away. Ching-niang fell to the ground, sobbing. Her parents urged her to go back to her room, complaining angrily to Chao Wen who, feeling both ashamed and angry, also left the house. When Chao Wen's wife heard his parents blaming her husband on her sister-in-law's account, she was displeased, but still forced herself to comfort her, though in somewhat disparaging terms.

"Sister," she said, "even though parting is painful, that man must be heartless to have accompanied you a thousand *li* and then taken off so suddenly. If he had any sense of righteousness, he should have consented to this marriage proposal. Anyway, you're young and beautiful; no need to worry about finding a good husband. Please stop fretting."

Ching-niang was speechless with anger, tears streaming down her cheeks. "Because of my miserable fate," she thought to herself, "I fell into the hands of ferocious bandits. Fortunately, a hero rescued me, and I hoped to entrust my life to him. Who could know that my wish would not work out, and instead my reputation would be soiled? Now even my parents, brother, and sister-in-law have misjudged me; how can I expect other people to understand me? Not only did I fail to repay Master Chao's kindness, but his good name suffered because of me. It's all my fault that his chivalry has been misinterpreted. With a fate as bad as this, it would've been better for me to have died at the Clear Oil Monastery, for at least I'd have been spared all the gossip and retained my good name. Now it's too late for regrets, but since death is only a matter of time, I might as well end my life now to affirm my chastity."

Ching-niang waited until the middle of the night when her parents were fast asleep before taking a brush and writing a quatrain on the wall. Then, taking a pinch of earth for incense, she gazed up at the sky, bowed four times to Chao, and hung herself with a white silk scarf from the beam.

What a pity that a fine daughter of a good family
Has become a woman of a short dream.

When the old couple got up the next morning and did not see their daughter come out of her room, they went inside and found her hanging from the beam. They were shocked and burst into tears. They saw a poem on the wall which read:

Heaven gave me beauty but no opportunity;
I've been disgraced and insulted.
Tonight I die to repay Master Chao,
So that our good names can be redeemed.

Ching-niang's mother took her daughter down. Chao Wen and his wife also came. Squire Chao thought over the poem and was convinced of his daughter's innocence. He then gave his son a sound scolding. They bought a coffin and a piece of land in which to bury her, but this is no concern of ours here.

Let us go back to Chao K'uang-yin, who rode off on the Red Unicorn throughout the night and arrived at T'ai-yüan, where he met his uncle Abbot Chao. Swiftfoot Ch'en Ming had already been there for three days, and told him that the last emperor of the [Later] Han had died and been succeeded by Lord Kuo,[60] who had changed the name of the dynasty to Chou and was recruiting heroes from all over the land. Chao was overjoyed, and after staying there for a few days, he bid Abbot Chao farewell and returned to Pien-ching with Ch'en Ming.

Chao was recruited as a minor officer. Following Emperor Shih-tsung[61] on various military campaigns, he was promoted to commander of the palace guards. Later, he succeeded the throne of Chou and became Emperor T'ai-tsu of the Sung Dynasty. Ch'en Ming was then made a regional commander for being a faithful follower.

After T'ai-tsu had ascended the throne, he conquered Northern Han.[62] Recalling the past affection he had had for Ching-niang, he sent a man to

---

[60] That is, Kuo Wei; see footnote 19.

[61] Emperor Shih-tsung (r. 954–959) was the adopted son of Kuo Wei. His original name was Ch'ai Yung.

[62] This is falsifying history. Chao K'uang-yin died in 976. Northern Han was conquered in 979 by the Sung founder's successor, Emperor T'ai-tsung (r. 976–997).

Chieh-liang County of P'u-chou to locate her. The envoy recorded the quatrain and reported back. Grief-stricken, T'ai-tsu granted her the posthumous title of "Madam Chastity" and built a shrine in her honor at the Little Prosperity Village. That deity by the Swift Stream Bridge in the Yellow Thatch Hamlet was granted the title of "The T'ai-yüan Deity." T'ai-tsu also ordered the local authorities to build a temple for this deity. To this day, the temple is never short of worshipers making offerings.

This story is entitled "Master Chao Disrupts the Clear Oil Monastery, then Escorts Ching-niang a Thousand *Li*." Later, a poem was written in praise of him:

Invulnerable to feminine charms as he was to physical danger,
He walked a thousand li *to escort Ching-niang home.*
In Han and T'ang times, the world was in chaos under
*   Empresses Lü and Wu;*
No one could compare with Chao in valor.

THE LADY KNIGHT-ERRANT

From *Liao-chai chih-i*

TRANSLATED BY LORRAINE S. Y. LIEU AND THE EDITORS

There was once a young man by the name of Ku, born of a poor family in Chin-ling.[1] He was talented and skilled in a variety of arts and crafts. However, since he could not bear to leave his aging mother, he made a simple living by selling calligraphy and paintings. He was single even at the age of twenty-five.

Opposite to where he lived was an empty house. One day, an old woman and a young girl came by to rent the place, but since there was no man in their family, Ku did not feel that it was appropriate for him to make a courtesy call.

One day when he returned home he saw the young girl coming out of his mother's room. She was about eighteen or nineteen, and of rare beauty and gracefulness. She made no attempt to hide when she saw Ku. There was an air of awe-inspiring composure about her. Ku went inside and questioned his mother. Mrs. Ku said, "That is the girl across the street. She came to borrow my scissors and ruler. She told me that only her mother lived with her. She doesn't seem to come from a poor family. When I asked why she isn't married, she said that she has to take care of her aged mother. I shall pay her mother a visit tomorrow, and sound her out. If they don't ask for too

[1] Modern Nanking, in the present Kiangsu Province.

much, perhaps you can take care of her mother for her."

The next day, she went over to the young girl's house. She found the mother hard of hearing, and when she looked around the house, there did not seem to be enough food there for the following day. She asked the old woman how they managed to get by, and the latter replied that they depended solely on the young girl's needlework. Finally, Mrs. Ku brought up the question of a possible marriage between the two families. The old woman seemed agreeable and turned around to seek the opinion of her daughter. Though the girl did not say anything, she was apparently not too happy about it. So Mrs. Ku returned home.

Later, as she thought about the girl's reaction, she said to her son, "Do you think we've been turned down because we're too poor? What a strange girl! So quiet and so straight-faced. Just as the saying goes, 'As beautiful as the peach and pear blossoms, but cold as the frost and snow.'" Mother and son exchanged their views on the matter for a good while and then ended their discussion with a sigh.

One day, Ku was at his studio when a young man came to buy paintings. He looked handsome enough, but his manner was rather frivolous. Ku asked where he came from, and the young man replied that he came from the neighboring village. From then on, he came over every two or three days, and became fairly close to Ku. Later, they started to tease and joke with each other; and when Ku embraced the young man, he made no more than a show of refusing. Thus they carried on a secretive relationship which was to become more intimate by the day.

One day, as the girl happened to pass by, the young man gazed at her for a while and asked Ku who she was. Ku told him what he knew about her and the young man said, "What a beautiful and fearsome girl she is!"

Later, when Ku went inside, his mother said, "The young girl just came over to borrow some rice. She said that they haven't eaten for one whole day. This girl is devoted to her mother; what a pity that she should be in such circumstances. We should try to help her."

Ku agreed with what his mother said, and carried a peck of rice over to the girl's house, conveying his mother's goodwill. The girl accepted the rice but did not say a word of thanks to him.

After that, she often went over to Ku's house, helping with his mother's sewing and other needlework. She took care of all the household chores like a housewife. So Ku held her in even higher esteem. Whenever he had some delicacies, he would bring a portion over to her mother. The girl never thanked him. Once, when Ku's mother got an abscess on her private parts which caused her to cry out day and night in pain, the girl frequently stayed by her bedside, looking after her, washing the wound, and applying medicine to it three or four times a day. Mrs. Ku felt uneasy, but the girl did not seem to mind the task at all. Ku's mother sighed and said to her, "Ah, where can I find a daughter-in-law such as you to see me through the end of my days?" As she said that, her voice was choked with tears.

"Your son is devoted to you," the girl comforted her, "so you're much better off than my mother, who has only a helpless girl to look after her."

"But surely even a devoted son can't do bedside chores like these! Anyhow, I'm old and could die any day. What I'm worried about is an heir for the family."

As she spoke, Ku came in. Mrs. Ku wept and said, "I'm grateful for all that this young lady has done for us. Don't you forget to repay her kindness."

Ku bowed deeply, but the girl said, "You were kind to my mother and I didn't thank you, so why should you thank me now?"

Ku's respect and love for her grew deeper; yet she remained just as cold and aloof to him as before.

One day, Ku had his gaze fixed on the girl as she walked out the door. Suddenly she turned around and smiled bewitchingly at Ku. Ku was overjoyed and followed her to her house. When he flirted with her, she did not rebuke him, so they went to bed happily and made love. Afterward, she cautioned Ku, "I hope you understand that this is a one-time thing." Ku returned home without saying anything.

The next day, he approached the girl again, but she flatly refused him and left. However, she went to Ku's place as frequently as before and met him quite often; but she did not give him the slightest encouragement. Any effort on his part to exchange pleasantries with her was met with unyielding sternness.

One day, when they had a moment to themselves, she abruptly asked Ku, "Who is that young man you were talking to the other day?" Ku told her and she said, "He has taken liberties with me several times. Seeing that you're quite close to him, I didn't want to mention it earlier. But please tell him this time: if he doesn't mend his ways, he won't live to see another day."

Ku relayed her message to the young man when he came in the evening, adding, "You must be careful. Don't offend her again!"

"If she's so chaste," the young man said, "how come the two of you are on such good terms?" Ku protested his innocence, but the young man retorted, "If there is nothing between the two of you, then why would she tell you improper things like these?" Ku could not answer, whereupon the young man said, "Well, tell her this for me, too. Tell her, don't be so self-righteous and try to put up such a chaste appearance; otherwise, I shall certainly spread this whole thing far and wide!"

Ku was extremely angry and his face showed it, so the young man left.

One night, when Ku was sitting alone at home, the girl came in unexpectedly and greeted him with a smile. "It seems that our love hasn't ended yet."

Ku was overwhelmed with joy and held the girl tightly in his arms. Suddenly they heard footsteps and both jumped up. The door was pushed open and the young man walked in. Startled, Ku asked him, "What are you doing here?"

The young man laughed. "I've come to watch the show of some virtuous and chaste people!" Then he looked at the girl and said, "You can't blame anyone now, can you?"

The girl scowled and flushed with anger. Without a word, she pulled up her topcoat and took out a shiny foot-long dagger from a leather bag, the sight of which frightened the young man so much that he immediately took to his heels. The girl gave chase, but there was no one in sight outside. She flung the dagger into the air; it rose with a loud twang and was as bright as a rainbow. Then something fell to the ground with a loud thud. Ku hurried to look at it by candlelight. It was a white fox with a severed head. Ku was terrified.

"This is your Boy Charmer!" the girl told him. "I've spared him time and again, only he didn't seem to care enough for his life."

As she was replacing the dagger in the leather bag, Ku pulled her toward the house, but she said, "I don't feel like it anymore. Your Boy Charmer has spoiled the game. Wait until tomorrow night." And she left immediately without looking back.

The next evening, the girl came as promised and they spent the night together. When Ku asked her about her magic, she said, "This is something you shouldn't know about. Also, keep what you saw last night to yourself; otherwise it will bring you only trouble."

Ku then brought up the subject of marriage again, and in reply she said, "I sleep with you in the same bed, and I do all the housework here; what am I if not a wife to you? Since we live like husband and wife already, why talk about marriage?"

"Is it because I'm poor?"

"If you're poor, I'm not any better off. It's only because I feel for you in your poverty that I'm here with you tonight."

Before she left, she reminded Ku again, "Meetings such as this can't be repeated too often. If I can come, I will; but if I cannot, it's no use forcing me."

Afterward, whenever they ran into each other and Ku wanted to talk privately with her, she avoided him. Yet she kept doing all the housework and needlework in Ku's house, as before.

Several months later, the girl's mother died. Ku exhausted all his resources to help the girl bury her. From then on, the girl lived alone. Ku thought that he could take advantage of the situation, so one day he climbed over the wall and called to her from outside the window. When there was no answer, he looked through the doorway and found the house empty. He suspected that the girl had gone out to meet someone else. He returned at night but again the girl was not there. He left his jade pendant by the window and departed.

The next day, they met in his mother's room. When Ku came out, the girl followed him out and said, "You seem to have doubts about me, am I right? Everyone has his own secrets that can't be shared with others. How can I make you believe me? Anyway, there is something urgent which I must discuss with you right now." Ku asked her what it was, and she said, "I'm already eight months pregnant and I'm afraid that the child might come any time. Since I have no legitimate position in your family, I can only give you a child; I can't raise it for you. You can tell your mother secretly to look for a wet-nurse, under the pretext that she herself wants to adopt a child. Don't tell anyone that the child is mine."

Ku agreed and relayed her wish to his mother. She smiled and said, "What a strange girl! She refused to marry you and yet she has no qualms at carrying on an affair with you!"

She carried out the girl's plan happily and waited for her delivery.

More than a month had passed, and when the girl failed to show up for several days in a row, Mrs. Ku became suspicious and went over to have a look. The door was tightly shut and all was quiet inside. She knocked for a long time before the girl came out, with her hair all disheveled and her face soiled. She opened the door for Ku's mother and closed it immediately. Inside her room, Mrs. Ku found a baby crying on the bed. The old woman was surprised and asked, "When was he born?"

"Three days ago," she replied.

Mrs. Ku unwrapped the baby and found it to be a chubby boy with a wide forehead. Overjoyed, she said, "You have given me a grandson, but what is a single girl like you going to do all alone in the world?"

"This is my secret, and I'm afraid I can't explain it to you," the girl replied. "You can carry the baby home at night when there is no one around."

The old lady returned and told her son, and both of them were puzzled. They went over and took the baby home at night.

Several nights later, the girl suddenly came over around midnight, carrying a leather bag in her hand. She smiled and said, "I've accomplished my goal. It's time for me to say good-bye."

Ku immediately pressed her for a reason, to which she answered, "I've always remembered your kindness in helping me to support my mother. I once told you that our bedding together was a one-time affair because one should not repay one's debt in bed. But since you're so poor and could not afford to get married, I tried to give you an heir. I was hoping to bear you a boy by taking you just once, but unfortunately my period came as usual afterward so I had to break my rules and do it again. Now that I have repaid your kindness, my wish is fulfilled and I have no regrets."

"What is inside that bag?"

"The head of my enemy."

Ku picked it up and looked inside. He saw a bearded head, all smashed and smeared with blood. Though frightened out of his wits, he managed to get the story from the girl, who finally took him into her confidence. "I've never mentioned it to you before because I was afraid that you might let the secret out inadvertently. Now that my work is finished, I can tell you about it freely. I'm originally from Chekiang Province. My father was a prefect. He was falsely charged and killed by his enemy, and our house was confiscated. I took my mother away and we lived quietly for three whole years under concealed identities. The reason why I waited so long before avenging my father was that my mother was still alive. And after my mother died, I was held up by my pregnancy. Remember the night you came by and I was out? Well, I went out to better acquaint myself with the ways in and out of the enemy's house. I didn't want to take chances." As she was leaving, she said these parting words to Ku: "Please take good care of my son. You yourself will not be blessed with long life, but this son of yours can bring fame and great honor to your family. Since it's so late, I don't want to wake your mother. Good-bye!"

Grief-stricken, Ku was about to ask her where she was going when, quick as a lightning flash, the girl disappeared. Ku sighed and stood there petrified for a long time.

He told his mother everything the next morning, but they could do no more than express their sorrow and admiration for her.

Three years later, just as was predicted by the girl, Ku died a premature death. His son later became a *chin-shih* at the age of eighteen, and he took care of his grandmother throughout her old age.

THE SELF-PROCLAIMED HERO

The self-proclaimed hero is usually someone who looks larger than he is. The bloated image of his strength and ability may be self-cultivated or attained incidentally. The latter can be said of Yang Wen in the first story. Coming from a family of generations of generals (even his father-in-law is a high military officer), Yang is naturally expected to be a martial-arts expert worthy of his family name, and considers himself to be one. In fact he is not. When he is robbed, he makes no resistance, and then makes no attempt to find the bandits, rescue his abducted wife, or even contact the authorities. He wins a staff tournament and then tarnishes what glory he has gained by hiding from his rival's angry followers. That victory is itself a paradox, for the adversary he has overpowered is later revealed to be an old man (Yang is in the prime of his youth, whereas the Shantung Yaksha is at least in his sixties). After repeatedly discrediting Yang, the storyteller dutifully dubs him a true hero in the end, but he has only succeeded in making him a mockery of heroism.

Yang Wen's blindness to his own incompetence is shared by the hero in "The Strong Kid of the Ch'in-huai Region." The only difference is that while Strong Kid finally learns his lesson when he is cut down to his actual size by a stronger man, Yang emerges as an even more bloated hero.

In the case of "The Sham Commander Reclaims His Beauty," the commander assumes an exaggerated image deliberately. Realizing that no one will come to his aid, Scholar Wang decides to pit himself against the odds. Of course he is not the person he claims to be, but given the circumstances, he has no other alternative. "Sham commander" though he is, his courage and resourcefulness are the envy of a true hero.

YANG WEN, THE ROAD-BLOCKING TIGER

From *Liu-shih chia hsiao-shuo*

TRANSLATED BY PETER LI

Preamble: [1]

The vast plain touches the clouds;
Endless reed-lined banks reach the well-tended fields.
Ancient forests of green trees and misty mountains;
Swiftly flowing waters beneath the broken bridge.
Winds blow from the mouth of the gorge. Monkeys cry.
The moon rises above the trees. The man lies awake.
He thinks, leaning alone on the balustrade, lost and
   bewildered.
The sound of a nearby flute brings back all his memories.

Yang Wen, the son of Yang Chung-li and great grandson of Yang Ling-kung,[2] was the third male child in the Yang family and was therefore known as Third Master Yang. He was skilled in the martial arts and learned in strategy. After reaching manhood, he took as his wife the daughter of Leng Chen, a marshal at the central court. A propitious date was chosen for the happy occasion

and the young lady was taken into the Yang family amid great celebration. Indeed:

Music of flutes and drums reaches the sky;
Sounds of pipes and songs shake the ground.
Carved candles shine on rows of pearls and jade;
The fairest of ladies is surrounded by a cluster of fair ladies.
Drums and music welcome her into the deep nuptial chamber,
Where, truly, her beauty matches her fame.
This Leng-shih is lively, refined, and poised.
She tidies her cloud-like phoenix hair,
And gently touches her fine eyebrows.
Her fragrant cheeks are like the peaches of Liu Yüan; [3]
Her smooth forehead is like the plum from Mount Yü. [4]
Her ruby lips are like cherries.
Her pearly white teeth are like rows of jade.
Her dainty shoes are like golden lotus treading on water;
Her thin waist is like the willow swaying in the wind.
It must be Ch'ang-e [5] *leaving her moon palace,*
Or a goddess descending from her jade terrace.

After he took Leng-shih as his wife, Yang Wen and his bride were as happy as can be. They were

---

[1] This is the only story in this anthology which, owing to the relatively primitive nature of the extant edition, still carries the label "preamble" (*ju-hua*).
[2] Yang Ling-kung is the fictionalized name found in popular literature for the legendary Northern Sung general Yang Yeh, well known for his actions against the invading Khitans. The saga of Yang Yeh, his descendants in the next two generations, and their spouses forms an exceptionally complicated tradition of Chinese popular literature which has continued to grow from Sung times to the present day.

[3] Liu Yüan should be Liu Juan, which stands for Liu Ch'en and Juan Chao of the Eastern Han period. The two of them, according to legend, went into the T'ien-t'ai Mountain and, after eating some peaches, spent half a year with two girls there. Upon returning home, they found that several generations had passed.
[4] In Kiangsi Province.
[5] A goddess of the moon.

inseparable and did everything together. Before they realized it, a few years had passed.

One day Yang went for a leisurely walk in town and saw a fortune-teller with a sign which read "The Future Is Known Before You Ask." Yang consulted the fortune-teller, only to discover that misfortunes were lying in wait for him. It was very, very odd indeed! He told the fortune-teller the year, month, day, and hour of his birth, and the fortune-teller laughed loudly and said, "The line in this diagram is moving, so there'll be great misfortune. It'll result in loss of money, catastrophe, quarrels, you name it. In the diagram, the flying dragon has entered your life, and the white tiger is upon you. The only way you can avoid disaster is to go one hundred *li* from here." After hearing the words of the fortune-teller, Yang was miserable. Days passed like years, food was tasteless, and he became ill.

Seeing her husband worried day after day, Leng-shih parted her ruby lips, revealing her pearly teeth, and asked, "Why have you been so moody for the past few days?" Yang told her everything. She listened for a while and said, "Even though the fortune-teller said that things do not look well, you need not worry. I'll go with you to the Eastern Mountains to make a vow and pray for a safe passage."

"You're right," Yang replied.

The next day, Yang and his wife bade farewell to his parents and his in-laws. They put their belongings in order, got ready all the money for the traveling expenses, the horses, and a sedan chair, and left the capital city by the east gate. Traveling by day, resting at night, eating and drinking as the need arose, they proceeded on their journey. Soon they arrived at a small place called the Immortals Dwelling Market which was not far from the Eastern Mountains. It was getting dark:

Shadows grow longer as the sun's rays slant.
In the distance, fishermen gather up their nets and hooks;
Close at hand, everywhere wooden gates are half closed.

On the distant waters several sails are homeward bound;
Listen to the call of the bugle horn from the tall towers!
A column of wild geese gently settles on the islet.
Four or five lonely boats lie helter-skelter on the bank.
Travelers return to their inns;
The herdboy on the calf rides toward home.

Since it was late, Yang and his wife stopped at the nearest inn and took a room for the night. Then in the middle of the night some bandits broke into the inn. Who were these bandits?

Great trees are used to build the bandits' lair;
Rapidly flowing waters form their moat.
Once their hot tempers are aflame,
They will leap from high city walls.
Their brandished swords glisten like gold;
At night they gaze out under a starry sky.
As the moon darkens, they look for golden clasps and hairpins;
When a high wind blows, fires are lit on the hilltops.

When these bandits broke into the inn, Yang was caught unprepared. He had no weapon close at hand. The bandits grabbed him and hit him over the head with the back of a knife, and he fell to the ground unconscious. Truly:

Even if you detour over a thousand li,
It's difficult to escape the disaster at hand.

Now Yang, being from a family of generations of generals, had no fear of bandits; it was only that he had no weapons at hand. The bandits entered their room and abducted his wife. They also took the luggage and jewels, the total value of which was one thousand in cash. After all this had happened, Yang said to himself, "I'm from a family of generals! How can I return home to face my family after I've been robbed?"

After having suffered this humiliation, Yang became very depressed; not knowing what to do, he left the inn and moved to Liu's Inn in the town. He thought to himself, "When I set out on my journey, there were the two of us; now I'm alone. I want to bring this case to court, but I don't have money." Feeling out of sorts, he fell ill for half a month at the inn. Fortunately, there were no complications, and he recovered.

Leaving the inn, he walked downtown where he saw a teahouse and went in. The attendant called out, "Sir, would you like tea or some fruit drink?"

"Either one will do, only I have no money."

The attendant said, "Have some tea anyway," and brought him some tea. This is what the tea was like:

Where the brooks are clear and cliffs are high,
Cut the cloud-touching tea leaves before the morning dew
    disappears.
Draw fine water from the jade well
And boil it to make good tea.
Taste once the tea of Monk Chao-chou [6] *and you'll never*
    forget it;
It penetrates into the mind and drives away the demon of sleep.

After Yang had finished his tea, the attendant asked, "Sir, where are you from?"

"I'm from the capital."

"Have you just recovered from an illness?" the attendant asked further. Yang answered yes.

The attendant then asked, "You've no money; what are you going to do? Suppose I told you a way to make some money; would you do it?"

"Of course," Yang answered. "I would be most grateful."

"My boss, the owner of this teahouse, is a rich man," the attendant continued. "We call him Squire Yang. He owns a jewelry shop and a pawnshop in addition to this teahouse. If one pays respects to him, he'll reward that person with money. Now this squire—" Before he had finished speaking, the squire himself came into the teahouse. Truly:

When you tend with too much care, the flowers do not bloom;
But casually stick a willow in the ground and it grows to be a
    full-blown tree.

[Later] Yang also composed a poem:

Treasures scattered, people separated,
I hadn't the face to return home.
If it were not for the teahouse attendant,
How could I make my name known?

[6] The celebrated T'ang monk Ts'ung-shen (778–897).

This Squire Yang had just eaten and had come to the teahouse to sit for a while. The attendant signaled to Yang to make his move. When the squire turned around, Yang greeted him with a great bow, and the squire returned the greeting. But our Third Master Yang, being a man of good upbringing, just could not open his mouth to ask for help. The attendant again nudged him, saying, "Go ahead!" At this time, the squire asked, "Sir, is there anything on your mind?"

Only then did Yang speak up. He said, "I'm a traveler, Yang Wen. I came from the capital specifically to make an offering at the Eastern Mountains. I fell ill at the inn and have no money to return to the capital. I humbly beseech your aid in enabling me to return home."

The squire listened to his story and then told the attendant to bring out some money. The attendant did as he was told, counted out the correct number of coins, then strung them together on three strings, and put the remainder back into a bamboo container. The squire then gave these three strings of cash to Yang for his traveling money. Truly:

It's easier to throw yourself to the tiger
Than open your mouth and ask for help.

This storyteller also has an appropriate verse:

If you must ask for help, ask the most generous man;
If you must help someone, help the most destitute.
When you are thirsty, a drop of water tastes like sweet dew;
But after you're drunk, another cup is as good as nothing.

After getting the three strings of cash from the squire, Yang put the money in his pearl-embroidered purse and was about to bid farewell to his benefactor when suddenly a group of villagers appeared surrounding a huge man. This huge fellow had a most fearful appearance:

He stands twice as tall as common man;
His waist is as broad as a trunk.
From his blue scarf hang four lengths of sash;
On his cap two golden rings hang dazzling in the sun.
A silk robe is bound tightly to his waist;

The pouches about his waist are filled.
The bags slung on his shoulder are stuffed with fowl;
His jade-studded belt is carved with rows of fish.
He's like the Wu-t'ung Bodhisattvas[7] descending from
    Heaven;
Like the god Erh-lang of Kuan-k'ou[8] leaving his court.

That fellow was mounted on a tall, handsome steed, and his servant leading the horse carried a wooden staff measuring the height of a man. At one end of the staff hung a silver-threaded reed hat. With a clip-clop, man and horse passed the teahouse and headed straight for the Eastern Mountain Temple to celebrate the birthday of the mountain god.

After exchanging a few more words with Yang, the squire suggested, "Tomorrow is the birthday of the mountain god; since you are from the capital, why don't you go there and give some kind of performance? Go to the temple tomorrow and give my friends a chance to help you. You may earn yourself twenty or thirty strings of cash."

"But I don't know that sort of thing," Yang replied.

"Mister, you're really stuffy," the attendant said.

But then Yang asked, "That man who rode past just now, who's he?"

"He's a specialist in the use of the staff," the squire answered. "His name is Li Kuei, nicknamed the Shantung Yaksha.[9] This fellow has been going up to the mountain for ten years, and has defeated all the staff fighters. For three years now he has had no opponents at all. If this year he meets no opponents again, the whole prize of a thousand strings of cash will belong to him. You see, on that poster over there, there's no other name."

"Sir, though at home I didn't learn how to

[7] The five bodhisattvas of the Kukkutarama Monastery built by the Indian ruler Ashoka.
[8] For a story related to this water deity, whose legends originated in Kuan-k'ou (in modern Szechwan Province), see "The Boot That Reveals the Culprit" in this anthology.
[9] Yaksha is a Buddhist term for the malignant demons in the earth, or in the air, or in the underworld.

make a living," Yang Wen then said, "I do know how to use the staff. Now that you've been so generous to me, I would like to have the village headman announce that Yang Wen will challenge the Shantung Yaksha. If I win I will consider the thousand strings to be a gift from you."

"You know how to use the staff?"

"Yes, I do."

"If you're as good as you say, then let me try you out first to see just how good you are. If you beat me, then I'll back you and arrange the match for you."

The squire then instructed the attendant, "Close the shop; we're through for today." The man did as he said.

Yang Wen followed the squire to the back of the teahouse, where he pushed open a side door that led into an empty courtyard. Yang Wen exclaimed, "What a beautiful courtyard. Just right for practicing the staff."

"You're weaker than I am," remarked the squire. So he ordered the attendant to buy a jug of wine and two catties of meat for Yang Wen to eat. After Yang had finished the food and the wine, he invited the attendant to have some.

Then the squire called out to the attendant, "Bring out the staffs." The attendant was not gone long before he returned with five staffs, which he spread on the ground.

The squire motioned to Yang, saying, "You pick a staff first." Yang took a look, and with a swift movement of the foot kicked one of the staffs high into the air. When the staff came down, he caught it with one hand.

The squire muttered to himself, "There was only one good staff in the five, and he picked the best one." He then called out, "Let's do it in the proper style and manner."

"Certainly," Yang responded.

The squire called out again, "You come first!" And Yang made the first thrust.

The attendant had no sooner picked up the remaining staffs and cleared the ground than one of the contestants was already defeated after two or three strokes. Truly:

Before you extend your cloud-grabbing hand,
Make sure you know what you're doing!

In the middle of the match, Yang called out to the squire, "I don't dare hit you. If I did, it would look very bad."

After a couple of thrusts, the squire cried out, "Guard yourself! You have a weakness."

"Sir, what weakness?"

"You hesitate, you don't follow through. How can you hit anyone if you keep stopping and starting?"

"Sir, you're slow and I'm fast. When my staff has already come down, I have to wait for you to block before I strike."

This is just as the ancients say:

Marvelous are the immortals of Lan-k'o;
How many springs pass during one game of chess? [10]
He who meets no challenge after mastering his art
Must be as generous as can be to his worthy foe.

However, the squire insisted, "I want you to hit me. I'd like you to hit me. Let's try again."

"If I hit you," Yang replied, "it would look very bad."

As they went at it again, there was a knock at the door. The attendant opened the door and greeted the caller. It was Sheriff Ma. "Where is the squire?" he asked.

"He's in the back practicing with the staff."

Sheriff Ma said teasingly to the squire, "So he's at it again! I've told him not to fool around with the staff, but he just won't listen."

The sheriff went inside and exchanged greetings with the squire. Yang also came over and bowed to the sheriff, who answered with a casual nod.

[10] The allusion is to a man of the Chin Dynasty who returned home after watching a game of chess and eating a date on Mount Lan-k'o (in Chekiang Province) to find that one hundred years had gone by.

The sheriff then said to the squire, "You should be able to recognize an expert when you see one. He's a bungler!"

"No, no!" the squire protested. "He wants to go up to the mountain to fight Li Kuei, the Shantung Yaksha. I heard him say that, so I'm trying him out first."

"This fellow wants to fight Li Kuei! Ha! How can he ever win? If he doesn't get a sound beating, then I don't know Li Kuei. I'll test him myself on the expert method of using the staff."

Yang listened in silence, but thought to himself, "What impudence! This fellow is insulting me."

Sheriff Ma then said to Yang, "I'm in charge of training men in the use of the staff. Do you care to fight a bout with me? If you win, I'll let you fight with Li Kuei. If you lose, then you'd better leave this place."

"I shall be most happy to," Yang replied.

The squire put aside his staff, while the sheriff took up a staff and struck a pose. Yang also assumed a stance and called out, "Sheriff, shall we have one bout or two?"

"Just one," the sheriff answered.

The staffs were raised not for two or three bouts, but for only one. Indeed:

When two hardy fellows meet,
It's best that none be hurt.
There's no need for two bouts or three;
One's enough to show who's strong and weak.

Sheriff Ma took one step forward and struck a blow at Yang Wen's midriff. With another half-step forward, he blocked the way with the staff. When Yang turned around to run, Ma raised his staff and took a downward swing at Yang's head. Yang side-stepped the blow. Not only did the staff fly past him but the sheriff also flew by. Yang turned and dealt a blow on his back and knocked him to the ground. Soon a swelling appeared on the sheriff's back. Yang said, "Sheriff, you're pretty good with the staff, and I'm not just a bungler."

The sheriff got up, adjusted his clothes, and said, "All right, you're really good." Truly:

Among the experts there is one better still;
There is another bull's-eye within the first bull's-eye.

He continued, "I'll let those involved know that you'll be available for the contest. They'll send you an invitation." After having said this, he left.

The squire said, "Brother! You're really good with the staff! You *did* spare me a while ago. Even Sheriff Ma isn't a match for you; how can I be? Why don't you stay in my teahouse? I'll take care of your needs. Take these two strings of cash to pay your bill at the other inn."

Thereupon, Yang Wen left the teahouse, went back to the inn, paid for his room and board, and returned. When the teahouse attendant saw him, he said, "Sir, you're quite a man. My boss doesn't care for anything but two things: wrestling and the staff."

The next day, after they had eaten, the squire and Yang were just having some tea when about twenty people came into the teahouse and addressed the squire, saying, "We heard that there is a fellow here who is going to fight Li Kuei. Tell him to come out!"

"He's right here, sitting in that chair," said the squire.

Yang got up and bowed, saying, "I'm Yang Wen."

Someone in the crowd said, "Yes, he's the one that's going to fight with Li Kuei."

Yang said, "Sheriff, I meant no harm yesterday."

"It was I who offended him yesterday," said the sheriff, "and he gave me a stroke on the back."

The village leaders took out three hundred strings of cash and said, "Third Brother Yang, this is for you." Yang thanked them and they left.

On the twenty-seventh day of the third lunar month, the officials in charge of the contest came to see the squire. Afterward, the squire said to Yang, "Brother, I'm going to the mountain." On the next day, Yang Wen dressed himself as a pilgrim and headed for the temple. When he arrived, indeed:

In the shade of the green pines,
The majestic temple is indistinctly seen;
Amid the old spruces,
There seem to be three tall gates.
The hundred flowers line
A footpath which leads to the temple.
Green bamboos all around;
Two streams flow like golden threads.
As you look to the left with the aid of Li-lou, [11]
A thousand li appear as if right before your eyes.
With Shih-k'uang [12] *on your right side,*
The distant sounds seem to be by your ear.
Weeds crowd the temple square;
In the vessels a hundred famous kinds of incense burn.
Offerings are made before the dais;
On the altar are placed the divination cups.
In the morning the wooden horses neigh;
In the evening the clay gods exchange greetings.

After arriving at this mountain temple, Yang burned incense and paid his respects to the various officials sitting on the stand. The leader of the group said, "This year Li Kuei has no opponent."

Li Kuei then bowed three times to the god of the Eastern Mountains, saying, "May Buddha be thanked for his protection." Looking at the officials, he bowed and said, "If this year I don't have an opponent, next year I shall not come again. It's not that Li Kuei is afraid to come, but when there's no opponent and I take all the prizes without a fight, I'm fearful of offending the deities." Li Kuei bowed once more to those in charge and looked at the two columns of soldiers trained in the use of the staff. He asked, "Do any of you

[11] Li-lou, a figure supposecd to have lived in the times of the early mythological ruler Huang-ti, was known for his ability to see minute objects at great distances.
[12] Shih-k'uang, a musician of the Spring and Autumn period, was able to predict the future through the analysis of sounds.

dare fight me?" No one made a sound; they didn't know what to do. Li Kuei then said, "If none of you dare fight me, then the prize is mine." After a pause, "All right, I shall take the prize."

Then suddenly a voice called out from the crowd, "Wait, wait! The prize doesn't belong to you!" Li Kuei looked up with surprise and saw a man in military garb who said, "I'm Captain Yang from the Western Capital;[13] I've come to burn incense and watch the fight. But I heard you say to the people here that you're going to take the prize without a fight. Now if you can beat me, then the prize is yours. If you lose to me, then the prize is mine. I challenge you to a match. Do you accept?"

"Good staffers all know one another," Li Kuei replied. "Whoever heard of a Captain Yang from the Western Capital?"

The officials said, "If you want to fight, go ahead. No one cares about your credentials. Proceed, proceed!"

The master of ceremonies read the rules and regulations, and the judges were ready. Now this captain was none other than Yang Wen, who had fought Sheriff Ma, one of those in charge of this contest. This fact was concealed from Li Kuei. Having accepted the challenge, Li Kuei called out, "Let him come!"

Yang Wen grabbed a staff, Li Kuei took up his, and the match was on. Now Yang was an expert, what would be regarded as a master by the other experts. When he saw a weakness in his opponent, he would move to complete the round. This Captain Yang raised his staff with both hands and was going to smash his opponent's head, the so-called "all-out" manuever. Li Kuei saw the staff coming down and used a blocking stroke. Before the staff fell, however, Yang took a step forward and instead of striking Li's head, with another half-step he struck his opponent on the calf. Li Kuei shrieked in pain and fell to the ground. Indeed:

A good rooster has no opponent;
The fast horse needs only one crack of the whip.

Li Kuei lost the match; Yang Wen went up to the platform and recited these lines:

Never has there been a fighter without foe;
Even among the strong, there is another stronger.
Even the overlord has his troubles at River Wu;[14]
Today, it is Li Kuei's turn to lose his fame.

Because Yang recited these lines, he aroused the wrath of some thirty young men who were Li Kuei's disciples. They were from families of the wealthy nobility. Seeing their master disgraced, they wanted to strike the young captain. Since "the few cannot withstand the many, and the weak cannot triumph over the strong," what was Yang Wen to do?

With claws you can burrow into the earth;
With the power to soar you can rise into the blue sky.
If you can't hide in the ground or rise into the sky,
Then how are you going to escape the danger at hand?

As the disciples were gathering around Yang Wen to attack him, the squire called out, "You can't hit him! All the heroes from different places have witnessed this game, and if the word spread that we had cheated him, then the next time it would be difficult to hold another contest. If you want to beat him, then come down to my teahouse; it still wouldn't be too late."

"The squire is right," they replied.

Yang returned to the teahouse and put the prize money in a back room. Just then Li Kuei's disciples called, "Sir, hand him over to us. We want to beat him to avenge our master."

The squire went to the back room and said to Yang, "Those fellows out there want to give you a beating. But let me ask, how old are you?"

"I'm twenty-four this year."

"I'm thirty, six years older than you. If you're

---

[13] The Western Capital (Lo-yang, in Honan Province) was one of the four capitals of the Northern Sung Dynasty, but it was not the seat of the central government.

[14] This alludes to the end of Hsiang Yü, the chief opponent of the Han founder, at the River Wu (Anhwei Province).

willing to pay respects to me as your elder brother, I'll save you from this beating."

Yang Wen thought to himself, "Since my intention is to present my case to the authorities and get back my wife, it would not do any harm to know a rich man"; so he consented.

The squire said, "I'll lead the way; you follow me."

Then the squire, whose full name was Yang Yü,[15] said to the young men outside, "That person who fought in the match is actually my brother; I hope that you'll be generous and forgive him."

Those people said, "Why didn't you say so earlier? Since he's your brother, why not have him come out, and let us greet him?"

The squire called to Yang, "Brother, come out and greet these gentlemen." Yang came out and bowed three times. Those fellows returned the greeting and said, "We hope you don't bear any grudge against us. In a little while, our master Li Kuei will come himself to pay you his respects."

Shortly afterward, Li Kuei came into the teahouse and greeted Yang, saying, "I haven't had an opponent for several years, and therefore I've become the champion. But today I've been defeated by you. Sir, you're not the same as the others. You must be from a family of generals; your skill is extraordinary! Please accept this expression of my respect."

Yang said, "There's no need for all this." Then he took out some of the prize money and gave it to Li Kuei. Li Kuei thanked him and left.

The squire then said, "My brother, you can live here if you like."

One day after breakfast, Squire Yang and Yang Wen were sitting in the jewelry shop when a big fellow riding on a horse came up to the shop. He

got off and bowed, saying, "Sir, your father is not well, and he wants you to come." With these words, he remounted and rode away. Yang Wen watched the proceedings and recognized the fellow as one of the bandits who had held the torch on the night he and his wife were robbed. But as he wheeled about to catch the fellow, the fellow leaped onto his horse and galloped away.

The squire turned to Yang and said, "Brother, can you watch the store for me for about a week while I go to see my father?"

"I would like to go with you and pay my respects to your father," Yang replied.

"You can't go. My father is a hot-tempered person; it's better that you don't go."

"There're too many valuables in the store; I don't dare take the responsibility."

"I trust you. What have you got to worry about?"

But Yang insisted, "Please let me go with you."

The squire finally gave in. "Since you want to go so badly, I suppose there's no harm."

The two rode off, and soon arrived at a place thirty *li* from the Immortals Dwelling Market. On this farmstead:

The haze slowly lifts;
The fog begins to dissolve.
In the distance, a moss-covered hill;
Close at hand, row upon row of rooftops stand.
Old juniper trees circle round like dragons;
Verdant pines stand like tiger tracks.
No travelers pass by for three years,
And during all four seasons no one comes.
Suddenly there is the smell of blood;
It is the hideout of the robber band.
Bowls hold human sauces;
Skulls become incense pots.
Children play with human heads;
Daughters learn the art of plundering tombs.

The two arrived at a farmhouse and dismounted. Someone inside announced, "Grand Master, the squire has come."

---

[15] The names of the squire and later of his father are given late in the story, which may cause some confusion for the reader. The nicknames of Yang Wen and the squire's father are also withheld until the end. Note the similarity of the nicknames, and the fact that all three major characters and one of the minor ones are Yangs.

The grand master replied from his seat in the hall, "Tell him to come in."

Yang Yü went in and bowed. The father asked, "How has business been these days?"

"Father, business has been good."

The father was about to speak when he noticed someone standing down the hall. He asked his son, "Who's that man in the hall?"

"Father, he is Third Brother Yang, a guest of mine. This fellow is an expert with the staff; he defeated Li Kuei!"

The father looked at Yang Wen and became irritated. He shouted an order: "Men, tie him up!"

At the moment, Yang Wen was like a dragon out of water, a tiger or leopard fallen over a cliff. The ancients had a poem:

Disaster issues from the people's mouths;
Do not be greedy for unrighteous goods.
Even if you know the stratagems of Heaven,
You cannot escape the disaster at hand.

The father told his aides to tie up Yang Wen. Fortunately, Yang Yü came to the rescue and told the men, "Leave him alone." They all withdrew.

Yang Yü said, "Let me tell you, father, this fellow is terrific with the staff!"

"How could he defeat Li Kuei?" the father said. "When I was young, I fought with him and couldn't beat him. How could a fellow like this subdue him? He must be a good-for-nothing from the brothels. You went to his place, squandered your money, and didn't want to return. I told you to come and this fellow was afraid to lose you, so he came with you."

"Father, this man isn't a bum," Yang Yü replied. "He's really good."

The father led his son down the hall and told his aides, "Put that fellow in the guest's quarters." And Yang Wen was led away.

Yang Wen went to the room, sat down, and thought, "The old man is a blackguard, and his son isn't a decent sort either. My wife must be here!"

After a little while, a woman appeared and said to Yang Yü, "You know that your father is not a reasonable man; why did you bring your friend here?"

Yang Yü said, "Mother, he wanted to come himself. I wanted him to stay at the jewelry shop, but he wouldn't; he insisted on coming."

The two of them talked until they came to Yang Wen's room and then went in. The woman brought in meat and wine, saying, "Here's some meat and wine for you. Don't be upset. It's really nothing. The boss is just troublesome." After this, both of them left.

After quite a while, Yang Wen heard someone come in to report, "Master, the band chief has sent a messenger here. He says that they're repairing their mountain fortress, and asks your permission to let his men temporarily camp at the old farmstead at Pei-k'an. They'll bring their own supplies and will not touch the villagers' food. After the fortress is repaired, he'll return everything. They also invited the master and the squire to come over. The chief recently captured a woman, the wife of a traveler. She is very beautiful, and they wish to make her the lady of the lair, so they've invited the master and the squire."

The grand master said, "Tell him that I'll visit him tomorrow at noon." Then the messenger left.

Yang Wen overheard this and was overjoyed. A smile broke over his face and he said to himself, "My wife is at the old Pei-k'an farmstead where the bandits are hiding out. This 'grand master' certainly is an evil man."

At dawn the next day, when:

The lamps half extinguished,
The morning tide has just come in;
Outside the window the light is just sufficient
For one to distinguish the faces of people.

Indeed:

The cock crows with the moon over the west river;
At the fifth watch the stars fill the sky.

93

As the east began to light, the cock crowed, and soon it was day. Yang Yü came to the guest's room and said, "Third Brother, why don't you go back? I'll return in a few days' time."

Yang Wen said, "Kind brother, may I borrow a staff for protection? From here to town is about a hundred and thirty *li*. Who knows what might happen on the way? I don't want to be caught empty handed."

Yang Yü lent Yang Wen a staff as requested. With the staff in hand, Yang Wen bade farewell and left.

Yang Wen left the village, walked for a short distance, and hid himself in some high bushes. He was waiting for Yang Ch'ing, the grand master, to pass. After a while, two men on horseback came along. Yang Wen let them pass by. Then he thought to himself, "Since I don't know where the old Pei-k'an farmstead is, I'll have to follow them." The man on the first horse was the grand master, Yang Ch'ing, nicknamed Bald-Tailed Tiger; the one following was Yang Yü. Yang Wen followed them for about two *li* and saw a farmstead:

The cold pierces the body;
The wind sweeps the face.
A few thatched huts, with stoves in front baking bread;
An unlimited space, with the back rooms stocked with axes and
    swords.
At sunrise, the flames of the lamps flicker;
At dusk, the winds in the ravines moan.
On these side roads, why should travelers ever come,
When in the mountains the sound of slaughtering is heard?

Yang Ch'ing and Yang Yü arrived at the farmhouse, dismounted, and went inside. Yang Wen was only a short distance away and hid himself in some tall grass. After the father and son entered the house, the four of them sat down: Yang Ta—the Thin-Waisted Tiger—and Leng-shih on one side, Yang Ch'ing and Yang Yü on the other. Yang Ta looked at the woman and found her calm and natural-looking, and concluded that she must be from a good family. Truly:

A cicada hairpin holds her cloud-like hair;
Fine eyebrows arch gently over her eyes;
Her ruby lips are like cherries;
Her pearly white teeth are like rows of jade.
Face like a flower,
Eyes like crystalline pools,
Natural and at ease;
Her spirit could not be more finely poised.

Indeed:

Even a killer bandit would turn his head,
And a meditating monk can't help but look.

Yang Yü broke out, "What a woman! She's worth all your trouble."

"My honored guests, I have nothing to entertain you with here," Yang Ta said. "We have only a few bowls of wine to mark the occasion of my taking a wife. As I've already mentioned to you, I'd like to use your old farmstead at Pei-k'an for a while. I put all the grain aside and won't touch a bit of it. After my fortress is repaired I'll move out immediately and won't linger."

"There's no problem; we're like one family," said Yang Ch'ing.

Meanwhile, Yang Wen was walking further away from the spot, thinking, "My wife is there. If I go to the authorities to report it, when will I be able to get her back? It would be better for me to take this staff in my hand and take her away myself." The ancients have observed:

If you don't hurry when you are going down hill,
Then it will be difficult to get to heaven.
If you fall into the ground with the wall,
Then you will both meet at the Yellow Springs.[16]

How could Yang Wen bear to wait? He left his hiding place in the tall grass and walked onto the road. Suddenly there appeared twenty or thirty rabble bandits who blocked his road and asked, "Who're you? What are you doing here?"

---

[16] This poem hardly makes any sense. The text is badly corrupt and there is only one extant copy.

"I'm a traveler; I've lost my way. I beg your pardon."

"This is no place for you. If you drop that staff in your hand, we'll let you go!"

How could Yang do a thing like that? He grasped his staff and was going to attack them when unexpectedly some of the rabble ganged up on him from behind, felled him, and tied him up. Then they led him to another farmstead in the distance. At this farmstead:

The forest shades the thatched huts,
Date and mulberry trees grow abundantly,
Tender grasses grow about the fence,
Sheep and cows graze in the pasture.
Under the bridge flows the cold blue water,
Strange jagged peaks stand beyond the gates,
Farmers line the banks of the stream,
And their chattering voices are wafted by the spring wind.

Indeed:

Wild grasses, fragrant flowers line the road,
But it doesn't lead you to Wu-ling.[17]

Yang Wen, who was tied up by the rabble gang, was brought to this farmhouse. Indeed:

Having escaped from the grasp of Heaven,
He fell into the mesh of Earth.

The rabble gang reported to their chief, who sat at a table in the hall with a great sword by his side. He called out, "Bring the man in and I'll question him."

When Yang Wen was hustled into the hall, the chief asked, "What is your name, and what are you doing here? If you tell the truth, you will be spared!"

Yang Wen replied, "Great chief, I'm from the capital. My name is Yang Wen; my great-grandfather is Yang Ling-kung, my grandfather is Yang Wen-su, and my father is Yang Chung-li. My wife and I had come to burn incense at the Eastern Mountains when we were robbed at the Immortals Dwelling Market and the robbers kidnapped my wife. Now she is with Yang Ta, the Thin-Waisted Tiger, at the old Pei-k'an farmstead. I've already found out the situation, and I was just about to take her away by force. I'm from a family of generals, nicknamed the Road-Blocking Tiger. Have you heard of me? Now that I've been captured, if I am guilty then put me to death. If not, please let me go!"

"I've long heard of your distinguished name," the chief replied. "I'm most honored to meet you." He ordered his men to untie Yang, then invited him to take a seat at his table and asked for forgiveness, saying, "I was a humble soldier under your father Yang Chung-li. My name is Ch'en Ch'ien. Later, because of unfortunate circumstances, I reluctantly became a bandit. But now that I've met my benefactor, who was robbed, of course I'll help you with whatever I have!" Indeed:

When there is a case of injustice,
Then bare your sword and set it right.

Ch'en Ch'ien brought out wine and invited Yang Wen to drink. Then, taking one hundred men along, they set out for the old Pei-k'an farmstead. When they arrived at the farmhouse, Yang Ta, Yang Ch'ing, Yang Yü, and Leng-shih were having a feast. Yang Wen grasped his staff and charged into the house. He aimed a frontal blow at Yang Ta and knocked him over and then escaped with his wife. In no time, Yang Ta recovered and called to his two hundred followers to give chase:

Half a thousand stout-hearted Tzu-lus,[18]
Five hundred fierce club-wielding guardian spirits.
Each one has the strength to raise the heavy cauldron;
Each one has the power to uproot a mountain.
All their swords are made with the finest metal;
Their coats of mail all use glistening bronze.

[17] This alludes to the discovery of the Peach Blossom Stream, a utopia celebrated in Chinese literature, by a fisherman from Wu-ling.

[18] Tsu-lu (551–479 B.C.) a disciple of Confucius, was well known for his knightly behavior.

Yang Wen, seeing the bandits coming, called to Yang Ta again to release his wife, at the same time trying to fend off the bandits. Fortunately Ch'en Ch'ien had a hundred men with him to help Yang Wen withstand the enemy. After two or three encounters, Ch'en Ch'ien and his men were defeated. The reason was that Yang Ta had more men than Ch'en Ch'ien. Yang Wen and his wife fled together with Ch'en Ch'ien and his men. Yang Ta and his men pursued. For Yang Wen, it was a case of:

Even if he can think of countless strategies,
It is difficult to avoid the disaster at hand.

As they were fleeing, they heard the banging of gongs. Yang Wen looked and saw some fifty archers from the district who were patrolling in the region. At the head of the archers was Sheriff Ma. Yang Wen bowed to him and told him the whole story. The sheriff told his men what had happened; then, together with Ch'en Ch'ien's men, they turned to meet the enemy.

Yang Ta rode ahead leading his men. Yang Wen came out to meet him. The two fought for less than one bout, and Yang Ta was felled by a severe blow. After this, Yang Wen and his wife returned to the capital.

Later, on account of his great accomplishments on the frontier, Yang Wen received a large promotion and became the regional commander of the Expeditionary Commandery[19] and an honorary tutor to the crown prince. It could be said that:

The general's wisdom and bravery pacify frontier regions,
And so his name is spread throughout the empire.

[19] The Expeditionary Commandery (*An-yüan chün*) was in the northeastern part of modern Hopei Province.

THE SHAM COMMANDER RECLAIMS HIS BEAUTY

From *Erh-k'o P'o-an ching-ch'i*

TRANSLATED BY DELL R. HALES

Some say that even thieves have their code of honor;
It's a brotherhood of many brave heroes.
If they happen to be in the company of truly chivalrous men,
They will readily identify with them.

When Chang Ch'i-hsien,[1] a prime minister of the Sung Dynasty, was still a commoner, he submitted ten policies for universal peace to Emperor T'ai-tsung [r. 976–997] upon the latter's visit to the Ho-pei Circuit.[2] T'ai-tsung was very pleased and immediately implemented six of Chang's proposals; the other four were reserved for subsequent consideration.

"Each of these ten policies," Chang stubbornly argued, "is a marvelous plan. They should all be adopted."

T'ai-tsung smiled at Chang's heady conceit, and on the day he returned to his court, he said to [the heir apparent] Chen-tsung [r. 998–1022], "When I was in Ho-pei, I met a man who has the potential talents of a prime minister. His name is Chang Ch'i-hsien and I have chosen him for your future use."

Chen-tsung kept this in mind until Chang was successful in the *chin-shih* examination. His name appeared, however, toward the end of the list. Observing this, Chen-tsung wanted to advance him to the top of the successful candidates, but as the list had already been decided, he issued a special decree conferring academic honors upon all the candidates. Later, Chang was promoted from one position to another until he became the prime minister.

Before this minister obtained any office, he had been lonely, poor, and down on his luck. However, he was generous and noble of spirit, with a free and unconventional manner about him. One day he came by chance to an inn where he decided to spend the night. At that time, a band of robbers stopped at the inn for food and drink as they returned from a round of pillage and plunder. With their weapons stacked as densely as a thicket, they appeared quite ugly and ferocious. Afraid of being caught by these ruffians, the local

---

[1] Historically, the author is off by one generation. The episode about Chang Ch'i-hsien (943–1014) described here is reported to have taken place between Emperor T'ai-tsu and his successor, T'ai-tsung, not between T'ai-tsung and Chen-tsung. Chang did serve as a prime minister from 991 to 993 toward the end of T'ai-tsung's reign. He also served briefly in the same capacity during the early years of Chen-tsung. The incident concerning Chang's "chivalrous" behavior is, of course, legendary.

[2] Not too different from the Hopei Circuit in T'ang times.

97

inhabitants, including the innkeeper, scurried away in all directions to hide. Chang was the only one who remained.

After watching this crowd imbibe until they were tipsy, he adjusted his cap, and with a solemn and dignified look, he greeted them with a bow.

"Gentlemen," he said, "I'm a poor student who is low on luck, and I'd like to ask you for some food and wine. May I?"

The group of bandits noticed that he was tall and robust, and that he spoke uninhibitedly. "If you're willing to demean yourself," they said merrily, "why not? But we're rough and crude. I'm afraid you might not find us fit company." They quickly rose and invited Chang to join them.

"People at large," responded Chang, "do not understand gentlemen like you. They call you 'thieves' without realizing that thieves are not made of ordinary stuff at all. You're all courageous men of the world and I myself share this chivalrous spirit, so it is fortunate that we've met today. Let's drink together; there shouldn't be any differences among us."

As soon as he had finished, he poured himself a large cup and drained it at one gulp. Observing him drink so briskly, the bandits refilled his cup, which he again quaffed in one draught. After three large cups in succession, he fetched a plate of pigs' feet from the table, quickly split them open, and wolfed down the entire platter with a fierce appetite.

The crowd of thieves looked on in amazement and said to Chang, "You really have the capacity of a prime minister! Any man who can disregard petty formalities is no ordinary person. Some day you'll be in charge of the nation; please remember that we reluctantly became bandits because of circumstances. Now in this humble place, we'd like to be friends with you first. Please don't say no."

Each one of them took out his money, and a large pile of valuables grew as they all struggled forward to offer their treasure. Chang did not even pretend to decline; he picked up the items

and tied them into a bundle with a cord. Holding this in his hand, he shouted, "Thanks!" and strode out of the inn. On this occasion he obtained things worth a hundred taels of cash, all of which Chang paid to the innkeeper to support himself in delightful and comfortable style for quite some time. But it was precisely his vigorous and bold spirit which set him apart from others even when he was destitute, and his daring enabled him to outwit the bandits. There is a poem in evidence of this:

The future minister is in a humble station;
His voracious appetite catches everybody's attention.
Simply because he is a man with such breadth of knowledge,
Even the bandits have learned to admire his courage.

In Yeh County of the prefecture of Lai-chou in Shantung Province, there was a powerful and fearless young man by the name of Shao Wen-yüan. His sense of honor and his chivalry were unexcelled, and when he saw an injustice, he would go forward to offer his help. But someone had slandered him before the county magistrate, saying that he relied on his strength to live as a robber. The magistrate, who was new in his post, found an excuse to have Wen-yüan beaten without making any investigations.

Later, the magistrate had to go to the capital for a meeting with his superior. No sooner had the magistrate left the district than a man armed with a sword approached on horseback and dismounted in front of him. The magistrate recognized him as Shao Wen-yüan and guessed that he had come to take revenge.

"Why are you here?" the magistrate asked in surprise.

"I've come for the express purpose of escorting you to the capital. There are many notorious bandits on the road ahead, and since they know my reputation, they will avoid us."

"I have been cruel to you; why are you so kind to me?"

"When you admonished and punished me the other day, you only meant good to me. Moreover, you're an upright official. I should do my best to repay you."

Only then did the magistrate breathe a sigh of relief. Shao Wen-yüan accompanied the official until he was halfway to his destination and then bade him farewell. Just as Shao had predicted, there was no sign of any outlaws.

One day while passing the gate of a grand mansion, Shao came upon a pack of over forty ruffians who had tied up the rich owner of the house and were pillaging his house. One of the bandits held his knife at the man's throat to intimidate him: "If the police come to save you," he cried, "I'll kill you first!"

The rest of the band finished ransacking the man's house for all the gold and silk. There was a heap of precious goods as high as the ceiling which the bandits figured they could not take with them. Finally, they beckoned to the local citizens to come and help themselves to the goods. "We might as well get rid of it for him," they said, laughing. Some of the people were too afraid of the consequences to leave their houses; some were curious and went to see what was taking place. But there were some greedy and bold enough to seize whatever they could and cart it away.

Shao heard all this commotion and decided to have some fun with the bandits. Twisting sideways, he shouldered his way in through the crowd and shouted, "What're you people doing here? What's going on?"

"There are many robbers here," the mob shouted in return. "Don't cause any trouble!"

Shao strode over to the neighbor's house, grabbed an iron pitchfork, and stood inside the gate. "Shao Wen-yüan is here!" he shouted. "Return the valuables that belong to this family and leave at once!"

The wealthy man heard him and was afraid that if his captor saw this response to his plight, he would quickly thrust his sword. "Good hero," he screamed, "please don't intervene! If you do, I shall be killed first!"

Shao understood and temporarily withdrew. The band of robbers then loaded twenty sacks of gold and silver on their horses and forced the bound victim to accompany them a distance of twenty *li* beyond the border before they released him. With his hair disheveled, the wealthy man returned home in great distress. But the outlaws did not anticipate that Shao Wen-yüan, who had left by himself and hurried after them at a distance, would gallop to overtake them as soon as he saw that the rich man had been set free. The bandits did not pay much attention when they perceived that only one man was after them.

"Put all the valuables by the roadside and be quick about it. Have you ever heard of Shao Wen-yüan?"

The robbers were so startled when they heard this name that they could make no reply.

"Since you're so slow about it," Shao went on, "I'll give you an example!" With a whizzing arrow he knocked one of them right off his horse. Greatly alarmed, the bandits all scrambled to dismount and kneel together at the side of the road to plead for their lives.

"Leave these things behind," ordered Shao, "and you may leave unharmed!"

The robbers all dropped their sacks and fled empty-handed on their horses. Shao borrowed several animals from the neighborhood to carry the plunder and finally reached the rich man's house to return the property. The rich man greeted him with a bow, saying, "This is something that you have won through your own efforts and is no longer mine. Without any regrets, I'd like to present it to you."

"I made the effort to help you." Shao scolded, "because I pitied your misfortune. Why should I covet these things?" He turned over everything and left without looking back. Truly he was a man powerful enough to subdue the thieves, as evidenced by the following:

Frightening it is indeed to see robbers in broad daylight,
But our hero subdues them with little effort.
Waving his whip, he retrieved Hsiang-ju's jade; [3]
Refusing any reward, he is really a man worthy of praise.

Now I am going to tell another story about a scholar named Wang who was resourceful enough to make fun of the outlaws. This will serve as the feature tale, but if you wish to know the details of this episode, readers, you must first listen to my "The Eight Scenes of the Hsiao and Hsiang Rivers": [4]

Dark dragon-like clouds above the ancient ferries;
Lakes connected by antler-like streams.
Tall willow trees hang low their heads at dusk;
Luxuriant grain stands in dense, long rows at dawn.
Men yearn for spring outings on days like this;
For anxious travelers, night's anchor seems a year away.
(To the tune of "The Evening Rain on the Hsiao and Hsiang Rivers.")

Consort Hsiang [5] *dressing her cloud-like hair;*
The dragon lady flashing her shining mirror.
The silvery moon on the water, flawless, translucent stream;
The elegant figure in reflection, natural, beauty supreme.
The sound of a flute in the cooling breeze;
Silence behind the lacquered doors on both shores.
(To the tune of "The Autumn Moon on the Tung-t'ing Lake.") [6]

South of Pa-kuei, [7] *the highway is dark;*
At Ts'ang-wu, [8] *few sounds come from the moonlit river.*
Last night the sky was in its natural cosmic charm;
Today a hundred sails are aloft in the wind.
Looking at the mirror, I watch my face;
Waiting in the tower, I long for my lover's return.
(To the tune of "The Returning Sail from the Distant River.")

The lake is smooth, with its water reaching the horizon;
Beaches and shoals stretch for a thousand li.
Marsh flowers with cool and lonely autumn faces;
Wild geese in scattered groups winging south.
Occasionally a small boat comes sailing by,
Sending startled flocks of birds into flight.
(To the tune of "The Wild Geese on the Sandbanks.")

At Tung-t'ing Lake the Hsüan Emperor [9] *expired;*
Gone is the goddess of the Hsiang River and her magic zither.
A deep, murky mist creeps over the waters;
The ancient temple on the mountain lies far away.
Bells chime at the new moon in the eastern grove;
A monk returns to the ferry by the chilly tide.
(To the tune of "The Evening Bells on the Misty Isle.")

At the lakehead the sky suddenly changed colors;
At the tower I linger to watch this scene.
The sudden squall has passed quickly over;
The setting sun shines brightly through.
The fishermen shift their boats from the eastern bank
To recast their lines in the western bay.
(To the tune of "The Fishing Village in the Evening Sun.")

A rustic inn by the harbor at midlake;
A plank bridge to the road past simple huts.
Young women with baskets of foxnut and wheat;
Old villagers with hampers of fish and shrimp.

---

[3] An allusion to Lin Hsiang-ju (fl. third century B.C.), a minister of King Hui-wen (r. 298–266 B.C.) of the state of Chao. The king of Ch'in wished to own the fabulous jade of Pien Ho, then in the possession of King Hui-wen. An offer was made to exchange fifteen cities for it, but in the final negotiations to complete the transfer, Lin suspected foul play and secretly sent the piece of jade back to Chao. The allusion is intended to emphasize the great amount of wealth involved and to praise Shao Wen-yüan's ability to preserve such a difficult prize.

[4] Both the Hsiao River (a tributary of the Hsiang) and the Hsiang River (a tributary of the Yangtze) flow through and meet in Hunan Province.

[5] The goddess of the Hsiang River.

[6] The Tung-t'ing Lake is in the northeastern part of Hunan Province, which literally means the province to the south of the lake. The lake is linked with the Yangtze River and several of its tributaries, including the Hsiang River. The size of the lake varies considerably according to the season. It reaches its maximum during summer and autumn.

[7] Near Kweilin in modern Kwangsi Province.

[8] At the border between the modern provinces of Kwangtung and Kwangsi.

[9] The Yellow Emperor, one of the earliest sage kings in the legendary period of Chinese history, is also known as the Hsüan Emperor as he was supposed to live at a hill in Hsüan-yüan, to the northwest of modern Hsin-cheng County in Honan.

Like a faint mirage reflected dimly in the water,
This beautiful scene seems so near yet so far.
(To the tune of "The Bright Mist at the Mountain
Village.")

The plums are now blooming in the countryside;
Cattails spread a floating blanket on the river.
Fine mansions crowd together like clumps of jade,
Where people dwell by the deep, clear lake.
All day long the white curtain hangs unfurled
As a lonely boat returns to its distant home.
(To the tune of "The Evening Snow in the River
Sky.")

These songs, which describe the wonderful
landscapes in Ch'u,[10] were composed by an official from Chekiang. In Ch'u, everyone praises
these melodies with enthusiasm and they are sung
everywhere. Surrounded by a multitude of mountains and connected by three rivers, the eight-
hundred-*li* stretch of the Tung-t'ing Lake makes a
good haven for thieves and robbers. In the early
period of our dynasty [Ming], Ch'en Yu-liang, a
pretender to the imperial throne, occupied the
Ch'u area and declared himself the emperor.[11]
He was later vanquished by Emperor T'ai-tsu [r.
1368–1398]. But his descendants now live in the
area between Jui-ch'ang and Hsing-kuo,[12] under
the family name of K'o-ch'en, and they are very
numerous.

For generations they had the practice of choosing an outstanding man to be the leader of their
clan, and were known for their skill in fighting
and their outlaw activities, such as robbing travelers and merchants. Their hideout became a

shelter for the criminals and rogues in the vicinity.
The authorities did not dare confront them. For
though there were district commanders who pa-
trolled this area to guard against any unusual in-
cidents, they had all become close friends with
these bandits. Removed from the jurisdiction of
local officials, their situation was not unlike that of
the outlaws at the Liang-shan Marsh in Sung
times.[13]

But let me tell how in Huang-kang County of
the Huang-chou Prefecture, there was a *hsiu-ts'ai*
named Wang who was preparing himself for
more advanced examinations. His family was very
rich, and had at its service several dozen male servants as well as numerous maidservants and concubines. A champion of justice who loved to roam
about the countryside, Wang was free and easy of
manner and much more resourceful than the
average man. Everything he managed was assured
of a good result. He was nicknamed Wang T'ai-
kung (Grand Duke Wang) because he was considered the equal of Lü Wang[14] in wisdom and ability.

Among his favorite concubines was one Hui-
feng, a woman whose beauty could truly sink a
fish, fell a goose, or cause the moon to hide and
flowers to blush for shame. Furthermore, she was
accomplished in poetry, racing horses, shooting
pellets, and all the rugged pursuits of youth. But
she was more than just a concubine, for Wang

[10] Ch'u is a collective term for the land covered by the two
modern provinces of Hupeh and Hunan. In Ming times this
area was taken as one provincial unit.

[11] Ch'en Yu-liang (1320–1363) was the son of a fisherman.
He first served under the banner of the rebel Hsü Shou-hui
and later, as leader of his own forces, conquered the territory
of modern Hunan, Hupeh, and Kiangsi. He proclaimed himself the emperor of Han, but was ultimately destroyed by Chu
Yüan-chang (T'ai-tsu), the founder of the Ming Dynasty.

[12] The locale is between southeastern Hupeh and northern
Kiangsi.

[13] Liang-shan Marsh, in western Shantung Province, was a
large swampy area which served at various times throughout
Chinese history as a bandit hideout. The story referred to here
is the *Shui-hu chuan* (The Water Margin), one of China's most
famous novels. It describes the adventures of a group of rebels
toward the end of the Northern Sung period. In the last few
hundred years, the waters in that area had already dried up.

[14] Lü Wang (eleventh to twelfth centuries B.C.), also known
as Lü Shang or Chiang Tzu-ya, was a virtuous old man of the
early Chou period. He was also named T'ai-kung Wang
(Grand Duke Wang) by King Wen. King Wen himself never
reigned; he was generally known by his posthumous title. According to tradition, Lü Wang was an extremely capable counselor to King Wen and he assisted his successor King Wu to establish the Chou Dynasty.

101

always took her along with him on his excursions. How beautiful was she?

Her temple locks are lightly combed into fine cicada wings,
Her painted eyebrows gently arched like the hills of spring.
Crimson lips glow like a ripened cherry;
Gleaming teeth form even rows of jade.
Flowers bloom in her blushing cheeks;
Eloquence flows from her expressive gaze.
Naturally graceful in bearing,
She has skills just as outstanding.
Stout heroes poised to kill would have to turn and look;
Meditating monks would have to pause and stare.

One day, Scholar Wang took Hui-feng traveling to Yüeh-chou, where they climbed the Yüeh-yang Tower. They looked out at the vast expanse of the Tung-t'ing Lake as it extended into the distance until the huge waves seemed to clap against the sky. It was winter, and as the water level was low, they could glance down from the tower and see that there was not a great measure of water between them and Mount Chün.[15] They left Yüeh-chou by the south gate and crossed the lake by boat, and after only a few *li* they were at the foot of the mountain. There they hired a sedan chair and traveled on for over ten *li* before they dismounted to visit the Shrine of the Hsiang Goddess. Several dozen paces to the right, within a thicket of overgrown thorns and brushwood, were the ancient sepulchers of the two imperial consorts. Wang fetched some wine, and he and Hui-feng poured a libation for them.

Walking on for half a *li*, they reached the outer gate of the Attainment Monastery where they saw the three characters meaning "Mountain of Predestination." Wang did not understand, and Hui-feng laughed at his puzzlement. "It means that one should visit this place only with a woman; otherwise, why would they use the term 'predestination'?"

Wang asked a monk, who replied, "The mountain spirits are very jealous of people who come here on excursions, and whenever someone tries to cross over, they cause ill winds and turbulent waves to stop them. Those who reach this place are predestined to come, and that is the reason for the name."

"If that is the case," chuckled Wang to Hui-feng, "this means that you and I are very fortunate to have reached this place today."

The monk then pointed with his finger to many grand sights, saying, "This is the Hsüan-yüan Terrace where the bronze cauldron of the Yellow Emperor was smelted. Over there is the Wine-Scent Pavilion, where Emperor Wu of the Han Dynasty [r. 140–87 B.C.] obtained the elixir of immortality; and there is the Verse-Chanting Pavilion, where we have found traces of the Immortal Lü.[16] Further beyond is the Liu Yi Well, where Liu passed on the message for the daughter of the Tung-t'ing lord."[17]

Wang said good-bye to the monk, and with Hui-feng left the place beside the abbot's room and climbed the Hsüan-yüan Terrace. As they leaned on the railing to look about in all directions, the water and sky seemed to be of one hue. The view was breathtaking. Further to their left was the Wine-Scent Pavilion. Circling out around to the left of the monastery gate, they climbed up to the Verse-Chanting Pavilion, then descended again to the Liu Yi Well, to the side of which was the Message Pavilion. In front of the latter was the Wild Tangerine Fountain and many other ancient landmarks.

They were just enjoying the scenery when suddenly they saw a huge fellow with a martial air about him coming up from below to take in the

---

[15] Of the many hills that dot the Tung-t'ing Lake, Mount Chün is among the most famous because of its link with the legends of the Hsiang goddess.

[16] Lü Tung-pin was, at a late age, trained by the immortal Chung-li ch'üan; later both of them were regarded as among the Eight Immortals. From the twelfth century, Lü became a prominent patriarch of religious Taoism.

[17] See "The Legendary Marriage at Tung-t'ing" in this anthology.

view. Although Hui-feng drew back under cover, there really was no place to hide. The man noticed her beauty and, focusing his attention on the two of them, he doggedly followed their every step. Wang felt ill at ease and quickly descended the mountain. But when they were almost to the boat, he noticed that the big fellow, who had also come down, whistled a signal. A boat nearby on the left responded. Ten or twenty fierce-looking men inside the boat jumped out and answered the man on the bank, who pointed to Hui-feng and cried, "Take that woman; we shall present her to our chief."

The band replied with a shout and moved together toward her like a hawk snatching a sparrow until they finally got her to their boat, hoisted full sail, and headed toward the middle of the Tung-t'ing Lake. Wang could only wail bitterly, for the outlaws in the lake area had many hideouts and dens, and he had no way of knowing which band of cutthroats had taken her away. He was in great distress and anxiety, and it was extremely painful for him to return alone along the route the two had taken. Truly:

He had no idea where his soul had gone;
It seemed to be chasing clouds over autumn streams.

Wang saw his beloved concubine abducted, but how could he let it end that way? He was a resourceful person and quickly sent men out everywhere to inquire in all the busy towns and marketplaces throughout the counties and prefectures of the province. A notice was posted which read [in brief]: "A reward of one hundred taels will be paid to anyone furnishing information [about this concubine]." The news soon spread that Scholar Wang had lost his concubine and had offered a large reward for her return.

From ancient times it has been said that, "A generous prize will always attract valiant men." One day Wang came to the provincial capital, where Hsiang Ch'eng-hsün, his good friend and regional military commissioner, invited him to a feast at the Yellow Crane Tower.[18] While they were drinking, Wang leaned on the railing and gazed at the unending panorama of river and mist. He thought of his beloved concubine Hui-feng, and wondered where she was among all these clouds and streams. Flicking the sleeves of his robe in anger, he rose to sing aloud a line from "Red Cliff," by Su Tzu-chan:[19]

I long for someone far away,
And look for my beauty at the other end of the sky.

Unaware that tears were flowing down his cheeks, he hummed these lines several times. Commissioner Hsiang noticed this and was about to question him when a servant nearby, acting as bodyguard, stepped boldly forward and said, "Sir, you don't look happy as you drink. Is it because you've lost your concubine?"

"How do you know about this?" asked Wang.

"You have notices posted on every street," replied the servant. "Everyone knows about it! Please enjoy your wine with my master; I'll tell you where she is later."

Wang bowed deeply, saying, "If I could discover her whereabouts, I would not refuse to drink a hundred cups."

"Is one woman worth all this bother?" said the commissioner. "But come, let's first drink a few cups before he explains."

Wang quickly took a large goblet and drained it three times without pausing. He again filled the cup and offered it to the servant. "Please tell me whatever you know; I'll reward you with one hundred taels."

"I am from the Hsing-kuo Prefecture," replied the servant. "My home is at Mount Ho-lü and I am well acquainted with the affairs of the K'o-ch'en clan there. The leader is called Master K'o-ch'en and he has several brothers, brave and pow-

---

[18] A famous tower, long cherished in traditional Chinese literature, to the southwest of Wuchang in Hupeh Province.

[19] Tzu-chan was the style of the celebrated Sung poet Su Shih (1036–1101).

erful men who specialize in smuggling and illegal activities around here. Their clan is the largest in this area, and while each locale among the rivers and lakes has a head man, they are all subordinate to him. The other day I heard that a beautiful woman was kidnapped on the Tung-t'ing Lake at Yüeh-chou and brought back to the leader of the clan. He was so pleased that he has been feasting and celebrating ever since. My home is not more than ten *li* from there, so I know all the details. She must be the young woman from your family."

"She was taken while we were at the Tung-t'ing Lake, and your information is correct."

"This man," said the commissioner, "is most generous and noble minded, and although he leads a band of outlaws, he has become good friends with the officials in our local government. He has also sent gifts to those in high official circles to strengthen these ties, and everyone responds to his bidding. He cannot be compared to a common bandit who can be forcibly arrested. If your concubine was taken by these people, I'm afraid you must give up any thought of a reunion with her. There're many beautiful women in the world and for you, my friend; it is better to forget about her. Just enjoy your wine, for it is useless to bear a grievance."

"How can anyone who regards himself as a real man allow his loved one to be kidnapped and, knowing where she is, not try to win her back with some scheme? Even though I have very little talent, I swear that I'll take her back, if only to give you an occasion for good laughter."

"I know that you are extremely capable; but how easy it is to talk, and how difficut to accomplish," said the commissioner.

From this moment, however, Scholar Wang relaxed, enjoyed his wine, and then left. The next day Wang sent fifty taels to the commissioner's servant to reward him for the information. Then he sought the commissioner's permission to use this man as a guide, and promised to give the servant another fifty taels to make the full one hundred when his woman was rescued. Commis-

sioner Hsiang laughed at the scholar for his romantic notions and ordered the servant to go along with Wang and do as he instructed. The servant was so overwhelmed with joy upon receiving the money that he was only too anxious to be of service.

Wang then obtained from him the names of the K'o-ch'en brothers for a plan that he had already formed in his mind. After writing out a formal complaint, he went directly to the office of the assistant military commissioner to present his case. When the assistant commissioner read his petition and saw the names of the K'o-ch'en brothers, including their leader, he was immediately apprehensive.

"It isn't wise to provoke these people," he said. "All that concerns you is a minor matter about a woman. If I issue a warrant and send someone to arrest them, it will inevitably stir up trouble, with tragic results. I simply cannot do it."

"I ask only for an official warrant," said Wang. "I myself will go to negotiate with them for her return. I won't need any of your soldiers, and you may rest assured there will not be any quarrel with them."

The assistant commissioner listened, as Wang made it sound so easy. "This warrant won't be a difficult matter, and I can approve your complaint right away. I'll issue orders with my official seal for you to take along."

"That's exactly how I would like to handle it," said Wang, "and I wouldn't presume to ask for anything else. With this document I can bring this case to a conclusion, and I will report to you afterward."

Only half convinced, the assistant commissioner had his clerks draw up the proper document and handed it to the scholar; Wang took it, acting rather pleased, as though he had already gotten his concubine back.

"My legal complaint has been approved," said Wang when he returned to Commisioner Hsiang, "and I have come to ask for your help."

"If you want us to go to the trouble of dispatching additional soldiers to fight with these outlaws," the comissioner said, shaking his head, "it's quite impossible."

"I've no use for any more men, so please set your mind at ease. I have my own people; I only want to borrow one of your official cruisers that you use regularly on the river. I also need two patrol boats and some ordinary equipment such as banners, flags, sun shades, and uniforms. Aside from this, I won't trouble you for any soldiers to help us, but will take only the servant who acted as my informant the other day. That will be enough."

"What do you plan to do?"

"I've my own way and I can't tell you now. You'll see after it's all over."

The commissioner complied with his request and loaned all the items to Wang. Quiet satisfied, Wang prepared over a month's supply of provisions and gathered together several dozen household servants. He had them dress as soldiers in the borrowed uniforms and they all boarded the boat to start up the river. Just like an important military official, he sailed out upon the waters amid the din of drums and horns. Truly:

Like a huge flotilla skirting the famous Red Cliff,
They glide up the river with their painted prow.
The mark of this commander was his naval cruiser;
It was time to throw down the pen of Pan.[20]

Wang ordered his men to make a wooden plaque bearing the insignia of a district commander as he sped along in his ship straight for the mouth of the river at Mount Ho-lü. When they were still more than four or five *li* from shore, he sent two men on ahead in a patrol boat. One of the men was the servant of Hsiang; the other was a trusted servant of his own, Wang Kuei. They were to bear the official insignia

[20] An allusion to Pan Ch'ao, a Han general who while working as a copyist threw down his pen in disgust and claimed that a hero should go forth to win glory and success in the battlefield, not work with brush and ink. He thereupon began a series of military campaigns which finally brought him to the attention of the emperor.

which would summon all the local citizens to greet the recently appointed district commander. They carried some red visiting cards on which a single stroke had been deleted from the surname "Wang" so that his name read "Chiang Wan-li." Their ultimate destination was the home of Master K'o-ch'en to present cards to each of the brothers. They were to explain that the new official admired the illustrious reputation of the brothers and wished to pay them a visit.

When the two of them had gone to carry out their orders, Wang instructed the boatmen to drift slowly ahead. Hsiang's servant was quite familiar with this territory; and after receiving such a generous reward, was there anything he would not do for Wang? He guided Wang Kuei in the patrol boat until they quickly reached the bank, where they carried the wooden insignia ashore to make the announcement. Soon everyone knew that the new official's ship had arrived and prepare to receive him. The servant then took Wang Kuei to a place which was in reality a farmstead. This is how it looked:

Freezing air assailing;
Icy winds buffeting.
Three winters with no passersby;
In a year few travelers are seen.
Clumps of juniper massed in dragon shapes;
Dense, bushy pine sharp as tigers' tracks.
Already high the red sun;
Inside the farmstead ghostly fires still flicker.
Long before the twilight comes,
Sad winds sigh by the old mountain streams.
Basins full of man-meat sauce;
Coin presses cover the minting stove.
Suddenly there's the smell of blood,
For this is, after all, a bandit's lair.

The servant was a local man who was well acquainted with many of the K'o-ch'en clan, so he went directly in to present the calling cards. Master K'o-ch'en recognized Commissioner Hsiang's servant and knew that he was employed by the government, so why should he suspect anything?

"This new official," said the leader as he discussed the matter with his brothers, "has shown us great honor, and since he has treated us so courteously, we should welcome him respectfully. Let's arrange a basket of fruit, take some mutton and wine, and make ourselves presentable to meet him at once. First, he'll see that we know the rules of propriety, and second, it'll show our strength and dignity. We can then entertain him in accordance with the kind of reception he gives us."

No sooner had this matter been settled than the announcement came that the official's ship had arrived at the estuary, and a group of sedan-chair bearers were ordered to take their conveyance to meet the guest. Of course, the K'o-ch'en brothers were all in martial array as they called out the names of twenty or thirty of their lackeys to bring the mutton and carry the wine; then, hoisting the flags and banners and burning candles, they went out to meet the official.

Wang's ship had reached its mooring and, dressed in the red silk cap and gown which he had borrowed, he called for the eight bearers to carry him ashore in a sedan chair. After the local citizens had shouted their greeting to him, the K'o-ch'en brothers stood on both sides to bow, and then led the way as Wang gave the order to go straight to their farmstead. When they arrived at the main hall, he climbed out of the conveyance while the brothers quickly brought a chair and placed it in the center of the room.

"Please sit down, sir," said the first K'o-ch'en, "and allow us to receive you properly."

"Let us dispense with these formalities right away," said Wang. "You brothers are noble and virtuous men of great fame, and I heard of your name long before I took up my office here. Now it is my good fortune to be assigned to this territory, and as I want to be good friends with gentlemen who have a true sense of honor, I have made this special trip to offer my greetings. How can I insist on maintaining the polite courtesies between officials and common citizens? Only if we act as guests and hosts can we have lasting friendship."

The K'o-ch'en brothers had knelt, and Wang raised them up with his hands, saying, "Please stop this nonsense. Heroes are not like ordinary people and don't require the usual amenities."

The brother humbly acquiesced and invited Wang to be seated. The three brothers stood in attendance, but Wang quickly ordered more chairs so they could sit on either side of him. Feeling very pleased at the way this official treated them, they hurriedly ordered wine to entertain him. Taking off his belt and robe, Wang, enjoyed himself fully at feasting and playing the finger-guessing game, without betraying the least trace of his real identity. As the wine was being passed around, he talked of chivalry and heroic deeds with flourishes and gestures of his hands and regretted that they had not met sooner.

The brothers were not only won over; they also felt flattered and grateful. "Since you've favored us with such kindness," they said, "we would indeed be willing to repay you with our lives. If you face some danger on the river, just shout and we will quickly respond, for our family would never want to invite evil retribution by forgetting your generosity toward us."

Wang was even more elated as he heard this and accepted the long succession of large cups filled with wine. From noon until late at night they drank before he finally said good-bye and went back to his ship. The banquet on this day was considered the first K'o-ch'en's party; the next day it was the second K'o-ch'en who acted as host; on the following day the third K'o-ch'en took his turn.

"Your arrival the other day was rather abrupt," said the first K'o-ch'en after the round had been completed, "so our first gathering did not count." He again entertained Wang with a day of feasting and gifts of gold and silk, which Wang accepted joyfully without much ado. When the feast was over and Wang had returned to the ship, the K'o-ch'en family all came to pay a courtesy call. Wang asked them to stay and quickly ordered wine.

"We're uncultivated men with a rustic way of

106

life," they said, declining. "It's already great fortune for us that you've deigned to accept our offer of wine and food. How dare we presume to accept your invitation?"

"Your courtesy demands a response," replied Wang. "How could it be possible that after I've put you to so much trouble to entertain me you would not allow me to reciprocate? Besides, our relationship shouldn't be bound by conventional rules. When I was at your place before, all of you acted as my hosts. Today you have visited me, and thus you will be my guests. Why can't we join in the spirit of the occasion without taking it so formally?"

The brothers found it difficult to decline, as the feast had already been arranged. After Wang had everybody properly seated, a group of theatrical entertainers were brought in to perform *The Oath of Brotherhood in the Peach Garden, The Long, Lonely Journey,* and other southern plays about the heroic aspirations of many a historical figure.[21] The K'o-ch'en brothers were unsophisticated people of the mountains, and when they looked at such gaiety and glamor, they were indeed spellbound. But they did not know that Wang had secretly ordered the boatmen to quickly and silently get under way upon the signal of the gongs and drums in the opera. Steering by moonlight, the boat drifted along with the current without those in the cabin being aware of it. They had gone several dozen *li* by the time the performance was finished, but their excitement had not flagged. As before, the men returned to the banquet tables to send the goblets flying with their drinking games.

Some entertainers joined in their songs, inciting greater delight as they toasted one another. Wang waited until he was sure that the boat had traveled some distance before he made his announcement:

[21] These two plays are based on episodes from the historical novel *San-kuo chih yen-i* (Romance of the Three Kingdoms). The first one is on the oath of brotherhood among Liu Pei, the founder of the kingdom of Shu, and his two sworn brothers Chang Fei and Kuan Yü; the second is on Kuan Yü's escorting his sisters-in-law single-handedly on a long journey to meet Liu Pei.

"It gives me great pleasure to enjoy the happy friendship we feel for one another. I've a small matter on my mind, however, which will greatly inconvenience you gentlemen, and I wish to discuss some wise solution with you."

"What is it? Please explain and we will do what you say," asked the startled K'o-ch'en brothers.

Wang asked a servant to bring over a small case, took out the official warrant, and held it in his hand. "A scholar by the name of Wang has lodged a complaint against you gentlemen, charging that you have kidnapped his concubine. Is this true?"

The brothers looked at one another in surprise, unable to conceal their secret very well. "There is a woman by the name of Hui-feng," replied the first K'o-ch'en, "who was taken at Yüeh-chou. She claims to belong to the Wang family and she is now at my place. We dare not hide anything from you."

"A woman is a small matter," replied the scholar, "but Wang is a man of heroic aspiration, by no means a common fellow. At present he wants to petition that you be eliminated as rebels and has already submitted this formal complaint to my superior. This warrant has been quietly processed and turned over to me for action. Since I'm a man abiding by the code of honor of the world, I wouldn't want to come against you with military force. Consequently, I invited you here so that tomorrow we can meet with my superior and give testimony about this affair with the scholar Wang."

The K'o-ch'en brothers were shaken at this and paled in fright. "We cannot take the matter of an audience with your superior so lightly! As soon as we get in court, we will surely be thrown in jail and in any event die there!" They all wanted to get away, but when they jumped up to push open the windows for a look, they saw they were far out in the middle of a broad, foggy, expanse of river. Since they had no boats, and were far from the shore or their hideaway, they were beyond help. Nor could they think of a way out. Truly:

With wings they could soar into the sky;
With claws they could penetrate into the earth.
But since they had no skills to burrow or fly,
How could they escape the present plight?

The brothers realized that they had been trapped and knelt down together. "Please save us," they implored.

"At this point, if you don't obey the summons, it will be difficult for me to report to my superior. If you do, it will mean trouble for you. We must make up a scheme which will enable me to cancel this document. Then you needn't go to court."

"We're not very clever," they admitted, "and would like to trouble you to think of a good plan for us."

"Wang is worried only about his concubine. It would be best to dispatch a patrol boat quickly to your place and bring the woman here. As soon as she is taken back, the authorities will return her to Wang. This warrant can then be withdrawn, and you gentlemen will avoid litigation."

"What is so difficult about that?" they said. "All we have to do is to write a note to the man in charge of our household and have her fetched here."

"Well, then, we mustn't delay. Do act quickly," said Wang.

The first K'o-ch'en scribbled out the authorization as Wang hurriedly sent for Hsiang's servant and Wang Kuei; one of them was familiar with the route, and the other knew the girl. Quietly he gave them their orders with the note, sent the two patrol boats off together, and prepared to wait for their return.

Meanwhile Wang enjoyed himself immensely as he drank wine to the continuous music of gongs and drums. The brothers saw that the scholar appeared to be calm and self-possessed, and although they had recovered somewhat from their initial shock, they still felt some emotional and physical strain. Wang's mood, however, was one of constant exhilaration marked by generous amounts of chatter, laughter, and incessant drinking. At dawn, the news spread quickly that the two patrol boats had returned with the young woman.

Wang promptly gave the order for Hui-feng to come aboard. Delighted, he sent her to a cabin amidships while he fetched four ingots of silver. He gave one ingot to each of the two men who had acted as messengers, and one ingot for each boat crew to share. After the money had been distributed, they all thanked him together. Only then did Wang order three more large cups of wine to bid the K'o-ch'en brothers farewell.

"This matter has been settled, and at last I can personally report to my superior. It is no longer necessary for you to stay here, so you may now return home."

The brothers thanked him profusely for his assistance and Wang replied with a playful tug at the first K'o-ch'en's beard.

"You really don't recognize who this scholar Wang is, do you? To tell the truth, I am Wang, and not the newly appointed district commander. I played this trick on you only because I couldn't give up my concubine. Now she has been returned, and I have tremendously enjoyed the pleasure of feasting with you these past several days. Wasn't this a matter of fate? Many thanks to you gentlemen; now it is time to say good-bye."

To the brothers, it seemed as though they were waking from a dream or sobering up from a drunk. At last their anxieties disappeared, and their laughter was spontaneous as they said, "Up to now, you fooled us so completely with such vigor and valor that you are in fact a true hero. We're simple fellows and it was our good fortune, as well as our destiny, to have the opportunity to serve you during these few days. As for the concubine, we offended you in our ignorance and we are quite ashamed!" Each took some silver from the purse at his waist, a little over thirty taels in all, and gave it to Wang. "This is for the young lady to expand her wardrobe."

Unsuccessful in repeated attempts to decline, Wang finally smiled and gave in. At their request, Wang ordered a patrol boat to escort them to a spot where the highway approaches the river bank and set them ashore. The brothers bid an attentive farewell to Wang, boarded the boat, and left.

Wang then called Hui-feng from the cabin to talk about that frightening affair of the other day, and she sobbed out the whole story.

"You're now with me again," he said, "and we needn't talk about it anymore. Have a cup of wine to calm yourself." Appearing to have missed each other very much, the two drank to their hearts' content, and then spent the night on the boat. When they rose the next day, they had already reached the pier at Wuchang, where Wang went to visit Commissioner Hsiang.

"I'm now finished with all the boats and equipment which I borrowed from you. I'm returning everything."

"What about your concubine?"

"Thanks to your assistance, she is already aboard the ship."

"How did you manage it?"

Wang told him in detail how he had deceived the bandit chief by disguising himself as a new official. "All this was due to your generosity," said Wang, "and I'm deeply in your debt for your influence and power."

"You were able to play such a clever trick in this strange episode only because of your extraordinary courage and wisdom. With your skills, you could be a great military leader."

At that time Wang presented another fifty taels to Hsiang's servant to complete the amount he had formerly promised. He hired another boat, put Hui-feng aboard, and requested from the commissioner a patrol boat as escort and as passage for all his servants. When all was arranged, he reported to the assistant commissioner and returned the warrant.

"How is the matter coming along?" the assistant commissioner asked. "Why are you giving this back?"

Again Wang related the entire adventure from beginning to end, and the assistant commissioner laughed. "Without raising a club or a spear, you were able to rescue someone from the lair of a tiger. That is really rare talent and imagination! The time can't be far off when the imperial court decides to use you for important tasks at the frontier, and I don't expect you to have any problems at all." For this high praise and regard, Wang modestly offered his thanks and left.

Wang took Hui-feng back to Huang-kang where the townspeople, as soon as they heard this news, all sighed in amazement: "This proves that Wang T'ai-kung's reputation is truly not just idle gossip!" And there is a poem to support this:

Our hero is truly of an extraordinary breed;
He was friendly with tigers, got along with wolves.
No need to tiptoe while the black dragon slept;
He soon took his pearl from the monster's jowls.

THE STRONG KID OF THE CH'IN-HUAI REGION

From *Li-weng i-chia yen*

TRANSLATED BY CONRAD LUNG

During the Chia-ching reign period [1522–1566], among the inhabitants who lived along the banks of the Ch'in-huai River[1] there was a lad. He was big and strong, and he had a dark complexion. Just a few months after he was born, he stopped taking milk and ate and drank with the grown-ups. When he was two years old, both his parents passed away, and he was brought up by his maternal uncle. He had great strength and was good at using his fists. He once killed a dog with a blow of his hand and, because of this incident, people called him Strong Kid.

Whenever Strong Kid fought with other children, nobody was his match. Even when a few score ganged up to attack him, since Strong Kid dealt out blows left and right with his fists, they all covered their heads and went home, crying or screaming, to complain to their fathers and big brothers.

The fathers and the brothers went to scold Strong Kid: "Which family's pig and dog are you that you dare to make trouble for us?"

"How could I dare to make trouble for you?"

Strong Kid said. "But to bear the burden of walking for my elders—that I can do."

So saying, he walked up to the group, grabbed the two legs of one of them with his two hands and lifted him up about two feet from the ground. He raised him high or brought him low while alternately walking and stopping. The man was afraid to do anything but giggle in fear of falling off. The incident created an uproar among the villagers.

Strong Kid had an active disposition and did not like studying. His uncle sent him to study under a teacher. He was rambunctious, and the teacher tried to punish him by flogging. But he seized the cane from the teacher and, with anger erupting from his eyes, said to him, "Fame and success should be achieved with my own bare hands. What use is there for these tedious writings?"

As soon as the teacher went out, he fought with the other children in the school, and none of the children managed to escape unscathed.

Furthermore, he often stole hairpins, earrings, and various articles of clothing from his uncle's house and exchanged them for drinks in taverns. When he was drunk, he would go wild and make

[1] This is a short river in Kiangsu Province, originating in Li-shui County and flowing through Nanking into the Yangtze River.

trouble. His uncle could not put up with him and threw him out. He hired himself out as a shepherd and time and again he falsely reported sheep lost on the forked roads when in fact he had stolen them and exchanged them for drinks. The owner was enraged, and once again he was dismissed.

By this time, he had already reached the age of twenty. He heard that the Japanese pirates were invading China and said in great delight, "Now my turn has come!" He immediately joined the army and rose from the minor ranks to assistant commander.

Once he drank with a fellow officer and, becoming tipsy, killed the officer while wrestling with him to find out who was stronger. Since the crime was punishable by death, he deserted his post, escaped to Ssu County,[2] changed his name, and lived in obscurity as a butcher.

He would steal out at midnight to help himself to others' cows. When he led out a cow from the stable, he would always call out, "I am riding away with your cow!" Having thus expressed his courtesy, he would ride the cow backwards and strike its buttocks with an axe. The pain would drive the cow to dash like the wind, and nobody could catch up with it. The next day, when the owner of the cow went to the marketplace to look for it, Strong Kid would say to him, "I'm the one who passed by your place and took away your cow yesterday. But since I announced to you beforehand what I was going to do, how could this be called theft?" If the owner pressed for the cow, he would only find that it had already been processed into dried beef and there was no proof that it belonged to him.

The hooligans in the marketplace selected Strong Kid to be their leader. In the daytime they gambled heartily, and at night they wandered in the courtesan's quarters. He became more egotistic by the day and once he even went so far as to

lament, "Nobody in this world is my match in strength. How unfortunate it is that I was born a thousand years too late to have a chance to challenge the hero who removed mountains and lifted cauldrons."[3]

Then city officials forbade the slaughter of cattle, and Strong Kid was out of business. He took the hides, bones, and horns he had saved, went to Kua-chou and Yangchow[4] to sell them, and got thirty pieces of gold. Before going home, he stopped by a tavern to buy some drink. He untied his purse of gold from his belt and put it on the table. The owner of the tavern saw it and said to him, "There're a lot of bandits on the road ahead. You should conceal your valuables properly."

Strong Kid threw away his cup, slapped the table, and said, "I've roamed the world for thirty years now, and I haven't yet met an opponent. I'll kowtow and submit to anyone who can take this gold from me!"

At the time, there were several youngsters eating at a table to the left of him. They were amazed when they heard what Strong Kid said. They rose and asked him his name and where he lived. Strong Kid said, "My name is not for you to know. I accomplished some great deeds at the border in earlier days, but now I've shunned official duties to be a commoner and I've become a leader of the gallants at Ssu."

"How many people can you deal with?" the youngsters asked.

"If ten thousand people are coming at me," said Strong Kid, "I'll take on ten thousand; if one thousand people are coming at me, I'll take on a thousand. I don't believe in worrying about how many people one can fight." The youngsters grew even more amazed.

[2] In modern Anhwei Province.

[3] The hero who claimed to be able to remove mountains and lift cauldrons weighing several thousand pounds was Hsiang Yü, the king of Ch'u. Hsiang lost to Liu Pang, the first emperor of the Han Dynasty, in the struggle for empire after the fall of the Ch'in Dynasty.

[4] Two adjacent prefectures in modern Kiangsu Province.

After his drink, Strong Kid packed up and rode off. He found a rider tailing after him at great speed before he had gone two or three *li*. Strong Kid thought to himself, "Can this be one of the bandits that we were just talking about?" The rider caught up with him and turned out to be just a youngster; so Strong Kid did not pay any attention to him. The youngster asked, "Where are you going?"

"Returning to Ssu," replied Strong Kid. The youngster said, "I'm your junior and also a native of Ssu. I've lost my way and I hope you'll kindly direct me home." Strong Kid rode ahead and led the way.

While they were riding, they conversed with each other rather amicably. Strong Kid asked the youngster, "You're carrying a bow and arrows. Are you good at archery?"

"I'm learning it but not yet good at it," replied the youngster.

Strong Kid took the bow and tried it out. Although he used all his strength, he could not draw the bow fully. He gave up and said, "This thing is good for nothing. What's the use of carrying it around?"

"Everything has its own use," the youngster said. "The difference is in who is using it." Then he tried the bow out himself. Just at that moment, a wild duck, squawking, was flying across the sky. The youngster let an arrow fly. The arrow shot through the feathers into the wild duck, and it fell dead in front of the horses. Strong Kid was surprised.

"You're carrying a knife; you must be good at knife work," said the youngster.

"Right. What I'm good at is this, not what you are carrying," replied Strong Kid. He took out his knife and handed it over to the youngster.

When the youngster saw it, he burst out laughing. "This is for killing chickens and slaughtering dogs. What use do you have for it?" With a twist of his hands, he bent the knife into the shape of a hook and with another twist he straightened it out as before.

Strong Kid lost his color and thought to himself, "He can surely take my gold with a snap of his fingers!" Although he continued to ride with the youngster, he was so afraid that gradually he could not keep his thighs from trembling. The youngster had to calm him down with comforting words.

After they had traveled on for some distance, the youngster, looking around and seeing no one in sight, raised his voice and yelled, and Strong Kid tumbled off his horse. The youngster first cut down Strong Kid's horse and then said to him, "If you disobey any of my orders, you will be like this horse." Strong Kid prostrated himself on the ground and inquired what the youngster wanted. The youngster said, "You good-for-nothing, untie the purse of gold from your belt and hand it all over!" Strong Kid emptied his purse and handed over all his gold to the youngster. He knocked his head on the ground and begged the youngster to spare his life.

"I have this bag of gold, which will be sufficient for me to buy ten days of drink," the youngster said. "You're like grass; you're not worth killing." He turned his horse and went back the way he had come.

Strong Kid was greatly depressed, and he could not move on, thinking to himself, "The thirty pieces of gold are not terribly important. But how can I go home and face my brethren after I, a hero for all my life, fell at the hands of a kid who still stank of milk?" Consequently, he did not return to Ssu but went away to a remote hamlet, built a thatched hut, and sold wine for a living. When he thought of what had happened, he often felt so ashamed that he wished he were dead.

One balmy spring day, some young men came in and ordered wine. Their fur garments were extremely fashionable and their horses impeccable;

they had the distinguished appearance of young gentlemen from great families. At the same time, they were spirited, free and easy, resembling the knights-errant from Ch'ang-an.[5] They sang wildly, thumping their table, oblivious of the people around them. Furthermore, they observed, "The man who is doing the dishes does not seem to be a common sort. Let's ask him to join us."

So saying, they dragged Strong Kid to their table and made him sit down with them. Strong Kid noted that nine of the young men were mere adolescents and the remaining one was still in his teens with his hair tied up in a knob.[6] This young man had a white and delicate complexion like that of a lady, and he did not speak much. However, whenever he spoke, all the others listened attentively. When they sat, they let him sit to their right,[7] and when they drank, they let him drink first. Strong Kid was somewhat puzzled by this.

One of the young men sitting at the end of the table looked familiar to Strong Kid. Strong Kid examined him carefully and found that he was the one who had cut down his horse and robbed him of his money. He said to Strong Kid, "Does the host still recognize his old friend?" Strong Kid dared not answer. Again the youngster said, "Who else could it be if you're not the one who untied your purse of gold from your belt and presented it to me as a gift? We're not the kind of people who would take other people's property by force. But we heard your boastful words and your scoffing at the world in the tavern by the fields, and that was why I went after you to challenge you. Surprisingly, you lost to me by a clear

margin. Now we have come to return the money."

Then he took thirty pieces of gold from his left sleeve, put them on the table, and said, "This is the original sum of money. It has been a year now, and the interest for this sum should be equal to it." He searched his right sleeve this time, took out another thirty pieces of gold, and gave them together with the first thirty pieces to Strong Kid. Strong Kid was afraid to take the money. A young man at the side threw down his sword and, with anger in his eyes, said, "When your belongings were taken away by others, you were not capable of retrieving them, and now even when they're being returned to you, you're afraid to take them back. What use is there for such a coward?" Strong Kid, in fear, quickly took the gold and put it inside his sleeve and left to prepare some chicken and corn to entertain the young men. However, they would not stay. The youngster who had returned the money said, "He's rather pitiful. He'd be very embarrassed if we refused his hospitality." Only then would the young men stay.

It happened that the stove was out of firewood, and Strong Kid wanted to ask his neighbors for some. The youngster who robbed him pointed at a dead tree by the house and said to him, "Why not use your hatchet?"

"It's what I need, but I don't have one," said Strong Kid.

The youngster thought for a long while and said, "I have to let my tenth brother solve this problem; none of us here is up to it."

The young man with his hair tied up in a knob embraced the tree with his arms and shook it left and right several times, and the tree fell over. He pulled out his sword and chopped off some side branches for the stove fire. After they had consumed an immeasureable amount of wine, they departed. There was not even a hint of what kind of people they were.

From then on, Strong Kid never matched his

---

[5] The site of the ancient city of Ch'ang-an, which was the capital city for quite a few dynasties, is near the modern city of Sian in Shensi Province. "Ch'ang-an" was frequently used in traditional Chinese literature simply to mean "capital city" instead of specifically designating the place. It is so used here, since Peking was the capital of the Ming Dynasty, the time setting of the story.

[6] The hairdo for boys under twenty.

[7] The seat of honor.

strength against that of other people. When others beat him up, he refused to hit back. When someone asked him where his old heroic spirit had gone, he gave the excuse that he was becoming old and weak. He was able to live out his natural life-span and died a peaceful death later, thanks, one may say, to the youngster.

THE INGRATE

The ingrate is one who repays kindness and generosity with exploitation or betrayal. To make excuses for his ingratitude, the ingrate normally belittles the benefit he has received (as in "The Shansi Merchant") or, by inverted reasoning, accuses his benefactor of being his enemy (as in "The Chung-shan Wolf"). Sometimes, however, the ingrate becomes an ingrate in spite of himself. Such is the case of the young servant Te-kuei in "The Case of the Dead Infant." That he is only an unintentional instrument of the downfall of his late master's wife does not negate the fact of his betrayal.

There is only one outcome for the ingrate in the moral cosmos of traditional Chinese fiction: his end is in direct proportion to his guilt—usually death. Justice is not necessarily administered by the local jurisdiction; the one who passes the verdict can be a resourceful outsider. This sometimes calls for a battle of wits, though in the end the ingrate is invariably brought to his knees. But the action of the ingrate in the entire event depends on one crucial factor—the simple-mindedness or even the stupidity of his benefactor. For technical reasons, however, this point is usually not emphasized. It is for this reason that in the moral parable "The Chung-shan Wolf" the benefactor is the personification of indiscriminate kindness.

THE CHUNG-SHAN WOLF

From *Tung-t'ien wen-chi*

TRANSLATED BY CONRAD LUNG AND THE EDITORS

Chao Chien-tzu[1] held a big hunt in Chung-shan.[2] The gamekeeper led the way, and falcons and hounds followed in throngs. The number of swift birds and fierce animals felled by the arrows was great.

A wolf, howling, stood upright like a man in their way. Chien-tzu unhurriedly mounted his chariot, drew his mighty bow, and shot a Su-shen arrow,[3] which buried itself completely in the wolf. Immediately, the wolf stopped howling and took flight. Enraged, Chien-tzu gave chase in his chariot. The dust raised veiled the sky, and the horses' hoofs sounded like thunder. It was difficult to distinguish between a horse and a man even at the short distance of ten paces.

Meanwhile, a Mohist,[4] Master Tung-kuo, was traveling northward to Chung-shan to seek employment as an official. The donkey he was riding was a poor one and he had a bagful of books with him. Traveling in the early morning, he had lost his way, and when he saw the cloud of dust, he was frightened. Suddenly the wolf ran up to him. It raised its head and said to him, "Is it not the master's vocation to render assistance to all those who need it? In the past, Mao Pao was ferried across the river [in time of danger] because earlier he had set free a tortoise,[5] and the marquis of Sui received a pearl because he had saved a snake.[6] Surely tortoises and snakes are not as intelligent as wolves. So, in the circumstances, why don't you let me get into your bag as soon as possible, so that I can preserve my endangered life? If I can escape from this peril, later on, what you've done will be like raising me from the dead. Certainly I'll follow the examples of the tortoise and snake and do everything I can to repay you."

"Dear me!" the master said. "If I helped you, wolf, I'd offend the lords and incur the wrath of

[1] Chao Chien-tzu was a minister in the court of the Duke Ting of Chin (r. 511–475 B.C.).

[2] Chung-shan was a state founded by a Tartar tribe (Hsien-pei) in the pre-Ch'in period at what is now Ting County in Hopei Province.

[3] Su-shen was a state of nomadic people inhabiting the region approximately covered by the modern provinces of Kirin and Heilungkiang. It was well known for producing fine arrows.

[4] A Mohist was a follower of Mo-tzu, a philosopher of the Warring States period who advocated the doctrine of universal love.

[5] The reference is to a story on Mao Pao, a prefect of the Western Chin Dynasty, who set free a white tortoise that had been captured by one of his soldiers. Later, when Mao Pao was defeated in a battle and fell into a river, the tortoise ferried him across to safety.

[6] Sui was a principality (in Sui County in modern Hupeh Province) in the Warring States period. The marquis of Sui once saved a wounded snake. In return, the snake searched for a large pearl in the river and gave it to the marquis.

the powerful. Since I don't know what kind of trouble I'd be getting into, how could I care about your reward? However, the fundamental principle of Mohist teaching being universal love, I must find some way to save your life. I certainly will not draw back even if I meet with misfortune."

Then he emptied his bag of books to put the wolf inside. He did this slowly and carefully: he was worried that in the front he would press too hard on the wolf's dewlap, and he feared that in the back he would expose its tail. After several attempts, he still couldn't put the wolf into the bag. As he was taking his time, trying this and that, the hunters were drawing closer and closer.

"No time to waste now," the wolf entreated him. "Would the master still be fastidiously courteous while saving people from fire or drowning? Would you leisurely ring the bells on your carriage if you were running away from bandits? Please act quickly!"

The wolf then offered its four legs for him to tie together, lowered its head clear down to its tail, bent its back, and hid its dewlap. It huddled up like a hedgehog, curled like an inchworm, coiled like a snake, held its breath like a tortoise, and gave itself up entirely to the Mohist scholar, who acted as the animal had suggested and put it in the bag. He then heaved it onto the donkey, using his shoulder as an aid. Afterward, he led the donkey to one side of the road and waited for Chao's hunting party to pass by.

Presently, Chien-tzu arrived. He looked for the wolf but could not find it. In a great fury, he drew his sword, cut off the tip of his chariot's shaft and showed it to the master, cursing: "Whoever dares to hide the whereabouts of the wolf will be like this shaft!"

The master prostrated himself on the ground, crawled forward, and on his knees said, "Unenlightened as I am, I've made up my mind to build a career in this world. For this reason, I've traveled a long way to this place and I've lost the right

direction myself. How can I find the track of a wolf and point it out to my lord's falcons and hounds? However, I've heard that 'a broad road will make a sheep go astray with its many forks.' Now a sheep is so docile that a boy can take care of it, and still we shall lose it if we leave it on a road with many forks. A wolf can hardly be compared to a sheep in its nature, and there are countless forked roads in Chung-shan on which even a sheep will get lost. But now you're only searching the broad road for the wolf; is this not like 'waiting for rabbits by a tree' or 'climbing a tree for fish'?[7] Furthermore, hunting is the business of gamekeepers. You should ask these men with the leather caps. I'm just a passerby; why should I be blamed? Unenlightened as I am, I know about the wolf. It has a greedy and vicious nature, and it gangs up with the jackals to do evil deeds. I certainly would like to offer you my assistance, no matter how slight it would be, so that you could get rid of it. Why should I hide anything from you?"

Chien-tzu was speechless. He turned his chariot and drove off. The master also spurred on his donkey to a fast pace and continued his journey.

After a long while, the shadows of the hunting banners had disappeared; the sound of the horses and chariots were heard no more. The wolf estimated that Chien-tzu had already gone some distance, so it said from inside the bag, "Master, please listen to me. Take me out of the bag, untie me, pull the arrow out of my leg, and I shall be on my way."

The master took the wolf out, and it growled at him, "It is my good fortune that I was rescued by you when the hunters were after me just then. I'm extremely hungry; if I don't get food, I shall die of starvation eventually. I'd rather be killed by the hunters and become the noblemen's food than starve to death by the roadside and become the

---

[7] Both of these allusions refer to those persons not only hoping for the impossible but also refusing to expend the least amount of effort.

prey of beasts. Since you're a Mohist who will work until your head is bald and your heels ache to try to do one good thing for the world, you'd not be stingy about offering me your body for food so that I can preserve my life, would you?"

Immediately, it smacked its lips and raised its claws, rushing toward the master. The Mohist hastily fought it with his bare hands and retreated, while fighting, to get behind the donkey. He ran around the donkey, using it as a buffer, and since he was trying his utmost to keep away, the wolf was unable to get at him.

Exhausted, they both paused to breathe with the donkey separating them. The Mohist said, "You're an ingrate! An ingrate!"

"I don't really want to be ungrateful to you," the wolf said. "But Heaven creates your kind to supply food for my kind."

There seemed to be no end to their battle, and the sun was slanting westward. The master thought to himself, "It's getting dark, and when the wolf pack arrives, I shall die for sure." Consequently, he decided to temporize with the wolf, saying, "It is a custom that we must consult three elders when in doubt. Let's go find three old men and ask them. If they say that I should be eaten, then I'm at your disposal; if not, then there's an end to it." Delighted, the wolf immediately set out with him.

They walked for some time, but met no passerby on the road. The wolf was starved. Seeing an old tree standing stiffly by the roadside, it said to the master, "Ask this elder."

"Since plants don't feel anything, what's the use of asking them?"

"Go ahead and ask. It will answer you."

The master had no alternative; he saluted the old tree, related the whole story, and then asked, "This being the case, am I still to be devoured by the wolf?"

A rumbling sound from inside the tree addressed the master: "I am an apricot tree. When the old gardener planted me years ago, all he had

spared was a pit. After one year, I flowered; in another year, I bore fruit. In three years' time, one could clasp my trunk in one's hands, and after ten years, one could embrace me. Now I am twenty years old. [All this time] the old gardener and his wife ate my fruit, and even guests from outside the family and lowly servants did the same. Furthermore, they sold my fruit in the market for a profit. My service to the old gardener has been immense. Now I am old. Since I can no longer put out flowers and bear fruit, the old gardener is mad at me. He has cut off my branches and stripped my leaves and is about to sell me to a carpenter for whatever I am still worth. Alas! Even a worthless tree in its old age cannot be spared the axe; what have you done for the wolf that you should hope to get off? Surely it should eat you."

As soon as the tree had finished its words, the wolf turned on the master with smacking lips and menacing claws.

"You're not acting according to the rule!" the master said. "We've agreed to ask three elders, and now we have only run into an old apricot tree. Why press me so soon?"

So they resumed their journey, and the wolf was getting all the more impatient. It saw an old cow basking in the sun among the remnants of some broken walls and said to the master, "Ask this elder."

"The nonsense of an ignorant plant just then already did enough damage. Now this cow is just an animal; what is the use of asking it?"

"Just ask it. Or I'll eat you."

The master had no alternative; he saluted the old cow, related the whole story once more, and asked for an opinion.

The cow frowned, opened its eyes wide in anger, licked its nose, opened its mouth, and said to the master, "The words of the old apricot tree are true indeed! When I was young and my horns were just beginning to grow, I was quite strong. The old farmer traded a knife for me and put me

119

to work in the field as a helpmate for the oxen. As I grew bigger and bigger, the oxen daily became older and weaker until I had to attend to everything myself. When the old farmer wanted to go somewhere fast, I pulled him in the farm cart, chose the shortest road to the destination, and ran there in a hurry. When he wanted to plow, I shed the cart and cleared the field of thorns and weeds for him. He depended on me as if I were his limbs. He relied on me for his food and clothing. He was able to marry because of me, and it was also because of me that he was able to pay his taxes and fill up his granary. On my part, I thought that when I died I would be buried with a mat over my body, like the horse or the dog. Formerly, he never had more than a picul or two of grain in his house; now he harvests more than ten times that amount. He used to live in poverty without any friends; now he promenades back and forth in the village hall. In the past, his wine jar and cup were covered with dust, and his parched lips never touched even an earthen pot that had wine in it. Today, he makes his own millet wine and shows off his wine jars, bragging about his wife and concubines. He used to wear short, coarse clothes, and his only companions were trees and rocks; he didn't know how to salute with his hands, and he was uneducated. At present, he goes to the village school and wears a straw hat, a leather belt, and comfortable clothes; and every grain and every thread comes from my labor. Now, because of my old age and frailty, he drives me into the wilderness where the wind ravages my eyes and the cold sun is my only company. Bones jut out like hills on my thin body; my old tears fall like rain. Spittle drops from my mouth helplessly, and I don't have the strength to raise my bent legs. My hair is gone and my skin is ruined by unhealed sores and wounds. The old farmer's wife is a ruthless sort. Day and night she reminds him, 'Every part of a cow's body is useful. We can dry the meat, remove the hair from the hide, and carve the bones and horns into utensils.'

And she points to the eldest son saying, 'You've been learning to be a butcher for a long time now. Why don't you sharpen your knife and get ready to use it?' This means that the writing is already on the wall; but I don't know where and when I shall meet my end. Now I have performed a great many services for them and still they are heartless; it seems I'll run into disaster before too long. What have you done for the wolf that you should hope to get off?"

As soon as the cow had finished speaking, the wolf again turned toward the master with smacking lips and menacing claws.

"Just a minute!" the master said.

Some distance away an old man, supporting himself with a staff, was seen coming their way. His beard and eyebrows were all white, and his garments were casual but in good taste; he appeared to be a cultured man. The master was surprised as well as delighted. He left the wolf behind and went up to the old man. He knelt down and said, weeping, "I beg the elder to speak and save my life." The old man asked why he said that, and the master said, "This wolf was pursued by hunters and it begged me to save it, but no sooner had I saved its life than it turned around and flashed its teeth at me. I entreated it earnestly without success and was going to be killed by it. I temporized with it by making a pact, insisting that the matter was to be settled by three elders. We first met an old apricot tree and the wolf forced me to ask it. The plant was ignorant and its answer almost cost me my life. We next met an old cow and the wolf forced me to ask it. The animal was just as ignorant and its answer almost cost me my life. Now we've run into you, sir. Could it be that Heaven is not going to let a scholar like me die? I dare to beg a word from you to save my life." Then he knocked his head on the ground, prostrating himself before the old man, and waited for his judgment.

When the old man had heard the story, he sighed again and again and struck the wolf with his staff, saying, "You are wrong! Nothing is more evil than turning against one's benefactor. The Confucians say that a person who cannot bear to turn his back on his benefactor is certainly going to be a devoted son. They also speak of the intimate father-and-son relationship among tigers and wolves. Now your ungratefulness is a denial of even the relationship of father and son." Then, in a harsh voice, he said, "Wolf, begone immediately! Otherwise, I'll club you to death."

"Sir," the wolf said, "you've only heard one side of the story. I'd like to tell you my version of the incident and hope that you will give me a hearing. In his attempt to save me, the master tied up my legs, shut me up inside the bag, and piled his books on me as I curled up and dared not breathe. He then carried on a pointless conversation with Chien-tzu. His intention was to profit from my suffocation in the bag. How can I not eat him?"

The old man turned to the master and said, "If that is indeed the case, then you are like Yi who was to be blamed for his own death."[8]

The master felt that he was being unjustly accused and gave a detailed description of his concern for the wolf and how he had struggled to put

[8] The reference is to a parable told by Mencius on P'eng Meng's apprenticeship with the famous archer Hou Yi of the Hsia Dynasty. After P'eng Meng had learned everything Hou Yi knew, he considered himself second only to his teacher. Consequently, he killed Hou Yi so that he could become the best archer in the world. Mencius considered that Hou Yi should also be held responsible for his own death because he failed to make a sound judgment before taking someone into his confidence.

it into the bag. The wolf for its part also tried its best to win the old man over with crafty argument. The old man said, "All that you two have said is not sufficient to convince me one way or the other. Let's try to put the wolf in the bag once more and I shall see if it is indeed cramped in there painfully."

The wolf gladly complied with this suggestion. It stretched out its legs for the master, who tied up the wolf, put it into the bag, and put the bag on the donkey without letting the wolf know what was actually going on.

The old man whispered in the master's ear, "Do you have a dagger?"

The master said, "Yes," and took one out.

The old man instructed the master with his eyes that the wolf had to be stabbed to death with the dagger. The master asked, "Won't it hurt the wolf?"

"The beast is so ungrateful and you still cannot bear to kill it," the old man said, laughing. "You're indeed a humane man but also extremely stupid. Going down a well to save a man or giving your clothes to a friend to save his life is good, but you should not endanger yourself in the process, should you? You belong to this kind. A superior man certainly will not consider it right to push humaneness to the point of stupidity."

As he finished talking, he laughed heartily, and the master laughed with him. Then he gave the master a hand in wielding the dagger. When the wolf was dead, they cast its carcass on the road and went on their way.

THE CASE OF THE DEAD INFANT

From *Ching-shih t'ung-yen*

TRANSLATED BY C. T. HSIA AND SUSAN ARNOLD ZONANA

Spring flowers and the autumn moon invite romance,
But how very soon rosy cheeks are crowned with white hair!
Let us compare frail humanity to the pine and cypress:
How many of us can thus withstand the winter's cold?

This quatrain speaks generally of how spring flowers and the autumn moon vex men's hearts, so that a young scholar will compose poems to lament the autumn and a beautiful maiden will sing songs to commiserate the spring. Frequently, these poetic puzzles of theirs imply regret that they have not met earlier, and the talk of their eyes conveys love. So in a rendezvous beneath the moon, a tryst among the flowers, they will only seek the romantic fulfillment of the moment, reckless of their lifelong reputations. In such cases, the couple shares a mutual love, each repaying a debt contracted in a previous existence, and so we need not be concerned with them.

There are also the situations in which the young man feels desire but the girl does not love him, or the girl loves him but the young man does not desire her. Although theirs is not a case of mutual love, still if one side is absolutely sincere, then the other, though as cold as the plaster god in a deserted temple, cannot help but be moved by the former's prayers and burning of incense morning and evening. If their union is destined to be brief, then they will eventually drift apart. But if their union is destined to be long lasting, then they will quickly become intimate. This also happens in the world of love, and we need say no more about it.

In addition, there are the cases in which a man remains unperturbed by beauty and a woman unmoved by love. Their virtue is like pure gold, and their hearts are like solid stone. Then, without cause, someone will set a snare to humiliate them, and in a weak moment they will lose their self-control and fall into the snare, to their undying regret. For example, the Buddhist abbot Yü-t'ung of Sung times had been an ascetic for fifty years. But because he offended Prefect Liu Hsüan-chiao, Liu schemed against him and ordered the prostitute Hung-lien to disguise herself as a widow and ask for a night's lodgings. She enticed him in a hundred ways and destroyed his asceticism.[1]

This type of encounter, and the resultant dalliance, is due to the victim's momentary failure to withstand temptation. Now I will tell a story about enticing a widow to lose her chastity; it could stand as a companion piece to the story of Yü-t'ung. Verily:

[1] The story given here is the summary of the first half of "Monk Yüeh-ming Redeems Liu Ts'ui" ("Yüeh-ming ho-shang tu Liu Ts'ui," *Ku-chin hsiao-shuo* 29).

*While tarrying on the mountain of love, do not ask for the
    Way;
If yet sunk in the sea of desire, do not sit in meditation.*

*To accomplish anything, one must stand on firm ground
And pay no heed to hollow reputation.*

It is said that during the Hsüan-te reign period
[1426–1436],[2] in Yi-chen County, a district of the
Yangchow Prefecture in the Southern Metropolitan Area,[3] there lived a commoner named Ch'iu
Yüan-chi, whose family was quite well off. He
married a girl of the Shao family (Shao-shih), an
outstanding beauty distinguished for virtue as
well. Husband and wife loved each other very
much. When they had lived together for six years
without issue, unexpectedly Yüan-chi fell sick and
died. Shao-shih, who was just then twenty-three
years old, was filled with grief and vowed to remain a chaste widow, never to marry again. Before she knew it, the three years of mourning had
passed. Because she was so young and had so
many days ahead of her, her parents urged her to
remarry. Her husband's uncle, Ch'iu Ta-sheng,
also repeatedly sent his wife over to reason with
her and ask her to change her mind. But Shao-
shih had a heart of stone and could not be moved.
She vowed, "Now that my late husband rests
below the Nine Springs, if I serve another family
and take a second husband, I shall either perish
under a knife or die by the rope." When everyone
saw how determined she was, who would dare
come to pressure her further? But the saying
goes, "If you can swallow three gallons of vinegar
at one sitting, you can live on as a lone widow."
Widowhood is not easily maintained. The best
long-term course for Shao-shih would have been
to take another husband openly. Although then
she would not have rated in the top category of
women, still she would not have missed being
counted in the middle group, and would not have
come to disgrace in the end. Verily:

After Shao-shih had made her boast, people,
according to their lights, either loudly praised her
or remained skeptical, watching what she would
do next. Shao-shih, however, was determined to
be chaste. She withdrew still further into the privacy of her own rooms and kept as her only companion the maidservant Hsiu-ku, with whom she
sewed for a living. There was also one ten-year-
old serving boy, Te-kuei, who guarded the middle
door leading to her inner apartment. It was also
his responsibility to fetch firewood and water and
make all necessary purchases. All the other serving boys, who had reached manhood, were now
dismissed. Thus there were no idlers in the courtyard, and inside and outside of her inner apartment a strict quiet and rectitude prevailed. After
several years of this, everyone was somewhat
awestruck and believed her. Who did not praise
Shao-shih for her steadfastness, in spite of her relative youth, and her maintenance of order and
discipline in her own household?

Time sped by like an arrow, and soon it was
time to observe the tenth anniversary of her husband's death. Shao-shih, cherishing his memory,
wanted to have a Buddhist memorial service conducted. She told Te-kuei to invite her uncle Ch'iu
Ta-sheng over to consult him about engaging
seven monks to recite the sutras for three days
and nights. "Uncle," Shao-shih entreated him, "as
a widow, I rely entirely upon you to make suitable
arrangements for the ceremonies." Ta-sheng
agreed.

Our story forks at this point. There was a man
named Chih Chu who had recently moved to the
neighborhood. A ne'er-do-well, he had always
been something of a troublemaker and did not
stick to a regular line of business. He just idled in
the streets and made a living by meddling in other
people's affairs. He heard people say that Shao-
shih was a young widow so very fair and chaste

---

[2] Hsüan-te is the only reign period of Emperor Hsüan-tsung
of the Ming Dynasty.
[3] Southern Metropolitan Area, so called for being under the
direct jurisdiction of Nanking (in modern Kiangsu Province).

that one could hardly find her equal in the world. Chih Chu did not believe this, and so morning and evening he was always hanging around the front gate of the Ch'iu house. There would be no other idlers around, of course; only the boy servant Te-kuei could be seen going in and out of the gate on his errands. So Chih Chu made his acquaintance, and came to be on familiar terms with him. One day, as they were chatting, he asked Te-kuei, "I have heard that your mistress[4] is very beautiful; is it true or not?"

As one serving since childhood in a family of strict propriety, Te-kuei was honest to the point of simple-mindedness. So he answered, "Beautiful indeed she is."

"Does your mistress ever come to the front gate to watch the street?" asked Chih Chu further.

Te-kuei waved his hand and said, "She has never gone past the middle door, let alone come out to watch the street—what a thought!"

Another day, as Te-kuei was shopping for vegetarian food, Chih Chu ran into him and asked, "Why is your household stocking so much vegetarian food?"

"It's needed for the Buddhist ceremonies observing the tenth anniversary of our master's death," replied Te-kuei.

"When?" asked Chih Chu.

"Starting tomorrow for three days and nights," said Te-kuei. "It's really a lot of work."

Hearing this, Chih Chu thought to himself, "Since she is commemorating her husband, she must come out to the central hall to offer incense. I'll just sneak in to see what sort of face she has, and if she really looks as chaste as a young widow should be."

On the following day, the seven monks, all ascetics, came at the invitation of Ch'iu Ta-sheng and set up an image of Buddha in the hall. With great solemnity they struck the cymbals and beat the drums, intoned the scriptures and performed

the ritual of penitance. Ch'iu Ta-sheng earnestly prayed to Buddha. Shao-shih came out to offer incense, but only once during the day and once at night. As soon as she had finished, she went back inside.

Taking advantage of all the ceremonial activity in the hall, Chih Chu got in several times to look, but not once did he see Shao-shih come out. Again by asking Te-kuei, he learned that she only came out once during the day at lunchtime. So on the third day just about lunchtime, Chih Chu again sneaked in, hiding behind the screen door. He saw the monks in their cassocks playing their musical instruments in front of the holy image and calling on the name of Buddha. On the ceremonial platform the monk in charge of the incense kept his hands and feet busy adding incense and changing candles. Of the members of the household there was only Te-kuei, who was coming and going, doing his best to respond to calls. When would he find time to check into what was going on elsewhere in the hall? Even Ch'iu Ta-sheng and several relatives were intently watching the monks pipe and drum; who would bother to see if there was a stranger in their midst?

In a short while Shao-shih came out to offer incense, and Chih Chu was able to watch her closely. A common jingle goes, "A widow in white/Ravishes one's sight." Dressed in plain white, Shao-shih appeared doubly striking in her unassuming beauty. Clearly she was

*The goddess of Kuang-han Palace suffused with moonlight,[5]
Or the fairy of Mount Ku-yeh, white as driven snow.[6]*

Chih Chu saw her and his whole body turned numb. Returning home, he could not stop thinking of her. The ceremonies having been completed that night, the monks departed at daybreak; and, as before, Shao-shih would not now

---

[4] The term "mistress" simply denotes the female head of the household. No secondary meaning is implied.

[5] Kuang-han is the palace in the moon where dwells the fairy Ch'ang-e.
[6] Ku-yeh, a mountain in present-day Shansi Province, is known as an abode of fairies.

venture as far as the central hall. Chih Chu could devise no stratagem that would work. Then he thought, "The boy servant Te-kuei is gullible. I'll just have to cast my hook carefully in his direction."

It was the fifth day of the fifth month,[7] and Chih Chu insisted on Te-kuei's coming home with him to drink some orpiment wine. "I don't drink," protested Te-kuei. "If my face gets red, I am afraid my mistress will scold me." "Even you don't drink, have some glutinous rice dumplings anyway," urged Chih Chu. So Te-kuei accompanied him home, and Chih Chu asked his wife to unwrap a plateful of dumplings, prepare a saucer of sugar, a bowl of pork, a bowl of fresh fish, two pairs of chopsticks, and two wine cups, and set them on the table. Chih Chu took the wine jar and was about to pour.

"I said I don't drink; don't pour me any," cautioned Te-kuei.

"It's fitting on this festival day to drink a cup of orpiment wine. This wine of mine is so weak it won't affect you," said Chih Chu. Unable to resist the pressure, Te-kuei could not help but drink. Chih Chu coaxed further, "A young fellow should never drink just one cup; you must have another to complete the pair." Te-kuei was unable to refuse and so drank another cup.

Chih Chu kept drinking himself, relayed the idle gossip of the streets, and then again poured a cup for Te-kuei. "I'm so drunk my face has turned all red. Now I really won't drink any more," said Te-kuei.

"Your face has turned red anyway. If you sit here a little while longer before you go home, it won't matter. Just drink this one cup; I won't force any more on you," said Chih Chu.

Altogether Te-kuei drank only three cups of wine. He had lived in the Ch'iu house since he

was very little, and had been under the strict control of his mistress. When could he ever have tried the taste of wine? Today, with three cups in his stomach, he was feeling woozy. Taking advantage of his inebriation, Chih Chu softly said, "Brother Te-kuei, I have a small matter to ask you about."

"Just tell me what it is," replied Te-kuei.

"Your mistress has been widowed for so long her desires must surely be stirring. If she could find a man to sleep with, wouldn't she be happy! Widows have always been anxious to have a man; it's just hard for them to meet one. You lead me there to give me a chance to tempt her, how about that? If it's a success, I'll reward you handsomely."

"What are you saying!" replied Te-kuei. "How can you be so wicked! My mistress is most proper and guards her place with vigilance. During the day no man is allowed to go through the middle door. At night, before she goes to bed, she and her maid carry a lamp and inspect everywhere to make sure that each door is locked. Even if I wanted to lead you in, where would you hide? Her maid never leaves her side. My mistress wouldn't permit one word of idle gossip, and yet you talk so impudently."

"If it's like this, do they come to inspect your room?" asked Chih Chu.

"Why wouldn't they?" said Te-kuei.

"Brother Te-kuei," said Chih Chu, "how old are you now?"

"Seventeen," he replied.

"A man is sexually ready when he reaches sixteen," said Chih Chu. "You are already seventeen. Do you mean to say you haven't thought of taking a woman?"

"Even if I had thought about it, it wouldn't do me any good," said Te-kuei.

"With such a beauty around the house for you to look at morning and evening, how can you not get excited!" said Chih Chu.

"You shouldn't talk like that!" he replied. "She is my mistress and at the least mistake she can hit me or scold me. Whenever I see her, I get so

---

[7] Tuan-wu, sometimes known as the "Dragon Boat Festival," when the traditional food is a pyramid-shaped pudding made of glutinous rice, and orpiment wine (a medicinal wine) is drunk to ward off evil spirits.

scared! How could you make fun of me like this?"

"Since you aren't willing to take me there," said Chih Chu, "I'll teach you a way so that you yourself may get your hands on her; how about it?"

Te-kuei shook his head and said, "This can't be done, can't be done! Besides, I don't have that kind of nerve!"

"Don't worry about whether or not it can be done," said Chih Chu. "I'll tell you a plan just to test her once. If you get her, don't forget my kindness today."

In the first place Te-kuei was under the influence of wine. In the second place he was just at the right age. Chih Chu's words made him itch inside. So he asked, "Tell me how to go about testing her."

Chih Chu said, "At night when you are ready to go to sleep, don't close your door, but let it remain open. Since it is now the fifth month and the weather is very warm, you can very well lie stark naked on your back and get that thing up nice and hard and wait until she comes to check your door. Then you pretend to be asleep. If she sees you, she must be aroused. After one or two times, she certainly won't be able to withstand her desire, and she will come to you."

"And if she doesn't, then what?" asked Te-kuei.

"Even if this doesn't work," said Chih Chu, "she still couldn't very well scold you. So you have everything to gain and nothing to lose."

"If I do as you say, elder brother, and it works, I won't dare forget to repay you," said Te-kuei. In a little while, when he had sobered up, he said good-bye. That night he acted according to the plan. Verily:

Under lamplight a heinous plot is hatched,
To turn around a woman's unturnable heart.

In all fairness, Shao-shih's household rules were extremely strict. Te-kuei, at the compromising age of seventeen, should have been sent away and another boy hired to serve her. Wouldn't that have been best! But because Te-kuei had waited on her in his clumsy and honest fashion ever since he was a child, and because Shao-shih herself, guileless and pure, had never thought of any embarrassing contingencies that might involve her in his company, she had let matters drift. That night, accompanied by her maid Hsiu-ku, Shao-shih lit the lamp and proceeded to check all the doors. When she saw Te-kuei lying naked on his back, she scolded, "This dog of a slave! His door isn't even closed, and he sleeps there stark naked! What impudence!" She then told Hsiu-ku to pull shut the door to his room.

Had Shao-shih acted decisively, called Te-kuei to her the next morning, told him of his lazy and outrageous behavior of the previous evening, and given him a sound scolding and beating, then Te-kuei would not have dared more. But she had lived alone for so long that it seemed to her the experience of seeing that rare thing would lengthen her life by a dozen years, and so she kept absolutely mum.

Te-kuei was emboldened. When evening came he repeated the act. Accompanied by her maid, Shao-shih again inspected the doors with a lamp. When she saw him, she again scolded, "This cur is getting even more impudent! Doesn't even cover himself with a quilt." She told Hsiu-ku to pull a sheet over the boy without waking him. This time she was somewhat aroused, but since Hsiu-ku was around she could not very well do anything.

On the third day Te-kuei went out and ran into Chih Chu, who asked him whether he had used the plan or not. Honest in his simpleminded way, Te-kuei detailed all the events of the two nights. Chih Chu said, "Since she told her maid to cover you and not to wake you, she must be feeling some love for you. I am sure you will be favored tonight."

That night, as before, Te-kuei opened the door, pretended to be asleep, and waited. Now that her mind was set, Shao-shih did not ask Hsiu-ku to accompany her on her tour of inspection. She took the lamp herself and went straight to Te-kuei's bedside. Looking at his supine body in all its nakedness and especially at that thing as hard and

firm as a spearhead, she could not but feel her
heart pounding wildly and her whole body afire
with lust. She took off her undergarment and
climbed onto the bed. Afraid that she might star-
tle Te-kuei, she noiselessly sat astride his body
and guided his entry. Then suddenly Te-kuei
clasped her, rolled over until he was on top, and
played with her the game of clouds and rain:

She had been long denied the pleasure of the bed;
He is experimenting for the first time with the joys of love.
She, reclaiming an old plaything, enjoys it with abandon;
He, delighting in the new taste of sweets, craves for more.
She, too hungry to choose her fare, doesn't mind the serving
*   boy with all his uncouthness;*
He, pampered and assured of favor, fears not his mistress's
*   authority.*
It's obvious he is but a noxious creeper;
Yet it intertwines on the trellis with a prized flower.
It's a pity that the ice and snow of her pure heart
Should melt like spring waters and flow eastward:
Her ten-year record of spotless chastity is rendered void—
She can never wash away her shame after a night's defilement.

After they had finished, Shao-shih told Te-kuei,
"I have endured widowhood for ten years. That I
should now lose myself to you must be repayment
for some wrong I did you in a previous existence.
You must keep your mouth shut and not let this
out to anyone. You can expect special favors from
me."

"How dare I not obey your command?" replied
Te-kuei.

From that night on, every evening Shao-shih
would use the inspection tour as an excuse to take
her pleasure with Te-kuei and then go back to her
own room. But she was afraid that Hsiu-ku might
find out, and so she connived to make it possible
for Te-kuei to seduce the maid. Shao-shih then
made a show of upbraiding Hsiu-ku so as to make
her confess her crime with Te-kuei and thus seal
her mouth. After that, the three of them were all
as close as water flowing in the same stream, and
did not hide anything from one another.

Grateful for the guidance of Chih Chu, Te-kuei

would often beg for this and that from Shao-shih
and take it as a present to him. Chih Chu, on his
part, was daily expecting Te-kuei to introduce
him to his mistress. Te-kuei, however, was afraid
that she might rebuke him, and did not dare
broach the matter. Repeatedly Chih Chu asked
for news, and each time Te-kuei just made excuses without denying him hope.

Shao-shih and Te-kuei lived like man and wife
for a few months, but even then it would seem
that they were fated for exposure and ruin. Shao-
shih, who had been barren during the six years of
her married life, now felt after only these few
months the imperceptible swelling of her breasts
and belly, for she had become pregnant. Fearing
that it would not do for people to find out, she
took some silver and gave it to Te-kuei, instructing him to go secretly to get some medicine for
abortion, so that she could miscarry the illegiti-
mate child and avoid future disgrace. But, in the
first place, Te-kuei was ignorant and did not
know what medicine was good for abortion. Second, ever since he received Chih Chu's guidance,
he had regarded him as his benefactor, hiding
nothing from him. So this time, too, he went to
discuss this confidential matter with him.

Chih Chu was nothing but a villain. He had
been highly resentful because Te-kuei was unwilling to bring him to his mistress. Now he welcomed this opportunity to work his will. Formu-
lating a plan in his mind, he deceived Te-kuei by
saying, "A certain pharmacy that I know has the
most effective medicine of this kind. I'll buy some
for you." So he went to a pharmacy, got four
doses of medicine to strengthen the womb, and
gave them to Te-kuei to take home.

Shao-shi took the medicine four times, but felt
no movement inside her womb. She told Te-kuei
to go to a different place to get some better medicine. Again Te-kuei came to Chih Chu and asked,
"How come the medicine you gave me last time
didn't work?"

"You can only abort once," said Chih Chu. "If
the first attempt is not a success, you cannot try

127

again. Especially since this medicine, which is of the highest quality and can only be obtained at that one place, did not induce an abortion, then the pregnancy is firm. If she now takes some harsher medicine to abort, I'm afraid it will harm her health." Te-kuei relayed these words to Shao-shih, who accepted them as true.

When Shao-shih was completing her last month of pregnancy, Chih Chu knew for sure that her time was due. He sought out Te-kuei and said, "I want to concoct some medicine to strengthen me, and I must use a newborn baby. Your mistress is about to come to term. When she gives birth to the child, she certainly won't raise it. Whether it's a boy or a girl, you can bring it to me. You owe me a lot; if you give me the child, you will be repaying my kindness without any expenditure on your part. Just keep it from your mistress, that's all." Te-kuei agreed.

A few days later, Shao-shih did give birth to a male child. After drowning it, she put it in a rush-bag and told Te-kuei to bury it in a secret place. Te-kuei acknowledged the order, but instead of burying the child, he took it secretly to Chih Chu. After stowing away the dead infant, Chih Chu clutched Te-kuei and shouted, "Your mistress was the wife of Ch'iu Yüan-chi, and he has been dead for many years. With a widow in charge of the house, where did the child come from? I am going to report this to the authorities!"

Te-kuei hurriedly covered Chih Chu's mouth, saying, "I took you to be my benefactor and talked over everything with you. How can you turn against me like this?"

Putting on a stern face, Chih Chu said, "You did a fine thing! You raped your mistress. Your crime deserves the punishment of being sliced to death. Do you mean to say that I should let you go just because you called me benefactor? Since you know that kindness should be repaid with kindness, what have you done for me? Now if you want me to keep my mouth shut, tell your mistress to give me one hundred taels of silver;

then I will conceal her evil ways and extol her virtues. But if there is no money, then I definitely won't end the matter. With this newborn baby as evidence, see if you can acquit yourself at court. Even your mistress will not have the face to live on in this world. I will await your answer at home; go now and come back right away."

On his way home, Te-kuei was reduced to tears in his state of fright. Realizing he could not conceal anything, he had no choice but to give the message to Shao-shih. She blamed him, saying, "What sort of thing is that to give somebody as a present! You have ruined me." As she finished speaking, she could not keep the tears from flowing.

"If it had been anybody else," said Te-kuei, "I wouldn't have given it to him. But because he was my benefactor, I couldn't very well refuse him."

"What sort of benefactor was he to you?" asked Shao-shih.

"It was he who taught me to lie naked on my back to arouse you," replied Te-kuei. "If it had not been for him, how could we have achieved our present love for each other? He said he wanted the child for medicine. Could I fail to offer it to him? How could I know that his intentions were not good?"

"What you have done," said Shao-shih, "was not very clever. At first it was my momentary weakness that made me fall for the trap of that villain; now it is too late to repent my folly. If I don't give the silver to ransom the child, he will certainly bring the matter to court. Then it would be too late to do anything." She had no choice but to take out forty taels of silver and instruct Te-kuei to take it to that villain in exchange for the child and then secretly bury it to remove the source of all danger.

Simpleminded, Te-kuei delivered the forty taels of silver to Chih Chu with both hands, saying, "There is just this much. Now give the child back to me."

Upon receiving the silver, Chih Chu was far

from satisfied. He thought, "This woman is beautiful, and her pockets are well lined. If I take advantage of this opportunity, it will be possible for me to move in and have her. Furthermore, I'll be in charge of her affairs. Won't that be lovely?" So he told Te-kuei, "I was only fooling when I said I wanted silver. But since you've brought it here, I can only accept. The newborn baby I have buried already. Why not commend me before your mistress and propose that she and I live together? If she agrees, I will manage the house for her so that no one would dare to take advantage of her. Won't that be lovely on both counts? Otherwise, I will dig up the child and inform on you still. Give me a reply within five days."

Te-kuei had no choice but to return home and relate all this to Shao-shih. She declared in rage, "Listen to that no-good ruffian! Don't pay any attention to him!" Te-kuei consequently did not dare bring up the matter again.

Meanwhile Chih Chu preserved the infant in lime, put it again in the rush-bag, and hid it. He waited five days without receiving Te-kuei's reply. He put it off another five days, making ten days in all. He reckoned that the woman would have recovered her strength by then. So he proceeded to the front gate of the Ch'iu house and waited for Te-kuei to come out. Then he asked him, "Is my proposal agreed to or not?"

"Can't be done, can't be done!" replied Te-kuei, shaking his head.

Chih Chu did not pause to ask another question, but heading toward the gate, he burst right in. Te-kuei did not dare stop him, but walked some distance from the house to the street corner to wait around and see what was to happen.

When Shao-shih saw someone walking into the central hall, she lashed out, "There are rules to observe in this house. Who are you, barging in like that?"

"My name is Chih Chu; I am Brother Te-kuei's benefactor," replied Chih Chu.

Knowing who he was, Shao-shih said, "If you are looking for Te-kuei, go outside. This is no place to rest your feet."

"I have admired you for a long time, as though I were hungry and thirsty," returned Chih Chu. "Although I am not worthy, I figure I'm not below Brother Te-kuei; so why do you so loftily repulse me?"

When Shao-shih heard these disagreeable words, she turned to walk away. Overtaking her, Chih Chu clasped her in his arms and said, "Your dead child is now at my place. If you do not obey me, I'll just report you to the authorities."

Shao-shih's fury knew no bounds, but unable to extricate herself, she could only use sweet words to beguile him, saying, "In the daytime I am afraid people will know. When night comes, I'll send Te-kuei around for you."

"You have made a promise in your own words. You'd better not break it!" warned Chih Chu. He loosened his grip, took a few steps, then turned his head and said, "I have a feeling you won't break your promise!" Then he walked straight out.

Shao-shih was so humiliated that she could not speak for some time as tears continued to stream down her face. Pushing open the door to her room, she sat down alone on a stool. Various thoughts ran through her mind, and she could not but admit that it had been all her own fault. In the beginning she had been unwilling to remarry, wanting to be a person of exemplary virtue. Now that she was threatened with exposure, how could she have the face to look upon her relatives? She thought further, "Previously I took an oath before them all, 'If I serve another family and take a second husband, I will either perish under a knife or die by the rope.' Now if I sacrifice my life to show my regret to my late husband below the Nine Springs, won't that be a good way out?"

Hsiu-ku saw her mistress sobbing, but did not dare go forward to calm her. She stood guard by the middle door, waiting for Te-kuei to return.

129

Te-kuei, on his part, did not return from the street until he had seen Chih Chu leave. Seeing Hsiu-ku, he asked, "Where is the mistress?" "In there," replied Hsiu-ku, pointing. Te-kuei pushed open the door to look for his mistress.

Taking a dagger from one end of her bed, Shao-shih had wanted to cut her throat with it, but was unable to lift her hand to perform the task. She sobbed awhile and put the dagger on the table. Then she loosened the eight-foot sash from her waist, made it into a noose, and hung it from a beam. She was about to slip her neck into the noose, but suddenly beside herself with anguish, she could not help sobbing violently.

All at once she saw Te-kuei push open the door and come in. A thought suddenly struck her: "Everything happened because this cur laid a trap to trick me into losing my honor and good name." No sooner had this thought occurred to her than she rose, her eyes glaring at her enemy. She lifted the dagger and struck a blow directly against his head. Because her strength was doubled in her state of fury, the dagger came down swiftly as the wind and split his skull in two. Te-kuei died instantly, his blood all over the floor. Frightened, Shao-shih guided her neck into the noose. As her feet stepped from the stool, her body swayed as if she were on a swing:

Two aggrieved ghosts find shelter underground;
A beautiful widow is lost to this human world.

As the saying goes, "Gambling is akin to robbery; lust is akin to murder." Today, two lives perished solely on account of the word "lust."

To resume our story: Hsiu-ku was accustomed from previous experience to withdraw to a distance whenever Te-kuei went into the lady's room, for he might have a special purpose in mind. But this time, when she did not hear a sound for a long time, she began to be suspicious. As she went in to look, she saw the one hanging above, the other stretched out below. She was for a while paralyzed by terror; then, gathering her courage, she shut the door to the room and hurriedly ran to the house of Shao-shih's uncle, Ch'iu Ta-sheng, to report the news. Greatly alarmed, Ch'iu Ta-sheng in turn reported to Shao-shih's father and mother, and together they all went to the Ch'iu house.

When the gate had been shut, they began to interrogate Hsiu-ku about the cause of the deaths. Hsiu-ku had known nothing of Chih Chu. Even his extortion of forty taels of silver as blackmail for the dead infant had been concealed from her. Because of this Hsiu-ku just gave a description of the illicit relationship between Shao-shih and Te-kuei, maintaining that she did not know why the two met their deaths that day. Though she was questioned over and over again, this was all she said.

When Mr. and Mrs. Shao heard of the adultery, they felt so ashamed that they went straight home, washing their hands of the matter. Ch'iu Ta-sheng could do nothing but take Hsiu-ku to the district tribunal to report the case. The magistrate made due examination of the two corpses: that of Te-kuei with a gash on the head and that of Shao-shih bearing evidence of death by hanging. He also heard Hsiu-ku's testimony. Then the magistrate declared: "It is quite obvious that Shao-shih and Te-kuei were adulterous lovers who had abolished the distinctions between mistress and servant. Te-kuei must have used affronting language; Shao-shih, enraged, momentarily lost self-control and unintentionally took his life. Frightened, she then hanged herself. There are no other facts in the case." He charged Ch'iu Ta-sheng with arranging for the funerals. Since Hsiu-ku had known of the adultery, she was sentenced to the cane and thereafter to be sold at public auction.

Meanwhile Chih Chu, foiled in his attempt to seduce Shao-shih, returned home and had every intention of seeing her that night. Hearing the news of the two deaths, he jumped in terror. For a long time he did not dare venture out his door.

Then early one morning, it occurred to him to pick up the rush-bag containing the lime-preserved infant and throw it in the river. An acquaintance named Pao Chiu, the foreman on the Yi-chen Lock of the [Grand] Canal,[8] however, caught him in the act of throwing and asked, "Brother Chih, what is it you have just thrown away?"

"Some pieces of salted beef, all wrapped up well to provide for a journey," said Chih Chu. "But unfortunately they have spoiled. Brother Chiu, if you are not too busy today or tomorrow, come over to my house for few drinks."

"Today we're very busy," replied Pao Chiu. "Lord K'uang Chung,[9] prefect of Soochow, is on his official journey to resume his post. His boat will be arriving any time now, and we're mobilizing our men to insure a speedy passage for him."

"If that's the case, we'll get together another day," said Chih Chu. Then he left.

K'uang Chung had originally been a tribunal clerk, and it was the minister of rites, Hu Ying, who had nominated him to be the prefect of Soochow. During the first year of his term the people called him Blue Sky K'uang for his impartial administration of justice. Then he returned to his native place to observe a period of filial mourning, but an imperial decree, superseding his personal feelings, soon recalled him and provided him with expeditious means of travel at government expense for his journey back to his old post.

Lord K'uang was in the cabin reading when his ship reached the mouth of the Yi-chen Lock. Suddenly he heard the crying of a baby coming up from the river, and he thought there must be an infant drowning. The servant whom he ordered to take a look returned with the report, "There's nothing there." This happened twice. Lord K'uang again heard the crying, but when he asked the others they all said that they heard nothing, causing him to exclaim "How strange!" Pushing open the window to see for himself, he noticed a small rush-bag floating on the water. Lord K'uang called to the sailors to pull it up. When they opened it to look, they reported, "It's a small child."

"Dead or alive?" asked Lord K'uang.

"It's been preserved in lime. It seems to have been dead for some time," answered the sailors.

"If it's dead, how could it cry?" mused Lord K'uang. "Moreover, if one were to toss away a dead child, that would be that; why should it have been preserved in lime in the first place? There must be a reason."

He told the sailors to place the dead child and the rush-bag on the prow of the ship, saying, "If anyone knows the story and secretly reports to me, I am offering a big reward." Upon receiving the instructions, the sailors took the child and the rush-bag and placed them on the prow.

It happened that the foreman Pao Chiu noticed the small rush-bag and recognized it as the one which Chih Chu had thrown away. "He said it was spoiled beef; how come it's really a dead child?" he mused. So he entered the cabin and reported to Lord K'uang, saying: "I don't know the story about this child; however, I know the man who threw it into the river. His name is Chih Chu."

"If we have the man, we'll have the story," said Lord K'uang.

On the one hand, K'uang ordered his men to quietly apprehend Chih Chu; on the other, he sent a messenger to invite the magistrate of Yi-chen to go to the district office of surveillance for a joint inquiry into the case.

Lord K'uang brought with him the dead infant and presided at court in the office of surveillance. By the time the local magistrate had arrived, Chih Chu had been brought in. Lord K'uang occupied

---

[8] In Ming times, the district of Yi-chen was situated close to where the Grand Canal met the Yangtze River; the Yi-chen Lock probably referred to a lock that controlled the water level in one of the canals in the area.

[9] K'uang Chung (1383–1443), is a historical figure whose career and fame as an upright official was largely as outlined here, except that he owed his appointment to the prefecture of Soochow to someone other than Hu Ying.

the seat of honor; the magistrate sat on his left. Because Yi-chen was not a district under his jurisdiction, Lord K'uang was unwilling to act on his own authority, and urged the magistrate to conduct the investigation. The magistrate knew that Lord K'uang had recently been favored with an imperial order and was, moreover, a man of somewhat unpredictable nature; how could he dare offend him? After the two had yielded to each other for some time, Lord K'uang finally had to start the questioning. He called out, "Chih Chu, this lime-preserved infant of yours, where did it come from?"

Chih Chu was about to deny any knowledge when he saw Pao Chiu to one side offering to tell what he knew. So he changed his line and said, "I noticed this dirty thing lying beside the road and thought it was quite unsanitary. So I picked it up and threw it in the river; really I don't know where it came from."

Lord K'uang asked Pao Chiu, "Did you see him pick it up by the roadside?"

"I first saw him as he was throwing it in the river," replied Pao Chiu. "When I asked him what it was, he said it was some spoiled beef."

Lord K'uang said in great anger, "Since he lied in saying it was spoiled beef, he must have been trying to hide something." He then shouted an order to his men to choose a heavy rod and give the suspect twenty strokes before resuming questioning. This rod of Lord K'uang's was merciless: its twenty strokes were the equivalent of more than forty strokes of another rod. Chih Chu was beaten until the skin split, the flesh ripped, and blood flowed. But he did not confess.

Lord K'uang shouted an order to apply the ankle-squeezers. His ankle-squeezers were also merciless. Chih Chu could bear it the first time, but not the second time. So he confessed, "This dead infant was the widow Shao's. The widow and her boy servant Te-kuei were having an affair, and she gave birth to this child. Te-kuei begged me to bury it for him, but a dog dug it up. So I threw it in the river."

Lord K'uang, seeing that his testimony was suspect, asked further, "Since you were willing to bury it for him, you must have been in collusion with the family."

"I was not," replied Chih Chu. "I was just on good terms with Te-kuei."

"If they had buried it, they would have wanted it to rot fast. Why has it been preserved in lime?" demanded Lord K'uang.

Chih Chu had no coherent answer to this; so he kowtowed and said, "Your Honor, I was the one who applied the lime. Knowing that the widow Shao was well off, I wanted to keep the dead infant to demand a few taels of silver. Unexpectedly, Shao-shih and Te-kuei both died. Since I couldn't follow through with my plan, I threw it in the river."

"Did the widow and her servant in fact die?" asked Lord K'uang.

The magistrate stood up bowing and said in reply, "They did. I personally conducted the inquest."

"How did they die?" asked Lord K'uang.

"The servant had his head split open by a knife; the widow committed suicide by hanging," replied the magistrate. "I investigated the case thoroughly. The two had been having an illicit affair for a long time, and the distinctions between mistress and servant had long been abolished. The servant must have used affronting language; enraged, the woman swung a knife and unintentionally killed him. Then, frightened, she hanged herself. There was nothing more to the case."

Lord K'uang pondered to himself, "Since they were lovers, how could a small verbal offense provoke her to such murderous acts! Earlier the dead infant cried out; there must be a reason." So he asked, "Was there anybody else living with Shao-shih?"

"There was also a maidservant named Hsiu-ku," replied the magistrate. "She has been sold at public auction."

"Since she has been publicly sold," said Lord K'uang, "she must be living hereabouts. May I

132

trouble Your Honor to have her summoned for questioning? Then we will know what really happened."

A short while after the magistrate had dispatched his runners, Hsiu-ku was brought in. Her testimony, however, coincided with that of the magistrate. After deliberating for a while, Lord K'uang stepped down from his seat and asked Hsiu-ku, pointing to Chih Chu, "Do you recognize this man?"

Hsiu-ku looked him over closely, then said, "I do not know his name, but recognize his face."

"I expected this," said Lord K'uang. "Since he was a close acquaintance of Te-kuei, he must have come to your house with him. You must tell the truth. If you depart from the truth ever so little, then your fingers will be put to the thumbscrew."

"In truth, I didn't ever see him come in until the very last," said Hsiu-ku. "He burst into the central hall on that day and forced his attentions on my mistress, but he left upon being repulsed. Later, when Te-kuei came in, the mistress was crying in her room. Te-kuei entered the room, and in a short time they were both dead."

Lord K'uang shouted angry words at Chih Chu: "Villain! If you were not in collusion with Te-kuei, how could you have dared to burst into the central hall? You were the sole cause of these two deaths!" He called his men, "I want to see him put to the ankle-squeezers again."

Under the stupefying pain of the torture, Chih Chu could not but confess from start to finish the whole story of how he guided Te-kuei in seducing his mistress, tricked him into handing over the dead infant, and blackmailed him for money; how he coerced him to serve as his accomplice in lust; how he stormed into the inner apartment of Shao-shih, embraced her, and begged for sexual favors; and how he was tricked into releasing her—all this he related in full detail. "The subsequent circumstances of the deaths," he added, "I truly know nothing about."

"These are the true facts of the case," pronounced Lord K'uang. He released Chih Chu from the ankle-squeezers, and told the clerk to take down a clear account of the confession. The magistrate by his side, realizing his own inferiority in intellect and ability, was chagrined beyond description.

Lord K'uang then wielded his brush and handed down the verdict in the following terms:

I find Chih Chu to be a lecherous villain.
First he stole a glance at the widow's beauty, at once giving
*   rein to his wicked heart;*
Then he seized upon the stupidity of her gullible servant,
*   artfully using words to entice him.*
The servant opened his door and lay down naked—a faithful
*   follower of his plan;*
The widow strengthened her womb and lost the dead child—
*   a total victim of his design.*
When unsuccessful at seeking adultery, he switched to
*   blackmail;*
Still not satisfied with the silver, he again sought adultery.
On account of her one moment of weakness, Shao-shih found
*   herself victim in a case of stealing the bell while trying to*
*   cover her ears;*[10]
By repeatedly resorting to tricks, Chih Chu was guilty of
*   ransacking other people's trunks and of climbing over the*
*   neighbor's wall to boot.*[11]
Through her hatred for Chih Chu, she came to hate Te-kuei—
*   a case of love turned into enmity;*
After slaying Te-kuei, she proceeded to hang herself—an
*   instance of shame lingering beyond death.*
Since mistress and servant are both dead, we will not deal with
*   them;*
Since the maid Hsiu-ku has already been beaten, she shall go
*   scot free.*
Unaccounted for yet is the archvillain,
Uncaught in the net of law.
Though Pao Chiu met him by accident,
The infant cried out with a purpose.
Since Heaven has had a hand in its detection,
The crime cannot be tolerated by man.
It is fitting, therefore,
That Chih Chu should be punished with death,
And his ill-gotten silver be recovered.

[10] A metaphorical saying signifying self-deception.
[11] A classical allusion about "climbing over the eastern neighbor's wall and embracing his virgin daughter" (*Mencius* 6.1), here signifying committing a sexual crime.

After Lord K'uang read this verdict, even Chih Chu was willing to accept the punishment. Lord K'uang submitted a report of the matter to his superiors, who were unanimous in praising his great sagacity. All the people spread his fame, not unjustifiably comparing him to Lung-t'u Academician Pao.[12] Also entitled "Prefect K'uang Judges the Case of a Dead Infant," this story is summarized in verse:

Lovely Widow Shao, tempted at heart, became confused;
Stupid Te-kuei, his good fortune over, met calamity.
Rascal Chih was the very devil in hatching plots;
Prefect K'uang resembled a god in passing judgment.

---

[12] The Northern Sung official Pao Cheng (999–1062), better known as Lord Pao in popular literature, once held the titular post of Auxiliary Academician of the Lung-t'u Pavilion. This anthology includes two Lord Pao stories, "The Jade-Faced Cat" and "Lion Cub Lane."

THE SHANSI MERCHANT

From *Yüeh-wei ts'ao-t'ang pi-chi*

TRANSLATED BY PAO-CHEN TSENG

There was once a merchant from Shansi who came to stay at the Honesty Inn in the capital. His attire was luxurious and his attendants and horses were richly equipped. He let it be known that his purpose in coming to the capital was to pay the fees for an official title, as others had done.

One day a very poor old man came to see him, but the merchant's servants would not even report this visit to their master. So the old man waited at the inn door until he saw the merchant in person. Only then was the old man received, but with cool indifference; he was offered a cup of tea without the usual civilities. The old man gradually hinted, in conversation, at his need for assistance; the merchant was annoyed and snapped, "I don't even have enough money for my fees; how can I spare any for you?"

Stung by this ingratitude, the old man turned to some nearby people at the inn and told them, "This merchant used to be very poor, and he depended on me for his living for more than ten years. I even gave him one hundred taels of cash to help him start a business, which made him a rich man. On my part, however, I have lost my office and find myself in bad straits. When I heard that he had come to town, I was as delighted as if I had been given a new life. My expectations aren't extravagant; I only want the same amount that I gave him in the past, so that I can clear up my debts and pay for the final trip home." After saying this, he wept. The merchant acted as if he had heard nothing.

One of the onlookers, a man from Kiangsi who said his name was Yang, introduced himself to the merchant and asked him, "Is it true, what the old man says?"

The merchant's face turned red and he replied, "Yes, it's true. I'm sorry, but I can't afford to repay him at this time."

Yang said, "You'll soon be an official, and it will be easy for you to borrow money. If someone would lend you this amount of money for one year without interest, would you be willing to borrow it to repay the old man?"

The merchant very reluctantly replied, "Well, all right. I suppose so."

"In that case," said Yang, "you write out a promissory note and I'll come up with the one hundred taels of cash."

Under the pressure of public opinion, the merchant did as requested. Yang accepted the note, opened his well-worn luggage and, taking out one hundred taels of cash, gave them to the merchant. The merchant unhappily passed the money to the

135

old man. After this transaction, Yang invited both men to a feast. The old man was delighted, but the merchant participated in the most perfunctory manner. Afterward, the old man expressed his gratitude and took his leave. A few days later, Yang also left. After that, there was no further contact between the merchant and Yang.

Later, when the merchant was checking his luggage, he found that one hundred taels of cash had disappeared. Since the locks on his trunk had not been tampered with, there were no grounds for further investigation. He discovered that he had also lost a fur vest and that there was a pawn shop ticket in its stead. The ticket was for two thousand coppers, which was the approximate amount Yang had paid for the feast. Then he realized that this Yang was a magician and had performed a sleight of hand to mock him. Everyone at the inn privately felt elated. The merchant, embarrassed and humiliated, soon left the inn. No one knew where he went.

THE HEARTLESS LOVER

It can be said categorically that no other love story in the T'ang period has generated as much scholarly discussion and pedestrian interest as "The Story of Ying-ying." To present-day readers, the ending of the story cannot be anything but a heartless betrayal of faith on the hero's part. In T'ang times, however, when consideration for marriage was not infrequently tempered with matters more practical than love, the hollow excuses invented by Scholar Chang for deserting his woman could have been construed as an act of "moral courage." For similar reasons, Li Chia (in "Tu Shih-niang Sinks the Jewel Box in Anger") betrays the confidence of Tu Shih-niang midway through their journey home, only to discover that he has been betrayed in his turn. By concealing her treasure until her lover decides to exchange her for silver, Tu Shih-niang shows herself to be just as practical-minded as Li Chia in her lack of faith in love. Examined in this light, the two stories presented here can be read not only as fiction but also as documents reflecting the rising aspirations and social values of T'ang and Ming China.

THE STORY OF YING-YING

From *I-wen chi*

TRANSLATED BY JAMES R. HIGHTOWER

During the Chen-yüan period [785–804][1] there lived a young man named Chang. He was agreeable and refined, and good looking, but firm and self-contained, and capable of no improper act. When his companions included him in one of their parties, the others could all be brawling as though they would never get enough, but Chang would just watch tolerantly without ever taking part. In this way he had gotten to be twenty-three years old without ever having had relations with a woman. When asked by his friends, he explained, "Teng-t'u tzu[2] was no lover, but a lecher. I am the true lover—I just never happened to meet the right girl. How do I know that? It's because things of outstanding beauty never fail to make a permanent impression on me. That shows I am not without feelings." His friends took note of what he said.

Not long afterward Chang was traveling in P'u,[3] where he lodged some ten *li* east of the city in a monastery called the Temple of Universal Salvation. It happened that a widowed Mrs. Ts'ui had also stopped there on her way back to Ch'ang-an. She had been born a Cheng; Chang's mother had been a Cheng, and when they worked out their common ancestry, this Mrs. Ts'ui turned out to be a rather distant cousin once removed on his mother's side.

This year Hun Chen[4] died in P'u, and the eunuch Ting Wen-ya proved unpopular with the troops, who took advantage of the mourning period to mutiny. They plundered the citizens of P'u, and Mrs. Ts'ui, in a strange place with all her wealth and servants, was terrified, having no one to turn to. Before the mutiny Chang had made friends with some of the officers in P'u, and now he requested a detachment of soldiers to protect the Ts'ui family. As a result all escaped harm. In about ten days the imperial commissioner of inquiry, Tu Ch'üeh,[5] came with full power from the throne and restored order among the troops.

Out of gratitude to Chang for the favor he had done them, Mrs. Ts'ui invited him to a banquet in

---

[1] Chen-yüan is the last of the three reign periods of Emperor Te-tsung of the T'ang Dynasty.

[2] Teng-t'u is an archetypal lecher. This allusion originates from the character ridiculed in Sung Yü's (fl. third century B.C.) rhyme-prose, "The Lechery of Master Teng-t'u."

[3] P'u-chou, also known as Ho-chung in T'ang times, was under the jurisdiction of Chiang-chou. It is modern Yung-chi County in Shansi Province, located east-northeast of Ch'ang-an.

[4] Hun Chen, the regional commander of Chiang-chou, died in P'u-chou in 799.

[5] Tu Ch'üeh, originally prefect of T'ung-chou (in modern Shensi), was appointed, after the death of Hun Chen, the prefect of Ho-chung as well as the imperial commissioner of inquiry of Chiang-chou.

the central hall. She addressed him: "Your widowed aunt with her helpless children would never have been able to escape alive from these rioting soldiers. It is no ordinary favor you have done us; it is rather as though you had given my son and daughter their lives, and I want to introduce them to you as their elder brother so that they can express their thanks." She summoned her son Huan-lang, a very attractive child of ten or so. Then she called her daughter: "Come out and pay your respects to your brother, who saved your life." There was a delay; then word was brought that she was indisposed and asked to be excused. Her mother exclaimed in anger, "Your brother Chang saved your life. You would have been abducted if it were not for him—how can you give yourself airs?"

After a while she appeared, wearing an everyday dress and no makeup on her smooth face, except for a remaining spot of rouge. Her hair coils straggled down to touch her eyebrows. Her beauty was extraordinary, so radiant it took the breath away. Startled, Chang made her a deep bow as she sat down beside her mother. Because she had been forced to come out against her will, she looked angrily straight ahead, as though unable to endure the company. Chang asked her age. Mrs. Ts'ui said, "From the seventh month of the fifth year of the reigning emperor to the present twenty-first year, it is just seventeen years."

Chang tried to make conversation with her, but she would not respond, and he had to leave after the meal was over. From this time on Chang was infatuated but had no way to make his feelings known to her. She had a maid named Hung-niang with whom Chang had managed to exchange greetings several times, and finally he took the occasion to tell her how he felt. Not surprisingly, the maid was alarmed and fled in embarrassment. Chang was sorry he had said anything, and when she returned the next day he made shamefaced apologies without repeating his request.

The maid said, "Sir, what you said is something I would not dare repeat to my mistress or let anyone else know about. But you know very well who Miss Ts'ui's relatives are; why don't you ask for her hand in marriage, as you are entitled to do because of the favor you did them?"

"From my earliest years I have never been one to make any improper connections," Chang said. "Whenever I have found myself in the company of young women, I would not even look at them, and it never occurred to me that I would be trapped in any such way. But the other day at the dinner I was hardly able to control myself, and in the days since, I walk without knowing where I am going and eat without hunger—I am afraid I cannot last another day. If I were to go through a regular matchmaker, taking three months and more for the exchange of betrothal presents and names and birthdates[6]—you might just as well look for me among the dried fish in the shop.[7] Can't you tell me what to do?"

"Miss Ts'ui is so very strict that not even her elders could suggest anything improper to her," the maid replied. "It would be hard for someone in my position to say such a thing. But I have noticed she writes a lot. She is always reciting poetry to herself and is moved by it for a long time after. You might see if you can seduce her with a love poem. That is the only way I can think of."

Chang was delighted and on the spot composed two stanzas of spring verses which he handed over to her. That evening Hung-niang came back with a note on colored paper for him, saying, "By Miss Ts'ui's instructions."

The title of her poem was "Bright Moon on the Night of the Fifteenth":

I await the moon in the western chamber
Where the breeze comes through the half-opened door.
Sweeping the wall the flower shadows move:
I imagine it is my lover who comes.

[6] To determine an astrologically suitable date for a wedding.
[7] An allusion to the parable of help that comes too late in chapter 9 of the pre-Ch'in philosophical work *Chuang-tzu*.

Chang understood the message: that day was the fourteenth of the second month, and an apricot tree was next to the wall east of the Ts'uis' courtyard. It would be possible to climb it.

On the night of the fifteenth Chang used the tree as a ladder to get over the wall. When he came to the western chamber, the door was ajar. Inside, Hung-niang was asleep on a bed. He awakened her, and she asked, frightened, "How did you get here?"

"Miss Ts'ui's letter told me to come," he said, not quite accurately. "You go tell her I am here."

In a minute Hung-niang was back. "She's coming! She's coming!"

Chang was both happy and nervous, convinced that success was his. Then Miss Ts'ui appeared in formal dress, with a serious face, and began to upbraid him: "You did us a great kindness when you saved our lives, and that is why my mother entrusted my young brother and myself to you. Why then did you get my silly maid to bring me that filthy poem? You began by doing a good deed in preserving me from the hands of ravishers, and you end by seeking to ravish me. You substitute seduction for rape—is there any great difference? My first impulse was to keep quiet about it, but that would have been to condone your wrongdoing, and not right. If I told my mother, it would amount to ingratitude, and the consequences would be unfortunate. I thought of having a servant convey my disapproval, but feared she would not get it right. Then I thought of writing a short message to state my case, but was afraid it would only put you on your guard. So finally I composed those vulgar lines to make sure you would come here. It was an improper thing to do, and of course I feel ashamed. But I hope that you will keep within the bounds of decency and commit no outrage."

As she finished speaking, she turned on her heel and left him. For some time Chang stood, dumbfounded. Then he went back over the wall to his quarters, all hope gone.

A few nights later Chang was sleeping alone by the veranda when someone shook him awake. Startled, he rose up, to see Hung-niang standing there, a coverlet and pillow in her arms. She patted him and said, "She is coming! She is coming! Why are you sleeping?" And she spread the quilt and put the pillow beside his. As she left, Chang sat up straight and rubbed his eyes. For some time it seemed as though he were still dreaming, but nonetheless he waited dutifully. Then there was Hung-niang again, with Miss Ts'ui leaning on her arm. She was shy and yielding, and appeared almost not to have the strength to move her limbs. The contrast with her stiff formality at their last encounter was complete.

This evening was the night of the eighteenth, and the slanting rays of the moon cast a soft light over half the bed. Chang felt a kind of floating lightness and wondered whether this was an immortal who visited him, not someone from the world of men. After a while the temple bell sounded. Daybreak was near. As Hung-niang urged her to leave, she wept softly and clung to him. Hung-niang helped her up, and they left. The whole time she had not spoken a single word. With the first light of dawn Chang got up, wondering, was it a dream? But the perfume still lingered, and as it got lighter he could see on his arm traces of her makeup and the teardrops sparkling still on the mat.

For some ten days afterward there was no word from her. Chang composed a poem of sixty lines on "An Encounter with an Immortal" which he had not yet completed when Hung-niang happened by, and he gave it to her for her mistress. After that she let him see her again, and for nearly a month he would join her in what her poem called the "western chamber," slipping out at dawn and returning stealthily at night. Chang once asked what her mother thought about the situation. She said, "She knows there is nothing she can do about it, and so she hopes you will regularize things."

141

Before long Chang was about to go to Ch'ang-an, and he let her know his intentions in a poem. Miss Ts'ui made no objections at all, but the look of pain on her face was very touching. On the eve of his departure he was unable to see her again. Then Chang went off to the west. A few months later he again made a trip to P'u and stayed several months with Miss Ts'ui.

She was a very good calligrapher and wrote poetry, but for all that he kept begging to see her work, she would never show it. Chang wrote poems for her, challenging her to match them, but she paid them little attention. The thing that made her unusual was that, while she excelled in the arts, she always acted as though she were ignorant, and although she was quick and clever in speaking, she would seldom indulge in repartee. She loved Chang very much, but would never say so in words. At the time she was subject to moods of profound melancholy, but she never let on. She seldom showed on her face the emotions she felt. On one occasion she was playing her zither alone at night. She did not know Chang was listening, and the music was full of sadness. As soon as he spoke, she stopped and would play no more. This made him all the more infatuated with her.

Some time later Chang had to go west again for the scheduled examinations. It was the eve of his departure, and though he had said nothing about what it involved, he sat sighing unhappily at her side. Miss Ts'ui had guessed that he was going to leave for good. Her manner was respectful, but she spoke deliberately and in a low voice: "To seduce someone and then abandon her is perfectly natural, and it would be presumptuous of me to resent it. It would be an act of charity on your part if, having first seduced me, you were to go through with it and fulfill your oath of lifelong devotion. But in either case, what is there to be so upset about in this trip? However, I see you are not happy and I have no way to cheer you up. You have praised my zither playing, and in the past I have been embarrassed to play for you.

Now that you are going away, I shall do what you so often requested."

She had them prepare her zither and started to play the prelude to the "Rainbow Robe and Feather Skirt."[8] After a few notes, her playing grew wild with grief until the piece was no longer recognizable. Everyone was reduced to tears, and Miss Ts'ui abruptly stopped playing, put down the zither, and ran back to her mother's room with tears streaming down her face. She did not come back.

The next morning Chang went away. The following year he stayed on in the capital, having failed the examinations. He wrote a letter to Miss Ts'ui to reassure her, and her reply read roughly as follows:

I have read your letter with its message of consolation, and it filled my childish heart with mingled grief and joy. In addition you sent me a box of ornaments to adorn my hair and a stick of pomade to make my lips smooth. It was most kind of you; but for whom am I to make myself attractive? As I look at these presents my breast is filled with sorrow.

Your letter said that you will stay on in the capital to pursue your studies, and of course you need quiet and the facilities there to make progress. Still it is hard on the person left alone in this far-off place. But such is my fate, and I should not complain. Since last fall I have been listless and without hope. In company I can force myself to talk and smile, but come evening I always shed tears in the solitude of my own room. Even in my sleep I often sob, yearning for the absent one. Or I am in your arms for a moment as it used to be, but before the secret meeting is done I am awake and heartbroken. The bed seems still warm beside me, but the one I love is far away.

Since you said good-bye the new year has come. Ch'ang-an is a city of pleasure with chances for love everywhere. I am truly fortunate that you have not forgotten me and that your affection is not worn out.

[8] After this Brahman music was introduced into China, it was dignified by the elegant name given to it by Emperor Hsüan-tsung of the T'ang Dynasty and by the performance of his favorite consort Yang Kuei-fei.

Loving you as I do, I have no way of repaying you, except to be true to our vow of lifelong fidelity.

Our first meeting was at the banquet, as cousins. Then you persuaded my maid to inform me of your love; and I was unable to keep my childish heart firm. You made advances, like that other poet, Ssu-ma Hsiang-ju.[9] I failed to repulse them as the girl did who threw her shuttle.[10] When I offered myself in your bed, you treated me with the greatest kindness, and I supposed, in my innocence, that I could always depend on you. How could I have foreseen that our encounter could not possibly lead to something definite, that having disgraced myself by coming to you, there was no further chance of serving you openly as a wife? To the end of my days this will be a lasting regret—I must hide my sighs and be silent. If you, out of kindness, would condescend to fulfill my selfish wish, though it came on my dying day it would seem to be a new lease on life. But if, as a man of the world, you curtail your feelings, sacrificing the lesser to the more important, and look on this connection as shameful, so that your solemn vow can be dispensed with, still my true love will not vanish though my bones decay and my frame dissolve; in wind and dew it will seek out the ground you walk on. My love in life and death is told in this. I weep as I write, for feelings I cannot express. Take care of yourself; a thousand times over, take care of your dear self.

This bracelet of jade is something I wore as a child; I send it to serve as a gentleman's belt pendant. Like jade may you be invariably firm and tender; like a bracelet may there be no break between what came before and what is to follow. Here are also a skein of multicolored thread and a tea roller of mottled bamboo. These things have no intrinsic value, but they are to signify that I want you to be true as jade, and your love to endure unbroken as a bracelet. The spots on the bamboo are like the marks of my tears,[11]

and my unhappy thoughts are as tangled as the thread: these objects are symbols of my feelings and tokens for all time of my love. Our hearts are close, though our bodies are far apart and there is no time I can expect to see you. But where the hidden desires are strong enough, there will be a meeting of spirits. Take care of yourself, a thousand times over. The springtime wind is often chill; eat well for your health's sake. Be circumspect and careful, and do not think too often of my unworthy person.

Chang showed her letter to his friends, and in this way word of the affair got around. One of them, Yang Chü-yüan,[12] a skillful poet, wrote a quatrain on "Young Miss Ts'ui":

For clear purity jade cannot equal his complexion;
On the iris in the inner court snow begins to melt.
A romantic young man filled with thoughts of love.
A letter from the Hsiao girl,[13] brokenhearted.

Yüan Chen[14] of Ho-nan[15] wrote a continuation of Chang's poem "Encounter with an Immortal," also in thirty couplets:

Faint moonbeams pierce the curtained window;
Fireflies glimmer across the blue sky.
The far horizon begins now to pale;
Dwarf trees gradually turn darker green.
A dragon song crosses the court bamboo;
A phoenix air brushes the wellside tree.
The silken robe trails through the thin mist;
The pendant circles tinkle in the light breeze.
The accredited envoy accompanies Hsi wang-mu;[16]

[9] An allusion to the story of the Han poet, Ssu-ma Hsiang-ju (179–117 B.C.), who enticed the young widow Cho Wen-chün to elope by his zither playing.

[10] A neighboring girl, named Kao, repulsed Hsieh K'un's (280–322) advances by throwing her shuttle in his face. He lost two teeth.

[11] Alluding to the legend of the two wives of the sage ruler Shun, who stained the bamboo with their tears.

[12] The poet Yang Chü-yüan (fl. 800) was a contemporary of Yüan Chen.

[13] In T'ang times the term "Hsiao-niang" referred to young women in general. Here it means Ying-ying.

[14] Yüan Chen (775–831) was a key literary figure in the middle of the T'ang period.

[15] The Ho-nan Circuit in T'ang times covered the area to the south of the Yellow River in both of the present provinces of Shantung and Honan, up to the north of the Huai River in modern Kiangsu and Anhwei.

[16] Hsi wang-mu, the Queen Mother of the West, is a mythological figure supposedly dwelling in the K'un-lun Mountains in China's far west. In early accounts she is sometimes described as part human and part beast, but since early post-Han times she has usually been described as a beautiful immortal. Her huge palace is inhabited by other immortals. Within its

From the cloud's center comes Jade Boy.[17]
Late at night everyone is quiet;
At daybreak the rain drizzles.
Pearl radiance shines on her decorated sandals;
Flower glow shows off the embroidered skirt.
Jasper hairpin: a walking colored phoenix;
Gauze shawl: embracing vermilion rainbow.
She says she comes from Jasper Flower Bank
And is going to pay court at Green Jade Palace.
On an outing north of Lo-yang's[18] *wall,*
By chance he came to the house east of Sung Yü's.[19]
His dalliance she rejects a bit at first,
But her yielding love already is disclosed.
Lowered locks put in motion cicada shadows;[20]
Returning steps raise jade dust.
Her face turns to let flow flower snow
As she climbs into bed, silk covers in her arms.
Love birds in a neck-entwining dance;
Kingfishers in a conjugal cage.
Eyebrows, out of shyness, contracted;
Lip rouge, from the warmth, melted.
Her breath is pure: fragrance of orchid buds;
Her skin is smooth: richness of jade flesh.
No strength, too limp to lift a wrist;
Many charms, she likes to draw herself together.
Sweat runs: pearls drop by drop;
Hair in disorder: black luxuriance.
Just as they rejoice in the meeting of a lifetime
They suddenly hear the night is over.
There is no time for lingering;
It is hard to give up the wish to embrace.
Her comely face shows the sorrow she feels;
With fragrant words they swear eternal love.
She gives him a bracelet to plight their troth;
He ties a lovers' knot as sign their hearts are one.
Tear-borne powder runs before the clear mirror;

Around the flickering lamp are nighttime insects.
Moonlight is still softly shining
As the rising sun gradually dawns.
Riding on a wild goose she returns to the Lo River.[21]
Blowing a flute he ascends Mount Sung.[22]
His clothes are fragrant still with musk perfume;
The pillow is slippery yet with red traces.
Thick, thick, the grass grows on the dyke;
Floating, floating, the tumbleweed yearns for the isle.
Her plain zither plays the "Resentful Crane Song";
In the clear Milky Way she looks for the returning wild goose.[23]
The sea is broad and truly hard to cross;
The sky is high and not easy to traverse.
The moving cloud is nowhere to be found—
Hsiao Shih stays in his chamber.[24]

All of Chang's friends who heard of the affair marveled at it, but Chang had determined on his own course of action. Yüan Chen was especially close to him and so was in a position to ask him for an explanation. Chang said, "It is a general rule that those women endowed by Heaven with great beauty invariably either destroy themselves or destroy someone else. If this Ts'ui woman were to meet someone with wealth and position, she would use the favor her charms gain her to be cloud and rain or dragon or monster—I can't imagine what she might turn into. Of old, King Hsin of the Shang and King Yu of the Chou[25] were brought low by women, in spite of the size of their kingdoms and the extent of their power; their armies were scattered, their persons butchered, and down to the present day their names

---

precincts grow the magic peach trees which bear the fruits of immortality once every three thousand years. This might be an allusion to Ying-ying's mother.

[17] The Jade Boy might allude to Ying-ying's brother.

[18] Possibly a reference to the goddess of the Lo River. This river, in modern Honan, is made famous by the rhyme-prose of Ts'ao Chih (192–232), "The Goddess of Lo" ("Lo-shen fu").

[19] In "The Lechery of Master Teng-t'u," Sung Yü tells about the beautiful girl next door to the east who climbed up on the wall to flirt with him.

[20] Referring to her hairdo in the cicada style.

[21] Again the goddess of the Lo River theme.

[22] This is also known as the Central Mountain; it is located to the north of Teng-feng County in Honan Province. Here the one ascending the mountain may refer to Chang.

[23] Which might be carrying a message.

[24] Hsiao Shih was a well-known flute-player immortal of the Spring and Autumn period.

[25] Hsin (Chou) was the familiar last ruler of the Shang Dynasty, whose misrule and fall are attributed to the influence of his favorite Ta-chi. King Yu (r. 781–771 B.C.), last ruler of the Western Chou, was misled by his consort Pao-ssu. The behavior of both rulers is traditionally attributed to their infatuation with the wicked women they loved.

are objects of ridicule. I have no inner strength to withstand this evil influence. That is why I have resolutely suppressed my love."

At this statement everyone present sighed deeply.

Over a year later Ts'ui was married, and Chang for his part had taken a wife. Happening to pass through the town where she was living, he asked permission of her husband to see her, as a cousin. The husband spoke to her, but Ts'ui refused to appear. Chang's feelings of hurt showed on his face, and she was told about it. She secretly sent him a poem:

Emaciated, I have lost my looks,
Tossing and turning, too weary to leave my bed.
It's not because of others I am ashamed to rise;
For you I am haggard and before you ashamed.

She never did appear. Some days later when Chang was about to leave, she sent another poem of farewell:

Cast off and abandoned, what can I say now,
Whom you loved so briefly long ago?
Any love you had then for me
Will do for the one you have now.

After this he never heard any more about her. His contemporaries for the most part conceded that Chang had done well to rectify his mistake. I have often mentioned this among friends so that, forewarned, they might avoid doing such a thing, or if they did, that they might not be led astray by it. In the ninth month of a year in the Chen-yüan period, when an official, Li Kung-ch'ui,[26] was passing the night in my house at the Pacification Quarter, the conversation touched on the subject. He found it most extraordinary and composed a "Song of Ying-ying" to commemorate the affair. Ts'ui's child-name was Ying-ying, and Kung-ch'ui used it for his poem.

[26] Kung-ch'ui was the style of the T'ang poet Li Shen (?–846).

145

TU SHIH-NIANG SINKS THE JEWEL BOX IN ANGER

From *Ching-shih t'ung-yen*

TRANSLATED BY RICHARD M. W. HO

*The barbarians were wiped out, and the imperial capital was
    founded;*
Where dragons fly and phoenixes dance, its features soar—
*To the left, it is embraced by the vast sea against the endless
    sky;*
To the right, it is flanked by the T'ai-hang Mountains.
*The might of spears and halberds at the nine garrisons
    pervades the distant frontier;*
The rule of inaction awes thousands of countries.
A time of peace, when everyone enjoys utopia come true;
Our empire, like a golden bowl, lasts with the shining sun.

This poem eulogizes the magnificence of having our capital established at Yen-ching. Speaking of the position of our capital: to the north it leans on strategic mountain passes, to the south it impinges on the central plains. It is indeed an impregnable city, a rich heavenly abode, a foundation not to be uprooted in tens of thousands of years. In the beginning, when the Hung-wu Emperor[1] swept away the barbarian dust, he established his capital in Chin-ling, which became Nanking, or the southern capital. Later on, the Yung-lo Emperor[2] raised an army in Pei-p'ing to subdue the rebellious forces from the south.[3] The capital was moved to Yen-ching; it was thus called Peking, or the northern capital. As a result of this move, this barren and bleak northern land was transformed into a flowery embroidered world.

After nine successions from the Yung-lo Emperor, the throne came to be occupied by the Wan-li Emperor.[4] He was the eleventh sovereign in our dynasty. This sovereign was discerning and inspired awe, being blessed with both grace and virtue. He acceded to the throne at the age of ten and occupied it for forty-eight years, during which he subdued three major insurrections. Which three? Those caused by Po Ch'eng-en of Hsi-hsia,[5] the Japanese *kanpaku* Hideyoshi,[6] and

---

[1] Hung-wu (1368–1398) is the reign title of Emperor T'ai-tsu, the founder of the Ming Dynasty.
[2] Yung-lo (1403–1424) is the reign title of Emperor Ch'eng-tsu of the Ming Dynasty.
[3] It was in fact a seizure of power in which the Yung-lo Emperor usurped the throne from the legitimate sovereign.
[4] Wan-li (1573–1620) is the reign title of Emperor Shen-tsung of the Ming Dynasty.
[5] Po Cheng-en, the deputy commander at Hsi-hsia (in modern Kansu Province), rebelled in 1592. His rebellion was soon suppressed.
[6] *Kanpaku* Hideyoshi (1536–1598), better known as Toyotomi Hideyoshi, was the key military and political figure during the Momoyama period of Japan. After being made *kanpaku*, or chief adviser to the emperor, in 1585, he exterminated the ruling Hōjō clan in 1590 and united the country. He then planned to subjugate Ming China and incited Korea to demand tribute from China. When Korea refused, Hideyoshi in-

Yang Ying-lung of Po-chou.[7] Hideyoshi invaded Korea. Po Ch'eng-en and Yang Ying-lung were provincial officials who plotted rebellions. One after the other they were all suppressed. This struck many foreign countries with fear and awe and they hurried to pay homage to China. Indeed:

When the emperor had Heaven's blessings all were happy;
The four seas were undisturbed, and peace reigned in the
country.

This story begins with the twentieth year of the Wan-li reign period [1592], when the *kanpaku* of Japan invaded Korea. The king of Korea submitted a memorandum to China to appeal for help. Our celestial dynasty thus sent an army across the sea to his aid. Meanwhile, the Ministry of Finance proposed that since provisions for the army were insufficient for the expedition, special revenues should be raised by the sale of positions in the imperial academies. The proposal received the emperor's consent.

Actually, this system offered several advantages to those with money: it facilitated their studies, their passing the examinations, and their making the acquaintance of influential people. It also guaranteed a comfortable future. Because of this, the sons of officials and wealthy families naturally preferred to take advantage of this step to become students of the imperial academies rather than going through the examinations. When this practice went into effect, the number of students in each imperial academy rose to over one thousand.

One of these students was Li Chia, styled Kan-hsien, a native of Shao-hsing in Chekiang Province. He was the oldest of the three sons of a provincial commissioner. He had been studying at local schools since childhood, but had failed to pass the prefectural examinations. Now, under the new regulations, he had purchased a place in the imperial academy in Peking. During his residence in the capital he went with a fellow student from his own province, Liu Yü-ch'un, to the pleasure quarters, and there he met a celebrated courtesan. The courtesan was called Tu Wei; because she was the tenth girl in her family, she was also known as Tu Shih-niang [Tu the Tenth Lady]. See just how beautiful she was:

Her elegance was seductive;
A bewitching fragrance flowed from her body.
Her arched brows were the color of distant hills;
Her clear eyes were moist as flowing tides of autumn.
Her face was like lotus—indeed she was a veritable Wen-
chün; [8]
Her lips were like cherries—she was comparable to Fan-su. [9]
Alas! A pity that this flawless piece of jade
Should have fallen into the streets of ill fame.

Shih-niang had become a courtesan at the age of thirteen. Now she was nineteen. In those seven years, she had met countless young men of rich and noble families who were so besotted by her charm that they never hesitated to spend all they had to win her attention. Thus in the quarters went the following four-line song:

If Shih-niang is at the feast,
Even the weakest drinker drains a thousand goblets.
When in the quarters Shih-niang appears,
All other pretty faces at once seem ghastly.

This Li Chia, a romantic young man, had never seen a true beauty. When he met Shih-niang he was absolutely captivated by her and fell head over heels in love with her, and since he was not only handsome and amiable but also open-handed and untiring in his pursuit of her, the attraction

---

vaded Korea in 1592 and ran into the Ming forces. He had to negotiate peace and withdraw his troops. This is known as the Bunroku Expedition in Japanese history. In 1597, Hideyoshi invaded Korea again, but he died before the expedition, known as the Keichō Expedition, reached its goal, and the Japanese forces were withdrawn. It was Hideyoshi who placed a ban on the newly introduced Catholicism.

[7] Yang Ying-lung, the border pacification commissioner of Po-chou (the present Tsun-yi in Kweichow Province), rebelled in 1598. He was defeated in 1600.

[8] Cho Wen-chün.
[9] A favorite concubine of the celebrated T'ang poet Po Chü-yi (772–846).

and the love soon proved mutual. Realizing that her procuress was greedy and heartless, Shih-niang had long wanted to get out by getting married; now that she saw how honest and devoted Li was, her heart became all the more set on him. Li, however, was too afraid of his father to commit himself. Even so, they fell more and more deeply in love, spending days and nights together enjoying each other's company, and remaining as inseparable as husband and wife. They solemnly exchanged a vow that they would never love anyone else. Indeed:

Was their love not as deep as the sea? Nay, it was
    unfathomable.
Was their faith not as high as the mountains? It was loftier.

Now let us return to the madam of the house. Since Li had become Shih-niang's lover, other wealthy men who heard of her had been trying in vain to see her. At first, when Li could afford to spend money lavishly on her, the madam, all smiles and obsequity, waited on him with the utmost attention. After more than a year, however, Li's means were nearly exhausted. He could no longer be as lavish as he wished, and the old woman began to neglect him. Meanwhile, news of Li's frequenting the courtesans' quarters reached the provincial commissioner, who immediately sent letter after letter to urge his son to come home. But the young man was so enamored of Shih-niang's beauty that he kept postponing his return. Later, when he heard how angry his father was with him, he was even more afraid to go home.

The adage has it: "Friendship based on profit ends once the money is spent." Shih-niang, however, loved Li so truly that the poorer he grew, the more passionately she became attached to him. The madam had told her repeatedly to send Li about his business, and seeing that the girl did not do so, she had tried several times to insult Li, hoping that he would leave in anger. But Li, who had by nature a gentle disposition, only returned with even milder words.

As a last resort, the madam began to berate Shih-niang. "In our profession we depend solely on our clients for food and clothing," she said one day. "It is the nature of our business to send an old customer out the front door while a new one is being received at the back. The more customers we have in our house, the wealthier we are. But with this Li Chia hanging around our place for over a year, not even the old customers are coming, let alone new ones. He must be Chung K'uei incarnate, scaring away even the smallest ghost who comes our way. Don't you see what he has given us? Smoke in our eyes instead of smoke in our chimney! What's to become of us?"

Shih-niang, however, was not one to quietly submit to such a reprimand. "Mr. Li didn't come here empty-handed," she retorted. "He has spent a fortune on us."

"That was one time, this is another. You tell him to give me a little money to buy firewood and rice to feed the two of you. In the other houses the girls are money-growing trees, they can live in style. It's just our bad luck that I'm keeping a white tiger who eats money. I'm the only one who has to worry every day about all the basic needs; I even have to support this tramp. Where do you think my food and clothes are coming from? You go tell that beggar of yours, if he still has some respect, ask him to give me a few taels of silver and I'd be happy to let you go off with him. I'll buy another girl to make my living. What do you say?"

"Do you really mean it?" demanded Shih-niang.

The old woman realized that Li Chia had not a penny left and in fact had pawned almost all his clothes; she was quite certain he would have no way to raise the money. "Have I ever lied?" she retorted. "Of course I mean it."

"Mother," said Shih-niang. "How much do you want from him?"

"If it were anyone else, I would certainly ask for a thousand taels. But I don't think that poor devil could ever afford to pay. Out of the goodness of my heart, I'll ask him for only three hundred. With that I could buy another girl to take your place. But there's one condition: he must pay me within three days. When he hands over the money, I'll hand over the girl. If he cannot pay me after three days, I don't care whether he's a gentleman or not, I'll beat the hell out of that wretch and drive him out of my house. You can't blame me for it then."

"Although he's away from home and has run out of money," said Shih-niang, "he probably could raise three hundred taels. But three days is too short. Can't you make it ten?"

"That pauper has nothing now but his bare hands," thought the madam. "Even if I gave him a hundred days, where indeed could he raise the money? If he fails to produce it, however shameless he is I don't think he'll have the nerve to turn up again. Then I can get my establishment under proper control once more, and Shih-niang will have nothing to say."

"Well, for your sake," she said, "I'll make it ten days, then. But if he doesn't have the money by then, I'm not to blame."

"If he can't find the money in ten days, I don't suppose he will have the courage to come back," said Shih-niang. "What I'm afraid of is that you might go back on your word if he comes up with the money."

"I'm already fifty-one," protested the madam. "I'm a devout Buddhist and I observe the monthly fast. How would I dare commit the sin of lying? If you don't trust me, let us clap each other's hands to make a pledge. May I become a dog or a pig if I go back on my word!"

How could the sea be measured with a cup?
The ill intention of this hag is laughable.
Sure that the poor scholar's purse was empty,
She purposely gave the lovely lady a problem with her demand.

That night in bed Shih-niang discussed her future with Li. "It's not that I don't want to marry you," said the young man, "but it would cost at least a thousand taels to buy your freedom, and where can I raise the money in my situation?"

"I've already spoken to mother. She wants only three hundred taels; but it must be paid within ten days. Although the money you brought with you has run out, you must have relatives and friends in the capital you can borrow from. If you can raise this sum, I'll be yours, and we won't have to suffer the old woman's temper anymore."

"My friends and relatives have all been avoiding me because I spend too much time here," said Li. "Perhaps tomorrow I'll tell them anyhow that I'm packing up to leave and coming to say good-bye, and then ask for money for my traveling expenses. I may be able to collect three hundred taels."

The next morning he got up, washed and dressed, and took leave of Shih-niang. "Return as quickly as you can," urged Shih-niang. "I'll be waiting for the good news." Li told Shih-niang not to worry and promised to do his best.

After he had left the quarters, Li called on a number of relatives and friends, pretending that he had come to say good-bye. They were pleased to hear that he was going home, but when he touched upon the subject of a loan for his homeward journey there was no favorable response from them. As the proverb says: "To speak of borrowing is to end a friendship." Citing good reasons, they all argued with themselves: "Li is a spendthrift whose infatuation with a courtesan has kept him away from home for over a year now, and his father is furious with him. Now all of the sudden he declares that he's going home; who knows if he's telling the truth? What if I lent him money for the journey and he spent it on girls again? When his father heard of it, what would he think? Since one way or the other I'll be blamed anyway, I might as well wash my hands of it."

"I'm very sorry," each of his relatives would say, "I happen to be short of cash at the moment. I'm afraid I can't help you." Everywhere he went, he received the same reply. Not one of his acquaintances proved generous enough to lend him even ten or twenty taels.

For three days he went from house to house without getting a penny. He dared not tell Shih-

149

niang the truth and had to parry her questions with evasive answers. The fourth day, however, found him in such despair that he was too ashamed to go back to the quarters. But after living so long with Shih-niang, he no longer had a dwelling place of his own. Having nowhere else to go, he went to Liu Yü-ch'un, a fellow student from his home town, to spend the night.

When Liu asked why he looked so worried, Li told him the whole story of Shih-niang's intention to marry him. Liu, however, shook his head and said, "I find this hard to believe. Shih-niang is the most prized courtesan in her profession. I think her price of redemption couldn't be less than ten pecks of pearls and a thousand taels in cash. The madam would never let her go for three hundred taels. I suspect this to be a trick of the old woman. She must have had enough of you because you are penniless and yet you're keeping her girl without paying her. This is her plan to get rid of you. As to Shih-niang, since she has known you for such a long time, she probably finds it hard to put it to you bluntly. Knowing you're short of money, she deliberately asks you for three hundred taels and gives you ten days to raise the sum. If you can't meet this deadline, of course you won't have the face to return; if you did, she would have all the more reason to sneer at you and insult you, making it impossible for you to stay. This is a trick people of her profession usually play. Do think it over; don't let them deceive you. In my humble opinion, the sooner you leave them the better."

When Li heard this, he was lost for words for quite some time. His heart was full of misgiving. Then Liu went on, "Don't make a wrong move. If you do want to go home and need money for the journey, your friends may be able to raise a few taels for you. But I doubt if you could get three hundred taels in ten months, let alone ten days. Nowadays, who would be interested in tiding over a friend in trouble? How well the two women know that you can never raise such a sum, to have devised such a plan to embarrass you!"

"I suppose you're right, my friend," Li at last replied.

But, still unwilling to give up Shih-niang, he continued to call on acquaintances for the loan and returned in the evening to stay at Liu's place.

He stayed with Liu Yü-ch'un for three days; thus six of the ten days had passed. Hearing no news from her lover for several days, Shih-niang had grown very anxious. She dispatched her little servant boy Ssu-erh to look for him. The boy found Li on the main street by chance.

"Master!" he called. "Mistress is expecting to hear from you!"

Li felt too ashamed to go back. He said, "I'm busy today. I'll come tomorrow."

But the boy had received instructions from Shih-niang. Taking hold of Li's coat, he would not let him go. "Mistress has asked me to find you," he said. "Please come with me."

On his part, Li also missed Shih-niang. Thus, half reluctantly, he followed the boy to Shih-niang's quarters. He couldn't find anything to say when he saw her.

"Has our plan worked out?" asked Shih-niang.

Tears fell from Li's eyes.

"Have people become so unfeeling that you cannot raise even three hundred taels?" she said.

With tears in his eyes, Li said, "Now I have realized it is easier to catch a tiger in the mountain than to seek help from one's friends. I've been running from house to house for six days, but I haven't been able to borrow a penny. It is because I was too ashamed to come to you empty-handed that I've stayed away for the last few days. Now that you've sent for me, I can only come to you with shame on my face. It's not that I haven't done my best, but this is the way of the world."

"Don't let the old woman know," said Shih-niang. "Please leave it to me for tonight. I might come up with an idea."

Thereupon she prepared a meal and they enjoyed the food and wine together before going to bed. In the middle of the night Shih-niang asked,

"Now that you cannot raise any money, what will become of us?" But Li had no answer for her except tears.

Soon it reached the fifth watch, near dawn. Shih-niang said, "Inside my mattress I've hidden one hundred and fifty taels of silver, all my savings. Take them. Now that I've taken care of half the sum, it should be easier for you to find the balance. Only four days are left now; there's really no time to lose."

When they got up, Shih-niang gave the mattress to Li. He was overjoyed. He asked the servant boy to carry the mattress for him and went straight to Liu's lodging, where he told Liu all that had happened the night before. When they tore up the mattress they found in the cotton padding many silver pieces which, when weighed, totaled one hundred and fifty taels. Liu was very much surprised and impressed. "This girl's devotion is not to be doubted," he said. "Now on your part you must not betray her trust. I'll do what I can to help you."

"Should you succeed in bringing us together, I shall be forever grateful to you!" Li exclaimed.

Thus Liu kept Li in his house while he went out himself to borrow the money. In two days he borrowed one hundred and fifty taels, which he gave to Li, saying, "I have put myself in debt not for your sake but for Shih-niang, whose devotion to you has deeply touched me."

Thereupon Li Chia, carrying the three hundred taels of silver, beaming with smiles, went to see Shih-niang. It was the ninth day—one day ahead of the appointed time.

"Two days ago you still could not borrow a penny," said Shih-niang. "How did you manage to raise one hundred and fifty taels by today?" When Li told her about his fellow student Liu, she pressed her hand to her forehead in token of gratitude. "Thanks to Mr. Liu, now our dreams can come true!" she exclaimed. Both of them were overcome with joy, and they passed the night in the quarters.

The next morning Shih-niang rose early and said to Li, "Once you have paid the money, I'll go with you right away. We should have all our travel arrangements made beforehand. Yesterday I borrowed twenty taels of silver from my sisters; you can take it to pay for our traveling expenses."

Li had, in fact, been worrying about where he was going to get the money for their journey, but had been too ashamed to broach the subject. Now he was truly delighted to have this twenty taels.

As they were talking, the madam knocked at the door. "Today is the tenth day, my child!" she called.

When Li heard this, he opened the door for her. "Thank you," he said. "I was just going to ask you over." Then he placed the three hundred taels on the table.

The madam had never imagined that Li could produce the money. She was dazed for a while and her face fell.

As she was about to retract her promise Shih-niang said, "Mother, during these eight years I've earned you a fortune worth several thousand taels. Today is the happy day on which I am to start a new life. You've given me your word. Here are the three hundred taels, delivered on time. If you change your mind, Mr. Li will take the money away, and I'll commit suicide on the spot. You'll then lose not only the money but me, too. Think about it before it is too late."

The old woman could make no reply. After some deliberation, she took out a scale to weigh the silver.

"Well, well," she said at last. "Since things have come to this, I don't suppose I can keep you any longer. But if you must go, go at once. Don't think you're going to take any of your clothes or ornaments with you." Immediately she pushed them out of the room, and called for a lock with which she padlocked the door.

It was the ninth lunar month, and the weather was getting cold. Shih-niang, just out of bed and not yet dressed, was still wearing her plain old

151

clothes. She knelt down twice before the madam. Li also made a deep bow to her. Then as husband and wife they left the old woman's place together.

The carp had freed itself of the golden hook;
Lithely it swam off, never to return again.

Li asked Shih-niang to wait for a while, saying, "Let me call a sedan chair so that we can go to Mr. Liu's place before deciding on what to do."

"My sisters have always been very kind to me," Shih-niang replied. "I ought to say good-bye to them. Besides, it is they who lent us the money for our traveling expenses the other day; we must thank them for that." So she went with Li to thank and take leave of the other courtesans.

Two of these girls, Hsieh Yüeh-lang and Hsü Su-su, lived in the neighborhood and were Shih-niang's closest friends. She called first on Yüeh-lang who, surprised to see her dressed in old plain clothes and without ornaments in her hair, asked what had happened. Shih-niang told her the whole story and introduced Li Chia to her. Then, pointing at Yüeh-lang, Shih-niang said to Li, "This is the sister who lent us the money the other day. You should thank her." Li bowed again and again in gratitude.

Yüeh-lang told Shih-niang to comb her hair and wash while she sent for Su-su. Then the two sisters brought out their emerald trinkets, gold bracelets, jasper hairpins, earrings, a brocade tunic and skirt, a phoenix girdle, and a pair of embroidered slippers, and with these they adorned Shih-niang until she was arrayed in finery from head to foot. Then they feasted together in celebration, and Yüeh-lang let the couple use her bedroom for the night.

The following day they gave another big feast to which all the girls in the quarters were invited. The girls toasted the happy couple, played music, sang, and danced, giving the best of their talents for the occasion. The feast lasted until midnight, when Shih-niang thanked each of her sisters in turn.

"Shih-niang, you've always been the one we all look up to," said the courtesans. "Now that you're leaving with your husband, we might never meet again. When you've decided on the day of your departure, we'll come to see you off."

"When the date is fixed, I'll let all of you know," said Yüeh-lang. "But since Shih-niang is going to travel thousands of *li* with Mr. Li, and their resources are scarce, we must make sure that she is equipped for the journey." Her suggestion met with unanimous approval before the girls retired for the night. Li and Shih-niang again spent the night in Yüeh-lang's room.

Shortly before daybreak Shih-niang asked Li, "Where are we going from here? Have you any definite plan in mind?"

Li replied, "If my father, in his anger, finds out that I've married a courtesan, not only will he make me suffer but you'll also suffer as a result. This has been worrying me for some time, but I haven't yet found a solution."

"The sacred bond between father and son must not be destroyed," said Shih-niang. "Since we can't expect to have his forgiveness in the immediate future, it might be better for us to go to the scenic Soochow and Hangchow area and stay for a while. You can then go home alone and ask some of your relatives and friends to intercede with your father on your behalf. When you two are reconciled, you can come to take me home, and all will be well."

"That's a sensible idea," Li agreed.

The next morning they said good-bye to Yüeh-lang and went to Liu Yü-ch'un's lodging to pack their luggage. When Shih-niang saw Liu she got down on her knees to make obeisance, and thanked him for his help. She said, "We'll do our best to return your kindness in the future."

Liu hastily bowed in return and said, "You are a remarkable woman, my lady, not to compromise your love in face of poverty. I was only fanning the fire in the direction of the wind. Such a trifling service is not worth mentioning."

The three of them spent the whole day drinking. The following morning they chose an auspicious day for the journey and arranged for the necessary sedan chairs and horses. Shih-niang also sent her servant boy with a letter to Yüeh-lang to thank her and bid her farewell. When they were about to leave, a host of sedan chairs arrived, bearing Yüeh-lang, Su-su, and the other courtesans coming to see them off.

"Sister, now that you two are leaving, and we know you are short of money," said Yüeh-lang, "we've prepared a small gift to express our affection for you. Please accept it. If you run short of cash on your journey, it might come in handy." Thereupon she instructed a servant to bring a gilt box; but since it was securely locked, its contents could not be seen. Shih-niang did not open the box, nor did she decline this gift. She just heartily thanked them all. By now the sedan chairs and horses were ready, and the couple was urged to start. Liu offered his friend and Shih-niang three cups, and then he and the ladies saw them to Culture Gate, where they all parted in tears. Truly:

To meet again in the future seemed unlikely;
Woeful it was to bid farewell at such a time.

In due course Li and Shih-niang reached the river Lu,[10] where they were to take a boat. They were lucky enough to find an official dispatch boat returning to Kua-chou,[11] and having settled on the amount of their fare, they booked a cabin. Once aboard, however, Li discovered that he had not a penny left. You may wonder how he had used up the money so quickly. The fact was that, although Shih-niang had given him twenty taels, he had used part of it to redeem a few of his clothes at the pawnshop, after having discovered that he did not have a single decent gown with him in the quarters. He also bought some new

---

[10] This river marks the northern end of the Grand Canal.
[11] Kua-chou, to the south of Chiang-tu in Kiangsu, is located at the junction of the Yangtze River and the Grand Canal.

bedding. Thus what was left of the money was sufficient only to pay for the sedan chairs and horses.

"Don't worry," said Shih-niang, noting his anxiety. "The gift my sisters gave us may now be useful." Thereupon she took a key and unlocked the box. Li, standing beside her, was too ashamed to look into the box as Shih-niang took out a scarlet silk bag and put it on the table.

"Would you open that and see what is in it?" Shih-niang asked.

Li picked up the bag, and immediately felt its weight; when he opened it he found pieces of silver which, after counting, totaled fifty taels. In the meantime, Shih-niang had locked the box again without saying what else it contained. Instead, she turned to Li and said, "The generosity of my sisters not only allows us enough money for our journey; it will also help defray our expenses when we stay in the south."

Surprised and delighted, Li said, "But for your help, I would have been stranded far away from home and died without a burial place. I'll never forget how much I owe you." From then on, whenever they talked of what had happened, Li would burst into tears of gratitude, and Shih-niang would always comfort him tenderly.

In a few days, the boat reached the Kua-chou harbor. Li hired a passenger boat, had their luggage transferred, and arranged to set sail the next morning at dawn. It was the middle of winter, and the full moon was as clear and bright as water. As the two sat together in the bow of the boat, Li said to Shih-niang, "From the time we left the capital we were shut up in the cabin with other people all the time, and were unable to talk freely. Now that we have the whole boat to ourselves, we can say whatever we want. As we're now leaving North China and coming to the Yangtze Valley, don't you think it's time we set aside our anxiety and had a really good time drinking?"

"I couldn't agree more, as I haven't had an opportunity to talk and laugh freely for a long while.

What you've suggested is exactly what I had in mind," said Shih-niang.

Li took out the wine cups, spread a rug in the bow, and started drinking with Shih-niang. When they were both warm with wine, Li, cup in hand, said to Shih-niang, "Your voice has always been the loveliest in all the quarters. I still remember that when I first met you and heard you sing so divinely, my soul seemed to take flight. But since then, we've been so beset by worries that I've long missed your heavenly songs. Now, with the bright moon shining on the clear river and with no one near in the depth of night, won't you sing for me?"

Shih-niang was in a happy mood, and so, clearing her throat and then tapping her fan on the deck to keep time, she sang. Her song was about a scholar offering wine to a girl. It was taken from the play *Moon Pavilion* by Shih Chün-mei of the Yüan Dynasty and was set to the tune of "The Little Red Peach Blossom":

As her voice soared into the sky, the clouds halted;
As her voice entered the deep river, the fish emerged.

Now in a neighboring boat there was a young man called Sun Fu, styled Shan-lai, a native of Hsin-an in Hui-chou.[12] His family had been in the salt business in Yangchow for generations and was extremely rich. He was now twenty years of age and a student in the imperial academy in Nanking. Sun was a dissolute young man whose habit it was to frequent the courtesans' quarters. Indeed, he was, with his frivolous nature, a leading personage in the business of pleasure.

It so happened that Sun's boat was also moored at the Kua-chou harbor on this particular evening. He was drinking alone and feeling bored when he heard a singing voice so clear and so exquisite that not even the song of a phoenix could match it. He stood up in the bow and listened for some time before he realized that the

singing was coming from the next boat. Just as he was going to make inquiries, the song ended. Thereupon he sent his servant to make secret investigations about the singer. The servant questioned the boatman, and was informed that the boat had been hired by a certain Mr. Li; nothing was known about the singer.

"The singer cannot be from a respectable family," thought Sun. "How can I get to see her?" Preoccupation with this problem kept him awake all night.

At the fifth watch a high wind sprang up on the river, and by dawn the sky was filled with dark red clouds. Soon snowflakes were flying madly. Vividly was the scene described in this poem:

Cloud-touching trees of the thousand hills disappeared;
On the numerous footpaths stirs not a soul.
From his little boat, an old man in straw hat and coat
Fishes alone on the chilly river, in snow.

Since the wind and snow made it impossible to sail, all boats had to remain in the harbor. Sun ordered his boatman to steer close to Li's boat; and then, putting on his sable cap and fox-fur coat, he opened the window pretending to watch the snow. It happened that Shih-niang had just finished dressing and, with her slender hands, she raised the curtain of the cabin window to empty her basin into the river. In so doing she was seen by Sun Fu, who was totally enchanted by her unearthly beauty. He fastened his gaze on the spot where she had appeared, hoping to catch another glimpse of her. But his patience was not rewarded. After some reflection, he leaned against his cabin window and chanted two lines from the "Plum Bossom Poem" by Scholar Kao:[13]

On the snow-clad hill sleeps the unworldly hermit;
From the moonlit woods emerges the beautiful lady.

When Li heard someone chanting poetry in the next boat, he leaned out to look, thus falling victim to Sun's plan. Sun's poetry chanting was pre-

---

[12] Hsi County in modern Anhwei Province.

[13] The well-known Ming poet Kao Ch'i (1336–1374).

cisely to attract Li's attention so that he could get acquainted with him. Now, hastily raising his hands in greeting, Sun asked, "What is your honorable name, sir?" Li introduced himself and then naturally asked the same question. Sun introduced himself, and they began to exchange gossip about the imperial academies. Very soon they became well acquainted.

"Heaven must have sent this snowstorm to hold up our boats so that we would meet," said Sun. "This is indeed my good fortune. Since we've nothing in particular to do in the boat, may I propose that we go ashore to a restaurant, so that I may have the benefit of your conversation? I beg you not to refuse."

"But we've just met," replied Li. "How can I put you to all that trouble?"

"You shouldn't say that," Sun protested. " 'Within the four seas all men are brothers.' "

Then he told his boatman to put down the gangplank and his servant boy to hold an umbrella to bring Li over to his boat. Then they performed obeisance in the bow and Sun politely asked Li to go first as they went ashore.

A few paces brought them to a restaurant. They went upstairs, chose a clean table by the window, and sat down. After the waiter had brought them food and drink, Sun raised his cup and toasted Li. Thus they drank and enjoyed the snow scene. After exchanging a few conventional phrases of courtesy, they gradually moved to topics surrounding the women of pleasure. Since both of them were old hands at this kind of life, their talk soon became more and more congenial until they had shared enough secrets to be in each other's confidence.

Before long Sun sent away all those who waited on him, and asked in a low voice, "Who is the girl who sang in your boat last night?"

Li Chia was only too eager to prove he was as good as his word, so he announced earnestly, "That is Tu Shih-niang, a well-known courtesan in Peking."

"If she was a girl in one of the quarters, how did you manage to get her?"

Thereupon Li told him the whole story: how they had met, how they had fallen in love, how Shih-niang had wanted to marry him, and how he had borrowed money to redeem her.

"It must be a pleasant thing to return home with a beautiful woman. But do you have your family's approval?"

"My wife is no cause for worry. What worries me is my very strict father," replied Li.

This at last gave Sun the opening he had been waiting for. So he asked, "Since your honorable father may not approve, where do you intend to install the lady? Have you discussed this with her?"

"Yes, I have," replied Li with a frown.

"Well then, she must have a good plan." Sun looked relieved.

"She intends to spend some time in the Soochow and Hangchow area and asks me to return home first. What I'm supposed to do is to have my friends and relatives intercede with my father for me. When, hopefully, his anger subsides, I'll think about getting her home. What do you think of this plan?"

Sun looked thoughtful for a while. Then he deliberately put on a worried look, saying, "Since we have only just met, I do fear you will take offense if I advise you on such an intimate matter."

"I need your advice," urged Li. "Please don't hesitate to speak frankly."

"Very well," said Sun. "As your father is a high-ranking provincial official, he is bound to be very strict in family discipline. If he has expressed displeasure over your spending time in low places, do you think he will allow you to marry a girl of easy virtue? As for your relatives and friends, who would not bow to your respected father's wish? If you seek their help, you're bound to be refused. Even if some of them are foolish enough to plead your cause, once they realize the old gentleman is against this marriage they are certain to change

155

their tune. As things are, you'll never bring about harmony in your family, nor will you have a satisfactory answer to give to your loved one. Even if you use delaying tactics and linger amid mountains and rivers, you cannot remain there indefinitely. When your resources were exhausted you would find yourself in a quandary."

Realizing that he had already spent more than half of the fifty taels he had possessed, Li nodded in agreement as soon as Sun touched upon the subject of his dwindling expense money.

"There is yet a sincere word of advice which I want to offer you," Sun went on. "But I don't know if you want to hear it."

"I'm only too grateful for your concern. Please don't keep anything back."

"I'd better not say it," declared Sun. "Who am I, a casual acquaintance, to come between you and someone dear to you?"

"Please say it; it's really all right," importuned Li.

"As the ancients said: 'Women are as fickle as water.' How much more so are the girls from pleasure houses! Since your mistress is a well-known courtesan, she must have paramours everywhere. There might be some former lover of hers in the south, and she might be employing your help in order to join him there."

"I don't think that can be the case," said Li hastily.

"Even if it is not," replied Sun, "the young southerners are notorious philanderers; if you leave your mistress by herself, there is no way to make sure she won't succumb to their temptation. On the other hand, if you take her home you will only further provoke the anger of your father. In fact, there doesn't seem to be an ideal solution to your problem at all.

"The sacred relationship between father and son is inviolable. If you offend your father and abandon your home for the sake of a courtesan, the whole country will condemn you for being a dissolute and reckless man. There will come a day when your wife will not consider you worthy of being her husband, your younger brothers will not consider you worthy of being their elder brother, and your acquaintances will not take you for a friend. How will you stand up to the world? You must think about it carefully right now."

This speech left Li at a loss. Hitching his seat nearer to Sun, he asked anxiously, "What do you think I should do?"

"I have an idea which you would do well to follow. But I only fear that you are too fond of your new love to carry it out," Sun replied.

"If you have a good plan to restore me to the bosom of my family, you are no less than my savior. Why should you hesitate to speak?"

Sun obliged, saying, "You have been far away from home for over a year. Your father is angry with you and your wife displeased. If I were you, I would be unable to eat or sleep. Your honorable father is angry with you only because you have let yourself become infatuated with a courtesan and are spending money like water. In short, he fears that you would squander the family fortune, once it came into your hands. Your returning home empty-handed would surely infuriate him. But if you are willing to give up your woman to make the best of a bad bargain, I'm willing to offer you a thousand taels of silver for her. With this sum, you can tell your father that you have been teaching in the capital and have not spent a penny of your allowance. He will certainly believe you. Peace will then be restored in your family. Now, as you can see, at a single stroke you might turn calamity into good fortune. Please consider my offer carefully. It is not that I covet your concubine's beauty; I only want to do what I can for you as a friend."

Li had always been of weak character, and was afraid of his father. Sun's words had succeeded in intensifying his worries. Rising from his seat, he bowed to Sun in gratitude. "Your judicious advice has opened my eyes," he said. "But since my concubine has followed me all these thousands of *li*, it would be unethical for me to sever relations with her too abruptly. Let me return to talk it over with her; I'll let you know as soon as I have her consent."

Sun reminded him, "Break the news tactfully. If she's so fond of you, how could she bear to estrange you from your father? I'm certain she'll help you to return home."

They went on drinking until dusk, when the wind and snow stopped. Then Sun told his servant boy to pay the bill, and walked hand in hand with Li back to the boat. Alas!

Be discreet when you speak to people;
Baring your heart to them is far from wise.

In the boat Shih-niang had prepared wine and food to enjoy with Li. But he was out the whole day. When dusk fell she lighted the lamp and continued waiting. At last Li returned. Shih-niang rose to welcome him, but noticed that he looked upset. She poured a cup of warm wine for him; he shook his head in refusal and went to bed without a word.

Shih-niang was disturbed. Having put away the cups and plates and helped Li to change, she asked, "What happened earlier today that has made you feel so bad?"

Li just sighed. By the time she had repeated her question several times he was asleep. She was so ill at ease that she was unable to close her eyes, so she remained seated on the edge of the bed. In the middle of the night Li woke up and heaved another great sigh.

"What is troubling you so badly that you keep sighing over and over again?" Shih-niang asked.

Li sat up, drew the quilt around him, and tried several times to speak; but he broke off each time and tears poured down his cheeks. Taking Li in her arms, Shih-niang comforted him with kind words, saying, "We have been in love for nearly two years and have gone through many difficulties to get where we are today. We have traveled thousands of *li*, and you've had no cause for sorrow. It truly perplexes me to see you so upset when we are about to cross the Yangtze to embark on a happy life. There must be a reason. Just as we shall live and die together as husband and wife, so should we discuss our troubles together. Please don't keep your worries from me."

After he had been pressed several times to speak, Li, with tears in his eyes, finally opened his mouth: "When I was poverty-stricken and far away from home you were so good as to share my hardships; for this I am immensely grateful to you. But I have been thinking things over: my father, holding a high provincial post, must follow convention, not to mention the fact that he is a very stern and severe man by nature. If he is so angry as to drive us out of the family, we shall be forced to wander, homeless. What will become of us then? If this happens, not only shall I lose my father's love, but the happiness of our marriage cannot be guaranteed either. Today my friend Sun from Hsin-an discussed this with me while we were drinking, and it really breaks my heart."

"What do you plan to do?" asked Shih-niang, greatly alarmed.

"As I am the one involved in this dilemma, I have been unable to see my way clearly. But Mr. Sun has thought out a good plan for me; only you may not agree to it," Li said.

"Who is this Mr. Sun?" Shih-niang was puzzled. "If his plan is good, why shouldn't I agree to it?"

"His name is Sun Fu, a salt merchant from Hsin-an and a gallant young scholar. He heard you singing last night and inquired about you, so I told him our story. When he heard that we would not be able to go home, he was willing to offer a thousand taels of silver for your hand, so that with the money I would find it less difficult to face my parents, and you would have a home, too. But I cannot bear to leave you; such a thought makes me weep." As he said this, his tears fell like rain.

Shih-niang withdrew her hands from him, smiling sardonically. "He must be a fine gentleman, indeed a hero, to have conceived this plan for you," she said. "You will have your thousand taels, and with me going to another man, you will no longer have any burden. This indeed is what is called 'initiated from feeling but kept within the proprieties.' Yes, this plan suits us both. Where is the silver now?"

"Since I had not received your consent," said Li, who had stopped weeping, "the money is still with him. It has not yet changed hands."

"Then you must close the transaction with him the first thing tomorrow morning," urged Shih-niang. "This opportunity is not to be missed. But a thousand taels is a lot of money; be sure the silver pieces are properly weighed and handed over before I cross to the other boat. You must not let that salt merchant trick you."

It was now the fourth watch. Shih-niang got up, lighted the lamp, washed, and adorned herself. "Today I am dressing to speed an old client and receive a new one," she said. "This is an important occasion." She applied rouge, powder, and scented oil with great care, and arrayed herself in splendid head ornaments and a magnificent embroidered gown. Her perfume scented the air, and her beauty was dazzling.

By the time she had finished dressing it was already dawn, and a servant arrived from Sun asking for a reply. Shih-niang stole a glance at Li and, seeing that he looked pleased, urged him to reply at once so that he could be in possession of the silver as soon as possible. Thus Li went to Sun's boat to announce that Shih-niang was willing.

"There's no difficulty about the money. But I must have some article as a pledge," said Sun.

When Li told Shih-niang of Sun's request, she pointed at her gilt box and said, "Let them take this."

Sun, in great exultation, promptly sent the thousand taels of silver to Li's boat. When Shih-niang had looked through the packages and satisfied herself that the silver was of full standard pu-rity and that the amount was correct, she held to the side of the boat and beckoned to Sun, who was immediately overwhelmed by her bewitching charm. Shih-niang then said, "May I have that box back for a moment? It contains Mr. Li's travel permit, which I must return to him."

Satisfied that Shih-niang was now his caged bird, Sun ordered his servant to carry back her gilt box and set it down in the bow. Shih-niang took her key and unlocked it, disclosing a series of small drawers inside, the first of which she asked Li to pull out. He did, and found it filled with precious ornaments to the value of several hundred taels of silver. To the consternation of Li, Sun, and the others in the two boats, Shih-niang immediately tossed them into the river.

Then she told Li to pull out a second drawer containing jade flutes and golden pipes, and a third drawer filled with curios of jade and gold worth several thousand taels. All these, too, Shih-niang threw into the water.

By this time the bank was thronged with spectators. "What a pity!" they all exclaimed.

While they were still mystified by her behavior, Shih-niang pulled out the last drawer, in which there was a casket. She opened the casket and they saw in it a handful of bright pearls; the rest of the casket was packed with other precious stones such as emeralds and cat's-eyes, the like of which they had never seen and the value of which they did not even dare guess. The onlookers let out thunderous cries of amazement and admiration. When Shih-niang was about to toss all these jewels into the river, Li was suddenly overcome by remorse and he threw his arms around her and wept bitterly, while Sun also came over to plead with her. But Shih-niang pushed Li away and turned angrily to Sun. "You know what Mr. Li and I have gone through to come this far! But you were cruel and heartless enough to tear us apart with your cunning words, only to gratify your lust. You are my greatest enemy! If my spirit survives after death, I will certainly take my case to the gods. You can stop dreaming about having your lustful will of me."

Then Shih-niang turned to Li and said, "I've been living in the mire as a courtesan for many years. For all these years I've saved something to support me for the rest of my life. Since we met we've sworn a love everlasting. When we left the capital I pretended that this box was a present from my sisters. Indeed, it was my intention to fit you out splendidly with the invaluable jewels it contained, so that when you returned to your parents they might appreciate my love for you and admit me into the family. I might then have remained happily with you and lived out my days without regret. But how was I to know that you did not trust me and were easily swayed by unfounded words? Now you've abandoned me halfway. In vain have I given you my true love. I've opened this box in front of all these people to show you that a trifling thousand taels means little to me. Like jade I have kept my heart and soul pure for you, but you have eyes that cannot see. Alas! I was born under the wrong star. I escaped from the bitter lot of a courtesan only to be cast aside by you. All those here today are my witnesses! I have not been untrue to you; it's you who have betrayed me!"

All those who had gathered were moved to tears. Bitterly they condemned Li for his ingratitude and disloyalty. Li, overwhelmed with remorse and shame, was about to turn to beg Shih-niang's forgiveness when, clasping the casket in her arms, she threw herself into the river. They shouted for help, but a thick mist obscured the river and the current was strong. She was nowhere to be found. How sad that such a beautiful courtesan of high renown should have found her way into the stomach of the fish.

Her lonely soul sank into the deep;
As if in a dream, she made for Hades.

The onlookers gnashed their teeth in rage and wanted to fall upon Li and Sun; the two men,

greatly frightened, immediately shouted to the boatmen to cast off and escaped in opposite directions. In the boat, Li caught sight of the thousand taels of silver and his longing for Shih-niang began to grow, his shame and regret growing with it until eventually he took leave of his senses, never to recover them for the rest of his life.

As for Sun, he fell ill with fright and was laid up in bed for over a month, constantly seeing Shih-niang standing by his bed reprimanding him. Little by little he wasted away until he died. People who knew of this took it to be a just retribution for the sin he had committed on the river.

Now we must come back to Liu Yü-ch'un. In good time he completed his studies in the capital and packed up to return home. When he reached Kua-pu[14] he moored his boat. While he was washing his face by the side of the boat, his brass basin fell into the river. He asked a fisherman to try to recover it, but the man drew up instead a small casket.

Liu opened the casket and found it full of priceless jewels, pearls, and other treasures. He rewarded the fisherman handsomely and placed the casket at the head of his bed, intending to look at its contents more closely when he was at leisure. That night, he saw a girl in a dream coming over the waves; as he looked at her, he recognized her as Shih-niang. She came up to him, curtseyed, and related to him how faithless Li had proved.

"You were generous enough to help me with one hundred and fifty taels," she said to Liu. "At that time I thought I could repay you after we had overcome our difficulties, not knowing what was to befall me. Although I was unable to repay you in person I have not forgotten your kindness. So this morning I sent you this casket through the fisherman to express my gratitude. Now farewell. We shall never meet again." Liu awoke with a start. Only then did he realize that Shih-niang was

[14] Kua-pu, to the southeast of Liu-ho in Kiangsu, is not the same place where the drowning incident takes place. Kua-pu is further upstream along the Yangtze River.

159

dead. For the next several days he could not but sigh for her.

Later generations, commenting on this incident, condemned Sun for his wickedness in his plot to obtain a beautiful girl for a thousand taels of silver. Li was no less than a common fool to have failed to appreciate Shih-niang's heart. For this he was not even worth one's contempt. As for Shih-niang, who was such an extraordinary woman, it was a tragedy that instead of finding a husband worthy of her and leading a life she deserved, she had to waste her affection on Li Chia. Indeed, it was like rendering bright pearls and rare jade to a blind man. It is truly pitiable that her love should have turned to hate, and that all her affection was gone with the flowing river. Appropriately, the following poem glosses the episode:

If you know not how to love, do not talk about it;
"Love," this single word, is too profound to comprehend.
If indeed you have fully comprehended it,
Call yourself a lover; you have no reason to be ashamed.

THE DEDICATED LOVER

With the possible exception of the oil peddler in the story of that name, none of the heroes in this group can make any real claim to being "dedicated" lovers. True to E. D. Edwards' observation, the Chinese "nominal hero is generally a quite unheroic person who, on finding a maiden in distress, sinks into a kind of physical and mental decline under the strain of trying to evolve a plan of rescue" (*Chinese Prose Literature of the T'ang Period,* II, 22). Quite naturally, it normally takes a woman to affirm the value of love. Such is the case of Pu Fei-yen. When waylaid by her husband during one of their rendezvous, her lover Chao Hsiang immediately takes to his heels, leaving Fei-yen to face the terrible consequence of adulterous passion. Not only does he fail to plan a rescue; he is never heard from again. Fei-yen, unrepentant, pays the dear price of love with her life. From her passion and suffering, she is certainly one of the most memorable of the female characters in traditional Chinese fiction who have experienced what Denis de Rougemont has called the "exquisite anguish" of love.

Sometimes, however, a woman's dedication to a man may result in a paradoxical form of love. Chu To-fu in "The Couple Bound in Life and Death" is one such example. Upon learning that her betrothed has contracted leprosy, she becomes all the more determined to serve Ch'en To-shou as a wedded wife, in spite of her mother's repeated remonstrations and the objections of her fiancé, who proposes canceling the marriage contract. Day in and day out she washes his wounds like a saint in Western hagiographical literature. In keeping with the Chinese cosmological scheme of a benign Heaven, her virtue is finally rewarded with the miraculous recovery of her husband, the birth of two beautiful children, and the success of Ch'en To-shou in the civil service examinations. To see To-fu as a "dedicated lover," however, is only one side of the story. She can be a totally different person if one chooses to examine her from a different perspective.

THE COURTESAN LI WA

From *I-wen chi*

TRANSLATED BY PETER RUSHTON AND THE EDITORS

Lady Ch'ien, Li Wa, used to be a courtesan in Ch'ang-an. Her behavior was so high-principled and exalted that it merits praise. It is for this reason that I, Po Hsing-chien,[1] an investigating censor, have made an account of her story.

During the T'ien-pao reign period [742–756],[2] the prefect of Ch'ang-chou[3] was a nobleman of Ying-yang.[4] His surname and given name I shall omit. His reputation was high among his contemporaries, and he was very wealthy. When he had reached the age of fifty, his only son was just twenty years old. His son was highly gifted in literature, and this marked him off from his peers. He was well thought of and praised by the people of his day. His father doted on him, and regarded him highly. He once remarked, "This is the thousand-*li* steed of our house."

After he had become a *hsiu-ts'ai* through the local examinations, he was about to set out [for the capital to take more advanced examinations]. His father amply provided him with all the accoutrements he would need, including horse and carriage; he also estimated his son's expenses in the capital and gave him funds accordingly. The father said, "When I look upon your talents, I'm sure that you'll make it in this first attempt. Now I've made provision for you for a full two years; I've given you more than needed to encourage you."

The young man was also confident of his own abilities. He saw his excelling in the examinations as a matter of course. From P'i-ling[5] he set out, and in little more than a month he reached Ch'ang-an. He settled in the Administration Quarter.

Once, as he was returning from touring the East Market, he passed through the east gate of the Blissful Quarter on his way to visit a friend in the southwestern section of the city. When he reached Jingle Lane he noticed a private residence whose gate and courtyard were not particularly large; but the house itself was deep and imposing. Only one of the doors of the gate was closed. A young beautiful girl, dressed in bluish green and with her hair arranged in a double knot, stood leaning on her maid. Her coquettish charm and manner were peerless. He caught sight of her and unwittingly stopped his horse, pausing

[1] Po Hsing-chien (776–826) was the younger brother of the poet Po Chü-yi.

[2] T'ien-pao is the title of the last of the three reign periods of the T'ang emperor Hsüan-tsung.

[3] Ch'ang-chou in modern Kiangsu Province.

[4] In central modern Honan Province, just to the south of the Yellow River.

[5] Another name for Ch'ang-chou (see footnote 3).

for a long while. In his indecision he could not bring himself to move on. He pretended to loose his grip on his whip, dropped it to the ground, and waited for his servant to pick it up. His gaze was fixed on the girl, who in turn looked back at him with an equally fascinated gaze. By now they were deeply drawn to each other. Finally, unable to summon the courage to speak up, he went on.

From then on, his mind was distracted. He secretly inquired about her among those friends of his who were familiar with Ch'ang-an. "That is the residence of the courtesan named Li," said a friend.

"Is she available?"

"She is rather rich. Most of her usual patrons are either nobles or from influential families; her income is sizable. If you aren't willing to spend a million in cash, you won't be able to move her."

"My only worry is that I may not be able to get acquainted with her. What's a million to me!"

One day he put on his best clothes and, with a host of attendants following, he set out for the house. A knock at the gate shortly drew forth a maid to open the door. "Can you tell me whose household this is?" asked the young man.

The maid did not reply, but quickly ran back in with the cry, "Here's the gentleman who dropped his whip the other day."

Greatly delighted, Li said, "Ask him in. Let me put on some makeup and change my clothes."

When he heard this, he was secretly flattered. He was led inside the courtyard, where he saw an older woman with long white hair and a somewhat hunched posture. She was Li's procuress. He bowed politely and said to her, "I've heard that you have a vacant apartment. If this is the case, I want to rent it for my lodgings."

"I fear that such a small, run-down place would not be good enough for you. How could I mention the rent?"

She then invited him into the guest's quarters, which were elegant. She sat down with him and began to chat. "I've a young daughter of limited talent, but she enjoys entertaining guests. I'd like you to meet her."

She then called for the girl to come out. She had bright eyes and white wrists, and carried herself with grace and charm. He got up nervously, not daring to look at her. After they had greeted each other, they began to chat casually. Such alluring beauty as this he had never seen before. Then they sat down again and had tea and wine together. The service ware was impeccable.

They talked for a long time until night drew on, and the sound of the watch drum could be heard from all directions. The older woman asked how far away he lived. He said mendaciously, "I'm staying several *li* outside the Lasting Peace Gate."

He hoped they would ask him to stay because of the distance. However, the mother said, "The drum has already sounded; you ought hurry back so as not to break the [curfew] law."

"This delightful conversation with you has been such a pleasure that I didn't notice the day had turned to night. It's such a long distance, and I've no relatives in the city. What am I to do?"

"Since you aren't put off by this rustic place and have already decided to move in here," the girl suggested, "what harm would there be in staying overnight?"

The young man anxiously looked at the old woman a few times, and she consented.

He then called for his valet to bring in two rolls of fine silk, requesting that they take these as compensation for the evening's fare. The girl laughed and refused: "That is not the proper way for guest and host. This evening's expenditure should be on the house. You may entertain us some other time." She firmly declined his offer, and stuck to her words all the way.

Shortly they moved to the western hall, where the curtains, screens, window, and couches were all of brilliant splendor, and the dressing-case, coverlets, and pillows were all of luxurious elegance. Presently candles were set forth and the meal brought in; the dishes were both plentiful and excellent. After supper, the old woman retired. Then the conversation between the young man and the girl grew more intimate, with jokes and laughter; there was no topic they would not touch upon.

"Since I happened to pass by your gate and saw you standing in the doorway the other day," he said, "my heart has been with you. Sleeping or eating I could not forget you."

"My heart has been like that as well," she responded.

"I didn't come here today simply in search of a place to live. Rather I wish to fulfill a lifelong ambition. Yet I don't know what my fate will be."

Before he had finished what he had to say, the old woman came in and asked what they were discussing. They told her everything. The old woman smiled and said, "It's only natural that a young man and a young woman should desire each other. If their feelings for each other are mutual, even their parents cannot call for restraint. But my daughter is so lowly; how is she fit to share a bed with you, sir?"

He got down from the dais, bowed and thanked her. "I'd like to take the responsibility of providing for you," he said.

So the old woman assented and took him as her son-in-law. They drank deeply and then parted for the evening. The following day the young man had all his belongings moved in, to live in the Li family.

From then on, he retreated from the circles of his friends and relatives. He spent his time in the company of muscians, entertainers, and the like, indulging in all sorts of wantonness. He grew intimate with the actors, and became something of a partygoer. When his money was exhausted, he sold his horse, carriage, and valet. In a little over a year he had squandered everything. Before long the old woman's attentions to him slackened, but

Li's affection remained as genuine and passionate as ever.

One day the girl said to him, "I've known you for a year, yet I'm still without child. I've heard that the god of the Bamboo Grove answers requests like an echo. Should we go and offer sacrifices to him?"

He had no idea that this was a scheme and was greatly delighted. He pawned his clothes at a shop in order to buy sacrificial meat and wine. Then they went to the temple to worship and lodged there for two nights before starting back. He rode a donkey behind the girl's carriage. When they reached the north gate of the [All Radiance] Quarter, she said to him, "My aunt's house is on the little street which turns east. Could we call on her and rest a bit?"

He agreed to what she proposed and, without walking more than a hundred paces, he saw a carriage gate. Through the gate he spied a spacious courtyard. One of the maidservants came up from behind the carriage and stopped him saying, "We've arrived." He got down off his donkey. Just then a maid came out and asked, "Who is it?" The girl responded, "It is Li Wa."

The maid then went in to announce their arrival. Shortly a woman, somewhat over forty, came out. Welcoming the young man she asked, "Has my niece come?"

Li Wa got out of the carriage. The woman greeted her, asking, "Why has it been so long since you last came?"

They looked at each other and smiled. Li Wa then brought the young man forward and asked him to bow. Then together they entered the side courtyard by the western gate. In the courtyard were artificial mountains, pavilions, bamboo trees, lush shrubbery, and ponds—truly a secluded place. He asked the girl, "Is this your aunt's private residence?"

She smiled and did not answer, but changed the subject. In a moment tea and fruits of exotic kinds

165

were served. A short time later, a man, sweating profusely, galloped up and reined in a Ferghana[6] horse to announce, "Your mother has suddenly fallen very ill. She can't even recognize us. You must return at once."

"I'm greatly disturbed," Li Wa said to her aunt. "I'll take the carriage and go back first. When I get home I'll send the carriage back; then the two of you can come along together."

He wanted to accompany her back. But the aunt and a maid whispered for a while and then signaled him to wait outside, telling him, "She might die at any time. We should discuss the matter of the funeral to help them through this crisis. What good will it do to go running off after her?" So he stayed, and together they calculated the cost of the funeral rites.

As night drew on and the carriage had not yet arrived, the aunt observed, "I wonder why no message has been sent back? Why don't you run along and find out what has happened? I'll be right behind you."

So the young man set out. When he reached the place the gate was locked tight and sealed with mortar. He was alarmed at this and inquired of the neighbors, who said, "They only rented this place. The lease was up and the landlord took back the house. The old woman has already been gone for two nights now."

"Do you know where they moved to?"

"We've no idea."

Then he intended to rush back to the All Radiance Quarter to check with the aunt, but by this time it was quite late. He figured that he would not be able to make it that evening, so he pawned his clothes for something to eat and a place to spend the night. However, he was so infuriated that from dusk to dawn he was not able to sleep. At dawn he urged his nag on. When he arrived, he pounded steadily on the door; but for a long

time there was no response. He then shouted loudly several times, which finally brought forth a servant who ambled out. He accosted the servant, asking, "Is the aunt in?"

"No such person."

"But last night she was here. Why is she hiding?"

When he asked whose home it was, he got the reply: "This is Minister Ts'ui's place. Yesterday someone rented it, saying they were receiving a cousin from afar. They left before dusk."

The young man was so shaken by this that he was delirious. Not knowing what to do, he went back to the old place in the Administration Quarter. The landlord took pity on him and offered him a meal, but he was so full of resentment that he could not eat for three days and became seriously ill.

Over the following ten days his illness grew even worse. The landlord began to fear that he would not recover, so he moved him to a mortuary. For some time, he appeared to be on the verge of death. The men at the mortuary took pity on him, and helped him out by offering him food. Later he recovered to the point where he could get up with the aid of a cane. The owner of the mortuary then put him to work. He was instructed to hold the ropes of the hearses. In this way he earned his keep. After some months he gradually regained his strength.

Each time he heard the funeral dirges, he would lament that he was not even as lucky as the dead, and he would sob and weep, quite incapable of restraining himself. When he returned home he would try to imitate the songs. As he was clever and intelligent, in a little while he could bring out all the subtleties of each song. There was not a singer in Ch'ang-an who could compare with him.

Now there were two mortuaries competing with each other. The one to the east had particularly elegant hearses, almost without peer. Their singers, however, were rather mediocre. The owner of the mortuary knew of this young man's

---

[6] Ferghana Valley in the Central Asian USSR. The Chinese province of Sinkiang borders the region in the southeast. Medieval China used to depend on this region for good horses.

talent. He came up with twenty thousand in cash and employed him. The veteran singers there all did their best to train the young man; they secretly taught him how to compose songs and sang in harmony with him. This went on for more than ten days without anyone outside knowing it.

The owners of the two mortuaries made an announcement: "Each shop will display its funeral supplies on the Heavenly Gate Street, so that the people can compare them and determine which one excels. The loser will pay fifty thousand to cover the cost of wine and food." The two parties agreed to this and drew up a contract which was signed by witnesses before they held the exhibition.

Men and women gathered by the tens of thousands. The neighborhood headmen informed the chief of police, who in turn reported it to the mayor of the capital. Men from all parts of the city came for the occasion, so many that the streets were deserted. From early morning until midday the exhibition went on. One after another the carriages, hearses, and ceremonial trappings were brought forward. The mortuary to the west was able to excel in nothing and its owner grew shamefaced.

So he set up a platform in the south corner of the ground. A man with a long beard came forward, holding a handbell and surrounded by several attendants. Swaying his beard and raising his eyebrows, he held his wrist, and then bowed and ascended the platform. He sang the "White Horse" lyric. With the air of assuming a sure victory, he glanced here and there as if no other singers of consequence existed. Unanimous was the sound of his admirers' praise. He thought himself to be without rival in his day, and that no one could humble him.

Later, the owner of the eastern mortuary assembled a platform in the north corner. A youth in a black cap came forward with a feather fan in his hand, accompanied by several attendants. It was none other than the young man of our story.

He adjusted his clothes and gazed up and down with composure. He then cleared his throat and began to sing with polished grace the elegy "Dew on the Shallots." His voice was clear and transcendent, even stirring the trees. Before he had finished, many in the audience wept.

As a result, the owner of the western mortuary became the object of mockery and he felt more humiliated. He quietly brought forth the amount he had lost and slipped away. Those present were all surprised by the outcome, as no one knew who this young singer was.

Previously the emperor had issued an edict, calling on the district administrators to appear once a year at court; this was known as the "Entry for Reckoning." It was during that time of the year that the young man's father was in the capital. Together with some of his colleagues he had changed into more common dress, and gone incognito to view the exhibition.

An old servant, the husband of the young man's wet nurse, seeing his movements and his voice, was about to accost him but did not dare. Unconsciously he wept; this startled the young man's father. He asked the servant about it, and the servant replied, "The singer's manner greatly resembles master's lost son."

To this the father replied, "My son was murdered by thieves for his wealth. How could it be he?" When he had finished speaking, he also cried.

After they had returned to their lodgings, the servant caught an opportunity and rushed back to check with some of the undertakers: "Who is the person who just sang? How could he be so superb?"

"Some noble family's son," they replied.

He asked for his name, but the young man had already changed it. The servant was shocked by this, but he managed to get close to the young man and examined him all over. Seeing the servant, the young man lost his poise and turned around to flee, trying to conceal himself in the

167

crowd. The servant grabbed his sleeve, "Are you not so-and-so?" They embraced each other and wept. The servant then took him home.

When they arrived, the father lashed out at his son: "Your behaving in this manner brings disgrace upon our family. How dare you show yourself here again!"

Whereupon the father took him out to a spot west of Crooked Creek Pond and east of Apricot Park. He stripped his son and used a horse whip to flog him several hundred times. The young man, overcame by pain, fell unconscious. The father left him for dead.

The youth's music instructor had asked some of his intimates to secretly follow him and keep an eye on him. They returned to report what had happened to his fellow singers; they all sighed with grief at his plight. Two men were ordered to go there with rush mats to bury him. When they arrived they found that his heart still had a bit of warmth. Some time after being helped up, he began to breathe slightly, whereupon they carried him back. They fed him some broth through a reed tube, and after passing the night he regained some consciousness. But for over a month he was unable to move his limbs.

The wounds on his body festered and burst, giving off such a vile stench that it bothered his companions. One night they abandoned him by the side of the road. The people who walked the streets all took pity on him. Often they would toss him some leftover food and in this way he was saved from starvation.

In about three months he could get up with the aid of a stick. His cotton robe, knotted in a hundred places, looked like a bunch of quails strung up together. With a broken bowl he roamed the neighborhood begging for food.

As autumn gave way to winter, at night he would take cover in the sewers and caves. During the day he went about the markets and shops. One day a heavy snow fell. Driven by cold and hunger, however, he still had to go out in spite of the snow. The sound of his begging was painfully moving and all who heard him could not help but be saddened by it. The snow was so deep that the doors of most households were shut. He reached the east gate of the Felicity Quarter. Turning north and following the wall, at the seventh or eighth house he found one gate with the left door open. This was Li Wa's house, though he had no knowledge of it. Cold and hunger made his wails still louder. It was a pathetic sound one could not bear to hear.

Li Wa heard it from her chamber, and said to her servant, "It must be him; I recognize the sound of his voice." She hurried out and saw him, wizened, thin, broken out in sores, barely looking human. Touched by his plight, she asked, "Is that you?"

He was so resentful and angry that he could not speak; he could only bring himself to nod at her. Li Wa came forward and embraced his neck. Bundling him in her embroidered robe, she took him to the western chamber. Almost speechless with grief, she said, "That he has come to this is all my fault." She then fainted.

When she revived, her mother, greatly agitated, rushed in: "What's going on?"

"It is he," replied Li Wa.

Her mother responded quickly, "Send him away. Why bring him here?"

But Li Wa pulled herself together and said, "Impossible. He is the son of a noble family. When he first came to our place, he drove a grand carriage and was in fine attire. In less than a year he spent all he had. We swindled him and threw him out. That was inhuman. We have ruined his career and made him an outcast from his family. The relationship between father and son is one of nature. We broke this bond of affection to the point where his father beat him and left him for dead. That's why he's come to these straits. Everyone knows who brought him to this. His relatives fill the court. One day those in power will look into this matter from beginning to end. Then calamity will fall upon us. What is more, if we deceive Heaven and turn our backs on men, the gods and spirits won't be on our side. Let's not give further cause for our ruin. Now I've been your daughter for twenty years, and I should have brought you no less than a thousand taels. You're over sixty. I wish to give you enough for twenty years of living expenses to redeem my freedom. We'll live in a place close by, so that we can still pay our respects to you daily. I should be most grateful to you if you would allow me to do this."

The old woman could see that the girl was not to be dissuaded; so she consented. After paying her mother, Li Wa had one hundred taels left. She rented a place a few houses north. She then bathed the young man and changed his clothes. She fed him some rich gruel to clean out his stomach; then she gave him some milk products to condition his intestines. Only after more than ten days did she dare offer him various delicacies from land and sea. The hats, shoes, and socks that she gave him were all of the finest quality. After a few months, he began to regain his weight. At the close of the year, he was fully recovered.

Li Wa on one occasion said to him, "Now your health is back to normal, and so is your will. If you spend some time collecting yourself, do you think you can still remember what you learned before?"

The young man thought this over: "I think I've retained two or three things out of ten."

Li Wa ordered a carriage and went out, with him following behind on horseback. When they reached the bookstores at the south gate of the Flag Tower, she told him to select whatever books he needed. This came to about one hundred taels. They loaded up all the books and drove back home.

She told him to forget about everything but setting his will on his studies. Turning night into day, he applied himself untiringly. Li Wa would often sit by his side, and they would not go to sleep until midnight. When she saw him growing tired of studying, she would tell him to compose some verse or rhyme-prose.

After two years, his study brought substantial results. He had read all the books available. "Now I should register for the examination," he said to Li Wa.

"Not yet. You must be thoroughly versed in your studies in anticipation of a hundred battles."

Another year passed, and Li Wa said he could now sit for the examination. He became a *chin-shih* of the first rank at the very first attempt, which made him known throughout the Ministry of Rites. The older scholars read his essays with great admiration. They wanted to befriend him, but did not have the opportunity of doing so.

"You still have a long way to go," Li Wa said. "Today, if one manages to become a *chin-shih* he thinks that he is entitled to an eminent position at court and has already attained renown everywhere. But your past conduct was scandalous, so in this respect you're not the equal of others. You must make further preparation to win again. Only then can you emerge supreme among the scholars and outshine the very best."

So he made even greater demands upon himself, and his reputation rose accordingly. That year happened to be the one for the special examination which was set up to recruit the best talents in the country. He took part in the examination for "Government Criticism and Advice to the Emperor"; his name came out first on the list. He received an appointment as the head of a bureau at the Ch'eng-tu Prefecture.[7] By then he had made many friends of various ranks and positions at court.

When it came time for him to take up his post, Li Wa said to him, "Now that you've been restored to your original station, and I've proven to you that I'm not an ingrate, for the rest of my years, I wish to return home to look after my

[7] The provincial capital of modern Szechwan Province, on the western side of the central Szechwan basin.

169

mother. You ought to marry a young woman of a prominent family, who can manage the household for you. Marriage is a serious business; don't ruin it for yourself. Think about it and take good care of yourself. It's time for me to say good-bye."

This brought him to tears: "If you leave me, I'll slit my throat."

Li Wa was determined to go. He did his best to convince her that he was unquestionably sincere in begging her to stay. She said, "I'll accompany you across the river [Yangtze] to Chien-men;[8] then you must let me go." He agreed.

In a little more than a month they had reached Chien-men. Before they set out again, the government gazette arrived. The young man's father had been summoned from Ch'ang-chou to the capital to be appointed prefect of Ch'eng-tu and simultaneously investigating commissioner of the Chien-nan Circuit.

When his father arrived ten days later, the young man sent his calling card and subsequently had an audience with him at the courier station. At first his father did not believe the caller was his son. But seeing his grandfather's and father's official titles and personal names on the card, he was astounded. He asked his son to ascend the dais; thereupon he took him into his arms and wept bitterly. It was some time before he could say, "Now we're father and son, just as it was before."

Since his father wanted to know what had happened, the young man give a detailed account from beginning to end. The father was astonished by it. He asked where Li Wa was.

"She has accompanied me this far, but she insists that I should send her back."

"You couldn't do that."

The next day the father ordered a carriage, and with his son first went on to Ch'eng-tu. He left Li Wa at Chien-men after acquiring a suitable residence for her. The following day he dispatched a matchmaker to arrange a formal marriage proposal and to prepare the six rites for the occasion.[9] Subsequently the young man and Li Wa were married.

Through the years, Li Wa proved herself to be a perfect wife. She kept the household strictly in order, so she was well loved by her relatives.

Some years later, the young man's father and mother both died. He maintained filial conduct to the utmost. In the hut he stayed in during the mourning period, a mythical stalk in the shape of a mushroom grew. The grain stalks in his district all had three blossoms. These events were duly reported to the higher authorities. There were also numerous white swallows nesting in his rafters. The emperor regarded these events as extremely unusual and accordingly he bestowed upon him many favors. After the mourning period, he was successively promoted from one illustrious post to another. In ten years he had attained several prefectships. Li Wa was honored with the title of Lady Ch'ien.[10]

They had four sons, and all of them attained high office, the lowest being prefect of T'ai-yüan. The sons all married girls of the most illustrious of families. Thus their entire household flourished, and no families were on a par with them. Ah, that a mere courtesan should comport herself so properly! Even the virtuous women of the past could not compare with her. How can one not marvel at this?

My great-uncle was once the prefect of Chin-chou.[11] Later he was transferred to the Ministry of Finance and finally to the post of commissioner of water and land transport. In these three posts he was the successor of the young man of this story. He was therefore fully acquainted with the details of this affair. In the Chen-yüan reign

[8] To the northeast of Chien-ko County in northern modern Szechwan.

[9] The six rites are the six stages from sending gifts to the bride's home to the final marriage ceremony.

[10] Ch'ien is Ch'ien-yang County in modern Shensi Province. Whether this place has anything to do with her title is not clear.

[11] Lin-fen County in modern Shansi Province.

period [785–806], I had occasion to talk with Li Kung-tso of Lung-hsi [12] about women of virtuous character, and so I told him the story of Lady Ch'ien. He clapped his hands and listened in awe.

[12] Lung-hsi in T'ang times covered the southeastern part of the present Kansu Province. Li Kung-tso (fl. 819) was the author of many famous *ch'uan-ch'i* stories, including "The Governor of the Southern Tributary State" ("Nan-k'o t'ai-shou chuan"), which is not included in this anthology because it is almost a direct descendant of "The World Inside a Pillow."

He insisted that I write it down. So I took up my brush, dipped it in ink, and sketched this story for the record. It was the eighth month in the autumn of the twelfth year of the calendar cycle [795],[13] the recorder being Po Hsing-chien of T'ai-yüan.

[13] This date is wrong. According to Tai Wang-shu, it should be the twenty-first year of Chen-yüan (805).

171

THE TRAGEDY OF PU FEI-YEN

From *San-shui hsiao-tu*

TRANSLATED BY JEANNE KELLY

Wu Kung-yeh of Lin-huai[1] was an administrative assistant of the Ho-nan Prefecture[2] during the Hsien-t'ung reign period [860–873].[3] His favorite concubine was called Fei-yen, from the Pu family. So delicate and fine were her looks and manner, she seemed barely able to support the weight of a garment of thin silk. She was good at singing the tunes of Ch'in,[4] enjoyed literary pursuits, and was especially skilled at tapping the pitch cups to the harmony of strings and flutes. Kung-yeh doted on her.

Adjacent to their house was the residence of Chao of T'ien-shui,[5] also a member of a prominent family. His son Hsiang, both handsome and learned, had just turned twenty and at this time was at home observing mourning rites.

One day Hsiang happened to spy Fei-yen through a crack in the south wall, and from then on became so despondent that he began to lose sleep and neglected his meals. He offered a generous bribe to Kung-yeh's doorkeeper to tell Fei-yen of his feelings. The doorkeeper appeared very reluctant at first, but finally gave in to the

generous offer and told his wife to wait until Fei-yen had an idle moment, when she could tell her of Hsiang's interest. When Fei-yen heard of this, she merely smiled and stared ahead fixedly without replying. The old servant conveyed all this to Hsiang, who went wild with joy, not knowing how to contain himself. He then chose a sheet of red, lined paper and wrote the following lines:

One look at your devastating beauty
Has thrown my mind in confusion.
Since I cannot fly to heaven to meet with you,
I hope instead you will descend to earth.

He sealed the poem and asked the doorkeeper's wife to take it to Fei-yen.

When Fei-yen read it, she sighed for quite a while and said to the old woman, "I, too, once had a glimpse of Mr. Chao. He is certainly talented and handsome. How unfortunate I am in this life not to have been given to him in marriage." This was because she despised Wu for his rude ways and violent temper, feeling that it was a poor match. She then reciprocated with a poem, writing on gilt phoenix paper:

The gloom that furrows my brows
Is only from the dark laments in the new poem.
Since your heart is so full of grief,
To whom will I unburden my passion?

[1] In modern Anhwei Province.
[2] Lo-yang was the site of the prefectural administration of the Ho-nan Prefecture in T'ang times.
[3] The only reign period of the T'ang emperor Yi-tsung.
[4] Approximately the present Shensi Province.
[5] In modern Kansu Province.

172

She sealed it and gave it to the old woman to deliver to Hsiang.

When Hsiang opened the letter, he chanted it aloud several times and, clapping his hands, cried joyfully, "My affair is going well!" Then, on jade-leaf paper, he wrote a poem to thank her:

Grateful I am to the lovely one who sent the welcome words.
Deep are the feelings in the tinted paper and scented ink.
On paper thin as cicada wings my grief is hard to convey.
In characters as tiny as a fly's head, I cannot tell all that is in
*   my heart.*
Perhaps the fallen flowers have covered the path to the cave of
*   the fairies.*
I only sense the light rain seep beneath my collar.
Your image comes to me a hundred times at rest, a thousand
*   times in my dreams.*
I cut out paper for a long verse in which to open my heart.

For ten days after the poem had been sent, the doorkeeper's wife did not return. Hsiang began to worry, fearing that either the affair had been discovered or Fei-yen had grown remorseful.

One spring evening, sitting alone in the front courtyard, he wrote a poem:

In the green and ruddy darkness, dim clouds rise.
I am alone with my grief in the small front yard.
Immersed in this deep and lovely night, whom can I speak to?
A star is parted from the Milky Way and the moon is alone
*   in the sky.*

Hsiang got up early the next morning and was just reciting this verse when the old woman arrived. She had a message from Fei-yen: "Don't feel upset because I've sent you no letter for the last ten days. I haven't been feeling well." She sent Hsiang a scented brocade purse and some green-tinted paper on which was written a poem:

Too weak to finish dressing, I lean on the decorated window
*   frame.*
Burdened with emotion, secretly I inscribe a poem on the
*   brocade.*
I have of late been afflicted with spring longing,
Becoming like the weak willows and leaning flowers that fear
*   the morning breeze.*

Hsiang tied the brocade purse close to his bosom. Carefully reading the note, he became fearful that Fei-yen's brooding would worsen her condition. He then cut a sheet of thin silk paper to write her a reply note:

Spring is so prolonged, while the heart is so full of cares. Since my first glimpse of you, your image has dominated my dreams. Even if you were a fairy, it would still be difficult for me, a groundling, to meet you. My heart, however, is as true as the bright sun, and I vow to fulfill my hopes. Yesterday the green messenger bird of the Jade Terrace[6] suddenly descended, bringing word from you. The gift of the scented, brocade purse, I wear close to my breast, where its sweet fragrance makes you seem closer to me. When I heard that you were overcome with passion, and have been indisposed, that your delicate nature is suffering, I was beside myself with worry, wishing I could fly to your side. I hope that you will relax and not become overwrought. Please do not be sparing with your short poems; I would rather break off some later appointment. How can I say everything in a letter with my mind so distracted? I enclose these meager lines of poetry and look forward to your reply.

You say you suffer at the coming of spring.
I imagine how you knit your dark eyebrows as you wrapped
*   the brocade.*
Respectfully I say to my dear Fei-yen,
This kind of involvement can cause the most pain of all.

The old woman went straight to Fei-yen's chamber with this reply. In his job as an administrative assistant, Wu Kung-yeh was extremely busy. Sometimes he would not return home for a whole day; sometimes he would have a night shift once every few days. At this time, it just happened that he was on duty at his office. Fei-yen opened the letter and read it through carefully to catch all the subtler meanings conveyed. She then heaved a long sigh and said, "The inclinations of his heart are the very thoughts on my mind. We're so alike

[6] An abode of the fairies.

173

in soul and spirit. Though we seem far apart, it is really as though we were very close." She then closed the door, let down the curtains and wrote him a letter in reply:

> I have been unfortunate in life. I was orphaned when young and later, deceived by a matchmaker, I was given to a despicable creature. On nights when the moon is bright and the breeze is crisp, I play the zither to unburden my heart. On bleak autumn days and dark winter nights, I entrust my grief to its tunes. Never had I expected that suddenly I would receive a message from you. When I read your letter, my thoughts flew to you; when I read your beautiful poems, I strained my eyes trying to see you. I only grieve that the Lo River has separated us. I would like to be the girl Chia Wu,[7] but the wall is too high to climb. Even traversing the clouds, I will never reach the Ch'in Tower.[8] The cavern where Ch'u encountered the goddess is beyond even my dreams.[9] I still hope Heaven will respond to my earnest plea, and the gods will grant us the chance to meet. Then should I die, it would be without regrets. I enclose a few short lines to confide my deepest feelings:

> *The spring swallows in the painted eaves must return together to nest.*
> *Would the ducks from the Lo riverbank ever fly alone?*
> *Often I grieve at how the maidens of the peach valley*
> *So carelessly sent their lover back home from amid the flowers.*

Sealing the envelope, she summoned the old maidservant and told her to give it to Hsiang.

When Hsiang had read the letter and the poem, he felt that Fei-yen was expressing even greater intimacy and could not control himself in his joy. Then, in a quiet chamber he burned incense and made offerings, preparing for the right moment to come.

Suddenly one day toward evening the old maid-servant arrived in haste. Smiling, she bowed and asked, "Does Mr. Chao wish to meet the goddess?" Startled, Hsiang plied her with questions. She then relayed Fei-yen's message: "Tonight my master will be at his office. This will be the most opportune time. Our rear garden adjoins your front wall. If your feelings for me still remain, I'll look forward to your coming. Ten thousand thoughts that fill my mind all await our meeting to be spoken."

When it grew dark, Hsiang climbed up the wall on a ladder. Fei-yen had already had thick bedding piled underneath. When he descended he saw Fei-yen, exquisitely attired, standing by the flowers. Exchanging bows, both were too over-joyed to speak. Arm in arm, they entered the house through the back door, lowered the curtains, covered the lamp, and gave themselves over to a night of consuming passion. Not until the morning gong sounded at the break of day did Fei-yen see Chao to the bottom of the wall. She took his hand and said amid tears, "Our meeting today was determined in a previous existence. Don't ever think that I'm not of an upright and pure nature, or that I'm dissolute in behavior. It is only because of your noble manner and bearing that I haven't been able to check my emotions. I hope you'll understand this."

Hsiang replied, "You're so beautiful and so kind. I've already given my solemn pledge to serve you forever in happiness." At this, Hsiang climbed over the wall and returned to his home.

The next day he asked the old maidservant to present Fei-yen with this poem:

Though the way to the dwelling of the goddesses is blocked,
One whose heart is true can still approach the Jade Terrace.
The breeze wafts a fragrance which recalls the deep night to mind,
And I know that in the palace of heaven the goddess is about to arrive.

Fei-yen smiled as she read it and then wrote the following poem in return:

---

[7] The girl Chia Wu of the Chin Dynasty stole some incense, given to her father by the emperor, for her lover.
[8] A tower built by Duke Mu of the state of Ch'in of the Spring and Autumn period for his daughter.
[9] This refers to the meeting between King Hsiang of the state of Ch'u and a goddess at the Wu Mountain.

Though we think of each other, I only fear we are barely
*   acquainted.*
When we meet, I still worry that in a moment we must part.
I wish I could become a crane beneath a pine tree,
And together with my mate fly up into the clouds.

After sealing the letter she gave it to the maidservant, asking her to tell Hsiang, "How fortunate it is that I have a little knowledge of poetry. Otherwise, who would there be to appreciate your great talent?"

After this, no more than ten days would pass without the two meeting in the back garden to confide their intimate thoughts and long pent-up feelings, thinking that even the gods and spirits knew nothing of their affair, while all on earth and in heaven were helping them. They gazed at the scenes around them, and composed poems to express their feelings, unable to put down all they felt despite constant visits together. A full year passed in this way.

It happened that Fei-yen had on several occasions beaten one of her maids over some trifling mistake. For this, the maid bore a secret grudge and took an opportunity to tell all to Kung-yeh, who cautioned her, "Don't speak of this. I'll spy on her."

Later, when it came time for him to be on duty, he made up an excuse and asked for a leave of absence. Toward evening, he set off for his office as usual but then hid himself near the outside gate. When the street gong sounded, he crept back along the wall to the backyard, from where he could see Fei-yen leaning against the window, humming softly. Then Hsiang peered at Fei-yen from over the wall. Unable to contain his rage, Wu lunged forward to seize him. Realizing what was happening, Hsiang fled. Kung-yeh grabbed at him but only caught hold of half his jacket. He then entered the room and called Fei-yen to question her. The color had drained from her face, and her voice trembled. But she would not tell him the truth. More incensed than ever, Kung-yeh bound her to a tall pillar and whipped her

until the blood flowed. All she said was, "Since my life has been blessed with love, I feel no regret at meeting death."

In the middle of the night Kung-yeh became tired and left to sleep for a while. Fei-yen called her favorite maid and said, "Get me a cup of water." When the water was brought, she drank it down and then expired. Kung-yeh arose and prepared to resume the whipping but found her already dead. He then undid the rope and carried her to her room where he called her name several times, and declared that she had died of a sudden illness. After several days, he buried her on the slope of the Pei-mang Hill.[10] All in the neighborhood, however, knew of her violent death.

Hsiang changed his clothes, assumed the name of Yüan, and escaped far away to the vicinity of the Yangtze and Che rivers.[11]

In Lo-yang were two scholars named Ts'ui and Li, who were regular companions of Wu. Ts'ui wrote a poem [when he heard the story of Fei-yen]. The last two lines were as follows:

After the flower-passing game,[12] the drinking guests departed;
On an empty bed the most luxuriant branch was thrown.

That night Ts'ui dreamed that Fei-yen came to thank him. "Though my face cannot be compared with peach blossoms, I have suffered a fate much more wretched. I receive your beautiful lines with shame."

The last lines of Li's poem were as follows:

Her sweet soul and charming spirit seem to be present,
When she should be ashamed to meet the faithful wife Green
*   Pearl.[13]*

During the night he dreamed that Fei-yen pointed her finger at him: "It is said, 'Scholars

[10] A hill outside the city of Lo-yang.
[11] In this context, "Chiang-che" cannot possibly stand for the present provinces of Chekiang and Kiangsu, though it refers to approximately the same geographical area.
[12] This was a party game. A bowl of lotus flowers was passed around, and each guest picked a petal. The first one to get the bowl after the last petal was gone had to sing.
[13] For the story of Green Pearl, see the preamble in the story

175

have a hundred virtues.' Do you, then, possess them all? Why do you malign others with such scathing remarks? You should be called down to the court below for cross-examination."

A few days later, Li passed away. His contemporaries found it all very strange.

Chao Yüan was later transferred to the Ju-chou Prefecture[14] to become the county registrar of Lu-shan; later when he was transferred again to another post, Li Yüan of Lung-hsi took over his old position. Toward the end of the Hsien-t'ung reign period, I in turn took over Li Yüan's position, and because I had been close friends with Li since our youth, I came to know of this secret affair that had happened at Lo-yang. Li made a record of it, and thus it came to be passed down.

"The Fellow from San-shui"[15] remarks; "Alas! Every age has its captiviting women, but one rarely hears of one who is truly pure and upright. Thus, just as scholars who boast of their own talents are lacking in virtue, those women who flaunt their beauty have illicit affairs. If both could be as cautious as one holding a full glass of water or one standing at the edge of a cliff, they would certainly become righteous men and virtuous women. Though one cannot disregard Fei-yen's crime, if one were to examine the inner reaches of her mind, one would indeed find tragedy!"

"Sung the Fourth Raises Hell with Tightwad Chang" in this anthology.

[14] In modern Honan Province.

[15] This is the pseudonym of the author, Huang-fu Mei. The location of San-shui is in the present Kansu Province.

THE OIL PEDDLER COURTS
THE COURTESAN

From *Hsing-shih heng-yen*

TRANSLATED BY LORRAINE S. Y. LIEU AND THE EDITORS

Young men love to boast of their romantic deeds,
But the arena of love is full of hazards.
Money without looks cannot guarantee affection,
While good looks without money are worthless.
Even one blessed with money and a handsome face
Mustn't forget the importance of attentiveness;
For only a thoughtful, understanding, and handsome youth
Will always be assured of the maiden's hand.

This poem, written to the tune of "The Moon over the West River," embodies the essential truth in matters concerning the arena of love. As the saying goes, "The courtesan loves a handsome face, but the madam will run after money." Thus if a patron of the brothels has the looks of P'an An and the riches of Teng T'ung,[1] he will naturally have no trouble in making everybody happy and will become the lord of the brothels and the leader of amorous excursions. But more important than good looks and money are the two words *pang-ch'en,* "sincere attentiveness." *Pang* is [as important as] the sole (*pang*) of a shoe, while *ch'en* is what the lining (*ch'en*) is to a garment.

With the help of *pang-ch'en,* a little good looks in a courtesan can become a great beauty. If she has a blemish, cover it up for her. In other words, if one wants the favor of a courtesan, one must be tolerant toward her, see to it that her needs are met, and go along with her likes and dislikes. This is what is meant by *pang-ch'en.* In the arena of love, it is those skilled in this art who usually get the upper hand in the competition and make up for their lack of good looks or money. Take Cheng Yüan-ho,[2] for example; when he was a beggar at a poorhouse, he was both poor and ragged. But when Li Ya-hsien saw him on that snowy day, she took pity on him. She clothed him in fine silk, fed him with delicacies, and eventually married him. Could this have been due to her desire for his money or her admiration for his good looks? It was rather because Cheng was the very personification of the art of *pang-ch'en* when he had money that she could not bear to abandon him. Just think of the time when Ya-hsien was sick and craved horse-tripe soup; Cheng immediately

---

[1] P'an An is the fictional version of the poet P'an Yüeh (247–300) who was reputedly exceedingly handsome. The early Han minister Teng T'ung was allowed to mint his own currency and was therefore exceedingly rich.

[2] For the story of Cheng Yüan-ho and Li Ya-hsien, see "The Courtesan Li Wa" in this anthology. The names of the hero and the heroine were added by later writers as the legend grew.

killed his mane-braided horse[3] and made soup for her. Isn't this enough to make her remember his love for her? Later on, Cheng came in first in the imperial examinations and Ya-hsien was given the title of Lady Ch'ien. The beggar songs "Lotus Petals" turned out to be proposals of great political value, and the poorhouse was replaced by mansions of marble. [Their past] was covered over by a quilt of the finest brocade, and the whole affair in fact became a fascinating anecdote in the arena of love. Truly:

When luck goes, even gold loses its sheen;
When luck comes, even iron has a glitter.

The incident took place in the Sung Dynasty, founded by Emperor T'ai-tsu. The throne was then passed on through the emperors T'ai-tsung, Chen-tsung, Jen-tsung, Ying-tsung, Shen-tsung, and Che-tsung—altogether seven reigns. They all discouraged military activities and promoted culture and the arts, and peace prevailed in the country. But when Hui-tsung [r. 1101–1125], or Emperor Tao-chün, ascended the throne, he was misguided by such ministers as Ts'ai Ching, Kao Ch'iu, Yang Chien, and Chu Mien;[4] he squandered a great deal of time and money on the construction of royal palaces for his pleasure, so much so that he completely neglected affairs of state. Consequently, resentment arose among the people. The Chin Tartars [the Jurchen] took advantage of this opportunity to attack, throwing this once prosperous and beautiful country into great turmoil. It was only after the two emperors Hui-tsung and Ch'in-tsung [r. 1126–1127] were captured, and Kao-tsung [r. 1127–1162] had

crossed the Yangtze River on a clay horse to reestablish the kingdom in the south,[5] thus dividing the country in half, that peace was restored. During these few decades, the people suffered so much hardship that it was a case of:

Making one's way in the crush of horses and armor,
Finding a home where swords and spears are rife,
Killing becomes like a sport, and
Plunder and pillage a way of life.

Now let me tell you the story of Hsin Shan and his wife Juan. They lived in Prosperity Village just outside the city of Pien-liang.[6] The two of them owned a store, and though their main line of business was rice, they also sold various other items, such as wheat, peas, tea, wine, oil, and salt. Their life was prosperous in a modest way. Although Hsin Shan was over forty, he had only one daughter by the name of Yao-ch'in. Even when she was a little girl, Yao-ch'in was as beautiful as she was clever. When she was seven, her father sent her to the village school, and she could memorize a thousand lines of text a day. At the age of ten, she was already skilled in composing poems. She once wrote a poem entitled "Thoughts of a Young Girl" which was highly praised by many:

All is quiet here after the curtain is drawn;
The incense in the duck-shaped burner glows low in this chilly
*   room.*
Moving the pillow, I'm afraid to frighten the mandarin ducks
*   huddling together;*
Trimming the candle light, I'm sad to see a pair of wicks
*   standing side by side.*

By the time she reached twelve, she had become equally adept in music, chess, calligraphy, and painting. When it came to needlework, her skills often amazed many. Her talents were surely endowed by Heaven; they could hardly have been taught. Since Hsin Shan had no son, he was anx-

---

[3] *Wu-hua ma,* literally "five-flower horse," has often been misinterpreted as a multicolored horse. It actually involves the customs of T'ang times in arranging the mane of a horse into a number of braids, usually either three or five (thus "three-flower horse" or "five-flower horse").

[4] Ts'ai Ching (1046–1126), Kao Ch'iu (?–after 1127), and Yang Chien (?–1121) were among the six notorious ministers, known as the "Six Bandits of Hsüan-ho," who served under Emperor Hui-tsung. Chu Mien (1075–1126), though not included, was equally notorious. Hsüan-ho (1119–1125) is the title of the last of the six reign periods of Hui-tsung.

[5] According to legend, Prince K'ang, in dodging the pursuing Jurchen soldiers, took refuge in a Taoist temple in which he found a horse and rode it across the Yangtze River. After the crossing he discovered that the horse was made of clay.

[6] Pien-liang, also known as Pien-ching or the Eastern Capital, was the capital of the Northern Sung Dynasty. It is modern K'ai-feng in Honan.

ious to find a son-in-law who would be willing to live with them and take care of them in their old age; yet because their daughter was so gifted, it was hard to find a suitable match for her. As a result, although there were quite a few suitors, none of them met with his approval. Unfortunately, Pien-liang was soon besieged by the Chin Tartars. There were many armies in the empire which were loyal to the emperor, but they were not allowed to engage in battles because the prime minister had already agreed to make peace with the invaders. The Chin Tartars thus became even more ferocious. They invaded the capital and captured the two emperors. All the people inside the city were scared out of their wits; carrying their young ones, helping their old ones, they abandoned their possessions and fled for their lives. Among them were Hsin Shan, his wife, and their twelve-year-old daughter.

Hurrying like dogs without a home,
Scuttling like fish slipped out of a net,
Suffering thirst, hunger, and hardships,
Once gone, where will they find a home?
Calling upon Heaven and Earth and their ancestors
To bless them so they won't run into the Tartars.

Indeed:

Rather be a dog in times of peace
Than be a human in times of separation and war.

They did not run into the Tartars on the way. Instead, they met with a group of defeated imperial troops. When the soldiers saw the bundles and bags which these refugees were carrying, they purposely cried out false alarms—"Tartars are coming!"—and set fires along the way. It was just about evening, and the refugees were so frightened that they scattered in confusion, each running for his own life. The soldiers took this chance to rob the people, killing those who were unwilling to yield. It was indeed multiplying confusion by confusion, and adding hardship to hardship.

Now back to Hsin Yao-ch'in. She was knocked down in the onrush of troops, and when she got

up again, she had lost sight of her father and mother. Not daring to call out for help, she hid herself among the graves by the road, where she spent the night. At daybreak, she ventured out for a look. All she saw was dust flying all over and corpses everywhere. The other refugees were nowhere to be seen. Yao-ch'in missed her parents and cried bitterly. She wanted to look for them, but did not know which direction to take. She finally headed south, crying as she went. She had walked about two *li* when she began to feel tired and hungry; so when she finally saw a thatched hut, she decided to go there and beg for some soup. By the time she reached it, she realized that the house was empty. The occupants had all fled. Yao-ch'in sat down by the mud wall and cried.

As the old saying goes, "No coincidences, no stories." It just happened that a man passed by at this very moment. His name was Pu Ch'iao, and he was a neighbor of Hsin Shan. He was a lazy and greedy man, often cadging meals from others as a means of living. Everyone called him Big Pu. He had also been separated from the main group of refugees and was walking alone. When he heard someone crying, he hurried over to take a look. Yao-ch'in had known him since she was a child, and now, at a time like this when she had no one to help her, she felt as if she had seen a relative when she saw him. She hurriedly wiped away her tears and rose to greet him: "Uncle Pu, have you seen my father and mother?"

Pu Ch'iao thought to himself, "The soldiers have taken away all my belongings and I was just worrying because I don't have any money for traveling. Now Heaven has sent me this priceless object. This is indeed a precious piece of merchandise, which I should invest in." So he lied, "Your father and mother were grief-stricken because they couldn't find you. Now they've gone ahead, but they told me that if I ever saw you I should be sure to take you to them. They even promised me a big reward."

Yao-ch'in was an extremely clever child, but at a helpless time like this, any guileless man could be fooled easily; so she left with Pu Ch'iao without suspicion.

Even if she had known that he was not the right companion,
Alas, any companion is better than none when one is desperate.

Pu Ch'iao gave her some of the food he had with him and told her, "Since your parents didn't stop for the night, we might not catch up with them until we reach Chien-k'ang[7] on the other side of the Yangtze River. So in the meantime, I'll call you daughter and you call me father. Otherwise people will think that I'm taking in lost girls, and this would be rather inconvenient."

Yao-ch'in consented readily, and from then on the two of them traveled together by land and by water under the guise of father and daughter. By the time they reached Chien-k'ang, they had heard that Wu-chu, the fourth prince of Chin,[8] had led his troops across the river and was fast approaching Chien-k'ang. They had also heard that Prince K'ang had ascended the throne and settled down at Hangchow, changing the name of the city to Lin-an.[9] So they went by boat to Jun-chou,[10] then passed through Soochow, Ch'ang-chou, Chia-ting,[11] and Hu-chou,[12] finally arriving at Lin-an, where they stayed temporarily in an inn.

By then Pu Ch'iao, having brought Hsin Yao-ch'in along with him for more than three thousand *li*, had already spent what little money he had. He had even given his outer clothes to pay the inn bill, and Hsin Yao-ch'in was the only mer-chandise left to him; so he decided to sell her. He discovered that Wang Chiu-ma, the madam of a brothel near the West Lake, was looking for a girl; so he brought Chiu-ma to the inn to take a look at Yao-ch'in and to bargain about the price. When Chiu-ma saw that Yao-ch'in was indeed a very pretty girl, she agreed to pay Pu Ch'iao fifty taels of silver for her. Pu Ch'iao took the silver and sent Yao-ch'in to Chiu-ma's house. It turned out that he was a rather cunning man: to Chiu-ma he only said, "Yao-ch'in is my daughter. It is most unfortunate that she has to enter such a business. I hope you'll be kind and gentle when you teach her. I'm sure she'll obey you if you'll just be patient with her." Then to Yao-ch'in, he said something else: "Chiu-ma is a close relative of mine, and I'm going to put you in her care temporarily. I'll come back for you as soon as I've found out where your parents are." Yao-ch'in believed everything and went happily.

What a pity that an extremely clever girl like her
Should fall into the snare of the brothels.

After Chiu-ma had taken Yao-ch'in in, she gave her a complete change of clothing, and kept her closed up in a room in the midst of the complex. Every day she served her with delicacies and comforted her with kind words. At first Yao-ch'in seemed to take all this quite naturally, but after several days, when there was no news from Pu Ch'iao, she began to miss her parents. With tears in her eyes, she asked Chiu-ma, "Why hasn't Uncle Pu come to see me?"

"Which Uncle Pu?" asked Chiu-ma in return.

"The Big Pu who brought me to your house," replied Yao-ch'in.

"He said he was your father," Chiu-ma said.

"But his family name is Pu and mine is Hsin!" And she proceeded to tell Chiu-ma in detail how she had fled from Pien-liang and become separated from her parents; how she had met Pu Ch'iao on the way and come to Lin-an with him, and the things he had said to coax her.

"I see," Chiu-ma said. "So you're an orphan

---

[7] Chien-k'ang is the present-day Nanking in Kiangsu Province.

[8] Yüan-yen Tsung-pi, the fourth son of the founder of the Jurchen Chin Dynasty, is commonly known as Chin Wu-chu, Wu-chu being one of his personal names.

[9] Lin-an (modern Hangchow), the Southern Sung capital, was officially known as the provisional capital because the Sung government was supposed to recover northern China from the hands of the invading Jurchen and resettle the seat of the government at the old capital Pien-ching. "Lin-an" literally means temporary dwelling.

[10] Chen-chiang in modern Kiangsu Province.

[11] To the southeast of Ch'ang-chou in Kiangsu.

[12] In northern modern Chekiang Province, to the southwest of the Tung-t'ing Lake.

now, just like a crab without legs. I might as well tell you the truth. That man Pu Ch'iao has sold you to me for fifty taels of silver. This is a brothel, and we all depend on the girls here receiving patrons for our living. There are several of them here, but none of them is of outstanding quality like you are. I'll treat you like my own daughter, and when you grow up, I can guarantee that you will enjoy every luxury for the rest of your life."

When Yao-ch'in heard this, she realized that she had been tricked by Pu Ch'iao and she cried bitterly. Chiu-ma comforted her for a long time before she finally stopped crying. From then on, [Wang] Chiu-ma changed the girl's name to Wang Mei, and everyone called her Mei-niang. She was taught to play different instruments and to sing and dance, all of which she excelled in. At fourteen, she was already a stunning beauty and was much sought after by the rich and noble young men of Lin-an, who came visiting with gifts in abundance. There were also others who appreciated the poetic gift in a woman, and so when they heard of her literary talent, they came to her door every day, asking for her poems and her calligraphy. Her name became more famous by the day, until they no longer called her Mei-niang; instead they called her "Queen of the Courtesans." The young men of the West Lake composed a *Kua-chih-erh* [13] song in praise of her:

Of all the courtesans,
Who is as beautiful as Wang Mei-niang?
She can write, she can paint, she can compose verses,
Not to mention her skills in singing and dancing.
People often compare the West Lake to Hsi-shih;
Certainly Hsi-shih is not as pretty as she.
If only one is lucky enough to embrace her,
Even death is a pleasure.

It was exactly because Mei-niang had acquired such a high reputation that someone made an offer for her first night when she was only fourteen. But since she was unwilling, and since Chiu-

ma regarded her as a potential money tree, naturally the latter took her refusal as a royal edict and did not force her. So another year passed, and Mei-niang was fifteen. Actually there were rules and regulations in this profession regarding a girl's first night. If it was done at the age of thirteen, it was considered too early; hence this was called "trying out the flower." It was a simple case of greed on the part of a madam who had no consideration for the girl's suffering. With regard to the patron, he, too, got very little pleasure out of it; he did it only to satisfy his vanity. At the age of fourteen, it was known as "blossoming of the flower." By that time, the girl should have already started to menstruate; so with mutual giving and taking, it could be done quite satisfactorily. At the age of fifteen, it was known as "picking the flower." Even though this was still thought to be rather young for ordinary girls, it was already considered past the right time for people in this business. Since Mei-niang had not yet taken a patron, the young men of the West Lake composed yet another *Kua-chih-erh* song:

Mei-niang is like a melon, just good for display;
At fifteen, she has never slept with anyone.
[A courtesan] in name but not in fact,
*   what use is there in having her around?*
If she isn't [an impenetrable] "stone girl,"
*   she must be [destined to be] bisexual.*
If that thing is still intact,
She must find its itching hard to fight.

Chiu-ma came to hear about all this and was afraid that it might give her business a bad name; so she came to persuade Mei-niang to receive visitors. Mei-niang refused flatly, saying, "Unless I see my own parents and they consent to it, I won't receive anyone."

Chiu-ma was displeased by her reply but at the same time did not have the heart to force her. Things dragged on for quite some time. Then by chance a rich man by the name of Chin was willing to pay Chiu-ma three hundred taels of silver for Mei-niang's first night. In face of such a large

[13] *Kua-chih-erh* is a type of folk song, mostly love songs, popular in Ming times.

181

sum of money, Chiu-ma immediately came up with a scheme and briefed Chin on when and how to achieve his goal. Chin agreed readily.

On the fifteenth day of the eighth month, Chin invited Mei-niang to his boat supposedly to watch the tides on the lake. Along with three or four accomplices, he drank and played the finger-guessing game, urging and persuading Mei-niang to drink until she was dead drunk. She was completely unconscious when they helped her back to Chiu-ma's house and laid her out on the bed. At the time, the weather was quite warm, and Mei-niang was not wearing that many layers of clothing. Chiu-ma personally stripped her naked for the convenience of her patron. Chin's weapon was no fantastic instrument, but with the help of a little saliva, he gingerly wedged open Mei-niang's thighs and pushed it in. Mei-niang was awakened by the pain, only to see that Chin had already gotten what he wanted. She wanted to struggle, but there was no strength left in her limbs. Thus Chin was able to do all that he desired, and the event ran its full course. Verily:

The petal has blossomed and withered amid the rain;
Already the beauty in the mirror is no longer herself.

At the fifth watch, Mei-niang awoke from her stupor and realized that she had been tricked by Chiu-ma and had lost her virginity. She could only lament her sad fate in meeting such brutality. She got up to go to the bathroom and put her clothes back on. Then she lay down on a rattan cot by the bed, turned her face toward the wall, and wept silently. When Chin came over and tried to embrace her, she did not hesitate to scratch him in the face, leaving several bloody trails on his cheeks. Chin was naturally put off; so as soon as day broke, he told Chiu-ma that he was leaving. Chiu-ma tried to make him stay, but he left in a huff.

Ordinarily, after a courtesan had spent her first night, the madam would be the first one to go into her room the next morning and offer her congratulations. Then courtesans from the other brothels would all come to congratulate her and there would be several days of feasting. The patron would stay on for a month or two, or at least two to three weeks. No one had ever left early the next morning the way Chin had. Chiu-ma was extremely puzzled; so she got dressed and went upstairs to look. She saw Mei-niang lying on the cot with a tear-stained face. Because Chiu-ma wanted to coax her to accept more patrons, she kept apologizing for what had happened. But Mei-niang did not pay any attention to her. Finally, Chiu-ma could only go back downstairs. Mei-niang cried all day, refusing to eat or drink anything. From that day on, she pleaded sickness and hid herself upstairs, turning her back on all visitors.

Chiu-ma was growing more impatient by the day. However, she dared not torture Mei-niang for fear of driving her to more desperate actions. Nor could she afford to let Mei-niang alone, because she had brought her up for the sole purpose of earning money. But if Mei-niang did not receive patrons, she would be useless even if she stayed there for a hundred years. Chiu-ma debated with herself for several days before she suddenly remembered her sworn sister and confidante Liu Ssu-ma: "She certainly has a clever tongue, so she might be able to persuade Mei-niang. Why not ask her over and let her try? If Mei-niang changes her mind, we certainly won't be short of business from now on."

Right away, she sent Pao-erh to invite Liu Ssu-ma over and told her all her troubles. Liu Ssu-ma said, "I'm a woman Sui Ho and a female Lu Chia.[14] I can talk an *arhat*[15] into falling in love, and I can persuade the fairy of the moon to consider marriage. You can count on me."

"If that's the case, I'll gladly kowtow to you even though I'm your elder sister," Chiu-ma said.

[14] Sui Ho and Lu Chia were two political advisers in the early second century B.C. who were famous for their eloquence.
[15] A Buddhist saint.

"Drink another cup of tea, so you won't be thirsty later."

"This mouth of mine can fill an ocean; I won't get thirsty even if I talk until tomorrow," Liu Ssu-ma replied.

She drank a few more cups of tea and then went to Mei-niang's room at the back of the house. The door was tightly shut, so Ssu-ma knocked softly, calling, "Niece."

Mei-niang heard that it was Ssu-ma, so she came to open the door. After the usual exchange of greetings, Ssu-ma sat down by the table and Mei-niang sat down next to her. Ssu-ma saw that there was a scroll of fine silk spread out on top of the table with a woman's face sketched in on it, though not yet colored.

"What a fine picture!" Ssu-ma praised. "How clever you are! How lucky Sister Chiu is to have such a clever daughter as you, so beautiful and so talented. Even with a cartload of gold, I don't think anyone could find a comparable girl in this entire Lin-an City."

"Don't make fun of me, auntie," Mei-niang said. "What wind had brought you over here?"

"I have often wanted to come and visit you," Ssu-ma answered. "But I'm always so busy with the work of my own house. Now that I've heard that you have just received your first patron, I have especially taken the time to come and congratulate Sister Chiu."

Mei-niang blushed when she heard the mention of her shameful experience; she bowed her head and said nothing. Ssu-ma knew that she was shy, so she moved her chair a little closer and, taking Mei-niang's hand in hers, said, "My child, a courtesan cannot afford to be as tender-skinned as a soft-shelled egg. You can never earn big money if you are so shy!"

"What do I want money for?" Mei-niang retorted.

"My child, even if you don't want money, think of your mother who has brought you up. She would at least like to get her investment back. As

the saying goes, 'Live by the mountain, live off the mountain; live by the sea, live off the sea.' Of all the girls here in Sister Chiu's house, who can compare with you? In her field, you are the only melon she can depend on for some seeds. That's why she treats you quite differently from the others. You are a clever girl, and you should know how to weigh and compare things. I've heard that ever since that night, you have refused to receive any clients. What is the meaning of that? If all the other girls were like you, who would provide this whole household of silkworms with mulberry leaves? Your mother has been kind to you, and you should try to return her kindness. Don't let the other girls have something to criticize you for."

"Let them talk. I'm not afraid of them!" Mei-niang retorted.

"My, my! Criticizing is a small thing; but do you know the rules of our trade?" Ssu-ma asked.

"What rules?"

"In this trade, we depend entirely on our daughters for our living. If we're lucky enough to take in a promising girl, it's just like a large family's acquiring a plot of fertile land or some form of profitable property. When she is young, we even hope that the wind blowing at her can make her grow faster. Her first night of receiving a patron is to us what the harvest is to the farmers. After that we expect to get the return on our investment: welcoming new customers at the front door, seeing old customers out at the back door; Chang bringing rice, Li sending firewood; all the hustle and bustle of coming and going. This is what we would call a prosperous brothel."

"How shameful! I don't want to do such things!"

Ssu-ma covered her mouth and chuckled, "You don't want to do such things! Do you think you're going to have your way? In the brothel, the madam is the boss. If a girl doesn't listen to her, she can beat her black and blue any time she wants to, and the girl will surely end up doing

183

what she says. Sister Chiu has always let you have your way because she knows that you are a clever and pretty girl, and have been pampered and spoiled since your childhood. She always wants to leave you some self-respect and tries to let you save face. But just now, she told me a lot of things; she said that you are ungrateful, and that you don't know the difference between what is good and what is bad for you. She's very displeased and has asked me to speak to you. If you insist on being so stubborn, she might get really angry and give you a sound scolding and beating. Where do you think you can go? Once she gets started, there will be no end to it, and sooner or later you'll have to give in to her wishes. But by then, your name would already have been ruined and you might even become the laughingstock among your sisters. Why don't you listen to me: since the bucket has already fallen into the well, you cannot pull it back up again. So why not go happily into your mother's arms and enjoy her favor while you can?"

"I come from a respectable family, and it was only through some ill fortune that I fell into this place. If you suggest to my mother that I be allowed to get out of here so that I can be properly married, you will be doing a greater good than building a nine-story pagoda for Buddha. But I would rather die than submit myself to this life of shame," pleaded Mei-niang.

"My child, getting out to be properly married is an admirable thing. Of course I'm in favor of it, too," said Ssu-ma. "But there are all sorts of getting-out."

"What are the differences among them?" Mei-niang asked.

"There are the 'real getting-out' and the 'false getting-out'; the 'bitter getting-out' and the 'happy getting-out'; the 'getting-out through a good chance' and the 'getting-out through forced circumstances'; the 'permanent getting-out' and the 'temporary getting-out'. Let me explain them to you one by one. What is the 'real getting-out'? If a talented young man marries a beautiful girl, and a beautiful girl weds a talented young man, then this is a good match. But perfect unions are often barred by many obstacles and are hard to attain. If by luck the two meet, he loves her while she loves him and neither can live without the other. He is willing to take her and she is willing to follow him—they are just like a pair of moths, inseparable even in death. This is the 'real getting-out.'

"What is the 'false getting-out'? The patron loves the courtesan but the courtesan does not love the patron. She doesn't want to marry him but uses the word 'marriage' to lure him into lavishing more money on her; and at the crucial moment, she backs out under some sort of pretext. There is also another kind of madly infatuated man who knows perfectly well that the courtesan doesn't love him, yet insists on marrying her. He spends a large sum of money to buy off the madam, so there is no room left for the courtesan to object. She is therefore forced into marrying him, but secretly bears a grudge. After the marriage, she will purposely disobey the family regulations, ranging from throwing tantrums to openly having affairs with other men, until the family can no longer tolerate her and after six months to a year has to let her go back. She becomes a courtesan again and goes right back to her old business. 'Getting-out' to her is but another way of making money. This is the 'false getting-out.'

"What is the 'bitter getting-out'? Similarly, the patron loves the courtesan while the courtesan does not love the patron, but she is in his power. The madam is afraid to cause trouble and has consented readily. The courtesan can do nothing except go, with tears in her eyes. Once married into the rich family with its strict formalities and proprieties, she finds that she has neither status nor freedom. She is like half a concubine and half a slave, toiling and suffering from day to day. This is the 'bitter getting-out.'

"What is the 'happy getting-out'? The courtesan is just searching for someone when she comes upon a gentle and good-natured patron from a rich family. His wife is kind but has no children, so he looks forward to marrying her to bear him a son. If she has a son, she will then become the heir's mother in the family. In such a marriage, she can hope for a comfortable life at present and in the future. This is the 'happy getting-out.'

"What is the 'getting-out through a good chance'? The courtesan, after enjoying a long time of popularity, feels that she has had enough. She decides to choose a suitable man and marry while she is still popular and has many suitors, thus beating a speedy retreat before it's too late, not having to suffer the neglect of others in her inevitable downhill days. This is the 'getting-out through a good chance.'

"What is the 'getting-out through forced circumstances'? The courtesan has no thoughts of getting out, but under circumstances such as being forced by some government officials, or having been bullied or cheated, or having too many debts which she is unable to pay, she decides to marry the first available man just to buy some peace and hide herself for good. This is the 'getting-out through forced circumstances.'

"What is the 'permanent getting-out'? The courtesan is already in her later years and has experienced all kinds of tumultuous experiences. By chance she meets a mature patron and finds that they have many things in common. So she wraps up her business and they live happily through their old age. This is the 'permanent getting-out.'

"What is the 'temporary getting-out'? He loves her and she loves him, but this red-hot affair is only a momentary flare of passion and has no long-term planning behind it. Either the family elders do not allow such a union; or the man's wife is jealous and, after several rough scenes, the courtesan is sent back to her brothel and the original payment returned; or his family is very poor and she cannot stand the hardship, so she returns to her old profession. This is the 'temporary getting-out.' "

"I would like to get out now, so what should I do?" asked Mei-niang.

"My child, let me teach you a foolproof way," Ssu-ma said.

"I'll never forget your kindness if you do," Mei-niang hastened to say.

"As for the matter of getting out, you will be considered clean once you are married into a family. Anyway, you have already done it with someone, so even if you get married tonight you cannot call yourself a virgin," Ssu-ma explained. "You can only blame your fate for bringing you into such a place. Your mother has already spent a lot of time and money on you; if you don't help her for a few years and earn some money for her, she won't let you go that easily. There's also another thing: even if you want to get out of here, you'll have to choose a desirable match first. Of course, you don't want to marry just anybody who happens to be around. But now you won't even receive a single patron; how would you know who to choose?

"If you insist on acting this way, your mother might be forced to sell you to someone who is looking for a concubine. This is one way of getting out, too, you know! Your husband might be old, or ugly, or illiterate as a country bumpkin. Wouldn't you be throwing your whole life away then? It would be better if you jumped into the river, for there might be someone nearby who would sigh 'What a pity!' when he heard the noise. Listen to me: why not go along with your mother and let her pick some clients for you? With your beauty and talent, I'm sure that ordinary patrons won't even dare to approach you. Your patrons will all be rich men or noble lords, and they will surely do justice to your beauty. Enjoy all you can while you're still young. Besides, you can also earn your mother a fortune and save yourself some money so that you won't have to ask for others' help later on. After five or ten years, pick out someone you like, someone who appreciates you, and then I'll personally arrange the match for you. You can be married off properly, and your mother won't stop you then. Wouldn't that be nice for both of you?"

When Mei-niang heard that, she smiled and said nothing. Ssu-ma knew that her words were taking effect, and so she continued: "All that I've said is for your own good. Listen to me now and you'll thank me later." After that, she got up to leave.

Chiu-ma, who was standing outside the door, had heard everything. When Mei-niang saw Ssu-ma out of her room, she bumped right into Chiu-ma; Mei-niang blushed and withdrew into her room hastily. Chiu-ma followed Ssu-ma back to the front of the house and they sat down again.

"Mei-niang is very stubborn," Ssu-ma said. "But now I've given her a good piece of my mind, I think she will change her own mind. So you just go ahead and look for a patron; I'm sure she'll be willing. I'll come again to congratulate you then."

Chiu-ma thanked Ssu-ma profusely and made her stay for dinner, and they parted only when both were stuffed with food and drink.

Later, the young men of the West Lake made up another *Kua-chih-erh* song to describe this episode:

Liu Ssu-ma, what a tongue you have!
Even a lady Sui Ho, a female Lu Chia, would have to adore
*   your wit.*
Lengthy in discourse, succinct in advice, never short of device,
You can make even drunkards sober.
As for the cunning ones, you can win them easily.
No wonder even our stubborn Mei-niang
Finally succumbs to your persuasion.

Now let us now go back to Mei-niang. After listening to Ssu-ma's advice, she thought it over carefully and found her argument quite reasonable. So from then on she began to receive visitors, who came in such numbers that she hardly had a moment left to herself. Her fame grew by the day, and even at ten taels of silver for a night, the patrons still fought eagerly for their turns. Chiu-ma was simply overjoyed at this sudden flow of income, while Mei-niang only had her heart set on looking for someone who could help her get out. But unfortunately this was not something that could be done in a hurry. Truly, as the saying goes:

Priceless objects are easy to acquire,
But loved ones are hard to come by.

Our story shifts at this juncture. Leaving Mei-niang for a while, let me tell you the story of Chu Shih-lao, an oil shop owner who lived outside the Clear Ripple Gate. Three years ago, he had adopted a young lad by the name of Ch'in Ch-ung, a refugee from Pien-liang. Ch'in's mother had died when he was still young; and his father Ch'in Liang sold him when he was thirteen while the old man himself went to work as an attendant at the Upper T'ien-chu Temple. Chu Shih-lao was old and childless, and his wife had died recently, so he treated Ch'in Ch'ung like his own son. He changed the boy's name to Chu Ch'ung and had him work in the oil shop to learn about the business. The two of them managed very well until Chu Shih-lao got a kidney disease which forced him to hire an assistant by the name of Hsing Ch'üan to help out in the shop.

Time passed by in a flash, and some four years went by. Chu Ch'ung had grown into a handsome young man of seventeen, and though he had already come of age, he was still unmarried. Chu Shih-lao had a maid called Orchid who was already over twenty. She had had her eyes set on Chu Ch'ung for some time, and on several ocasions had tried to seduce him. Now Chu Ch'ung was a good and honest youth; besides, he found Orchid distasteful and ugly. Thus Orchid's advances were not reciprocated. Frustrated, she began to switch her attention to Hsing Ch'üan, a bachelor near forty, who proved to be an easy catch. After many a clandestine meeting, they came to feel that Chu Ch'ung was often in their way and decided to think of a way to get rid of him. One day, Orchid went to Chu Shih-lao and accused Chu Ch'ung: "Young master has often made advances to me. He is very untrustworthy."

Since Chu Shih-lao had had an affair with Orchid earlier, he could not help feeling a little sour. Hsing Ch'üan, on his part, put away some money in the shop and then went to report to Chu Shih-lao, "Young master has been gambling and losing money. The cash in the shop has been short several times. He must have stolen it."

At first Chu Shih-lao did not believe them, but being old and gullible, he was finally taken in by the repeated accusations. He summoned Chu Ch'ung before him and gave him a severe scolding. Being a clever boy, Chu Ch'ung realized immediately that it must have been Hsing Ch'üan and Orchid's doing. He wanted to explain, but on second thought he decided that he would only make himself look bad if the old man chose not to believe him. Then he thought of a solution and suggested it to Chu Shih-lao: "Since business has been slow in the shop, there's really no need for two men to stay there; so why not let Hsing Ch'üan take care of the shop while I go and peddle oil in the street? I'll report all the sales to you every day. This way we'll have two incomes at the same time. Does it make sense?"

Chu Shih-lao was about to give his consent when Hsing Ch'üan said to him, "He doesn't really want to peddle oil in the streets! He has been stealing quite a bit of money from your shop in the last few years, so he has some savings now. He is also angry with you for not finding him a wife. Thus he's unwilling to help out here any longer and is just using this as an excuse to get out, to pick himself a wife, and to set up his own household."

Chu Shih-lao sighed. "I've treated him like my own son, and yet he has such bad intentions toward me. Since I don't have the blessing of Heaven I might as well give up. After all, he's not my own flesh and blood, and he'll never be on my side. There's nothing I can do except let him go his own way."

So he gave Chu Ch'ung three taels of silver and told him to leave. He was kind enough to let Chu Ch'ung take all his clothes and bedding. Chu

Ch'ung knew that it was no use for him to argue, so he kowtowed four times to Chu Shih-lao and left, crying bitterly. It was simply that:

Hsiao-chi lost his life because of slander;
Shen-sheng killed himself to satisfy his father.[16]
If such calumnies beset even one's own son,
No wonder an adopted son must suffer more.

It turned out that Ch'in Liang had never told his son that he was going to work at the Upper T'ien-chu Temple; so after Chu Ch'ung had left Chu Shih-lao's house, he rented a small room by the All Peace Bridge where he kept all his belongings. Then he locked his door and went from place to place inquiring about his father. After searching for several days and finding out nothing, he put the matter aside for the time being. During those years with Chu Shih-lao, he had always been faithful and honest, and therefore had not a single penny of private savings. The three taels of silver which Chu Shih-lao had given him was not enough for capital. What kind of business could he do? He thought about it for a long time, and finally decided that selling oil was the only kind of business he was familiar with. Besides, the oil dealers all knew him well; it would indeed be the least risky business for him to go into. He bought himself the necessary equipment and gave all the remaining money to one of the oil dealers to supply him with oil. The owner there had known Chu Ch'ung to be an honest fellow. He also remembered how at a very young age Chu Ch'ung used to take care of the oil shop for Chu Shih-lao but now had had to become a peddler because he had been slandered by the other worker and forced out of the shop. Consequently, he sympathized with Chu Ch'ung for the injustice done to him and had set his mind on helping him. He gave him the best quality oil, measuring it out

[16] Hsiao-chi, the crown prince to King Wu-ting (1339–1281 B.C.) of the Shang Dynasty, and Shen-sheng (?–654 B.C.), the heir apparent of Duke Hsien of the state of Chin of the Spring and Autumn period, were both victims of calumny by the consorts of their fathers.

for him generously. Chu Ch'ung, in turn, was able to treat his customers the same way; so his oil was usually sold much faster than that of the other peddlers. He lived frugally on a careful budget. Very soon, he was able to save up enough money to buy himself some daily necessities and clothes. The one thing which still preoccupied his thoughts was his father. He thought, "Everyone knows me as Chu Ch'ung, so who would know that my real name is Ch'in Chung? If my father happens to come and look for me, he won't even have a clue."

Thereupon he changed his family name back to Ch'in. This storyteller has this to say: when a man of position wants to change his name, he has to present a petition to the court, or notify the Ministry of Rites, the imperial academies, and other appropriate authorities so that his action becomes a matter of public record. But what can an oil peddler do so as to let the others know that he wants to resume his original family name? Ch'in thought of a way: on one side of the oil buckets, he painted a big character "Ch'in" and on the other side, he painted the characters "Pien-liang" in order that everyone could see at a glance who he was. From then on, the people in Lin-an came to know his original name and all referred to him as Oil Peddler Ch'in.

At the time, the early spring weather was neither too cold nor too hot. Ch'in heard that the monks at the Monastery of Manifest Blessings were going to hold a nine-day service and he thought that they would probably need a large quantity of oil, so he went there with his oil load. The monks had heard of him as a peddler whose price was reasonable and whose oil was of the finest quality, and they all brought oil from him. Therefore, for nine days, Ch'in did his business only at this monastery. It was simply that:

Trickery won't bring you profit,
Honesty won't cause you loss.

On the ninth day, Ch'in Ch'ung left the monastery after having sold all his oil. The weather was extremely good on that day, and there were many sightseers strolling around. Walking along the bank of the lake, Ch'in Ch'ung saw the Ten View Pond in the distance with its red peach blossoms and green willows. There were also many decorated boats with musical bands playing on the lake. All in all, there was much to admire and enjoy all along the way. After walking for a while Ch'in Ch'ung felt tired, so he went back to an open space to the right of the Monastery of Manifest Blessings. Putting down his load, he sat down on a rock to rest. There was a house nearby, facing the lake. Its fence was painted, and inside the red hedges there were bushes of fine bamboo. Before one had a chance to view the inner chambers, one was already impressed with its appearance of tidiness. Ch'in Ch'ung saw several men dressed in fine clothes coming out, followed by a young girl. They bade one another good-bye at the door, and then the girl returned inside. Throughout all this time, Ch'in Ch'ung was unable to take his eyes off the girl, because he had never seen such beauty or such grace before in his life. He was overwhelmed with excitement. But Ch'in Ch'ung was an innocent youth and did not know that the place was actually a brothel. As he was wondering to himself, a middle-aged woman and a young maid came out and stood by the door, gazing idly around. When the woman saw the oil load, she said, "Ah, we were just going to send for some oil, and here is an oil peddler. Why not buy some from him?"

The maid took an oil bottle from the house and approached Ch'in, but he did not notice her until she called to him, "Oil peddler."

"I have no more oil today," Ch'in replied, "but I'll bring some over tomorrow if you want it."

The maid could read a little, and when she saw the character "Ch'in" on the oil bucket, she said to the woman, "The oil peddler's name is Ch'in."

The madam had also heard the others talk about a certain Oil Peddler Ch'in and what an honest man he was. So she told Ch'in, "We need oil every day. If you're willing to carry it over, we'll be your regular customer."

"Thank you. I'll bring it over promptly every day," Ch'in promised.

After the woman and the maid had gone back inside, Ch'in thought to himself, "I wonder who this woman is to the young girl? I'm going to deliver oil to them every day, and I shall at least get to see her, whether I make money or not. What luck!"

As he was about to put the load back on his shoulder and start out again, he saw two men carrying a sedan chair with blue silk curtains approaching with speed, followed by two pages. Stopping in front of the house, the two men put down the sedan chair and the pages went inside. Ch'in Ch'ung thought, "I wonder what's happening? Who are they waiting for?"

A little while later, he saw two maids coming out, one carrying a scarlet cushion and the other carrying an inlaid bamboo box, both of which they handed to the sedan-chair bearers to put under the seat. Then the young girl whom he had seen earlier came out, followed by the two pages, one carrying a lute case and the other carrying several scrolls, with a flute hanging from his wrist. She mounted the sedan chair and the bearers carried it back the way they had come, while the maids and the pages all followed on foot. With this second and closer look, Ch'in Ch'ung was even more puzzled. Carrying his oil load, he walked away slowly.

After a few steps, he saw a tavern by the river. Ch'in Ch'ung was not in the habit of drinking, but after seeing this young girl, he felt both happy and troubled; so he put down his load and went into the tavern. He picked a small table and sat down. The waiter asked him, "Are you expecting company or are you drinking alone?"

"I'm drinking alone," Ch'in Ch'ung replied. "Bring me some good wine and few dishes of fresh fruit, but no meat."

While the waiter was pouring the wine, Ch'in Ch'ung asked him, "Who lives in that house with the gilded gates?"

"That's the villa of young Master Ch'i, but it's now occupied by a woman by the name of Wang Chiu-ma."

"I've just seen a young lady going off in a sedan chair. Who is she?"

"She is the famous courtesan Wang Mei-niang, but everybody calls her 'Queen of the Courtesans.' She comes from Pien-liang but was stranded here as a refugee. Whether it's music, singing, dancing, chess, calligraphy, or painting, she's skilled in every one of them. All her clients are rich and well known, and she asks ten taels of silver for an overnight stay. Ordinary fellows cannot possibly hope to get near her. The place they used to live in outside the Golden Flood Gate was too small, so young Master Ch'i, one of her intimates, lent them this house about a half a year ago."

When Ch'in Ch'ung heard that she was also a native of Pien-liang, his homesickness was aroused, but at the same time he felt even more drawn toward her. He drank a few more cups and paid the waiter. As he was walking home, he thought to himself, "What a beautiful girl, and what a pity that she should have fallen into a brothel." Then he laughed to himself, "How would I have seen her if she had not fallen into a brothel!" The more he thought, the more infatuated he became. "Man has but one life; grass sees but one autumn. If I could hold her in my arms for one night, I would die without regrets." Then he rebuked himself: "Bah! I carry this load all day long, and I only make a few pennies. How can I think of such impossible things? I'm just like a toad in a ditch, wanting to eat the flesh of the swan. How can he get his bite? All of her clients are either rich or noble lords; I don't think she'd receive an oil peddler like me even if I had the money." But a new thought occurred to him: "I've heard that the madams care only about money, and they're willing to take a beggar as long as he can pay the price. Moreover, I'm in a respectable trade, so why shouldn't she receive me if I have the money? But where can I find the money?"

He daydreamed and mumbled to himself all the way home. It makes one wonder, how could there be such a foolish man? A peddler with only three taels of silver for his capital, and yet he was thinking of spending ten taels for a night with a famous courtesan. What dream! But as the saying goes, "If there's a will, there's a way." After wracking his brain, he finally figured out a way: "From tomorrow on, I shall put aside money to buy oil according to the business of the day and save up the balance. If I save one penny a day, I shall have three taels sixty cents at the end of one year. So I shall have enough money in three years' time. If I save two pennies a day, it'll only take me one and a half years. If I save even more, about one year will be sufficient."

While he was thinking, he had reached home. He unlocked the door and went inside; but because of all the thoughts that had occupied his mind on his way home, he found the room, otherwise the same, sad and lonely. Without eating his dinner, he climbed into bed, where he tossed and turned all night long and could not quite forget the beautiful girl.

Because she is as fair as a flower or the moon,
He has completely lost his willpower.

The next morning, he got up at dawn, filled his oil buckets, ate his breakfast, and headed straight for Chiu-ma's house. He went in through the front gate but dared not venture any further. He stuck out his head and looked around. Chiu-ma had just gotten up, and her hair was still disheveled. Ch'in recognized her voice telling Pao-erh

what to buy in the market, so he called out to her. Chiu-ma looked outside and saw Oil Peddler Ch'in; she smiled and said, "What an honest man! You kept your word."

She asked him to bring the oil in, and he weighed out a bottle of about five catties. She named a price which was quite reasonable, and Ch'in Ch'ung accepted without argument. Chiu-ma was very pleased with his attitude and so she said, "This bottle of oil is good only for two days. If you will come every other day from now on, I won't buy from anyone else."

Ch'in Ch'ung agreed and left. His only regret was that he did not have a chance to see the Queen of the Courtesans. "Anyway," he thought to himself, "I'm glad that they have become my regular customers. If I don't see her the first time, I may see her the second time; if I don't see her the second time, I may see her the third time. There's one thing though; if I have to come all this way just to sell one bottle of oil, this is certainly no way to do business. The Monastery of Manifest Blessings is on my way; even though they're not holding services today, they probably need oil just the same. Why don't I go over and take a look? If I can get some more customers there, I can sell all my oil along this route."

As luck would have it, the monks there were just hoping that he would call, and all bought oil from him. Ch'in Ch'ung made agreements with each of them to deliver oil there every other day. That day was an even-numbered day, so from then on, Ch'in Ch'ung did his business in other places on odd-numbered days and only called on the Ch'ien-t'ang Gate route on even-numbered days. Once outside the Ch'ien-t'ang Gate, he always headed for Chiu-ma's house first, hoping to see the Queen of the Courtesans, and occasionally was successful. When he did not see her, he felt that his longing was in vain; but when he did see her, his longing became all the more intense. It was a case of:

Heaven and earth may end one day,
But this passion will never die.

With Ch'in Ch'ung calling at Chiu-ma's house every other day, everyone in the house soon got to know him. Time passed quickly, and soon more than a year had gone by. In the meantime, Ch'in Ch'ung had selected the better pieces of silver from his sales every day—thirty cents, twenty cents, or at least ten cents—and saved them up. Every time he had accumulated a certain amount, he would have the pieces changed into larger ones. Saving in this way, he had eventually put aside a large bag of silver of whose value he himself had lost count. One rainy odd-numbered day, he decided not to do business. Since he was rather pleased with his savings, he thought, "I have nothing better to do today; why don't I weigh them and find out exactly how much I have saved?"

So he took out his umbrella and went over to the silversmith's shop to borrow a scale. The silversmith was a snobbish man and thought to himself, "A mere oil peddler and he wants to borrow a scale to weigh his silver! Even if I give him a five-tael weight, I don't think the scale will tip!"

When Ch'in Ch'ung opened his bag and showed the large number of small pieces of silver, even though there were only a few large pieces, it was an impressive sight. The silversmith, being what he was, immediately changed his opinion and attitude toward Ch'in Ch'ung. He thought, "One really cannot judge a man by his appearance, just as one cannot measure the sea with bushel baskets."

He then hurried to set up the scale and took out a bunch of weights in various sizes. The silver in the bag came to exactly sixteen taels, the scale tipping at the one catty mark. Ch'in Ch'ung thought to himself, "Leaving the three taels of capital aside, there is still more than enough for a night at the brothel." Then he thought of something else: "How can I pay with all these little

pieces of silver? People will look down on me if I do. Since it's so convenient here, why don't I change them into larger pieces? It'll certainly look more presentable."

So he had the silversmith make for him one large ingot of ten taels and one small ingot of one tael eighty cents. He used part of the remaining four taels eighty cents to pay the silversmith and bought a new hat and new pairs of shoes and socks for himself. When he returned home, he washed and starched his clothes and then perfumed them over and over again with Persian incense. On the first bright and sunny day, he got up early and dressed himself up.

Even though he is no rich and noble lord,
He is certainly a romantic lad.

After Ch'in Ch'ung had groomed himself carefully, he put the silver in his sleeves, locked the door, and headed straight for Wang Chiu-ma's house. He was in high spirits all the way, but by the time he reached their front door, his sense of shame caught up with him, and he thought, "I've always come here as the oil peddler, and today I've come here as a patron. How can I approach them?"

As he was pondering, the door opened with a creak and Chiu-ma came out. When she saw Ch'in, she said, "Master Ch'in, why aren't you doing business today? And you are all dressed up! Where are you going?"

Since it was already too late for Ch'in to retreat, he had to brace himself and go forward to greet her. Chiu-ma returned his bow.

"I've come to pay you a visit, auntie," Ch'in Ch'ung said.

Chiu-ma was an old hand at the game, and also a good judge of the human heart, so she immediately guessed what his real intentions were; she thought to herself: "He must have taken a fancy to one of my girls and wants to meet her or even stay for the night. Though he is no big spender,

191

as the saying goes, 'Whatever is in the basket is good for food.' We can make enough out of him to buy a bunch of scallions. Why not earn his money? His silver is certainly as good as any other man's."

So she put on a big smile and said, "Thank you, Master Ch'in. But I'm sure there must be something that you want to see me about."

"I have an impudent request which I'm too embarrassed to mention," ventured Ch'in Ch'ung.

"Why not say it?" encouraged Chiu-ma. "Please come inside, and we can talk about it."

Even though Ch'in Ch'ung had come to Chiu-ma's house more than a hundred times before as an oil peddler, this was the first time he had ever sat on these chairs reserved for the guests. Chiu-ma invited him into the reception room, made him sit in the place of honor, and called the servants to bring tea. Soon, a maid brought the tea out. She recognized that the guest was none other than Oil Peddler Ch'in, yet she could not figure out why Chiu-ma was treating him so cordially. With bowed head, she could not help giggling to herself. Chiu-ma saw it and scolded, "What's so funny? Where are your manners?"

The maid stopped her giggling and went inside after collecting the tea cups. Then Chiu-ma asked Ch'in, "Master Ch'in, what is it that you want to tell me?"

"Nothing of great importance," Ch'in replied. "I would like to invite one of the girls in your house for a cup of wine."

"Just for a cup of wine? Of course you would want to spend the night, too. I've known you to be a steady young man; what has aroused such romantic interest in you?"

"I've had this wish for a long time now."

"You know all my girls; which one do you like?"

"I don't want anyone else. I just want to spend one night with the Queen of the Courtesans."

Chiu-ma thought that he was making fun of her, and her countenance changed immediately.

"What an outrageous request! Are you trying to insult me?"

"I'm an honest man, and my wishes are sincere," Ch'in Ch'ung hurried to say.

"Even the manure buckets have two ears.[17] Don't you know the price of my Mei-niang? You can't afford to spend half a night with her even if you empty all your oil buckets. Why don't you choose someone else?"

Ch'in Ch'ung shrugged and made a face, "Wow! May I ask how many thousand taels of silver you ask?"

This remark convinced Chiu-ma that he was only joking, so she smiled and said, "Not much, only ten taels of silver—that is, not including food and other expenses."

"If that is all, I think I can afford it." He took out the biggest ingot and handed it to Chiu-ma. "This one weighs ten taels and is of the standard purity and weight. Please accept it, auntie." Then he took out another smaller ingot and also handed it to Chiu-ma, saying, "This smaller one weighs two taels, which I hope will cover the food and the other miscellaneous expenses. If you can grant this small request of mine, I shall never forget you and will repay you whenever I can."

Chiu-ma was overwhelmed by the sight of the shiny ingots and could not bear to see them leave her hands again. Still a little worried that Ch'in had done this on an impulse and would later regret loosing his capital, she decided to make sure: "It's not easy for a small businessman like you to save up so much money. Why don't you think it over carefully?"

"I have made up my mind. Please don't worry about it," Ch'in Ch'ung assured her.

Chiu-ma put the silver into her sleeves and said, "All right, but there are some difficulties."

[17] This means that even if Ch'in Ch'ung were as dumb as a manure bucket, he should have heard about the price for spending a night with Mei-niang.

"Auntie, you are the head of the family. What problems can there be?"

"The people whom my Mei-niang frequents are all rich and noble. Really, 'Prominent scholars are among her companions, while illiterate men have no place in her circle.' She will recognize you as Oil Peddler Ch'in and may not want to entertain you."

"Surely you can bring her around with your skillful persuasion," Ch'in Ch'ung pleaded. "I will never forget your kindness if you would help to make my wish come true."

As she saw that he was quite determined, an idea suddenly struck Chiu-ma, so she grinned and said, "I have thought of a way to help you, so now it all depends on your own luck. If you succeed, don't let it go to your head; if you don't, don't blame me. Mei-niang went to a dinner party at Scholar Li's house yesterday and has not returned yet. Today, young Master Huang has already made an appointment with her to tour the lake. Tomorrow, Hermit Chang and some of the other scholars have invited her to a gathering of their poetry society. As for the day after tomorrow, the son of Minister Han already arranged several days ago for a party to be held here. Why don't you come back three days from now? Oh yes, don't deliver oil here during these few days. You'll get more respect that way. And one more thing: you don't look like a high-class patron wearing those cotton clothes. Wear a silk robe next time, so the maids won't recognize you as Master Ch'in. It'll make it easier for me to cover up for you." Ch'in promised to follow all her instructions, and left.

He rested for three days and did not go out to peddle oil. Instead, he bought a half-new silk robe from a pawn shop and after putting it on, strolled idly around the streets and practiced acting like a man of class and distinction. Indeed:

Before learning the ways of the brothels,
First practice the etiquette of the Confucians.

Let us go right on to the fourth day. On that day, Ch'in woke up at dawn and went to Chiu-ma's house; but since it was still early, he found the door still closed. He thought about taking a walk before coming back again, but he was afraid that the monks at the Monastery of Manifest Blessings would ridicule him if they saw him in such unusual attire. So he strolled around the Ten View Pond instead and returned only after a long time. The door of Chiu-ma's house was open, but a carriage was parked before it and many servants were sitting idly inside the gate. Even though Ch'in Ch'ung was unfamiliar with the ways of the world, he was at least discreet enough not to venture inside right away. Instead, he asked the carriage driver, "Whose carriage is this?"

"We're from the Han Estate, waiting for our young master," the man replied.

Ch'in realized that young Master Han had stayed overnight and had not left yet. So he turned back again and went into a restaurant for some food. He stayed there for as long as he could before going back to Chiu-ma's house. This time the carriage was gone, but he was greeted by Chiu-ma as he was walked in with: "My apologies, Master Ch'in. I'm afraid we can't make it today. Young Master Han has dragged her off to view the early plum blossoms at East Village. He is a steady customer so I couldn't say no. I heard that they're going to the Monastery of Soul's Retreat tomorrow, to visit a chess master for a few games with him. Then young Master Ch'i has also sent over several invitations, and since he is the owner of this house, I can't very well refuse him. When he comes, he may stay for several days; I can't say for sure. Master Ch'in, if you really want to meet Mei-niang, why don't you wait patiently for another few days? Otherwise, I'll gladly return your money."

"I'm only afraid that you won't help me," said Ch'in. "Better late than never! As long as I can fulfill my wish, I'm willing to wait even if it takes ten thousand years."

"If that is the case, I'm sure I can help you," Chiu-ma said.

Ch'in bade her farewell and was getting up to leave when Chiu-ma said to him, "Master Ch'in, there's another thing which I would like to remind you of. Don't come too early next time; late afternoon will be about right. By then, I can tell you for sure if she'll be free or not. Actually, the later you come, the better it will be. I have good reasons, so just have faith in me and I won't let you down."

"Of course, of course." Ch'in nodded repeatedly.

Ch'in Ch'ung did not do any business that day. Starting from the next morning, he peddled oil in other places without passing the Ch'ien-t'ang Gate area; and when he finished with his business each day, he dressed up and went to Chiu-ma's house around evening for news. For more than a month, he had no luck.

On the fifteenth day of the twelfth month, a snowstorm had just cleared up and the west wind had just blown over. The fallen snow had turned to ice, and it was very cold, but the ground was dry. Ch'in tended to his business for most of the day and then dressed up as usual to go to Chiu-ma's house. Chiu-ma greeted him with a big smile and said, "You're in luck; the chances are ninety-nine out of a hundred you're going to succeed."

"What is still missing?" Ch'in asked.

"Mei-niang is not yet home."

"Will she be back?"

"Today Marshal Yü has invited her to view snow on his boat in the lake. He is an old man of seventy, and he has no part in amorous affairs. He said earlier that he'd send her home before dark," Chiu-ma assured him. "So why don't you go into the bridal chamber[18] and drink a few cups

of wine to keep yourself warm while waiting for her return?"

Ch'in Ch'ung agreed happily. Chiu-ma led him through many twists and turns and finally came to the place. It was a one-story structure with three rooms which was both bright and airy. On the left was an unoccupied room for the maids, with the usual furniture and bedding prepared for the guests. The room on the right was the bedroom of the Queen of the Courtesans, and it was locked. There were other side chambers attached to the sitting room in the center. Above the guest seats in the middle of the sitting room, there hung a landscape painting by a well-known artist. Wisps of fragrance were rising from the incense burner on the high stool. Several antique pieces decorated the tables on both sides, and many poetry scrolls were hung on the walls. Ch'in was ashamed that he was no accomplished scholar and dared not inspect them any more closely. He thought to himself, "If even this sitting room is so elegant, the layout of Mei-niang's room must be even more elaborate and luxurious. I can enjoy all this to my heart's content tonight, so ten taels for one night really isn't too much."

Chiu-ma invited Ch'in Ch'ung to sit on one of the guest seats, while she took the hostess' position to keep him company. A little later, the maid brought in the lamp; then the table was set with six bowls of seasonal fruit and one large plate of assorted delicacies, whose inviting aroma began attacking his nostrils even before he had touched anything. Chiu-ma held the wine bottle and urged him, "All my girls have guests today, so I'm afraid I'm the only one left to keep you company. Please enjoy yourself and drink your fill."

Ch'in was unaccustomed to drinking, and since he had something more important in mind, he drank very little and refused to drink more.

"Master Ch'in, you must be hungry; please eat something and then we'll drink some more," Chiu-ma suggested.

The maid brought out two bowls of rice, one of

---

[18] The procuress uses this language to give her patrons the feeling that they are bridegrooms for the day.

them as a second helping, and placed them in front of Ch'in Ch'ung along with a bowl of soup. The madam, of course, was used to drinking, so she kept him company by having more wine. Ch'in Ch'ung put down his chopsticks after finishing only one bowl. Chiu-ma said, "The night is long; eat some more."

Ch'in Ch'ung ate another half of a bowl. The maid came in with a lantern and said, "The bath is ready. Will the guest please come with me?"

Ch'in Ch'ung had bathed before he came out, but did not think it polite to refuse; so he went to the bathroom, washed thoroughly with soap, and scented himself again. When he came back, Chiu-ma ordered the delicacies taken away and used a hot-pot to warm the wine. By then, it was completely dark outside, and the Monastery of Manifest Blessings had sounded its evening bells, but Mei-niang still had not returned.

Lovely lady, where are you dallying?
Your lover is waiting impatiently.

As the saying goes, "It's the one who waits who is impatient." Seeing that the girl had not yet returned, Ch'in Ch'ung was both anxious and bored. He was stuck with the madam, who bombarded him with a lot of nonsense and poured him one cup after another. Soon another watch passed. Suddenly, there was a great commotion outside, and the maids came in to announce that Mei-niang had returned. Chiu-ma and Ch'in Ch'ung both got up to receive her. Mei-niang was drunk and was helped into the room by the maids. At the door, she saw hazily that the room was brightly lit and that the remnants of a feast were spread all over the table. She stopped and asked, "Who's been drinking here?"

"My child, it's the Master Ch'in I've been telling you about," Chiu-ma explained. "He admires you and has constantly sent presents over. We've kept him waiting for more than a month already because you didn't have the time. Luckily you're free tonight, so I have asked him to keep you company."

"I've never heard of a Master Ch'in here in Lin-an City. I don't want to meet him!" So saying, she turned around to go.

Chiu-ma stretched out her arms to stop her, saying, "He's a very nice man. I'm telling you the truth."

Thus Mei-niang turned around, and as she was stepping into the room again, saw Ch'in Ch'ung and found him rather familiar. But because she was drunk, she could not quite remember who he was at the moment. She said, "Mother, I know this man. He's a nobody. People will laugh at me if I receive him."

"My child, this is Master Ch'in who owns a silk shop at the Golden Flood Gate. I think you met him before when we used to live there. That's why you find him so familiar," Chiu-ma persisted. "Don't mistake him for someone else. I saw that he is very sincere and so I have promised him already. Please don't make me break my word. For my sake, let him spend the night. I know I'm in the wrong; I'll make it up to you tomorrow." She pushed Mei-niang gently toward Ch'in Ch'ung as she spoke, so Mei-niang could do nothing except go into the room and meet him. Indeed:

You cannot outtalk the procuress even if you have a thousand
*   tongues;*
You cannot wriggle free from the procuress even if you have
*   ten thousand arms.*
So even if you're equipped with a thousand tongues and ten
*   thousand arms,*
You'd better just let the procuress lead you by the hand.

Ch'in Ch'ung had heard every word that was said but pretended that he had heard nothing. Mei-niang greeted him and sat on one side. The more she looked at him, the more suspicious she became. Feeling displeased, she said nothing to him; instead, she asked the maids to bring some wine and poured it into a large cup. Chiu-ma thought that she was going to offer it to Ch'in

Ch'ung, but she finished it herself in a single gulp. Chiu-ma tried to stop her: "My child, you're drunk. Don't drink any more."

But Mei-niang would not listen to her. Insisting that she was not drunk, she drank more than ten cups. Since she was already quite drunk to begin with, naturally she soon became too dizzy even to sit upright. She told the maid to open up the bedroom and light the lamps. Then, without letting down her hair, she just kicked off her shoes and slumped onto the bed with all of her clothes on. Chiu-ma was rather apologetic when she saw her daughter behaving thus, and said to Ch'in Ch'ung, "My daughter is rather spoiled and is given to having her way. Something is bothering her today. It has nothing to do with you, so please don't be offended."

"Of course not," Ch'in Ch'ung assured her.

Then Chiu-ma persuaded Ch'in Ch'ung to drink some more, but he refused firmly; so she sent him into the bedroom and whispered in his ear, "She's drunk; please make allowances." Then she called out to Mei-niang, "Get up, my child, and take off your clothes. You can sleep better that way."

Mei-niang was already fast asleep and did not answer, so Chiu-ma had to leave. The maids cleared the table and said to Ch'in Ch'ung, "Master Ch'in, good night now."

"I would like to have a pot of hot tea if I may," Ch'in Ch'ung said.

The maid brewed a pot of strong tea and brought it into the room; then, closing the door behind her, she went to rest in her own room. Ch'in Ch'ung turned to look at Mei-niang and found her sound asleep with her face toward the wall, lying on top of her quilt. He was afraid that she might catch cold, especially being drunk, but he did not want to wake her. Suddenly, he saw a red silk quilt on the bedstead, so he took it down and gently covered Mei-niang. Then he made the lamp as bright as possible, took off his shoes, and went to bed with the pot of hot tea. Sliding in be-side Mei-niang, he lay down with his left hand cuddling the tea pot and his right hand on Mei-niang. He dared not even close his eyes for a minute. Verily:

Even though he didn't have a chance to command the clouds and the rain,
Nevertheless, he had smelt the fragrance and caressed the jade.

Mei-niang woke up around midnight and felt the wine acting up. A burning in her chest made her sit up in bed, retching. Ch'in Ch'ung hurried to sit up, too, and knowing that she was about to vomit, he put down the teapot and stroked her back gently. After a long while, the nausea suddenly overcame Mei-niang and faster done then said, she threw up. Ch'in Ch'ung was afraid that she might soil the bedding, and immediately used the sleeves of his robe to cover her mouth. Mei-niang was not aware of that and vomited without reserve. When she had finished, she asked for some tea to rinse her mouth, still with her eyes closed. Ch'in Ch'ung got down from the bed, took off his robe quietly and put it on the floor. Feeling the teapot and noting that it was still warm, he poured a cup of strong tea and handed it to Mei-niang. Mei-niang drank two cups in succession. Although she still felt a little heartburn, she was so tired that she immediately fell back to sleep. Ch'in Ch'ung took off his robe, rolling up his soiled sleeve, and laid it by the bedside.[19] Then he climbed back into bed and embraced Mei-niang as before.

Mei-niang did not wake again until daybreak. When she turned around and found Ch'in Ch'ung lying beside her, she asked, "Who are you?"

"I'm Ch'in Ch'ung," he answered.

Mei-niang thought about the night before but could only vaguely recall what had happened. She said, "I must have been dead drunk last night."

[19] Evidently there is textual corruption here, since it is mentioned in an earlier sentence that Ch'in Ch'ung has already taken off his robe.

"No, not really."

"Did I throw up?" she asked again.

"No," Ch'in Ch'ung replied.

"That's good." But on the second thought, she said, "I remember having vomited and also drinking tea. Was I dreaming then?"

Ch'in Ch'ung then told her, "Yes, you did throw up. I thought you might vomit so I was prepared for it. I held the tea against my body to keep it warm and when you did throw up and asked for tea, I poured you some. I'm glad you didn't refuse and drank two cups."

Mei-niang was shocked. "Oh, how filthy! Where did I throw up?"

"I was afraid that you might soil the bedding, so I held it with my sleeves."

"Where is your robe now?"

"I rolled everything up inside the robe. It's over there."

"What a pity that your robe is soiled."

"I'm only too glad that my robe could be of some service to you."

When Mei-niang heard that, she thought to herself, "What a thoughtful man!" and already liked him quite a bit.

But then, it was already bright daylight. Mei-niang got up to go to the bathroom. As she looked at Ch'in Ch'ung, she suddenly recognized him as Oil Peddler Ch'in, so she said, "Tell me frankly. Who are you? And why were you here last night?"

"Since you bother to ask me, of course I'll tell the truth. I'm actually Ch'in Ch'ung who comes to your house to deliver oil quite often." Then he proceeded to tell her in detail how he first saw her seeing the guests out and later mounting the sedan chair, how much he had longed for her ever since, and how he had saved up the money just to spend the night with her. "How fortunate I am to have spent a whole night being so close to you. I'm very happy and more than contented."

Mei-niang was more moved than ever when she heard this. She said, "I was drunk last night and didn't take care of you. Don't you regret that you've wasted your money for nothing?"

"You are like a goddess from heaven. I consider myself lucky that you don't scold me for not serving you better. How would I dare to have other improper desires?"

"People in a small business like yours should save up some money to support their families. You really shouldn't have come to this kind of place."

"I'm single and I have no family," Ch'in Ch'ung explained.

Mei-niang thought for a while and asked, "Will you be back again?"

"Being so close to you for one night will sustain me for the rest of my life; I would not dare to hope for more."

"Where could I find such a good man?" Mei-niang thought. "So honest, so kind, and above all so understanding, covering my weaknesses and praising my merits. I don't think it's possible to find another like him in a million. What a pity that he's a mere peddler; otherwise I wouldn't hesitate to marry him."

As she was pondering, the maids brought in water for them to wash their faces, and also two bowls of ginger soup. Ch'in Ch'ung washed his face, and since he had not undone his hair the night before, he did not have to comb it. He took a few sips of the ginger soup and was prepared to leave. Mei-niang said, "Why don't you stay a while longer? I still have something to say to you."

"Since I admire you so much, nothing will make me happier than to stay with you for as long as I can. But one must know one's position. It was already impudent of me to have come here last night, putting your reputation in jeopardy. It's best that I leave as soon as possible."

Mei-niang nodded and told the maids to leave the room; then she opened her makeup box, took out twenty taels of silver, and handed them to Ch'in Ch'ung, saying, "I'm sorry to have caused you all the trouble last night. This money is to help you with your business. Don't tell anybody, though!"

Ch'in Ch'ung would not take the money, so Mei-niang added, "I get this money quite easily. This is but a token of my appreciation for your kindness last night. Please take it. If you need more capital, I can be of assistance to you in the future. As for the dirty robe, I'll ask the maid to wash it and then return it to you."

"Please don't bother with this cheap robe. I can wash it myself. It's only that I really shouldn't take your money."

"Don't mention it." Mei-niang stuffed the silver into Ch'in Ch'ung's sleeves and pushed him out. Ch'in Ch'ung realized that it would be impossible to refuse, so he bowed deeply, rolled up the dirty robe, and left the room.

A maid saw him as he passed Chiu-ma's room. She announced, "Madam, Mister Ch'in is leaving."

Chiu-ma was just inside the bathroom, so she called out, "Master Ch'in, why are you leaving so early?"

"I have some personal matters to attend to. I shall come back to thank you some other day," Ch'in Ch'ung called back.

We will speak no more of Ch'in Ch'ung for the present. After his departure, Mei-niang felt ill at ease for some time. Even though nothing had happened between her and Ch'in Ch'ung, she was apparently touched by his sincerity. She called off all her engagements that day and rested at home because she was still under the influence of the wine from the previous night. Though she had received many men since she became a courtesan, she thought of no one but Ch'in Ch'ung during that day. There is another *Kua-chih-erh* song to show this:

Loved one,
Even though you're no rich man's son,
And you're only a small businessman,
Yet alone you've treated me gently, talked to me tenderly;
You alone know my heart.
I think you're not one of those temperamental ones;

I think you're not one of those unfaithful ones.
Several times I've tried to get you off my mind
And realized that it's harder than I thought.

Now let us leave Mei-niang and Ch'in Ch'ung for a while and return to Chu Shih-lao. Since Ch'in Ch'ung was no longer around, Hsing Ch'üan and the maid Orchid carried on their affair openly, completely ignoring the old man, who was now sick in bed. Chu Shih-lao became extremely angry several times, so the two of them came up with a plan. They waited until the dead of night, took all the money in the shop, and ran away together. Chu Shih-lao did not find out until the next morning. The neighborhood was alerted and a list of losses was made out. They looked around for several days without result. It was then that Chu Shih-lao regretted deeply having listened to Hsing Ch'üan earlier and having driven away Chu Ch'ung. Time had now proven who was the faithful one. He had heard that Chu Ch'ung was living by the All Peace Bridge and peddled oil for a living. He thought of asking him back so he could have someone to look after him in his old age, but he was afraid that Chu Ch'ung might bear a grudge against him. Hence, he asked his neighbors to speak to Chu Ch'ung, asking him to "remember only the good and forget the bad," and to come back to him. When Ch'in Ch'ung heard that, he immediately packed his belongings and moved back to Chu Shih-lao's house. Both cried bitterly when they met. The old man took out all his money and handed it over to Ch'in Ch'ung. Adding this to the twenty some taels which he had saved, Ch'in Ch'ung renovated the oil shop and again took charge of the business there. Since he had returned to Chu Shih-lao's house, he went back to his former name, Chu Ch'ung.

Within a month, Chu Shih-lao's illness worsened and he soon died. Chu Ch'ung was grief-stricken and made the funeral preparations just as if Chu Shih-lao had been his own father. The ancestral graves of the Chu family were outside the Clear Ripple Gate. There, Chu Ch'ung again performed all the burial ceremonies with due respect and was greatly praised by his neighbors for his loyalty to Chu Shih-lao. After everything had been properly taken care of, Chu Ch'ung reopened the shop. This oil shop was one of long standing and business had always been good. It was only when Hsing Ch'üan ran it in his dishonest way that many of the customers left. Now, when they saw that young Master Chu was in charge again, they were more than willing to do business with him, and the shop increased in prosperity by the day.

Since Chu Ch'ung had to handle all the business single-handedly, he was anxious to find someone familiar with the trade to help him. One day, a middleman by the name of Chin Chung brought over a man in his early fifties. He turned out to be none other than Hsin Shan, the man who used to live in Prosperity Village outside the city of Pien-liang, the one who had lost his daughter Yao-ch'in during the retreat of the government troops. Since then, the couple had been left in a pitiful state, running from one place to another during those year of chaos. They had heard about Lin-an's prosperity and that more than half of the refugees who had crossed the river had settled there. They thought that their daughter might have been stranded there, too, and had come especially to look for her. They found no news, but had spent all the money they had. They also owed the inn some money and were about to be evicted any day. It was in this helpless situation that they accidentally learned from Chin Chung that Chu Ch'ung's oil shop was looking for an assistant. Hsin Shan himself had once owned a store and was quite familiar with the oil trade. Moreover, this Master Chu was from Pien-liang, too, which made them fellow villagers. So he pleaded with Chin Chung to recommend him. Chu Ch'ung asked Hsin Shan a few questions and was moved when he heard that the latter was also from

Pien-liang, so he said, "Since you have nowhere else to go, why don't the two of you move to my place? I'll treat you like my own relatives, and you can take your time looking for your daughter."

He gave Hsin Shan two strings of cash to pay off his inn bills. Hsin Shan's wife was also brought over to meet Chu Ch'ung, who cleaned up one room for the old couple to live in. From then on, the two of them also did their best to help Chu Ch'ung in the shop as well as in the house, so Chu Ch'ung was very happy about the arrangement.

Time flashed by, and more than a year passed. Many people, seeing that a dependable and well-off young man like Chu Ch'ung was still unmarried, were more than willing to give him their daughters. But Chu Ch'ung had already seen the beauty of the Queen of the Courteans; the ordinary girls could hardly catch his fancy. He was determined to find a girl with outstanding qualities before settling down. This matter was thus delayed day after day.

You cannot talk about water to those who have seen the sea,
Nor about clouds to those who have seen the mist over Mount Wu.

We shall now go back to Wang Mei-niang. Her reputation grew steadily and she led an extravagant life. Yet when she was moody, when a drunken patron threw tantrums, when rival patrons quarreled over her, or when she woke up in the middle of the night feeling sick and nauseated without anyone to comfort her or take care of her, she could not help thinking of Ch'in Ch'ung and his thoughtfulness, and longed for another chance to meet him. About a year later, an incident completely changed her fate.

There lived in Lin-an a young man named Wu, the eighth son of Wu Yüeh, the prefect of Foochow.[20] Now this young man had just returned from a visit to his father in Foochow and was loaded with money. A frequent visitor to gam-

[20] On the seaboard of modern Fukien Province.

199

bling dens and houses of pleasure, he had long heard of the Queen of the Courtesans but had not had a chance to meet her, even though he had sent over several invitations to her. Mei-niang, however, had heard that he was a man of dubious character had therefore refused him with all sorts of excuses. Even though Wu himself had been to Chiu-ma's house several times with his friends, he had never seen Mei-niang even once. One day around the time of the Ch'ing-ming Festival,[21] when most people were out visiting their ancestors' graves and enjoying the spring scene, Mei-niang, partly because she was tired of the numeous spring excursions and partly because she had many promised poems and paintings to do, decided to have a day off by not receiving any visitors.

She closed the door, lit some fine incense, set the stationery in order, and was just about to start writing when she heard a commotion outside. It was Wu, bringing with him a dozen insolent servants to get Mei-niang for a boat party. When Chiu-ma made excuses for Mei-niang, he became angry and proceeded to vent his displeasure by breaking the furniture and household utensils as he made his way to Mei-niang's room, where he found the door locked. Actually, the brothels had a way of turning away unwanted guests: the courtesan would hide inside the room and the door would be locked from the outside; then the guest would be told that she was not in. The innocent ones would be tricked, but Wu was an old hand at the game and naturally was not deceived by this. He ordered his servants to break the lock while he himself kicked open the door. Mei-niang did not have time to hide and was caught. Without further ado, Wu ordered two servants to drag her, one holding each arm, from the room, as he himself stood there swearing and cursing. At first Chiu-ma wanted to go forward and make apolo-

gies, but seeing that the situation was getting out of hand, she decided to slip aside. Soon the entire household became empty. Wu's servants then dragged Mei-niang out of Chiu-ma's house and ran down the streets with no consideration whatsoever for her small bound feet. Wu followed behind, thoroughly enjoying the scene. They went all the way to the West Lake and forced Mei-niang onto the boat before letting go of her.

Ever since she had entered Chiu-ma's house at the age of twelve, Mei-niang had always been brought up among silks and brocades, and was looked upon as a gem and a jewel. Never in her life had she suffered such humiliation and mistreatment. Once on the boat, she turned away by herself and started to wail. When Wu saw that, his countenance fell, not unlike the forthrightness of Kuan Yün-ch'ang in charging single-handedly into the meeting.[22] Without preliminaries, he sat on an armchair facing the lake with his servants flanking him, then ordered the boat to start sailing amid curses and insults: "Bitch! Whore! Ingrate! Make another sound and you'll be flayed!"

Mei-niang, of course, was not frightened, and she kept on crying. The boat soon reached the pavilion in the middle of the lake. Wu told the servants to set up the food in the pavilion and himself went first, telling the servants, "Ask the little bitch to come and keep me company."

But Mei-niang held on to the railing and refused to go, wailing even louder. By then, Wu had lost his interest, so after drinking only a few cups, he returned to the boat to pounce on Mei-niang. She stamped her feet with all her might and screamed more defiantly. This made Wu so furious that he ordered the servants to take away Mei-niang's hairpins. With her hair all disheveled, Mei-niang ran to the bow and would have jumped

[21] A spring festival roughly equivalent to the Easter time, around April 5th, at which the Chinese worship at the graves of their ancestors.

[22] In chapter 66 of the novel *San-kuo chih yen-i,* Kuan Yü, despite the fact that he might be trapped, goes to attend a bargaining meeting in the state of Wu. It turns out to be really a trap. But Kuan manages to get hold of the chief adviser of Wu as a hostage and easily escapes.

into the water if the pages had not stopped her in time. Wu then told her, "Don't think you can frighten me with your temper. Even if you killed yourself, I'd probably only have to spend a few taels and that's all there would be to it. But it would be indeed a pity if you lost your life this way, so I'll let you go if you stop crying, and I won't give you any more trouble."

When Mei-niang heard that he was willing to let her go, she immediately stopped crying. Wu told his servants to sail to a deserted spot outside the Clear Ripple Gate, where he had Mei-niang's shoes and foot-bindings stripped off, thus exposing a pair of feet like two strands of jade bamboo shoots. After his men had helped her ashore, he broke into more abuses: "Little bitch, see if you can walk home by yourself. I have no time to see you home!" Then the boat was poled away and sailed into the lake. Indeed:

There are those who would burn a harp and boil a crane,[23]
But you can't find one who has pity on the fragrant and
*   beautiful one.*

Barefoot, Mei-niang could hardly move an inch. She thought, "I have both beauty and talent, yet I have to endure such humiliation because I have fallen into this business through ill fortune. I have indeed known all the noblemen and highly placed people in vain. None of them are on hand when I need them. Having been shamed like this, how can I live with it even if I do manage to get back? I think I'd be better off dead. But then I would be dying because such a worthless incident that it would make a mockery of my reputation. At a time like this, I think even the village women are far better off than I. It's all because of that big-mouthed Liu Ssu-ma! If it weren't for her, I wouldn't have fallen in the first place, not to men-

tion all these troubles. It's true that ever since times of old beautiful girls have been ill fated, but I don't think they were ever as pitiful as I am now."

The more she thought, the sadder she felt, and she burst into tears again. What a coincidence that on this very day Chu Ch'ung had gone outside the Clear Ripple Gate to visit Chu Shih-lao's grave. After sweeping the grave, he sent the sacrificial materials back by boat while he himself returned on foot. He heard someone crying as he was passing through and went over to take a look. Even though Mei-niang's hair was disheveled and her face was soiled, her beauty was still unaffected, so how could Chu Ch'ung fail to recognize her? In great shock he hastened to ask her, "Mei-niang, what happened to you?"

Mei-niang was crying bitterly when she heard a familiar voice. She stopped her sobbing, looked up, and found that it was the thoughtful Master Ch'in. Under circumstances like these, she felt as if she had seen a relative, so she poured out her heart to him. Chu Ch'ung was so pained to see her suffer like this that he also shed tears of sympathy. He took out a long white silk handkerchief, tore it in half, and bound up Mei-niang's feet. Then he wiped away her tears, helped her to straighten her hair, and comforted her with many kind words. When Mei-niang had finally stopped crying, he went and called a sedan chair for her, while he himself walked all the way to escort her home.

Chiu-ma was in a flurry, looking everywhere for some news of her daughter, when she saw Master Ch'in bringing her home. This was just like the recovery of a precious pearl to her, so naturally she was overjoyed. Besides, she had not seen Ch'in Ch'ung peddling his oil for quite some time, and had heard that he had inherited Chu Shih-lao's business. Since he had more money at his disposal now and was in a much more respectable position than before, naturally she received him with a new deference. Seeing her daughter in

---

[23] Playing the harp was one of the four cultivated pastimes of a traditional scholar (the other three were chess, calligraphy, and painting). The crane was considered one of the most graceful creatures. To burn a harp or to boil a crane was something only the most rustic person would do.

such a state, she asked Mei-niang for the reasons and learned that she had suffered a great deal, and that it was only thanks to Ch'in Ch'ung that she had been saved. Chiu-ma thanked him profusely and a feast was prepared in his honor. Since it was getting late, Ch'in Ch'ung only drank a few cups and got up to leave. Mei-niang, of course, would not hear of it; she said, "I have always had feeling for you, and have often regretted not being able to see you again. I certainly will not let you go like that today."

Chiu-ma also got up to detain him. Ch'in Ch'ung was overjoyed at his unexpected good fortune and accepted gladly. That night, Mei-niang played various musical instruments, sang, and danced—displaying every one of her skills to the fullest so as to please Ch'in Ch'ung. Ch'in Ch'ung felt as though he were having a dream rendezvous with a goddess. They feasted into the night, and then the two of them retired to bed in each other's embrace. Naturally, the perfect bliss of their union was beyond doubt:

One is a young man in his prime;
One is a young woman well versed in the art she plies.
He relates how the three years of longing have occupied his
*   soul and his dreams;*
She tells him her share of yearning, and is only happy now to
*   be so close to him.*
She thanks him for his past patronage, as well as today's
*   deliverance;*
He thanks her for this night, more loving than the first.
The courtesan upsets her powder box, staining the silken
*   kerchief;*
The oil peddler spills over his oil jar, soiling her quilt.
If you've laughed at this village boy who once squandered his
*   capital,*
Witness how he has succeeded in the greatest romance ever
*   told.*

When it was over, Mei-niang said, "I have something very important to confide to you, and I hope you won't make any excuses."

"If there is anything I can do for you, I will never refuse even if it means going through boil-ing water and raging fire. Why should I make excuses?"

"I want to marry you!"

Ch'in Ch'ung laughed and said, "You will have married ten thousand times before you'll think of me. Please don't make fun of me. It'll only make Heaven jealous and take away what I have."

"I speak from the bottom of my heart. How can you say I'm making fun of you? Ever since I was tricked by my mother into losing my virginity, I've always wanted to get out of this business. But since I didn't have much experience in dealing with men at that time, and couldn't really distinguish the good from the bad, I dared not make a hasty decision and thereby ruin my whole life. Later on, even though I met a lot of men, they were either spendthrifts or playboys. They only cared about their momentary pleasure, and had hardly any goodwill or consideration for my welfare. You're the only sincere and dependable man I've found after looking for so long. I've heard that you're still single, so if you don't look down on my shameful past, I'm willing to marry you and serve you for the rest of my life. But if you refuse me, I shall hang myself with three feet of white silk right here in front of you to prove my sincerity. It would certainly be better than dying so worthlessly at the hands of that vulgar creature yesterday and making myself an object of ridicule." Having finished, she started to cry.

"Mei-niang, please don't feel so sad," Ch'in Ch'ung comforted her. "I'm more than honored to have you bestow your love upon me, for this is more than anything I can ask for. But you are a woman of great fame and worth, while I'm a poor and powerless peddler. I'm afraid I might not be able to gather enough money to redeem you no matter how hard I try."

"That's no problem. To tell you the truth, I started a long time ago to save valuables and have put them away in other places for this very purpose. You don't have to trouble yourself about the problem of money."

"But even if you're able to redeem yourself, you are sure to miss your life of luxury, and I'm afraid you will find life quite unbearable in my house."

"I am ready to wear cotton clothes and eat coarse food without a word of complaint."

"Even if you are willing, I wonder if auntie will consent to it."

"I have my ways. Here's what I'll do . . ." The two of them talked about this and that until daybreak.

Mei-niang had in fact stored away many trunks and boxes of valuables with several of her intimates, such as the sons of Academician Huang, Prime Minister Han, and Marshal Ch'i. Now, under the pretext that she needed them, she gradually took them back and had Ch'in Ch'ung secretly move them over to his house. This done, she mounted a sedan chair to see Liu Ssu-ma, and told Ssu-ma about her plan to get out of the business.

"I did mention this before, but you're still young now and I don't know who you want to marry," Ssu-ma said.

"Auntie, never mind who he is. Anyway, I've followed everything you said, so it'll be a real getting-out, a permanent getting-out, and it won't be a half-true half-false, temporary, or unfinished thing. I'm sure mother won't object if you go and talk to her. I have nothing to offer you to show my gratitude except this ten taels of gold, which you can use to make some small hairpins. Please try your best to convince mother. There will be additional matchmaker presents if the matter is successful."

As soon as Ssu-ma saw the pieces of gold, she was smiling with her eyes in two tiny slits. She said, "You're like my own daughter, and this is a nice thing; so how can I take anything for it? I'll keep this for you for the time being. I'll take care of the whole thing for you. But since your mother thinks that you're her money tree, I don't think she'll let you go that easily. She might ask for more than a thousand taels of silver. Is your man

willing to pay that much? Maybe I should meet him and talk things over with him," Ssu-ma offered.

"You don't have to worry about those details. Just consider that I'm buying my own freedom."

"Does your mother know you're here?"

"No."

"Why don't you stay here for lunch while I go over to your house and talk to your mother. I'll let you know the outcome afterward."

Ssu-ma hired a sedan chair and went over to Chiu-ma's house. Chiu-ma welcomed her inside, and when Ssu-ma inquired about the incident with young Master Wu, Chiu-ma told her the whole story.

"For those of us who are engaged in this kind of business," said Ssu-ma, "it is better to have daughters of average beauty and talent, for they can make money for us and will not cause any trouble. They can receive any kind of guest and have steady business every day. But my niece is so famous that she's just like a piece of dried fish that has dropped on the ground, which even the ants will not leave alone. It may appear to be good business, but actually it is by no means easy business. Although you can charge a high fee for the night, she brings you only an empty name. Every time those noble young lords come, they inevitably bring along with them several followers, and the whole party usually stays the whole night long. What a nuisance! And you have to play up to every single one of them. Any slip on your part and they'll come up with all sorts of foul language, and even break the things around the house. You can't even tell their masters. Then there are all those scholars and poets with their poetry societies and chess clubs, and those government officials whom you must entertain several times each month. Finally, your rich young clients are always fighting over Mei-niang. If you promise her to Chang, you inevitably offend Li. If one side is happy, the other side is naturally offended. Take this incident with young

Master Wu; what a close shave! One careless slip and you may even lose your capital. You can't bring a lawsuit against these noble lords, so what can you do except swallow your anger and forget about the whole thing! You're lucky that this bolt of lightning has passed overhead and no one was hurt. If something does happen, it'll be too late for regrets afterward. I've heard that Wu's anger has not yet died down, and he wants to make more trouble for you. So long as my niece has such a bad temper and refuses to play up to the patrons, this will always be a source of trouble."

"That's exactly what I've been worried about," agreed Chiu-ma. "Actually this fellow Wu is a man of some importance and is by no means a nobody, yet that girl absolutely refused to meet him and therefore brought all this trouble upon herself. She used to listen to me a little when she was younger, but now that she's famous, with all those rich young men flattering her, spoiling her, indulging her, she has become so puffed up and headstrong about getting her way. When guests call, she'll receive only those she wants to; not even a team of nine oxen could drag her to those she doesn't care to see."

"All the courtesans are like this once they have some sort of a name," Ssu-ma said.

"I want to discuss something with you. If someone is willing to buy her, do you think I should sell her? It'd save me a lot of trouble, and I wouldn't have to be on edge all day long."

"What an excellent idea!" exclaimed Ssu-ma. "If you sell her, you can buy five or six others with the money you get—and maybe even ten if you can lay your hands on some inexpensive ones."

"I have thought about it quite carefully. As a rule, rich and powerful men usually don't want to spend much; they only want to use their position to take advantage of us. As for those who are willing to spend the money, my daughter always manages to find fault with them, putting on all sorts of airs and refusing with all sorts of excuses. If there's someone suitable, I hope you can be the intermediary and make the match. Also, if that girl refuses, you must talk to her for me, for she listens to you more than she does to me."

Ssu-ma laughed heartily and said, "Actually, I've come here today precisely with someone in mind for Mei-niang. How much do you want before you'll let her go?"

"Well, you know how things are. In our profession, we always try to buy cheap and sell high. Furthermore, Mei-niang has been famous for some years now here in Lin-an; who hasn't heard of the 'Queen of the Courtesans'? How can I let her go at a mere three or four hundred taels? I must have at least one thousand taels."

"Let me go and talk it over with the client. If he's willing to pay the price, I'll be back to let you know; if not, I won't bother to come back." Before she left, she asked purposefully, "Where is my niece today?"

"Don't talk about it," Chiu-ma sighed. "Ever since the day she was bullied by that fellow Wu, she's been afraid that he might be back for more and has been visiting all her intimates, telling them about the incident. The day before last, she was at Marshal Ch'i's; yesterday she was at Academician Huang's; and I don't know where she is today."

"You're the boss as long as you put your foot down. I'm sure Mei-niang will give in. But in case she refuses, I'll talk her into it. Just don't put on all sorts of airs when I do bring you the client."

"I give you my word," Chiu-ma promised.

Chiu-ma saw her to the front door where Ssu-ma hastily bade her farewell and mounted the sedan chair. In truth:

This woman Lu chia can turn black into yellow;
This female Sui Ho can turn short into long.
If everything were like the mouth of a procuress,
A foot of water could stir up a wave three thousand feet long.

When Ssu-ma arrived home, she told Mei-niang how she had persuaded Chiu-ma, and added, "Your mother has already given her consent, so as soon as the money passes hands, everything will be settled."

"The money is ready now. Could you please come to my house tomorrow so that we can settle this matter? Let's strike while the iron is hot; otherwise we might have to start all over again."

Ssu-ma said, "If it's all arranged, of course I'll come."

Mei-niang bade Ssu-ma farewell and went home. She did not say a word about the matter to anyone.

Around noon the next day, Ssu-ma came to Chiu-ma's house as agreed. Chiu-ma asked her, "How is the matter going?"

"It's almost settled. Now it's time for me to talk to Mei-niang," replied Ssu-ma.

Ssu-ma went into Mei-niang's room. After greeting each other, they chatted for a while, and then Ssu-ma asked, "Has your patron arrived yet? Where is the money?"

Mei-niang pointed at the trunks by her bed and said, "Inside there." She opened all five or six of them and took out thirteen or fourteen packets with fifty taels of silver in each. Together with the jewels which she also counted out from the trunks, they amounted to exactly a thousand taels. Ssu-ma was so overwhelmed with amazement that her eyes almost burst with flame and her mouth watered. She thought, "What foresight for such a young girl! I wonder, how did she manage to save up so much? Those girls over in my house receive patrons just like she does, but none of them can even come close to this. What little they have in their pockets they squander on dried seeds and candies. I even have to buy cloth for them when their foot-bindings get worn out. What a blessing for Sister Chiu to have bought her. She must have earned a fortune during these years, and now she's going to get such a handsome sum for letting her go. All this easy money for Sister Chiu!"

When Mei-niang saw Ssu-ma pondering, she thought that the latter was not satisfied with what she had already given her, so she hurried to take

out four scrolls of fine silk, two hairpins, and a pair of phoenix jade pins, and put them on the table, saying, "These few things are to thank you for your trouble."

Ssu-ma accepted happily and went to inform Chiu-ma, "Niece is willing to buy her own freedom with exactly the same amount you've asked. It's even better than having someone else buy her, since you can now avoid all the feasts and presents which you otherwise would have had to give to go-betweens and idlers."

Chiu-ma appeared displeased when she heard that her daughter actually had so much in private savings. Do you know why she was displeased? In this world, there are none as greedy as the madams. They won't feel satisfied until all the things which the courtesans get are in their hands. There are some courtesans who try to keep their private savings in their trunks, but if the madams hear about it, they wait until their daughters are out and then break the locks of the trunks and take away all the valuables. It was only because of her reputation, because Mei-niang was such a money tree for Chiu-ma, because all her patrons were either rich or influential men, and because she had a rather stubborn character that Chiu-ma dared not do it to her. How could she have known that Mei-niang had stored away such great wealth if she dared not even go into the latter's room? When Ssu-ma saw the color change in Chiu-ma's face, she guessed what was in her mind and hastened to say, "Sister Chiu, please don't think too much about it. Niece has saved up all this from her own proper share, and it doesn't belong to you. If she had wanted to spend it, she would have spent it all by now; if she had been dumb enough to give it to her poorer lovers, you wouldn't even know about it. It's nice that she has some money. You can't very well let her go naked! If she had no money, you'd at least have to fit her out decently so she could get married respectably. Now that Mei-niang is taking care of everything, you don't have to worry about a thing, and you

205

can keep the entire sum of money for yourself. Furthermore, even if she does buy back her freedom, she's still your daughter; if she makes good, she will surely come back to visit you on festivals and other occasions. Also, even if she gets married, she still has no real father or mother, and you will probably be honored as the grandmother and other such things when the time comes."

All this talk made Chiu-ma feel better, and she agreed to keep her part of the deal. Ssu-ma went inside to bring out the silver, checking every packet and appraising each piece of jewelry before handing it to Chiu-ma.

"I've purposely put down the price on each item; I'm sure you can get more money if you sell them," she told Chiu-ma.

Even though Chiu-ma was a madam, she was quite an honest one, so she believed everything Ssu-ma said. After Chiu-ma had accepted everything, Ssu-ma asked Chiu-ma's husband to write a letter of release for Mei-niang.

"Since auntie is here, I would like to take leave of father and mother right now, and live at auntie's place for a few days until I can pick an auspicious day to get married. I wonder if auntie will grant me this wish?" Mei-niang asked.

Since Ssu-ma had already taken the many presents given to her by Mei-niang, she was eager to get Mei-niang out of Chiu-ma's house so that the latter could not go back on her bargain. So she agreed, "That's the right way to do it."

Mei-niang immediately packed up her makeup box and jewelry boxes, trunks, and bedding, leaving everything that belonged to Chiu-ma untouched. She then followed Ssu-ma out, took leave of her adopted parents, and called upon all the sisters to say good-bye. Chiu-ma shed a few tears as was customary. Mei-niang hired several men to carry her belongings and mounted a sedan chair happily to go to Ssu-ma's house. Ssu-ma cleared a nice quiet room for her, and all the courtesans there came to congratulate her.

That night, Chu Ch'ung sent Hsin Shan over

for news and learned that Mei-niang had already bought her freedom. He picked an auspicious day and came for her with all due pomp and ceremony. Liu Ssu-ma was of course the official matchmaker. Chu Ch'ung and Mei-niang passed their wedding night in bliss and happiness. Indeed:

Even though their love affair was an old one,
Yet on this occasion their happiness increases a hundredfold.

The next day, when Hsin Shan and his wife came to meet the new bride, they were all in for a great shock. After a few exchanges, it came out that they were the long-separated parents and daughter, and everyone cried for joy. When Chu Ch'ung realized that the old couple were actually his father and mother-in-law, he immediately asked them to sit down while he and Mei-niang paid their due respects to them. The neighbors were all amazed when they heard about it. That day, they prepared a big feast to celebrate this dual happiness, drinking and enjoying themselves to the fullest. After three days, Mei-niang asked her husband to prepare several sets of presents to send over to her various intimates' houses, thanking them for keeping her trunks and also giving the news of her marriage. This showed how thorough and thoughtful Mei-niang was. There were also presents for Wang Chiu-ma and Liu Ssu-ma, who were both extremely grateful.

One month later, Mei-niang opened her trunks. They were filled with silver, gold, and fine silk amounting to about three thousand taels in value. She gave the keys to her husband, who made good use of this money to acquire land and property and also to expand his business. The oil shop was now under the care of his father-in-law Hsin Shan. In less than a year, Chu Ch'ung had made enough money to enable him and his family to live in style with a number of servants waiting on them.

To show his gratitude to the gods for their blessings, Chu Ch'ung made a vow to make offerings of candles and a three-month supply of oil at all the monasteries in the region. At each monastery, he himself took to feasting and participated in all the ceremonies. He started from the Monastery of Manifest Blessings and went on through the Monastery of Soul's Retreat, the Monastery of Buddhist Incarnation, the Cleansing Mercy Monastery, and the T'ien-chu Monastery. Let us single out the T'ien-chu Monastery for mention. It was a monastery of the Goddess of Mercy, Avalokiteshvara,[24] and had three separate but all very popular temples, namely the Upper, Middle, and Lower T'ien-chu Temples. But since they were all in the mountains, they were not accessible by boat, so Chu Ch'ung had the servants carry the loads of candles and oil while he himself went in a sedan chair. They first came to the Upper T'ien-chu Temple. The monks there received him into the main hall, while the attendant Old Ch'in lit the candles and incense. At that time, Chu Ch'ung's physical appearance and mannerisms had both changed as a result of his prosperity. Now he looked quite stout, quite different from when he was young. Naturally Old Ch'in could not recognize him, but the big characters "Ch'in" and "Pien-liang" on the oil buckets attracted his attention. What a coincidence it was that these two buckets should be used for this trip! When Chu Ch'ung finished offering the incense, Old Ch'in brought out the tea and the abbot offered it to Chu Ch'ung.

"Sorry to bother you, but can you please tell me why these three characters are on the buckets?" asked Old Ch'in.

When Chu Ch'ung heard the thick Pien-liang accent of the man asking the question, he quickly asked in return, "Old attendant, why do you ask? Are you a native of Pien-liang, too?"

"That's right," answered Old Ch'in.

"What is your name? Why did you come to work here? How long ago was it?"

[24] Avalokiteshvara, Goddess of Mercy, was in all probability a male deity originally.

Old Ch'in told him in detail: "I came here as a refugee a few years ago, but I gave up my thirteen-year-old son Ch'in Ch'ung to Chu Shih-lao for adoption because I could not support the two of us. It has been eight years now, but since I'm old and weak, I didn't go down the mountain to look for him."

Chu Ch'ung embraced him and burst into tears. "I'm Ch'in Ch'ung! I used to peddle oil for Chu Shih-lao and have put the three characters on the buckets in the hope that you might one day see them and recognize them. Who could have known that we would meet here! This must be the will of Heaven."

When the monks saw this miraculous reunion, they all murmured in astonishment. Chu Ch'ung spent the night at the Upper T'ien-chu Temple and slept with his father, exchanging news of past events. The next day, he changed his name on the written invocations at the Middle and Lower T'ien-chu Temples from Chu Ch'ung back to Ch'in Ch'ung. After performing all the ceremonies at the two temples, he returned to the Upper T'ien-chu Temple and asked his father to go home with him, so that he could look after him. But Old Ch'in was accustomed to the way of life of a devout Buddhist, and was unwilling to go back to the mundane world. Ch'in Ch'ung persuaded him: "We've been separated for eight years, so I must make up for those times when I wasn't able to take care of you. Furthermore, I have recently been married, and you must let your new daughter-in-law pay her respects to you."

Old Ch'in had to agree, so Ch'in Ch'ung had his father sit in his sedan chair while he himself walked all the way home. He took out a new set of clothes for Old Ch'in to change into, and then had him sit down in the main hall so he and his wife could pay their respects to him. The Hsins were also introduced, and a large feast was arranged for the day, with only vegetable dishes and wine served at the insistence of Old Ch'in. The next day, the neighbors all came to congratulate them, bringing along many presents. Indeed, this was a fourfold happiness: the new marriage, the reunion of the bride's family, the reunion of father and son, and Master Ch'in's resuming his original name. The celebration lasted for several days.

Old Ch'in was unwilling to stay with his son and only wished to live quietly at the Upper T'ien-chu Temple. Ch'in Ch'ung dared not go against his father's wish, so with two hundred taels of silver, he built a new room at the temple for his father to live in. He sent over the expense money punctually every month; he himself went to visit his father every ten days, and brought his wife along once every season. Old Ch'in lived to be eighty and passed away peacefully. He was buried in the mountains as he wished. But all this happened later, and really does not concern us here.

Let us now go back to Ch'in Ch'ung and his wife. They lived happily until their old age, and their two children both became famous scholars. Even to the present day, when someone is skilled in the art of *pang-ch'en*, he is still referred to as "Master Ch'in" or the "Oil Peddler" in the pleasure quarters. There is a poem to prove it:

When spring comes, a hundred kinds of flowers blossom anew
*   everywhere;*
Bees and butterflies race to enjoy spring.
What a pity that so many of Mei-niang's young and rich
*   patrons*
Are not half as fortunate as the oil peddler.

THE COUPLE BOUND IN LIFE AND DEATH

From *Hsing-shih heng-yen*

TRANSLATED BY JEANNE KELLY

The frenzied world of men is like a game of chess,
Where both players stay locked in battle until the final move.
Then in a moment, the game is over, the pieces put away.
That day, who really was the loser and who the winner?

These lines compare a game of chess with the course of world affairs. The great multitude of crises and changes encountered in the world are reduced to nothing in the wink of an eye, just as in a game of chess where reddened eyes and parched throats mark a life-or-death struggle as fierce as the Sun-P'ang contest[1]—or the Liu-Hsiang contention for the crown,[2] never abating until the last pitched battle at River Wu. But when the game is at an end and the pieces put away, one merely laughs it all off. Thus, the scholar-gentleman and the recluse often release their excitement at the chessboard, here finding relaxation and enjoyment. The poems and songs written on this theme are too numerous to mention.

[1] Sun Pin of the state of Ch'i and P'ang Chüan of the state of Wei studied military tactics together. Later, P'ang became a general of Wei and grew jealous of Sun's talent. He had the latter's feet cut off and his face tatooed. Sun managed to escape to Ch'i, where in a battle with Wei he had P'ang's forces surrounded. P'ang then killed himself.

[2] Liu Pang defeated Hsiang Yü, his chief rival, and founded the Han Dynasty in 206 B.C.

Only the poem of the *chuang-yüan* Tseng Ch'i,[3] written at the emperor's request, is truly excellent:

The two foes have each pitched their battle tents,
And sit plotting stratagems to decide life or death.
Swift steeds gallop across the occupied domains,
And gilt armor stirs up the river waves.

The songs and dances of Consort Yü lament the scene at Kai-hsia;[4]
The banners of the Han generals close in on the city under Ch'u.
When the excitement is over, all schemes exhausted, and the battle at an end,
Shadows of pines and flowers soon extend across the chessboard.

Though this poem is good, there are those who criticize the couplet referring to Consort Yü and the Han generals for hackneyed phrases; and as for the seventh line, "The excitement is over, all schemes exhausted, etc.," they find the idea there to be quite insipid. Poems written on command are meant for the eyes of the emperor and should be imbued with more spirit. We also have a poem

[3] Tseng Ch'i (1372–1432) lived in the early Ming period. He became a *chuang-yüan* in 1404.

[4] Consort Yü was the favorite of Hsiang Yü; Kai-hsia was the scene of the last battle between Hsiang Yü and Liu Pang.

209

of the Hung-hsi Emperor,[5] which far surpasses the ordinary in the grandeur of the sentiment expressed:

The two contending states resort to arms,
Marshaling their troops to gain the upper hand.
A row of horses is first to make a move,
While generals defend secluded camps against attacks from far
*   away.*

Defying danger, out go the chariots to take stray soldiers,
And from across the river cannon balls fall on the guarded
*   camp.*
At leisure one grasps the strategy of the campaign,
And a single victorious move brings peace at last.[6]

So why should we be saying all these things about chess today? It is because there were once two families who on the basis of a few chess moves became inseparable friends and contracted a marriage alliance between their two children. Later this was told in a colorful tale. Truly:

A husband and wife are not matched just in this life;
Their marriage was determined centuries before.

In the Fen-yi Prefecture in Kiangsi Province there lived two landed gentlemen on opposite sides of the street. One was Ch'en Ch'ing and the other was Chu Shih-yüan. Though they were not wealthy men, the estates left them by their ancestors gave them ample resources. Both Ch'en Ch'ing and Chu Shih-yüan were in their forties, and their families had been neighbors for generations. They shared similar views and interests, and both kept to their station in life, minding their own business and doing nothing to stir up gossip. Each day after their meals, they would

---

[5] Hung-hsi is the title of the single brief reign period of the Ming emperor Jen-tsung (1425).
[6] The Chinese chessboard is divided by a "river." In the center of the two opposite ends of the board, a "camp" is formed by four squares. The pieces of Chinese chess are roughly translated, the "general," "governor," and "counselor" who must stay within the "camp," and the "horse," "chariot," "cannon" and "foot soldier," who may cross the "river." Pieces in the two camps are differentiated by colors, usually red and black.

meet together and while away their leisure time playing chess. Sometimes they would take turns playing the host, but they made a practice of serving nothing more elaborate than tea and a simple meal. The neighbors nearby would also drop in to watch the games when they had a leisure moment. Among them was a man named Wang San-lao, now over sixty, who had been an enthusiastic and skillful player in his youth. In recent years he had been afflicted with high blood pressure and so never took part for fear of becoming overexcited. As he had nothing to do all day, he found his only enjoyment in watching the games, and of this he never tired.

Generally speaking, chess players do not take kindly to spectators, for as it is often said, the onlookers see clearly while the players are in a fog. If a spectator fails to hold his tongue and lets slip a few words at a crucial point in the game, the outcome might be completely reversed. Good manners do not allow the loser to display anger over such a trivial matter, but if he tries to accept it in silence, he may find his resentment hard to swallow. The ancients have a good way of putting it:

A true gentleman remains silent at a chess game.
The cad chatters away over a glass of wine.

Fortunately, Wang San-lao possessed the virtue of never opening his mouth before the game was over; and when the outcome was decided, he would then remark on which move had been decisive for the victor, which move had meant defeat for the loser. Chu and Ch'en both appreciated his analyses and did not find them offensive.

One day Chu Shih-yüan was playing chess at Ch'en Ch'ing's house, with Wang San-lao looking on. After lunch, the pieces were set up again on the board and the game was about to begin when a lad walked in. And what sort of child was he?

His face looked as though powdered;
His lips as though rouged.
His shaven head indigo,

And he had hands as delicate as jade.
His air was graceful and refined;
His step serene and dignified.
One might have thought him an angel,
And not an ordinary child of this earth.

The lad was To-shou, the son of Ch'en Ch'ing. He came in carrying a satchel. As he entered the sitting room, he calmly set the satchel down on a chair and then greeted Wang San-lao, bowing deeply. Wang San-lao was about to return the civility when Ch'en Ch'ing pressed the old man down firmly in his chair, saying, "You musn't be so formal with him. To treat him like this will only compromise his fortune!"

"What kind of talk is that?" Wang San-lao replied. But despite this protest, he was held down by Ch'en Ch'ing and had to content himself with making a gesture of courtesy by slightly raising his hips from his seat and bending a bit at the waist. The lad then turned to Chu Shih-yüan, greeted him, and bowed. As Ch'en was sitting across the chess table from Chu when the latter returned the bow, he could not very well pull him down, and so had no choice but to accept the bow. Having greeted the two guests, the lad then went to greet his father. Straightening up, he reported, "Father, as tomorrow is the Ch'ung-yang Festival,[7] my teacher has suspended classes and gone home for a couple of days. He told us we are not to play while at home but to do our assignments and study." Then picking up his satchel from the chair, he solemnly withdrew to the inner quarters.

Impressed by his graceful carriage, clear speech, and perfect manners, Wang and Chu both praised him to the skies.

"How old is your son?"

"Nine," replied Ch'en Ch'ing.

"It seems only yesterday that a party was given to honor his birth," remarked Wang San-lao. "All of a sudden nine years are gone. Truly, time is

like an arrow. How are we to keep from growing old?" He then said to Chu Shih-yüan, "If I remember correctly, your daughter was born in the same year."

"Why, yes," replied Chu. "In fact, my daughter, To-fu, is also nine years old now."

"Forgive me for speaking out of turn," said Wang, "but as you two have become chess partners for life, why not make yourselves in-laws through the marriage of your son and daughter? In ancient times there was a Chu-Ch'en Village in which lived only two clans who had been intermarrying for generations. Your surnames coincide so exactly that it must be the will of Heaven. Besides, with such a fine boy and girl, as everyone well knows, what could be more perfect?"

Chu Shih-yüan had already taken a liking to the lad, so before Ch'en Ch'ing had a chance to reply, he said, "Why, that's a wonderful idea! Only I'm afraid Brother Ch'en would not agree to it. If he were willing to go along with the idea, there's nothing I'd like better."

"Since Brother Chu doesn't disdain my humble circumstances," Ch'en said, "as the father of the boy, what objections could I have? We have but to trouble San-lao to act as go-between."

"Tomorrow is the day of the Ch'ung-yang Festival," Wang San-lao said, "and happens to be an inauspicious day, but the following day is a particularly good one, so I shall come visit you then. As this seems to be the sincerest wish of both of you gentlemen, we shall consider the matter settled as of now. I ask nothing more for my services than a few cups of nuptial wine."

"There's a story I must tell you," said Ch'en Ch'ing. "Once the Jade Emperor[8] wished to make a marriage proposal to the Emperor of Earth. After some deliberation, he said, 'Both parties involved are emperors, so someone with the status of an emperor must be invited to act as go-between. Let's ask the Kitchen God to descend to

[7] Ch'ung-yang Festival falls on the ninth day of the ninth month by the Chinese calender. This day is traditionally celebrated by climbing mountains.

[8] The Jade Emperor is the supreme god of the Taoist pantheon.

earth and arrange the match.' When the Emperor of Earth saw the Kitchen God, he cried in astonishment, 'Why is the matchmaker so black?' To which the Kitchen God replied, 'Since when has there ever been a matchmaker willing to offer his services for nothing?' "[9]

Wang San-lao and Chu Shih-yüan both laughed heartily. Chu and Ch'en resumed their game and played on until evening.

Merely because of a game of chess,
A bond lasting several lifetimes was made.

On the following day, the day of the Ch'ung-yang Festival, nothing of note occurred. On the tenth, Wang San-lao changed into a newly tailored suit of clothes and set off for the Chu residence to formally arrange the marriage. Chu Shih-yüan had already spoken of it to his wife, Liu-shih, praising the fine qualities of their future son-in-law. That day they agreed without further ado and paid little attention to the matter of betrothal gifts. It was understood that when it came time for the marriage, whatever amount was deemed proper would be given from either side and would be taken without complaint.

When Wang San-lao conveyed these words to Ch'en Ch'ing, he was delighted. Ch'en then selected an auspicious day and formalized the agreement by sending the betrothal gift. The Chu's sent over their daughter's betrothal card,[10] and a banquet was held to celebrate the occasion. From this time on Chu and Ch'en addressed each other as relatives, and their chess games continued as before.

Time is fleeting, and before they knew it six

[9] This joke hinges upon a pun. "[Not] willing to offer his services for nothing" (*pu shih pai tso te*) can possibly be taken as "[matchmaking] cannot be done by a white fellow [someone with a fair complexion]" because the word *pai* means both "nothing" and "white."

[10] The bethrothal card is a document on which are written four pairs of cyclical characters to indicate the hour, day, month, and year of birth. The exchange of these cards constitutes a formal engagement. These eight characters are used by the fortune-teller as a basis for predicting one's fortune.

years had passed. Ch'en To-shou was now fifteen and had mastered all the classics. It was expected that he would pass the imperial examinations, placing high on the list of successful candidates, and bring honor to his family. Who could have foreseen the misfortune which awaited him? He was suddenly afflicted with the vile disease of leprosy. In its initial stages it was assumed to be only a case of scabies, and no one gave it much thought. After a year, however, the disease had become much worse and his whole appearance had changed beyond recognition.

His flesh turned the color of parchment,
And the skin became chapped and wrinkled.
The poison within his whole body
Developed into blotches and ugly sores.
The worms writhed throughout his body,
And morning and evening he itched in agony.
Scabies, however terrible, was nothing in comparison.
If it was not leprosy,
It was in fact no different.
This beautiful child was transformed into a toad;
The young lad took on the look of a withered tortoise.
His fingers itched from a fetid pus,
And the filth of his body gave off a foul odor.

Ch'en Ch'ing had only this one child, and he meant more to him than life itself. Seeing him in this state, he was of course beside himself with worry. Even chess lost its appeal for him. He called in doctors and fortune-tellers, burnt incense and carried out vows made to the gods. There was nothing he did not try. In this way they suffered through a whole year, during which time sizable sums of money were spent, but the boy's condition showed not the slightest improvement. Needless to say, the parents were sorely distressed. As the future father-in-law, Chu Shih-yüan was equally upset, and morning and night he was at the doorstep inquiring about the boy's health.

Over three years went by without a single hopeful sign. When Chu Shin-yüan's wife learned of her future son-in-law's condition, she cried and wept and complained to her husband, "Our daughter doesn't stink. Why were you so anxious to promise her at the age of nine? Now what are we to do? It'd be just as well if that leprous toad dropped dead and let our daughter go free! He's neither alive nor dead now, and here our daughter is about to come of age; yet we can neither marry her nor break it off. Surely she can't be expected to live like a widow while that leper keeps hanging on! It's all the doing of that [ugly] turtle Wang San-lao. His meddling has ruined our daughter's chances for life!" And she heaped abuses on Wang San-lao, over and over again calling him a turtle, while alternating her curses with fits of weeping.

Now the fact was that Chu Shih-yüan was afraid of his wife, and while she let fly with all this foul abuse, he dared not put in a single word to stop her.

One day, as his wife Liu-shih was putting the kitchen cupboard in order, her eyes fell upon the chess pieces and chessboard and she suddenly flew into a rage, cursing her husband. "You turtles! Just because you saw eye to eye over a game of chess you had to go and make a match at our daughter's expense. Why keep this source of trouble around?!" As she spoke, she strode to the gate and flung the chess pieces out into the street. The chessboard she likewise smashed against the ground.

Chu Shih-yüan was a meek man. When he saw his wife venting her rage in this way, he did not dare to interfere but slipped out of sight. Their daughter, To-fu, being too bashful to come plead with her mother, let her carry on until finally she had had enough. As the saying goes:

Walls have ears,
And windows eyes.

Ch'en Ch'ing had already gotten wind of Liu-shih's day-long tirades against the matchmaker and her husband, but had been unwilling to believe it. When the whole street became littered with chess pieces, however, he had a good idea as to the reason.

He talked the matter over with his wife. "We must judge others' feelings by our own. To our great misfortune, our son has contracted this horrible disease. It is quite evident that he will never be cured. To demand that this lovely girl be given in marriage to a leper would be a sin indeed. The girl herself would no doubt bear us a grudge for it. And were she to be forced into our house against her will, we could hardly expect her to be dutiful. In the beginning, when this engagement was made, there was good feeling on both sides. No great fortune was spent. If we are to acquit ourselves honorably in this, we must act honorably to the very end and not turn a good thing into a tragedy. If we take the long-range view, the best course would be to return the girl's betrothal card to her family and let them make another suitable match for her. If Heaven takes pity on our son and he recovers one day, there shouldn't be any problem in finding a wife for him. Now the whole thing has caused a rift between Chu and his wife. With her crying and nagging, why even I cannot bear it." Having reached a decision, he hurried over to see Wang San-lao.

Wang happened at that moment to be sitting in front of his gate chatting leisurely with some friends. Seeing Ch'en Ch'ing approach, he hastily stood up and bowed, asking, "Has your son's condition improved in these past few days?"

Ch'en shook his head and replied, "No, not at all. There's something I'd like to speak to you about. Could you please come by my house?"

Wang followed Ch'en immediately to the latter's house and each took a seat in the sitting room. When tea had been served, Wang asked, "What can I do for you?"

Ch'en Ch'ing brought his chair up closer to Wang and then poured out everything that was on his mind. He began by describing how dreadful his son's condition was. Then he told how Liu-shih had been complaining. This Wang San-lao

213

himself had heard something about, but outwardly he could only remark casually, "I don't think what you heard is true."

"How could I presume to speak so freely of such things if they weren't true? I don't blame them, because I've been feeling ill at ease myself. I'm willing to return the betrothal card so that the Chus can be free to arrange another match. This would suit both parties and certainly is the only natural course to take."

"But I'm afraid that cannot be done! After all, my business is to bring couples together, not to part them. If one day you come to regret your decision, you'll put me in a most uncomfortable position."

"I've already discussed this several times with my wife," Ch'en Ch'ing assured him. "We'll never regret it. As for the small present given at the time of the engagement, there is no need for it to be returned."

"Since you're returning the betrothal card," Wang San-lao put in, "the betrothal gift must of course be returned. But Heaven always smiles on the virtuous. Your son will one day recover from his illness. You must consider this carefully before you act."

"Looking for my son's recovery," replied Ch'en Ch'ing, "is certainly like groping for a needle in the ocean. You never know when you'll have it in your grasp. In the meantime, how can we stand in the young girl's way?" With that he pulled the betrothal card from his sleeve and, with tears in his eyes, handed it over to Wang San-lao.

Wang was also grief-stricken and said, "As your mind is made up, I must carry out your wish. Nevertheless, your relative is a man with a strong sense of propriety. He will no doubt refuse."

Ch'en Ch'ing dried his tears and replied, "I do this of my own accord, not under any pressure from my relative. If he should hesitate, I'll leave it entirely up to you to persuade him. Let him know that this is my earnest desire and no empty gesture."

"As you wish," said San-lao. He then stood up and went off to the Chus.

Chu Shih-yüan welcomed him in and offered him a seat. Before either spoke, Chu called several times for tea. The reason behind this was that Liu-shih had been cursing the matchmaker by name all day long, and though this had never come to Wang's ears, Chu was feeling shameful, afraid that San-lao would take offense. Thus he made a great show of calling for tea. Unfortunately, Liu-shih now so thoroughly detested Wang San-lao for ever having made such a wretched match that no matter how many times her husband called her, she would not bring out the tea. This is an example of how petty-minded women can be.

After a while, Wang San-lao said, "There is a delicate matter that I've come especially to talk to you about. I must begin by apologizing. Please don't be offended by what I have to say."

"Please feel free to speak. How could I be offended by an old gentleman like you?"

Wang San-lao then proceeded to give a detailed account of Ch'en Ch'ing's decision to dissolve the engagement. "This was all your relative's idea," he concluded. "I am merely conveying the message. The final decision rests entirely with you."

Now Chu had already reached the end of his tether with his wife's constant nagging and would have liked to set himself free of it, except that he could not be the one to broach the subject. To him Wang San-lao's announcement was like a letter of pardon handed down from the emperor. He was, of course, delighted. But he said, "Though Mr. Ch'en has acted with great virtue, I'm afraid that he'll live to regret it and only make things more awkward."

"I've mentioned all this to him, but his mind is made up. There's no reason to doubt his sincerity. Here is your daughter's betrothal card. Please take it."

"How can I accept this before the betrothal present is returned?"

"He said that such a small gift was not worth considering, but I blurted out that since he was returning the betrothal card, of course the betrothal gift should also be returned."

"That is only natural," agreed Chu Shih-yüan. "The twelve taels that we received will be returned in full. There are also two silver hairpins which my daughter has in her keeping. When I've gotten them from her, I'll return everything together. I'll leave the card with you for the time being."

"No matter," Wang San-lao said. "You may as well keep it yourself. I'm going home now. Tomorrow I shall be back to get the betrothal gift; then I'll go give the word to your relative." With this he took his leave. There is a poem which testifies to this:

Today the matchmaker's binding cord was untied again
The words the go-between once spoke have all proved untrue.
The good Wang San-lao of Fen-yi,
His was the doing and the undoing.

Chu immediately went in to tell his wife the news Wang San-lao had brought concerning the cancellation of the marriage contract. Liu-shih was overjoyed. She counted out the twelve taels, partly from her own savings, and gave them to her husband. Then she asked for the pair of silver hairpins from her daughter To-fu. Though her daughter had never studied the classics, the quality of her mind was praiseworthy. She had been listening to her mother's harangues for some time and had already grown quite dejected. When she was now asked to return the betrothal gift of the hairpins, she knew it meant the annulment of the marriage. Without a word, she went straight to her room, locked the door, and burst into tears.

Seeing the expression on her face, Chu Shih-yüan realized at once what was disturbing her, and he said to his wife, "It must be the cancellation of the marriage which is upsetting her. You must try to coax her gently. If you're hasty and try to put too much pressure on her, she may do something rash, and we'll always regret it."

Heedful of her husband's advice, Liu-shih went and knocked at her daughter's door, calling to her in a subdued tone of voice, "My daughter, whether you give us the hairpins or not is up to you. There's no need to be upset. Now, open the door. If there is something bothering you, tell your mother about it. I'm ready to listen to whatever you say."

At first the girl would not open the door, but after her mother had called her several times, she finally unbolted it, called, "It's open," and then went and sat down on a stool, seething with anger.

Liu-shih pulled another stool up close to her and sat down. "My daughter," she began, "your mother and father have been feeling miserable about the unfortunate match we made for you. Fortunately, the boy's parents are now willing to cancel it. No greater blessing could be asked for. There is no hope that that leper will ever recover. The marriage would only ruin things for you. We must return the hairpins to their family and sever all ties. A girl of your beauty need never worry that no one else will ever come ask for you, so you mustn't be stubborn. Now give me the hairpins so that they can be returned.

The girl remained silent and merely continued to weep.

Liu-shih went on coaxing her a bit and then, seeing the state her daughter was in, said gently, "We're only trying to do what's best for you. Now tell me frankly whether or not you're willing. Can't you see how bad it makes us feel when you keep your suffering to yourself like this?"

"It's best! What's best?" To-fu burst out hatefully. "It's still early to be asking for the hairpins!"

"Good heavens!" exclaimed Liu-shih. "Such a fuss over a couple of hairpins! They couldn't weigh more than two or three taels altogether. If you become engaged to a wealthy man, you can have hairpins of gold or jade."

215

"Who cares about hairpins of gold or jade!" the girl cried. "What respectable girl ever takes the betrothal gift of two houses? Poverty, wealth, sorrow, or joy, they're all predestined. I was born to be the wife of Ch'en To-shou and I shall die a ghost of his family. And these silver hairpins will go with me to the grave. You can just forget about returning them!" After this outburst, she again began sobbing her heart out.

Liu-shih saw it was pointless to continue. All she could do was report to her husband the state that their daughter was in. "There's just no way out of this marriage," she added.

Because of his close friendship with Ch'en Ch'ing, Chu Shih-yüan had never wanted to renounce the marriage in the first place. But because his wife had put up such a fuss, he had had no choice but to try to dissolve it for the sake of his own peace of mind. Such a display of ardor from his daughter was unexpected and even somewhat gratifying.

"If that's the way it is," he said, "there's no sense in making it harder on the girl. Tell her that the engagement still holds as before."

When Liu-shih relayed this to her daughter, she at last wiped away her tears. Truly:

Three winters won't change the lone pine's uprightness.
Ten thousand hardships won't alter the noble girl's heart.

The rest of that evening was uneventful. The next day Chu Shih-yüan, without awaiting the arrival of Wang San-lao, went himself to inform Wang of his daughter's stubborn refusal, and returned the betrothal card to him.

"Remarkable!" exclaimed Wang. "Truly remarkable!" He set off at once to report all this to Ch'en Ch'ing.

Ch'en Ch'ing had been quite loath to cancel the marriage, so when he heard that his future daughter-in-law had held firmly to her resolve, he was more than pleased. Bowing repeatedly to Wang San-Lao, he said apologetically, "I've put you to too much trouble! Nevertheless, I'm afraid that my son will not be cured and that that will ul-

timately make the union difficult. I'll have to trouble you to bring this matter up at a later date."

Wang dismissed him with a wave of his hand. "After this, I won't want to do it again."

We shall make no more idle comments, but instead tell how, when Chu Shih-yüan saw that his daughter refused to renounce the marriage, he became more anxious than ever about his son-in-law. He made inquiries everywhere about noted physicians and specialists and provided for their traveling expenses to come and administer treatment.

At first the physicians always promised a cure, and even the patient's spirits rose as he took the medicine. But later, when it all proved ineffective, he gradually lost heart. There were some who came with letters of recommendation and were full of grandiose promises and boasts, demanding high fees and writing guarantees. But it all came to nought. One day followed another, and soon more than two years were gone. By then all the doctors agreed that it was a chronic disease which was beyond cure.

Heaving a sigh, To-shou called his mother and father to him, and said, with tears in his eyes, "My father-in-law would not consent to cancel the contract and instead called in noted physicians to administer medicines in the hope that one day I would recover. Now that the medicines have all proved ineffective, it's obvious I will never be cured. Don't be unfair to the girl. I definitely wish to renounce this engagement."

"This was suggested once, and your in-laws were both agreeable," said the father, "but your fiancée stubbornly refused, so the betrothal card was returned to us."

"If she knew that I wished to cancel it, she'd no doubt be ready to give in."

The mother, Chang-shih, admonished him. "My son, just take good care of your health. Don't concern yourself with such trivial matters."

"It'll be a burden off my mind," replied To-shou, "if the engagement is called off."

"Let's wait until your father-in-law gets here,

216

and then you can tell him yourself," suggested his father.

He had barely finished speaking when the maid announced, "Mr. Chu has come to visit Master Ch'en."

The mother slipped away. Ch'en Ch'ing invited him into the study. When To-shou saw his father-in-law, he thanked him profusely for his visit. Chu Shih-yüan was quite dismayed to see that his son-in-law looked more like a ghost than a human being. After they had had some tea, Ch'en Ch'ing found an excuse to withdraw. To-shou then poured out everything that was on his mind. He said he would never recover from the disease, that it would make marriage difficult, and that he was determined to cancel the engagement. From his sleeve he pulled out a card on which a poem had been written. Chu Shih-yüan opened it and read:

By a stroke of ill fate, a dread disease befell;
A good match is a good match no more.
The binding thread was on this morning untied,
So that the future of a young girl can be freed.

It had not been Chu's wish to cancel the engagement the first time; he had been pressured into it by his wife. Now that he had seen his son-in-law's sickly state, read the poem in his own hand, and heard the resolution in his voice, the wish began unconsciously to stir in his mind. Nevertheless, he said, "Don't say such things! What's most important is to take care of yourself." He folded the poem carefully and tucked it away in his sleeve. Then he took his leave.

Ch'en Ch'ing met him in the sitting room and said, "My son's remarks just now were spoken in all sincerity. I hope that you'll find a way to persuade your daughter to go along with this. In the meantime, I'll return the betrothal card to you."

"As you both so earnestly insist," Chu Shih-yüan said, "I'll keep it for the time being, but later you must allow me to return it."

Ch'en Ch'ing then saw him out the gate.

When Chu Shih-yüan returned, he told his wife what his son-in-law had said.

"As our son-in-law doesn't want her to be his wife," Liu-shih said, "there's no point in her remaining bound to him. Explain to her what the poem says, and she'll surely change her mind."

Chu Shih-yüan then gave the card to his daughter saying, "Master Ch'en will not recover from his illness and has said as much to me himself. He wishes to cancel the contract. This poem then is his bill of divorce. My daughter, you must think of your future. Don't be stubborn."

To-fu read the poem, then returned without a word to her room, where she took out her brush and inkstone and wrote the following poem after To-shou's:

Though misfortune has brought a dread disease,
A marriage bond is a marriage bond no less.
A woman's duty is to remain true to her betrothed.
Let no one speak to me about the beauty of youth!

It has always been said that good news never goes beyond the gate, while bad news spreads far and wide. The word soon spread that Master Ch'en had rejected his fiancée and had himself informed his father-in-law of his decision. Immediately Aunt Chang, Granny Li, and a host of those who depended for a living on matchmaking appeared at the Chus' door to propose a match, bringing along lists of prospects. They talked of sons of prominent and wealthy families and of opulent betrothal gifts. Though a matchmaker's words are not to be trusted, they were enough to put Liu-shih in a fever of excitement, just like the mother of Ch'ien Yü-lien,[11] who barely had time to turn away the Wangs and promise the Suns. But to everyone's surprise, her daughter's mind remained as firm as iron and stone, and she did not waver from her original position. When she saw her mother entertaining the go-betweens with the finest tea and wine, she knew what was in

---

[11] Ch'ien Yü-lien is the heroine of a famous Ming tale. Her betrothed, Wang Shih-p'eng, is demoted when he refuses to marry the prime minister's daughter. Ch'ien's stepmother then seeks to marry her to Sun Ju-ch'üan. She jumps into the river rather than submit, but is rescued and later reunited with Wang.

store for her. Her fiancé would never recover, and her parents would not permit her to remain faithful to him. After giving it considerable thought, she finally came to the conclusion that death was the best way out. At night, by the light of the lamp, she took out To-shou's poem, placed it on the table, and read it over. She sat weeping through nearly two watches. Then, while her parents lay sound asleep, she untied the silk sash from around her waist and hanged herself with it from a beam. Truly:

There are a thousand things one can do while alive,
But a mishap can suddenly bring everything to an end.

By then it was already the third watch, and To-fu was not, as it turned out, destined then to die. Chu Shih-yüan suddenly felt as though someone had wakened him from his dreams. The only sound that came to his ears was his daughter's sobbing. Startled, he rubbed his eyes and woke his wife, saying, "Just now I heard our daughter weeping. Could something have happened? Let's go look in on her."

"Our daughter is sound asleep in her room," his wife replied. "You're imagining things. Go ahead and look, if you want, but I'm going to sleep."

He threw on some clothes and got up. In the darkness he opened the door and groped his way to his daughter's bedroom. There he pushed at the door with both hands, but it did not open. He called her name several times but got no response. All he could hear was a strange sound of phlegm rattling in the throat. In alarm, he summoned all his strength and broke open the door with one kick. There in the dim light of the lamp on the table, he beheld his daughter dangling from a high beam, turning round and round like a horse on a wheeling lantern. He gasped in astonishment. Hurriedly pulling up the wick of the lamp, he shouted, "Wife, come quickly. She's hanged herself."

When Liu-shih heard these words in her dreams, it was as though cold water had been splashed over her. Without taking the time to get dressed, she threw a blanket over herself and dashed into her daughter's room, crying for her dear one. Chu Shih-yüan at least had had the presence of mind to take her down, bracing his knees against her buttocks while he slowly untied the noose from around her neck. He then began massaging her. Liu-shih stood shivering and calling her daughter's name. After quite a while, signs of life gradually returned and she began breathing faintly. Liu-shih gave thanks to Heaven and Earth. She went back to her room to put on her clothes and warmed some water, which she then poured down her daughter's throat. Slowly To-fu regained consciousness. When she opened her eyes and saw her parents standing before her, she burst into loud weeping.

"Daughter!" cried her parents. "Why, even the lowly cricket and ant cling to life. How could you do such a foolish thing?"

"In death I could preserve my name and my chastity," To-Fu replied. "So why have you brought me back to life? Though this time my attempt failed, sooner or later I shall surely die. It would have been better to let me go now and save yourselves further worry. Then it'd be as though you had never had me to begin with." With these words she fell to weeping piteously. Chu Shih-yüan and his wife pleaded with her again and again but in vain. This kept up until daybreak. Then Chu instructed his wife to stay by To-fu's side as she rested, while he went to the temple of the city god to draw a divination lot. The lot read:

The times are unpropitious;
Disasters strike year after year.
The clouds will eventually part to reveal the sun,
As fortune and longevity are prearranged in Heaven.

He studied the prediction carefully. The statements in the first two lines had already come true. The third line, "The clouds will eventually part to reveal the sun," perhaps meant that things were about to take a turn for the better. And as for the last line, "As fortune and longevity are prearranged in Heaven," with the words "fortune" (*fu*) and "longevity" (*shou*) contained in the names of his daughter and son-in-law—could there still be hope for Master Ch'en's recovery? Could he one day marry To-fu, and could theirs be a match "prearranged by Heaven?" He couldn't resolve his doubt.

When he returned home, his wife was still sitting in his daughter's room. When she caught sight of her husband, she hurriedly waved her hand at him, cautioning, "Don't make any noise! She's just stopped crying and fallen asleep."

The night before, when Chu Shih-yüan had pulled up the wick of the lamp, he had noticed a card on the table but had not had time to take a closer look. Now he picked it up and looked at it. It was the poem written by his son-in-law. Next to the poem was another one which he recognized to be in his daughter's handwriting. He read it through and then said with a sigh, "What a virtuous girl! As her parents, we should be helping her cultivate her virtue instead of forcing her to do what is against her wish."

He then explained the words on the divination lot to his wife. "*Fu* and *shou* are made in Heaven, and are determined by the gods. If we change things to suit our own selfish ends, Heaven will certainly not extend its protection. Besides, our daughter has made a vow in her poem and would die for it. We can't keep watch on her forever. If we relax our guard for a second and she takes her life, it would only bring us dishonor, or worse yet make us the butt of ridicule. If you ask me, the best thing to do would be to marry her to Ch'en. This would prove our good intentions on the one hand and comply with our daughter's own wishes on the other. It would also absolve us of the responsibility. What do you think?"

Liu-shih's heart was still pounding from the fright her daughter had given her. She replied, "Do whatever you like. I'm in no state to deal with such things!"

"We still have to ask Wang San-lao to talk to them," he said. By coincidence, as Chu Shih-yüan was stepping out the gate, Wang San-lao chanced to pass by. Chu stopped him and invited him in, and then recounted everything that had occurred in detail. "We are willing to marry our daughter now. Please convey the message for us."

"As I've said before, my job is to bring people together, not to part them. Since what you've said is in a worthy cause, it's my duty to be of service."

"When my daughter saw our son-in-law's poem, she composed one to match it expressing her feelings. If the Ch'ens still decline, you can show them this poem."

Wang San-lao took the card from him and set off at once. Since the two families lived directly opposite each other, he had but to step out of Chu's house to enter the Ch'ens.' When Ch'en Ch'ing heard that Wang San-lao had arrived, he assumed that he had come to confirm the cancellation of the contract, and hastened forward to greet him. "I suppose that you are bringing word from Mr. Chu?" he asked.

"I am indeed," replied Wang San-lao.

"As the cancellation of the marriage is the wish of my son this time, my relative has nothing further to say, I presume."

"My visit today is not to cancel the match but to affirm it."

"Please, San-lao, this is no time for joking!"

Wang San-lao then told him of the Chu daughter's suicide attempt and how anguished the parents had been. "If the girl is left at home, there is no telling what might happen. It's their wish that she come to look after Master Ch'en. This, to my mind, would be of benefit to both parties. Your relative would then be free of worry and would earn a good name besides. Your wife would have someone to assist her, and your son would have a trustworthy person to take care of him. What more could you ask for?

"Though I appreciate my relative's good intentions," said Ch'en Ch'ing, "I must still ask my son how he feels about this."

Wang San-lao then gave Ch'en Ch'ing the card with the matching verses, saying, "Your daughter-in-law has written a response to your son's verse. She has a fervent nature. Should your son refuse, she would surely take her life. That would be a terrible pity indeed!"

"I'll bring word to you shortly," Ch'en said. He then consulted first with his wife. "A girl of such ardor would certainly show virtue and filial piety. How much better even than parents to have the devoted care of such a wife! And if by chance there should be issue from such a union, then even if our son did not live, it wouldn't be the end of the Ch'en line. Once we have made a decision, our son certainly couldn't say no."

The two of them then went to the study and told To-shou all this. At first To-shou refused, but when he had read the matching verses, he fell silent, and Ch'en Ch'ing then knew that his son was willing. He gave word to Wang San-lao, chose an auspicious day, and sent some gifts of clothing and jewelry. When To-fu learned that she was to marry into the Ch'en family, she was content. On the appointed day, the bride was brought to her new home accompanied by the music of flutes, pipes, and drums. When the neighbors heard that the leprous son of the Ch'en family had married, they spread the news around that "the day has come for 'the toad to eat the meat of the swan.' " And some cruel pranksters made up a ditty about it:

Strange to be called Longevity
When doomed to die so young.
And strange that a fair sweet-scented girl
Should follow so foul a smell.

Under the red silk coverlet,
In raptures they lie,
While the stinking fumes of pus
Vie with the flowery fragrance.

But enough of this chatter. To-fu, from the moment she was brought to her husband's home, was in every way amiable and obliging, giving To-shou her loving care and attention. And how did she show this?

With concern and solitude,
She strove to fill his every need,
Preparing his medicines and boiling his herbs,
Which first she would try on herself.
Early to rise and late to bed,
She would not have time to undo her dress.
Every ache and itch in his body
She rubbed and massaged each time.
And the blood and foul pus on his garments
She carefully washed away.
She nursed him as a mother would a child,
All but offering him the breast;
And like the devoted daughter to her mother-in-law,
Was ready to cut off her own flesh for soup.[12]
Though deprived of the pleasures of the conjugal bed,
Never once did she complain of the toil.
A wife she was no more than in name;
How pitiful, this young woman with few joys and many cares.

Two years passed in this way, with both parents-in-law quite pleased. Only one thing seemed to be unusual. For while the young couple's filial piety was beyond reproach during the day, at night they slept separately, never sharing the same quilt or pillow. To-shou's mother Chang-shih, though she wished to have them consummate the union, did not quite know how to broach the subject.

One day she happened to enter their room and, noticing that her daughter-in-law was absent, she remarked, "My son, your pillow is soiled. Let me take it and have it washed for you." Then she added, "Your quilt is also dirty." Rolling them up into a bundle, she carried them out, leaving but one pillow and quilt on the bed. It was obvious she wished the couple to sleep together under the same quilt in the hope that a son might be born to carry on the family name. Who could have guessed what went on in the minds of the young couple? To-shou thought to himself, "It is more

[12] Human flesh was considered in traditional China to be an effective medicine for otherwise incurable wasting diseases. Since human flesh was not commercially available, devoted children would cut a few slices from their buttocks so as "to move Heaven," i.e., they hoped that Heaven would intervene and bring about a miraculous cure.

than likely that I shall die; so our union will not be a long one. What right have I to soil her virginity?" And To-fu thought to herself, "In the weakened condition my husband is in, how could he have the energy for carnal pleasures?" For these reasons they had gone on sleeping separately since their marriage, both having their own quilts and pillows.

On that night, there was only the one quilt and pillow, which both belonged to the wife. It was her habit, after her husband had gone to sleep, to sit under the lamp to do her needlework, not retiring herself until her parents-in-law had both gone to bed. That night, when To-shou asked his mother for another pillow and quilt, she had put him off. "They're not dry yet. Why not make do for just one night by sleeping together?"

To-fu gave her own pillow to her husband, but as he was afraid of soiling his wife's bedding, he slept in his clothes. To-fu likewise did not undress, so they slept separately as usual.

The next day, when Chang-shih learned of this, she mistakenly blamed her daughter-in-law for putting on airs, interpreting her good intentions as an act of malice. She made a terrible scene, casting veiled accusations and aspersions about. To-fu was an intelligent girl and had no trouble taking her meaning, but for fear of upsetting her husband, she feigned ignorance and concealed her tears. To-shou realized to a certain extent what was happening and was quite distressed. In this way another year rolled by.

The disease had been contracted at the age of fifteen. It had set in at the age of sixteen. At nineteen, the offer to cancel the engagement had been refused, and at twenty he had married. It had now been nearly ten years since the first onset of the disease. How depressing it was to have to linger on like this, neither dead nor alive!

To-shou got word that a blind fortune-teller had recently arrived from Chiang-nan.[13] He went by the name of Mr. Divine, and he was known for

[13] Chiang-nan refers to the area to the south of the Yangtze River.

his willingness to speak frankly. To-shou wanted to have him cast a horoscope so that he might know how close he was to his death. Now from the time he had taken ill, To-shou had loathed his ugly appearance and rarely left the house. Today, in order to have his fortune told, he took special care to dress neatly, and then made his way to the booth of Mr. Divine. The fortune-teller arranged his horoscope and divined his fortune from his "five planets."

"Which one in your household is the subject?" he then asked. "I'm afraid what I'm going to say is not pleasant. Only if you promise not to take offense will I speak frankly."

"I only want to know the truth," To-shou replied. "There's no need to hold anything back."

"The subject's fortune can be told from the fourth year on," the fortune-teller began. "From the age of four to the age of thirteen, his childhood is uneventful. The ten-year period from age of fourteen through twenty-three is an ill-fated time. He is due to suffer from a terrible disease which leaves him more dead than alive. Am I correct so far?"

"You are," Ch'en replied.

"During the last ten years," the fortune-teller continued, "the water element is lacking, but he still manages to escape. The period from twenty-four to thirty-three are years of worse luck. The oars and rudder of the ship are lost in a perilous storm; the horse's saddle and bridle break at the edge of a precipice. An early death is indicated. If you have a better horoscope, I'll be glad to do another one for you, but this one is not worth discussing."

When the young man heard these words, he fell glumly silent. Hurriedly giving the man his fee, he took his leave and departed. As he tried to collect his thoughts, without his knowledge the tears rolled down his cheeks. He thought to himself, "The fortune-teller was right about the past ten years. If during the next ten years my luck is even worse, they are bound to be full of misery. My own death is of little consequence, but what a pity it is that my good and virtuous wife should have served me for three years without a single night's enjoyment. How can I involve her further in my sufferings? Since life has not been any different from death for me, what good would it do even if I could live a few more years? The best thing would be to die as soon as possible and set her free, for she can then start all over again while she is still young and beautiful." Thus he conceived the idea of committing suicide. At an herbalist's along the way home he bought some arsenic and hid it in his clothes. When he reached home he said nothing about his visit to the fortune-teller.

That evening as he got into bed, he said to his wife, "We were betrothed to each other at the age of nine. I always hoped that when we grew up we'd have a harmonious marriage and good children. Who could have foreseen that I would come down with a horrible and incurable disease? For fear of ruining your future, I offered twice to cancel the contract. But out of kindness you refused and insisted that we get married. Though it has been over three years now, we have been married in name only, for I wouldn't want to cripple you with my disease. This is one point on which my conscience is clear. After I die and you become betrothed to another, then you can say this in all truth and no one can call you a 'soiled woman.'"

"When I was betrothed to you, I was prepared to share with you all joys and sorrows. That you are now stricken with this disease is part of my fate. We shall live together and die together, that's all there is to it. Please speak no more of my finding a better match elsewhere."

"You have a nature as ardent as fire," Ch'en said, "but there can be no future in a union such as ours. As it is, you have already far exceeded your wifely duty in the care you have given me over these years. I'm afraid I won't be able to repay your kindness in this life, but we shall certainly meet again in the next."

"How can you speak so dishearteningly? Is it proper for a husband and wife to talk of repayment?"

The two continued their arguing well into the night before finally falling asleep. Truly:

A husband and wife speak only but a small portion,
Never pouring out everything that lies in their hearts.

The following day, To-shou spoke with his parents for some time. With the idea of death firmly on his mind, he wanted to express his feelings on how hard it was for children to break away from their parents.

Toward evening, To-shou said to his wife, "I'd like some wine."

"You usually don't drink wine for fear of itching. What makes you want some now?"

"I feel somewhat out of sorts today, and thought I might try some wine. Would you heat a pot for me?"

Although she had had misgivings about the morbid turn his conversation had taken the night before, she didn't have the least idea what he had in mind. She asked her mother-in-law for a pot of good wine, heated it to boiling, and set it on the table along with a tiny cup and two plates of delicacies.

"I don't want a small cup," To-shou said. "A bowl will be fine."

To-fu then fetched a bowl and prepared to pour out the wine, when he said, "Don't bother. Let me pour it myself. I don't care for any delicacies, but I'd like some fruit with the wine if possible."

Having sent To-fu from the room with this request, he removed the lid of the pot, took the arsenic from the package, and emptied it into the pot. Then, pouring himself a bowl, he hurriedly gulped it down. After she had taken a few steps, To-fu became uneasy; turning her head, she noticed that her husband appeared agitated while trying to make his actions seem casual. At this her suspicions became greatly aroused. Fearing that

222

something was wrong, she hastened back, but he had already swallowed one bowl of the wine and poured out another. Noting a strange color to the wine, she caught hold of the bowl to prevent him from drinking it.

"To tell you the truth," To-shou said, "the wine has arsenic in it. I mean to kill myself and relieve your suffering. I've already taken a bowl and am beyond help. Let me get drunk and be done. It'll save you further toil." He then wrested the bowl from her hand and drank it down.

"I've said I'd live with you and die with you," To-fu said. "Now that you've taken the poison, I cannot live on alone." Whereupon she grabbed the pot nearby and drank it down to the last drop. By this time he was feeling the effects of the poison and could give no attention to what his wife was doing. In a moment both had collapsed together on the floor. A contemporary lamented over this in his verse:

Though while ill he never neglected to thank her for her
*   attention,*
Only at her death was he fully aware of the degree of her
*   devotion.*
The two were so much in love they were willing to die for each
*   other;*
No measure of gold could buy two such hearts.

Meanwhile, hearing that her son wished to drink some wine, Chang-shih personally prepared a dish of dainties to take to him. When she heard the two words "take poison" from outside his door, she gasped in astonishment and quickened her pace. Catching sight of the two of them lying prostrate on the floor, she knew something dreadful had happened, and immediately began to cry in lamentation.

Ch'en Ch'ing, when he got there, discovered some of the arsenic still left in the wine pot. He had once heard of an antidote for this. One could be saved by drinking the blood of a freshly killed lamb. And so the two were fated to be saved, for as luck would have it, their neighbor on the left was a butcher dealing in lamb. He was at once told to slaughter a lamb and collect its blood.

At this point, Chu Shih-yüan and his wife both appeared on the scene. Ch'en Ch'ing and his wife set to work pouring the blood down their son's throat while Chu Shih-yüan and his wife attended to their daughter. As a result of the lamb's blood they had been given, they soon began vomiting and finally revived. The poison remaining in their stomachs burst their skin and the blood flowed in streams.

After more than a month of convalescence, they were able to ingest food and liquids normally. Such an extraordinary occurrence! That To-fu should recover was already surprising. To-shou, however, had been suffering from leprosy for ten years, during which time a number of well-known physicians had been called in and medicines had been given him, all to no avail. This time, to everyone's surprise, his taking poison had served to verify the old medical axiom, "Fight poison with poison." The venomous blood gushed out through the skin, completely draining the poison, and then even the leprous scars gradually healed. By the time he had completely recovered, the sores had completely disappeared and once again his complexion was smooth and lustrous and his skin was delicate and shining. Even his own parents could not recognize him. He had truly shed his skin and changed into a new frame, becoming reborn. The pure hearts of a noble husband and devoted wife had moved Heaven and Earth. Thus poison was no longer poisonous and instead death was escaped. Misfortune brought blessings, and tears turned to laughter. The lines of the verse of the temple divination lot which read, "The clouds will eventually part to reveal the sun, as fortune and longevity are prearranged in Heaven," had come true.

Ch'en To-shou and his wife went off to the temple to burn incense and give thanks. To-fu offered the silver betrothal hairpins as an oblation. When Wang San-lao heard the news, he came

223

over leading the neighbors from all sides and bringing pots of wine and boxes of food to celebrate. They feasted for several days. To-shou, now twenty-four years old, resumed his studies and reviewed the classics and histories. At the age of thirty-three he passed the imperial examination and at thirty-four his name appeared at the top of the list of successful candidates. The ten-year period during which Mr. Divine had predicated he would die turned out to be the happiest years of his life. But then how can the common mortal ever penetrate the subtle workings of fate? Predictions of misfortune or blessing can never be completely trusted. From this time on, Ch'en Ch'ing

and Chu Shih-yüan became closer friends than ever. They played chess for many more years, and both passed away when they were well into their eighties. Ch'en To-shou rose to become a censor, and his wife To-fu remained forever devoted. A son and daughter were born to them. They themselves lived to venerable ages and left numerous descendants down to this day. The title of this story is "The Couple Bound in Life and Death," and indeed as the following poem says:

Chu and Ch'en became to all a byword for devotion—
A match that was settled at a mere game of chess.
So true and virtuous, this husband and his wife,
Aided by Heaven, they remained united in life and in death.

THE LEPER GIRL

From *Yeh-yü ch'iu-teng lu*

TRANSLATED BY DENNIS T. HU

Mount Yü-chi[1] to the south of River Huai[2] was a secluded and densely wooded region, the haunt of mythical creatures such as the dragon. It was not until the late Ming period that it became inhabited, developing by and by into quite a populated area. A young man called Ch'en Ch'i, styled Lü-ch'in, together with his father Ch'en Mao and his mother Huang-shih, were among those who made their homes on the lower slopes of the mountain. The Ch'ens were farmers and merchants, managing a comfortable living. Ch'i, at fifteen, was an able student. His mother had only one, younger brother, Huang Hai-k'o, who, once traveling to a certain county in Kwangtung, made some money as a salesman and stayed.

One day Ch'i's mother was seriously ill. While they were alone she grasped Ch'i's hands and between sobs, said to him, "After I die, father's sure to remarry. Stepmothers are all alike. If times become too hard for you, go to Kwangtung, look for your uncle, and stay with him." So saying, she gave the weeping son her personal savings, which amounted to more than thirty taels in cash, for traveling expenses.

After his mother's death, his father remarried. The stepmother, Wu, turned out to be as ruthless to Ch'i as his mother had predicted. He went and cried bitterly on his mother's grave and, leaving a note by his father's pillow, left home.

Close to six months of traveling brought him to Kwangtung but also exhausted his funds and left him nowhere near finding his uncle. He checked everywhere in the busiest thoroughfares and marketplaces but his uncle was not to be found. Drifting alone through the villages, Ch'i was gradually reduced to becoming a beggar. More and more he came to regret his impulsiveness and his hasty move, yearning every day to go back home. Wandering to the east of the city one day, he came across a betel-nut tree, half-hidden behind which was a door made of unhewn wood. As he started singing loudly the beggar's melody, "The Falling of the Water Lily Petals," an old man emerged. He had short whiskers, a reddish complexion, and hair that had half turned white. Ch'i's outward appearance amazed him. "Little beggar boy! How refined and well-mannered your looks, my goodness, and yet how depressed you sound!"

[1] There is a Mount Yü-chi to the southeast of Wu County in southern Kiangsu, but this place is far away from the area of River Huai.

[2] This river originates in southern Honan. It flows through Anhwei Province and northern Kiangsu to join the Yangtze River via the Grand Canal.

225

"Since I've read the classics, is it surprising that I look refined? Lost, frustrated, and fallen on hard times, how can I help being depressed?"

"How did it all come about?" the old man asked. Ch'i thus told him where he had come from and how he had been trying to locate his uncle.

"Your uncle's the man by the name of Huang Hai-k'o," said the old man, looking intently at Ch'i. "He had a light complexion and quite a few pockmarks."

"Yes, that's him!"

"Well, he died here a long time ago. He used to be an accountant for a wealthy family and was also a good businessman. He married a prostitute, but after he had died of an illness, the woman took his money and ran away with a servant. Since I was a drinking friend of his, I bought a simple coffin and buried him under a big tree right next to the convent on the east side of the city. The grave with the short tombstone is the one."

Ch'i knelt to thank him. He then followed the directions and located his uncle's grave. What the old man had told him was confirmed by the nuns. Wailing and crying for his uncle, Ch'i swore an oath: "If you hear me in the other world, uncle, give me all your blessings on my trip home. I promise to carry your remains back to your home."

The nuns took pity on Ch'i and fed him with bean gruel. "The elderly gentleman you met is Ssu-k'ung Hun, and had known your uncle for quite some time. You can try to get him to help you. But don't let him know we nuns told you this."

On seeing the man the next day, Ch'i called him "Uncle Ssu-k'ung" with unceremonious abruptness.

Startled, he asked, "How did you get to know my name?"

Ch'i lied, "I spent the night by the grave, and uncle told me everything in a dream. He gave me instructions to ask for your help."

Ssu-k'ung was taken aback. "Actually, your uncle and I were nothing more than acquaintances. Nevertheless, I'll see what I can do for you." Three days later, he came back with a gift of a silk gown for Ch'i, brimming with the smugness of a benefactor. "I'm just a poor man and can't afford expensive gifts for you. I hope you understand. Fortunately, in a mountain district of the neighboring county there's a wealthy man called Elderly Ch'iu, a distant relative of mine. The old couple has a darling of a daughter, called Yüan-mei, also known as Li-yü, about your age. Her looks are just divine. The Ch'ius have set such a high standard for a match that so far nobody's been good enough to be chosen as her husband. You're poor, but with your brilliance, talents, and refined manners, you beat everybody in the area. Let me be matchmaker and write you a letter of introduction. You go ahead and get yourself married into their family. Ch'iu's definitely going to reward you handsomely; enough, certainly, for you to ship your uncle's coffin home."

Hearing such a proposal, Ch'i asked for some time to give it more thought and consideration, but Ssu-k'ung failed to see why that was necessary. Ch'i went on, "You see, I'm born of a humble family and have lived off the countryside all this time. We've always led simple lives close to the soil. I'm afraid that it wouldn't be easy for a pampered daughter of the rich to adjust. Besides, the marriage being a formal and well-publicized affair, how could they let me do what I like and just leave afterward?"

"You prig! You are a dumb scholar. What you're going to do is just cheat him of his money. Where in this whole wide world will he hunt for a son-in-law who's run away?"

Ch'i could not think of anything better to do himself and, somewhat passively, took the letter and went along. Ch'iu's place turned out to be a complex of imposing mansions, with large, well-secured compounds. The attendant at the gates, seeing that Ch'i could not be someone with im-

226

pressive credentials, ordered him to stay well away from the property. However, after the letter was presented and delivered inside, two young men emerged and greeted the visitor courteously: "Father has ordered us to bid you welcome." So, Ch'i thought, these were the old man's sons, and followed them into the estate. The buildings and gardens that he saw bore the class and style of a well-established family of means. A giant of a man, with beard hanging all the way down to his waist, was standing at the top of a short flight of steps, Ch'i hurriedly approached and exchanged greetings with him. As they took their seats inside, his host asked after the health of Ssu-k'ung. Soon the lady of the house was announced. An attractive woman in her forties appeared, with two maids-in-waiting at her sides.

"This is my wife. Since your family and Ssu-k'ung's are long-time friends, you and we are like relatives, too. May I take the liberty of introducing my wife to you?"

Ch'i bowed to greet the lady. Taking a good, hard look at him, she smiled, and turned to her husband: "Cousin Ssu-k'ung is really a good judge—the young man's quite a person."

A feast was instantly prepared, and Ch'i was offered cup after cup of wine. While they were eating, the host asked him a little about his background; then he said, "I wonder if Ssu-k'ung has mentioned this to you. We have always loved our young daughter Li-yü very dearly. We don't want to see her married off to some faraway place. And then, to choose an ideal mate, with superb grace and the best of other qualities, has so far been next to impossible. Now by a happy stroke of luck, you have been introduced to us. Isn't this tie predestined? We'd like to marry our daughter to you without further ado."

As he compliantly gave assent, Ch'i left his place at the dinner table to thank them solemnly. "I'm a worthless nobody," he went on to explain humbly. "To marry above myself into your family is something I'd be more than happy to do. However, it is for the purpose of locating my uncle that I traveled to this area. I'd very much like to go home for a short while about three or four days after the wedding. As soon as my uncle's reburial is properly taken care of, I'll come back here. These plans I have to tell you, my elders, ahead of time."

The woman smiled. "Oh, young man, why are you in such a hurry?"

Her husband was quick to stop her. "The young man's filial piety should by no means be discouraged," he said, interrupting. "Let me fetch you five hundred taels in cash right away for traveling expenses." Ch'i was delighted, and respectfully accepted the arrangement.

Soon music started to flow, and there was not a corner of the house that was not as brightly lit as day. Senior servants proceeded to lead Ch'i to secluded quarters. After having changed there into brand new attire, he was directed to a carpeted area. From the inner chambers, several young maids brought out a beautiful girl in her mid-teens. She was clad in the finest of silks and elaborate jewels. Conducting herself with poise and charm, she completed with Ch'i the traditional ceremonial greeting rites of the betrothed. Together they went into their wedding suite. Ch'i pushed aside his bride Li-yü's fan to take a look at her, only to discover that even dewdrops on the lily, and the pinkish glow of the peach, could not match the dazzling beauty that was in front of him. Feeling his heart racing feverishly, Ch'i regretted the rash thoughtlessness with which, just a moment ago, he talked about a temporary absence shortly after the weddng. He now intended to maneuver to postpone his plans, so that he could stay and enjoy conjugal love with Li-yü.

The feast had drawn to a close, and the lamps were growing dim. As the timepieces chimed a late hour the maids and servants retired. Leaning on a table, Ch'i was lost in melancholy. From time to time Li-yü brushed aside the brocade curtains to steal a look at her bridegroom. There seemed to be a trace of anguished pallor in her countenance. With no inkling of what was on her mind, Ch'i went near to speak to her in sweet, tender words. But as he tried to help her remove her ornaments and makeup, he was stopped by a gesture of her frail hands. Tears started rolling down her cheeks when he leaned closer. Getting up, she first snuffed out the candle and checked to see that no one was nearby; then she closed the door. She whispered, "Do you realize that you don't have long to live?"

"What?"

"Where do you come from, and where are you planning to go? Tell me all the details, please."

Ch'i did as he was asked. Li-yü, amid her sighs, was about to speak, but changed her mind. Ch'i knew that something was really wrong, and knelt down to plead for mercy.

Li-yü explained, "I'm so impressed by your elegant charm that I can't bring myself to keep this secret from you. Now, listen. I am a leper. You see, this place is located in the westernmost part of Kwangtung, and for generations girls of the area have been known for their stunning beauty. But they all inherit this dreadful disease. When they grow to be fifteen, their rich parents lure male visitors from afar with gifts worth thousands of silver dollars. It's not until the infection is completely transferred to these men that the families begin looking for a genuine match. If the latent illness is not gotten rid of at that point, it will soon break out. The girls' skin will start to dry out and crack, and their hair will curl up. Of course, after that, no man would ever take a second look at them. The visitors who, because of their greed for money, and not knowing what's going on, consummate the marriage, get a pinkish rash on their necks within three or four days. It's only about a week before a terrible itch develops all over the body. Then, after a little over a year, they have sustained convulsive seizures. Though in some cases the onset may be mild, there is still no chance of survival."

Only upon hearing this did Ch'i realize the kind of situation he was in. He wept. "I'm all by myself, tens of thousands of *li* from home, and I'm charged with a heavy responsibility. Won't you let me escape? Please have pity on me."

"You might as well forget it. It's so difficult to get hold of men here; as soon as you came in, the place was surrounded with our armed guards to make sure that you stayed."

"Actually, my own life doesn't matter so much," Ch'i said, still weeping. "What grieves me is that I do have an aging father at home."

"Although I'm a woman, I'm not ignorant of the importance of honor and integrity. Because of its doomed circumstances, this place doesn't allow a woman to remain virtuous. I've always resented it so much that I don't think this life is worth living at all. Why don't you just lie in bed with me, both of us fully clothed. Then after three days take the money and go home immediately. Once the infection attacks, I won't live for too much longer anyway. The only thing I ask of you is that you set up the traditional memorial tablet back home, with an inscription to the memory of Ch'iu Li-yü, your wife by first and formal marriage. Then I could rest in peace." When she had finished, she embraced him and began to sob.

"Oh! If we go through with the marriage I'll die, and if not you will. Why don't we get hold of some poison and commit suicide together, and just hope for a reunion in our next life?" Ch'i was bitter and distressed.

"No, that won't do. Instead, write down your full address for me, and I'll sew it into the hem of my dress. When the day comes that my errant soul starts to wander to faraway places, I may have a chance to greet my in-laws. And perhaps even take a simple meal from you, too."

Ch'i managed to give her the address, but he was already in a fit of weeping. They got into bed and slept together. Unable to control himself, time after time he tried to make love to Li-yü, but she gently refused and tried to comfort him instead. Thus it was a marriage in name only, unconsummated: the situation was as frustrating and regrettable as the case of those born frigid or impotent.

The very next day, Ch'i's parents-in-law ignored him completely, as if he were a total stranger. That same night Li-yü bit and sucked lightly at his neck until pinkish marks appeared in several places. "This will do," she said. Then she gave him two bangles of gold and two of jade, as personal gifts. Ch'i was about to fix a date for reunion, but as though in mourning for herself, she said, "By the time you come this way again, I'd probably have already spent quite some time in my grave!"

Next morning her father did as he had promised and motioned for Ch'i to leave immediately. When Ch'i arrived at the convent, the nuns noticed the marks on his neck and would not even let him in. He lost no time in hiring a huge boat, dug up his uncle's coffin, and sailed south.[3] During the night Ch'i could not help weeping. The boatman thought that his grief must have been caused by the loss of a well-loved uncle and was both impressed and moved, paying him all the more respect. Ch'i finally arrived home and was reunited with his father. It turned out that his stepmother had passed away, and a maid was taken as concubine. His father was more than delighted to see him again. He noticed the money Ch'i had but thought that it must have been a legacy from his uncle, and so did not question him about it. They reburied his uncle and bought some farm land. Ch'i's father was a master brewer, and set about cultivating grains for the manufacture of wine. His wine shop prospered and brought in so much profit that it became possible for Ch'i to attend school and concentrate on his studies.

[3] Here the direction is questionable. From Kwangtung, Ch'i should head north for his home. Perhaps the rationale is that there is no direct water route between Kwangtung and the Huai area, and Ch'i might have had to sail south through the Pearl River to reach the sea and then travel along the coast to reach central China.

Meanwhile, Li-yü's father, on Ch'i's departure, had no doubt in his mind that his daughter was completely cleansed of her infection. As he was busy engaging the services of matchmakers to find a son-in-law, however, Li-yü's disease flared up. On close examination, it proved indeed to be leprosy. With tears in his eyes, her father sternly questioned her. Meanwhile the women of the household checked up on her and found her to be still a virgin. "Oh, you little fool!" they shouted at her all at once, "Don't you want to live?"

A month passed; Li-yü grew weaker and weaker. They sent her off to a leper house established by philanthropic officials. Since the illness had always been recognized as contagious, to such an extent that one patient in a family was enough to contaminate the entire household, even a favorite daughter had to be cast out. No love or bonds of sentiment could save her. After her admission into the institution, she made repeated attempts on her own life. Each time, however, an aged, pockmarked man who spoke with a heavy southern accent appeared to intervene and save her. Then she started to consider flight. The old man turned out to be more than willing to show the way. "My name is Huang, and I'm from south of the River Huai. Isn't it your wish to locate Ch'en Lü-ch'in? I vaguely remember that he and I have somehow met before. I'm about to travel east anyway, so why don't you come with me?"

Li-yü figured that she was seriously ill anyhow, and since the man was so open and magnanimous, she was delighted to go along. The doors, one after another, seemed to fling themselves open for them. When they reached the suburbs, the old man applied saliva to her small feet, at the same time softly chanting as if casting a spell. As soon as they resumed their journey, Li-yü found herself speeding along like a runner in perfect condition. She was therefore deeply grateful, and treated him as she would her father. In order to pay their traveling expenses, she unhesitantly sold her silver bangles. However, the funds only lasted until they got to the area of Hupeh and Hunan. They then had no alternative but to beg for a living. The old man played the flute while Li-yü composed the song "The Chaste Evergreen" and sang from door to door collecting alms.

The chaste evergreen, how exuberant its boughs!
It must be misconduct in her last life
That causes her to be born a girl—
And into such a forsaken place as Kwangtung.
A leper at birth, and leprosy will grow with her:
What injustice, what lamentable fate!
How brightly the ornamented candles shine
Upon the nuptial cup
As she hides her tears, stealing a look at her lover.
Handsome is Ch'en, with supreme grace and bearing.
Snuffing the candle as I steal a look at you,
I can't suppress the excitement within me.
I am a leper girl,
But a leper you are not to become.
My leprosy, through you, may be cured: I shall live.
But the leprosy passed on to you: for me you will die.
You're about to die for me and you don't know it;
In the wedding suite, in the adorned chambers,
You drink from the golden goblet.
Peacocks, dance no more.
Cuckoos, stop your calling.
The parakeets, lost for words, are ready to fly away.
You fall into the trap, and how my heart weeps for you!
You— Oh, don't you see?
A worthy steed cannot take two saddles;
So is a chaste woman determined to stay on with but one name,
Though she may have to give her life for it.
Your appearance will remain heavenly;
This wretched fate of mine: flimsy as paper.
The skin dries out; the tissues crack,
The hair that used to be smooth, natural curls
Turns yellow and falls.
Hiding her face, she runs into the leper house,
Not wanting to infect and harm her relations.
A treasure of a daughter before,
Now she is left to die.
Amid silken finery she lived before—
Into a prison she now falls.
The moonlight shines on a bare beam.
There a white piece of cloth hangs,

And with it a girl's life
That is going, going, nearly gone.
Though I am still alive,
I shall not stay in my home any longer.
Since I am still alive,
I shall look for my husband.
Oh, a life such as this
Is no better than death.
What will come out of such living death?
The chaste evergreen, how luxuriant its boughs!
Home for the birds and shade for the fishes.
There are birds that fly in pairs, wing to wing,
And fish that are inseparable couples,
Sharing a coverlet in life, sharing the grave in death.
Even if coverlet and grave may not be shared,
However, my mind is made up,
Clear and unclouded as the brilliant moon.
The peach flowers are ablaze in the moonlight.
The plum tree perishes for the peach flowers;
It is attacked by worms.
The chaste evergreen, how red its boughs and leaves!
All that is blood
From the eyes of the leper girl!

The song, telling of her plight and fidelity to Ch'i, was a sad one, matched only by the weeping music of the flute. There was not a single person who was not moved to tears. They were all eager to offer them food, doing so with compassion untainted by overtones of condescension or patronage. Half a year's journey finally brought them south of the River Huai. As they approached the foot of a mountain, an endless stretch of old houses came into view, and above the treetops extended green banner signs of various shops. The old man pointed into the distance: "That one facing the south with a heap of yellowish stones in front is the place you're looking for. Go ahead by yourself. I'm going to have to disappear from now on. But please bring a message to the Ch'ens: say Hai-k'o thanks them." At these words he vanished from sight. Recovering from her bewilderment, Li-yü approached the shop. An aged gentleman sitting by the side of the wine oven bore a resemblance to Ch'i; she had a feeling that he was Ch'i's father. Li-yü thus sang her "Chaste Evergreen" song. The man threw her a coin. She repeated it, and he threw her another.

"Your son Ch'en Ch'i," she said, starting to weep, "while he was in the west of Kwangtung, contracted a debt that he didn't repay. I've come all this way to call him to account. How are a couple of coins going to pay for all that's due me?" Taken aback, the old man asked her the details, and she promptly explained everything.

"Ch'i is my son all right," he said. "But I can't just take your word for it. Right now he's at the autumn examinations in Nanking, but he should be back here soon. This can be checked out with him in person easily enough, and then we'll know for sure." Hearing this, Li-yü knelt to greet him in the proper manner of a daughter-in-law. He sent her to a convent to be cared for, and had maids assigned to her service. But they all spat and went away. Fortunately, an elderly nun sympathized with her and greatly relieved her misery and suffering.

It was more than a month before Ch'i returned. When his father confronted him with the matter, he was shocked out of his wits. "We are certainly under an obligation," his father said. "And since we can afford to keep her here for the rest of her life, that's what we're going to do. Even though you won't be sharing a bed with her like husband and wife, we owe it to her." Thanking his father, Ch'i scurried off to look in on Li-yü.

"I didn't come all the way here in the hope of leading a normal married life with you." Li-yü clutched his clothes and wept. "All I expect is to be buried in your family cemetery!"

Sobbing, Ch'i tried to comfort her. "How did you manage to travel here all by yourself?" he asked. She began telling him about the old man with the yellowish complexion—how he looked, and everything they did. Ch'i was startled. "Why, that's uncle! But wouldn't that mean he's an earthbound spirit?"

Ch'i brought Li-yü home. He cleared out enough space amid the vats in the wine cellar so she could stay there. All the domestic staff, however, kept a safe distance; not one of them dared get anywhere near except for a young maid by the name of Kan-chiao. She alone provided toilet care and other services for Li-yü. As for meals and medicines, they were all served by Ch'i himself. After a while he even packed his bedding to sleep by her side, making Kan-chiao do the same. Neither of them as a consequence contracted the disease.

Presently the results of the examinations were announced: Ch'i won top honors in his district. Instantly he became the prime target for local matchmakers, whom he nevertheless adamantly refused one after the other. To his father's gentle persuasions, he replied, sobbing, "I'm barely twenty-one, and the leper girl doesn't have long to live. Why don't we wait until she's taken away by her illness before I get married? That won't be too late at all, will it?" And, afraid that if he left home there would be no one to take care of Li-yü, Ch'i feigned sickness to avoid a more advanced examination. Li-yü, distressed, beat her head against the earthen wine vats. "All because of me, he's delaying the continuation of the ancestral line. Besides, I'm a hindrance to his career. How am I to face, on my death, the ancestors in the other world? I might as well be dead!" Again she beat her head against the vats. If it were not for Kan-chiao she would have been dead.

One day Ch'i went to visit a relative, had a few drinks there, and because of rain, decided to spend the night. Kan-chiao, on the other hand, was not feeling well, and stayed in bed in the house. Li-yü had nothing better to do than listen to the rain and snuff the candle, meanwhile tossing and scratching because of the itch.

Suddenly there came a crisp, swishing noise from up on the main beam. There, a monster of a black snake, thick as a child's arm and measuring about seven feet long, swept through the air. At first Li-yü was rather scared. But then, on second thought, she thought that if she could get herself eaten by the snake, it might just be better than killing herself. So she decided to let things take their own course. With its body coiled around the beam, the snake dipped its head downward to lift the wooden cover of one of the vats. The cover fell as if forcibly dashed onto the floor. It started drawing wine from the vat, and feeding thus, before long became full. Then it tried to recoil upward, but by then its body was stiff as a dried-out creeper bough. In a matter of moments it fell into the vat, where it turned and wallowed and finally exhausted. All of a sudden silence returned. Fetching a light, Li-yü struggled up to take a look. The snake was dead. It occurred to her that maybe the snake's venom was just as good as the most deadly of poisons. So, cupping her hands, she helped herself to the wine. By the time she had drunk more than a jugful, she began to feel awake and refreshed, her depresson gone. The itching of her infected skin, however, took a sharp turn for the worse. But as she washed it with the wine, it subsided instantly. The next day she again, without anybody knowing about it, drank and washed with the wine. Her illness all but disappeared: the skin that had been cracking dry before had now turned moistly lustrous as jade; the hair that had curled up hung down now as freely as clouds. Moreover, the peeling and blistering face and limbs had changed into the natural beauty of blossoms, of the moon, fine and tender now as newly sprouting bamboo shoots.

Kan-chiao, in elated amazement, reported to Ch'i. When asked how it had all happened, Li-yü told him about the wine with the dead snake in it. Ch'i took a close look at the reptile and saw that the black scales that covered its entire body took the pattern of calligraphy from an accomplished hand. On its head grew a single horn bearing a bright red color. So this was none other than "Black Wind," the king of snakes in the local mountain district.

Ch'i dressed Li-yü in embroidered silks and lace clothing, adding flower-shaped hairpins, pearls, and jade, to present her to his father and the young female relatives of the house. Everyone was overwhelmed by her heavenly charm. "When I was a child," Ch'i's father said, "I heard that the king of snakes has been around these mountains for just about a thousand years. There was once a foreign monk who needed only one or two pieces of its scales for a case of skin disease, but he never did get them. How could one know that Heaven on high had it especially reserved for me to cure my fine daughter-in-law?"

That same day presents and ritual paraphernalia were readied and preparations made for formal wedding ceremonies. The house was crowded by people in pearl-sequined shoes; there was feasting to the accompaniment of woodwind and drum music. People raced to the place from as far as a hundred *li* away just to look at Li-yü, and returned home feeling proud and honored.

Three years later she gave birth to a child and, being thankful of the good service Kan-chiao had given her, insisted on taking her on as Ch'i's concubine. He refused, but to no avail. In the spring of the same year, Ch'i took the court examinations and was named a fellow of the imperial academy. Subsequently, he was appointed a prefect to take charge of social welfare and relief efforts for the homeless, dispossessed, sick, and needy. It did not take him long to become as loved by the populace as if he were their own dear father.

His promotion to governor-general of Kwangtung and Kwangsi soon followed. There he summoned Li-yü's father and asked for his daughter. In feigned sobs the father-in-law said, "My daughter was fated to die young, and passed away a long time ago. You mean, sir, you intend to look for your wife of old times?"

Ch'i then demanded to be given Li-yü's remains so they could be sent home for burial. The old man was frightened, and offered one thousand taels in cash as a present on the occasion of Ch'i's father's birthday. Ch'i turned him down. Then he called upon Ssu-k'ung and inquired about the girl; the latter told him, "Li-yü, while escaping in fright, fell to her death down a steep cliff."

Ch'i scoffed, "So they really think that I am so mean and small-minded!" He promptly ordered the maids to present his wife. Li-yü appeared, properly dressed as a titled lady, wife of an official of the first rank, beaming and radiant. Her father was so startled that he almost fell to his knees. Only after he had taken a better look was he convinced that it was none other than his own daughter. With tears in her eyes, she asked after the good health of her parents. He could not believe what was happening, and felt so ashamed that he could have died.

Thereafter Li-yü visited with her parents frequently. She not only had medicine made from the poisoned wine, but also established a clinic for the lepers of the two provinces. Numerous lives were saved. When Ch'i was in his forties, his father still enjoyed good health. Ch'i asked to be relieved of his official duties so that he might personally serve his father in his final years. On his return home he refurbished his uncle's grave. In the convent he installed a stone plaque in honor of his wife Lady Ch'iu, recording on it a summary of her life. To this day the medicinal wine from this mountain area is still keeping its fine reputation.

THE BROKEN HAIRPIN

From *Hsin ch'ing-nien*

TRANSLATED BY LIU WU-CHI

On the fifth day of my arrival at the West Lake, I went up immediately after breakfast to the southern verandah of the inn. As I paced back and forth, the sound of the monastery bell wafted across; it lingered, then vanished. The West Lake from a distance looked as beautiful as ever, but the friends who accompanied me there were different at different times. This was my thirteenth visit. I came alone nine times; on other occasions, I came once with the Buddhist monk T'an-ti, once with the Ch'an master Fa-jen, and at another time with Teng Sheng-hou and the recluse Tu-hsiu.[1] This time I was with Chuang Chih.

A dark, gloomy day—rain threatened but didn't fall. There were no sightseers at the lake, only a few lotus-gathering boats that emerged and disappeared. Suddenly, I noticed a light boat sailing toward the shore across the blue waters and red lotus flowers under a long line of drooping willows. Taking a closer look, I saw a casually dressed young woman in the boat. I thought to myself: she was certainly in good spirits to be on the lake all by herself. Soon the boat was an-chored by the stone jetty in front of the inn. As she walked up, she looked so uncommonly beautiful that she seemed like a fairy.

The young woman came straight to the inn and asked the doorkeeper for me; he took her upstairs. Before my astonishment had subsided, she was already in front of me; she curtsied graciously and said, blushing, "Sir, please excuse my intrusion. I've heard that you are here with Mr. Chuang. Is that true?"

"Yes," I replied casually.

"I'm a friend of his and have come here expressly to visit him. May I ask if Mr. Chuang is around?"

"He left on horseback early this morning," I replied, "perhaps for a trip to the Ling-yin and T'ien-chu mountains. He could be back this evening, but I'm not sure. Is there any message I could give him?"

The young woman pondered for a moment, and then she said, "My name is Tu Ling-fang. I'm staying at the Lakeside Hotel, room 6. Kindly ask Mr. Chuang to visit me tomorrow morning. I'm sorry to have disturbed you."

"I'll be glad to deliver the message."

Blushing again, she thanked me and left by the same boat.

The young woman's visit had left me in a state

[1] Ch'en Tu-hsiu (editor of the *Hsin Ch'ing-nien* and later one of the founders of the Chinese Communist Party) and Teng Sheng-hou were respectively dean and principal of the Anhwei High School, An-ch'ing, Anhwei, where Su Man-shu, the author of this story, taught in 1912–1913.

234

of bewilderment. First of all, my friend Chuang Chih was a man of integrity. He was respectable, prudent, and studious. I had never heard of his being the romantic sort. Then where did this girl come from? Second, since I had never met her before, how would she know my name? And how did she come to know that I was with Chuang? Third, the girl was in her teens; why did she want to invite Chuang over to her hotel? One would suspect that she came from the pleasure houses, like female entertainers and musicians, but that could not be the case because she had proper manners and looked so *distinguée*. On the other hand, if she were Chuang's family friend, why did she come alone to see him? Would she not fear gossip? Sitting quietly, I pondered these matters for a long time before I said fearfully to myself: "All women in this world are a source of calamity!"

Since I had made up my mind, when Chuang returned in the evening, I did not mention the girl's visit to him, at least for the time being. The next day, I called up the Lakeside Hotel and inquired, "How many people are there in room 6?"

"Three: a young lady, her mother, and a maid."

"Where did they come from?"

"Shanghai."

"How long are they staying?"

"They're leaving by express train after lunch."

It would be too late, I thought, for Chuang to keep the appointment. This was, after all, a trifling matter. It would not be a betrayal of a friend's trust if I didn't inform him of the girl's visit. A day later, on the eighteenth, friends asked us to go to the head of the [Ch'ien-t'ang] River to watch the tides and to see how three oxen would pull a boat downstream against the onrushing bore. Chuang was tired and did not go. When I returned in the evening, I couldn't find him in the room. The doorkeeper told me, "He got a letter at six o'clock. When supper was served, he simply sat there without eating. He soon left the inn as if he had something urgent on his mind."

I went at once to look for him. I walked along the embankment and located him at the Broken Bridge. He was all by himself, gazing vacantly into the wind.

"The dew is heavy and the wind gusty. You'd better go back," I said.

Without replying, Chuang merely held my hand and followed me back to the inn. After we got there, I was completely exhausted and went to bed right away without telling him of the girl's visit.

I woke up suddenly at midnight and found the moonlight seeping through the curtain. Putting on my clothes, I peered out. A splendid moonlit scene of the lake and the mountain came to my view. I wanted to wake Chuang to join me. Adjusting my clothes, I walked over to his bed. It was empty. I went out to look for him and found him standing dejectedly and motionlessly before the railings. As I tapped his shoulder from behind, I discerned in the moonlight tear stains on his face.

"Why are you so deep in thought?" I asked.

Chuang gave no reply, but quietly wiped away his tears with a handkerchief. Deeply disturbed, I knew not how to comfort him and could only urge him to go back to bed. I had no way of finding out whether he actually went to sleep; I myself was only half asleep.

The next morning, I noticed that Chuang's face was ashen gray, his eyes slightly reddened, and his appetite gone. These could have been the thoughts in his mind: "There's just no end to my sorrow. I have little chance of recovering sufficiently to enjoy with my friend the beauty of the lake and mountains, the wind and moon."

After lunch, I said to him earnestly, "You have changed a great deal since yesterday. Perhaps you have some hidden grief that has been touched off by something I don't know about. Why don't you tell me? We are good friends, and if you were in my place, what would you feel if you had seen me like that last night?"

Even though I tried over and again, I could not

coax any answer from him. Not wishing to upset him further, I took him for a boat ride in the hope that it would relieve his distress. Still, he would not open his heart to me. I figured that for such a sincere and trusting person as Chuang Chih, something truly unspeakable must have happened to keep him from confiding in me. The letter mentioned by the doorkeeper—could it have come from the girl? I did not want to talk to him about her because I knew that he had an affectionate nature, and at such an impressionable age, he could have easily stumbled if once he took the wrong step. I do not mean that people shouldn't talk about love. But, judging from his present state of mind, I could readily see that there must have been a close relationship between Chuang and the casually dressed girl. I myself had long been nurtured in affliction. Why should I let myself be reminded of the agony of love on account ·of Chuang?

On Solitary Hill, where I had taken Chuang Chih, we saw a group of foreigners strolling about in the Crane-Releasing Pavilion. Suddenly, a blue-eyed girl sang out aloud: *Love is enough. Why should we ask for more?*[2]

At the end of her song there was an echo from the valley: *Love is enough. Why should we ask for more?*

Then a young man added: *Oh, you kid! Sorrow is the depth of love.* And the valley echoed as before. All the visitors laughed heartily. Chuang also smiled, but it was a forced smile that merely increased my concern for him.

Afterward, a succession of fine days followed. The sky was clear and the lake placid. I urged Chuang Chih to come with me whenever I went out. Gradually, the swelling grief in his heart sub-

---

[2] This and all the subsequent sentences and phrases printed in italics in this story are in the original Chinese text. It marks perhaps the first time a Chinese novelist incorporated a number of English sentences and phrases in his fictional writings. No sources have been found for the English "quotations" in this story; quite probably they were composed by Man-shu.

sided and peace was once more restored to him. But he looked weak and fragile as if after a long illness. As for myself, I felt adrift in a vast sea and could only hope that the waves would subside and my friend would regain the equanimity of his heart.

Unexpectedly, Chuang asked me one day, "That day when I went horseback riding, did an old man come to see me?"

"No," I answered right away. "It was a young lady who came looking for you." Chuang was greatly astonished. "A young woman?" he asked. "What did she say?"

Only then did I tell him of the girl's visit. "Who is she?" It was my turn to inquire.

"I know her but have never met her before," Chuang replied after a brief pause.

"At that time," I said, "I didn't want to distract you from your trip with such trivial matters. So, I didn't tell you. Now, I can't help asking what made your face change that day when you read the letter. It must have come from the girl, didn't it?"

"No," Chuang answered hastily. "The letter was from my uncle."

"So, there is little relationship between the letter's content and the girl's visit?" I pursued the question further.

"I never expected that she'd come to see me," Chuang said. "I had no knowledge of her visit until you told me just now."

I asked again, "Would you have been willing to see her if you had been here?"

"No," Chuang replied.

"Why is it then that you wanted to know whether an old man had come to see you, and who is he anyway?"

"I was afraid I might have missed my uncle if he had showed up here."

Not long afterward, about late autumn or early winter, Chuang packed his luggage and left the place. I had to stay on to recuperate from a recurring intestinal trouble. I read and fished. Occasionally, I smoked a Manila cigar, though in fact that was no way to cure my sickness.

One day, another girl came and wanted to know if Chuang was here.

"He left long ago," I told her.

As I spoke, I watched her closely and was impressed by her beauty and grace. She was a girl in her mid-teens. When she learned that Chuang had gone, she was disappointed and left immediately in her carriage.

After she left, I thought for a while and sighed: "This girl and the earlier one, who came to see Chuang, are both unusually beautiful. Even putting aside the question of their relationship with Chuang, you could readily conclude from their disappointment at failing to see him that he must have been the object of their affection. One wonders, however, to whom is Chuang's heart attached?"

I also wondered why Chuang had expressed reluctance to see the first girl. Would he be willing to meet the one who had just come? Unfortunately, I had no way of finding out. Alas! Love is the hardest knot to untie. When he hid his tears late that night, I knew that he must have been entangled in love. Yet, for all I knew, he had never been involved with any women. I was also sure that Chuang was not a fickle man. True, as an old saying goes, "Once the thread of love is fastened, even death cannot untie it." This could be said of Chuang Chih. Now two beautiful girls had called on him; so Chuang's misery could well be imagined! Sad it was indeed, for I was afraid that my good friend would not live out the allotted span of his life! That's why I was so convinced that "All women in this world are a source of calamity!"

Half a month later, I also returned to Shanghai. After I had unpacked my things, I went straight to see Chuang. His aunt met me and said, "He had a sudden attack of fever a few days ago and is now staying in the French hospital."

I went there immediately to look for him.

Seeing me, Chuang held my hand silently without smiling.

"Are you better now?" I asked.

Chuang merely nodded his head. I felt his forehead and was assured that he didn't have a high fever. In such a situation, I thought, he was not ready for the news of the second girl's visit. So I kept quiet and sat silently in the room for almost half an hour as Chuang closed his eyes and dozed off. Just then, the doctor came in. I asked him in a hushed voice about his patient's condition. He told me that Chuang's case was not dangerous, but his nerves had been badly affected. Thus he warned me not to mention to Chuang anything in the past that would upset him. After the doctor had left, I looked at my watch: it was already ten past eight in the evening. Chuang was still comfortably asleep. I stood up and was about to leave when he suddenly opened his eyes and said to me, "Please don't go so soon. I'd like to have a long talk with you."

"You should rest quietly," I said. "I'll come to see you tomorrow morning."

"I'd like to tell you something tonight," Chuang insisted. "Please sit down. I want to bare my heart to you—that will surely work better than medicine. As a matter of fact, I felt better as soon as I saw you. Well, this is the situation: today I got a letter from Tu Ling-fang. She's coming here at nine o'clock. I've told the doctor about the visit and gotten his permission to talk to her for an hour. You saw her at the lake, but this is our first meeting. So I beg you to stay with me, and if I fail to communicate my feelings to her, you'll have to help me out. You're my dearest friend, and so is she even though I've never seen her before. At our meeting tonight, you'll render me a great service if you testify to her my sincere feelings for her; later you could also help by telling my uncle about her virtuous conduct and gracious manner when I plead my case with him."

Chuang became quite animated as he talked. I was relieved that he did not appear sick at all.

Still, in all my life I had never found myself in the kind of situation I was in tonight. It is well known that love between man and woman can result only in anxiety, grief, and pain. So how could I put in a word between him and the girl? But Chuang was sincere in his request, and I could not very well refuse him. Silently, I sat down again.

In a short while, the visitor arrived. She stopped outside the room. Chuang managed to sit up and invited her to enter. I bowed to her in greeting.

Chuang said solemnly to the girl, "My admiration for you has grown with time. How happy I am to have a chance to meet you at last!" Hearing this, the girl blushed. She was shy, embarrassed, and did not know how to answer.

"This is my friend Man-shu," continued Chuang. "He is a kind and understanding person. Please don't stand on ceremony with him."

"All right." Only then did the girl answer in a low voice.

"All this time, my thoughts have been constantly with you," Chuang said. "But unfortunately, things often went wrong and I was prevented from seeing you on several occasions. I suppose your brother must have relayed my message to you in his letters."

"Yes, he did," answered the girl, as tense as before.

"While I was visiting the West Lake," Chuang said, "My uncle wrote me that you were engaged to a Mr. Lin and that the date of your marriage had been set. Is that true?"

"No," said the girl in a tremulous voice as her face paled.

"If what I just said were true," pursued Chuang, "what would you do—?"

Before he could finish, the girl interrupted him. "By the blue sea and the azure sky, I swear that even death could not change my heart!"

Upon hearing these words, Chuang was extremely moved and didn't utter a word for a long time.

Suddenly, the girl asked, "Did your uncle know that I went with my mother to watch the tides at Ch'ien-t'ang in mid-autumn?"

"I suppose he did," said Chuang.

"Did he know that I tried to see you at the lake?"

"Only Man-shu and I knew it."

"Your uncle left for T'ung-chou[3] today. When will he be back?"

"I have no idea."

At this point, the girl was about to ask another question but refrained. Finally, she said timidly, "Have you ever met Lien-p'ei before? She and I came from the same village and we went to school together. Her tenderness and modesty are indeed commendable."

"When I was in Tsingtao," said Chuang, "I met her three times. My aunt introduced us."

"It was she who told me about your visiting the West Lake with Mr. Man-shu. She is now in Hangchow.[4] Didn't you meet her at the lake?"

"I had no idea she was there," said Chuang.

It was only then that I had a chance to put in a word. "After you left," I said to Chuang, "there was indeed another young lady who came."

The girl was surprised and said to me, "Please, sir, did she put up her fine dark hair in a bun, and carry herself most gracefully?"

"That's she," I said.

Hearing these words, Chuang was deeply affected; tears welled up in his eyes. Equally affected, the girl went over to Chuang's couch and, holding his hand, said weeping, "You know where my heart lies, and I know yours!" While speaking, she took from her hair a jade hairpin and gave it to Chuang, saying, "If Heaven should thwart our desires, break it!"

These were dark, ominous words. I could not bear to listen any further. I took out my watch. It

[3] In Kiangsu Province.
[4] The Chinese text has "Wu-lin," an old name for Hangchow.

was already ten o'clock. I urged the girl to leave early so that Chuang could have a good night's rest. She silently shook hands with me and departed in grief. Alas! This was my friend's first meeting with Ling-fang, and it was also to be their last!

Upon returning home that night after having witnessed the meeting between Chuang Chih and Ling-fang, I pondered over it time and again but failed to make out the exact relationship between the two. I had personally observed Chuang's sudden emotional disturbance when he learned from his uncle's letter of Ling-fang's impending marriage to another man. This proved that Chuang truly loved Ling-fang. I also perceived that during the short time they were together, the girl had displayed deep feelings of love for him beyond the few words they exchanged with each other. When she shook my hand, I recalled, her palm was extremely hot—an indication of the excitement she had felt in her first visit with Chuang. From their conversation one could also make out that it was the uncle who stood in the way of their love. According to Chuang, it was through his aunt that he had met Lien-p'ei three times. Apparently, she was the choice of his uncle and aunt. When Ling-fang asked me about the girl with the pretty coiffure and graceful bearing, the description could fit only the second girl who came to look for Chuang on the lake. So actually I had also seen her, with her fresh, sprightly looks. But I didn't know whether Chuang loved Lien-p'ei as much as he loved Ling-fang, and whether Lien-p'ei also loved Chuang as much as Ling-fang did. As I pondered these questions, I suddenly realized how absurd I had become! Certainly, it was an emotional affair for my friend, a crisis in his life, but it was none of my business. Why should I speculate on other people's love affairs in my own fantasy? I took off my clothes and went to bed. Soon, I came to a dream land that bore great resemblance to reality. Indeed, the things I dreamed were even more intriguing than what had actually transpired. So let me relate to you my dream:

Together with Chuang Chih, Ling-fang, and Lien-p'ei, I took a boatride from the Brocade Ribbon Bridge on the Inner [West] Lake. As we paddled along, I saw some withered, decaying lotus leaves trembling in the wind. Often, they shed their watery tears as if to complain sadly to the Creator. I took pity on them and watched them closely. One of the leaves shook its head and said, "Don't be so conceited as to think that I am begging for your pity."

When we were under the West Freshet Bridge, Ling-fang, pointing to the bank, said to Lien-p'ei, "Those tiny flowers are rather pretty in their red petals, almost like the color of goldfish. Earlier, I saw them bloom, and now with my own eyes I see them wither. What kind of flowers are these?"

"I don't know," said Lien-p'ei.

"Could they be duckweed flowers?" Chuang then asked me. I told him, "This plant is of the same species as the duckweed but of a different variety. Its common name is 'ghost lantern.' It is used sometimes as medicine." Just then, the boat emerged from under the West Freshet Bridge, and Ling-fang and Lien-p'ei broke into a song, singing in unison:

Together with female companions we tread on green grass,
Avoiding Su Hsiao-hsiao's grave[5] on the roadside."

Gradually, the sound of singing died away in the distance and I found myself in a small armchair as the morning sun shone on the trees outside. Fresh from my dream, I lost myself in the dawn breeze.

After lunch I went back to the hospital, taking with me a dozen white and purple flowers for Chuang. He was lying quietly on the bed. As I had no desire to mention the events of the night before, I chattered away about our last visit to the West Lake. There was little else I could do, though I knew full well he was not in the least interested in what I was saying.

I saw the hairpin the girl had left by his bedside last night and I told him, "You'd better keep it in

[5] Su Hsiao-hsiao was a renowned courtesan in the late fifth century.

a safe place." His eyes half open, Chuang merely shook his head. I took a handkerchief from him, wrapped the hairpin in it, and placed it under his pillow.

After a while he said to me, "This morning, my aunt came to tell me that uncle is about to return and would like to have me stay with them at their country residence."

"How old is your uncle?" I asked.

"Sixty-one," he replied. Then he continued, "Even now I can hardly make out why he always prevented me from seeing Ling-fang. But I love Ling-fang as much as I love my uncle."

"Who is Ling-fang's elder brother?" I asked.

"My schoolmate, a wonderful friend."

"Where is he?"

"Switzerland."

"Has he written to you?"

"Yes, always about Ling-fang and me."

"What did he say?"

"He urged me to ask my aunt's permission for an early engagement with Ling-fang, but my aunt still has her heart set on my marrying Lien-p'ei."

"What kind of person is Lien-p'ei?" I asked.

"She is my aunt's maternal niece. Even early in her childhood she was already skillful in embroidery; she was also well read in the classics and history. Aunt loves her dearly."

"Do you love her as much as you love Ling-fang?" I asked.

Sighing slightly, Chuang answered, "I love her as much as I love my aunt."

"So you are in love with two beautiful girls at the same time," I concluded.

"You'll understand my feelings better if you know what is implied in the saying that 'plentiful is the water in the Jo,[6] but all one wants is a dipperful.' "

"May I ask then," I said, "on whom did you first set your heart?"

"Ling-fang."

"You saw Lien-p'ei before Ling-fang, and yet you came to love Ling-fang first. How could this be?" I asked.

"In the year when Yüan[7] was about to declare himself emperor, I happened to be in Peking for a visit. A friend of mine, who was a high official under Yüan, summoned me to his residence. After a few drinks, he took out a document and asked me to translate it into French. I read that thing—a diplomatic message for distribution in foreign countries. It was full of high-sounding passages from memoranda sent to the government by representatives of the various provinces as testimony of the nation's support for Yüan as emperor. That kind of obsequious writing was hard to bear. Worse still, it would become all the more absurd and ludicrous once rendered into a foreign language. So I declined. The man said, 'If you don't do it, that's all right. But how about signing your name there?' I told him, I am neither a diplomat nor an official of the former dynasty, so why bother to have the signature of a nobody on a document such as this? After that, I said good-bye to him immediately. Three days later, the police came. I was arrested and taken to an unknown destination. At that time Tu Ling-yün [Ling-fang's brother] was a secretary in one of the government bureaus. When he learned that I had been implicated by some corrupt official, he did his best to get me released. Afterward, he resigned his position and traveled around the world until he finally settled in Switzerland. Ling-yün was orphaned when he lost his father at twenty. He studied in Rome for four years with Ling-fang and both made names for themselves.

"Right after I returned to Shanghai from Peking, Ling-yün came to live with me at Bubbling Well Road. We shared everything from sleek

---

[6] Jo-shui, a fluid between air and water, found in fairyland.

[7] Yüan Shih-k'ai (1859–1916), a powerful warlord in Peking, succeeded Sun Yat-sen (1866–1925) as president of the Chinese Republic in 1912. Later, he attempted to establish a constitutional monarchy with himself as the emperor. He died shortly after the failure of his attempt.

horses to light fur coats. When he was about to take the trip abroad, we had a picture taken as a souvenir. A few days later, he gave me some intimation of his sister's feelings for me. Tapping me on the shoulder, he asked, 'What do you say, my friend?' I was so happy and grateful that I almost wept. At that moment, even though I did not say it openly, I secretly pledged my heart to her. After I had thought it over for three days, I told my uncle and aunt about this matter. But they remained noncommittal and I didn't want to push it further. Then one day, Ling-yün quietly left. Since then, I have always cherished in my heart what he did for me. Thus, although I never had any occasion to meet his sister face to face, I've given my heart to her, and no lapse of time can make me change my mind."

"Since you love her, why is it that you refuse to see her?" I asked.

"Because I dare not go against the wish of my uncle," Chuang replied.

"That's fine," I said, "and proper for a nephew. Now I understand why your uncle didn't want you to meet Ling-fang. It was because he feared that with your honest and trusting nature, you could fall under the spell of her lovely gazes. This clearly indicates your uncle's loving concern for you rather than his displeasure at Ling-fang. I wonder if you would mind a bit of advice from me? It seems obvious that your uncle and aunt plan to arrange a proper marriage for you. Even though you refuse to change your mind, you are bound to marry Lien-p'ei in the end. Moreover, if in time you could reverse your position and shift your love from Ling-fang to Lien-p'ei, your problem would be resolved most satisfactorily for everyone concerned. Ling-fang, too, I believe, will eventually come to forgive you. Otherwise, sorrow will pursue you endlessly even unto your grave, and remorse will come too late for you."

After listening to my talk, Chuang's face suddenly turned livid and his body shivered as though suffering from ague. I regretted my

words but there was little else I could say under the circumstances. I waited until he had calmed down before I left.

A few days later, as he had said, his uncle and aunt came to take him to their country residence at Chiang-wan.[8] I went to visit him. His uncle was sitting on a rattan chair, holding a volume of the *Tung-lai po-i* (Critical Writings of Tung-lai),[9] swaying his knees back and forth as he read. Chuang introduced me to him: "Uncle, this is my friend Man-shu, who went to Hangchow with me."

Hearing these words, his uncle slowly took down his big tortoiseshell spectacles, stood up, and nodding slightly to me, asked, "Did you come from Shanghai?"

Upon hearing my answer in the affirmative, he continued, "I've heard that you've traveled a lot around the country. That's fine! That's fine! The weather is nice today, so just walk around and take a look at this place."

"Thank you, sir," I replied.

At that time a maidservant came in and laid on the rattan side table a tea service. Chuang invited me to sit down as his uncle urged me solicitously to eat some of the pastry. He took into his own hand some pieces of hill-haw cake and candied lotus seeds to offer me and Chuang. I took a furtive glance at his long, blackened fingernails and told myself that he must have been an expert in finger calligraphy.[10]

After tea, Chuang Chih took me to the western part of the garden. As we walked, I said to him, "Your uncle seems to be a kind and reasonable person. If you opened your heart to him, you might find him sympathetic."

"Uncle has been most benevolent and gracious to me," said Chuang. "I'll do whatever he wishes, but this affair is different. I'm afraid I'll have to

[8] On the outskirts of Shanghai.
[9] *Tung-lai po-i,* by the Southern Sung scholar Lü Tsu-ch'ien (1137–1181), styled Tung-lai, is a collection of Lü's opinions on the early historical work *Tso-chuan* (The Tso Commentary).
[10] He wrote with his right index finger (dipped it in the black ink) instead of using the brush.

disobey him one day. That's why I've been in a state of anxiety all this time. My uncle, I think, must have also realized it. Lately, he has been showing special consideration for me. But he still regards this kind of independence in love and marriage as something uncivilized, and hence not to be tolerated."

At that moment we heard the rumbling sound of a carriage. Chuang and I went to the garden gate to take a look. As the carriage door opened, a young woman stepped down, her shoes small and dainty. I stood there quietly to look at her; she was none other than the second girl who had come to see Chuang at the lake.

After a sidelong glance at me, the girl turned her gaze on Chuang. Half blushing and half smiling, she was about to say something. I knew Chuang must have been trembling inside though he appeared to be calm outwardly. Finally, the girl said, "I hear that you've been unwell. Are you all right now?"

"It's kind of you to ask, but I've recovered now," replied Chuang.

"As soon as I returned from Tsingtao," the girl said, "I went to Hangchow to see you but you were already back in Shanghai." She stopped after these words; then casting her lovely glance at me, she asked, "Mr. Man-shu, how long have you been back here?"

"Six days," I answered.

After a short pause, the girl turned to Chuang again and said, "Did you see Ling-fang at the lake?"

"I happened to be out, and didn't see her."

Immediately the girl continued, "So you haven't seen her even now?" It seemed that she had been ready with the question for some time. Chuang Chih found it difficult to answer, so he remained silent. The girl stared at him as if to communicate with her eyes: "I know very well she gave you her hairpin at your bedside in the hospital."

Shortly afterward, a maid came to invite the girl inside while Chuang and I continued our stroll on the lawn, looking around as we walked. Momentarily, Chuang's face paled and he stood where he was, frozen. To my questions, he answered, "I feel badly whenever I think of Lien-p'ei's affection for me and my aunt's kindness, especially because the direction of my love runs counter to their wish. I also recall your admonishment the other day. I feel torn."

Realizing that his sorrow must have been deep, though his words were mild, I comforted him. "Don't feel so upset. Someday, I'll plead your case with your uncle, and who knows, it might turn out well!" I had little confidence in what I said. But those who are blinded by love are like children— these words appealed to him as much as talk of sweets to a child. How could Chuang know the worry in my heart?

On my way back after I left Chuang, I caught sight of a carriage passing by. The rider inside was none other than Lien-p'ei; her eyes were red from crying. I sighed in my heart that this was a girl so totally given to love that she didn't know how to control her passions.

Nowadays, people's mores and morals change with the times. Womenfolk of a questionable and seductive nature vie with one another in pursuit of lust and luxury. They appear to be obsessed by the idea of women's emancipation, but what they do is to commit excesses and transgressions in the name of liberation, just like men who scheme for profit and gain in the name of patriotism. These so-called liberated women and patriotic men, indeed, are even worse than depraved females and deceitful shopkeepers, and I cannot imagine where their souls are, if they have any.

When I came back to Shanghai this time, none of the things I heard and saw pleased me. True, I have quite a few old friends who continue to be optimistic, and I will readily admit that they have intelligence and talent, though they lack the opportunity to display them. In this modern age, their words cannot save the world and their knowledge is useless for the times. However, in

242

view of the infinity of the universe, they can only put on a cheerful countenance. While their true feelings are roiling within them, they pretend to be optimistic outwardly. If we can realize how they feel, we will certainly disagree that only the elderly statesmen are concerned with the affairs of the state and the welfare of the people.

When I got to the Huangpu riverbank, it was already 10 o'clock in the evening. I fumbled in my pocket and found only nine coppers inside. It was too late to find overnight lodging with friends. Years ago, when I stayed abroad and had no place to spend the night, I often went to the waiting room in the station and waited for dawn as I smoked. But I could not do that in Shanghai, so I went straight to a friend in his newspaper office. His head was buried in a confused pile of papers and he was writing madly. When he saw me, he laughed and said, "Don't accuse me of being the kind of person who writes a thousand words in one sitting but hasn't a single idea in his head."

"That's exactly what I think you are," I said. "What concerns me is that I have no place to go at such a late hour. So I've come here to impose on you."

"That's all right," he said. "I have a day couch here where you can rest for a while. As soon as I finish writing, I'll come chat with you. I get tired of writing every day about 'nobility,' 'cabinet ministers,' and the like, and would love to have a chance for some heart-to-heart talk with an old friend."

"When will you go to bed?" I asked.

"About five or six in the morning," he said. "Don't you know that we in the newspaper business generally get up and go to bed at about the same time the Americans do on the other side of the globe?"

"Well, let me sleep here," I said. "At five or six tomorrow—that's the time I'll get up."

"In that case," he said, "go on to bed and I'll continue with my writing."

So I went to bed with my clothes on.

The next morning, I got up early and went to another friend's house. Seeing me, he said, "You don't have your winter clothes on. By the way, when are you going back to the West Lake?"

"I don't know yet," I replied.

The friend handed me a hundred-dollar bill[11] and said, "Take it and buy something with it."

After receiving the money, I went straight to a store in the British Concession to buy a watch, for which I paid seventy dollars. I figured that when I was about to leave Shanghai I would return my friend's favor by giving the watch as a present to his son for use at school. After I made the purchase, I bought twenty dollars' worth of Manila cigars and then returned to where I had been lodging with my friend.

The next day, I got a letter from Chuang inviting me to go to his place right away. When I arrived, he took me to his bedroom and whispered to me, "Tomorrow, my aunt is going to ask Lien-p'ei to stay with us. I just don't know what to do. It'd be wonderful if you could come here to keep me company so we could chat together in the morning and at night. If I were alone, she'd often come in to disturb me. The other day, I treated her coldly and she left in a flurry. I know she must have complained to my aunt."

"What else did your aunt say to you?" I asked.

"I learned the news of Lien-p'ei's visit from the maid, not from my aunt," he said.

"In a week's time I'm going back to the West Lake with a friend from Szechwan. Sorry I can't oblige you."

"It would be fine if you just stayed here for a week," pleaded Chuang. "Otherwise, I'll have to flee from her to somewhere else."

"Where will you go?" I asked him immediately.

"I've considered the matter carefully," he said. "If things get bad, I'll take Ling-fang with me to Soochow or any other city along the Yangtze."

"Does Ling-fang know anything about this?"

[11] This equaled about 500 1978 U.S. dollars in terms of buying power.

"I haven't seen her since our meeting in the hospital."

"All right," I said. "I'll come to keep you company. Then we can talk it over carefully. It would be rash of you to take off like that. I don't think you should do it."

I moved over to stay with Chuang Chih the same day. His uncle and aunt treated me kindly and I was grateful to them.

The next day, Lien-p'ei also moved in, to a room on the south side of the garden. From the simple baggage she brought with her, one could see that she did not plan to stay long. Every time Chuang met Lien-p'ei, I noticed, he said nothing to her but merely greeted her with a nod. Sometimes when he saw Lien-p'ei alone in front of the hall, he would walk away to avoid her. Lien-p'ei, of course, was aware of it but there was little she could do.

One cold, gloomy day, while I was talking idly with Chuang in the study, a maid came in with a "hundred-layer crystal cake" and said to Chuang, "This is from Miss Yen. She made it herself for you and your friend." Chuang accepted it.

Not long after the maid had gone, Lien-p'ei herself came smiling into the study, in her easy, graceful way, to inquire after Chuang's health. He showed little surprise at the visit but also little attentiveness to the visitor. He said casually, "Thanks for the cake, Miss Yen. Please sit down by the stove where it's warm. It is cold today."

Lien-p'ei waited until Chuang Chih and I had returned to our seats. Then, adjusting her skirt, she sat down in front of the fire. She was dressed in a western outfit: a snow-white woolen blouse, its collar fastened by a large pink necktie like a scarf; a short dark-green velveteen skirt; long black stockings; a pair of dark velvet shoes with a pink *ribbon* bow on the top, like the kind fashionable in eighteenth-century Europe. She did not wear a hat. Her hair was tied up in a bun and her ears were adorned with two diamond pendants, each like a shiny star piercing through the dark clouds of her hair. Seeing that Chuang sat there nonchalantly without saying a word, I tried to make a little conversation: "Miss Yen, have you ever been to Europe or America?"

"No," answered Lien-p'ei, lowering her head. "I would like to go to Europe in two or three years to visit the recent battlefields. But I have little desire to go to America, where there are few historical sites worth visiting. Moreover, the Americans believe that to *make money* is their most important business, as shown in the saying, '*Two dollars is always better than one dollar.*' They look down upon us Chinese as if we were dogs. How could I have the face to go to their country? People speak highly of the materialistic civilization in America, but they do not know that American millionaires are just misers who take advantage of their industrial technology to make the common people even poorer every day. Some advocates of humanitarianism have said, 'If the atmosphere on this great earth could be had for a price, it would be completely taken over by the Americans.' How painfully true are these words!"

After she had finished speaking, she stretched out her white hand to put some coal into the stove. In the meantime, Chuang had taken up a book to read. After she had put in some coal, Lien-p'ei said good-bye to us and, adjusting her skirt, went away.

"Such a nice girl," I said to Chuang, "so amiable and courteous!"

Chuang heaved a deep sigh without uttering a word. I took out a Manila cigar and began to puff away. Before I had smoked half of it, he suddenly threw down his book and said to me, "This girl is quite conversant with English and French literature. For five and half years she learned phonology from Charles, a Scotch gentleman. So she is not only beautiful in looks but could be my mentor as well. I regret I met her too soon and now I have no desire even for her company. Alas! How unpredictable is fate!" As he spoke, Chuang's eyes were moist with tears.

Later, he said to me, "Let's both go and visit Ling-fang. I've been worried about her brother, as I haven't heard from him for a long time."

"That's a good idea," I said.

So we went together to Rue Batz to call upon Ling-fang, but learned from the maid that Ling-fang and her mother had gone to K'un-shan[12] several days earlier. We left in disappointment. When we returned to the house, Lien-p'ei greeted us outside the garden gate. She took a letter from her pocket and showed it to Chuang: "This is from Ling-fang. She wrote that she had gone to K'un-shan but would return soon."

The next day, the weather was gorgeous. After breakfast, Chuang's aunt took us for a ride. They had two [single-horse] shays on the estate. For that occasion, a second horse was harnessed to each vehicle to make two two-horse carriages. When we drove out, the passersby on the street all raised their heads to stare at us, dazzled by Lien-p'ei's beauty. She was most attractive in the purple suit which she had put on for the occasion.

It was already noon when we got to Nanking Road. We rested and had lunch in the Shanghai Restaurant. As I looked down from the balcony of the restaurant, I saw Ling-fang drive by in a carriage. Apparently she had also seen us, but Chuang was engaged in a conversation with Lien-p'ei and did not see her; nor did I mention it to him.

After lunch, we went shopping at Whiteway and Weiss, since Lien-p'ei's things were all purchased in foreign department stores. Lien-p'ei was in especially good spirits that day, her charm increasing with her happiness. Chuang waited upon his aunt attentively, and it could not be said that he was unhappy. As for me, a satellite revolving round the constellations, I felt neither elated nor depressed. Lien-p'ei bought two silver pens-and-pencil sets and gave Chuang and me a set each; she also presented us each with a pair of binoculars.

[12] Near Soochow, in Kiangsu.

Shopping done, we visited the parks: the Hsü Garden, Zikawei,[13] the Liang Garden, and the Ts'ui Orchard. Rather fatigued after these trips, Chuang suggested to his aunt, "Could we stay in the city overnight instead of going back to the country?"

"It's all right with me," said the aunt, "but the hotels are not clean."

"There is the St. George, operated by westerners," he said. "It is elegant and secluded. Later, if aunt wishes it, I'd like to invite you all to the opera."

"That will be grand," said the aunt, "but you have to ask Miss Yen to interpret for me."

"I'll ask her," he said.

In the evening we went to the Museum Theater. By the time we got there, the place was already crowded with westerners, both men and women, this being the night when a celebrated opera was to be performed. During the performance, Lien-p'ei translated the words of the arias so clearly that they seemed to be spoken by the singers themselves. Her extraordinary intelligence greatly impressed me. We had been in the theater for almost two hours, and yet she continued unceasingly her eloquent presentation. Suddenly, an actor dressed in a dark costume came onto the stage. Gazing angrily at the audience, he spoke in a refined but tremulous voice:

What the world calls love I neither know nor want. I know God's love, and that is not weak or mild. That is hard even unto the terror of death; it offers caresses which leave wounds. What did God answer in the olive grove when the Son lay sweating in agony, and prayed and prayed: "Let this cup pass from me!" Did He take the cup of pain from His mouth? No, child; He had to drain it to the depth.

At these words, Lien-p'ei paused and abruptly stopped her flowing stream of words. Chuang's aunt asked, "Why have you stopped translating?" She repeated the question several times without

[13] Zikawei (also spelled Siccawei) is well known for the Jesuit Mission established there and its garden.

getting an answer from Lien-p'ei, who looked wooden. Both Chuang and I knew what had so deeply moved Lien-p'ei, but Chuang's aunt thought that the actor was saying something obscene. Displeased, she ordered us to return to the hotel. Only then did I learn that it was Lien-p'ei's birthday.

Early the next morning, Lien-p'ei took Chuang and me for a walk on the lawn. After a while, she suddenly put her hand on Chuang's left arm. Her head lowered and her mouth closed, she looked tired and flushed. Chuang, on the other hand, was pale in countenance, but he continued to walk on.

When we got back to the porch, I went up the steps and led the others to a small sitting room. I said to Chuang, "It's still an hour and a half before breakfast. Let's rest here for a while. Just listen to the birds singing! They seem to say that the year is drawing to an end."

Hearing these words, Lien-p'ei craned her neck to look outside; then she said to Chuang, "Here, out in the country, the leaves are half fallen and the birds gone without a trace. Pretty soon we'll have a snow scene before our eyes." As she talked, she fixed her gaze on Chuang, but the latter appeared to be hard of hearing and merely played with his watch chain.

At that moment a hotel guest burst into the room, a tennis racket in hand. He was on his way out to the porch; so I followed him outside to watch him play. Two girls and a man were already waiting for him on the lawn. As they were expert players, I turned back to call Chuang and Lien-p'ei to come out and watch the game.

Who could have expected the scene I then witnessed? Chuang was still sitting there, silent and motionless, on a sofa, his eyes staring vacantly at the carpeted floor, while Lien-p'ei nestled her body toward Chuang's right side, her long hair flowing down over his shoulder, her cherry lips pouting, and her eyelashes tear-stained, while she folded her drenched handkerchief with both hands.

Apparently, they were both aware of my presence. But in Lien-p'ei's case, it seemed as if she were saying to herself, "My behavior is only proper—even God would approve of it. As for my love, my tender passion—there's no reason why I should hide it!" On his part, Chuang's heart was as cold as ice at that moment. He had his reason for being unmoved by the love of such a beautiful creature. But it was exactly this point that Lien-p'ei failed to understand, and the reader, probably, will come to sympathize with her. The fact was, Chuang could not have helped being affected by the display of such tenderness and affection. However, as he recalled the words, "With God looking down from above, be not fickle in thy heart," he became so firm in his resolution and so noble in his bearing that none dared to encroach upon his private feelings.

"Has your aunt awakened?" I ventured.

"I'll go and look," he murmured, and then excused himself and left.

By that time, Lien-p'ei had risen from the chair. While she was fixing her hair before the mirror, she wiped her cheeks with a silk handkerchief. I had great sympathy for Lien-p'ei but I also felt that this is the kind of frustration we can't do anything about.

Immediately after our return to Chiang-wan, Chuang Chih appeared terribly upset. He sighed over and again; he also questioned his maid several times.

That night when I went to the study to look for a book I found Chuang sitting there with his face to the lamp, weeping. I sat beside him, and as I was about to console him, he said suddenly to me in a mournful voice, "Ling-fang's hairpin is broken!"

Startled, I asked, "When was it broken? By whom?"

"I don't know," he replied. "I found it broken soon after returning home." He had barely finished his words before he burst into sobs.

Just at this juncture, Lien-p'ei came in and, standing in front of Chuang Chih, exclaimed,

"You are crying! Why? Did I do anything to offend you? Please tell me." But there was no reply from Chuang even though Lien-p'ei repeatedly pressed him with questions. Lien-p'ei knew, of course, that he was upset because of her; she, too, hid her face and cried as she sat beside Chuang. After a long while, a maid came in to help Lien-p'ei to her bedroom. Chuang was still trembling all over. I knew he must be terribly sick and urged him to go to bed right away.

Next morning, when I went to see Chuang, he acted as if he did not know me at all but only stared at me fixedly without uttering a word. I hurriedly left him and asked for permission to see his uncle. I told him of Chuang's serious condition and hinted delicately about Chuang's love affair with Ling-fang in the hope that my intercession might be of some help to his nephew. His uncle, however, said angrily to me, "This young man has ignored my advice and acted most outrageously! Will you please tell him that it was I who broke the jade hairpin? Being young and licentious, he has failed to heed the instructions of the ancients that 'a coquette is without chastity and a libertine without loyalty.' " He then wrote out a prescription to give to me, saying, "This young man's illness comes from an attack of evil influences in the liver. Get three-tenths of a tael each of ginseng, white peony root, and Pinellia tuberfera; two-tenths of a tael each of Arisaema japonicum and coptis root; one-tenth of a tael each of dried mandarin orange peel, liquorice root, and white mustard seeds. Boil them slowly in water and ask him to drink the medicine. He'll get well after two or three doses. Please take good care of him for me." As he spoke, he continuously heaved deep sighs.

I took the prescription, said "Yes, sir," and withdrew. When I called the waiting maid and asked her to go to the herbalist to fill the prescription, she told me in a hushed voice, "Miss Yen died last night in her bedroom. Such a strange incident! The mistress forbids me to tell the young master."

"Did you find out how Miss Yen died?" I asked.

"I only saw it this morning," the maid replied. "She cut her throat with a knife."

"By all means hide it from the young master. Go quickly and get the medicine," I told her.

When I got back to Chuang's bedroom, I found him lying there motionless. He stared vacantly at me; his face had become purplish and his lips ashen white. I asked him repeatedly how he felt, but he acted as if he had not heard me. I sat down quietly beside him, waiting for the maid to return. Suddenly, Chuang shook his head as if to say that he already knew about Lien-p'ei's death. I could not figure out how he had discovered it, as nobody could have told him about it.

Later, the maid returned with the medicine. At the same time, she handed Chuang a letter. After reading, he gave it to me, his face having turned leaden. I leaned toward him and laid my hand on his shoulder. Tears began to roll down his face. I knew the letter was from Ling-fang but I had no time to read it at present.

Half an hour later, the maid entered with the concoction. Chuang drank it in small sips and then rested quietly. Only then did I have a chance to read Ling-fang's letter:

Dear Mr. Chuang:

After our meeting in the hospital, we were like stars in opposite corners of the Milky Way on the distant horizon even though we were actually close to each other. Whenever I thought of your great kindnesses and the grace of your feelings, I could only nod my head and sigh.

The ties of our affection are now severed! The day before yesterday, I went to visit you at your residence—it was also the time you took Lien-p'ei out for a ride. Your uncle graciously exhorted me with his sincere advice. After listening to him, I asked your uncle to break the hairpin which I left you the other day in fulfillment of our pledge. Now that the hairpin has been broken into halves, I, too, have changed my mind.

I hope you will renounce your love for me, this humble one, and devote yourself to Lien-p'ei. May the eternal sun bear witness that henceforth I shall forswear my affection for you! I also hope you will comply with the wishes of your uncle and aunt so that you can enjoy the life of a happy and united family. If you do, even I, unfortunate as I am, will feel relieved and comforted. Alas! If only we could be united in wedlock in the next world, and cherish our conjugal happiness in a future existence!

At present, we are doomed to be parted in this life. What else could I say to you?

Once again, my respects to you.

Ling-fang

After I had finished reading the letter, I knew that Chuang Chih could never find happiness in his life again. It had left him like flowing water. I also mourned that Lien-p'ei could not be recalled to life. As to Ling-fang's future, for the present I had no time to think of it.

Chuang Chih suddenly woke up and vomited. I stroked his back gently. Soon afterward, he said to me, "Ling-fang has cut me off. This I understand, for I can well perceive her feelings. It's a pity that I'll have no chance to see her again, but—" When he came to these words, he was so choked with grief that he could hardly make himself heard. I quickly helped him to lie down, and he lay there without uttering a word.

I asked the maid to take good care of Chuang. I then left him to return to my room, hoping that someday we could again have good times together after he had recovered his senses and his spirit. But I myself was so greatly perturbed that I just sat there quietly and smoked. I chain-smoked more than ten cigars before I undressed and went to bed. It had become half past one by my watch without my realizing it.

As I was about to close my eyes, I heard someone opening my bedroom door. It was the maid. She was holding a candle in her hand, and sobbing uncontrollably, she said to me, "The young master has breathed his last."

I got up at once, ran to Chuang's room, and felt his body, which was already ice cold. Soon his uncle and aunt came in. Except for long sighs, his uncle said not a word, but his aunt, crying in a trembling voice, tenderly stroked the dead body and said, "Why have you become so unfeeling as to involve us in such deep sorrow and trouble!" She cried again as she finished talking.

Immediately after dawn, I hurried out in a rickshaw to a pawnshop at the Rainbow Bridge to pawn my new watch which, after all, I did not have to give away as a present.

I got back forty dollars for the watch. As I left the shop, I met a girl whom I recognized as Ling-fang's maid by the red mole (as big as a watermelon seed) on her right cheek. So I asked her, "How is Miss Ling-fang?" The maid restrained her tears and gave no answer. I knew something must have gone wrong with Ling-fang.

The maid took me to a corner of the pawnshop and said, "The young lady hanged herself last night. Oh, how pitiable! Now there isn't even enough money in the house for her funeral. That's why the old mistress sent me here."

I was deeply saddened by these words, as much as Chuang would have been.

Three days later, Chuang Chih's funeral was held, but only a distant relative and a schoolmate of his came. Neither knew the cause of his premature death.

After he had been buried in the Cemetery of the Multiple Blessings, I gave a generous sum of money to the keeper and asked him to place fresh flowers before the grave in all seasons so that Chuang would be spared the sorrow of having to look at wilted blossoms. Now that the fated relationship between Chuang Chih, Ling-fang, and Lien-p'ei has come to an end, the three may yet get together one day in their next existence. But this is something about which I am unwilling to speculate.

THE REUNITED COUPLE

Whenever forced to separate because of unforeseen disasters, the loving couple in traditional Chinese fiction can be expected to take their departure in the hope of ultimate reunion. However, if the force that separates them is willful and authoritarian, the couple may react defiantly, even at the risk of death. Loach Fan and his wife belong to the first category. Separated by war, they divide the double mirror between them as a pledge of love and look forward to the day when the mirrors can be matched again. But when Han P'ing and his wife are forced to part, they register their defiance by the only form of protest available to them: suicide.

The separation and eventual reunion of Chiang Hsing-ko and San-ch'iao ("The Pearl Shirt Reencountered") can be read not only as one of the most touching "reunited couple" stories, but also as a good example of the *pièce bien faite* in traditional Chinese fiction. This story is also unique for its tolerant view of adulterous love. Thanks to its well-constructed plot, in which the storyteller has carefully incorporated a set of extenuating circumstances for San-ch'iao to move within, her reunion with her husband is not only structurally inevitable but also morally acceptable.

One persistent feature of this type of story is that there is always an object or phenomenon to signal the stages of separation and reunion of the couple. The mirror of Loach Fan and the "pearl shirt" are good cases in point. The twin tree trunks symbolize the unending tie of the Han P'ing couple. The jade Avalokiteshvara in "Artisan Ts'ui and His Ghost Wife" functions as a sort of matchmaker in bringing the couple together.

HAN P'ING AND HIS WIFE

From *Sou-shen chi*

TRANSLATED BY CONRAD LUNG

Han P'ing, a retainer of King K'ang of the state of Sung,[1] married a girl from the Ho family who was very beautiful. King K'ang seized her for himself, and Han P'ing was filled with resentment. The king imprisoned him and sentenced him to hard labor at a fortress. P'ing's wife secretly sent him a letter with the following ambiguous words:

The rain falls on and on;
The river is broad, the water deep.
But when the sun appears, it is like my heart.

The king got hold of the letter and showed it to his attendants. None of them understood its meaning. A minister, Su Ho, met the challenge and answered, " 'The rain falls on and on' means that she grieves and yearns for him. 'The river is broad, the water deep' represents the barriers between them. 'But when the sun appears, it is like my heart' means that she intends to take her own life."

Before long, P'ing killed himself. His wife surreptitiously allowed her clothes to rot. Then when the king walked to the top of a tower with her, she jumped from it. The attendants grabbed at her, but her clothes gave way in their hands. She left a letter in her belt saying:

The king would like me to live, but I wish to die. I hope the king will grant that my bones be buried with P'ing in the same grave.

The king was angry and did not heed her supplication. He gave orders to their relatives that they be buried in separate graves that faced each other. He said, "Since you two will not stop loving each other, I shall not stop you if you can bring the graves together."

Before long, a large catalpa tree grew on the top of each grave. In ten days, they were large enough to embrace. Their trunks bent toward each other, their roots intertwined below, and their branches interlocked above. Furthermore, a pair of mandarin ducks, one male and one female, were found living in the trees. They remained there constantly and never left, day or night. Side by side, they emitted cries that were sad and moving.

The Sung people grieved for the couple and called the catalpa "the tree of mutual love (*hsiang-ssu shu*)." This was how the term "mutual love" originated. Southerners said that the birds were the reincarnated souls of Han P'ing and his wife. Nowadays, there is a Han P'ing Town at Sui-yang,[2] and a song about the story is still preserved.

[1] A notorious tyrant who ruled the state of Sung (between modern Honan and Kiangsu) toward the end of the Warring States period.

[2] The capital city of Sung, near the modern town of Shang-ch'iu in Honan.

ARTISAN TS'UI AND HIS GHOST WIFE

From *Ching-shih t'ung-yen*[1]

TRANSLATED BY CONRAD LUNG

*The color of the mountains and the bright mist make for a
    lovely scene.*
*Basking in warmth, the returning geese lift off from the level
    sand.*
In the eastern wilderness, flowers swarm before one's eyes;
In the southern fields, the grass is sprouting everywhere.
Willows on the embankment
Are still free of the ravens.
*My search for fragrant flowers has led me to a house in the
    mountains.*
On the edge of the fields, red plum flowers are falling,
*But the apricot branches are yet to be covered with red
    blossoms.*

The *tz'u* poem, to the tune of "A Sky of Par-
tridges," describes the scenery of early spring.
But, truthfully, it is not as well written as "The
Song of Middle Spring":

In drunken dreams in the courtesans' quarters every day,
*They are unaware that outside the city spring is once again
    advancing.*
The apricot flowers have just begun falling in the light rain;
The willows are swaying softly in the gentle breeze.

Painted barges are drifting;
Piebald horses are galloping;
The green shade is dark over the little bridge outside the door.

Into this land of the immortals no traveler would go;
Behind how many bead curtains can people be found?

This *tz'u* poem describes the scenery of the second month of spring. In truth, it is not as well
written as "The Song of Late Spring" composed
by Lady Huang,[2] which is even better:

Spring's charm is as intoxicating as wine:
*From time to time, swallows' words can be heard through the
    window screens;*
The willows by the little bridge let fly their fragrant catkins;
*Here and there blossoms fall from the peach trees
    of the mountain monastery.*
The orioles grow old;
The butterflies fly east and west.
*Endless is the sorrow when spring departs and is nowhere to be
    found.*
The color of the grass over the steps blurs in the morning rain;
*The pear flowers everywhere on the ground chase after the
    morning wind.*

But none of these three poems can be compared to the one composed by Wang An-shih, the
duke of Ching,[3] when he saw the flower petals

---

[1] The *Ching-pen t'ung-su hsiao-shuo* (Capital Version of Popular Stories) version of this story is entitled "The Jade Avalokiteshvara" ("Nien-yü kuan-yin").

[2] Lady Huang (*Huang fu-jen*) is often identified as the early
Southern Sung poetess Sun Tao-hsün. But in that case
"Huang" would have to be her husband's name, and since the
usual practice is to use the woman's own (maiden) name in
such a title, this identification is doubtful.

[3] Wang An-shih (1021–1086) was a famous politician and
man of letters of the Northern Sung period.

252

being blown to the ground one after another by the wind and realized that it was the eastern wind that rushed spring away. This poem says:

There are days in spring when the wind is sweet;
There are days in spring when the wind is foul.
The flowers cannot bloom without the spring wind;
But alas! they bloom just to be blown away.

But Su Tung-p'o[4] said, "The eastern wind does not make spring depart; the spring rain does." He had a poem in testimony:

It is before the rain that the flower pistils are first seen,
But after the rain no flower can be found under the leaves.
One after another the bees and butterflies fly over the wall,
Thinking that spring is in the neighboring house.

Ch'in Shao-yu[5] said, "Neither the wind nor the rain is responsible. It is the willow catkins that carry spring away." He had a poem:

Light and scattered are the willow flowers in the third month;
Flying effortlessly, wandering carelessly, they carry spring
    away.
These flowers themselves are heartless things,
Since one flies east and one flies west.

Shao Yao-fu[6] said, "The willow catkins are not responsible either. It is the butterflies that chase spring away." He had a poem in evidence:

Just as the flowers bloom in the third month,
Hustling, bustling come the butterflies
And carry spring away to the end of the world,
Increasing the sorrow of the traveler on the road.

Minister Tseng[7] said, "The butterflies are not responsible either. It is the singing of the oriole that drives spring away." Here is his poem:

The flowers are blooming in all their glory.
Why does the spring night have to be sorrowful?
Why have the fragrant blossoms aged in this spring night?
The singing of the oriole has driven spring away,
And in no time, the gardens and the woods have all turned
    barren.

Chu Hsi-chen[8] said, "The oriole is not responsible either. It is the crying of the cuckoo that causes spring to depart." He had a poem saying:

The crying of the cuckoo has made the spring depart
While the blood it spits out is still wet on its beak.[9]
The day is long in the courtyard, quiet and empty;
People are afraid of the coming of the evening.

Su Hsiao-hsiao[10] said, "None of these things is responsible. It is the swallow that carries spring away in its beak" As proof, she wrote the following *tz'u* poem to the tune of "Butterflies Love Flowers":

I used to live on the banks of the Ch'ien-t'ang River.
Flowers bloomed, flowers fell—
I never paid attention to the passing of the years.
The swallow is carrying away the colors of spring;
Gusts of apricot rain[11] are falling on the gauze window.
My cloud-like hairdo still half done; the horn comb stays in my
    hair slantingly
As I gently clap the sandalwood boards
And sing to the end the song of "The Gold-Threaded Dress."[12]

---

[4] Tung-p'o was the style of the poet Su Shih.

[5] Ch'in Kuan, styled Shao-yu (1049–1100), was one of the "Four Scholars of the Su School," a literary circle of poets centered around Su Shih.

[6] Yao-fu was the style of the noted Northern Sung philosopher Shao Yung (1011–1077).

[7] The identity of Minister Tseng is uncertain. Tseng Kung-liang (998–1078), Tseng Pu (1035–1107), and Tseng Chao (1047–1107) are among the possibilities.

[8] Hsi-chen was the style of the Sung philosopher Chu Tun-ju (1081–1159), but there was also a Sung poetess with the same name. It is uncertain which person the story is referring to here.

[9] A cuckoo that cries out blood is an allusion to the legend that the bird was a reincarnation of Tu Yü, the king of state of Shu (modern Szechwan) of the Warring States period. He killed himself after he had wronged one of his retainers, and when he was reincarnated as a cuckoo, he kept crying for his misdeed until he coughed up blood.

[10] The *Ching-pen t'ung-su hsiao-shuo* version replaces Su Hsiao-hsiao, a famous Six Dynasties courtesan, with Su Hsiao-mei, who, according to popular tradition, was the younger sister of Su Shih and the wife of Ch'in Shao-yu. Su Hsiao-mei was actually a product of imagination.

[11] The apricot rain is the kind of drizzle that usually falls continuously for days during the late spring and early summer in southern China.

[12] "The Gold-Threaded Dress" was an anonymous song popular in T'ang times. It sang about ephemeral youth and stressed the *carpe diem* theme.

When I finish, the colorful clouds are already nowhere to be found,
And when I wake from my dream, the moon is rising from the southern shore.

Wang Yen-sou[13] said, "Neither the wind, nor the rain, nor the willow catkins, nor the butterflies, nor the orioles, nor the cuckoos, nor the swallows has anything to do with it. It is just that the ninety-day season of spring has come to an end and spring departs." He once wrote a poem which reads as follows:

Blaming the wind and blaming the rain are both wrong;
Even if the wind and rain do not come, spring will still depart.
The red has disappeared from the cheeks of the plum, but the green fruits are still small;
The yellow is gone from the corners of their bills and the young swallows are flying.
The soul of Shu[14] cries so strongly that the shadows of flowers disappear;
The silkworms of Wu[15] eat so heartily that the mulberry trees become thinly leaved.
I am vexed that spring has departed and is nowhere to be found,
Leaving behind floating on the rivers and lakes this one fisherman in his straw raincoat.

Why should this storyteller be talking about all these poems on the departure of spring? Well, during the Shao-hsing reign period [1131–1162],[16] in the provisional capital,[17] there lived a man who was a native of the Yen-an Prefecture[18] in Kuan-hsi. He was the prince of Hsien-an,[19] a military commander of three com-

manderies. One time, accompanied by many of his family members, he went out to enjoy spring, fearing that it would soon depart. When evening arrived, they turned toward home and came to the Carriage Bridge inside the Ch'ien-t'ang Gate. After the sedan chairs of his family had all crossed the bridge, the one that belonged to the prince arrived. Suddenly a man could be heard calling out from inside a picture-mounting shop beside the bridge: "My child, come out and look at the prince." At that moment the prince saw who was coming out and called out to his aide-de-camp, saying, "I've wanted to find that girl for some time. Now she is here. See that she is brought to my place tomorrow."

After receiving this command, the officer went to find out the identity of the girl who had come out to look at the prince. Indeed:

While it is uncertain when the dust behind carriages will stop,
The binding love between people is bound to disappear sooner or later.

He saw a house beside the bridge with a signboard hung outside. On it was written: "The Chü Family—Old and New Calligraphy and Paintings Mounted." Inside the shop were an old man and his daughter. What did she look like?

The cloud-like hair above her temples is like a cicada's wings;
Her moth eyebrows, lightly painted, are like the mountains in spring.
A cherry forms her red lips;
Two rows of jade chips are her white teeth.
Her bound feet in small bow-like shoes walk with lily steps.[20]
Like the trills of an oriole is her voice, sweet and charming.

As soon as he discovered that she was the one who had come out to look at the prince, he went into a teahouse across the street and sat down. An old woman brought him tea, and he asked her, "Please, granny, go across the street to the mounting shop and invite Mr. Chü over for a talk." The old woman immediately went to invite Chü over.

[13] Wang Yen-sou (1042–1092) was a scholar-official in the Northern Sung period.
[14] The soul of Shu is a circumlocution for the cuckoo (see footnote 9).
[15] Sericulture was and still is one of the most important industries of the Wu region, the present Kiangsu Province.
[16] The second of the two reign periods of Kao-tsung (r. 1127–1130), the first emperor of the Southern Sung Dynasty.
[17] Lin-an.
[18] Yen-an in modern Shensi Province.
[19] The prince of Hsien-an was the famous Southern Sung general Han Shih-chung (1089–1151). He was ennobled in 1143.

[20] "Lily steps" is a conventional expression used to describe a beautiful woman's graceful way of walking.

254

After he and the officer had bowed to each other, they sat down, and Artisan Chü asked, "Sir, is anything the matter?"

"Nothing important; I just want to talk to you. Is the girl you called out to see the prince just then your daughter?"

"Yes, she is my daughter—there's three of us in the family."

"How old is she?"

"Eighteen years old."

"Are you going to marry her off or present her to an official?"

"My family is poor," said Artisan Chü. "Where can I find the money to marry her off? I shall have to present her to the household of an official one of these days."

"What skill does the young lady have?" the officer asked, and the artisan told him his daughter's skill. This can be described in the following *tz'u* poem, to the tune of "The Eyes Are Enticing":

A secluded chamber with a small courtyard early in the day.
A beautiful girl in a silk dress.
Without wanting to rival the creation of the Lord of the
*   East,* [21]
She has embroidered a flower pattern with a golden needle.
The open pistils, surrounded by slanting branches and young
*   leaves,*
Lack only a fragrant scent.
In the innermost recesses of gardens and woods,
They attract throngs of butterflies and bustling bees.

Now that he knew the girl was good at embroidery, the officer said, "Just now, the prince noticed an embroidered apron on your daughter from his sedan chair. We're looking for an embroiderer for our household, so why don't you present her to the prince?"

After Chü went home and told his wife about this, he prepared a written agreement for the presentation of his daughter and brought her to the prince's residence the next day. The prince paid the price, made her a maidservant, and gave her the name of Hsiu-hsiu.

[21] The Lord of the East is the god of spring.

One day, the prince received a warrior's robe embroidered with a round flower pattern from the emperor. Hsiu-hsiu at once embroidered another robe, following the same pattern. The prince, seeing this, was pleased and said [to himself], "The emperor has bestowed upon me a warrior's robe with a round flower pattern, but what rare and unusual thing can I give him in return?" He went to the storehouse and found a piece of translucent jade the color of sheep's-suet.

He immediately summoned the jade carvers under his command and asked them, "What can this piece of jade be carved into?"

"It's good for a goblet," one of them said.

"What a waste!" said the prince. "Such a piece of jade; how can I just make a goblet out of it?"

"Since this piece of jade is pointed at the top and round at the bottom, it is good for making a *Mohoulo* doll," [22] suggested another jade carver."

"A *Mohoulo* doll is useful during the festival on the seventh day of the seventh month," responded the prince. "Otherwise, it is useless."

Among the jade carvers was a young man twenty-five years of age named Ts'ui Ning. He had served the prince for several years and was a native of the prefecture of Chien-k'ang in Sheng-chou. At this moment, he bowed to the prince and stepped forward, saying, "Your Highness, the shape of this piece of jade, pointed at the top and round at the bottom, is extremely awkward. The only thing it can be carved into, really, is the Avalokiteśvara of the Southern Seas."

The prince exclaimed, "Excellent! That's exactly what I had in mind," and he immediately told Ts'ui Ning to start working.

In less than two months, the jade Avalokiteśvara was finished. The prince at once wrote a memorandum and presented the piece to the emperor, who was greatly pleased. Ts'ui Ning's pay

[22] The *Mohoulo*, usually made of wood or wax and in the shape of a child, was a popular toy for the festival on the seventh day of the seventh month. The term is a transcription of Mahakala, the great black deity of Buddhism.

was increased and he also won the favor of the prince.

The days went by and it was spring again. Artisan Ts'ui was drinking in a tavern with several friends after a spring outing; but when they had downed only a few cups, they heard a great din in the streets. As they opened the windows and looked out, they saw people yelling amid great commotion, "There's a fire at the Well-Pavilioned Bridge!" The drinking stopped; and when they came down from the tavern to take a look, here is what they saw:

At first it was like a firefly,
And then it was like the gleam of a lamp.
The flame of a thousand candles could not match it;
The blaze of ten thousand pyres could not rival it.
The Liu-ting God had overturned the heavenly furnace, [23]
And the eight powerful guards had set the fire that scorches
*   mountains.* [24]
If this had been the beacon lit at the assembly of Mount Li,
We should think that Pao-ssu would be delighted with it. [25]
If this had happened at the Red Cliff,
We would think that it was Chou Yü carrying out his
*   marvelous plan.* [26]
[Perhaps] the Wu-t'ung God was dragging along his gourd of
*   fire,* [27]
Or the red donkey of Sung Wu-chi had been hurrying along
*   and fell over.* [28]
Since neither wax nor oil had been spilled,
Why was the smoke rolling up and the fire burning fiercely?

[23] The Liu-ting God is a fire god in folk beliefs.
[24] The word "eight" is used to form a pair with the word "six" (*liu* in Liu-ting) in the preceding sentence. "Eight powerful guards," therefore, does not necessarily carry any special implication.
[25] This is a reference to the story of King Yu of the Western Chou Dynasty who lighted the beacon unnecessarily and assembled all the feudal lords at Mount Li (in modern Shensi) just to induce a smile from his favorite consort, Pao-ssu.
[26] The fire at Red Cliff is a reference to the battle fought on the Yangtze River to the northeast of Chia-yü County in modern Hupeh between the joint forces of Wu and Shu and the armada of Wei during the Three Kingdoms period. Chou Yü, the admiral of the Wu-Shu joint forces, set fire to the armada of Wei and won a decisive victory.
[27] The Wu-t'ung God is another fire god in popular beliefs.
[28] Sung Wu-chi was a Taoist immortal who rode a red donkey and was believed to be the god of fire.

When Artisan Ts'ui saw this, he said anxiously, "It's not far from the prince's residence!" But by the time he had run to the prince's mansion, he saw that everything had already been moved away, and the place was quiet and deserted. Unable to find anyone, he entered from the left corridor. The place was lit up like day by the fire. From the other side of the left corridor, a woman, muttering to herself, staggered out from the main hall and ran right into Ts'ui Ning. Ts'ui Ning recognized her as the maid Hsiu-hsiu. He backed up a couple of steps and greeted her with a mumble. The fact was that the prince had once promised Ts'ui Ning, "When Hsiu-hsiu's term is up, I shall marry her to you." All the people then cheered them and exclaimed, "What a fine couple!" Ts'ui Ning had on many occasions thanked the prince for this promise. Ts'ui, being still single, was naturally infatuated with Hsiu-hsiu, while on her part Hsiu-hsiu, seeing that he was such a fine young fellow, was looking forward to marrying him.

On that day, when this fire broke out, Hsiu-hsiu, holding in her hand a kerchief full of gold, pearls, and other valuables, came out from the left corridor. When she bumped into Ts'ui Ning, she said, "Mr. Ts'ui, I was slow in leaving. All the maids in the house have run away already, and no one is in charge now. You'll simply have to take me out of here to shelter." Ts'ui Ning and Hsiu-hsiu at once left the prince's residence and walked along the river until they reached the Lime Bridge.

"Mr. Ts'ui, my feet hurt." Hsiu-hsiu said. "I can't walk anymore."

"A few steps more and we'll reach my place," Ts'ui Ning said, pointing ahead. "Let's get in there before you rest."

After they arrived at Ts'ui Ning's house and settled down, Hsiu-hsiu said, "I'm hungry. Mr. Ts'ui, buy something for me to eat. It'd be even better if I could have a cup of wine to calm myself down."

Ts'ui Ning immediately went to buy some wine,

and after two or three cups, they could best be described by the following couplet:

After three cups of wine reach their stomachs,
Two petals of peach blossom rise to their cheeks.

Isn't there a saying that "Spring is the master of flowers and wine is the catalyst of lust"?

"Do you remember the time when we were enjoying the moon on the terrace?" Hsiu-hsiu said to Ts'ui Ning. "I was betrothed to you and you just kept on thanking the prince. Do you remember or have you forgotten?"

Ts'ui Ning clasped his hands and could only reply with "Eh."

"At the time, all the people were congratulating you saying, 'What a fine couple!' How come you've forgotten about it?"

Ts'ui Ning again could only reply with "Eh."

"Rather than keep on waiting, why don't we become husband and wife now, tonight? What do you think?"

"How would I dare?"

"You're afraid of the consequences? What if I call out and ruin you? People will wonder why you brought me home. I shall report you to the prince tomorrow."

"Let me explain to you," Ts'ui Ning said. "It's all right that we become husband and wife, but there's just one thing: we must leave this place. We have to make use of this fire and the confusion to run away tonight—only then shall we be safe."

"Since I'm going to be your wife, I shall do what you say."

That night, they became husband and wife.

They left home after the fourth watch with their belongings and valuables. It goes without saying that they ate when hungry, drank when thirsty, rested by night, and traveled by day. Eventually, they reached Ch'ü-chou.[29] Ts'iu Ning said, "Five roads intersect here; which road should we take? Why don't we take the one to

Hsin-chou?[30] I'm a jade carver and I have several friends there in the same trade. Maybe we can settle down there." And so they took the road to Hsin-chou.

After they had been living there for a few days, Ts'iu Ning said, "There are merchants who go to the capital from here often. If they mention in the capital that we are here, the prince will surely send people to track us down and arrest us. It's not safe here. Whey don't we leave Hsin-chou and go someplace else?" The two set out on the road again and headed for T'an-chou.[31]

In a few days, they arrived at T'an-chou. They had really run far enough this time. They rented a house in T'an-chou City and put up a sign: "Artisan Ts'ui, the Jade Carver from the Capital." Ts'ui Ning then said to Hsiu-hsiu, "This place is over two thousand *li* from the capital, and I don't expect any trouble. We can feel safe here and be husband and wife forever." There were also a few officials living in T'an-chou temporarily. Seeing that Ts'ui Ning was an artisan from the capital, they gave him enough work to keep him busy every day.

Ts'ui Ning secretly sent people to gather information about his former employer. Someone who had been there told him that a maid had been missing from the prince's household since the night when the fire broke out. A reward had been offered for her some time ago, but her whereabouts were still unknown. No one knew that Ts'ui Ning had taken her away and that they were now living in T'an-chou.

Time flew like an arrow, the sun and moon shuttled back and forth, and more than a year went by. Suddenly early one day, just as the shop opened, two men dressed in black who looked like officers came in and sat down. They said, "Our lord has heard about an Artisan Ts'ui from the capital. We were told to ask him over to take on a job." Ts'ui Ning gave his wife a few instructions and then followed these two men to Hsiang-t'an

[29] Near the present Ch'ü County in Chekiang Province.
[30] Near the present city of Shang-jao in Kiangsi Province.
[31] The present city of Ch'ang-sha in Hunan Province.

County.[32] He was brought to meet the official in his residence and received a commission to work on some jade.

On his way home, he ran into a man wearing a bamboo hat. He had a cotton jacket with a double collar made of white satin, and the cuffs of his trousers were tied up with black and white puttees. On his feet were a pair of hempen sandals, and he was carrying a load on a long pole over his shoulder. This man was coming from the other direction and he looked at Ts'ui Ning. Ts'ui Ning did not see this man's face, but the man saw Ts'ui Ning's and strode after him. Indeed:

Whose young child is it that sounds the fisherman's board
And frightens a pair of mandarin ducks into flight in
different directions?

Who this man was, hear the next session tell.[33]

The cows are being guided by bamboo sticks, and flowers are
strewn over the street.
The moonlight is sifting through the cracks in the fence of my
thatched hut.
Inside the crystal cup is home-brewed wine;
Inside the white jade tray are pickled prunes.
Don't be sad,
But be merry!
Struggling all my life, I have won only a happy
face.
I cannot find a friend within three thousand li,
But I have been the commander of a hundred thousand
soldiers.

This *tz'u* poem to the tune of "A Sky of Partridges" was composed by the General Liu[34] of the Brave and Fierce Commandery (*Hsiung-wu chün*) at Ch'in-chou[35] in Kuan-hsi. Since participating in the battle of Shun-ch'ang,[36] he had led an idle life in his temporary home in Hsiang-t'an County in T'an-chou in the Hu-nan Circuit.[37] He was a famous general, but he did not covet money and so he lived in poverty. He often went drinking in the village taverns. People in these taverns did not know that he was General Liu and often teased him. General Liu said, "A million Tartars have been as nothing to me and yet I am now mocked by my own people." So he composed this poem to the tune of "A Sky of Partridges," and it found its way to the capital.

At the time, the commander-in-chief in attendance at the central court was the prince of Yang-ho.[38] When he saw the poem, he was extremely saddened by it and said, "I didn't know that the general had come to this poor state." He then ordered the comptroller to send someone to take some money to the general.

At the same time, after Ts'ui Ning's former superior had heard how poor General Liu was, he also sent someone to take some money to him. It just so happened that this messenger passed through T'an-chou and saw Ts'ui Ning on the road from Hsiang-t'an. He followed Ts'ui Ning all the way home and saw Hsiu-hsiu right there behind the counter. He therefore burst in on them and said, "Mr. Ts'ui, I haven't seen you for a long time, and I'm happy to run into you. So Hsiu-hsiu is with you, too! The prince ordered me to deliver a letter to someone in T'an-chou, and that's why I'm here. Well, I can see that Hsiu-hsiu is now your wife, and that's not bad at all." Both Ts'ui Ning and his wife were terrified now that they had been discovered.

---

[32] The present city of Hsiang-t'an in Hunan.

[33] These two lines, crucial evidence of the way professional storytelling was conducted in Sung and Yüan times, have been dropped in the *Ching-pen t'ung-su hsiao-shuo* version of this story.

[34] The General Liu referred to here was Liu Ch'i (?–1162).

[35] The present T'ien-shui County in Kansu Province.

[36] Near the present Fu-yang County in Anhwei Province. The battle, fought in 1141, was one of the last major confrontations between the Jurchen and the Chinese before the situation of having these two contending states separately occupying northern and southern China became a settlement that lasted for almost another hundred years. The Jurchen were conquered by the Mongols in 1234.

[37] The Hu-nan Circuit in Sung times covered most of the area of modern Hunan Province plus the northern tip of modern Kwangsi Province.

[38] The prince of Yang-ho was probably the general Yang Ts'un-chung (1102–1166) of the Southern Sung period.

Who was this man? He was a guard in the prince's household and had been serving the prince since he was a child. The prince found him honest and trustworthy, and that was why he was sent to deliver the money to General Liu. His name was Kuo Li, and people called him Private Kuo. The Ts'uis at once invited Private Kuo to stay, prepared some wine to entertain him, and entreated him, "When you return home, please don't tell the prince about this."

"There is no way the prince could find out that you are here," Private Kuo said. "It's no business of mine; why should I tell on you two?" Thereupon he thanked them and left.

When he returned home, he reported to the prince and handed over the letter of reply. Then he looked at the prince and said, "I passed by T'an-chou the other day on my way back after I had delivered the letter and I saw two people living there."

"Who are they?"

"They are Hsiu-hsiu and Artisan Ts'ui. They entertained me and asked me not to report them to you."

Upon hearing this, the prince said, "What impudence! But how could they have managed to run all the way there?"

"I don't know the details either. I only saw them living there, and Ts'ui Ning has put up a sign and is earning a living at his trade as before."

The prince thereupon sent a clerk to file a complaint with the tribunal of Lin-an. An inspector and some officers were immediately sent to the prefecture of T'an-chou in Hu-nan, taking with them money for traveling expenses. After they had presented their warrant to the local authorities, they went to look for Ts'ui Ning and Hsiu-hsiu, like

Black eagles in pursuit of purple swallows
And fierce tigers preying upon helpless lambs.

Within two months, the two were apprehended and brought back to the prince's residence.

The prince held court as soon as they arrived. Now during his campaigns with the Tartars, the prince had fought with a sword called "Small Green" in his left hand and a sword called "Big Green" in his right. Countless number of Tartars had been cut down with these two swords. They were now kept in their sheaths hanging on the wall. When the prince came into the main hall, all bowed to him, and the two fugitives were brought in immediately and made to kneel down. The prince was in a great fury and in a flash he took down the Small Green from the wall with his left hand and pulled the sword out [of its sheath] with his right. His eyes were as wide as when he was killing the Tartars and his teeth were grinding noisily.

His wife was frightened to death and remonstrated with him from behind the screen: "Prince, this is the capital, the emperor's city; it is different from the border areas. If they are guilty of a crime, you can just send them to the Lin-an tribunal for punishment. How can you just slaughter people at will?"

Hearing this, the prince said, "I can't tolerate the impudence of these two runaway beasts. Now that they've been captured and I am in a fury, indeed I want to kill them. But since you advise against it, then I'll just have Hsiu-hsiu taken to the back garden and Ts'ui Ning sent to the Lin-an tribunal for punishment." Thereupon, he ordered that those who had made the arrest be rewarded with money and wine.

Ts'ui Ning was handed over to the local authorities of Lin-an, and he confessed everything from the beginning: "It happened on the night of the fire. I came to the prince's residence and found that everything had been removed. I saw Hsiu-hsiu coming out from the corridor, and she grabbed me saying, 'Why do you put your hand on my breast? If you don't do as I say, I shall ruin you.' She demanded that we elope together. I couldn't help it but ran away with her. This is the truth."

259

The local authorities handed over Ts'ui Ning's confession to the prince. The prince was an upright man. After reading the confession, he said, "Since this is the case, be lenient to Ts'ui Ning and give him a light sentence. but he should not have tried to escape, so he should be beaten and banished to the Chien-k'ang Prefecture."

Some officers were then assigned to escort Ts'ui Ning there. As they left the North Pass Gate and reached the Gooseneck Point, they saw a sedan chair carried by two bearers coming up behind them and heard a voice calling, "Wait a minute, Artisan Ts'ui!" Ts'ui Ning recognized the voice as Hsiu-hsiu's. He wondered why she was trying to catch up with him in such a hurry and he was full of misgivings. Like a bird that had been wounded by an arrow, he dared not get involved any further, and so he hastened on his way with his head down. Before long, the sedan chiar behind them 'caught up and stopped. A woman came out of it, and she was none other than Hsiu-hsiu. She said, "Artisan Ts'ui, now that you are going to the Chien-k'ang Prefecture, what is going to happen to me?"

"What can be done?" Ts'ui said.

"After you were taken to the Lin-an tribunal for punishment, I was brought into the back garden and beaten thirty strokes with a bamboo stick. Then I was thrown out. I found out that you were going to Chien-k'ang, so I tried to catch up with you in order to go with you."

"That's good," Ts'ui Ning said.

So they rented a boat and went straight to Chien-k'ang. The escorting officers then returned by themselves. If these officers had been busybodies, then there would have been more trouble. But they knew that the prince had a hot temper and would not easily let off anyone who annoyed him. Since they were not members of the prince's household, why should they meddle in other people's business? Furthermore, Ts'ui Ning had been buying them wine and food throughout the journey and had been most respectful to them. So, when they went back to the capital, not only they did not breathe a word of Hsiu-hsiu's sudden appearance, but instead they made up something nice to say about Ts'ui Ning.

Now let us say more about Ts'ui Ning and his wife, who were now living in Chien-k'ang. Since they had already paid for their offenses, they were no longer afraid of running into people who knew their past. They opened up a jade-carving shop as before. [One day] the wife said, "We surely are living comfortably here, but my father and mother have suffered quite a bit since you and I ran away to T'an-chou. When I was brought back to the prince's place, the two wanted to kill themselves. Now it's only proper that we send someone to Lin-an to bring them here to stay with us."

"That would be fine indeed," Ts'ui Ning replied.

Thereupon, he sent a man to the capital to fetch his in-laws. He wrote down the address and gave a description of the old couple to this man.

When the man arrived at Lin-an and found the address, he checked with a neighbor, who pointed at the house and said, "That's it." When the man went up to the door, he saw that it was locked and barred with a bamboo stick. He asked the neighbor, "Where have the old couple gone?"

"Don't bring this up. They have a daughter as beautiful as a flower and she was presented to a family of great importance. But instead of enjoying her good fortune, this daughter ran away with a jade carver. The other day, they were captured and brought back from T'an-chou in Hu-nan. The man was punished by the Lin-an tribunal and the daughter was taken into the back garden of the prince's residence. When the old couple heard that their daughter had been arrested, they wanted to kill themselves. Since then, we don't know their whereabouts. The door has been locked all this time."

When he heard this, there was nothing the man sent by Ts'ui Ning could do but to return to Chien-k'ang.

While this man was on his way, let us turn back

to Ts'ui Ning. [One day] as he was sitting in his house, he heard someone saying outside, "This is the residence of the Artisan Ts'ui you're looking for."

When the wife, summoned by Ts'ui, went out to take a look, she saw none other than old Chü and his wife. When they saw one another, they embraced in happiness. The man who was sent to Lin-an to bring back the old couple did not return until the next day. He told Ts'ui what had happened, that he could not find the old couple and that he had made the journey in vain. [He learned that] the old couple had come here on their own.

"We have indeed given you a lot of trouble," the old couple said. "Since we didn't know that Ts'ui Ning and our daughter were living in Chien-k'ang, we've been looking here and there for them until we came here."

Needless to say, the four people lived together from then on.

Meanwhile, at the imperial court, the emperor went to an adjoining palace one day to amuse himself with the treasures there. When he picked up the jade Avalokiteshvara to look at it, a jade bell accidentally fell off. He immediately asked an attendant close by, "How can this be repaired?"

The attendant examined it a couple of times and said, "What a beautiful jade Avalokiteshvara! What a pity the jade bell fell off!" As he examined the bottom, he saw the following words carved there: "Made by Ts'ui Ning." "If this is the case, it is simple. Since we know who made this, all we have to do is to summon this man and tell him to repair it."

An edict was sent to the prince's residence to summon the jade carver Ts'ui Ning. After reporting back to the emperor that Ts'ui Ning had committed a crime and was now living in Chien-k'ang, the prince at once sent someone to Chien-k'ang to bring Ts'ui Ning back to Lin-an. After Ts'ui Ning had found a place to leave his luggage, he was summoned to appear before the emperor. The emperor gave him the jade Avalokiteshvara to take home for repair. After thanking the em-

peror, Ts'ui Ning went to find a piece of jade of a similar kind, carved it into a bell, and restored the bell to the figurine. When he returned it to the emperor, he was paid for the job, which was without precedent, and he was told that it would be all right for him to live in Lin-an. Ts'ui Ning said to himself, "Now that I am favored by the emperor, I am respectable again. I shall rent a house and once again open a jade-carving shop in the area near the lower course of the Clear Lake River. I am no longer afraid to be seen by anyone."

Well, it happened by coincidence that just two or three days after he opened the shop, a man came in from outside who was none other than Private Kuo. When he saw Artisan Ts'ui, he said, "Congratulations, Mr. Ts'ui. So you're living here." Then he raised his head and saw that standing behind the counter was Artisan Ts'ui's wife. He was startled and immediately ran out with long strides.

The wife said to her husband, "Stop that guard for me, for I have something to say to him." Indeed:

If one does not do anything despicable in life,
No one will harbor hatred for him in this world.

Artisan Ts'ui immediately caught up with Kuo Li and held him back. He saw that the guard just kept shaking his head and mumbling to himself, "Strange! Strange!" Unable to get away, Kuo Li had to return with Ts'ui Ning, and sat down in his house.

As soon as the wife saw him, she asked, "Private Kuo, formerly, it was with the best of intentions that we asked you to stay to have wine with us. But after you went home, you reported us to the prince and ruined our happiness. Now that we have been favored by the emperor, we're no longer afraid of your reporting us."

Private Kuo could not find anything to say to defend himself; he could only mutter, "I'm sorry."

After he left Ts'ui Ning's place, he went

straight to the prince's residence and reported to the prince, "A ghost!"

"What's wrong with this man?" the prince said.

"Your Highness, a ghost!"

"What ghost?"

"Just now, I passed by the area near the lower course of the Clear Lake River and I saw Ts'ui Ning's jade-carving shop there. Then I saw a woman behind the counter, and she was Hsiu-hsiu!"

"You're talking nonsense," the prince said impatiently. "I had Hsiu-hsiu beaten to death and buried in the back garden. You yourself must also have seen what happened. How can she be there now? Aren't you playing a joke on me?"

"Your Highness, how would I dare play a joke on you? Just now she stopped me and made accusations for some time. I know you don't believe me. Let me write you a military pledge[39] and I'll go and bring her back."

"If she really exists, you write me a military pledge."

That man was indeed destined to suffer, for he wrote the military pledge. After the prince had taken it, he ordered two sedan bearers on duty to bring a sedan chair and said to them, "Bring the girl back. If she is really still alive, I'll cut her down with my sword. If not, Kuo Li, you shall be cut down in her place."

Kuo Li then went with the two sedan bearers to get Hsiu-hsiu. Indeed:

Two ears of grain have ripened on a single wheat stalk,
And a farmer cannot tell one from the other.[40]

Kuo Li, a native of Kuan-hsi, was a straightforward man and he did not know that a military pledge should not be made so easily. The three went straight to Ts'ui Ning's house, and there Hsiu-hsiu was still sitting behind the counter. She saw Private Kuo coming in quite a hurry—but she did not know that he had made a military pledge to get her!

"Young lady, by the order of the prince, we've come to get you," Private Kuo said to her.

"If this is the case, wait for me a little while and let me comb my hair and wash up. Then I'll go with you."

At once she went inside, combed her hair, washed, and changed her clothes. Then she came out and got into the sedan chair, leaving a few instructions for her husband. The two bearers carried the sedan chair straight to the front of the prince's residence, and Kuo Li went in first.

The prince was waiting in the main hall. After Kuo Li had made his bow, he said, "I've brought Hsiu-hsiu back."

"Tell her to come in," the prince said.

Kuo Li came out and said, "Young lady, the prince tells you to go in."

He lifted up the curtain and felt as if a bucket of water had been poured over him as he looked inside. Hsiu-hsiu had simply disappeared from the sedan chair. He asked the two bearers, and they replied, "We don't know. We saw her get into the sedan chair and then carried her here. We haven't gone anywhere else."

Screaming, Kuo Li went running in. "Your Highness, there is indeed a ghost!"

"How impudent!" the prince said. "Tie this man up! Bring me the pledge and let me cut him down this very moment." And at once he reached for his Small Green.

Since Kuo Li had been in the service of the prince, he had accumulated quite a few merit points. But because he was a boorish fellow, he remained a private. Now he was really frightened, and said, "I have the two bearers as witnesses. I beg you to summon them and ask them."

The two sedan bearers were at once sent for

---

[39] A military pledge is an agreement made between an army officer and his superior that the officer would be severely punished if he could not successfully carry out a special mission. The mission, unlike a regular commission, is usually taken by the officer on his own initiative.

[40] The author is hinting that this Hsiu-hsiu, though nearly identical, is not quite the same Hsiu-hsiu that Private Kuo used to know.

and questioned. They answered, "We saw her enter the sedan chair, but when we arrived here, she disappeared."

Hearing what they said, the prince began to believe that Hsiu-hsiu was indeed a ghost. Now he just wanted to question Ts'ui Ning to find out a little more. He immediately sent someone to summon Ts'ui to his residence. Ts'ui related the whole story from the beginning to the end.

"If this is the case," the prince said, "Ts'ui Ning had nothing to do with the whole business. Let him go."

Ts'ui took his leave, and the prince became so irritated that he had Kuo Li beaten fifty times on the back with a stick.

After Ts'ui Ning heard that his wife was a ghost, he went home to question his in-laws. The two looked at each other and then went out the door. With a splash, both of them jumped into the Clear Lake River. Ts'ui Ning immediately yelled for help. People tried to find their bodies in the river but the corpses were nowhere to be found. The fact was that when the old couple heard that Hsiu-hsiu had been beaten to death, they had thrown themselves into the river and were already dead. They, too, were ghosts.

Ts'ui Ning returned home in a depressed mood. He went into his room and saw his wife sitting on the bed. Ts'ui Ning said, "My wife, please spare me."

"I was beaten to death by the prince because of you and was buried in the back garden," Hsiu-hsiu said. "What hatred I have for that Private Kuo for his talking too much! I've avenged myself now—the prince has beaten him fifty times on the back with a stick. Now that everybody knows that I am a ghost, I can't stay here anymore."

After she said that, she got up and grabbed Ts'ui Ning with both hands. He just screamed and fell to the ground. When the neighbors came to look, here is what they saw:

The pulses on both wrists ended, everything has stopped;
His life has already returned to the yellow earth.

Ts'ui Ning was also dragged away to become a ghost like the other three—his own wife and her parents. Later, people had a good comment on this story:

The prince of Hsien-an could not calm his fiery temper;
Kuo Li, the guard, could not control his idle tongue;
The girl Chü Hsiu could not bear to part with her husband,
And Artisan Ts'ui could not get away from his ghost wife.

THE PEARL SHIRT REENCOUNTERED

From *Ku-chin hsiao-shuo*

TRANSLATED BY JEANNE KELLY

No honor comes with the riches of high office,
And to live past seventy is rare.
After death who remembers an empty name?
Like idle games, in the end all is vain.
Do not fritter your youth away in wanton excess,
Nor crave the quick satisfaction of women and wine.
Cast aside worries over right and wrong;
Content yourself with your lot and be satisfied.

The *tz'u* poem, set to the tune of "The Moon over the West River," exhorts everyone to be content with his lot, finding joy in what fate brings, and not to sap his vitality or ruin his conduct in drink, lust, riches, or anger. If happiness has to be sought, it is not true happiness; where advantage is gained, there will be loss. Of the four words, none is so dreadful as lust. The eyes are the go-between of passion; the heart is the seed of desire. In the beginning, you will be in a state of anxiety. In the end, you will lose your heart and soul. If occasionally some wayside flower should capture your fancy, no harm will come of it. If you should set your mind to scheming, going against the canons of society while seeking only a moment of pleasure for yourself with no regard for the long-cherished love between a husband and a wife—in short, if your own charming wife or favorite concubine were lured astray by the clever artifices of

another, how would you feel? The old saying puts it well:

Though men's hearts may be blind,
The way of Heaven does not err.
If I do not defile the wives of other men,
They will not violate mine.

Dear audience, listen today while I tell you the tale of "The Pearl Shirt." You will see that retribution is inevitable, and this should be a good lesson for all young men.

In this story I will set forth only one person, a man by the name of Chiang Te, known also as Hsing-ko, of Tsao-yang in the prefecture of Hsiang-yang in the Hu-kuang Province.[1] His father, Chiang Shih-tse, from youth had traveled throughout Kwangtung as a merchant. As he had lost his wife, Lo-shih, he was left with but one child, a son named Hsing-ko, who was just nine years of age. He could not bear to part with the boy, yet neither could he give up the source of his livelihood in Kwangtung. He gave much thought to the matter but in the end could find nothing for it but to take his nine-year-old son along as a companion on the journey, teaching him a few

---

[1] Consisting of the modern provinces of Hupeh and Hunan.

264

tricks of the trade. Despite his youth, the child was born with:

Clear brows and lovely eyes,
White teeth and red lips,
A dignified step
And clever speech,
Intelligence surpassing a student's
And the ingenuity of a full grown man.
Everyone called him "a little cherub,"
And all admired this priceless gem.

Fearing the envy of others, Chiang Shih-tse would never reveal that this was his own son, but wherever they went, he would say only that this was Master Lo, his wife's nephew.

Now it happened that the Lo family also plied their trade in the Kwangtung area. But whereas the Chiangs had been at it for only one generation, the Los had been in the trade for three. All the innkeepers and brokers of the region had known the Los for generations and treated them as part of their own families. When Chiang Shih-tse began traveling, it was in fact his father-in-law who had first started him off. Because the Los had of late been beset with a succession of unjust lawsuits against them, the family had fallen into financial straits, and for several years they had been unable to get away. Thus, at the sight of Chiang Shih-tse, there was not a one of the various innkeepers and brokers who failed to ask for news of the Los, voicing the greatest concern. When Chiang Shih-tse appeared this time with a child whom they discovered to be a relative of the Los, and who was besides so handsome and alert, they recalled their friendship extending over three and now four generations, and there was not a single one but was filled with delight.

Enough of this idle chatter. Let's tell instead of how Chiang Hsing-ko, after making several trips with his father, proved to be so quick to learn that he soon had grasped all the various intricacies of the business. His father was of course delighted by this. Who then could have anticipated that

when he was seventeen, his father would die of a sudden illness? The elder Chiang should be thankful at least that he was at home at the time and thus was spared becoming a ghost of the road. Hsing-ko wept for a spell but eventually had to dry his tears and arrange for the funeral. Besides the funeral rites, needless to say, he made offerings and had prayer services said to insure the safe passage of his father's spirit to the next world.

During the forty-nine days of mourning, the relatives from both sides of the family all came to mourn and offer their condolences. There lived in the prefecture a Mr. Wang, who was to be the father-in-law of Hsing-ko. He also called to offer sacrifices. Naturally the Chiang family members engaged him in conversation, during which they remarked on how capable Hsing-ko had proved to be for his age. All on his own he had managed to conduct the entire funeral. One thing led to another, and finally someone suggested, "Mr. Wang, now that your daughter has also come of age, why not choose this sad occasion to complete the match? With a wife to keep him company, things will be easier for him." Mr. Wang, however, would not consent to this, and on that same day he took his leave.

After the burial rites had been completed, a number of the relatives tried to prevail on Hsing-ko. At first, Hsing-ko, too, refused, but at their repeated urging, he began to reflect on how lonely he would be by himself, and reluctantly agreed. He asked the original matchmaker to go speak for him in the Wang household. Mr. Wang flatly refused, saying, "Our family also has to prepare a simple dowry. How can this be done at a moment's notice? Besides, as the year of mourning is not yet completed, it would mean violating the rites. If there is to be a marriage, let's wait until the year of mourning has passed before discussing it." When the matchmaker brought back the reply, Hsing-ko realized he spoke quite sensibly and did not force the issue.

Time went by like an arrow and before he knew it, the anniversary had arrived. After Hsing-ko had observed the sacrifices before his father's memorial tablet and had taken off his coarse hemp garments of mourning, he again commissioned the matchmaker to speak to the Wangs, and finally consent was given.

After no more than a few days, the six rites were all completed and he brought his bride home. The poem [to the tune of] "The Moon over the West River" testifies to this:

White mourning curtains are exchanged for ones of red;
Colored garments replace the hempen cloth.
Decorated rooms are resplendent with candles blazing;
The nuptial wine and wedding feast are all prepared.
Why wish for an opulent dowry,
When a wife of charm and beauty is more rare?
Tonight the joys of the bridal bed suffice;
Tomorrow, congratulations will be said.

The new bride was the youngest daughter of Mr. Wang, nicknamed "Third Eldest." Since she was born on the festival date of the seventh day of the seventh month, she was also called San-ch'iao, or "Blessed Third."[2] The Wang's two previously married daughters were both of unusual beauty. In Tsao-yang County, they were admired by all around and a four-line ditty was even made up about them:

Wives are easy to come by,
But such beauties as the Wang girls you never saw.
Better to have one as a bride
Than to be imperial son-in-law.

As a common saying has it, "If business goes bad, it's for a short time. If a marriage goes bad, it's for a lifetime." Many families of wealth and influence seek only their equal in station, or pursue

an alliance with a family of great means. With never a regard for the rights and wrongs of the matter, they agree on a match. Later they find the bride they have brought home is of uncommon ugliness, and when it comes time to show her to the various relatives and family members, the parents-in-law are only in for embarrassment. Added to this, the husband himself, unhappy with his lot, will probably begin to roam about on his own. Unfortunately it is the ugly woman who knows best how to control her husband. If he is like most, he will then become querulous. If, for the sake of appearances, he gives in to her a few times, she will begin to put on airs. As none of these alternatives is particularly appealing, Chiang Shih-tse, when he heard that Mr. Wang had a knack for turning out fine daughters, had sent over lavish gifts and concluded a marriage pact between his son and the youngest daughter while the children were still very young. Today at last she was brought to her new home, and indeed she was of great charm and beauty. One could even say she was twice as beautiful as either of her older sisters. Truly:

Hsi-tzu of Wu was not so lovely.
Nan Wei of Ch'u could not compare.[3]
If placed beside the Avalokiteshvara watching the moon in the water
She would share in the bows and the homage.

Chiang Hsing-ko also had his share of looks and ability; and now that he had taken such a lovely bride, together they were like a pair of jade carvings turned out by a master craftsman, more happy and loving than ever a couple could be. After the third day, Hsing-ko changed into clothes of a lighter hue and, saying that he was in mourning, had no more to do with outside affairs. He passed his time entirely in the company of his wife in the chamber upstairs, giving himself over to pleasure from dawn until dusk. In truth, whether walking or sitting, they never left each

[2] This festival originates from the romantic legend of the Herdboy and the Weaving Maid (Altair and Vega, respectively), who are permitted to meet only once a year across the Milky Way on the seventh (*ch'i*) day of the seventh month. This festival is known as *ch'i-ch'iao*, or the Blessed-Seven Festival. The third daughter of the Wang family, born on that date, was thus San-ch'iao, "Blessed Third."

[3] A beautiful girl of the Spring and Autumn period.

other's side, and while they dreamed, their souls were together. It has always been the case that days of hardship are difficult to endure and happy times pass by quickly. The warmth of summer passed and cold weather came. The period of mourning had already been completed, and we need say no more about their removal of the mourning gowns and the setting up of the memorial tablet.

One day Hsing-ko began thinking about the trade in Kwangtung his father had engaged in while alive. It had been neglected now for over three years, and a number of credit slips remained there uncollected. That night he talked it over with his wife, indicating his desire to make the trip. At first she agreed that he "should go." Later when they began talking about the distance he would have to travel, loving couple that they were, how could they bear to part? Unconscious tears began rolling down both her cheeks, and Hsing-ko, too, was loath to leave her. Both of them were sunk in gloom for a while, then abandoned the idea. This happened more than once.

Little by little time slipped away. Without their realizing it, another two years passed by. This time, Hsing-ko made up his mind to go. Keeping it secret from his wife, he packed his bags on the outside, chose a propitious day, and finally informed her five days before his departure.

"It's often said, 'If left to sit idle, one can even consume a mountain.' Now that there are two of us, I must set up a business to support the family. There's no sense in tossing away this means of making a living. The weather during the second month is not too hot or cold. If I don't get started now, what better time can I expect?"

His wife could see he was not to be dissuaded and asked only, "When will you be returning?"

"In any case the trip must be made. Whatever happens, I'll return in a year, even if it means next time I'll have to stay away longer."

Pointing to a cedar tree in front of their house, his wife said, "Next year when this tree puts forth buds, I'll be expecting your return." With these words, her tears began flowing like rain. Hsing-ko wiped them away for her with his sleeve, unaware that his own tears were falling. Their remorse at parting and deepened affection for each other cannot be conveyed in a few words.

On the fifth day, husband and wife, amid tears and sobs, talked the whole night through, renouncing all thought of sleep. At the fifth watch, Hsing-ko got up and packed his things. He placed in his wife's care all the jewels and valuables left by his father, taking along only the business capital, copies of the accounts, a change of clothing, bedding, and the like, as well as a few gifts he had prepared. All was arranged and packed with care.

They had in their house two male servants. He took with him the younger one, leaving the older one at home to attend to his wife's needs and run the daily errands. Two older women tended solely to the kitchen. In addition there were two maids, one called Bright Cloud, the other Warm Snow, who were to serve only in the upper chamber, under orders not to go too far from their mistress's side. When all the orders had been given, he said to his wife, "Now you must pass your time patiently. The neighborhood is full of idle trash, and you're so pretty. Don't invite trouble by standing at the front gate to gaze about."

His wife replied, "You needn't worry. Go quickly now and come back soon." The two hid their tears and bade farewell. How true it is that:

Of all the sad occasions in the world,
None matches that of parting or separation through death.

As Hsing-ko set off, he was thinking only of his wife, and he remained oblivious to all else the whole day. After a number of days he arrived in Kwangtung and put up at an inn. All his old acquaintances came over to see him. Hsing-ko handed out his gifts, and one after another they gave feasts to welcome him. This went on for the better part of a month without a pause for rest. Now Hsing-ko had quite depleted his health while at home, and had since endured the drudgery of the road. In addition, he was subjected to a period of irregular eating and drinking. Finally, he contracted a case of malaria which kept up all summer, developing into dysentery in the autumn. Every day he had the doctor check his pulse and administer medicine to him, but it lingered on through autumn, when at last he recovered his health. In the meantime, his business had been neglected, and he could foresee that it would be impossible to return home within a year. Truly:

For only a tiny fly's head of profit
He abandoned the love nest and a happy marriage.

Though Hsing-ko missed his home, as time went on, he decided he would have to give up any idea of returning.

Let's leave the subject of Hsing-ko's travels and instead turn our attention to his wife, San-ch'iao. Ever since the day her husband gave out his instructions, she had not for several months cast a glance out the window nor moved one step from the upper chamber. Time went as swiftly as an arrow, and before she knew it, the year had drawn to a close, and every house was noisily engaged in burning pine wood in braziers, setting off firecrackers, holding feasts, and playing games. The sight of all this filled San-ch'iao with grief, and she thought of her husband. What a dismal night it was! It was exactly as described by the poet in the poem:

Winter ends, but not the melancholy.
Spring has come, but not her husband;
As the day dawns, she bewails her loneliness,
Unwilling to try on her new clothes.

The next day was New Year's Day, the first day of the first month. The two maids, Bright Cloud and Warm Snow, did all they could to persuade their mistress to go to the front room to view the scene on the street.

The Chiang's residence had two interconnecting wings, front and rear. The first faced out on the street and in the second were the bedrooms. San-ch'iao normally spent all her time in the second. Today, unable to resist the urgings of the maids, she finally walked across the corridor to the front wing and had them open the windows and let down the curtain. The three of them then watched from behind the curtain. How crowded and noisy the street was that day!

"All these people coming and going," San-ch'iao remarked, "yet there's not a fortune-teller among them. If there were, it'd be nice to call him in to ask news of my husband."

"Today is New Year's Day," said Bright Cloud. "Everyone wants to relax and have fun. Who'd want to be out telling fortunes?"

"Depend on us," declared Warm Snow. "We promise within five days we'll have one in here to tell your fortune."

After breakfast on the fourth day, Warm Snow had just gone downstairs to relieve herself when she suddenly heard the sound of knocking in the street. The object producing the noise, called an "announcer," was the blind fortune-teller's trademark. Without waiting to finish her business, Warm Snow hurriedly pulled up her pants and dashed outside calling the blind man to stop. Then in the same breath she turned on her heels and ran up the stairs to inform her mistress. San-chiao ordered her to call him in to take a seat in the parlor. After his asking price had been agreed upon, San-ch'iao went down to hear his pronouncements. as the blind man picked a lot, he asked what it was for. At that moment, the kitchen maids, having heard the commotion, came running in, and speaking for their mistress said, "This diagram is to ask about the traveler."

"The wife is asking about her husband, then?" asked the blind man.

"That's right," replied the old women.

"When the green dragon rules the world," declared the fortune-teller, "the sign of wealth is set in motion. If the wife is asking about her husband, the traveler is halfway home. With him he has gold and silks filling a thousand chests, and there is no sign of a storm in his path. The green dragon belongs to the wood element, and wood thrives in the spring. Around the time of the beginning of spring[4] he started off. By the end of this month or the beginning of the next, he is sure to return home, laden with riches besides."

San-ch'iao instructed the male servant to give him three pennies and send him off. Beside herself with joy, she went up to her room. It was a true case of "thirst allayed by the sight of plums" and "hunger satisfied with a picture of cakes."

Most people, as long as they don't cherish high hopes, will remain untroubled. Once they get their hopes stirred, then all sorts of foolish wishes and silly ideas start coming to them, making the time drag by. Merely because she put stock in the words of the fortune-teller, San-ch'iao now thought of nothing but her husband's return, and from this time on often went to the front of the house, where she sat gazing up and down the street from behind the curtain.

This went on right up until the beginning of the second month, when the cedar trees began to put forth their buds, and still there was no sign of her husband. Remembering his promise at departure, she grew more and more anxious. Several times a day she would peer outside. And then it happened that she met her handsome young man. Truly:

If there is a bond between them, the two will meet across a
*   thousand li.*
Without a bond, they will not meet though face to face.

And who was this handsome young man? As it turned out, he was not a native of the area, but came from Hsin-an in Hui-chou, a man by the name of Ch'en Shang, also called "Big Happy Brother," which was later changed to Ta-lang, "Big Boy." He had just turned twenty-four and was a fine-looking fellow. Though he would not

[4] Either the fourth or the fifth day of the second month.

have surpassed Sung Yü or P'an An in looks, neither would he have ranked beneath them.

This young man, who had lost both parents, got together a sum of two or three thousand taels in cash and began making trips to Hsiang-yang to buy rice, beans, and such, usually going once a year. His quarters were outside the city, but on this particular day, he had happened to enter the city to check at Pawnbroker Wang's shop on the Great Market Street for letters from home. The pawnshop was right across from the Chiangs', and so he came to pass by. You ask how he was dressed? On his head was a Soochow-style palm-leaf hat, and he wore a robe of Hu-chou silk, white as a fish's belly, which happened to be just like the one Hsing-ko usually wore. Catching sight of him from a distance, San-ch'iao thought that he was her husband returning, and she lifted the curtain and fixed her gaze on him. When Ch'en Ta-lang raised his head to find a beautiful young woman in an upper story staring at him unblinkingly, he assumed that she had taken a fancy to him, and he, too, threw a glance in her direction. Who could have known there would be this misunderstanding on both sides? When San-ch'iao realized that it was not her husband, both cheeks turned bright red with shame, and hastily pulling the window shut, she ran into the back room where she sat down on the edge of the bed. However, her heart would not stop pounding wildly.

Meanwhile, Ch'en Ta-lang's soul had already been snatched away by the woman's gaze. When he reached his quarters, he still could not get her off his mind. He said to himself, "Though my wife at home is rather pretty in her own way, how could she ever compare with this woman? I must get a message to her somehow, but I've no way to get in. If I could just spend a night with her, even though it cost me my entire capital, this life would not have been lived in vain." He began to sigh, then suddenly remembered that in the East Alley of the Great Market Street, there was a pearl seller named Granny Hsüeh with whom he had done business before. This old woman had a clever tongue, and besides she was out day after day traveling through the streets and alleys. Was there a family she did not know? He would have to talk over the matter with her. Surely she would have some suggestion to make.

Tossing and turning, he finally got through a restless night. The next day he was up bright and early, and saying that he had business to attend to, called for some cold water so he could wash and comb his hair. Taking along one hundred taels' worth of silver and two ingots of gold, he hurried into the city. As the saying goes:

If you're after enjoyment in life,
You have to put in an all-out effort.

When Ch'en Ta-lang entered the city, he made straight for the East Alley and there knocked on the gate of Granny Hsüeh's. She was in her yard selecting her pearls, her hair in disarray. When she heard the knocking, she gathered up the bundle of pearls, asking at the same time, "Who is it?" When she heard the three words, "Ch'en of Hui-chou," she hurried to open the gate and invite him in, saying, "I haven't washed yet, so I won't try to stand on ceremony with you. What honorable business brings you here at such an early hour?"

"I made a special point of coming early, for I was afraid I'd miss you if I came later," replied Ch'en Ta-lang.

"You want to buy some pearls or trinkets from me?"

"I do want some pearls, but there's a bigger business that you'd be interested in."

"Anything out of my line, I'm not used to handling."

"Is it safe to talk here?"

Granny Hsüeh shut the gate and invited him in to take a seat in her small room; then she asked him, "Now what's on your mind?"

Seeing that no one was around, Ta-lung fished in his sleeve for the silver and opened his cloth bundle, spreading its contents out on the table, as he said, "Only after you've accepted these one hundred taels will I presume to speak."

Not knowing what was afoot, the old woman could not be induced to take them. Ta-lang said, "Is it too little for you?" Hurriedly he took out two ingots of shining gold which he also placed on the table, saying, "Please take these ten taels of gold. If you refuse again, I'll take that to mean you're intentionally turning down my request. Today I'm the one who has come seeking your help and not the other way around. This is a matter I can't do without your help; that's why I've come to you especially. If you should try but fail, the gold and silver will still be yours to keep. I certainly won't come back to ask for it, nor will I hold any grudges against you. I'm not such a petty sort!"

Tell me, dear audience, has there ever been a procuress without greed for money? How could the sight of those gold and white pieces fail to stir her desire? At this moment, her face was all smiles, and she said, "Now you mustn't get me wrong, sir. Never in my life have I asked for a cent of any money which I don't deserve. Today I'll accept whatever your assignment is and put this aside for the time being. If it turns out I can't be of service, I'll return the money to you." As she finished speaking, she put the gold ingots in with the bundle of silver pieces and wrapped them up together, saying, "I'm being much too bold." She went to stash it away in her bedroom, then hurried back and said, "I'll not presume, sir, to express my thanks yet. You must tell me what do you want me to do."

"I'm searching desperately for a certain life-saving jewel," said Ch'en. "It's to be found only in the house of a certain family in the Great Market Street. Go and borrow it for me please."

The old woman broke into laughter and exclaimed, "You're just up to mischief! I've been living in this alley for more than twenty years now, yet I've never heard of any life-saving jewel in the

Great Market Street. Please tell me, sir, who owns this jewel?"

"Who lives in that big house across from the pawnshop of Wang from my country?"

The old woman thought for a moment, then replied, "That's the house of Chiang Hsing-ko of this region. Chiang has been away traveling for over a year, now. Only his wife is at home."

"His wife is the very one I must borrow this life-giving jewel from," he said, and with this he pulled his chair up closer to the old woman and told her just what was on his mind. When the old woman had heard him through, she hurriedly shook her head and exclaimed, "Now, that's quite a difficult matter! The girl has been married to Chiang Hsing-ko for less than four years, and the couple are like fish and water. They're never so much as an inch apart. Now that he's had to go away, the young mistress has never left the upper story, so chaste is she. Hsing-ko has some peculiar ways and is quickly angered over trifles, so I've never once gone near their door. I've no idea what the young lady even looks like, so how could I possibly agree to take on such a task? Your gift has proved too high a blessing for me to enjoy."

At these words Ch'en Ta-lang fell to his knees. When the old woman tried to pull him up, his hands gripping her sleeves held her down firmly in her chair so she could not budge. "My very life is in your hands," he implored. "You just have to come up with some clever plan, so that I can take her and save this wretched life of mine. If this is successful, there'll be another hundred taels for you. If you refuse, then I may as well end my life this very moment."

The old woman was too startled to know what to do, and she said, "All right, all right! You're overwhelming me with all this. Now, please get up. There is something I have to say."

Ch'en at last rose and, holding his hands together in a respectful salute, said, "Whatever clever plan you have, please tell me at once."

"This will take time," Granny Hsüeh replied.

"If you want it to work out, you can't figure in terms of months or years. If a time limit is set, then I won't be able to accept the assignment."

"If indeed it can work out, then what difference will a few days make? Only, how do you plan to go about it?"

"After breakfast tomorrow, be sure to meet me at Wang's pawnshop. Don't be late. Bring a little extra cash along with you, saying only that you're doing business with me. Now, there's a reason for all this. If I can get these feet of mine past the Chiang's threshold, you're in luck. You must then hurry back to your lodgings. Don't loiter around the front door. Should you be recognized, everything will be ruined. If I make any headway, I'll come myself to report to you."

"I'll do everything you say," Ch'en said. And with a deep bow, he happily opened the door and departed. Truly:

Before the defeat of Hsiang Yü and before the crowning of Liu Pang,
Altars have already been set in honor of the generals.

Nothing else worth mentioning happened that day. The next day Ch'en put on a fine suit of clothes, took out a few hundred taels in cash, which he placed in a large leather box, and ordered a young servant to carry the box along behind him to the Wang's pawnshop in the Great Market Street. Noticing that the windows of the house opposite were tightly closed, he guessed that the mistress was not in. Then, greeting the pawnshop keeper, he asked for a wooden stool and sat down in front of the door, gazing off toward the east. Presently Granny Hsüeh came in sight, clutching a wicker case in her arms. Ch'en stopped her and asked, "What's in the case?"

"Pearls and jewelry," she answered. "Would you be interested, sir?"

"Just what I'm after."

The old woman entered the pawnshop and, seeing the shopkeeper, apologized for her intrusion and then opened the case. Inside were ten or more bundles of pearls as well as some smaller boxes, all filled with novel varieties of flower clusters speckled with blue, ingeniously designed to give delight, bright and dazzling. Ch'en selected a few strings of thick white pearls along with various hairpins and earrings, and placing them all in one pile, said, "I'll take all of these."

The old woman gave him a look and said, "Please take what you want; but I'm afraid the price may be more than you're willing to pay."

Ch'en had already gotten the message, and opening the leather box, he began stacking up the glittering white pieces of silver, shouting, "With all this silver, you think I can't afford those things of yours?!"

By this time, quite a few neighborhood loafers had strolled over and stood watching in front of the pawnshop.

"I was merely joking," the old woman said. "How could I presume to take you lightly, sir? You must be careful with your silver. Please put it away. I'm asking only to be paid a fair price."

The two of them bickered back and forth, the one demanding a high price, the other countering with a smaller sum, as far apart from each other as heaven and earth. The one setting the price would not waver from her original demand. In the meantime, Ch'en Ta-lang, holding on to the things and refusing either to put them down or raise his offer, deliberately stepped out of the shop. He turned the pieces over one by one to get a good look at them, remarking on which was genuine and which was fake, appraising their value as they sparkled in the sunlight. This eventually drew the entire market crowd over to watch, and there were continuous shouts of appreciation.

"Buy them if you're going to," the old woman burst out. "If not, then leave them. What's the point in just wasting someone's time like this!"

"Who's not buying?" retorted Ch'en, and the two went off on another round of haggling over the price. Truly:

A mere dispute over the price,
And the lady upstairs was aroused.

Hearing all the commotion going on opposite her door, San-ch'iao was drawn in spite of herself to the front room, where she pushed open the window and peeked out. All that caught her eye was the sparkling of pearls and the brilliance of gleaming gems—a lovely sight. When she noticed the old woman and the stranger wrangling interminably over the price she instructed her maid to go summon the old woman over so she could have a look at her things. Bright Cloud crossed the street as instructed and gave Granny Hsüeh's sleeve a tug, saying, "My mistress would like to see you."

"Which family is that?" the old woman asked deliberately.

"The Chiangs across the street," replied Bright Cloud. At this the old woman swept up the pearls and other items in one deft motion and hurriedly wrapped them up, saying, "I've no time to carry on this nonsense with you!"

"All right then, I'll raise my offer a little," Ch'en said.

"I'm not selling. For that kind of price, I could have sold them long ago." As she spoke, she placed them into the case and locked it up again. Taking it in her arms, she started off.

"I'll carry it for you, old lady," Bright Cloud offered.

"No need," replied Granny Hsüeh, and without a backward glance, she strode straight across to the house opposite. Secretly rejoicing, Ch'en gathered up his silver pieces and, saying good-bye to the pawnshop keeper, returned to his lodgings. Indeed:

His eyes gazed after the victory flag;
His ears listened to the glad tidings.

Bright Cloud led Granny Hsüeh up the stairs, where she met San-ch'iao. When the old woman caught sight of the young wife, she thought to herself, "Truly a heavenly creature! No wonder

Ch'en has lost his head over her. If I were a man, I'd be in a tizzy myself." She then said, "I've often heard of your virtue and intelligence and have only regretted never getting a chance to make your acquaintance."

"What is your honorable name, old lady?" asked San-ch'iao.

"My name is Hsüeh. I live over in the East Alley, so I'm a neighbor of yours."

"Why wouldn't you sell those things of yours just now?"

Laughing, the old lady said, "If they weren't for sale, I wouldn't have taken them out. But what a fool that stranger turned out to be, despite his fine appearance! He can't recognize a thing of worth!" At this she proceeded to open her case and take out a few hairpins and earrings which she handed to the woman for inspection, exclaiming, "Madam, can you imagine what it cost just to make such pieces? Why, the prices he offered are ridiculous! How could I ever account for the loss to my employer?" And she held up some pearl pendants, saying, "Top-notch goods like these. He must be dreaming!"

San-ch'iao inquired what the asking price and the price offered had been, and then said, "That was really putting you out some."

"Well, after all, you're from a good family," said the old woman, "and have a wide experience with such things. Your eye is ten times sharper than a man's."

San-ch'iao instructed the maid to serve tea, but the old woman put in, "Don't bother with tea. I've an important matter to attend to over in the West Street. Too much of my time was wasted dealing with that man. The saying is certainly true that 'When a deal falls through, it holds up the work.' Would you mind if I left this case along with the key in your care? I'm going off for the time being but will return shortly." So saying, she left. San-ch'iao ordered her maid to see her down the stairs. She left the house and struck off toward the west.

San-ch'iao had fallen in love with the pieces and waited eagerly for the old woman's return so she could bargain with her. The woman did not appear for the next five days. On the afternoon of the sixth day, there was a sudden heavy downpour. Before the sound of the rain had died out, there was a knocking at the door. San-ch'iao ordered the maid to open it to see who was there, and in came Granny Hsüeh, her clothes half soaked and with a tattered umbrella in her hand. She recited, "Don't leave under clear skies, but wait instead for the rain to start." She set the umbrella at the bottom of the stairs and went up. Offering her blessings, she said, "Madam, the other day I broke my promise to you."

San-ch'iao hastened to return her greeting and asked her, "Where have you been these past few days?"

"My daughter has just been blessed with a son, so I went to look and stayed a few days. I just returned this morning. On my way back the rain started, so I stopped at the house of an acquaintance to borrow an umbrella, a tattered one at that. What luck!"

"How many sons and daughters do you have, old lady?"

"Only one son, who's already married. But I've four daughters. This is my fourth. She was made the concubine of Mr. Chu of Hui-chou. He runs a salt shop just outside the North Gate here."

"You have many daughters, so you don't consider them worth bothering about. But this place has no lack of suitable husbands; how could you bear to marry her off to an outsider as a concubine?"

"Now you don't understand. This man, though he comes from other regions, is a very kind person. Though my daughter is a concubine, the first wife remains at home and it's my daughter who stays at the shop, where she has servants and maids to serve her. Every time I go there, he treats me with the respect due an elder, and is never in the least neglectful. Now that she's given him a son, it's even better."

"Then it's a real blessing for you that you found her such a good match," said San-ch'iao. As she finished speaking, Warm Cloud brought in some tea.

"On a rainy day like this I've nothing to attend to," said the old woman. "May I be so bold as to ask to look at your jewelry? I might come across some interesting designs which would be good to keep in mind for the future."

"They're all just ordinary ones. You must promise not to laugh." So saying, San-ch'iao took out a key, opened up a chest, and one after another removed a large number of hairpins, filigree, tassels, and the like.

At sight of them, Granny Hsüeh could not find words enough to praise their beauty. "When you have such rare treasures as these, you must surely find those few things of mine unworthy of your notice."

"That's very kind of you to say. How much do you really want for those things of yours?"

"You're a good judge of value, madam. What need is there for me to waste my breath?"

San-ch'iao picked up her own pieces, then brought out Granny Hsüeh's wicker case, set it on the table, and handed the old woman the key, saying, "Please open it, old lady, and check your own things."

"There's really no need to."

Granny Hsüeh then opened the case and removed the items one by one for San-ch'iao's inspection and assessment. The prices San-ch'iao offered proved to be quite near the mark. The old woman made no effort to argue with her, but cried joyfully, "This way, no one will lose out. Even if I make a few strings less, it'll be a pleasure."

"There's just one thing. At present I've no way to get all the cash needed. The best I can do is offer you half now, then settle with you in full when my husband returns. He'll be back any day now."

"A few days will make no difference," the old woman replied. "But as I've given in considerably on the price, the silver must be of the finest grade."

"That'll be no problem," San-ch'iao said. She picked up the few ornaments and pearls she liked best, then ordered Bright Cloud to bring out some wine and drank with the old woman.

"How can I let you go to so much trouble?" said the old woman.

"I've plenty of time on my hands," said San-ch'iao, "and it's so seldom that I have a chance to enjoy your company. If you don't mind the little I have to offer, I hope you will often come to visit."

"Thank you, madam, for your kindness to one so undeserving. My house is so unbearably noisy, while here it is quiet."

"What business is your son in?" San-ch'iao asked.

"Oh, he handles the gem dealers. They're in every day clamoring for wine and soup. The racket they make is more than one can stand. Luckily for me, I'm out making the rounds of all the houses, so I need spend little of my time at home. Otherwise, if I had to stay cooped up in six feet of space, I'm afraid I'd go out of my mind."

"Our house is quite close to yours. Whenever it gets too much for you, then just come on over for a chat."

"I'm just afraid that I might outstay my welcome."

"Not at all," San-ch'iao assured her.

In the meantime the two maids in turn had been busily moving back and forth, and had laid out two sets of bowls and chopsticks, two plates each of smoked chicken, smoked pork, and fresh fish, along with bowls of fruit and plates of vegetables, sixteen dishes altogether.

"What a feast!" exclaimed the old woman.

"These are the only things we have on hand. Please don't blame me for my lack of hospitality." So saying, San-ch'iao poured some wine and passed it to Hsüeh, who took the cup and toasted her health. Then they sat down across the table and began drinking. Now it happened that San-ch'iao's capacity for wine was considerable, while the old woman was something of a wine jug herself, and as they began to drink, they became more and more congenial, regretting only that they had not met earlier. That day they continued eating until evening came and the rain finally let up. The old woman expressed her thanks and prepared to return home. San-ch'iao brought out a large silver goblet and urged Hsüeh to have another few rounds. She then had supper with her and said, "Stay a while longer, old lady. I'll get the first half of the money for you."

"It's getting late," the old woman said. "Please relax and don't worry about it tonight. I'll come and get it tomorrow. I won't take along this wicker case, either. That'll save me from having to lug it over the muddy roads."

"Then tomorrow I'll be expecting you," San-ch'iao said.

The old woman said good-bye and went down-stairs, picked up her tattered umbrella, and left the house. Truly:

Nothing like the tongues of these cunning old hags
To cause much upset in other peoples' lives.

During all this time Ch'en Ta-lang waited list-lessly in his lodgings, not having heard a word from the old woman. At the sight of the rain that day, he guessed that she would be at home and made his way through the wet and mud into the city to see if there was any news, only to find she was not at home. At a tavern he had three cups of wine with something to eat, and then went to Granny Hsüeh's place to inquire again; but still she had not returned. Noticing how late it was getting, he was on the point of turning back when he caught sight of the old woman, her face beaming, staggering and reeling into the alley.

Ch'en approached her, and bowing, he asked, "How are things coming along?"

The old lady said with a wave of her hand, "It's still too early. The seeds are just now being sown. No sprouts are up yet. It'll be another five or six years before the blossoms open and the fruit is ready for you to taste. So you needn't come nosing about here. I'm not the type to gossip."

Seeing how drunk she was, Ch'en Ta-lang had no choice but to turn around and go back.

The following day the old woman bought some fresh fruit, as well as chicken, fish, pork, and the like, which she ordered the cook to prepare and pack into two boxes. She then bought a jug of fine wine and, asking her neighbor boy, Hsiao-erh, to carry it for her, arrived at the front gate of the Chiangs'.

Seeing no sign of Granny Hsüeh yet that day, San-ch'iao had just ordered Bright Cloud to go out and look up and down the street for her; so she chanced to see the old woman as she approached. The old woman bade Hsiao-erh set down the boxes downstairs and then sent him off. Bright Cloud meanwhile had already announced her arrival to her mistress, who received her as an honored guest, going out to the top of the stairs to meet her. The old woman was full of thanks and greeted her by saying, "I happened to have some wine, so I brought it along for your enjoyment."

"You really shouldn't have spent so much money," San-ch'iao said. "Why should I deserve all this?"

The old woman asked the two maids to carry the things upstairs and lay them on the table.

"Old lady, you're much too extravagant, making such a display as this!" San-ch'iao said.

The old woman replied with a laugh, "I'm afraid our poor house cannot prepare anything good. Please take it merely as an offer of a cup of tea."

Bright Cloud then went to fetch bowls and chopsticks and Warm Snow got the brazier going. In a moment the wine was warmed and the old woman said, "Today is my little treat. Now you must take the guest's seat."

"Though you've gone to much trouble on my

account, how can you expect me to accept the seat of guest in my own house?" protested San-ch'iao. Each continued to yield the seat politely to the other for some time until finally Granny Hsüeh was obliged to sit in the guest's position.

As this was their third meeting, they felt on even closer terms than before. In the midst of drinking, the old woman said, "Your husband has been away for a long time now and still hasn't returned. How could he abandon you like that?"

"Indeed, you're right. He said he'd be back in a year. I can't imagine what could be keeping him."

"If you ask me," said the old woman, "when one has put aside a rare gem like you, even if he found himself piles of gold and heaps of jade, they would not be anywhere near as precious." She went on, "For most of those accustomed to be constantly on the road, the inn is their home and their home an inn. Take my fourth daughter's husband, Mr. Chu, for example. Now that he's got himself a concubine, he's stayed happy morning and night. How's he ever going to miss home? Perhaps in a span of three or four years, he'll return once, and then before one or two months are up, he's off again. His wife at home is left in charge of his neglected children and lives like a widow. How would she know what he's up to on the outside?"

"Oh, but my husband's not like that."

"This is all just idle chatter, of course. How could one possibly compare heaven and earth?"

The two spent the day guessing riddles, rolling dice, and getting themselves pleasantly intoxicated before they said their good-byes.

On the third day Granny Hsüeh came with Hsiao-erh to get the dishes and at the same time picked up the first half of the promised sum. San-ch'iao had her stay once more for a snack.

From then on, using the half-unpaid sum as a pretext for asking news of Hsing-ko, she often came to visit. The old woman had a gift for chatter, and besides was given to cracking jokes and carrying on like a crazy fool with the maids, so that she had endeared herself to servants and mistress alike. If a day went by without her appearing, San-ch'iao would feel lonely, and so had her old servant find out where she lived. Then she would invite her over at all hours, so that they became more and more intimate.

There are in the world four kinds of people whom one should never get involved with. Once they become familiar with you, there's no stopping them. Who are they? Wandering priests, beggars, vagrants, and procuresses. The first three are bad enough, but the procuress is even more dreadful, if only because she will worm her way into one's home. When the women of the household grow weary of the monotony, they will go round her up. Grannie Hsüeh was a bad sort to begin with, full of honeyed words and gentle phrases, and now she had become the bosom friend of San-ch'iao, who could not do without her for a minute. How true that:

Painting a tiger's skin is easy, but not so the bones.
A man's face one can know, but not his heart.

To Ch'en Ta-lang's repeated inquiries, Granny Hsüeh replied only that it was still too early. It was now the middle of the fifth month, and the weather was steadily becoming hotter. The old woman chanced to mention to San-ch'iao how cramped she was in her snail-sized quarters, which a western exposure made particularly unsuitable for summer weather. They could not be compared with the spacious airiness of the upper story of San-ch'iao's house.

"Why not spend your nights here if you can leave your family in the evening?" said San-ch'iao.

"That would be very nice indeed. I'm only afraid that your husband might come back."

"When he does return, it probably won't be in the middle of the night!"

"Well, if you don't mind the trouble—I'm really being very forward now—how about my moving my bedding over and keeping you company tonight?"

"Oh, we have plenty of bedding," said San-ch'iao. "You needn't bring your own. Why not go back and let your family know, then spend the rest of the summer over here?"

The old woman did, indeed, tell her son and daughter-in-law of her intentions, and then came back carrying only a box of toilet articles. San-ch'iao remonstrated with her. "You've gone to unnecessary trouble. Surely you don't think we've no combs here? Why have you brought this?"

"One thing I've always hated is sharing a washbasin and comb. I'm sure you have a set of the finest combs, but how could I ever dare use such things? And the same goes for those belonging to the maids. It's better I bring my own. But now you must tell me which room I should sleep in."

San-ch'iao indicated a tiny wicker couch in front of her own bed and said, "I've already arranged a place for you to sleep. We'll be close together so that we can chat during the night if we have trouble sleeping." She pulled out a green gauze curtain, which she asked the old woman herself to hang up. They then had a drink of wine together before finally settling down to sleep.

Normally the two maids laid out their bedding in front of the bed to keep the mistress company, but now that the old woman was there, they were sent off to sleep in the next room.

From this time on, the old woman would go about the streets doing her trading by day and after nightfall return to the Chiang's to sleep. Often she brought a jug of wine along to provide a little merriment.

The couch and the bed were arranged in the shape of the letter T; and though the women were separated by a curtain, it was as though they were sleeping in the same bed. During the night they would chatter endlessly, leaving out none of the lewd talk that was heard on the streets. The old woman, at times feigning intoxication or madness, would go into the details of her own youthful affairs in order to stir up the young wife's longings, getting her roused to such a point that her tender cheeks alternately flushed and paled, paled and flushed. The old lady was well aware that the young woman's feelings were aroused but that she could not bring herself to voice her thoughts.

Time sped by, and soon it was the seventh day of the seventh month, San-ch'iao's birthday. Early in the morning the old woman prepared two boxes of birthday gifts for her. San-ch'iao thanked her and tried to make her stay for a bowl of noodles, but the old woman said, "I have some pressing business to attend to today, but in the evening I'll come keep you company and we can watch the Herdboy pay his visit to the Weaving Maid."[5] She then departed.

She had gone no more than a few steps from the door when she ran into Ch'en Ta-lang. Not wanting to hold a conversation there in the street, they retreated to a quiet, secluded alley. Contracting his brows, Ch'en complained to the old woman, "What a dawdler you are! Spring went and summer came and now here it is the beginning of autumn. Today you say it's too early and tomorrow you'll be saying it's too early again. You don't seem to understand that a day is like a year for me. If we put this off any longer, her husband will be back, and the whole thing will be thrown to the winds. That will be nothing less than murdering me! When I get down to the court of hell, you can be sure I'll see that you pay for it with your life!"

"Don't get so excited and so impatient," the old woman said. "You're here at just the right time, for I was about to go looking for you. Now the success or failure of our plan all depends on what happens tonight, but you must do everything just as I say." And she told him that thus and so was to be done, in such and such a manner. "Everything must be kept very quiet. Don't give me trouble."

Ch'en nodded and exclaimed, "A marvelous plan! When it has succeeded, I'll certainly reward

[5] For Herdboy and Weaving Maid, see footnote 2.

you handsomely." With this he went off in high spirits. Truly:

He marshals his forces to seize the jade,
Exhausting his energies on the fulfillment of his desires.

Granny Hsüeh had set that evening to bring the matter to a successful conclusion. In the afternoon a fine rain had fallen and the sky had become overcast. By evening neither moon nor stars were visible. The old woman led Ch'en through the darkness and concealed him off to the left while she went to knock on the door. Bright Cloud opened the door and came out with a lighted paper lantern. Intentionally, the old woman groped in her sleeve, saying "I've dropped a Lin-ch'ing[6] handerchief. Could you please help me find it?" Taken in by this, Bright Cloud shone the lantern down on the pavement. The old woman seized this opportunity to motion Ch'en over and whisked him through the door, leading him to an empty space underneath the stairs where he could hide. She then cried out, "I've got it. You needn't look anymore."

"Just in time, too," Bright Cloud said, "for the fire's gone out. I'll go light another one to show you in."

"Oh, I can find my way by now. No need for a light." In the darkness they closed the door and groped their way up the stairs.

"What did you drop?" San-ch'iao asked.

Granny Hsüeh pulled a small handkerchief from her sleeve and said, "This is the culprit. It's not worth anything, but it was given to me by a customer from Peking. Don't they say, 'a meager gift but a generous wish?'"

"I'll bet it's a keepsake from a lover," San-ch'iao said teasingly.

"That's about right," the old woman said with a chuckle.

That night they drank and made merry.

"There's more than enough wine and food," the old woman remarked. "Why not offer some to

---

[6] In modern Shantung Province. A Lin-ch'ing handkerchief is especially valuable.

---

the maids and servants in the kitchen and tell them to really enjoy themselves as on a festival night?"

San-ch'iao went ahead and put aside four dishes of food and two jugs of wine, which she told the maids to take downstairs. The two serving women and the male servant ate and drank for a while and then went off to bed. But of this we need speak no more.

To continue, the old woman in the course of her drinking asked, "Why hasn't your husband returned yet?"

"It's been a year and a half now all together," said San-ch'iao.

"Even the Herdboy and the Weaving Maid meet once a year. But you've been apart now for half a year longer than they. As the saying goes, 'Once the man is on the road, you don't have any more control.' A traveler never lacks opportunities for romance. The only one who has it hard is the wife at home."

San-ch'iao sighed and lowered her head, making no response.

"But I'm just full of prattle," the old woman said. "Tonight is a celebration for the Herdboy and the Maid. One should drink and be merry instead of making unpleasant remarks." With that she poured out some wine and urged the lady to drink.

Well in her cups at this point, the old woman pressed more wine on the two maids, saying, "This is the nuptial wine of the Herdboy and the Weaving Maid. You must drink some more, and one day you will marry loving husbands who'll never leave your side." Unable to resist her urgings, the two maids forced it down, and as neither were good drinkers, they began to stagger and reel about. San-ch'iao ordered them to shut the staircase door and go on to bed while the two of them continued drinking by themselves.

As the old woman drank she babbled on, "Madam, how old were you when you got married?"

"Seventeen," replied San-ch'iao.

"My, you were late in having your first experience! You weren't taken advantage of. I was thirteen when I first experienced it."

"You were married that early?"

"Well, now, as for getting married, that was at the age of eighteen. You see, I was learning needlework at the house next door, and the young master began flirting with me. Smitten by his good looks, I gave in to him. At first it was quite painful, but then after two or three times I came to enjoy it. Was it that way with you, too?"

San-ch'iao only giggled in reply.

"It's better never to have had a taste of what it's like," the old woman went on. "Once you've experienced it, you can't give it up. Sometimes you get such an itch deep down inside. It's not too bad during the day, but oh, is it ever hard to bear at night!"

"You must have known quite a few men while you were still at home. How did you ever pass as a virgin when you got married?"

"My mother had a notion of what was going on and was afraid it would lead to disgrace, so she gave me a prescription for restoring virginity, an infusion of guava peel and alum. Washing with this will tighten things up. I just made a big fuss about how painful it was and that way it was kept secret."

"As a girl, you must have had to sleep alone at night."

"I still remember when I was at home and my older brother was away, I used to sleep with my sister-in-law in the same bed. We took turns playing the man's part."

"What's the good of two girls sleeping together?"

The old woman walked over and sat down close beside San-ch'iao. "You may not realize it," she said, "but as long as the two of you have a good understanding, it can be enjoyable for both and give you some release, too."

San-ch'iao gave the old woman's shoulder a shove. "Oh, I don't believe it. You're telling lies."

The old woman could see her desires had been stirred and purposely tried to rouse her. She continued, "I'm fifty-two this year, and often during the night the old itch comes over me, and I can't bear it. Lucky for you you're able to manage so well despite your youth!"

"If you can't bear it, why not get yourself a man?"

"This withered old flower? Who'd want me now? I may as well tell you, I've my own means of getting satisfaction, an emergency measure."

"Oh, you're lying. What sort of way could that be?"

"Just wait until we're in bed," the old woman said, "and I'll tell you all the details." She had just finished saying this when a moth began hovering over the lamp. She raised her fan and struck at it, deliberately smashing the lamp with her fan. "Oh, dear!" she cried. "I'll go light another one." Then she went over and opened the staircase door. Ch'en Ta-lang had already made his way up the stairs, and had been lying in wait behind the door for some time. All this was in accord with the old woman's prearranged scheme. She then declared, "Oh, I forgot to bring a light for the lamp," and turning around, led Ch'en Ta-lang to her own couch, where she concealed him. The old woman went downstairs for awhile, then came back up and announced, "It's quite dark outside, and all the lights in the kitchen have gone out. What should we do?"

"I'm used to sleeping with a light on," said San-ch'iao. "I get really terrified in pitch darkness."

"How about if I sleep with you to keep you company?"

San-ch'iao, who had wanted to ask her about her "emergency measure," replied, "Splendid."

"Madam, you go on and get in bed. I'll be there as soon as I shut the door."

San-ch'iao undressed first, then got into bed and called, "Hurry to bed, granny."

"I'm coming," replied the old woman. But instead she dragged Ch'en up from her couch and pushed him stark naked into San-ch'iao's bed. San-ch'iao touched his body and remarked, "My, your skin is smooth for your age." The other made no reply but wriggled down under the covers, then putting his arms around her, he kissed her. Still thinking it was the old woman, she embraced him. All at once he rose up on top of her and began. Now, for one thing, the young woman had had a little too much to drink, which had left her in a haze, and for another, her longings had been stirred up by the old woman. At this point she had no time to demand explanations, but let him have his way with her.

One, a young woman languishing lovesick in her chamber,
The other, a handsome young man, away from home and
craving romance.
One had endured for so long—
Like Wen-chün at her first glimpse of Hsiang-ju.
The other, waiting long in anticipation—
Like Pi-cheng finally meeting with the Ch'en girl.[7]
Clearly a long drought brought to an end by a sweet rain,
A joy to exceed meeting an old friend away from home.

Ch'en Ta-lang was a man familiar with the world of sensual pleasures, and he explored all its mysteries and savored its every delight, setting the girl's soul adrift from her body. It was not until the rain had stopped and the clouds dispersed that San-ch'iao at long last asked, "Who are you?"

Ch'en Ta-lang then recounted to her in detail how he had yearned for her, and how he had implored Granny Hsüeh to devise a plan. Now here at last he had fulfilled his lifelong wish and could die without regret.

The old woman came up to the edge of the bed and said, "It's not that I was overbold, but that first of all, I pitied the young lady spending her nights alone in the springtime of her youth, and second, I wanted to save the life of Mr. Ch'en. You two were destined for union. It had nothing to do with me."

"Now that things have come to this," said San-ch'iao, "if by chance my husband should find out, what should I do?"

"Only you and I know of this," said Granny Hsüeh. "We have only to buy the silence of the two maids, Bright Cloud and Warm Snow, and then who else could let it out? Leave it to me to see that your nights are merry, and there will be no problem. But later on you mustn't forget all I've done for you."

At this point, San-ch'iao ceased to consider the matter any further, and the two continued their wild delights until the fifth watch had died away and the sky had begun to brighten, and even then they were loath to part. The old woman urged Ch'en up and sent him off.

From then on, not a night passed that they did not spend together. Sometimes the old woman came with him; sometimes the young man came alone. As for the two maids, the old woman cajoled them with sweet words, frightened them with threats, and had their mistress reward them with gifts of clothing. When Ch'en came he would often give them some money to buy things. Thus kept in a state of contentment, they became a party to the undertaking. Upon his arrival at night and departure at dawn, at each coming and going, the two maids were always there to usher him in or send him off with never a hindrance. Ch'en and San-ch'iao were truly a loving couple, joined as though by glue, and close as husband and wife. Wishing to secure their relationship, Ch'en often gave her gifts of fine clothes and jewelry, and paid off the rest of the money she owed the old woman. With another hundred taels in cash he showed his gratitude to the old woman. After more than half a year's time, he had paid out approximately one thousand taels in cash, and San-ch'iao also had given the old woman things worth over thirty taels in cash. It was only because of the old woman's relish for such ill-gotten gains that she was willing to mastermind their affair. As the ancients have said, "All parties must come to an end":

The evening of the first moon after the New Year had no
sooner passed

---

[7] Another well-known pair of lovers: P'an Pi-cheng and Ch'en Chiao-lien.

280

Than already the Ch'ing-ming season of the third month had come.

Ch'en Ta-lang began to reflect that he had let his business slip for a long time now, and that he should be returning home. That night, when he spoke of this to the young woman, so deep was their attachment that neither could bear the thought of separation. On the other hand, she would gladly have packed a few of her valuables and run off with him, to be his wife forever. But Ch'en said, "It cannot be done! Every detail of our affair from start to finish is known to the old woman. Even my landlord, Mr. Lü, who has seen me come into the city every night, can't but have his suspicions. What's more, there are always crowds of passengers aboard the ships. We can deceive no one. And the two maids cannot be taken along either. When your husband comes back and finds out the true facts, he certainly won't let the matter drop. Please be patient for the time being. Next year at this time, I'll find some quiet, secluded lodgings and get a message to you in secret. Then the two of us can secretly leave without anybody's knowledge. Won't that be a better solution?"

"But if you don't come back next year, what then?"

At this Ch'en made her a vow, and she said, "As your heart is sincere, I, too, will remain true to you. Once you are back home, if there is someone available, have him take a message to Granny Hsüeh's home, so that my mind can be at rest."

"I know what to do. Don't worry," Ch'en assured her.

After another few days, Ch'en hired a boat, loaded it with provisions, and came back to say good-bye to the young woman. That night their affection was redoubled. They talked for a while, then wept for a while, then gave themselves up to pleasure, not sleeping a wink the whole night. At the fifth watch they rose, and the young woman went and opened a chest from which she took out something precious called a "pearl shirt," which she handed to Ch'en, saying, "This shirt is an heirloom of the Chiang family. If you wear it in the summertime, you will feel a coolness through to your bones. You are setting off at a time when the heat is increasing, so it is just what you'll need. I'm giving it to you to remember me by. When you wear this shirt, it will be as though I were pressed close to your body."

Ch'en felt himself go limp and he could not speak through his sobs. She then put the shirt on him, and ordering the maid to open the gate, went herself to see him out. After repeated entreaties for him to take good care of himself, she bade him farewell. As the poem goes:

Years ago amid tears she bade her husband farewell.
Today, she cries with grief as she sees off her new love.
Deplorable indeed is the fickle nature of women.
She calls a wild bird to supplant the gentle dove.

Our story now divides in two. We shall tell how Ch'en Ta-lang wore this pearl shirt every day close to his skin. Even at night when he took it off, he laid it beside him in his bed, never letting it out of his sight.

All along the way he met with favorable winds, and so in less than two months he reached Feng-ch'iao in the Soochow Prefecture. Feng-ch'iao was a gathering place for brokers in fuel and rice, so he was certain to find a dealer to whom he could dispose of his cargo. But we will speak no more of this.

One day he attended a banquet given by a man from his own county, and there met a merchant from Hsiang-yang, elegant and handsome in appearance. It was none other than Chiang Hsing-ko himself. Hsing-ko had done some trading in jewels, tortoiseshell, sappanwood, aloeswood, and the like in Kwangtung, and then set off with some companions. After some discussion among themselves, the group of them all decided they wanted to go to Soochow to do some selling. Hsing-ko had often heard the saying that "Up above there

281

is Paradise, down here there are Soochow and Hangchow," and he thought he would visit this large bustling city, do his trading, and then finally wend his way home.

Chiang Hsing-ko had arrived in Soochow in the tenth month of the preceding year. As he was known to everyone in his business circle as Master Lo, Ch'en Ta-lang did not have the least reason to suspect anything. These two men, meeting as they did quite by chance and being of nearly the same age and of similar appearance, in the course of their conversation developed a mutual respect and admiration. During the banquet each asked where the other was staying and they exchanged visits, subsequently becoming good friends and getting together quite often.

When Hsing-ko had finished settling the accounts with all of his customers and was about to depart, he stopped in at Ch'en's lodgings to bid him farewell. Ch'en brought out some wine to entertain him, and soon they found themselves carrying on a pleasant conversation. It was toward the end of the fifth month, and the weather was stifling. Both of them loosened their clothing as they drank and Ch'en exposed the pearl shirt to view. Hsing-ko was astounded. Still, he could not very well let on that he recognized it, and so he merely remarked on its beauty. Presuming on their close friendship, Ch'en then asked, "On the Great Market Street of your county lives a man named Chiang Hsing-ko. Perhaps you know him?"

Cleverly choosing his words, Hsing-ko answered, "I've been away for a long time. Though I know there is such a person in our town, I'm not acquainted with him. Why do you ask?"

"To tell you the truth," Ch'en replied, "I became rather involved with his family." He then told of his love for San-ch'iao, and pulling the shirt out to look at it, said with tears in his eyes, "This shirt was a gift from her. When you go back, I have a letter I'd like you to deliver for me. Tomorrow morning I'll take it over to your inn as early as possible."

"Of course," replied Hsing-ko. But in his heart he was saying, "Could such a thing be! But the pearl shirt here is proof. This couldn't be just idle chatter." At that moment, it was as though needles were jabbing into his stomach. Finding some pretext to stop his drinking, he hurriedly rose and took his leave.

Back in his lodgings, he was overtaken by the alternate moods of pensiveness and fretfulness, wishing he could learn some means of shrinking distance that would bring him home in an instant. He packed his bags that very night, and the following morning boarded the boat, ready to set off. Suddenly on the bank someone came rushing up all out of breath. It was Ch'en Ta-lang. He handed a large packet to Hsing-ko, exhorting him repeatedly to be sure to deliver it. Hsing-ko was so angry that his face turned ash gray and he was unable to speak a word. He waited till Ch'en Ta-lang had left and then looked at the letter. On the outside was written, "Please deliver to the house of Granny Hsüeh in the East Alley of the Great Market Street." His anger mounting, he tore open the letter with one hand. Inside was a peach-pink sash of silk gauze, two yards or so in length. With this there was also an oblong paper box, containing a phoenix hairpin of fine white-tallow jade. A note read:

Granny Hsüeh, would you be so kind as to deliver these two small gifts to my dearest San-ch'iao as a remembrance? I will see her without fail next spring. Tell her to take good care of herself.

In a rage, Hsing-ko tore the note to shreds and flung them in the river. Picking up the jade hairpin, he hurled it to the deck where it broke in two. Then suddenly it occurred to him: "How stupid of me! I should keep this as evidence." He then picked up the pieces of the hairpin and, wrapping them up together with the sash, packed them away. Next he pressed the boatmen to get the boat under way.

He hurried home in a fit of impatience, but as the front gate of his house came into view, without his realizing it, tears began to fall and he thought, "In the beginning there was such love and affection between us. That this horrible thing should have happened is due entirely to my greed for a pittance of profit, which caused me to go off and leave her living virtually the life of a young widow. I'm to blame for this disgrace, but it's too late for regrets now." He was getting more and more impatient, and he had wished he could reach home in a minute. But now that he was there, he was filled with bitterness and remorse. His pace slowed with each step he took. As he entered the door of his house, he had to swallow his anger and steel himself to meet his wife. Hsing-ko uttered not a word. San-ch'iao herself, overcome with guilt, felt her face flood with shame, and she dared not come forward to express her wifely solicitude. When Hsing-ko had finished moving his baggage, he stated only that he was going to see his parents-in-law. In fact, he went out and spent the night on board the boat.

The next morning when he returned home, he said to his wife, "Your mother and father have both fallen ill. Their condition is grave. Last night I was obliged to stay over to keep watch on them. You are uppermost on their minds, and they wish to see you. I've already hired a sedan chair, which is now waiting at the gate. You must go over there with all speed. I'll follow immediately behind."

When her husband had not come back the whole night, San-ch'iao had grown worried. Hearing that her parents were ill, she assumed it to be serious and was naturally alarmed. Hastily handing the keys to the chests over to her husband, she summoned an old maidservant to follow her and then got into the sedan chair and departed. Hsing-ko stopped the servant and, drawing a letter from his sleeve, instructed her to deliver it to Mr. Wang. "When you have delivered the letter, come back in the sedan chair."

San-ch'iao returned home and to her surprise, found both parents in good health. Seeing his daughter return on her own like this, Mr. Wang, too, was amazed. He took the letter from the maidservant, opened it, and found that it was a document of divorce. It read:

I, Chiang Te, the undersigned of this Document of Divorce, a native of Tsao-yang in the Hsing-yang Prefecture, through the arrangements of a go-between was formally betrothed in youth to the woman Wang. Contrary to expectations, after entering her husband's home, this woman committed numerous misdeeds, as defined by the seven statutes of divorce.[8] Out of consideration for the affection between husband and wife, a statement of these is not made public. I willingly consent to her return home and have no objections to her marrying again if she so wishes. I certify that this Document of Divorce is genuine.

Dated this ____ day, of the ____ month, second year of the Ch'eng-hua reign period [1466].[9] Palm print [of Chiang Te].

Also contained in the envelope were a peach-pink sash and a broken white-tallow jade phoenix hairpin. Wang read all this with great consternation, and then called his daughter over to ask for an explanation. When San-ch'iao heard that her husband had divorced her, without uttering a word, she burst into tears. Fuming with indignation, Wang marched straight over to his son-in-law's. Chiang Hsing-ko came forward hurriedly to greet him with a bow. Mr. Wang returned the courtesy, then said, "Son-in-law, my daughter was pure and innocent when she married you. Now, what sort of misdeeds has she committed that has made you divorce her? You owe me an explanation."

"It is not for me to say," Hsing-ko replied. "You had best ask your daughter to tell you."

"She does nothing but cry, and won't say a word," Wang said. "It's unbearable! My daughter has always been an intelligent girl. I can't imagine

[8] The seven grounds on which a wife could be divorced in traditional China were: (1) failure to give birth to a son; (2) adultery; (3) disobedience to parents-in-law; (4) quarreling; (5) stealing; (6) jealousy; (7) contracting a malignant disease.
[9] Ch'eng-hua (1465–1487) is the title of the only reign period of Emperor Hsien-tsung of the Ming period.

her ever committing an untoward act. If it's a matter of some small slip of hers, I hope that for my sake you will forgive her. You two were betrothed at the age of seven or eight and since you have been married have never had so much as a quarrel between you, but have lived in good harmony. Now you've been home from your trip no more than a few days. What fault of hers has suddenly come to your attention that makes you so heartless? You'll certainly be ridiculed by all for your injustice and lack of consideration."

"I won't presume to say much, father-in-law. Only, there was handed down in our family a pearl shirt, which was kept by your daughter. Ask her now if it is still there. If it is, I will say no more. If it is not, then you must not blame me."

Wang returned home at once and questioned his daughter. "Your husband is asking you only for some sort of pearl shirt. Tell me the truth, who have you given it to?"

What her father relayed to her hit her right in the face, and she flushed crimson with shame. She could not bring herself to speak, but began to wail louder than ever, giving her father such a fright that he did not know what to do.

"You mustn't go on crying like that," Mrs. Wang entreated her. "Tell your mother and father the truth so we can help you sort things out."

But the girl would not tell and continued her dolorous sobbing without cease. Mr. Wang had no choice but to hand the divorce paper along with the sash and hairpin over to Mrs. Wang and ask her to try to coax their daughter into telling the truth.

In a state of perplexity, Mr. Wang went over to chat with the neighbors. Noticing how red and swollen her daughter's eyes had become, Mrs. Wang began to grow fearful that she had endangered her health. Comforting her with a few words, she went down to the kitchen to warm some wine to try to help dispel her grief.

Alone in her room, San-ch'iao began to wonder to herself how on earth the incident of the pearl

shirt had ever slipped out. Nor could she figure out where the sash and hairpin could have come from. After pondering for some time, she said to herself, "Oh, I understand. This broken hairpin means 'the mirror is broken and the hairpin is rent,' and the sash is obviously intended for me to hang myself. He remembers the affection we once shared and could not bear to make it public. It is because he wishes to preserve my good name. To think that four years of love and affection could be destroyed in a single day! And the fault is all mine for turning my back on my husband's devotion. Even if I were to live on in this world, there's little chance that I would ever know a moment of happiness. Better to hang myself now and put an end to it once and for all." With that she shed more tears. Then placing stools one atop the other, she tied the sash to a beam and prepared to hang herself. But her span of years had not yet been completed. She had left the door of her room open, and just at that moment Mrs. Wang happened to enter with the jug of fine wine she had heated. The sight of what her daughter was preparing to do threw her into a panic. Without setting the wine jug down, she dashed forward to pull her down. In her rush, she kicked over the stools, and mother and daughter were sent sprawling in a heap while the jug of wine overturned with a splash. Mrs. Wang scrambled to her feet and helped her daughter up.

"How foolish you are!" she cried. "A girl in her twenties—a flower not yet in full blossom. How could you do such a stupid thing? Who's to say your husband won't one day have a change of heart? And even if he does divorce you, with your looks, do you think no one will want you? No doubt you will find some other good match, and can then be assured of a life of comfort ever after. Now try to take things easier. There's no need to be so distressed."

When Mr. Wang came back and learned of his daughter's suicide attempt, he, too, tried to reason with her for a while and directed his wife to make

284

sure she was prevented from making any further attempts. After several days, San-ch'iao saw the futility of it and gave up the idea. Truly:

Husband and wife were once birds in the forest.
As the ultimate fate comes upon them, each flies away.

As the story continues, Chiang Hsing-ko, taking two pieces of rope, bound Bright Cloud and Warm Snow, then questioned them about the case under torture. At first they refused to admit anything, but unable to endure the lash, they finally confessed everything in detail from beginning to end. By then it was plain to see that it was all brought about by the evil enticements of Granny Hsüeh, and that no one else was to blame.

The next morning Hsing-ko got together a band of men and they descended on Granny Hsüeh's place, sending the things in her place flying about like falling snow. They stopped just short of tearing the house down. The old woman knew she was in the wrong and stayed out of sight. Not a soul came forward with the slightest protest. Seeing how things were, Hsing-ko felt himself vindicated. Returning home, he called in a procuress and sold her the two maids. For the chests of valuables in the upper rooms, numbering sixteen altogether both large and small, he wrote out thirty-two sealing strips and sealed them up with the strips placed crosswise, never once opening them. And why was this? Once Hsing-ko and his wife had been deeply in love, and though it had ended in divorce, he was still in great anguish. The sight of these objects would recall their owner to mind. How could he bear to open them and look inside?

At this point our story forks. Let us talk about a certain Wu Chieh, a *chin-shih* from Nanking, who was appointed county magistrate of Ch'ao-yang in Kwangtung. His journey over the waterways to his post took him past Hsiang-yang, and as he had not brought his family along, he decided he would choose for himself a pretty concubine. Along the way he had looked at a number of girls

but had found none to his liking. Hearing that San-ch'iao was famed throughout Tsao-yang for her beauty, he set aside a gift of fifty taels and commissioned a go-between to negotiate with her family. Wang delightedly agreed, but fearing that his former son-in-law might raise objections, he went himself to the Chiang residence to inform Hsing-ko. Hsing-ko raised no objection, and on the eve of the wedding he hired men to deliver the sixteen trunks from the upper rooms, the original seals left intact and the keys included, to Magistrate Wu's boat to be handed over to San-ch'iao for her dowry. At this she was overwhelmed with embarrassment. When others came to hear of it, some praised Hsing-ko for his generosity, some ridiculed him for his foolishness, and others reviled him for his spinelessness—so different are the minds of men.

But enough of this chatter. Let's go back to Ch'en Ta-lang, who, after disposing of his cargo in Soochow, returned to Hsin-an, with San-ch'iao uppermost on his mind. Morning and night he would look at the pearl shirt and then moan and sigh. His wife, P'ing-shih, suspected that there was something strange about this shirt, and so, when her husband had fallen asleep, she quietly stole it and hid it in the ceiling beams. In the morning when Ch'en got up and was ready to put it on, he could not find it and demanded it from his wife. She denied having any knowledge of it. He flew into a rage, upending boxes and emptying out chests in an all-out search. But finding it nowhere, he assailed his wife with a stream of wild abuse. Driven to tears, she launched into a noisy quarrel with him. This raged on for several days.

Finally, in a state of exasperation, Ch'en hastily gathered up his money and, taking along a young servant, set off again [by boat] to Hsiang-yang. As he approached Tsao-yang, he was suddenly set upon by a band of robbers who made off with his entire capital and murdered his servant as well. Ch'en was quick-witted enough to make his way to the prow of the boat where he managed to hide himself above the helm, and thus narrowly escaped. Seeing that going back home was now out of the question, he planned to put up at his old lodgings and get a loan from San-ch'iao to tide him over until he could set himself up again. Heaving a sigh, he resignedly left the boat and went ashore. When he arrived at Mr. Lü's house outside the city of Tsao-yang, he explained what had happened. Now, he said, he was going to go ask Granny Hsüeh to borrow some money from an acquaintance so that he could carry on with his trade.

"You perhaps haven't heard about it," said Lü. "That old woman got herself into a scrape from leading Chiang Hsing-ko's wife astray. Last year when Hsing-ko came home, he demanded some sort of pearl shirt from his wife. Apparently she had given it to her lover and couldn't produce it. Hsing-ko divorced her on the spot and sent her home. Now she's been remarried as the concubine of a *chin-shih* Wu of Nanking. The old woman's house was knocked to pieces by Chiang. After that she didn't feel it was safe around there for her anymore, so she cleared out to a neighboring county."

All this came to Ch'en as no little shock. He felt as though a bucket of cold water had been poured on his head. That night fever and chills set in and he fell ill. The illness carried with it symptoms of melancholia and lovesickness as well as of nervous shock. He lay stricken in bed for over two months. Though occasionally he showed some signs of improvement, he was nowhere near a complete recovery. He became a burden to the host and servants, who grew impatient waiting on him. Made uneasy by this, he roused himself enough to write a letter home and called Lü in to talk it over. What he wished was to find someone who could deliver the letter to his home, pick up money for traveling expenses, and come back with a relative to look after him. This all suited the host perfectly, and as luck would have it, he had an acquaintance who was an official courier on a commission to deliver some documents to the Hui-Ning area.[10] Traveling over land and water from station to station, he could make the trip quite quickly.

Lü took Ch'en's letter and gave it to the courier along with a little cash provided on his behalf, asking him to deliver it at his convenience. As the saying goes, "A lone traveler is free to choose his own pace. A courier on a mission hasn't a moment to lose." In a few days, he reached Hsin-an. After locating the house of Ch'en Ta-lang, the courier delivered the letter and flew off on his horse. How true that:

All because of a letter worth a pile of gold,
Another predestined marriage is brought into being.

Let us return to P'ing-shih, who opened the letter to find that it was in her husband's handwriting. It read:

Regards from Ch'en Shang to his worthy wife, P'ing-shih. After taking leave of you I ran into brigands at Hsiang-yang who robbed me of my capital and murdered my servant. I fell ill from shock and have been confined to bed in my old quarters at Mr. Lü's for two months now with no sign of improvement. Please ask a trusted relative to come see me right away, bringing along enough money for traveling expenses. Written from my bed in haste.

P'ing-shih read this with a mixture of credulity and disbelief, thinking to herself, "The last time he returned home, he had lost a thousand taels of his capital. In view of that pearl shirt business, it's certainly the result of some sort of improper dealings. Now here he is again with this story about being robbed, wanting more money for traveling expenses. I'm afraid it's all lies."

Then she reflected, "He wants some trusted relative to come right away to see him. His condition must really be serious. There's no way of knowing whether he's telling the truth or not. At any rate, who should I ask to go?" She turned it over in her

[10] Hui-chou and Ning-chou. Ning-chou is in northern Kiangsu.

mind, unable to allay her anxiety. Then after discussing the matter with her father, Mr. P'ing, she packed up her valuables and family possessions, taking the servant Ch'en Wang and his wife along with her. With her father as her companion, she hired a boat and set off toward Hsiang-yang to see her husband. When they arrived in Ching-k'ou,[11] the old man came down with a respiratory ailment and someone was found to escort him home.

Meanwhile, P'ing-shih, with the rest of her party in tow, continued on her way. After several days they arrived on the outskirts of Tsao-yang and through inquiry found the house of Ch'en's old landlord, Mr. Lü. As it turned out, Ch'en had passed away ten days previously. Mr. Lü had put out enough money to have him placed in a makeshift coffin. P'ing-shih burst into tears and fell over on the floor in a faint, not regaining consciousness for some time. She then hastily changed into mourning clothes and repeatedly begged Mr. Lü to let her open the coffin for a look and transfer the body to a better coffin. Mr. Lü adamantly refused. P'ing-shih had no other recourse but to buy some wood and have an outer casing made for the coffin. She also engaged Buddhist priests to say prayer services and burnt large quantities of paper money. Lü had already demanded twenty taels in cash to compensate him for his trouble, and let her fuss about as she liked while he remained silent.

After more than a month, P'ing-shih decided to choose an auspicious day to escort the coffin back home. Taking note of how young and attractive she was, Lü guessed she would not remain a widow for long and, furthermore, as she seemed quite well off, he began reflecting that here his son, Lü Erh, was still unmarried. Why not keep her here and arrange a match? After all, wouldn't it suit the purpose of both parties? Mr. Lü bought some wine and invited Ch'en Wang over for a drink. Asking Ch'en's wife to put the suggestion

[11] Modern Chen-chiang County in Kiangsu.

to P'ing-shih in a tactful way, he promised rich rewards. But Ch'en's wife was a complete simpleton. What did she know of tact? With no regard whatever for what was proper, she came straight out with it before her mistress. P'ing-shih was furious and gave her a sound scolding along with several slaps in the face. The landlord also received his share of the abuse. Angered though he was at this rebuff, Lü could not very well say anything. Truly:

Before the mutton dumplings reach your mouth,
You've already gotten the stench all over you.

Lü then began to incite Ch'en Wang into running away. Ch'en also saw no point in his staying around, and so he talked it over with his wife and made her his accomplice. With one on the inside and the other on the outside working in cooperation, they stripped P'ing-shih clean of all her money and jewelry, and then the pair of them absconded during the night.

Fully aware of what had happened, Lü turned his criticisms on P'ing-shih: "You should never have brought such scoundrels along with you. Luckily, they stole their own mistress's things. What a mess it would have been if it had been those of someone else!" Grumbling that the presence of the coffin was hurting his business, he told her to have it removed right away. Furthermore, remarking that since it was not good for a young widow to be staying there, he pressed her to leave. P'ing-shih had no counter to his arguments and was obliged to rent another place and have the coffin moved over and installed there. The bleakness of these circumstances can well be imagined.

Next door to her there lived a woman named Seventh Aunt Chang, who was as active as she was sociable. Hearing P'ing-shih sobbing, she often came over to comfort her. P'ing-shih often asked her to pawn a few articles of clothing to help meet expenses and was very grateful for her help.

Before a few months were out, all her clothes had been pawned. Since as a girl she had learned to sew quite well, she began to consider teaching needlework in a wealthy family to get by until she could decide what to do next. When she discussed this with Seventh Aunt Chang, the latter said, "It's not for me to say, of course, but a wealthy family is no place for a young woman like you. The dead are gone, but the living must keep on living. You've a long life ahead of you. Surely you don't want to spend the rest of your days as a seamstress? Besides, such people have a poor name and are looked down upon. And here's another thing: what are you going to do about this coffin? That, too, is quite a burden for you. To go on paying rent is no solution."

"All this has crossed my mind before, but I can think of no other way."

"Well, I have a plan, but you must not be offended when I tell you. Here you are, a lone widow, hundreds of *li* from home, without a penny to your name. You've no hope of ever moving the coffin back. Aside from the difficulty of making ends meet, it'll be hard enough just to maintain your widowhood. And even if you do hold out for a time, what good will that do? In my humble opinion, your best bet would be to put your youth and good looks to advantage, find a good mate for yourself, and then get married to him. With the money you get from betrothal gifts, you can buy a plot of land for your husband's burial, and you'll be well taken care of besides. That way, neither you nor your dead husband will have any regrets."

P'ing-shih found this all sensible, and after pondering the matter for a while, she sighed and said, "All right, then. No one can ridicule me for selling myself to bury my husband."

"If you've made up your mind, then I have a prospect already lined up for you. He's about your age, very nice looking and quite wealthy besides."

"If he's very wealthy, then I'm afraid he wouldn't want someone who's been married before."

"He himself is marrying for the second time. He even told me, 'It makes no difference whether this is her first or second marriage, as long as she's presentable.' Now, how could someone of your grace and charm fail to please him?"

As it turned out, Seventh Aunt had been commissioned by Chiang Hsing-ko to find him a wife. Since his previous wife was of such outstanding beauty, he wanted only to find someone equally pretty. Though P'ing-shih was not as attractive as San-ch'iao, she was more than her match in ability with her hands and with her mind.

The following day, Seventh Aunt entered the city and spoke with Chiang Hsing-ko about it. When he heard P'ing-shih was from the lower Yangtze region, Hsing-ko was especially pleased. In all of this, P'ing-shih was not asking for a cent in the way of bethrothal gifts. All she wanted was to buy a plot of good land for the burial of her husband.

After a few trips back and forth by Seventh Aunt Chang, the two parties agreed.

We won't become tedious here, but will tell instead how P'ing-shih attended to her husband's burial, and wailed loudly when the sacrifices were over. Eventually she resigned herself to setting up her husband's memorial tablet and put aside her clothes of mourning. Before the appointed day, Chiang sent over clothes and jewelry and had all her clothing redeemed from the pawn shop. On the wedding night, drums and flutes were loudly played, and the bridal chamber was lit with colorful candles. In fact:

Though from past experience the rites have grown familiar,
The warmth and depth of feeling is greater than before.

Chiang observed the dignity of the bride's manner and felt a deep respect for her. One day when he happened to come in from the outside, he found her in the midst of straightening out a trunk of clothing. Inside there was a pearl shirt. Recognizing it, Hsing-ko asked in astonishment, "Where did that shirt come from?"

"There's something strange behind this shirt," replied P'ing-shih, and she proceeded to tell him how her former husband had carried on about it and how they had quarreled and parted in bitterness. She then added, "Before when I was in need, I thought several times of pawning it, but since I didn't know its origin, I was worried lest it start a scandal, so I didn't dare let it be seen. To this day I myself have no idea where the thing came from."

"Was your former husband Ch'en Ta-lang, also known as Ch'en Shang? Fair-complexioned and beardless, with long fingernails on his left hand?"

"Yes, that's him all right," replied P'ing-shih.

Hsing-ko's tongue hung out in astonishment and, pressing his palms together, he raised his eyes to heaven and said, "From this becomes manifest the laws of Heaven. How truly fearful it is!"

P'ing-shih asked him what he meant, and he told her, "This pearl shirt was once an heirloom of my family. Your husband seduced my wife and received from her this shirt as a remembrance. I first knew about the affair when I met him in Soochow and saw the shirt. I returned home then and divorced her. Who could have foreseen that your husband would die away from home? When I remarried this time, I heard only that my new bride was the former wife of a Ch'en, a trader from Hui-chou. Who would have guessed this was none other than Ch'en Shang! Isn't this a case of retribution paid out in kind!"

When she heard all this, P'ing-shih felt her hair stand on end. From then on, their affection for each other deepened.

This, then, is the story of Chiang Hsing-ko's reencounter with the pearl shirt. As the verse goes:

Fully manifest are Heaven's laws, which must not be ignored.
In the exchange of wives, who benefited most from the trade?

Clearly, the debt has been returned with interest paid.
A marriage destined for a hundred years, suspended only for a time.

We will now go on to tell how, a year after Hsing-ko had found himself a wife, he set off again for Kwangtung to do his trading. Then fate came to intervene. One day he was at the pearl dealers' in Ho-p'u [12] and had just concluded a deal, whereupon the elderly dealer proceeded to pick out one particularly large pearl from the lot and take it for himself, refusing to give it up. Irked by this, Hsing-ko yanked at the old man's sleeve, trying to get at the pearl, but the force he exerted was more than he realized, and it knocked the man over. He fell to the ground and lay there still. Hsing-ko hurried to help him up, but found that he had already breathed his last.

The old man's family and neighbors rushed over in a swarm, yelling and screaming, and seized Hsing-ko. Without waiting for an explanation, they gave him a severe beating, then locked him up in an empty room. That same night an accusation was written out and at the break of day, when the county magistrate called the morning session of court, the accusation was presented together with the defendant. The magistrate accepted it for consideration, but because of other official business which had to be attended to that day, he gave orders that the accused be kept in custody to await judgment the following day.

Can you guess who this magistrate was? His name was Wu Chieh, and he was a *chin-shih* from the Nanking area—none other than the second husband of San-ch'iao. His original appointment had been to Ch'ao-yang; when his superiors saw how upright he was, they had him transferred to a post in the pearl-producing region of Ho-p'u.

That night Wu Chieh sat carefully examining the accepted cases beneath his lamp. San-ch'iao was there idly looking over his shoulder when her eye chanced to fall upon the charge of homicide

[12] Formerly a pearl-producing area in western Kwangtung.

brought by Sung Fu against one Lo Te, a trader from Tsao-yang. Who else could it be if not Chiang Hsing-ko! She felt a sudden painful twinge as she recalled their love in former days. Tearfully she began pleading with her husband, "This Lo Te is my elder brother. He was brought up by my mother's family, the Los. Somehow while on his travels he committed this grave offense. Please, for my sake, spare his life and let him return home."

"It'll have to depend on how the trial goes. If the charge of murder is proved valid, I'll be in no position to pardon him." Her eyes brimming with tears, San-ch'iao dropped to her knees and beseeched him piteously.

"Now, don't get upset. I have a way," he comforted her.

The next morning when court was in session, San-ch'iao again clutched at the magistrate's sleeve and said through tears, "If my brother cannot be saved, I, too, must end my life, and we'll never meet again."

As the magistrate took his seat on the bench, he called this case to be tried first. Sung Fu and Sung Shou appeared, crying and demanding vengeance for their father's death. They submitted, "Angered in a dispute over some pearls, the defendant at once beat him unconscious, whereupon he fell to the ground and died. Your Honor, we await your judgment."

The magistrate asked for the testimony of the witnesses. Some said he was knocked down, others that he fell when pushed.

"Their father stole one of my pearls," Chiang Hsing-ko argued. "Angered at this, I began to dispute with him. Because of his old age, he was not so sure on his feet. He fell down on his own and died. It had nothing to do with me."

"How old was your father?" the magistrate asked Sung Fu.

"Sixty-seven."

"The elderly are prone to faint," observed the magistrate. "It was not necessarily due to a beating."

Sung Fu and Sung Shou insisted that he had been killed by a blow.

"Whether an injury was sustained or not must be determined by examination. As you say he was beaten to death, have the corpse submitted to the morgue, and we will hear the results of the examination during the evening session of the court."

Now the fact was that the Sungs were a prominent, respected family, and the old man had been a district alderman. How could the sons ever allow an autopsy on their father in a morgue? Together they kowtowed and said, "Our father's death occurred in full view of everyone. We beseech you, Your Honor, to come and inspect the body at our home. We do not want a public examination."

"If there is no visible sign of injury to the bones, how can one expect the accused to admit his guilt? Without a postmortem report, how am I to report this case to the higher authorities?"

The two brothers merely persisted in their pleading. The magistrate became irritated with this and snapped, "As you won't allow an examination, I cannot very well proceed with the case either."

Greatly alarmed by this, the two brothers began rapidly kowtowing and said, "We await Your Honor's verdict."

"When a man is approaching seventy," began the magistrate, "death is to be expected. Now, supposing it turned out that he did not die from a blow and that an innocent man was wronged. Then it would only increase the guilt of the deceased. How could you, his sons, be at peace with yourselves, if after having seen your father reach such a venerable old age, you were to give him an ill name after his death? But if it is not true that he was beaten to death, it is true that he was pushed and fell. If Lo Te is not severely punished, then you will be left with no vent to your anger. I therefore sentence him to don hempen clothes of mourning and conduct the rites in the manner expected of a son. He is to bear all expenses for the funeral. Do you agree to this?"

"We don't dare to disobey Your Honor's verdict," the two brothers replied.

When Hsing-ko saw the magistrate had settled the case once and for all without resorting to punishment, he was overjoyed. At that, the defendant and plaintiff all kowtowed and expressed their gratitude.

The magistrate then declared, "I will not make a record of the trial. The defendant will be put under escort and when the matter is concluded will report back to me, at which time I shall cancel the complaint." Truly:

An easy matter it is to do wrong in court.
Accumulating hidden merit is likewise not difficult.
Just look what Magistrate Wu has this day achieved.
He righted a wrong and released the innocent, leaving both
      parties jubilant.

Meanwhile, from the time her husband went to court, San-ch'iao had felt as though she were sitting on a blanket of needles. As soon as she heard he had left the session, she went to meet him to learn the outcome.

The magistrate told her just how he had settled it. "For your sake," he said, "I didn't subject him to a single blow of the stick."

San-ch'iao thanked him over and over and then said, "My brother and I have been apart for a long time, and I'm anxious to see him again to ask news of our parents. If you could in some way arrange for us to meet, it would be a great kindness."

"That should be easy enough."

Dear audience, San-ch'iao, after all, had been divorced by Hsing-ko, bringing all feelings of love and obligation to an end. So, you will ask, how could there be so much emotional involvement? As husband and wife, they had, in fact, been deeply in love, and it was because of her wrongdoing that Hsing-ko could do nothing else but divorce her, unbearable as it had been for him even then. That was why on the eve of her remarriage, he had presented her with all sixteen trunks. Because of this, her heart had nearly melted. Now that she was in a position of wealth and honor, upon seeing him in trouble, how could she not come to his aid? This is what is known as returning kindness for kindness.

We now go on to tell how Chiang Hsing-ko carried out the magistrate's orders, scrupulously observing all the rites and not sparing himself any expense in the funeral. The Sung brothers could make no complaints. When the funeral services were over, he was escorted back to the tribunal to report. The magistrate called him in to his private chambers and offered him a chair. Then he said, "If it hadn't been for your sister's repeated entreaties, brother-in-law, I would have come close to treating you wrongly in this case."

Hsing-ko was bewildered by this and could make no reply. After a moment, when they had had their tea, the magistrate invited him into his study and asked his wife to come out to meet him. Wouldn't you say this fortuitous encounter was just like a scene from a dream? Neither of them bowed nor spoke, but they flew into each other's arms in a tight embrace, and burst into loud sobs. Wailing over a mother or father was never so heart-rending. Even the magistrate looking on found it more than he could bear and said, "Don't be so grieved. I can see you are not just brother and sister. Come on and tell me the truth. Perhaps there's something I can do."

They ceased their crying somewhat, but neither would speak. Finally unable to hold out against the magistrate's questioning, San-ch'iao knelt and told him, "I deserve ten thousand deaths for my sin. This man is my former husband."

Realizing that he could hide the truth no longer, Hsing-ko also knelt and told him everything from their love for each other to their divorce and the subsequent remarriage of each. When he had finished, they fell to weeping again and even Magistrate Wu felt the tears streaming down his cheeks. He then said, "As you love each other so much, how could I bear to tear you apart? Fortunately there has been no child born during these years, so you've my permission to be reunited at once."

They bowed their heads to the floor many times to express their thanks to the magistrate.

The magistrate quickly called a sedan chair and escorted San-ch'iao out of the tribunal. He then summoned some men to carry away the original sixteen chests that had accompanied her and bade Hsing-ko accept them. Finally he ordered a member of his staff to escort the couple to the border of his district. Such was the goodness of Magistrate Wu. Truly:

The pearls returned to Ho-p'u shine brightly once
*   again.* [13]
The swords reunited in Feng-ch'eng are twice as
*   wondrous as before.* [14]

[13] The pearl industry almost came to an end because of the insatiable greed of local magistrates. When Meng Ch'ang of the Eastern Han Dynasty became magistrate, he put an end to such exploitation and the pearls could be seen in the region again.

[14] Chang Hua (232–300) once asked Lei Huan to interprete the phenomenon of a purple aura in the sky. Lei took it to

The great virtue of Mr. Wu is something all admire.
Would such a man crave riches or be driven by desire?

This man, who had heretofore been without a son, was later made minister of personnel. In Peking, he took a concubine who gave him three sons in succession, each of whom passed the imperial examinations. All agreed this was his reward for his good deeds. But all this came later.

Let's go on and tell how Chiang Hsing-ko brought San-ch'iao home, where she met P'ing-shih. As the first in marriage, Wang-shih [San-ch'iao] took precedence. But whereas she had been divorced, P'ing-shih had become his wife through formal arrangement and ceremony. Besides, she was a year older. Thus, P'ing-shih was given the position of first wife and Wang-shih became second wife. They addressed each other as "sister," and from this time on, the husband and the two wives remained united. There is a verse which testifies to this:

A loving couple are joined for a lifetime.
But how shameful when the wife returns as a concubine.
Blessings and misfortunes come not without design.
Heaven above is the just official easiest to come by.

mean two precious swords buried somewhere in Feng-ch'eng. Having dug out the pair of swords, Lei gave one to Chang. After both of them died, the two swords changed into two dragons and reunited.

292

LOACH FAN'S DOUBLE MIRROR

From *Ching-shih t'ung-yen* [1]

TRANSLATED BY EARL WIEMAN

At the mansion on the west bank the curtain is raised,
And we sing a new tune in the doggerel fashion.
Only lost dreams of youth remain of the lusty life;
Stop the song—
And empty the cup while life still lingers.
Tomorrow we will board the boat again,
And tonight's revelry becomes only a memory.
We are both strangers in a far-off land;
Stop grieving–
The crescent moon casts its light on a vast land!

The last sentence of the *tz'u* poem is a borrowing from a Soochow folk song which, in full, runs as follows:

The crescent moon casts its light on a vast land!
How many families are rejoicing, and how many are torn by
* sorrow?*
How many married couples are lucky enough to be in the
* same bed?*
How many are separated and scattered to different places?

This song, which was composed during the Chien-yen reign period [1127–1131] [2] of the Southern Sung Dynasty, describes the distress of people separated by war. Misgovernment during the Hsüan-ho reign period [1119–1125] had allowed authority to fall into the hands of villains. This situation had lasted into the Ching-k'ang reign period [1126–1127] [3], when the Chin Tartars [the Jurchen] seized the capital, capturing the two emperors Hui-tsung [4] and Ch'in-tsung and carrying them off to the north. Prince K'ang crossed the [Yangtze] River on a clay horse and, abandoning Pien-ching, established his rule in only one part of the country and changed the reign title to Chien-yen.

The people on the roads at that time, fleeing the Eastern Capital in fear of the Tartar incursion, followed the emperor south. Pursued by the Tartar cavalry, the people were caught up in the fighting and fled in whatever direction they could. Who knows how many families were split up this way! Countless fathers and sons, husbands and wives, never saw one another again. But a few among them were separated and then reunited, and news of such happenings spread among the populace. As a poem puts it:

---

[1] The *Ching-pen t'ung-su hsiao-shuo* version of this story is titled "The Reunion of Feng Yü-mei [and her Husband]" ("Feng Yü-mei t'uan-yüan"), in which the surname of the heroine and her father in the feature story is changed from Lü to Feng.

[2] Chien-yen is the title of the first of the two reign periods of Emperor Kao-tsung of the Southern Sung period.

[3] Ching-k'ang is the title of the only reign period of Ch'in-tsung, the last emperor of Northern Sung.

[4] See "The Boot That Reveals the Culprit" in this volume for a story about Emperor Hui-tsung.

The swords were separated and brought together again;
Water drops from the lotus shatter and form anew.
All things transpire by the hand of fate,
And the smallest matter is ordained by Heaven.

The story is about a man of Ch'en-chou [5] named Hsü Hsin, who since childhood has been skilled in the martial arts. He took a wife of the Ts'ui family, a girl of some beauty, and their means were sufficient to support the two of them comfortably. But then the Chin army invaded and carried the two emperors off to the north. Hsü Hsin and his wife talked the matter over and decided that they were not safe where they were; so they packed what property they could carry in two bundles and, each carrying one of them, fled day and night with the rest of the masses.

When they reached Yü-ch'eng [6] they heard earthshaking cries behind them and assumed that the pursuing Tartars must be closing in, but actually it was the remnants of the routed Sung forces. Because of the steady erosion of discipline, the soldiers had lost their morale. When ordered to engage the rebels, to a man they would desert in fear without staying to fight. Whenever they came upon the common people, however, they would flaunt their prowess, robbing them of their property, and carrying off their sons and daughters. Skilled though he was in combat, Hsü Hsin was no match for the routed troops pouring in and so he fled for his life. Hearing only the sounds of wailing on all sides, he soon lost track of his wife Ts'ui-shih and, finding it impossible to search for her in the tumult, he could only press on ahead. After traveling for several days he sighed and gave up hope. There was nothing he could do.

Arriving at Sui-yang and feeling the pangs of hunger and thirst, Hsü entered a village inn and ordered some food and wine. In this time of such turmoil, the inn was not what it had once been. It had no wine; even the food, which was of the coarsest variety, was served only after it was paid for, out of fear that it would be snatched. As Hsü was counting out the money, he suddenly heard a woman weeping. Truly, as the saying goes, "Never mind what is not your proper business. If you do, you will be distracted." Hsü stopped counting the money and rushed out of the inn to see what was the matter. What he saw was a woman with disheveled hair sitting there on the open ground, wearing only a single garment. The woman was not his wife, yet she resembled her in both age and appearance. Hsü's compassion was aroused and judging her by his own experience, he said to himself, "This woman must have met with misfortune, too. I should go and ask her what has happened."

[To his inquiry], the woman answered, "I'm a daughter of the Wang family of Cheng-chou [7] and my name is Chin-nu. I became separated from my husband while fleeing from the fighting. Left alone, I was seized by stray soldiers. After walking for two days and a night we arrived here. My feet are so swollen that it's hard for me to move even an inch; so the blackguards stripped me of my clothing and abandoned me here. Since I have only this one garment and nothing to eat, and am away from all my kin, I see only death in store for me. That's why I'm crying here."

"I lost my wife in the commotion, too," Hsü said, "so we're truly in the same boat. Fortunately, I have some money for traveling expenses with me. You had best stay in this inn for a few days and rest yourself, and when I make inquiries about my wife I'll ask about your husband as well. What do you say?"

The woman held back her tears and said gratefully, "That would be fine."

Hsü opened his bundle and gave her some clothing to wear, and after they had something to eat in the inn, he rented half a room for their lodgings. He brought her food and tea dutifully

---

[5] In modern eastern Honan.
[6] In eastern Honan, close to the border with Shantung.

[7] In northern Honan, near K'ai-feng.

every day, and she was moved by his kindness. They realized how difficult an undertaking finding the husband and wife would be. Fate had caused them to meet—a woman without a husband and a man without a wife—and with two warm bodies thus thrown together, things were bound to run their natural course.

After a few more days, when her feet no longer hurt, they became husband and wife and set out again for Chien-k'ang. This was just after Emperor Kao-tsung [Prince K'ang] had crossed the river, ascended the throne, and changed the reign title to Chien-yen. Notices were posted for the recruitment of soldiers, so Hsü enlisted in the army as an officer and made his home in the Chien-k'ang City.

The days and months flew by, and before they knew it, it was the third year of the Chien-yen period [1129]. Late one day, as Hsü Hsin was returning with his wife from visiting relatives outside the city, she became thirsty, so he took her to a teahouse for some tea. A man sitting there saw the woman enter, and he stood to the side and watched her stealthfully without ever turning his eyes away. The woman kept her eyes lowered and paid no attention to him, but Hsü considered his behavior exceedingly strange.

After finishing their tea, they paid and left the teahouse. The man followed them at a distance, and after they got home he stood by their gate and would not leave.

Hsü's temper flared and he asked, "Who are you? Why are you spying on someone else's woman?"

The man addressed him apologetically with folded hands and said, "Don't be angry, sir. I have something to ask you."

Hsü Hsin, whose anger had not yet subsided, replied, "Then out with it!"

"If you won't get mad at me, sir," the man said, "let's step to the side, for I have something to tell you. Otherwise, I won't dare to speak."

Hsü went with the man to a secluded lane, but he seemed too embarrassed to say what was on his mind. "I consider myself a man of generosity," Hsü said. "If you've something to say, feel free to speak."

Only then did the man dare to ask, "Who was that woman just now?" he asked.

"She is my wife."

"And how long have you been married to her?"

"Three years."

"Isn't she Wang Chin-nu, from Cheng-chou?"

"How did you know that?" Hsü responded, much surprised.

"This woman is my wife," the man said. "We were separated in the war. I had no idea that she was with you."

Hsü felt extremely uncomfortable when he heard this. He recounted in detail how he had been separated from his own wife at Yü-ch'eng, and how going on to Sui-yang he had met this woman at the village inn. "At the time, it was truly because I took pity on her for being all alone with no one to turn to," he said. "I didn't know then that she was your wife. What are we supposed to do now?"

"Don't worry," the man replied. "I've already taken another wife myself, and my former marital ties need not be mentioned again. But we were torn apart so quickly that there was no time for even a word of farewell. If I could only see her for a moment and tell her of my sorrow and suffering, then I could die with no regrets."

Hsü was deeply touched by this story. "Real men must be forthright with one another," he said, "and there is nothing that we cannot talk over. I'll expect you at my house tomorrow. Since you have remarried, bring your new wife along and we can all be as kin; that way the neighbors won't take it amiss."

The man thanked him joyfully, and as they were about to part, Hsü asked him his name. "I'm Lieh Chün-ch'ing of Cheng-chou," he answered.

That night Hsü told his wife Chin-nu the details of his encounter. Remembering the affection between herself and her former husband, she secretly shed tears and lay awake the whole night. The following morning, just after they had finished washing, Lieh and his wife arrived. Hsü went out to receive them. When he and Lieh's wife saw each other, they were both taken aback and were moved to tears—for she was, in fact, none other than Hsü's former wife, Ts'ui-shih!

After they were separated in Yü-ch'eng, Ts'ui-shih had searched for Hsü, but her efforts proved to be in vain. So she had gone with an old woman to Chien-k'ang, where she pawned her hairpins and earrings and rented a place to live. After three months had passed, there was still no news of her husband. Seeing that Tsu'ui-shih could not go on that way, the old woman talked her into agreeing to marry Lieh Chün-ch'ing.

Who would have thought that the two couples would meet so unexpectedly this day? Truly it was a coincidence arranged by Heaven! They all embraced their former spouses and wept. Hsü and Lieh then performed the ceremony of eight kowtows and swore brotherhood with each other, and a banquet was set out. That evening they switched wives, each taking back his original partner. From that time forth there was unceasing friendship between the two families. There is a poem in evidence:

Husbands switch wives, wives switch husbands;
What a curious transaction this is!
Such meetings as this are the work of Heaven;
So they laugh in the lamplight as they reclaim their old spouses.

This story, entitled "Interchanging the Marital Bonds," is a tale of the Chien-k'ang City in the third year of the Chien-yen period. There is another story of the same period called "The Double Mirror Rejoined." Though not based on so remarkable a coincidence, when it comes to being considered as a moral exemplum of "righteous husbands and virtuous wives," it is far superior to the above story. In truth:

To spread afar, tales must have popular appeal;
And to move listeners, words must relate to moral conduct.

The story goes that during the fourth year of the Chien-yen period of the Southern Sung, an official from Kuan-hsi named Lü Chung-yi was appointed tax commissioner of Foochow. At that time the Min region[8] was still at the height of its prosperity, and Lü brought his family along as he went to take up his office. For in the first place Foochow, backed by mountains and overlooking the sea, was a leading metropolis of the southeast; and in the second place, the turmoils of the central plains could be avoided there. In the spring of the year after Lü set out, his journey took him through Chien-chou.[9] Of this city the *Yü-ti chih* (Geographical Gazetteer) says: "Chien-chou, with its green streams and vermilion mountains, has some of the finest scenery in eastern Min." But an ancient saying applies well here:

During the third month, flowers in Lo-yang are brilliant as
*   brocade;*
Alas! I missed the springtime when I came.

From ancient times, the words "war" and "famine" have gone together. The Tartar forces crossed the [Yangtze] River and laid waste to the Liang-Che area.[10] Min's fate was such that although the war did not reach there, the region encountered a year of famine. Stories of the famine in Chien-chou tell how a peck of rice sold for a thousand in cash, and the people had no means of subsistence. And since the central government was carrying on a military campaign and provisions for the troops took precedence over everything else, the local government was too busy collecting the levies for higher authorities to pay any attention to the destitution and suffering of the people.

As the saying goes, "Even the cleverest wife cannot cook gruel without rice." Since the people

---

[8] Approximates modern Fukien Province.
[9] Modern Chien-ou County in Fukien.
[10] Liang-Che was the collective name for the Che-tung Circuit and the Che-hsi Circuit in Sung times. Together they covered the present Chekiang Province plus the area to the east of Chen-chiang County and south of the Yangtze River in Kiangsu Province.

were being goaded and harrassed by the local government although they had no more money or grain to give, they finally could endure it no longer and escaped into the mountains, there to gather into bands of robbers. "A snake cannot move without a head," as the saying goes, and consequently a "local emperor" emerged. This man was Fan Ju-wei, who spoke of justice and came to save the people from their plight.[11] The robbers streamed to him in droves, assembling at his call until they numbered over a hundred thousand strong. What they did was nothing other than:

Setting fires when the wind was high,
And killing when the moon was dark;
They hungered together when food was scarce,
And shared alike when there was meat.

The government troops were unable to resist them and suffered several defeats in succession. Fan then occupied Chien-chou and, proclaiming himself field marshal, sent his troops to plunder in all directions. All the men of the Fan clan were given false titles and were made officers over the soldiers. Among Fan's relatives was a twenty-three-year-old nephew named Fan Hsi-chou. From childhood he had been well acquainted with the nature of water and could stay beneath its surface for several days and nights. Because of this talent he had been given the nickname of "Loach" Fan. He was actually a scholar but had not yet passed any imperial examinations. Under pressure from Fan Ju-wei—members of the Fan clan who would not follow him in rebellion were beheaded as a lesson to the public—Hsi-chou, in order to preserve his life, had no choice but to join him. Although he lived among the rebels, however, he took it upon himself to help people whenever he could, and he took no part in the plunder and intrigue. Seeing how timid he was in everything, the rebels derided him by changing

his nickname to "Blind Loach," thus making fun of his uselessness.

Let us return to Lü Chung-yi. He had a daughter whose pet name was Shun-ko, just sixteen years of age. A girl of lovely appearance and gentle demeanor, she was traveling with her mother and father to his post in Foochow. As they approached Chien-chou a party of the rebel Fan's soldiers happened upon them; their luggage and valuables were seized, and they themselves were scattered to the four winds. Lü became separated from his daughter, and being unable to find her, he sighed with grief for a time and finally had to go on to take up his appointment.

But we will only tell how Shun-ko, unsteady on her tiny feet, could not run and was captured by the rebels. She wept bitterly as they were taking her to Chien-chou. Fan Hsi-chou, seeing her on the road, took pity on her. He asked about her family and Shun-ko told him that she was the daughter of an official, whereupon Hsi-chou drove the soldiers away and untied her hands. Taking her to his home, he comforted her with kind words, telling her his most intimate feelings: "I'm not really a rebel," he said. "I was forced into it by my kinsmen. Some day, when we are pardoned by the government, I'll be a loyal citizen again. If you do not despise my lowly station and consent to be my wife, that would be the best thing that could happen to me in three incarnations." Shun-ko did not really want to go along, but as she had fallen into his hands and had no recourse, she could only agree.

The next day Hsi-chou reported the matter to the rebel chief Fan Ju-wei, who was delighted. Hsi-chou then took the girl to his official residence and chose an auspicious day for the presentation of betrothal gifts. He had an heirloom mirror—two mirrors, actually, joined together into one. This clear, bright mirror reflected a distinct image and could be opened and closed. On the inside of the mirror two words were cast, meaning the male and female mandarin duck, respectively, and so it was called the "mandarin

---

[11] The uprising of Fan Ju-wei described in this story is largely historically true.

297

duck mirror." Hsi-chou gave the girl this mirror as his betrothal gift. All the members of the Fan clan were invited, and the couple was properly united in matrimony.

One the descendant of a gentry family,
The other a jewel of a prominent clan;
One with the manner of a refined scholar,
The other with a character warm and tender;
One who, though among bandits, had not lost his lofty bearing,
The other who though a captive, had not altered her elegant
    air—
Outlaws toasted them as bride and groom that day,
And the fair maiden was matched with a good husband that
    night.

After that the couple lived in harmony as husband and wife, treating each other as respectfully as guests.

From ancient times it had been said: "A pot that stays at the well will surely end up in pieces." Fan Ju-wei was able to commit his great transgression only by taking advantage of the central court's occupation elsewhere, so that its military forces could not touch him. But he did not take into account the famous generals Chang Chün [styled Te-yüan], Yüeh Fei, Chang Chün [styled Po-ying], Chang Jung, Wu Chieh, Wu Lin,[12] and the others, who inflicted repeated defeats on the Chin army and began to stabilize the country. Emperor Kao-tsung then established his capital at Lin-an and changed the reign title to Shao-hsing [1131–1162]. In the winter of that year the emperor ordered Prince Han of Ch'i, whose personal name was Shih-chung,[13] to lead a great army of a hundred thousand soldiers against the rebels.

[12] With the exception of Chang Jung, all these were famous military figures during the interregnum between the Northern Sung and the Southern Sung. But the roles they played could not be so sweepingly summed up as they are in the text. Chang Chün (styled Po-ying) was actually the right-hand man of Ch'in Kuai (1090–1155), who betrayed the country's interests to negotiate a peace treaty with the Jurchen.

[13] The Southern Sung general Han Shih-chung also appears in "Artisan Ts'ui and His Ghost Wife," included in this anthology, under the title of the prince of Hsien-an. The title used in this story (Prince Han of Ch'i) was given to him posthumously.

Being no match for Prince Han, Fan Ju-wei could do nothing but close the city gates and defend himself. Prince Han thereupon built an encirclement and laid siege to the city.

Prince Han and Lü Chung-yi were old friends from their days in the Eastern Capital. Now with Han leading the army against the rebels, he knew that Lü, being the tax commissioner posted at Foochow, would be familiar with the customs and sentiments of the people of the Min area. In those days military commanders usually carried blank letters of imperial appointment when on expeditions and could give commissions to local talent on their own authority. Han accordingly appointed Lü deputy commander in his army, and the two of them stayed together outside the city of Chienchou to direct the siege.

Within the city there was weeping and wailing day and night. Fan Ju-wei made several attempts to break out through the city gates but was beaten back each time by the government troops, until the situation became desperate for him. Shun-ko said to her husband, "I've heard that 'A loyal minister does not serve a second sovereign, and a chaste woman does not serve a second husband.' When I was captured by the rebels I swore to die; but you rescued me and made me your wife, and I became yours. Now the government army is outside the gates and the city will surely fall. Once the city is taken, as a member of the rebel leader's clan, you will certainly not be spared. I want to die before you do, for I could not bear to see you executed." She drew out the sword at the head of the bed and made to cut her throat with it.

Hsi-chou hastily put his arms around her and, taking away the sword, comforted her: "I did not join the rebels by my own design. I know that there is no way to vindicate myself, and I've committed myself to my fate, for the destruction here will be total and no one will be spared. But you are the daughter of an official and are a captive here; you have nothing at all to do with the rebels. Furthermore, the officers and men under Field

Marshal Han are all northerners just as you are, and you speak the same dialect as they do. For this reason, they certainly will have sympathy for you. And you might meet a relative or friend who will pass a message on to your father so that you can be reunited with him. Your situation is by no means hopeless. Life is so precious; how can you seek a needless death?"

"Should I survive to live another day," Shun-ko said, "I swear never to remarry. I fear only that I might be captured by some officer, and I would rather die by the sword than lose my chastity."

"With your vow of determination and moral fortitude, I will be able to die content. If by some chance I should escape like a fish from the net and go on living, I, too, swear not to take another wife, thus to reciprocate your devotion."

"Let each of us take one side of the mandarin duck mirror that you gave me as a betrothal gift and keep it securely on our person. Some day, when the mirror is put together again, then we, too, will be reunited as husband and wife," Shun-ko continued. After this, they wept together.

This conversation took place in winter, in the twelfth month of the first year of the Shao-hsing reign [1131]. In the spring, during the first month of the second year of Shao-hsing, Prince Han broke through the walls of Chien-chou and Fan Ju-wei burned himself to death in desperation. Han then raised the yellow imperial flag and proclaimed amnesty for the surviving outlaws; members of the Fan clan alone were not pardoned. Half of the clan members were killed in the fighting and the rest were captured by the government troops and sent to Lin-an as prisoners. Seeing how desperate the situation was, Shun-ko felt certain that Hsi-chou would not have a chance to escape. In a panic she ran into a deserted house, removed her kerchief, and hanged herself with it. Truly:

Better to seek an early but chaste death
Than to live a full life as a shamed woman.

But her alloted span of life was not yet complete. Just then Deputy Commader Lü led some soldiers by and saw that a woman was hanging herself in the deserted house, so he ordered an officer to have her taken down at once. He approached to get a better look—and saw that it was his own daughter, Shun-ko! She soon regained consciousness, but it was a long time before she recovered her voice. A simultaneous outpouring of joy and grief accompanied this reunion of father and daughter. Shun-ko told him how she had been captured by the rebel soldiers and then saved by Fan Hsi-chou, whose wife she became. Lü listened to her story and was silent.

The story is told how, after pacifying Chien-chou and restoring peace to its people, Field Marshal Han and Deputy Commander Lü went back to Lin-an together to personally report their victory to the emperor. How the Son of Heaven rewarded them for their services need not be described here.

One day Lü spoke with his wife about their daughter being young and without a mate, and how something should be done about it. Together they went to her and urged her to remarry. But Shun-ko told them of the vows she and her husband had exchanged and was adamant in her refusal.

"You're the daughter of a good family," the father said, "and you married that rebel because at the time you had no choice. Now by Heaven's favor he has died and you have been set free, so why must you still think of him?"

Tears filled her eyes as Shun-ko replied, "My husband was a scholar and a gentleman. He was forced by his clansmen to join the rebels. Although he was with the rebels, he helped people whenever he could and never did anything against the law of Heaven. If Heaven is not blind, he'll surely have escaped from the tiger's jaws and, like duckweeds adrift on the sea, we might meet again some day. Until that time I want to lead a religious life and stay at home serving the

THE REUNITED COUPLE

two of you. Even if I live in widowhood for the rest of my life, I won't have any regrets. But if you must have me remarry, it'd be better if you let me kill myself now and remain a chaste woman." Her father saw the rationality of her argument and pressed her no more.

Time flew by like an arrow and before they knew it, it was the twelfth year of the Shao-hsing reign [1142]. By then Lü Chung-yi had risen repeatedly in rank to become regional commander-in-chief, leading the troops garrisoned at Feng-chou.[14]

One day the commandant at Canton sent Commander Ho Ch'eng-hsin to deliver an official dispatch to the regional high command at Feng-chou. Lü invited Ho into his hall and quizzed him about local conditions in Canton, talking with him at length before letting him depart.

Shun-ko watched them secretly from behind the curtain in the inner hall and, when her father went back into the residential quarters, she asked, "Who was the man who brought the dispatch just now?"

"A commander from Canton, Ho Ch'eng-hsin."

"How strange! In the way he speaks and walks, he looks just like my husband Fan Hsi-chou of Chien-chou."

"None of the Fan family were spared when Chien-chou was captured," her father said, laughing. "Some may have died unjustly, but they have all died, nevertheless. Furthermore, this officer from Canton is named Ho, and he serves by official appointment. There is nothing at all to connect him with your husband. You're just dreaming; how the maids will laugh if they find out about this!"

Thus chastened by her father, Shun-ko flushed with shame and she dared say no more. Truly:

The deep affection she held for her husband
Created discord between father and daughter.

Half a year later, Ho Ch'eng-hsin brought another military dispatch to Lü's headquarters.

[14] Modern Feng-ch'uan County of Kwangtung.

Again Shun-ko watched in secret from behind the curtain, and her mind was again filled with suspicions. "Since I've led a religious life and am done with the affairs of the world," she said to her father, "I'm no longer susceptible to feelings of love anymore. But I've watched this Ho from Canton carefully, and he's the very image of my husband. Why don't you invite him into the inner hall and offer him something to eat and drink, and question him closely? My husband has a nickname 'Loach,' and that year in the besieged city, when it was clear that it would fall, we each took one side of a mandarin duck mirror as a keepsake. If you call him by his nickname and test him with the mirror, you'll surely find out the truth about him." Her father agreed to go along with her request.

When Ho came to the headquarters the next day to get the return dispatch, Lü invited him into the inner hall for some food and drink. While they were drinking, Lü asked him about his family and his place of birth. Ho was evasive and seemed ill at ease.

"Aren't you nicknamed 'Loach'?" Lü asked. "I know everything already, so you might as well speak up."

Ho asked Lü to dismiss his attendants and then he knelt hastily, saying, "I deserve to die."

Lü helped him to his feet and said, "You needn't act this way."

Only then did Ho dare to bare the truth. "I'm from Chien-chou and my real family name is Fan," he said. "In the fourth year of the Chien-yen reign [1130] my clansman Fan Ju-wei stirred up the starving masses, took the city as his base, and revolted. I joined the rebels simply because I had no choice. When the imperial forces came to suppress the rebellion, all of the rebel leader's clan were executed; but since I had always made a habit of helping people, there were people who protected me. Afterward I changed my name to Ho Ch'eng-hsin and took advantage of the amnesty to enlist in the army. In the fifth year of the Shao-hsing reign, I was assigned to the troops under the junior guardian of the heir apparent, Yüeh Fei, and went with him on his expedition against the rebel Yang Yao [15] at the Tung-t'ing Lake. Being all from the northwest, Yüeh's troops were not used to fighting on water, whereas I'm a southerner and have been familiar with water from childhood. I can stay underwater for three days and nights at a time. That's why I'm called Loach Fan. Junior Guardian Yüeh, therefore, personally chose me to be in his vanguard and to lead the troops into each battle. Finally, the rebel Yang Yao was crushed. Because of my service, Junior Guardian Yüeh recommended me for a military appointment and, after several promotions, I'm now a commander at Canton. During these past ten years I've told this story to no one. Now that you've asked, I dare not conceal it from you."

"What is the name of your wife?" Lü asked. "Is she your first wife or your second?"

"While I was with the rebels, I happened to run into the daughter of an official on the road and took her as my wife. The following year the city was captured and we were separated in our flight. But we vowed that if we survived, I'd not take another wife and she'd not marry another husband. Later on I went to Hsin-chou and found my aged mother again. To this day my mother and I live together, keeping only a maidservant to do our cooking. I haven't remarried."

"When you and your wife made your vows, what did you use as a keepsake?"

"We had a mandarin duck mirror which could be put together into one or taken apart; each of us kept one side of it."

"Do you still have this mirror?"

"I keep it with me morning and night. I can't bear to part with it for even an instant."

"Let me see it."

Ho loosened his coat and from his girdle untied an embroidered pouch in which the mirror was kept. Lü took the mirror and examined it; then from his sleeve he took another mirror which he put together with it. When Ho saw that the two mirrors matched perfectly, he burst into tears. Lü was so touched by this show of emotion that he, too, could not restrain the tears as he said, "The girl you married is my daughter, and she's here in the quarters right now."

Thereupon he took Ho into the parlor to be reunited with his daughter, and they both wept profusely. Lü consoled them and ordered a banquet in celebration, and that night he kept Ho back to sleep in his residence.

A few days later Lü was ready to send his return dispatch. His son-in-law therefore set out on the return trip with his wife. Lü told his daughter to go with Ho and live with him at his post in Canton. When Ho's period of appointment was up the following year and he was going to Lin-an, he and his wife stopped at Feng-chou again to take leave of her father. Lü prepared a costly dowry for her and dispatched officers to escort them to Lin-an.

Figuring that what had happened to him was far enough in the past to have been forgotten and feeling that he could not allow the Fan family to have no descendants, Ho submitted a petition through official channels to the Board of Rites requesting that his surname—but not his given name—be restored. This meant that his original given name was changed while his original surname remained the same, so that he became known as Fan Ch'eng-hsin. Later on, successive promotions elevated him to viceroy of the Huai region,[16] and he and his wife grew old together. It is said that the double mandarin duck mirror was passed down by their descendants from generation to generation as a treasured heirloom.

---

[15] The rebellion of Yang Yao (?–1135) was a continuation of the earlier uprising of Chung Hsiang (?–1130). As described in the story, Yang Yao's rebellion was suppressed by the general Yüeh Fei (1130–1141).

[16] This is apparently a geographical misplacement. In Sung times the administrative chiefs of the three subsidiary capitals (Western Capital, Northern Capital, and Southern Capital) were viceroys. The Huai region was not the site of any of these capitals and was, for that matter, too close to the territory occupied by the Jurchen.

THE REUNITED COUPLE

When people of later times talked about how Loach Fan remained unsullied by the rebels while in their camp and how his fondness for helping people resulted in many lives being saved, they said that he was able to escape the jaws of death and be reunited with his wife as a reward for his good deeds and his accumulated virtue. A poem lends proof to the story:

Apart for ten years like . ds on the horizons,
The ducks are united again in the rejoined mirror;
Never say they met by chance like duckweeds on the sea—
It was in truth Heaven's reward for their secret virtue.

THE *FEMME FATALE*

The beautiful but morally questionable woman regarded as a source of trouble is a theme as old as literature itself. She is not only dangerous to others but also destructive to herself. No one having an amorous association with her is likely to emerge intact. A woman of this type can be as talented and beautiful as she is jealous and venomous. The woman who combines all these qualities in this anthology is the poetess Yü Hsüan-chi. Indeed jealousy typifies much of the relationship between a *femme fatale* and the man in her life. When such conflicts occur, even two sisters ("Empress Chao Fei-yen") cannot coexist in peace. Sex is always involved. To the *femme fatale*, sex is an instrument for power, enabling her to dominate and control the man in her life. Along with jealousy comes greed, which is another characteristic of the *femme fatale*. In this respect, the avarice of Judge Wei's wife (in "The Henpecked Judge Who Loses a Governorship") is just as destructive to her husband's career as the unquenchable sexual drive of the consort Chao-yi (in "Empress Chao Fei-yen"), who literally drains the emperor of his life.

The man in the *femme fatale*'s life is generally a weak but lecherous man. Indeed, it is due to the weakness of his character that Wu Shan (in "Han Wu-niang Sells Her Charms at the New Bridge Market") almost loses his life, and the failure of Judge Wei as a judge is attributable to his failure as a spineless man.

THE POETESS YÜ HSÜAN-CHI

From *San-shui hsiao-tu*

TRANSLATED BY JEANNE KELLY

At the Universal Temple in the Western Capital there lived a nun, Yü Hsüan-chi, styled Yu-wei. She was a courtesan in Ch'ang-an, and her beauty was such as could overthrow a realm, while she was all the more admirable because of her literary accomplishments. She liked to read and write and was especially given to the art of poetry. At the age of sixteen, she decided to dedicate herself to the Taoist teachings.

At the beginning of the Hsien-t'ung reign period [860–875], she became a nun at the Universal Temple. Meanwhile, her beautiful lines describing the delights of amour spread widely among the literati. However, she was by nature as frail as the orchid, and she could not keep herself under control. She would receive the flirtations of the young gallants and spend her time with them. Thus, the romantic young men would compete with one another to adorn themselves and try to win her favor. Some would visit her bringing along wine, and she would always sing verses to the accompaniment of the lute. From time to time on such occasions banter was unrestrained. The less sophisticated ones felt humble before her. Her poetry had lines such as:

Over the scenic farm paths a distant view of spring;
Under the bright moon, autumn thoughts abound.

And:

Too deeply in love to speak;
Red tears flow in pairs.

And:

With burning incense I mount the jade altar;
Holding the tablet solemnly, I perform the rituals toward the
*   gate of the palace.*

And:

Such passion and melancholy all come from dreams.
The divine face and everlasting fragrance surpass the flowers.

These couplets were unrivaled.

She had a maidservant named Lü-ch'iao who was as clever as she was attractive. One day Hsüan-chi was unexpectedly invited to a neighboring temple. She reminded Lü-ch'iao as she was about to go, "Don't go out. If an old patron should come, just tell him where I am."

Hsüan-chi was detained by her companion and did not return to the temple until the evening. Lü-ch'iao met her at the door and said, "A little while ago a guest came. When he learned that you were not in, he went on without dismounting."

It happened that the guest in question was an old patron of Hsüan-chi's, and she suspected that Lü-ch'iao had betrayed her. That night she hung out the lanterns and bolted the doors. Then she ordered Lü-ch'iao to her bedroom, where she questioned her. The maid replied, "I have waited on you for many years now and have always conducted myself properly. I would never allow such a thing to happen and thus incur your displeasure. When the patron came and knocked at the door, I told him through the door that you were not in. Without a word, he rode away. As for romantic sentiments, it has been years since I had such feelings. I pray that you will not suspect me." Hsüan-chi became even more incensed. She stripped Lü-ch'iao naked and gave her a hundred lashes, but the latter still denied everything. Finally, on the point of collapse, Lü-ch'iao asked if she could have a cup of water. Pouring it on the ground in libation, she said, "You seek the way of the Taoist triad[1] and of immortality, yet cannot forget the pleasures of the flesh. Instead you become suspicious and falsely accuse the chaste and the righteous. I will certainly die by your evil hands. If there is no Heaven, then I have no recourse. If there is, who can suppress my fervent soul? I vow never to sink dully into the darkness and allow your lascivious ways to go on." Having spoken her mind, she expired on the floor. Frightened, Hsüan-chi dug a pit in the backyard and buried her, assuring herself that no one would know of it.

The time was the first month of spring of the *wu-tzu* year of the Hsien-t'ung reign [868].[2]

---

[1] The Taoist triad stands for the three supreme deities in the profuse Taoist pantheon.

[2] The *wu-tzu* year of the Hsien-t'ung reign period was the ninth year of that reign. *Wu-tzu* marks the sequential order of the year in the lunar calendar cycle. Each cycle covers sixty years.

Whenever someone asked about Lü-ch'iao, Hsüan-chi would reply, "She ran away after the spring rains had ceased."

A guest once dining in Hsüan-chi's room happened to go urinate in the backyard on the spot of the burial. There he saw a swarm of black flies clustered over the earth. Though he chased them off, they came back. Taking a closer look, he saw what seemed to be traces of blood. Besides, there was a stench. The guest left presently and confided this to his servant, who went home and told his brother. His brother, a watchman, had once asked Hsüan-chi for money and she had rejected him, so he had harbored a grudge against her. On hearing of this, he hurried to the temple gate to spy. He noticed people about conversing casually, but was surprised not to see Lü-ch'iao around. He called the other watchmen and, carrying shovels, they forced their way into Hsüan-chi's yard and uncovered the body. Lü-ch'iao looked just as she did when alive. The watchmen then reported Hsüan-chi to the city authorities of the capital area. An official questioned her and she wrote a confession.

In court circles there were many who spoke in her behalf. The city authorities reported the case to the emperor. In autumn, nonetheless, she was executed. While in prison she still wrote poetry:

It is easier to obtain a priceless treasure
Than it is to find a lover who is true.

[And:]

The bright moon shines into the dim corner;
The crisp breeze opens the short lapel.

These were among her beautiful lines.

EMPRESS CHAO FEI-YEN

From *Ch'ing-so kao-i*

TRANSLATED BY RACHEL L. LIANG AND THE EDITORS

In my native place, there was a young man named Li who came from a family with generations of Confucian scholars. In recent years his family had become poorer. Once while I was visiting him I saw in the corner of his room a broken bamboo basket containing several old books. Among them was "The Story of Empress Chao Fei-yen." Even though some of the pages were mixed up and some missing, it was still readable. I obtained Li's permission to take the book home and, after some editorial work, I had a complete story ready for circulation.

Empress Chao had an exceedingly slender waist and her gait was so light that her graceful carriage, which was beyond imitation, was compared to the single stem of flower dangling in the grasp of a human hand. While in the household of a princess,[1] she was given the name Fei-yen, "Flying Swallow." After she was summoned to the palace, she managed to have her sister admitted as well.[2] Her sister won the favor of the emperor[3] and was given the title Chao-yi, "Chief Consort." Chao-yi was endowed with good humor and blessed with a delicate frame and smooth skin. The Chao sisters were both reigning beauties, surpassing all the girls in the place.

Ever since Chao-yi had entered the palace, the emperor seldom visited the Eastern Palace.[4] At that time Chao-yi resided in the Western Palace and the queen mother occupied the Central Palace.

Empress Chao was hoping to have a son so she could be assured of her position and secure the emperor's perpetual favor. To achieve this, she often had secret affairs with young men smuggled in inside a cart loaded with calves. One day, the emperor, accompanied only by a few attendants, came to visit the Eastern Palace. Empress Chao was making love to a young man at that moment. After the attendants hastily announced the emperor's arrival, the startled empress hurried out to greet him. Seeing her head gear askew, her hair tousled, and her speech rambling, the emperor became quite suspicious. After a while, he heard coughing coming from behind the drapes, so he left the palace. After that time, he nursed the intention of having the empress killed, but suppressed it for the sake of Chao-yi.

One day, while drinking in the company of

[1] Princess Yang-an, a sister of the emperor.
[2] The given name of her sister was Ho-te.
[3] Emperor Ch'eng of the Western Han Dynasty [r. 32–7 B.C.].

[4] The residence of the empress in traditional China was generally know as the Eastern Palace.

Chao-yi, the emperor suddenly rolled up his sleeves and stared fiercely at her. Seeing his steaming anger, Chao-yi immediately left her seat and kneeled before him, saying, "I came from a lowly family, without anyone especially dear to me. Ever since I came to the palace and was placed under your service, Your Majesty has given me undivided attention and placed me above all others. This apparently invited others' jealousy. Besides, my ignorance must have been a source of your irritation. I beg for an immediate death if it would somewhat alleviate your anger." With these words, her tears flowed.

The emperor held her up by the arm and said, "Please sit down and listen to me. You are not guilty," he continued. "It is your sister whose head I wish to chop off, whose hands and limbs I wish to sever and throw in the dung heap; only so would I feel happy."

"What has my sister done to deserve such severe punishment?" inquired Chao-yi.

After the emperor related to her the incident, Chao-yi pleaded with him. "It is because of the empress that I had the chance to come here. How can I live if she has to die? Your Majesty will certainly invite rumors if the empress is killed for no reason. I would rather die in her place, however brutal the torture." Then she burst into tears and threw herself onto the floor.

The startled emperor helped her up immediately and appeased her: "Because of you, I'm not going to persecute the empress. I just mention it for your information. There is no need to blame yourself so harshly." Quite a while later, Chao-yi returned to her seat.

The emperor ordered a secret investigation to find out who the man behind the drapes was. When it was learned that he was the son of a palace guard, Ch'en Ch'ung, the emperor sent someone to kill him at his residence and dismissed the father.

Chao-yi went to pay the empress a visit, told her all she had learned, and said, "Sister, don't you remember our days of poverty when we had nothing to depend upon? You sent me to weave straw shoes with the girl next door and sell them to get rice. One day I came home with the rice, but we couldn't cook because the stormy weather left no wood to start a fire. We were so hungry and cold that we couldn't sleep. You told me to hold tight to your back to keep warm and we wept together. Don't you remember that? Now we're lucky to have all this luxury, second to none, and yet you are destroying yourself. If another incident happens to provoke His Majesty's anger, there will be no way to save you. You will be beheaded and become the laughingstock of the whole world. I can save you today, but life itself is so unpredictable. If I die first, whom can you depend upon?" She wept and wept, and so did the empress.

After the incident, the emperor never visited the Eastern Palace again and his love was with Chao-yi alone. Once when Chao-yi was taking a bath, the emperor peeked at her. The palace maid informed her of his presence, and she hurried to hide herself away from the candlelight. Seeing this, the emperor became even more infatuated. Later, Chao-yi was taking a bath again and the emperor secretly bribed the maids not to warn her. He peeked through the screen and saw Chao-yi sitting in a tub filled with fragrant water, reminding him of a piece of white jade immersed in a stream of deep chilled water. He was so aroused that he was beyond himself. He said to a nearby attendant, "No emperor ever has two empresses. If there were such a precedent, I would make Chao-yi my empress as well."

When Empress Chao learned that the emperor's affection for Chao-yi had deepened after seeing her in the bath, she also prepared her own bath and invited the emperor over. When he arrived, she went to take her bath, stripping herself nude and playfully sprinkling water on him. The more she tried to become intimate with him, the more unhappy he became. Finally he left before she finished the show. In tears, she said, "His affection is for one person only. There's nothing I can do."

On Empress Chao's birthday, Chao-yi went to the celebration, as did the emperor. In the midst of the feast, the empress decided to take advantage of the situation, and so she dropped a few tears. The emperor asked her, "Wine usually gives us some happy moments, yet you alone appear to be so sad. Is there anything you're not happy with?"

"In the days when I was serving the princess, Your Majesty came to visit the palace. I was standing behind the princess, and Your Majesty's eyes often lingered on me. The princess knew your wish and sent me to your service. I was lucky to have earned your affection. Once I made Your Majesty's clothes dirty; when I tried to wash them, you wanted to keep them as a remembrance. A few days later, with your teeth marks still fresh on my neck, I was made the empress. I'm crying because the memory of those days comes to my mind." The emperor, greatly touched at the reminiscence of the old days, looked at her and sighed deeply. At this point, Chao-yi excused herself, knowing that the emperor wanted to stay. Indeed, he stayed until dusk.

The empress, taking advantage of the opportunity, devised a scheme. After three months, she announced her pregnancy in a memorandum:

After serving for some time in the palace, I was blessed with the love of Your Majesty and was made the empress. This has been so for quite a few years. Recently on the occasion of my birthday, Your Majesty was so kind as to send me your blessing and to make a special visit to the Eastern Palace. I had the honor of your presence at the banquet and once again Your Majesty bestowed your love upon me. These few months I have felt the fullness of my body, my period has stopped, and I enjoy a delightful craving for all kinds of delicacies. Knowing that the future emperor is within me, I feel as if I am carrying the sun. As the sign of a rainbow crossing the sun stands for a good omen, the resting of a dragon in my bosom means a blissful prosperity. At the day of earnest expectation, I will give birth to the divine heir and will present him to Your Majesty at the court. With the sincerest congratulations, this is a special memorandum for the announcement of this joyful event.

At that moment, the emperor was at the Western Palace. Overjoyed at the news, he replied:

We are greatly pleased at your announcement. The relationship between husband and wife is an inseparable one. The heir to my throne is of great importance to the country. Please take good care of yourself in your early pregnancy. Avoid any strong medicine and give yourself all the necessary nourishment. If you have any requests in the future, do not bother to send them in writing. An oral message through the attendants would suffice.

Both the queen mother and Chao-yi sent messengers to offer their best wishes.

Fearing that the emperor might come and discover the lie, Empress Chao planned a cover-up with the help of the eunuch Wang Sheng. He advised her to announce: "A pregnant woman should not go near a man, for fear that his presence means contact and this, in turn, endangers the child and may cause a miscarriage." Accordingly Empress Chao sent Wang to convey this message to the emperor. From then on, the emperor never went to her place and only sent messengers to inquire about her health.

As the time of birth drew near, the emperor prepared presents for the coming Newborn Bath ceremony. The empress sent for Wang Sheng (and the other eunuchs).[5] She told Wang, "You came to the palace as a eunuch. Because of me, both you and your father enjoy wealth and power. I'm feigning pregnancy to secure my position. Now the time is near. Could you find a way out

---

[5] These words, not in keeping with the context, seem to be an interpolation.

for me? If everything works out, you'll benefit from this for many years to come."

"I'll look for a newborn baby outside and bring him here to be your son," replied Wang. "Of course, everything will be kept secret."

With the empress's consent, Wang paid one hundred taels in cash for a baby born only a few days earlier on the outskirts of the capital and brought him into the palace in a container. But when they opened it, they found the baby already dead.

Startled, the empress said, "The baby is dead. What is the use of it?"

"I know it. The container is airtight, and so the baby suffocated," Wang replied. "I'll go find another one and place him in a container with holes to allow the air to get in. The baby will stay alive."

Wang found the baby, but the baby started crying just before they got to the palace. Wang did not dare to go inside. Later, he tried again and the baby cried again. Wang never got into the palace with the baby, for the inner palace had been tightly guarded since the incident of the man behind the drapes.

Wang went to see the empress, informing her of what had happened. She wept, saying, "What am I going to do?"

At that time, the pregnancy was over twelve months long and the emperor began to get suspicious. Some explained to him, "The mother of King Yao [6] was pregnant for fourteen months before he was born. The baby the empress is bearing must be a sage."

The empress, finding no way to cover up her lie, finally sent a messenger to inform the throne: "Last night I dreamed of a dragon sleeping in my bed and I suffered a miscarriage." The emperor felt very sorry about it.

Chao-yi knew the trick, and therefore sent word to her sister: "You claimed a miscarriage. Do you mean that you haven't carried the baby long

[6] A ruler in the early legendary period of Chinese history.

enough? Your trick can hardly fool a child, not to mention the emperor. If your trick is revealed, I'd hate to predict the manner of your death."

Meanwhile, Chu-shih, an attendant responsible for serving tea, gave birth to a son. The eunuch Li Shou-kuang announced the news while the emperor was having dinner with Chao-yi. In great anger, she said to the emperor, "I remember one day you told me that you had spent some time with the queen mother. Now, Chu-shih has a son. Where did the baby come from?" She rolled on the floor, crying madly. The emperor helped her back to her seat.

Chao-yi summoned the eunuch Chi Kuei and commanded, "Bring the baby here." Chi did as he was told. Again Chao-yi commanded him, "Kill him for me." Chi hesitated. She scolded him in anger: "Why do I support you with high pay? If you don't do what I say, I'll kill you, too." Chi threw the baby against the palace pillar until he was dead and disposed of the carcass in the inner palace. From then on, all the pregnant maids were ordered killed.

Later, the emperor's health deteriorated; he had difficulty walking, and became impotent. A Taoist monk presented him with some pills. It was said that the pills were concocted under extremely high heat for a hundred days. When a pill was dropped in a large jar of water, the water would boil immediately. The water was then replaced, and the process was repeated for a period of ten days until the water did not boil when a pill was dropped in. Only then was the pill ready for consumption. The emperor took one each day, so he could still make love to Chao-yi.

One evening, while they were together at the Great Prosperity Palace, Chao-yi, half drunk, gave him ten pills. For the early part of the night, the emperor, holding Chao-yi in a bed shaded with red satin drapes, chuckled continuously. By midnight, he began to feel dizzy. Knowing that he could not go on, he tried to sit up but failed. Chao-yi, frightened, held the candle up to watch him. The emperor was lying there, ejaculating incessantly. He died after a while. The queen mother sent an officer to question Chao-yi about the cause of death, and she pressed hard for the reason. Thereupon Chao-yi committed suicide.

Empress Chao, still in the Eastern Palace, had long been neglected by the emperor. Once she cried in her sleep for quite some time until the maid awakened her. She explained, "I dreamed of the emperor emerging from a cloud; he offered me a seat and demanded that tea be served. The attendants refused, saying, 'The empress does not deserve the tea because she never served you well.' I was so displeased. I asked, 'Where is Chao-yi?' The emperor said, 'She was condemned to becoming a giant turtle suffering perpetual cold in the icy water of the North Sea to pay for the murder of my sons.' " With this, she cried in deep grief.

Years later, the king of the northern state Great Yüeh-chih[7] went hunting at sea. He saw emerging from a cave a giant turtle with jade hair ornaments on its head, gazing at the waves, seemingly with a yearning for the human world. He sent a messenger to Emperor Wu [r. 502–549] of the Liang Dynasty inquiring about this matter and was told the story of Chao-yi.

[7] A federation of Indo-Scythians roughly occupying the modern region of Kashmir and Afghanistan; hence "northern" in the text should be "western."

311

HAN WU-NIANG SELLS HER CHARMS AT THE NEW BRIDGE MARKET

From *Ku-chin hsiao-shuo*

TRANSLATED BY ROBERT C. MILLER AND THE EDITORS

When the emotions are trapped by beauty, then there is no
* freedom.*
On Mount Li signal fires were lit to fool the feudal lords.
No sooner had that famous smile toppled the empire
Than the jade terraces were covered with the dust of the
* invading barbarian armies.*

This is a historical poem by Hu Tseng[1] which relates how King Yu of the Chou Dynasty was infatuated with a consort by the name of Pao-ssu, and how he tried by every means to please her. Just to win a smile from her, he lit the warning beacons on the top of Mount Li which were used to summon the feudal lords in time of distress. The feudal lords, thinking that King Yu was in danger, assembled their troops and came to his rescue. But when they arrived at King Yu's halls, all was peaceful. At this Pao-ssu indeed laughed very hard. Later, when the western tribes raised armies and came to attack, the feudal lords did not come to his aid, and the invaders killed King Yu at the foot of Mount Li.

Again, in the Spring and Autumn period, there was a Duke Ling of Ch'en who seduced Consort Hsia, the mother of Hsiao Cheng-shu, and with

his retainers K'ung Ning and Yi Hsing-fu spent days and nights at her house carousing. In shame and resentment, Cheng-shu shot Duke Ling with an arrow.

Later, in the Six Dynasties period, the last emperor of the Ch'en Dynasty was infatuated with Chang Li-hua and Lady K'ung, and himself composed the song "Flowers of the Inner Court" in praise of their beauty. Heavy with wine and dissolute idleness, he paid no attention to matters of government. When, pursued by the Sui armies, he could find no place to hide, he and his two consorts jumped into a well and were captured by the Sui general Han Ch'in-hu. Thus he lost his kingdom. As the poem says:

In the midst of pleasure, disaster suddenly arises in the stable
* of the Hsia.[2]*
In a dry well, the "Jade Tree" song is still heard.
Just witness that the two Ch'ens ended up in the same course,
And you will realize that warfare brought by women has
* always caused a country's downfall.*

During his reign [605–617], Emperor Yang of the Sui Dynasty was enamored with the beauty of Consort Hsiao. Wishing to view the beauty of Yangchow, he made Ma Shu-tu[3] overseer, con-

---

[1] Hu Tseng (fl. 860) was a T'ang scholar-official who wrote a collection of historical poems entitled *Yung-shih shih* (Poems on Historical Events). This poem is in *chüan* 2 of the said collection.

[2] The duke was shot in a stable.
[3] A fictitious character.

scripted one million commoners, and dredged the Pien River,[4] which was more than a thousand *li* long, losing countless lives in the process. He built phoenix warships and dragon boats and made the palace maids pull them. Along the shore, sounds of gaiety could be heard for a hundred *li*. Later, Yü-wen Hua-chi[5] rebelled in Chiang-tu[6] and beheaded Emperor Yang at the Wu-kung Terrace. His empire was thus overthrown. There is a poem which verifies this:

Once the thousand-li canal was opened
Waves destroying the Sui came from Highest Heaven.
The brocade sails were still furled when the battle cries were
 heard.
Alas, alas, the dragon boats would not return again.

Now Emperor Ming-huang of the T'ang Dynasty[7] was infatuated with the beauty of Yang Kuei-fei [Consort Yang]. His springs were spent dallying with her and his nights in wild pleasure. Who could have expected that Yang Kuei-fei would be having an affair with An Lu-shan, who was presented publicly as her adopted son? One day, just following their intimacy, when Yang's hairpin was skewed and her hair in disorder, Ming-huang surprised them with an unexpected visit. Yang Kuei-fei got by with lame excuses, but from that time on Ming-huang became suspicious and eventually sent Lu-shan away to Yü-yang[8] to be regional commander. But Lu-shan still longed for Yang Kuei-fei and raised an army in revolt. Truly:

Out of Yü-yang war drums advance shaking the earth,
Tearing apart the melody of "Rainbow Skirt and Feathered
 Cloak."

[4] This river changed course several times in history. In Sui times, it drew its water from the Yellow River at Ying-yang in modern Honan and flowed eastward through Shantung to Kiangsu. The work described in the text is part of Emperor Yang's Grand Canal project.
[5] A usurping subordinate of Emperor Yang.
[6] Near Yangchow in modern Kiangsu.
[7] Ming-huang (the Bright Emperor) is a more familiar name for the T'ang emperor Hsüan-tsung.
[8] In northern Hopei, just south of the Great Wall.

Ming-huang had no alternative but to gather his court and flee. At the foot of Mount Ma-wei[9] his troops mutinied and demanded the death of Yang Kuei-fei. Ming-huang then fled to Shu. It was only because of the years of bloody fighting led by General Kuo[10] that the two capitals[11] were recovered.

All the rulers of whom we have spoken lusted after feminine beauty so much that they lost their kingdoms and ruined themselves. How can their catastrophes fail to give us common folks a warning against the danger of lasciviousness?

You may well ask, "Storyteller, why all this talk about the danger of lasciviousness?"

Today I will tell you of a young man who, because he did not heed the warning and went chasing after a woman, nearly destroyed his own body, squandered his family's wealth, and caused a commotion in the New Bridge Market. This episode, which has been made into a romantic story, is truly a case of:

Citing the errors of the past
For the benefit of future generations.

It is said that, in the Sung Dynasty, ten *li* outside the prefectural city of Lin-an was the town of Hu-shu and that five *li* farther on from Hu-shu was the New Bridge Market, in which there lived a rich man known to his neighbors as Squire Wu. His wife, P'an-shih, had given him a son called Wu Shan, who had in turn married a girl of the Yü clan and had a four-year-old son. The family turned the front portion of the house into a silk shop, but they also lent money and speculated in grain, and as a result had become extremely wealthy. Five *li* outside the New Bridge Market there was a town called Gray Bridge Market. Squire Wu had recently built a house there and put his son Wu Shan, assisted by a manager, in

[9] To the west of Hsing-p'ing County in Shensi.
[10] General Kuo Tzu-yi (697–781) was primarily responsible for suppressing the An Lu-shan Rebellion.
[11] Ch'ang-an and Lo-yang.

313

charge of a retail store for the distribution of silk floss to the local weavers.

Wu Shan was clever and handsome. Furthermore, he was as civil in his manner as he was practical-minded in managing business affairs. He had no mind for frivolity. For this reason his father never worried that his son would bring trouble on himself.

Wu Shan left home early every morning to go to the shop and conduct business, returning home in the evening. The shop occupied only the front portion of the building, the rooms at the rear [which faced the river] being empty. One day Wu Shan had extra things to attend to at home and only arrived at the shop toward noon. As he entered, he saw two barges loaded with many boxes, baskets, tables, chairs, and other household effects anchored behind the building, and several men were moving those items into the empty rooms. From one of the barges there emerged three women—a fat middle-aged one, an old woman, and a young girl. After they had disembarked, they entered the house. It is because of this event that Wu Shan was brought to this:

A body, like the moon at dawn, falling prey to mountain peaks;
A life like a midnight lamp, its oil exhausted.

Wu asked the manager, "Who are they? How could they move into my house without permission?"

"They came from the city," the manager replied. "The man of the family has just been sent here on duty. Because they can't find anyplace to stay on such short notice, they asked Old Fan next door to beg leave to stay for only two or three days. I was just going to inform you when you came in."

Wu Shan was about to fly into a rage when he saw the young girl, who straightened her sleeves, came forward, and bowed deeply in greeting. "I beg you, sir, not to be angry. It's not your manager's fault, but rather our own forwardness. Since this was such an urgent matter and we had

no choice, it was impossible for us to go to your place to seek your permission first. I beg you to forgive our impropriety and allow us to stay for a few days; once we find a house, we'll move. Needless to say, we'll pay the rent."

At this, Wu Shan's temper subsided and he said, "In that case, you can stay as long as you like. Please make yourself at home!"

After this short exchange, the girl hastened to help her companions carry the boxes and baskets. Seeing this, Wu Shan was driven by an inexplicable urge to offer her a helping hand.

"Storyteller! You say that Wu Shan was by nature straightforward and not frivolous. How do you explain that upon seeing this young girl his anger turned to pleasure to such extent that he gave her a hand in moving the furniture?"

What you don't know is that when Wu Shan was at home, he was strictly watched by his parents, who allowed him no chance to get near any place of ill repute. Since he was not dumb, but an intelligent, handsome, and industrious fellow in the prime of his youth, how could he help being moved at the sight of such a beautiful girl right in his shop, especially when his parents were not around?

Both the fat woman and the young girl coaxed him, saying, "We can't trouble you to exert yourself, sir."

"Since you're staying here," Wu Shan replied, "it's as if we were all in one family. So let's behave accordingly."

With that everyone was happy.

When evening came, Wu Shan, before returning home, asked the manager to make arrangements with the newly arrived tenants and draw up a lease for him. The manager did as instructed. When Wu Shan arrived home, he of course did not mention the matter to his parents. All night his thoughts were with the young girl.

The next morning he got up early, dressed neatly in his best clothes, and calling his valet Shou-t'ung to accompany him, strutted off to the shop. Indeed:

Downcast, one drinks on credit in the tavern;
Out of luck, one runs into a lover.[12]

Wu had arrived at the shop and made a few sales when in walked the servant working for the girl's family; he invited Wu Shan to go in for a cup of tea and for the lease. Wu Shan had wanted to go in and thought it most fortunate that the servant had come with an invitation. When he entered he saw the young girl, her smile beaming, come to greet him: "Sir, please come in and have a seat."

After he had entered one of the side rooms and taken a seat, the old woman and the fat one also came in, so he sat there in the company of the three women. Wu began, asking, "Lady, may I ask your family name, and why there are no men in your household?"

"My husband is surnamed Han," the fat woman replied. "He and our son are employed at the tribunal, and since they leave early and return late, you've never seen them."

Some time later, Wu lowered his head to steal a look at the girl and found that her beautiful eyes were resting on him. "May I ask how old you are, sir?" she ventured.

"I'm twenty-four. May I ask the same question, miss?"

"I'm as old as you are, twenty-four. How true is the saying that 'those who are destined for each other will eventually meet regardless of the distance that separates them.' Why, I've moved out of the city only to come upon a gentleman like you, not to mention the fact we're of the same age."

At this point, the old woman and the fat one saw what was going on, made some excuse, and left. Only the two of them remained, sitting opposite each other. The girl began trying to excite Wu Shan with suggestive talk. Wu had, at the

beginning, thought that she was of a decent family. He had allowed her to stay in the house thinking that he might flirt with her. Who would have thought that once they became somewhat acquainted she would be so aggressive? Only then did he realize that things had gone too far. He had decided to leave immediately when the young girl walked over, sat down beside him, and began to make advances to him.

"Sir, your hairpin—may I take a look?"

Wu took off his cap and was about to remove the hairpin when the girl, holding his hair with one hand and grasping the pin with the other, said as she rose, "Sir, let's go upstairs and talk." Saying this she immediately went upstairs; he followed, asking for his pin. Indeed:

Even if you are as cunning as a demon
You still have to drink the water from the footbath.[13]

Wu Shan climbed the stairs and called out, "Miss, please return my hairpin. I've business at home and need to go back right away."

"You and I in a former life were fated to be lovers, so don't go on pretending. Come, let's have some fun."

"Please don't," Wu Shan replied. "If people find out, it wouldn't look good. Besides, this place isn't at all private."

He was about to go downstairs when she, resorting to all sorts of seductions, embraced and clung to him. As her smooth slender fingers loosened his garments, his passion rose like fire and could no longer be held back. Falling onto the bed, they immediately conjured up a storm of clouds and rain.

When their passion abated, the two sat there embracing. Surprised and delighted, Wu asked, "What's your name?"

"In my family I am the fifth child [thus I am called Wu-niang]. When young I was called Sai-chin, but when I was older my parents just called

[12] This couplet means additional problems for someone already in trouble. To drink on credit only increases one's debts, and to run into a lover in a moment of distress causes further suffering.

[13] Drinking water from the footbath means having no choice at all and being completely under someone else's control.

me Chin-nu. May I ask what is your seniority in your family and your occupation?"

"I'm the only child. My family is in silk as well as in the moneylending business. Ours is quite a respectable concern at the New Bridge Market. The silk shop here is under my management."

Chin-nu was secretly pleased and thought to herself, "Having such a rich fellow on my hook now isn't a bad deal at all."

Now the truth of the matter is that Chin-nu was actually a disguised prostitute, or, if you will, a "private convenience." Her family, without any official status, had no other means of support but depended solely on this personal enterprise. The old woman was the fat woman's mother and Chin-nu was her daughter. Originally, the fat woman was from a good family, but because her husband was a good-for-nothing, she herself had reluctantly turned to this profession.

Chin-nu was attractive and had some education. She had been married for some time, but because she did not behave properly in her husband's home and had affairs with others, she was sent back to her mother. As it happened, the fat woman was close to fifty at that time and her customers were decreasing. Her daughter, then, took over the family business and did it on an even larger scale.

They used to live in the city, but someone had had them reported to the authorities and, becoming nervous, they had moved away to escape. It was then, alas, that Wu Shan fell into her hands. Her trap was laid and only awaiting the prey, and he took the bait. Why was no man ever seen at their place? When the father and son saw a customer coming, they would take cover, as a matter of course. Anyone who showed an interest in this woman would fall into her net; thus she had beguiled quite a number of men.

At this time Chin-nu said "Having moved so hurriedly, we're a little short of money. If possible, I beg you to lend me five taels of cash. Please don't say no."

Wu gave his assent, rose, and straightened his clothes and cap. Chin-nu returned his hairpin and the two of them went downstairs and resumed their seats in the side room.

Wu thought to himself, "I've been here a long time. I'm afraid the neighbors are talking." He drank another cup of tea; when Chin-nu asked him to stay for lunch, he said, "I've stayed too long. I can't stay for lunch. In a little while I'll send the money to you."

"This evening I'll prepare some food and wine especially for you. You must come," she said.

At this Wu Shan went out into the shop.

Actually, Wu's visit to Chin-nu's room had been seen by one of the neighbors. The building was divided into two six-room units, and Chin-nu only occupied one of them. The other unit of the building was the silk shop, and the upper story was vacant. This busybody, seeing that Wu Shan had not come out for a long time, hid himself next to the partition in the empty floor, whence he had clearly heard and seen all that had taken place.

Thus, when Wu came out and sat in the shop, he saw several neighbors coming to taunt him saying, "Congratulations, Mr. Wu!" At this he began to suspect that they knew what had happened. Then, when he saw everyone laughing, he blushed and said, "What's the reason for this? What is there to congratulate?"

Among them was the one Shen Erh-lang, the owner of the general store across the street, who had spied on him. He called out, "So you're going to deny it. After she took your hairpin, what did you go upstairs for?" This struck right to the heart of the matter, and Wu Shan, unable to respond, made up an excuse and rose to leave. But they blocked his way saying, "We'll chip in to give you a celebration party." Wu Shan had no ears for what they were saying and walked off sulkily toward the west.

He walked all the way to the house of his maternal uncle and had lunch there. After he left the place, he borrowed a set of scales from a shop-keeper to weigh out two taels from the silver he had with him for buying silk and put it in his sleeve. He lingered there until afternoon[14] before he returned to the shop.

"The tenants inside were just here to invite you to have a cup of wine," said the manager.

At that moment the servant came out. "Sir, where have you been? I couldn't find you any-where. We've prepared a feast especially for you. Besides the manager, there are no other guests."

When Wu Shan and the manager went into the room, everything was already laid out—the usual treat of fish, meat, wine, and fruit. Wu was placed in the seat of honor, Chin-nu sat opposite, and the manager sat on the side. When the three of them were seated, the servant served wine. After drinking several cups, the manager understood what was going on, excused himself to close the shop, and left.

Wu Shan's usual wine capacity was slight. After the manager left, he relaxed and drank ten or so cups with Chin-nu, and soon he felt the influence. He then gave the silver from his sleeve to Chin-un. Rising and taking her hand he said, "I have something to tell you. I think our relationship is going to run into some problems. The neighbors all know about us and have been making fun of me. If word should get to my parents, what could I do? The people here have piercing eyes and wagging tongues and are unforgiving. They might become jealous of us and spread rumors around. You can hardly live here quietly. What I'd like to suggest is that you find a quiet place to live and I will come often to visit you."

"What you say is true," Chin-nu replied. "I'll discuss it with mother."

At this moment, the servant brought in two cups of tea. After they had drunk them, they turned to their usual pastime again.

"After I leave this time, I won't come here

again, to prevent further gossip," Wu Shan said as he was leaving. "When you've found a place, send the servant to bring me word. I'll come myself to see you off." After this he went into the shop, gave the manager some instructions, and went home.

After Chin-nu had seen Wu off, as it was getting dark, she went upstairs to take off her makeup. Coming downstairs to have supper, she reported to her parents all Wu Shan had said about moving to another place to avoid gossip. After that, they all went to sleep.

The next morning, the fat woman instructed the servant to go out discreetly and gather what-ever information there was from the neighborhood. He stood outside the door for a moment and then went and sprawled in the doorway of Chang Ta-lang, the rice seller next door. He sat there for some time, and heard nothing but excited gossip from several neighbors concerning the affair of Wu Shan and Chin-nu. He then returned home and reported to the fat woman, "With busybodies like that in the neighborhood, it's no place to make a living."

"Because we didn't have any peace in the city, we moved here in the hope of settling down in a place where we could be left alone and live rather permanently. Who would have thought that we would again run into such neighbors?" She sighed after saying this. On the one hand, she told her husband to go out and look for another house; on the other, she kept watch on what the neighbors were saying before making any move.

Since the day Wu Shan returned home, he had been wary of people's gossip. Feigning sickness to his parents, he did not go back to the shop again, leaving his business to his manager.

Chin-nu was not used to being so quiet about the house. Soon the servant was at his trade again soliciting former customers and the place became quite busy. At first the neighbors thought that the traffic was coming only from Wu Shan, and they did not realize that the business was flourishing

---

[14] The text has "midnight," an apparent textual error.

until they saw the sudden surge of new customers. Among the neighbors were some troublemakers who observed, "This is a decent residential area. How can we tolerate such trash living here? There's an old saying 'Whoring breeds killing.' Just imagine, if a fight breaks out and someone gets killed, we'll all be involved."

This, of course, was not lost on the servant's ears, and he duly reported to his mistress. The fat woman listened to this, and then, having no object for her anger, exploded at the old woman: "You senile old fool, what are you afraid of? Why don't you go out and give them hell, the yapping sons of bitches?!"

At this, the old woman got up, went outside, and shouted, "Don't you fart at us, you yapping sons of bitches! If any of you answers me back, I'll teach him a lesson if I have to die for it! What family doesn't have relatives coming and going?"

"That thieving, law-breaking old bitch!" some of the neighbors remarked. "As if it weren't enough that she has that kind of business in her home, now she has to use her foul mouth."

Shen Erh-lang, the grocery store owner, was on the point of shouting back when someone who didn't want to meddle in others' business put in, "Just ignore her! Don't waste your time on someone who's already lost half her senses. Just drive her out."

After her insulting outburst, seeing that no one was coming forward for another round, she went back inside. At this point all the neighbors went to speak with the manager: "You must have no brains, letting such shady people live here. Instead of admitting their own shortcomings, they turn around and send the old woman to abuse others. You must have heard her. If we all go and speak to the squire, it won't reflect well on you."

"Good neighbors," the manager said, "there's no need to bring the matter up again; I'll ask them to move out soon."

When the neighbors had finished speaking and left, the manager immediately went inside and said to the fat woman, "You must quickly find a place and move out. Don't get me involved. Since things have come to this, even if you stay you won't be happy."

"You needn't have said anything," the fat woman replied. "My husband is looking for a place in the city, and we'll be moving before long."

At this the manager left. The fat woman, speaking to Chin-nu, said, "Tomorrow we'll move into the city. Today we'll have the servant secretly go and tell Master Wu, without, of course, letting his parents know."

Having received his instructions, the servant went to the silk shop of Squire Wu at the New Bridge Market. Not daring to go inside, he walked over and waited beneath the eaves of a doorway across the street and kept an eye on the entrance to the shop. Before long Wu Shan came out; seeing the servant, he hurriedly came over and led him away from the gate of his own house to the place of a weaver, where they sat down.

"Is anything the matter?" Wu asked.

"I've been instructed to come over to inform you that Wu-niang, acting according to your wish, is moving into the city tomorrow."

"That's fine. Don't you know where in the city you'll be staying?"

"We're moving to Cross-Bridge Street to the south of the Wool Fort of the Patrol Barracks."

Wu Shan took out a small piece of silver weighing about one-fifth of a tael and gave it to the servant, saying, "Use this to have a cup of wine. Tomorrow noontime I'll come myself to see you off."

The servant took the money, expressed his thanks, and went home.

The following morning Wu Shan asked Shou-t'ung to follow him, stopped in a food shop by the Brocade Bridge and bought two packages of dried fruit, giving them to Shou-t'ung to carry, and then went to the shop at the Gray Bridge Market. There he spoke with the manager and went over the sales accounts of the previous days;

then he went inside to see Chin-nu and her mother. Taking the fruit from Shou-t'ung and a packet of silver from his gown, he said, "The two packages of dried fruit are for you, to go with your tea.[15] These three taels of silver are to help defray your moving expenses. When you've settled down, I'll come to see you again."

Chin-nu took the fruit and the silver, and then she and her mother rose to thank him, saying, "We are now even further in your debt. How can we deserve it?"

"There is no need for thanks," Wu Shan replied. "We'll be in touch." Rising, he saw that the boxes, baskets, and furniture had already been loaded onto the barges.

"When will you come to see us?" Chin-nu asked.

"Probably after four or five days."

Then the girl and her family bade farewell to Wu Shan and moved into the city that same day. Truly:

If this place is uncongenial,
There are others which are better.

Wu Shan used to suffer from a summer sickness, and during the hot season he always became weak and thin. As it was the beginning of the sixth month, he had called in an acupuncturist to give him moxabustion treatments on several places on his back. Now resting at home, he did not go to the shop. Although his thoughts were always on Chin-nu, the pain of the treatments was so severe that he could not leave the house.

Chin-nu had been living on Cross-Bridge Street since the seventeenth day of the fifth month. In the neighborhood there lived mainly the families of soldiers, and thus the environment was not good for her sort of work. Also, the road was lightly traveled, and a long period could pass with not a soul to be seen.

"The other day Master Wu said that he would

---

[15] People in Sung and Ming times served tea by mixing tea leaves with dried fruits.

come within a few days," the fat woman said to Chin-nu. "It's been a month now, and we haven't even seen him once. If he comes to the city, surely he'll drop in to see us."

"We could send the servant to the shop at the Gray Bridge to inquire after him," suggested Chin-nu.

So the fellow went, leaving by the Mount Ken Gate, and upon arriving at the Gray Bridge went to the silk shop to see the manager.

Seeing him, the manager said, "Well, what brings you here?"

"I've come to see Master Wu."

"The master has had some moxabustion treatments at home and has not recovered, so he hasn't been around."

"If you go there, could I trouble you to take him a message? Say that I came but didn't find him." Without delay the servant took leave of the manager and, returning home, reported to Chin-nu.

"Now we know he didn't come because he had moxabustion treatments at home," said Chin-nu.

That same day, after talking it over, Chin-nu and her mother told the servant to buy two pieces of pork tripe and clean them. Then, stuffing them with a mixture of glutinous rice and lotus seed, they cooked them until tender. Early next morning Chin-nu, in her room, prepared some ink and wrote the following letter on some fancy paper:

Greeting to you, my dear friend Master Wu. Ever since I saw you last, my heart has been with you, full of anxious longing. Waiting for your visit I stand in the doorway but have not seen you come. Yesterday I sent the servant to convey my greetings, but he returned without meeting you. Since moving to this place, it has been desolate, but hearing of your suffering from moxabustion treatments has given me no peace, sitting or lying down. All I can do is sit here helplessly, knowing that I cannot suffer on your behalf. I have cooked two stuffed tripe as a small indication of my good wishes toward you. Please accept them. My feelings need not be expressed.

The twenty-first day of the second month of summer

Humbly yours,
Sai-chin

When she had finished writing she folded the paper into a letter, packed the tripe into a box, wrapped it in a cloth, and gave both the box and the letter to the servant, instructing him, "Go to his house and seek out Master Wu. You must find him and hand these to him in person."

Picking up the box and placing the letter in his bosom, the servant went out the door, down the boulevard, out through the Wu-lin Gate, and straight to the New Bridge Market, where he sat on a curbstone outside the house of Squire Wu. It happened that Shou-t'ung was just coming out. "Grandpa," he called out, "where have you come from? Why are you sitting there?"

The servant, pulling Shou-t'ung to a deserted spot, said, "I've come to speak with your master. I'm just waiting here. Would you go and tell him I'm here?"

Shou-t'ung went back inside, and before long Wu Shan came out. The servant quickly bowed. "Master, I'm so happy that you're all right."

"Thank you. What's in the box?"

"Wu-niang, thinking anxiously of your moxabustion treatments but having nothing better to offer, especially prepared these two pieces of tripe for you."

Wu Shan took him to a restaurant and took a seat upstairs. Then Wu asked, "Is the new place all right?"

"It's terribly desolate," the servant replied. Taking the letter from his bosom he gave it to Wu Shan who, after having opened and read it, refolded it and hid it in his sleeve. Then, opening the box, he took out one of the tripe, asked the waiter to cut it up, and ordered that two pots of wine be heated.

"You stay here and eat. I'm going back to write a reply for you to take back."

"Thank you."

Wu Shan returned to the house and went to his bedroom, where he secretly wrote a reply and weighed out five taels of silver. Then, returning to the upper floor of the restaurant, he drank several cups of wine with the servant.

"Thank you very much for the good wine," the servant said. "I've had enough now."

At this, Wu Shan gave him the silver and the letter, saying, "These five taels of silver are for expenses; convey my fondest greetings to Wu-niang. In two or three days I will definitely go over to see her."

The servant, with the silver and the letter, got up and went downstairs, where Wu Shan saw him off from the restaurant. Returning home when it was already dark, he immediately handed the money and the letter to Chin-nu who, opening the letter and holding it under the lamp, read:

> Shan humbly writes in reply to his dearest lady Han Wu-niang. The gracious reception I received as well as the loving favors you bestowed I have never forgotten. Since then I have wanted to meet with you, but because of moxabustion treatments I have been forced to disappoint you. Not only have you sent someone to inquire about me but you have also taken the trouble to prepare all these delicacies for me. For this I am more than grateful. Within two or three days it should be possible for me to visit you. This five taels of silver is a trifling token of my feelings, which I humbly beg you to accept.
>
> Wu Shan bows again.

Needless to say, Chin-nu and her mother were very happy with the five taels of silver.

Now Wu Shan stayed at the restaurant until evening, and then, taking the box with the tripe, he sneaked into the bedroom and said to his wife, "Look at this. A weaver, hearing of my treatments, today gave me two stuffed tripe. One of them I ate with a friend while I was out, and the other I brought home for you."

"Tomorrow you must be sure to thank him," his wife replied.

That evening Wu Shan and his wife ate the tripe in their room and never mentioned it to his parents.

Two days passed. On the third day, the twenty-fourth of the sixth month, Wu Shan got up early and said to his father and mother, "I haven't gone to the shop for quite a while. Today I feel better, and I think I should go over and have a look. Besides, there are several weavers on the Shrine Lane whose accounts I want to settle. I'll return home once I get back from the city."

"Go if you want to, but don't overexert yourself," his father said.

Taking leave of his father, Wu Shan called for a sedan chair and got in, and, with Shou-t'ung following carrying an open umbrella, he set out. Now Wu Shan's life was almost ruined by Chin-nu with this visit to the city. Truly:

This damsel of sixteen, with a body as smooth as cream,
Has a sword hidden in her loins to slay supreme idiots.
Though no head is seen to fall,
The marrow in their bones is dry as straw.

Wu Shan, riding in the sedan chair, arrived in the Gray Bridge Market almost before he knew it. Alighting, he entered the shop and exchanged greetings with the manager. His thoughts, however, were only with Chin-nu, and he had stayed only a short while when he said to the manager, "I'm going into the city to settle some of the weavers' accounts. When I return we'll go over the regular accounts."

The manager guessed where Wu was going but dared not stop him. He merely said, "Since you've just recovered, it may not be a good idea to go out so soon, lest you become ill again." But Wu Shan would not listen and got into the sedan chair. The bearers, as they had been previously instructed, set off, entering the city at the Mount Ken Gate and winding their way to Cross-Bridge Street near the Wool Fort. There he inquired after the Han family who had just moved there

from the Lake Market.[16] Someone in the neighborhood pointed to a house adjoining the medicine shop. As Wu Shan got out of the sedan chair, Shou-t'ung knocked on the door. The servant came out to open the door, and when he saw Wu Shan, he hurried back inside to report his arrival. As Wu Shan entered, Chin-nu and her mother came out together, all smiles, and welcomed him: "Rare guest indeed! What wind has blown you here today?"

When Wu Shan and the two women had finished exchanging greetings, they all went inside to sit and drink tea. "Would you like to take a look at my room?" Chin-nu asked. So Wu Shan and Chin-nu went upstairs to her room. Indeed:

When agreeable friends visit, one is never bored.
Among intimates, confidences are exchanged without restraint.

Chin-nu and Wu Shan were as happy in their reunion as a fish in water and inseparable as lacquer and glue.[17] What they said to each other was the usual sort of love talk. Naturally, a feast was prepared and the servant brought it upstairs. Moving the mirror stand, Chin-nu spread it out on the dressing table. Then the servant went downstairs again and only dared go up when Chin-nu called for more wine. The two of them sat side by side. Chin-nu poured a cup of wine and offered it to him in studied formality, saying, "Since the time of your treatments, there has not been a single moment when I was not thinking of you."

Wu accepted the cup and said, "It was because of the treatments that I did not keep our appointment." When he had finished the wine, he poured a cup for Chin-nu in return. When they had drunk more than ten cups, their desire was kindled like a flame and they could not but fulfill it as before, and the height of their passion was limitless.

[16] This may be the town of Hu-shu referred to at the beginning of the story.
[17] Lacquer and glue, both pasty and sticky, would be inseparable once mixed together.

When done, they rose, washed their hands, and drank a few more cups. Inebriated though they were, their desire had still not been exhausted. Confined in bed by his illness, Wu Shan had abstained from sex for a whole month. Seeing Chin-nu, how could he be content with just one throw? He should have died. All his life force had been drawn out and distracted by Chin-nu. When his desire rose again, he went through another round. Truly:

Too much of even the best food will make one ill;
Excessive pleasure will bring disaster.

Afterward, Wu Shan felt that his mind was dazed and his body exhausted. Unable to keep his eyes open, without eating he lay down on the bed and went to sleep. Seeing Wu sleeping, Chin-nu went downstairs and announced to the bearers outside, "The master has had some wine and is now resting upstairs. You two gentlemen please wait here, and don't hurry him."

"We wouldn't dream of hurrying him," they replied. Having given these instructions, Chin-nu went back upstairs and went to sleep at Wu's side.

Wu Shan, on the bed, had barely closed his eyes before he heard someone call several times, "Master Wu, how comfortably you're lying on bed!" Through his wine-sodden eyes Wu Shan saw that it was a fat monk wearing an old ragged robe, with a silk sash around his waist and a pair of monk's sandals on his bare feet. After the monk had greeted him, Wu rose to return the gesture, saying, "Master, where is your monastery, and why are you calling me?"

"I'm the abbot of the Water Moon Monastery at the Mulberry Garden. Because my student is dead, I've come to enlighten you. I can see from your countenance that your share of fortune in life is thin, and that you are not destined to enjoy wealth and fame. The best thing for you to do is to renounce the world, cast aside desires, become a monk, and be my student."

"You're being rather unreasonable. My father and mother are in their fifties and have just me,

the only child, to carry on the family line. How can I become a monk?"

"The best thing for you to do is to become a monk," the priest reiterated. "If you continue to seek wealth and fame, you won't live long. Follow this poor monk's advice and come with me."

"Nonsense!" Wu Shan said. "Anyway, this is a woman's bedroom and you are a monk. What do you think you're doing here?"

The monk opened his eyes wide and shouted, "Are you coming with me or not?"

"You bald ass! You're out of your mind. Stop bothering me," Wu retorted.

At this the monk became angry and dragged him off. When they reached the staircase, Wu cried out, but the monk pushed him vigorously, making him tumble downstairs. Startled, he woke up to find himself covered with a cold sweat. He opened his eyes and saw Chin-nu, still asleep. It had been just a dream. Feeling confused, he pulled himself together and sat on the side of the bed for some time. Chin-nu awoke and said, "Did you sleep well? It is so seldom that you come; why not stay overnight and go back tomorrow?"

"My parents will be anxious," he replied. "I have to go. I'll come again another day."

Chin-nu got up and called for a snack, but Wu Shan said, "I don't feel well, and I don't feel like eating."

Chin-nu saw that the color of his face was not good and dared not insist that he stay. Wu adjusted his clothes and cap and went downstairs, where he took leave of Chin-nu and her mother and hurriedly got into the sedan chair.

The sky was already dark. In the sedan chair, Wu Shan gave the matter some thought: "Having a dream in the daytime is very strange." Frightened and worried, he gradually felt a sickness in his stomach, but as he was riding in the sedan chair, there was nothing he could do about it. Much as he wished to be at home at once, he could do no more than order the bearers to hurry. When arriving at the gate of his house, he could bear it no longer; he jumped out, went inside, and hurried upstairs. As he sat on the night stool, first there was pain and then diarrhea—what he had discharged was all blood. After sitting there for a long time, dizzy and delirious, he climbed onto his bed, weak and in pain. His present condition was due to the fact that his vital force had already been weakened and he had compounded the problem with sexual excess.

His father, having seen that Wu Shan's face had lost its color, hurried upstairs and shouted in alarm, "Son, what happened to you?"

"I drank several cups of wine at the house of one of the weavers and slept there. When I awakened I was so thirsty that I drank a bowl of cold water. This brought on the cramps that later changed into diarrhea." His teeth clattered even before he had finished speaking. His whole body was bathed in a cold sweat, while at the same time it was as hot as burning coal. His father ran downstairs and called a doctor to come and examine him.

"His pulse has almost stopped," the doctor said. "This illness is difficult to cure."

Over and over his father pleaded with the doctor to try his best to save his son. The doctor said, "This is not a case of diarrhea. It is a case of sexual exhaustion resulting from the dissipation of the vital force. Such cases are usually beyond cure. I'll give him a prescription to help him restore his vital force. If after he takes this medicine, his fever drops and his pulse returns, there may be some hope." The doctor wrote out a prescription and left.

Wu Shan's parents questioned him over and over, but he would only shake his head and did not reply. About the time of the first watch that night he took the medicine, lay back on the pillow, and rested. Suddenly he saw the monk who had appeared to him that day standing by the side of the bed. "Wu Shan," he said, "why do you torture yourself so much? It would be better to follow me."

"Get out of here! Leave me alone!"

Then, without further ado, the monk tied his yellow silk sash around Wu Shan's neck and began to drag him away. Wu held onto the bed frame, cried out loudly, and awakened in fear; again it was a dream. When he opened his eyes, and his parents and wife were all standing in front of him.

His parents asked, "Son, why were you so frightened?" Wu Shan, his mind greatly confused, became aware of the fact that he was about to die. Thus he related all the details of the affair with Chin-nu and the monk he had seen in the dream to his parents. After this he cried in great choking sobs, his parents and wife all shedding tears also. Squire Wu saw that his son's illness was indeed critical and dared not blame him. He said some comforting words to him instead.

After Wu Shan had told his parents everything, he swooned several times. When he revived, he tearfully addressed his wife, saying, "Serve my parents well and look after our son. The income from the silk business should be enough for your expenses."

"Just set your mind on recovery," his wife said, crying, "and don't worry anymore."

Sighing and asking a maid to help him sit up, Wu Shan said to his parents, "I cannot recover. You've brought me up for nothing, an unworthy and disobedient son. Perhaps this is the year that I was fated to run into this woman and meet my nemesis, so what is the use of my repentance now? Let my example of losing life through improper conduct be a lesson to all young men. Life is indeed man's most valuable possession. Let those who are attracted to licentiousness know what has happened to me. After I have died, throw my body into the river. Only then can I hope to atone for my sin of neglecting my wife and my son as well as failing to fulfill my own responsibility as a son to my parents."

After speaking, he had just closed his eyes when the monk was again before him. Wu Shan implored him, saying, "Master, what wrong have I done to you that you won't let go of me?"

"Because I broke my vow of chastity and ended

my life in the place where you were, I've been kept in hell for a long time, and there is no way for me to escape. When that day I chanced to see you indulging in sexual pleasure in broad daylight, I decided at once to make you my companion." Having said this, the monk left.

Wu Shan awoke and related all this to his parents. His father said, "Obviously you're possessed by a malevolent spirit." He hurried outside into the street where he burned incense and candles and offered sacrificial food, praying to heaven, saying, "Have compassion for my son's life. I will personally go to the place where you died and have sacrifices made for your peace." When the prayers were finished he burned paper money.

When Squire Wu went back inside, it was already dark and Wu Shan was asleep facing the inside of the bed. Suddenly he sat up, opened his eyes and said, "Squire, I violated Buddha's injunction against lust and I killed myself at the Wool Fort. When your son went there to engage in lustful pursuits, I could not but think of my former actions and I wanted to make your son my substitute in order to bring about my salvation. Now that I've received your sacrificial food and money and your promises to sacrifice for my release, I'll relinquish him and won't create any more trouble. I will now go to the Wool Fort and await your offering. If I obtain release I'll never come again." When he had finished speaking, he folded his hands in salutation and then Wu Shan suddenly awoke. His color returned; when his wife felt him,

the fever had gone. Rising, he went to the toilet; there was no more diarrhea. The entire family was exhilarated. The doctor who had come before was again asked to examine him.

"His six pulses have returned to normal,"[18] the doctor said. "There is hope now." Then he wrote out a prescription. After several days of care, Wu Shan gradually recovered.

His father invited several monks to make an all-night sacrifice at Chin-nu's house, and Chin-nu's family had a dream in which they saw a fat monk, holding a staff, leaving the place.

Wu Shan recuperated for a half a year and then resumed his business responsibilities at the New Bridge Market. One day he discussed this incident with the manager, full of remorse: "People living in the world ought not do anything against their own consciences. Just as there are people who take you to task openly, there are spirits who censure you in the dark. I almost lost my life for not taking heed of this."

From that time on he mended his ways and never went to Chin-nu's place again. Among family and friends who knew him, there were none who did not respect him for this. Indeed:

Though deeds of passion seem delicious,
When viewed objectively, such actions are indeed deplorable.
Once perception of this is achieved, all evil thoughts end,
And all of life will be at ease and in peace.

[18] There are three pulses in each wrist for the balance of the *yin* and *yang* elements in the body.

THE HENPECKED JUDGE WHO LOSES A GOVERNORSHIP

From *Tsui-hsing shih*

TRANSLATED BY TAI-LOI MA

What do purple banner and yellow imperial edict matter?
Accumulating virtue is better than wealth or position.
Soon pretty clothes will fall apart like butterflies.
Snails haunt the vermilion doors of the once powerful.
Besides the coffin, what does one possess?
For what does one strive?
Well may we laugh at misers.
Money only passes through one's hands for a limited time.

It is most difficult for people to overcome greed. People obsessed by it will consider only their own aggrandizement and ignore all social properties and human relationships. Worse still, they no longer have any sense of shame. They respect neither the law nor moral retribution. The situation is even more acute for officials. The greed of those engaging in farming and trade is limited, no matter how hard they try to enrich themselves. Such, however, is not the case with officials, who can punish and order people at will. Once their operations are established and their avaricious natures are recognized, they will be surrounded by hangers-on who will offer them ways and means for aggrandizement. There is no end to their activities. They will use various pretexts for robbing the people, such as raising the quota applied to making up fiscal deficits, impos-

ing heavy taxation, and extorting money from the rich. When giving out government loans, they favor merchants with property deeds as security. Those who extort in the open are of course wicked, but the most malignant ones are those who make gains behind the scenes. How many would willingly give away expensive seasonal presents, birthday gifts, drinking cups of rhinoceros horn or gold, brocade, gilded screens, old paintings and vases, famous calligraphy and curios [to their superiors for free]? Such things are actually extortions received under the name of "gifts."

Gifts are sent in every morning,
And the sound of beating can be heard daily.
The official is in residence,
While nine out of ten households suffer as in hell.

Nevertheless, the officials cannot do otherwise. Once they get their appointments, each day in office is a day for spending money. They are expected to donate part of their salaries to the government, subscribe to the public granary, contribute to army rations and public works, not to mention buying horses and meeting the household expenses, sending one gift here and giving two presents there. With all these expenses, how can a poor scholar without any assets manage? Nowadays there are some officials who, just after leaving their administrative duties, will send in memoranda criticizing their former colleagues for taking bribes and buying recommendations and promotions through expensive parting gifts and the like. May I ask these people if they have really cut themselves off from social functions? When evaluation and selection times come, do they not entreat their fellow townsmen and superiors with gifts? Still, it is better for one to antagonize men of position than the common people. It is better to regret gifts than to be left all alone feeling sorry for oneself. Small gifts will suffice. Why should one ruin one's integrity to curry favor? As far as wealth is concerned, it is up to Heaven. It is mentioned in the *T'ang-shu* (The History of the T'ang Dynasty) that in the netherworld there are officials in charge of confiscating surplus wealth. The prime minister Li Ch'iao was poor, whereas his colleague Chang Yüeh was rich.[1] A monk offered this explanation: "Chang is the lord of the insatiable spirits. There are ten furnaces in the netherworld to mint him all the money he needs." Everything is thus controlled by fate.

Both poverty and wealth are in the hands of the Creator.
Who else can strike a balance between the clumsy and the
*   ingenious?*
The clever man will let fate be his guide,
Pausing and advancing as it dictates.

In the Ming Dynasty there was a censor who told his disciples, "Wealth is regulated by fate and can't be obtained through unjust means. Once on an inspection tour through Yunnan, I stayed at an official residence for the night. I had an uneasy feeling and couldn't sleep. 'Is there any injustice that needs to be redressed?' I asked. In a daze, I saw a god in golden armor appear before me.

" 'Your Honor,' the god told me, 'has a thousand taels in cash hidden here. I have come especially to inform you of this.'

" 'Where?' I asked.

" 'Beneath the bricks by your seat.'

"I removed the chair and bricks, and found twenty pieces of silver, totaling one thousand taels.

" 'How can I bring it home?' I asked.

" 'All you have to do is write down your name, your native place, and your present address. I'll deliver it for you,' replied the god.

"I did as I was told, placed the piece of paper on the silver, and put the bricks back.

"Later, when the inspection tour was about to be completed, a classmate of mine,[2] who was then on leave because one of his parents had passed away, came and asked me to give a favorable recommendation for [a friend of his], a county magistrate. He and I were to get two hundred taels each for the effort. I declined firmly to receive anything. But my classmate insisted. 'If you don't take it, you might forget the whole business afterward. Unless you take the money now, I wouldn't feel at ease.' So reluctantly I accepted the money.

"I returned home after the tour of duty. By chance I recalled my encounter with the god in golden armor. I had the servants prepare some dishes of fish, pork, and fowl for sacrificial purposes, and I prayed silently. Suddenly the god appeared and told me, 'The silver is under the long table in your study.' The next day, I asked the servants to remove the table, and indeed the silver was there. But there were only eight hundred taels. 'Originally there were one thousand taels. Now there are only eight hundred. Where have the two hundred taels gone?' I wondered. That night, the god appeared again and said, 'The outstanding two hundred taels is the share of your classmate.' I was so frightened by this revelation that I was sweating.

"It is evident that every little step we take is

---

[1] As given in the story, Li Ch'iao (644–713) and Chang Yüeh were two contemporary officials in the T'ang period.

[2] In traditional China people passing the civil service examination in the same year had a special intimate relationship among themselves and with the examiner, not unlike those among classmates and between student and mentor.

known to the gods and spirits. What we gain in one place is to be paid off in another. Our fate is predetermined. From what I experienced, isn't it clear that it would be futile to attempt to get more than one's share?"

Merchants become rich not because of sheer calculation.
The poor are predestined.
The greedy contrive in vain.
No human ingenuity can circumvent Heaven's design.

I've heard about a certain *chin-shih* from Kwangtung surnamed Wei. When he was still a student, he was so poor that he did not even have the means to support his family.

Without a lamp, he used to read under the moon.
Wind passed freely through his empty door.
The cooking utensils were usually covered with dust.
The purse was often without cash.

He devoted himself completely to study and did not pay much attention to household affairs. Fortunately, his wife's family was quite well off and she was also rather diligent. She worked hard from dawn to dusk to support the family. Every now and then she would grieve that his study had depleted her dowry and complain about their poverty. Each time Wei tried his best to comfort her: "Don't worry. When I pass the examinations, I guarantee that you'll have all the food you can eat and all the dresses you can wear. I won't mind repaying you ten times your dowry."

As expected he passed the provincial examination, and was again successful in the subsequent examinations to become a *chin-shih*. He was placed on the third list and was to be appointed as a prefectural judge. But first he was assigned as an trainee in the Censorate. Immediately there were the expenses for employing valets, hiring horses, and social functions. After serving his apprenticeship, he had to wait for some time before he could be appointed. Since it was inconvenient to travel back and forth over a long distance, he stayed at the capital.

Half a year passed. To pay for rent and board, congratulatory and consolatory gifts, and presents to superiors when selection time came, Wei got into debt. On the twenty-fifth of an even month,[3] through a drawing of lots, he received an appointment to the Chiang-ling Prefecture[4] in Hu-kuang Province. This drawing of lots is no routine affair.[5] Whenever there is an assignment for an important prefecture, some officials serving in the capital, the classmates, and even the examiners will pay the appointee a visit to establish a friendly relationship with him so as to make it easier for them to ask special favors once the new official takes up his post. They even see to it that their colleagues in charge of appointments give the opening to their favorite person. Nine out of ten positions are filled in this manner. Usually the lots are divided either into the south, the north, and the central, or into the upper, the middle, and the lower. For example, Wei was a Cantonese, so only two tallies, for Chiang-ling and Kwangtung, were placed in the lottery holder. Even if Wei drew the tally for Kwangtung, he would be appointed to Chiang-ling since the rule against conflict of interest prohibited his serving in his native province. Or, arrangements would be made for a native from Hu-kuang to draw the lots with Wei. The latter could not be appointed to Chiang-ling. So again Wei would get the post.

Bureaucratic abuses are like heavy clouds
That dim even the bright moon.
People of low ability accumulate in the system
As pieces of firewood are placed over one another.
No wonder Feng T'ang had reason for grievances.[6]

[3] The second, fourth, sixth, etc., months of the lunar calendar.

[4] In the present Hupeh Province.

[5] This is a case of anachronism. Appointment through drawing lots was first introduced in 1594 by the minister of personnel Sun P'i-yang (1532–1614). Since this story mentions Chang Chü-cheng (1525–1582), a predecessor of Sun, as occupying the same position, the system could not have been in effect at that time.

[6] A Han official who admonished Emperor Wen (r. 179–157 B.C.).

After he received his appointment, Wei hired a sedan chair and went to Hsü.[7] From there he sailed across River Huai and the Yangtze River, and got to Kwangtung via Chekiang and Kiangsi. Having offered sacrifice to his ancestors and bid farewell to his relatives, he left with his wife to take up his post.

For long his wife had heard about the advantages of being an official and expected to receive an ocean of silver and a mountain of cash. When they arrived at the destination, runners and lackeys came out to welcome them by the roadside, creating an imposing spectacle. By the time he entered the tribunal, members of the gentry from the prefecture and subordinate counties were paying their respects with various gifts, creating quite a bustling scene. Nevertheless, since he was new to the office, Wei acted with reserve. Only when his visitors insisted on his acceptance would he take one or two items. From then on, Wei was busily occupied with, among other things, directives from the governor, regional inspector, surveillance commissioner, and circuit intendant, and documents from the prefect. Actually, [without his knowing it], his duty at the tribunal proved to be more one of serving the profit-seekers around him than filling his office as a judge.

After more than a year later, he was sent on an inspection tour for the regional inspector. Instead of parting presents and feasts, the prefects and county magistrates gave him about a hundred taels. In contrast, what he got from the county magistrates in the form of gift for the Dragon Boat Festival and the New Year was about four taels from each magistrate. Moreover, those of distant or small counties might dodge the occasions and not give anything. "Alas!" his wife would say, "The education officer's only chance is the festivals. But even he has more visitors than you; and each time that students are admitted to

the school, he gets tuition fees." These casual remarks, spoken as if unintentionally, are most annoying and act as a goad. All gifts were received by his wife, who often asked for jewelry and new clothes. Because he had spent her money when he was poor, and she was a wheedler who would not stop crying unless her demands were met, Judge Wei reluctantly had to let her have her way. Indeed:

He had made up his mind to be righteous,
But had no way to discourage her foolish greed.

Furthermore, whenever she bought pearls, jade, or silk, she would not only lower the price but would also demand a discount for the purity of her silver. All this helped to create a rapacious image for Judge Wei.

A fierce tiger may have all the power;
But if he is submissive to the cunning fox
Which as his surrogate subdues all other animals,
The tiger can only lament the loss of his power.

Among the tribunal clerks there was one Shan Kuei, a cunning underling. It was he who had been sent to Kwangtung to escort the newly appointed official and his family. He offered presents to both the mistress and the butler, thereby gaining the judge's favor. He also observed closely the character and habits of the judge. It did not take long for him to realize that the mistress was the real master of the household and that she had a craving for money.

Meanwhile, there was a local mogul named Ch'en Ch'ih, who was at once a rich man and a criminal. He kept scores of retainers to conduct illegal business along the Yangtze River and raid neighboring villages. One day they robbed an official vessel of a classmate of the circuit intendant in charge of military affairs. The intendant was putting pressure [on the local authorities] to have the culprits caught. The constables had to report the progress to the magistrate and the prefect every three days and to the intendant every fort-

---

[7] The northwestern part of modern Kiangsu Province.

night. In the past, when his retainers brought back jewelry, satin, and the like, Ch'en Ch'ih would give them some cash in exchange and then sell the loot in the neighboring provinces. In this way, the bandits would not carry any stolen goods that might attract suspicion.

However, this time they got a lot in the robbery, and since they were not satisfied with the meager reward that Ch'en Ch'ih used to provide, they kept some of the booty themselves and wanted to dispose of it immediately. Some ventured to sell the goods, but they had no knowledge of their value. Their action did not escape the observation of some keen constables. The bandits also visited the brothel of Chou Ying, where the pretty Hsüeh-erh, Ch'u-yün, and the other courtesans all knew how to squeeze money from their clients. Because they had come by the money easily, these bandits spent lavishly at the brothel and gave away some of the jewelry as presents. Thus they were arrested by the constables. When they admitted they were Ch'en Ch'ih's retainers, about a dozen more accomplices were apprehended at Ch'en's place. However, through bribery, Ch'en Ch'ih had the blame shifted to the pander, and the case was so reported to the higher authorities.

Being an extremely cunning person, Ch'en Ch'ih was very generous when in trouble and promised anything. But once the danger subsided, he would not honor whatever pledges he had made. Well aware of his character, the tribunal clerks purposely left some grounds for future litigation. They left intact in the constables' initial report a sentence which mentioned that among those arrested was the adopted son of Ch'en Ch'ih, who was not summoned.

When the case was sent back by the intendant for review, Judge Wei, being one dedicated to his work, scrutinized the documents carefully. "Bandits who committed such serious crimes must have a lair," he thought. "The brothel was only a place for them to enjoy themselves. It was quite natural for the pander not to report the case to the author-

ities because of the money they spent. The boss must have been their master for years and cannot be a pander whom they have known for only a few days." Therefore he issued a warrant for the arrest of Ch'en Ch'ih.

To catch the guilty, one has to exhaust all means.
To eliminate the villain, one has to show one's determination.
When a fair and upright judge is in office,
People may travel in safety.

While he was going to have Ch'en Ch'ih arraigned, the acting regional inspector asked him to investigate a case at Wuchang[8] on his behalf. So Judge Wei had to put the case aside.

Soon after Wei took up his post, he made a trip to call upon the governor, regional inspector, surveillance commissioner, and circuit intendant. Because of a head wind, he had the boat anchored at a small inlet. Alone and with nothing to do, he looked around and noticed some buildings behind a distant wood of pine and bamboo. The wind also carried the chiming sound of bells. He asked the boatman and was told that it was the Royal Longevity Monastery. Judge Wei said, "This place is next to my jurisdiction. It would do no harm to spend some time there." With a few attendants and without the usual ado of an official visit, he went to the woods. Over there:

Bamboo clusters welcome the guests;
Lofty pines seem to attract visitors.
Few people frequent this river village.
A footpath cuts through the luxuriant turf.

As he passed through the woods, he heard not only the intermittent chiming sound but also music from pipes. Some young novices carrying musical instruments and a dozen or so monks holding incense sticks came out to welcome him. At the gate, a monk with white hair and a bright face greeted him deferentially. After paying respects to the icons in the main hall, Judge Wei went to the abbot's room. It was a bamboo hut

---

[8] A prefecture in Hupeh Province.

with paper-pasted windows. The atmosphere was rather casual. There were also some small plants and rare flowers. It was a perfectly quiet place for retreat. The furniture and utensils were clean and orderly, without the slightest trace of dust. Covering the walls were paintings and couplets complimenting the abbot Tao-chi. One of them had this to say:

The hundred-year-old tree knows the monk's age.
The bright moon shines over the venerable heart.

Another:

Leaving behind earthly turmoil for twenty years;
Transversing the ages with one heart.

And:

The banner waves in the wind only because one thinks so.
Enlighted, there's no mirror in one's heart to be cleansed.[9]

Also:

Wisdom comes from meditation.
With perception, one serves as the light of the world.

Seeing this, Wei said to himself, "So this old monk must be Tao-chi. Since he is a renowned cleric, I should treat him as my equal." The abbot, however, inspite of Wei's insistence, would only take a side seat. Presently tea was brought in together with some fresh fruits and pastries. The two then had an impromptu discussion on Ch'an Buddhism, and complimented each other.
An official able to say something about Ch'an Buddhism has already transcended the common lot. As the monks hoped to obtain favors from the judge, the conversation went on genially. After quite a while, Judge Wei was invited to a vegetarian feast with ingredients from distant places. It seemed that much preparation had been done in advance.

"Your Reverence, you're a renowned cleric;

[9] Both lines refer to the sayings of Hui-neng (638–713), the Sixth Patriarch and the founder of the Southern School of Ch'an Buddhism.

isn't it more appropriate for you to ignore temporal matters?" asked the judge. "Just then you came all the way to greet me. I surely don't deserve it!"

A fun-loving, quick-tongued young monk, standing by the side, blurted out, "Ordinarily our master doesn't receive visitors and is rather lax in etiquette. Three days ago, while in meditation, he foresaw that Your Honor would come and sent me on a special errand to town to prepare the dishes. And this morning, he also sent people out beyond the gate to welcome you. That's how things happen."

"Is it true that Your Reverence can foretell the future?" asked Wei.

"Not at all. This young monk is only joking," Tao-chi replied.

Wei also thought that the young monk was only joking. That night he stayed at the temple, and soon became a good friend of the abbot. A large piece of red paper with Judge Wei's name on it was pasted in the hall [so that he could share the benefits of others' prayers]. Though he did not take the quick-tongued monk's words seriously, Wei was intrigued. On his return trip and subsequently whenever he passed by, he would visit the abbot. Every time he was treated in the same respectful manner. This time Wei again called on the abbot.

When he arrived at Wuchang, all he had to perform were some routine duties at the prefectural and the county tribunals: checking the granaries and treasuries, calling the muster-roll of runners, hearing cases, and on the advice of some tribunal clerks recommending to the regional inspector the acquittal of a few prisoners against whom the incriminating evidence was rather circumstantial. He also asked the prefect and the magistrates to evaluate their subordinates and report any clerks who should be reprimanded. All these names were then submitted to the regional inspector for action. It happened that Chang T'ai-yüeh was back home because his mother had passed away.[10] The chief provincial officials all went to Chiangling to pay their respects. Judge Wei, too, returned to his own office.

The work is as routine as copying pictures of the gourd.
The clerks work to no purpose.
Who really cares for the public?
Only the one who examines with an open mind.

When Judge Wei resumed his unfinished business, Ch'en Ch'ih had already contacted Shan Kuei, hoping to have his case dismissed. Shan suggested that if he were willing to part with a thousand taels, then everything could be settled.

"I've heard that Judge Wei has never taken any bribe. If we approach him untactfully and infuriate him, the situation may get worse. Unless we can count on some intimate friend of his, perhaps we should get in touch with Grand Secretary Chang's scion[11] instead," Ch'en said.

With a wry smile, Shan replied, "You should be grateful that I'm willing to take up this case. As for the young Chang, three thousand taels won't be enough for him to open his eyes."

Convinced by Shan, Ch'en Ch'ih gave him a thousand taels. Taking advantage of Wei's absence, Clerk Shan first talked with the butler.

"Sure, our mistress is crazy about money. Once she promises, our master'll have to do as he's told," the butler said.

"As I see it, our master is most impartial," said Shan, trying to provoke the butler deliberately. "I'm afraid that even his mistress can't help. However, if this can be done, it's possible to get ten thousand taels. As to your share, you can get at least a thousand."

"It takes a special method to tie an ox. We can count on our mistress," the butler replied.

When the butler told the mistress about the case, she promised to take it upon herself as predicted. However, Shan Kuei gave her only six hundred taels, the butler sixty taels, and the intermediaries thirty taels. Shan kept the rest for himself.

With a thousand taels one gets help from the roar of the
*   lioness.[12]*
When three sides of a net are left open, cunning owls escape
*   easily.[13]*

Returning from his tour, Wei spent an evening with his wife and both drank a little. After the dishes were removed, she told her husband jubilantly, "You've been an official for over one year, and it's only today that we've made a fortune."

"Are you speaking of the gifts I brought back from my tour?" asked Wei.

"You call those things a fortune?" His wife returned his question with a question. Then taking out Ch'en's petition from her sleeve, she continued, "This man has given me six hundred taels. You should exonerate him."

"The man can't be spared. I'm about to arraign him to establish my reputation," said the judge.

"It's better to seek wealth than fame. You've been talking about the advantages of being an official all these years. But you haven't saved enough even to pay back your debts accrued at the capital. Now that we have this money, I'm not going to return it."

"An official will get rich eventually. Please don't interfere with this case," Wei pleaded.

"An official will get rich eventually? You've been a *chin-shih* for two years and a prefectural judge for one. What've you got now? If one doesn't grab money when given the chance, one'll

---

[10] T'ai-yüeh was the style of Chang Chü-cheng, the leading politican of the early Wan-li period. Here the storyteller committed another error. Chang's mother outlived her son and witnessed his posthumous disgrace. However, in 1578 Chang did go home briefly to see to his father's funeral.
[11] The son of Chang Chü-cheng.

[12] A euphemism for a dominating wife.
[13] This means that the captives are deliberately set free.

never live to old age. Do what you like, I'm going to keep the money."

"Who brought in the money?" Wei asked.

"It's heaven-sent!" she blurted out. "Don't be silly! You may not want any money. But when you're up for promotion, those bastards will ask for your money. Let me ask you, if you don't get some money to pay back your debts, who will lend it to you in the future? Furthermore, this case has already been decided; why do you create trouble by reopening it?" Her temper had risen and she was ready to make a scene.

The tiger has a fierce temperament,
Yet the jackal is more greedy.
Not understanding reputation nor righteousness,
It indulges itself in material gains.

His wife then went straight to sleep without even showing him the money. With feigned indignation, Wei summoned the butler [and other servants] and scolded them: "You shameless slaves! Now who did it?" Since everyone had gotten some money, they just looked at one another and did not speak out. When he was about to beat the doorkeeper, his wife again jumped up and cried, "Are you going to beat him to spite me, because you dare not lay your hands on me?" Wei had to back out when his wife became hysterical. He would have liked to grill the flunky assigned to his residence, but he was afraid that might create a commotion. So all he could do to vent his anger was to give the fellow a beating of twenty-five strokes when he found the pretext of the latter's not attending to his duty.

For the next few days, Wei was depressed. When his superior pressed for his opinion, he had no alternative but to endorse the previous verdict. To show off his influence, Shan Kuei had the mistress force her husband to exonerate Ch'en Ch'ih completely and to fix the guilt on the pander. Consequently, Ch'en Ch'ih had nothing to worry about, and the pander was awaiting execution.

He does not intend to kill,
But he has to because he gets the bounty.
His endorsement goes down like a halberd;
Spirits of people wrongly executed are crying in the Nine
*   Springs.*

Because of this incident, Wei was afraid that his wife might try her hand again, so he tightened the security of his residence. He even seldom went out to drink. Not long afterward, he was again assigned by the regional inspector to Wuchang. This time he took precaution of sealing off his residence and assigned two flunkies from the tribunal to perform errand duties. He also cautioned his wife, "Please don't repeat what you did before." But she retorted, "You really deserve to be poverty stricken for life! Just wait and see!" Before he left, he reminded the doorkeeper to keep a careful watch.

Wei was a dedicated official at heart. Feeling guilty over the whole affair and fearing others might know it, he became very depressed. As his boat approached the Royal Longevity Monastery, he wished to be on land at once so that he could talk with the abbot. However, he did not hear the sound of any musical instrument even after he had passed through the woods. Fortunately, a young monk saw him when he reached the gate. Others were quickly notified. A few monks came out to greet the judge, but their apparel was in disarray. Some did not have their clerical caps, while others were not wearing their gowns. None of them had the time to carry any incense sticks. Inside the abbot's place, he found there was thick dust on the table and the chairs were in disorder. After a while, Tao-chi came out and apologized, "Please excuse our negligence!" They had some tea and a vegetarian feast of some rather common fare. It happened that the same fun-loving, quick-tempered monk was assigned to serve the official.

"Why couldn't the master foretell my coming this time?" Wei teased the young monk.

"Our master didn't inform us this time, so we're

unable to treat Your Honor properly," explained the young monk.

"There's a reason for what happens. Even I don't understand why it turns out this way," Tao-chi cut in quickly to apologize.

"What's the reason? It won't hurt to tell me," demanded Wei.

"The whole thing may sound incredible. The guardian god of our humble temple is miraculous. Whenever an illustrious person passes by, it'll inform me three days in advance through a dream. Once, when Grand Secretary Chang was on his way to Wuchang to take the provincial examination, he stopped by our humble temple to take shelter from strong winds; and we were informed beforehand by the guardian god. After Grand Secretary Chang rose to prominence, he donated ten *mou* of land to the temple for maintenance and gave us a tablet praising the miraculousness of the guardian god. In the past, Your Honor's arrivals were all announced beforehand. Only this time, things went wrong. I don't know whether the guardian god has gone elsewhere or for some reason it just didn't want to inform us."

"Is that so?" asked Wei.

"I wouldn't dare to lie to you," replied Tao-chi.

"It'll take me only ten days or so to go to Wuchang and return. Will Your Reverence please ask the guardian god to give an explanation?"

When he made this request, Wei was not sure whether he should believe in what he was told. But the old monk did speak to the statue: "You're the master of this temple. Whether it will flourish or decline all depends on you. How could you fail to notify us beforehand of the arrival of the illustrious person? Now we've offended Judge Wei. If he really got upset, it would bring harm to the temple. Be quick and tell me why you didn't inform us the last time." He repeated his question several times as if the earthen idol had ears to hear.

Perturbed by the complexity of the matter,
One tends to make repetitive statements.

This god was really miraculous. After the abbot prayed, it appeared to him that night in a dream and gave a detailed explanation. The old monk was stunned by the revelation.

Don't say Heaven is far above.
The god notices every action below.

Half a month later, Wei returned. Again no one came out to greet him. Noticing this, Wei said jokingly, "So the guardian god is not miraculous now."

"It is," the old monk muttered.

"If so, why didn't it notify you? And what was its reply to my last inquiry?"

Tao-chi hesitated, not knowing whether he should speak out.

"So the guardian god is just a pretext," Wei said with a hearty laugh.

Tao-chi pondered for some more time. He would like to tell the judge, but was afraid that would antagonize him. On the other hand, if he did not tell, then the judge might think he had been lying all along. He found himself in a dilemma. Finally he said, "I'd better not tell you."

"We've been such close friends. You can tell me anything," pleaded Wei.

"The guardian god told me so. But I dare not believe it," the monk said. Pulling his chair closer to Wei and speaking in a low voice, he continued, "The guardian god said that Your Honor was to govern Ch'u and become the minister of personnel. This place would be under your jurisdiction."[14]

"I'm afraid it won't happen this way," Wei said with a smile.

"That was why it announced your arrivals in the past," added the monk.

[14] Perhaps the monastery, as suggested by its title, was supported by government funds.

333

"Now it no longer announces my arrival; does that mean that I am not going to govern Ch'u?"

"I don't know how to explain to you," answered the monk. When further pressed by the judge, he said, "The god said that recently Your Honor had received six hundred taels from a man and had substituted an innocent person for the guilty one to be executed. A heavenly mandate had been proclaimed revoking your governship because of this false verdict. So the god will no longer announce your arrival."

Judge Wei was stupefied. Indeed:

Just as when standing on the top of the Hua Mountains,[15]
Just as when standing by the side of a deep ocean,
Sweat soaks through the outer garment.
He no longer can control himself.

Fighting to keep his composure, the judge said, "I'm a self-disciplined person. At times I may make some false judgment and punish the innocent. But I've never received any bribe or twisted the law." Finding it impossible to stay a moment longer, he rose up and wanted to return to his boat. Tao-chi tried his best to convey his regret, but failed to persuade the judge to stay. He saw the judge off at the gate.

Holding the monk's hands, Wei entreated his friend, "Please treat what you've just told me as confidential."

"Of course, of course," the monk replied immediately.

On his way home, Wei was very depressed. He thought of asking someone to urge the pander to appeal, and then he himself could entreat his colleagues to change the verdict. Yet he was afraid of the action Ch'en Ch'ih might take if he found out. "Furthermore, this case has already reached the Ministry of Justice. But if I just ignore the case, then the real culprit will go free while the wrongly accused will be executed. All this is due to the bribe I've accepted!"

Because of poverty, one is forced to play the role of a helpless
*   cub.*
In remorse, one discovers only too late that he is a scapegoat in
*   the end.*

As soon as he reached home, he ordered the doors opened and went straight to his study and sat there silently in a melancholic mood. His wife had been waiting impatiently for his return because she had taken in some more cases. "That's strange!" she cried out when told the judge had gone to his study. She went there and heard Wei stamp his feet twice and lament, "How carelessly I have thrown away a ministerial seat!"

With a smile, his wife went in to greet him and asked, "What minsterial seat have you thrown away? If it is still intact, we can ask someone to bring it back."

"For your six hundred taels, my post of minister of personnel was sold."

"If the post of minister of personnel can be bought and sold, surely it'd be better to have money."

Then Wei related at length all that had taken place, and added, "Everything had been watched closely by the gods. It's too late to do anything now." He became so grieved that he almost burst into tears.

Don't be too hasty in rejoicing over bountiful goods;
Heavenly order is evident everywhere.
To exhaust the iron ore from Wei-chou
And forge the character "mistake" won't help.

Finding herself resented, his wife blurted out, "You made up this ghastly tale because you think I've taken up some new cases. It must be the ghost of poverty in your student days who is now speaking through your mouth." She left spitefully without giving her husband a chance to answer.

Not long afterward, new ordinances were set by Chang Chiang-ling[16] that called for immediate execution after sentencing of pirates in the south

---

[15] A mountain range (also known as the Western Mountains) in Shensi Province.

[16] That refers to Chang Chü-cheng because Chang was a native of Chiang-ling.

and highwaymen in the north.[17] When the imperial edict and ministerial directive were received, the pander and the bandits were all beheaded in the marketplace. What a pity:

He is only a commandant of prostitutes,
Having nothing to do with bandit chiefs.
All plants are mowed down without discrimination.
The color brush of the judge raises a storm.

When Wei heard about the execution, he became even more worried. He became so ill that he was unable to serve out his term. He asked for a leave of absence and returned to his native place. Within a few years he died.

Thus we see that he who gains through improper means will not only be censured by mortals but also punished by the gods. A man with a righteous disposition will not take the slightest advantage of others. Even if there were no gods, one should not act improperly, not to mention hurting others for material gain. How can the woman whose mind is the most shallow be allowed to be the master? The origin of this malady can be traced to the time when people's minds become set on wealth and eminence, even before they take up their studies to become officials. When these people become officials, nothing can restrain them from exploiting their fellow men. Let me pose this question to the misers. Granted that one covets money in order to support one's wife and to purchase office; but if one cannot even save one's own life, and one's destined official position is taken away, should one not take heed?

[17] Usually executions were carried out only in the autumn. Although Chang Chü-cheng opposed any delay in execution, he did not set rules for immediate execution after sentencing.

Although not everything that has been said about the netherworld should be taken too seriously, yet at the same time one should not be too skeptical. But certainly one should not bend the law and exploit the people. As for reviewing cases, even though one does not accept the bribe personally, one still cannot cast off his official responsibility. If he takes things as they come, even though he is not personally involved in the administration of the graft, he is still derelict of his duty as an official for obstructing justice, for failing to redress grievances. Recently, some officials have sided with the yamen clerks, allowing them to manipulate the law. Thus the true criminals become the plaintiffs, whereas the innocent lose their property or even their lives. Wrongdoings are forgiven; scholars are treated contemptuously. Warrants are issued without any grace period and appeals are rejected *en masse,* so as to insure that sentences will be irrevocable. Since the work of reviewing cases has fallen into the hands of tribunal clerks, the official only acts as he is ordered to. However, if an official heartlessly refuses to redress a wrong which will cause an innocent person's life and ruin his family, I am afraid that he cannot escape moral judgment and heavenly anger. Therefore, there is an ancient saying that a judge should steer clear of official influence, retributive sentences to either benefactor or enemy, requests by wife or friends, bribery, and letters seeking various favors; and he should dispense justice impartially. There is no difference between actually killing a person and executing one through a violation of justice. Those who are responsible for reviewing cases should take heed and tremble at this!

THE SUPERHUMAN MAIDEN

If one member of a loving couple is not an ordinary mortal, normally it is the woman who plays the superhuman role. She is usually an animal (both Miss Jen and Red Jade are foxes) assuming a human form after hundreds of years of self-cultivation in supernatural magic. This does not mean that she has no limit to her power. Miss Jen, resourceful as she is, loses her life in the jaws of the hounds, and the powerful white lady (in "Eternal Prisoner under the Thunder Peak Pagoda") is eventually subdued by the more powerful monk. Their limitations, indeed, have much to do with their human quality. When she falls in love with a young man, the superhuman maiden can never free herself from the human bondage; both Miss Jen and the white lady are victims of their own passion.

Another notable quality of the superhuman maiden is that though she is not of humankind, she is more often a stickler for the moral codes of society than her human sister. It is precisely owing to her respect for the sanctity of human marriage that the daughter of the dragon king (in "The Legendary Marriage at Tung-t'ing") is willing to submit herself to the brutal treatment of her husband. Miss Jen serves the interests of two men, but she offers herself only to the one who claims her first. Red Jade finds it improper to stay on with her loved one after the young man's father has accused her of misconduct.

Except for the story of the dragon king's daughter, indeed most of the stories about superhuman maidens before the Ch'ing period conclude rather tragically, either in death or with the leading lady being forced to return to her original form. The moral implication is simple: the superhuman maiden, however lovely and exemplary her looks and manners are, is, after all, unhuman and accordingly should not be treated as our kind. For this reason, the collection from which "Red Jade" is taken, P'u Sung-ling's *Liao-chai chih-i,* in which marriage between the human and the superhuman is allowed to run its happy course, is truly revolutionary (see the sectional introduction to "The Ghost Wife" for a comparable comment).

MISS JEN

From *I-wen chi*

TRANSLATED BY WILLIAM H. NIENHAUSER, JR.

Miss Jen was a fox-fairy.

There was a certain prefect, Wei Yin, who was the ninth son in his family. His maternal grandfather was Li Wei, the prince of Hsin-an. Since his youth he had been uncontrolled and fond of drinking. His cousin's husband, Cheng the Sixth (I can't remember his given name), had previously been a practitioner of martial arts and was also fond of wine and women. Cheng was poor and had no family left, so he threw his lot in with his wife's relatives. He became friends with Wei Yin and they always caroused together.

In the middle of summer of the ninth year of the T'ien-pao reign period [750] they had been riding through the streets of Ch'ang-an and were going to stop for a drink in the New Prosperity Quarter. When they reached a point south of the Peace Prevailing Quarter [immediately to the west of New Prosperity], Cheng said he had some business and, asking his companion to go on alone, promised to follow him to the tavern. Wei then rode his white horse on to the east, while Cheng turned south on his donkey into the northern gate of the Peace Prevailing Quarter.

There Cheng happened upon three women walking in the street. Among them was one dressed in white and of an enchanting beauty. When Chang saw her he was delightfully sur-prised and whipped his donkey up alongside them, staying a bit behind or in front, wanting to dally with her but not daring to.

The one in white kept on making eyes at him as if she were interested in him. Cheng jested with her: "A beautiful girl like you shouldn't be walking."

"When someone has a mount but won't let me use it, what else can I do?" the girl replied, smiling.

"Though my nag's not good enough to carry you, I'd like to offer it to you at once and follow along on foot."

They looked at each other and laughed, and with the two maids taking turns leading him on, the couple was soon on quite intimate terms. By the time Cheng had followed them east to the Pleasure Gardens, night had fallen. He could see a mansion and, through a carriage gate in the earthen wall, the dignified arrangement of the household. As the girl in white was about to enter, she turned and asked him to linger a bit, and then went in. One of the maids who had accompanied her stayed in the gateway and asked his name and age. Cheng told her and asked similar questions about the lady in white.

"Her name's Jen and she's the twentieth child in her family," the maid replied.

After a little while he was invited in. He hitched his donkey at the gate and placed his hat on the saddle, before noticing that a woman in her early thirties was bidding him welcome. This was Miss Jen's elder sister. Candles had been lit and a feast was laid out. By the time Cheng had drunk several goblets of wine, Jen appeared, freshly made up. They drank heartily and were content. Far into the night they went to bed. Her lovely appearance and beautiful body, each song or smile, her manners and movements, all were captivating, almost otherworldly!

Just before dawn Jen said, "You must go! My sister and I are associated with the imperial music bureaus and serve in the Southern Tribunal.[1] We have to go out at dawn, so you can't tarry." So they arranged another rendezvous and he left.

He walked along until he reached the gate which led out of the quarter, but it was still barred. To one side there was a Tartar bakery. The proprietor had just lit a lamp and was preparing to start a fire in his stove. Cheng sat down to rest under the eaves of his shop to wait for the morning drums,[2] and he spoke with the man.

"If you go east from here, you'll come to a gate in the wall," Cheng said, pointing to the place where he had spent the night. "Whose residence is that?"

"There's only some broken-down walls, and grounds which have been let go—no house."

"But I just stopped there. How can you say it's not there?"

He argued obstinately with the man until the latter suddenly understood. "Ah, ha! I see! There's a fox spirit around there who often beguiles men into spending the night with her.

She's been seen three times already. You met her, too?"

Cheng blushed, but to conceal it from him said simply, "No."

After it had become light, he went again to examine the place and found the earthen wall and the carriage gate as before. When he peered in, however, there were only overgrown fields and abandoned gardens.

When he had returned to Wei Yin's, the latter upbraided him for failing to keep their appointment. Cheng did not reveal his secret but replied that he had been engaged in some other matter. But whenever he remembered the girl's bewitching beauty, he wanted to see her again. He just could not bring himself to forget her.

After a fortnight or so, Cheng was out for a stroll, and as he went into a clothing stall in the Western Market, he caught a glimpse of her. She was attended by the same maids as before. Cheng hurriedly called to her, but she turned around and spun into the crowd to hide. Cheng continued to call her and pressed after her. She just turned her back to him and, speaking from behind her fan, said, "You know all about me. How could you come to me again?"

"What does that matter?"

"This whole affair is shameful. I find it difficult to face you."

"The way I long for you with all my heart, how can you bear to leave me again?"

"I wouldn't dare. I'm just afraid you'll find me repugnant."

Cheng vowed his love in words even more sincere. Jen then glanced around at him and lowered her fan, revealing a ravishing beauty as brilliant as before. "I'm not the only one of us in the world of men," she said. "It's just that you can't recognize the others. Don't feel that I alone am strange."

Cheng demanded another rendezvous.

"People dread us because of the harm we do," she went on. "But I'm not like that. If you won't

[1] In T'ang times, the Southern Tribunal referred collectively to the offices of the prime ministers because the departments of the Chancellery, the Secretariat, and State Affairs were all located at the southern portion of the imperial palace complex. The two imperial music bureaus were also located there.
[2] The morning drums signaled the opening of the gates.

despise me, I'll wait on you hand and foot forever. Should I ever incur your displeasure for one reason or another, I'd pack and go without your telling me to."

Cheng promised to find a place for her to stay. "East of here," she said, "there is a huge tree growing out of the ridgepole of a house on a quiet, secluded lane. We can rent it and live there. Last time we met someone riding off eastward from the south side of Peace Prevailing on a white horse. That was your wife's cousin, wasn't it? His house had a lot of superfluous furniture. We can borrow some of it."

At that time Wei Yin's uncles were all at posts in every corner of the country and three households of goods had been stored away there. Cheng made inquiries about the house as she had instructed him and went to Wei Yin about the furnishings. His cousin wanted to know what he planned to use them for. Cheng replied, "I've recently acquired a beauty, and have already rented a place. I want to borrow these things to put it in order."

Wei smiled. "With your looks, you must have got hold of some hag! How could she be that beautiful?" Then he loaned him everything—curtains, draperies, bedding, and mats—and had a clever young servant boy tag along to get a peek at the girl. Before long the boy came running back to report, out of breath and covered with sweat. Wei greeted him with a question, "Was she there?"

"Yes."

"What'd she look like?"

"Uncanny! Like nothing in the world you've ever seen!"

Now there were a good many women in Wei Yin's clan, and he had of old followed such indulgent ways that he knew many beauties. So he asked, "Is she as beautiful as so-and-so?"

"She can't be compared to her!"

Wei reeled off the names of four or five beautiful women for comparison, but the reply was always: "Can't be compared to her!"

At that time Wei's sister-in-law, the sixth daughter of the prince of Wu, was as captivating as a fairy. Among the girls in the clan she was considered the most beautiful. Wei asked, "How would she stack up against Prince Wu's sixth daughter?"

Again the answer was: "Can't be compared to her!"

Wei clapped his hands in astonishment. "How on earth could there be such a person?" He hurriedly ordered water, washed his face and neck, put on a new turban, daubed some color to his lips, and set off for Cheng's.

He arrived as Cheng had just left. Upon entering he saw a young manservant with a broom in his hands sweeping up, and a maid standing near the door. No one else was to be seen. He questioned the lad, who smiled and replied that no one was at home. Wei looked around and saw a red skirt protruding from under a door. He stepped forward to take a closer look and saw Jen crouched in hiding behind the leaf of the door. He led her out into the light to get a better look—she was even more beautiful than she had been reported to be. Wei nearly went out of his mind with passion. He took her into his arms, intending to ravage her, but she would not submit. He restrained her physically, and when he had nearly forced her, she said, "I'll give in, but please let go of me for a moment!" As soon as he acquiesced, she struggled as hard as in the beginning. It went on like this several times. Then Wei held her tight with all his strength. Jen was exhausted, and she was sweating as if drenched in rain. Since she knew there was no way to avoid him, she relaxed and resisted no longer, but her expression became very sorrowful.

"What are you so unhappy about?" Wei asked.

She sighed and then replied, "I really feel sorry for Cheng!"

"Why do you say that?"

"Though he's a full six feet tall, he can't even protect a woman. He's no real man! You've had courage and wealth since youth, and have taken many beauties, most of whom must have been better than I. But Cheng is poor and I am all that he can call his contentment. How can you, in seeking to indulge yourself even further, take from someone who has never had enough? I feel sorry, because he's poor and hungry and can't support himself, because he wears your clothes, eats your food, and is humiliated by you. If he could earn his own living, things would never have gotten this way."

When Wei, who was an honorable and righteous man, heard this speech, he immediately let her go. He bowed and said, "Please accept my apology." Soon Cheng returned and they met one another joyously.

From this time on, Wei provided Jen with all her daily necessities. She often stopped by Wei's home on her way in or out, whether by carriage, on horseback, in a sedan chair, or on foot—she did not make a practice of staying at home. On those days when Wei took part in her daily excursions, they enjoyed each other's company very much. Even though intimate, they never went beyond the bounds of propriety. Thus Wei loved and respected her, and never grudged anything she needed. Even when eating or drinking, he never forgot her. Since Jen understood his love for her, she professed her thanks to him. "It shames me to be so loved by you, but I see myself too rude and unrefined to requite your magnanimity. Moreover, since I can't forsake Cheng, I can't act according to you wishes. I come from Ch'in, born and raised here in the capital—from a line of entertainers. Among my cousins there are many mistresses and concubines. Thus I know the gay quarters of Ch'ang-an very well. If there is an attractive young lady you've admired, but have not yet been able to meet, I could carry her off for you. I would like to do this to repay your kindness."

"That would be perfect!" Wei exclaimed. In the market there was a girl who sold clothes named Chang the Fifteenth. She looked fair and pure. Wei had long admired her and therefore asked Jen if she knew her.

"She's one of my cousins. It will be easy to arrange."

And, indeed, in less than two weeks it was set up. After several months he grew tired of her and ended the affair.

"Market girls are easy enough to procure," Jen professed. "They don't serve to demonstrate my resources. If you know of some girl who is secluded and difficult to get at, please let me know. I would like to try my very best."

"The other day during the Cold Food Festival,[3] as a couple of friends and I were strolling by the Temple of a Thousand Blessings, we saw General Tiao Mien's women giving a musical performance in the hall. There was one who was skilled at the flute, about sixteen years old, with braided hair hanging down about her ears. She was exquisitely beautiful. Do you know her by any chance?"

"She is [the general's favorite mistress] called Ch'ung-nu. Her mother is my elder sister. I can get her for you."

Wei bowed down to her, and she again promised him help. Then she began to frequent the Tiao residence, and this continued for more than a month. When Wei pressed her to learn of her plans, Jen requested two rolls of fine silk to be used as a bribe. He supplied them to her as ordered. Two days later, just as they had sat down to a meal, one of the general's servants leading a black steed came to pick up Jen. At the news of this invitation, she smiled and said to Wei, "Things are falling into place!" Jen had previously tainted Ch'ung-nu with an infection which neither acupuncture or medicine could alleviate. Both the girl's mother and the general had become so worried that they resorted to the help of a

[3] The day before the spring festival Ch'ing-ming, when no fire is lit and only cold food is served.

number of shamanesses. One of them had been secretly bribed by Jen to indicate the area in which Jen lived as an auspicious place to move the patient. As soon as she had examined the girl, the shamaness said, "It is not good for her to stay here. She should be moved to a certain place to the southeast, so that she can regain the vital forces necessary for life."

The general and the girl's mother paid a visit to the area and realized that Jen lived there. General Tiao then asked if his mistress might live there. Jen began to exaggerate the cramped nature of her quarters, but after the general had repeatedly entreated her, she finally consented. Then, in a carriage together with her clothing and other essentials, and accompanied by her mother, the lady was carried to Jen's. On her arrival there she began to recover. Before a few days had passed, Jen had secreted Wei in the house and brought them together. After a month the girl became pregnant. Her mother took fright and immediately brought her back to General Tiao. Thus the affair was broken off.

One day Jen said to Cheng, "Can you get hold of five or six thousand in cash? I could help you make a good profit."

"Sure," Cheng replied. Then he got a loan of six thousand from someone.

"There's a horse trader in the market who has a horse with a blemish on one haunch," she explained. "Buy it and bring it home."

Cheng went to the market and there, indeed, he saw a man leading a horse with a dark blemish on its left haunch, which he was trying to sell. Cheng bought it and returned. His brothers-in-law all jeered at him. "That's a no-good beast! What did you buy it for?"

After a little while Jen told him that the horse could now be sold and that he should get thirty thousand for it. Cheng then took it out to sell. Someone offered him twenty thousand, but he refused. The entire marketplace buzzed with talk like "Why is he offering so much?" and "Why won't the other sell?" Cheng mounted and went home. The buyer followed him to his door, repeatedly raising his offers, until he had reached twenty-five thousand. Still not giving in, Cheng told him, "I won't sell for less than thirty." His brothers-in-law all railed at him. Cheng could not stand any more and, in the end, he sold it for under thirty thousand.

Later Cheng went on the sly to question the buyer and find out his true motives. He learned than an imperial horse with a blemish on its haunch kept at the Chao-ying County[4] had died three years ago. This man who had been the functionary in charge was about to leave the post and he would have to pay sixty thousand for the horse at the value set by the government. He had reckoned that if he could buy a substitute horse for half the price, his savings would be considerable. And, with this horse he could claim provisions for the horse for the past three years, making his losses quite minimal. For these reasons he had to buy it.

Since Jen's clothes were old and shabby, she asked Wei Yin for new ones. Wei thought he should buy a roll of silk for her, but she did not want it: "I'd rather have ready-made clothes." Wei summoned a salesman, Chang the Eldest, to buy for her, and sent him to learn what she had in mind. After Chang had seen her, he came to Wei in a state of bewilderment. "She must be a fairy or someone from the royal household whom you've stolen away. She can't belong to this mundane world! You should send her back right away; don't get yourself in trouble." Such was the effect that her beauty had on men. But what her reasons for buying ready-made clothes rather than sewing them herself actually were, Wei had no way to find out.

More than a year later Cheng received his reassignment to become Courageous and Intrepid Deputy Commander of the Huai-li Militia[5] in

[4] In modern Shensi Province.
[5] Huai-li Militia is a fictitious invention of the author.

343

Chin-ch'eng County.[6] At that time Cheng had taken a lawful wife and, although he was free to go where he pleased during the day, at night he had to sleep at home. He often regretted that he could not devote his nights to Jen. As he was about to go to his new post, he entreated Jen to come along. She did not want to go: "We'll be on the road for half a month or so. That won't make for any fun. I beg you to leave me what you think I'll need for food and expenses, and I'll wait here for your return."

Though Cheng earnestly beseeched her, she only became more insistent. Cheng then went to Wei Yin for help. Wei exhorted her once more, and pressed her for her reasons. After some time she replied, "A shamaness told me it would be unlucky for me to travel west this year. So I don't want to go."

Though Cheng was greatly puzzled, he did not press for further explanations. Together with Wei, he laughed at Jen: "How can anyone be as intelligent as you are and yet so superstitious?" Then he entreated her the more firmly.

"If the prophecy comes true," she reasoned, "I'll die in vain for you. What good will that be?"

The two men merely replied, "That's ridiculous," and they begged her as earnestly as before. Since she could see no way out, Jen finally agreed to go. Wei lent her a horse and saw them as far as Lin-kao,[7] where they drank some wine in farewell and parted.

After a couple of days they came to Ma-wei Slope.[8] Jen rode in front, with Cheng close behind on his donkey. The maids on other beasts trailed along after them. At that time some of the grooms of the imperial West Gate Stables were training dogs to hunt at Lo-ch'uan.[9] They had been at it for more than ten days. It so happened that just as they ran into one another on the road, a black dog sprang out from the grass. Cheng saw Jen suddenly drop to the ground, change back into her original shape, and race away to the south. The black dog followed. Cheng ran along after shouting, trying to stop them, but he could not. After a little more than a *li,* the dog caught her.

Fighting back tears Cheng took money from his pack to redeem the body for burial, and cut some wood to make a marker. When he turned and looked at her horse, it was grazing alongside the road. Her clothes lay in a heap on the saddle and her shoes and stockings still hung from the stirrups, like the empty shell of a cicada. Only her jewelry had fallen to the ground. No other traces were to be seen. Her maids were also gone.

About ten days later Cheng returned to the capital. Wei was delighted to see him back and asked him, "Is Jen well?"

With tears in his eyes Cheng replied, "She's dead."

When Wei heard this he was greatly upset. Inside the house they gave in completely to their grief. Slowly Wei began to ask about the cause of her death. Cheng answered that she had been killed by a dog.

"Even if the dog was fierce, how could it kill a human?" Wei queried.

"She wasn't human."

"Wasn't human! What then?"

Cheng then told him the whole story, from beginning to end. Wei was speechless. On the following day he ordered his carriage made ready and went with Cheng to Ma-wei Slope. He had the grave opened to look at her, and then re-

---

[6] Near the present Kao-lan County in Kansu Province.

[7] A courier station to the west of the T'ang capital.

[8] Ma-wei was a courier station well known in Chinese history as the location at which the celebrated T'ang beauty Yang Kuei-fei was put to death. See the preamble in "Han Wu-niang Sells Her Charms at the New Bridge Market" in this anthology for a summary of the event.

[9] Lo-ch'uan, a probable corruption of Lo-shui (Lo River), flows northwest from the junction of the Wei, Lo, and Yellow rivers east of Ch'ang-an. It would not be likely that Cheng's route would take them near this river, and there seems to be a geographical inconsistency here.

turned, sorely moved. When they recalled the events of the recent past, they realized that only in her not having clothes tailored was she much different from mortals.

Thereafter Cheng became a superintendent of imperial grounds. His household prospered; he kept a stable of a dozen or so horses, and lived to the age of sixty-five.

During the Ta-li reign period [766–779],[10] I, Shen Chi-chi, was in Chung-ling.[11] Since I often went out with Wei Yin, and since he frequently told me Jen's story, I am most familiar with all the details. Later on Wei became a censor in the Bureau of State Affairs of the Censorate and concurrently prefect of Lung-chou.[12] He died there in office.

Ah, the principles of man can be found in the emotions of supernatural beings! To be accosted and not lose one's purity, to follow one man until death—even among the women of today there are those who could not measure up to this. Unfortunately, Cheng was not a very sensitive man. He only enjoyed Jen's beauty, and never fathomed her character. Had he been a man of truly deep understanding, he might have twisted the strands of fate, investigated the limits between spirits and humans, and written it all up beautifully to transmit his more abstruse feelings, rather than just surfeiting himself with her manners and appearance. What a pity!

During the second year of the Chien-chung reign period [781] General P'ei Chi of the palace guards, Deputy Mayor Sun Ch'eng of the capital, Secretary Ts'ui Hsü of the Ministry of Finance, Censor Lu Ch'un of the Department of the Secretariat, and I, at that time a censor in the Department of the Chancellery, were all banished to the southeast. On our way from Ch'in to Wu,[13] we traveled over land and water together. Chu Fang, a former censor, purposely arranged a trip so that he could go along with us. As we floated down the Ying River and crossed the Huai River, we lashed our boats together and flowed with the current, feasting by day and talking all the night, each one summoning forth some bizarre tale. When the group had heard the events surrounding Jen, they were all dismayed. They asked me to write them up as a record of the unusual. Thus I came to write this account.

---

[10] Ta-li is the title of the third reign period of the T'ang emperor Tai-tsung (r. 763–779).

[11] In modern Kiangsu Province.

[12] In modern Shensi.

[13] Approximates the present Kiangsu Province.

THE LEGENDARY MARRIAGE AT TUNG-T'ING

From *I-wen chi*

TRANSLATED BY RUSSELL E. MC LEOD

In the Yi-feng reign period [676–679][1] a scholar named Liu Yi went up [to the capital] for the examinations and failed. He was about to return home to the shores of the Hsiang River when he recalled that a man from his own area was temporarily living in Ching-yang,[2] and he went there to make his farewells.

He had gone six or seven *li* when a bird flew up from the ground and frightened his horse, so that it galloped wildly down the left side of the road for another six or seven *li* before he was able to stop it. He saw a woman tending sheep by the roadside.

Yi gazed in wonder; she was extraordinarily beautiful. Still, she had a troubled look about her and her clothes were shabby. She stood listening intently as if she were waiting for someone. Yi asked her, "What misfortune has made you demean yourself in this way?"

The woman at first smiled evasively, but finally she wept and turned to him, saying, "I am most unfortunate indeed, and now, sir, I've even become a cause for concern to a gentleman like you. Still, my grievance is such that I can't avoid you, shamefaced. I'd be grateful if you would hear me! I am the youngest daughter of the dragon ruler of [Lake] Tung-t'ing. My father and mother gave me in marriage to the second son of the Ching River[3] lord, but my husband was devoted to pleasure and was led astray by some of the servants and maids. He grew tired of me and was always treating me badly. I finally complained to my parents-in-law, but they are very fond of their son and will not restrain him. When I continued pressing my complaint I finally offended my parents-in-law. They humiliated me and I ended up in this situation." Having said this, she sobbed and wept in unrestrained grief.

"Tung-t'ing," she continued, "is I don't know how far from here, such a vast distance that my letters and messages have no way to get through. I understand that you are returning to Wu and will be passing close by Tung-t'ing. I wonder if I might trouble one of your servants to deliver a letter for me?"

"I'm a man of honor," said Yi. "What you have told me stirs my blood. I am sorry that I have no

[1] Yi-feng is the title of the ninth of the fourteen reign periods of the T'ang emperor Kao-tsung.
[2] Ching-yang County in modern Shensi.

[3] A small river flowing from Kansu to Shensi.

feathers, cannot spread some wings and fly! It isn't a question whether I'm willing or not. But the waters of Tung-t'ing are deep, and I travel on land. How can I transmit your message? Since traveling underwater is different from traveling on land, I fear that I shall fail in my own sincere commitment and go against your wishes as well! Have you some art to guide me?"

The woman wept sadly and thanked him, saying, "My profound gratitude goes without saying! If I could get some word of reply I would, even dead, express my thanks! If you had been unwilling I would not dare to speak, but since you are willing and have asked me about it, I must tell you that there is no real difference between Tung-t'ing and the capital city itself."

Yi asked to hear more. The woman said, "On the south shore of Tung-t'ing there is a large orange tree. The local people call it the 'Sacred Orange.' At this place, you should remove your belt and bind it around some object. Then strike the belt three times on the tree and someone will respond. If you let him guide you, you will have no difficulty. Aside from what is written in my letter, I trust you will also convey the words from my heart. Please, please do not fail me!"

"I will certainly do as you wish," Yi said.

The woman then removed a letter from her inner garment, bowed twice, and presented it to him. She seemed almost overcome with grief as she looked off toward the east and wept. Yi was deeply touched. He placed the letter in his bag and then inquired further, "I don't understand why you tend these sheep; do the supernatural beings actually do slaughtering?"

"These are not sheep; they are rainworkers."

"What are rainworkers?"

"Things like thunder and lightning."

He looked closely at them and saw that they all had a proud air and spirited gait, and that their manner of eating and drinking was unusual; still their size, their coats, and their horns were just like those of ordinary sheep.

"Since I am acting as your messenger," Yi said finally, "I hope you will not avoid me if you should sometime return to Tung-t'ing."

"Not only will I not avoid you, but I will treat you as a relative," she replied.

The conversation ended, and Yi took his leave and went east. He had gone only a dozen yards or so when he looked back: the woman and the sheep had all vanished. That evening he reached the town and said farewell to his friend. In just over a month he arrived home and made inquiries around Tung-t'ing. There was indeed a "Sacred Orange" on the south shore of the lake. He removed his belt and struck it three times against the tree. Suddenly a warrior came up from the waves, bowed twice, and inquired, "Honored guest, where do you come from?"

Yi did not answer directly but said, "I would pay my respects to the great lord."

The warrior parted the waves and, indicating the route, permitted Yi to enter. He said to Yi, "You must close your eyes; you will be there in a few moments."

Yi followed the instruction and soon arrived at a palace. There he saw ranked towers and great halls, a million gates and doorways, and every kind of strange plant and rare tree. Then the man stopped Yi at the corner of a huge edifice and said, "Please be seated and wait."

"What place is this?" Yi asked.

"This is the Divine Void Hall."

When Yi looked closely he saw every kind of treasure known to the world of men: pillars of white jade, staircases of green; couches of coral, screens of quartz; cut glass set in green lintels and amber laid in rainbow-hued beams, all of a strangeness and wonder beyond words.

Still after a long while the king had not arrived. Then Yi asked the warrior, "Where is the Tung-t'ing lord?"

"My lord is presently at the Dark Pearl Pavilion. He is discussing the *Fire Canon* with the Sun Priest. They should be concluding shortly."

"What is the *Fire Canon* about?"

"My lord is a dragon. The spiritual power of the dragon relates to water; with a single droplet he can cover mountains and valleys. The priest, however, is a man. The spiritual power of man relates to fire; with a single torch he can burn down the O-fang Palace.[4] Since these two types of spiritual genius are different in their functions, the mystic transformations are also distinctly different. The Sun Priest is clever about the ordinances of mankind and my lord has invited him and is listening to him."

Just as he finished speaking the palace gate opened; with attendants following close as shadows and clustered like clouds, there appeared a man clothed in purple and grasping a scepter of green jade. The warrior rose abruptly and said, "This is my lord!" Then he went forward to report.

The lord gazed down at Yi and asked him, "Are you from the world of men?"

"Yes," Yi responded. He then bowed and the lord also bowed and asked him to sit inside the Divine Void Hall.

"This watery precinct," he said to Yi, "is dark and remote, and we ourselves are ignorant. There must be some reason, sir, for you to disregard a distance of a thousand *li*?"

"I am a native of the same area as Your Majesty," said Yi. "I was raised in Ch'u but went off to Ch'in to study. Recently I failed in the examinations and went for a ride by the banks of the Ching River. There I saw Your Majesty's beloved daughter tending sheep in the fields. The winds blowing about her and the rain pelting her made a sight difficult to bear. I therefore asked about the matter. She said to me, 'This has happened because of my husband's rude neglect and the disregard of my parents-in-law.' Her sad tears falling

pell-mell truly linger in one's mind! She entrusted me with a letter and I accepted it. I have it with me now." He then brought out the letter and presented it.

After the Tung-t'ing lord had surveyed it, he covered his face with his sleeve and wept, saying, "This is my fault as her father; I was not able to examine and listen, but instead acted as one deaf and blind and caused this little one from the ladies' chambers to suffer slanders and wrongs in a faraway place. You, sir, were a passerby, yet you were able to take the matter to heart. For as long as I have hair and teeth I will never dare to forget your kindness!" With this, he grieved and sighed for a long while more. The attendants all shed tears.

There was a eunuch in close attendance on the lord. The lord gave the letter to him, ordering him to take it to the inner palace. In a few moments all within were loudly weeping. The lord said in alarm to his attendants, "Tell them quickly not to make a sound; Ch'ien-t'ang may learn what has happened!"

"Who is Ch'ien-t'ang?" Yi asked.

"Our beloved younger brother. He was responsible for the Ch'ien-t'ang [River], but he has now 'withdrawn from office.' "

"Why must he not be informed?"

"He is overly bold. The nine-year flood in the time of [the Sage King] Yao was due to one of his rages. Recently he quarreled with the generals of heaven and flooded the Five Mountains.[5] Because of our own meager virtue in the past and at present, the Lord on High[6] was lenient with our relative. But he is under confinement here and thus the people of Ch'ien-t'ang await him day by day."

Before his words had ended, there was all at

[4] A magnificent palace built by the first king of Ch'in (for a fictional account of him, see "Prince Tan of Yen" in this anthology) near the modern city of Sian in Shensi. It was burned down by Hsiang Yü.

[5] Eastern, Western, Southern, Northern, and Central Mountains; all have been referred to in the notes to previous selections.

[6] A general reference to the supreme deity without any particular religious connotation, usually taken as the equivalent of Heaven.

348

once a great sound splitting the heavens and rending the earth. The palace buildings shook and clouds and mists rolled and rolled. Suddenly there appeared a red dragon more than a thousand feet long with eyes flashing lightning and a tongue blood-red, vermilion scales and a flaming beard. The neck bore a gold lock and from the lock dragged a jade pillar. Thousands of lightning bolts and tens of thousands of thunderclaps issued violently around its body, while sleet and snow, rain and hail all fell at the same time. Then it broke through the azure sky and flew away.

In his fear, Yi had fallen prostrate to the ground. The lord personally helped him to rise, saying, "Don't be afraid, you will certainly not be harmed."

For a long while Yi was fairly shaken, but then he regained his composure and asked to leave, saying, "I would like to return while I still have life, so that I will not be here when he comes again."

"It won't happen again," the lord said. "His departures are thus, but his arrivals are not. We should be happy if we might slightly represent to you our feelings of fond esteem." Then wine was ordered and toasts exchanged in a manner according with the proper reception of guests.

Presently, with an auspicious breeze and favoring clouds, mild, soft, peaceful, and mellow, with splendid and brilliant flags and pennants, and pan pipes following at the last, there came thousands and tens of thousands of lovely ladies, laughing, chattering, pleased, and happy. Finally there came a person of inborn beauty who was covered with bright jewels and layered silks and gauzes. When he looked closely, Yi saw that it was the woman who had asked him to take the message. Yet she seemed both happy and sad and her tears fell like silk threads. In a few moments, she entered the palace, a red mist covering her right side, a purple vapor unrolling at her left, and fragrant scents all around her.

The lord smiled and said to Yi, "The Ching River prisoner has arrived!" Then he excused himself and returned to the inner palace. In a few minutes a sad complaint was heard; this continued for a long time.

The lord came out again and drank and ate with Yi. There was also a man wearing purple clothing and holding a green jade. Of commanding appearance and a vigorous demeanor, he stood to the left of the lord, who said to Yi, "This is Ch'ien-t'ang."

Yi rose and hastily paid his respects. Ch'ien-t'ang also observed the formalities and said to Yi, "My niece was so unfortunate as to be humiliated by a heartless youth. It was only thanks to your sense of honor and righteousness, worthy of a gentleman, that she was able to make her grievance known to us. Otherwise she would have become dust in a grave by the Ching River. Words cannot express the gratitude we feel in our hearts for your kindness."

Yi deprecated this and bowed respectfully. Then Ch'ien-t'ang reported to his elder brother, "I left the Divine Void Hall in the early morning and by late morning I was at Ching-yang. I fought at noon there and returned here in the early afternoon. Before returning I flew up to the Ninth Heaven[7] to report to the Lord on High. The Ruler understood the grievance and pardoned me. I am also excused from my former banishment. However, in my impetuous outburst I did not stop to take my leave. I upset the inner palace and was also rude to the guest. I am mortified and deeply ashamed. Then he stepped back and bowed twice.

"How many did you kill?" the lord asked.

"Six hundred thousand."

"Damaged crops?"

"Eight hundred *li*."

---

[7] "Chiu-t'ien" has two possible meanings: the nine heavens or the ninth heaven. In ancient times the Chinese used the same numerical number to designate two different systems of the heavens, vertical and horizontal. Here the context seems to refer to the vertical system.

"Where is the heartless fellow?"

"I ate him."

The lord said in distress, "That the ruthless boy acted as he did was certainly insufferable, but you yourself were very rash. Fortunately, the Lord on High in his divine wisdom understood the extremity of the grievance. Now what could I have said if this had not been the case? Hereafter, don't do anything like this again!" Ch'ien-t'ang again bowed twice. That evening Yi was lodged in the Aureole Hall.

The next day Yi was again feasted in the Emerald Palace. Friends and relatives were gathered, a great music troupe was assembled, fine wines were set out and delicate foods arranged. To begin with, ten thousand men danced on the right with reed whistles, horns, snares, war drums, banners, flags, swords, and halberds. One of the men stepped forward and said, "This is 'Ch'ien-t'ang's Victory Music.' " The heroic atmosphere of the flags and weapons, the violent glances and fearsome movements of the warriors made the hair on those who watched stand on end.

Then a thousand women dressed in light and patterned silks, pearls, and jade danced on the left with bells and chimes, stringed and wind instruments. One woman came forward from among them and said, "This is the 'Princess Returns to the Palace Music.' " The pure tones were compelling, like grievances or affectionate longings. As the seated guests listened, they wept without knowing they were weeping.

When the two dances had ended, the dragon lord was pleased and he gave out fine silks to reward the dancers. Then all the guests sat down together and drank freely with great enjoyment.

When they had drunk their fill, the Tung-t'ing lord struck the mat and sang:

Blue, blue the broad skies; wide, wide the vast earth!
Men all have their ideals, but who can judge their measure?
The fox spirit and the rat sage live near altars and hide in
*   walls.*

One burst of thunder and lightning, and who will dare to
*   stand?*
Give thanks to an upright man, his good faith and altruism
*   strong!*
He has brought our flesh and blood back to her own home!
We speak respectfully and in deep gratitude: "We will never,
*   ever forget!"*

When the Tung-t'ing lord had sung his song, the Ch'ien-t'ang lord bowed twice and sang:

High heaven ordains matches, and birth and death come from
*   fate.*
Hers was not to be his wife, nor his to be her husband.
Our dear one was sad and bitter close by the River Ching,
Hair swept with wind and frost, rain and snow on clothes
*   of silk.*
She trusted an exalted gentleman who sent her missive hither.
Our flesh and blood is restored to our home.
Say thanks forever, and end no more!

When the Ch'ien-t'ang lord's song had ended, he and the Tung-t'ing lord both presented cups to Yi. Yi accepted with deference, quaffed the wine, and in turn offered cups to the two lords. Then he sang:

Under blue skies wide, wide, Ching water flows east.
Sad the fair one, a rain of tears, a blossom mourning.
A letter arrived from far away; this to end the lady's sorrow.
Her bitter grievance is now redressed; here she enjoys a happy
*   ease.*
Respectful thanks for lofty music; also for a splendid feast.
My rustic home is silent; I cannot stay here long.
I shall say my farewell, while sadness binds me round.

When the song had ended, all cried, "Hurrah!" Then the Tung-t'ing lord set forth a green jade casket filled with horn of the 'water-parting rhinoceros,' and the Ch'ien-t'ang lord in turn set out a red amber dish filled with luminous pearls. The two stood and presented these to Yi. Yi declined at first but then accepted them. Then the people from the inner palace placed figured silks, pearls, and white jade near Yi until they stood in gleaming heaps which in a short time completely surrounded him. Yi laughed and talked with everyone around, bowing modestly all the while. When he had drunk his fill and enjoyed himself to the limit, Yi excused himself and again rested in the Aureole Hall.

The next day Yi was again feasted in the Pure Light Pavilion. The Ch'ien-t'ang lord, under the influence of wine, took on a serious expression and said to Yi haughtily, "Surely you know 'a hard rock can be split, but can't be rolled; a righteous man can be killed, but not put to shame'? I've got an idea I'd like to put to you. If you agree, we'll all be up in the clouds; if not, we'll be in a mess of shit! Now, what do you say?"

"I would like to hear about it," Yi said.

"The wife from Ching-yang is the beloved daughter of the Tung-t'ing lord," said Ch'ien-t'ang. "She's a gentle person of fine character, esteemed by all her relatives and in-laws. Unfortunately she was humiliated by a scoundrel, but now that has come to an end. We would like to appeal to your high principles and ask you to be our relative forever. Then the one who has received your kindness will have some place to turn to, and those who love her will know to whom she has been entrusted. Surely, this would accord with the way of a gentleman from first to last?"

Yi stood up solemnly and then laughed, saying, "I truly did not know that the Ch'ien-t'ang lord was so petty-minded and provoking! In the beginning I heard how you had spanned the nine parts of the country, held the Five Mountains close to you, to vent your anger. And then I saw you break the gold lock and drag the jade pillar when you went to the rescue. It seemed to me that in resolve and firmness, in wisdom and rectitude, no one was your equal. That in righting a wrong you did not fear death, that in acting for one you loved you had no regard for your own life—this is in keeping with the ideals of a true man of honor. Now, how, when the pipes are just playing sweetly and relatives and guests are enjoying themselves, can you ignore your own principles and intimidate someone? This is quite unexpected! If I

should meet you among towering waves or in the darkness of mountains, your scales and beard bristling and clouds and rain about you, and you should threaten me with death, I would look upon this as something done by a brute beast and would certainly not have any feeling of resentment. Now, as you are wearing hat and clothes, sitting down to discuss propriety and altruism with me, your character displays the five principles to the fullest and you have a thorough understanding of human relationships. Even sages and heroes in the human world cannot match you in these respects, still less the spirits of the rivers. Does it in any way seem right that you should now want to intimidate someone, with your body sprawled out rudely, your temper flaring, and your courage drawn from wine? My physical form cannot match the size of even one of Your Majesty's scales, yet I will dare to resolutely withstand Your Majesty's wayward mood! Will Your Majesty please reflect on this!"

Ch'ien-t'ang drew himself back and apologized. "We were born and raised in the palace rooms and have not heard forthright moral discourse. Just now we spoke arrogantly and rudely offended a person of quality. When we step back and consider this, we realize it was unpardonable. We should be fortunate if you do not regard this as an affront."

That evening they again feasted happily and Yi and Ch'ien-t'ang became intimate friends.

The next day Yi announced his departure for home. The Tung-t'ing lord's consort gave a farewell banquet for Yi in the Hidden View Hall. The men and women servants were all in attendance. The consort wept and said to Yi, "Our daughter has received your great kindness and she regrets that she has not been able to express her gratitude. Now the time of parting is here." She ordered the Ching-yang woman to come forward to join the banquet and to bow to Yi to express her thanks.

The consort also said, "With this parting I

351

wonder if there shall ever be a day for another meeting?"

Though Yi had earlier refused Ch'ien-t'ang's request, at this banquet he nevertheless had a certain feeling of sad regret. The banquet ended, good-byes were said, and the palace was filled with sadness. The treasures presented to Yi were of a wonder beyond description. He retraced his steps to the shores of the river with more than ten men, who carried his baggage to his home and then left. Yi went to the jewelers' shops in Kuang-ling[8] to sell what he had gotten. Before he had sold a hundredth part, his wealth already totaled millions. He was richer than any of the wealthy families on the upper course of River Huai.

He married a girl of the Chang family; she died. He married another girl from the Han family; after several months she also died. He moved to Chin-ling. He was melancholy because of his solitary state and made plans to marry again. A go-between informed him, "There is a woman of the Lu family, of Fan-yang.[9] Her father's given name is Hao. He was once magistrate of Ch'ing-liu.[10] In his old age he has become fond of Taoism and wanders alone among 'clouds and springs.' No one knows where he is now. Her mother is Cheng-shih. The year before last the girl married Chang of Ch'ing-ho,[11] but unfortunately Chang soon died. Cheng-shih is concerned about the girl's [being widowed at such a] tender age and wants to find a virtuous mate who will be worthy of her intelligence and beauty. What do you think?"

Yi then chose an auspicious date and the ceremony was carried out. Since both parties were from prominent families, everything used in the ceremonies was of the finest quality. All the gentlemen of Chin-ling were envious.

After more than a month, Yi entered his room late one evening and had the strong impression, while gazing at his wife, that she resembled the dragon woman, though she surpassed her in beauty and plumpness,[12] so he spoke to her about what had happened before.

"What a strange story!" she responded. "In any case, you and I are going to have a child." Yi was more devoted to her than ever. The child was born, and a month later the wife changed her clothes, put on fine jewelry, and entertained the relatives. When they had a moment, she smiled and said to Yi, "Don't you remember me from before?"

"In the past I carried a letter for the daughter of the Tung-t'ing lord; I still remember it."

"I am the Tung-t'ing lord's daughter. You erased that grievance by the Ching River. I was grateful for your kindness and swore to repay you. When you did not agree to my uncle Ch'ien-t'ang's proposal, we were separated, each at a different corner of the world, and I had no way of communicating with you. My parents wanted to marry me to a young boy of the Cho-chin [River].[13] It was hard to change the secret vow I had made and also hard to go against my parents' orders. Since you had rejected me, I understood well that you and I would never be able to see each other again. Still, although my original grievance had been reported to my parents, my intention of repaying this had not been fulfilled. I often wanted to fly to you and tell you everything, but it happened that you married and remarried. First you married Chang; after that you married Han. When Chang and Han had died in succession, you chose to live in this place. Therefore, my parents were happy to let me follow my wish to repay your kindness. Today I have the opportunity to serve you and I shall live out my life in happiness and die without any regrets." Then she sobbed and her tears fell.

[8] Near Chiang-tu in modern Kiangsu Province.
[9] The area around Ta-hsing in modern Hopei.
[10] Ch'u County in modern Anhwei Province.
[11] Ch'ing-ho County in Hopei.

[12] Plumpness was a mark of beauty in T'ang times. Yang Kuei-fei is a well-known example of a plump beauty.
[13] A small river at Ch'eng-tu in modern Szechwan.

She looked at Yi and said, "I didn't talk about this with you before because I knew that you weren't one who cared much for romantic adventures. I mention it now because I know you have some feeling for me. An unworthy woman, I was not fit to hold your love forever. So I am relying on your love for the child to make up for my own inadequacy. Not knowing how you feel makes me sad and fearful; and I can't overcome those feelings. When you took my letter, you smiled and said to me, 'If you should sometime return to Tung-t'ing, do not avoid me!' It is really not clear; at that time did you have in mind the situation which we are in today? Later, when my uncle made his request of you, you refused firmly. Was your refusal sincere, or were you just indignant? Please tell me!"

"All this must have been fated," Yi said. "When I first saw you there by the Ching, you seemed so oppressed and haggard that I truly had a strong feeling about the injustice done to you. But the only thing that I permitted in my mind at the time was simply taking the news of your grievance—nothing more than that. When I said 'don't avoid me,' it was just a casual remark and I didn't mean anything by it. When Ch'ien-t'ang importuned me, it was so unreasonable that it made me angry. If a man sets out to act from a motive of righteousness, can he kill someone's husband and take his wife? That was the first impossibility. If my ideal was to be upright and sincere, and to be honest in my conduct, then could I have bowed to the circumstances and concealed what was in my heart? This was the second impossibility. When I expressed myself in a free manner, returning toasts all around, I was thinking only of what was proper. I was not concerned about escaping harm. But on the day when I was going to leave and I saw your look, as if you were unwilling to part, I felt very sorry about it. In the end I was caught in the rules of conduct and could not show my gratitude. Ah, but now that you belong to the Lu family and live in the human world, I no longer have any misgivings. From now on, let us live together in happiness; don't let your heart be troubled by small worries!"

His wife was deeply moved and wept tears of happiness. It was some time before she stopped. Finally she said to Yi, "Don't consider that because I am of another kind, I have no feelings. I will certainly requite you. The dragon has a life-span of ten thousand years. We share this now. We shall travel freely on the land or in the waters. Don't think I am speaking recklessly."

"I didn't know that having been a guest in your kingdom I should also join the company of the immortals!" Yi said happily.

Then together they called at Tung-t'ing. The warm exchanges between hosts and guests cannot be adequately recorded. Later they lived in Nan-hai[14] for forty years. Their residence, their carriages and horses, rare objects, and household goods were not inferior to those of marquises and counts. Yi's relatives were also favored with blessings. The people of Nan-hai were all amazed that the passage of years had no effect on Yi's appearance.

During the K'ai-yüan period [713–741] His Majesty[15] turned his attention to matters concerning spiritual beings and immortals, and he made a thorough search for Taoist techniques. Yi was discomfited, so the couple returned to Tung-t'ing. For more than ten years nothing was seen of him.

At the end of K'ai-yüan, Yi's cousin Hsüeh Ku was an official in the capital, but was banished to the southeast and passed across Tung-t'ing. As he gazed off on a clear day, he saw a green mountain suddenly emerge from the waves ahead. The boatmen all stood back and said, "There was never any mountain here! This could be the doing of some water monster!" Soon the boat was close by the mountain island and a brightly decorated vessel floated out from it to welcome Ku.

14 Most of the area in modern Kwangtung Province.
15 Since the reign period is given here, "His Majesty" apparently refers to Emperor Hsüan-tsung.

One of the men called out to him, "Master Liu has come to welcome you." Hsüeh at once recalled Liu Yi and quickly got to the foot of the mountain, where he lifted his robes and stepped ashore. There was a palace on the island which looked like one in the human world, and Yi was standing in one of the palace chambers. Musicians were ranged before him, and behind him were gathered beautiful maids. Rare and precious objects were there in numbers far exceeding what is known in the world of men. In his speech Yi had grown more profound, and his appearance was younger. He met Ku at the steps of the palace and said, as he grasped Ku's hand, "It is only a brief time since we parted, yet your hair is already gray!"

Ku laughed and said, "The elder is an immortal and the younger some dried bones. This is fate!"

Yi then brought out fifty pills and gave them to Ku, saying, "One of these pills will increase your life by a year. Come back when they are gone. Don't make yourself unhappy by staying too long in the human world." After a joyous banquet, Ku took his leave. Yi was never seen again.

Ku often told this story. After some forty years Ku's whereabouts also became unknown.

Li Ch'ao-wei[16] of Lung-hsi recorded this and then he sighed and said, "The principal members of each of the five categories in the animal kingdom[17] have spiritual natures, and their differentiations are here apparent. The man belonged to the bare-skinned category, yet his sincerity and trust were extended to the scaly creatures. Tungt'ing was possessed of the greatest rectitude; Ch'ien-t'ang was impetuous and straightforward. All this can be explained. Ku told the tale but did not record it. He was only able to draw near the borders of that other region. I wrote this because I found some meaning in the story."

[16] The name of the author.
[17] The five categories are: bare-skinned (man); feathered (birds); furred (beasts); scaly (fish); shelled (tortoise).

ETERNAL PRISONER
UNDER THE THUNDER PEAK PAGODA

From *Ching-shih t'ung-yen*

TRANSLATED BY DIANA YU

Hill stretches beyond green hill, tower beyond tower;
Here by the West Lake, when will dancing and singing ever
    cease?
The warm breeze has cast such drunken spells on our sightseers
They think this Hangchow scenery is their old capital, Pien-
    chou! [1]

The West Lake, our story's setting, is well known for the serenity of its hills and waters. In the Hsien-ho reign period [326–334] of the Chin Dynasty, when a big mountain torrent swept past the West Gate, an ox was seen amid the waves whose entire body was the color of bright gold. Later it went in the wake of the receding flood and mysteriously disappeared near the North Hill. This caused a sensation among the inhabitants of Hangchow, who were all convinced that it was a miracle. In memory of it, they erected the Golden Ox Monastery. At the West Gate, now called the Golden Flood Gate, there is a temple dedicated to the General of Golden Splendor.

In those times a foreign monk bearing the ordination name of Hun-shou-lo roamed to these parts of the Wu-lin Prefecture and, on seeing the hill scenery, remarked, "Here it is, the small peak that suddenly disappeared from the Divine Vulture Mountain." [2] None at that time believed him, but the monk said, "I remember that somewhere in a cave in the Divine Vulture Hill, facing the Divine Vulture Mountain, there lives a white gibbon. Let me call it out, to prove that I am right." Sure enough, the animal came out at his call. There is a pavilion in front of this peak, now called the Cold Fount Pavilion.

The Solitary Hill rises in the middle of the West Lake. This was where the Honorable Lin Ho-ching [3] spent his hermit days. At his order earth and stone were assembled and a road was built, leading eastward to the Broken Bridge and westward to the Sunset Peak. This is now called Solitary Hill Road.

In the T'ang Dynasty, the prefect Po Yüeh-t'ien [4] constructed a causeway that went as far as the Jade Screen Hill in the south and the Sunset Peak in the north. This is now known as the Po Causeway. From time to time torrents rushing down the hills would damage it, and it was more

[1] Another name for Pien-ching.

[2] The Divine Vulture Mountain referred to here is Gridhrakuta, a mountain frequently visited by the Buddha.
[3] The Sung poet Lin P'u (967–1028).
[4] Yüeh-t'ien was the style of the T'ang poet Po Chü-yi.

355

than once repaired with money from the official coffers. Then, in the Sung Dynasty, Su Tung-p'o came here to take up the prefectship. Seeing the damage done by the water, he purchased wood and stone, hired laborers, and thoroughly strengthened the two roads. Su's workmen painted the railings on the six bridges a bright red and lined the causeway with plum and willow trees, converting the spot into extremely pleasant scenery, quite worth the painter's brush when the warm spring weather arrives. Posterity called it the Su Causeway. Two stone bridges [with dikes] were also erected side by side on the Solitary Hill Road to divert the flow of the water. They are the Broken Bridge in the east and the Western Calm Bridge in the west. Here, as they say:

Hidden in the hills are three hundred monasteries,
And locked in the clouds, two tall, distant peaks.

That is about as much as most storytellers will tell you—the beautiful scenery of the West Lake, the fairy haunts of olden days. Today, however, let me tell you a story about a handsome young man who, just because he made a pleasure trip to the West Lake, came upon two women and got himself involved in a scandal that shocked many a pleasure alley in quite a few cities. It is just the sort of story that a clever writer can weave into an engaging tale. Here, then, I will tell you the name of the lad, what manner of women he encountered, and the rest that followed. But first of all, a poem for your pleasure:

How endless is the gentle rain in this Ch'ing-ming season!
And how sad our wayfarer, as he plods along the road.
"Pardon," he says, "can you tell me a place where wine is
served?"
"There's Apricot Village in the distance," says a little buffalo-
tender.

Our story goes back to the time of the Emperor Kao-tsung of the Sung Dynasty, when the capital had been moved to the south of the Yangtze. In the Shao-hsing reign period [1132–1162], in Black

Pearl Lane near the Garrison Bridge in Hang-chow [the site of the prefectural administration] of the Lin-an Prefecture, there lived a petty official Li Jen, who served as a levy officer in the army, while at the same time he kept accounts for Marshal Shao's house. His wife had a younger brother, Hsü Hsüan, whom they called Hsiao-yi [The Second]; he was the eldest son in the family. Hsü's father used to own a shop that sold medicinal herbs, but both parents had died when Hsü Hsüan was still a boy. Hsü Hsüan was now twenty-two years old, and he worked as an assistant in an herb shop that belonged to a distant uncle. The herb shop was situated at the corner of Officials' Lane.

One day, when Hsü Hsüan was busy dealing with customers, a monk came up to their shop. He made a sign of greeting and said, "I'm from the Pao-shu Pagoda Monastery. The other day I sent dumplings and a circular about almsgiving to your house. The Ch'ing-ming Festival is at hand, and it's time to offer prayers to the ancestors. Don't forget to come along to our monastery to perform the incense-burning ceremony."

"I'll be there," Hsü Hsüan assured him.

At that the monk left.

In the evening Hsü Hsüan went home to his brother-in-law's place, for that was where he lived, being yet unmarried and without a family. That night he told his sister, "Today a monk from the Pao-shu Pagoda Monastery asked me to go and perform the paper-burning ceremony at their place. I shall go tomorrow, and make offerings to our ancestors."

The next morning he rose early and went out to buy all the things required—paper images, candles, pennants, paper money, and the like. Then he ate, changed into new clothes, shoes, and socks, tied the paper offerings up in a piece of cloth, and went to his uncle's place at the corner of Officials' Lane. His uncle looked at him and asked where he was going.

"Today I have to go to the Pao-shu Pagoda

Monastery to burn paper offerings to our ancestors. With your permission, I'd like to take a day off."

"All right. Come back as soon as possible."

Hsü Hsüan left the shop, made his way through the Blissful Lane and the Flower Market Street, crossed the Well-Pavilioned Bridge, passed the Ch'ien-t'ang Gate, which was behind Clear River Street, went over the Stone Receptacle Bridge and past the Tablet of Creatures Set Free, and came to the Pao-shu Pagoda Monastery. There he looked up the monk who had sent him the dumplings, said his confessions, performed the paper-burning ceremony, and then stayed a while in the main hall to watch the monks chant the sutras. After partaking of the devotional meal, he bid farewell to the monk and left. He strolled along at a leisurely pace to the Western Calm Bridge, Solitary Hill Road, and the Temple of the Four Sages, thinking he might pay a visit to Lin Ho-ching's grave and spend some time at the Six-in-Unity Fountain.

But all of a sudden clouds gathered in the northwest, and a mist hung over the southeast. Then came a sprinkling of rain which soon grew to something of a drizzle. In keeping with the Ch'ing-ming season, Heaven has not failed to bring down the good rain that will hasten the flowers' blooming! As the rain went on and on, Hsü's shoes were soaked. He took off his new socks and shoes and came out of the Temple of the Four Sages to look for a boat, but none was to be seen. Just as he seemed stuck in this situation, he spotted an old man rowing a boat toward him. What luck, to see that it was none other than Old Chang! He shouted, "Old Chang, give me a lift!"

The old boatman heard his call and, recognizing Hsiao-yi, brought the boat to shore. "So you're caught in the rain," he said. "Where do you want to go?"

"I would like to get off at the Golden Flood Gate."

The old man helped him into the boat and they went off in the direction of the Harvest Joy Restaurant.

They had gone no more than a hundred feet on the water when they heard someone call from the shore, "Grandpa, boat please!" Hsü Hsüan looked and saw that it was a woman calling. Her raven hair was done up in mourning fashion, with a white hairpin and comb stuck in at the side, and she was wearing a white silk blouse and skirt of fine flax. By her side stood a young maid, dressed in green, her hair combed into two horn-like tufts held in place by two pieces of red hair-strings and pins, and carrying a bundle in her hands. They were eager to get into the boat.

"Since it is so little trouble on our part, we might as well give them a lift, too." Old Chang said.

"Please ask them to come along," Hsü responded.

So Old Chang moored by the shore, and the woman came onto the boat with her maid. Seeing Hsü Hsüan, she unpursed her rosy lips, showing her white teeth, and gave a deep bow. He hurriedly rose and bowed in return. Then the two women seated themselves in the cabin.

When they had settled down, the woman kept glancing at Hsü Hsüan again and again. At the sight of such a fine beauty and her pretty attendant, he could not help feeling attracted, though he had always been innocent and inexperienced.

"Allow me to ask, sir, what is your name?" she asked.

"My name is Hsü Hsüan, the eldest in the family."

"Where do you live?" she asked again.

"In Black Pearl Lane, near the Garrison Bridge. I work in an herb shop."

Since she had asked so many questions, Hsü thought, "I should ask her something in return." So he stood up and said, "Will you let me know your name, and where you live?"

"I'm the younger sister of Captain Po of the imperial guards, and I'm married to Master Chang.

357

Unfortunately, my husband is already dead. He is buried just over there at the Thunder Hill. Since the Ch'ing-ming Festival is getting near, I took my maid along with me to sweep his grave. On our way back we were caught in the rain. What a time we would have had if you had not taken us in!"

They chatted on a while, and then the boat neared the shore. The woman said, "We came out in such a hurry today that I forgot to bring money. Could you kindly pay our boat fare for now? I'll certainly return it."

"Please don't worry about it, madam." Hsü said. "It's just a trifling sum."

He paid the boat fare. But the rain just would not stop. Then he escorted the two of them ashore.

"My home is just at the entrance to Twin Tea-house Lane, near the Arrow Bridge," the woman said. "If you don't mind, come to our house for tea, and I shall pay you back the boat fare."

"Please forget about the trifle. It's getting late. I shall visit you some other time."

After this exchange, the woman and her maid went away by themselves.

Hsü made his way past the Golden Flood Gate, keeping under the eaves as he went, and arrived at the Three Bridges Street, where his younger uncle ran an herb shop. He came up to the shop and saw his uncle just in front of the door.

"Hsiao-yi, where are you going so late?" his uncle asked him.

"I went offering at the Pao-shu Pagoda Monastery and got caught in the rain. I've come to borrow an umbrella."

Hearing this, his uncle called, "Old Ch'en, bring Master Hsiao-yi an umbrella!"

Old Ch'en soon brought one out. Opening it, he said, "This one was made by the Honest Shu Manufacturers, at the Clear Lake of the Character-Eight Bridge. It's a fine umbrella with eighty-four ribs and a purple bamboo handle, and not the slightest tatter in it yet. Take it and don't break it, mind you!"

"Certainly, certainly," Hsü said. He took the umbrella, thanked his uncle, and walked outward in the direction of the Sheep Dike.

At the corner of the Rear Market Street Lane, somebody called to him, "Master Hsiao-yi!" Turning around, Hsü Hsüan saw, there under the eaves of the little teahouse at the entrance to Lord Shen's Well Lane, a woman standing—none but the lady in white, his boat companion!

"Madam, why are you here?" he asked her.

"The rain won't stop, and my shoes are all wet. I sent Ch'ing-ch'ing home to fetch an umbrella and stockings. Since it's getting late, could you walk some distance with me?"

Under the same umbrella they went as far as the Sheep Dike. He asked her, "Which way are you going?"

"Over that bridge, in the direction of the Arrow Bridge."

"I'm going to the Garrison Bridge and it's a short way. You had better take the umbrella. I'll come for it tomorrow."

"I've given you a lot of trouble. You are certainly most kind!" the lady in white said.

Then Hsü Hsüan walked home in the rain, keeping under the eaves of the houses. Reaching home, he met his brother-in-law's servant Wang An, who had just come back with an umbrella after a vain search for him. Later he had supper at home. That night thoughts of the woman completely occupied him, and he kept tossing and turning in bed. When he fell asleep he dreamed of the same episode that had occurred during the day, with the same romantic atmosphere, but the shrill crow of the cock broke his sweet dreams. As our poem describes it:

Now that his heart and fancy have soared to the utmost heights,
Butterflies and bees madly raid his early hours.

When dawn finally came, he rose, washed and ate, and went to the shop, but he was so distracted that he could not concentrate on doing business.

When it was past midday he pondered, "If I don't forge a lie, how can I get the umbrella back and return it?" He asked his uncle sitting at the counter, "My brother-in-law tells me to go home earlier to deliver a present for him. May I take half a day off?"

"Go, but be back early tomorrow!"

"Of course!" answered Hsü Hsüan, and straightaway he headed for the entrance to Twin Teahouse Lane near the Arrow Bridge, to inquire about the white lady's house. But no one could offer him any help, even after half a day's asking.

Just when he was at a loss what to do, he saw Ch'ing-ch'ing, the white lady's maid, coming from the east in his direction. He approached her and asked, "Miss, where exactly is your house? I've come to get my umbrella."

"Follow me, sir," Ch'ing-ch'ing said. They went a short distance and then she said, "Here we are."

Hsü Hsüan looked up and saw a two-story building with a large double door, which had four peepholes and a fine red bamboo curtain suspended from above in the middle. Behind it was the central hall, with twelve black lacquer armchairs neatly arranged on the sides, and four landscapes by ancient masters on the walls. The house faced the residence of Prince Hsiu.[5]

Ch'ing-ch'ing went behind the curtain and said, "Sir, please come in and sit down." Hsü followed her. Then she called softly, "Madam, Master Hsiao-yi is here."

From inside came the white lady's reply: "Show the gentleman in, and serve tea."

Hsü Hsüan hesitated, but at Ch'ing-ch'ing's repeated beckoning he went in. His eyes confronted a row of four intricately carved lattice windows. When a blue curtain was lifted, it revealed a small parlor, with a table decked with a pot of tiger lilies, four paintings of ladies hung on either side and, on the central wall, a picture of a deity. On

[5] Prince Hsiu was the father of Emperor Hsiao-tsung (r. 1163–1189) because Kao-tsung, the first emperor of Southern Sung, had no son of his own.

another table stood a bronze vase that looked like an incense burner.

The white lady came forward and made a deep bow. She said, "Dear sir, thank you so much for helping us out yesterday. We were only just acquainted then, which makes me all the more grateful."

"It's hardly worth mentioning."

"Stay a while, and we shall have some tea." After tea was served, she added, "We'll have a little wine, as a token of my appreciation."

Before Hsü could refuse, Ch'ing-ch'ing had brought out an array of delicacies and fruits. He said, "Thank you for your generous hospitality. Please don't let me cause you too much trouble." After taking a few cups, he rose, saying, "It's getting dark, and I have a long way to go. It's time for me to leave."

"Oh dear," she said, "last night a relative of mine borrowed your umbrella and took it away. Let's drink a few more cups, while I send someone to fetch it."

"It's getting late," he insisted, "and I must go."

"Just one cup more."

"I'm quite full. Thank you ever so much."

"If you insist on going, will you take the trouble to come again for your umbrella tomorrow?"

Hsü had to consent to this and go home.

The next day he went to the shop and did some business; then he found another excuse and went to the white lady's place again to fetch his umbrella. Seeing him come, she again invited him to drink a few cups of wine.

"Please return the umbrella to me, and spare the rest of your trouble."

"It's all prepared. Please have just one cup."

He was obliged to sit down, and she filled a cup of wine and presented it to him. She then spoke in a seductive voice: "Dear sir, in front of an honest gentleman like you I might as well not pretend. My husband is dead already. In some past incarnation you and I must have been a married couple, for at our first meeting you were immediately so good to me. It's true, isn't it, that we're mutually fond of each other? If you will find us a matchmaker, we can be married and be a happy couple the rest of our lives. Wouldn't that be wonderful?"

Listening until she finished, Hsü thought to himself, "Certainly, this is a good match! To have such a wife would be more than I can ask for! Of course I'm absolutely willing. Only one thing is in the way—I work at my uncle's as an assistant in the daytime and I lodge at my brother-in-law's at night. Though I have some savings, they're barely enough for my own clothes. Where can I get money to set up a family?" So he held back his answer.

"Why don't you answer me?" she pressed him.

"Thank you very much for bringing this up, but, to be frank with you, my circumstances are embarrassingly difficult. I don't think I can say yes."

"That's easy. My purse is loaded. You need not worry about that," she said. Whereupon she ordered Ch'ing-ch'ing, "Go and bring me an ingot of silver."

As he watched, Ch'ing-ch'ing held on to the banisters and went upstairs, took down a bundle, and handed it to her mistress.

"Sir, take this and spend it. If you need more, just come again," the white lady said as she handed the bundle to Hsü Hsüan.

On opening it, he saw that it contained fifty taels of glittering silver. He put it away in his sleeve and rose to go. Ch'ing-ch'ing gave the umbrella back to him, and he took it and went home. He hid the silver away, and the night passed without further ado.

The next morning he rose and went to the Officials' Lane entrance and returned the umbrella. Then, with a little silver, he bought a nice big roast goose, fresh fish, lean pork, a young chicken, and fruits and the like. He took all these home and bought a bottle of wine, and told the waiting woman and the maids to prepare some dishes. That day his brother-in-law Officer Li

happened to be at home. When the wine and dishes were laid out, Hsü invited his brother-in-law and sister to come to the table. Officer Li was surprised at such a treat, and asked, "Why are you squandering money today? You usually don't take to the winecup. Today's a bit odd!"

The three of them sat down in order of seniority. When they had drunk a few cups, Officer Li said, "Well, dear brother, you couldn't have lavished all that money for nothing."

"Please don't make fun of me. This is nothing worth mentioning. I owe you a great deal—all these years you and sister have taken care of me. As the saying goes, 'No guest should give trouble to two hosts.' Now that I'm grown up, the time will come when you two can no longer look after me. Lately, a marriage proposal was made to me. I would like you and sister to make the decision for me. This is a lifetime matter."

Hearing these words, his sister and brother-in-law pondered, "Usually Hsü Hsüan will hardly part with a penny. This much generosity today and he expects us to get him a wife!" Husband and wife eyed each other and just would not answer him. After the meal was over, Hsü Hsüan went back to his business.

A few days passed, and Hsü Hsüan began to wonder, "Why doesn't my sister bring the matter up?" When he saw her, he asked her, "Have you talked about it with brother-in-law yet?"

"No," she answered.

"But why not?"

"This matter is not like other things. You cannot hurry about it. Furthermore, your brother-in-law has been looking quite ill-tempered these last few days, and I'm afraid I might irritate him. So I refrained from asking."

"But you're not pressing hard enough, sister," said Hsü Hsüan. "What's so difficult about it? The truth is, you're afraid I'd make him spend money. That's why you didn't take me seriously!"

He got up and went into his bedroom, opened the case, and took out the white lady's silver. Handing it to his sister, he said, "Here, no more excuses please! All I want is brother-in-law's consent."

"So my brother has saved up this much working for uncle—no wonder you want to marry! All right, you go off, and leave it to me," his sister replied.

When Officer Li came home, his wife said to him, "Husband, what do you know! Your brother-in-law wants to get married, because he has quite a bit of savings! Now he asks me to help myself to some small change. We will have to settle this matter for him."

Hearing this, Officer Li exclaimed, "So that's why! Well, it's good he has his own savings. Show it to me."

His wife took out the silver and handed it to him. Holding it in his hands, Officer Li looked at it this way and that. All of a sudden he saw the inscription mark on it, and cried aloud, "Alas! We're all finished!"

His wife, shocked, asked him, "Why, what's so terrible about it?"

"Several days ago, fifty ingots of silver were stolen from Marshal Shao's treasury." Officer Li explained to her, "It was a mystery, because the seals were all intact, and there was no tunnel that could lead in. He ordered the local authorities to dispatch urgent orders to catch the thief, but there isn't the slightest clue. Already many people have been implicated, and now they have put out a notice stating the mark and numbers of the ingots. Whoever captures the thief and retrieves the loot will get a reward of fifty taels. But anyone who withholds information, or hides the thief—his whole family will be banished to the frontier, while he himself will get due punishment. This silver here exactly fits the description on the notice, so it is definitely the silver from Marshal Shao's treasury. The police are hot on the scent now. As the saying goes, 'In a fire there's no time to care for relatives.' We must make a move; otherwise if it leaked out tomorrow we would never be able to explain. Whether he stole it or borrowed it, I'd rather see him punished than get involved myself. I'll take the silver to the authorities and own up, to save our family."

His wife, hearing these words, could only gape and stare in horror.

Immediately, the silver was surrendered to the authorities. The prefect, on receiving this information, could not sleep a wink the whole night. The next day, he lost no time in dispatching Inspector Ho Li, who, taking along his assistants and a number of smart constables, rushed to Li's herb shop at the entrance to Officials' Lane to arrest the main culprit, Hsü Hsüan, in the name of the law. They came up to the counter, gave a shout, put a rope around Hsü, and tied him up neatly. He was brought to the tribunal to the sound of gong and drum. Prefect Han happening to be holding court that moment; Hsü Hsüan was taken in and made to kneel.

"Beat him!" sounded the order.

"Sir, hold your punishment! I don't even know what I'm guilty of!" Hsü cried.

"Loot and thief are both here," the prefect shouted impatiently. "How can you explain yourself, and how can you plead not guilty? Without breaking a seal or lock, someone has stolen fifty ingots of silver from Marshal Shao's treasury. Officer Li has already owned up. I'm sure you are keeping the other forty-nine ingots as well. Let me see—the seals and locks were not damaged, but the silver was stolen—then you must be an evil sorcerer! All right, don't take him away yet!"

Then he called out for them to bring some foul blood.[6] Only then did Hsü Hsüan understand what it was all about.

"I'm not a sorcerer! Let me explain!" he yelled.

"All right, then say where this silver comes from," the prefect said.

Then Hsü Hsüan related carefully, bit by bit, that incident—how he had lent out his umbrella, and how he had gotten it back.

---

[6] Foul blood is the blood of a cock or a dog. It is believed to have the power to subdue sorcery, as the crucifix is thought to have comparable strength in the Western tradition.

"Who is this white lady? Where does she live?" the prefect again asked.

"According to her, she is the younger sister of Captain Po of the imperial guards. She lives in the black house opposite the residence of Prince Hsiu. It's on a slope, at the entrance to Twin Teahouse Lane, near the Arrow Bridge."

Immediately the prefect sent Ho Li to take Hsü Hsüan, under guard, and go to the Twin Teahouse Lane to arrest the culprit.

Bearing the command, Ho Li and his men went directly to the black house opposite the residence of Prince Hsiu at the entrance to Twin Teahouse Lane. At the front of the house, they saw four windows looking out onto the street, and a big double door, but the flight of steps leading up to the gate was strewn with garbage, while the gate itself was barred by a stick of bamboo! They were astounded at the sight. The neighbors were summoned at once—the florist Ch'iu the Elder to the left, and the cobbler Old Sun to the right. This frightened Old Sun so much that he had a rupture and fell to the ground.

The other neighbors came forward and said, "There has never been any white lady here. Not more than five or six years ago this house was inhabited by Commander Mao, but the entire family caught the epidemic disease and died. Even in broad daylight, ghosts often come out of the house to buy things, and no one dares move in to stay. A few days ago we saw a madman standing in front of the door, saying hello to passersby."

Ho ordered them to remove the bamboo stick that was barring the door. The inside seemed deserted. Suddenly a gust of wind blew out a stinking, rancid smell. It startled them all, and they retreated a few steps. Seeing this, Hsü Hsüan was rendered speechless. Among the constables, there was a daring fellow nicknamed Drunkard Wang the Second because he came second in the family and loved liquor. He shouted, "Come with me, all of you!"

They gave a cry and rushed in together. Inside they saw a fully furnished place, with panels, screens, tables, and chairs. When they came to the staircase, they made Wang the Second go up first, and the rest followed. On the upper floor, a coat of dust three inches thick had settled on everything. They came up to the entrance of a room, pushed open the door, and looked inside. The bed was curtained, and there were chests and boxes and all. On the bed sat an attractive-looking woman, dressed in white. Seeing this, no one dared go forward.

"Is madam a goddess or a spirit?" they addressed her. "We have orders from the prefect of Lin-an to summon you to bear witness with Hsü Hsüan."

The woman remained motionless. Drunkard Wang the Second said, "Does no one dare go up? Then how shall we settle this? Let me gulp down a jug of something strong, and then I'll take her to the prefect."

A few men were sent off at once to bring back a jug of liquor for Wang. Wang unsealed it, drank the last drop, and then, crying, "You won't scare me!" hurled the jug toward the curtain. If only he had not done that! No sooner was the jug hurled than they heard a loud crash—a peal of thunder from the blue! The terror of it shook them to the ground. When they rose to their feet and looked, the woman had vanished from the bed. Instead, they saw there a pile of glittering silver. They went forward and examined it, and then exclaimed, "Oh good!"; for on counting there proved to be forty-nine ingots in the pile. "We'll take it to the prefect," they said; so, carrying the silver on a pole, they made their way back to the office.

Inspector Ho reported the incident to the prefect. The latter said, "Then she must be an evil spirit. Well, let it be. The neighbors are not guilty, and may go home in peace." He then ordered the fifty silver ingots to be returned to Marshal Shao, together with a report carrying a full explanation of the case. As for Hsü Hsüan, under the serious charge of "committing an act which should not be committed," he was given a beating, spared the punishment of tattoo on the face, and sentenced to hard labor in a prison camp in the Soochow Prefecture.

Officer Li, feeling uneasy because he had given Hsü Hsüan away, gave all fifty taels of Marshal Shao's reward to his brother-in-law to equip him for his journey. Uncle Li wrote two letters of introduction for Hsü Hsüan, one to be presented to Head Clerk Fan, the other to Master Wang who ran the inn beside the Fortune Bridge. After a great deal of weeping, Hsü Hsüan bade farewell to his sister and brother-in-law, put on his cangue and, under the escort of two guards, departed from Hangchow. They took the boat at the East New Bridge and reached Soochow in a few days' time. There they visited Head Clerk Fan and Master Wang. The latter offered money on Hsü's behalf to the upper and lower ranks of officials, and directed the two guards to the Soochow city tribunal, where they made their report and delivered the prisoner. Then, having collected the return slip, the guards went home. Head Clerk Fan and Master Wang brought Hsü Hsüan out of jail on bail and arranged lodgings for him upstairs at Master Wang's. Feeling very sad, Hsü composed a poem, which he wrote down on the wall:

Alone in this high tower, I look toward home;
Sadly I watch the sun set through the gauze window.
Having been sincere and honest all my life,
How could I fall in with a woman so evil!
O white lady, I no longer know where you are;
And in what part of the land is Ch'ing-ch'ing now?
Forsaking my bone and flesh, I have come to Soochow,
But my heart breaks in pieces as I remember home.

Our tale, hitherto eventful and therefore lengthy, now skips over a period with little to relate. Quite unnoticeably, time shot by like an arrow and the days and months sped as quickly as the shuttle on a loom. More than half a year had passed since Hsü Hsüan settled down in Master Wang's house.

Toward the end of the ninth lunar month, as Master Wang was standing idly in front of the door, watching people in the street come and go, he saw a sedan chair coming along in the distance, attended by a young maid at one side. The maid came up and asked, "Please, sir, is this the house of Master Wang?"

Master Wang bowed in haste and said, "This is it. Who are you looking for?"

"We're looking for Master Hsü Hsiao-yi, who came from Lin-an."

"Wait a minute, and I'll tell him to come out."

The sedan chair stopped at the door. Master Wang went inside and called, "Hsiao-yi! Someone is looking for you!"

Hearing the call, Hsü Hsüan came along hurriedly and followed Master Wang to the door. He looked—who could it be but Ch'ing-ch'ing, attending a sedan chair in which sat the white lady! Seeing them, Hsü Hsüan poured out a torrent of words: "You wicked devil! Since you smuggled the silver from the treasury, you've put me into such hot water! My wrong was never righted! Now that I have come to this, what business would you have to come here? I feel ashamed for you!"

"Sir, please don't blame me," the white lady said. "I've made this trip especially to explain the matter to you. Let's go inside and I'll tell you all about it." She told Ch'ing-ch'ing to get their luggage and alighted from the sedan chair.

"You're an evil spirit. You're not allowed to come in!" Hsü declared. He barred the doorway and would not give way.

The white lady made a deep bow to Master Wang and said, "I am speaking the truth, sir; please believe me. Can I be an evil spirit? My dress has seams, and I cast a shadow under the sun. Unfortunately, I have lost my husband, and I am thus ill treated! Whatever was done was my husband's doing, not mine. Now, afraid that you might blame me, I have come especially to explain. When it is clarified, I will leave content."

"Show the lady inside, and sit down before you talk," Wang said.

In response she said, "Go in with me and we'll

reason it out before Mrs. Wang." Only then did the watchers-on at the door disperse.

Inside the house, Hsü Hsüan explained to Master Wang and Mrs. Wang, "She stole money from the treasury, passed it on to me, and got me in trouble with the law. And here she comes again. What more can she say?"

"My late husband left me that silver," she protested, "and I gave it to you with all good intent. I myself did not know where it came from."

"Why is it that when the constables came to arrest you there was nothing but garbage in front of the gate? And why is it that we heard one loud crash inside the curtain and you were gone?"

"When I heard you had been arrested because of the silver, I was afraid you might tell on me; then I would be taken to court and made a fool of in front of everybody. It would be so humiliating! So I ran away and hid in my aunt's house near the Splendid Treasure Monastery. Then I sent someone to heap a pile of garbage in front of our gate. Leaving the silver on the bed, I begged the neighbors to cover up for me."

"You simply ran away, and left me there to face the law!"

"I left the silver on the bed thinking that it would settle everything. Never did I guess there could be such a hullabaloo! Learning that you had been banished here, I took some money and came in the boat to look for you. Now that is is all explained, I'll go away. Perhaps you and I were never fated to be husband and wife."

Then Master Wang put in, "But madam has come all this way. Don't tell me you are going off right away! Come, you must stay a few days first, before deciding what to do next."

Ch'ing-ch'ing also said, "Since the good master insists, madam should stay a couple of days. After all, you once gave your word to marry Master Hsiao-yi."

The white lady at once retorted, "Shame, shame! As if I were all that desperate about getting married! I came only to clarify what is true and what is not."

"Since you promised to marry him," said Master Wang, "why go away? We must keep you here!"

Needless to say, the sedan chair was sent away.

In only a few days' time, the lady's flattery had won over Master Wang's wife so completely that the latter urged her husband to offer himself as Hsü Hsüan's matchmaker, and the eleventh day of the eleventh month was chosen for the occasion of the grand union. In a flash the happy day came. The white lady took out some silver and bade Master Wang prepare their wedding feast. She and Hsü Hsüan went through the matrimonial ceremony, and their union was sealed. When the feast was over, they entered the gauze-curtained chamber together. The myriad charms of her voice and body so overwhelmed Hsü Hsüan that he was as elated as if in the presence of a fairy, and only regretted that they hadn't met sooner. The wonderful hours passed so quickly that, before they knew it, the cock had crowed thrice, hailing the dawn. Indeed:

To happy lovers, the night is regrettably short;
Only lonely souls would dread the dragging of the hours.

From that day on they became an inseparable pair, like fish and water. In Master Wang's house they reveled all day long, deliriously enamored of each other.

Days and months went by, and soon half a year had elapsed. Springtime, that lovely warm season, arrived, bringing the flowers into gorgeous bloom. Carts and horses flooded the streets, and the townfolk were as busy as ever. That day Hsü Hsüan asked Master Wang, "Why is everyone coming out looking so happy today? Such a hustle and bustle everywhere!"

"This is the fifteenth day of the second month," Master Wang told him. "Men and women alike are going to pay respects to the Reclining Buddha. Why don't you make a round to the Heavenly Heritage Monastery, too?"

"I'll leave word with my wife and go watch the fun," Hsü said.

He went upstairs and said to the white lady,

"Today is the fifteenth day of the second month, and men and women alike are going to pay respects to the Reclining Buddha. I'll make a brief trip and be right back. If anyone asks for me, just say I'm not home, and don't come out and show yourself in public."

"What is there in him to see?" she asked. "Wouldn't it be better to stay at home? I don't see any reason for going."

"I'm going just for the fun of it. Don't worry. I'll be right back."

Leaving the house, Hsü joined several people whom he knew, and together they went to the monastery to see the Reclining Buddha. Walking along the cloisters, he made a tour of the various halls of worship. On coming out of the monastery, he caught sight of a man dressed in a Taoist robe, with a cap on his head, a yellow silk band wrapped around his waist, and hemp sandals on his feet. The man was sitting in front of the monastery, selling medicine and giving away charms and holy water. As Hsü was standing there to watch, the priest declared, "I am a priest from the Chung-nan Mountains;[7] I travel everywhere, distributing charms and holy water, saving people from illness and calamities. Come forward here, anyone who has trouble!"

The priest saw in the crowd a trail of black fog looming over the head of Hsü Hsüan, and he knew some evil spirit must be hanging about him. He cried, "Of late you have been haunted by an evil spirit, which is doing you more than a little harm! I'll give you two charms to save your life. This one you should burn up at the third watch, and this one you should insert in your hair."

Accepting the charms, Hsü made a deep bow, thinking to himself, "I've suspected all along that my wife is an evil spirit. So it's true." After thanking the priest, he returned to the house.

When night fell and the white lady and Ch'ing-ch'ing were asleep, Hsü got up and muttered to himself, "It's probably the third watch already."

He inserted one charm in his hair, and was just about to put a flame to the other when the white lady heaved a sigh and said, "Hsiao-yi, we've been husband and wife for so long, and yet you still don't have confidence in me. Instead you listened to a stranger's words, and deep in the night you now burn a charm to exorcise me! All right, burn it up and see!"

She snatched the charm and burned it up in a jiffy, but nothing happened. She said, "Really, how can you say I am an evil spirit?!"

"Don't blame me," Hsü said. "That Taoist priest in front of the Monastery of the Reclining Buddha is sure that you are."

"Tomorrow I'll go along with you and see what kind of a priest he is," she replied.

The next day she rose early, finished her toilet, decked herself with hairpins and earrings, and put on a plain-color dress. She told Ch'ing-ch'ing to take good care of the house, and then husband and wife went to the Monastery of the Reclining Buddha. There in front of the monastery they saw a big crowd gathered around the priest, who was giving away charms and holy water.

Opening wide her witchy eyes, the white lady walked right up to him and shouted, "How impertinent can you be! Being a Taoist, yet going to such an extreme as to tell my husband that I am an evil spirit! As if that weren't enough, you wrote him a charm to trap me!"

"What I practice is the method of the Five Heavenly Thunderbolts,"[8] the priest retorted. "Any evil spirit who swallows my charm immediately changes into its true form."

"In the presence of everyone here, you can write me a charm and I will swallow it!"

He wrote one and handed it to her. She took it, and gulped it down. They watched but nothing happened; so they all said, "She's a woman all right! How can you call her an evil spirit?" Together they heaped abuses on the priest, who was rendered speechless and could only stare and gape shamefacedly.

[7] A mountain range that stretches from western Honan through the southern portion of Shensi to eastern Kansu.

[8] A type of witchcraft.

"You've all witnessed, gentlemen," she then announced, "that he failed to catch me. I know a little trick which I learned in childhood. Let me try it on the reverend master, for your entertainment."

Whereupon she muttered something which none of them could catch. All of a sudden the priest, as if caught by someone, shrunk to a heap, and rose into mid-air, where he was suspended. All who saw it were greatly amazed, and Hsü Hsüan was dumbfounded.

"If not for the sake of you gentlemen," the white lady said, "I'd hang the reverend master up there for a year."

She blew a puff of breath, and down came the priest. He fled, only lamenting that he lacked a pair of wings. Then the crowd dispersed. Our couple went home, needless to say, and the white lady continued to pay for all their expenditures from her own pocket. They were truly happy together.

He sings and she follows, and thus they pass
Their days in mirth, their nights in merriment.

Time flew like an arrow, and all too soon the eighth day of the fourth month, the Birthday of Buddha Shakyamuni,[9] had arrived. In the streets people could be seen carrying statues of the bathing Buddha under cypress canopies, and stopping at every house to ask for alms. Hsü said to Master Wang, "This is indeed much like Hangchow."

A youngster next door, called Ironhead, said, "Master Hsiao-yi, today they're holding a Buddhists' gathering at the Heavenly Heritage Monastery. Go and have a look."

Hsü went inside and told the white lady about it. She said, "What's there to see? Don't go!"

"I'm making the trip just to kill time," Hsü pleaded.

"If you must go, the old clothes that you have on now would not look decent. Let me dress you up."

[9] The principal Buddha, the founder of religious Buddhism.

Ch'ing-ch'ing was ordered to bring some new, stylish things for Hsü to try on. They turned out to be just the right l   gth, as if tailored to fit. He had a black silk hat on his head, behind which dangled a pair of white jade rings at the back, and he wore a blue silk robe. On his feet were black boots, and in his hand a fanciful folding fan, decorated with a coral pendant and with gilded figures of lovely girls painted on its thin gauze surface. His attire was thus complete. In her melodic voice the white lady reminded him, "Come home early. Don't let me worry about you!"

Hsü got Ironhead to accompany him, and along they went to the Heavenly Heritage Monastery to watch the Buddhists' gathering. Everyone marveled at the sight of such a fine-looking gentleman. Then someone was heard to say, "Last night an amount of jewelry and cash worth four or five thousand strings of cash was stolen from Squire Chou's pawnship. They have listed the stolen goods and made a report to the authorities. Police are searching, but the thief is nowhere to be found." Hsü heard these words but did not know what they meant. Together with Ironhead he hung around the monastery, watching the great bustle of men and women, of different walks of life, who had come to burn incense.

Eventually he told himself, "She wants me to go back early. I had better be off." As he turned around in the crowd he lost sight of Ironhead, so he walked out of the monastery alone.

There at the gate several men were standing, dressed as constables, with badges hanging at their waists. One of them spotted Hsü Hsüan and said to his companions, "What this man has on him looks pretty much like it."

One of them who knew Hsü called to him, "Master Hsiao-yi, let me have a look at your fan." Unaware that the man was playing a trick, Hsü handed the fan to him.

"Look, this fan and the pendant on it exactly fit the description on the list!" the man said.

"Get him!" they all shouted, and put a rope

around Hsü Hsüan and tied him up. What a scene! It was like:

Several black vultures darting after a sparrow;
A pack of hungry tigers devouring a lamb.

"Gentlemen," Hsü cried, "don't be mistaken! I have done nothing wrong!"

"We shall soon find out about that from Squire Chou's shop facing the prefect's tribunal!" the constables said. "They lost five thousand strings' worth of jewlery and clothes, together with white jade rings, a fanciful folding fan and a coral pendant—will you say you have done nothing wrong? Both loot and thief are here; how will you defend yourself? You certainly have guts, to take us for good-for-nothings! Everything on you from head to toe is Squire Chou's, and yet you show yourself in public so boldly!"

Hsü Hsüan was petrified. After a moment's silence, he said, "So that is why. Well, no bother, no bother. There must be a real thief."

"You'll do your own explaining at the tribunal," they said.

The next day the prefect conducted the hearing and Hsü Hsüan was brought in. "Where did you hide the jewelry and valuables you stole from Squire Chou's shop?" the prefect asked him. "Tell the truth, to spare yourself the rod!"

"Believe me, Your Honor, what I have on me, clothes and all, belongs to my wife. I don't know where it came from. Use your discreet judgment, I beg you!"

"Where is your wife now?" the prefect shouted.

"She's upstairs at Master Wang's inn, near the Fortune Bridge."

The prefect at once sent Inspector Yüan Tzuming along, with Hsü under guard, to bring the white lady back under arrest.

Their arrival at the inn gave Master Wang a shock. He asked hastily, "What's all this about?"

"Is my wife upstairs?" Hsü asked.

"Shortly after you and Ironhead went off to the Heavenly Heritage Monastery, she said to me, 'My husband is off to the monastery to enjoy himself, and tells me and Ch'ing-ch'ing to mind the house. Since he's not back yet, I'll go with Ch'ing-ch'ing to look for him. Please look after the place for us.' Then they went out, and when evening came they were not back. I thought she had gone with you to visit relatives. She hasn't been back today."

By order of the constables Master Wang made a thorough search for the white lady, but she was nowhere to be seen. So Yüan Tzu-ming brought Master Wang to the prefect, who asked, "Where is the white lady?"

Master Wang then reported the entire matter in detail and said that the white lady must be an evil spirit.

After some careful interrogation the prefect ordered, "Detain Hsü Hsüan."

Master Wang, however, spent some money and bought himself out, to await the final verdict.

Now Squire Chou was sitting at leisure in the teahouse opposite his house when a household servant made him this report: "The jewelry and the rest of the things have been found in an empty chest upstairs in our shop." Hearing this, the squire hurried back to take a look—and sure enough, there they were, with only the hat, the rings, the fan, and the pendant still missing. He said, "Then obviously they have done Hsü Hsüan an injustice. It is not right that an innocent man should be ruined." He secretly spoke to the authorities concerned, and begged them to charge Hsü with only a minor offense.

At that time it happened that Officer Li was sent by Marshal Shao to Soochow on business, and he lodged at Master Wang's inn. Master Wang told him all about Hsü Hsüan, from his arrival there up to his involvement in the lawsuit. Officer Li thought, "After all, he's one of the family. How can I not help him?" So on Hsü's behalf he went begging for favors and paying bribes high and low, until the day came when the prefect obtained a complete confession from Hsü, blaming everything on the white lady. Then Hsü's trial was concluded: he was guilty of "not owning up to the presence of an evil spirit, and other similar charges," and his sentence amounted to a hundred strokes of the rod and banishment to a hard-labor camp in the Chinkiang[10] Prefecture three hundred sixty *li* away.

"Going to Chinkiang is all right for you," Officer Li said. "I have a sworn uncle there by the name of Li K'o-yung, who owns an herb shop near the Needle Bridge. Let me write him a letter; then you can go to him for help."

So Hsü Hsüan borrowed some roadfare from his brother-in-law, expressed his gratitude to him and Master Wang, treated the two escort guards to a meal, packed his things, and went on his way. Master Wang and Officer Li accompanied him for some distance, and then parted and went home separately.

Hsü Hsüan and the guards sped along on the road, eating when hungry and drinking when thirsty, traveling by day and resting by night, and in a few days' time reached Chinkiang. The first thing they did was to look for Li K'o-yung's herb shop near the Needle Bridge. On arriving there, they saw an assistant selling goods at the front of the shop, while the old squire himself was just coming out from behind. Hurriedly the two guards and Hsü Hsüan stepped forward and greeted him. Hsü said, "I'm a relative of Hang-chow's Officer Li; here is a letter from him."

The assistant handed the letter to the old squire, who opened it, read it, and said, "So you are Hsü Hsüan."

"Yes, I am," Hsü replied.

Li K'o-yung gave the three of them a meal, and then sent a servant with them to the prefectural tribunal, where they made their report and paid some graft money to bring Hsü out on bail. The guards obtained their return slip and found their own way back to Soochow, while Hsü followed the

servant back to Li's place. There he expressed his thanks to the squire and presented himself to Mrs. Li. Having read Officer Li's letter, Li K'o-yung knew that Hsü had been an assistant in an herb shop, so he put him in his shop to help with the business, and arranged lodgings for him on the upper floor of the beancurd vendor Old Wang's place in the Fifth Lane. Li K'o-yung became very fond of Hsü because he worked so conscientiously.

There were originally two assistants in the shop, one by the name of Chang, the other named Chao. Whereas Chao had been a quiet, honest man all his life, Chang all along was greedy and cunning. Counting on his own seniority, he liked to bully the younger shoptenders. The addition of Hsü Hsüan to the staff greatly displeased him, for he feared his own dismissal. His jealousy drove him to wicked schemes. One day, when Li K'o-yung came to the shop to look around, and asked how the newcomer was performing, Chang said to himself, "Here he comes into my trap!" So he answered, "He's fine—except for one thing."

"What is that?" asked Li.

"He's most attentive to the big customers, but just won't bother about the petty ones; so people say he is no good. I've talked to him several times about it, but he won't listen."

"That's easy. I'll tell him myself. He cannot disobey me."

After overhearing their conversation, Chao spoke to Chang in private: "We should all try to pull together. Hsü Hsüan is a newcomer. You and I should help him along. If he makes a mistake, we should point it out to him rather than mention it behind his back. What if he learns about it? He'll think we're jealous."

But old Chang retorted, "You young people, what do you know!"

As it was already late, they went home separately, but Chao went along to Hsü Hsüan's place and told him, "Old Chang is spreading jealous words about you in front of the boss. From now

---

[10] At the junction of the Yangtze River and the Grand Canal in Kiangsu.

on you must be more careful and treat all customers alike, be they big or small."

"Thank you for your advice," said Hsü. "Let's go for a drink together."

They went into a tavern and sat down. The waiter brought dishes and delicacies, and they had a few cups. Then Chao said, "The old squire has the bluntest of tempers. He can't stand any contradiction. You just follow the dictates of his temper, and be patient in your work."

"Sir, you are so good to me; how can I thank you enough?"

They had a few more cups. As it was getting dark, Chao said, "It's dark and the roads are difficult. We can meet again some other time." Hsü paid for the wine, and they parted.

Feeling somewhat dizzy with the wine, Hsü was afraid he might bump into people, so he groped his way home under the eaves of the houses. As he was walking along, there on an upper story some window was pushed open, and ashes from a clothing iron rained down on his head. He stopped in his tracks and yelled, "Who's the blind fool up there? This is really outrageous!"

He saw a woman come down with hurried steps. She said, "Sir, please don't be cross. That's my fault. I was much too careless!"

Hsü Hsüan, half drunk, raised his head and looked into her eyes—and who could it be but the white lady! Anger and fury swelled in his bosom, and his flames of wrath could find no control. He snarled, "You thief, you bitch, you evil spirit! You've given me such trouble, dragged me into two lawsuits!"

Indeed, if one does not react according to one's natural temper, one falls short of being a real man. As coincidence would have it:

After all that frenzied searching, to no avail,
They should meet here—by casual working of fate!

He yelled, "So you have come after me again! Doesn't this prove you are an evil spirit?" He charged into her house and grabbed her tight,

shouting, "Shall we settle it in court or in private?"

The white lady said with a smile, "As the saying goes, 'Husband and wife for one night,/ Love lingers on for a hundred nights.' Will you listen to me? All those clothes were originally left me by my husband. As I love you so, I made you wear them. But in return for my love I was spited; then we became enemies."

"That day when I went home to look for you, why were you not there? The innkeeper said you and Ch'ing-ch'ing had gone to the monastery to look for me. Why are you here now?"

"When we arrived at the monastery, we heard that you had been caught, and Ch'ing-ch'ing was unable to get any further news. We assumed you made good your escape. Fearing they might come after me, I told Ch'ing-ch'ing to rent a boat, and we went to my uncle's place in the Chien-k'ang Prefecture. We arrived here only yesterday. I know very well I got you into trouble with the law twice, and I felt such misery and shame that I didn't even dare face you! But even though you blame me now, it's no use. We were in love, and we are man and wife. We used to get along so well; why must we run away from each other now? We have a love bond between us, as constant as the T'ai Mountains and the Eastern Sea,[11] and we must live and die together. Please, since we are already married, take me back, and let's stay together the rest of our lives. Wouldn't that be wonderful?"

At her persuasion, Hsü was instantly gladdened and stopped fretting. He only pondered a second and then, overcome by her charms, gave up the idea of going home and spent the night at her place upstairs.

The next morning he went back to Old Wang's house in the Fifth Lane up the river, and told Wang about the arrival of his wife and her maid from Soochow and the rest of the story, adding,

---

[11] Referring to the open stretch of water to the east of the coastal provinces of Kiangsu, Chekiang, and Fukien.

"I'd like to have them move in here to stay with me."

"That's fine. There's really no need to ask," said Wang.

That very day the white lady and Ch'ing-ch'ing moved into their new lodgings upstairs in Old Wang's house. The following day they threw a tea party for the neighbors, who showed their welcome on the next day with a jolly feast. The fourth day, Hsü Hsüan got up early, combed his hair and washed, and said to the white lady, "I'll go express our thanks to the neighbors, and then I have to go back to work. You and Ch'ing-ch'ing just stay upstairs and mind the house; don't go outside." After leaving these instructions, he went on his way to do business in the shop and return home at night.

In this way, leaving early and turning in late, he was unaware of the swift passage of the days and nights. A month passed, and one day Hsü Hsüan suggested to the white lady that she should pay her respects to his employer Squire Li and his wife and their household. She said, "Since you're an assistant in his shop, maybe I should present myself to him, if only for the sake of getting along."

The following day a sedan chair was hired. The white lady seated herself in it, asked Old Wang to carry their boxes of presents on a pole, told Ch'ing-ch'ing to follow behind, and went to Squire Li's house. She descended from the sedan chair, entered, and asked to see the squire, who hurriedly came out to receive her. Courteously she gave her greeting, made two bows each to the squire and Mrs. Li, and then presented herself to the other ladies of the household.

The truth is that Li K'o-yung, although advanced in years, was singularly fond of lusty pleasures. At the sight of the white lady with such extraordinary charms:

His three souls no longer stayed seated in his body,
While his seven spirits flocked over to her side.

He simply could not take his eyes off her. As wine and dishes were then laid out to entertain them, his wife said to him, "What a smart little lady she is! Such good looks and gentle conduct, and so modest and well behaved, too!"

"Indeed. Hangchow girls are really handsome," he answered.

After the meal, the white lady thanked them for their hospitality and went home.

Meanwhile, Li K'o-yung pondered to himself, "If only I could spend a night with this woman!" He knitted his brows, and an idea came into his mind. "My birthday falls on the thirteenth day of the sixth month. That's it! The little bird will fall into my trap!"

Sure enough, almost before we know it, the rapid succession of days and nights now brings us past the Dragon Boat Festival right into the sixth month. The squire said, "Wife, the thirteenth is my birthday. Let's give a dinner party and invite our relatives and friends to spend a day here. It would be a happy occasion."

That same day invitations were sent to all relatives, neighbors, friends, and assistants in the shop. The next day presents of candles, noodles,[12] handkerchiefs, and the like flooded in from every household that was invited.

On the thirteenth, the [male] guests came to the feast, which lasted a whole day, and on the following day it was the female guests' turn to come and offer birthday greetings. More than twenty ladies came, including the white lady. She appeared in full array, in a blue blouse that was brocaded with gold thread and a bright red chiffon skirt, and on her coiffure she wore an extremely fanciful headdress of jewels, jade, gold, and silver. With Ch'ing-ch'ing escorting her, she went into the inner chamber and delivered her birthday greetings to the squire and paid her respects to Mrs. Li.

The feast was laid out in the east wing of the

[12] Noodles, a symbol of longevity, are usually eaten on birthdays in China.

house. The truth is, Li K'o-yung was a man who even when he was eating a flea would save a hind leg, and only because the white lady was such a beauty did he design such a grand feast. While the guests passed around the cups and made merry with the goblets at the table, the white lady rose from her seat to go to the toilet. Now the squire had already given orders to his trusted waiting woman, saying, "If the white lady should want to retire, you should take her to the quiet room at the back of the house." As the plan was already set, he went there before her, and hid there waiting, for certainly:

What need for him to tunnel or climb a wall?
His trap is set, and she is sure to fall!

As soon as she saw the white lady get up, the waiting woman, as instructed, directed her to a quiet, out-of-the-way room at the back of the house. After the woman had gone, the squire, restless with lascivious thoughts, could control himself no longer, but he dared not charge in immediately. Instead, he peeped into the room through a crack in the door. If only he had not peeped, for that one single peep gave him the scare of his life! Turning around, he dashed away, only to collapse on his back when he reached the rear quarters.

Is there still life in him? That is hard to tell,
But already strength from all four limbs is gone.

For what he saw in that room was no pretty female form, but a big, coiling white snake, whose body was as bulky as a water bucket and whose two eyes, like lanterns, were gleaming with golden light. It shocked him half to death, and he turned around and fled, but slipped and fell.

When the maids helped him up from the floor, they saw that his face was pale and his lips had lost all color. Hastily the housekeeper made him swallow a nerve-calming pill, and only then did he come to his senses. Mrs. Li and the guests all arrived. Seeing him in such a state, they asked, "What happened? What was the matter?"

Instead of telling them the truth, Squire Li said, "I got up too early today. These few days I've been quite tired out. I felt an attack of dizziness and fainted."

They escorted him to his room and put him to bed, after which the guests returned to the table and had a few more cups. Then the banquet was concluded, and they expressed their appreciation, took their leave, and went home.

After coming home, the white lady turned the matter over in her head. She was afraid when they met in the shop the next day Squire Li would tell Hsü Hsüan about her true identity, so she conjured up a plan. While taking off her clothes she proceeded to sigh. Hsü asked, "You've just come back from a party. What's all this sighing about?"

"Husband, how shall I tell you? That Squire Li had an ulterior motive in giving this birthday party of his. When he saw me rise from my seat to go to the toilet, he hid in there and tried to rape me, tugging at my skirt and pants to make me yield. I would have yelled, if not for my fear that it would cause a scandal in front of all those people. I gave him a push and he fell on the floor. He was afraid of losing face, and gave them a false story, saying he had had a fit and had fainted. What a terrible time I had. If only I knew how to get my revenge!"

"Fortunately, he had not managed to overpower you," said Hsü. "As he is my employer, we can do nothing but tolerate it this once. But in future stay away from him."

"So you will not stand up for me! But I still have to face the world!"

"My brother-in-law wrote to him and I came to him for help, and he was so good as to take me in as an assistant. What do you say I should do now?"

"A fine man you are!" retorted the white lady.

371

"He has insulted me, yet you will still work for him!"

"But where else can I go? How shall we earn a living?"

"Shop assistant is after all a lowly post. Why don't we open an herb shop of our own?"

"Fancy your suggesting it! Where's the money?"

"Don't worry. It's simple. Tomorrow I'll give you some silver and you can go rent a house first."

Well, in past ages as in the present, there have been those who are eager to perform good deeds for others. It happened that their next-door neighbor Chiang Ho was one such helpful fellow. The very next day Hsü Hsüan, having received some silver from the white lady, enlisted Chiang Ho's help, and the latter rented a house for him near the Chinkiang ferry pier. They bought a set of herbalist's cabinets and, bit by bit, gradually laid in a stock of medicinal herbs. By the time the tenth month came, everything was ready. They chose an auspicious day and opened the herb shop. Hsü Hsüan stopped going to the squire's shop, and the squire, having his own qualms, did not dare to call upon him.

The new shop did good business from the moment it opened, and as the days went by, the profit grew. One day, as Hsü Hsüan was selling herbs at the front of the shop, along came a Buddhist monk, with a donation register in his hand. He addressed Hsü, saying, "I come from the Golden Hill Monastery. The seventh day of the seventh month is the birthday of the Illustrious Dragon King. You are cordially invited to come to our incense-burning ceremony, and to donate to our coffers."

"You need not put down my name," said Hsü. "But I have a piece of fine lakewood incense[13] here which I can give to you as an offering."

He took it out of the cupboard and handed it to the monk, who repeated his invitation by saying, "We expect you at ＿ r incense-burning ceremony that day," and went away with a greeting.

The white lady, who saw this scene, said, "You stupid fool! Such a nice piece of incense, and you had to give it to that ass of a monk! I'm sure he will spend it on liquor and meat!"

"I gave it to him in all sincerity. If he squanders it, the fault is his," said Hsü.

Soon the seventh day of the seventh month arrived. While Hsü was opening up the shop, he saw that the streets were particularly busy. Chiang Ho, the busybody, said, "Master Hsiao-yi, that day you made an offering with your piece of incense. Why don't you make a trip to the monastery today?"

"Wait a minute while I settle my things, and then I'll go with you."

"I'll keep you company for sure."

Quickly, then, Hsü put things in order and went inside and told the white lady, "I'm going to the Golden Hill Monastery to join their incense-burning ceremony. You take care of the house."

"As the saying goes, 'No one visits the temple unless he has a purpose.' What's your purpose?"

"Well, first, I've never been to the Golden Hill Monastery and should like to see the place. Second, I already made one offering that day, and they expect me to go and burn incense today."

"Since you're bent on going, I can't stop you. But you must promise me three things."

"Which three?"

"One: not to venture into the abbot's cell. Two: not to talk to any monk. Three: come right back afterwards. If you come back late, I'll go there to look for you."

"That's easy. I'll do as you say."

Then he changed into clean clothes, shoes, and socks, tucked his incense box in his sleeve, and, together with Chiang Ho, went down to the riverside. There they boarded the ferry, which brought them to the Golden Hill Monastery.

---

[13] Lakewood (*Acronychia laurifolia bixme*) is grown in Sumatra and South China. The wood is cut to size, dried, and burned for its fragrance. It is usually used as an incense in religious ceremonies.

They first went to the Hall of the Dragon King and burned incense. Then they made a routine tour of the monastery and, following the crowd, came to the door of the abbot's cell. All of a sudden Hsü remembered, "My wife has told me not to go in." Whereupon he halted and stayed outside.

"What does it matter?" Chiang Ho said. "She's at home all by herself. When you go back you can just tell her that you haven't been inside."

Then they went in and took a look, and came out.

Now sitting on the high seat in the center of the abbot's cell was a monk of great spiritual accomplishment. With neat, elegant brows and clear, bright eyes, a round shaven head and a monk's habit, his very looks were those of a true master. When he caught sight of Hsü Hsüan passing by, he immediately called to his attendant, "Quick, tell that young man to come in here!" The attendant searched for a while, but there being thousands of people moving about noisily, and no way of identifying Hsü in the crowd, he reported that the gentleman was nowhere to be found. On hearing that, the monk took up his staff and came out of the abbot's cell to look for Hsü himself. But neither at the front nor at the back could Hsü Hsüan be spotted.

When the monk came out of the monastery, he saw that a crowd of people had already gathered there, waiting to board the ferry. But a storm was mounting, and as it raged more and more fiercely everyone exclaimed, "We're stuck!" In the midst of such a scene, a boat came into sight, moving in the river toward them as fast as if borne on wings. Hsü Hsüan remarked to Chiang Ho, "The storm has already held up the ferry. How could that boat get here so fast?" Even as they were wondering, the boat came nearer, and they saw on it a woman dressed in white clothes and a girl all in green. When the boat came to shore, they saw clearly and recognized the two as the white lady and Ch'ing-ch'ing. Hsü was more than a little

startled. The white lady came up to the edge of the shore and called, "Why don't you come home? Get in the boat, quickly!"

Just when Hsü Hsüan was about to board, he heard someone shout from behind, "Evil creature, what is your business here?" Turning round, he heard a general mutter, "The great monk Fa-hai is here!"

"Evil creature," the monk said, "how dare you show yourself again so insolently and wreak havoc on mortality! Mark it: I've come here especially for you!"

At the sight of the monk, the white lady rowed away from the shore. Then she and Ch'ing-ch'ing turned the boat over, dived under water together, and were lost to sight. Hsü turned around to the monk and bowed earnestly, saying, "Holy master, save my worthless life!"

"How did you get involved with that woman?"

Starting from the very beginning, Hsü related to him all that had happened. When he heard the story, the monk said, "She's an evil spirit. You must go back to Hangchow at once. If she should impose herself on you again, you can come to the Cleansing Mercy Monastery to the south of the lake to see me. As the poem goes:

She was an evil spirit, disguised in female form;
By the West Lake she made a show of her charms.
Not knowing what she was, you fell into her trap;
When misfortune befalls you, then come to me south
　　of the lake.

Hsü Hsüan expressed his gratitude to Fa-hai. Accompanied by Chiang Ho, he crossed the river by ferry and found his way home. At home, neither the white lady nor Ch'ing-ch'ing could be seen. He was then convinced that they were evil spirits. When evening came, he invited Chiang Ho to pass the night with him, but he was so unhappy that he did not sleep a wink.

The next morning he rose early, told Chiang Ho to take care of the house, and came to Li K'o-yung's place at the Needle Bridge. There he told the squire what had lately happened, whereupon the squire confessed, "That day at my birthday party, completely unprepared, I bumped into her when she was in the toilet. The sight of her grotesque form scared me so badly that I passed out. I didn't dare tell you at that time. Since it has come to this, why don't you move in and stay with us before making further plans?" Hsü thanked the squire, and moved in.

He had lived there for more than two months when suddenly, standing at the door one day, he saw the community headman come along, ordering all households to prepare incense, flowers, lanterns, and candles to welcome the issuance of the emperor's grand amnesty. The reason was that in that year the Emperor Kao-tsung installed Hsiao-tsung[14] as his heir apparent, and an amnesty was issued throughout the country to celebrate the occasion. Except for homicides and other serious crimes, all convicts would be released from their sentences and allowed to go home. This sudden bestowal of freedom so overjoyed Hsü Hsüan that he composed the following poem:

Thanks be to our Emperor for bestowing this decree;
The net of mercy open, I can now reform.
No longer fated to die in an alien place,
I shall return to my native town, alive and well.
What distress, to be tied up with that evil creature!
And what relief, to have all sins forgiven!
When I reach home, I shall burn incense in holiest reverence,
And thank Heaven and Earth, for granting me new life!

After this poetic outburst, Hsü Hsüan asked Squire Li to facilitate things by paying money to those high and low in the prefectural tribunal. The prefect granted him an audience, with the result that he was given a permit to go back home. He bade farewell to his neighbors, the squire and Mrs. Li and their household, as well as the squire's two assistants. Then he asked the helpful Chiang Ho to purchase some indigenous products for

[14] See footnote 5 above.

him and, laden with these, returned to Hang-chow.

When he reached home, he found that his sister and brother-in-law were in. He bowed four times in front of them. On seeing him, Officer Li scowled and said, "You're certainly quite incorrigible! I wrote letters of introduction for you twice, to help you find employment and shelter, yet you never wrote home to tell us that you have married at Squire Li's place! What a heartless, faithless brat you are!"

"I never married anyone!" Hsü Hsüan protested.

"Two days ago a woman came to us," his brother-in-law said. "She was attended by a maid, and she said she is your wife. She said that on the seventh day of the seventh month you went to the Golden Hill Monastery to burn incense, and hadn't been home since then. She had looked everywhere for you, and learned only just now that you have come back to Hangchow; so she and the maid made their trip here ahead of you. They have been here two days already."

Then Li ordered a servant to inform the woman and her maid and ask them to come out. They confronted one another again—it was indeed the white lady and Ch'ing-ch'ing! At the sight of them, Hsü stared and gaped, and was scared stiff. But he dared not tell his story to his sister and brother-in-law, and could only yield himself to their scolding.

Li ordered Hsü to stay in the same room with the white lady. Seeing that it was getting dark, Hsü was terrified. He dared not approach her, but knelt on the floor before her and said, "What fairy or spirit are you? Please spare my life!"

"Husband, why talk so? We have been married all this while, but never have I harmed you in any way. Why do you come with such unpleasant words?"

"Since I came to know you, you have gotten me into two lawsuits. When I went off to the Chin-kiang Prefecture, you followed me in hot pursuit.

That day at the Golden Hill Monastery, just because I lingered a while too long, you and Ch'ing-ch'ing came on the scent again. Then at the sight of that monk you jumped into the river. I thought you were dead—but here you are again! Have some pity on me, please. Let me go!"

The white lady glared at him with witchy eyes and said, "Husband, everything I did was for our good. I never expected it would make you so bitter. You and I are married. We have shared the same bed, and spent wonderful hours together. What now? You believed in other people's idle words, and kept quarreling with me! Here and now let me tell you: listen to what I say and we shall be happy, past issues brushed aside. But if you've other thoughts, I'll cause this entire town to be flooded with blood, and the deluge will drown all the townspeople and bring them the most horrible of deaths."

This announcement made Hsü Hsüan tremble all over. For a moment he was speechless. He dared not reply or walk away. Then Ch'ing-ch'ing broke in, "Master, mistress loves you so much because you're as handsome as a Hangchow gentleman should be, and also because of your deep affection for her. Now do as I say: be good to her, and don't have any more suspicions."

Hsü Hsüan could not prevail against the two of them. He could only exclaim, "Oh, the misery of it!"

His lamentation was heard by his sister, who was out in the courtyard enjoying the cool of the evening. Hearing him exclaim so, she came up to their door but, thinking that the young couple were having a lovers' quarrel, dragged Hsü out of the room, while the white lady shut the door and went to bed by herself. Then Hsü disclosed to his sister the whole story from beginning to end. She then asked her husband, who was just coming in from the courtyard, "The young couple has just had a row. I wonder if she has gone to bed now? Will you go take a look and tell me?"

Officer Li tiptoed up to their room, and saw a half-glimmer in that dark interior. He licked on the window's paper screen and made a hole in it, and took a peep inside. If only he had not peeped! For sleeping there on the bed, with its head resting against the skylight to catch the cool evening breeze, was a giant python, its body as bulky as a water bucket, its coat of scales shining with a silver glitter that lit up the room like day. Shocked by the sight, Li turned around and fled back to his own room. He kept quiet about the matter, though, and just said, "She's asleep. There is no sound at all." Hsü Hsüan, however, hid in his sister's room and would not go out. Nor did his brother-in-law question him.

The night passed. The next day, Officer Li took Hsü Hsüan to a quiet spot and asked him, "Where did you get that wife of yours? Tell me the whole truth, and don't hide anything from me. Last night I saw with my own eyes what she is—a big white snake! It is only because I feared it would terrify your sister that I didn't come right out with it."

Then Hsü told it all to his brother-in-law, who said, "If it's so, let's call upon that snake charmer Mr. Tai who usually stations himself in front of the White Horse Temple, for he has a way with snakes. I'll go with you to fetch him."

The two of them then hurried to the White Horse Temple, where they found the man standing in front of the entrance. They said, "Hello there!"

"What can I do for you, gentlemen?" the man asked.

"There's a big python in our house," explained Hsü. "We have come to ask you to catch it for us."

"Where is the place?"

"It's Officer Li's house in Black Pearl Lane, near the Garrison Bridge," Hsü said. Meanwhile he took out a tael of silver and handed it to the man, saying, "You can take this in advance. After you have caught the snake, we'll reward you more."

The man took it and said, "Go home first, gentlemen; I shall be with you in a minute."

Li and Hsü then went home, while the man filled a bottle with orpiment solution. Armed with that, he came straight to the Black Pearl Lane and asked for Officer Li's house. He was told it was the two-story building just ahead. Coming up to the door of the house, he lifted the curtain and gave a cough. No one came to answer. He knocked on the door for a little while, and out came a young lady. She asked him, "Who are you looking for?"

"Is this Officer Li's house?" asked Tai.

"It is."

"There's a big snake in your house, the two gentlemen told me just now. They asked me to come and catch it."

"A snake in our house? You must be mistaken."

"The gentleman has already given me a tael of silver. He said after I've caught it I'll be handsomely rewarded."

"There's nothing of the sort in here! You shouldn't believe them. It's just a joke."

"Why should they want to play a joke on me?"

Again and again the white lady tried to send him away, but could not succeed. Getting impatient, she said, "Even if you are a snake charmer, I'm afraid you would be helpless against this one!"

"We boast of seven or eight generations of snake charmers in our family. I don't see how one particular snake can pose a problem."

"That's what you say. But when you see it, you'll run away."

"I won't run, I won't run. If I run you can fine me one tael of silver."

"All right, come with me."

He followed her into the courtyard, where she turned a corner and disappeared, leaving him standing there in the open, with the bottle in his hand. After a little while, there rose a gust of bleak wind, and where it swept past there appeared a big python, with a body as big as a water bucket. It shot forward toward him. Indeed:

The tiger is all ready for attack,
Though you may mean him no harm.

Tai was horrified, and fell backward, breaking even his orpiment bottle. The python opened wide its blood-red gorge of a mouth, showing its snow-white teeth, and came forward as if to bite. He scrambled up and fled, and only wished he were born with two more legs. In one breath he ran the whole distance across the bridge and bumped into Officer Li and Hsü Hsüan. They asked, "How did it go?"

He said, "Gentlemen, you had better know this!" and related the episode from beginning to end. Then he took out the tael of silver and gave it back to Officer Li, saying, "If it hadn't been for these two legs of mine, I wouldn't even be alive! Here, save this for someone else!" Then he was gone as fast as his legs could carry him.

"Brother-in-law, what can I do now?" Hsü said.

"We see now that she is really an evil spirit," Li said. "Well, in Ch'ih-shan Port[15] there lives a man called Chang Ch'eng, who owes me a thousand strings of cash. You can go there, find a quiet spot, and rent a room to stay in. When that devil doesn't see you anymore, she'll be gone."

Since he could think of no other way, Hsü agreed to the arrangement. When they reached home, the house was as quiet as ever, and nothing at all was stirring. Officer Li wrote a letter, enclosed the credit note to his debtor in it, and told Hsü to be off to Ch'ih-shan Port.

At that the white lady called Hsü into their room and said, "You certainly have guts! So you summoned that what's-his-name snake charmer, eh? Now listen: if you're good to me, I'll have mercy. If you're bad, you'll bring disaster to the whole town, and everyone will be killed!"

These words set Hsü trembling all over, and he dared not utter a sound. In low spirits he took the credit note with him and went to Ch'ih-shan Port. There he sought Chang Ch'eng out, and dug his hand into his sleeve for the note, but it was not there. Exclaiming in distress, he turned around and went all the way back to look for it, but it was

[15] On the southern side of the West Lake.

nowhere to be found. In this miserable state of mind he arrived in front of the Cleansing Mercy Monastery.

Then all of a sudden he remembered the words of the monk Fa-hai, the abbot of the Golden Hill Monastery: "If that evil spirit should follow you to Hangchow, come to the Cleansing Mercy Monastery to see me." Well, there couldn't be a more opportune time for paying such a visit! Hastily he entered the monastery and asked the preceptor, "Pardon me, reverend, can you tell me if Reverend Fa-hai is in or not?"

"He's not in," the monk replied.

Hearing this, Hsü felt more miserable than ever. He turned around and went along to the foot of the Long Bridge. There he muttered to himself, "The devil is after me. Why should I care to live on?" He fixed his eyes on the clear water of the lake, and was going to jump in there and then, for, as the saying goes:

If the Yama King[16] *expects you at the third watch,*
You cannot be late—if only by an hour!

Just when he was about to jump into the water, Hsü heard somebody call from behind, "My good man, why this folly? Death is cheap—ten thousand dead lives are only counted as five thousand pairs.[17] If you're in trouble, why not come to me?"

Hsü turned around and looked—there stood Reverend Fa-hai! Cassock and begging bowl on his back, and his monk's staff in hand, he had indeed only just arrived—just in time to save Hsü Hsüan. If he had come only a little later, say the amount of time required to eat a bowl of rice, Hsü Hsüan would have been no more. At the sight of the monk, Hsü immediately bowed and cried, "Master, save my life!"

"Where is that evil creature now?" the monk asked.

Hsü narrated in detail all that had happened

---

[16] The supreme ruler of hell.
[17] The death of someone unrelated hardly matters at all. The numerical impact of ten thousand lives can easily be reduced by counting them in pairs.

since, and added, "Now she's after me again. I beg you, master, save my life and redeem me."

Fa-hai took out an alms bowl from inside his sleeve and handed it to Hsü Hsüan, saying, "Don't let the woman know when you get home, but steal upon her unawares and throw this over her head with all your strength. Then press it down firmly and don't be afraid. Now you can go home." So Hsü thanked the master for his kindness and made his way home.

At home, Hsü saw the white lady sitting there muttering curses: "Wonder who it was who made me and my husband become enemies? If I find out, I must settle it with him!" Cautiously he waited until he caught a moment when she was not looking. Creeping up from behind her, down he came with the bowl and settled it on her head. With the strength of his life he pressed on it. Then the woman's form disappeared as the bowl was pushed down. Not for a moment loosening his grip, he pressed down steadfastly. From inside the bowl he heard her say, "I was your wife these several years; won't you consider that at all? Come on, open up a little!"

Hsü Hsüan was at a loss what to do when it was reported that a monk had shown up, saying he had come to capture the evil spirit. Hsü Hsüan at once asked Officer Li to show the venerable priest in. When he had entered, Hsü said, "Master, save me!" The monk muttered some incomprehensible words and gently lifted the bowl. Sure enough, there was the white lady, shrunken to a minute size of seven or eight inches, looking like a puppet. Her eyes were closed and, curling herself into a heap, she cowered on the floor.

"What manner of evil creature or spirit are you," the monk shouted, "who dare haunt human beings? Explain yourself!"

The white lady then made her confession. "Grand master," she said, "I'm actually a python. One day, seeking refuge from the raging storm, I came to the West Lake with Ch'ing-ch'ing. I never expected to meet Hsü Hsüan, but meet we did, and I fell in love with him. Unable to control myself, I violated the rule of Heaven. But I was never responsible for any killing of life. Have mercy on me, grand master!"

The monk then asked what kind of creature Ch'ing-ch'ing was. The white lady answered, "Ch'ing-ch'ing is a thousand-year-old green fish from the pool under the third bridge in the West Lake. We met by chance, and I made her my companion, but she has not had a single day of joy. Have mercy on her, too, grand master."

"Considering that you've spent a thousand years in spiritual devotion," Fa-hai said, "I'll spare your life. Now show your true form."

But the white lady was not willing, whereupon the monk flew into a rage. He muttered some chant, then shouted aloud, "Come to my aid, Guardians of the Sky! Bring the spirit of the green fish before me, and let the white snake show herself in true form, to await my verdict!"

After a second, up swept a violent gust of wind before the court. As it swept past, a crashing sound was heard, and down from mid-air dropped a green fish over ten feet long. It made several leaps and darts on the ground, then shrank to just over a foot—for sure, a little green fish. As they looked at the white lady, they saw that she had also changed back into her true form—a three-foot-long white snake—and even then it still raised its head and fixed its gaze on Hsü Hsüan. The priest put these two creatures into his alms bowl, tore off a piece from his garment, and sealed the mouth of the bowl with it.

This he brought to the Thunder Peak Monastery. He laid it in the open ground before the monastery and ordered men to bring bricks and stones and erect a pagoda over it.

Later, Hsü Hsü raised a lot of alms money and made the pagoda into a beautiful piece of architecture seven stories high. Thus tamed and imprisoned under it, the white snake and green fish would no longer be able to enter the human world for centuries and centuries to come. Indeed, the following chant from the monk tells their future fate:

Not until the West Lake dries up,
Not until the ripples cease,
Not until the Thunder Peak Pagoda collapses,
Not until then, will the white snake be free.

After making the above proclamation, Reverend Fa-hai wrote a poem of eight lines, as a piece of advice for the world:

The world should heed my advice: love not the beauty of
*   women,*
For beauty casts spells on beauty's lovers.
Be pure in mind—that will ward off evil spirits;
And behave properly—then no harm can come your way.
Look at Hsü Hsüan—he loved a beautiful woman,
And what was his lot? All trials and tribulations!
If I had not come personally to his rescue,
That snake would have swallowed him, bones and all!

After Reverend Fa-hai had recited this poem, the onlookers went away. Hsü Hsüan alone made up his mind to renounce the world and follow the priest and honor him as his master. There at the Thunder Peak Pagoda he put on a monk's robe and was shaven, and after several years of devotion, one evening he passed into nirvana. His fellow monks put him in a coffin and cremated him, and kept his ashes in a tower, to be preserved for a thousand years. Before he passed away, he also left these lines of poetry for the edification of later generations:

My master delivered me from this vainglorious world;
Like an iron-tree in blossom, I am finally reborn.
As incarnation succeeds incarnation in recurrence,
Life is transformed, life upon life renewed.
In truth, is beauty constant? Or is it vanity?
Know then: that it is formless, yet in various forms appears.
For the two, beauty and vanity, are interchangeable,
But between vanity and beauty, the line should be clearly
*   drawn!*

RED JADE

From *Liao-chai chih-i*

TRANSLATED BY HSING-HUA TSENG

In the Kuang-p'ing Prefecture,[1] there lived an old man named Feng and his son Hsiang-ju. Both of them were *sheng-yüan*. Feng was almost sixty and he was an upright person, even though the family was poor. Within the span of a few years both his wife and daughter-in-law passed away. Thereafter, he and his son had to take care of all the housework.

One night, when Hsiang-ju was sitting outside in the moonlight, he suddenly saw a young woman from the house on to the east peering at him over the wall. She appeared to be quite beautiful. She smiled as he walked toward her. He beckoned her over, but she did not respond. When he became more ardent, she finally gave in and with the help of a ladder came across. Then they spent the night together. He asked her name, and she replied, "I'm your next-door neighbor, Red Jade." Hsiang-ju was happy and pledged eternal love to her. She accepted his love vows and thereafter came to his room every night.

Half a year passed in this way until one night when the elder Feng got up in the night and heard a woman's voice and laughter. Peeping through, he saw a young woman in his son's room

and became infuriated. The old man called his son out and chided him: "You stupid fool, what do you think you're doing? We're so poor, and yet you don't work hard; instead you're leading a life of dissipation. If other people found out, your reputation would be ruined. Even if no one should discover this, your life will be shortened as punishment." Hsiang-ju knelt before his father, wept, and confessed his guilt.

Feng then berated the woman: "A woman who behaves in this way not only strains her own reputation but she also hurts others. If this affair were discovered, our family wouldn't be the only one disgraced." Having spoken his mind, he returned to bed still fuming.

Red Jade wept and said, "Your father's reprimands have made me ashamed. Our relationship must end."

Hsiang-ju replied, "As long as my father is alive, I cannot make my own decisions. But if you really love me, I hope very much that you can put up with this humiliation."

She was determined to leave, and Hsiang-ju began to weep. Red Jade tried to comfort him. "Since our relationship has never been properly arranged—I merely climbed over the wall to meet you—how can we possibly expect to become husband and wife? I know, however, of a good pro-

---

[1] Part of Chihli Province in the Ch'ing period (modern Hopei Province).

379

spective bride for you in this neighborhood. You can ask a matchmaker to make arrangements for you." Hsiang-ju replied that he did not have the wherewithal for such an arrangement. Red Jade said, "Tomorrow evening, wait for me. I'll come and help you."

The next evening she brought with her forty taels of silver and offered them to Hsiang-ju. "Sixty *li* from here, in the village of Wu, there's a young woman named Wei who is eighteen years old. Because her parents are asking too much for betrothal money, she is still unmarried. If you give them enough money, then you'll surely have their permission to marry their daughter." And then she left.

Later Hsiang-ju sought an opportunity to speak with his father about going to see this young woman, but he did not tell his father about the silver. His father, knowing only too well what their financial situation was, tried to discourage him, but the son pleaded, "I just want to give it a try." The father finally agreed. Hsiang-ju borrowed a few servants and horses and went to the Wei's place.

Wei had once been a farmer. Hsiang-ju took him out for a conversation. Wei had been aware that Hsiang-ju came from a good family and, seeing that the young man was handsome and well mannered, was already disposed to accept this man as a suitor for his daughter. But he was still not sure that this suitor could afford the betrothal gift. Hsiang-ju, sensing the hesitation in Wei's words, took out all his silver and put it on the table. Wei was most pleased; he then asked a neighbor to act as matchmaker and write the marriage contract on red paper. Hsiang-ju went inside to pay his respects to his bride's mother. Their house was small and crowded. There he found the girl hiding behind her mother, and he stole a look at her. Though she wore only ordinary cotton clothes, the girl was attractive. Hsiang-ju was delighted. Wei invited him to stay overnight and said, "You don't have to come in person to fetch our daughter. When the small

trousseau and dowry are ready, we will send her to you."

Hsiang-ju set a date with him for the wedding and later returned home. Once there, he only told his father that Wei cared more about the suitor's family background than his wealth. His father was extremely pleased.

On the date set for the marriage, Wei sent his daughter to the groom's house as promised. This young woman proved to be hard working, thrifty, and virtuous, and their life together was harmonious. Two years later, they had a son whom they named Fu-erh. At the Ch'ing-ming Festival, Hsiang-ju and his wife took Fu-erh to their ancestors' tombs. On the way, they ran into a local dignitary named Sung who had once been a censor but later was dismissed for accepting bribes. Even now he was only a private citizen in the country; he had not mended his rapacious ways. On that day, he was returning from visiting his family tombs and was struck by the beauty of Hsiang-ju's wife. He asked the villagers nearby about her. Upon discovering who she was, he thought that since Hsiang-ju was poor, he could be tempted with money; so he sent a servant over to hint at his intentions. Hsiang-ju was deeply offended by this unexpected proposition, but realizing that Sung was a powerful man, he restrained himself and received the messenger with forced smiles. When he reported this matter to his father, the old man was enraged; he rushed over to Sung's servant and, gesturing wildly, shouted ten thousand curses at him. Frightened, the servant ran off.

Sung also took great offense. Immediately he dispatched several of his men to Feng's place to beat up the father and son. Hearing the commotion, Hsiang-ju's wife left the baby on the bed and screamed for help with her hair in wild disarray. The men abducted her and left for Sung's house. Feng and his son groaned and moaned on the ground, while the baby cried in the room. The neighbors took pity on them and came over to help the old man and son to bed. It was one full day before Hsiang-ju could stand up again, with aid of a cane; but his father was so angry that he could not eat. He began to cough blood and died shortly thereafter. Hsiang-ju broke into loud wails and, taking his son in his arms, brought his suit all the way to the governor, but to no avail.

Later he learned that his wife had died preserving her chastity; this distressed Hsiang-ju even more. However, he could find no one who could help him to redress his grievances. He often thought of ambushing Sung on the road and assassinating him, but Sung was always well protected. Furthermore, there was no one to whom he could entrust his son. Day and night he mourned and was so depressed by the injustice he had suffered that he could not even close his eyes.

Unexpectedly, one day a burly man with a curly beard and a wide jaw came to Hsiang-ju's house to offer condolences. Hsiang-ju had never met this man before, but he invited him to sit down. Before he could ask where he came from, the guest spoke: "You have the death of your father and the abduction of your wife to avenge. Have you forgotten about this?"

Hsiang-ju suspected the man to be a spy sent by the Sung family; so he replied evasively. The stranger was so infuriated by his manner that his eyes flashed with anger. He abruptly walked out, saying, "I thought you were a real man, but now I see that you're a worthless coward."

Hsiang-ju realized that his suspicions were unfounded, and so he fell on his knees, trying to prevent the stranger from leaving, and said, "I was afraid that you were sent by Sung to discover my intentions. Now I'll speak frankly. For a long time I've been planning my revenge, but I was concerned about my child, the only one who can carry on the family line. You are a generous friend; would you take care of my child?"

The stranger replied, "That's a woman's job. I can't do it. What you're asking me to do, please do it yourself; and what you intend to do yourself, I'm willing to do for you."

Hsiang-ju bowed his head to the ground in gratitude, but the stranger ignored him and walked out. Hsiang-ju rushed after him, asking for his name. The stranger replied, "If I fail, I don't want your blame; and if I succeed, I don't want your gratitude." Then he left. Hsiang-ju, fearing reprisals, took his child and ran away.

That night, after the Sung family had gone to bed, someone climbed over the wall to get inside the house and killed Sung, his two sons, a daughter-in-law, and a maid. The Sung family reported these murders to the authorities. The magistrate was shocked. Because the Sungs insisted that Hsiang-ju had done this deed, the magistrate sent men to arrest him, but he was not to be found. His absence seemed to confirm his guilt. The Sung servants and government officers searched everywhere for Hsiang-ju. That night, in the hills to the south, they heard a baby crying; they traced the sound and caught Hsiang-ju. They bound the man, but the baby cried even louder. Then they snatched the baby from Hsiang-ju and threw him on the ground. Hsiang-ju was so distraught that he wanted to die.

Brought before the magistrate, he was asked, "Why did you murder these people?"

"I've been unjustly accused," Hsiang-ju replied. "They were killed in the night, but I left in the daytime. Furthermore, I was carrying a baby. How could I climb walls and murder them?"

"Why did you try to run away if you didn't murder anyone?" the magistrate asked.

As Hsiang-ju could not reply, he was put in prison. Hsiang-ju wept, saying, "I don't care if I die, but the baby is innocent."

The magistrate said, "You killed other's sons; why should you complain if your son dies?"

Hsiang-ju's name was removed from the list of *sheng-yüan,* and he was then subjected to questioning and torture.[2] But he did not confess.

That night, after the magistrate had retired, he heard the thud of something striking his bed. He

[2] *Sheng-yüan* were exempted from punishment short of penal servitude; therefore Hsiang-ju's name had to be removed from the list first.

shouted in fear and the entire household was aroused. They all gathered in his room and by candlelight they found a dagger, glittering like frost, which had penetrated more than an inch into the wooden frame of the bed and was stuck so deep it could not be removed. The magistrate was frightened out of his wits. He sent armed guards to search everywhere but could find nothing. He felt discouraged from pursuing the murderer, and furthermore, since Sung himself was dead, there was no one to pressure him; therefore he sent a report to his superior, who pardoned Hsiang-ju. Thus Hsiang-ju was finally released.

When Hsiang-ju returned home, his house was bare and his rice jar was empty. He was all alone. Fortunately, his neighbors were all sympathetic toward his plight and brought him food. Though he took comfort in the thought that the revenge had been carried out, he could not hold back his tears when he recalled the series of disasters which had nearly destroyed his entire family. No sooner had his tears stopped than he realized how poverty-stricken he had been, and the fact that he was the last in his family line; then he again cried aloud uncontrollably in his solitude.

In this way half a year elapsed. Since the government had gradually relaxed its investigation of the case, Hsiang-ju asked the magistrate for permission to obtain his wife's remains. After he returned from the burial, his grief was so overwhelming that he tossed and turned on his bed, despairingly thinking that there was no reason to go on living, when suddenly he heard a knock on the door. He listened intently and heard someone outside who seemed to be talking to a child. He quickly jumped out of bed and peered out. The speaker seemed to be a woman. As soon as he opened the door, she said to him, "I'm glad that your revenge is accomplished and that you are safe." Her voice sounded familiar, but he could not recall immediately who she was. He lit a candle and discovered that this was Red Jade, holding a child by the hand. The little child was smiling and seemed happy by her side. Without taking time to ask her any questions, Hsiang-ju immediately embraced her and wept. Red Jade also looked disconsolate.

After a while, she pushed the child toward Hsiang-ju and said, "Don't you remember your father?" The child held tightly to Red Jade's skirt and looked at his father. Hsiang-ju looked closely at the child and found that it was indeed Fu-erh. He was greatly surprised and asked, "Where did you find him?"

Red Jade replied, "Let me tall you the truth. I once told you that I was your neighbor, but that wasn't true. I'm really a fox spirit. One evening while I was taking a stroll, I found this child crying in a valley. I took him to Shensi and raised him. As soon as I learned that your misfortunes had ended, I brought him here to be reunited with you." Hsiang-ju was very moved; he wiped his tears and thanked her profusely. Fu-erh clung to Red Jade as though she were his mother; he could not remember his father.

Before the day dawned, Red Jade sat up abruptly, and Hsiang-ju asked where she was going. She answered, "I'm leaving." Hsiang-ju quickly knelt in front of the bed, still undressed, and wept so hard that he could not raise his head. Red Jade smiled and said, "I'm only teasing you. Because we're just starting a home, we have to rise early and retire late."

From then on she worked as hard as a man, doing everything in the house. Hsiang-ju was worried about their poverty, but Red Jade said, "Please don't worry about the money; just concentrate on your studies. I don't think we'll starve to death." Red Jade took out some money, bought a loom, rented a few *mou* of land, and hired laborers to work in the field. Red Jade herself also went out to till the fields, and made repairs around the house. These were her daily tasks. When the neighbors saw that she was such a good housewife, they were all happy to help her.

Half a year later, the household was flourishing

and resembled a noble family's. Hsiang-ju said, "It's as though our home had been destroyed by fire and you've rebuilt it from the ashes; but one thing remains to be done. I don't know what to do about it."

Red Jade asked what it was, and he replied, "The provincial examination is drawing near but my name has not been restored to the list of *sheng-yüan*."

Red Jade smiled and said, "Some time ago I sent four taels of silver to the commissioner of education, and your name was restored to the list. If I had waited until you mentioned it, it would have been too late." Hsiang-ju thus became all the more impressed by her. He took the examination and passed with honors.

Thus at thirty-six years old, he already had a large piece of land and a big house. Red Jade looked so delicate that it seemed as if the wind could blow her away, yet she worked harder than a farmer's wife. Even in the bitterest winter, her hands were soft and as smooth as cream. She herself told everyone that she was thirty-eight years old, but she only looked a little over twenty.[3]

[3] Comments at the end of the story are not translated here because they cannot be considered part of the narrative.

THE GHOST WIFE

The ghost wife, unlike the superhuman maiden, is a human being in an after-death existence. To readers unfamiliar with Chinese literature, this may evoke a comparison with the Gothic novel in the tradition of Ann Radcliffe (1764–1823). But the Gothic element (if we may use the term) in traditional Chinese fiction is not usually associated with horror. Indeed, the only story in this section that can be regarded as mildly frightening is "A Mangy Taoist Exorcises Ghosts." In the other stories, whether the heroine is a ghost ("Scholar T'an" and "Nieh Hsiao-ch'ien") or a living person possessed by a ghost ("The Golden Phoenix Hairpin"), she is invariably charming and accommodating. In many respects, the ghost wife resembles the superhuman maiden: she is just as gifted in her limited supernatural powers, just as traditionally bound in her respect for social order, and just as tragically disqualified from leading a long and happy life with her earthling husband or lover. Only under most unusual circumstances is a marriage between a ghost wife and a human made possible, as in the case of "The Golden Phoenix Hairpin" which, strictly speaking, is a marriage by proxy (through Wu Hsing-niang's sister).

It is again to P'u Sung-ling's credit (see the sectional introduction to "The Superhuman Maiden") that he breaks away from all previous practices and allows Nieh Hsiao-ch'ien to lead a normal happy life with her husband. Nieh's marriage to Ning Ts'ai-ch'en is extraordinary not only because such a case is unprecedented but also because of her guilty past: she is responsible for a number of murders committed while she was under the control of the demon. In arranging this marriage between Ning and Nieh, P'u Sung-ling has added a human as well as humanitarian dimension to what can be loosely called the Gothic tradition of Chinese fiction.

SCHOLAR T'AN

From *Lieh-i chuan*

TRANSLATED BY DENNIS T. HU

There was once a scholar by the name of T'an. Being almost forty and yet still unmarried, he was often disgruntled, and was moved to study the *Shih-ching* (Book of Songs).[1]

Late one night, a matchless beauty fourteen or fifteen years old, clad in finery that was beyond compare, came to offer herself as his wife.

"I'm not quite the same as anybody else," she told him. "Don't shine any lights on me. Only after three years can you do so."

Thus they became husband and wife, and she gave birth to a son. When the child was two years old, T'an could no longer control his curiosity. One night, lurking and waiting after his wife had gone to bed, he stealthily shone a light on her. From the waist up she was just like any human being, but from that point downward there was no flesh, only dried-out bones.

The woman, awakening to what had happened, said to him, "You let me down. I was just about to come to life—why couldn't you wait another year? Why did you have to shine a light on me now?"

T'an apologized to her.

Now in an uncontrollable fit of weeping, she continued, "Although our relationship is forever ended from this time on, I am worried about our son. Since you're too poor to manage a livelihood, come along with me for just a while. I'll give you something."

So T'an followed her. They went into a gorgeous mansion, in which the rooms and everything in them were of extraordinary excellence. Handling him a pearl-sewn robe, she said, "You can live on this." Then she tore off the lapel of T'an's garment to keep, and left.

Some time thereafter T'an took the robe and sold it to the prince of Sui-yang, who bought it for ten million in cash. The prince, however, recognized the robe, saying, "This belonged to my daughter. He must be a graverobber." He therefore had T'an brought in to be questioned.

T'an withheld nothing and told him the truth. Nevertheless, the prince remained unconvinced and proceeded to inspect his daughter's tomb, which turned out to be the way it had been, untampered with. On exhuming the coffin, they discovered that beneath its lid there was indeed the lapel from a garment. The prince next asked to see T'an's son. Noting how much the child looked like his daughter, he had no more doubts. He called T'an in immediately, returning to him the robe that had originally been given him, and duly recognized him as son-in-law. Moreover, he presented a memorandum to the emperor recommending that T'an's son be given the honorific title of palace attendant.

[1] *Shih-ching* is the earliest collection of Chinese poetry. It includes more than three hundred examples of different types of regional folksongs and ceremonial songs of northern China compiled around 600 B.C.

387

A MANGY TAOIST EXORCISES GHOSTS

From *Ching-shih t'ung-yen* [1]

TRANSLATED BY MORGAN T. JONES

Apricot blossoms after the rain
Are fallen and withered, the color of rouge.
On the flowing river the fragrance drifts away.
Gradually the one I love moves farther off; these spring
*   thoughts are hard to put aside.*
I take leave of you regretfully.
My gaze lingers on the shadow of the wall.
Who will pick the green plums?
Where is the golden saddle now?
Green willows, as of old, line the path in the southern field.

The clouds and the rain have dispersed for only a moment.
With such feelings, why such light disregard, such casual
*   parting?*
The swallows talk in a thousand voices.
Could they be bringing some news of him?
Our solemn promises and deep vows—
If I could only see that man again!
If I saw him again, only then would it all seem real.
But now, helpless,
Piling up a thousand sorrows in my heart, I vex
*   myself to no end.*

This is a *tz'u* poem [to the tune of] "The Charms of Nien-nu." It was written by a scholar named Shen Wen-shu who had gone to the capital to participate in the imperial examinations. Actually, it was not his composition but a compilation of lines from various writers of the past. Why do I say this? Let me explain it to you from the beginning.

The first line is "Apricot blossoms after the rain." Ch'en Tzu-kao [2] wrote a "Song on the Cold Food Festival" to the tune of "Making a Call at the Golden Gate." It reads:

Green willow twigs—
Beneath the willow trees people are eating cold food.
Orioles chatter restlessly; the flowers are left alone.
The spring grass on the jade steps is damp.
In idleness, I lean listlessly on the warmer.
Who knows what matters lie within my heart?
Incense smoke winds about the window and turns against the
*   wall*
After the rainwater drips from the wilted apricot blossoms.

The second line: "Are fallen and withered, the color of rouge." Li Yi-an [3] wrote a "Song of the Late Spring" to the tune of "P'in-ling." It goes:

Fallen and withered blossoms,
Their color red as rouge.
Another year's spring has come again.
From the willow trees light catkins fly out;
On bamboo stalks new shoots are added.
Lonely,

---

[1] The *Ching-pen t'ung-su hsiao-shuo* version of this story is titled "A Den of Ghosts in the West Hill" ("Hsi-shan i-k'u kuei").

[2] Ch'en Hsien, styled Tzu-kao, was a Sung poet.

[3] Li Ch'ing-chao (1084–1147), styled Yi-an, was one of China's best female *tz'u* poets.

In solitude I face the tender greenness in this tiny garden.
Climbing up mountains and gazing down at streams does not
    suffice.
Would that I could hasten the end of your roaming!
In clear dreams of another year
I will travel a thousand li to the bend in the stream to the south
    of the city,
Treading gently on the ripples,
For my old friend, from time to time, to fix his eyes on me.

The third line: "On the flowing river the fragrance drifts away." A certain Li of Yen-an wrote a "Song of Spring Rain" to the tune of "Washing Brook Sand":

Red roses drooping, powerless beneath the burden of the
    raindrops.
Butterflies, full of passion, sporting from flower to flower.
On the flowing river the fragrance drifts away; the young
    swallows sing.
Spring did not mind that at Nan-p'u [4] my soul was rent,
Though the mirror was first to know of Tung-yang's sickness
    as his clothes grew smaller. [5]
Tonight the moon hovers by the small tower.

The fourth line: "Gradually the one I love moves farther off; these spring thoughts are hard to put aside." The Ch'an Buddhist monk Pao-yüeh [6] wrote a "Song of Spring" to the tune of "The Willow Tops Are Green." It goes:

Laden with passion and yearning, my heart.
Gradually the one I love moves farther off;
This sorrow of parting is hard to put aside.
After the rain, the chill;
Before the wind, the soft fragrance.
Spring is in the pear blossoms.
Leaning on a table the traveler gazes at the horizon;
Waking from my wine-rapt sleep I watch the setting sun, the
    scattering crows.

Outside the gate, a rope swing.
Atop the wall, a woman.
This deep courtyard, whose is it?

The fifth and sixth lines: "I take leave of you regretfully. My gaze lingers on the shadow of the wall." Ou-yang Yung-shu [7] wrote a "Ch'ing-ming Song" to the tune of "A Bushel of Pearls":

Painful, these spring thoughts.
Ch'ing-ming past, how fine are the orioles and blossoms!
I bid you, do not tell the melancholy one
The green grass has again been crushed by perfumed wheels.
Night came, the wind and moon lasted 'til dawn.
On the shadow of the wall my stare was fixed, but no one came.
I hate this parting from you; how great my sorrow!
As though spring were arrested, the cold will not relax; but
    blossoms and branches still grow old.

The seventh line: "Who will pick the green plums?" Ch'ao Wu-chiu [8] wrote a "Song of Spring" to the tune of "Regrets in the Pure Shang Tune":

Pitching wind,
Shrouding rain,
On pliant jade-green stalks blossoms droop heavily.
In a tight spring gown,
Delicate, languishing,
I remember in days past
I picked green plums with him.
It is all like a dream.
When will we meet again?
How pitiful, crooked and broken, my phoenix hairpin.
Barred by mountain passes.
As the evening clouds turn blue
The swallows come,
Yet I'm still without news of him.

The eighth and ninth lines: "Where is the golden saddle now? / Green willows, as of old, line the path in the southern field." Liu Ch'i-ch'ing [9]

---

[4] Nan-p'u was the site of a sorrowful parting in "Pieh-fu" by Chiang Yen (444–505).

[5] This is a reference to the Six Dynasties literary figure Shen Yüeh (441–513) whose style was Tung-yang and who was reputed to be in constant poor health. The couplet means that even the mirror, an inanimate object, is more intimately connected with human feeling than is spring.

[6] A monk of the Five Dynasties period.

[7] Ou-yang Hsiu (1007–1072), styled Yung-shu, was a celebrated statesman, historian, and literary figure of the Northern Sung period.

[8] Ch'ao Pu-chih (1053–1110), styled Wu-chiu, was a Northern Sung poet.

[9] Liu Yung (ca. 990– ca. 1050), styled Ch'i-ch'ing, was a well-known poet.

once wrote a "Song of Spring" to the tune of "Pure and Peaceful Joy" which reads:

Clear or cloudy, it's not yet certain
As the thin sun burns away the shadows of the clouds.
What fragrant path is the golden saddle now seeking out?
The green willows, as of old, line the quiet path through the
*   southern fields.*
Stifled and dissatisfied; so much spring emotion.
Pitifully, I am growing too old to achieve my dream.
I watch myself, tweezers in hand, pluck the remaining frost
*   from my temples.*
I will not come to life again with the fragrant grasses.

The tenth line: "The clouds and the rain have dispersed for only a moment." Yen Shu-yüan[10] wrote a "Song of Spring" to the tune of "The Beautiful Lady Yü":

Even flying blossoms follow their feelings to another place;
They are not bound to their branches.
The morning breeze scatters them thin—my melancholy is so
*   hard to bear—*
And follows the river flowing east past the Ch'in tower;
But to my grief, the clouds, the rain have dispersed for only a
*   moment, and*
Idly leaning against the balustrade, I watch.
Two drops of tears spring out and dampen the red blossoms.
Secretly I lament this jade-like face, its prospect that of the
*   flowers.*

The eleventh line: "With such feelings, why such light disregard, such casual parting?" Lady Wei[11] had a "Song of Spring" set to the tune of "Rolling Up the Pearl Curtain" which goes:

I remember when you came, it was not yet late in spring.
Holding hands, we plucked flowers,
Our sleeves soaked by the dew-tipped blossoms.
Secretly we prayed to the flowers for our love;
We raced to be the first to find a double-blossomed stalk.
With such feelings, why should we be estranged?
Such light disregard, such casual parting.
Where shall I tell my grief?

[10] Yen Chi-tao (ca. 1031– after 1106), styled Shu-yüan, was a famous poet.
[11] Lady Wei was the wife of the Sung minister Tseng Pu and a poet in her own right.

Tears moisten flower and branch on the crab-apple tree.
The Lord of the East instructed me in vain.

The twelfth line: "The swallows talk in a thousand voices." There is a "Song of Spring" by K'ang Po-k'o[12] set to the tune of the shortened form of "Magnolia Blossoms" which reads:

Willow blossoms all blown away,
Now clouds press down on the green shade; the wind is still.
The curtain hangs motionless.
Swallows chatter in a thousand voices as they fly past.
The small tower is deeply tranquil.
After I rose I did not straighten my disordered hair.
In my dream you could not return.
Spot upon spot—teardrops stain my gold-threaded dress.

The thirteenth line: "Could they be bringing some news of him?" Ch'in Shao-yu wrote a "Song of Spring" to the tune of "Roaming in the Palace at Night":

Why does the Lord of the East leave again?
The deserted courtyard is filled with fallen blossoms and flying
*   catkins;*
Though the swallows prattle on intently,
They have not brought any news of him to me.
With this broken heart
I am longing for someone gone far away.
After I woke from my lovesick dream
It rained the whole night through.
All the more is this unbearable
When I hear the call of the cuckoo.

The fourteenth and fifteenth lines: "Our solemn promises and deep vows—/If I could only see that man again!" There is a "Song of Spring" by Huang Lu-chih[13] set to the tune of "Pounding Whitened Silk" which goes:

Powder falls from the plum tree;
Gold flutters from the willow.

[12] K'ang Yü-chih (?– after 1159), styled Po-k'o, was a Sung poet.
[13] Huang T'ing-chien (1045–1105), styled Lu-chih, was a Northern Sung poet and was one of the "Four Scholars of the Su School."

A gentle rain and a light wind cut the dust on the path
    through the field.
Of our solemn promises and deep vows, to whom can I
    complain?
If I could only see that man again.

The sixteenth line: "If I saw him again, only then would it all seem real." Chou Mei-ch'eng[14] has written a "Song of Spring" to the tune of "Drop after Drop of Gold." It reads:

From plum blossoms leak out tidings of spring.
The willow branches are long,
The grass shoots green.
Without my knowing it, over the years, my temples have
    whitened.
Thinking of the passage of time is almost more than I can bear.
In the orchid hall, wine cup in hand, I recall my good guest
And knit my eyebrows.
I am growing melancholy over this spring scenery.
News of him cut off by a thousand li;
If I could see him again, only then would it all seem real.

The seventeenth and eighteenth lines are: "But now, helpless, / Piling up a thousand sorrows in my heart, I vex myself to no end." Ou-yang Yung-shu once wrote a *tz'u* to the tune of "The Butterfly Loves Flowers":

Inside the curtain the chill spring wind from the east still bites
    at the flesh.
Within the snow the plum blossoms make the first report of
    spring's early arrival.
But now, helpless, my heart is yearning;
Piling up a thousand sorrows, I vex myself to no end.
Warming up the golden stove, I heat my fragrant bath.
In boredom I cut fragile paper figures with my gold knife.
Beneath the embroidered quilt, finally at the fifth watch, I drift
    into a sweet sleep,
Behind the silk panel unaware that dawn is on the gauze
    window screen.

Now we have mentioned that Shen Wen-shu was a scholar. Today I will tell you about another scholar who came to the capital, Lin-an, to sit for the imperial examinations and thereby became involved in a bizarre story of numerous episodes. Now I ask you, what is the name of this scholar? To proceed with our story, he was a student from the Majestic Commandery (*Wei-wu chün*) in Foo-chow named Wu Hung who, in the tenth year of the Shao-hsing reign period [1140], left his home and came to Lin-an seeking to obtain merit and fame, hoping:

In one attempt to reach the top of the Dragon and Tiger
    Board,
And in ten years to arrive at the Phoenix Pool.[15]

How could he have known that luck was not with him and that in this attempt he would fail? Scholar Wu fell into a boundless depression. He lacked money for traveling expenses and, besides, was too ashamed to return to his home; so for the time being he could only open a small school at the foot of the present-day Prefecture Bridge in order to earn a livelihood. He planned to wait for three years until the examination took place again in the spring, until the examination halls opened and he could once again go forth to seek merit and fame. Month after month, he was able to eke out a living by tutoring some students in the neighborhood, and before he knew it, over a year had gone by since he first opened his school. It was his good fortune that the people in that area all took their children to his school, and so he prospered even to the point of having some savings.

One day, as he was teaching in the schoolroom, he heard the ringing of the bell attached to the blue cloth curtain hanging in the doorway. Then someone walked in. Schoolmaster Wu looked at the person and saw that it was none other than his former neighbor, Granny Wang, a go-between who relied on matchmaking for her livelihood.

Schoolmaster Wu, with hands folded before

---

[14] Chou Pang-yen (1056–1121), styled Mei-ch'eng, was a celebrated Sung poet.

[15] The Dragon and Tiger Board was the list of successful *chin-shih* candidates. The Phoenix Pool stood for the prime ministership.

him, bowed to her and said, "I haven't seen you for a long time. Where are you living now, granny?"

"I'd have thought that the schoolmaster would have forgotten all about me," the old woman said. "I'm now living by the city wall at the Ch'ien-t'ang Gate."

"How old are you?" asked the schoolmaster.

"I'm seventy-five. How about you?"

"I'm twenty-two."

"You're just twenty-two? But you look like you're over thirty! To think how you must wear yourself out every day! In my humble opinion, you really mustn't be without a wife to care for you."

"I've made a few inquiries," the schoolmaster said. "But none of the girls strikes my fancy."

"This is a case of 'Only the ones with mutual bonds will be thrown together.' Now let me tell you, I have a very good match for you. She has a dowry of one thousand strings of cash and she'll bring along a maidservant. She's beautiful, and what's more, she's good at all sorts of musical instruments. She can write and she can do some accounting, too. And that's not all. She comes from the family of an illustrious official and wants only to marry a scholar. Now are you interested?"

When the schoolmaster heard this, a smile spread over his face as though his joy were sent from Heaven. He answered, "If indeed there is such a person it would, of course, be wonderful. But where is this young lady now?"

"Let me tell you, schoolmaster," said the old woman. "Since she left the household of the deputy prefect, the third son of Grand Preceptor Ch'in,[16] two months ago, I don't know how many betrothal cards have been sent to her. Officials from the Three Departments,[17] from the Six Min-

istries,[18] and from the Bureau of Military Affairs have come to propose to her. Also officials from the various palace bureaus have come to pay court, not to mention the merchants and shopkeepers. But she's too choosy. Either they're socially too high for her or they're too lowly. The young lady says, 'I just want to marry a scholar.' Furthermore, she is bereft of both father and mother and has only a maid, Chin-erh. Because of her unusual musical talent, she was given the name Li Yüeh-niang [Li the Lady Musician] in her household. Just now she is staying with a former neighbor at the White Goose Pond—"

The two had not yet finished talking when they saw the wind blow open the cloth curtain which hung in the doorway and noticed a person walking past. Granny Wang said, "Schoolmaster Wu, did you see that person who just walked by? Now you may have the chance to take the young lady as your wife—" Hastening out the door into the street, Granny Wang overtook and returned with the person who had just walked past. It was none other than the one at whose house Li Yüeh-niang was staying. Her surname was Ch'en, and people called her Godmother Ch'en. After Schoolmaster Wu and Godmother Ch'en had exchanted bows, Granny Wang asked, "Godmother Ch'en, is the young lady at your house engaged yet or not?"

"Engaged?" Godmother Ch'en answered. "Not a chance! True, good suitors have never been lacking, but you just don't know how stubborn she is. Why, all she says, is 'I just want to marry a scholar.' I can only wish her luck."

"I have a good match in mind," said Granny Wang, "but I don't know whether godmother and the young lady would approve or not."

"Whom do you have in mind?" asked godmother.

Pointing her finger at Wu, Granny Wang said, "This gentleman. What do you say?"

[16] This expression suggests someone from a renowned and powerful family; the actual son of Ch'in Kuai is probably not intended by the storyteller here.

[17] Departments of the Chancellery, the Secretariat, and State Affairs.

[18] Ministries of Personnel, Rites, Revenue, War, Punishments, and Public Works.

"You must be joking!" godmother said. "Why, if she can marry this gentleman, she's really in luck."

Wu could not bring himself to finish teaching for the remainder of that day, so he dismissed his pupils, who bowed and left for their homes. The schoolmaster then locked the door and went out with the two old women. He was obliged to treat them to some wine, and after several cups, Granny Wang rose to her feet and said, "Since the schoolmaster does desire this union, I think it is necessary to ask godmother to find a betrothal card."

"I happen to have one on hand," said godmother, slipping her hand into her stomacher and producing a card.

"Godmother," said Granny Wang, " 'One doesn't give empty promises before an immortal, just as one doesn't swim on dry land.' Pick a date and bring the young lady and her maid, Chin-erh, to the tavern by the Mei Family Bridge so that the schoolmaster and I can take a look at her and see if she's a suitable match."

Godmother assented. Then she and Granny Wang thanked Schoolmaster Wu and departed, whereupon he paid the bill for the wine and returned home.

Let us skip the other trifling matters.

On the appointed day, Wu changed into some new clothes, released his students from class, and set out for the tavern by the Mei Family Bridge. From a distance Granny Wang greeted him; they entered the tavern together and went upstairs, where Godmother Ch'en received them. Schoolmaster Wu immediately inquired, "Where is the young lady?"

"The child and Chin-erh are sitting in the eastern compartment," godmother informed him.

The schoolmaster broke a small peephole in the paper panel of the room by licking it with the tip of his tongue. Taking a look inside, he almost exclaimed, "The two of them simply aren't human!" In what way were they not human? The young lady was so beautiful that he thought of her as the Avalokiteshvara of the Southern Seas and he saw the maid Chin-erh as the incense-bearing Jade Maiden in the palace of the Jade Emperor. Why did he say they were not human? When he looked at Li Yüeh-niang, he saw:

Eyes like pools of clear water,
Cheeks like red blossoms;
Hair softly combed into cicada's wings,
Moth eyebrows penciled lightly like spring mountains;
Vermilion lips forming a fresh cherry,
White teeth like two rows of jade pieces.
Her bearing naturally graceful,
She was unsurpassed among her peers.
Like the Weaving Maid descended from the Jade Terrace,
Like Ch'ang-e departed from the moon palace.

When he looked at the maid Chin-erh, he saw:

Eyes clear and lovely,
Temples high and full, arresting one's eye.
Eyebrows like new moons,
Cheeks like spring peaches.
Her bearing like a delicate flower not yet fully blossomed,
Her flesh and skin soft and fine as though exuding fragrance.
Embroidered slippers adorned her tiny golden lotuses
And a short purple hairpin of gold was stuck in her hair.
It was like plucking the green plum and peeking at the
*   handsome youth,*
Like riding by the red apricots and poking one's head over the
*   wall.*

From that day, when he stuck the hairpin in her hair,[19] it naturally followed that the dowry was sent, a goose was presented, and the documents were exchanged. Shortly thereafter she and Schoolmaster Wu were married. Their wedded life was blissful. It was just like:

A pair of phoenixes over the bland clouds at the edge of
*   heaven,*
Mandarin ducks in deep water crossing their necks.
They wrote an agreement in this life never to part,
And a pair of sashes bound them together for future lives.

[19] "Sticking in the hairpin" indicates engagement. A goose was traditionally presented to the groom.

But let us now tell of one day in the middle of the month when all the students were to come early to worship Confucius. Schoolmaster Wu said to his spouse, "Wife, I'll get up first and go to officiate." But when he passed before the stove, he saw the maid Chin-erh there, with her hair spread across her back, her eyes rolling; and the nape of her neck was smeared with blood. When the schoolmaster saw this, he screamed and fell to the ground in a dead faint. His wife immediately rushed to his side to revive him and Chin-erh came to help him to his feet.

"What did you see?" his wife asked him.

Now Schoolmaster Wu was the head of the household, and on no account would it do for him to say, "I saw Chin-erh in such and such a condition." All he could say for the moment was that he must have been seeing things. He made an excuse, saying "I got up this morning and didn't put on enough clothing. As a draft of cold air struck me, I became dizzy and fell to the ground."

Chin-erh hurriedly prepared a decoction to calm his nerves, and before long all was well. But from this time on, Schoolmaster Wu came to harbor some vague suspicions.

But let us skip over these trivialities. It was during the time of the Ch'ing-ming holiday recess, and there was no class. After giving his wife some instructions, Wu changed his clothes and went out to take a stroll. He set out, passing over the Ten Thousand Pines Ridge, and went to what is the present-day Cleansing Mercy Monastery, where he looked around for a little while.

When he was about to leave, Schoolmaster Wu saw a man bowing and saluting him, and he returned the greeting. This man was the waiter from the tavern opposite the Cleansing Mercy Monastery. He told the schoolmaster, "A gentleman in the tavern has asked me to invite you in, sir."

Wu entered the tavern with the waiter and saw that this man was none other than Wang Ch'i, the secretary of the Lin-an Prefecture. He was known in the area as Third Master Wang Ch'i. After the two of them had exchanged greetings, Third Master Wang Ch'i said, "I saw you just as I arrived, but I could hardly presume to shout at you, so I sent the waiter out to invite you over."

"Where are you going now?" Wu asked.

Wang at first said nothing, but thought to himself, "He has just married. Let me play a prank on him!" So he said, "I'd like to invite you to go to my family cemetery with me, because this morning the caretaker came by and told me, 'The peach trees are in bloom and the wine that I make is ready to be sampled.' How about going there and having a few cups?"

"That would be just fine," said the schoolmaster. So the two of them left the tavern and took the road leading to the Su Causeway. They saw people roaming about on their holiday outings, taking in the sights of spring. Truly:

People are clustered together like the spokes on a wheel;
Carts and horses are everywhere, side by side.
The gentle wind fans the landscape.
The sun becomes ever more brilliant.
Orioles are warbling in the shade of green willows,
Butterflies playing on the stalks of exotic flowers.
Flutes and strings sound out—
In whose hall is this banquet?
A clamor of talk and laughter
Here and there in spring towers and summer pavilions.
Perfumed carriages race,
Horses with jade bridles competing.
The sound of fair-faced young gentlemen striking their stirrups
*   peals out,*
And young maidens dressed in red lift up embroidered screens
*   to look on.*

At the end of the South New Road they found a boat for hire. They took it and headed for the Mao Family Pier where they went ashore and walked about, passing by the Jade Springs and the Dragon Well.

Wang Ch'i's family cemetery was directly at the foot of Camel Ridge of the West Hill. Truly a lofty peak! [Having made the climb up and crossed over the peak], they began their descent from the ridge, and after they had walked on for one *li* they arrived at the cemetery. Chang An, the caretaker, came out to meet them. Wang Ch'i immediately directed Chang An to prepare some food and wine; then he and the schoolmaster went into a small garden nearby. There they sat down and proceeded to get thoroughly drunk on the homemade wine. After a time, when they noticed the color of the sky, they realized that they had been there for quite a while:

The sun had fallen in the west;
The moon had emerged in the east.
Beautiful women, lamps in hand, had returned to their
    chambers.
Fishermen on the banks of the river had put aside their hooks;
Fish peddlers had sold the catch and returned home along
    bamboo-lined paths.
Herd boys, riding on calves, had entered the flowery villages.

The hour was indeed late and Schoolmaster Wu wanted to start on the journey homeward, but Wang Ch'i insisted, "Let's drink another cup and then I'll go with you. We can cross over the Camel Ridge and spend the night with whores at a brothel on the Nine Mile Pine Road."

Schoolmaster Wu said nothing but thought to himself, "I've just gotten married; if I'm forced to stay out all night, she'll certainly be home waiting for me to return. What should I do? But then, at this late hour even if I were to rush to the Ch'ien-t'ang Gate, by the time I arrived, the gate would have been locked for the night." He had no alternative but to allow Wang Ch'i to lead him off by the hand, and thus they struck out over the Camel Ridge.

Now wouldn't you say that there is much coincidence between human affairs and in natural occurrences? When they reached the top of the ridge, clouds massed from the northeast, fog emerged from the southwest, and a heavy rain began to fall. Indeed, it was as though the Milky Way had turned over and had begun to leak, and

as though the vast sea had overturned like a water basin. Truly a great downpour! There was no place where they could seek shelter in this deluge. So, braving the pouring rain, they walked on for a space until they caught sight of a small bamboo tower. Wang Ch'i said, "Let's go in there for a while." But they were not entering the tower to seek shelter from the rain, they were:

Like pigs and sheep entering a butcher's shop,
Step by step seeking the road to extermination.

When the two of them went running in to get out of the rain, they saw that it was in reality an unkept cemetery. There were no buildings inside, only the tower at the entrance. So the two of them just sat on the stone steps waiting for the rain to stop. In the midst of this great downpour, they saw a man dressed as a jailer jump over the bamboo fence into the cemetery and walk over to a grave mound.

"Chu Hsiao-ssu, you're being called. Today's your day to come out and show yourself," he shouted.

From within the grave mound there was a slow response: "I'm coming, sir."

Before long the earth above the grave mound opened and out jumped a person whom the jailer took in tow and dragged off. When Schoolmaster Wu and Wang Ch'i saw this, they were petrified with fear; their legs straightened and their backs stiffened. Their feet were motionless and their entire bodies were shaking convulsively.

Noticing that the rain had stopped, the two of them got up and left. The ground was slippery and their hearts were filled with fear. As they fled, their hearts leaped like little fawns, and their feet were as unsteady as those of vanquished fighting cocks. As though there were a thousand troops and ten thousand horses bearing down on them from behind, they were too terrified to turn their heads and look back.

When they reached the hilltop, they strained their ears to listen. They heard echoing out of the deserted valley the sound of someone in the forest being struck with a beating rod. After a short time they saw the jailer coming toward them in pursuit of the man who had leaped out of the grave mound. Seeing this, the two of them once again began to run. To the side of the ridge there was an old, tumbledown temple of the mountain god. They entered the temple, hurriedly slammed the door, and blocked it with the weight of their bodies. Indeed, so frightened were they that they dared neither gasp nor fart.

Listening intently to the goings on outside, they heard the voice of a man screaming, "You're beating me to death!"

Another voice responded, "You felonious demon! Making promises and then not giving me my due! Why shouldn't I beat you?"

Wang Ch'i said in a hushed tone to Schoolmaster Wu, "Those you hear outside there passing by are the jailer and the man who leaped out of the grave."

As the two sat inside, huddled together and shaking, Wu complained to Wang, "You've brought me all the way out here only to scare me to death. My wife is probably waiting at home right now not knowing what to do—" But before he had finished speaking they heard someone outside knocking on the temple door and demanding, "Open the door!"

"Who's there?" the two asked.

As they listened, they realized it was a woman's voice. "Well done indeed, Third Master Wang Ch'i!" she cried. "You dragged my husband out here, keeping him out all night, and made me come all the way out here searching for him. Chin-erh! Let's force this door open and get your master."

When Schoolmaster Wu heard this voice outside, he realized that it could be no one else. He thought, "It's my wife and Chin-erh! How did they know that Wang Ch'i and I were here? Could it be that they, too, are ghosts?"

He and Wang Ch'i didn't dare make a sound.

They heard the voice outside say, "If you don't open the door, I'll just have to squeeze myself through a crack in it to get in." When Wu and Wang Ch'i heard this, all the wine that they had drunk that day turned into cold sweat.

Shortly they heard another voice outside. "Mistress, I don't mean to be presumptuous, but perhaps it would be better if you went home now. I'm sure the master will come back tomorrow by himself."

"Chin-erh," said Wu's wife, "you're right. Let's go back home. We'll settle this later." Then she shouted, "Third Master Wang Ch'i, I'm going home now, but tomorrow morning you had better see to it that you send my husband home!"

How could the two of them dare answer her?

When Wu's wife and Chin-erh had finished speaking and left, Wang Ch'i said, "Schoolmaster Wu, your wife and her maid Chin-erh are both ghosts, and this is no place for people to be. Let's get out of here."

When they opened the temple door, they realized that it was nearly the fifth watch, and there was still no one around. As the two of them began their descent from the ridge, they were still a little over a *li* from the foot of the hill when they saw two people come out into the open from a grove. The first one was Godmother Ch'en; the second, Granny Wang. They hailed him; "Schoolmaster Wu, we've been waiting a long time for you. Where have you and Third Master Wang Ch'i been?"

Wu and Wang looked at them and exclaimed, "These two old hags are also ghosts. Let's run!" Indeed, fleeing like roebucks, leaping like deer, jumping like apes, flying like falcons, they descended from the ridge. Behind them the two old women were still slowly pursuing.

"After all this running around all night long without a thing to eat, we're now half starved. I wish we could meet a real human being after a whole night of encountering so many ominous things." No sooner had they said this than they spotted a house at the bottom of the ridge. Seeing a pine branch hanging in front of the gate,[20] Wang Ch'i remarked, "I think we can probably buy some locally made wine here. Let's go in and have a cup or two to fortify ourselves and at the same time stay away from those two old hags."

As they dashed into the tavern, they saw the wine seller:

Wrapped about his head, a green turban the color of cow's
    gall;
Wrapped about his body, a red waistband the color of pig's
    liver;
A pair of old trousers,
And on his feet straw sandals.

"How much for the wine?" Wang Ch'i asked.

The man answered merely, "It's not heated yet."

"Then bring us a bowl of cold wine!" said Schoolmaster Wu. But the man stood there without saying a word, without breathing.

"There's something odd about this wine seller, too," Wang said. "He must also be a ghost! Run—" But before he could finish, a blast of wind rose within the tavern:

Not the scream of a tiger,
Nor the roar of a dragon.
In broad daylight, [too weak] to strip the willow or make
    flowers blossom,
In its darkness mountain goblins and water demons are
    concealed.
Blowing open the earth before the gate of hell,
It raises the dust before the Feng-tu Mountain.[21]

After the wind had subsided, neither the wine seller nor the tavern was to be seen, and the two of them found themselves standing atop a grave mound. This frightened them as greatly as if their souls had left their bodies. Hurriedly they followed the road, took a boat in front of a brewery on the Nine Mile Pine Road, and went directly to the Ch'ien-t'ang Gate, where they went shore. Wang Ch'i returned to his own place, but Schoolmaster Wu first headed straight for Granny Wang's house by the Ch'ien-t'ang Gate. Upon arriving he saw that the door was locked. He inquired at the neighbors' and they told him, "Granny Wang died a little over five months ago." This so shocked him that he simply stood there stupefied, eyes unblinking and mouth agape, not knowing what to do.

He left the Ch'ien-t'ang Gate and passed by what is today the examination hall in the Chingling Temple complex, crossed the Mei Family Bridge, and arrived by the edge of the White Crane Pond, where he sought out Godmother Ch'en's house. When he came to her door, he found it barred by a pair of bamboo poles set crosswise. In front of the door was a government lantern, and above the door were written the words: "The heart of man is like iron; the law of the land is like a forge."[22] He inquired about Godmother Ch'en and learned that she, too, had died more than a year ago.

Leaving the White Crane Pond, he returned home by the Prefecture Bridge to find the door of his own house secured with a lock. He asked at a neighbor's house, "Where did my wife and the maidservant go?"

"Yesterday morning as soon as you left," the neighbors told him, "your wife told us, 'Chin-erh and I are going to visit my godmother.' They have not yet returned."

Schoolmaster Wu just stood there staring blankly, unable to utter a word. Suddenly there appeared on the scene a mangy Taoist priest. After scrutinizing Schoolmaster Wu, he said, "I've observed that you, sir, have come under the influence of malevolent spirits. Let me exorcise them for you so as to prevent misfortunes from befalling you."

[20] The conventional sign of a tavern.
[21] Feng-tu is the capital of hell and is located at the mountain of that name in Szechwan.

[22] The bamboo cross sealing Godmother Ch'en's door and the government lantern placed in front of it indicate that the state was handling her estate.

Schoolmaster Wu immediately invited the Taoist priest inside and prepared for him some incense, candles, and some water for spells. The priest immediately began his conjury. He mumbled an incantation and then shouted out, "Quick!" whereupon there appeared a celestial general:

Yellow silk kerchief is tied about his forehead,
Brocade belt wrapped around his waist;
A long gown of black silk, round floral patterns embroidered
*   on the sleeves.*
Gold armor bound tightly around his body,
A sword slung crossways flashing clear and bright like an
*   autumn stream;*
Boots shaped like lions' heads.
Above, he could penetrate into the blue heavens,
Below, into the nine regions of death.
Should a dragon wreak harm,
He could plunge to the ocean floor to capture it.
Should an evil spirit cause a disturbance,
He could enter its mountain cave to apprehend it.
By the altar of the Liu-ting God,
He was given the name "Officer of Spells";
Before the steps of the Lord on High,
He is called "Attendant of Heaven."

Bowing, the celestial general asked, "Where would the immortal dispatch me on my mission?"

"Malevolent spirits are active in Wu Hung's house and are also at large on the Camel Ridge. Apprehend them for me and bring them here."

As soon as the celestial general received these orders a wind arose in Wu's house:

Formless, shadowless, penetrating into the bosom of man,
With the power to make peach trees blossom in the second
*   month.*
On the ground it pinches away the yellow leaves;
Entering the mountains, it pushes away the white clouds.

When the wind had subsided, the celestial general seized and brought back several of the ghosts who had been causing the disturbances. [It turned out that] Schoolmaster Wu's wife, Li Yüeh-niang, had been the concubine of the deputy prefect, the third son of Grand Precepter Ch'in, and had died in childbirth. The maid Chin-erh had been beaten severely by the wife of the deputy prefect, who was jealous of her beauty. Chin-erh consequently had cut her own throat. Granny Wang had died of dropsy. Godmother Ch'en, the guardian, while washing clothes at the edge of the White Crane Pond had fallen into the water and drowned. Chu Hsiao-ssu, who leaped out of the grave mound on the Camel Ridge when summoned by the jailer, while still alive had been the caretaker of a cemetery; he had died of consumption. The one who ran the tavern had died of typhoid. Having thus established the identities of the ghosts and causes of their deaths, the priest removed a gourd from his waist. To a human, this was a mere gourd, but to a ghost it was hell. When the priest began his conjury, the ghosts all grabbed their heads and began to scatter and flee like mice, but he caught them and forced them all into the gourd. He then directed Schoolmaster Wu, "Take this and bury it at the foot of Camel Ridge." The mangy Taoist then cast his staff into the air, whereby it was transformed into a white crane, which he mounted and thereupon departed.

Schoolmaster Wu flung himself to his knees and began kowtowing. "My eyes are but of flesh and I did not recognize you as an immortal. I'm willing to renounce the world and leave my household to follow you. I only hope that you'll take me as your disciple so that I may attain deliverance."

The Taoist priest then reappeared and said, "I am Immortal Kan of the Upper World. In days gone by you were my herb-gathering disciple; but your mortal mind was not pure, and midway on the path you showed regrets and thought to backslide. Because of this you fell into the Lower World. As punishment, in this present life of yours, you were reborn as an impoverished Confucian scholar and taste to the full the sufferings owing to ghostly doings and the vicissitudes of indulgence in carnality. Now, having seen through it, you may leave the world of dust [this world] and discipline yourself in the Way. If you'll only wait until a complete cycle of twelve years has passed, I'll come to deliver you." After he finished speaking he vanished, turning himself into a gentle, soothing breeze.

From then on, Schoolmaster Wu renounced the world to follow the Way, and he drifted all around the country. After twelve years he encountered Immortal Kan at the Chung-nan Mountain and followed him away.

A poem states:

Single-mindedly disciplining yourself in the Way, reject the world of dust.
How then could evil spirits venture to disturb you?
Good and evil are merely distinctions produced by the mind.
Recalling the ghosts of the West Hill, quickly make a new resolve and change your ways.

THE GOLDEN PHOENIX HAIRPIN

From *Chien-teng hsin-hua*

TRANSLATED BY PAUL W. KROLL

During the Ta-te reign period [1297–1308],[1] there lived in Yangchow a rich man by the name of Wu who was a district defense commandant. He lived next to the Loft of Vernal Breezes, and was a neighbor of Master Ts'ui, an official with whom he had a deep bond of friendship. Ts'ui had a son named Hsing-ko and Wu had a daughter called Hsing-niang, both of whom were still in their infancy. Ts'ui sought the girl as a future wife for his son, and when Wu gave his consent Ts'ui presented him with a golden phoenix hairpin as a pledge. Shortly thereafter Ts'ui was transferred to a post in a distant region, and for fifteen years not a word was exchanged between the two families.

In this time the girl reached her nineteenth year in the seclusion of her chambers. Her mother said to Wu, "The young master of the Ts'ui family has been gone now for fifteen years with no news at all, and Hsing-niang has fully matured. I don't believe that we should hold to the previous accord and waste her youth."

Answered Wu, "But I've given my word to my friend; the convenant has already been made. How can I go back on it?"

The girl likewise yearned for the arrival of her betrothed, became sick, and was confined to bed. Within half a year she died. Her parents wept in grief.

As Hsing-niang was being prepared for burial, her mother, holding the golden phoenix hairpin, stroked the corpse and said tearfully, "This is a token from your husband's family. Now that you are gone, what use is there in my keeping it?" Thereupon she fastened it in her daughter's hair to be interred with her.

Two months after the burial, young Ts'ui arrived. Wu received him and inquired of his affairs, to which Ts'ui replied, "My father died in the post of the prefectural judge of the Hsüan-te Prefecture.[2] My mother, too, passed away several years ago. Having now completed the mourning period, I've hastened here in spite of the thousand-*li* distance."

With tears falling, Wu told him, "It was Hsing-niang's bad fortune to fall ill because she yearned for you so. Two months ago, she died without fulfilling her wishes. She has already been buried."

Wu thereupon conducted him into the girl's chambers and burned sacrificial money before her

---

[1] Ta-te is the title of the second reign period of Emperor Ch'eng-tsung of the Yüan Dynasty (r. 1295–1307).

[2] In modern Hopei Province.

memorial tablet to inform her of Ts'ui's arrival. Every member of the household wept bitterly.

Then Wu said to Ts'ui, "Your parents are dead, and your home is so far away. Now that you are here, please make yourself at home at my place. The son of an old friend is just like my own son. You need not be a stranger to me because of Hsing-niang's death." He then ordered Ts'ui's baggage moved in, and the young man settled down in a small studio beside the gates.

Half a month passed, and the Ch'ing-ming Festival came. Because of the recent death of Wu's daughter, the entire family paid a visit to the grave. Hsing-niang had a younger sister by the name of Ch'ing-niang, who was in her seventeenth year, and also went along on that day. Only Ts'ui remained at the house to look after things.

When the family returned in the evening, the sky had already darkened. Ts'ui greeted them, standing to the left of the gates. When the first of the two sedan chairs had entered and the second was before him, something seemed to fall out of it with a tinkling sound. He waited until the sedan chair had passed by and then hurried over to pick it up. It was a golden phoenix hairpin. He wanted to return it to the inner quarters immediately, but the central gate had already been secured and he could not gain entrance. So he went back to his little studio and sat alone before a lighted candle, reflecting on his unconsummated betrothal and his loneliness. Considering that there was no future in living with someone else's family, he sighed deeply.

Just as he was about to retire for the night he suddenly heard a light knocking at the door. He called out to see who it was, but there was no reply. After a short pause, the knocking resumed. This sequence was repeated three times before Ts'ui finally unlatched the door and peered out. Standing out there was a lovely young girl who, upon seeing the door open, hitched up her long dress and stepped into the room. Ts'ui was shocked, but the girl lowered her head and with

bated breath spoke to him in a low voice: "You don't recognize me? I'm Hsing-niang's younger sister, Ch'ing-niang. A while ago I threw a hairpin from the sedan chair. Did you retrieve it?" She then pulled him toward the bed, but Ts'ui, remembering her father's hospitality, refused her, saying, "I don't dare." And he firmly resisted her repeated advances.

Suddenly the girl's face flushed and she raged at him: "My father has treated you with the propriety he would show his own brother's son, and has taken you into his own household. But now in the deep of the night you entice me here! What are you up to? If I report this to my father he will surely take you to the magistrate, and will not let you off!" Ts'ui, taken aback by this threat, could only comply with her wishes. When dawn came she left.

From this time on, each evening she would come in secret to the little studio next to the gates and each morning would depart in secret. A month and a half passed in this way. One night Ch'ing-niang said to Ts'ui, "I live in the ladies' quarters while you live in an outside studio. Fortunately, no one has yet learned of this affair, but I only fear that a 'good cause will meet many obstacles and the wedding day can easily be delayed.' For if one day our secret is discovered, I'll be condemned by my family, shut up, and caged like a parrot. Then, 'once the ducks are struck, the love-birds will be frightened as well.'[3] Even though I'm quite willing to face this, I'm afraid that your good name would be compromised. It would be better to flee with our valuables before the matter is discovered. Rendering ourselves unknown in far-off villages and hiding our identities in other districts, we can grow old together without care and never be separated."

Ts'ui was rather happy with her suggestion and said, "What you have said is indeed sensible. Let

[3] This adage means that when one person is punished the fears of someone else will also be called forth. Ch'ing-niang implies that her punishment would involve Ts'ui as well.

me think about it." Whereupon he mused, "I'm an orphan, miserably alone, and have long lacked relatives and close friends. Even though I wish to flee with her, where could we go? But once I heard my father remark that our old servant Chin Jung was a faithful and honorable man. He dwells in Lü-ch'eng in the Chinkiang Prefecture,[4] and tills the earth for a living. We shall throw ourselves on his kindness; surely he will not refuse us!"

The next night, the two of them left at the fifth watch, carrying with them only the simplest luggage. They hired a boat and passed by Kuachou, whence they continued to Tan-yang.[5] There they inquired of the villagers and succeeded in finding Chin Jung, whose family had prospered and become wealthy, while he himself had been made headman of the village. Ts'ui was delighted and went directly to Chin's place, but he was not recognized at first. However, when he mentioned his father's name, official rank, and native place, and his own childhood name, Chin finally remembered him. Chin set up a memorial tablet for his deceased master and wept. Then he seated Ts'ui and respectfully made obeisance, saying, "Here's my former young master." Ts'ui fully informed him of his reason for coming, whereupon Chin had the main quarters cleared and lodged the two there. He attended them as though he were attending his former master, providing them with all the clothing and food they required.

After they had resided with Chin for nearly a year, the girl said to Ts'ui, "At first I dreaded the censure of my parents, so I, like Lady Cho,[6] fled with you. I did it because there was no other way out. Now the old grain has been consumed and the new grain is sprouting—time passes like a flowing stream, and a year's time has already gone by. All parents love their offspring, and if we return now of our own accord they will be so happy to see us once again that they certainly will not reproach us. No kindness is greater than that of our parents wh⁻ give us life, so how can they bear to break off from their children? Why not go and see them?" Ts'ui assented, and together they crossed back over the Yangtze River, returning to the girl's native town.

As they drew near her home she said to Ts'ui, "Having run off for a year, I fear I may meet my father's wrath if I go with you. It would be better if you went on ahead and took a look first. I'll moor the boat here to wait for you." As he was about to leave, she called him back and gave him the golden phoenix hairpin, saying, "If he doubts you, show him this."

When Wu heard that Ts'ui was at his gate, he was overjoyed and went out to welcome him, making unexpected apologies: "My lack of hospitality must have caused your uneasiness and subsequent departure for elsewhere. It's all my fault! I hope you will not take offense." Ts'ui prostrated himself and, not daring to look up, repeatedly asked for Wu's forgiveness.

"What crime have you committed to call forth such alarming words? Please explain yourself and allay my doubts."

"Behind drawn curtains your daughter and I carried on a secret affair," Ts'ui said, bowing. "Our affection for each other grew, and turning our backs on the name of righteousness, we committed the offense of having a clandestine relationship. Without informing you I took her as my wife and we stole away to hide in the far wilderness. The months stretched on, and for a long time we made no effort to keep in touch with you. And though our affection is more devoted even than that of husband and wife, how can one forget the kindnesses of father and mother? Now I've brought your daughter back with me. Humbly I implore you to behold the depth of our feelings and forgive our serious offense, so we may grow old together and be forever united. The blessing of your fond love and our happy family

---

[4] In the present Kiangsu Province.
[5] Both of these two places are in Kiangsu. The town of Lü-ch'eng is just a short distance to the east of Tan-yang County.
[6] Cho Wen-chün.

life are what we seek. I hope you will take pity on us."

On hearing this, Wu replied in amazement, "But my daughter has been bedridden for almost a year, unable to take thin gruel, and even needed help to turn over. How could such a thing be?"

Ts'ui concluded that Wu was afraid of bringing disgrace to his family and was covering up the truth in order to put him off; so he answered, "Ch'ing-niang is at this moment in my boat. You can send someone to bring her here."

Though Wu did not believe him, he commanded a servant to hasten there. When the servant arrived he saw no one. Wu thereupon became angry at Ts'ui and berated him for this sham. But Ts'ui brought forth from his sleeve the golden phoenix hairpin and showed it to Wu. When Wu beheld it he was utterly confounded: "This token was interred with my deceased daughter, Hsing-niang. How could it possibly turn up here?"

As they were feeling perplexed, Ch'ing-niang unexpectedly rose from her bed and went directly to the hall. She made obeisance to her father and said, "I'm Hsing-niang, whose ill fortune it was to leave you so early in my life and be cast into the wilderness. But my predestined bond with the young master of the Ts'ui family was not yet broken. I've come here now desiring only to have my beloved younger sister Ch'ing-niang continue the union. If you concur with this wish, her ailment will be cured instantly; if not, she'll expire now before you."

The entire household was petrified. They could see that the body was indeed that of Ch'ing-niang, but the voice and mannerisms were those of Hsing-niang.

Her father rebuked her: "You're already dead. By what right do you return to the human world and cause this turmoil?"

She replied, "After I died, the Courts of the Underworld did not find me guilty of any crime and therefore did not restrain me with the usual prohibitions. I was put under the tutelage of Lady Hou-t'u,[7] and put in charge of forwarding messages. Since my earthly destiny had not been fulfilled, I was granted a special leave for one year in order to consummate my marriage with Master Ts'ui."

Her father, realizing her sincerity, assented. She immediately composed her countenance and made obeisance to him in gratitude. Then she clasped Ts'ui's hand, sighing tearfully over their parting: "My parents have granted my wish. Be a good son-in-law, and take heed not to forget your old love because of the new." After speaking these words she cried bitterly and fell to the ground. She appeared dead.

Quickly an herb broth was forced between her lips, and in a brief while Ch'ing-niang revived. All symptoms of her sickness were gone, and her actions seemed normal. When asked about what had happened, she apparently remembered nothing, as if she had just awakened from a dream. An auspicious day was then chosen for Ts'ui's marriage.

Moved by Hsing-niang's affection, Ts'ui sold the hairpin in the marketplace. With the twenty taels of silver he received for it, he purchased incense, candles, and paper money for offerings and presented them at the Hydrangea Monastery, where he enjoined the Taoist monks to erect an altar for making sacrifices and prayers for three days and nights to thank Hsing-niang.

She appeared to Ts'ui once more in a dream and said, "Thanks to your prayers, I have gained my salvation. My love for you is undying, even though we are in separate worlds. I feel deeply grateful and have great admiration for you. My younger sister is gentle and meek; please treat her with kindness." Ts'ui awoke in wonderment and grief.

From this time on there was no further communion between the two of them.

Ah! How strange!

[7] The cult of Lady Hou-t'u (*Hou-t'u fu-jen*) became popular during the T'ang period, and remained alive until the present century, especially in the Yangchow area.

NIEH HSIAO-CH'IEH

From *Liao-chai chih-i*

TRANSLATED BY TIMOTHY A. ROSS

Ning Ts'ai-ch'en, of Chekiang Province, was generous and candid by nature and scrupulous in maintaining the rectitude of his character. He would often say to people, "I've never loved another woman in my life."

On one occasion, he traveled to Chin-hua.[1] When he reached the northern suburbs, he rested at a monastery. The halls and pagodas in the monastery were magnificent, but the grounds were overgrown with vegetation, as though the place were deserted. On either side of the main hall were the residential quarters, with their doors hanging ajar. Only to the south was there one room with a fairly new lock on the door. To the east beyond the main hall, there were tall bamboos which were so large that they could not have been encircled with a man's hands. Wild lotus were in bloom in a large pond beneath the bush of bamboos. He was pleased with the tranquility of this place. Since the official examiners had arrived to conduct the imperial examinations, rents of lodgings in the city were high. He thought of staying where he was, and strolled about waiting for the monks to return.

At dusk, a gentleman came to the monastery and went to open the door of the southern room.

Ning Ts'ai-ch'en hastened to greet him and stated his intentions. The gentleman said, "There's no one in charge of these premises. I've been temporarily staying here myself. If you enjoy the solitude and would frequently honor me with a visit, I should be fortunate indeed." Ning was delighted. He gathered some straw to make his bed and propped up some boards for a table; he planned to remain there for some time.

That night, when the moon was as clear and pure as water, the two men sat together in the monastery corridor and started their conversation by exchanging names. The gentleman said that his surname was Yen and his style was Ch'ih-hsia. Ning thought that the man might have come to take part in the provincial examinations, but his accent did not identify him as a native of Chekiang. When asked, the man said that he was a native of Shensi Province. He seemed to be truthful and sincere. When they had exhausted their topics for conversation, they bowed to each other and parted, retiring to their own rooms.

Ning, being in a new place, could not get to sleep for a long time. He heard voices from the north of his room as though some members of a family were talking. He got up and concealed himself beneath the stone window in the northern wall. By carefully peeping out, he saw, in the

[1] Prefecture in Chekiang Province in the Ch'ing period.

small courtyard beyond the low wall, a woman of forty-odd years. There was another, elderly woman who wore a faded robe of dark red silk, and had a few ornaments in her hair; she was hunchbacked and showed signs of aging. Both of them were chatting under the moonlight.

"Why isn't Hsiao-ch'ien here yet?" asked the middle-aged woman.

"She'll be here soon," the old woman said.

"Has she said any angry words to you, granny?"

"I haven't heard any, but she seems upset," the old woman said.

"That girl doesn't deserve to be treated well—" said the woman. Before she had finished speaking, a girl of seventeen or eighteen appeared, and she was lovely indeed.

"Don't talk about people behind their backs!" the old woman said, laughing. "We were just speaking of you, you little witch, and you sneak up here without a sound. It's a good thing we weren't criticizing you."

"You're as beautiful as someone in a painting," the old woman continued. "If I were a man, you'd surely win my heart."

"If you don't flatter me, granny," said the girl, "who will?"

Thereafter Ning could not tell what the woman and the girl said. He thought that they were neighbors, so he went back to sleep and no longer listened to them. It was after a long while that silence returned. Just as he was about to fall asleep, he realized that someone had come into his room. He quickly got up and looked around. It was the girl of the northern courtyard. When he questioned her in alarm, the girl laughed and said, "It's a moonlit night and I couldn't sleep, so I came over here to be your wife for the night."

Ning said sternly, "Aren't you afraid of what others would say? I am. It only takes one little slip to ruin one's honor."

"No one knows what goes on at night," the girl said. When Ning continued to chide her, the girl appeared hesitant, but it seemed that she still wanted to say something. Ning shouted at her, "Get out immediately! Otherwise I'm going to call the scholar in the southern chamber!"

Frightened, the girl withdrew from his room. But then she came back again and laid an ingot of gold on his mattress. Ning picked it up and flung it onto the porch in the courtyard, saying, "Such ill-gotten things will only soil my purse!"

The girl was ashamed and left. Picking up the gold, she said to herself, "This man is really as hard as iron."

The next morning, a scholar from Lan-chi[2] who had come with his servant to await the examinations took lodging in the eastern chamber. He died suddenly during that night. There was a tiny puncture on the sole of his foot, as though it had been jabbed by an awl, and a small strand of blood was oozing out. But the cause for all this was unknown. The following night his servant also died the same way. Toward evening, Yen returned and Ning asked him about this. Yen said that it was probably the work of a demon. Ning, being a bold and upright man, did not pay much attention to it.

At midnight, the girl came again and said to Ning, "I've had much experience with men but I've never met anyone as firm as you. You are truly a sage, so I wouldn't dare deceive you. My name is Hsiao-ch'ien and I'm from the family of Nieh. At the age of eighteen I died and was buried beside this monastery. A demon has often forced me to serve it in its lowly deeds. I really take no pleasure in seeking men out so shamelessly. Since there is no one else to kill in the monastery, I'm afraid that the demon will send a yaksha for you at night.'

Ning was terrified, and begged for her advice. "Stay in the room with Yen," said the girl, "and you can avoid harm."

"Why doesn't the demon bewitch Yen?"

"He's an extraordinary man and the demon doesn't dare go near him."

[2] A county in the Chin-hua Prefecture.

405

"How do you bewitch people?" he asked.

"When a man becomes intimate with me, I secretly pierce his foot with an awl and he becomes unconscious. Then I suck out his blood and give it to that demon to drink. Sometimes I use the gold—actually it's not gold at all, but the bones of the rakshas.[3] The demon will cut out the heart and liver of anyone who keeps the gold. These two methods are used because women and gold are what men are after."

Ning thanked her and asked when he should put himself on guard. She told him it would be the following night. When they were about to part, she wept and said, "I've fallen into the sea of sorrow, and though I seek the shore I can't reach it. You're a man of exemplary righteousness and I'm sure you can save me from this bitterness. If you are willing to wrap up my rotten bones and move them to some peaceful spot for reburial, I'll be as grateful to you as if you'd given me a new life."

Ning readily consented and asked where she was buried. She said, "Remember the aspen with a crow's nest in it; that's the spot." When she finished speaking, she went out the door and in no time at all disappeared.

The next day, fearing that Yen would go elsewhere, Ning went early to his room and invited him over. Later that morning he served Yen food and drink, at the same time observing him closely. He finally asked Yen to allow him to stay for the night, but Yen refused, citing his own eccentric addiction to solitude. Ning would not listen and carried his bedding over. Yen could do nothing except shift the bed and make room for him. Then he told Ning, "I know you are a reliable man and I admire your character. I have a little secret which is difficult to explain in a hurry. Please don't pry into my boxes and parcels. If you do, the consequences will be unfortunate for both of us."

Ning solemnly assented. When they went to bed, Yen placed a small box on the windowsill. He fell asleep at once, snoring heavily. But Ning was fully awake.

About the first watch, a man's shadow indistinctly appeared outside the window. Suddenly it approached the window and peered inside. Its eyes flashed and Ning was frightened. He was about to call Yen when something as dazzling as a strip of white silk ripped open the box and emerged. It struck the stone window frame and shot forth sparks; then it withdrew into the box as swiftly as lightening. Yen awoke and got up. Ning pretended to be asleep and watched him secretly. Yen opened the box and took something out of it; he looked at it and smelled it in the moonlight. It was white and bright as crystal, about two inches in length and as broad as a leek leaf. When he was finished, he wrapped it up again with several layers of cloth and put it back in the broken box.

"What old demon was that," he said to himself, "so impudent as to break my box?" Then he went back to bed. Ning was greatly amazed and got up to question Yen. He also told Yen what he had seen. Yen said, "Since we're good friends, how would I dare keep you in the dark? I'm a knight-errant. If it hadn't been for that stone window frame, the demon would have been killed right there. Anyway, he's wounded."

"What's the thing you're hiding in the box?" Ning asked.

"It's a sword," replied Yen. "Just then I smelled the odor of a demon on it."

Ning expressed a wish to see it and Yen accordingly took it out of the box and showed it to him. It was a small, glittering sword. Ning respected Yen even more.

The next morning, Ning found traces of blood outside the window. When he went out to the north of the monastery, he saw a deserted cemetery with graves. Sure enough, there was the aspen tree with a crow's nest among its topmost branches. When he had done what he had come

---

[3] Rakshas are the fierce demons that are sometimes considered not as violent as yakshas, sometimes similar.

to Chin-hua to do, Ning packed his baggage in a hurry to return to his home. Yen prepared a farewell feast for him and both men felt deep friendship for each other. Then Yen presented Ning with a worn leather case and said, "This is a sword case. Take good care of it; it can ward off demons."

Ning wished to study his arts with him, but Yen said, "As you are a man of righteousness and principle, you are qualified to learn this. But since you're to belong to the world of wealth and prestige, you're not meant to become a man of my profession."

Ning then excused himself, saying that he had his sister's burial to attend to. He dug up the girl's bones and arranged them in burial garments; then he rented a boat and returned to his home. His study faced an open pasture, so he built a tomb there for the girl. He sacrificed and prayed, "Taking pity on your lonely spirit, I have buried you near my humble dwelling. Here we're able to hear each other's songs and sobs. May you never again be oppressed by cruel demons. Here is a bowl of wine for you to drink; though it is not very good, I hope you won't mind."

When his prayer was finished, he started to leave. From behind him someone called, "Please wait for me. We'll go together."

He turned to look, and it was Hsiao-ch'ien. Full of joy, she thanked him: "You've kept your word. Were I to die ten times over, it would still not be sufficient recompense for your kindness to me. Please let me go home with you, so I may pay my respects to your parents. I am ready to be your servant or your concubine with no regrets."

Ning looked at her closely, and found her skin smooth, her feet delicate and slender. She was exquisitely beautiful when viewed in broad daylight.

He led her into his study and told her to sit down and wait a little while. Then he went in to inform his mother. His mother was startled. Ning's wife had been ill for a long time and his mother warned him to say nothing of this to her for fear that it might alarm her. While they were talking, the girl came lightly into the room. She was on her knees and kowtowed.

"This is Hsiao-ch'ien," Ning said. His mother was taken aback and did not know what to do.

"I was all alone, without parents or brothers," Hsiao-ch'ien said to her. "Your son showered me with the dew of his benevolence and I wish to offer you my humble service in order to repay his great kindness."

Only when Ning's mother had seen how beautiful and lovable the girl was did she pick up enough courage to speak to her: "I'm overjoyed that you want to take care of my son. But I have only this one son and he must carry on the family line. I wouldn't want him to take a ghost for a wife."

"Truly I've no other intentions," the girl said. "Since you don't trust a dead person, let me treat him as a brother and serve you as my mother morning and night. How about that?"

Ning's mother, sympathizing with her sincerity, consented. The girl wished to pay her respects to Ning's wife, but the mother refused on the grounds that her daughter-in-law was ill, and the idea was dropped. The girl immediately went to the kitchen to replace Ning's mother, and she went about the household as though she had always lived there.

That evening, Ning's mother grew fearful. She told the girl to go back to her own quarters, unwilling to have her stay there for the night. The girl knew the mother's feelings and left. Passing Ning's study, she wished to enter, but instead retreated and paced about nervously, as though she were afraid of something. When Ning called her, the girl said, "The smell of a sword in the room frightens me. That's why I didn't enter on the way back here."

Ning realized then that it must have been the shabby leather case that frightened her and went to hang it in another room. The girl then came in and sat down beside the candle. For a long time she remained silent and finally she asked, "Don't you read at night? When I was young, I used to read the *Surangama Sutra (Leng-yen ching)*,[4] but by now I've forgotten more than half of it. May I ask you to find a copy for me? I have time at night and you can help me."

Ning agreed, and she sat in silence until the second watch was nearly over without saying a word about leaving. When Ning urged her, she said forlornly, "Being a lonely ghost in a strange place, I'm really afraid of my solitary grave."

"There's no other bed in my study," Ning said, "and besides, as brother and sister, we should avoid suspicion."

The girl got up, frowning in distress, as though she wanted to cry. Reluctantly, she walked slowly out the door. As she crossed the threshold, she disappeared. Ning secretly felt sorry for her and wished that he had kept her in his room and prepared another bed for her. But he was also afraid of his mother's anger.

The girl waited upon Ning's mother every morning. She drew the water for toilet, managed the affairs of the household, and performed everything according to Ning's mother's wishes. Every evening after she had informed his mother that she would retire, she went at once to the study where she read the sutra by candlelight. When she felt that Ning wanted to sleep, she then sadly took her leave.

Some time before, Ning's wife had been bedridden and Ning's mother had had to work so hard she could scarcely bear it. Now, with the girl's help, she was able to take her ease. Her heart was touched and as the days passed, she came to love the girl as if she had been her own daughter. She even forgot that Hsiao-ch'ien was a ghost. She could not bear to let the girl leave at night and wanted her to stay with her in her bedroom.

At first, Hsiao-ch'ien neither ate nor drank. But after six months, she gradually took some thin rice-gruel. Mother and son both doted on her. They avoided mentioning that she was a ghost, and of course outsiders would not be able to tell.

Shortly after, Ning's wife died. His mother secretly wished to take the girl as her daughter-in-law, but was afraid that it would do her son harm. The girl realized this and took an opportunity to say to the mother, "I've lived here for more than a year and you ought to know my feelings. I came away with your son because I did not want to harm travelers; I had no other purpose in mind. Your son's honorable character has won everyone's approval. I only hope that by staying with your son for a few years, I may be able to get an imperial recognition through him. This will be to my credit in the underworld."

Ning's mother was aware that the girl had no evil intentions but feared that she would not be able to provide descendants for the family.

"Sons and daughters are bestowed by Heaven," the girl said. "Your son is destined for good fortune and he is allotted three sons to bring honor to the family. Having a ghost wife will not deprive him of that."

Ning's mother believed her and discussed it with her son. Ning was exhilarated. He arranged a banquet and invited his relatives and friends. Some of them asked to see the new bride, so the girl adorned herself and came out. Everyone was stunned by her beauty. None of them had the least idea she was a ghost; instead they took her to be a fairy. The female relatives of his family all sent her presents and vied with one another in making her acquaintance. The girl excelled at painting orchids and plum flowers on small scrolls, which she frequently gave them in return. Those who received them treasured them.

One day Hsiao-ch'ien stood at the window, with bowed head and a melancholy air on her face. Suddenly she asked, "Where is that leather case?"

"Since you were afraid of it," he replied, "I put it in another place."

"I've been around living people for a long time

---

[4] *Surangama Sutra* is a work of Tantric Buddhism translated into Chinese as the *Leng-yen ching* by Paramiti, a monk from Central India, in 705.

now," she said. "So I'm no longer afraid of it. It would be best for you to hang it up at the head of the bed."

When Ning asked her the reason she said, "I've felt quite uneasy for the last three days. I think the demon of Chin-hua will sooner or later come for me because it hates me for running away."

So Ning brought in the leather case. The girl inspected it closely, and observed, "It was used by the extraordinary swordsman to carry human heads. Since it's so worn out, I wonder how many people he has killed! Seeing it today, I couldn't help feeling goose pimples."

Ning hung the case up once more. The next morning, she asked him to hang it up over the door. That night, as they sat by the lamp, she asked Ning to keep vigil with her. Suddenly there was a sound as though a bird in flight had fallen to the ground. The girl was frightened and hid behind the curtains. Ning looked out and saw what seemed to be a yaksha, with glowing eyes and a bloody mouth. It advanced with gleaming teeth and waving arms, but it halted at the door. After hesitating for quite a while, it slowly approached the leather case. It plucked at the case with its claws, as though it wanted to rip it open. Suddenly with a loud noise the case swelled up to the size of a basket. A ghostly thing appeared with its upper body exposed; it seized the yakhsa and pulled it inside. The great sound died down and the case shrank back to its former size. Ning was astonished. The girl came out and said happily, "Now our troubles are over!"

They both looked into the case and found in it only a few quarts of clear water.

Some years later, Ning became a *chin-shih* and his ghost wife gave birth to a son. After he had taken a concubine, each woman again gave birth to one son. All his sons became well-known officials.[5]

[5] Comments at the end of the story are not translated because they are not part of the narrative.

THE ALMOST FORTUNATE MAN

In traditional China the concept of Heaven functions with the persuasion and rigidity of a religion. The idea of fate, therefore, has been accepted passively as an expression of the will of Heaven, a manifestation of the operation of the cosmic order. Any unpredictable turn of event is explained as beyond the control of man. To challenge this is to violate the mandate of Heaven.

The inexorability of fate is all the more obvious when a golden opportunity slips right out of one's hand. The old man in "A Taste of Immortality" and Scholar Ts'ui in the story of that name are good examples in that both men are teased by the capriciousness of Heaven. The irony is that they fail not because of any wrongdoing on their part, but precisely because they react to an unusual situation in their normal human way: the old man devoted to Taoism refuses to eat what appear to him to be human and animal remains, while Ts'ui, being a devoted son, acts according to what his mother told him.

Similarly, Tu Tzu-ch'un in the story of that title regains his humanity as soon as he lets out a cry when his son is smashed to death. Perhaps a small comfort Tu-Tzu-ch'un and those like him can draw is that to be chosen for the heavenly test at all is a sure sign of fortune. For, even though in the end no one is allowed to win out over the will of Heaven, each man has reaped a small windfall in his own way.

411

SCHOLAR TS'UI

From *Hsüan-kuai lu*

TRANSLATED BY DONALD E. GJERTSON

During the K'ai-yüan and T'ien-pao reign periods [713–755], there lived near the entrance to Lo Valley in Tung-chou a scholar by the name of Ts'ui.[1] He delighted in the cultivation of beautiful flowers, and in late spring the luxuriant fragrance of their blossoms would carry as far as a hundred paces. Every morning, Ts'ui would regularly go to water and look at his flowers.

One day a young woman came riding by unexpectedly from the west, followed by several maidservants of all ages. The young woman was of exceptional beauty, and her mount was a splendid animal. But before Ts'ui had the chance to get a closer look, she had already passed by.

The next morning the young woman again passed by. This time Ts'ui had prepared in advance some fine tea and wine, and had arranged mats and cushions among the flowers. He approached her and bowed. "I'm by nature quite fond of flowers and trees," said Ts'ui, "and all the things growing here in this garden I planted with my own hand. This is their most luxuriant and fragrant season, and they are truly worth your attention and appreciation. I've noticed that you pass by here every day, and thinking that your

servants and animals must be tired, I've prepared a simple meal for your refreshment."

The young woman rode right by without looking back, but one of the maidservants following her said to Ts'ui, "If you've prepared good food and good wine, don't worry, we'll be there!"

At that, the young woman turned and scolded her maid: "Why are you talking to others so freely?"

The next morning Ts'ui again went first to the garden to wait for the young woman; when she came by he whipped his horse and followed after her. When they came to his country house, he dismounted and again bowed to the young woman, inviting her in. After some time, an old maidservant said to the young woman, "The horses really are tired; there's no harm in stopping for a short rest." Thereupon she took the horse's rein and led it over to Ts'ui's house.

"If you would like to marry our young mistress," the old maidservant said to Ts'ui, "I could act as your go-between. How would that be?"

Ts'ui was greatly pleased, and bowing again and again, he knelt down to ask her to do so. The old maidservant continued, "There's no question that the matter can be arranged. In fifteen or sixteen days from now there'll be a most auspicious day. On that day you have only to prepare everything

---

[1] These places are fictitious.

413

necessary for the marriage ceremony and arrange a feast right here. Young mistress's elder sister over in Lo Valley has been indisposed lately, and that's why we've been going to see her every day. After we get there, I'll inform her of the arrangements, and when the day arrives, we'll all come here for the ceremony." At that, they all left.

Remaining behind, Ts'ui arranged everything for the wedding just as he had been instructed. When the day arrived, the young woman and her sister both came. The elder sister was also extremely beautiful, and she gave her younger sister away in the marriage ceremony.

Ts'ui's mother was still living in the family house, and knew absolutely nothing about the marriage. Since he had married without informing his mother, Ts'ui merely explained that he had taken a concubine. Nevertheless, his mother noticed that the new bride was very pretty.

After more than a month had passed, one day a man unexpectedly arrived with gifts of food for the young woman; the food was exceptionally delicious.

Later, Ts'ui came to notice that his mother was beginning to look tired and worried, so he prostrated himself before her and asked the reason. "You're my only child," his mother explained, "and I've always prayed for your well-being. Now this new bride that you've taken is truly a beauty without peer. Even in statues and paintings I've never seen one so beautiful. I'm sure she is some kind of a fox demon and will bring harm to you. This is what I've been worrying about."

Ts'ui returned to his chambers, where he found his wife crying. "From the beginning I've wanted to serve you as a wife should, and hoped to do so forever," she said, "but I hadn't realized that your mother would consider me a fox demon. I'll leave you tomorrow morning." Also crying, Ts'ui was unable to speak.

The next morning the young woman's retinue came for her. The young woman mounted a horse, and Ts'ui mounted another to accompany her on the way. When they had traveled some ten *li* into Lo Valley, they came upon a stream between the mountains where rare fruits and exotic flowers wondrous beyond description grew. Before them stood halls and mansions more splendid than those of the royal palace. More than a hundred maidservants came out to greet the young woman, and asked, "Why did you bring along this ungrateful fellow?" Thereupon they assisted the young woman in, leaving Ts'ui outside the gate.

Before long, a maidservant came to deliver a message from the young woman's elder sister: "You've returned the bride. Besides, your mother is suspicious and interfering. The matter should therefore be brought to an end, as it does not seem appropriate for the two of you to see each other. My younger sister has, however, served you as wife, so I suppose we should receive you."

After a little while, Ts'ui was summoned in. He was scolded and reprimanded over and over again, but the criticisms were always delivered in an orderly and gentle manner. Ts'ui could only bow down, prostrate himself, and accept the reproaches. He was then led into the main hall where, sitting across from the two sisters, he had dinner with them. When the meal was finished, wine was ordered, and musicians were summoned to play gentle music, which was most pleasing in its endless variations. When the music came to an end, the elder sister said to her sister, "We must ask Ts'ui to go home now; do you have anything you wish to give him?" The young woman then took a white jade casket from her sleeve and presented it to Ts'ui, who also gave her a memento in return.

Both of them sobbing, Ts'ui went out the gate. When he arrived at the entrance to Lo Valley and turned around to look back, he could only see a thousand peaks and a myriad ravines; the road through the valley was no longer there. Weeping bitterly, he returned home.

Afterward, he would often hold the jade casket

in his hands, feeling melancholy. One day, a foreign monk knocked on his door, seeking a meal. "You're in possession of a great treasure," said the monk, "I beg you to show it to me."

"I'm but a poor scholar," replied Ts'ui, "how could I possess such a thing?"

The monk continued, "Was there not a marvelous being who presented it to you? I knew of its existence when from a distance I saw its aura enveloping your house."

Ts'ui then thought of the jade casket and showed it to the monk. The monk stood up, offered to buy the casket for a million in cash, and then left.

[Before he left,] Ts'ui asked the monk, "Just who is the young woman?"

"The woman you took as your wife," replied the monk, "Is Lady Yü-chih, the third daughter of the Queen Mother of the West. Her elder sister is also famed for her beauty in the world of immortals, let alone the world of men! What a pity that the two of you did not remain married longer. If you had stayed married for an entire year, then you and your family would have gained immortality!"

TU TZU-CH'UN

From *Hsü Hsüan-kuai lu*

TRANSLATED BY JAMES R. HIGHTOWER

Tu Tzu-ch'un lived, apparently, around the time of the Chou[1] and Sui dynasties. As a young man he was extravagant and unmindful of his patrimony. Being a man of free and easy spirit, he gave himself over to drinking and dissipation until he had squandered all his wealth. When he appealed to his relatives, they disowned him, one and all, as irresponsible.

Winter was coming on, his clothing was in rags, and his belly was empty. As he walked about Ch'ang-an, the sun set and he still had had nothing to eat. He found himself at the west gate of the East Market, uncertain where to turn. His hunger and chill were obvious, and he looked up to heaven and sighed.

An old man there leaning on a staff asked him, "What are you sighing about, sir?"

Tzu-ch'un said what was on his mind. As he grew eloquent over the shabby treatment he had received from his relatives, his indignation showed on his face.

"How many strings of cash would you need to feel well off?" the old man asked.

"With thirty or fifty thousand I could get along."

"That's not enough."

"A hundred thousand."

"Still not enough."

"A million."

"Still not enough."

"Three million."

"That should do," the old man said at last, and drew from his sleeve a single string of cash, saying, "This is for tonight. Tomorrow at noon be waiting for me at the Persian Hostel in the West Market. Don't be late!"

Tzu-ch'un went at the appointed time, and the old man actually delivered the three million, leaving without telling his name.

Now that he was rich, Tzu-ch'un's profligate nature flared up again; he was convinced that he would never again be a pauper. He rode sleek horses and dressed in light furs; he assembled drinking companions, hired musicians, singers, and dancers in the gay quarter with never a thought for the future. Within a year or two he had gradually exhausted his resources. Fine clothes and carriage were replaced by cheap ones, he surrendered his horse for a donkey, and then gave up the donkey and walked. In no time he was as destitute as before.

At his wits' end, he stood at the gate to the market, bemoaning his lot. As if in response to his

---

[1] This is the Northern Chou Dynasty (557–581), the last of the non-Chinese regimes that occupied North China during the Northern and Southern Dynasties period.

416

sighs, the old man appeared. Seizing Tzu-ch'un's hand he exclaimed, "Amazing, that this should happen again! I will help you again—how much do you need?"

Tzu-ch'un was too embarrassed to reply and, to the old man's urgings, he could only shake his head in shame.

"Come again at noon tomorrow, the same place," the old man said.

Swallowing his shame, Tzu-ch'un went, and was given ten million strings of cash. Before receiving them, he was filled with determination to invest his money wisely in the future, putting Shih Chi-lun and Yi Tun[2] quite in the shade. But once the money came into his hands, his resolve grew unstable and his irresponsible character reasserted itself. Within a couple of years he was poorer than ever.

Again he ran into the old man in the same old place. Humiliated past endurance, he covered his face and fled. The old man seized the skirt of his robe and stopped him. "Too bad!" he said. "You have had bad luck." And he offered him thirty million, with the warning, "If this does not cure you, poverty is in your blood."

Tzu-ch'un thought, "When I lost all I had through extravagance and dissipation, my relatives and high connections spared me not a glance. Yet this old man has come to my aid three times—how can I repay him?" And to the old man he said, "With what you have given me I can put my affairs in order. It enables me to provide for widows and orphans and restore my name as a man of honor. I am deeply touched by your great generosity, and when I have accomplished this task, I will be at your disposal."

"It is what I had hoped. When you have taken care of your affairs, meet me next year on the fif-teenth of the seventh month[3] by the twin junipers at the [Temple of] Lao-tzu."

Reckoning that most widows and orphans [of his clan] were to be found in the area to the south of River Huai, he transferred his capital to Yang-chow, where he bought some fifteen hundred acres of good land. Within the city he built a large house, and on the main roads he erected over a hundred hostels, in which he lodged the widows and orphans of the whole region. He married off his nieces and nephews and had the unburied re-mains of his relatives moved to the clan cemetery. He requited those who had been kind to him and avenged his wrongs. When this was all done, the date was approaching, and he went to the ap-pointed place, where he found the old man whis-tling in the shade of the twin junipers.

Together they climbed the Cloud Terrace Peak in the Hua Mountains. When they had gone forty *li* or so, they came upon an imposing edifice, not the dwelling of any ordinary person. High over-head were colored clouds, and wary cranes were soaring about. The main hall stood out; inside was an alchemist's furnace over nine feet high emit-ting purple flames that lit up the door and win-dows.

Nine jade damsels[4] stood around the furnace, which rested on a green dragon in front and a white tiger behind. Just before sunset the old man appeared, no longer in ordinary dress, but now wearing the yellow cap and red robe of a Taoist priest. In his hands he held three pills of horn-blende and a cup of wine, which he gave to Tzu-ch'un, instructing him to swallow them. Then he spread a tiger skin against the inner wall on the west side and seated him on it, facing east.

---

[2] Shih Ch'ung, styled Chi-lun, was a legendary rich man of the Chin Dynasty. The long preamble in the story "Sung the Fourth Raises Hell with Tightwad Chang," included in this anthology, is on this man. Yi Tun was an exceptionally rich salt merchant of the Spring and Autumn period.

[3] The Taoist term *chung-yüan,* literally the "mid-cycle day," refers to the fifteenth of the seventh month. This day is also the Avalamba Festival. The two other accompanying terms, *shang-yüan* (the upper-cycle day) refers to the fifteenth of the first month, and *hsia-yüan* (the lower-cycle day) refers to the fifteen of the tenth month.

[4] The Taoist fairies.

"Be careful not to speak," he warned. "Though you see imposing spirits or fearful demons, or yakshas, or fierce wild beasts or hell itself—even though your dearest relatives are bound and tortured, none of it will be real. Through it all you must neither move nor speak; quiet your heart and fear not, and in the end you will suffer no harm. Just put your mind on what I have said." And he went out.

Tzu-ch'un looked around in the hall. There was only a large earthen jar filled to the brim with water, and nothing else. No sooner had the Taoist departed than the slopes of the hillside were covered with armed men carrying flags and banners, a thousand chariots and ten thousand horsemen. The roar of their shouts shook heaven and earth. One of them they addressed as "Great General"; he was over ten feet tall, clad, as was his horse, all in golden armor of a dazzling radiance. His bodyguard of several hundred men, all holding swords or drawn bows, dashed into the hall shouting, "Who are you that dare face the Great General?"

On both sides they raised their swords and advanced, demanding to know Tzu-ch'un's name and what sort of person he was, to which he made no response. Enraged, they made a great uproar as if they were about to slash him, and shoot arrows into him, but he paid them no attention. The general left in a fury.

All at once there were all sorts of creatures—fierce tigers and poisonous dragons, griffins and lions, cobras and scorpions—roaring and snatching as they rushed forward to seize and bite, even leaping into the air over his head. Tzu-ch'un remained unperturbed, and in a little while they were all gone.

Then a great rain fell in torrents, with thunder and lightning in the murky air, and fire wheels racing by to the left and the right, the lightning striking in front and behind, until he could not open his eyes. In a moment the water in the hall was over ten feet deep, lightning came in an unbroken stream, and the thunder roared, as though the very hills and rivers were split open.

In no time the waves had reached the place where Tzu-ch'un sat, but he did not budge at all and paid no attention to anything around him.

Before long, the general appeared again, leading a troop of ox-headed jailers and demons of extraordinary appearance. They carried a huge cauldron which they placed in front of Tzu-ch'un. They surrounded him on all sides with long, forked spears. He was given an ultimatum: if willing to tell his name, he would be set free. If not, he would be impaled through the heart and thrust into the boiling cauldron. He made no response.

Next they brought in his wife and dragged her to the foot of the steps. Pointing to her the general said, "Tell your name and we will let her go."

When he did not respond, she was whipped until the blood flowed. They shot her with arrows, cut her with knives, poured boiling water on her, and seared her flesh with irons until she could not endure it and screamed and wept, "I am of no account, a disgrace to a gentleman like you. But I have after all had the good fortune to serve you more than ten years as your wife. Now I am tormented past endurance by these demons. I would never expect you to get down on your knees and beg favors of them, but all it would take to save my life is just one single word!" Her tears rained down as she alternately prayed and cursed.

When Tzu-ch'un persisted in paying no attention, the general shouted, "You think we can't hurt your wife?" And he ordered them to bring the knife and block and slice her, inch by inch, beginning with her feet. She screamed and wept even more desperately, but to the end Tzu-ch'un never once paid her the slightest attention.

The general then announced, "This villain has perfected his black magic and cannot be allowed on earth any longer." He ordered the attendants to behead him, and when it was done, they led his ghost before the Yama King, who said, "Is this the sorcerer of the Cloud Terrace Peak? Deliver him to the tortures of hell."

There he experienced in complete form all the

tortures—swallowing molten bronze, being beaten with an iron cudgel, pounded in a mortar, ground in a mill, buried in a fiery pit, boiled in a cauldron; he climbed the mountain of knives and the tree of swords. Through it all he remembered the Taoist master's injunction, and it all seemed bearable, so never a sigh escaped him. The torturers reported that he had suffered all the punishments, and the Yama King said, "This man is a secret villain. It is not fitting that he should be reborn a man; we will have him born a daughter in the family of Wang Ch'üan, the deputy magistrate of Shan-fu County in Sung-chou."[5]

From birth the little girl was sickly, and hardly a day passed without acupuncture or moxa burning or some nasty medicine. And she was always falling out of bed or into the fire, but whatever the pain she never made a sound. Soon she was grown into an extraordinarily beautiful girl, but because she never spoke, she was thought by her family to be dumb. Her relatives would take liberties with her and offer her all sorts of insults, but she would not respond.

In the same town was a *chin-shih* named Lu Kuei who, hearing of her beauty, sought her through an intermediary for his wife. The family declined on the grounds that she was dumb, but Lu said, "If my wife is worthy, what need has she for speech? She will serve as a reproach to sharp-tongued women." They agreed to the match, and Lu married her as his wife, with all the six rites.

For several years their love was very deep. She bore him a son, who at two years was unusually bright and clever. His father held the child in his arms and talked to her, but she did not respond. He tried all sorts of ways to get her to talk, but never a word would she say. In a fury he exclaimed, "Minister Chia's wife [of the Spring and Autumn period] despised her husband and would never smile, until he shot a pheasant, which made her feel better about him. I cannot do as well as

[5] In modern Kiangsu Province.

he did, though I should think my accomplishments as a man of education were better than any mere archery. If you are not ever going to speak, what use to a man of honor is the child of a wife who despises him?"

And he took the child by its two feet and dashed its head against a stone, spattering blood for several paces around. In Tzu-ch'un's heart love welled up, and for an instant he forgot his vow, inadvertently letting slip a sound of distress: "No—"

The sound was still in the air as he found himself sitting in his old place, the Taoist standing in front of him. It was just the beginning of the fifth watch. He saw the purple flames shoot up through the roof and all at once they were surrounded by a fire. Roof and walls were all in flames.

"You have failed me!" the Taoist said with a sigh.

He seized Tzu-ch'un's hair and threw him in the water jar, and the flames subsided.

"My son, your heart was purged of joy and anger, grief and fear, loathing and desire," the Taoist said to him. "It is only love that binds you still. If you had not uttered that cry, my elixir would have been ready, and you, too, could have become an immortal with me. It is hard, alas, to find someone with the capacity for immortality. I can smelt my elixir again, but your body must remain earthbound. Take heed!"

Pointing out the distant road back, he sent Tzu-ch'un on his way. Tzu-ch'un climbed up on the platform to look. The furnace split apart and inside was an iron rod thick as a man's forearm and several feet long. The Taoist had put off his robe and was cutting at the rod with a knife.

When Tzu-ch'un got back home, he was filled with shame that he had forgotten his vow, and resolved to go back and try to make amends. He went to the Cloud Terrace Peak, but there was no sign of anyone, and he returned home again, sighing and chagrined.

A TASTE OF IMMORTALITY

From *Erh-k'o P'o-an ching-chi*

TRANSLATED BY DELL R. HALES

Immortality has always been shaped by one's fate;
Struggling is vain if you're not marked for longevity.
But how many foolish dreamers in this mortal world
Stir their crucibles daily for the elixir of life?

Our story tells how once there lived an old man who was extremely devoted to Taoism. Whenever he saw a Taoist priest pass by, he would treat him with the utmost respect and courtesy.

One day, a priest with his hair bound up in a double knot came to pay him a visit. His clothing was tattered, but the expression on his face was healthy and pleasant. Surmising that this priest was someone extraordinary, the old man welcomed him into his home with considerable cordiality. The priest ate and drank great quantities, which the old man furnished him with unflagging diligence. Afterward the priest came and went several times, while the old man received each visit in exactly the same manner.

One day the priest said to him, "I've enjoyed your hospitality for some time now, and I'm very grateful that you haven't begrudged me anything. Would you please come to my place, so that I may serve you a few country dishes as an expression of my appreciation?"

"I've never asked where you live," said the old man. "May I now ask how far it is, and can an old fellow like me make it there?"

"My retreat is hidden in the mountains, but it's not too far from here. If you'll come along with me, we'll soon be there."

"In that case, I would certainly like to go."

With the priest leading and the old man behind, they left the busy streets of the village and walked carefully across the fields and rustic trails until they turned into a mountain path. The region was secluded and abounded with thick, luxuriant growth. After they had traveled over a few low mountain ridges, several thatched huts came into view within a small valley among the hills.

"That's my mountain hideaway," said the priest, pointing.

In a few more steps they were in front of his shack. He opened the door and helped the old man inside. The latter looked around and saw that:

It wasn't a mansion with a splendid red gate,
But it smelled of magic blossoms from fairyland.

After inviting him to sit down in the front room, the priest went alone to the back rooms for a time.

"The meal is ready," said the priest as he returned. "Please rest here for a new moments while I invite a few companions to join us in pleasant conversation."

420

The old man was delighted to learn that there were other priests close by and replied happily, "Please do as you wish, and I'll wait here by myself."

The priest went directly out while the old man sat there absent-mindedly. When after a long delay his host had still not returned, he became somewhat impatient and rose to look around. By now he was rather hungry and wanted to find something to eat. Anticipating that there would be something edible in the pantry, he went through a side door and reached the kitchen. He was not prepared to see that there was no cookstove there at all, but only a few date-wood spoons and some ladles made of coconut shells. There were also two earthenware water jars covered with bamboo lids.

When the old man walked over and looked, he was surprised to find that one jar actually contained a small white dog, with its hair plucked clean, immersed in water. "No wonder," thought the old man, "that this priest doesn't abstain from regular meats and wine; he also eats dog meat." When he lifted the other lid to look, he was even more startled to find a tiny dead baby, complete with hands and feet, submerged in water. The old man became quite suspicious now.

"This priest couldn't be a good fellow. He takes meat and wine, and lives out here in this mountain wilderness with no life in his hut, only these two things. I might forget the dog, but certainly not the dead baby. Is he some sort of murderer who sets people's houses on fire? I've been making a mistake in being friendly with him. Even to stay here is dangerous."

He wanted to leave, but he had forgotten the way home and would have to wait there patiently. At this moment of uncertainty the priest arrived with several other Taoist priests, all of whom had white hair and shaggy eyebrows. They entered the hut, greeted the guest courteously, and sat down. The old man felt strongly apprehensive and waited to see what would happen.

"I'd like all of you to know," he heard the priest say, "that this gentleman has been my benefactor, but I've been unable to repay his kind hospitality until now. To express my appreciation, I've given all of you a special invitation to come enjoy with us two delectable dishes that I've been fortunate enough to obtain today."

As the priest finished speaking, he went into the kitchen. He took the two things from the earthenware containers and set them on the table; then before each person he placed a pair of wooden spoons. He then turned toward the old man and said, "This fare is considered rather uncommon. Please try some."

The old man saw that the two dishes on the table were indeed the small dog and the baby which had been soaking in the water crocks. The crowd of priests all parted their beards and clapped their hands.

"Brother!" they cried. "Where did you get two such unusual things?" They all prepared to start eating and politely pushed the dishes first toward the old man, who became quite frightened.

"Ever since I was very young," the old man said, "I've never broken my vow to forego eating dog meat, not to mention human flesh! Now that I'm old, how could I go back on my word?"

"These are merely vegetable dishes," observed the priest, "and it's quite all right to eat them."

"Even if I were starving," said the old man, "I wouldn't dare."

"Naturally," said the other priests, "if he is so determined, we cannot force him to dine."

"Please forgive us for being so impolite," they said, bowing with their hands folded.

The priests then gathered around and ate up every bit of the meal. Even the remaining drops of juice that had spilled on the platter were also licked clean. The old man just stared at them in silence, for he had not the courage to utter a sound.

"Since you haven't eaten with us," said the priest, "you've wasted your visit. I haven't any-

421

thing proper to serve, but how can I let you go hungry?" He went into the kitchen again and brought out some white pastry for the old man. "This is some homemade cake which will satisfy your hunger. Please have a piece."

The old man saw that it really was cake, and since he was rather hungry, ate it. The flavor seemed a little bitter to him, but he was so famished that he did not care how it tasted. No sooner had he finished it than he began to feel healthy, robust, and vigorous. "Although Ch'ang-an is nice," he thought, "it isn't a place I should stay in.[1] Now that I'm no longer hungry I should leave." The priest did not try to detain him as he came to say good-bye, but only replied, "I'm sorry that I've treated you so rudely on this occasion, and I feel badly about it. Of course, I'll escort you home myself."

They went out with the other priests, who expressed their thanks and left. The priest accompanied him until they approached a busy spot where he knew that the old man could find his way alone. He then left without saying good-bye. As the old man continued on toward home, he suspected that they were a bad lot. He saw they were accustomed to eating dog meat and human flesh; it was likely that this group of priests practiced sorcery, and were wicked thieves and murderers.

After a couple of days had passed, the priest with the double knot in his hair again arrived at the old man's home.

"I offended you the other day," he said with a bow.

"After seeing such a strange meal," replied the old man, "even today I'm still afraid."

The priest laughed. "That's because it was not your destiny. I'd gone through a lot of trouble to obtain these two items and did not dare enjoy them by myself. I recalled your kindness and especially invited you to my retreat so that we could share the meal with my colleagues together. How could I have known that you were not ordained for immortality!"

"How can you consider that small dog and child as immortal food?"

"Those were potent medicinal herbs that were of extremely ancient vintage. They only looked like a small dog and baby, and were not really flesh and blood. The one with the shape of a dog was the root from an ageless medlar tree;[2] if you ingest the root, you can live for a thousand years. The tiny baby was a ginseng root[3] that required ten thousands years to form; eating this will add thousands of years to your life. You shouldn't cook these things but eat them in their natural state. [If I were lying to you,] how could we humans consume the raw flesh of dogs and people, just like wild animals, without even spitting out a single bone?"

Only then did the old man recall the circumstances of that meal the other day. Of course, everyone had taken the food uncooked, and he had seen no bones. Then he was convinced that the priest was telling the truth.

"I was so stupid the other day," he said remorsefully. "Why didn't you explain?"

"This is a matter of one's fate. If you weren't appointed to this end, how could I reveal the secrets of Heaven? Now that the affair is over, I can talk about it."

The old man beat his breast and stamped his feet. "I missed the chance to become an immor-

---

[1] The source of this metaphor is the Chinese veneration for the fabulous T'ang capital of Ch'ang-an. It was considered one of the most beautiful sights to see. To most medieval Chinese, a journey to Ch'ang-an amounted to a pilgrimage.

[2] An old legend indicates that, like ginseng, the root of the medlar (*Lycium chinensis*) can take the shape of certain things, and that eating it will prolong a man's life.

[3] Miraculous curative powers are attributed to the ginseng plant. It has long held a leading position in Chinese herbal medicine. The root of the plant is the most valued part, becoming gnarled and strangely shaped. The more it resembles the form of a man, the more valuable it is considered.

tal," he cried, "even though it was right before my eyes! But it's too late to grieve over it. If you have some more, could you give me another herb to eat?"

"Those herbs came from magic roots and cannot be found again under ordinary circumstances! But though you didn't have any of the vegetables the other day, you did taste some of the thousand-year tuckahoe.[4] From now on, you'll never be sick during your lifetime, and you'll live to be over a hundred."

"What is tuckahoe?" asked the old man.

"That was the white cake you ate. That was all that was provided for in your destiny; it's not that I don't want you to join me in immortality."

The priest left after he finished speaking and never came again. And from that time on, the old man did indeed live over a hundred years without a single illness before his death.

Obviously, some people have the good fortune to become immortals. But in spite of the fact that the elixir of life may be right before you, and someone deliberately points it out, if it isn't your lot, it will never touch your lips. There are imbeciles, however, who have heard the Taoist sermons and hope to make the pill of immortality. When the poisons they extract from deadly elements, such as arsenic and mercury, flow into their stomachs, they are soon beyond saving. This is why the ancients had the saying: "When taking drugs in search of immortality, there are many who misinterpret the prescription."

Ever since men of the Chin Dynasty popularized elixirs like the "Five-Stone Powder" and the "Cold-Resisting Powder," who knows how many intelligent victims have been destroyed by these toxic potions? There have been many ministers of state, even emperors, who could not be revived from the effects of these toxins. Why were they so blind? Because the dosages they prepared always followed the directions left behind by immortals. In concocting the elixir, however, the immortals insisted on perfect harmony between mind and body, eliminating every particle of greed and lust. Therefore, when they swallowed the potions, the water and fire elements in their bodies automatically refined the ingredients evenly into a medicinal concentrate which made their physical powers firm and unyielding, enabling them to live forever.

The people who compound these elixirs nowadays are those who nourish evil thoughts about women and wealth. They use drugs precisely for the purpose of obtaining life so they can indulge in their lustful desires. This idea is wrong to begin with. Moreover, their bodies are weary and dissipated when they are exposed to the dangerous chemicals made from these powerful elements, so how can they survive them? This is why nine out of ten persons fail in their quest. There is an occasional poem by Chu Wen-kung[5] which says:

I drifted along seeking immortality,
Left the world to dwell in mountains and clouds.
Like a thief who opens the secrets of Heaven,
Slipping past the gates of life and death.
Bright golden pot emblazoned with tiger and dragon,
Three years in making those wondrous pills.
When a pinch of elixir goes into the mouth,
You soar through the sky in bright sunlight.
To take the path I yearn to follow
Is as easy as casting off my shoes.
But I was afraid of opposing natural laws;
Even living longer will bring no peace of mind.

This verse is proof that there is such a thing as the elixir of life, but when the product was ready, the poet was apprehensive about violating the principles of creation. Therefore, he did not want to continue his study of Taoist mysticism. But how

---

[4] The *fu-ling*, or China root, a large edible fungus which grows on the roots of fir trees.

[5] The famous Southern Sung philosopher Chu Hsi (1130–1200).

could one anticipate that people who are ignorant of these principles would indulge in the reckless preparation and consumption of these harmful mixtures? Do they think that Heaven would be so indiscriminate as to allow them to join the true immortals? Thus, even the life that is given them is snuffed out.

[This is only the preamble; it is followed by the long main story on a futile and a fatal attempt to make immortality drugs.]

THE FAITHLESS SEEKER

If the almost fortunate man fails because he refuses to surrender his humanity or to compromise his moral principles, the faithless seeker fails because he is unwilling to make a necessary sacrifice, or simply because of his lack of faith. In most cases the faithless seeker is a hypocrite. He pursues his aims deceptively and selfishly, only to discover at the end that he has cheated no one but himself. The fate of Yang Tsung-su's father (in "In Search of a Heart") is one such example. The painful lesson that Wang and Huang, respectively learned, in "The Taoist Priest of the Lao Mountains" and "The Monk's Magic" cannot be measured in terms of financial loss alone: it is their ego that has suffered most. Worse still, unlike the almost fortunate man the faithless seeker has no reward whatsoever to compensate him for his ordeal.

IN SEARCH OF A HEART

From *Hsüan-shih chih*

TRANSLATED BY HSING-HUA TSENG

At the beginning of the Ch'ien-yüan reign period [758–759],[1] there lived an old man named Yang in K'uai-chi.[2] He was so rich that he could easily be the richest man in the prefecture. One day,he became seriously ill; he seemed to be dying, and he was confined, moaning, to his bed. However, he lingered on for quite a few months.

His son, Tsung-su, who was known in the vicinity for his filial piety, spared no expense to obtain the best medical care for his father. He consulted a doctor named Ch'en, who examined the father and concluded, "The illness stems from the heart. Because your father is too rich and his life has been so obsessed with moneymaking, he no longer has a heart. The only cure is for him to eat a live human heart. But where in this world can you get a live human heart? Besides this, I know of no cure."

When Tsung-su heard this, he realized that there would normally be no possible way to obtain a live human heart; the only thing that could be done was to appeal to the Buddha, and this piety, perhaps, might bring results. He asked the monks to chant sutras and commissioned some craftsmen to paint and carve images of Buddha. Later, he

himself took offerings of food and clothing to the monks of the temples in the prefecture.

One day when he was carrying food to one of the temples, he lost his way and mistakenly took a path which led to a mountain. At the foot of the mountain, he saw a stone niche. Seated inside was a foreign-looking monk. The monk appeared very old, withered and lean, and wore a cassock made of rough wool. He sat on a rock in the lotus position. Tsung-su thought that this monk must be an extraordinary man. He approached, bowed reverently to him, and asked, "Master, where are you from? Why do you make your home in this desolate place where no one ever comes and where you have no one to attend to you? Aren't you afraid of being hurt by wild animals? Or are you a monk who has already attained the power of Buddha?"

The monk replied, "My family name is Yüan.[3] My ancestors lived at the Pa Mountains[4] for generations. Later a branch of the descendants moved to Yi-yang[5] and scattered to different places in the various mountains. We all follow our family tradition, living as hermits in the mountains

---

[1] Ch'ien-yüan is the title of the second of the four reign periods of the T'ang emperor Hsiao-tsung (r. 756–763).
[2] Modern Shao-hsing in Chekiang Province.

[3] This is a pun on the word for "ape."
[4] A mountain range that runs through the present provinces of Szechwan and Shensi.
[5] In modern Kiangsi Province.

where we can be free to chant and cry out[6] as long as we like. Many poets have praised our cries, for which we are fairly well known as of this day. There was another branch of our clan named Sun.[7] They liked to play up to rich and famous people; they knew what people liked and how to please them. They could be taken to the marketplace to do tricks and earn money for their masters. But I alone prefer Buddhism; I want to set myself apart from the vulgar lot and retire like a hermit in the valley. I've been living here for many years. I admire Ashoka,[8] who was willing to cut the flesh from his body [to feed animals]. I also admire Buddha, who was willing to jump off a cliff to feed the hungry tigers. I eat acorns and drink the spring water. I only regret that no tiger or wolf has come to eat me: I can only wait for them."

"You're indeed a sage!" Tsung-su said. "You would go all the way to sacrifice yourself for the wild animals. You're wonderfully brave and godlike! My father has been ill for several months. Medicine doesn't do him any good, and I worry day and night to no avail. One doctor said the trouble is in his heart. He cannot be cured unless he eats a live human heart. Now, master, since you're willing to sacrifice yourself to feed wild animals, wouldn't it be better if you gave your life to save a human being? Please consider it carefully."

The monk replied, "If I can do so, that's what I really want. Since you want my heart for your father, how can I refuse? If I'm willing to sacrifice

my life for animals, why wouldn't I do so for a human being? But, I haven't eaten anything yet today. First, give me a meal and then I will die."

Tsung-su was very happy and thanked him profusely. He offered the monk all the food he had brought. The monk quickly gobbled down the food and then said, "Now I'm full, and I should fulfill my promise, but wait until I have worshiped the gods in all four directions." He straightened out his cassock and emerged from the stone niche. After he worshiped the gods in four directions, he suddenly jumped onto a tall tree.

Tsung-su thought that he was preparing to show off a magic power which no one could predict. But a little while later, the monk asked Tsung-su to come to the foot of the tree and shouted at him rudely, "What was that you asked me for?"

Tsung-su replied, "I wanted to get a live human heart to cure my father's illness."

"The thing that you want I have already promised you, but I want to explain to you some lines from the *Diamond Sutra*.[9] Will you listen?"

"I've always believed in Buddhism. Since today I had the good fortune to meet you, my master, how could I refuse to listen?"

The monk said, "The *Diamond Sutra* has this to say: 'The heart of the past cannot be had, the heart of the present cannot be had, the heart of the future cannot be had.' Now you want to take my heart, but that cannot be had either!" When he finished talking, he jumped around, shouted, suddenly changed into an ape and disappeared. Tsung-su was both frightened and astonished but managed to find his way home.

---

[6] Yelling, in the manner of Tarzan, was considered very good for releasing pent-up emotions.

[7] This is a pun on the word for "monkey."

[8] The term "Yu-li wang" given in the text is badly corrupt. It should be "A-yu wang" (or "A-yu-chia" and other similar variants), the Chinese translation for Ashoka who, from his original position as the ruler of the Mauryan Empire of North India in the third century B.C., united India and became the first famous patron of Buddhism.

[9] The *Diamond Sutra* is the short translated title for a treatise of Mahayana Buddhism. Its original title is *Vajracchedika-prajnaparamita-sutra* and it was first translated into Chinese by the eminent Indian translator Kumarajiva (ca. 344–412).

THE TAOIST PRIEST OF THE LAO MOUNTAINS

From *Liao-chai chih-i*

TRANSLATED BY JEANNE KELLY

There lived in our village a man named Wang, the seventh son of an old family, who from youth had longed to take up Taoism. Hearing that in the Lao Mountains[1] there were many immortals, he shouldered a pack and set off in that direction.

At the top of a peak of the mountains, he came upon a secluded temple. A Taoist priest with white hair down to his neck and of lofty demeanor was sitting on a rush mat. Wang bowed low, spoke with him, and found the doctrines he expounded abstruse but profound. Wang asked the priest to take him as a disciple. The priest said, "I'm afraid you're too soft and spoiled to put up with the hardships." Wang assured him that he could.

The disciples of the priest were quite numerous. Toward evening they all assembled together. Wang made obeisance to all of them and then stayed on in the temple.

Early the next morning, the priest summoned Wang, gave him an axe, and sent him off with the others to gather firewood. Wang respectfully did as he was told. More than a month passed and his hands and feet had become heavily callused. Un-

able to endure this hardship, he had secretly made up his mind to go home.

Returning one evening to the temple, he saw two men drinking with the master. The sun had already set, but no lamps or candles had been lit. The master cut some paper in the shape of a round mirror and pasted it on the wall. In a moment, bright moonlight filled the room, by the light of which even a hair was visible. All the disciples crowded round to wait upon them. One of the guests said, "On such a lovely night, the joy should be shared by all." He then took a jug of wine from the table and gave it to the disciples, bidding them drink their fill. Wang wondered to himself how this one jug of wine could serve seven or eight people. Everyone then found himself a cup or bowl and raced to drain his cup first, fearing that the supply would soon be exhausted. But again and again wine was poured out without ever seeming to diminish. Wang marveled at this.

A moment later, one of the guests said, "You have provided us with bright moonlight, yet we drink alone. Why not call [the moon goddess] Ch'ang-e to come?" He then threw a chopstick into the moon, and there, a beautiful girl came forth from the light. At first barely a foot high,

---

[1] A famous mountain range on the seaboard of the eastern Shantung Peninsula.

upon reaching the ground she attained full stature. She had a slender waist and a beautiful neck, and gracefully she fluttered through the steps of the Rainbow Robe Dance. When this was over, she sang:

Fairies! Oh, Fairies! Have you returned,
Leaving me shut up in the Palace of the Moon?

Her voice, as beautiful as the notes of a lute, was clear and far-reaching. When the song was finished, she whirled around, jumped up on the table, and before the astonished gaze of the company, turned back into a chopstick. The three men laughed heartily.

Then the other guest said, "This has been a happy evening, and we've had enough wine. How about treating us to a feast in the Palace of the Moon?" Leaving their seats, the three gradually walked into the moon, where all could see them sitting and drinking, their beards and eyebrows as plainly visible as images in a mirror.

After a while, the moon gradually dimmed, and when the disciples lit some candles, they found the priest sitting alone; the guests had disappeared. The food still remained on the table, while the moon on the wall was nothing but a piece of paper, round as a mirror. The priest asked, "Have you all had enough to drink?" "Quite enough," they replied. "In that case, you should get to bed early so that you won't be late in gathering firewood tomorrow." They all obeyed and withdrew. Wang was secretly delighted and all thoughts of returning home vanished.

Another month passed. The hardships had become more than Wang could endure, and besides, the Taoist priest had not taught him any magic skill. Unable to wait any longer, he took his leave, saying, "I came a long way to receive your instruction. Though I cannot obtain the secret of immortality, perhaps if you could impart some small skill, it would satisfy my desire for knowledge. Already I've been here two or three months, and I

have done nothing but go out early in the morning to collect firewood and return in the evening. I never experienced such hardship at home."

The priest laughed and said, "Didn't I tell you that you couldn't stand the hardships? Now since this has been borne out, I'll send you on your way tomorrow morning."

Wang said, "I've worked for you for many days. If you could impart a little of your skill, I wouldn't have come in vain."

"What skill do you seek?"

Wang replied, "I've noticed that wherever you go, walls are never an obstacle in your path. If I could only learn the secret of that, it would be enough." The priest laughed and assented. Thereupon he taught Wang a magic spell which he had him recite through to the end. Then he cried, "Go on through!" Wang faced the wall, not daring to approach it. Again the priest said, "Try going through." Wang advanced cautiously, but when he reached the wall, he stopped. "Lower your head and rush through. Don't hesitate," commanded the priest. Wang accordingly stepped back several paces from the wall and rushed forward. When he reached the wall, it seemed as though there was nothing there. Turning to look back, he found he was indeed outside the wall. Overjoyed he returned to thank the priest, who told him, "When you return home, your heart must remain pure; otherwise the spell will not work." He then gave him money for traveling expenses and sent him home.

Back at home, Wang bragged that he had met an immortal and now solid walls could not obstruct his path. His wife did not believe him, so Wang prepared to repeat his performance. Stepping back several feet from the wall, he rushed forward. His head struck the hard wall, and abruptly he fell down flat. His wife helped him up and looked him over. His forehead had swollen into a lump the size of a huge egg. She made great fun of him and Wang, shameful and indignant, cursed the old priest for being a scoundrel.

THE MONK'S MAGIC

From *Liao-chai chih-i*

TRANSLATED BY LORRAINE S. Y. LIEU

Once there was a man named Huang who was the descendant of a once-prominent family. Huang was both talented and full of high aspirations, and he had been on good terms for a long time with a monk who lived in the monastery outside the village.

The monk went on a trip one day and did not return until more than ten years later. When he saw that Huang's situation had not improved a bit, he sighed. "I thought you would have prospered long ago! How come you're still the same old self? I guess you're simply not destined for an auspicious future. Let me bribe the lord of hell for you. Can you raise ten strings of cash?"

Huang replied that he could not, and the monk said, "Try your best to get half the amount. I'll borrow the rest for you, and we'll meet in three days' time."

Huang agreed and pawned all he had to raise the money. Three days later, the monk gave Huang the five strings of cash as promised.

There was a well in Huang's house which had never dried up, and people said that it went all the way to the sea. The monk told Huang to string up all the money and place it by the well; then he instructed him, "Drop the money in when you think I'm about to arrive back at the monastery. Wait for about half the time it takes to cook a meal, and when a coin floats up, you must kowtow to it." Then the monk left.

Huang knew nothing about sorcery and thought that since there was no guarantee of success, it would be such a waste to throw ten strings in all at once. So he hid nine strings and threw down only one. After a short while, a large bubble floated up, and with a loud bang it burst open, showing a large coin as big as a cart wheel. Huang was terrified. After he kowtowed to it, he took out another four strings to throw in. But they all fell onto the large coin noisily and were blocked from sinking down.

At dusk, the monk came and scolded him: "Why didn't you throw them all in?"

"I did!" Huang protested.

"The messenger of hell has only taken one string," the monk said. "Why are you lying?"

So Huang had to tell him the truth. The monk sighed, "A stingy man can never achieve anything significant. You're now destined to become only a senior *hsiu-ts'ai;* otherwise, you could have gone as far as *chin-shih.*

Huang deeply regretted what he had done and

431

asked the monk to exercise his magic power again. The monk sternly refused and left.

Huang saw that the money was still floating in the well, so he hooked it up with a rope. Then the large coin sank.

That year, Huang was selected to be a senior *hsiu-ts'ai* on a supplementary basis,[1] just as the monk had predicted.

[1] This was mainly a ̇. ̇. orative title. The person concerned was, in effect, being placed on a permanent waiting list. He would be given an official post only when no other suitable candidates were available.

THE DREAM ADVENTURER

The experience of the dream adventurer can be both conventional and unconventional. The conventional pattern, as represented by adventure of Scholar Lu (in "The World Inside a Pillow"), is close to being a formula. With the help of a magic pillow, Lu leaves the primary world of daily reality to enter the secondary world of fantasy. After a lifelong prominent career in this realm, he wakes up to the world of actuality only to find out that the duration of his dream is as brief as is suggested in the story: "The millet which the host had been steaming was not yet ready." In line with the parabolic scheme of the story, this experience is supposed to have helped him realize the emptiness and the transience of worldly glory. Simple as it is, the story is related in a three-part structure, giving prominent attention to the dream adventure. What needs to be noted in this connection is that the dream itself does not purport to be a vision of another world: it is presented in all seriousness as "real life" by frequent citations of historical facts and other concrete data. Since the central action is focused on the realistic concerns of human beings, the dream-like quality and allegorical elements are minimized. In this respect, the adventure of Scholar Chang is strikingly unique in its absence of any allegorical intent. The dream world in "Scholar Chang" is truly three-dimensional in that the shared experience of the different dreamers happens at the same clock time in the same place involving the same people. To the knowledge of the Editors, there are no comparable examples (other than a few similar T'ang tales) in the vast repertoire of Chinese dream stories.

THE WORLD INSIDE A PILLOW

From *Wen-yüan ying-hua*

TRANSLATED BY WILLIAM H. NIENHAUSER, JR.

In the seventh year of the K'ai-yüan reign period [719] there was a certain old Taoist monk named Lü who had acquired the arts of the immortals. While traveling on the road to Han-t'an,[1] he stopped at an inn to rest. Taking off his cap and loosening his belt, he sat down and leaned up against his pack. Suddenly he saw a young traveler, one Mr. Lu. He was wearing a short robe[2] and riding a black colt, and had also stopped at the inn on his way to the fields. He sat down on the same mat as the old man and they chatted and laughed amicably.

After a while Lu, looking at the shabbiness of his own dress, sighed and said, "A great man born out of his time; such is my distress!"

"To look at you, you don't seem to be suffering or ill," the old man said. "Just now we were chatting away happily; why do you suddenly moan about your distress?"

"But mine is such an insignificant life! How can you speak of being happy?"

"If yours can't be called a happy life, then what is a happy life?"

"A man is born to do great deeds and build a name for himself, to be a general in the field and a minister at court, to eat from lavish dishes, listen to beautiful sounds, to bring glory to his clan and prosperity to his family. Only after this can one speak of happiness! I've 'set my heart upon learning' and have been enriched by engaging in the arts.[3] All these years I've considered that the blue and purple official robes were mine for the taking. Now I'm already at my prime and still I toil in the fields and ditches. If this is not distress, what is it?" Having finished this speech the young man's eyes grew blurry and he felt sleepy.

At that time the innkeeper was steaming some millet. The old man reached into his pack, took out a pillow, and gave it to Lu, saying, "Rest your head on this pillow. It'll surely allow you to experience a kind of success as full of splendor as that which you've set your heart upon."

The pillow was made of blue porcelain, and

[1] Han-t'an, located in the southwestern part of the present Hopei Province, was the capital of the state of Chao in the Warring States period. This placename alludes to the story told by Prince Mou of Wei to the logician Kung-sun Lung about a young boy from Shou-ling (of the state of Yen) who went to Han-t'an to learn the local style of walking. Before mastering it, however, he forgot his former method and was forced to crawl home (see the "Autumn Floods" chapter of *Chuang-tzu*). The lesson of this parable is reminiscent of that taught by the old Taoist in the present story and may be intended to reinforce the message.

[2] Such apparel indicated the status of a commoner; officials wore long robes.

[3] Paraphrasing maxims of Confucius in the *Analects*.

there was an opening at each end. The young man nodded his head and lay down on it; then he noticed that the apertures were becoming large and bright. He stood up, walked into the pillow, and found himself getting back to his own home.

Several months later he married a girl of the Ts'ui family from Ch'ing-ho.[4] The girl was extremely beautiful, and the young man became wealthy. He was greatly content. His clothes and equipage grew daily more bright and splendid. The following year he participated in the *chin-shih* examination, passed, and put on the robe of collator in the Department of the Imperial Library. By imperial order he was then transferred to be the magistrate of Wei-nan County.[5] Soon he was promoted to investigating censor, and then moved to be a diarist of imperial activity and repose and the director of decrees. Three years thereafter he was sent out to take charge of the prefecture of T'ung-chou,[6] then transferred to become the prefect of Shen-chou.[7] He had a natural proclivity for construction work and built a canal from Shen-chou to a point eighty *li* west to bypass some impassable spots in the river. The people of the area so profited thereby that they erected a stone tablet to record his accomplishments. He was given charge of the prefecture of Pien-chou,[8] then received the position of the investigating commissioner of the Ho-nan Circuit, and was later summoned to be the mayor of the capital.

That year the Spiritual and Martial Emperor[9] planned to engage the western and northern barbarians and thereby increase his lands. Then the Tibetan generals Stagra [Konlog] (Hsi-mo-lo [Kung-lu]) and Čogro Manpoči (Chu-lung Man-

pu-chi) attacked the prefectures of Kua-chou and Sha-chou.[10] The regional commander, Wang Chün-ts'u, had just recently been killed,[11] and the entire area between the Yellow River and the Huang River was in turmoil. The emperor, in search of a capable commander, appointed Lu as vice-president of the Censorate and regional commander of the Ho-hsi Circuit.[12] Lu routed the barbarian rabble, cutting off seven thousand heads and opening up nine hundred *li* of land. Then he had three great fortifications built to protect the strategic positions. The people living along the frontier set up a tablet at the Chu-yen Mountain[13] to commend him. When he returned to court, his merits were recorded by the official historians and his rewards were extremely handsome. He was transferred to be the second minister of the Ministry of Personnel, and was later made concurrently the head of the Ministry of Finance and the president of the Censorate. His contemporaries viewed him as pure and dignified; the people loved his bearing and majesty.

His success, however, was envied by the prime minister, who attacked him with unfounded slander and caused his demotion to prefect of Tuan-chou.[14] After three years he was summoned to become a counselor to the emperor, and before long became the prime minister. Together with Hsiao Sung, the president of the Department of the Secretariat, and P'ei Kuang-t'ing, the president of the Department of the Chancellery,[15] he

---

[4] This clan from Ch'ing-ho (in modern Hopei) was one of the "seven great surnames" of the T'ang period. Marriage to a girl of one of these families was considered a most important first step to making one's career and fortune.

[5] In modern Shensi Province.

[6] In modern Shensi Province.

[7] In modern Honan Province.

[8] The modern K'ai-feng in the present Honan Province.

[9] A reference to Emperor Hsüan-tsung (r. 712–756).

[10] Both of these places are in the present Kansu Province, with Sha-chou much better known under its later name, Tun-huang. Given the high degree of actuality in the historical data used in this story, "Kua-Sha" may be the corruption of "Kua-chou," as historically only Kua-chou was attacked by the Tibetans in 727.

[11] Historically, Wang Chün-ts'u was indeed killed in 727.

[12] The Ho-hsi Circuit refers to the area to the west of the Yellow River, covering parts of modern Shensi, Kansu, and Inner Mongolia.

[13] In modern Kansu Province.

[14] In modern Kwangtung Province—a very remote area in T'ang times.

[15] Historically, Hsiao Sung was appointed the president of the Department of the Secretariat in mid-729, and P'ei Kuang-

controlled major policy for the next dozen years. He saw the emperor three times a day with excellent plans and secret orders, and by presenting what needed to be revised or renewed, he became recognized as a capable prime minister.

Then his colleagues cast aspersions on him, accusing him of being in league with border commanders and plotting rebellion. An edict ordered that he be imprisoned; officers led their men to his door, and he was quickly restrained. He was extremely frightened at this sudden turn of events and said to his wife, "At my home in Shantung I have about five hundred *mou* of fine land, enough to protect us from hunger and cold. What affliction could have caused me to seek an official's salary? Now that things have come to this, I long to put on that short coarse robe again and ride that black colt back down the road to Han-t'an, but it's impossible." Then he drew his knife and was about to slit his throat, but his wife stopped him in time. All others implicated died, but he was protected by the eunuchs so that his death sentence was commuted. He was then banished to the prefecture of Huan-chou.[16] After a few years the emperor learned that the charges were false and again sought him out to be the president of the Department of the Secretariat, enfeoffed him as duke of Yen, and favored him exceedingly.

He had five sons—Chien, Ch'uan, Wei, T'i, and Yi—all capable and talented. Chien passed the *chin-shih* examination and became an auxiliary secretary in the Bureau of Scrutiny in the Ministry of Personnel. Ch'uan became a censor in the Bureau of General Affairs of the Censorate. Wei was made an assistant in the Office of Imperial Sacrifices, and T'i the magistrate of Wan-nien

County.[17] Yi was most virtuous, becoming a vice-president of the Department of State Affairs at the age of twenty-eight. Lu's in-laws were all of the most respected families in the empire, and he had over a dozen grandsons.

Twice banished to the barren frontiers, Lu returned both times as a pillar of the state. Into the provinces and back to the capital, roundabout the various offices and ministries, for over fifty years mighty and grand, Lu was naturally inclined to extravagance and luxury, fond of indulgence and pleasure. The sounds and sights of his harem were all of the uppermost beauty. Those fine lands, excellent mansions, beautiful women, and celebrated steeds presented to him through the years were too numerous to tally.

In his later years he gradually became debilitated and often asked to be relieved of his posts, but this was not allowed. When he was ill, envoys from court would come to ask after him so frequently that they trod in one another's footsteps. Every famous physician and exalted medicine made its way to him. On the point of dying, he submitted the following memorandum:

Your servant was originally a student from Shantung, with fields and gardens as his pleasures. By chance he encountered this divine fate and has obtained a series of official posts. Too many have been the special rewards received, of particular bounty the extensive favor shown. As he went out from the capital he was thronged by banners of an imperial representative; on returning he was elevated to be the prime minister. In handling business both in and out of the central court, he has passed through many years. Ashamed of the imperial favor he has enjoyed, he has been of no aid to the morally efficacious emanations of Your Majesty. A base fellow playing a gentleman's role, he has bequeathed only plunder; treading as if on thin ice, he has increased his misgivings, so that, as each day he dreads the next, old age has arrived unawares.[18] This year he will pass eighty still holding highest possible govern-

---

t'ing was made the president of the Department of the Chancellery in early 730. The use of such data greatly enhances the reality of the dream world described in this story and tactfully places Lu's prime ministership at the same time, a time slot that neatly fits the chronological sequence of the story.

[16] In modern Vietnam.

[17] In the present Shensi Province.
[18] Again paraphrasing Confucius.

ment post. His time has already run out; muscle and bone have already grown infirm. He senses that there will be no recovery; his health is failing fast, his time of service nearing its end. He considers that there is no deed which can repay the blessings of Your Majesty. In vain has he carried the imperial favor. Now he takes leaves forever of the saintly reign. Although his feeling of attachment is unbounded, he respectfully offers this memorandum to express his gratitude.

The reply read:

With your eminent virtue you have served as our chief support. Outside the central court, you have screened us like a hedge, upheld us like a buttress. In the central court, you have assisted us in bringing about harmony and prosperity. The tranquility and peace of the last two dozen years have truly been in your trust. When you contracted this illness, we daily expressed our hope of your recovery. Not expecting this grave infirmity, we are truly taken with sympathy. Now we have ordered the Grand General of Cavalry, Kao Li-shih,[19] to go to your house, ask after you,

and report to us. May we press you to take extra care of yourself for our sake. We especially hope for nothing rash, and await your recovery.

That evening he died.

With a yawn Lu stretched and awoke to find himself lying in the inn. The oldster was sitting beside him and the millet which the host had been steaming was not yet ready. Everything was as before. He got up with a start. "Could it all have been a dream?"

"The happinesses of human life are all like that," the old man replied.

Lu sat lost in thought for a long time, and then thanked the old man; "Of the ways of favor and disgrace, the vagaries of distress and prosperity, the patterns of accomplishment and failure, the emotions of life and death, I have thoroughly been made aware. In this way, sir, you have checked my desires. How could I dare fail to profit from this lesson?"

Then he bowed and left.

---

[19] Kao Li-shih was the most trusted eunuch of Emperor Hsüan-tsung. He was given this lavish title in 748. The mention of his name is significant in this context because it suggests the esteem the emperor had for Lu.

SCHOLAR CHANG

From *Tsüan-i chi*

TRANSLATED BY DONALD E. GJERTSON

There was once a man by the name of Chang who lived at Red Castle Slope, northeast of Chung-mou County in Pien-chou. Since he was very poor, he parted with his wife and children and went to the north of the Yellow River.[1] Five long years passed before he returned. On his way from north of the river to Pien-chou, he went out of the gate of Chen-chou in the evening; by the time he reached Pan-ch'iao, it was already dark. So he left the main road and took a shortcut along the hillside to return home.

Suddenly off in a thicket he saw some brightly burning lamps and five or six people in the midst of a drinking party. Chang got down from his donkey and approached them; while he was still more than ten paces away, he saw his wife among them, joking and laughing happily with the others. Chang then hid himself among some white poplars to spy on them.

He saw a man with a long beard who raised his cup and said, "Please, madam, sing for us."

Chang's wife was from a scholarly family, and from an early age she had studied literature. She therefore knew a great many songs. She did not want to sing for them, but being earnestly entreated from all sides, she finally sang:

Sighing for the withered grass,
How mournful is the cricket's tune.
My husband has gone and not yet returned.
Tonight, as I sit in sadness, my temples are as white as snow.

"In appreciation of your song, I'll cheer you up with a cup of wine," said the man with a long beard.

When she had finished drinking, the wine was passed to a young man with a light complexion. He again asked her to sing.

"Once is more than enough," Chang's wife protested. "How can you ask me again?"

The man with a long beard gestured with a bamboo chopstick and said, "Set out the pitcher! Anyone who refuses a request to sing has to drink a cup. And anyone who sings any humorous parts out of old songs has to pay the same penalty." Thereupon, Chang's wife sang again:

Have a drink;
Don't decline.
Falling blossoms have encircled the branch in vain;
Flowing waters will never return.
Trust not your youth;
How long can it last?

The wine came to a man in purple dress, and he, too, raised his cup and requested a song.

[1] Apparently to make a living.

439

Chang's wife was not pleased, but after pondering for a while, she finally sang:

I hate the empty chamber,
And in autumn, the days never seem to end.
No news from my groom,
And in the distant sky, the wild geese travel in vain. [2]

The wine came to a foreigner in black dress, who also requested a song. Chang's wife had already sung three or four songs in a row and was slightly out of breath. When she was still hesitating, the one with a long beard pushed the pitcher toward her and said, "You shouldn't refuse, so you're fined a cup!" Chang's wife sobbed and drank, and then sang while passing the wine to the foreigner:

Mournful and urgent is the evening wind;
Dew has moistened the grass in the courtyard.
My husband has gone and not yet returned;
How could he know that I often cry in my closed chamber?

The wine came to a youth in green dress. He raised his cup and said, "The night is already late. I fear we cannot linger for much longer, so please don't refuse to sing us another song." Again Chang's wife sang:

The light of the fireflies threads through the white poplars;
The sad wind pierces the wild grass.
I wonder if I'm traveling in a dream,
And grief has pervaded the old garden path.

The wine came to Chang's wife, and the man with a long beard sang as he passed it to her:

[2] The wild goose, in addition to being associated with the autumn season, is believed to be the carrier of messages between travelers and their folks, back home or elsewhere.

Before the blossoms we met
Beneath the blossoms we parted.
Why must you speak of being in a dream,
When all of life is but a dream?

When the wine came back to the foreigner in purple dress, he again requested a song. "This time, make it seductive," he added. Chang's wife lowered her head, and before she began to sing, the man with a long beard again pushed the pitcher toward her.

At that Chang became angry, and feeling around his feet, he found a tile. He threw it and hit the fellow with a beard right on the head. He threw a second tile, but this time it hit his wife on the forehead. Suddenly everything became quiet, and there was nothing to be seen.

Chang thought his wife had died; so crying bitterly he resumed his journey throughout the night. In the morning he reached home. Members of his household came out to welcome him in astonishment and delight. When he inquired about his wife, a maidservant said, "Mistress has had a headache since last night." Chang went into the room and asked his wife the cause of her complaint.

"Last night," his wife said, "I dreamed that I was in a thicket, where there six or seven fellows who one after another kept pressing me to drink and urging me to sing. In all, I sang six or seven songs. There was a fellow with a long beard who kept pushing the pitcher to me. While we were drinking, some tiles came flying in. The second one hit me on the forehead. I awoke with a start, and had a headache."

Chang then realized that what he had seen the night before had been his wife's dream.

THE ARCHETYPAL QUESTING MAN

The archetypal questing man is a selfless seeker of supernatural power through an exceedingly difficult journey for the salvation of someone else. Although not quite identical to quests in Western literature, the journeys of Maudgalyayana and Lord Pao do share a number of similarities with their Western counterparts: departure from the human world, elaborate preparation (in Maudgalyayana's case, nothing less than the attainment of arhatship), initial failures and eventual success in enlisting help from the supreme deity (in both cases, none other than the Buddha), the acquisition of power to overcome the obstacles (the cat in the Lord Pao story, the ability to change the attitude of his mother in the Maudgalyayana story), return to the starting point (Lord Pao) or journey on to another place of guaranteed happiness (Maudgalyayana).

What makes their journeys remarkable is the selfless nature of their goals. The seekers in question are not after anything for their own benefit, and they gain little after the journey. Lord Pao is Justice Incarnate, the Bestower of Light in a world of darkness. Maudglyayana's purpose may be more personal, for the one he originally intends to redeem is his mother. But as he descends into hell, he is moved by the sorrowful sight of the condemned. Thus, besides saving his mother, Maudglyayana is instrumental in bringing about the eventual salvation of many a pitiful soul on the River of Futility. Their objectives being so honorable, assistance from the supreme deity is only a formality once their sincerity has been tested and proven. Their initial failures and obstacles can thus be seen more as initiation rites for the archetypal questing man than as a trial of faith.

THE GREAT MAUDGALYAYANA RESCUES HIS MOTHER FROM HELL

From the Tun-huang *Pien-wen* Manuscript P2319

TRANSLATED BY EUGENE EOYANG

Now on the fifteenth day of the seventh month, the heavens open up, the gates of hell swing wide, the karma of the Three Paths [of Pain][1] is dissolved, and the Ten Commandments[2] overflow. The assembly of monks [*sangha*] has set down this date as a holy day of thanksgiving, and so the eight classes of supernatural beings[3] all come to observe this occasion. The assembly makes offerings of its worldly goods so that those who have passed away may change their fate and improve their lot. For this reason, on the Avalamba Festival[4] we offer up a hundred tasty sacrifices to the Honorable Triad[5] in supplication for divine mercy on the entire congregation, and first to rescue those who hang upside down from their distress.[6]

Long ago, when Buddha lived in this world, he had a disciple, Mu-lien [Maudgalyayana],[7] whose secular name, before he joined the order, was Lo-pu. Mu-lien was deeply committed to the Three Treasures,[8] and revered the Greater Vehicle [Mahayana].[9] Once he wanted to go to another country for new adventures, so he divided up his

[1] They are the hell of fires, the hell of blood, and the Asipattra Hell of Swords.

[2] They are the opposites of killing, stealing, adultery, lying, speaking with a double tongue, slandering, filthy language, covetousness, anger, and perverted views.

[3] They are the eight classes of supernatural beings mentioned in the *Lotus Sutra: deva* (celestial spirits), *naga* (dragons), *yaksha* (demons in earth, air, and hell), *gandharva* (musicians of the Shakra heaven—one of the eight heavens), *asura* (war demons), *garuda* (mythical birds), *kinnara* (musicians with men's bodies and horses' heads), and *mahoraga* (demons shaped like the boa).

[4] This festival of all souls (*Yü-lan hui* in Chinese) takes place on the fifteenth of the seventh month, when prayer services are said by Buddhist monks and Taoist priests and elaborate offerings are made to the Buddhist triad (see footnote 5) for the purpose of releasing from the purgatory the souls of those who have died on land and sea.

[5] The Buddha, the Law, and the Ecclesia.

[6] Hanging upside down refers to the condition of certain condemned souls, especially those for whom the Festival of Avalamba is held.

[7] Maudgalyayana (or Maha-Maudgalyayana, or Maudgalaputra), noted for his miraculous powers, was one of the ten disciples of Shakyamuni (*Shih-chia-mou-ni* in Chinese), the principal Buddha. Formerly an ascetic, Maudgalyayana agreed with Shariputra, another major disciple of the Buddha known for his wisdom and learning, that whoever first found the truth would reveal it to the other. In Buddhist iconography, Shariputra appears on Buddha's right, Maudgalyayana on his left.

[8] Same as the Buddhist triad.

[9] The Mahayana school is one of the main traditions of Buddhism. It is now made up of various syncretistic sects found chiefly in Tibet, Nepal, China, and Japan. Emphasis is placed on compassion, universal salvation, enlightenment, and wisdom.

443

worldy possessions. He instructed his mother to initiate offerings, supplying provisions to wandering Buddhist monks as well as any other mendicants who came by. But after Lo-pu left, his mother became stingy and selfish, and the wealth which had been entrusted to her was secretly hidden away. Her son, in the course of time, completed his travels and returned home. The mother told the son, "I have, as you instructed, given alms and built up our blessings." And so, because she had deceived both the secular and the holy community, she dropped straight away down to the Avichi Hell[10] to suffer innumerable tortures after she died.

Lo-pu, after three years of mourning, offered himself to the service of Buddha, was admitted into the holy order, and devoted himself to religious practices. By obeying the Law, he attained the blessed state of an arhat in the end.[11] Then, with his transcendent eyes, he looked all over for his dear mother, but in all the six realms of life and death,[12] there was no trace of her. Mu-lien consulted the World-Honored One [the Buddha]: "Where is my good mother enjoying eternal bliss?"

To this, the World-Honored One answered Mu-lien, "Your mother has already descended down to the Avichi Hell, where she is suffering innumerable tortures. Although you've attained the heights of arhatship, what can you do? Only the efforts of the assembled monks from all directions[13] on the day of the summer sacrifices, with their cumulative strength, can save her. This is why the Buddha, in his compassion, instituted this means, and established the Festival of the Avalamba especially for this purpose."

Lo-pu from the time his parents died[14]
Mourned three years until the obligation was over.
To hear music and not rejoice spoils one's appearance;
To eat delicacies and not find them tasty is bad for flesh and bone.
It is said that the Tathagata [the Buddha], when he was in the Deer Park,[15]
Took pity at once on all the people of the world.
Today, I search for the Way in order to find the Tathagata,
And go to the Twin Grove[16] to ask the Buddha, etc., etc.[17]
[40 lines][18]

On the day when Mu-lien went to the trees in the Twin Grove, he [had already] become an arhat. How did this come about? Truly the *Lotus Sutra* says, "The ranks of the poor first accept the value, then dispose of the wastes." This is it. First one attains arhatship, then one follows the Way. Look at Mu-lien, sitting deep in the mountains in attitudes of meditation! His father was living in Devapura.[19]

Mu-lien cut off his hair, shaved his head,
And thereupon went deep into the mountains.
Dark and deep, where it was quiet, with no one around.

[10] The Avichi Hell, the last and deepest of the eight hot hells (vs. the eight cold hells), is the place where the condemned go through endless cycles of suffering, death, and rebirth without intermission.

[11] An arhat is one who has acquired transcendent powers over nature, matter, time, and space. Arhatship is to be succeeded either by buddhahood or by immediate entrance into nirvana (the state of perfect freedom and the absorption of the individual into the supreme spirit).

[12] These represent the six directions of reincarnation, i.e., three upper forms (the spirits of heaven, men, and awesome demons), and three lower forms (animals, hungry ghosts, and denizens of hell).

[13] The text reads "the ten directions," which include the four cardinal and the four intercardinal directions as well as "up" and "down."

[14] In the manuscript P2319, the verse lines appear in a run-on pattern, with no space between the lines.

[15] The Deer Park (also known as Mrigadava), the site of the Buddha's famous first sermon, was a retreat of the wise.

[16] The sal trees under which the Buddha entered nirvana.

[17] "Etc., etc." (*yün, yün* in Chinese) is a formula used in the text to indicate either an opportunity for further elaboration or an omission.

[18] The figure indicates the number of lines found in the other scrolls, particularly the contextually more complicated S2614, but not in P2319.

[19] Devapura (or Devaloka) is the palace of the devas (the heavenly beings) and the abode of the gods. This sentence is not in the *Tun-huang pien-wen chi*.

There he sat down, facing the void, in meditation, etc., etc.
[20 lines]
From the moment Mu-lien emerged from meditation,
He quickly achieved supernatural power.
He came as suddenly as a clap of thunder,
And went away like the whirlwind.
[4 lines]
With the supernatural status, he achieved spontaneity;
Throwing his magical begging bowl [in the sky], he leaped into
heaven.
In almost no time, he went
All the way up to the realm of Brahma,[20] etc, etc.
[39 lines]

Mu-lien went to Devapura to look for his father. At one gate, he met an old man, to whom he said, "I, a poor monk, was named Lo-pu when I was young. After my parents passed away, I left home and entered the order of Buddha, cutting off my hair and shaving my beard. I'm now known as Great Maudgalyayana, and I'm well known for my supernatural power."

When the old man was told Mu-lien's childhood name, he knew that he was his son. "It's been so long since we last saw each other. How have you been?"

Lo-pu, or Mu-lien, recognized his good father and, after inquiring as to his welfare, asked, "And my good mother, where is she now receiving the rewards of happiness?"

"Your mother's karma," the old man answered, "while she lived, was different from mine. I observed the Ten Commandments, and obeyed the Five Prohibitions,[21] and so when I died my spirit lived on in heaven. But your mother, all the days of her life, committed numerous sins; so when she died, she dropped down to hell. Ask around for your mother in the dark alleys of Jambudvipa."[22]

After hearing this, Mu-lien said farewell to his father and descended from heaven. But he was

unable to find his mother. Instead, he saw eight or nine men and women who were wandering around with nothing to do. Mu-lien stepped forward and asked their business and where they came from:

"No, no! Don't bow toward me.
Good souls, who are you?
Why are you all milling around here,
Wandering about with nothing to do?"
[3 lines]
They replied, telling the monk:
"It's only because we have the same surnames and given
names,
That our names were confused, and we were summoned here.
We wandered around for a few days.
Proven innocent, we were released, and then went home,
But we had been buried prematurely by our families.
[11 lines]
To moan and bewail our fate does no good in the end.
[1 line]
Please go to tell the men and women in our families,
Tell them to perform good works to save the dead from
misfortune," etc., etc.

Mu-lien remained silent for a while, and then he said, "Do you know [a certain] Lady Ch'ing-t'i?"

"No one among us knows her," they replied.

"Where does the Yama King live?" Mu-lien then asked.

"Your Reverence," they answered, "go north several steps further, and you'll see in the distance a triple-layered gate, guarded by thousands of strong men, all wielding swords and staffs. This is the gate of the Yama King."

Mu-lien, upon hearing this, went north several paces and then saw the triple-layered gate, where the strong men were herding and prodding numberless sinners and driving them in. Mu-lien went forward looking for his mother and, not being able to find her, he stood by the side of the road and cried loudly. Afterward he dried his tears and proceeded forward. After explaining why he was

[20] Brahma is the father of all living beings.
[21] The first five of the Ten Commandments.
[22] Jambudvipa is the southern one of the four continents which, according to Indian mythology, comprise the world.

445

there, he was permitted an audience with the king. The gatekeeper let him in to see the king, who asked him to state his business.

When the king saw Mu-lien come in,
He clasped his hands, shrank back, and nearly stood.
"Your Reverence, you couldn't have any business here!"
Then, hastily behind the desks, the two bowed to each other,
    etc., etc.
[*29 lines*]

When Mu-lien had finished, the king called him up the dais to meet the Bodhisattva Kshitigarbha,[23] and Mu-lien paid his respects.

"You've come to look for your mother?"

"Yes, I've come to look for my mother."

"Your mother committed many sins when she was alive; she was completely and utterly evil, and must have dropped down to [hell]. You just go on, I'll be there right away."

The king then summoned the keeper of karma, the commissioner of fate, and the custodian of records, who all responded immediately and came before him.

"This monk's mother is Lady Ch'ing-t'i. How long ago did she die?"

"Your Majesty," the keeper of karma said, "Lady Ch'ing-t'i has already been dead now for three years. The record of her penance is filed with the recorder of the Heavenly Court as well as the commandant of the T'ai Mountains."[24] The king summoned the two boys who respectively record good and evil deeds and sent them to the T'ai Mountains to check out which hell Lady Ch'ing-t'i was in. The king added, "Your Reverence, you'd better go along with these two boys,

and ask the General of the Five Ways.[25] He should know where she's gone."

When Mu-lien heard this, he took his leave of the king and went out. Before he had gone but a few steps, he came upon the River of Futility.[26] There he saw countless sinners who had doffed their clothes and hung them up on the trees, crying over and over again in loud lament, wanting to cross the river but unable to, pacing back and forth, at sixes and sevens, holding their heads and sobbing. Mu-lien asked them what had happened:

"The waters of Futility rush toward the west;
Shattered rock, jagged cliffs—the way is rough.
Clothes taken off and hung on tree branches;
We have not been transferred, and must stay here.
By the riverbank we ask that our names be called;[27]
Without our knowing it, our chests are soaked through.
Only today we've come to realize what death means.
Two by two, under the trees, our tears of grief stream down.
[*18 lines*]
Oxhead demons, staffs in hand, on the southern bank;
Hell's guardians, wielding tridents, on the northern shore.
The eyes of those in the water bulge out;
The tears of those on the riverbank gush forth.
Had we known how bitter death would be,
How would we not have cultivated good deeds in life!"

Mu-lien then asked those who stood under the trees by the River of Futility:

So heaven and hell are no fairy tale!
For those who sin and do not care, the punishment of heaven.
[*1 line*]
"I had a mother without much merit.
Her departed soul, therefore, dropped down here to the Three
    Paths;
After hearing this, I've ventured to come down to hell.
Tell me if you have any news of her."
The sinners all looked at Master Mu-lien,

[23] Kshitigarbha, one of a group of eight Dhyani or Meditation Bodhisattvas, is the savior of lost souls and the deliverer from hell.

[24] Since the Han period, the worship of the T'ai Mountains was combined with the Buddhist concept of hell to place the god of the T'ai Mountains as the counterpart of the Yama King on earth; hence it is his line of duty to administer matters concerning life, death, reincarnation, the government of men and spirits.

[25] He is a general in the retinue of the ten kings of the underworld responsible for keeping the book of life. After the Sung period, this term is used to designate five individual spirits who were bandits in their former existence.

[26] This is the inevitable river in purgatory to be crossed by all souls.

[27] P2319 shows spaces between verse lines beginning at this point.

All weeping and sobbing both eyes sore:
"We have been dead only a very short time;
Your mother, good monk, we really don't know.
In life we all committed many sins;
Only in suffering today do we begin to repent.
You may have wives and concubines by the droves,
But who would be willing to die in your stead?
When you have departed from these depths,
Please report this to our sons and grandsons:
'Never mind the white jade for our coffins;
In vain, the yellow gold buried in our tombs.
Persistent mourning, signs of sorrow are of no use,
And tabor music, stringed dirges, we can't hear.
If you want to end our torment and suffering,
Nothing is better than works of charity to save lost souls.' "

"Your Reverence, please pass on the message for us, asking them to do more charity works in order to save the deceased. Aside from the Buddha himself, no one is able to save us. Good monk, we hope very much that [the boats of] your bodhi [perfect wisdom] and nirvana [perfect freedom] will constantly appear to deliver all the living beings. The sword of wisdom is to be constantly sharpened, and the grove of worries is to be cut down, so that majesty spreads to all the hearts of the world. This may well be the fulfillment of the ideal of all the Buddhas. If we are to be delivered from the mire and the mud, this is indeed due to the great benevolence of your kind mother."[28]

Mu-lien, after making inquiries, again went on.

[28] The reading adopted here is vastly different from that of the *Tun-huang pien-wen chi*, so far the most authoritative collection of *pien-wen* tales. The editors of that collection treated this paragraph as a descriptive passage rather than dialog, and made the following paragraph (as it is treated here) an uninterrupted part of the same passage. Their reading not only requires Mu-lien to go back to the human world right at this point (an illogical move according to the situation) to transmit the message, but also requires the speaker and the tone of all the subsequent sentences to be changed. On top of that, they mispunctuated quite a few sentences in the middle of the passage. That this passage is written in the direct speech and repeats in part the essence of the preceding rhyme passage is a good illustration of the fact that, in *pien-wen* literature, the contents of the rhyme passages and the prose passages often overlap.

In a short while, he arrived at the place of the General of the Five Ways; there he asked for news of his mother:

The General of the Five Ways had a hateful mien;
His gold armor glimmered and his sword dazzled,
Intimidating millions of souls around him—
All took flight on their hands and feet.
His call sounded like thundering earthquake;
His angry eyes flashed like blinding light.
Some had their chests cut open, their hearts exposed;
Others had the skins of their faces peeled.
Although Mu-lien was a sage,
He was scared to death.
[19 lines]
The general clasped his hands and said to the monk:
"Don't let tears spoil your manners;
Those who come this way are as many as the sands in the
*   Ganges.*
If I ask them about Lady Ch'ing-t'i, who may know the
*   answer?" etc., etc.*
[8 lines]

"Have any of you seen Lady Ch'ing-t'i?" the general asked those around him.

From the left, a chief officer answered, "General, three years ago, there was a certain Lady Ch'ing-t'i whose name was inscribed on the tablets of the Avichi Hell. Now she is suffering there."

Mu-lien, upon hearing this, said to the general, "Would you please tell me, although all sinners receive judgment before the [Yama] King before they are sent down here, why my mother has never been brought before the king?"

"Good monk," the general replied, "there are two kinds of people in the world who are not allowed an audience with the king. One includes those who have observed the Ten Commandments and the Five Prohibitions—these don't have to meet the king after their death, for their spirits will live on in heaven. The second category includes those who in their lives did not practice good deeds, but gave themselves to evil karma, so that when they die, they are sent forthwith into hell. They also do not see the king. Only those who are half good and half evil get to see the king to have their fate judged. They will first go through reincarnation, and then they will be rewarded or punished according to what they deserve."

After Mu-lien had heard this, he started to search through the various hells for his mother.

Mu-lien's tears flowed as he thought of the past;
The fate of all creatures seemed tossed on the wind.
His good mother came to death's vale of suffering;
Her spirit had long been wasted away, etc., etc.
[15 lines]

When Mu-lien had finished, he moved on, and in a wink, he reached one of the hells. Mu-lien inquired of the guardian, "Does this prison have a Lady Ch'ing-t'i or not? She is my mother, which is why I've come looking for her."

"Your Reverence," the guardian replied, "this prison is full of men; there are no women here. A little further ahead, there is the Asipattra Hell of Swords. If you ask there, you will, no doubt, get to see her."

Mu-lien went on, and came upon another hell; the left side was called the Mountain of Knives, and the right, the Forest of Swords. In this hell, the tips of swords were locked in confrontation, with blood dripping down. There [Mu-lien] saw the guardian pushing countless sinners into this hell.

"What is this hell?" Mu-lien asked.

"This is the Asipattra Hell of Swords," a raksha replied.

"What sins have been committed by the sinners here that they should be in this hell?" Mu-lien then asked.

"These sinners," the guardian said, "when they were alive, violated the temples, defiled the monasteries, and were fond of picking the fruits of the temples and stealing firewood and kindling from the temples. Now let them attempt to pull the sword trees with their hands; see if their limbs and joints can stay together."

The Mountain of Knives, bleached bones here and there;
The Forest of Swords, human heads by the millions.
If you want to put an end to the sinners' climbing the
*   Mountain of Knives,*
Nothing's better than cultivating the temple grounds.
Planting fruit trees within the monastery walls,
Liberally sowing seedlings to grace the temple.
Of course, you can't give pleasure to these sinners,
Who will forever suffer torments numberless as the sands of
*   Ganges.*
[9 lines]
Bronze-tipped arrows whizzing by straight into the eye—
Mountain of Knives, Forest of Swords, will cut us down.
Although they cannot return to life in a thousand years,
They still must suffer incessantly in the jungle of iron [knives
*   and swords].*

Mu-lien, when he heard this, broke down in tears and went forward to ask the guardian, "In this hell, is there a Lady Ch'ing-t'i?"

"Good monk, is she related to you?"

"She's my mother."

"Your Reverence," the guardian then replied, "in this hell there's no Lady Ch'ing-t'i, but if you go a little further, there is a hell which is only for women. You should get to see her there."

Mu-lien, on hearing this, went on ahead until he reached a hell that was a *yojana*[29] high from top to bottom, with black smoke gushing up, and a stench to stink up the sky. He came upon a horse-headed raksha with an iron staff in his hand, standing there looking haughtily.

"What's the name of this hell?" Mu-lien asked.

"This is the Hell of Bronze Pillars and Iron Beds," the raksha replied.

"What sins did these poor souls commit in life that they should have dropped down to this hell?"

"In life," the guardian replied, "girls who seduced boys, boys who lured girls, as well as parents and children who had incestuous rela-

[29] *Yojana* was a rather ambiguous unit of measurement. It has been described as the distance covered by a day's march of an army, and as forty, thirty, or sixteen *li*, and as eight *kroshas* (four *kroshas* being equivalent to nearly thirty *li*).

tions, teachers and students who had affairs, and masters and servants who had liaisons—they have all dropped down into this hell, where the east is separated from the west with men and women each occupying one division."

The women lie on the iron beds, their bodies nailed down:
The men are wrapped around the bronze pillars to rot.
[6 lines]
The knives cut bone and flesh, pierce right through;
The swords cut liver and gall into little pieces.
[3 lines]
Their parents, if still alive, are building up blessings for them,
But only one out of seven may be saved.
Even let the Eastern Sea turn into a mulberry field:
The sinners will have yet to be released, etc., etc.

When Mu-lien finished his inquiries, he went on ahead. In a twinkling of an eye, he was at another hell. There, he asked the guardian, "Does this place have a Lady Ch'ing-t'i in it?"

"Good monk," the guardian said, "is Lady Ch'ing-t'i your mother?"

"Yes, she's my mother."

"Three years ago, there was a Lady Ch'ing-t'i who was among those who dropped down here, but she was put on the roster for the Avichi Hell. So now she is over there."

Mu-lien fainted for a moment. He resumed his normal breath after a long while, and then slowly went on ahead. Then he ran into a raksha, who guarded the way. Mu-lien questioned him [and the raksha replied]:

[24 lines]
"It appears we have a Lady Ch'ing-t'i here,
Though I can't completely confirm that report.
[2 lines]
Bodies of new arrivals were strewn about.
Please take my advice and go back home.
To look for someone here is to look in vain.
You'd better go quickly to see the Tathagata;
What use is there in beating your breast in despair?"

After Mu-lien learned of all these obstacles in the [various] hells, he immediately turned back.

Then, sailing up with his magic begging bowl, in a wink, he was in the Grove of Brahma, where he circled the Buddha three times before sitting down in front of him. He looked up in reverence at the honored visage, his eyes not wavering. There, he spoke to the World-Honored One:

It's been a long time since I received instructions from the
*   Tathagata;*
Throughout heaven and earth, I've constantly searched.
Only my father has been able to live in heaven,
But my mother I haven't been able to meet face-to-face.
When I heard she was suffering torments in the Avichi Hell,
The mere thought of her wrenched me inside.
Raging fires, dragon serpents obstruct my progress:
In my consternation, I can think of no other way.
The Tathagata's holy power moves mountains and oceans.
All living creatures usually benefit from his benevolence.
So I have hurried here to have you explain
How mother and son can meet once again."
The World-Honored One comforted the Great Maudgal-
*   yayana:*
"Now, please, stop your tears of grief.
The sins of the world are drawn out like string:
They don't result from outside pressures.
Someone hurry to bring him my abbot's staff;
It can ward off the Eight Obstacles,[30] the Three Calamities.[31]
As often as possible, chant my name;
All the hells should be accessible to you."

Mu-lien assumed the Buddha's power, soared away, and went down as fast as a windborne arrow. In a wink, he reached the Avichi Hell. Still in the sky, he saw fifty oxhead, horse-brained rakshas and yakshas, with teeth like jagged stumps, mouths like bowls of blood, voices like thun-

[30] This term refers to the eight conditions in which it is difficult for someone to see the Buddha or to hear his Dharma (Law)—in the hells; as hungry ghosts; as animals; in Uttarakuru (the northern continent where all is pleasant); in the long-life heavens; as deaf, blind, and dumb; as a philosopher on earth; in the intermediate period between a Buddha and his successor.

[31] There are two kinds of calamities. The minor three calamities, appearing during a decadent period in the world, are war, pestilence, and famine; the major ones, for the destruction of the world, are fire, water, and wind.

449

derclaps, eyes like flashes of lightning on their way to heaven to report for duty. When they encountered Mu-lien, they yelled at him from afar: "Good monk! Don't come to these regions. This is not a good place to come to. This is the road to hell. In the west, there is black smoke full of hell's poisonous vapors; if you inhale it, Your Reverence, here and now you will turn to ashes and dust."

"Good monk, haven't you heard about the Avichi Hell?
Even iron and rock, in passing through it, will not be spared.
Where is the hell one speaks of?
Toward the west, black fumes spurt forth over there."
Mu-lien chanted Buddha's name countless times;
"Hell was once my domain."
Then he wiped his tears and shook the staff in the air,
And all the demons fell like puffballs on the spot.
Sweat poured out like moisture from rainfall;
Bewildered, hardly conscious, they could not help but sigh.
Three-pronged halberds dropped from their hands;
Six-pointed pitchforks flew out of their arms.
"Buddha has sent me to see my mother,
To save her from the calamities of the Avichi Hell."
Mu-lien did not stay still, but soared right over;
The lictors of hell looked, but didn't dare block his way.

Mu-lien went on ahead until he reached another [part of the Avichi] hell. When he was about one hundred steps away, he was so overcome by fire and smoke that he almost fainted away. This Avichi Hell had iron walls that were high and steep, so tall that they almost touched the sky. The horrors within were beyond description.[32] All of [the lictors] were oxheads and horsefaces. Even hearts of iron and stone would quake with fear and lose their souls.

Mu-lien, holding his staff, moved forward to listen,
To learn something about the turns for the better in the Avichi
* Hell.*
In most hells there would normally be some rest,

[32] This sentence seems to occur only in P2319, which does not have the more than five lines of prose represented by lines 2–7 of the text (largely based on S2614) on p. 731 of the *Tun-huang pien-wen chi.*

But in this Avichi Hell, there was no such respite.
[32 lines]
Suddenly, they spied the monk standing there;
Moreover, they had never made his acquaintance.
Certainly no one person could be held to account,
Only the merciful power of the Three Treasures.

"Good monk," the guardian of this hell asked, "what business do you have here that you should open the gates of hell?"

"The World-Honored One gave me the means to open them."[33]

"What did he give you to open them with?"

"He gave me his twelve-ringed abbot's staff to open the gates."

"Good monk," the lictors, too, asked, "what is your reason for coming here?"

"My mother is named Lady Ch'ing-t'i," Mu-lien replied, "and I have come to look for her."

When the guardian heard this, he went up to a high tower in the hell compound, raised a white flag, and beat on an iron drum. "Is there a Lady Ch'ing-t'i in the first cell?"

No answer from the first.

He went to the second cell, then to the third, the fourth, the fifth, and the sixth—and the answer was no each time.[34] The lictors went to the seventh cell and saw Lady Ch'ing-t'i nailed down on a platform with forty-nine spikes, and called out, "Are you Lady Ch'ing-t'i?"

"Yes," she said.[35]

Then the guardian told her, "There's a monk outside who claims to be your son."

[33] The *Tun-huang pien-wen chi* reads: "If I didn't open them, who would? The World-Honored One gave me the means to open them." P2319 omits the first sentence.

[34] The corresponding passage in the *Tun-huang pien-wen chi* is much more complicated. In this text the guardian checks through the second cell all the way to the sixth one, asking the same question and going through the same flag waving (though with different flags at different cells) and drum beating procedure. He received the same negative answer.

[35] Here the *Tun-huang pien-wen chi* reads:
"If you're looking for Lady Ch'ing-t'i, that's me."
"Why didn't you answer me earlier?"
"I was afraid that you might want to take me to another place for torture. That's why I didn't answer your call."

Ch'ing-t'i, when she heard this, replied, "Guardian, I have no son who is a monk. He must be mistaken."

When the guardian heard this, he returned to the high tower to report: "Your Reverence, how could you have made such an error, taking that sinner in the hell as your mother? What's the reason for this nonsense?"

Mu-lien, when he heard this, broke down in tears. He told the guardian, "I was called Lo-pu when I was small. After my parents passed away, I entered the order of Buddha and became a monk, assuming the name of Great Maudgalyayana. I hope that you've not been put out and would go back once more to make the inquiry."

When the guardian heard this, he went back to the sinner: "The monk outside claims his name was Lo-pu when he was small."

"If he was called Lo-pu as a child," Ch'ing-t'i said, "then he is my son, my precious offspring, this sinner's own flesh and blood!"

Hearing this, the guardian helped lift Ch'ing-t'i up, drawing out the forty-nine spikes, tied iron chains around her waist, put shackles on her, and drove her outside the gate. This was how the mother and the son met.

The shackles around her, full of pricks as fish scales.
A thousand years of punishment that cannot be imagined.
From the seven apertures in the head, blood spurted forth;
Fire flared out from the woman's mouth.
[4 lines]
Oxheads held the cangue on both sides;
Stepping and stumbling, she came forward.
Mu-lien embraced his mother, bursting into tears,
And crying: "This comes from my not being a devoted son!"
etc., etc.
[97 lines]

His mother was then driven back into the cell.[36] When Mu-lien saw his mother go back in, his bones snapped, his heart broke, and he choked on his sobs. Then he stood up and beat his breast, as if the Five Mountains trembled, and the seven apertures in his head all gushed blood. In the end, he seemed to die, but in time revived, and he pushed himself off the ground with his arms and put his clothes in order. He then leaped into the sky and to the place of the World-Honored One.

Mu-lien's feelings were all in a turmoil.
What others said seemed blurred: he heard not at all.
After a long while, he woke with a revelation;
Throwing his begging bowl and leaping to the sky, he went to ask the Buddha.
Mu-lien told the Buddha all about his sorrow and suffering,
And spoke of the Mountain of Knives and the Forest of Swords.
"By the grace of Buddha's overwhelming power,
I have managed to see my mother in the Avichi Hell."
[16 lines]
"Your mother committed many sins in the life before,
So her soul went straight down to the Avichi Hell.
She can not absolve herself from sin, after all this time;
And no one but the Buddha, no ordinary mortal can understand all this."
Then he called Ananda [37] *and the other disciples:*
"I must go down to save her myself."

The Tathagata, leading the eight groups of supernatural beings, surrounded in front and back, shining forth radiance, shaking the ground, went to release the souls from suffering in hell:

The exalted wisdom of the Tathagata is equitable,
And in his compassion, he saves the multitude in hell.
Innumerable worthies, a congregation from all eight sectors,
Followed in procession and moved as one.
Deep and hidden [was the procession],
Heaven above, heaven below—nothing quite so extraordinary!
On the left, it was overwhelming; on the right, devastating:
Like mountain peaks peeking out from above the clouds.
High and lofty,
The vaults of heaven and of hell opened together;
Moving like rain, shaking like thunder,
Just like the moon rising round over the sea.
[2 lines]
In the clouds, heaven's music wafts on the willows;
On the air, a flurry of plum-blossoms floats down.

---

[36] This line only occurs in P2319.

[37] Ananda was the most learned disciple of the Buddha.

The Buddha-king steps forth, the jade tablet in hand;
The Brahma-lord from the rear holds the golden tablet.
What can't be fathomed can't be fathomed:
The transcendent power of the Tathagata liberates the hell.
Left and right, the supernatural beings of all classes;
Here and there, imperial guards of all directions.
In the Buddha's eyebrows flashed a thousand hues;
Behind his head, a halo-cloud in dazzling colors.
When the radiance permeates hell, it disintegrates—
The Forest of Swords, the Grove of Knives, crushed into dust.
The lictors of the hells, accepting grace, bow down on their
*   knees*
And clasp their hands in supplication to the Buddha.
[9 lines]
The sinners all gain rebirth in heaven;
Only Mu-lien's mother still goes hungry.[38]
Hell then is totally transformed;
In the end, the majesty of Shakyamuni prevails.

Mu-lien, beneficiary of Buddha's power, once again saw his beloved mother. But her sin was too deeply rooted, and her karma was difficult to cast off; although she was able to avoid the stench of hell, she nevertheless fell into the realm of the "hungry ghosts." Although the misery is greatly reduced, there is no comparison between the conditions of [the realms of] bitterness and happiness. If one walks ahead on the road [and anticipates her life], one feels the hardship increase a thousandfold. The throat feels like the tiny aperture of a needle, so small that water cannot drip through, while the head is like the T'ai Mountains, which [the waters of] three rivers are not enough to cover. Without one's even hearing so much as a hint of water and drink, the months go by, the years pass, and the miseries of starvation must be endured. From a distance, pure, cool, refreshing waters can be seen, but up close, they turn into a pus flow. Delicious food, delectable meals, turn into blazing fire.

[Lady Ch'ing-t'i told her son,] "Your mother is suffering from hunger-pangs, and her life is

hanging by a thread. If you don't take pity on me, how can you possibly be called a devoted son? The paths of life and death are blocked off, and any future meeting is beyond prediction. If you wish to rescue someone from the perils of such emergency, the matter shouldn't be delayed. The life of monkhood is to rely on faith and devotion. Even though there will always be enough sustenance, I still fear that it is difficult for me to consume. Please, son, leave me, go to Rajagriha,[39] and see that I get something to eat."

Mu-lien took leave of his mother, tossed up his begging bowl, and ascended into the heavens. In a wink, he arrived in the city of Rajagriha. At one house after another, he begged for food, and came to the residence of an elder. Seeing that it was not the hour for begging, the elder stopped him and asked him the reason: "Good monk, breakfast is over and the time for eating has passed. What are you going to do with this food you're begging for?"

Mu-lien responded to him, "Worthy elder,

After she passed away, this monk's mother's
Soul was sent directly down to the Avichi Hell.
Of late the Tathagata saved her,
Her body all withered bones, her breath a wisp.
This poor monk's heart broke, bit by bit;
How could a bystander know the pain?
I know I have come at the wrong time to beg;
I only intend to bring my mother some food to eat."
When the elder heard this, he was startled,
His thoughts unsettled, his feelings uneasy.
[The elder's subordinates (?) said:]
"Golden saddles cannot touch the pearl-bright heart.
No reason to add makeup to a pretty face.
So, let us sing, let us be happy;
A man's life is as uncertain as a flickering candle.
No one sees those enjoying bliss in heaven;

---

[38] The *Tun-huang pien-wen chi* reads: "Only Mu-lien's mother became a hungry ghost."

[39] This ancient Indian city, a little to the southwest of the present city of Bihar, was important in early Buddhism. It was the site of the council that is said to have been held right after the death of the Buddha for the purpose of verifying the sayings of the Buddha and for establishing the basic disciplinary code.

We only hear of crowds of sinners in hell.
There's time to eat and time to clothe oneself.
Don't learn to hoard things like a fool:
Better build up karma for the time to come.
For who can guarantee life from day to day?
When two people meet, no one thinks of death;
Wealth and riches must not be spared for the body.
One day, we pass away and are placed in coffins.
What use is it to water the graves in vain?
Those who are wise use wealth to do charity,
Whereas fools use money to buy land and property.
All through life, one struggles in search of riches;
But after death, in the end, others will portion them out."
The elder, hearing these words, was started by doubt:
"The blessed land, the Three Treasures, are difficult to meet."
Hurriedly, he urged his subordinates not to waste any more
*   time;*
From the house, they took out food for the monk.
All of a sudden, hell disintegrated and dissolved,
Which even the bright-minded Buddhas find inconceivable.
The elder held offerings of food in his hands,
Went over to the monk, and wished him well:
"This is not just for Your Reverence to give to your mother,
But so that all the sinners can eat their fill."
After Mu-lien had received the delicious food,
He put the food in the begging bowl to tend to his mother.
Then he went to the wilderness [to meet his waiting mother],
And with a golden spoon, he fed her himself.

Although Lady Ch'ing-t'i had suffered the ordeals of hell, her stinginess and greed, in the end, had not been rooted out. When she saw her son coming with food, she succumbed to her miserliness and avarice: "The monk who comes is my son, and he is bringing for me the food he has collected from the world of humans. Now all of you have to be patient. I will tend to myself. There is little I can do for the rest of you."

Mu-lien took the food and offered it to her in his begging bowl. But his mother was afraid that someone might snatch it from her; so, glaring out at the companions all around her, she used her left hand to cover up the bowl, and scooped up the food with the right hand. Before the food reached her mouth, it turned into raging flame.

The devotion of the elder who had donated the food had been profound, but it was not enough to expiate a selfishness that was deeply ingrained.

When Mu-lien saw his mother like this, his insides were unstrung: "I have but the puny strength of a lowly monk; my ability is limited, and I am but an insignificant man. Only by consulting the World-Honored One can one know the road to salvation." Now, let us take a look at how his mother ate:

When she saw the food, she went forward to take it.
Even before she ate it, out of greed, she had already
*   started defending it.*
"My son had brought food from the world of humans,
With which he intended to cure my hunger pangs.
The food does not seem to be enough for myself;
All of you, be patient and wait."
Ch'ing-t'i's karma of greed and selfishness was deep,
So when she put food in her gullet, it caught fire.
And when Mu-lien saw his mother touched by flames,
He became hysterical, beat his breast as if to level a mountain.
From his ears and nose, blood came streaming out,
And he cried out, "Oh, my poor mother!"
[24 lines]
"Now, the food cannot be put in my mouth,
And the fire, for no apparent reason, hurts me.
Those who are covetous should remember this;
They will encounter a hundred or more misfortunes.
Good monk, you are my most devoted son;
Get me some cold water to salve my empty stomach."

Mu-lien, when he heard his mother asking for water, her breath scorched, her voice hoarse, remembered in a flash that south of Rajagriha there was a great river, with vast expanses of water without end, named the Ganges, where he could find relief for his fire-singed, suffering mother. When people in the southern [continent] Jambudvipa saw this water, it was pure, clear, refreshingly cool river; when the mortals of heaven saw this water, it was a crystal pond; when the fish and the tortoises saw it, it was a babbling brook; but when Ch'ing-t'i saw this water, it became a pus flow with fierce fire. She went to the water's edge and, without waiting for her son's blessings, out of greed supported herself on the shore with her left hand, and out of avarice dipped her right hand into the water, because her greed and avarice knew no bounds.[40] The water had not reached her lips when it turned into fire.

When Mu-lien saw the food his mother ate turn into fire, and the water she drank also turn into fire, he pounded his head and beat his breast in loud lamentation and tears. He came before the Buddha, paid homage three times, and addressed him: "World-Honored One, in your grace and mercy, please rescue my mother from her misery. Now when she eats food, it turns into fire, and when she drinks water, it also turns into fire. How might she be spared this ordeal of fire?"

"Mu-lien," the World-Honored One replied, "your mother cannot eat anything, and there is no way to overcome this without first celebrating, one year from now, on the fifteenth day of the seventh month, the Festival of the Avalamba. Only then can she begin to eat."

Mu-lien, seeing his mother starve, said, "World-Honored One, can this be achieved on the thirteen or fourteen day each month? Must she wait for the fifteenth day of the seventh month each year before she can eat?"

"It is not just for your mother that the Festival of Avalamba has been established on this day; it is also for meditative exercises, the day for the arhats to attain the Way, the day of absolution for Devadatta,[41] the day of rejoicing for the Yama King, the day when all the hungry ghosts eat their fill."

When Mu-lien heard the Buddha's instructions, he went to a temple tower on the outskirts of the city of Rajagriha and recited the sutras of the Mahayana school to broadly establish the blessings of the Avalamba, so that his mother might have a meal to eat from that offering.

Once she was fed, mother and son again lost sight of each other. Mu-lien looked for his mother all over the place, but could not found her; so mournfully, with tears streaming down both cheeks, he came before the Buddha. Paying homage to him three times, he stood in front of him, his hands clasped together, and, on his knees, said, "World-Honored One, when my mother took food and it turned to fire, drank water which also turned into fire, it was possible for me to save her from her ordeal of fire only through the compassion of the World-Honored One. So, on the fifteenth day of the seventh month, she was able to eat a meal. But since then, my mother and I have not seen each other. Is it because she has dropped down to hell and is again on the way to becoming a hungry ghost?"

"Your mother has not fallen into hell nor into the realm of hungry ghosts," the World-Honored One replied. "Because you attained merit from reciting the sutras and establishing the blessings of the Avalamba Festival, your mother has been transformed from the form of a hungry ghost into that of a black dog in Rajagriha. If you wish to see her, you must go, without any discrimination, begging at each house, whether rich or poor, until you arrive at the gate of a very wealthy elder, where a black dog will come out and nip at your cassock, mouthing words as if it were human. This, then, is your mother."

Mu-lien received these instructions and took his begging bowl and plate to look for his mother. Without any regard to the wealth or humbleness of the dwelling, he went through every lane and alley, all around, but could find no trace of her. Then he came upon the residence of an elder and saw a black dog running out of the house, which began nipping at Mu-lien's cassock, at the same time making sounds very much like human speech: "Oh, my own devoted son, if you could save your mother from the realm of the un-

[40] The middle portion of this sentence does not make too much sense; this may be a case of textual corruption.

[41] Devadatta was a cousin of Shakyamuni and his enemy. For his plots against the Buddha, he is said to have been swallowed up alive in hell.

derworld in no time at all, why can't you release me from this miserable state of being a dog?"

"Dear mother," Mu-lien said, "because your son was not devoted, calamity has befallen you, and you have descended down to the Three Paths. Now, don't you prefer life in this form as a dog, or would you rather go on in the world of the hungry ghosts?"

"Obedient son," his mother answered, "in this dog's life, I can yap, move about, stay in one spot, sit, or sleep. If I am hungry, I can always go to the sewage pit and eat human offal; if I am parched, I can always drink from the gutters to quench my thirst. In the morning, I hear the elders chanting praises of the Three Treasures; in the evening, I hear the women reciting scripture. Of course I prefer this life as a dog, even if I have to pick up filth from all over, just so long as I don't have to hear the word 'hell' in my ears anymore."

Mu-lien then took his mother to the front of a Buddhist stupa in Rajagriha, and for seven days and seven nights he chanted the Mahayana sutras, made his confessions, and recited the abstinences. His mother, having benefited from these devotions, was able to shed her dog skin and hang it up on a tree, once again assuming the body of a woman.

"Mother," Mu-lien said, "it is not easy to achieve human form; it is not easy to be born in China; it is not easy to hear the law of Buddha; and it is not easy to develop a good heart. I ask you, mother, now that you have attained human form, to perform good works."

Mu-lien then took his mother beneath the sal trees in the Twin Grove, where he performed his homage to Buddha three times and, standing in front of him, said, "World-Honored One, would you look at the course of my mother's karma, examine it from the beginning, and see if there is any sin left still?"

The World-Honored One did not refuse to do what Mu-lien asked. He looked over the three realms of karma, checking her out for the slightest bit of sin.

Mu-lien saw that his mother's sins were expiated and was overjoyed. He said, "Mother, you should go to where you belong. The world of Jambudvipa is no place for you. Birth and death, there is no end to it. But in the west, the Land of the Buddha is most perfect."

Then, she felt herself spirited away by the *devas* and dragons and escorted by the Heavenly Maidens, and taken to the Trayastrinsha Heaven,[42] there to enjoy everlasting bliss.

The first time this sutra was chanted, there were eighty thousand bodhisattvas, eighty thousand monks, eighty thousand male deacons, and eighty thousand female deacons, performing the ritual around and around, in joy and in the faith that this teaching would prevail.

The Great Maudgalyayana *pien-wen,* one scroll.[43]

[42] Trayastrinsha is the heaven of Indra, one of the twelve spirits associated with the cult of the Master of Healing. The capital of this heaven is situated on Mount Sumeru, the central mountain of the nine mountain ranges of the universe.

[43] In the *Tun-huang pien-wen chi,* this line is followed by two additional lines: "The sixteenth day of the fourth month of the seventh year of the Chen-ming reign period [921], which is the eighteenth year of the calendar cycle, copied by Hsüeh An-chün, a trainee at the Pure Land Monastery. The script [of this scroll, namely, S2614] being of Chang Pao-ta."

THE JADE-FACED CAT

From *Lung-t'u kung-an*

TRANSLATED BY GEORGE A. HAYDEN

In Ch'ing-ho County[1] lived a young scholar, Shih Chün, whose wife, Ho Sai-hua, was a woman of stunning beauty and consummate skill in embroidery. One day Shih Chün, at the news that imperial examinations were to be held in the Eastern Capital, said, "After a decade of uninterrupted study, it would be a shame to miss this opportunity." He said good-bye to his wife and set out on his way. He was accompanied by his valet, Hsiao-erh, and they traveled by day, rested by night, and stopped for food and drink only when they felt the need. After several days, they arrived at an inn before a mountain range, where they stayed the night.

Now these mountains stretched for over six hundred *li* to the border of the Western Capital. It was a region of dark forests, deep valleys, and soaring cliffs and crags, unfrequented by man but abounding in spirits and demons. Living there was a pack of five rats who had descended from the Western Paradise;[2] they were able to transform themselves by magic and appear and disappear at will. Sometimes they would change into old men and emerge to cheat traveling merchants of their goods. Or perhaps they would appear as young girls to beguile men or as men to seduce beautiful women from wealthy families. These demons addressed one another by the order of seniority, such as "Rat Number One," "Rat Number Two." They lived in a cave at the foot of Seaview Cliff.

On that very day, Rat Number Five happened to be in the mood to play some tricks, and so he changed himself into an innkeeper. While greeting his guests by the mountain pass, he by chance met with Shih Chün. He noticed that Chün was a handsome man and went about making inquiries as to his home and other personal matters. Shih Chün told him not only where he lived but also his plan to take the examinations in the capital, and at this news the demon was inwardly pleased.

That night the rat prepared a feast to entertain Shih Chün. While they were drinking and talking, they touched upon a great variety of subjects. To each question by Shih Chün, the demon had an immediate reply. Amazed, Shih Chün thought to himself, "This man is only an innkeeper. How in the world did he come by such a wide store of knowledge?" He therefore asked, "I wonder, sir, if you might have been engaged in scholarship yourself at one time or other?"

---

[1] During the Sung Dynasty as well as the Ming, two counties bore this name: one in present day Hopei Province, the other in modern Kiangsu Province. The route Shih Chün takes to the capital seems to indicate the former.

[2] The paradise of the Buddha Amitabha (*O-mi-t'o fo* in Chinese).

At this the demon smiled. "I might as well tell you. Three years ago I took the examinations myself, but since my bad luck prevented me from having any success, I threw my books away and opened this little inn here, where I just manage to get by."

Shih Chün urged him to keep him company well into the middle of the night, whereupon the demon hatched a plot. He blew a puff of noxious breath into the wine and handed it to the young scholar. All would have been well for Shih Chün had he not drunk that wine, but once the wine went down his throat, he fell to the floor in a daze. Hsiao-erh hurried over to help him up and lead him into their room to lie down. The pain was unbearable, and Hsiao-erh began to panic. No doctor was available, and by daybreak, the innkeeper of the previous night was nowhere to be found. With considerable effort, he supported his master and went on for a short distance until he came upon an inn where they could rest. By this time it was clear to him that some spell was at work.

Meanwhile the demon had immediately shed his former likeness and changed into that of Shih Chün. He ran to Chün's home, where Sai-hua was just doing her morning toilet. Hearing of her husband's return, she hurried out and saw Shih Chün standing there, wreathed in smiles. To her question why, after only twenty or so days away, he had come home so soon, the demon answered, "As I was approaching the capital, I came upon an examinee, who told me that the examinations were over and the candidates were leaving the capital. When I heard that, rather than go into the city, I turned around and headed back."

"Why didn't Hsiao-erh come back with you?"

"He found the journey too rough. I left our things with a friend of his and told them to bring them back later."

Believing this story, Sai-hua prepared breakfast. Later, several relatives came by and, without exception, they took him for the real Shih Chün.

From this time on, Sai-hua was as accommodating to the demon as a wife could be, blind as she was to the fact that her true husband was suffering in an inn.

A couple of weeks later, Shih Chün obtained a pill from a Taoist named Tung which brought him to full recovery. But when at last he was ready to proceed to the capital, he heard that the examinations were over. With Hsiao-erh he started a slow homeward journey that took him over twenty days.

Hsiao-erh went ahead into the house first. Sai-hua and the demon happened to be drinking in the rear of the main room, and when she heard Hsiao-erh returning, she got up and came out, asking him why he was so late in getting back.

"Getting back late?" said Hsiao-erh. "That's nothing! The master nearly lost his life!"

Sai-hua asked him which "master" he was talking about, and Hsiao-erh said, "Why, the one I went to the capital with. What do you mean, 'which master'?"

"You took your own sweet time loafing along the way," Sai-hua laughed. "Your master's been here over twenty days now!"

Hsiao-erh was shocked. "That's impossible! My master and I have been with each other day and night, never so much as an inch apart. How can you say he's back home already?"

At this reply Sai-hua was perplexed. Just then Shih Chün came in, and when he caught sight of his wife, he embraced her and broke into tears. Hearing what was going on, the demon strode out to the front of the main room and shouted, "Who do you think you are, taking liberties with my wife?" Shih Chün in a rage came forward, struggled with the demon, and ended up by being driven out of his house. All the neighbors were shocked to see this.

At his wits' end, Shih Chün finally told his father-in-law about the entire matter; the latter, deeply troubled by what had happened, had him prepare a complaint for the tribunal of Prime

Minister Wang.[3] After examining the complaint, Wang thought the case very strange and immediately dispatched some clerks to bring in the demon and Sai-hua for questioning. When this was done, Wang saw that indeed there were two Shih Chüns. His counselors around him all said that Magistrate Pao[4] was the only one who could settle the affair, but unfortunately he was not back from the border yet. Wang called for Sai-hua to step forward, and in response to his detailed questions, she related the facts as she knew them, one by one. Wang asked her, "Have you by any chance noticed any distinguishing marks on your real husband's body?"

"There is a black mole on my true husband's right arm," was the reply.

Wang first summoned the false husband up front and had him remove his clothing to the waist. Inspection of his arm failed to reveal a black mole, and Wang thought to himself that this was the imposter. He then called the actual husband forward for inspection and found, as he had expected, a black mole on his arm. At this point Wang ordered the real Shih Chün to kneel on the left and the false one on the right and commanded the constables to bring in a long cangue, telling them, "Examine those two. The one with a black mole on his right arm is the real Shih Chün, and the one without is a devil. Put the long cangue on him and send him off to jail."

By the time the constables had come forward to make their examination, both men had a mole on the arm, and no one could tell the real one from the imposter. Wang exclaimed, "What deviltry is this? On first inspection only one of them had it; now they both do!" He had both men imprisoned for the time being and declared that the investigation would resume the next day.

In prison the demon, finding this treatment hard to swallow, took out his "emergency incense" and lit it, sending the four rat spirits beneath Seaview Cliff into a council of action. They decided on a rescue mission, and Rat Number Four took on the form of Prime Minister Wang, assuming his seat in the tribunal at earliest light on the following day. He brought out both Shih Chüns from beneath the steps to the dais for interrogation and had the real Shih Chün beaten severely. Shih Chün, humiliated by such injustice, called out his grievances in loud wails. Presently, the real Prime Minister Wang entered the courtroom and was shocked to discover someone else sitting in his place. He at once ordered the constables to seize him, but the pretender rose in fury and screamed for the constables to arrest the genuine Wang. Instantly the courtroom was in an utter confusion, and the constables, again at a loss to determine the real one from the pretender, dared not make the slightest move. At the sight of two Prime Minister Wangs wrangling away with each other, everyone was absolutely dumbfounded.

One resourceful senior member of the tribunal stepped up and offered a suggestion. "We've no way of knowing which of Your Excellencies is the real Prime Minister Wang, and we could go on arguing for days on end, all to no avail. Why not rush the case to His Majesty for deliberation?"

Upon learning of the case, Emperor Jen-tsung summoned the two ministers into audience. Once in court the demon performed some of his magic and with a whiff of his breath clouded Jen-tsung's eyes, robbing him of his usual clarity of vision. The emperor ordered that both men be placed in the Pan-Celestial Prison to await the ascendance that night of the Northern Dipper,[5] when the false minister would definitely be exposed. The fact is that Jen-tsung was the avatar of the Great

---

[3] A fictitious character.
[4] The fictionalized version of the Northern Sung official Pao Cheng.

[5] The connection of the Big Dipper with fate and celestial adjudication has existed in Chinese mythology since at least the Han.

Barefoot Immortal,[6] and he could see things in heaven during the midnight hours.

Now that both Prime Minister Wangs were in prison, the demon was afraid that he would be found out and immediately lit up his emergency incense. At a sniff of this, the three rat spirits beneath Seaview Cliff went into conference and sent the third rat off to the rescue. Rat Number Three, performing his bit of magic, changed himself into Jen-tsung and was sitting in the Grand Hall of Audience even before the final watch of the night. He was assembling the various officials for adjudication when the real Jen-tsung made his appearance in the hall. When the officials spied their august lord in duplicate, every one of them, civil or military, turned pale and rushed to make a report to the Dowager Empress at the inner palace. In great consternation, she brought out the Jade Seal and followed the officials into the hall, determined to find out the truth once and for all. She told them, "Don't be alarmed. On the emperor's left palm are patterns of mountains and rivers and on the right palm patterns of grain and soil. See which of them has these and you'll know the real one from the false." Together the officials examined, and as she had said, the real Jen-tsung had the markings and the other did not. The Dowager Empress ordered that the imposter be put into the Pan-Celestial Prison for interrogation.

The counterfeit emperor began to panic and burned his emergency incense. This left Rats Number One and Two in a state of some irritation. Their conclusion was that Rat Number Five was an idiot to have stirred up such an extreme criminal case involving the central court itself. Rat Number Two said, "Well, there's nothing to do but go on ahead and get them back." He accord-

ingly exercised his magic powers, transformed himself into a bogus Dowager Empress, and ascended the hall, where he tried to have all of the prisoners released. As coincidence would have it, an order from the Dowager Empress instructing the jailers not to allow the demons to escape also came at the same time. When the officers learned of the orders of the two Dowager Empresses, one for release, the other for imprisonment, they had no idea which was from the real Dowager Empress. This caused Jen-tsung so much anxiety that he lost both sleep and appetite for days.

The ministers petitioned His Majesty to send an envoy to the border to bring Prime Minister Pao back; for he alone could clear matters up. The emperor gave his assent and at once issued a proclamation directing an envoy to hasten to the border. After the order was read, Lord Pao returned to court for an audience. He informed the throne that he wished to straighten out the case for good. When he had retired from court and entered the K'ai-feng tribunal, he summoned twenty-four merciless lictors, carrying thirty-six instruments of punishment, to form ranks beneath the courtroom. He then had the suspects brought out of prison for investigation. There were indeed two Prime Minister Wangs, two scholar Shihs, one Dowager Empress, and one Emperor Jen-tsung. Lord Pao smiled and said, "Here in this tribunal I admit I have some doubt concerning the Prime Minister and Shih Chün, but about the Dowager Empress and the Emperor I have none at all. For now I shall imprison everyone here and report to the City God tomorrow; then I shall announce my verdict."

The four rat spirits, finding themselves in the same cell, looked at one another and started to talk things over in secret. "Lord Pao said he'd report to the City God; that means he's going to uncover our original identities, and that's going to put our lives in jeopardy. Since this business has stirred up the anger of Heaven, we're not going

---

[6] Legend during the Sung had it that Jen-tsung was an immortal brought to earth in answer to Emperor Chen-tsung's prayers for an heir. As a child, Jen-tsung loved to go barefoot.

to get away with it very much longer. We'd better ask Number One to come here for consultation." They then lit a stick of emergency incense.

Rat Number One happened to be around the K'ai-feng Tribunal when the incense was burned. He soon found out that Lord Pao was judging the case; laughing, he said, "Let me be Prime Minister Pao, and we'll see how well he can handle it!" He changed himself by sorcery into a false Lord Pao and, taking his seat in the tribunal, initiated proceedings.

But the real Lord Pao had just returned from the Temple of the City God, and at the sudden report that a Lord Pao was already sitting in session, he smiled and said, "Accursed vermin! Can you go further than this?!" He headed straight into the courtroom and ordered the attendants to arrest the demon, who came down to where Pao was standing and became identical with him. Having no inkling as to which was the real Pao, the constables were hesitant to act. Lord Pao's temper flared, and he gave instructions to his confidential clerks: "Keep a close watch at the doors; word of this must never leak out. Wait until I leave the courtroom before you go inside to attend to his orders." Only after he had heard them acknowledge these orders did Pao make his departure. The false Pao, still in the courtroom, tried his best to manage the case from there, but the constables were far too puzzled to respond to his commands.

Meanwhile Pao had gone home to see his wife, Li-shih, to whom he said, "This case is so involved with devils and magic that I can't make any sense out of it. I'll have to appeal to the Lord on High to exorcise those foul creatures. Cover me up tightly on the bed with the quilt and take no action from that point on. In two days and nights at the most, I shall be back." Thereupon Pao drank a few mouthfuls of the peacock blood with which he had daubed his face when he was on duty at the border. He then lay down on the Netherworld Bed and went directly to the Court of Heaven.

The celestial precepter escorted him to the Jade Emperor who, having heard his report, ordered the inspectorate to discover what kind of being was responsible for the disturbances. The answer was that five demonic rat spirits from the Thunder Peal Temple [7] in the west had descended to the world below to make trouble. The Jade Emperor thought of raising a celestial army against them, but the inspector counseled, "A celestial army could never bring them under control, for if we pressed them, they would only enter the sea and stir things up even more. One thing only can subdue them: before the Hall of the Buddha at the Thunder Peal Temple, in the Jewel-Covered Basket, is the Jade-Faced Cat, which would put an end to the demons far better than a hundred thousand celestial soldiers." The Jade Emperor thereupon sent a heavenly envoy to Thunder Peal Temple to get this Jade-Faced Cat.

With the heavenly petition in hand, the envoy arrived at Thunder Peal Temple in the west and obtained an audience with the Buddha. After the petition was read, the Buddha conferred with his disciples. One of them came forward and said, "The cat really can't be spared from the Hall of the Buddha; we need it to keep rats away from all the sutras. If we lend it out, the sutras will suffer."

"It is the will of the Jade Emperor," said the Buddha. "We can't very well disregard it."

The same disciple replied, "We could always lend them the Golden-Eyed Lion instead. If the Jade Emperor started to quibble, we could say that we need the cat to protect the sutras. He couldn't possibly take offense at that."

The Buddha gave his approval and sent the Golden-Eyed Lion on with the heavenly envoy. The Jade Emperor summoned Pao in order to present him with the animal. Observing this, the inspector voiced his objection. "Lord Pao, the Star

[7] In the Ming novel *Hsi-yu chi* (Journey to the West), Tripitaka, Monkey, and the other pilgrims obtained the sutras from the Tathagata Buddha at this temple.

460

of Civil Virtue,[8] has come to us because of disaster in the Eastern Capital. If the animal we give him is not the Jade-Faced Cat, it'll result only in wasted effort on his part. I'd hope that Your Majesty will show pity and lend him what he really needs." The Jade Emperor assented and sent the heavenly envoy off to Thunder Peal Temple once again, this time in the company of Lord Pao.

They made their obeisance to the Buddha and presented their request. At first the Buddha was adamant against the idea, but an arhat of the Mahayana school[9] stepped forward and said, "The Star of Civil Virtue has undergone immense trouble and pain for the sake of the people. With your devotion toward the people in the human world, we really should make him the loan." The Buddha agreed to this and had an acolyte take the sacred cat out of the Jewel-Covered Basket. At the recitation of a chant, the cat shrunk in size and hid itself in Lord Pao's sleeve. After receiving instructions on how to capture the rats, Pao took leave of the Buddha and returned with the heavenly envoy to inform the Jade Emperor that he had obtained the Jade-Faced Cat. Vastly pleased, the Jade Emperor commanded the god T'ai-yi[10] to give Lord Pao some willow water as an antidote for the poison.[11] When the time came for the heavenly envoy to see him through the Gate of Heaven, Lord Pao awoke on his bed. Five days had already passed.

Mrs. Pao with considerable relief fed her husband some broth, and Lord Pao told her that he had borrowed an instrument of exorcism from the Buddha of the Western Paradise and that she

was to reveal this secret to no one. She asked, "What do you intend to do now?"

"Go into the palace tomorrow," he said, "and ask the Empress Dowager to choose a certain day on which to build a tower in the Southern Outskirts.[12] When that is accomplished, I can finally bring this case to a conclusion."

Following his instructions, Mrs. Pao entered the palace the next morning and made her request to the Dowager Empress. The Dowager Empress gave her consent and ordered Ti Ch'ing,[13] commissioner of military affairs, to see to the construction of the tower in the Southern Outskirts without fail. Ti Ch'ing had his troops proceed to the Southern Outskirts, where they completed the tower according to specifications. At the tribunal, Lord Pao ordered the twenty-four stalwarts to go to the tower for the trial on the appointed day. The resulting commotion drew every citizen of the capital out for a look.

On that day, everyone was standing beneath the tower: the true and the false Jen-tsungs and Dowager Empresses and the two prime ministers and Shih Chüns. The civil and military officials were in ranks on either side. The real Lord Pao sat alone on the tower, while his pretender remained below, arguing for his own cause. Toward noon, Lord Pao took out the holy scripture of the Buddha from his sleeve, and at the sound of his chanting, out of his sleeve came the Jade-Faced Cat, with the size and ferocity of a ravenous tiger. The stench of the rats brought a golden gleam to its eyes, and it sprang down from the tower, sinking its teeth first into Rat Number Three, the false Jen-tsung. Rat Number Two, by now in its true form, tried to escape but was held fast by the extended left paw of the sacred cat. The cat caught Rat Number One with its right paw, then opened

---

[8] In Ming and Ch'ing popular literature, Pao is given as an incarnation of this star.

[9] It has to be noted that *arhats* (*Lo-han* in Chinese), the equivalent of the Taoist *chen-jen* (the perfect ones), are essentially connected with the Hinayana school of Buddhism.

[10] Elsewhere in Chinese mythology this stellar god (literally "Supreme Unity") ranks on a par with the Jade Emperor. Here his position might be regarded as subordinate.

[11] The poison the willow water is supposed to counteract may be the peacock blood which Pao drank before heading for the Court of Heaven.

[12] The location south of the capital in which the emperor sacrificed to Heaven on the winter solstice.

[13] A historical general (1009–1057) of the Northern Sung. In popular literature, two incarnations of astral deities are the right-hand men of Jen-tsung: Pao as the Star of Civil Virtue and Ti as the Star of Martial Virtue.

its jaws and felled this rat demon with one bite. This produced a roar from the crowd beneath the tower. The two rats posing as the prime minister and Shih Chün transformed themselves and lit out for the clouds, but the sacred cat bounced up and sent Rat Number Five tumbling down with a bite. This left Rat Number Four still free, but, hot on the chase, the Jade-Faced Cat ran after it like a shaft of golden light. Seeing the destruction of the demons, the civil and military officers all cheered.

Lord Pao came down from the tower and observed the four rat spirits. They were approximately ten feet long, with hands and feet like those of humans. From their wounds poured a white creamy substance. Lord Pao reported to the throne, "These rats subsisted on human essence and blood. Let each soldier cook and eat them to increase his strength." Emperor Jen-tsung agreed and sent soldiers to gather the carcasses up.

The imperial entourage then entered the court, where the officials all offered their congratulations. The emperor in great joy had Lord Pao brought up to the throne for personal commendation. He held a feast for the officials and ministers of the court and ordered the historian to record the marvels that had occurred. Lord Pao then left the court and returned to his tribunal.

Shih Chün was released, and he took his wife back home to enjoy their happy reunion. Later, however, Sai-hua experienced constant pains in the abdomen from being poisoned by her intercourse with the demon. When Shih Chün gave her a pill which he had obtained from the Taoist Tung, she recovered by vomiting the noxious essence.

Later, Shih Chün became a *chin-shih* and worked his way up the officialdom until he headed the Ministry of Personnel. He had two sons who were established figures in their own right.[14]

[14] The last paragraph is based on a 1809 edition of the *Lung-t'u kung-an* printed together with the *Kang-feng kung-an* (The Cases of Lord [Hai] Kang-feng) in two horizontal columns, under the collective title *Lung-t'u Kang-feng kung-an ho-pien*.

THE JUDGE

In traditional China the local prefect or magistrate played a crucial role in the life of the ordinary citizens. As the head of the local administration, it was his duty to pass judgment in the event of a civil dispute. His role as judge provided him more contacts with the people under his jurisdiction than his function as administrator. Appeal to higher authorities for a "grievances hearing" was uncommon, and his judgment was usually final. This image of the judge has figured in a large body of Chinese fiction.

The judge is usually cast as a defender of truth and administrator of justice, and as such he is expected to do more than simply solve lawsuits. For the insulted and the injured, he is looked upon as no less than a savior. Lord Pao, who appears in "Lion Cub Lane," is the perennial symbol of the savior judge.

Occasionally a judge, despite his good intentions, may err in judgment because of impatience, lack of experience, or simply prejudice; the story in "The Jest That Leads to Disaster" presents a good example of the tragic consequences of hasty judgment. But the imperfect side of the so-called "upright officials" (*ch'ing-kuan*), Lord Pao included, is seldom revealed. When they err in judgment or willfully commit a wrongdoing, rarely do they have to meet the same just punishments that criminals receive at their hands. "Magistrate T'eng and the Case of Inheritance" is an amusing illustration; though the storyteller reveals T'eng's trickery, he is allowed to get away with the spoils without being identified as a villain.

Even small officials have power
* PEOPLE LISTEN
- by social law (written)
- not really by law
- not until Ching Dynasty is law clear.
- in Tang Dynasty laws were made

463

NIEH YI-TAO THE MAGISTRATE

From *Shan-chü hsin-hua*

TRANSLATED BY CONRAD LUNG

Nieh Yi-tao, a native of the Chiang-hsi Circuit,[1] was the magistrate of a certain county.[2]

Early one morning, a vegetable peddler went to the market to buy vegetables. While on his way, he accidentally found a bundle of paper money. At the moment, it was not yet dawn. He hid himself in an out-of-the-way place and waited. When dawn came, he counted the money. The value of the bills was equivalent to fifteen taels of silver. There were some bills in the denomination of five thousand in cash in the bundle, and the vegetable peddler took out one, bought two thousand in cash worth of meat and three thousand in cash worth of rice, placed them in the baskets hanging on his shoulder pole, and returned home without buying any vegetables.

When his mother saw that there were no vegetables, she asked him about it. He replied, "Earlier, I found these bills on my way to the market. So I bought some meat and rice and came home."

"You're lying to me," the mother said angrily. "People would drop one or two bills but not a whole bundle of them. You must have stolen them. If you've indeed found them, you should return them." She admonished him over and over again, but he would not listen.

"If you won't do as I say, I'm going to report the case to the authorities," she said finally.

"The money is something I picked up on the street," the son said. "I don't know whom to return it to."

"You can wait at the place where you found it," she said. "When the owner of the money comes and looks for it, return it to him." Then she added, "Our family has never had the money to buy so much rice and meat. Now, suddenly, you found this money; it does not bode well."

The son then took the money to the place where he had found it. Indeed, someone came along and looked for it. The vegetable peddler was just a simple villager; he did not even ask the man how much money he had lost but simply said "Your lost money is here" and returned it to him. All the bystanders asked the owner of the money to reward the peddler. But the owner was stingy and did not want to do it. Instead, he said, "The money I lost is equivalent to thirty taels of silver and now half of it is still missing. How can I reward him?" A quarrel broke out on the difference between the sum of money lost and the sum

---

[1] The Chiang-hsi Circuit in Yüan times is equivalent to the area along the Yangtze River in the northern part of the present Kiangsi Province.

[2] In the present text there are two blank squares before the word county; presumably the name of the county was given in the original edition.

found, and the case was brought before the local authorities.

Magistrate Nieh cross-examined the peddler and found his testimony quite trustworthy. Then he secretly summoned the mother, asked her the same questions, and found that her answers matched her son's. Consequently, he ordered affidavits to be made of the testimony by both parties. The owner affirmed that he had indeed lost a sum of money equivalent to thirty taels of silver, while the peddler's version stated that he had in fact only found a sum equivalent to fifteen taels.

After viewing the affidavits, the magistrate announced the verdict: "If this is the case, the money found is not the money lost. The fifteen taels of silver must be a gift from Heaven to a virtuous mother for her livelihood in her old age." He gave the money to the mother and son and ordered them to leave. He told the man who had lost the money, "You must have lost your thirty taels of silver somewhere else. Go and look for it yourself." Then, with a harsh voice, he ordered the man to leave. People who heard about the incident were all satisfied with the settlement.

THE JEST THAT LEADS TO DISASTER

From *Hsing-shih heng-yen* [1]

TRANSLATED BY JEANNE KELLY

Intelligence and quick wit are bestowed by Heaven,
And muddled thinking and stupidity may not be what they
*   seem.*
Jealousy is all in the thinness of the eyebrows;
Fights start up in the thick of gossip and laughter.
The heart is more treacherous than the Yellow River's nine
*   bends,*
And even under ten coats of armor, a hated face will show.
Nations have perished because of women and wine.
But has the love of learning ever caused a good man's decline?

This poem merely points up how difficult it is for a man to get on in the world, for life's path is narrow and men's hearts are hard to fathom. The Great Way [2] recedes ever further away and man's nature is infinitely varied. Men all hustle and bustle about in the pursuit of gain, but in their ignorance and foolishness they bring along nothing but calamity. All this must be pondered carefully if one wishes to maintain himself and protect his family. Thus the ancients had a saying, "There is a time for frowning and a time for laughing. In either case it is a serious matter."

This story tells of a man who, merely because of a few jesting remarks made under the influence of wine, ended up losing his life, bringing ruin to his family, and sending several others to their deaths. But first, by way of preamble, I shall tell a story.

In the Sung period, there was a young scholar by the name of Wei P'eng-chü, styled Ch'ung-hsiao, who at the age of eighteen took as his bride a girl as pretty as a flower. But he had hardly been married for a month when the examination period began. So, bidding his wife farewell, Wei packed his bag and set off for the capital to take the examination. Before his departure, his wife said to him, "Whether you receive an official appointment or not, come back as soon as possible. Don't abandon your loving wife."

"Honor and fame are as good as in my pocket, so there's no need for you to worry," Wei replied.

He then set off for the capital, where he did indeed achieve immediate success on the examination, placing second on the posted list of graduates. He presently became a well-known person in the capital and was accorded great pomp and ceremony. He did not neglect to write a letter home and sent a servant to bring his family to the capital.

The letter began with the usual greetings and the news of his official appointment. At the end of the letter was one line which read:

[1] The *Ching-pen t'ung-su hsiao-shuo* version of this story is titled "The Wrongly Executed Ts'ui Ning" ("Ts'o-chan Ts'ui Ning").

[2] This refers to the utopian golden age supposed to have existed in the legendary early period of Chinese history.

As I have had no one to look after me here in the capital, I have already found myself a second little wife. I await your arrival so that we can share in the glory.

The servant took the letter along with money for traveling expenses and went straight home. When he met his mistress, he offered his congratulations and then presented her with the letter, which she opened and read immediately. Then she exclaimed to the servant, "Why, that ingrate! No sooner has he received an official post than he takes a concubine!"

"But no such thing had happened while I was at the capital," said the servant. "I think the master must be joking. You'll see for yourself when you get there. You mustn't worry about it."

"Well, if that's the case," she said, "I'll forget about it."

Then, as there were no passenger boats available, she began packing her things for the trip while she looked for someone who could deliver a letter to the capital. When the bearer of the letter reached the capital, he asked the way to the lodgings of the new graduate Wei and delivered the letter. Needless to say, he was treated to food and wine before he started his trip back.

When he received the letter, Wei opened it and found that it contained nothing but:

While you have found yourself a second little wife in the capital, I have taken a second little husband at home. We will soon set off together for the capital.

When he read this, Wei thought that it must have been said in jest and so paid no further attention to it. Then, before he had time to put the letter away, the arrival of a fellow examination graduate was announced. Wei's accommodations at the capital were not as spacious as his own home, and as the visitor was a good friend and knew, moreover, that Wei did not have his family with him, he went straight in and took a seat. After they had exchanged a few pleasantries, Wei got up to go relieve himself.

Glancing over some of the correspondence on

Wei's desk, the friend chanced to come across his wife's letter. It so amused him, he deliberately read it out aloud.

Taken by surprise, Wei blushed crimson and said, "It's just a silly thing. I teased her, so she wrote that as a joke."

The friend broke into loud laughter and remarked, "That's hardly something to joke about." He then took his leave.

This fellow was also young, and loved to gossip. In no time at all the incident of the letter was spread all over the capital. There were, moreover, a group of officials who, jealous over Wei's early success on the examination, seized upon the incident and wrote a memorandum to the throne, charging that Wei was young and undisciplined, that he was not fit for high office, and that he should be demoted and sent off to a provincial post. Wei was overcome with remorse. Subsequently things did not go well for him, and he thus let slip an opportunity for a brilliant career.

This then is how a fine post came to be thrown away all because of a joke.

Now my main story concerns another man who, also because of a jest made after a few drinks, was sent to an untimely death, and along with him a few other persons unjustly lost their lives. And why was this? The following poem is cited in testimony:

Life's rough and rugged paths are truly forbidding;
The mouths of others open readily for a laugh.
The white clouds are unfeeling creatures;
But then they are drawn out by the wild winds.

During the Southern Sung period, the capital was situated at Lin-an, which was in no way inferior in wealth and splendor to the old capital of K'ai-feng. To the left of Arrow Bridge in this city, there lived a man named Liu Kuei, styled Chünchien. His family had once been well to do, but in Liu Kuei's hands it had fallen on bad times. At first he had been able to study, but later, seeing that the situation had become impossible, he dropped his studies to take up business. In this he was like a man learning to walk in his middle years. As he was inexperienced in this line of work, he soon lost all his capital. Gradually his large house was exchanged for a smaller one until he was renting only a few rooms.

He and his wife Wang-shih were both young and shared a mutual respect. Later, when there was no son born, he took the daughter of Ch'en the cake vendor as his concubine. Both of them called her Erh-chieh, "Second Sister." This took place before he became completely destitute. Now there were no others in the household, only the three of them. Liu Kuei was an amiable man, well liked by the neighbors, who were always telling him, "Mr. Liu, you have run into bad times and so are down on your luck, but after a while, things will surely take a turn for the better."

Though they talked on like this, nothing of the sort ever occurred, and he merely sat around dejectedly at home unable to see a way out.

One day while he was idling at home, Old Wang, a servant of his father-in-law and a man close to seventy years of age, arrived and said to Liu, "It is the squire's birthday, and I've been especially instructed to come escort you and the mistress back for a visit."

"Here I've been so immersed in my own day-to-day worries, I've even forgotten it was my father-in-law's birthday!" Liu replied.

Liu and his wife then gathered up a few articles of clothing and packed them into a bundle which they gave to Old Wang to carry. Erh-chieh was instructed to look after the house: "It's too late to return today, but we'll be back by tomorrow evening." With this said, they departed. After going more than twenty *li* from the city, they reached the residence of Squire Wang and paid their respects. That day, surrounded by guests, Liu and his father-in-law had no opportunity to discuss all the details of his straitened circumstances. When the guests had all gone home, Liu and his wife spent the night in the guest room.

At dawn, Wang came to have a talk with his son-in-law. "Son, you can't go on like this," he began. "After all, 'sitting idle one can eat up a mountain of gold,' for 'the gullet is as deep as the sea, and the days and months pass as quickly as the weaver's shuttle.' You must think of a long-range plan. My daughter committed herself to you for life with the expectation that you could provide her with ample food and clothing. Surely this isn't the best you can do?"

"You are right, of course," Liu said, sighing. "But 'It's easier to go up the mountain and catch a tiger than to ask another for money.' In my present circumstances, who will take pity on me as you do? The only thing for me to do is bear up under my difficulties. Asking for help from others would only be labor wasted."

"I don't blame you for feeling like that. But I can't sit by and watch you go on this way, so I'm going to give you a little capital, and you can try opening a grocery store. Wouldn't it be better if you could earn a little something to help make ends meet?"

"That's very kind of you. Of course it would."

They then had supper, and afterward Wang took out fifteen strings of cash which he gave to Liu, saying, "Son, use this to set up the store. When you are ready to open it, I'll give you another ten strings. Your wife can stay here for a few days. When the time comes to open the store, I'll bring her myself to your home and offer you my congratulations. How does that sound?"

Liu thanked him again and again and, shouldering the money, departed forthwith. When he reached the city, the sky had already darkened. As his route took him past the house of an acquaintance who also wished to go into business, he thought it might be a good idea to stop by and discuss the matter with him a bit. He went up and knocked at the fellow's door. There was an answering shout from within, then the man came out, bowed, and asked, "What can I do for you?"

Liu explained the situation to him in detail. The man then said, "I've nothing to do at home. If I can be of use, I'll certainly come help."

"That would be splendid," said Liu.

They discussed a few business matters, and then the fellow invited Liu to stay for some dishes that had already been prepared, and they also drank a few cups of wine. Liu, who had little capacity for wine, began to feel giddy. He stood up to go, saying, "I've disturbed you too much today. Please come by my place tomorrow so that we can discuss our plans."

The fellow saw Liu to the end of the block then said good-bye and returned home. Of this no more need be said.

Now, if this storyteller had been born in the same year and grown up shoulder to shoulder with Liu, he could have grasped him tightly around the waist and dragged him away, and then perhaps he would not have suffered such a calamity. But instead Liu died an unworthy death,

Like Li Tsun-hsiao [3] as seen in the Wu-tai shih (History of the Five Dynasties),
Or P'eng Yüeh [4] as recorded in the Han-shu (History of the Western Han Dynasty).

With the money slung on his back, Liu made his way home step by step and knocked at the door. By then it was already time for the lamps to be lit. The concubine, Erh-chieh, was alone in the house. Having nothing to do, she had kept watch until dusk and then bolted the door and dozed off under the lamp. How could she have heard Liu rapping at the door? He had to knock for some time before she finally awoke and called, "Coming," and then rose and opened the door.

When Liu had come into the house, Erh-chieh took the money from him and laid it on the table.

She then asked, "Where did you get this money from? What's it for?"

Now, in the first place, Liu had had a bit too much to drink, and second, he was annoyed at her for being so slow to open the door. He decided he would scare her with a little joke, and so he said, "If I tell you, I'm afraid you'll take offense. But if I don't, you'll have to be told eventually, anyway. It's just that I've been unable to see a way out of my difficulties, and so have had to pawn you to a merchant. But being loath to part with you, I've only pawned you for fifteen strings of cash. If luck comes my way, then I can redeem you with interest. If things go as badly as they have before, I'll just have to give you up!"

The concubine could not believe this when she heard it, but there were the fifteen strings of cash piled up in front of her. But how could she believe it? "He has never said a cross word to me," she thought, "and I've always been on good terms with elder sister. How could he suddenly become so callous and cruel?" Bewildered, all she could say was, "Even so, my parents should still be notified."

"If your parents had been told," said Liu, "the whole deal would have been off. Tomorrow, after you have gone to the man's house, I'll see about getting someone to notify your parents. I'm sure they won't blame me for it."

"Where were you drinking today?" she then asked.

"The person I pawned you to treated me to some wine after we had signed the contract."

"Why hasn't elder sister come back?"

"She couldn't bear to see you go, so she's waiting until tomorrow after you've gone to come back. I had no choice in this. It's all been settled." He couldn't help laughing to himself as he said this. He then lay down on the bed without undressing and had soon fallen asleep.

The concubine could not get it off her mind. "I wonder what sort of man he's sold me to? I should first go and tell my parents about it. Even

---

[3] Li Ts'un-hsiao (?–894) was the adopted son of Li K'o-yung of the late T'ang period. He distinguished himself in battle, but later suffered slanderous charges and was put to death by Li K'o-yung. In 923, Li Ts'un-hsü, the son of Li K'o-yung, established the Later T'ang Dynasty which lasted until 936, with three more emperors.

[4] P'eng Yüeh (?–196 B.C.) was a famous general of the early Han period. He was accused of plotting against Liu Pang after Liu had conquered all of China to establish the Han Dynasty. Liu Pang had him sliced to pieces.

if someone comes all the way to my place to look for me tomorrow, it still has to be settled this way."

After pondering the matter for a while, she took the fifteen strings of cash and set them in a pile at Liu's feet. Taking advantage of his drunken stupor, she quietly collected a few articles of clothing, slowly opened the door, and slipped out, pulling it shut behind her. She then went over the neighbors on their left, the house of Chu San-lao, and asked Mrs. Chu to let her stay for the night, explaining, "Today my husband for no reason sold me, and I must go tell my parents. Would you please let him know tomorrow? Since now I belong to someone else, he can go with my husband to my parents' place and clarify the matter, for I must know where I am to go."

"That seems most sensible," the neighbor said. "You go ahead. I'll see to it that your husband is informed."

After spending the night, she said good-bye and left. We won't go into the details. Truly:

When the sea tortoise frees itself from the hook,
It wiggles its tail and shakes its head, never to return again.

We'll leave this for the moment. Liu meanwhile slept until the third watch. When he awoke, he found the lamp still burning and his concubine absent from his side. He assumed she was still in the kitchen clearing things up and called for her to bring some tea. After calling for a while and getting no response, he made an effort to get up but, still groggy from the wine, soon fell asleep again.

At that moment, a certain burglar, made desperate by losses at gambling during the day and out to see what he could pick up that night, came by chance upon Liu's door. Since the concubine had pulled the door shut without locking it when she went out, with only a light shove from the thief it swung open. He stole his way into the bedroom without being discovered. When he reached the head of the bed and took a look about him in

the still-bright light of the lamp, he could see nothing worth taking. Groping around on the bed, he noticed a man sleeping there with his face toward the wall. At his feet was a pile of copper coins. He picked up a few strings but in the process woke Liu, who rose up shouting, "Hey, you've no right to take that! I borrowed those few strings from my father-in-law to support myself. If you steal them, what will I do?"

Instead of replying, the man struck at Liu's face with his fist. Liu dodged to one side and then got to his feet, ready to fight with him. When the robber saw how nimble Liu was, he fled from the room. Liu raced after him out the door and straight into the kitchen where he was about to cry out for the neighbors to come seize the thief. Becoming frantic and seeing no way out, the burglar suddenly caught sight of a gleaming axe for chopping firewood near at hand. In desperation, he picked it up and swung it at Liu, striking him squarely in the head and knocking him to the ground. Again he swung, chopping him on the side. Liu clearly was dead. Alas! May his soul be blessed!

"I couldn't stop once I'd started," the man said. "But then you chased after me. I wasn't out after your life!" Turning, he went back into the bedroom and picked up the money. Pulling out a sheet from the bed, he wrapped it up and adroitly tied it. He then went out, pulling the door shut behind him.

When the neighbors rose the next morning and noticed Liu's door shut and his house silent, they called, "Mr. Liu! You've overslept!" But there was no response. They then pushed at the door and entered, surprised at finding it unlocked. They went straight in and there discovered Liu's corpse on the floor. "His wife went to her father's home two days ago, but what has become of his concubine?" A cry was raised.

Then the neighbor Chu San-lao, at whose house the concubine had spent the previous night, spoke up: "His concubine came over to our house yesterday evening to spend the night. She said that Liu had sold her for no reason. She went straight off to her parents, asking me to tell Liu that since she now belonged to another, they could go to her parents' and explain the situation. Now someone must be sent to overtake her and bring her back so that we can account for her whereabouts. Another must go notify his wife and have her return. Then we can decide what to do."

Everyone agreed that this was best.

First someone was sent to Squire Wang's residence to break the terrible news. The old man and his daughter burst into tears, and the former said, "Yesterday he left in such fine shape. I gave him fifteen strings of cash to start a business with. How then did he come to be murdered?"

"This is what happened," said the messenger. "It was already dark when Mr. Liu returned yesterday, and he was slightly drunk. No one knows whether he had any money with him or exactly when he returned. But this morning Mr. Liu's door was ajar, so several of us pushed it open and went in. There he was dead on the floor. We saw no trace of either the fifteen strings of cash or his concubine. A cry was raised and the neighbor on the left, Chu San-lao, came out and said that Mr. Liu's concubine had come over yesterday evening to spend the night. She told him that Mr. Liu had for no reason pawned her to another man and that she wanted to let her parents know. She stayed overnight and went off this morning. We decided that you and his wife should be notified, and at the same time someone was sent after the concubine. If he didn't overtake her on the way, he was to go straight on to her parents' place and in any event bring her back to be questioned. You and Mrs. Liu had best come back and avenge the death of Mr. Liu."

The squire and his daughter hastily got ready, treated the messenger to food and wine, and then hurried to the town as fast as they could go.

Now the concubine had left the neighbor's house early in the morning and set off toward home. Before she had gone more than one or two

li, her feet became too sore to continue, so she sat down by the side of the road. She then caught sight of a young man coming toward her wearing a swastika-shaped turban and a loose jacket. A shoulder bag full of coins was slung on his back and on his feet were silk shoes and clean socks. As he drew opposite the girl, he took a look at her. Though no great beauty, her bright eyes and sparkling teeth, fresh complexion and clear gaze made her quite attractive. Indeed:

Wildflowers always dazzle the eye,
And country wine is most intoxicating.

The young man set down his pack and gave her a deep bow. "I see you are traveling alone, miss. Which way are you going?"

She greeted him and said, "I'm going to my parents' place. I was too tired to go on, so I stopped here to rest for a while." She then asked, "Where have you come from, sir? And where are you going?"

Respectfully clasping his hands in front of his chest, he replied, "I'm from the country. I've been to the city to sell my silk and am going toward the Chu Family Shrine with the money I received."

"Why, my parents' house is to the left of the Chu Family Shrine. I'd be very happy if you would take me along with you."

"Of course. Since that is the case, I'd be delighted to escort you there."

The two set off on their way, but before they had gone more than two or three *li,* two men came sprinting toward them from behind, dripping with sweat and out of breath, with their shirts pulled open in front. They called out, "Hey, you up there, young lady, slow down! I have something to say to you." Sensing something strange in their urgency, the concubine and the young man both halted in their tracks. The two men rushed up to them and, without offering any explanation, each grabbed hold of one of them, saying, "A fine thing you've done! Where do you think you're going?"

Taken aback, the concubine looked up to find

two of their neighbors, including the one at whose house she had spent the previous night.

"Surely I must have told you last night," she said. "My husband sold me for no reason and I'm going to notify my parents. Why do you come rushing up like this?"

"I'm not a busybody," Chu San-lao said, "but there was a murder in your family. You have to come back to testify."

"But my husband has sold me," she insisted. "He brought the money home yesterday. What's this about a murder? I'm not going!"

"Well, sure of yourself, are you? If you refuse to go, I'll call the constable and have you arrested! Otherwise we'll all be brought into this and there'll never be any peace around here!"

Seeing the ugly turn events had taken, the young man said to the concubine, "Under the circumstances, you had better go back. I'll just go on by myself."

The two neighbors both cried out, "If you hadn't been here, it would be all right, but since you're traveling along with her, you can't get away!"

"But that's ridiculous!" cried the young man. "I met her along the road and happened to go part of the way with her. Nothing improper happened on the way. How can you force me to go with you?"

"There was a murder at her house," said Chu San-lao. "Do you think we're going to let you go and then try to settle the case without a suspect?"

At this point the young man and the concubine were left with no choice. A crowd of onlookers was steadily gathering and all were urging him, "Young man, you had better go! As the saying goes, 'He who has done nothing shameful by day need not be alarmed by a knock on the door at night.' Why not go along?"

The neighbor who had overtaken them put in, "If you refuse to go, you're admitting your guilt. Don't think we're going to let you off!" The four of them then went back together.

When they reached the door of Liu's house, what a commotion they found! The concubine went in and there was Liu hacked to death on the floor; the fifteen strings of cash on the bed were nowhere to be seen. Her jaw dropped and her tongue hung out in amazement.

The young man was also appalled. "How unlucky I am!" he exclaimed. "I joined up with the woman for no special reason and now I'm involved in a crime."

People were still milling around in confusion when Squire Wang and his daughter came staggering up. At sight of his son-in-law's corpse, Wang burst into tears. Then, turning to the concubine, he asked, "Why did you kill your husband and make off with the fifteen strings of cash? Today the will of Heaven has prevailed. What do you have to say for yourself?"

"There were indeed fifteen strings of cash," the concubine said. "But when my husband came home last night, he told me he was pressed for money, so had pawned me to someone for fifteen strings and that today I was to go to that man's house. Not knowing what sort of man he had pawned me to, I decided to go notify my parents first. So, in the dark of night, I piled the fifteen strings near his feet, pulled the door closed, and went over to Chu San-lao's house to spend the night. This morning I went to inform my parents. When I left, I asked Chu San-lao to tell my husband that since I now belonged to another, they should both go to my parents' place to settle it. I don't know how he could have been murdered."

"How can you tell such a tale?" cried Mrs. Liu. "Yesterday my father gave him fifteen strings of cash to take back and set up a business to help support the family. Why would he want to trick you into thinking it was money received from pawning you? [What has happened is that] while alone in the house for two days, you took up with another man. You saw how poor the family had become, and couldn't stand it any longer. The sight of all that money gave you ideas, so you killed your husband and stole the money. Then you contrived to spend the night at the neighbors, and plotted with your lover to run off together. You were traveling with a man just now. What do you have to say for yourself? Do you deny that?"

The crowd shouted in unison, "Mrs. Liu is right!" And to the young man they said, "Young man! How did you plot with her to kill her husband? You secretly agreed to wait in some secluded place and then run off somewhere together, didn't you? Just what was your plan?"

"My name is Ts'ui Ning," the man said. "I have never met this woman before. Yesterday evening I went into the city to sell silk for several strings of cash, which I have here. I happened to meet her along the road and asked her where she was going. She was then traveling by herself. It turned out we were going the same way, so we set off together. I knew nothing of what had happened."

But the crowd refused to listen to his explanations, and when his shoulder bag was searched, exactly fifteen strings of cash were found, not a penny more nor a penny less. The crowd all began shouting, " 'The net of Heaven is wide; though it is not fine, nothing slips through.' You acted with the girl to kill him, made off with his money, abducted his wife, and set off with her for another district, intending to involve us all in a lawsuit left without a clue."

At this moment Mrs. Liu seized hold of the concubine; Squire Wang seized Ts'ui Ning and, with the neighbors on all sides acting as witnesses, they went in a group to the tribunal in Lin-an. When the prefect learned there was a murder case before him, he immediately opened a session of court and called each of those involved in turn to tell his or her story from the beginning.

Squire Wang was the first to testify. "Your Honor, I come from a village of this district and am nearly sixty years of age. I have but one daughter, whom I gave in marriage some years ago to Liu Kuei of this city. Later, because no son was born, he took as concubine a girl of the Ch'en family, called Erh-chieh. The three of them have lived together ever since without a cross word. As the day before yesterday was my birthday, I sent a messenger to bring my daughter and son-in-law back to spend the night. On the following day, seeing that my son-in-law's family was destitute and without means of support, I gave him fifteen strings of cash so that he could open a shop and make a living. Erh-chieh was then at home looking after the house. Last night, when my son-in-law arrived home, for some reason she hacked him to death with an axe and then ran away with a young man by the name of Ts'ui Ning. They have been caught and were brought back. I hope Your Honor will pity the tragic death of my son-in-law. The scoundrel and adulteress are here with the stolen money as evidence. I beg Your Honor to pass judgment on this!"

The prefect heard him through and then called, "Will the woman Ch'en come forward! How did you come to plot with this scoundrel to murder your husband, steal the money, and run away together? What do you have to say for yourself?"

"Although it was as a concubine that I was given to Liu Kuei," Erh-chieh submitted, "he always treated me kindly. His wife is also most virtuous. So how could I ever wish him harm? But when my husband returned last night, he was rather drunk and came in carrying fifteen strings of cash. When I asked him where it came from, he said that since he was no longer able to support his family properly, he had pawned me to someone for those fifteen strings of cash. He had not notified my parents of this, but expected me to go to my new home on the following day. I was upset about it and left the house that same night to go over to a neighbor's to spend the night. The first thing this morning I set off for my parents' place. I asked the neighbor to tell my husband that since I now belonged to someone else, he should go to my parents' place to settle the matter. I had only gone part of the way when I saw the neighbor at whose house I had spent the night come rushing up. He seized me and brought me back. I don't know the reason for my husband's murder."

"Nonsense!" roared the prefect. "Those fifteen

strings of cash were obviously given to him by his father-in-law, and here you're trying to tell me it's the money he received from pawning you. This is clearly an outright lie. Furthermore, what was a woman doing out in the middle of the night? You were planning to run off! This whole business couldn't be the work of a woman alone. There must certainly have been someone who helped you plot to murder and rob. Come on, tell the whole truth!"

The concubine was about to protest when some of the neighbors knelt down together and said, "Your Honor's words are truly wise and just! This concubine did indeed spend the night at the second house on the left and went off this morning. When we found that her husband had been murdered, some men were sent to overtake her. When they caught up with her, she was walking along with that young man and absolutely refused to come back. We seized them and brought them back by force. Someone else was sent to fetch his wife and father-in-law. When they arrived, the father-in-law stated that yesterday he had given his son-in-law fifteen strings of cash to start a business. But the son-in-law is now dead and the money has disappeared. Under repeated questioning, the concubine said that before she left the house, she had piled the money on his bed. A search of the young man then turned up exactly fifteen strings of cash. Who else but the concubine and the young man could have plotted the murder? With such clear evidence, how can they deny it?"

This all seemed to make sense to the prefect, who then called the young man to come forward. "How can such outrageous conduct be tolerated here in the imperial capital?! Just how did you abduct the concubine, steal the fifteen strings of cash, and kill Liu Kuei? And where were you going together today? Confess the truth!"

"My name is Ts'ui Ning and I come from the country," the young man answered. "Yesterday I went to the city to sell my silk, for which I received fifteen strings of cash. This morning I chanced to come upon this lady along the road. i didn't even know what her name was. How could I have known a murder had been committed in her household?"

"Nonsense!" roared the prefect. "I can't believe there could ever be such a coincidence. They lost fifteen strings of cash, while you sold your silk for exactly fifteen strings of cash. It's clear that you are lying. Besides, it's said, 'Do not covet another's wife nor ride another's horse.' If you had nothing to do with this woman, why were you traveling and putting up together? You cunning rogue! What else but a beating will bring a confession from you?"

A group of men then gave Ts'ui Ning and the concubine such a beating that they passed out. Old Squire Wang, his daughter, and the neighbors all insisted over and over again that these two were the guilty ones. The prefect, too, was anxious to conclude the case. After being questioned under torture, poor Ts'ui Ning and the concubine, unable to endure the punishment, finally broke down and confessed that, tempted by the sight of the money, the latter had murdered her husband, stolen the fifteen strings of cash, and fled with her lover. The neighbors on both sides all made their marks on the confession. The couple were then put in large cangues and taken off to cells for prisoners condemned to death. The fifteen strings of cash were returned to their original owner [Wang], who handed them over to the men in the tribunal for presents, only to find they were not enough!

The prefect wrote up a report of the case and submitted it to the imperial court. The ministry concerned, after due consideration, sent its conclusions to the emperor. An edict was then issued:

Ts'ui Ning abducted another man's wife and murdered for money; he should by law be decapitated. The woman, Ch'en, conspired with this villain to perpetrate the most heinous of crimes, the murder of one's husband, and is to be sliced to death as an example to the public.

The confessions were then read out, and the two were led from the prison to be sentenced in court, one to decapitation and the other to slicing. They were then taken under escort to the market-place and there the sentences were carried out as an example to the populace. Had they mouths all over their bodies, they could not have spoken out in protest. Truly:

The dumb tastes the gentian root;
He has no way to tell others of the bitterness.

Now listen, dear audience, if the concubine and Ts'ui Ning had in fact murdered for money, they would certainly have fled on that same night. Is it likely that she would have gone and spent the night at a neighbor's house? Would she have gone to her parents' place the following morning only to be seized on the way? This injustice could have been brought to light with a close examination of the facts. But who expected the judge to be so muddled, intent only on concluding the case without ever realizing that under pain of torture, one would confess to anything? In the netherworld, accounts are kept of one's misdeeds. Whether [retribution] be as far removed as his descendants or as near as his own lifetime, the spirits of the two who were wronged will not let him go. Thus, an official must never pass judgments according to whim nor mete out punishment as he pleases. Rather, he must strive to make just and proper decisions. It is all too true that the dead can never be brought back to life nor the broken be made whole. Alas, the pity of it! But no more idle talk.

Meanwhile, when Mrs. Liu arrived home, she set up a memorial tablet for her husband and began her mourning. After some time, her father, Squire Wang, urged her to remarry, but she replied, "Even if I don't observe the three-year period of mourning, I should at least wait until after the anniversary rites of his death." Her father assented and went away.

Time passes swiftly. Mrs. Liu managed to maintain herself at home for nearly a year. Seeing that she could not hold out much longer, her father sent Old Wang to bring her back. "Tell the mistress to gather her things and come back home. She can remarry as soon as she has observed the anniversary of Liu's death."

There was nothing she could do and so, after thinking over her father's words, she decided this was most sensible. She tied up her belongings in a bundle which she gave to Old Wang to carry and said good-bye to the neighbors, promising to return soon.

It was autumn, and as they left the city, they were caught in a sudden rainstorm which forced them to leave the road and seek cover in a forest. Somehow they took a wrong path, and so it was that:

Like pigs or sheep on their way to the butcher's,
With each step they went farther along the path toward death.

As they entered the woods, they heard a loud shout from behind some trees: "I am the king of the Ching Mountain. Wayfarers, halt and pay me the toll!" Mrs. Liu and Old Wang were terrified. Then suddenly a man leaped out:

On his head he wore a red concave turban,
On his body an old soldier's jacket.
Around his waist was a sash of red silk.
On his feet were a pair of black leather boots,
And in his hand he held a broadsword.

He came toward them brandishing his sword. Old Wang, who was doomed to die, cried, "You worthless brigand! I know what you're up to. This old life isn't worth much. Let's have it out!" And he charged toward him, head down. But the bandit dodged aside, and the old fellow, carried forward by the force of his thrust, plunged to the ground.

"Impudent old mule!" roared the bandit in a rage, and he stabbed him twice with his sword. Blood gushed out over the ground and it was obvious that Old Wang had met his end. When Mrs. Liu saw how fierce the man was, she knew she would never escape with her life, and so she decided to put on an act. Clapping her hands, she cried, "Well done!" At this the bandit stopped short and stared at her wide-eyed. "Who was this man to you?" he shouted.

"I was unlucky," she lied. "My husband died, and then I was tricked by a matchmaker into marrying this dotard who can do nothing but eat. Now you've killed him for me and rid me of the nuisance!"

When the bandit saw how prudent she was, and that she was not bad looking besides, he asked, "Would you be willing to be the wife of a brigand?"

Unable to think of a way out, she replied, "I would be happy to serve a hero like you."

The bandit's angry expression turned to one of delight, and after sheathing his sword, he threw Old Wang's corpse into a stream and then led Mrs. Liu along a winding path to a large country house. Picking up a few clods of mud from the ground, he tossed them on the roof, whereupon someone from inside came out and opened the gate. When they had entered the hall, he called for a sheep to be killed and wine to be brought out, and thus they became man and wife. The two got along well enough together, for:

Though it was obviously no match,
She was bound to him by circumstances.

Less than a year after the outlaw had married Mrs. Liu, he made a series of rich hauls, and they found themselves quite well off. His wife was provident and constantly exhorted him with wise sayings: "It has always been said that 'An earthen jug will break at the well, and a general is bound to die in battle.' There is enough now for the two of us to live on for the rest of our lives, but if you keep on flouting the will of Heaven, you will surely meet a bad end. Isn't it said that 'Though the Liang Garden⁵ is splendid, it's still not like

home?' It would be better for you to change your ways and start a small business that could provide enough income to live on."

Her constant entreaties finally won out against him, and he did abandon his old ways and go off to the city, where he rented a room and opened a general goods store. During his leisure time, he often visited the temple to chant Buddhist sutras and fast.

Then one day while he was relaxing at home, he said to his wife, "Though I grew up as a bandit, I was always aware that wrongs were never forgotten nor debts ever canceled. But I went on every day frightening and robbing people in order to provide for the future. Then later I got you. Things never went too smoothly, but now I've changed my ways. Sometimes I think back to how I wrongly took the lives of two men and brought ruin to two others, and it preys on my mind. I wish I could perform prayer services for their spirits. This is something I never told you about before."

"How did you happen to kill two people?" she asked him.

"One was your husband. He charged at me that day in the forest and so I killed him. He was an old man and I bore him no grudge. Now I've taken his wife besides. He could hardly rest easy over that."

"But if it hadn't been for that," she said, "how could we be together now? It's all over with now, so just forget about it." She then asked, "And who was the other man you killed?"

"As for the other one, Heaven will find it even less forgivable. It involved, besides, two innocent people who paid with their lives. It was a year ago. I had lost money gambling and was without a penny to my name. I went out during the night to see what I could lay my hands on, and chanced to pass by a door which was unlocked. I

---

⁵ Liang Garden was a magnificent park built by Prince Hsiao of Liang of the Western Han Dynasty for the entertainment of his favorites. The place was nice, but his guests could not stay there forever.

pushed it open and went in. There was not a soul around. Groping my way inside, I saw a man lying drunk on a bed with a pile of copper coins at his feet. I went over and helped myself to a few strings and was about to set off when I woke the man, who then sat up and said, 'My father-in-law gave me that to start a business. If you steal it, my whole family will starve!' He then got up and raced out the door ready to raise a cry for help. I realized I had no time to lose. It happened that an axe for cutting firewood was lying near my feet, and in a moment of desperation I picked it up and shouted, 'It's either you or me!' And cut him down with two strokes of the axe. Next I went to the bedroom and picked up all the fifteen strings of cash. Later I heard that his concubine and a young man named Ts'ui Ning were implicated. They were unjustly accused of murdering him for money and executed. Though I've been a robber all my life, there have been only these two murders, which neither the laws of Heaven nor the hearts of men can ever forgive. Some day I must conduct services for their spirits."

When his wife heard this, she groaned to herself, "So my husband, too, was killed by this brute! And Erh-chieh and that young man were unjustly executed. I can see now that I should never have insisted on their paying with their lives. They will never forgive me in the court of hell!" For the time being, however, she kept up an appearance of gaiety and said nothing more.

The next day, at the first opportunity, she slipped out and went straight to the Lin-an tribunal to seek justice.

A new prefect had taken over the post only a half a month before and had just opened court when his attendants brought in the woman seeking justice. Mrs. Liu kneeled at the steps and burst into sobs. When she had stopped crying, she recounted all that the outlaw had done: "He killed my husband, Liu Kuei, but the prefect who tried the case refused to make a thorough investigation, concluding it carelessly and sending Erh-chieh

and the man Ts'ui Ning off to their deaths. Later he also killed Old Wang and took me away with him. Today Heaven's will has prevailed and he has confessed everything. I beseech you, Your Honor, judge this case properly and right the wrong which has been done!" When she had finished speaking, she wept again.

Moved to pity by her statement, the prefect sent someone to seize the king of the Ching Mountain. When he was questioned under torture, his answers were found to coincide exactly with Mrs. Liu's statement. He was immediately sentenced to death, and the case was reported to the authorities. After the required sixty-day waiting period, an imperial edict was issued stating:

It has been found that since the king of the Ching Mountain murdered for money and implicated innocent people, he should by law be executed without further delay for the murder of three people. The original prefect who decided the case without securing the truth is to be stripped of all official rank. Out of pity for the unjust deaths of Ts'ui Ning and the woman Ch'en, their families are to be interviewed and given proper compensation. Since the woman Wang was forced by the bandit into becoming his wife and was able to clear up the false charges surrounding her husband's death, half of the bandit's property is to be given to her for support, and the other half is to be confiscated by the state.

That day Mrs. Liu went to the execution ground to witness the execution of the king of the Ching Mountain. She then took his head to be offered as a sacrifice to her dead husband as well as to the concubine and Ts'ui Ning. She wept there for a spell. Her half of the [bandit's] property she donated to a convent, and she herself, morning and evening, chanted the Buddhist sutras and prayed for the souls of the departed, living to a venerable old age. As the verse goes:

The good and evil alike lost their lives.
From a mere jesting remark, disaster ensued.
So when you speak, pray be true and honest,
For the root of all misfortune lies in the tongue.

LION CUB LANE

From *Lung-t'u kung-an*

TRANSLATED BY GEORGE A. HAYDEN

In Iron Hill Hamlet, Virtue Village, in Ch'ao-shui County of Ch'ao-chou,[1] there lived a young scholar, Yüan Wen-cheng, who had from childhood applied himself to preparation for the imperial examinations. His wife, whose maiden name was Chang, was a woman of both beauty and good character. By the time their only son was three years old, Yüan heard that examinations were about to be held in the Eastern Capital. When he advised his wife of his intention to take part in the examinations, she said, "We're not very well off, and our boy is so small. If you go, who will support us?"

"My ten years of hard study have been dedicated to success in this single moment," replied Yüan. "Rather than your staying home without support, it would be better if you gathered up your things and came along with me."

The two of them, traveling by day and resting by night, arrived in the capital after a good many days and set their baggage down at the inn of Granny Wang, where they spent the night.

The next day, once the morning preparations and breakfast were over, Yüan took his wife and son into the city to see the sights. Suddenly with a shout of "Make way!" the advance party of a pro-cession drew near. Husband and wife dodged to one side and saw a rather flashy aristocrat on horseback who was none other than the younger Imperial Brother Ts'ao.[2] From his horse Ts'ao caught sight of the wife's beauty and was seized with desire. He had his guards invite Yüan to be entertained at his mansion, and since it was an invitation from a brother-in-law of the emperor, Yüan did not dare refuse.

Upon the Yüans' arrival at the residence, Ts'ao came out in person to greet them. After the introductions were over and everyone was seated, Ts'ao asked Yüan his background, and Yüan told him of his journey to take part of the examinations. Ts'ao was greatly pleased at this and first told a maid to conduct the wife to the rear chambers and see to her wishes. He then had the servants set out wine and a full banquet and saw to it that Yüan eventually drank himself into a stupor. He secretly ordered the servants to escort Yüan to an out-of-the-way place and strangle him with a rope, and to beat the three-year-old boy to death as well. This was the tragedy that befell scholar Yüan, whose lifetime of learning ended like a dream.

[1] In the northeastern part of modern Kwangtung Province.

[2] One of the brothers of Empress Ts'ao and hence brother-in-law to Emperor Jen-tsung. He and his elder brother as depicted in this story appear to be fictional.

When the wife came out again to go back to the inn with her husband, Ts'ao said to her, "The scholar has had a little too much to drink for the time being, and I've helped him into the bedroom to lie down." The wife was perturbed by this. After all, she could not very well go on into the residence to be with her husband; so she decided to wait for him to wake up. Toward dusk, Ts'ao commanded the maid to tell her of Yüan's death and urge her to be Ts'ao's wife. At this Mrs. Yüan cried bitterly, and she wished to die. Ts'ao, realizing that she was not about to go along with his wishes, had her imprisoned in the inner chambers and sent the maid in day after day to plead with her, to no effect whatsoever.

[Here the story breaks off.] One day Lord Pao, after having rewarded the armies at the border, was now back at court. Having discharged all his duties, he was passing by a stone bridge on the way back to his tribunal when an extraordinary gust of wind arose in front of his horse and twisted around and around without cease. "This must be a sign of some injustice," he thought to himself. He immediately sent his attendants. Wang Hsing and Li Chi, after the wind to see where it came to ground. Receiving their orders, Wang and Li followed the wind, which descended right in the middle of Imperial Brother Ts'ao's residence.

The two saw four high walls towering above them on all sides. On a doorway in the center of one wall were the words, "Onlookers will have their eyes gouged out, and whoever points here will lose the hand he pointed with." The two attendants went back in fright to report to Lord Pao, who said angrily, "That's not the imperial palace; who do they think they are to come out with nonsense like that?" When he went to take a look for himself, he found that it was indeed the house of some noble family, but he had no idea which one it might be. He had his soldiers search out an old man in the vicinity and learned from him that it was the mansion of the Ts'aos, the imperial brothers-in-law. Lord Pao remarked, "No imperial relative's residence is as enormous as this, and they are nothing but brothers by marriage. Look at the extravagance of this place!'

The old man sighed and said, "I wouldn't have dared say this if Your Honor hadn't broached the subject, but they have even more power than the one now on the throne. Offenders who fall into their clutches get the iron cangue, and beautiful women they kidnap and violate. I don't know how many men they've killed, and because of all the people they've murdered, their home has recently been haunted. The imperial brothers found it impossible to live there any longer and have now moved the entire household to new locations."

Upon hearing this, Lord Pao dismissed the old man with a gratuity and set his guards to breaking open the lock on the gate. He went straight inside and took the seat above the great hall, which he found to be as imposing as the imperial palace itself. He then called for Wang Hsing and Li Chi to summon as a witness the whirlwind ghost that had appeared in front of his horse. The two, once outside the gate, pondered the matter but could think of no plan. They waited until evening and then, by the entrance to the Ts'ao mansion, shouted at the top of their voices for any victims of injustice to speak up. At once a gust of wind arose, and with it a wraith holding in its arms a three-year-old child. When it had followed the attendants inside, Lord Pao saw that its hair was tousled and its body bathed in blood. He asked it, "How did you die? Tell me everything that happened."[3] The spirit told the whole story of how he had taken his wife and son to the capital to attend the examinations, how he had been murdered by the Ts'ao family, and how his corpse had been sunk in the well of the garden at the back of the house. "Your wife is alive," Lord Pao said.

---

[3] At this point, all the available Ch'ing editions have a physical lacuna. This sentence is taken from a recent reprint which otherwise abounds in textual problems.

"Why didn't you have her come to make the accusation?"

"My wife was taken away to Cheng-chou three months ago," answered Wen-cheng. "How could she manage to see Your Honor?"

"You may go now," said Pao. "I'll settle your grievance." At this reply, the spirit changed into a gust of wind as before and left.

The following day Pao, back at his tribunal, ascended the dais and gathered the attendants together, telling them, "Last night the spirit said that a thousand taels of gold were stored away in the well in the garden behind the Ts'ao mansion. Anybody willing to go down and get it will receive half." Wang and Li offered to enter the well and recover the gold, and once there they came upon a dead body. They climbed out of the well in alarm and informed Lord Pao, who said, "I find that hard to believe. Bring the corpse up here so that I can have a look at it." Back down the well shaft went the two, much against their will, and up came the corpse. Lord Pao ordered it carried to the K'ai-feng tribunal and placed it in the west wing. He then asked his guards where the elder Ts'ao had moved to and was told that he was now living in Lion Cub Lane. With some mutton and wine he had commanded Li Wan and Chang Ch'ien [4] to prepare, Pao went off to pay him a visit.

When Pao arrived at the Ts'ao residence, the elder imperial brother had not yet returned from court, and his mother, Matriarch Ts'ao, was angry with Pao and would not accept the gifts. Humiliated, Lord Pao was just about to head for his office when he ran into the elder imperial brother-in-law coming home; at the sight of Lord Pao, he dismounted and engaged him in conversation. On being told of what had just happened, he asked for Pao's pardon.

After the two men parted company, the elder Ts'ao returned home in a troubled mood and said to his mother, "I met Lord Pao just now. He told me that he has been treated improperly. If Pao should find out that my brother has committed a crime, his life might be in danger."

His mother laughed. "My daughter is the empress; what do we have to fear from him?"

"He wouldn't hold back even if the emperor himself violated the law, not to mention the empress," he replied. "We'd better write a letter to brother telling him to do away with the scholar's wife to avoid repercussions."

Giving her approval, the mother wrote the letter and had a man take it to Cheng-chou. When he had read it, the younger Ts'ao had no recourse but to force wine upon Yüan's wife. He had just grabbed hold of a knife and stepped into her room to dispose of her when he caught a glimpse of her beautiful face. Unable to go through with it, he left the room and came upon the servant Old Chang, to whom he revealed everything. Chang said, "I'm afraid that if you kill her, her wronged spirit will stay and haunt us. In my garden there is an old well, so deep that you can't see the bottom. The best thing to do would be to push her into the well, and your problems would be over." Delighted, Ts'ao rewarded Chang in advance with ten taels in cash. He had the maid tie up Yüan's wife and with Chang's help took her to the garden at the back.

Now Old Chang was intending all along to save her life and merely bided his time until she awoke. When after a while she did come to, he listened to her story and felt all the more pity for her. In stealth he opened the rear gate and gave her the ten taels in cash for traveling expenses to go to the Eastern Capital and report the case to Lord Pao. She bowed her thanks and went out the gate.

She, a woman of gentle upbringing, would have had no hope of reaching the capital on her own if it had not been for the fact that the star T'ai-po,[5]

---

[4] Two of Lord Pao's confidential attendants.

[5] The god of the planet Venus.

moved by her anguish, transformed himself into the shape of an old man and conducted her to the Eastern Capital. There he left her, changing himself into a rush of wind. She looked up in bewilderment and discovered that she was standing before the gate of the inn of Granny Wang. She went in to seek lodging for the night and was recognized at once by the old woman. When she heard what had happened, Granny Wang wept and said, "I've just heard that Lord Pao has gone out early to offer incense. When he comes back, you can step in front of his horse and press your charge."

Yüan's wife asked someone to write out the complaint and then went out into the street, where she met with an official. Thinking that he was Lord Pao, she went up to him and presented the accusation. She had no way of knowing that he would turn out to be the elder imperial brother-in-law. The sight of the complaint gave him a shock, and on the charge that she was willfully impeding his way, he beat her senseless with his iron whip. A search of her person revealed the ten taels of silver, which he took with him after throwing her body into a deserted alley. When news of this reached Granny Wang, she came at once and saw that Mrs. Yüan still had some breath in her. She lost no time in carrying her back to the inn and bringing her back to consciousness.

A few days later, having learned that Lord Pao would be passing by the inn, Yüan's wife blocked his way and gave him her accusation. Lord Pao accepted the complaint and ordered his attendants to take her to the wing of the tribunal to identify the corpse. She certified that this was indeed her husband. Pao next had Granny Wang brought in for questioning and in that one session got all the facts he needed for the case. He sent Yüan's wife into the rear chambers in the company of his own wife, Lady Li, and released Granny Wang.

Lord Pao thought that he would first of all arrest the elder Ts'ao and then wait to see what further steps to take. He took to his bed with a feigned illness. When the report that Pao was sick reached the emperor, he assembled his ministers to plan a personal visit. Out stepped the elder Ts'ao, who suggested, "Let me go first to make inquiries; Your Majesty can always make the trip in good time later on."

The emperor agreed, and the next day the elder Ts'ao was announced at Pao's tribunal. Lord Pao ordered his servants to get ready, and no sooner did Ts'ao step down from his sedan chair in front of the main hall than Lord Pao appeared to invite him in. The condolences lasted for some time, following which wine was brought in. They were well into their drinking when Lord Pao stood up and said, "Imperial brother, I've just received a written complaint stating that someone's husband and son were murdered and that she herself was kidnapped. Later she escaped to the Eastern Capital and made her complaint to a certain official, who beat her unconscious with an iron whip. Fortunately, Granny Wang brought her back to life, and her accusation has now found its way into my hands. I have given it my authorization and would now like to take the matter up with you. I wonder what the name of that official might be?"

At these words the imperial brother-in-law felt a chill from his hair to his bones. From behind the screen appeared Yüan's wife, in tears, charging, "This is the man who tried to beat me to death!"

"Are you aware of the penalty for baseless slander?" shouted Ts'ao.

Furious, Lord Pao had his guards seize Ts'ao, remove his cap and gown, and send him off to jail in a long cangue. Fearful that word of this would leak out, he ordered the gates shut and Ts'ao's attendants detained. He then laid plans for the arrest of the younger imperial brother-in-law.

He wrote a counterfeit letter and, after stamping it in cinnabar with a seal that he had confiscated from the elder Ts'ao, sent a man to Cheng-chou to say that Matriarch Ts'ao was seriously ill and that the younger Ts'ao was to hurry back to the capital. Ts'ao recognized his older brother's seal on the letter and instantly started off for the capital. As luck would have it, he ran into Lord Pao, who invited him into the tribunal. After some wine and pleasantry, Ts'ao got up in a state of semi-intoxication and said, "A letter from my brother said that my mother is very sick. May we continue this some other time?"

Just then from the back of the hall Yüan's wife stepped out and, weeping, gave her account of the past events. When his eyes fell upon her, Ts'ao's face turned the color of mud. He soon found himself under arrest and in jail wearing a cangue. Some attendants notified Matriarch Ts'ao, who anxiously took a directive straight to the K'ai-feng tribunal. There she came upon the two imperial brothers-in-law being strung up for questioning beneath the dais of the great hall. She went forward to Lord Pao and related the substance of her directive, but an attendant snatched it from her hands and tore it to pieces. As a last resort, she hurried back to report the matter to Empress Ts'ao, who in turn informed Emperor Jen-tsung. The emperor, however, refused to take action. In panic, Empress Ts'ao surreptitiously left the palace for the K'ai-feng tribunal to plead for her two brothers.

"The imperial brothers-in-law have committed a capital crime," said Pao, "and you have left the palace without permission. Tomorrow I am going to report this to the throne." The empress had no reply to this and could do nothing but return to the palace.

On the following day, Matriarch Ts'ao herself addressed Emperor Jen-tsung, and he finally dispatched the senior ministers of the court to the K'ai-feng tribunal to bring about some kind of compromise. Lord Pao had anticipated this and sent his guards out to announce that every official had his own tribunal and whoever so much as

stepped into his would suffer the same punishment as the Ts'aos. Upon learning this, the high ministers could only turn back. The emperor knew that Lord Pao would not allow any favoritism. However, as Matriarch Ts'ao wailed day and night before him, he reluctantly made a personal visit to the K'ai-feng tribunal. Lord Pao received the emperor and, once the latter had taken his seat, he stepped forward to make a petition by biting the jade belt of the emperor three times. "Today is not the day for sacrifice to Heaven and Earth or for encouragement of agriculture; how could you leave the court so casually? This is the omen for a three-year-long drought."

"I have come expressly on behalf of my two brothers-in-law," said Jen-tsung, "in the hope that in all things you will bear some consideration for me."

Lord Pao replied, "Since Your Majesty is eager to commute the sentence of your two relations, a single order of clemency would have been sufficient; why go through all the trouble of a personal visit? As a matter of fact, the crimes of your brothers-in-law fill the dockets, and if I am not going to be permitted to pass judgment, I would just as soon hand in my resignation and retire to my farmstead."

Jen-tsung returned to court, and Lord Pao ordered the executioners to lead the two Ts'aos to the execution ground. This news sent Matriarch Ts'ao into court to ask the emperor to pardon her two sons. The emperor assented and sent an edict of clemency in the care of an envoy for him to read to Lord Pao on his knees at the place of execution. Pao received the imperial instruction to pardon only criminals in the Eastern Capital, along with the two imperial relatives. Lord Pao observed, "All are equal before the law. Why not pardon the whole empire as well?" He ordered the younger Ts'ao executed right away and a postponement of the execution of the elder Ts'ao until noon.

When Matriarch Ts'ao learned of this, she hurried off to appeal before the emperor in tears. Prime Minister Wang suggested, "Your Majesty will have to pardon the whole empire if you want to guarantee the safety of your elder brother-in-law." The emperor gave his consent and drafted a proclamation for circulation throughout the empire, to the effect that all were to be pardoned regardless of the gravity of offense. After learning of this general clemency, Lord Pao immediately ordered the cangue removed from the elder Ts'ao and set him free.

Ts'ao returned home to his mother, whom he tearfully embraced, saying, "Your unworthy son has deeply disgraced his parents. Now that I have returned to life from the very clutches of death, and knowing that you will be well provided for, I would prefer to relinquish my official rank and perfect my inner nature in the mountains." His .mother could do nothing to dissuade him. Later,

Ts'ao received instruction from a sage and took his place in the ranks of the immortals.[6]

After having brought the case to a successful conclusion, Lord Pao saw to Yüan Wen-cheng's burial on the northern slope of South Mountain[7] and sent Yüan's wife back to her home district with a gift of gold and silver from his treasury. By this time every member of the various families graced by the pardon offered praise to Lord Pao for his humanity. In this single case, Lord Pao, by executing one imperial brother-in-law, had resolved the grievous injustice of an entire household and, by saving another imperial brother-in-law, had released the condemned of a whole empire. Truly was he the swift thunder that enriches the meadowlands with sweet rain.

[6] He becomes in later legends one of the Eight Immortals—Ts'ao the Imperial Brother-in-Law.
[7] Another name for the Chung-nan Mountain.

MAGISTRATE T'ENG AND THE CASE OF INHERITANCE

From *Ku-chin hsiao-shuo*

TRANSLATED BY SUSAN ARNOLD ZONANA AND THE EDITORS

Young men of the Hsieh family stand like the orchids and the
*   ash trees in the courtyard.*[1]
Three T'ien brothers stand below the flowers of the Judas tree.[2]
When brothers are in harmony, as pipe and flute,
Their parents' hearts are filled with delight.
Many who stem from the same root bitterly harass one another
As they fight over property and possessions.
The snipe and the mussel grip each other voraciously, but in
*   vain,*
And fall to the benefit of the fisherman.[3]

This *tz'u* poem, to the tune of "The Moon over the West River," exhorts all brothers to live in harmony. Now let me mention the teachings of the three religions, all of which show men how to be virtuous. Confucianism has the thirteen classics, the six classics, and the five classics. Buddhism has the various items in the *Tripitaka*. Taoism has the *Chuang-tzu* and the *Lieh-tzu* (*Nan-hua Ch'ung-hsü ching*).[4] If you were to amass all the various esoteric teachings until they overflowed chests and covered tables, you would find upon examination that all their thousands of thousands of words are redundant.

In my opinion, to be a virtuous person it is sufficient to follow the teaching of two characters: *hsiao-ti*—"filial piety and brotherly love." Of these two, it is sufficient to take note of the single character *hsiao*, "filial piety."

When one displays filial piety toward his parents, he observes what they love and loves it, observes what they honor and honors it. In the interaction between brothers who are like branches from the same tree, this love and honor should run even deeper if only for the sake of their parents. As to the question of family property, since it all comes from the same parents, why should it be divided between what is yours and what is mine, what is fertile and what is barren?

Suppose you are born into a poor family and inherit not a single penny; you will undoubtedly be resolute in your struggle to earn a living. But if

[1] Hsieh An (320–385) once asked the young members of his family why people would like to have respectable children. Hsieh Hsüan (343–388), his nephew, answered that everybody expected his children to stand like orchids and ash trees (symbols of transcendence and elegance) in the courtyard.

[2] When the three T'ien brothers of the Han period wanted to cut up the Judas tree in the courtyard in dividing the estate, the tree withered and died. Seeing this, the brothers were moved and decided to live together. Then the tree came back to life again.

[3] This refers to a famous parable used by the fourth century B.C. statesman Su Tai. Su was advising the king of Chao to stop fighting with the state of Yen, for he feared that the state of Ch'in would take advantage of the situation to conquer both of them.

[4] *Nan-hua ching* and *Ch'ung-hsü ching* are respectively the alternative titles for *Chuang-tzu* and *Lieh-tzu*. These titles were introduced in T'ang times.

485

you see that there are lands in the family already, then you will be afraid that you will get too little and you will certainly fight for more. You will infer without cause that your parents loved one brother more than the other and that the division was not equal. The parents who now dwell below in the Nine Springs must surely feel sorrow in their hearts. How could devoted sons behave this way? The ancients, therefore, had a fine saying:

Brothers are something hard to come by.
Land is something easy to obtain.

Why are brothers hard to come by? Let me give you an example. In life there can be no relationship more intimate than that between parents and their children. But when the parents give birth to a child, they have at least reached the prime of life. How can it be possible for them to live long enough to die with their children? At best they may be able to live together until the children reach middle age. Now, granted that the love between a husband and wife has no equal, since they keep each other company unto old age. But what about that period of time before they were married in which they were total strangers?

Only brothers, born of the same family, accompany one another from youth through old age. They discuss matters together and help one another out in difficulties. They are as close to one another as the left hand is to the right. How extraordinary is this relationship! Land and property, however, are different: if you lose them today, you still have a chance to get them back one day. Such is not the case for a brother. If you lose one, it is as if you have cut off a hand or severed a foot; you will be deformed for the rest of your life.

Now that I have said this much, do you not agree that "Brothers are something hard to come by, while property is something easy to obtain?" If you ruin the brotherly relationship for the sake of property, it would have been better for you to be a poor man without inheritance, for that would have saved you from future envy and disputes.

Today I am going to tell a story of this dynasty [Ming], "Magistrate T'eng and the Case of Inheritance." The story urges men to value morality and disdain property, not to forget the two-character rule, "filial piety and brotherly love." Honorable readers, it is none of my business whether or not you have brothers. What is important is that each of you should follow what your conscience dictates and learn to be a good man, that's all. Verily:

When a good man hears this story it pierces to the center of his heart.
To an evil man, it is a mere breeze passing by his ear.

It is said that in the Yung-lo reign period [1403–1425] of this dynasty, there lived in Hsiang-ho County in the Shun-t'ien Prefecture of the Northern Metropolitan Area [5] a certain Prefect Ni, whose personal name was Shou-ch'ien and style Yi-chih. He had great wealth, fertile lands, and magnificent dwellings. His wife, Ch'en-shih, had given birth to an only son named Shan-chi.

After Shan-chi had married and Ch'en-shih had passed away, Prefect Ni retired from office and lived alone as a widower. Although he was old, he had an unusually high spirit and good health. Every matter, such as collecting rents or loaning money, he attended to himself, unwilling to live his days in idleness.

When Prefect Ni reached seventy-nine, Ni Shan-chi said to his father, " 'Men who reach the age of seventy have always been a rarity.' This year you are seventy-nine, father. Next year you'll be fully eighty years old. Why don't you let me relieve your burden so that you can enjoy your life more?"

The old man shook his head and explained, "Live a day, work a day. Let me plan and labor for your sake. When my feet stretch rigid in death, then, it is none of my concern."

---

[5] So called for being under the direct jurisdiction of Peking.

Every year in the tenth month Prefect Ni made a trip in person to the village to collect the rents. He stayed there the entire month, while his tenants filled him with tender chickens and good wines. That particular year he went again and stayed a few days.

One day by chance he had nothing to do after lunch, and so he strolled leisurely around the village to take in the rustic scenery. Suddenly he caught sight of a young girl and an old, white-haired woman as they approached the bank of the creek to pound clothes on the rocks. The girl, dressed in country fashion, had many attractive aspects to commend her:

Hair as black as lacquer,
Eyes as sparkling as clear water,
Slender fingers like young scallions,
Curving eyebrows that seemed daubed black.
A lovely body in a plain cotton gown,
As fine as any dressed in silk.
Lovely little rustic flower,
Whose grace and beauty need no adornment.
Her small figure is well proportioned.
Sixteen years is just the right age.

Prefect Ni gaped foolishly as old passions suddenly stirred in him. After the girl had finished her washing, she left with the old woman. The old man watched carefully as they went by several houses and passed through a little white plaited gate.

Without delay, Prefect Ni turned around and summoned the head of the village. He told him all he had seen and instructed him to inquire into her background, particularly her marital status. "If she hasn't been betrothed, I would like to take her as my concubine; I don't know whether she would be willing or not."

The village headman, eager to ingratiate himself with his master, set off as soon as he had heard his instructions. He found out that the girl's family name was Mei. Moreover, her father had passed the prefectural examinations. Both her parents had died when she was young, and she lived with her maternal grandmother. She was seventeen years old, and still not betrothed.

After the village headman had ascertained the facts, he spoke with the old woman, saying, "My master has observed the good qualities of your granddaughter and he wishes to take her as his concubine. But she is to be his concubine in name only, because his first wife has been dead for a long time and there'll be no one to boss her around. Naturally, I needn't mention that once your granddaughter is married, not only will she be well provided for, but even your own daily needs will also be taken care of by the Ni family. When you die, you'll get a decent funeral. I'd hate to see you miss out on this good fortune."

The old woman listened to his embroidered speech, and consented at once. The marriage must have been fated, for no sooner was it mentioned than agreed upon. Prefect Ni was elated when the village headman returned with this news. After the betrothal gifts were discussed and settled, he consulted the imperial almanac for an auspicious day. Since he was afraid that his son would interfere, Ni simply presented the betrothal gifts and completed the marriage ceremony in the village. When they had been married, they were indeed a handsome pair. There is a poem to the tune of "The Moon over the West River" in witness of this:

One wears frosty hair wrapped in dark gauze,
The other, rosy cheeks amid jet black locks.
Imagine a withered vine curling up to the fragrance of a
*   flower bud,*
And you have a picture of our groom drooping by the bride's
*   side.*
One is a heart full of sorrow,
The other, privately overcome with trouble,
Fearing that his weapon is not enough for a handful.

That evening Prefect Ni braced himself up to discharge the duty expected of a husband. Truly:

Remember that this first night of married love is the best.
And on this night their passion was equal to that of young
*   lovers.*

When three days had passed, he summoned sedan chairs and carried Mei-shih back home to meet his son and daughter-in-law. The entire household came to kowtow and call her "young mistress." The prefect made gifts of fabric to everyone. All were delighted except his son Ni Shan-chi, who was inwardly dissatisfied. He said nothing openly, but behind his father's back he and his wife carped. "The old man has really gone too far. At his age, he's like a candle in the wind; he should consider the consequences of his actions. He should know he has perhaps five, or at best ten years left in this world; and yet he goes off and makes a fool of himself. Having sought out this young woman in full bloom, he himself should also have the sexual potency to match hers. Don't tell me he'll just let her sit there, and be married only in name.

"Another thing: many an old man has a young wife by his side. When he cannot satisfy her, the young wife can't suppress her desires any longer. She'll simply steal men by hook or by crook, thus becoming the disgrace of the family.

"And that's not all: a young woman who follows an old man is comparable to a man leaving home in time of famine. She'll wait until the time is right and then run away. She'll pilfer here, filch there, concealing the booty in different places as she goes along. Meanwhile, she'll act the part of a foolish coquette to make her huband provide her with clothing and more jewelry. When the time comes for the tree to fall and the bird to fly away, she will then turn around and marry someone else, gathering up her booty to use for her own gratification. This parasite is a worm in the wood or an insect in the rice. To have such a person around in the house is most devastating."

After a short pause, they continued, "This girl is so flirtatious. She looks more like a courtesan than a girl from a good family. You can see that she just uses coyness as a bait to entice father. If her position at our father's side were to be only half concubine, half maidservant, that wouldn't be so bad, for she'd still be in our control afterward.

It is ridiculous that father doesn't understand this and tells everyone to call her 'young mistress.' I guess it would make him even happier if we called her 'mother'! Let's simply ignore her; otherwise she'd get notions of being the first lady of the house, and turn around to vent her anger upon us tomorrow." There seemed to be no end to their grumbling.

Soon some busybody spread the words around and Prefect Ni got wind of this. Although he was disturbed, he kept it to himself. Fortunately, Mei-shih was of a warm and complaisant nature. She served the old and treated the young in a pleasant and genial manner, so that everyone lived harmoniously.

After two months Mei-shih became pregnant. She concealed her knowledge from everyone, and informed only her husband. As days grew into weeks and weeks into months, a boy was born in the tenth month, to the great astonishment of the family. As the birthday was precisely the ninth day of the ninth month, he was accordingly given a pet name, Ch'ung-yang [Double Ninth]. Prefect Ni's birthday happened to be on the eleventh of the same month, and this year he had the fortune of reaching eighty years old. Guests bringing congratulations filled the house. The prefect gave a feast both for his own birthday and for the celebration of the third day of the baby's birth.

All the guests said, "Venerable sir, at your age you've fathered a son, a sure sign of your vitality as well as your guarantee to attain great age." Prefect Ni was most pleased.

Behind his father's back Ni Shan-chi again said, "When a man reaches sixty, his virility fails; how much more must this be true of one who is eighty! Where does one see a withered old tree putting forth new flowers? I do not know the origin of this half-breed boy, but he definitely is not the blood descendant of my father. I certainly do not acknowledge him as a brother." Such remarks eventually reached the old man, but again he hid them in his heart.

Time sped by like an arrow, and before they

knew it, another year had passed. Ch'ung-yang had reached his first birthday. The family made ready for him to choose from the First Birthday Tray.[6] Both family and distant relatives came to offer congratulations. Ni Shan-chi walked out of the house, and did not return to entertain the guests. The old man understood his reasons well and did not make any attempt to bring him back. He took it upon himself to entertain the guests and drank a full day's wine. Although he never mentioned it, he could not help feeling discontent. As the saying goes, "Filial piety by the son sets the father's heart at ease."

Now this Ni Shan-chi was an avaricious and cruel man. What he dreaded most was that when the little boy grew up he would be allotted a share of the father's estate. Therefore, he was unwilling to acknowledge the boy as a brother. He spread wicked rumors about the mother and son, so that he could put them in their place later on.

But as the prefect was an educated man and former official, how could he fail to discern this design? His only regret was that he himself was aging, and that he would be unable to see Ch'ung-yang grow into manhood. Since later on the child would have to ask for living expenses from his brother, he had to force himself to have patience in order to avoid conflict with his older son. How it pained him to look at the little boy! And when he looked at Mei-shih, so very young, he was full of pity for her! Thus he was in turn meditative, melancholic, angry, and remorseful.

Four more years passed. The small child had now grown to be five years old. Noting that he was intelligent and quick, but also much too playful, Prefect Ni wished to start him at school. Since the boy's brother was called Shan-chi, he was given the school name Shan-shu.[7] The prefect selected an auspicious day, prepared some fine wine

and delicacies, and led the child to make obeisance to his teacher.

This teacher, in fact, had been hired by Prefect Ni to teach his grandson, Shan-chi's son. The prefect reasoned that if the young uncle and nephew were to go to school together, they would both benefit. Ni Shan-chi, however, did not see things the same way. To begin with, he was not happy with Ch'ung-yang's school name, because this had placed the boy on a par with him as a brother. Now if his son were to study together with Shan-shu and call him "uncle," they would become accustomed to this relationship from a young age. Later his son might even be tyrannized by him. He felt that he had better pull his son out and find him another teacher.

That day, he called his son out on the pretext of sickness. The following days the boy was absent from school. At first Prefect Ni thought it was a real illness, but a few days later, the teacher spoke to him, saying, "Mr. Ni Shan-chi has hired a different teacher for his own son. I don't know why."

Had the prefect not heard about this, it would have been all right. But when he heard these words, he became so furious that he wanted to seek out his older son and interrogate him. Then a second thought occurred to him, "If Heaven has produced such an unfilial seed, to speak with him would do no good. I shall simply let him have his way."

Heavy with sorrow, he was returning to his rooms when by accident he tripped over the threshold and fell. Mei-shih hurriedly helped him up and supported him to a recliner, but he was already unconscious.

She urgently summoned a doctor, who declared that he had had a stroke. Some ginger broth was forced down his throat in order to rouse him. Then he was taken to bed. Although Ni was conscious, his whole body felt numb, unable to move. Mei-shih sat at the head of the bed warming medicines and attentively waited on him. She offered him several doses of medicine in succession, all without effect. The doctor felt his pulse and said,

---

[6] At a boy's first birthday, a large tray full of various objects is given to him. The first object he grasps is taken to indicate the direction of his destiny.

[7] Chinese families used to name their children in a systematic way, using an identical character in the composition of the given names of all of them.

"At best he'll linger on for days, but there's no hope for recovery."

When Ni Shan-chi got word of this, he, too, came several times to look on. Seeing that the old man was gravely ill and showed little sign of recovery, he started shouting orders around the house, striking and cursing the servants, as if he were already the master. Hearing this, the old man became more distressed. Mei-shih could do nothing but grieve. Even the little lad did not go to school but remained in the room, attending to the old man.

The prefect realized the gravity of his illness and summoned his older son. He took out the account book wherein the family lands, houses, and accounts of outstanding loans were all listed, and enjoined his son, "Shan-shu is only five years old; he couldn't even get dressed without someone helping him. Even Mei-shih is too young to manage a household. It'd be useless for me to allocate part of the estate to her. Now, I'm handing all the accounts over to you. Later, when Shan-shu reaches maturity, you should, just for my sake, get a wife for him and allocate to him a small house and fifty or sixty *mou* of fertile land, so that he won't have to suffer from hunger and cold. These instructions I've written in the account book of the estate, to serve as my will. You can use it as testimony.

"Should Mei-shih choose to remarry, act according to her wish. But if she wishes to devote her life to taking care of her child, you must not force her to remarry. If when I am dead you comply with what I've said on every point, you'll have been a devoted son. And I, resting in the Nine Springs, will be able to close my eyes."

Ni Shan-chi took the account book and opened it to have a look. All was indeed written there precisely. His face lit up in smiles, and he said several times, "Don't worry, father, I'll follow your instructions without fail." He left joyfully clutching the book in his arms.

When Mei-shih saw that he had gone a safe distance, streams of tears fell from her eyes. Pointing to her child, she said, "Do you mean to say that this little one is not your own blood? Why, you've so freely handed everything over to your older son! Tell me: what would you have the two of us live on in the future?"

"There is something you do not understand," the prefect said. "Don't you see that Shan-chi is not a good person? If I were to divide my estate equally, it would be difficult even to guarantee this little one's life. There is no better alternative than to let him have his way and give him everything. Then he will have no cause for jealousy."

Mei-shih continued to cry as she said, "That may be true, but there is a saying, 'As far as the children are concerned, there are no distinctions between those by the concubine and those by the legal wife.' For others, this gross disparity will be cause for ridicule."

The prefect replied, "I can't afford to worry about that. Since you're so young, and I'm still alive, let's place the child in Shan-chi's care. After my death, wait for half a year or at most a year before choosing for yourself a husband who will take good care of you for the rest of your life. Don't stay here, as they'll give you nothing but harassment."

"What are you saying? I, too, am a daughter of a Confucian family. A wife should remain faithful to her husband until death, not to mention the fact that I've this little child with me. How could I part with him? Come what may, I'll stay with my boy."

"You mean you really want to live out your life as a widow? Wouldn't you have regrets later on?" the prefect asked her.

Mei-shih then swore a solemn oath.

Prefect Ni said, "If you're so determined, don't worry that you and your child are not provided for." As he was speaking he groped for something underneath the pillow and handed it to Mei-shih. At first she thought that it was just another account book of the estate, but in fact it was a small scroll, one foot wide by three feet long.

"What is this scroll for?"

490

"This is my portrait. There is a secret within it. You should quietly hide it away. Don't let anyone else see it. Just wait until your child has grown. Even if Shan-chi does not take care of him, don't show your feelings. Wait until a wise and upright judge appears; then take this scroll to him and plead for justice. Tell him the details of my will, and implore him to carefully and thoroughly investigate. There will be, I'm sure, a settlement which will provide the two of you with complete comfort." Mei-shih accepted the scroll.

After that Prefect Ni lingered on a few more days and then choked on phlegm one night and passed away at the age of eighty-four.

Three breaths of life serve a thousand purposes.
Death comes one day, and your myriad affairs cease.
If you knew early that nothing could be taken to the Nine
    Springs,
Why did you work so hard to save money?

Meanwhile, after Ni Shan-chi had obtained the estate account book, he demanded the keys to each and every granary and storehouse. Every day he went to check the list of miscellaneous goods on the estate. How could he find the time to go to his father's house to ask after him! Only after his father had died and Mei-shih had sent a maidservant to convey the news to him, did he and his wife come running, sobbing out a few cries of "Father, father." In a couple of hours they had turned and gone. It was left to Mei-shih to keep vigil by the body. Fortunately, all the preparations for the funeral such as burial clothes and coffin had been prearranged, so Shan-chi did not need to trouble himself.

After the body had been prepared for burial, and mourning garments had been donned, Mei-shih and her child kept vigil in the hall of mourning. From dawn to dusk they grieved and never left his side. Shan-chi merely made a list of the mourners and received them; he displayed no feelings of grief or pain. Before the customary forty-nine days were over, he selected a day for the burial.

On the very night of the burial service, Shan-chi and his wife took Mei-shih's rooms by storm, emptying chests and trunks, for they suspected that his father had laid some private wealth aside in them. The clever Mei-shih, fearful that they would confiscate his portrait, took out several old, worn-out garments from the two trunks she had originally brought with her from home and asked the two of them to search and see. Seeing that she was quite willing for them to be searched, they did not bother to look in those trunks. The two of them created havoc for a while and then left.

As she reflected on her sad plight, Mei-shih began to wail. Seeing his mother like this, the child, too, began to weep uncontrollably. The situation was such that:

Even a clay figure would respond with tears;
Even a daredevil would grieve in his heart.

The next morning Ni Shan-chi called in a carpenter to have a look at Mei-shih's house. He wanted to remodel it for his son, who was about to marry. He moved Mei-shih and her boy into three storage rooms in the rear courtyard, giving them only one small simple bed and a few coarse stools and tables. There was not even a single decent utensil.

Originally there had been two maidservants in Mei-shih's service. Shan-chi took the older one for his own household, leaving behind only the young one, eleven or twelve years old. It was she who fetched the food for Mei-shih and the child from the kitchen every day, and she could not care less whether there was enough food. Mei-shih was well aware of the problem and took it upon herself to ask for her ration of rice, make a brick oven, and prepare the food. She sewed from morning until night to make some money for a few small dishes as well as to make ends meet. The little lad went to the neighbor's house for schooling, and Mei-shih paid the teacher's salary herself.

Ni Shan-chi not only asked his wife many times to urge Mei-shih to remarry, but he also sought out a matchmaker to discuss marriage with her. However, having been convinced that Mei-shih was dead set against remarriage, he realized that he could do nothing but leave her alone. Mei-shih was all patience; she had never uttered a word of complaint. Therefore, ruthless as Shan-chi was, there was nothing he could do about this mother and child.

Time sped by like an arrow. Before they knew it, Shan-shu had grown to be fourteen years old. Mei-shih had been a discreet woman, so much so that she had not spoken a word about the past to her son, fearing that the child might make an occasional slip of the tongue which would cause all sorts of trouble. The problem was, now that he was fourteen, he had a mind of his own and could no longer be kept in the dark.

One day he went before his mother to ask for a new silk robe. Mei-shih replied that there was no money, and Shan-shu said, "My father was once a prefect, and he had only two children. Now you see how rich my brother is. All I want is a garment, and yet we can't afford it. Why is that? Since you've no money, mother, I'll go and ask my brother." He finished what he had to say and started to leave.

Mei-shih grabbed him and said, "My son, what is so important about a silk garment that you must go begging for it? There are these common sayings: 'If one is sparing with his happiness, he accumulates happiness,' and 'When young, wear cotton; when grown, wear silk.' If you wear silks when you're young, then when you're grown you won't even have cotton to wear. Let a few more years go by. Wait until you've advanced in your studies. Then your mother will gladly sell herself to buy clothing for you to wear. Your brother is not one whom it is wise to provoke. Why bother him?"

"You're right, mother," Shan-shu replied.

Although he said so, in his heart he did feel he was right. He thought, "My father's estate of ten thousand strings of cash ought to be divided be-

tween both brothers. Besides, I'm not a stepson. Why won't my brother take care of me at all? It's funny that mother should have talked that way, selling herself to buy even a single bolt of silk for me! How very strange indeed! Since my brother is not a tiger, why should I be afraid of him?"

An idea then occurred to him, and without telling his mother, he went directly to the main house, sought out his brother, and greeted him. Shan-chi really gave a start, and asked why he had come. Shan-shu replied, "I'm the son of an official, and yet I dress in blue hemp. I don't want to be laughed at by others, so I've come specifically to ask you for a piece of silk to make a robe."

"If you want that," said Shan-chi, "go ask your mother."

Shan-shu said, "Our late father's estate is under your management, brother, not mother's."

When Shan-chi heard the expression "the estate," his eyes opened wide and his face flushed crimson as he asked, "Who told you to say those words? Did you come here today to ask for clothing to wear, or did you come to fight over the family property?"

"The estate is bound to be divided someday," Shan-shu said. "Now I just want a robe to look a little more respectable."

"A bastard like you," said Shan-chi, "why do you want to look respectable? Even if father did leave an estate worth ten thousand strings of cash, he had only one son by his legal wife, and one legitimate grandson; so what business is it of yours, bastard! What evil influence have you been listening to that you come here to seek trouble with me? You'd better not make me lose my temper, or you and your mother will soon find yourselves living in the streets!"

"We're both father's offspring," said Shan-shu, "so why am I a bastard? So what if I anger you? Do you mean to say you would plot against mother and me and keep all the estate for yourself?"

Greatly provoked, Shan-chi cursed, "You little

beast, don't you dare to contradict me!" Shan-chi grabbed the boy's sleeve and gave him a series of blows, until the boy's head was all bruised and swollen.

Breaking free from his brother, Shan-shu dashed out to his mother in tears and told her everything that had happened. She chided him: "I told you not to go stirring things up! You didn't listen to me, so it serves you right to get a good beating!" Although she talked like this, as she was rubbing the bruises on his head with her blue gown, tears were falling in spite of her. There is a poem in evidence:

The youthful widow shelters her forsaken, orphaned child,
Making do with meager food and threadbare clothes.
Just because the family is lacking in filial regard,
A branch of the tree is snapped in two, part to flourish, part to
*   perish.*

After giving this matter some further thought, Mei-shih became fearful that Shan-chi might seek revenge. Accordingly, she sent her maidservant to offer him an apology for her son's offense, saying that the young lad was innocent of the ways of the world. But this still did not mollify Shan-chi's anger.

Early the next morning, Shan-chi invited several clansmen to the house, took out his father's handwritten testament, and asked Mei-shih and her son to come so that they could examine the document together in public. Then he said, "Venerable elder clansmen, it is not that I'm unwilling to care for the two of them, or that I intended to ask them to leave; I'm doing this only because Shan-shu had words with me yesterday and quarreled over the family property. I'm honestly afraid that when he grows up, he'll have much more to say. Today I'm sending them to live elsewhere. In the eastern village there is a house with fifty-eight *mou* of land. All is in accordance with father's will; I'm not acting in the slightest on my authority. Venerable elder clansmen, I humbly beg you to bear witness."

This group of relatives had always recognized Shan-chi as a merciless person. Besides, there was his father's handwritten testament. Who dared say anything to incur Shan-chi's enmity? They all acted most diplomatically. Those who toadied to Shan-chi said, " 'A thousand pieces of gold will not buy a dead man's pen.' According to the will, there is no room for further argument." Even those who pitied Shan-shu and his mother would only say, " 'A man does not eat only the food of his inheritance; a woman does not wear only the clothes she has when she marries.' There are many who, though empty-handed, have risen in life through their own efforts. Now that you have a place to live and fields to till, you already have something to start with. The rest all depends on your own efforts. Even if you only manage to get rice gruel, don't complain, for each man has his own fate."

Realizing that their stay in the rooms of the rear courtyard could be no more than a temporary arrangement, Mei-shih could only abide by their decision. After expressing their thanks to the clan elders, she and her son took leave of the ancestral hall and bade farewell to Shan-chi and his wife.

As soon as Mei-shih had given instructions for a few old furnishings to be moved along with the two trunks she had brought with her as a bride, they rode on hired animals and headed for the house in the eastern village. There they saw a dilapidated house with overgrown weeds covering the ground. It had been in a state of disrepair for years. The roof leaked; the floor was damp; it was completely uninhabitable. Making the best of the situation, Mei-shih cleaned up a room and made up the bed. When she called in the farmers for some information, she learned that even these fifty-eight *mou* of land were of the lowest quality. In a good year, if these fields produced half a crop it should be considered a full harvest. In a year of drought, one might not even get back the original seed. Mei-shih could only lament their bitter fate.

493

Her son, however, had a sudden turn of mind: "Since both my brother and I are my father's off-spring," he asked his mother, "then why is the will so one-sided? There must be a reason for it. Could it be that it is not really father's own hand-writing? As the saying goes, 'Rank and status do not bear on property division.' Why don't you bring the case before the officials, mother? Even if the authorities' decision still turns out to be in my brother's favor, we wouldn't have any reason for complaint."

Having thus been reminded, Mei-shih then disclosed to her son all the feelings she had hidden for over ten years. "My son, you must not doubt the words of the will," she said, "for they really are from your father's hand. He said that because you were young, you might be taken advantage of by your brother; that is why he allocated all the estate to him so that he would be appeased.

"When he was nearing his end, he gave me a scroll with his portrait on it and reminded me again and again that a riddle was concealed in it, and that I should wait until an upright, intelligent official was around before presenting it to him for examination. He said that this portrait would enable us to live a life free from poverty."

"Since there was such a thing," said Shan-shu, "why didn't you mention it earlier? Where is the portrait? Go get it quickly and let me have a look!"

Mei-shih opened her trunk and took out a cloth parcel. Removing the cloth holding the bundle, she uncovered a piece of oiled paper, bound and sealed. They broke the seal, rolled out the one-by-three-foot-long scroll, and hung it on a chair. Mother and son together knelt and made obeisance. Apologizing to her late husband, Mei-shih said, "Since we cannot obtain incense and candles in the village, please forgive our improprieties."

When Shan-shu had finished his obeisance, he rose and examined the portait carefully for a while. He saw a seated man, white-haired, wearing a black silk cap. He was painted with life-like

grace: he was embracing an infant in his bosom and pointing to the ground with one hand. Shan-shu mulled it over in his mind for some time, but could not solve the riddle at all. He could only roll up the scroll and put it back in the parcel, greatly puzzled.

Several days later Shan-shu set out for a nearby village in the hope of finding someone who could explain the meaning of the scroll to him. He happened to pass in front of Kuan-ti Temple,[8] where he saw a procession of villagers ceremoniously raising high a lamb and pig to be sacrificed to the god Kuan-ti.

Stopping to watch for a while, Shan-shu happened to notice a passerby, an old man leaning on a bamboo staff, who was also looking on idly. "What's the ceremony for?" asked the old man.

"We had suffered an injustice," answered someone in the crowd. "Fortunately, we had a most judicious official who helped us settle the case. We had made promises to the gods, and so we've come today especially to repay our debt in worship."

"What injustice? And how was it settled?" asked the old man.

One of them answered, "The magistrate of our district had received from superior officials clear, written directions that each ten families should form a tithing group. I, Big Ch'eng, was the leader of my tithing group. Within our group there was a certain Chao, who was a first-class tailor. He frequently worked all night in others' houses, and would not return home for several days. One day he suddenly disappeared, and had not returned after more than a month. His wife Liu-shih enlisted the assistance of all the neighbors and friends to search for him everywhere, but not a trace was found.

"A few days later a corpse with its head crushed floated up in the river. After the headman of the ward had reported this to the authorities, some-

[8] A temple for the worship of Kuan Yü. Kuan-ti means God Kuan.

one recognized the clothing to be that of Chao the tailor.

"The day before Chao had left home, he and I had had a spat over nothing after drinking some wine. Having lost my senses, I went to his home and destroyed some of his furniture, nothing more than that. However, his wife accused me of taking his life! The former county magistrate Ch'i, influenced by her one-sided testimony, sentenced me to death. Since the magistrate was not happy with the fact that the people in my tithing group had not stepped forward to turn me over to the authorities, they were also implicated because of me. Having no one to turn to for vindication, I spent three years in prison.

"Fortunately, our new official, Lord T'eng, came to my rescue. Although he entered the officialdom as only a *chü-jen,* he is a most astute man. When the time came for the reexamination of cases during the torrid days of summer, I prostrated myself and poured out my grievances before him. He, too, had his doubts and thought to himself, 'A drunken brawl is no great feud. Why would one commit homicide just for this?' He allowed me to file a petition and issued warrants for the witnesses in order to reexamine the case.

"Lord T'eng fixed his eyes on Chao's wife and confronted her with a direct question whether she had remarried. In reply, she said, 'Because the family was poor, I have already remarried.'

"He further asked whom she had married. 'He is also a tailor, Shen Pa-han,' replied the woman. In no time Shen Pa-han was apprehended by Lord T'eng's order.

" 'When did you marry this woman?' he asked him.

" 'I married her more than a month after her husband died,' said Pa-han.

" 'Who served as go-between?' asked Lord T'eng. 'What betrothal gifts were given?'

"Pa-han said, 'When Chao the tailor was alive, he had borrowed seven or eight taels in cash from me. When I heard that he had died, I went

around to his house to convey my condolences and to collect my money. His wife was not able to repay the loan and promised to marry me in recompense. We didn't even have a go-between.'

"Lord T'eng further asked, 'Since you're a tailor, how did you acquire seven or eight taels in cash?'

" 'I saved it up little by little and gave it to him,' answered Pa-han.

"Lord T'eng gave him a pen and paper, and instructed him to carefully itemize his loans. Pa-han began to make a list, noting whether the loan was in rice or in cash. In all he had made thirteen separate loans [to Chao] totaling seven taels and eighty cents.

"When Lord T'eng had examined the writing, he shouted, 'Beat this man to death! How dare you falsely incriminate an innocent person?' He then ordered that the torture of squeezing staffs be applied. But Pa-han still refused to confess.

" 'I shall now show you the evidence of your crime, so that you will have no choice but to confess,' said Lord T'eng. 'Since you're a moneylender, you don't mean to tell me that you made loans to no one but Tailor Chao? It must be that you've had an illicit relationship with his wife, and because Chao felt that courtesy was due your wealth, he chose to close one eye.

" 'Thus, by the time you started considering a permanent alliance with his wife, getting rid of Chao became a logical solution. Then you helped his wife prepare a legal accusation against Big Ch'eng. The words you have just written on this list match [the handwriting of] those on the original accusation paper submitted by Chao's wife. Now if you didn't take his life, who did?'

"After that he ordered the woman's fingers stretched to make her confess. When she heard the pronouncement of Magistrate T'eng, with every sentence supported by facts, she recognized that he was clearly in a class with Master Kuei-ku.[9]

[9] A philosopher of the fourth century B.C., famous for his clairvoyance and skill in divination.

495

She was so disarmed by his intelligence that she did not even dream of denying anything. She confessed as soon as the finger racks were applied. Pa-han could only plead guilty also.

"The fact is, when Pa-han first began his affair with the woman, no one was aware of it. Later, however, Pa-han's frequent comings and goings made Tailor Chao worry about others' gossip, and so he began to wish to put an end to their relationship. On Pa-han's part, he secretly discussed the matter with Liu-shih, planning to kill Tailor Chao and marry her. However, Liu-shih did not agree.

"Acting alone, Pa-han took advantage of the tailor's return from work at someone's house and coaxed him into a tavern. Seeing that the tailor was dead drunk, he walked him to the river's edge, where he overpowered him, smashed his forehead with a rock, and dumped his corpse into the bottom of the river. He figured that as soon as the furor had cooled down, then he would marry the woman.

"Later the corpse drifted up and was identified. Pa-han had heard of our quarrel and talked Liu-shih into making an accusation against me. She found out only after she was remarried that Pa-han was responsible for the murder of her husband. Since they had already become man and wife, she couldn't say anything.

"When Lord T'eng's investigation exposed the true facts of the case and placed the blame on them, I was released to return to the peace of home. My relatives and friends collected enough money so that I could hold this procession for the god. Sir, could there be a more blatant injustice than this?"

The old man replied, "Such a righteous and judicious official is really hard to come by. The people of this district are indeed fortunate!"

Ni Shan-shu listened up to this point, and then turned toward home to relate every detail to his mother. "Now that we have such a fine official with us, we should waste no time and take the portrait to him."

To this his mother agreed, and they started making inquiries about the date for petitioning the court. That day she arose before dawn; bringing her fourteen-year-old son and carrying the scroll, she arrived at the tribunal and called out at the gates.

When the magistrate saw that she had no legal petition, just a very small scroll, he thought it was strange. After he asked the reason, Mei-shih gave him a detailed account of Ni Shan-chi's behavior, and the old man's instructions as handed down to her in his final days. After accepting the scroll, T'eng told her to go home first. After they had left, he entered his chambers and examined the scroll carefully. Thus:

A single portrait holds the mystery to the hunt
For a family treasure of a thousand pieces of gold.
The bitter suffering of the widow and orphan
Brings the brilliant magistrate to the test of his intellect.

Now that Mei-shih and her son are on their way home, let's leave them for the moment and turn our attention to Lord T'eng. When the magistrate had finished with the petitions for the day, he returned to his private quarters and took out the small scroll for further examination. It was a portrait of Prefect Ni who had one hand embracing an infant and the other hand pointing to the floor. He studied it for a long time and thought, "This infant is undoubtedly Ni Shan-shu. As regards the hand pointing to the ground, could it be that he wants an official to read his thought below the ground and render service for his sake?"

He thought further, "Since he left his will in his own handwriting, it'd be difficult even for an official to make any changes on his behalf. But as he said that there is a mystery concealed in the scroll, there must be a reason for it. If I don't resolve this mystery, my lifetime's reputation for brilliance will be jeopardized."

Every day, after he had left the courtoom, he unrolled the portrait to examine it. He pondered over it day after day but to no avail.

496

Now it seems that few mysteries remain unresolved forever. In Lord T'eng's case, an opportunity offered itself when one day after lunch, as he was looking at the scroll again, a maidservant brought in tea for him to drink. Stretching his hand to take the tea cup, he accidently knocked against it and spilled some tea on the scroll. T'eng put down the cup, went out to the verandah and spread the scroll to dry in the sun. Suddenly he saw under the sunlight traces of several characters inside the scroll. Intrigued, he peeled off a layer only to discover that a piece of paper with characters was concealed inside the painting. It turned out to be a will written by Prefect Ni:

I am an official holding the rank of prefect. At my advanced age of over eighty, I would have no regrets even if I should meet my end the very next hour. What worries me is that Shan-shu, my son by the concubine, is only one year old, and it will be a long time before he can stand on his own feet. Shan-chi, my older son by the legal wife, is a man not known for filial love. I fear he might hurt his brother in the future.

The two recently acquired mansions and all my land properties, I bequeath to Chi. Only the small old house on the left side [of the estate] is allotted to Shu. Though the house is not large, there are five thousand taels of silver buried in five jars below the left wall. Beneath the right wall are buried six jars, containing five thousand taels of silver and one thousand taels of gold. This is equivalent to the value of the lands and houses I bequeathed to Chi.

Whoever is the discerning official who acts on this case in the future and sees to it that justice is done, Shu should reward him with three hundred taels of silver.

Written in his own hand by Ni Shou-lien in his eighty-first year.

Dated and sealed

The truth is, this portrait had been commissioned on the occasion of Ni's eighty-first birthday and the child's first. This confirms the old saying that "No one knows a child like his father."

Now Magistrate T'eng was a most opportunis-

tic man. He could not keep his mouth from watering at the mention of the great amounts of gold and silver listed in the will. He knit his brows and came up with a plan. He secretly sent a runner to apprehend Ni Shan-chi in order to speak with him.

Ni Shan-chi, complacent in his monopoly of the family property, happily spent day after day at home. Suddenly a tribunal runner arrived with summons to take him to court. Ni Shan-chi was not granted a moment's hesitation, and unable to refuse, he could only go along to the tribunal.

The magistrate was attending to official matters when the runner announced, "We have brought Ni Shan-chi." The magistrate called him before the bench and asked, "Are you then the older son of Prefect Ni?"

"Yes, I am."

"Your stepmother has filed a complaint against you," said the magistrate. "She said that you expelled your brother and her and appropriated all lands and houses. Is this true?"

Ni Shan-chi replied, "I kept Shan-shu, my brother by the concubine, by my side and fostered him from childhood to maturity. Recently, the mother and son have chosen to live separately. I never expelled them! With regard to the family property, father settled the division with a will written in his own hand in his last days, and I surely dare not disobey."

"Where is your father's handwritten testament?" asked the magistrate.

"Now it is at home. Allow me to fetch it for your inspection, Your Honor."

The magistrate said, "In her complaint, your stepmother reports that the property is worth ten thousand strings of cash, no ordinary small amount. The authenticity of the will has yet to be verified. Since you are the heir of an official, I do not wish to make things difficult for you. Tomorrow I shall summon your stepmother and her son. I will personally come to your house to make an official review of the estate. If there is, in fact, an

497

unequal distribution of the wealth, justice will take the precedence over any personal consideration in this matter." He shouted for the runners to take him out quickly, and then go summon Mei-shih and her son to appear for a hearing the next day.

Since Shan-chi had bribed the runners, they released him without further ado. Then they went to the eastern village to summon his stepmother and half brother.

Now the severity of Lord T'eng's tone had already frightened Shan-chi out of his wits, because he had not really divided the estate at all, even though he had his father's testament for his protection. To strengthen his position, he would need all the clansmen to bear him witness. Throughout the night he distributed taels of silver among relatives on his mother's, father's, and wife's sides of the family, and urged them all to come the next morning. He implored them to back him up with one voice, should the official ask about the matter of the will.

Ever since Prefect Ni died, no one among these relatives had received the slightest favor from Shan-chi. They had not even once been invited for meals or drinks. Now, he was handing them large amounts of money. Truly: "In quiet times he burned no incense; but now he anxiously clasps the feet of the Buddha." Though each one laughed secretly, they accepted the money that fell into their laps nevertheless. The next day, before committing themselves, they would observe the manner of the official before taking a stand. A contemporary composed this verse:

Do not accuse the stepmother of readily making complaints.
As an elder brother you served your own selfish purposes.
Now you use silver to buy allegiance from your clansmen,
When you could have just presented an orphaned child with a
*   single bolt of silk.*

As for Mei-shih, she knew already that the magistrate had assumed responsibility for her case when she saw the tribunal runners summoning her. After the night had passed, mother and son left for the tribunal at the break of day and went in to see Magistrate T'eng.

"I have pity for you, an orphan and widow," he said. "Naturally it is my duty to speak on your behalf. But I have heard that Shan-chi holds a will, handwritten by his late father. What should we do?"

"Although there is that will," said Mei-shih, "it was written as a device to preserve the child's life, and it does not reflect my late husband's true wishes. If Your Honor examines the amounts in the estate account book, you will understand clearly."

The magistrate replied, "The common jingle goes, 'An honest official has difficulty settling family affairs.' However, today I may manage to provide the two of you with enough clothing and food for a lifetime. But you must not set your hopes too high."

Mei-shih thanked him and said, "If we are able to avoid hunger and cold, that will be sufficient. How could we hope to put ourselves in a class with Shan-chi as scion of a wealthy family?"

Thereupon T'eng ordered Mei-shih and her son to go first to Shan-chi's house and await him. Earlier Ni Shan-chi had had the great hall swept clean. There he set out an armchair draped with a tiger's skin and lit some fine incense. Then he urged his relatives to come early and await the official. In the meantime, Mei-shih and her son arrived. Seeing this whole crowd of relatives before them, they greeted them one by one and asked them to speak on their behalf. Although Shan-chi was filled with anger, he knew that this was not the time to give vent to it, as each was privately preparing a few words of greeting for the official.

They had not waited long when they heard shouting in the distance, and guessed it was the magistrate arriving. Shan-chi adjusted his clothes and hat and went to welcome him. The older men among the relatives made ready to advance and meet the official, while the younger and timid ones all huddled behind the outside wall and peered out to see what would happen. They saw two ranks of officials carrying insignia, and behind them a state umbrella of blue silk which sheltered the wise and talented Magistrate T'eng.

When they arrived at the entrance to the Ni house, the insignia bearers knelt down and gave a shout. Mei-shih and the brothers Ni all knelt together in welcome. A retainer shouted to all of them to stand up. The chair-bearers set down the sedan chair, and Magistrate T'eng, calm and unhurried, emerged from it. As he was about to enter the gates, he suddenly addressed the sky with repeated salutations, and made replies as if he were engaged in greetings with his host. Everyone was alarmed to see him behave in such a manner.

They observed the magistrate continue to bow ceremoniously all the way into the hall. While he performed his successive bows, he uttered words of polite conversation. First, with folded hands, he saluted the tiger-skin chair that faced the south, just as though there were a person inviting him to take a seat. Without delay he turned and pulled up another chair which he placed facing the north as though for a host. After he had repeated a few more courteous remarks to the sky, he took his seat of honor.

When the assembled people saw him acting as though he were seeing a ghost, they dared not advance before him, but stood along the two sides gaping. They saw the magistrate, seated in the place of honor, bow and begin to speak. "Your wife," he said, "has placed the matter of your estate in my humble hands. How would you like this matter to be settled?"

When he had finished speaking, he cocked his ear in a posture of listening. After a good while, he shook his head, his tongue hanging out [in surprise], and said, "Your older son has really gone too far." After that he listened quietly for a while, and then spoke again: "What provisions do you wish made for your second son?"

He stopped awhile, and then said, "A small house on the right side. What plans do you have for his livelihood?" Then he answered repeatedly,

"Thanks for your instructions." Again, he stopped awhile, and then resumed, "I will hand over this item also to your second son. I will carry out all your instructions."

After pausing for a short time, he once more bowed and said, "How could I dare to accept your bounty!" He gestured refusal for a good while, and then said, "Since you are so earnest in your esteemed command, I am obliged to accept. I shall give your second son a certificate with the official seal for him to retain as proof." Rising and bowing several times, he said, "I shall see to it immediately that your instructions are carried out." Everyone around was dumbfounded.

They watched the magistrate stand up, look around, and ask, "Where has Prefect Ni gone?" The runners answered respectfully, "We haven't seen any Prefect Ni!"

"How strange!" said the magistrate. He summoned Shan-chi and told him, "Just now your venerable father himself welcomed me outside the gate and sat facing me, and we held a lengthy discussion. You all must have heard."

Shan-chi replied, "I didn't hear anything, sir."

"The gentleman whom I just talked to," said the magistrate, "was very tall, had a thin face, high cheekbones, small eyes, long eyebrows, big ears, several thin strands of beard, silver-white hair, a silk cap, black boots, a red robe, and a gold belt. Does Prefect Ni fit this description?"

Horrified, everyone was drenched in cold sweat. All knelt and said, "That is truly how Prefect Ni looked when he was alive."

"How could he suddenly disappear?" asked the magistrate. "He said that there are two large residences in the family and an additional small old house on the eastern side. Is that true?"

Shan-chi could only tell the truth. "Yes, it's true."

The magistrate said, "We shall now proceed to the small house on the eastern side to have a look. I shall have something to say."

Everyone had seen the magistrate carry on a lengthy conversation with himself in such earnest-

ness, and his description of Prefect Ni was so un-
nervingly accurate, that all believed that the old
prefect had indeed appeared. Their tongues
hung out in great amazement. Who could have
known that it was all made up by Magistrate
T'eng, who had studied the portrait and was
therefore able to give an accurate description of
Prefect Ni? There was, of course, not a sentence
of truth in what he said. There is a poem in evidence:

The title "sage" is itself empty;
Ghosts and spirits are the only ones we dare not offend.
Were it not for the magistrate's phony tale,
The rebellious son would not have been so easily subdued.

With Ni Shan-chi leading the way and the
others following behind the magistrate, they soon
reached the old house on the east side. This old
house had been Prefect Ni's dwelling before he
passed the examinations. Ever since the great residences were built, this house had been left empty,
serving merely as a granary for rice and wheat.
Only one servant and his family lived there.

They watched the magistrate walk around the
house and then walk directly into the main room
and sit down. He said to Shan-chi, "That must
have been your father's spirit. He has given me a
detailed account of your family's problems and
has entrusted me to make a decision. What would
you say if I gave this house to Shan-shu?"

Shan-chi kowtowed and said, "Everything according to your judgment, Your Honor."

The magistrate then demanded the estate account book and looked it over carefully. He said
over and over, "That is quite a large family estate!" He read through the testament written at
the end, laughed loudly, and said, "Your father
wrote this settlement himself. Yet just now he
stood before me and recounted Shan-chi's many
failings. The old gentleman seems to be quite unpredictable."

He summoned Shan-chi to come before him.
"Since the will is recorded in writing," he said, "all
the lands and accounts are given to you. There

should be no room for Shan-shu to dispute this."

Mei-shih secretly cried out in anguish. She was
on the point of going before the magistrate to
plead with him when she heard him continue,
"This old house is allotted to Shan-shu. Whatever
is in the house, Shan-chi shall not claim."

Shan-chi thought to himself, "There is nothing
here but broken furniture, not worth anything. I
sold most of the grain stored here a month ago.
There is not much left, and I have all the advantage." Then repeatedly he said, "This is an extremely wise judgment, Your Honor."

The magistrate said, "Now that the two of you
have given your word in agreement, neither of
you can have any complaints in the future. Since
all those present are your relatives, they will
please serve as witnesses. When Old Mr. Ni stood
face to face with me just now, he instructed me,
'Buried below the left wall of this house are five
thousand taels of silver in five jars which you
should give to my second son.'"

Shan-chi was unbelieving, and announced, "If it
does exist, even if it were ten thousand taels of
gold, it belongs to my younger brother. On no account would I dare to disagree."

"Even if you want to, I wouldn't let you," said
the magistrate.

Then he sent the servants in search of hoes and
shovels. Mei-shih and her son were all eyes as the
workers were led over to the east wall to dig up
the foundation, where in fact they uncovered five
large jars. They lifted them out. The jars were
brimming with shining silver. When one jar of
silver was set on the scales, it weighed sixty-two
and half catties, or exactly one thousand taels.

Everyone was dumbfounded when they saw
this. Shan-chi was now more convinced that his father's spirit had made an appearance. Otherwise,
how would the magistrate have known about this
hidden silver that even the family was unaware
of? He just watched as Magistrate T'eng ordered
the five jars spread out in a row before him. Then
the magistrate gave further instructions to Mei-
shih. "Near the wall on the right there are five

more jars which contain an additional five thousand taels," he said. "In addition to this, there is one jar of gold pieces which I have just been commanded to receive as my reward. I do not think I deserve this, but since Prefect Ni was so persistent, I can only oblige."

Mei-shih and Shan-shu kowtowed and said, "The five thousand from the left side have already exceeded our hopes. If the right wall yields even more, how could we dare not to comply with the will of the master?"

"I can't be sure of this myself," said Magistrate T'eng. "I only relied on the late Prefect Ni's instructions, which have already been proven correct."

Again he ordered the men to excavate near the western wall, where there were indeed six large jars, five with silver and one with gold.

As Shan-chi gazed upon these piles and piles of gold and silver, his eyes blazed with fury. How he wished he could snatch away just a single ingot! But there was his earlier promise, and he dared not utter a single word.

Magistrate T'eng wrote out a document and gave it to Shan-shu as evidence. The servant in charge of the house was also given to the mother and the son.

Mei-shih and Shan-shu were filled with exhilaration and together kowtowed in thanks. Though filled with great resentment, Shan-chi could only also kowtow several times and force himself to say, "Many thanks, Your Honor, for your disposition of the case."

The magistrate wrote out several seal strips to cover the jar of gold and had it placed in his sedan chair to be carried back to his tribunal for his personal disposal.

Everyone thought that since Prefect Ni had promised the gold to the magistrate, it was only natural that he should take it with him. Who would dare to raise any objection? Such an outcome is a good illustration of the saying, "When the snipe and mussel grasp each other, the fisherman gains the profit."

Had Ni Shan-chi been kind and considerate, and had he lived in peace with his younger brother and been willing to divide the estate equally, then each brother would have had a fair share of the thousand taels of gold, which had now fallen into the hands of Magistrate T'eng. Shan-chi had thus helped along some stranger with a free gift and brought sorrow on himself at the same time, not to mention the ill reputation he had now earned as an unfilial son and an unbrotherly brother. In all his plans to scheme against others, his schemes against others turned against him in the end.

Let us stop this idle gossip and speak further of Mei-shih and her son. The next day they went to the tribunal to thank Magistrate T'eng. He had already removed the will from the portrait and had it remounted before returning it to Mei-shih.

Only then Mei-shih and her son understood that the hand in the portrait pointing to the ground was referring to the gold and silver below the ground. They spent the ten jars of silver on acquiring land and consequently became a wealthy household.

Later, Shan-shu married and had three sons who all made names for themselves in their studies. Within the Ni family only this branch enjoyed such great prosperity. Shan-chi's two sons both turned out to be profligates, and the estate was finally dissipated. After Shan-chi died, the two great houses were sold to Uncle Shan-shu. All those in the neighborhood who knew the story of the Ni family from the beginning were convinced that the family had received divine justice. Indeed:

There has never been partiality in the Way of Heaven.
The foolish ways of Old Brother Ni are fit for ridicule.
From his position as heir, he rudely oppressed his stepmother,
And caused the dead father to plot against his own son.
The characters hidden in the scroll are there for good reason.
Gold concealed under the ground now belongs to the judge.
Wouldn't it have been better if the heir had had a little sense of
*   fairness?*
Then there would have been no qurrel and no legal suit.

501

THE DETECTIVE

Unlike Western detective fiction, a *kung-an* story usually reveals the identity of the criminal at the very beginning (see "Lion Cub Lane" in the previous section). The reader is thus given more knowledge of the crime than the law-enforcement officer. The two stories selected here, as in the case of "Magistrate T'eng and the Case of Inheritance," represent a refreshing exception to the rule: in the beginning the reader is left as much in the dark as the detective with respect to the actual circumstances of the crime. The solution of such a case generally calls for a mixture of brain and muscle. When the regular administrative official plays the detective, his activity is primarily confined to the courtroom. When the guesswork fails and out-of-courtroom action is required (as in the story "The Boot That Reveals the Culprit") the sedentary official is soon found to be not as useful for the administration of justice as the low-ranking inspectors and constables, if only because the culprit, from this point on, has to be confronted not only mentally but also physically. As a representative of this type of resourceful detective, Big Jan in the "Boot" story, small as his role is, is one of the most successfully drawn characters in traditional Chinese stories of crime and detection.

THE BOOT THAT REVEALS THE CULPRIT

From *Hsing-shih heng-yen*

TRANSLATED BY LORRAINE S. Y. LIEU AND THE EDITORS

The time of the first darkening shades of willows:
Last winter's chill become soft as water,
Wisps of rain flying like motes of dust,
A gust of east wind
Rustling through corn husks,
Rippling in the emerald pond—
Celestial maidens, spirits of the flowers and the moon,
Sound their pipes and flutes to celebrate renewal,
Cheering "Long live the Emperor"
In the cup of Nine Clouds,
Drunk forever on the fragrant spring.

This poem, sung to the tune of "Greenish Willow Tips," was composed by a scholar of the Sung Dynasty. The Northern Sung was founded by Emperor T'ai-tsu [r. 960–976].[1] The eighth emperor who succeeded to the throne was Emperor Tao-chün, with the temple title of Hui-tsung [r. 1101–1125].[2] He was actually the reincarnation of Li Yü [r. 961–975], the last emperor of the Southern T'ang. One day, when his father, Emperor Shen-tsung [r. 1068–1085], was admiring the portraits of the various emperors of past dynasties, he was most impressed by the one of Li Yü, whose majestic air and distinguished appearance easily set him apart from the rest. Shen-tsung could not stop marveling at that portrait. Then he dreamed of Li Yü entering the palace, and later the empress gave birth to Emperor Tao-chün. [This reincarnation of Li Yü] was given the title of Prince Tuan when young, and was of a most charming and romantic nature. There was nothing at which he did not excel.

When his elder brother Emperor Che-tsung [r. 1086–1100] passed away, Prince Tuan, with the support of the ministers, succeeded to the throne. After he had established his reign, peace prevailed in the country, and since there was nothing urgent to be dealt with in the court, he spent a great deal of his time in the royal gardens. During the first year of the Hsüan-ho period [1119–1125], he ordered extensive construction at the northeastern corner of the capital—digging ponds, and landscaping gardens which he called Longevity Hill and Silver Mount. All this was placed in the charge of the eunuch Liang Shih-ch'eng.[3] He also commissioned Chu Mien to collect and transport to the capital all the exotic flowers and rare plants, quaint bamboos and strange rocks from the area of the three Wu's,[4]

---

[1] For a story about this first emperor of the Sung Dynasty, see "The Sung Founder Escorts Ching-niang One Thousand *Li*" in this anthology.

[2] Hui-tsung was a celebrated artist and was well known for his romantic temperament.

[3] Liang Shih-ch'eng (?–1126) was one of the "Six Bandits of Hsüan-ho" mentioned further on in the story.

[4] There are three different explanations for the three Wus. One of them is: K'uai-chi, Wu County, and Wu-hsing all in modern Chekiang Province.

the Erh-Che Circuits,[5] the area of the Three Rivers,[6] and Kuang-nan East and Kuang-nan West Circuits.[7] He called this the Special Collection of Plants and Rocks. It was truly the collection of collections, and the choicest of the choice.

The work took several years to complete and the place was then named the Mountain of Ten Thousand Years. It was filled with all kinds of strange flowers and beautiful trees, as well as rare animals and strange beasts. Words are simply powerless to suggest the beauty and magnificence of the pavilions built within the imperial compounds. The countless sights included Jade Hall, Jasper Forest Hall, Serenity Chamber, Immaculacy Chamber, Wonders Chamber, Mountain Chamber, Mist Pavilion, and Phoenix and Hanging Cloud Pavilion. The six ministers Ts'ai Ching, Wang Fu, Kao Ch'iu, T'ung Kuan,[8] Yang Chien, and Liang Shih-ch'eng, who toured and admired this beautiful scenery thoroughly, were known as the "Six Bandits of Hsüan-ho." Truly:

Buildings of fine jade are numerous as the trees in the forest;
When bamboo and cypress cross, their luxuriant foliage makes
*   ample shade.*
The emperor has kindly allowed his ministers to stroll around
*   from time to time;*
It makes them feel as if they have lost themselves among the
*   clouds.*

Among all these magnificent buildings, there was a True Jade Studio, situated southwest of the Peace Hall. This studio was the residence of the emperor's favorite concubine, Consort An. It was decorated with golden doorknobs, hanging chains, and dainty jade railings, and its grandeur was indeed a delight to the eyes. Ts'ai Ching and

a few other ministers had often been the emperor's guests at royal banquets there, and they left some of their writing on the wall. There is a poem in evidence of this:

The new Peace Hall complements the autumn glory;
The emperor has invited the ministers to his royal concubine's
*   dwelling.*
Elegant feasts and mellow wine enhance the refined interest
In seeing Consort An in the True Jade Studio.

We will now leave Consort An to enjoy the many blessings of the emperor and attend to our story proper, which concerns a certain lady-in-waiting by the name of Han Yü-ch'iao. She was barely fifteen when she was selected to enter the palace. As she walked, her jade ornaments would jingle and her light silk skirt would sway like clouds. Her complexion subdued the shine of white snow and her face excelled the beauty of a hibiscus. For all her beauty and grace, however, Lady Han was still very much a neglected woman, if only because the emperor showered all his favor on Consort An.

The story took place at a time when the glory of spring and the beauty of the landscape intensified the loneliness of Lady Han's plight—lying on the red bedding only made her bitter, and sleeping in her emerald quilt made her feel chilly. When the moon cast its soft rays onto the palace steps, she grew sad and would not play her flute. When the insects were humming by the painted wall, she grew restless in her mandarin-duck-embroidered quilt. She was weary of dressing up in the morning and gradually became a victim of her spring desires. She sighed and lamented all day until she was finally overcome by illness. There is a poem to summarize her situation:

The east wind has come and gone,
Yet the teardrops on her face remain undried.
Each early spring, late spring,
Cold spring, warm spring,
Rainy spring, shiny spring,
Has all but drained the life of a beauty.

---

[5] Same as the Liang-Che Circuits described in an earlier footnote.

[6] There are three different explanations for the Three Rivers. One of them is: the rivers Ching, Wei, and Lo. Ching flows into Wei, while Wei flows into Lo.

[7] Covering the area of modern Kwangtung and Kwangsi.

[8] With the exception of Wang Fu (1079–1126) and T'ung Kuan (1054–1126), all the "Six Bandits of Hsüan-ho" have been referred to in previous footnotes.

Only the flowers fallen randomly still hold on to the essence of
  spring.
Fragrant grass confuses the dancing butterfly;
Green willows court the oriole in vain.
Even though she has both hoped and tried,
Alas, the loved one is gone forever.
So she is as if drunk, as if dazed,
As if crazy, as if dancing,
As if dreaming, as if awakened.

Slowly her spirit waned and she wasted away considerably—just like a frowning willow or a wilting flower. An imperial physician was summoned to examine her, but the medicine he prescribed proved to be to no avail.

One day, when Emperor Tao-chün was in a side hall, Marshal Yang Chien was summoned for an audience: "Lady Han is not feeling well. Since you brought her here, please take her back [to your place] for recuperation. Let her rest until she is fully recovered before sending her back. Her meals and her medicine will be delivered to her from the palace. Keep me informed of her progress."

Yang Chien kowtowed and withdrew. He immediately sent for some attendants to arrange for the transportation of Lady Han's belongings. They carried Lady Han in a closed sedan chair, and with two waiting women and two maidservants, went to Marshal Yang's residence. [When they arrived,] the marshal himself went inside first to inform his wife of the matter so she could welcome Lady Han in the front hall. He then divided his quarters into two parts and cleaned up the West Garden for Lady Han to live in. He also put a lock on the door, only allowing the physician and his own servants to pass through. The marshal and his wife went over to visit her once a day. During the rest of the time, the door remained locked. A bucket was left by the door to pass on news and meals. Indeed:

Green grass reflected upon the steps naturally conveys the
  colors of spring;
Yellow oriole on the other side of the leaves sings in vain.

After nearly two months, Lady Han's complexion was beginning to regain its original color, and her appetite seemed to have increased slightly. The marshal and his wife were most pleased. They prepared a feast to celebrate her recovery and at the same time to bid her farewell. In the middle of the banquet, the marshal and his wife said together, "Lady Han, we're very happy that you've fully recovered from your illness. This is indeed a joy and a blessing. We shall report to the palace and choose a day for you to go back there. What do you think?"

Lady Han clasped her hands and said to Lady Yang, "I'm indeed an unfortunate woman to have brought on myself so much sorrow and suffering. After lying sick in bed for two months, I'm only beginning to feel a little better. For this reason, I'd like to have your permission to stay a few more days. Please don't report my present condition to the palace yet. I'm aware that my staying here has caused you a lot of inconvenience, and I can only look forward to the day when I can repay your kindness."

The marshal could do nothing but give her his consent.

After two months, Lady Han prepared a feast in return for the hospitality she had received from the marshal and his wife. For entertainment she had story recital by a storyteller. One of the stories narrated happened to be about another Lady Han in the inner palace of Emperor Hsüan-tsung [r. 847–860] of the T'ang Dynasty.[9] Like the real-life Lady Han, she was also a frustrated and unhappy woman because she was ignored by the emperor. Not knowing what to do, she had scribbled a poem on a red leaf, which then floated out of the palace along the gutter. The poem read:

Water, why flow so swiftly?
Inside the forbidden palace, there is nothing to do all day long.

[9] Though the transliteration is identical, this emperor (*hsüan* "to proclaim") is different from the other T'ang emperor we have seen a number of times in the other selections, Hsüan-tsung (*hsüan* "mystic"), who ruled from 712 to 756.

I sincerely urge the red leaf
To go all the way into the world.

A man by the name of Yü Yu, who had come to the capital to take part in the imperial examinations, picked up the red leaf. He responded with a poem and let it float back into the palace along the gutter. Later this scholar became famous. When the emperor learned about this, he married Lady Han to Yü Yu. The two lived very happily ever after.

When Lady Han heard this story, she suddenly thought of something and she sighed deeply. She did not say anything, but inside her heart, she wondered, "If I could be as lucky, then I wouldn't have lived my life in vain!"

After the feast, they all retired separately to their rooms. In the middle of the night, Lady Han felt a severe headache and her face was flushed. All the strength left her limbs and there was nowhere in her entire body which did not ache and itch. For no apparent reason at all, she became sick again. This time, the sickness was even worse than before. Alas, she was:

A leaking house under many nights of rain;
A late ship against a gust of adverse wind.

When Lady Yang came to visit her in the morning, she said to Lady Han, "We haven't reported to the palace that you could be taken back. Since you're here, why not stop worrying, cheer up, and put your mind at ease; this is the way to a speedy recovery. In the meantime, don't worry about going back to the palace."

"I'm grateful for your kindness," Lady Han told her. "It's just that my illness is already beyond cure. I can see that though I'm not good enough to go to heaven, quite soon I'll be buried under the earth. Since I can't repay your kindness in this life, I'm willing to be a horse or a dog in my next life to pay my debt to you." After she had said this, her breath became short and faint.

Feeling sorry for her, Lady Yang said, "Lady Han, don't say that. Heaven has always been partial to the good and virtuous. I'm sure you will recover very soon. Come to think of it, the medicine will only do you harm if it doesn't have the desired effect on your illness. I wonder if you've made any vows to the gods but failed to carry them out, thus incurring their wrath?"

"Ever since I entered the palace, I've been miserable every day. When have I had the heart to make vows?" replied Lady Han. "But since my illness is so serious and taking medicine seems useless, I wonder if there is any god who is most ready to answer people's prayers. I'd like to make a vow to him. If I come through this time, I'll honor my promise."

"Lady Han, both the Lord of the North Pole and the god Erh-lang at the temples here are known for their speedy answers to prayers. Why don't you set up an altar and make a vow to them for your early recovery? Once you get well, I wouldn't mind taking you there to give thanks to them. What do you think?"

No sooner had Lady Han nodded her consent than the maids brought out the altar. Since she could not get up, Lady Han lay back on the pillow, and with her hands pressed against her forehead, she prayed, "Your maidservant Han entered the palace at a very young age, but unfortunately has never enjoyed any attention from the emperor. This is the cause of my present illness, which forces me to take up temporary residence at Marshal Yang's. If I am lucky enough to deserve your blessing, and if my health is restored, I shall embroider two long banners and go personally to your temples to present them, along with other offerings, as a token of my gratitude." Lady Yang also took sticks of incense and prayed for Lady Han.

Strange as it would seem, from the time she made the pledge, Lady Han's health began to show signs of improvement. She was fully recovered after a month's rest. The marshal and his wife were overjoyed and again gave a feast to celebrate her recovery.

During the feast, Lady Yang said to Lady Han, "The gods have responded to your prayer, and they proved to be much more effective than the medicines. But you mustn't be ungrateful and forget your vow."

"How would I dare to do that?" replied Lady Han. "I'll go as soon as I have finished embroidering the long banners. Also, I wonder if you would be so kind as to accompany me there?"

"I'd be more than happy to," said Lady Yang.

After the feast, Lady Han took out some money for making the arrangements for the sacrifices and at the same time began embroidering the four long banners. As people of old have observed so aptly:

When there is fire, the pig's head will be properly cooked;
When there is money, things will naturally go through.

No matter how strange or difficult the things are, so long as there is money, they can surely be obtained or accomplished. So, within a few days, the long banners were ready. When hung on long bamboo poles, they looked dazzling. An auspicious day was chosen, and the servants, both from the palace and from the marshal's household, had packed all the incense and other offerings together. They accompanied the two ladies to the temple of the Lord of the North Pole. When the temple keeper learned that these two illustrious ladies were coming, he immediately came out to welcome them in the front hall. A prayer was read and the long banners were hung up. Lady Han knelt down to read a prayer. After the ceremony, they toured the temple. When the temple keeper served tea, the ladies asked one of the servants to reward him with some money. Then they mounted their sedan chairs and returned home.

The night passed peacefully, and they woke up early the next morning to go the temple of the god Erh-lang. This visit caused a series of strange and bizarre happenings. Truly:

Words are like hooks and threads,
Pulling out intrigues from bygone times.

Let us digress no more. The two ladies and their servants went to the temple and were received by the temple keeper, who then performed the usual ceremonies of reading a prayer and burning incense.

It happened that Lady Yang had just gone over to a side room when Lady Han quietly went forward, lifted a corner of the gilded curtain of the altar, and looked inside. Everything would have been different had she not done that. For there she stood transfixed. This was what she saw:

His headgear is stitched with golden flowers;
His body is covered by a brown embroidered robe.
The waistband is made of the finest Lan-t'ien [10] jade;
His boots are decorated with designs of flying phoenix.
Even though he is only an image made of mud and wood,
Yet he looks so handsome and so majestic,
With his bright eyes and shiny teeth,
All he lacks is breath
To make him move.

When Lady Han saw the statue, her eyes were dazzled and her heart quivered. In spite of herself, a wishful thought slipped out of her mouth: "If I'm to have a bright future, I only hope that I can marry someone in your image. Then my lifelong wish would be fulfilled."

She had barely said that when Lady Yang returned and asked her, "Lady Han, what are you praying?"

"I didn't say anything," Lady Han immediately answered.

Lady Yang did not question her anymore. They went on sightseeing until the evening and then returned home and retired to their own rooms. Indeed:

If you want to know what the heart is thinking,
Just listen to what comes out from the mouth.

Let us return to Lady Han. She retired to her room and took off her formal attire, arranged her hair, and put on her daily clothes. With her chin

[10] A mountain to the southeast of modern Lan-t'ien County in Shensi Province, a well-known jade-producing area.

in her hands, she was silently thinking of the image of the god Erh-lang. Suddenly, an idea occurred to her, and she asked the maids to set up the altar in a quiet corner of the garden. Then she prayed to the sky, "If I'm to have a bright future, I only hope that I will marry someone just like the god Erh-lang. It'd be so much better than the lonely and sad life I've lived in the palace."

As she said that, her tears were already flowing down her cheeks. She bowed and prayed, then prayed and bowed again. Evidently she had lost herself in her fantasy.

Strange though it may sound, just as Lady Han had finished praying and was about to pack up to return to her room, a loud clang was heard among the flower bushes. Then a god-like figure appeared, standing right in front of her. One could see:

Dragon-like brows, phoenix-like eyes,
Bright teeth, crimson lips,
Carefree manner above this mundane world,
Gentle, yet with awe-inspiring features.
If he is not a guest of the gods' dwelling,
Then he is surely someone who feasts on evening clouds and
    morning dew.

On closer examination, there was not the slightest difference between him and the statue of Erh-lang in the temple. He had a bow in his hand and resembled a great deal the god Chang Hsien.[11]

Lady Han was both frightened and pleased—frightened because there was no telling whether this descent of the god meant disaster or blessing; pleased because the god had a pleasant face and a congenial smile. He even started to talk; so she immediately approached him and greeted him demurely. Opening her crimson lips and showing her pearl-like teeth, she said, "Since I'm so honored by your presence, please come into my room and allow me to pay my respects."

Erh-lang went smilingly into Lady Han's room and seated himself comfortably. After observing

[11] A deity who is usually regarded as a fertility god.

all the proprieties, Lady Han stood waiting before him.

"I'm much obliged to you for your generous offerings," said Erh-lang. "By chance I was strolling in the sky today when I heard your most sincere prayers. I've learned that you were originally a member of the divine realm banished temporarily into this mundane world by the Jade Emperor because your earthly desires had not been cleansed completely. But you were allowed to enter the palace to live a life of luxury and ease in the world. Once your time is up, you'll be permitted to go back to the divine realm. Then you'll know for sure that you're no mortal being."

When Lady Han heard that, she was filled with joy. She bowed and prayed, "Honorable god, I don't wish to go back to the palace. If I'm to have a meaningful future, I'd like to marry a good man in your divine image and spend the rest of my life with him. Only then would I feel that the spring flowers and the autumn moon have not existed in vain for me. I couldn't care less for richness and luxury."

"That can easily be arranged," said Erh-lang with a smile. "I'm only afraid that Your Ladyship is not determined enough. Marriages are predestined, and so if it is your fate to meet someone, you'll meet him whatever the distance." After he said that, he got up and leaped over the windowsill, disappearing with a loud clang.

If not for this visitation, Lady Han might have reconciled herself to her fate. But now she had seen her god with her own eyes. She became so bewildered that she went to bed without taking off her clothes. Indeed:

When one is enjoying oneself, the night is too short;
When lonely, it seems to hang on forever.

She tossed and turned, but still could not suppress her aroused passion. Murmuring, she thought to herself, "Just a while ago when the god Erh-lang looked me in the eyes, he seemed so passionate. But then why was he gone so suddenly? Perhaps as a god he is more intelligent and straightforward, unlike us mundane human beings. I must have been mistaken!"

But after thinking a while longer, she said to herself, "What I don't understand is that, judging by his demeanor, he talks and carries himself just like a human being; so why wasn't he affected at all by my beauty? Or have I been remiss in something that he decided to leave me? Come to think of it, I should have been more considerate and affectionate to him; that way, even if he's a man made of iron and rock, I think he'll finally melt. Now that I've missed the chance this time, I wonder when we will meet again?"

She simply could not shake off these thoughts, but could only wait until dawn before doing anything. But by dawn, she was asleep and did not wake until nearly noon. She felt listless and moody the whole day and was impatient for evening to come. When it finally became dark, she set up the altar again and went to pray in the garden as she had done the day before: "If I can see the Honorable One once again, I shall be as happy as if I had achieved salvation for three lives to come."

No sooner had she finished praying than the god Erh-lang appeared before her with a bang. Lady Han was thrilled, and the day's sorrow and worry immediately vanished like melting ice and crumbling tiles. She approached him, bowed, and said, "Can I trouble you to come to my room? There is something confidential I'd like to tell you."

Erh-lang smiled most obligingly and went into Lady Han's room, holding her hand. After Lady Han had gone through the usual formalities, she waited upon Erh-lang, who had seated himself in the middle of the room.

"You have the essence of an immortal within you," Erh-lang said to Lady Han, "So you can sit down with me."

So Lady Han sat down across from him and ordered the maids to bring in wine and fruit. As they exchanged a few cups of wine, Lady Han told Erh-lang what lay deep in her heart, yielding to:

Spring, the master of flowers;
Wine, the catalyst of lust.

Right there and then, Lady Han took off her clothes and kissed Erh-lang. "If you do not look down upon me as being defiled, then I hope you'll forget your celestial responsibility for the time being, so that we can enjoy the pleasures of the mundane world for just a short while." Erh-lang gladly agreed, and they went to bed hand in hand. They lingered until the fifth watch in the morning before Erh-lang got up, bade Lady Han to take care of herself, and promised to visit her again. He got out of bed, put on his clothes, picked up the bow, and climbed over the windowsill. Then with a zoom he disappeared.

In her happiness, Lady Han did not doubt for a single moment that this was an actual visitation of her god. Apprehensive that Lady Yang might send her back to the palace at any moment, she had to feign sickness and put on a sorrowful countenance in the daytime. But as soon as nighttime came, she became the picture of life and vitality, hardly able to hide her joy. When Erh-lang arrived, they would first exchange a few cups of wine before sporting until dawn. This went on for some time.

The weather had suddenly turned cool one day. Emperor Tao-chün was distributing autumn clothes for the entire palace when by chance he thought of Lady Han. So he dispatched a palace official to Marshal Yang's residence with a gown and a jade waistband for Lady Han. After Lady Han had set up the altar and thanked the emperor for the gift, the court attendant informed her, "I'm glad that Your Ladyship has gotten well. His Majesty the Emperor has thought of you often, and has sent you this gown and jade waistband. If Your Ladyship is fully recovered, please

511

get ready to return to the palace as soon as possible."

Lady Han entertained the official and said, "I'm afraid that I must trouble you to report for me that I'm only half recovered from my illness, and that I wish His Majesty would allow me to stay a little longer. I shall be greatly obliged to you for this favor."

"That shouldn't be any problem," replied the official. "Since His Majesty has enough company in the palace, when I go back I'll simply report that you've not yet recovered. All Your Ladyship has to do is take good care of yourself." Lady Han thanked him again and he left.

At night, when the god Erh-lang came, he said to Lady Han, "I'm glad that the emperor's love for you has not diminished. May I take a look at the gown and the jade waistband?"

"How did you know that?" asked Lady Han.

"I'm aware of everything that happens. How can a small thing like this escape my attention?" At this Lady Han immediately took out everything for his inspection.

"One should not keep such precious things to oneself, you know," said Erh-lang. "It just happens that I need a jade waistband. If you're willing to give it up to me, you'll accumulate merit in heaven."

"Since I belong to you already," replied Lady Han, "how could I begrudge you a mere jade waistband? Take it, by all means."

Erh-lang thanked her and then they went to bed as usual. Shortly before the fifth watch of the morning, he got up, picked up the bow, and put on the waistband. Then, as before, he disappeared through the window. But then:

If you don't wish anyone to know what you've done,
It is better not to have done it in the first place.

Even though Lady Han and the marshal were living in a residence divided into two separate units, still, because the former was from the palace,

many extra precautions were taken. It was expected that no idler would dare to venture into this closely guarded area. But recently, lights in the West Garden had been seen throughout the night, and whispers and murmurs could be heard, as if people were moving about and talking. Lady Han also seemed to be much more energetic than before, with a smile on her face constantly. The marshal had been wondering to himself for some time before he asked his wife, "Do you see anything unusual about Lady Han?"

"I was also a little suspicious," his wife answered. "But then I thought that since the security in this place is so tight, nothing could happen! But since you're also suspicious, it can easily be looked into. Wait until it's dark, and then we can send a dependable servant to climb up on the roof and see what's really going on inside. This will also avoid any hasty conclusion on our part."

"That sounds reasonable," the marshal said. Immediately two able servants were summoned and given specific instructions: "Don't go through the door. Use a ladder against the outside wall, and wait until all is quiet before climbing over to Lady Han's room. See what is going on inside and report immediately." He also warned them that it was a matter of great importance, and urged them to be extremely careful. Having received their orders, the two servants left, while the marshal waited for their report.

Within a few hours, they had found out what was happening in Lady Han's room. They asked the marshal to dismiss all the servants before telling him that they had just seen Lady Han drinking with a man in her room. "Lady Han kept referring to him as the Honorable God. We thought about the matter quite carefully, too. Since the walls of the residence are so high and security so tight, how can any miscreant get in there unless he has wings? Maybe he really is a god."

The marshal was so taken aback by what he heard that he exclaimed, "How strange! How very strange! So that's it! But are the two of you telling the truth? Remember this is a matter of grave importance!"

"Everything we said is the absolute truth," they replied.

"Let this be just between you two and me," the marshal reminded them. "Not a word is to get out!"

The two servants left as instructed. The marshal then went in and informed his wife of the situation. "Despite what they said, I don't think I can believe it unless I see it with my own eyes. Tomorrow night, I'll go there and find out what this god looks like."

The marshal waited until the next evening and sent for the two servants who had gone spying the night before. He then ordered them, "One of you will go with me and the other will wait here. Don't let anyone know about this."

After he had given these orders, the marshal and one of the men stole over to a point outside Lady Han's window. The marshal peeped into the window, and lo and behold, there was the god seated inside the room looking as real as the two servants had described him. He wanted to cry out but had to swallow his anger, being afraid that he might get into a spot he couldn't get out of. Upon returning to his place, the marshal again reminded the two servants not to discuss this matter with anyone. He then returned to his room and said to his wife, "It must have been the infirmities of Lady Han's youth and her unstable state of emotion that attracted the evil spirit. No ordinary human being could have dared to violate the chastity of a royal consort. We must send for a Taoist exorcist. In the meantime, you must go and notify Lady Han, and I'll go personally to invite the priest."

Lady Yang assented.

Early the next morning, Lady Yang got up and went over to the West Garden. After Lady Han had served tea, the marshal's wife sent away all the servants. "There is something I wish to say to you," she said to Lady Han, coming right to the point. "Who is it that you have been talking to every night? Some gossip has already reached my ears. This is no small matter, Lady Han; you must tell me everything and speak only the truth."

On hearing that, Lady Han blushed and said, "I haven't been talking to anyone in my room at night, except maybe chatting with the maids and the waiting women. Who could have come here?"

Lady Yang told her in detail everything her husband had seen there the night before. Lady Han was stupefied and did not know what to say or do.

"Don't be afraid," Lady Yang comforted her. "The marshal has already gone to look for an exorcist and in no time we shall know whether he is a man or a ghost. Only one must be very careful during the night. Anyway, there's no need to be afraid." After this, Lady Yang left, but Lady Han had already broken into cold sweat. It was just approaching dark when Erh-lang arrived, earlier than usual, with his bow next to him all the time.

Let our story turn to the Taoist priest whom the marshal had hired. He was Priest Wang, the famous disciple of Priest Lin of the Efficacy Monastery. He was now in the front hall making preparations for his performance. By evening, someone came in to report that the god had arrived. Priest Wang then put on his robe and, brandishing his sword, charged right toward Lady Han's room.

"What kind of evil spirit are you?" he shouted, entering the room with large strides. "How dare you defile a lady from the palace! Meet your punishment from my sword!"

"Don't be impudent!" Erh-lang said calmly, and behold,

As if holding the T'ai Mountains in one hand,
And carrying a baby in the other,
He drew the bow taut until it looked like a full moon,
Sending out pellets like shooting stars.

One pellet hit Priest Wang in the middle of the forehead, and blood immediately oozed down. He flopped backward, his sword flung aside. The servants hurried forward to carry him back to the front hall, while Erh-lang evaporated from the windowsill as before. What was it like then? Simply:

Even the sky and the earth are frightened by the mere mention of Erh-lang;
Even the ghosts and the gods are scared by his presence.

Let us now go back to Lady Han. Since she had seen the god Erh-lang defeating the Taoist priest, her belief that a genuine god had descended upon her was strengthened even more. So she stopped worrying.

As for Marshal Yang, he realized that Priest Wang was useless, so he gave him some money as compensation and sent him away. Then he sent for Priest P'an of the Five Mountain Monastery. P'an was an expert in the method of the Five Heavenly Thunderbolts and was also a judicious and resourceful man. On Marshal Yang's invitation, he came immediately. The marshal had to recite the whole story from beginning to end.

"First, I wish to be taken to the West Garden. I shall be able to tell whether he is a ghost or a man by the surroundings," said P'an.

So P'an left the marshal and went to look all around Lady Han's bedroom. He then asked permission to look at Lady Han's complexion. Turning to Marshal Yang, he said, "According to my observation of Lady Han's complexion, I don't think that she is harassed by any evil spirits. It's simply the doings of some sorcerer. I have a way to deal with him. There's no need to use charms or exorcizing water, and it won't be necessary to beat the drums or ring the bell. When he comes, I'll catch him as easily as catching a turtle in a jar. I'm only afraid that he has already seen through our plans and will not come again. Then there's nothing I can do."

"I shall be more than happy if he doesn't come back," said the marshal. "Do stay for a while and have some tea."

In the opinion of this storyteller, if that knave had watched the development of the situation carefully and had acted accordingly, he would have escaped like a kite with a broken cord, never to return again. He would then have had his good time without ruining his name and his chances at other places. It would have been perfect indeed if he had known the saying:

Things from which you've gotten a good deal,
Don't try them again.
Places where you've stolen an advantage,
Don't go there again.

Now at this point, we really have no way of telling whether this Erh-lang was a man or a supernatural being. All we know is that after tasting the forbidden fruit, he wanted more. So he came as usual that night.

"I didn't know beforehand what was to happen last night, and I'm sorry for their impertinence," Lady Han said to him. "But I'm glad that you were not harmed."

"I'm a true god from heaven and have only come down to you because it was predestined. Sooner or later, I'll help you rid yourself of your mortal frame and ascend to heaven in broad daylight," he replied. "How presumptuous that idiot was! He couldn't get close to me even if he was equipped with a whole army." Lady Han admired Erh-lang all the more and treated him with redoubled affection.

Meanwhile, someone had already reported to the marshal, who in turn informed Priest P'an. P'an asked the marshal to quietly order a waiting woman to go to Lady Han's room under the pretext of waiting on them, and then try to steal the god Erh-lang's bow to disarm him. After the waiting woman had gone, P'an tightened his attire. He did not put on his Taoist robe, nor did he take along his sword. He then asked for a brow-high staff and two servants to light up the place from afar with two torches.

"If you're afraid of his pellets, then hide yourselves beforehand," he instructed them. "Let me go there first, and see if his pellets can come close to me!"

Both men laughed to themselves, "See how he brags! He'll probably get a pellet himself!"

In the meantime, the waiting woman had gone as instructed to Lady Han's room. She slowly edged her way toward Erh-lang while he and Lady Han were busy toasting each other. She stole the bow and hid it in a side room. At the same time, the servants who were taking Priest P'an to Lady Han's room had already arrived. After telling him, "This is the place," they immediately withdrew.

P'an pushed aside the curtain and took a quick look around. Right before his eyes the god Erh-lang was sitting comfortably inside the room. P'an gave a loud cry, lunged with his staff, and struck at Erh-lang's head. Erh-lang reached out for his bow but it was no longer there. Shouting, "I've been tricked!" he hastened onto the windowsill. But in an instant P'an's staff had already hit him on the back of the leg, and something fell on the floor. Nevertheless, Erh-lang made his escape among the flowers.

P'an picked up the fallen object from the floor and took a look at it under the light. It was a quadruple-stitched black leather boot. He took it and reported to the marshal: "In my opinion, this affair must have been the work of some sorcerer. It has nothing to do with the real god Erh-lang. The question is how to catch him."

"Thank you, but we don't have to trouble you anymore. I'll see to it that he answers for what he has done," replied the marshal. He paid P'an and sent him away.

Next we see Marshal Yang on his way to the residence of Grand Preceptor Ts'ai [Ching] in his sedan chair. He went straight into Ts'ai's study and told him Lady Han and Erh-lang's story from the beginning. "We can't simply let him go like this. We'll become a laughingstock!" he concluded.

"That shouldn't be any problem," said Ts'ai. "I'll ask Magistrate T'eng of the K'ai-feng district to use this boot as a clue, and send some capable constables to locate the whereabouts of the culprit. Then he'll be punished according to the law."

"Thank you for your advice," said Marshal Yang.

"Stay for a while," said the grand preceptor.

He then dispatched his servant Chang to go and invite Magistrate T'eng to come over as soon as possible. After greetings were exchanged, the grand preceptor dismissed all the servants. Then he and the marshal said together, "How can we tolerate such license under the rule of His Majesty the Emperor! Magistrate T'eng, you must be very careful. This is a matter of utmost importance. Don't let a word leak out; otherwise the impostor will be on the run."

When he heard that, Magistrate T'eng's face turned ashen and he immediately replied, "Certainly, certainly, I'll be very careful about it."

Taking the boot with him, he returned to his tribunal and immediately assembled his officers. Inspector Wang, the head detective officer on duty that day, was summoned and, after the hall had been cleared, given every detail about the case. "I'll give you a three-day deadline to capture this culprit at Marshal Yang's residence," he ordered. "Be discreet about it. If the case is solved, you'll be rewarded handsomely. If not, you'll be severely punished!" After saying this, he dismissed the officers.

Inspector Wang took the boot into the detectives' office, gathered all the officers together, and sighed. You can see:

There is a double lock between his brows;
There are a hundred pecks of newly added sorrow in his heart.

There was a detective officer by the name of Jan Kuei whom everyone called Big Jan. He was both quick-witted and resourceful, and had solved quite a number of difficult cases for the inspector.

Wang liked him very much. That day, when Jan saw that the inspector had locked brows and a worried look on his face, he did not bother him or ask him what the matter was. He only spoke of irrelevant matters.

Wang, seeing that they all seemed completely unconcerned, took out the boot, threw it on the table, and said, "What a hard life it is to be a officer! How can there be such a stupid magistrate? This boot cannot talk! But he gave me a three-day deadline to catch the man who has committed a crime at the Yang residence. Don't you all find it rather ridiculous?!"

Everyone took turns in inspecting the boot. When it was passed to Jan Kuei, he seemed disinterested and only commented, "Difficult! Very difficult indeed! The magistrate is quite stupid, Inspector. I don't blame you for being worried!"

When Wang heard such a comment coming quite unexpectedly from Jan Kuei, he said, "Big Jan, even you are saying that it is difficult. You don't mean to suggest that we leave the matter as it is? Aren't you putting me on the spot? What am I going to say to the magistrate? You all earn your living from this place, yet all you say is 'Difficult! Very difficult indeed!'"

"We might do something about it if it were an ordinary burglary or theft," the others said. "But since the culprit is a man capable of sorcery, how can we even get near him? If anyone could get close to him, then Priest P'an would have caught him long ago. Even he could do nothing but knock a boot off him; what else can we say except that it's our bad luck to get involved with this kind of case? There is simply nowhere we can start looking."

Wang had been only a little worried before, but after hearing what they said and finding their arguments all too reasonable, he was really troubled. Fortunately, Jan Kuei broke his silence and said in his most confident manner, "Inspector, let's not be so pessimistic. After all, he's just another human being; he certainly doesn't have

three heads or six arms! As soon as we can find some kind of slip he has made, we can certainly get to the bottom of the whole thing!" Thereupon he examined the boot again very thoroughly.

The others all laughed and said, "Big Jan is at it again! This boot isn't an antique. It's simply a piece of leather dyed black, sewn together by thread, with a blue cloth lining, a sole added, and water sprayed on, to make it stiff and good looking."

Jan Kuei did not bother to argue with them. He continued to examine the boot carefully under the lamp. The four lines of stitches on the boot were all tightly sewn. It was only when he examined the tip of the boot that he saw a slight loosening in one of the lines of stitches. Jan Kuei flicked his small finger and accidentally broke two threads. The leather flipped up and the blue cloth lining inside could be seen under the light. Jan Kuei took another look and found a slip of paper, which he examined carefully. Ah, it would have been a different story if he had not looked into this slip of paper! His reaction at that moment was like someone who had discovered gold or some hidden treasure in the middle of the night. When Inspector Wang saw it, he, too, broke into a big smile. The others all crowded around to see the slip of paper. The words on it read, "Made by the shop of Jen Yi-lang, on the fifth day of the third month of the third year in the reign of Hsüan-ho."

Wang said to Jan Kuei, "This year is the fourth year in the reign of Hsüan-ho. So this is a boot made less than two years ago. Now if we can lay our hands on Jen Yi-lang, this case will be more than half solved."

"Don't go to him today," said Jan Kuei. "Wait until tomorrow and then send two men to tell him that there is some work you would like him to do. Tie him up as soon as he gets here and we won't have to worry about him not telling the truth."

"Splendid. Now you're talking!" said Wang.

They all stayed and drank the whole night long.

No one dared to leave. As soon as it was dawn, two men were sent to arrest Jen Yi-lang. Within two hours, Jen was brought over to the detectives' office. They played it rough and tied him up.

"You swine, how dare you do a thing like this?"

Frightened out of his wits, Jen said, "What thing? Do let me know what I'm guilty of before tying me up!"

"What else do you have to say? Wasn't this boot made in your shop?" asked Wang.

Jen took the boot and looked at it carefully. He then replied, "Inspector, this boot was made by me. But there's one thing which I'd like to mention: ever since the time when I opened the shop, no matter whether shoes are ordered by the ministers' houses or bought by passing customers, I've always kept each and every transaction in a ledger at home. It clearly notes down the years, months, and days on which the shoes are ordered by the different clerks of the ministers' residences. The number and other specifications on the slip of paper inside this boot should tally with the entry in the ledger. If the inspector doesn't believe me, just cut open the boot and look at the slip of paper; then you'll know that I've told the truth."

Wang saw that Jen Yi-lang had accounted for everything in detail, so he said, "He's an honest man. Release him and we'll have a nice talk."

After Jen was untied, the constables said, "Jen Yi-lang, please don't take offense. We're only following orders from our superiors."

Then they showed him the slip of paper. Jen took a look at it and said, "Inspector, no problem at all. Not to mention that this boot was made within the last two years, even if it had been made within the last three or four years, the ledgers are still at home. Please send someone with me to get them, so everything can be cleared up."

So two men were sent to follow Jen Yi-lang. They went to his house, took the ledgers, and were back at the detectives' office in no time at all. Wang examined the ledgers personally, and when he reached the fifth day of the third month of the third year, the entry exactly matched the one on the slip of paper. He was stunned when he saw that the boot was ordered by the clerk of Grand Preceptor Ts'ai's residence. So Wang took Jen Yi-lang, the boot, and the ledgers and hurried over to the tribunal to report on the case.

They were immediately received by Magistrate T'eng in the hall, as this case was his direct responsibility. Wang informed him of the progress he had made and handed him Jen Yi-lang's ledger. The magistrate then personally went over the data and found that indeed they agreed with Inspector Wang's report. Visibly shaken, he uttered a sigh: "So this is what it is!" But still not fully convinced, he pondered for a while and said, "At any rate, this case has nothing to do with Jen Yi-lang. Release him right now." Jen bowed, expressed his gratitude, and left. The magistrate called him back again and reminded him, "We'll let you go only on the condition that you don't speak a word of this outside. If someone should ask you, just change the subject. Don't make a mistake on this."

"I certainly won't." So saying, he left happily.

Magistrate T'eng took the ledgers and the boot, mounted his sedan chair, and headed for Marshal Yang's residence with both Wang and Jan Kuei. The marshal had just returned after the daily audience with the emperor and received them in the hall after the doorkeeper reported their arrival.

"This is not the place to talk," said the magistrate. So the marshal led them into the study on the west side and dismissed everyone except Wang and Jan Kuei, who were to wait on them. The magistrate repeated what had happened from the beginning and asked, "What am I supposed to do now? In my humble position, I don't dare to make any decision."

In view of the evidence before him, the marshal was stupefied for some time before he thought to himself, "The grand preceptor is a prominent minister in the state, rich and powerful. How could he have done such a thing? But then this

517

boot is clearly from his residence. It must have been someone close to him that has done such an ignoble thing."

They discussed the matter for a while. At one point, they even thought of taking the boot to the grand preceptor's residence and confronting him with the question directly. But they were aware that this might harm the grand preceptor's honor and dignity; the consequences of offending him need not be mentioned. Then they thought of dropping the whole case; but it was too serious a matter, and it had already involved two Taoist priests and the arrest of Jen Yi-lang. Since this case was now more than half public, they could not pretend that it had not happened. How could they deny their knowledge once it came out into the open in the future? If the emperor were to become angry, they could well imagine what kind of punishment would be waiting for them. After much consideration, the marshal decided to ask Wang and Jan Kuei to leave first. Then, without calling for his sedan chair, he took up the boot and the ledgers and hurriedly left with the magistrate. Truly:

You wear out pairs of iron shoes without discovering what you
    want to find.
Then suddenly out of nowhere what you've been looking for
    appears.

Marshal Yang and the magistrate rushed over to the grand preceptor's residence. They waited for a long time outside the door before the grand preceptor received them in the study. After the formal greeting ceremonies and the tea, the grand preceptor asked, "Have you made any progress?"

"We know who the culprit is already," Marshal Yang replied. "But for fear of damaging your good name, we haven't yet made the arrest."

"This is certainly no small matter. How could I presume to protect the guilty one?"

"Even if you don't intend to protect him, I'm sure you will be in for a little shock."

"Just name the culprit. What's the big problem?"

"I beg you to dismiss the servants; I'll tell you who he is."

After the grand preceptor had sent away all the servants, Marshal Yang opened the briefcase and handed the ledgers over for the grand preceptor's inspection, saying, "You're the only one we could approach for a decision, Grand Preceptor."

"Strange! how strange!" the grand preceptor muttered.

"Please don't bear a grudge against us, since this is an official matter of the utmost importance."

"I'm not blaming you. I'm only puzzled by the mysterious origin of the boot."

"But it was clearly recorded in the ledger that it was Steward Chang who ordered it. There can be no mistake about that."

"This boot was indeed ordered by Chang Ch'ien, my steward, but as soon as he had delivered it, he had nothing to do with it anymore. Come to think of it, all the clothes, shoes, and socks in my house are handled by different waiting women, whose duty is to see that each item is clearly recorded, whether it is to be used by the household or to be sent out as a gift. A detailed report has to be made at the end of each month, to account for everything passing through. Let me have someone check the ledgers and then everything will be clear."

He sent a servant to call the waiting woman who handled all the shoes. She immediately came, with a ledger in her hand.

"This is a boot from my house. How come some outsider has gotten hold of it?" asked the grand perceptor. "Check it immediately."

The waiting woman checked through the ledger item by item, and found that this boot had been ordered in the third month of the preceding year.

Soon after it was delivered, a student of the grand preceptor by the name of Yang Shih, also known as Master Kuei-shan,[12] happened to be around to pay his teacher a visit. He had been recently promoted prefect of a place near the capital, and as he was on excellent terms with the grand preceptor, he decided to stop by on his way to his new job. More an unkempt Confucian scholar than a government official, he dressed quite shabbily and his shoes had holes in them. So the grand preceptor had sent for a round-collar gown, a silver waistband, a pair of boots, and four fans, and gave them to him as a farewell present. This was the very boot which the grand preceptor had given to Prefect Yang. It was clearly recorded, and the grand preceptor showed it to the Marshal Yang and Magistrate T'eng.

"This certainly has nothing to do with your house," said the two apologetically. "Please forgive our presumptuousness in bringing this matter up with you. It was all because of the burden of our responsibility."

"How could I blame you? You've done what you're supposed to do," the grand preceptor said, laughing. "But now what shall we do with Prefect Yang? I think there must be a reason for it. Luckily his prefecture is not far away; I can send for him for questioning and get to the bottom of all this. You two can leave now, but don't let anyone know about this." The two took their leave and returned to their own residences.

The grand preceptor immediately sent an attendant to bring Prefect Yang. Within two days, they had returned to the capital and reported to the grand preceptor.

After tea was served, the grand preceptor said, "Being a prefect, you're just like a parent to the people. How could you do such a thing? This is an unpardonable crime against His majesty."

After this, he gave an account of Lady Han's

[12] Yang Shih (1053–1135) was a well-known Sung philosopher.

story to Prefect Yang. The latter bowed slightly and replied, "My honorable teacher, after I had taken your generous gifts last year, I caught some kind of eye disease at the inn before I left the capital. People told me that there is a temple of the god Erh-lang around here which responds to people's prayers readily and works great miracles. So I made a pledge that as soon as my eye ache was gone, I would immediately go to burn incense and to make a sacrifice to the god. Later, when I was cured, I kept my pledge and went to the temple. I noticed that the god Erh-lang's whole attire looked neat and tidy, with the exception of his black boots, which had a ripped seam. It looked most out of place, so I immediately took off this pair of boots and offered them to the god. What I'm saying is the absolute truth, for I have never done anything deceitful in my life. Having committed myself to the study of the classics, how would I dare to commit such an abominable crime? I hope the grand preceptor will examine the evidence carefully."

The grand preceptor had always known that Yang Kuei-shan was a devoted Confucian scholar, and definitely would not dare to do anything against the law. So upon hearing Yang's explanation, he said, "Of course, I'm aware of your honorable reputation. I asked you here to answer for yourself only to satisfy the official formalities." He then treated the prefect to food and drink. After the meal, he told the prefect that he could leave but bade him not to let a word out to any outsider. Thus:

If you do not do anything against your own conscience during the day,
Then there is no need to be frightened at the knocking of the door during the night.

The grand preceptor then asked Marshal Yang and Magistrate T'eng to come over and declared in a forthright manner, "This matter has nothing to do with Prefect Yang, so I can only hope that you people will work harder to solve this case."

There was nothing the magistrate could say; he took back the boot and returned to his office. He sent for Inspector Wang and told him, "At first I thought we were really on to something, but now it has turned out to be nothing at all! Take this boot back and I'll give you another five days to catch the culprit."

Wang was greatly troubled upon receiving this order. He returned to the detectives' office and said to Jan Kuei, "What rotten luck! Everything was fine when you found a clue in Jen Yi-lang, and since it turned out that the shoe belonged to the grand preceptor's house, I thought that he would act as most officials do: cover up. How could I know that they would want to go on with the matter? They don't know that there is simply no way to solve this case. Come to think of it, if it is true that Prefect Yang offered the boot to the god Erh-lang, could it be that that was indeed the shoe left by his romantic adventure? But where can I find some evidence to show the magistrate?"

"Even if you don't say so, I know the crime has nothing to do with Jen Yi-lang, or Grand Preceptor Ts'ai, or Prefect Yang," said Jan Kuei. "You said that it might have been done by the god Erh-lang; I don't believe that a god would commit such an immoral act! It must have been done by some sorcerer in the vicinity of the temple. Why don't we go around the neighborhood and see if we can find some clues? Don't be overjoyed if we catch him, and don't be distressed if we don't."

The inspector then gave the boot to Jan Kuei. Jan Kuei prepared two baskets of sundry goods and carried them on a long pole across his shoulder. Rattling an "awaken the maidens," a small drum used by street hawkers to attract the attention of their customers, he went to the temple of the god Erh-lang. He put down his load, lit a stick of incense, and prayed, "Divine one, please lend me your assistance in apprehending the scoundrel so that your own name can be cleared."

After he had made his genuflection, he drew three lots for divine guidance and they all proclaimed favorable auspices. Jan Kuei thanked the god and left the temple. Lifting the load back onto his shoulder, he took a walk around the temple with his eyes wide open, on the lookout for anything suspicious. He passed by a house with a single door and a half window next to it. A half-new mottled bamboo curtain was hanging on the door, which had been left ajar. He heard someone calling him from the inside: "Over here, peddler."

Jan Kuei turned around and saw a young woman, so he said, "Yes, madam. What can I do for you?"

"You do collect miscellaneous items, don't you? I have something here which I'd like to sell for a few pennies so I can buy some candies for my little boy. Do you have any use for it?" asked the woman.

"My basket has a name, 'Catch Them All.' So you know I buy almost everything," replied Jan Kuei. "Why don't you bring it out and I'll have a look at it?"

The woman asked her little boy to bring out the object and show it to Jan Kuei. What did the little boy bring out? Truly:

The Ch'in ministers had difficulty separating a deer from a horse;
Chuang-tzu found it hard to tell whether he was really a man or a butterfly.

What the boy took out turned out to be a quadruple-stitched black leather boot, exactly the same as the one which Priest P'an had struck off the other day. Jan Kuei was secretly overjoyed, but told the woman, "Since you have only one, it won't be worth anything. How much do you really want? Just don't go too high."

"I only want some cash to buy something for the child to eat. So I'll let you name the price, as long as it is fair."

So Jan Kuei pulled out one and a half strings of cash, and handed them to the woman, saying, "It's up to you! If you take this, then I'll take that. If you don't think it's enough, then forget it. You know I really haven't much use for one boot."

"Just a little more and you have a deal."

"No, I can't." So saying, Jan Kuei picked up his load to go.

The little boy started to cry, so the woman had to call Jan Kuei back, and said to him, "I don't care how much, but just give me a little more."

So Jan Kuei took out another twenty pennies and said, "All right! All right! It's really more than I should pay."

He took the boot, pitched it into one of his baskets, and left. He was secretly thrilled: "At last this case is half solved. I won't say anything yet. I'll wait until I've found out in detail the background of this woman, and then I'll have some ground for action."

That night, after he had left the load in the custody of a friend who lived near the Tientsin Bridge, he returned to the detectives' office. When Wang came to inquire, he just replied that there was no news.

The next day after breakfast he retrieved the load from his friend and again went to the woman's house. He saw that the door was locked, so the woman must have gone out. He thought for a while and suddenly an idea occurred to him. He put down the load and started to look around from door to door. He saw an old man sitting on a small stool, making ropes with hay. Jan Kuei approached him and, after apologizing to him for interrupting his work, asked, "Uncle, can you please tell me where has that lady who lives on your left gone to today?"

The old man stopped working, and then looked up at Jan Kuei and asked in return, "Why do you ask?"

"I'm a peddler of sundries," Jan Kuei replied. "Yesterday I bought an old boot from the lady. I didn't take a good look at it and it turned out to

be a bad bargain for me. Today, I've come back just to ask her for my money back."

"I'd advise you to rather suffer the loss than provoke that woman. She is the mistress of Sun Shen-t'ung, the keeper of the Erh-lang God Temple. That Sun Shen-t'ung knows all kinds of sorcery and is really a menace. This old boot must have been taken from the statue of the god and given to his mistress so that she could sell it for some money and buy the child some candies to eat. Today, the woman has gone to her grandmother's place. She has known the temple keeper for quite some time. For some reason or other, they didn't see each other much for two to three months; but recently, they seem to have made up again. If you ask her for your money back, she definitely will not return it to you. Instead you'll only infuriate her and she'll tell her lover about it. Then he'll use his sorcery against you and there'll be nothing you can do about it!"

"Since that is the case, I think I'll take your advice. Thank you, uncle."

Jan Kuei left the old man, put the load back on his shoulder, and returned with a smile on his face to the detectives' office. Wang immediately said inquiringly, "You must be in luck today!"

"I think you can say that," replied Jan Kuei. "Will you please show me the boot so that I can have a closer look at it?"

Wang took out the boot and Jan Kuei compared it with the one which he had bought. They were indeed identical.

"Where did you get that boot?" Wang asked anxiously.

Jan Kuei then gave him a detailed account of his investigation. "Did I tell you that the god Erh-lang is not responsible for this? Now it is quite obvious that Sun Shen-t'ung is the true culprit. There is no doubt about it."

Wang was beside himself with joy. He immediately burnt some incense to thank the gods, and toasted Jan Kuei as a gesture of appreciation.

"Now how are we going to catch him?" he

asked. "I'm afraid that word will get out and that rascal will already have run away. Then we wouldn't know where to catch him."

"Where's the problem?" replied Jan Kuei. "Tomorrow we'll prepare the three kinds of sacrificial animals and other presents, and then go to the temple under the pretext of thanking the god and carrying out our pledges. When we arrive at the temple, the temple keeper naturally will come out to welcome us. Then a wine cup can be thrown as a signal, and we can catch him without wasting any effort at all."

"That's a good idea," said the inspector. "But first I must report to the magistrate before taking any action."

So Wang reported to the magistrate, who was also overjoyed. "This is your job. Only be very careful and don't make any mistakes. I've heard that sorcerers can escape by making themselves invisible, so you must bring along some counteragents, such as a mixture of pig's blood, dog's blood, garlic, and human manure. Pour these on him and surely he won't be able to escape."

Wang received the instruction and left to make preparations.

Early the next morning, they came to the temple, having secretly ordered some people to carry the four counteragents and stand ready at a distance. When the time for action came, they would then come forward to join him. After giving out all the orders, Wang and Jan Kuei changed their clothes, and with their followers they went into the main hall to burn incense. The temple keeper Sun Shen-t'ung came out as expected to receive them and to read a prayer. Barely had he finished reading the first sentences when Jan Kuei, who was pouring wine next to him, dashed the wine cup to the ground. The others immediately came around to arrest the temple keeper. They were indeed as

Majestic as a black eagle chasing a purple sparrow,
Ferocious as a fierce tiger devouring a meek lamb.

Then they emptied the four kinds of counteragents on his head. The temple keeper knew that once this was done, he had no hope of escape, no matter how powerful he was. They clubbed him all the way back to the K'ai-feng tribunal.

When Magistrate T'eng heard that the god-imposter had been caught, he immediately opened the trial.

"What an impertinent scoundrel!" shouted the magistrate. "How dare you use sorcery to seduce an imperial lady and cheat her of the precious royal gift! What do you have to say?"

At first Sun Shen-t'ung still wanted to deny the charges, but under heavy torture he realized that he could not get free and had to admit his guilt. He confessed, "When I was young, I started learning sorcery while wandering around the country. Later I became a priest in the Erh-lang God Temple, and bought my position as the temple keeper. Because I had overheard that Lady Han would like to have a husband exactly like the god Erh-lang, I couldn't help getting the idea of disguising myself as the god in order to seduce her and subsequently to cheat her of the jade waistband. What I've said is the complete truth."

The magistrate decreed that he be put in a large cangue and thrown into prison. He also ordered the prison guards to watch him carefully while waiting for the emperor to pass down the verdict. The magistrate then put the case records in order and reported to Marshal Yang. The two then conferred with Grand Preceptor Ts'ai at his residence, and sent a memorandum to Emperor Tao-chün.

The imperial edict finally came: "The criminal is guilty of two crimes: the defilement of an imperial lady and the acquisition of imperial property by fraudulent means. He is therefore sentenced to a lingering death. His wife will enter the palace as a maid. The jade waistband will be returned to the palace if it still has not been used. Lady Han is guilty of improper conduct, and is therefore expelled from the palace. It will be up to Marshal Yang to marry her off to a civilian."

Even though Lady Han had been greatly shaken by this turn of events, her lifelong wish was fulfilled and her passionate longing was finally satisfied. Later, she married some merchant from a distant town who owned a shop in the capital. He promised not to bring her back to his home district. So he traveled between the two places, and they were able to live harmoniously together until old age. But this is no immediate concern of ours here.

The magistrate of K'ai-feng brought Sun Shen-t'ung out from the prison and the verdict was read aloud in court. A notice listing his crimes was also posted on the bulletin with the sentence: "Death by slicing." He was carried to the marketplace, where he was executed before the public. Verily:

All retributions of one's former deed
Come rushing when one's luck has gone bad.

That day, the marketplace was swarming with spectators. After the supervisor of executions had read out the list of his crimes, the executioners evoked the Lords of Punishment before laying their hands on Sun Shen-t'ung.

This story was originally circulated by the storytellers in the capital, and it has now become part of the unofficial history of the Sung Dynasty.

One must abide by Confucian law,
And live up to Hsiao Ho's demands.[13]
For adultery brings a violent death,
Which no sorcery can help one avoid.

[13] Hsiao Ho (?–193 B.C.) was one of the chief advisers of the Han founder.

YEN-CHIH

From *Liao-chai chih-i*

TRANSLATED BY AMY LING

In Tung-ch'ang,[1] there lived a veterinarian named Pien. He had a daughter whose childhood name was Yen-chih. She was both intelligent and pretty, and her father loved her dearly. He wanted his daughter to marry a scholar, but families of scholars looked down upon him as their inferior and did not favor such an alliance. Therefore, Yen-chih was already fifteen and still remained unengaged.

A family named Kung lived across the street. The wife, whose own surname was Wang, was a frivolous person and enjoyed jokes. She was a friend of Yen-chih.

One day when Yen-chih saw Wang to the door after the latter's visit, a young man happened to pass by on the street, wearing white clothes and a white cap. He was so strikingly handsome that Yen-chih could not help staring at him, following him intently with her eyes. The young man, embarrassed, lowered his head and hastened away. When he had already gone some distance up the street, her gaze was still following him. Seeing this, Wang said playfully, "You're such a pretty, intelligent girl; if you could be married to him, that would be wonderful." Yen-chih blushed and could not say a word.

"Do you know him?" Wang asked.

"No, I don't," she answered.

"He's a *hsiu-ts'ai* by the name of E Ch'iu-chun; he lives in the South Lane. His father was a *chü-jen*. I was once their neighbor; that's why I know him. He is the most gentle of men. Now he's wearing white in mourning for his wife's death. If you really like him I can pass the word along and ask him to send over a matchmaker."

Yen-chih said nothing. Wang walked away with a smile. When several days had passed and nothing had happened, Yen-chih wondered if Wang had not had time to deliver the message or if the young man's family had not approved of her. Torn between her anxieties and fears, she lost interest in eating and drinking and finally became seriously ill.

Just at that time Wang came to see her and asked why she was ill. Yen-chih said, "I don't know why, but I didn't feel well the day after you left. I feel I'm just lingering on, and death is only a matter of time."

Wang said in low tones, "My husband has been away on a business trip, so no one has been able to go over to E Ch'iu-chun's place to speak for you. Is this the cause of your illness?"

Yen-chih's face was flushed for a long time.

Wang teased her, "If this is the real reason, since

[1] A prefecture in the western part of Shantung Province.

524

you're so sick now, you need not worry about propriety. Perhaps we should just invite him over tonight. How could he refuse?"

The girl sighed and said, "Since things have come to this stage, there's no going back for me. If he doesn't consider me too inferior, please ask him to send a matchmaker to arrange a wedding. That will help me get well. Under no circumstances would I want him to come see me secretly." Wang nodded and took her leave.

When Wang was young, she had a lover, Su Chieh, who lived next door. After her marriage, Su came to see her whenever her husband was not home. That night Su came, and Wang told him what Yen-chih had said. The two laughed about it, but she asked Su to go to E's place to deliver the message. Having known for a long time that Yen-chih was beautiful, Su was pleased to hear this news, thinking it an opportunity for himself. At first he wanted to plot his scheme with Wang, but on second thought he changed his mind, afraid that she would be jealous. Therefore, in the course of the conversation, he elicited from Wang the vital information about the layout of Yen-chih's place.

The next evening, he climbed over the wall of the Pien residence, went directly to the girl's room, and knocked on the window. "Who is it?" the girl inside asked.

He answered, "This is E."

"I think of you as a partner in marriage," said Yen-chih, "not just as someone for one night. If you truly love me, you should quickly get a matchmaker. If you're only interested in having an affair, I won't have anything to do with it."

Su pretended that he agreed with her, and begged only to hold her hand. The girl, not wanting to be too hard on him, struggled to open the window. Su pushed his way in, took her in his arms, and wanted to make love with her. She was too weak to resist and fell to the floor, breathless. Su quickly raised her and Yen-chih said, "Where are you from, you scoundrel? You couldn't be Mr.

E, for he would be much more gentle. Knowing the reason for my illness, he would not have treated me this way. Leave me alone now or I'll scream. Then your reputation will be ruined and mine as well."

Afraid that his deception would be discovered, Su did not dare to force her any longer but asked her when they would meet again. The girl answered that their next meeting would be on their wedding day. Su thought that was too far away and pressed her again. The girl grew tired of his insistence and said that it had to wait until her recovery. He asked her for a token, but she would not give him anything. Then he grabbed her foot, took off her embroidered shoe, and began to leave. The girl called him back, saying, "Since I've already promised to be your wife, why should I begrudge you anything? I'm only worried that if our marriage never took place, I'd become a laughingstock. Now that you've taken my shoe, I doubt I can ever get it back. Thus, if you should change your mind, the only way left for me is to die."

After leaving the girl, Su went over to Wang's house. He lay down but was worried about the embroidered shoe. To reassure himself, he felt in his sleeve where he had hidden it, but it was gone. He lit a light and looked all over for it. Wang asked him what he was looking for, but he did not answer. He then suspected that she had hidden it. She only smiled, making him even more suspicious. Su knew that he had no alternative but to tell her the whole story. He then took a lantern and searched outside but found nothing. He returned, discouraged, and retired, thinking that since it was in the middle of the night and with no one around, the slipper should still be on the street. The next morning, he went out to look again, but there was no trace of it.

In the meantime Big Mao, a hanger-on in the area who had long been interested in Wang without success, came to know that Wang and Su were together. He then planned to catch them red-handed so that he could blackmail Wang. That night he passed by Wang's place and, finding that the gate was unlocked, walked in. As he was approaching her window, he felt something soft as cotton under his feet. He picked it up and examined it; it was a girl's embroidered shoe wrapped in a handkerchief. He eavesdropped on them and heard everything Su said. Delighted, he ran off.

Several days later, Big Mao climbed the wall of the Pien house. Being unfamiliar with the layout, he stumbled upon the room of Yen-chih's father. Seeing a man outside his window, the old man thought that he had come for his daughter and became very angry. He grabbed a cleaver and rushed out. Big Mao was frightened and turned back to run out. As he was attempting to climb over the wall, the old man caught up with him. Mao, in desperation, snatched the cleaver from the old man's hand. At this time, Yen-chih's mother had also been aroused and was screaming. Afraid that he could not escape, Big Mao struck out at the old man with the cleaver. Having become stronger, Yen-chih got up when she heard all this commotion. The entire household came out and saw by candlelight that the old man's head had been split open. He could no longer speak and died shortly thereafter. They found an embroidered shoe by the wall. The mother examined it and recognized it as Yen-chih's shoe. She questioned her. Yen-chih wept and told her the whole story. She did not want to involve Wang, so she merely said that E ch'iu-chun had come of his own accord.

The next morning they reported this matter to the authorities and had the *hsui-ts'ai* arrested. E Ch'iu-chun was a very quiet person. Even though he was nineteen years old, he was as shy as a child when he met a stranger. When arrested, he was frightened to death. He could not say a word before the county magistrate, but trembled all over. The magistrate took this as a sign of guilt and had him tortured. Unable to stand the torture, he confessed and was sent to the prefectural seat. The prefect also had him tortured. Indignant at being so wronged, he tried to talk to the girl face to face, but each time he met her at court, she unleashed such a torrent of anger and bitterness that he could not get in a word. Then he was sentenced to death.

This case was brought to court several times under several officials, but the verdict remained the same. This case was finally transferred to the Tsinan Prefecture for retrial. The prefect was Wu Nan-tai.[2] Judging by E Ch'iu-chun's person, Wu did not think that this young man could be a murderer. Wu secretly sent a person to talk to him informally so that he would be more at ease to tell the truth. As a result, he became more convinced that the *hsiu-ts'ai* was innocent. He pondered the matter for several days before he began the trial.

First he questioned Yen-chih: "After you had planned the next meeting, did anyone else know about it?"

Yen-chih answered, "No."

Again he asked, "Was anyone present when you met E Ch'iu-chun for the first time?"

Yen-chih again said, "No."

Then Wu summoned the young man and questioned him very gently. E then informed Wu, "Once I passed by the Pien residence and saw a former neighbor, Wang, and this girl coming out of the house. I hurriedly walked away and didn't speak to her at all."

Prefect Wu admonished Yen-chih, "Why did you just say there was no one else when he says his former neighbor was there?" He ordered arrangements for her torture.

The frightened girl then confessed, "Wang was there at the time, but she had nothing to do with any of this." Wu stopped the questioning and ordered the arrest of Wang.

Several days later, Wang was brought to him. Having made sure that the two women were kept apart, Wu immediately questioned her. The first

---

[2] Wu Nan-tai (*chin-shih* 1633) served as the prefect of Tsinan (Chi-nan) in 1655; this gives the story an exact time setting.

question he asked was, "Who was the murderer?"

"I don't know," Wang replied.

Wu then tried to trick her, "Yen-chih said that you know everything about the Pien murder. Why are you lying?"

The woman cried out, "That's not true! This lewd girl wanted a man, and although I told her I would make the arrangements, I was only teasing her. She herself brought the scoundrel into her house. How could I know anything about it?"

It was only after further interrogations that Wang disclosed the jokes she had made on different occasions. The prefect called in Yen-chih and asked her angrily, "You said that Wang didn't know anything, but why did she herself admit that she would undertake marriage arrangements for you?"

In tears, Yen-chih replied, "Because of my unworthiness, my father died. Since I didn't know this case would drag on, I couldn't bear to involve Wang."

The prefect asked Wang, "After you teased the girl, whom did you tell?"

Wang replied, "No one."

This infuriated Wu, and he said, "Since husband and wife share the same bed, there shouldn't be any secrets between them. How could you say you've told no one?" Wang explained that her husband had been away on business.

Wu retorted, "Those who enjoy teasing people always laugh at others' foolishness just to show off their own cleverness. Who is going to believe you that you didn't tell anyone?"

He ordered her fingers put to the rack. Wang, out of fear, told the truth: "I told Su Chieh." Prefect Wu then released E and arrested Su.

When Su came, he also said he did not know anything. Wu said, "If you can get involved with a lowly woman, you can't be an honest person." Therefore, he had him tortured.

Su Chieh then admitted, "It is true that I tricked the girl, but after I had lost the shoe, I never returned to her again. I really don't know anything about the killing."

Prefect Wu said, "What else wouldn't a person do if he could go so far as to climb over walls to enter another person's house?" He had Su Chieh tortured again. Unable to stand the pain, Su admitted to the murder. The case was then sent to a higher authority and everyone was full of praise for Prefect Wu's wisdom. Since his decision was considered final, Su now had only to wait until autumn to be executed.

Despite his loose morals, Su was a well-known scholar in the Shantung area. He heard that the commissioner of education, Shih Yü-shan,[3] was a most virtuous and capable official who had a high regard for men of talent. Su therefore sent him a very moving appeal. The commissioner requested his record of confession and, after examining it very carefully, pounded the table and said, "He has been wronged!"

He then asked the various offices concerned to transfer all the materials on file to him so that he could reopen the case. He asked Su, "Where did you lose the embroidered shoe?"

Su replied, "I don't know, but when I knocked on Wang's door, the shoe was still in my sleeve."

Shih asked Wang, "Besides Su Chieh, how many other lovers do you have?"

"None," she replied.

Shih said, "How can a loose woman have only one lover?"

"I knew Su Chieh when we were young," Wang replied, "so I couldn't refuse him even after mar-

[3] Shih Jun-chang (1619–1638) was a noted scholar of the early Ch'ing period. He became a *chin-shih* in the same year as Wu Nan-tai; they were therefore classmates in the traditional sense of the term. Historically, he held the post of commissioner of education for Shantung from 1656 to 1661. Shih was also the mentor of P'u Sung-ling, the author of the short story collection, *Liao-chai chih-i,* from which this selection comes. Shih passed the special 1679 examination for the best scholars of the time (only one such examination was held throughout the entire Ch'ing period) and later took part in the compilation of the *Ming-shih* (The History of the Ming Dynasty).

riage. Later, there were other people interested in me, but I had nothing to do with them."

Shih asked her to name some of the others. Then she said, "Big Mao, who lives in the neighborhood, has made advances to me several times, but I always refused him."

Shih asked, "What made you so chaste?" He gave orders to have her beaten. Then Wang knocked her forehead against the ground until it bled and insisted that she had no other lovers. When she was released, Shih asked her, "While your husband was away, weren't there any other people who came to your house for one reason or another?"

"Yes, there were a few who came to my house once or twice either to borrow money or to bring gifts."

It happened that those few she named were rascals from the neighborhood who were interested in Wang but never dared to express themselves openly. Shih took down their names and gave orders to have them arrested. When they were all assembled, he took them to the Temple of the City God, where he made them kneel down in front of the altar and said to them, "I had a dream a few nights ago, and the City God told me that the murderer is one of you. Now, before this god, you cannot lie. If you are willing to confess, then I will reduce your punishment. Otherwise, there will be no mercy."

These people simultaneously claimed that they had not killed anyone. Shih then ordered torture instruments for the neck, hands, and feet to be placed on the ground before them and threatened to use all of these. He ordered their clothes removed and had their hair bound. They all cried out that they were being treated unjustly. Shih ordered them released and said, "Since you won't confess willingly, I'll have to seek the help of the gods."

He asked that all the windows be covered with blankets so that no light could leak in. In the dark, he ordered the suspects to expose their backs and then gave them water in a basin to wash their hands. Then he tied them along the wall and gave them the order, "Sit facing the wall and don't move. The murderer will be identified by the god's writing on his back."

After a while he called them all out, examined them, pointed at Big Mao, and said, "This one is the real murderer."

Before this took place, Shih had arranged that ashes be spread on the wall and that soot be mixed in the water. Afraid that the god would write on his back, the murderer sat with his back against the wall and thereby rubbed ashes onto his back. When he walked out, he used his hands to cover his back, leaving smudges of soot. Shih had suspected all along that Big Mao was the murderer; now he was convinced. He proceeded to have Mao tortured in earnest, and Big Mao confessed in full detail. The final verdict read:

In the case of Su Chieh, because of his amorous escapades he was accused of homicide and became a notorious lecher. His love for Wang began in childhood; so he treated the lover as if she were his wife. From one sentence which indiscreetly slipped out, his passion for another woman was aroused. Thus, he climbed over the wall of the girl's house and deceived her into letting him in. Such behavior for a scholar is truly disgraceful. Fortunately for her, the girl was sick; therefore he had pity on her and did not take further advantage of her. This behavior is evidence that some of the conscience of a scholar still remained. However, he then snatched the shoe from her foot. Isn't this again the most despicable behavior? While his going over the walls is not beyond others' knowledge, the shoe he took away disappeared like a fallen lotus petal without a trace. One deception breeds another; who would believe that this was the most unjust of all injustices? This disaster was decreed by Heaven, and Su Chieh was almost tortured to death. Because of the wrong he did, he brought retribution upon himself and almost lost his head. Though he tarnished his reputation as a scholar by climbing over others' walls, to sentence him to death for a crime he did not commit would be injustice indeed. Thus his sentence should be reduced to make up for what he has already endured. It should suffice that his academic titles be removed, but that he be given another chance to start over.

In the case of Big Mao, that cunning wretch and city gangster, despite a harsh rejection by the neighbor woman, his lecherous passion was not extinguished. He spied another man committing an error and that gave him a wicked idea. He opened the door, thinking he would have the happiness of meeting a woman. Since he had asked for soup and received wine, he dreamed of satisfying his lust. Who could know that Heaven would intervene and send him to the wrong room? There his fiery lust was extinguished and the sea of passion became turbulent. The old man attacked with a cleaver without considering his own safety. A robber when cornered will fight back desperately, and even a rabbit will bite when trapped. He jumped over the wall hoping to be taken for the girl's lover, but when he snatched the weapon, he lost the shoe. Therefore, the fish escaped the net, but the swan was caught. It is a pity that such a devil should exist on the road of romance! And what place has the devil in the lover's nest? He should be beheaded to everybody's satisfaction.

In the case of Yen-chih, she was already of marriageable age but not yet engaged. Since she is as beautiful as the goddess in the moon, she deserves a lover as pure as jade. Her beauty would certainly have insured a good marriage, but she was anxious to make a match herself. Unfortunately, everything turned out to be an empty dream. When her desires were unsatisfied, lovesickness overtook her. Her impatience had attracted devils who all came for red cheeks and were afraid they would lose "rouge."[4] Birds circle around her and both claimed to be "au-

tumn falcon."[5] A single lotus petal was picked and the flower's fragrance was diminished. Her house was broken into again and again, and its treasure was nearly stolen. Her lovesickness had become the cause of all these troubles. All this led to the death of her father and further disaster. Fortunately, she maintained her purity like jade without a blemish. Her true love was imprisoned but after much struggle he was finally released. Her resistance even after a man was in her room is worthy of praise. She is still as pure as snow. Now it would be a fine thing to help her dream come true. I will ask the magistrate to serve as the matchmaker.

After the case was closed, the story spread far and wide. Ever since Prefect Wu took up the case, Yen-chih had begun to realize that E Ch'iu-chun had been wronged. During each court hearing, when their paths crossed, she agonized over his suffering. With tears in her eyes, she seemed desirous of saying something, but no words came. Moved by her unalterable love, E had fallen in love with her himself, but the thought of her modest family background and the fact that she had been seen in court every day had deterred him. He was afraid that people would laugh at him should he marry her. Day and night he was troubled by such conflicts, but did not know how to resolve them. Now that the verdict had been passed, he was relieved and pleased. The magistrate acted as matchmaker, and the two were happily united at last.[6]

---

[4] "Rouge" is the literal meaning of *yen-chih*.

[5] "Autumn falcon" is the literal meaning of *ch'iu-chun*.
[6] Comments at the end of the story are not translated because they do not constitute part of the narrative.

THE MASTER THIEF

The master thief is so smugly confident of his skill that he may find it unchallenging to pick an ordinary citizen as his target. He would rather, as can be seen in "The Wit of the Master Thief," try his hand on an official who is supposed to be alert and clever. The real challenge, however, is to outwit his own peers. To demonstrate the master stroke of a thief, the storyteller usually employs the method of comparison. Sung the Fourth is given the opportunity to establish his credentials in breaking into the heavily guarded storehouse of Tightwad Chang (no ordinary citizen who takes few precautions) and in dodging the detectives. But just as this titular hero is about to claim the honor of being a master thief, he is defeated by Chao Cheng, a former student of his, three times in a row. The outcome of this contest of wits makes clear to the reader who is the real master thief. Worth noting in the story are not only the various tricks these thieves play on one another but also the appalling lack of honor among thieves. If Wei Chiu (in the first story in "The Wit of the Master Thief") had not taken precautions, he would have been decapitated by his partner. In return, Wei Chiu traps his dishonorable accomplice. The relationship between Sung the Fourth and his two students hangs on the constant tension of betrayal. What keeps them together is the common bond of self-interest on the one hand, and the necessity of protecting themselves from their common enemies on the other, even though more often than not they are enemies themselves.

THE WIT OF THE MASTER THIEF

From *Liang-hsi man-chih*

TRANSLATED BY AMY LING

It's a common saying that although a thief is a low-class person, his wit is often sharper than a gentleman's. This may seem ridiculous, but there are times when the thief's cunning is so far beyond people's expectations that he deserves to die for it.

A man named Wei Chiu from Kao-yu County[1] could run so fast that in one day he could cover a few hundred *li*. He would run with such force that only a tree blocking his path could stop him. As a thief, his activities were not confined to his own county; all the people in the Huai region suffered from his ventures. He lived in the marketplace of Kao-yu, running a small restaurant by day and stealing by night.

One morning soon after he got up, a Taoist priest came to the restaurant to see him. After having some noodle soup, the Taoist invited Wei to a quiet place, bowed to him, and called him "master." Wei was startled and asked why he did that. The Taoist replied, "I also have a little skill, but it's nothing to compare with yours, master. I've heard that outside the city of Ch'u-chou[2] there is a rich family. I came to ask you to go with me so that I can be sure of a large haul." Wei

agreed to help and told the Taoist priest to go first. The Taoist then hurried off.

That night Wei closed his restaurant, lit a lamp, and began to beat his servant for negligence. The servant was so angry at this unjust treatment that he shouted for the constables. The authorities arrested both of them and kept them in jail overnight, intending to send them to court the next day. Wei spoke to a constable secretly: "We're good friends, and my family is here. I won't run away. If you let me go tonight, I'll come back tomorrow." The constable agreed and let him go.

As soon as Wei was released, he climbed over the city wall and ran two hundred *li* to the outskirts of Ch'u-chou. It was just the second watch. The Taoist priest was already there. Each was happy to see the other. Wei asked the Taoist to be the lookout while he climbed in through the window. Inside, he saw gold, pearls, and silk in abundance; he threw a hundred pieces of fine silk out the window. The Taoist divided these into two bags and carried them on his back. A little later, when Wei came out of the window, the Taoist thought that since Wei was the only person in the world who was a better thief than he, it would be best to kill him. He drew his sword and cut off Wei's head. When the head dropped to the ground, the priest found that it was made of

[1] In the present Kiangsu Province.
[2] Modern Huai-an in Kiangsu.

533

paper. Actually Wei himself had escaped from another door and had run back to Kao-yu and returned to the jail.

It was now dawn. Because the Taoist was carrying a heavy burden, he could not move fast; so he was caught and sent to jail in Ch'u-chou. The Taoist described how he and Wei had worked together on this robbery. A Ch'u-chou official sent a summons to Kao-yu for Wei's arrest, but the authorities at Kao-yu testified that Wei and his servant were arrested for fighting and had been put in jail that night. Thus it was impossible for Wei to have been involved in the robbery. Trapped by Wei's trick, the Taoist alone was punished. Wei was very cunning and could always find a foolproof alibi; he committed many burglaries, but there was no way the authorities could arrest him.

Once there was an official who was transferred to the capital. The front part of the inn where he stayed was a teahouse, and across the street was a dye shop. Whenever he had nothing to do, he would sit at a table watching the passersby.

One day he noticed with great surprise that several people were walking back and forth in front of him, watching the dye shop in a suspicious manner. One of them came to him and whispered, "We're doing business, and we're going to steal the silk they're dyeing. I came to ask you not to mention it."

"That has nothing to do with me," the official replied. "Why should I say anything about it?"

The fellow thanked him and left. The official thought to himself, "The dye shop has all its silk hanging high up on a busy street. In this broad daylight, with ten thousand eyes watching, if they have the skill to steal, then they're smart thieves indeed." So he watched carefully to see how they would manage it. But what he saw was only the same group of people walking back and forth in front of him, sometimes on the left, sometimes on the right. As the hours passed, the number of people decreased. At dusk, everyone was gone. "Those fools," the official said smiling. "They've put me on." Then he returned to his room to order some food, and he found that all his belongings were gone.

SUNG THE FOURTH RAISES HELL WITH TIGHTWAD CHANG

From *Ku-chin hsiao-shuo*

TRANSLATED BY TIMOTHY C. WONG

Money comes and goes like a never-ending stream;
Don't be miserly with widows and paupers.
Look at the site of Shih Ch'ung's Golden Valley:
Once towering pavilions, now brambles and briars.

It is said that in the Chin Dynasty there lived a man Shih Ch'ung, styled Chi-lun. Before he became prosperous, he spent his time on a little boat along a large river, fishing with a bow and arrow for a living.

One time unexpectedly in the dead of night, someone banged on his boat and pleaded, "Chi-lun, save me!" Shih Ch'ung heard him and opened the mat window, sticking his head out to see what was the matter. Moonlight was setting the sky aglow and the water sparkled in reflection. In the moonlight, on the water's surface, stood an old man.

"What urgent business has brought you here in the middle of the night?" Shih Ch'ung asked.

"Save me!" the old man cried out again.

So Shih Ch'ung promptly told him to get into the boat and asked him again what this was all about.

"I'm not a human being," the old man answered. "I'm the old dragon king of the upper course. As I'm aged and weak, I've been bullied by the little dragon from the lower course of the river who, taking advantage of my years, picks fights with me. I've lost to him time and again and there's no place for me to run to. He has challenged me to fight him again tomorrow, and I'm sure to get whipped once more. That's why I've come to ask you a favor. Aim your bow toward the river at noon tomorrow where there'll be two large fish battling each other. The one in front will be me, while the one pursuing from the rear will be the little dragon. I hope you'll agree to help me out. Shoot an arrow at the big fish in the rear. If you can finish off the little dragon, I'll naturally repay you richly for the favor."

After hearing this, Shih Ch'ung solemnly agreed to do as he was told. The old man bade him farewell and, turning away, leaped into the river and disappeared.

At noon the following day, Shih Ch'ung readied his bow and arrow. Sure enough, just as it was getting to be noontime, he saw two large fish speeding along the surface of the river. Shih Ch'ung put his arrow across his bow and, keeping his eye on the fish in the rear, zinged it directly into its belly. The river turned crimson as the fish expired on the water's surface. Then the wind

535

and the waves died down and nothing else happened. At midnight that night, the old man again came to the boat to offer his thanks. "Because you've done this good deed for me, I can now live on peacefully," he said. "Come noon tomorrow, bring your boat to the seventh willow tree on the south shore at the foot of Mount Chiang[1] and wait for me. I'll repay you well." Then he was gone.

The next day Shih Ch'ung did as he was told: he brought his boat to the designated willow tree at the foot of Mount Chiang, [and went ashore] to wait. He saw three ghostly messengers emerge from the water surface and pull the boat toward them. Presently, the boat was returned, filled with such things as gold, silver, pearls, and jade. The old man also came out of the water and said to Shih Ch'ung, "If you want more treasures, you can bring your empty boat back here and wait." Thereupon he took his leave.

And so whenever Shih Ch'ung brought his boat to the willow tree and waited, he received a boat-load of precious things. In this way, he became an immensely rich man. He built up connections with the powerful with his wealth and repeatedly rose in the ranks until he became a marshal, thus achieving status as well. Subsequently he bought a stately residence in the city and constructed behind it the Golden Valley Gardens with pavilions, terraces, towers, and halls. Using thirty pecks of large pearls, he purchased a concubine named Green Pearl. He also secured other concubines, a number of maidservants, and maids-in-waiting, and cavorted with them day and night, enjoying to the full his wealth and position. He cultivated the friendship of court officials and relatives of the emperor. Even the embroidered silk draperies in his house measured over ten *li* in length. In all of heaven and earth, one could not find luxury and splendor to compare with his.

One day he gave a banquet solely in the honor

[1] A hill to the east of Nanking.

of the imperial brother-in-law Wang K'ai, whose sister was the empress. When both Shih Ch'ung and Wang K'ai were half tipsy, Shih ordered Green Pearl to come out to pour wine for his guest. She was indeed dazzlingly beautiful. Once Wang K'ai saw her, he could hardly contain himself and licentious thoughts immediately stirred within him. When Wang K'ai took his leave at the end of the feast, his heart was so enthralled with Green Pearl's charms that he longed for the chance to possess her. Now Wang K'ai had often matched his precious possessions with Shih Ch'ung's, but Wang's things never measured up. Because of this Wang had secretly harbored ill will toward Shih and wanted a chance to ruin him. But since Shih Ch'ung continued to entertain him lavishly, Wang could find no excuse to carry out his schemes.

Then one day, the empress invited Wang K'ai to a banquet at the palace. When Wang saw his sister he tearfully told her, "In this city there is a rich man whose familial wealth runs into the billions and whose precious and rare possessions are too numerous to even be described. He often invites me to banquets in order to compare our treasures, but even one or two of his things are superior to any hundred items of mine. So take pity on me, dear sister, and help me salvage my pride. Borrow some rare things from the imperial treasury so that I can compete with him."

On hearing this the empress summoned the eunuch in charge of the imperial treasury. A large coral tree was brought out measuring three feet eight inches high. It was the pride of the palace. Without asking permission of the emperor, the empress ordered it transported to Wang K'ai's residence. Wang K'ai thanked his sister and, upon returning home, covered it carefully with layers of Shu brocade.

The following day Wang prepared a large feast of rare delicacies and, transporting everything to the Golden Valley Gardens, invited Shih Ch'ung to join him. Beforehand he had ordered the coral tree taken to an empty pavilion in the gardens. When the two were enjoying the feast, Wang K'ai said, "I've a treasure for your perusal; I hope you won't find it worthless." Shih Ch'ung asked that the brocade be removed and smiled when he saw it. Then, with one whack of his walking stick, he shattered it to pieces.

Greatly agitated, Wang K'ai cried out in agony, "This is the pride of the imperial treasury! Just because you can't measure up to me this time, you've destroyed it out of jealousy! What am I going to do?"

Shih Ch'ung broke into loud laughter and said, "Don't you worry. This is by no means an irreplaceable treasure."

Thereupon he invited Wang K'ai to a garden in the rear to look over his own coral trees. In varying sizes, they numbered over thirty, some as tall as seven or eight feet. He took one of equal size to the one he had shattered and gave it to Wang to be returned to the treasury. He also took a larger one and presented it to Wang as a gift. Wang retired in shame, convinced that there were no treasures in all the land to match Shih's. So in his jealousy, he formulated a wicked plan.

One day, Wang K'ai had an audience with the emperor and he informed His Majesty: "There is in this city a rich man named Shih Ch'ung who holds the post of marshal. His wealth rivals the nation's, and he lives in extreme extravagance. I'm afraid he's even better off than Your Majesty. Unless he is removed quickly, he will probably be a source of unforeseen danger."

This convinced the emperor, who issued a verbal edict to his guards to have Marshal Shih Ch'ung arrested and thrown into prison. All his possessions were confiscated. Wang K'ai was determined to get Green Pearl for himself and sent soldiers to surround her quarters and seize her. But Green Pearl thought to herself: "My husband's life has been ruined by this man's slander and I don't even know whether he's dead or alive. Now that this man wants to take me by force, how could I submit to him? I'd rather die than suffer such shame!" Thereupon she leaped to her death from her upper-story dwelling in the Golden Valley Gardens, to the profound regret of all.

When Wang K'ai heard about this, he became furious and ordered Shih Ch'ung executed in the marketplace. At the moment of his execution, Shih remarked with a sigh, "It's all because you people covet my riches."

"Since you knew that excessive wealth can bring about one's ruin," the executioner replied, "why didn't you get rid of it earlier?"

Shih Ch'ung was unable to answer him and, stretching out his neck, received the blade. Master Hu Tseng wrote a poem which says:

From the moment the beauty fell from her jade-like pavilion
Unending sorrow descended on the house of Chin.
Even the trees, sole remnants of the Golden Valley Gardens,
Were bent with mourning against the setting sun.

I've just related how Shih Ch'ung met with calamity because of his wealth and how in the course of flaunting his treasures and his women he met his nemesis in the person of Wang K'ai, the imperial brother-in-law. Now I'll tell you about a rich man who minded his own business and never went about looking for trouble. Nevertheless, because of his unrepenting miserliness, he brought upon himself some unusual happenings that make for an entertaining story. And what was this rich man's name? Listen and I'll tell you: this rich man's surname was Chang and he was called Fu. His home was located in K'ai-feng, the Eastern Capital. For generations, his family had been well known as pawnbrokers, and he was addressed as Squire Chang. This Squire Chang had a foible; he would even want to:

Pluck tendons from the backs of fleas,
Cut the thigh from the leg of a paddy-bird,
Peel the gold leaf off the face of an old buddha statue,
Scrape the black from the skin of a black bean [for paint],
Save the spittle to use as lamp fuel,
Rub a pine tree for frying oil.

This man had four great wishes:

First, that his clothes would last forever,
Second, that his food would stay in his stomach forever,
Third, that he would pick up valuables in the streets,
And fourth, that he could have his sexual pleasure with the
devils in his sleep.

In sum he was a real skinflint who would not ever think of spending a solitary cent. If he should chance upon a penny on the ground, he would seize it and shine it up like a mirror, knead it as if it were a musical stone, nip it out as if it were a saw. He would call it "my baby," kiss it, and stick it in his purse. When the people saw how tight he was, they gave him the nickname of Squire "Tightwad" Chang.

It was about noon one day, and Chang was lunching on cold rice and water in the back of his shop while his two clerks were counting cash out front. Then a man appeared wearing nothing on his entire upper body, which was tattooed with designs and writing so that it resembled brocade. He had on trousers of white gauze cinched up in a sloppy manner. Clutching a bamboo ladle in one hand, he peered around Boss Chang's place, bowed deeply, and begged for alms, saying, "Please have mercy on this beggar." Seeing that Chang was not around, one of the clerks flung a couple of pennies into the ladle.

Just then, from behind the latticed screen, Chang noticed what had gone on and hurried forward. "Aha!" he glowered. "What do you think you're doing, Mr. Clerk, throwing two pennies to him? Two pennies every day and in a thousand days there'd be two whole strings of cash!" Striding forward hurriedly, he seized the man with the ladle and, in one quick motion, emptied all the money in the ladle onto the shop's pile of cash. Moreover, he ordered his shopkeepers to give the beggar a beating, so that even the passersby felt indignant when they saw it. The man with the ladle took all the blows without daring to resist; he merely stood in front of Chang's door, wagging his finger and cursing.

Just then a man called out, "Brother, come here. I want a word with you." Turning his head, the beggar man saw an older person dressed like a jailer. The two greeted each other.

"Brother," the older man said, "this Squire 'Tightwad' Chang is an unreasonable man; don't you scrap with him. I'll give you two taels of cash. Even if you wind up selling turnips with this capital, at least you'll be your own boss."

The beggar man took the money, made his obeisances, and went off, and I'll say no more about him for now.

The older man was a native of the Peaceful Commandery (*Feng-ning chün*) in Cheng-chou. His name was Sung, and since he was the fourth eldest among his siblings, people called him Sung the Fourth. He was a footloose vagabond.

Around midnight that night, Sung the Fourth bought two fried dumplings for four pennies on the Gold Bridge, stuffed them inside his shirt, and went over to Tightwad Chang's place. There was nobody else walking the streets, and the moon was covered by dark clouds. Sung took out a strange-looking, rope-like contraption and, hooking it to the eaves, clambered up to the top of the house. Having secured the contraption at the roof, he jumped into the courtyard. There were rooms on either side of the courtyard, and he saw lamplight in a room off to one side. While he listened for noises there, he heard a woman saying, "What's the matter with Third Brother? He still isn't here."

"Ah!" said Sung to himself. "This woman must have set a secret tryst with someone." He took a peep at the girl and saw:

Silky, silky raven locks,
A glittery, glittery pale forehead,
Curvy, curvy seductive brows,
Pretty, pretty flirtatious eyes,
A cute, cute straight nose,
Bright, bright red cheeks,
A bubbling, bubbling fragrant mouth,
A gentle, gentle smooth chest,
Round, round white breasts,

Dainty, dainty jade-like hands,
A slim, slim tiny waist, and
Shapely, shapely arched feet.

Sung went up and covered her eyes with his two sleeves. "Third Brother, what do you think you're doing, frightening me like that?" she giggled. With a jerk, Sung secured her by the waist and, brandishing his sword, warned her, "Quiet! You make any noise and I'll kill you!"

The woman turned into a mass of shudders. "Sir, please spare my life," she begged.

"I'm here on business," Sung told her. "Let me ask you: how many traps are there between here and the storehouse?"

"Ten paces or so from my room," she answered, "you'll come across a deep pit in which there are two ferocious dogs. Beyond that there are five guards, drinking and gambling, who take turns at the watch. The storehouse is over there. Once inside, you'll find a paper figure holding a silver globe in its hands. Beneath the figure are triggering mechanisms. If you step on them, the silver globe will tumble to the floor and roll along a predesigned rut straight to the squire's bed to wake him up for your arrest."

"Is that so?" said Sung. "Who's that coming over behind you?"

Unaware of the trick, the girl turned her head. Sung dispatched her with a blow of his sword down her shoulder, and she crumpled in a splash of blood.

Coming out of the room, Sung took about ten steps and went around the pit from the west. When he heard the two dogs barking, he took the dumplings from his bosom, filled them with a special kind of drug, and, advancing closer, tossed them to the dogs. Their delicious smell was irresistible, and the dogs downed them in two gulps and soon rolled over unconscious. Sung went on and heard the shouts of about five or six people rolling dice. Taking out a small vase, Sung placed some of the drug into it, struck a flame with a piece of flint, and set the contents on fire. Every-

one's nose filled with the incense-like smell. "It really smells good!" the five people remarked. "At this late hour, it must be the squire burning incense." They sniffed here and sniffed there until one by one they tumbled head over heels. In a twinkling all five had fallen over from the fragrance. Sung went over to them and noticed some leftover wine and food and helped himself to all of it. The five watched him with their eyes wide open, but they could not even utter a sound.

Then Sung went over to the storehouse door and saw that it was secured by a triple lock as thick as a man's arm. He took out a master key called "Openall" which could unlock anything, regardless of size. With one twist, Sung opened the lock and went into the storehouse to look around. There he encountered the paper figure holding the silver globe. First taking the globe into his own hands, Sung set off the trigger mechanisms with his feet. He then gathered together goods worth fifty thousand strings of cash which Chang had stashed away—all top grade pearls, gold, and such—and wrapped everything into one bundle. Taking out a brush, Sung wet it with his saliva and wrote these four lines on the wall:

The Sung Dynasty's free and easy vagabond
Throughout the Four Seas enjoys reknown.
He has been to the top of the Cauldron of Peace;
Here, as everywhere, his fame resounds.

This done, Sung found his way out of Chang's house without even bothering to close the storehouse door. "Though the Liang Garden is a nice place," he thought to himself, "one can't stay there forever." And despite the lateness of the hour, he went directly back to Cheng-chou.

When the sun came up the next morning at Squire Chang's residence, the five guards regained consciousness to find the storehouse door wide open, the two dogs drugged to death, and the woman murdered; and they hastily reported everything to the squire. The latter made an official complaint to the authorities and Magistrate T'eng assigned Officer Wang Tsun to the case. When the constables saw the four lines on the wall, Chou Hsüan, one of the more experienced among them, said, "This man, sir, is none other than Sung the Fourth."

"How do you know?" Officer Wang asked.

"In line one," Chou replied, "we need to note the word 'Sung,' while in 'throughout the Four Seas' of line two we should take out the word 'four.' In line three, we find the words 'has been,' and line four begins with the word 'here.' Taken together, these words would form the sentence 'Sung the Fourth has been here.' "

"I've long heard that among professional thieves there is one called Sung the Fourth who is a native of Cheng-chou and who is greatly skilled in his trade," said Wang. "He must be the culprit." So Wang dispatched Chou Hsüan and a group of constables to Cheng-chou to arrest Sung the Fourth.

After an arduous but uneventful journey, they arrived at Cheng-chou and asked for directions to Sung's place. [When they got there], they saw a small tea shop in front of his house. They went in for some tea and an old man went to the stove to brew it for them. "While you're at it," they told him, "why don't you invite Sung the Fourth out to have tea with us?"

"The master has been laid up with a slight illness," the old man replied. "I'll go in and convey your message."

The old man went inside and presently they heard Sung shouting from within: "I have a splitting headache and can't even get you to get me three cents worth of rice gruel! I spend all kinds of money every day keeping you alive, but can't even count on your help! What do I keep you around for?" Then—slap! slap!—the sounds of the old man being struck.

Soon they saw the tea brewer again, clutching a bowl in his hand. "Please wait a few minutes, sirs," he muttered. "Sung the Fourth has asked me to buy him some gruel; he'll join you after he has eaten it."

The constables waited anxiously, but the old man who went off for gruel never returned, and Sung the Fourth never appeared. They grew impatient, and when they finally entered the house to look, they found an old man all tied up. They took him to be Sung the Fourth and were coming up to arrest him when he spoke up. "I'm the tea brewer for Sung the Fourth," he said. "The one who went off with the bowl to buy gruel is Sung himself."

Everyone was shocked on hearing this. "He's really as good as his name," they sighed. "We've been remiss. He's hoodwinked us."

There was nothing they could do but hurry out the door to chase him. But there was not the slightest chance they could catch up with him. All they could do was split up and go after him in different directions, and I needn't go into any more detail about this.

What happened was that when they were busy having tea, Sung the Fourth, from his inner quarters, noticed their Eastern Capital accents. He stole a peak at them and found them to be constables. He thought something was up and so he put on a show of cursing and scolding. Meanwhile, he exchanged clothes with the son of the old man and, lowering his face, came out pretending to be in a hurry to buy rice gruel. Because of this, no one suspected anything.

Now let me tell you about Sung who, having escaped, thought to himself: "Where should I go now? I have a student, a native of the P'ing-chiang Prefecture,[2] named Chao Cheng. I've had a letter from him saying that he is now in Mo County. I might as well go stay with him."

So Sung changed his clothes, put on the costume of a jailer, and covered up his face with a fan, pretending to be blind. Taking his time, he gradually made his way to Mo County. When he got there, he came across a small tavern:

[2] Soochow in modern Kiangsu Province. Soochow is also known as Ku-su, after Mount Ku-su outside the city.

Clouds waver in the enshrouding mist, wine pennants flutter;
The time languishes in these peaceful days.
Here the warrior can bolster his heroic courage;
The beauty can dispel her melancholic ennui.
In the early dawn three-foot willows droop along the banks
Where a sign-stick slants out from among the apricot blossoms.
A man may not have fulfilled as yet his life-long dreams,
But let him enjoy his song and enter into the realm of wine.

Sung felt hungry and entered the tavern to buy himself a few drinks. The waiter had brought him his order and Sung had downed a few cups when he saw a bright-looking youth enter the tavern. As to this fellow, how do you suppose he was dressed?

A brick-shaped cap, tied at the rear;
A single-breasted black silk gown with belt.
Broad trousers below,
And silken shoes at a slant.

"Greetings, sir," the youth called out and Sung recognized him as none other than his student Chao. Because people were around, Sung did not dare address him as an old acquaintance, but simply invited him to sit down. Chao exhanged a few pleasantries with Sung and took his seat, ordering an additional tumbler from the shopkeeper and helping himself to a drink. "Where have you been all this time, sir?" Chao asked in a low voice.

"Have you had any business lately?" Sung asked in return.

"Some. But I've already spent whatever I made on wine and women. I heard you came up with something yourself in the Eastern Capital."

"It wasn't much," Sung replied. "Only got forty or fifty thousand strings of cash out of it." Then he asked Chao, "Where are you heading right now?"

"I want to take a little trip to the Eastern Capital and have a little fun along the way. I'd like to have something to talk about when I go back to the P'ing-chiang Prefecture."

"You can't go."

"Why not?"

"For the following three reasons, you mustn't go," said Sung. "First, you're a native of northwestern Chekiang, and you know nothing about the Eastern Capital. There're very few in our line of business who know you there. To whom would you turn for help? Second, the hundred-eighty-*li* wall surrounding the Eastern Capital is called 'Wall of the Leaning Ox.' Now we are no more than 'hayseed thieves,' and it has been commonly said that 'when hay enters an ox's mouth, it is not long for this world.' Third, there're five thousand sharp-eyed constables there, and a general inspector heading three investigative offices."

"None of these things scares me. Sir, don't you worry," said Chao. "I won't be nabbed so easily."

"Since you don't believe me and insist on making the trip, I'll tell you what," said Sung. "I'll go to an inn and put this package of small valuables I got from Tightwad Chang next to my pillow; if you can steal it from me, you may go ahead to the Eastern Capital."

"As you say, sir," said Chao. The discussion thus concluded; Sung the Fourth paid the bill and went to an inn with Chao. The clerk there, seeing Sung come in with another person, greeted the two of them. Chao went into the room with Sung, and then said good-bye and went off by himself. By that time the sky was getting dark. What did it look like?

Darkening mist veils the distant peaks,
And a thin fog curls up in the glowing sky.
Crowds of stars sparkle together, and the moon glows in
*   competition.*
The emerald brilliance of the distant river vies with that of the
*   mountains.*
In the deep forest, an ancient temple
Scatters a few notes from its bell;
By the meandering shoreline, from a tiny skiff
Dots from fishermen's lamps flicker.
On a branch, a cuckoo calls to the moon;
Among the flowers, butterflies rest in fragrant clusters.

When Sung saw that night was near, he thought to himself: "Chao Cheng is crafty. I'm his teacher;

if he's really able to steal this stuff from me, I won't be able to live it down. So I'd better get to bed early."

As he was retiring, however, Sung worried again about what Chao might do, but he could think of of no better plan than to place the package of valuables next to his pillow while he reclined on the bed. He heard squealing sounds from the roof beams. "Strange," he thought. "The night watch hasn't even begun and the rats are already out to harass people." As he looked up at the beams, a bit of dust fluttered down, and Sung sneezed twice. In a while, the rats no longer made any noise, and Sung could only hear a couple of cats meowing and fighting and finally trickling urine down squarely into his mouth! Phew! Still, Sung gradually became tired and drowsy and dozed off.

When he got up the following morning, the package by his pillow had disappeared. As he was feeling lost, the desk clerk came in. "The gentleman who came here with you last night is here to see you," he announced.

Sung the Fourth came out and saw that it was none other than Chao Cheng. They bowed toward each other and Sung invited him into his room and secured the door. Chao Cheng took out a package from his bosom and returned it to his master. "Let me ask you," said Sung. "Since neither the walls nor the door have moved, how in the world did you manage to come in and take it away?"

"I shan't conceal the truth from you, sir. All the barred windows with tar-paper shades by the bed in the room are pasted over with rice paper. Well, I first got onto the roof and made noises like a bunch of rats. The dust which fluttered down in your eyes and nostrils and caused you to sneeze was merely a kind of anesthetic. The 'cat urine' which followed was my own piss."

"You beast!" Sung exclaimed. "You weren't playing fair."

"I then sneaked up to your room," continued Chao, "where I peeled off the paper and, with a tiny saw, cut off two bars from the window. Then I eased myself inside, went over to your bed, took the package, and climbed back out the window. I reconnected the bars with tiny nails. Then I pasted the paper over them once more and, look as you may, you won't detect any signs of tampering."

"All right! All right!" cried Sung. "You're sharp. I won't deny you're pretty clever. If you can steal this package of mine again tonight, then I'll admit you really are something."

"Fine," said Chao. "That'll be a cinch." He returned the package to Sung. "I'll leave you for now, sir; see you tomorrow." He drifted away as soon as he had finished speaking.

Sung remained silent, but he was thinking to himself: "Chao Cheng is as skilled a burglar as I am. Now that I've let him take away my package, things look really bad for me. I might as well pack up and run." So he summoned the desk clerk and said to him, "Friend, I'm moving on now. Here's two hundred in cash. May I trouble you to buy a hundred in cash worth of roast pork, and ask for extra pepper and salt. Also buy fifty in cash worth of steamed cakes. The remaining fifty in cash is for you to buy yourself a drink."

The clerk thanked him, went downtown, and bought the meat and cakes. On his way back, someone accosted him from a teahouse some ten doors away from the inn: "Mr. Clerk, where are you heading?"

The clerk looked up and saw that it was the friend of Sung the Fourth. "Listen, sir," said the clerk, "the old man wants to leave. He asked me to buy roast pork and steamed cakes for him."

"Let's have a look," Chao Cheng said and opened up the lotus-leaf wrapping for an examination of the contents. "How much cash worth of pork is this?"

"A hundred," was the reply.

Chao then took out two hundred in cash from his bosom and said, "Leave this meat and these cakes here. I'm giving you another two hundred in cash. Will you do me the same favor and buy me the same things you've just bought? You can keep the balance for a drink."

The clerk thanked him and went off, returning presently with the food. "Sorry to have troubled you," said Chao. "Let me wrap that meat up again for the old man. When you see him, tell him for me to be a bit careful tonight." The clerk nodded and left.

Returning to the inn, he handed over the meat and steamed cakes to Sung. Sung took them and thanked him. "The gentleman who was with you earlier told me to warn you about being careful tonight," the clerk told Sung.

Sung packed his bag, settled his bill, and slung his bedding on his back. Carrying in his hand the package of things he had stolen from Tightwad Chang, he left the inn. Walking a short distance, he was soon on the road to Pa-chiao Town.[3] He reached a river crossing, but the ferry boat was on the opposite shore. He waited, but it did not come over and his stomach began to feel the pangs of hunger. He sat down on the ground, placing the package of valuables in front of him. Then he opened up the wrapping of the roast pork, split open one of the steamed cakes, added more pepper and salt to a few fatter pieces of meat and, rolling them in the cake, took a couple of bites. Suddenly everything turned topsy-turvy, and he fell over right where he was sitting. All Sung could see then was someone dressed as an army captain seizing the package of valuables and going off. He could only open his eyes wide and watch him go. Unable to either shout at him or chase him down, Sung had to let things happen as they would. The captain took the package, crossed the river, and was gone.

After a long time, Sung regained his faculties. "Who in the world is that captain who made off with my package?" he tried to think. "The roast

pork that the clerk bought for me must have been drugged." Containing his anger, Sung hailed the ferry boat, crossed the river, and went ashore, thinking all the while about where he should go to look for that captain. Down at the mouth and in need of food and drink, he chanced upon a village tavern, and this is what he saw:

A wooden gate, half open, a tattered pennant drooping low.
The rustic wine seller, how was he to know about a man named
*   Hsiang-ju who had worked as a dishwasher?*
The uncouth tavern maid who keeps silkworms, it's hard to
*   compare her to Cho-shih,[4] who presided over the wine*
*   warmer.*
The large characters on the wall are the poem written, while
*   tipsy, by the village schoolmaster.*
The hempen gown on the hanger was left as security by a
*   farmer, a lover of wine.*
The earthen couch is lined with coarse brew and broken bottles.
Faintly on the wall, covered with dust, a polychrome drawing
*   of drunken immortals.*

Sung thought he might as well go in and drown his cares in a bit of wine. The tavern waiter greeted him and brought the wine, which he drank glumly. When he was on the third cup, he saw a woman come into the tavern:

Shiny hair, a powdered face; white teeth, ruby lips.
A turban tied at eyebrow level; a silken skirt touching the floor.
Flowers at an angle on the side of her hair,
A smile adorning her face.
She may not be the equal of a pampered beauty,
But she's at least a winsome tavern maid.

The woman entered the shop and greeted Sung the Fourth. Then she sang a song, clapping her hands in rhythm. Sung looked at her closely, and her face seemed somehow familiar. Taking her for a prostitute, he invited her to sit down. The woman settled herself opposite Sung and, calling for another order of wine, downed a cupful. Sung took her into his arms, gave her a

---

[3] To the southwest of K'ai-feng.

[4] Cho Wen-chün.

543

pinch or two, and began to caress her. Then he started to feel her chest and exclaimed, "Hey, little girl, you haven't got any breasts!" He proceeded then to touch her privates, but felt only a dangling tool. "Dammit!" Sung blurted out. "Who the hell are you?"

"I'm no prostitute," the one in disguise, with arms akimbo, said. "I'm merely Chao Cheng from the P'ing-chiang Prefecture in Soochow."

"You sneaky, insolent bastard!" Sung screamed. "I'm your teacher, and you made me feel your privates! Now I know it, that captain must have been you."

"Sure. That was me all right."

"My package of valuables, where have you put it?"

Whereupon Chao Cheng ordered the waiter, "Return the package to the gentleman." The waiter brought it out and Sung took it. "How did you manage to get this from me?" Sung asked.

"I was sitting in the teahouse a few doors from the inn when I saw the clerk carrying a package of roast pork. I asked to see it and then told him to get some for me also. Then I added some drug to it and wrapped it up again, telling him to take it along to you. After that I made myself up like a captain and tailed you. When you fell over, I took the package away and waited for you here."

"You're really smart," said Sung. "You deserve to go to the Eastern Capital."

They quickly paid the bill and left the tavern together. Going on to an uninhabited area, Chao removed the flowers, washed his face in a stream, and changed back into male attire, complete with a dark, silken cap.

"Now that you're going to the capital," said Sung, "I'll give you a letter of introduction to see someone who is also a student of mine. He lives on the bank of the Pien River and he sells dumplings stuffed with human flesh for a living. He's called Hou Hsing, and since he's second among his siblings, he is known as Hou the Second."

"Thanks, master," said Chao. Then they went

to a nearby teahouse where Sung wrote the letter and gave Chao some final instructions, and the two said their farewells, each going his separate way. Sung the Fourth stayed behind in Mo County.

That night, Chao checked into an inn, and when he opened Sung's letter, he saw that it said:

Dear Second Brother and Sister:
   How have you been since we parted company?
   There is presently a crook from Ku-su called Chao Cheng who wants to go to the capital to do business. I purposely am sending him to you. This fellow is not one of our members. His flesh is just right for use in your family business. Three times I have suffered from his insolence. So you must by all means get rid of this person, so that he will never be troublesome later to our brotherhood. . . .

After reading this letter, Chao's tongue hung out so far in shock that he could hardly pull it back. "Other people might be cowed and dare not go," he thought finally, "but I'll just see what he can do to me. I'll know how to take care of myself." So he folded up the letter again and sealed it as before.

At dawn, he left the inn and went ahead to Pa-chiao Town. Then he set out for Flatbridge and reached Ch'en-liu County. He went along the Pien River and, toward noon, saw a dumpling shop on the bank of the river. In front of the door stood a woman, her waist cinched with a scarf in a "jade well" pattern. "Sir, have some dumplings before you go on," she shouted out. On the sign outside the door was written: "The Hou Family Restaurant. Excellent Dumplings."

Chao figured that this must be Hou Hsing's place and went on inside. The woman greeted him and asked him to order. "Wait," said Chao, and unslung a pack from his back. It was full of gold and silver hairpins, some with ornamented heads, some with two or three links, some plain— all swiped along the way.

When Hou Hsing's wife saw them, her greed

544

was stirred. "This customer has some hairpins," she said to herself. "Even though I sell human-flesh dumplings and my husband's a thief, we never have that much. Just wait. In a while when he'll order some dumplings and I'll slip in a heavy dose. All those hairpins will be mine."

"Bring me five dumplings," Chao called.

"Right away," answered Hou's wife, taking up a dish. She put five dumplings in it and added to them pinches of a drug powder from a box by the stove.

"The drugs must be in that box," murmured Chao to himself. He took a packet of drugs from his bosom and called, "Please get me some cold water for my medicine." Hou's wife brought him half a bowl of water and placed it on the table. Saying he would eat the dumplings afterward, Chao swallowed the medicine and then took his chopsticks to break open the dough. He took one look at the filling and said, "My father told me not to buy dumplings on the banks of the Pien River because they are all made with human flesh there. Look at this piece. There's a fingernail, and it must be part of a human finger. And on this piece of skin are all sorts of little hairs; it's got to be flesh from the pubic area."

"Seriously, sir," protested Hou Hsing's wife, "how can you say such things?"

Chao Cheng ate the dumplings and heard the woman say "Fall!" while she stood in front of the stove, watching for Chao to topple over. But nothing happened. "Bring me another five," ordered Chao.

"I guess it's because there was too little of the drug. This time I'll put more inside," thought Hou's wife. Chao Cheng again took out his packet and took some medicine. "What kind of medicine are you taking?" the woman could not help asking.

"It's something dispensed by the judge of the P'ing-chiang Prefecture called 'cure-everything pills,'" Chao replied. "It's good for whatever ails a woman, whether it be headaches or troubles with pregnancy or childbirth, or for malfunction in the spleen, or for gastric pain."

"If you could spare a dose," said Hou's wife, "I'd like to try it."

Chao Cheng took out a different packet from inside his robe and gave a hundred or so tiny pills to Hou's wife, who took them all and passed out in front of the stove. "This woman was going to do me in," said Chao. "But I've now taken care of her. Someone else might run away at this point, but I'm going to stay right here." With deliberate nonchalance, he loosened his belt right there and began to pick fleas off his body.

Presently a man carrying a load of goods returned. "He must be Hou Hsing," said Chao. "Let's see what he'll do."

Hou and Chao nodded to each other and Hou asked, "Have you had your dumplings yet, sir?"

"I've had them," answered Chao.

"Wife," Hou called, "have you figured out the bill?" He looked here and there for her. Finally he found her on the floor in front of the stove, spittle rolling out one side of her mouth, mumbling incoherently something about being drugged.

"I know now," said Hou Hsing. "This woman was unable to recognize a business comrade and must have been tricked by that customer outside." So he went to Chao Cheng and apologized, "Brother, my country wife was blind not to know you. I hope you'll forgive us."

"What is your name, brother?" asked Chao.

"I'm Hou Hsing."

"And I'm Chao Cheng of Ku-su."

The two bowed toward each other, and Hou Hsing gave his wife an antidote.

"Here," said Chao, "my teacher Sung the Fourth has a letter for you."

Hou Hsing took it and opened it to read its content, including the final part which said "You must . . . get rid of this person." When Hou finished, he was filled with anger and hatred and said to himself, "He was insolent three times to my teacher. Tonight I must take his life."

To Chao Cheng he simply said, "I've been aware of your lofty reputation for a long time, and it's fortunate that I can meet you." He promptly prepared a feast to serve his guest and, after supper, settled Chao down to sleep in the guest room. He and his wife then went about serving their late-night customers outside.

Meanwhile, in his room Chao noticed an offensive smell and, looking around, found a big basin underneath the bed. Sticking his hand there, he felt a human head and then a hand and a foot. He moved all this out to the back door and, stringing the pieces together on a rope, hung everything up on the eaves over the entrance. Then he shut the door and went back to the room just in time to hear the woman say, "Husband, let's begin!"

"Not yet, wife," Hou cautioned. "Let him sleep a little more deeply."

"I saw him take out two or three hundred gold and silver hairpins today. After we do away with him tonight, I'll stick them all over my hair and, tomorrow, show them off to people."

"Aha!" thought Chao Cheng on hearing this. "The two of them want to take my life after all. But it doesn't worry me."

Now Hou Hsing had a son about ten years old called Pan-ko who, sick with malaria, was confined to bed. Chao Cheng went into his room, carried him to Chao's own bed, covered him with blankets, and then sneaked out the back door. Before long, Hou Hsing's wife, carrying a lamp, and Hou a huge firewood axe, pushed open the door to Chao's room. Seeing a sleeping figure under the covers, they hacked him, blankets and all, into three pieces with a couple of whacks. When Hou lifted up the covers to look, however, he could only exclaim, "Heaven help us! The person we've killed is our own child, Pan-ko." The couple started to wail as Chao shouted at them from behind the back door: "Why have you murdered your own child for nothing? Chao Cheng is right here!"

Hou Hsing was naturally furious when he heard this and, taking up his axe, he sprinted out the back door after Chao. Pop! Pop! His forehead banged into some objects which turned out to be a human head, a foot, and a hand, all hung together on the eaves like parts of some giant toy. Ordering his wife to move them back into the house, Hou continued his chase. Chao saw behind him Hou closing in and in front of him a creek. Now Chao, as a native of P'ing-chiang, was used to the water. With a leap, he plunged into the creek. In pursuit Hou also jumped into the water. With a stroke and a kick, Chao was on the opposite bank. Hou also knew how to swim but was somewhat slower. Reaching land first, Chao took off his clothes and wrung them dry. Hou went after him and, from the fourth watch to the beginning of the fifth, tailed him for about twelve *li*, all the way to a bathhouse by the Heaven-Obeying Gate (also known as the Hsin-cheng Gate) of the capital. Chao Cheng went in to wash his face and dry his clothing over the fire. As he was washing, someone pulled both legs from under him and flipped him to the floor. When Chao saw that it was Hou Hsing, he knocked the latter down with his two bare knees and, holding him down, pummeled him thoroughly.

It was at that moment that an old man dressed as a jailer appeared and, coming up, told them to "break it up, for my sake." Chao Cheng and Hou Hsing lifted their heads to see that it was none other than Sung the Fourth. They both greeted Sung and immediately bowed to him. Sung reconciled the two of them and took them to an herb-tea shop for a cup or two. There, Hou reported to Sung what had happened.

"Let's let bygones be bygones," said Sung. "Chao Cheng is going into the Eastern Capital tomorrow. The fellow selling fried dumplings at the foot of the Gold Bridge there is also a member of our brotherhood. His name is Wang Hsiu and, in the ability to get up and around on rooftops, he has no peer. That's why he's been given the nickname 'Sick Kitten.' He lives in the rear of the Great Hsiang-kuo Monastery.[5] Now he has on his peddler's stand a large gold-flecked jar with a glaze fired in the kilns of the Chung-shan Prefecture in Ting-chou.[6] He values it as much as his own life. Do you think you can steal it from him?"

"No problem," said Chao Cheng. "Wait until the city gate opens; then I'll meet you at Hou Hsing's place around noon."

Chao Cheng put on his brick-shaped cap tied at the rear and his double-breasted black silk gown and went ahead to the foot of the Gold Bridge. There he saw a vendor's stand with a large gold-flecked jar on it. Behind the stand stood an older fellow:

With a single-layer green gauze cap from Yün-chou[7]
And a willow-patterned cotton shirt.
Around the waist, a scarf of the "jade well" pattern.

"This must be Wang Hsiu," said Chao to himself.

He crossed over the bridge and swiped a bit of red rice from a rice shop. Then he plucked a few leaves from a vegetable stand. He put the rice and the leaves into his mouth and chewed them. Then he went over by Wang's stand again and, tossing down six pennies, bought a couple of fried dumplings while purposely letting a penny fall to the ground. When Wang bent over to pick it up, Chao spat the chewed-up rice and leaves onto his cap, and then ambled off with his dumplings. He hung around the Gold Bridge until he saw a youngster skipping by. "Hey, little boy," Chao called. "Here's five pennies. You see that dumpling seller, Mr. Wang? On his cap is a pile of insect and ant droppings. Go tell him about it, and don't say I told you to."

Sure enough, the child went over and said, "Mr. Wang, look what's on your cap."

Wang Hsiu took off his cap and, thinking the

mess was really insect droppings, went into a teahouse to wipe it off. But when he came out to look at his stand, the gold-flecked jar had disappeared. For when Chao Cheng saw Wang Hsiu go into the teahouse, he was quick to take advantage of the latter's momentary inattention; snatching the jar and tucking it up his sleeve, he sped away.

He went directly to Hou's place. Both Sung and Hou were startled to realize what had happened.

"Hell, I don't want his stuff," said Chao. "I'll just return it to his wife."

Then he went into his room to change into an old, tattered cap, a pair of old hempen shoes, and a worn-out cotton shirt. Clutching the gold-flecked jar in one hand, he went straight to the rear of the Great Hsiang-kuo Monastery. He sought out Wang's wife and greeted her saying, "Your husband told me to come back here to ask you for a new shirt, an undershirt, a pair of pants, and new shoes and socks. The gold-flecked jar here is to show I'm telling the truth."

The wife had no idea that it was a trick. Taking the jar, she brought out the various items of clothing and turned them over to Chao. Chao took them and once more went to see Sung the Fourth and Hou Hsing. "Master," he said, "I exchanged the gold-flecked jar at his house for all the clothing here. In a while, let's all go together and return everything as a joke. Meanwhile I'll just put them on and go have a bit of fun."

Chao then dressed himself in Wang's things and went back to the city. He went to the Sang Family Pleasure Grounds for a stroll and bought some wine and pastries. Then he left the area and was crossing the Gold Bridge when he heard someone call out, "Chao Cheng!" He turned to see that it was Sung the Fourth, along with Hou Hsing. The three of them went together to the Gold Bridge where they saw that Wang Hsiu was still selling fried dumplings.

"How about having some tea with us, Wang Hsiu?" said Sung.

Wang greeted his teacher and Hou. Then he

---

[5] A magnificent Buddhist temple in K'ai-feng.
[6] A famous porcelain-producing area in Ch'ü-yang County in modern Hopei Province.
[7] To the northwest of Tung-p'ing County in Shantung Province.

looked at Chao Cheng and asked Sung who he was. Sung was about to tell him when Chao dragged him aside and told him not to give away his name: "Just say I'm a relative of yours. You'll see my reasons later."

"What is his name?" Wang asked again.

"He is a relative of mine. I brought him here to the capital for some fun," Sung replied.

"In that case," said Wang Hsiu, "I'll leave my dumpling stand at the teahouse for a while. Let's all go for some wine at a quiet tavern outside the Heaven-Obeying Gate."

They went into the tavern. The waiter brought out the wine, and they all downed a few rounds. "Master, I was so upset this morning," said Wang Hsiu. "I had just carried my stand out there when a man buying dumplings dropped a penny on the ground. I went to pick it up and didn't know that some kind of insects crapped on my cap. When I went into the teahouse to wipe it off, the gold-flecked jar disappeared. I've been stewing all day."

"That man has an awful lot of gall," said Sung. "But we must count him clever to have succeeded in pulling a trick on you. Don't get all worked up about it. When we have time tomorrow, all of us will help you look for this jar. It's only a simple matter, and we'll find out what happened no matter what. You won't lose anything." Chao Cheng only chuckled to himself at this. All four of them had had their fill of wine and, as it was already dark, each headed for home.

Now let's talk about Wang Hsiu. When he got home, his wife asked him, "Husband, some time ago did you ask someone to bring the gold-flecked jar home?"

"I never did," said Wang.

"Well, it's here," said his wife, bringing it out. "But he took a few clothes away."

Wang could not guess who it might have been when, suddenly, he recalled: "Today that relative of Sung the Fourth's was wearing a set of clothing that looked very much like mine." He kept wondering about it and the whole thing depressed him. Presently he took some wine and, putting aside all his cares, drank himself into a stupor with his wife. Then he took off his clothes to go to sleep, saying to his wife, "Wife, we two haven't done anything together for a long time."

"You're an old man," said the wife. "So don't go having wild ideas."

"Haven't you heard, wife," said Wang, "that 'Youth can curb desire, but the aged burn like fire'?"

He had by then moved alongside his wife and started in on his business. He was still at it when Chao Cheng, taking advantage of their drunkenness, opened the door and sneaked in under the bed. He flung the chamber pot against the bedroom door when he realized the two of them were having their sport. Startled, Wang Hsiu and his wife jumped up as if they had seen a ghost. They saw someone crawl out from underneath their bed, carrying a package in his hand. In the lamplight, Wang could make out the man with whom he and his companions had been drinking that afternoon. "What are you up to?" he asked.

"Sung the Fourth told me to return your package," said Chao.

Wang took it and saw that it contained a pile of clothes and demanded again, "Who are you?"

"I'm Chao Cheng of the P'ing-chiang Prefecture in Ku-su."

"Ah, so that's it," said Wang. "I've heard of your fair name for a long time now. It's a great pleasure to make your acquaintance." Then Wang kept Chao there to spend the night.

The following day, they took a casual stroll together. "You see that great mansion at the foot of the White Tiger Bridge?" said Wang Hsiu. "It is Prince Ch'ien's residence. There's quite a store of wealth there."

"We'll work on it when it gets darker," said Chao.

"All right, then."

Around the third watch that night, Chao Cheng

dug a tunnel to Prince Ch'ien's storehouse and made a haul of thirty thousand strings of cash and one ivory-white jade belt with a muted flower pattern in an encircling dragon design. Wang Hsiu kept watch on the outside, and returned to hide out with Chao in his home.

The following day, Prince Ch'ien wrote a letter to Magistrate T'eng, and the latter reacted angrily when he read it. "How can we tolerate this kind of burglary right here in the capital?" he fumed. Right away he dispatched the inspector Ma Han and ordered him to catch the robber of the Ch'ien residence within three days.

When Inspector Ma received his orders, he made all the constables work around the clock. In returning home, he passed by the Great Hsiang-kuo Monastery. There he encountered a man with a brick-shaped cap tied at the rear and wearing a purple shirt who came up and asked, "Some tea, Inspector?" Together they went into a tea-house, and a waiter brought them tea. The man in the purple shirt took out a packet of pine nuts and walnut kernels and put them into the two cups.

"May I have your name, sir?" said the inspector.

"My surname is Chao and I'm called Cheng," replied the man. "I'm the one who robbed the Ch'ien residence last night."

When Inspector Ma heard this, he felt a chill running down his spine, but he could do no more than wait for other constables to come by and help arrest the man. He drank the tea and suddenly everything turned upside-down: he'd been drugged! "The inspector is drunk," Cheng called out and, holding him up, took out a pair of trusty scissors and snipped off half of one of the inspector's sleeves, [which contained his money,] tucking it into his own. He paid the bill and told the waiter that he as going out "to get someone to take care of the inspector." Then he went off by himself.

After quite a while, the effect of the drug in Ma's stomach wore off and he came to, only see

that Chao was gone. He returned home for the night.

At dawn the following day Inspector Ma escorted Magistrate T'eng to the palace for the morning audience. Riding his horse, the magistrate was just on the point of entering the Gate of Proclaiming Virtue when he saw a man in a black shirt and a wraparound hat with curved corners blocking the way. This man shouted out a loud greeting and said, "Prince Ch'ien has an official letter to present to you." Magistrate T'eng accepted it; the man bowed and went off. But even as the magistrate, still mounted, was reading the letter, he discovered that the buckle of the official goldfish belt around his waist had disappeared.

The letter read as follows:

The Ku-su thief Chao Cheng humbly informs the honorable magistrate:

All the articles lost from the Ch'ien residence were really stolen by me. If Your Honor wants to find my hideout, it is as far as the ends of the earth, and as near as your hands before your eyes.

On reading this the magistrate became even more aggravated. When he returned to his tribunal after the audience, he immediately went to his courtroom and sought out official complaints from the people. Those who had written depositions were to have placed them in a special box. When he had read about ten documents, he noticed that one of them did not accuse or complain about any injustice, as was normal procedure. On that document was written only a little ditty, to the tune "The Moon over the West River":

As surely as waters return to the ocean
Outlaws to the capital flow.
Inspector Ma, the inspector-in-chief, now knows
The vest is not the main suit.[8]
I've even taken the prince's belt of jade,
And, lifting his goldfish, dealt the magistrate a blow.

[8] In other words, a petty officer shouldn't behave as if he were the big boss.

Now who in the world is that so-and-so?
An earthly bolt of cloth, beside the little moon's glow.

"It's Chao Cheng again," the magistrate said when he finished. "What a master thief he is!" So he immediately sent for Ma Han to ask him about the progress of the case.

"Because I couldn't recognize the thief Chao Cheng," Ma reported, "I had a run-in with him yesterday. He's really a pro. I did find out, however, that he's the student of Sung the Fourth of Cheng-chou. If we can apprehend Sung, then we'll have Chao as well."

This suddenly reminded Magistrate T'eng of the case in which Sung had robbed Chang Fu's storehouse, a case not yet solved. So he summoned Officer Wang Tsun and told him to cooperate with Ma Han in seeking out and apprehending the thieves Sung the Fourth and Chao Cheng.

"It's hard to trace down those culprits," reported Wang. "I beg Your Honor to set a longer time limit, and you must also post an official reward. If someone greedy for the reward money comes forward with information, this case will be easily settled."

T'eng agreed to this and set one month as the deadline for the apprehension of the criminals. He accordingly wrote out an official proclamation:

> Anyone who discovers and reports the whereabouts of the stolen goods will receive one thousand strings of cash from the government.

Ma Han and Wang Tsun took the document and went to Prince Ch'ien's residence to report to him and to beg him to add to the reward money. So Prince Ch'ien pledged another thousand strings. Then the two went to Squire "Tightwad" Chang's place to ask him to also post a reward. But considering that he had already lost valuables worth fifty thousand in cash, how could he possibly be willing to put out any reward?

"Squire, you'll lose a lot if you don't spend a little," everyone told him. "If the robbers can be apprehended, the great pile of lost goods will revert back to you. Even the magistrate has put out a reward on your behalf, and the prince has also signed up for a thousand. If you're nonetheless unwilling, it won't look good for you when the magistrate finds out."

Squire Chang was unable to argue with this and so he wrote out yet another reward poster, reluctantly pledging five hundred strings. Inspector Ma took all the posters and posted them outside the tribunal, and then he conferred with Officer Wang and each of them went off to carry out their investigations.

Large hordes of people gathered to read the posters. Sung the Fourth also read them and went off to confer with Chao Cheng. "Damn that Wang Tsun and that Ma Han," said Chao Cheng. "There's been no ill-feeling between us in the past, but they insist on increasing the reward money to get us. And damn Squire Chang the tightwad. All the others put up a thousand strings of cash; he alone posts only five hundred. He really rates us cheaply! Let's give him something else to worry about; only then will I be satisfied."

Sung the Fourth also resented Officer Wang for having sent the constables to arrest him and Inspector Ma for reporting to the authorities that Chao Cheng was in league with him. So they pooled their ideas and came up with a plan they both approved with enthusiasm. Chao then handed over the ivory-white jade belt stolen from Ch'ien's place to Sung, and the latter, in turn, picked out a few of the most renowned pieces of jewelry from the package of valuables from Tightwad Chang and handed them over to Chao. The two then went their separate ways, each to carry out his own part of the plan.

Now let's follow Sung the Fourth who, having just started on his way, ran into the man with the bamboo ladle who had been begging outside Chang's door that day. Sung got hold of him and took him outside the Heaven-Obeying Gate, all the way to Hou Hsing's place, for a rest. "I need your help today," he then told him.

"Whatever my benefactor might want of me, I wouldn't think of saying no."

"There's a thousand strings of cash in it for you, to feed your family."

The man was startled. "My goodness," he cried. "I'm not worthy of receiving all that."

"Just do as I say," said Sung, "and you'll do all right."

He took out the jade belt and told Hou Hsing to dress up as a palace officer. "Take this belt to Tightwad Chang's pawnshop and pawn it for money. This belt is priceless, but just ask for three hundred strings of cash and say to him, 'I'll come back to redeem it in three days; if I can't make it, I'll ask for a final payment of another two hundred strings. Meanwhile you keep it in your shop and guard it with care.'"

Hou Hsing went off and did everything he was told. Now Squire Chang was a greedy sort and, once he laid eyes on the belt and saw the prospect of earning some interest, he did not bother about the article's origin and accepted it as security for the three hundred strings of cash.

After Hou Hsing took the money and reported back to Sung the Fourth, Sung told the beggar to go take down the poster on Prince Ch'ien's gate and claim the reward. When Prince Ch'ien learned that the stolen article had been located, he ordered the beggar to be brought before him so that he could interrogate him personally. "When I went to the pawnshop to pawn something," the man told him, "I just happened to see the clerk selling the white jade belt to a customer from the north and asking a price of a thousand five hundred taels. Someone was saying that it came from Your Highness's residence, and so I've come to report."

Prince Ch'ien dispatched more than a hundred soldiers and, with the beggar showing the way, they hurried to Tightwad Chang's residence. Before anyone could say anything, they searched the

pawnshop's storeroom and came up with the white jade belt. When Squire Chang came out to explain, these soldiers—now why would they bother with reasons?—slipped a noose around his neck and brought him along with his two chief clerks to face the prince. After Prince Ch'ien had examined the belt and found that it was the genuine article and that the informant had not lied, he wrote out an order for the beggar instructing his treasury to give the latter the thousand strings of reward money.

Mounting his sedan chair, Prince Ch'ien then went personally to the K'ai-feng [tribunal] to pay a call on Magistrate T'eng, delivering Chang and his subordinates for questioning. Because he had been unable to arrest the culprits himself, the magistrate was extremely embarrassed to have the prince deliver them. "You reported to our court the other day that you were robbed and listed all kinds of valuables," he chided Chang. "I've been wondering how you, a commoner, could have accumulated all that wealth. Now I know that it's because you're involved with thieves! Now speak honestly: who stole this jade belt for you?"

"My possessions are inherited from my ancestors, and I've never been a thief or a fence," Chang replied. "This belt was brought to me by a palace officer late yesterday afternoon and pawned for three hundred strings of cash."

"Didn't you know about Prince Ch'ien's losing an ivory-white jade belt with a muted flower pattern and an encircling dragon design?" pursued the magistrate. "How is it you didn't consider its origin and just gave out the money? Where is that palace officer now? It's clear your explanation is sheer nonsense!"

He shouted for the jailers to apply torture to Chang and his two clerks; they were beaten until their skin split open, their flesh curled, and blood flowed freely. Chang was unable to bear the pain and volunteered to accept the responsibility of locating the man who had pawned the belt within three days. If he proved unable to meet the time limit, he agreed to accept the blame. The magistrate did have some doubts of his own; so he only had the two clerks held in jail and, putting Chang under guard, granted him permission to report within three days.

His eyes brimming with tears, Chang left the tribunal and went to sit down in a tavern, offering his guards a few drinks. They were just lifting their cups when an old man strolled in from outside to ask, "Which one of you is Squire Chang?"

Chang put his head down and dared not reply. The guards asked, "Who are you, sir, and why are you looking for Squire Chang?"

"I have some good news for him. I made a special trip to his pawnshop and heard that there was a trial going on at the tribunal. So I came on over."

Only then did Chang get up to say, "I'm Chang Fu. What kind of good news do you have for me? Please sit down right here and tell me about it."

The old man drew close to Chang and sat down. "The things you lost from your storehouse," he asked, "did you ever find out where they went?"

"I never did."

"I know a little something, and I've purposely come to tell you about it. If you don't believe me, I'm willing to show you the way. Only after you've seen the stolen articles will I dare to claim the reward."

Squire Chang was overjoyed. "If I can recover those fifty thousand strings worth of goods," he thought, "even if I have to pay a fine to Prince Ch'ien, I'll still have something left over. If I use a little bribe here and there, I can get free of all these troubles." So he asked, "Since you are so sure of yourself, may I have the thief's name?"

The old man whispered a few things into Chang's ear and Chang became greatly surprised. "That's not possible!" he exclaimed.

"I'm willing to go to the tribunal and write out an accusation. If I can't furnish the genuine booty, I'll accept the blame for the crime myself."

Chang could not have been happier. "I'll trouble you to have a few drinks here with me," he said. "When the magistrate holds his night court, we can go and report together."

The four of them drank until they were slightly tipsy. The time soon came for the magistrate to hold his court. Squire Chang brought out a piece of paper, had the old man write out an accusation, and the four of them went together to the tribunal to report.

Magistrate T'eng looked over what the old man, whose name was Wang Pao, had written; it said that Inspector Ma and Officer Wang had stolen Chang Fu's treasures. "The two of them have served for many years," T'eng thought to himself. "How could they do such a thing?" So he asked Wang Pao, "Aren't you making false accusations over some private grudge? What proof do you have?"

"I was working as a broker in Cheng-chou," said Wang Pao, "when I saw a couple of people selling a lot of gold and jewels there. They said that they had more stashed away at home and would bring them when they wanted to do more business. I recognized them as constables from this prefecture and wondered how they came by so many valuables. I've now seen Chang Fu's list of stolen items, and they coincide with the things sold; so I want to take Chang Fu to their houses for a search. If we don't find anything, I'm willing to accept the blame."

Magistrate T'eng had his doubts about all this. Nevertheless, he sent Inspector Li Shun to lead a group of alert constables and go along with Wang Pao and Chang Fu.

At this time Inspector Ma and Officer Wang were running around the various counties investigating the two robbery cases and thus were not home. The group first went to Officer Wang's place, made an outcry, and rushed in. Wang's wife, carrying their three-year-old child, was munching a piece of date cake in front of the window and amusing herself with the baby. She was startled at the commotion and wondered what was going on. Afraid that all this racket would frighten the child, she covered his ears with her sleeve and took him into another room. The intruders followed on her heels and, surrounding her, demanded to know where she had hidden the stolen goods from Squire Chang's house.

The woman's eyes became glazed, and she did not know what to say. Impatient at her silence, the constables proceeded to open up chests and overturn trunks, rummaging all over the place. They found a few silver hairpins and some clothes, but there were no stolen goods. Inspector Li was about to vent his frustration on Wang Pao when he saw the latter duck down and crawl beneath the bed. From a leg on the side of the bed next to the wall, he untied a package and, grinning from ear to ear, brought it out. The group opened it up and saw that it contained a pair of gold cups with a flower design inlaid with various kinds of jewels, ten tortoiseshell cups rimmed in gold, and a string of prayer beads of pearls from the North Sea. Squire Chang saw that these were from his storehouse and, feeling a sudden shock of recognition, cried out loudly.

The woman herself had no idea where these things had come from. Doubled over with fright, she could hardly close her mouth nor lift her drooping arms. The crowd did not bother to listen to explanations in any case and, taking a rope, tied a noose around her neck. Moaning and weeping, she entrusted her child to her neighbors and had no choice but to go with the group.

The group then went to Inspector Ma's home and searched around; and it was again Wang Pao who poked around and located in the scaffolding under the eaves a package of pearls, along with such items as gold bracelets inlaid with precious stones—all of which Squire Chang identified.

So the wives of both spouses were brought to the tribunal where Magistrate T'eng was still sitting on the bench waiting for answers. He saw everyone rush in and line up the many stolen ar-

ticles on the floor, and he listened to the report that the goods had been found on the leg of a bed and under a roof and had all been properly identified by Chang Fu. T'eng was greatly surprised. "I've often heard that it takes a thief to catch a thief," he thought. "But I couldn't imagine Wang Tsun and Ma Han really doing this kind of thing."

He shouted out orders to lock up the two wives, and set a time limit for catching the culprits; the recovered booty he sent to the government storehouse for temporary safekeeping. The informant waited outside and, when the stolen articles were properly identified, received his promised reward.

"I'm someone from a family with means," pleaded Chang Fu to the magistrate, kowtowing all the while. "Regardless of what has happened, I really know nothing concerning the jade belt from Prince Ch'ien's residence. As for the stolen goods from my home, they've already been identified. But I'm loath to claim them and would be willing to offer them in restitution to Prince Ch'ien. I hope Your Honor will expedite the matter and release me and my two clerks, and may the gods bless you and your posterity forever if you do so."

Since Magistrate T'eng knew in his heart that Chang was innocent, he allowed him to leave on bail. Wang Pao followed Chang to his home, collected his five hundred strings' reward, and left.

Now Wang Pao was none other than Wang Hsiu, the "Sick Kitten," who was without peer in negotiating rooftops of tall structures. It was Sung the Fourth who designed the plan, deliberately sending Wang Hsiu to hide the things stolen from Squire Chang under the bed and the eaves of the two houses. It was also Sung who told Wang to change his name to Wang Pao, so that when he made his accusations and fished out the stolen goods, the government would have no way of knowing who he really was.

As for Wang Tsun and Ma Han, I can now relate how, having heard the news about the arrest of their wives, they hurried back from their work in the outlying counties to see Magistrate T'eng. The magistrate did not bother with explanations but started right in with torture, beating them until their flesh ripped open and demanding that they confess to having stolen Chang Fu's goods. But through it all the two refused to confess. The magistrate then ordered the two wives brought out from jail, and the four of them could only gape at one another, completely at a loss for words. Even the magistrate did not know what to do and simply sent all of them to jail.

The following day he again summoned Chang to the tribunal and urged him to use his own resources to pay back Prince Ch'ien for his lost articles and to wait for an eventual settlement from the government for his own losses. Unable to resist this pressure, Chang could do nothing other than accept this proposal. But when he thought over everything later at home, he became tremendously frustrated and depressed. Moreover, he really could not bring himself to part with his pos-

sessions. So, in the end, he hanged himself in his storehouse. Alas for the famous Squire "Tightwad" Chang! Because of his stubborn miserliness, he wound up bringing great calamity upon himself, losing even his own life. As for Officer Wang and Inspector Ma, they both eventually died in jail.

The gang of thieves, on the other hand, openly perpetrated crimes in the Eastern Capital, drinking good wine and bedding famous courtesans, and there was no one to stop them. During that period, the capital was in turmoil; no household enjoyed peace. It was not until Lung-t'u Academician Pao became the magistrate that these thieves began to feel some fear and finally disbanded, allowing the city to experience peace for the first time. As evidence there is a poem:

Parsimony and greed bring calamity;
The Eastern Capital was overrun by robbers and fiends.
Only when Magistrate Pao arrived at last
Did we know that peace comes only with good officials.

LIU LING

From *Shih-shuo hsin-yü*

TRANSLATED BY CONRAD LUNG

Liu Ling[1] had a weakness for wine. He was extremely thirsty and asked his wife for some wine. His wife poured away the wine, broke the container, and tearfully admonished him, "You drink too much. It's bad for your health. You must stop it for your own good!"

"Very well," said Liu Ling. "But I cannot restrain myself. The only way is to pray to the spirits and the gods and swear to them that I shall give up drinking. Prepare the sacrificial meat and wine now."

[1] Liu Ling (221–300) was one of the "Seven Sages of the Bamboo Grove," a group of poets and Neo-Taoist thinkers known for their eccentric behavior and predilection for wine.

"As you wish," his wife replied.

She then placed the wine and the meat before the gods and asked Liu Ling to make his pledge. Liu Ling knelt down and prayed:

Heaven gives life to me, Liu Ling,
Who is famed for wine drinking.
I can down ten dipperfuls at a sitting,
And five dipperfuls will cure my drunken sickness.
One must not listen
To the words of a woman.

Then he drank the wine, ate the meat, and soon was drunk.

HOU PO

From *Ch'i-yen lu*

TRANSLATED BY MORGAN T. JONES

When [Hou] Po was a *san-kuan* official,[1] he was subordinate to Yang Su,[2] who was fond of Hou's ability in witty conversation. Whenever Hou went to the government offices Yang Su would engage him in talk and make him discuss various kinds of dramatic performances. At times this would last from morning until night before Hou could finally return home.

[After one such day], Hou had just left the offices when he ran into Yang Su's son, Hsüan-kan, who said to him, "Scholar Hou, could you tell me an amusing story?"

Hou Po was thus detained, having no alternative but to do so. Thereupon he said, "There was once a tiger who, desiring to search for meat, ventured out onto the plain. He saw a hedgehog lying on its back and, mistaking it for a piece of meat, was on the verge of biting into it when suddenly the hedgehog seized him by the nose. In a state of panic the tiger ran, giving no thought to stopping or resting, until he reached the mountains. Exhausted, he collapsed and, falling into unconsciousness, slept. The hedgehog then released the tiger's nose and left. When the tiger woke up, he was delighted [that he was free again]. Walking over to a spot beneath a chestnut tree, the tiger lowered his head and saw a chestnut burr.[3] He thereupon leaned over to speak to it: 'I met your father in the morning; would the young master please step aside and yield the road?' "

[1] *San-kuan* was a honorific title which did not carry with it any specific duties.

[2] Yang Su (?–606) was a trusted high official of Emperor Yang (r. 605–617) of the Sui Dynasty.

[3] The fruit of the chestnut is in the form of a large prickly burr in which the nuts are encased.

THE FAKE KNIGHT-ERRANT

From *Lo-yang chin-shen chiu-wen chi*

TRANSLATED BY PAO-CHEN TSENG

Po T'ing-hui of Wan-chou,[1] a *t'ai-pao*,[2] was the eldest son of the retired president of the Secretariat, Po Wen-ko.[3] T'ing-hui held the post of keeper of the imperial estates; at the same time, he was the acting superintendent of the five bureaus of imperial auxiliary services, and the local military inspector.[4] Later he was appointed the prefect of Wan-chou as a reward for putting down a rebellion in Shu. After retirement, he died at Ching-nan.[5]

Po T'ing-hui was fascinated by the unusual and was especially interested in the magic of the Taoists.

He had a cousin, T'ing-jang, who was a military officer[6] but was a libertine. T'ing-jang liked to wander about the business districts. Once a friend asked him, "Have you ever heard of knights-errant?"

"Of course," he answered.

"Have you ever seen one?" the friend continued.

"No, I haven't," he replied.

"Now there is a man staying at the Prosperity Inn in town whom everyone calls 'master.' He's a knight-errant. Let's both go and visit him."

T'ing-jang agreed to this proposal and the next day they went together to the inn. There they saw several persons seated in a circle on a mat. Among them was a person with deep-set eyes, thick eyebrows, a dark complexion, and a brown beard. When T'ing-jang arrived, only the brown-bearded man remained seated.

"You should pay your respects to him," his friend urged.

T'ing-jang kowtowed, but the brown-bearded man acknowledged without getting up, and asked slowly, "What family is this boy from?"

The friend answered, "This is Minister Po's nephew. He has come with me, master, to pay his respects to you."

The brown-bearded man smiled and said, "Since he brought you here, sit down and drink with us."

After a little while, someone brought in a

---

[1] In modern Szechwan Province.
[2] This honorific title may be literally translated as "the grand guardian."
[3] Biographical details unknown.
[4] The place in question is given as Shui-pei in the text. Its location in Sung times has yet to be identified. But given the fact that Po's other duties were confined to the Sung capital, Shui-pei might reasonably be taken as in the same region.
[5] The area around the counties of Chiang-ling and Kung-an in the present Hupeh Province. This paragraph, copied from Po T'ing-hui's only available biography, sums up practically all that is known of him.
[6] The title given in the text is *chin-shih tu-chiang*, but the actual duty of this funtionary has yet to be clarified. In all likelihood, this was not a high military post.

wooden basin. The brown-bearded man took out several bottles of wine and, after filling the basin with wine, set a porcelain bowl in front of each person. Then a serving table was brought in with some donkey meat at one end of it. One of the men drew a knife and cut the meat into big chunks. Everyone helped himself to wine with a wooden ladle, and a large dish for the meat was set down in front of each person. Seeing this, T'ing-jang showed great uneasiness. The brown-bearded man raised his wine bowl and emptied it in one gulp. The others followed suit. Using their hands, they helped themselves to the meat. The men looked at T'ing-jang with raised eyebrows and expressions of displeasure. Then T'ing-jang very reluctantly drank half a bowl of wine and ate a little meat. When they had finished, the others rose to leave. T'ing-jang watched them closely and realized that they were all dog butchers and street wrestlers. Only his friend and he stayed behind to chat with the brown-bearded man.

The friend introduced him to the brown-bearded man, saying, "Mr. Po is a man of high aspirations. Please feel free to talk with him."

The brown-bearded man removed a dagger from his bed, unsheathed it, and played with it. He flicked his nails several times against the blade, showing off the resonance of the metal. Seeing this, T'ing-jang was convinced that the man was a real knight-errant. He left his seat and repeatedly kowtowed, saying, "It is a great privilege to meet you, sir, and I hope to be your student some day."

The brown-bearded man told him, "This dagger has taken a few scores of lives. They were all stingy, oppressive, wicked people. I cooked their heads and they tasted like pigs' and lambs' heads."

T'ing-jang, hearing this speech, felt as though thorns were pricking him all over; he took his leave in great alarm.

At home, he recounted the entire story to his cousin T'ing-hui. Like the sons of most influential families, T'ing-hui was fascinated by this kind of unusual personalit   so he said to T'ing-jang, "Is there a way for me to meet him?"

"I can talk this over with my friend."

T'ing-jang informed his friend, who replied, "Just prepare a feast and wait at home."

The next morning, the friend came with the brown-bearded man. The Po cousins invited them in, and both kowtowed to the bearded man, who received this homage without returning the courtesy.

After the feast, the brown-bearded man asked T'ing-hui, "Do you have any good swords here?"

T'ing-hui brought out several dozen swords and placed them in front of him. The brown-bearded man examined them one by one and said, "These are all ordinary stuff, nothing special."

"I have two more in my room," T'ing-jang said. "Let me show you."

When the brown-bearded man saw them, he threw one on the ground, saying, "This one is ordinary stuff." Then he examined the other one and concluded, "This one is all right." He ordered the blacksmith to sharpen the blades and asked that fire tongs be brought to him. He raised the sword and cut the tongs in two. The blade remained unchipped.

Then he said, "This one looks all right." He played with it and swung it for a long while before he announced his intention to leave.

Fascinated, T'ing-hui asked him to stay with them. He was given a room by the hall and was treated with deference. But he seldom spoke, and in his conversation with others, he limited his response to a few words.

One day he borrowed a steed [from T'ing-hui]. Several days later he returned on foot explaining, "The horse took fright and ran away." Ten days later, someone had the horse returned.

A month or so after this, the brown-bearded man told T'ing-jang, "Borrow ten ingots of silver, a leather case, a good horse, and two servants for me from your brother. I'm going to Hua-yang[7] for a few days. When I return, I'll return the money and the horse."

T'ing-jang thought for a while and was reluctant to give the man what he asked, but he remembered that he had killed many stingy people in the past. If he were given everything he asked for, however, there was the possibility that the man would never return. He hesitated and could not decide what to do. Then the brown-bearded man became angry and threatened to leave. The cousins apologized and said, "The ten ingots of silver and the horse are no problem. The problem is how to choose the attendants who would best serve you."[8] The brown-bearded man simply looked around and picked out two servants; thus he was given everything he wanted. The brown-bearded man accepted all this without a word of thanks, mounted the horse, and left. The two cousins could not understand what this man was doing.

A few days later, one of the servants returned, saying, "The master led us to the city wall and sent me back because he thinks I walk too slowly." Ten days after this, the other servant returned and said, "We arrived at Shan-chou,[9] where the

---

[7] Hua-yang County in modern Szechwan.
[8] Apparently there had been a time gap between the bearded man's request and the response of the two cousins.
[9] In the present Honan Province.

master became angry with me and sent me back." The Po cousins believed that the man was a knight-errant, so they dared not criticize his actions for fear that he might hear about it and take revenge.

A year passed and there was still no sign of him. Then one day, a merchant passed by the Po residence, riding the horse borrowed by the bearded man. Po's servants all recognized the horse and reported the matter to Po [T'ing-hui], who questioned the merchant about it. The merchant said that he had bought the horse at Hua-chou[10] with eighty strings of cash. He showed them his receipt, which indicated this transaction very clearly, but the seller's name was different. Only then did the Po cousins realize that they had been deceived. Three or four years later, someone saw the brown-bearded man in Shan-chou and discovered that he was an experienced ironsmith.

A man may seem honest and sincere, yet he still cannot be trusted too readily. The brown-bearded man made a living with his fake swordsmanship; it was only natural that the Po cousins should fall into his trap. The reason for recording this here is to have it serve as a lesson, so that any readers running into comparable situations will know what to do. This type of fraud is indeed the worst one can ever expect. All should take heed of the lesson.

---

[10] In the present Shensi Province.

THE SWINDLER ALCHEMISTS

From *P'o-an ching-ch'i*

TRANSLATED BY WILLIAM L. JENNY AND THE EDITORS

In worn-out clothes and shabby gown was the one
Who claimed he could turn metals to silver.
He should have made some for his own expenses
Instead of selling water to others for household use.

This quatrain was composed by T'ang Po-hu,[1] a scholar of the present dynasty [Ming]. What it refers to here is a group of alchemists who set ingenious traps to trick the greedy and gullible. They claim that they are able to change herbs into immortality drugs, lead into gold, and mercury into silver. This they call the "Art of the Yellow and White," or simply "smelting." They ask that you lend your silver to be the base, and then at the first opportunity, they make off with it. This they call "lifting the lid."

Once an alchemist approached T'ang Po-hu with such a scheme. "Sir," he said, "you're a man of celestial qualities and, as such, you may be sure that we shall not fail."

T'ang rebuked him: "You go about wearing rags. If you possess such a skill, why don't you make some silver and gold for yourself? Why labor for others?"

"Because I possess these arts, fate has turned against me. Consequently I must seek out those destined for great wealth; it is only to them that

[1] T'ang Yin (1470–1523), styled Po-hu, was a well-known painter and literary figure of Ming China.

my learning can be of service. Since I am not so destined, I may not turn my arts to my own profit. It is because I see that you are so well favored by fate that I ask you to be my partner. We alchemists refer to this as 'seeking outside assistance.'"

"May I make a proposal to you?" T'ang replied. "You proceed with the transmutation without any material assistance from me. I'll merely contribute a share of my luck, and if the experiment succeeds, I shall be happy to give half of the silver to you."

Hearing T'ang speak in this way, the alchemist realized that he was making fun of him. He knew that T'ang would not be a customer on whom he could play tricks, and left right away. Thus it came about that we have this poem, which T'ang Po-hu wrote to put us on our guard. Yet among these scoundrels there are some suave ones who would not be so easily out-talked. How is it so?

They would say, for example, "The spirits' magic is for the world's salvation; we mustn't use our powers for our own profit. Rather we must find a man of surpassing virtue, favored by the gods, and employ our alchemy for mutual benefit. Since the spiritual essence of such a man is perfect, we may be sure that the elixir of immortality can also be perfected."

They could go on endlessly in this way. Such reasoning, is it not perfectly true? As to alchemy, is it not a sacred art? It was the Taoist sages, after all, who taught us to transmute cinnabar into gold, but only for the benefit of mankind. Master Lü [Tung-pin] did have his worries that the gold [acquired through Taoist alchemy] might return to its original substance after five hundred years, thus causing trouble for posterity. Therefore he never said "I'll help you acquire property or support a family."

There are men, however, like Tu Tzu-ch'un,[2] who was invited by a Taoist to act as the "outside assistance." But when the drug was about to be completed at the Cloud Terrace Temple, he ruined it because he still could not completely rid himself of his attachment to love [for his son].

As for the greedy people today, they surround themselves with wives and concubines, acquire land and houses, enrich themselves at others' expense, and cheat in business dealings. What kind of consciences do they have?! They seek depraved Taoists and expect them to successfully turn out immortality drugs for their lifelong enjoyment and for the benefit of their descendants. Isn't that idiotic? Such men should be told that "The perfection of the spiritual essence is the prerequisite for the perfection of the immortality elixir." They act as if they could completely give up the cultivation of the spirit and concentrate on the making of the silver! With such cheap intentions, there is absolutely no hope of their ever succeeding in their alchemic experiments. Dear audience, wouldn't you agree that whoever hears this, no matter how ignorant he is, should realize that such absurd things cannot be done? However, it is always the cleverest men on earth who fall into these traps. Why is it so?

Now let me tell you about a wealthy man of Sung-chiang[3] by the name of P'an, who was a student of the imperial academy. He was learned, articulate, and considered an amiable man by all who knew him. But he had one strange obsession in life: his passion for alchemy. There is a common saying, "Birds of a feather flock together." Because he had this preoccupation, one after another the alchemists came, and P'an was every so often duped into giving away quite a bit of money.

Undiscouraged, he just explained this by saying he had not been lucky enough to meet a first-class alchemist. It was his conviction that since alchemy had such a long tradition, failure was unthinkable. Sooner or later, he would meet with success. Why worry over a little loss? So he went on searching with ever greater fervor. As a result, his name became well known among the alchemists far and near; those who were around him were all of the same mind: to take advantage of his gullibility.

One autumn P'an took a pleasure trip to the West Lake at Hangchow and rented a place to stay. He happened to notice in the neighboring garden a man, accompanied by a woman, who like himself had evidently come to relax at the lake. The man was traveling with much luggage, his servants were all well dressed, and the woman who accomapanied him was exceptionally beautiful. Upon inquiry, P'an learned that she was the man's concubine. Every day the man hired a luxurious pleasure boat and regaled himself with the most sumptuous meals and drinks, in the company of his concubine and a group of musicians. The table was covered with an endless display of finely wrought vessels of gold and silver. At nightfall he would return to his quarters surrounded by lantern carriers, and present a generous tip to all the members of his entourage before retiring.

P'an observed all this with the keenest interest. "Rich as I am, I could scarcely afford his extravagance. He must be the equal of T'ao Chu[4] and Yi Tun." Finally his admiration prompted him to send his respects to the stranger, and this led in

---

[2] See the T'ang tale "Tu Tzu-ch'un" in this anthology.
[3] Southwest of modern Shanghai.

[4] A legendary rich man of the Spring and Autumn period.

turn to a personal meeting. They introduced themselves and exchanged the usual amenities. When he felt somewhat at ease, P'an said, "Sir, your wealth is certainly unequaled."

"Oh, it's really nothing to speak of," replied the man.

"But surely, for your manner of living a man would need a mountain of gold. Otherwise he would soon be bankrupt."

"Even a mountain of gold can be leveled easily enough. What is needed is an inexhaustible supply."

This quickened P'an's interest. "What sort of inexhaustible supply?"

"I've known you such a short time that I don't feel I can tell you."

"But I would want to know sooner or later."

"If I told you, perhaps you wouldn't understand. Or perhaps you wouldn't believe me."

P'an saw that the man was testing him, and all the more fervently he begged to be told. The man finally sent away his servants, leaned over to P'an, and whispered into his ear, "I am in possession of the 'powder of nine cycles.' I can turn mercury and lead into gold. If one can be successful in this art, gold is just as cheap as tiles. Why should it be highly valued?"

The very mention of alchemy set P'an's blood racing. In excitement, he cried, "So you're an expert alchemist! I've long wanted to learn that art but have found no one to teach me. If you do practice this art, I want to learn it from you whatever the cost."

"Well," said the man, "it's not something that can be casually spread around, but I guess there's no harm in doing a little smelting for our own amusement." With that he ordered his valet to start a fire. They melted a small quantity of lead. From a pouch hanging from his belt, the man took out a small paper packet. He opened it and revealed a small lump of powder. Lifting some with the nail of his finger, he flicked it into the pot. When they emptied the pot, the lead had

disappeared and in its place were small bits of fine-grade silver, glittering like snowflakes.

Now dear audience, you may say that since the powder could change base metal into silver, how could the skill not be real? Actually there is a way of hiding the silver. He had previously extracted the essence of some silver by firing it together with some chemicals. Every tael of silver is reduced to about one-tenth of its weight. Then when he melted the lead with this powder, the lead evaporated and only some residue remained. With the essence of silver, all took on a silvery color. But there was not one bit more silver than was originally in the powder. This is the way alchemists deceive their victims, who invariably believe in the validity of what they have seen. Indeed, this rich man was enthralled when he saw the transformation.

"No wonder he lives in such luxury, when silver comes to him as easily as this. All my previous efforts ended in loss of capital, but now I've met a real master. I must beg him to give me some help."

"How do you make this powder?" he then asked the alchemist.

"This powder is called 'seed of silver.' First you take silver as a base, whatever its amount, and then smelt it together with chemicals. You must smelt it in the cauldron for nine cycles. When the heat has reached the required temperature, the mixture will first send out yellow filaments and then turn white as snow. Then you may remove the lid and gather up the powder which has been produced. One particle of it, the size of a grain of rice, will transform base metals into gold or silver. The silver which you use as a base remains completely unaffected."

"How much silver is necessary?"

"The more you use, the stronger will be the powder. With half a box of this powder, you can be as rich as the nation itself."

"Although I'm not rich," P'an replied, "I believe I could manage to raise several thousand taels. If you would do me the honor of coming to my home, instructing me in your method of smelting, and helping me to perform a transmutation, the desire of my life will be satisfied."

"Novices in the art must be carefully chosen, and I do not usually perform transmutations for others. But you are a sincere man and one of obvious spiritual superiority. Moreover, I confess to feeling that our meeting here must have been predestined. So there should be no harm in doing it for you just once. Just let me have your address and I shall call on you sometime."

"I live in Sung-chiang, a journey of two or three days from here. Since you're willing to visit me, why not gather your things and come now? If we part like this and are unable to meet again, just like that I'll have missed the opportunity."

"I'm a native of Chung-chou,[5] where I live with my mother. I had heard such praises of the beauty of Wu-lin that I came here with my concubine to enjoy the scenery. I brought no money but have been relying on my alchemic transmutations to meet my expenditures, so I have been able to tarry here for some time. Now that I've met you and that we have something in common, it'd be rude of me not to share my knowledge with you. However, if you'd permit me, I'd like to take my concubine home first and see to the needs of my mother before going to your place. It would not be much of a delay."

"My home has guest quarters, and the lady would be welcome to stay there. Why don't you bring her along? You can work at the same time. Wouldn't it be convenient? My home is a humble place, but you're most welcome, and we would do our best to make the lady feel comfortable. If you can come immediately, I shall be most grateful."

"Since you're so earnest, allow me to speak with my concubine and then we can make ready to leave."

P'an was ecstatic. That afternoon he sent a note

to the alchemist inviting him to dine on the lake the next day. On that day he received the man at the boat with great ceremony. Each one of them made a great display of his learning, praised the other's accomplishments, and regretted that they had not met sooner. The day was spent in merriment and [after they returned], P'an had a complete dinner sent to the alchemist's concubine. On the following day the alchemist in turn invited P'an to a feast, which was exceedingly sumptuous. The dinnerware, as might be expected, was all of gold and silver.

The two of them took a liking to each other, and after all the sightseeing, they made arrangements to move on to Sung-chiang. They hired two large boats, loaded on their belongings, and sailed together all the way. During the journey P'an occasionally caught a glimpse of the young concubine as she gazed out the cabin window of the other boat. He observed her secretly and was struck by her graceful beauty. But alas:

The river surged between them,
And the words lay locked in his heart.

The poem sent by P'ei Hang to Lady Fan[6] expresses much of his sentiment:

Even Wu and Yüeh[7] thought of the other party when in
*   the same boat;*
How much more so when separated from the goddess
*   by only a screen.*
I'd have us meet in the City of Jade[8]
And fly far away, with the luan[9] and the crane, into the
*   depths of the sky.*

P'an, gazing at the beauty on the other boat, found himself in exactly the same situation. What

---

[5] In modern Honan Province.

[6] According to legend, P'ei Hang of the T'ang period once met the beautiful Lady Fan on a boat. Through her assistance, he later married Lady Fan's sister, and both he and his wife eventually became immortals.

[7] Even these two rival states of the Spring and Autumn period would think of the well-being of the other side when they realized that they were interrelated.

[8] In Taoist mythology, the City of Jade is the dwelling place of the Lord on High.

[9] *Luan* is a fabulous bird in Chinese mythology.

a pity there was no one to act as messenger for him.

But let us return to the story. In a few days the two boats arrive at Sung-chiang. P'an went to his home first and then went back to the alchemist with his invitation. After the usual courtesies, P'an said, "This is my humble place. It's rather inconvenient with all the people coming and going. Not far from here I have a villa; there you and the lady would find it much more peaceful. As for myself, I could sleep in the study there. It'd be both quiet and secluded, and you could work undisturbed. What do you think?"

"It is most important that I be protected from any outside intruders when performing alchemic transmutations. And since my concubine is with me, privacy is all the more desirable. Yes, your villa will certainly be a much better place."

P'an ordered the boatmen to take the boats to the villa, while he and the alchemist walked hand in hand.

Over the doorway of P'an's villa was a plaque which read "The Garden of Pleasure." Inside were:

Old trees projected against the sky,
New bamboo groves surrounding the place.
Majestic beams stretching across the spacious buildings;
Stylish indeed are these mansions and pavilions.
Deep inside the houses
Are secluded rooms and quiet quarters.
Hosts of artificial mountains,
Secure enough to hoard the works of history.
Caves, and beyond more caves;
Could it be that they are the sanctuaries of the immortals?
The sound of music
Might be able to bring in the phoenix;
To watch a game of chess here
Would bring time to a standstill.[10]

Seeing the scenery of the villa, the alchemist exclaimed in delight, "Truly a magnificent and secluded place! Just the right place for transmuting metals and for settling my concubine. My mind will be at ease when I work for you. It seems you have been richly blessed by fate."

P'an gave orders for the concubine to be shown in. Playing her role, she took her two maids, Spring Cloud and Autumn Moon, and walked seductively toward the pavilion in the garden. P'an discreetly bowed and was about to withdraw, but the alchemist said, "You and I are like brothers now, so it is only proper that she pay her respects to you." He introduced P'an to her. Seeing her closely, P'an felt that her beauty would make the moon and flowers hide in shame.

Now are there any rich men in this world who are not greedy and lascivious? At that moment P'an was like a snowman before a fire, about to fall. The transmutation immediately dropped to second place in importance. He turned to the alchemist and said, "The apartments in the garden are all large. If madam will select whichever one she likes, as soon as possible I will send some maidservants to wait on her."

As the alchemist was going off with his concubine to view the apartments, P'an rushed home, fetched a pair of golden hairclasps and a pair of golden bracelets, and then presented them to the alchemist. "May I present these humble gifts to madam on the occasion of our first meeting?" he said. "Please don't refuse because of their small value."

The alchemist in one glance saw that they were made of gold and declined to accept, saying, "You're too generous. Gold is easy for me to acquire but for you it means great expenditure. I could not in good conscience take these things."

"I realize that they are nothing to you. But in honor of the young lady, I beg you to accept them as a token of my sincerity."

---

[10] These two lines illustrate a celestial setting. The daughter of Duke Mu of the state of Ch'in of the Spring and Autumn period learned music from her husband Hsiao Shih. She played it so well that the music brought in the phoenix. The second allusion stands for the timelessness at Mount Lan-k'o, where enough time to pay a game of chess meant the passing of several generations in the human world.

"Since you're so generous, it would be rude of me to refuse," the alchemist replied. "I'll do my best to create the transmuting powder as a way of repaying you." With a smile on his face he went into the apartments and handed the gifts over to a maid. He then called his concubine out and told her to express her thanks.

On seeing her again, P'an felt that the money he had spent had already been handsomely rewarded. In his heart he thought: "This fellow not only knows how to change lead into gold; he also has this beautiul girl! I wonder if any man can be happier than he? Fortunately, it's only a matter of time until I learn the tricks of smelting from him. What concerns me now is whether I'll have a chance to become more familiar with this woman. I certainly won't feel content unless I can go to bed with her. But for the time being I'll be the picture of propriety. If I don't get a chance, at least I won't ruin the whole thing. There's no need to hurry anyway. I had better take care of the smelting first."

He turned to the alchemist. "May I ask when we can begin the smelting?"

"When we get the silver we need as a base, we can begin any time."

"How much silver do we need to begin?"

"The more the better—the more base you have, the more powder it will produce. Moreover, you will save yourself the trouble of going through the smelting again later."

"In that case," said P'an, "I'll provide two thousand taels of silver. Tonight I'll stay at the main house and put everything there in order. Tomorrow I'll move over here and we can begin work."

That evening he treated the alchemist to a lavish dinner in the garden, and later, of course, had a dinner sent to the concubine in her apartments.

The next day P'an measured out two thousand taels of silver. He had been pursuing the art of alchemy for a long time and had all the utensils needed for the transmutation. All he had to do was have them moved to the alchemist. P'an was indeed familiar with this business. With all the ingredients ready, he went over to see the alchemist.

"I appreiate your thoughtfulness in bringing these things," said the alchemist, "but my method is different from those of other alchemists, as you will find out once we begin the firing."

"It is precisely that method which I wish to learn," said P'an.

"My method is known as 'the nine cycles.' Each cycle consists of nine days. After nine such cycles, that is, eighty-one days, the lid of the cauldron may be opened and the finished product taken out. On that day you will be a very rich man."

"It will all be due to your kindness," said P'an.

The alchemist ordered his valet to begin the preparations. They fired up the cauldron and slowly placed the silver pieces inside. The alchemist brought out the prescription and handed it over to P'an. Then he placed several rare chemicals in the cauldron. When the colored smoke rose up, they sealed the lid.

The alchemist then called his servants, who had come with him, and said, "Since I'll be here for three months, I want some of you to return home and report to my mother what I'm doing here." Only the few who could help with the smelting stayed on, while the others went home as instructed.

The firing began and went on day and night. The alchemist frequently went to check the fire, but never once did he open the cauldron. When he was not busy, he chatted with P'an; sometimes they played chess, sometimes they drank together. It goes without saying that they got on very well together.

Occasionally P'an sent some small gifts to the concubine to win her favor, and she would reciprocate by sending an appropriate gift in return.

Things went on this way for more than twenty days. Suddenly one day a man appeared at the gate. He was panting and sweating and dressed in mourning clothes. He rushed into the garden and it was soon discovered that he was one of the servants who had been sent back to the alchemist's home earlier. He ran up to the alchemist, began kowtowing and crying, and said, "Your mother has passed away and you must hurry home to attend to the funeral."

The alchemist turned pale and fell on the ground sobbing. P'an was alarmed and tried to calm him. "Your mother was bound by her allotted life-span," he said. "You must restrain your grief; excessive mourning won't do you any good."

The servant continued to plead with the man: "There's no one at home to manage things, sir. You had better set off as soon as possible."

The alchemist ceased crying and said to P'an, "I had looked forward to completing this with you to show my gratitude. Now that this misfortune has overwhelmed me, I can't stay any longer. On the other hand, the smelting is not yet finished; worse still, the process cannot be interrupted. This is a dilemma. But my concubine, though a woman, has been with me for a long time and is fully informed as to the smelting procedure. I could leave her here to supervise things. My only worry is that she is so young. With no one to watch over her, I am afraid that she will be an inconvenience to you."

"You and I are just like brothers," said P'an. "Why should it be an inconvenience to me? As long as she stays here where the cauldron is, no one will be around to bother her. I'll have some older maidservants keep her company, and at night they can accompany her to my wife's place to sleep. I'll be here to keep watch over the villa until you return, so there shouldn't be any inconvenience at all. And of course, her meals will be well taken care of."

The alchemist pondered a while and said, "My mother's death has thrown me into a state of confusion. I've heard that the ancients would often entrust the care of their wives and children to their friends. Since you're so sympathetic about my situation, I can only follow your advice. I shall leave her here to attend to the firing, while I myself return home to attend to my business. As soon as possible I will return to open the cauldron. That way I can fulfill both obligations."

When P'an saw that the alchemist was willing to let the concubine stay, he was beside himself with joy. With broad smiles he responded, "In that case, it'll be perfect."

The alchemist went inside to tell the concubine of the new developments, and that she was to stay and watch over the firing. He then brought her out to see P'an, who was to be her guardian. "You are only to watch the cauldron," he told P'an. "Under no circumstances are you to open it. If anything is done incorrectly, the whole process will be ruined."

"Supposing," P'an asked, "that your return trip is delayed and the eighty-one days are up. What shall we do?"

"After the nine cycles are completed, leaving the powder in the cauldron for a few more days won't hurt anything; the powder will be all the stronger."

After some words in private with his concubine, the alchemist quickly took his leave.

Since the concubine had stayed behind, P'an was sure that the alchemist would return before too long. He was not worried about the firing, as the silver was bound to materialize. What was foremost in his mind was that he should not miss the opportunity of the alchemist's absence and the concubine's living in the garden to make advances. He occupied himself with searching for an opportunity to make his first move.

As he was pondering the problem, Spring Cloud came in and said, "My mistress asks you to please escort her into the smelting room to check the cauldron." With great haste P'an smoothed his gown, adjusted his cap, and hurried to her apartments.

"Your maid just told me that you wished me to accompany you to inspect the cauldron."

"Please go first. I shall walk behind you." Her

voice was as sweet as the singing of birds. Then, in her graceful way, she walked out of the room and bowed to him.

"You are a guest here," P'an said. "It would be rude of me to go first."

"I am a woman; it would be presumptuous of me [to precede you]."

In the few moments it took to exchange those words, though they never touched each other, they were able to look directly at each other quite intently. Finally P'an prevailed upon her to go first, accompanied by her maids. Walking behind her, P'an grew excited as he watched the way she walked.

When they came to the firing room, she turned to her maids and said, "Only those authorized are permitted to approach the cauldron. You two will have to stay outside. Mr. P'an will go in with me." On hearing this, P'an rushed ahead and together they went into the room where they inspected the cauldron. P'an gazed ever more ardently at the girl, completely entranced by her beauty. He couldn't care less about the fire. Unfortunately, the presence of the valet who tended the fire prevented his uttering any amorous words, so he could only express his heart with his eyes.

When they reached the door, he brazenly said, "Thanks for coming over. You must be lonely in your room, now that your husband has gone." In answer, the concubine said nothing but only smiled. She did not back away this time, but turned and slowly walked off to her room.

P'an was wild with passion. "If only that boy had not been there, I could have had her," he thought. "Tomorrow I must get rid of him, and when I go with her to check the cauldron, I can make my move."

That evening he gave an order to one of his servants: "Tomorrow prepare a feast for that valet who watches the fire. Tell him that he has worked hard and I want him to have a rest. Get him good and drunk."

Later that night, he sat alone drinking. The events of the day ran through his mind and he thought of the concubine in her room. His desire made him restless, so he composed a poem:

The splendid flowers of the magnificent garden,
Transplanted to the humble home.
Think not on the world you left behind,
For spring days are swiftly slipping by.

He moved nearer to the door leading to the apartments, and again chanted the poem several times, deliberately—hoping that it could be heard inside.

Soon Autumn Moon came out carrying a cup of tea and said, "My mistress heard your chanting, and fears that your throat might be dry. She offers you this tea." A smile of delight broke across P'an's face, and he thanked her profusely.

Shortly after Autumn Moon withdrew, he heard a poem being chanted inside.

Who is the master of this lovely flower?
It's only a flower flying in the east wind.
If the god only takes pity on her plight,
Her intention will be the same as his.

P'an knew very well what the poem was intended to mean, but he could not rush in to her then and there. He also heard a door close inside, so he withdrew to his study and went to sleep.

The next morning one of his servants, following P'an's orders, invited the alchemist's valet to a feast. The lad was bored with his work and so threw himself into the drinking with great gusto. Before long he was dead drunk and fast asleep outside.

As soon as P'an learned that the valet was elsewhere, he went to accompany the girl to inspect the cauldron. She left her room, and as before, walked in front of him. When they arrived, the maids, as on the previous day, stayed outside and the concubine went in. P'an kept close behind her. When she saw that the valet was gone she feigned alarm and said, "What's happened to the boy? Leaving the fire unattended!"

"There's another fire here that needs to be fed, so we'll let that one go out," said P'an.

She pretended that she did not understand. "The fire must not be permitted to go out!"

"Then you and I can generate some real fire to light it up."

"How can a man dedicated to the sacred art of alchemy think such thoughts, much less give utterance to them," she said in the most serious manner.

"You sleep with your husband," said P'an, "and he's an alchemist. Do you mean to say that you two do nothing together?"

The girl could not refute him but only said, "This is a serious matter, and you want to fool around."

"We were destined to meet in a former life; that makes it a serious matter for us, too." So saying, he embraced her and fell to his knees.

The girl bade him get up and said, "My husband is a very strict man and I dare not misbehave. But since you're so earnest, I can't bring myself to refuse you. Perhaps we might arrange to meet somewhere tonight."

"I implore you to grant me your favors here and now. Why should we wait until evening?"

"Someone might come in," she said. "It's impossible to do it here."

"I've taken every precaution. The valet is away at a party. Everyone else is forbidden to enter. This place is secluded. No one will know."

"This room is only for the firing. I'm afraid something would go wrong and we would regret it. No! We can't do it here!"

But P'an was driven by such passion that he lost all concern for the firing. He held her tight and said, "I wouldn't care if it meant danger to my life. I only beg you to save me." Regardless of whether she was willing or not, P'an dragged her to a couch, pulled down their pants, and wriggled his way into her. His happiness was celestial:

The one-string harp opens and closes;
The holeless flute lifts up and drives down.

The fire is stirred up in the glowing stove
And the lead is thrust in through the door.
Tongue thrashing in the flowery pool,
Mouth full of subtle fragrance,
He sips the juice of the jade,
Whereas his own liquid enters the lady's chamber.
Drowned in pleasure he drinks the jasper waters;
No need to wait for other spiritual attainment in the Ninth
   Heaven;
Such ecstasy as this transports him to supreme happiness.

After they were finished, P'an, straightening his clothes, thanked her. "I am most grateful to you. But we had so little time together. Can we meet again tonight?" He bowed before her.

"I had originally promised to meet you tonight, but you couldn't wait. Such things shouldn't be done near the cauldron, you know."

"I was afraid to let the opportunity pass me by. I felt I had to take it while I could."

"Shall I come to your study tonight," she replied, "or do you want to come to mine?"

"Whatever you suggest."

"Since my maids must sleep in my room, it would be awkward for you to come there. I'll make an excuse and come to you tonight. Tomorrow I'll make proper arrangements so that you can come to my room."

That night, after everyone was asleep, she left her room and went to P'an's. Together they sported there with great delight. After that, in his room and in hers, they enjoyed the pleasures of love without restraint. P'an took it as the strangest of his adventures and only wished that the alchemist would never return. He did not care whether the transmuting powder was ever completed.

They went on enjoying each other's company for half a month. One day the doorkeeper announced: "The alchemist has returned." P'an was taken aback, but he received the man, and after they had exchanged amenities, the alchemist went in to talk with his concubine. After a while he came out again and said, "She told me that the firing proceeded with no difficulties. Since the nine cycles have passed, the powder is finished and we

570

can open the cauldron. We're sort of hungry now; let's wait until tomorrow, when we can make sacrifices to the gods before unsealing the lid."

That night, though P'an was deprived of his new-found pleasure, he was nevertheless excited over the prospect of opening the cauldron the next day and finally possessing his long sought-for prize. The next morning after offering paper horses and a few other sacrificial items, they proceeded to the firing room.

Immediately upon entering, the alchemist said, "Why is the atmosphere so strange in here? Something's wrong!" He unsealed the lid of the cauldron and, looking inside, jumped back in surprise. "It's ruined! It's ruined! The powder is ruined and even the silver has turned to dross! There must have been lewd acts performed in this room, and their evil influence ruined the smelting!"

P'an turned pale and was unable to speak, for the alchemist had spoken the truth and he was terrified. The alchemist meanwhile was in a rage. P'an could even hear the gnashing of his teeth. The alchemist questioned the valet: "Who has come into this room?"

"Only Mr. P'an and the young lady. They came once a day to check the fire."

"Then why is it the preparation has been ruined?" demanded the alchemist. "Go tell her to come here!"

The boy went to fetch her, and when she came, the alchemist shouted, "What did you do while you were here watching the fire? Everything has been ruined."

"I came every day with Mr. P'an. We never touched the seal on the cauldron. I don't know what could have happened."

"Who said anything about touching the seal? Oh, I see. That must be what you did!" He looked at the valet: "Were you ever away when they came?"

"Only once," said the valet. "Mr. P'an had me treated to a feast because he thought I was working too hard. I drank too much and fell asleep

outside there. That was the only day that they were here alone."

The alchemist let out a horrible laugh. "So that's it!" He went to his traveling bag, got out a leather whip, and turned to the concubine. "There's no use trying to hide what you've done, you little harlot."

He raised his whip and lashed at her, but she dodged it and cried out, "I didn't want to do it, but he forced me!"

P'an all the while looked on petrified, wishing there were a hole in the ground he could crawl into. The alchemist glared at him. "What great promises you made when I entrusted her to you! And you did this the moment I was away. What a vile dog you are! An unprincipled man like you, how can you ever dream of performing transmutations! Out of my sight! This little slut—I'm going to beat her to death so she won't bring any more shame to my door!" He dashed at her with his whip, and she turned and fled into her room. Her two maids tried to restrain the enraged man and begged him to forgive her. Instead he gave each of them a lash and his whip broke.

P'an watched all this helplessly, and then knelt before the alchemist and pleaded with him: "It was all my fault. I'm willing to forget the loss of my silver if only you can forgive us."

"You're getting what you deserve," said the alchemist. "You had your fun and you lost the powder. You've got nothing to complain about. But my concubine, is she for you to enjoy? You've spoiled her for me; what can be done now? I'm still of a mind to beat her to death and let you pay for her life."

"I'll make it up to you," cried P'an. He sent a servant to fetch two large silver bars. He took them, bowed down, and held them up in front of the alchemist, who only scoffed: "What are they to me! I can get silver easily enough."

P'an kowtowed again and offered two hundred more taels of cash.

"If you take this money, you can get yourself another concubine. I know I was stupid, but for the sake of our past friendship, please forgive her."

"Your money means nothing to me. But a scoundrel like you should be taught a lesson. Otherwise you'll return to your old ways. I'll take the money and donate it to charity."

He took the three hundred taels and packed it away. Then he ordered his concubine and the servants to pack their belongings. In a great rush they moved everything down to the same boat on which the alchemist had arrived the day before. As they pulled away from shore he could still be heard cursing P'an. "Despicable wretch! To think that he so disgraced me!"

P'an had been terrified that the alchemist would bring disaster on his house; so even though he had lost some money he felt himself fortunate to be rid of the man. As for the silver in the cauldron, he really believed that he had ruined it by his improper behavior. "I was too impatient," he said regretfully. "I should have waited until the powder was finished, kept her here under some pretense or another, and figured out a way to have the affair with her. Then I could have had it both ways. Or I simply should never have made love to her in the firing room in the first place. That way everything would have been all right. But I was stupid, and it's my own fault that I lost the money. I had finally met an alchemist who really knew how to make silver and I fouled it up!" Yet he consoled himself: "She is such a rare beauty, and I had her for quite some time. It was quite an adventure and I enjoyed it tremendously. There is certainly nothing to regret."

But poor P'an never realized that it was all a trick by the alchemist. When he was at the West Lake, he heard that P'an was also vacationing there. He then set up the scheme to trap him. By the time he came to stay at P'an's house, he had managed to make it all appear so natural. Later, when the servant arrived announcing the death of his mother, he secretly "lifted the lid" of the cauldron, removed the two thousand taels of silver,

and rushed off, leaving the concubine with P'an to avoid suspicion. The seduction, too, was part of the scheme. P'an was made to appear the guilty party and was unable to answer the charge in any way but to confess. It could well be the working of the gods that he fell into the trap. Even at the very beginning he was so impressed with the man's wealth that he felt he must be a genuine alchemist. He had no idea that the dazzling dinnerware was in fact copper and lead plated with liquid gold and silver. But under the influence of the strong wine and the dim light, who would think of testing it? And so, in that one moment of carelessness, P'an made a serious mistake. The scheme was truly the brainwork of a wicked genius.

Nevertheless, after being so cheated, P'an still did not learn his lesson. He just said that he had ruined a golden opportunity through his own fault and continued all the more in his devotion to alchemy. One day, another alchemist came along and got P'an talking on the latter's favorite subject. Greatly impressed, P'an invited the alchemist to stay at his home. "Not long ago," P'an said, "I had a guest who knew how to change metals into gold. I asked him to show me how. He agreed and was even doing the smelting for me. Unfortunately, I insulted him and he left before it was finished. It was, of course, a great disappointment to me."

"He's not the only one around who can do it!" exclaimed the guest, and he called for P'an's servants to make a fire under a cauldron. Then, just like the alchemist before him, he sprinkled a little powder onto some lead and changed it into silver.

"Wonderful," said P'an. "Last time was a failure but this time will be a success." He managed to put together a thousand taels of silver and turned them over to the man. The alchemist meanwhile called in several of his own friends to act as assistants. P'an, seeing how easily the lead turned to silver, was not the least suspicious. That night, however, the lid was lifted; the next day [the alchemist and his friends] were nowhere to be found.

After such consecutive losses, P'an found himself in financial straits. Angry and ashamed, he said to himself, "How much time and energy I've spent on this business! The first time the loss was my own mistake. Who was to know that this time, when I thought I was at last about to succeed, I would turn out to be the victim of a fraud? Where can I track those scoundrels down? No doubt they're off somewhere playing their tricks on another hapless soul. Maybe I'll run into them. Even if I don't, there's always the chance I'll meet a real alchemist and acquire some of the transmuting powder. One never knows!" With that, he gathered together a few belongings and set off on his journey.

One day, in a crowd of people near the Heaven Gate of Soochow, he came across them. He was about to begin shouting at them, but they were unalarmed and smiled at him, just as if he were an old friend. They came up and invited him to a restaurant for a meal. Apologizing profusely, they said, "We realize we repaid you poorly for your generosity. We felt badly about it, but that's just the way we are. Please don't think badly of us. There's a way we can repay you and settle everything."

"What way?" asked P'an.

"Since we spent all your money soon after taking it, we can't give that back. But there is a rich man in Shantung who wants us to transmute some metals for him. Everything has been agreed upon and we are only waiting for our master to come and accompany us. Now he has a long way to travel and won't arrive here for quite a while. So if you'd be willing to pose as our master, when the rich man gives us the silver we can reimburse you for your losses. It's just as easy as that. However, if you don't do it, there's no other way we can repay you. What do you say?"

"What kind of person is your master?"

"He's a monk. Please shave your hair, and we'll treat you accordingly as our master. Then we'll go straight to that place."

Since P'an was anxious to get his money back, he cut his hair and went off with them. They treated him with great courtesy all the way to Shantung, where they arrived at the home of the rich man. They introduced P'an as their master. The rich man invited him into the main hall and began to converse about the alchemic arts. P'an, with all his knowledge of alchemy and his wide learning in general, was able to impress the man, and by evening the man willingly turned over two thousand taels of silver. They agreed to begin the smelting on the next morning. The rich man then treated his guests to a feast at which they all got thoroughly drunk and were carried into the study to sleep.

The next morning they began preparations for the smelting, and P'an, who knew a little about the routine, now and then pretended to give instructions. When the silver was placed in the cauldron, the gang members, playing the part of dutiful disciples, sat down to keep watch over it. The rich man was interested in learning the lore of alchemy from P'an and monopolized his time with drinking and chatting, so that P'an was unable to get away. His accomplices, however, took the first opportunity to lift the lid, and ran away leaving their master behind.

The rich man had not been suspicious at first, but the next morning when he saw that the others had left, he seized P'an and was about to take him to the authorities in order to have the others apprehended. P'an broke down in tears and said, "My name is P'an and I'm from Sung-chiang. I'm not really a member of that gang. Because of my devotion to alchemy, I was cheated by them. Lately I ran into them on the road. They said they were coming here to transmute metals and that I could recover my losses if I came along. They cut my hair and had me pretend to be their master. I only wanted to get my money back. How was I to know that they would swindle you and leave me stranded here as well?" He finished and wept bitterly.

On questioning him, the rich man discovered that P'an was indeed telling the truth. He was, as he said, from a prominent family in Sung-chiang. In fact their two families had had dealings with one another some years before. Seeing that P'an had been so badly deceived, the man did not have the heart to turn him in and released him. P'an was left penniless on his journey back to Sung-chiang. So, relying on his shaven head and his monk's robe, he posed as a mendicant and begged his way home.

He passed through Lin-ch'ing, and there, near the wharf, was a boat. In the window he saw the face of a beautiful woman peering from behind the curtains, gazing out at the street. She seemed familiar, and upon looking more carefully, P'an recognized her as the alchemist's concubine with whom he had had the love affair. "What's she doing on that boat?" he wondered. He went to the boat, inquired of one of the men there, and learned that a certain scholar from Honan, accompanied by a well-known courtesan, was on his way to the capital to take the examinations. "Can it be that the alchemist sold her?" thought P'an. "Or is it just that this woman looks like her?"

He kept walking up and down by the side of the boat, watching [the window] all the time. Suddenly someone came out of the boat's cabin and said, "Our mistress would like to ask if you are from Sung-chiang."

"Yes, I am."

"Would your name be P'an?"

P'an was startled and asked, "How did she know that?"

At that point a voice called out from inside, "Ask him to come alongside the boat."

P'an went up as told. "Yes," said the voice inside, "I'm indeed the woman who came to your home with the alchemist. I am actually a courtesan from Honan. When I was at your place, I had been hired by the alchemist to act as his accomplice in cheating you. But I truly feel sorry for what I did to you. How do you happen to be here anyway?"

P'an poured out his sorrow, told her how he had repeatedly been duped and why he was now returning from Shantung.

"I feel obligated, if only for some sentimental reason, to offer you something to help you complete your journey," the voice inside said. "Take it, go straight home, and from now on, whenever you meet one of those so-called alchemists, don't put any faith in them whatsoever. I have lived among them, so I know very well that they are all frauds. If you heed my words, I will feel that I have repaid you for the few nights of affection you showed me." She finished speaking and had a servant present P'an with a packet containing three taels of cash.

P'an, in no position to refuse, expressed his profound gratitude. Only then had P'an finally come to understand that his deception by the alchemist had been assisted by "the wiles of beauty." And it was thanks to this same courtesan that he was able to return home. For the rest of his days he remembered her words and never again sought riches through alchemy. But his arriving home with a shaven head and the story of his folly gave his friends a hearty laugh at his expense.

So let this be a lesson to those who are also fond of alchemy.

In performing alchemy, one must first abjure lust,
For alchemy and worldly desire are as separate as water and
fire.
Hoping to obtain alchemy with a sinful heart
Is like longing for the swan's meat while dwelling in a sewer.

BIOBIBLIOGRAPHICAL NOTES

Since the source of each selection is given immediately after the translated title, the following biobibliographical checklist is arranged alphabetically for easy reference. As most traditional Chinese fiction writers are minor figures in history, almost all the available biographical information about them remains sketchy and at times controversial. For this reason, only the most essential facts about their lives are given here. With regard to textual data, our list serves no other purpose than to help the reader to locate the best of available texts. The reference works from which the notes are taken are also omitted, as a complete documentation of these materials would make this section unduly lengthy. A number of basic references, however, are listed in the "Suggested Reading."

Chüan 卷 is a rather ambiguous unit of book-division. It could be a chapter, a volume, or a section. For this reason, we have preferred to use the romanized form.

The five forms of traditional Chinese story, *pi-chi* 筆記, *ch'uan-ch'i* 傳奇, *pien-wen* 變文, *hua-pen* 話本, and *kung-an* 公案, are described in the Explanations at the beginning of the book.

Ch'i-yen lu 啓顏錄 (Records of Jokes), ten *chüan*, was originally written by Hou Po 侯白 (fl. 606), a scholar known for his quick wit and humor. Although Hou held a number of minor posts, he is better remembered as a court jester in the early Sui period.

Ch'i-yen lu has long been lost, but a number of passages survive in several sources. The most complete collection of these fragments can be found in Wang Li-ch'i 王利器, ed., *Li-tai hsiao-hua chi* 歷代笑話集 (Jokes from the Various Dynasties) (Shanghai: Ku-tien wen-hsüeh ch'u-pan she 古典文學出版社, 1956), pp. 9–43. In passing, it must be noted that some portions of the *Ch'i-yen lu* are about the events of the T'ang period, presumably added anonymously by Hou's admirers. The translation of the selection "Hou Po" (originally untitled) is based on the text in *T'ai-p'ing kuang-chi* (q.v.) 248.

Chien-teng hsin-hua 剪燈新話 (New Tales Written While Cutting the Wick) represents the revived interest in *ch'uan-ch'i* in early Ming after a decline of this type of story in Sung and Yüan times. Its author, Ch'ü Yu 瞿佑 (1341–1427), was an accomplished poet as well as a parallel-prose stylist who spent most of his life as a schoolteacher. Ch'ü was a productive writer, but most of his works have not survived.

According to the information given in the authorial preface (dated 1378), this story collection should have been larger than it is. The extant version containing twenty-two stories in four *chüan* represents apparently only a small portion of the original work. As is typical of earlier *ch'uan-ch'i* stories, most of the pieces are on recent or contemporary events.

The popularity of the *Chien-teng hsin-hua* can be attested to by the two imitation sequences prepared by other Ming writers: *Chien-teng yü-hua* 剪燈餘話 (More Tales Written While Cutting the Wick) by Li Ch'ang-chen 李昌祺 (1376–1452), completed ca. 1420, with twenty-two stories in five *chüan*, and *Mi-teng yin-hua* 覓燈因話 (Tales Written While Searching for a Lamp) by Shao Ching-chan 邵景詹, published in 1592, with eight stories in two *chüan*. Many stories in these three collections were used as sources by later *hua-pen* writers, notably Ling Meng-ch'u 凌濛初. In Japan, the popularity of these three collections, particularly the *Chien-teng hsin-hua*, can be seen in the writings of Asai Ryōi 淺井了意 (1612–1691). Many stories in his *Togibōko* 伽婢子 (1666) are clear imitations of *Chien-teng hsin-hua*.

The best edition of these three titles is the combined volume collated by Chou Yi 周夷, *Chien-teng hsin-hua (wai erh-chung)* 剪燈新話（外二種）(New Tales Written While Cutting the Wick [Plus Two Other Works]) (Shanghai: Ku-tien wen-hsüeh ch'u-pan she 古典文學出版社, 1957). Our selection, "The Golden Phoenix Hairpin" 金鳳釵記, is in *chüan* 2 (Chou's edition, pp. 26–30).

Ching-shih t'ung-yen 警世通言 (Comprehensive Words to Admonish the World), published in 1624, is the second collection in Feng Meng-lung's 馮夢龍 (1574–1646) *San-yen* 三言 (The Three Words) series. As with the two other collections in the same series (*Hsing-shih heng-yen* and *Ku-chin hsiao-shuo*, q.v.) *Ching-shih t'ung-yen* comprises forty *hua-pen* stories composed at different times and by different hands. The earliest pieces date back to Sung times, while a number of the later ones were written by Feng Meng-lung and his associates. The themes and contexts of these stories are equally diversified. Many early *hua-pen* stories are preserved thanks to the publication of the *San-yen* series.

Feng Meng-lung, a minor late Ming official, was indisputedly the most knowledgeable connoisseur of Chinese popular literature and its most dedicated champion. Besides the *San-yen* collections, he edited and wrote a number of historical novels; collected and edited folksongs, *pi-chi* tales, and plays; and published other works of a less unorthodox nature for a Confucian scholar. He had a large private collection of popular literature from which the *San-yen* volumes originated.

The appearance of the *San-yen* series, along with the *Erh-p'o* 二拍 collections (*P'o-an ching-ch'i* and *Erh-k'o P'o-an ching-ch'i*, q.v.) of Ling Meng-ch'u is responsible for bringing the vogue of *hua-pen* literature to its height toward the end of the Ming period. Scores of similar works were published following the success of the *San-yen* stories. What makes Feng's anthologies unique and valuable, however, is not only their higher literary merit, but also their inclusion of both old and new stories. All subsequent *hua-pen* collections are the works of individual authors. Since the *San-yen* stories represent the best of the *hua-pen* tradition, the Editors feel justified in making more selections from this series.

Two editions are recommended for the *Ching-shih t'ung-yen*, one for good printing, helpful notes, and easy availability, the other for textual completeness. The 1956 modern edition published by Tso-chia ch'u-pan she 作家出版社 of Peking in one volume (and subsequent Hong Kong reprints), with notes prepared by Yen Tun-yi 嚴敦易, is accurate enough for general use. But it is an expurgated version with a number of erotic passages bowdlerized. For those who do not like to have the stories tampered with willfully by modern editors, the two-volume photographic edition of the 1624 text published by Shih-

chieh shu-chü 世界書局 of Taipei in 1958 is the answer. Our selections are based on this earliest known edition. The textual purist, however, has to be warned that this and the two other *San-yen* titles photographically reproduced by Shih-chieh shu-chü in the late fifties are mere photostatic reprints of uncollated texts and that none of these Ming editions are free from typographical errors.

This present anthology includes seven stories from the *Ching-shih t'ung-yen*: "Artisan Ts'ui and His Ghost Wife" 崔待詔生死冤家 (no. 8); "Loach Fan's Double Mirror" 范鰍兒雙鏡重圓 (12); "A Mangy Taoist Exorcises Ghosts" 一窟鬼癩道人除怪 (14); "The Sung Founder Escorts Ching-niang One Thousand *Li*" 趙太祖千里送京娘 (21); "Eternal Prisoner under the Thunder Peak Pagoda" 白娘子永鎮雷峯塔 (28); "Tu Shih-niang Sinks the Jewel Box in Anger" 杜十娘怒沉百寶箱 (32); "The Case of the Dead Infant" 況太守斷死孩兒 (35).

Ch'ing-so kao-i 青瑣高議 (Remarkable Opinions under the Green Latticed Window), twenty *chüan* (plus seven *chüan* in the sequel) in the version prepared by Tung K'ang 董康 (1867–1947), is a miscellany compiled by Liu Fu 劉斧 (ca. 1040–after 1113) of the Northern Sung period. Although we know next to nothing about Liu Fu, it seems certain that most of the materials included in this work were taken from previous sources. Some sections of this work are devoted to collecting the *ch'uan-ch'i* stories written by Sung writers. About a dozen of the *ch'uan-ch'i* included therein bear the names of the original authors. Ch'in Ch'un 秦醇 (fl. ca. 1086) is one of these identified authors; he is credited with four pieces, including our selection, "Empress Chao Fei-yen" 趙飛燕別傳 (*chüan* 7). No biographical data on Ch'in are available.

The recommended edition of this work is the modern punctuated text published by Chung-hua shu-chü 中華書局 (Peking) in 1959, based on Tung K'ang's version.

Erh-k'o P'o-an ching-ch'i 二刻拍案驚奇 (The Second Collection of Striking the Table in Amazement at the Wonders), published in 1632, is the second story collection put out by Ling Meng-ch'u 凌濛初 (1580–1644). Collectively, this work and *P'o-an ching-ch'i* (q.v.) are known as the *Erh-p'o* 二拍 (The Two Strikes). After the fashion of the *San-yen* (see *Ching-shih t'ung-yen*), each of these collections had forty *hua-pen* stories. However, even the most complete extant edition of the *Erh-k'o P'o-an ching-ch'i* has only thirty-nine stories, with the last piece replaced by a play. Unlike Feng Meng-lung's *San-yen* collections, all the stories in the *Erh-p'o* were written by Ling Meng-ch'u himself, making good use of the materials in previous *pi-chi* collections. The model set by Ling Meng-ch'u, in turn, stimulated the production of many similar works before the end of the Ming period.

Ling Meng-ch'u was a local official as well known for his knowledge in other areas as for his story writing. He was a renowned playwright as well as one of the best late Ming publishers, specializing in multicolor printing. Works printed by Ling Meng-ch'u are generally considered rare books today.

Since many of the stories written by Ling Meng-ch'u are rather erotic (a special feature of late Ming literature), most of the modern editions are heavily expurgated. For the *Erh-k'o P'o-an ching-ch'i*, two editions are recommended: one is the thirty-eight-story edition prepared and adequately annotated by Wang Ku-lu 王古魯 and published by Ku-tien wen-hsüeh ch'u-pan she 古典文學出版社 (Shanghai) in 1957; the other is the thirty-nine-story edition prepared by Li Tien-yi 李田意 (in which Ling's marginal notes are retained) and published by Cheng-chung shu-chü 正中書局 (Taipei) in 1960. Two stories are selected from this collection: "A Taste of Immortality" 仙境無緣 (preamble of no. 18; the title is supplied by the Editors), and "The Sham Commander Reclaims His Beauty" 僞漢裔奪姜山中／假將軍還珠江上 (27).

Hsin ch'ing-nien 新青年 (The New Youth, 1915–1926) is one of the most influential periodicals of the May Fourth Movement (1919) era. Edited by Ch'en Tu-hsiu 陳獨秀 (1879–1942), one of the founders of the Chinese Communist Party, this periodical served as a channel for the *avant garde* in political thought, in literature, and in other cultural activities. Su Man-shu's 蘇曼殊 (1884–1918) story "The Broken Hairpin" 斷簪記 was first published in *Hsin ch'ing-nien*, 2:3 (Nov. 1916), 1–9, and 2:4 (Dec. 1916), 1–7. Ch'en Tu-hsiu and Su Man-shu had been intimate friends since their school days in Japan in the early 1900s.

Su Man-shu's original name was Chien 戩; later he changed it to Hsüan-ying 玄瑛. Man-shu is his Buddhist name, by which he is known to posterity. At once a poet, a scholar, a story writer, an essayist, a translator, a romantic, a Buddhist monk, a patriot, and a friend of many important literary and political figures, Su Man-shu was something of a legendary figure, appearing in the last phase of traditional China. His Sino-Japanese parentage, eccentric be-

havior, and familarity with several foreign languages have all helped to accentuate the mystery of an already mysterious character. His fictional writings in classical Chinese are, of course, excessively sentimental and puerile by modern standards. He is represented here chiefly for his historical role: one of the last of China's traditional writers commanding a traditional style in celebration of a traditional sentiment—the Chinese respect for one's elders even at the cost of one's happiness.

Hsing-shih heng-yen 醒世恆言 (Lasting Words to Awaken the World), published in 1627, is the last collection in Feng Meng-lung's *San-yen* series (the other two collections are *Ku-chin hsiao-shuo* and *Ching-shih t'ung-yen*, q.v.) In a number of respects this work is rather different from the two previous collections. Since Feng Meng-lung apparently did not have an overall plan when he started publishing this series (see the discussion in the *Ku-chin hsiao-shuo* entry), the distribution of the earlier *hua-pen* stories in the three works is rather uneven. The result is that *Hsing-shih heng-yen* contains primarily Ming compositions. As revealed by the recent research of Patrick Hanan, even Feng's own writings, which figured prominently in the two earlier collections, are no longer as significant in his last volume. Feng has included *en masse* at least twenty-two stories by Hsi Lang-hsien 席浪仙, the author of *Shih-tien t'ou* 石點頭 (The Nodding Stone), presumably for the sake of keeping the uniform format of forty stories for each volume. This at least explains in part why Feng Meng-lung did not publish a fourth collection. As the average Ming *hua-pen* is longer than its predecessors, the *Hsing-shih heng-yen* is about one-third thicker than the two earlier collections.

For general use, the modern annotated edition by Ku Hsüeh-chieh 顧學頡 published by Tso-chia ch'u-pan she 作家出版社 in 1956 is adequate enough. The censored passages can be retrieved from the 1959 Shih-chieh shu-chü 世界書局 (Taipei) photographic reprint.

This anthology includes five stories from the *Hsing-shih heng-yen*: "The Oil Peddler Courts the Courtesan" 賣油郎獨占花魁 (no. 3); "The Couple Bound in Life and Death" 陳多壽生死夫妻 (9); "The Boot That Reveals the Culprit" 勘皮靴單證二郎神 (13); "The Jest That Leads to Disaster" 十五貫戲言成巧禍 (33); "Old Servant Hsü" 徐老僕義憤成家 (35).

Hsü Hsüan-kuai lu 續玄怪錄 (More Accounts of Mysteries and the Supernatural), by Li Fu-yen 李復言 (fl. 830); the extant versions are believed to be only a portion of the original work, since a number of the stories cited in the *T'ai-p'ing kuang-chi* (q.v.) cannot be found in these editions. As late as the early Sung, *Hsü Hsüan-kuai lu* was available in both a five-*chüan* version and a ten-*chüan* version. No biographical information on Li Fu-yen is known except that he was a junior contemporary of Niu Seng-ju and that his work was inspired by Niu's example (see the next entry).

The selection "Tu Tzu-ch'un" 杜子春 can be found in *T'ai-p'ing kuang-chi* 16; the recommended text is the one in Wang Kuo-yüan 汪國垣, *T'ang-jen hsiao-shuo* 唐人小説 (T'ang Tales) (Hong Kong: Chung-hua shu-chü 中華書局, 1958), pp. 230–33 (originally published in Shanghai in 1936).

Hsüan-kuai lu 玄怪錄 (Accounts of Mysteries and the Supernatural), ten *chüan*, by Niu Seng-ju 牛僧孺 (778–847), no longer survives. Thirty-three of its stories are preserved in *T'ai-p'ing kuang-chi* (q.v.). It is generally believed that it was the *Hsüan-kuai lu* that generated the interest in and the popularity of supernatural tales in the T'ang period.

Niu Seng-ju, a courageous and upright T'ang official (he held the post of prime minister from 823 to 824), is best remembered in history for his part in the rivalry between his faction and that of another major political figure, Li Te-yü 李德裕 (787–849). This strife, with its endless rounds of incriminations and counter-incriminations involving several generations for well over forty years, hastened the collapse of the once prosperous T'ang Dynasty.

The story selected for this anthology, "Scholar Ts'ui" 崔書生, can be found in *T'ai-p'ing kuang-chi* 63; the translation is based on the collated version in Wang Kuo-yüan 汪國垣, *T'ang-jen hsiao-shuo* 唐人小説 (T'ang Tales) (Hong Kong: Chung-hua shu-chü 中華書局, 1958), pp. 196–97.

Hsüan-shih chih 宣室志 (Records of a Palace Chamber), ten *chüan* (plus one *chüan* of appendix), was written by Chang Tu 張讀 (?–ca. 853). Like the *Hsüan-kuai lu* by his maternal grandfather Niu Seng-ju, Chang Tu's work is a story collection primarily on the supernatural. His great-great-grandfather was the well-known literary figure Chang Tsu 張鷟 (657–730) who wrote the famous *ch'uan-ch'i* story, "A Visit to the Fairy Lodge" 遊仙窟. Chang Tu's intellectual precocity is evidenced by his passing the *chin-shih* examination at the age of nineteen. He once held the post of assistant in the Department of State Affairs during the reign of Emperor Wen-tsung 文宗 (r. 827–840).

The selected story, "In Search of a Heart" 求心錄 (a title made up by a later editor) is in *chüan* 8. The recommended edition is *Pi-chi hsiao-shuo ta-kuan* 筆記小説大觀 (Collected *Pi-chi* Fiction), Series I (Taipei: Hsin-hsing shu-chü 新興書局, 1960).

I-wen chi 異聞集 (A Collection of Strange Events), ten *chüan*, is a collection of T'ang *ch'uan-ch'i* stories compiled by Ch'en Han 陳翰 (fl. 874). This work has long been lost, but the strange worlds created in the extant stories continue to fascinate us and they are frequently cited as representing the best of T'ang *ch'uan-ch'i* tradition. Many of these stories are preserved in the *T'ai-p'ing kuang-chi* (q.v.).

On the basis of *T'ai-p'ing kuang-chi*, Tseng Ts'ao's 曾慥 (?–after 1163) *Lei-shuo* 類説 (Fictional Works in Classification) and other sources, Wang Meng-ou 王夢鷗 has recently put together an annotated collated anthology of forty-one stories from the *I-wen chi*; see his *T'ang-jen hsiao-shuo yen-chiu, erh-chi* 唐人小説研究、二集 (Studies of T'ang Stories, Second Volume) (Taipei: Yi-wen yin-shu kuan 藝文印書館, 1973). Five of our selections originate from the *I-wen chi*. All of them can be found in the *T'ai-p'ing kuang-chi*, but the titles in the *I-wen chi* are usually different. In the following list, the titles of these five stories are given as they appear in the *I-wen chi*, with the *T'ai-p'ing kuang-chi* titles added in parentheses wherever they differ:

Shen Chi-chi 沈既濟 (ca. 741–ca. 805), "Miss Jen" 任氏傳 (任氏) (Wang Meng-ou, pp. 186–92), *T'ai-p'ing kuang-chi* 452.

Shen Chi-chi, "The World Inside a Pillow" 枕中記 (呂翁) (Wang Meng-ou, pp. 196–200), *T'ai-p'ing kuang-chi* 82.

Li Ch'ao-wei 李朝威 (n.d.), "The Legendary Marriage at Tung-t'ing" 洞庭靈姻(柳毅) (Wang Meng-ou, pp. 169–79), *T'ai-p'ing kuang-chi* 419.

Po Hsing-chien 白行簡 (776–826), "The Courtesan Li Wa" 汧國夫人傳 (李娃傳) (Wang Meng-ou, pp. 238–46), *T'ai-p'ing kuang-chi* 484.

Yüan Chen 元稹 (775–831), "The Story of Ying-ying" 鶯鶯傳 (Wang Meng-ou, pp. 255–62), *T'ai-p'ing kuang-chi* 488.

I-wen chi is cited as the source in the *T'ai-p'ing kuang-chi* versions of "The World Inside a Pillow," "The Legendary Marriage at Tung-t'ing," and "The Courtesan Li Wa"; no source is mentioned in the *T'ai-p'ing kuang-chi* for the two other stories. The translations in this anthology are based on the collated texts of Wang Meng-ou and those in Wang Kuo-yüan's 汪國垣 *T'ang-jen hsiao-shuo* 唐人小説 (T'ang Tales) (Hong Kong: Chung-hua shu-chü 中華書局,

1958), in that order of preference. For "The World Inside a Pillow," however, we have used Wang Kuo-yüan's edition, which in turn is based on the text in the *Wen-yüan ying-hua* (q.v.).

Ku-chin hsiao-shuo 古今小説 (Stories Old and New), published in 1620 or 1621, is the first collection in the *San-yen* series. In the editor's preface, Feng Meng-lung (using Lü-t'ien kuan chu-jen 綠天館主人 as a pseudonym) explained that the publication of these forty stories culled from his large private library was prompted by his friends. As the general nature of the title suggests, it seems certain that Feng had no definite plans to publish subsequent volumes. The immense success of the *Ku-chin hsiao-shuo*, however, gave him enough incentive to put out *Ching-shih t'ung-yen* (q.v.) and finally *Hsing-shih heng-yen* (q.v.). By then the title *Ku-chin hsiao-shuo* seemed to be inharmonious, so it was replaced in later editions by the title *Yü-shih ming-yen* 喻世明言 (Illustrious Words to Instruct the World). Since all these three titles contain the character *yen* (words), these anthologies are collectively known as the *San-yen* (The Three Words). Though *Ku-chin hsiao-shuo* and *Yü-shih ming-yen* have been used interchangeably by scholars, the former is used in this anthology, as our selections are based on the earliest known edition.

The one-volume edition edited and annotated by Hsü Cheng-yang 許政揚 and published by Jen-min wen-hsüeh ch'u-pan she 人民文學出版社 of Peking in 1958 is recommended for its general accuracy and copious notes. Again, the two-volume photographic edition published by Shih-chieh shu-chü 世界書局 of Taipei in 1958 remains the only uncensored edition, even though typographical errors are not corrected and no notes are provided.

Five stories are selected from the *Ku-chin hsiao-shuo* for this anthology: "The Pearl Shirt Reencountered" 蔣興哥重會珍珠衫 (no. 1); "Han Wu-niang Sells Her Charms at the New Bridge Market" 新橋市韓五賣春情 (3); "Wu Pao-an Ransoms His Friend" 吳保安棄家贖友 (8); "Magistrate T'eng and the Case of Inheritance" 滕大尹鬼斷家私 (10); "Sung the Fourth Raises Hell with Tightwad Chang" 宋四公大鬧禁魂張 (36).

Li-weng i-chia yen 笠翁一家言 (Li-weng's Own School of Thought), ten *chüan*, is a miscellany of the early Ch'ing literary figure Li Yü 李漁 (1611 – after 1680). Besides being a noted playwright-producer and the author of two fairly erotic story collections— *Shih-erh lou* 十二樓 (The Twelve Towers) and *Wu-sheng hsi* 無聲戲 (Plays Without Sounds)—Li Yü is best remembered as China's foremost drama critic.

Recently the German sinologist Helmut Martin 馬漢茂 put together most of Li Yü's extant works, some of which only survive in one or two copies, and published the fifteen-volume *Li Yü ch'üan-chi* 李漁全集 (The Complete Works of Li Yü) (Taipei: Ch'eng-wen ch'u-pan she 成文出版社, 1970). This is naturally the text we recommend. Volumes I–IV are the *Li-weng i-chia yen*; our selection, "The Strong Kid of the Ch'in-huai Region" 秦淮健兒傳, is in *chüan* 2 (I, 242–50).

Liang-hsi man-chih 梁溪漫志 (Casual Remarks at the Liang Stream), ten *chüan*, is a miscellany by Mi Kun 費袞 (*chin-shih* 1205) of the Southern Sung period. The contents of this work are truly miscellaneous and the quality of the various parts differs accordingly. But some sections are so high in documentary value that the Sung government historians used them as source material for the compilation of the official history for the period of the first three Southern Sung emperors (1127–1194). However, nothing substantial is known of Mi Kun himself.

"The Wit of the Master Thief" 俚語盜智, the story included in this anthology, is in *chüan* 10. The recommended edition is the one in the *Chih-pu-tsu chai ts'ung-shu* 知不足齋叢書 (Works Published by the Never-Learning-Enough Studio) (Ch'ing period).

Liao-chai chih-i 聊齋志異 (Tales of the Unusual from the Leisure Studio) by P'u Sung-ling 蒲松齡 (1640–1715) is unquestionably the most important collection of stories ever written by a single author in the classical language, in terms of quality, influence, and sheer size. Written soon after the golden age of *hua-pen* literature, it succeeded not only in achieving an immense popularity but also in weeding the vernacular stories out of the literary scene for good. Except for the circulation of the *Chin-ku ch'i-kuan* 今古奇觀 (The Wonders of the Present and the Past), an anthology based entirely on the *San-yen* (*Ku-chin hsiao-shuo, Ching-shih t'ung-yen,* and *Hsing-shih heng-yen,* q.v.) and the *Erh-p'o* (*P'o-an Ching-ch'i* and *Erh-k'o P'o-an ching-ch'i,* q.v.), the production and publication of *hua-pen* stories virtually came to an end after the appearance of the *Liao-chai chih-i*, which represents a good combination of both *ch'uan-ch'i* and *pi-chi* stories.

Although from the Sung through the Ming period, the use of classical language in story writing never reached heights comparable to T'ang times, it would be an underestimation of P'u Sung-ling to attribute his success to his imitation of the T'ang taste. Most of

P'u's longer stories (there are many short *pi-chi* stories in the collection) are demonstrably different from T'ang tales in that few of the common characteristics of the T'ang *ch'uan-ch'i*—such as the liberal use of poetry, the narrator as the witness of the event, the refusal to identify the major characters, the employment of fiction writing for calumnious purposes, and the denial of a happy ending to an animal-turned-beauty—are present in *Liao-chai chih-i*. In many respects, *Liao-chai chih-i* can be seen as having created a tradition of its own, such as the incorporation of minor historical facts through painstaking research, affirmation of the value of love and personal freedom beyond the extent to which most traditional story writers would like to or dare to go, and systematic but subtle criticism of the social ills and political problems of the day. This is all the more remarkable in view of P'u Sung-ling's rather limited social experience. His stories are brought to life with rich local color and contemporary events, and his fox-beauties, charming and assertive, earthly yet superhuman, are among the most beloved heroines in traditional Chinese story.

P'u Sung-ling himself was a rather obscure figure in his own time, who would have left no mark in history if he had not written the *Liao-chai chih-i*. Following the career of a local schoolteacher and living in constant poverty, he only once traveled outside his native area in western Shantung Province and had little connection with other scholars of his day. Thanks to his posthumous fame, many of his writings have been preserved for posterity. Besides *Liao-chai chih-i*, P'u is also credited by Hu Shih 胡適 (1891–1962) with the authorship of the early Ch'ing novel *Hsing-shih yin-yüan chuan* 醒世姻緣傳 (A Marriage to Awaken the World). Though widely accepted, Hu's argument is rather shaky.

The *Liao-chai chih-i* was circulated in manuscript form when P'u Sung-ling was still alive and was not published until half a century after his death. This can perhaps explain in part why so many stories were missing in the first printed versions and editions based on them. The arrangement of the table of contents in these editions is also different from the original manuscript. The tremendous work of restoration was not done until Chang Yu-ho 張友鶴 brought out his variorum edition, *Liao-chai chih-i p'ing-chu* 聊齋志異評注 (The annotated "Tales of the Unusual from the Leisure Studio") (Peking: Chung-hua shu-chü 中華書局, 1962), in three volumes, which is based on the first

half of P'u Sung-ling's own manuscript copy (discovered in 1948 and now available in photostatic reprints) and nearly all the major editions. This edition has five hundred stories in twelve *chüan* plus an appendix (about seventy stories more than the earlier editions); the stories are also arranged in an order as close to the original as possible. Chang's edition, needless to say, is the one we strongly recommend.

Six stories are selected from the *Liao-chai chih-i*. Their locations and paginations in Chang's edition are as follows: "The Taoist Priest of the Lao Mountains" 勞山道士 (*chüan* 1; I, 38–41); "Nieh Hsiao-ch'ien 聶小倩 (*chüan* 2; I, 160–68); "The Lady Knight-Errant" 俠女 (*chüan* 2; I, 210–16); "Red Jade" 紅玉 (*chüan* 2; I, 276–83); "The Monk's Magic" 僧術 (*chüan* 7; II, 968–69); "Yen-chih" 臙脂 (*chüan* 10; III, 1367–79).

Lieh-i chuan 列異傳 (Records of Marvels), three *chüan*, is attributed to Ts'ao P'i 曹丕 (187–226), the first emperor (r. 220–226) of the kingdom of Wei of the Three Kingdoms period. Ts'ao P'i, like his father Ts'ao Ts'ao 曹操 (155–220) and his younger brother Ts'ao Chih 曹植 (192–232), was a noted poet, and he had the distinction of being one of China's earliest critics, with his own formulation of literary theory. However, attribution of the *Lieh-i chuan* to him is rather questionable.

The work itself has long been lost, but the extant passages are now conveniently available in Lu Hsün 魯迅 (Chou Shu-jen 周樹人, 1881–1936), ed., *Ku hsiao-shuo kou-ch'en* 古小說鈎沉 (Fragments of Ancient Fiction) (Shanghai: Lu Hsün hsien-sheng chi-nien wei-yüan hui 魯迅先生紀念委員會, 1941), I, 133–48. The story "Scholar T'an" 談生 (a title made up in later years) selected for this anthology is in I, 144–45, of Lu Hsün's collection.

Liu-shih chia hsiao-shuo 六十家小說 (Sixty Stories) is the collective title for six story collections, ten stories each, published by the Ming scholar-official Hung Pien 洪楩 in the years 1541–1551. Unless more new discoveries are made, this is the earliest *hua-pen* collection as far as the extant texts are concerned, since the so-called Sung collection *Ching-pen t'ung-su hsiao-shuo* 京本通俗小說 (Capital Version of Popular Stories) is a forgery. Hung Pien, who saw his role only as a publisher, did not take it upon himself to make any serious editorial changes. In consequence, these stories are much closer to the stage of professional storytelling than the stories in the later collections published by Feng Meng-lung, who took much liberty to make changes in the stories he included in the *San-yen* (*Ku-chin hsiao-shuo*, *Ching-shih t'ung-yen*, and *Hsing-shih heng-yen*, q.v.).

So far only twenty-nine of the sixty stories have been discovered; we do not even know the titles of all the sixty stories. When these stories were first discovered and subsequently published in photographic editions in 1929 and 1934, the original collective title and the individual titles of the six collections were still unknown. The title used, *Ch'ing-p'ing-shan t'ang hua-pen* 清平山堂話本 (*Hua-pen* Stories Published by the Ch'ing-p'ing-shan Studio), refers to the name of Hung Pien's studio. All the later editions, including the collated edition with modern punctuation by T'an Cheng-pi 譚正璧 (Shanghai: Ku-tien wen-hsüeh ch'u-pan she 古典文學出版社, 1957), use this made-up title. Now that the true history of Hung Pien's work is known, we would like to refer to this collection by its original name, though the substitute title is still commonly used in library catalogs. T'an's collated edition is fairly reliable and easy to read. It contains twenty-seven stories; the two remaining pieces were not included because of serious textual corruption. In all the editions, the stories are not numbered. Our selection, "Yang Wen, the Road-Blocking Tiger" 楊溫攔路虎傳, is on pp. 169–86 in T'an's edition.

Lo-yang chin-shen chiu-wen chi 洛陽縉紳舊聞記 (Stories about the Officials of Lo-yang), twenty-one stories in five *chüan*, was written by Chang Ch'i-hsien 張齊賢 (943–1014), who served as prime minister from 991 to 993 during the reign of Northern Sung emperor T'ai-tsung 太宗 (r. 976–997) and also served briefly in the same capacity during the early years of Chen-tsung 眞宗 (r. 998–1022). Most of the stories in this work are set in the late T'ang and Five Dynasties periods and are supposed to be based on facts. The present anthology includes a story on Chang himself (see the first story in the preamble of "The Sham Commander Reclaims His Beauty").

"The Fake Knight-Errant" 白萬州遇劍客, the story selected from this work, is in *chüan* 3. The recommended edition is the one in the *Chih-pu-tsu chai ts'ung-shu* 知不足齋叢書 (Works Published by the Never-Learning-Enough Studio) (Ch'ing period).

Lung-t'u kung-an 龍圖公案 (The Cases of Lung-t'u) is a collection of *kung-an* stories with Lord Pao 包公, the glamorized version of the Northern Sung official Pao Cheng 包拯 (999–1062), as the titular hero. Early complete editions (Ch'ing) carry one hundred stories in varying *chüan* divisions (five, eight,

ten *chüan*). Later editions usually have a much smaller number of stories and carry more popular titles, such as *Pao-kung an* 包公案 (The Cases of Lord Pao).

Lung-t'u kung-an is the patchwork of a late Ming scissors-and-paste editor who copied verbatim most of the stories from a few earlier *kung-an* collections. The voluminous Lord Pao literature since the early Ch'ing is almost entirely derived from this collection.

No Ming editions of the *Lung-t'u kung-an* have been known, and even early Ch'ing editions are not easy to locate. One recommended edition easily available is the "T'ing-wu chai" 聽五齋 edition photographically reproduced by T'ien-yi ch'u-pan she 天一出版社 of Taipei in 1974. The two selected stories, "The Jade-Faced Cat" 玉面貓 and "Lion Cub Lane" 獅兒巷, can be found in almost all editions, although their locations in terms of *chüan* and order are not the same.

P'o-an ching-ch'i 拍案驚奇 (Striking the Table in Amazement at the Wonders), published in 1628, is the first collection of Ling Meng-ch'u's *Erh-p'o* series. All the forty stories, as in the case of the *Erh-k'o P'o-an ching-ch'i* (q.v.), were written by Ling Meng-ch'u himself.

The recommended edition is the two-volume set prepared by Li Tien-yi 李田意 and published by Yu-lien ch'u-pan she 友聯出版社 of Hong Kong in 1967. It is the only edition with all forty stories, along with the original authorial marginal and interlinear notes. It also has the distinction of being the only unexpurgated edition. There is, however another Yu-lien edition in which all the erotic passages have been bowdlerized. For those who would like to have the benefit of well-prepared notes, consult the edition prepared by Wang Ku-lu 王古魯 and published by Ku-tien wen-hsüeh ch'u-pan she 古典文學出版社 of Shanghai in 1957. This edition, besides having all the erotic passages taken out, lacks chapters 37, 39, and 40. The last four chapters are missing in all other editions.

The story selected for this anthology is "The Swindler Alchemists" 丹客半黍九還／富翁千金一笑 (18).

San-shui hsiao-tu 三水小牘 (Records [by the Fellow from] San-shui), three *chüan*, was written by the minor late T'ang official Huang-fu Mei 皇甫枚. The work, completed in 910, is based largely on contemporary events.

This work no longer survives in its original form. The most complete editions are the two-*chüan* version (plus an appendix) edited by Miao Ch'üan-sun 繆荃孫 (1844–1919) and included in his *Yün-tzu-tsai k'an ts'ung-shu* 雲自在龕叢書 (Works Published by the Spontaneous Clouds Shrine), and the punctuated edition (also in two *chüan* plus an appendix) published by Ku-tien wen-hsüeh ch'u-pan she 古典文學出版社 in 1958. The 1958 edition has a total of forty-six stories. However, as far as the two selected stories are concerned ("The Tragedy of Pu Fei-yen" 步飛烟 and "The Poetess Yü Hsüan-chi" 魚玄機箸韠綠翹致斃), the texts provided by Wang Kuo-yüan 汪國垣 in *T'ang-jen hsiao-shuo* 唐人小說 (T'ang Tales) (Hong Kong: Chung-hua shu-chü 中華書局, 1958), pp. 293–97, are the most complete (Wang only selected seven stories), especially toward the end of the Pu Fei-yen story. Although the authenticity of these extra passages has yet to be verified, we chose to use the fullest texts for our translations.

Shan-chü hsin-hua 山居新話 (New Talks at the Mountain Retreat), one *chüan*, was written by the minor Yüan scholar-official Yang Yü 楊瑀 (1285–1361). Based largely on recent and contemporary events, this work offers one of the few reliable sources for the study of Chinese life under the Mongol rule. In this anthology, this is also the only work selected to represent the Yüan period.

The selection "Nieh Yi-tao the Magistrate" 聶以道 originally did not have a title. The recommended edition is the one included in the *Chih-pu-tsu chai ts'ung-shu* 知不足齋叢書 (Works Published by the Never-Learning-Enough Studio) (Ch'ing period).

Shih-chi 史記 (The Historical Records) is the first of the long series of official histories in China (twenty-four to twenty-six dynastic histories depending on how the works are counted). Unlike most of the Official histories prepared by a group of government historians, *Shih-chi* is basically a one-man work by Ssu-ma Ch'ien 司馬遷 (145–86 B.C.?). *Shih-chi* is also the only official history which covers more than a dynasty or a historical period: it covers the first two thousand years of Chinese history all the way down to the days of Ssu-ma Ch'ien's own life. Its one hundred and thirty *chüan* of over half a million words are divided into five main sections: (1) "Basic Annals" (*Pen-chi* 本紀); (2) "Chronological Tables" (*Piao* 表); (3) "Treatises" (*Shu* 書); (4) "Hereditary Houses" (*Shih-chia* 世家); (5) "Biographies" (*Lieh-chuan* 列傳). With only slight modifications, this pattern of classification has been faithfully followed by later official historians.

Like his father, Ssu-ma Ch'ien was a court historian, and this gave him access to the imperial libraries. But he was not content with the use of archival sources. He traveled far and wide in search of materials both written and oral. But his *Shih-chi* was not only done largely in an unofficial capacity but also under extremely tragic circumstances. In arguing for the loyalty of a Han general who surrendered to the Huns, Ssu-ma Ch'ien incurred the anger of the emperor and was punished by imprisonment and castration. He was subsequently released in 96 B.C. and appointed palace secretary, a post he held until his death. *Shih-chi* was completed in ca. 91 B.C.

There are many excellent editions of *Shih-chi*, including a fairly large number of Sung editions. For practical purposes, the one we would like to recommend is the modern punctuated edition published by Chung-hua shu-chü 中華書局 of Peking in 1959. The selection included in this anthology ("The Biography of Yü Jang" 豫讓) is in *chüan* 86, being one of the "The Biographies of Political Assassins" 刺客列傳.

Shih-shuo hsin-yü 世說新語 (New Anecdotes of Social Talk), by Liu Yi-ch'ing 劉義慶 (403–444), for its size and its influence on the later development of Chinese fiction is easily the most important story collection of the Six Dynasties period. It is a collection of anecdotes about scholars, officials, and other members of the upper social strata from late Han to the close of the Eastern Chin period. Erudite and yet entertaining, in both language and style the *Shih-shuo hsin-yü* represents the *pi-chi* tradition at its best and deserves to be regarded as a landmark of Chinese fiction. Its contents cover a great variety of subjects, reflecting quite truthfully the social aspirations as well as the philosophical trends in one of the most chaotic periods of China's political history. Not only does it make a good source book for the social historian; the linguist also will benefit a great deal from its sentence patterns, especially in conversation. Furthermore, no study of humor and satire in traditional China could be complete if it did not take this work into account.

Liu Yi-ch'ing, prince of Lin-ch'uan 臨川 (in modern Kiangsu Province), was the nephew of Emperor Wu 武帝 (r. 420–422) of the (Liu) Sung Dynasty. A man of gentle character who must have seemed out of place amid the flaunted eccentricity of the time, Liu Yi-ch'ing was a literary patron as well as a famous man of letters. Besides *Shih-shuo hsin-yü*, he is credited with at least the following fictional works: *Yu-ming lu* 幽明錄 (Records of the Dead and the Living), *Hsüan-yen lu* 宣驗錄 (Records of Divine Manifestations), and *Hsiao-shuo* 小說 (Fiction).

Shih-shuo hsin-yü was originally in eight *chüan*. The annotated edition done by Liu Hsiao-piao 劉孝標, the famed Liang Dynasty commentator, was originally in ten *chüan*. The present versions, current since Sung times, is in three *chüan* subdivided into thirty-six sections.

Shih-shuo hsin-yü was perhaps originally titled simply *Shih-shuo* 世說 (Social Talk). In T'ang times, it was also known as the *Shih-shuo hsin-shu* 世說新書 (The New Book of Social Talk). In all likelihood, the extant version, at least in the order of the stories, is rather different from the original work.

The edition we have used is the one annotated by Yang Yung 楊勇 (Hong Kong: Ta-chung shu-chü 大衆書局, 1969). The two selected stories, "Hsün Chü-po Visits His Friend" 荀巨伯 and "Liu Ling" 劉伶, are in section 1 (Yang, pp. 8-9) and section 23 (p. 550), respectively.

Sou-shen chi 搜神記 (In Search of Deities) was compiled by Kan Pao 干寶 (fl. ca. 317), an official and government historian of the Chin period. Kan Pao also wrote the historical work *Chin-chi* 晉紀 (Records of Chin) in twenty *chüan* to register the events of the Chin Dynasty.

According to Kan Pao's preface to this work, *Sou-shen chi* was prepared as testimony of the power of the supernatural, in which the compiler deeply believed. But the extant work, in the opinion of Lu Hsün 魯迅 (Chou Shu-jen 周樹人, 1881–1936), may not be the one Kan Pao compiled, since it is mostly concerned with the search for immortality and it shows traces of Buddhist influence.

The present editions of the *Sou-shen chi* are divided into two major groups with corresponding differences in contents: the twenty-*chüan* editions, and the eight-*chüan* editions. The story "Han P'ing and His Wife" 韓憑夫婦 (a made-up title) selected for this anthology is in *chüan* 11 of the twenty-*chüan* version. For this version, we recommend the one contained in the collection *Hsüeh-chin t'ao-yüan* 學津討原 (Tracing the Sources of Scholarship) (Ch'ing period).

T'ai-p'ing kuang-chi 太平廣記 (Grand Gleanings Compiled during the T'ai-p'ing Reign Period); our knowledge of Chinese fiction before the Sung period in general, and the T'ang in particular, would have been more scanty if this voluminous work had not

been compiled in the early Sung, when a number of these works were still in circulation. One of three extensive compilations ordered by Emperor T'ai-tsung, *T'ai-p'ing kuang-chi* was designed to cover fictional works published before the early Sung. Under the able editorship of Li Fang 李昉 (925–996), the compilation of this work of five hundred *chüan* only took about a year and a half to complete. No fewer than five hundred sources had been consulted. Since 70 percent of these sources no longer exist today, the value of the *T'ai-p'ing kuang-chi* as a fiction anthology and a source book cannot be overexaggerated.

Li Fang also served as the chief editor of an even more ambitious government-sponsored project, the *T'ai-p'ing yü-lan* 太平御覽 (Imperially Reviewed Encyclopedia Compiled during the T'ai-p'ing Reign Period). Totaling one thousand *chüan*, this work is truly an encyclopedic storehouse of information drawing from over one thousand six hundred varied sources.

Most of the T'ang stories selected for this anthology are preserved in the *T'ai-p'ing kuang-chi*. We have listed these stories separately under their own sources as indicated in the *T'ai-p'ing kuang-chi* itself. Of the stories we have chosen from this Sung compilation, only two are without source identification: "Feng Yen" 馮燕 by Shen Ya-chih 沈亞之 (782?–831?) in *chüan* 195, and "Wu-shuang the Peerless" 無雙傳 by Hsüeh Tiao 薛調 (830–872) in *chüan* 486. "Feng Yen" is also available in *chüan* 3 of the original author's collected work, *Shen Hsia-hsien wen-chi* 沈下賢文集 (The Prose Writings of Shen Hsia-hsien [Shen Ya-chih]) (*Ssu-pu ts'ung-k'an* 四部叢刊 [The Collected Writings of the Four Basic Branches of Literature] edition, 1919); but the text therein is not as complete as the one in the *T'ai-p'ing kuang-chi*. Therefore, for both "Feng Yen" and "Wu-shuang the Peerless," the translations are based on the collated texts in Wang Kuo-yüan 汪國垣, *T'ang-jen hsiao-shuo* 唐人小說 (T'ang Tales) (Hong Kong: Chung-hua shu-chü 中華書局, 1958), pp. 165–73. The modern punctuated edition of the *T'ai-p'ing kuang-chi* published by Chung-hua shu-chü 中華書局 of Peking in 1961 is highly commendable. But the editions prepared by Wang Kuo-yüan and Wang Meng-ou (see the next entry), wherever available, have proven to be more accurate.

Tsüan-i chi 纂異記 (Bizarre Events Recorded), one *chüan*, by Li Mei 李玫 (fl. 827), has been lost perhaps since the end of Sung times. A number of stories are preserved in the *T'ai-p'ing kuang-chi* (q.v.) and some other titles, from which Wang Meng-ou has recently compiled a collated collection of twelve stories as part of his *T'ang-jen hsiao-shuo yen-chiu* 唐人小說研究 (Studies of T'ang Stories) (Taipei: Yi-wen yin-shu kuan 藝文印書館, 1971), pp. 1–70. No new discovery, however, has been made regarding the life of Li Mei. Our selection "Scholar Chang" 張生, preserved in *T'ai-p'ing kuang-chi* 282, is available in Wang Meng-ou's book, pp. 28–30.

Tsui-hsing shih 醉醒石 (The Waking Drunken Stone), comprising fifteen stories, is one of the dozens of late Ming *hua-pen* collections that appeared after the works of Feng Meng-lung (see *Ching-shih t'ung yen*) and Ling Meng-ch'u (see *Erh-k'o P'o-an ching-ch'i*). With only one exception, all the stories in this work are on events of the Ming period. As can be seen from the examples in this work, *hua-pen* literature in the late Ming had lost all its early vitality. The stories in these late Ming collections are invariably loosely constructed, didactic, and thematically repetitious. The author of the *Tsui-hsing shih* is known to us by his pen name, Tung-Lu ku k'uang-sheng 東魯古狂生, which literally means "The Old Mad Scholar from Eastern Shantung."

There is a reliable 1956 Ku-tien wen-hsüeh ch'u-pan she 古典文學出版社 edition, which has been duly pirated by Taipei's Shih-chieh shu-chü 世界書局. Our selection, "The Henpecked Judge Who Loses a Governorship" 惟內惟貨兩存私/削祿削年雙結證, is the eleventh story in this collection.

Tun-huang *pien-wen*: *Pien-wen* 變文 texts, along with other Tun-huang 敦煌 manuscripts, are scattered throughout the world. As far as *pien-wen* are concerned, the main collections are located at the Peking Library, the British Library, and the Bibliothèque Nationale. Some are in Leningrad. The most complete modern edition of *pien-wen* is the two-volume set prepared by Wang Chung-min 王重民, et al., *Tun-huang pien-wen chi* 敦煌變文集 (Peking: Jen-min wen-hsüeh ch'u-pan she 人民文學出版社, 1957); a Taiwan pirate edition is also available. This collection has seventy-eight stories and ballads, some of which are different versions of the same stories. *Pien-wen* texts recently published for the first time in Russia are not included in this collection.

The manuscript (available on microfilm) we used for the translation of "The Great Maudgalyayana Rescues His Mother from Hell" 大目乾連冥間救母變文 is in the Bibliothèque Nationale, catalog number "Pelliot 2319." *Tun-huang pien-wen chi* has three ver-

sions of this story; the longest one (II, 714–55) is actually a composite version prepared by the editors based primarily on the Stein 2614 manuscript in the British Library. Thus, strictly speaking, it cannot be counted as a *pien-wen* text. Pelliot 2319 is chosen because it is the most complete text of the story and it is probably much closer to the actual style of storytelling than the other versions. The ellipses (duly indicated in the translation) in this manuscript are supposedly the places where expansion and elaboration could have occurred. Though highly acclaimed by scholars in the field, the *Tun-huang pien-wen chi*, the reader will note by carefully comparing the translation with the text in the said edition, is not free of serious punctuation errors.

Tung-t'ien wen-chi 東田文集 (The Prose Writings of Tung-t'ien) is a work by the Ming censor Ma Chung-hsi 馬中錫 (1446–1512). The story "The Chung-shan Wolf" 中山狼 is taken from *chüan* 3. The edition in the *Chi-fu ts'ung-shu* 畿輔叢書 (The Collected Writings of the Imperial Domains, 1930), is recommended.

Wen-yüan ying-hua 文苑英華 (Fine Blossoms from the Garden of Literature), like the *T'ai-p'ing kuang-chi* (q.v.), is another government-sponsored project prepared in the early Sung period. To supplement the areas not covered by the *T'ai-p'ing kuang-chi* and the *T'ai-p'ing yü-lan*, this work is devoted to the incorporation of prose essays. In organization it is modeled after the famous collection *Wen-hsüan* 文選 (Anthology of Literature) edited by Hsiao T'ung 簫統 (501–531). It even starts where *Wen-hsüan* left off, at the end of the Liang Dynasty in mid-sixth century. This one-thousand-*chüan* collection, however, is not as expertly edited as the two previous works; it was revised almost immediately after it had been compiled. The compilation was begun initially under the experienced editorship of Li Fang, but Li was soon transferred to another duty and the work was subsequently completed by constantly changing editors.

The story "The World Inside a Pillow" 枕中記 is based on *Wen-yüan ying-hua* 833 because this version is textually much better than the *I-wen chi* (q.v.) version preserved in *T'ai-p'ing kuang-chi* 82. *Wen-yüan ying-hua* is available in many good editions; one commendable one is the photographic reprint published by Chung-hua shu-chü 中華書局 of Peking in 1966.

Yeh-yü ch'iu-teng lu 夜雨秋燈錄 (Writings Done in the Rainy Nights and under the Autumn Lamp), written in classical Chinese and in sixteen *chüan*, is one of the story collections popular in the late Ch'ing period. The style is close to that of the *Liao-chai chih-i*, but the thematic emphasis is on romantic affairs of the human world rather than on those between human beings and superhuman maidens.

Nothing is known of its author, Hsüan Ting 宣鼎. His surname suggests that he could be a Manchu. The early editions of this work carry an authorial preface dated 1895, which at least gives us an idea of his active years. His preface also identifies him as a native of Anhwei Province.

This work has altogether one hundred and thirteen stories. The selection "The Leper Girl" 麻瘋女邱麗玉, in *chüan* 3, is the nineteenth story. In the 1950s Kuang-chih shu-chü 廣智書局 of Hong Kong published a modern edition (n.d.) of this work, which is generally free of serious typographical errors.

Yen Tan-tzu 燕丹子 (Prince Tan of Yen), by an anonymous writer, has always been considered a very rare piece of fiction handed down to us from as early as the second century B.C. In view of its stylistic sophistication, it would be nothing short of a miracle if it were indeed dated from such antiquity. To dismiss this traditional dating, however, has proven difficult. Back in the 1930s, the study by the noted literary historian Lo Ken-tse 羅根澤 argued that this story could not have been written in such an early time. But his point has never been seriously taken into consideration in later histories of Chinese fiction. In this anthology, we have subscribed to the view of Kuo Wei-hsin 郭維新 who, following Lo, is of the opinion that this story was probably written in the period from 479 to 502.

Nearly all the modern editions of this story are based on the collated edition of Sun Hsing-yen 孫星衍 (1753–1818) as incorporated in his *P'ing-chin kuan ts'ung-shu* 平津館叢書 (Works Published by the P'ing-chin Studio) (Ch'ing period).

Yüeh-wei ts'ao-t'ang pi-chi 閱微草堂筆記 (Jottings from the Thatched Abode of Close Observations) is the collective title of five story collections written by the early Ch'ing scholar-official Chi Yün 紀昀 (1724–1805). The five separate works are seldom published independently. Chi Yün is largely remembered today as the chief editor of the all-inclusive government-sponsored project *Ssu-k'u ch'üan-shu* 四庫全書 (The Complete Library of the Four Basic Branches of Literature).

Living in an age when the popularity of the *Liao-chai chih-i* (q.v.) was overwhelming, Chi Yün was one of P'u Sung-ling's few strong critics. He took P'u to task for mixing the two different styles and traditions of *ch'uan-chi* and *pi-chi* in the same collection, and for giving too many detailed descriptions without identifying the sources. Chi's charge, of course, does not make much sense today by our literary standards, but the extent to which he held his purist convictions can be seen by the trouble he took in writing the *Yüeh-wei ts'ao-t'ang pi-chi*, which was modeled upon the examples of the Six Dynasties period.

The selection for this anthology, "The Shansi Merchant" 山西商, is taken from *chüan* 4 of the *Luan-yang hsiao-hsia lu* 灤陽消夏錄 (Records of Passing a Summer at Luan-yang County), which is the first collection in the *Yüeh-wei ts'ao-t'ang pi-chi*. Most of the easily available Ch'ing editions of this work are accurate.

SUGGESTED READING

This list is confined to books and articles written in English that have some bearing, either directly or indirectly, on the selections in this volume. Not all areas of traditional Chinese stories have received scholarly attention, and this unbalance is clearly reflected in the studies available. Therefore, only basic references are given here. Y. W. Ma is now preparing, with the support of the National Endowment for the Humanities, a comprehensive bibliography of modern studies in Chinese, English, Japanese, French, German, and Russian on all aspects of traditional Chinese fiction. Those who would like to seek more complete information on reference materials may consult this guide when it becomes available, hopefully in 1980.

Bauer, Wolfgang. "The Tradition of the 'Criminal Cases of Master Pao' Pao-kung-an (Lung-t'u kung-an)," Oriens, 23–24 (1974), 433–49.

Birch, Cyril. "Some Formal Characteristics of the Hua-pen Story." Bulletin of the School of Oriental and African Studies, 17:2 (1955), 346–64.

—— "Feng Meng-lung and the Ku-chin hsiao-shuo." Bulletin of the School of Oriental and African Studies, 18:1 (1956), 64–83.

Bishop, John Lyman. The Colloquial Short Story in China: A Study of the San-yen Collections. Cambridge, Mass.: Harvard University Press, 1956.

Bodde, Derk. "Some Chinese Tales of the Supernatural: Kan Pao and his Sou-shen chi." Harvard Journal of Asiatic Studies, 6 (Feb. 1942), 338–357.

Ch'en, Li-li. "Pien-wen Chantefable and Aucassin et Nicolette." Comparative Literature, 23:3 (Summer 1971), 255–61.

—— "Outer and Inner Forms of Chu-kung-tiao with Reference to Pien-wen, Tz'u and Vernacular Fiction." Harvard Journal of Asiatic Studies, 32 (1972), 124–49.

Crawford, William Bruce. " 'The Oil Vendor and the Courtesan' and the Ts'ai-tzu chia-jen Novels." In Critical Essays on Chinese Literature, edited by William H. Nienhauser, Jr. Hong Kong: The Chinese University of Hong Kong Press, 1976, pp. 31–42.

Edwards, E. D. Chinese Prose Literature of the T'ang Period, A.D. 618–906. London: A. Probsthaian, 1937–38, 2 vols.

Eoyang, Eugene. "The Immediate Audience: Oral Narration in Chinese Fiction." In Critical Essays on Chinese Literature, pp. 43–57.

Fan, Ning. "Early Vernacular Tales." Chinese Literature, 1955, no. 3 (March 1955), 86–89.

Hales, Dell R. "Dreams and the Daemonic in Traditional Chinese Short Stories." In Critical Essays on Chinese Literature, pp. 71–88.

Hanan, Patrick. "The Development of Fiction and

Drama." In *The Legacy of China,* edited by Raymond Dawson. Oxford: Clarendon Press, 1964, pp. 115–43.

——— "The Early Chinese Short Story: A Critical Theory in Outline." *Harvard Journal of Asiatic Studies,* 27 (1967), 168–207. Reprint in *Studies in Chinese Literary Genres,* edited by Cyril Birch. Berkeley and Los Angeles: University of California Press, 1974, pp. 299–338.

——— "The Authorship of Some *Ku-chin hsiao-shuo* Stories." *Harvard Journal of Asiatic Studies,* 29 (1969), 190–200.

——— *The Chinese Short Story: Studies in Dating, Authorship, and Composition.* Cambridge, Mass.: Harvard University Press, 1973.

——— "The Making of *The Pearl-Sewn Shirt* and *The Courtesan's Jewel Box.*" *Harvard Journal of Asiatic Studies,* 33 (1973), 124–53.

——— "The Nature of Ling Meng-ch'u's Fiction." In *Chinese Narrative: Critical and Theoretical Essays,* edited by Andrew H. Plaks. Princeton: Princeton University Press, 1977, pp. 85–114.

Hayden, George A. "The Legend of Judge Pao: From the Beginnings through the Yüan Drama." In *Studia Asiatica: Essays in Felicitation of the Seventy-fifth Anniversary of Professor Ch'en Shou-yi,* edited by Laurence G. Thompson. San Francisco: Chinese Marerials Center, 1975, pp. 339–55.

Hightower, James R. "Yüan Chen and 'The Story of Ying-ying.' " *Harvard Journal of Asiatic Studies,* 33 (1973), 90–123.

Hrdličková, V. "Some Questions Connected with Tun-huang pien-wen." *Archiv Orientalní,* 30:2 (1962), 211–30.

Hsia, C. T. " 'To What Fyn Lyve I Thus?'—Society and Self in the Chinese Short Story." *Kenyon Review,* 24:3 (Summer 1962), 519–41. Revised version under the title "Society and Self in the Chinese Short Story" reprinted as an appendix to C. T. Hsia, *The Classic Chinese Novel: A Critical Introduction.* New York: Columbia University Press, 1968, pp. 299–231, 372–75.

Hsu, Wen-hung. "The Evolution of the Legend of the White Snake." *Tamkang Review,* 4:1 (Apr. 1973),109–27; 4:2 (Oct. 1973), 121–56.

Hung, William. "The Last Four Lines of the Mulan Ballad." In *Studia Asiatica: Essays in Felicitation of the Seventy-fifth Anniversary of Professor Ch'en Shou-yi,* edited by Laurence G. Thompson. San Francisco: Chinese Materials Center, 1975, pp. 357–62.

Idema, W. L. "Storytelling and the Short Story in China." *T'oung Pao,* 59:1–5 (1973), 1–67. Reprint in W. L. Idema, *Chinese Vernacular Fiction: The Formative Period.* Leiden: E. J. Brill, 1974, pp. 1–67.

Knechtes, David R. "Dream Adventure Stories in Europe and T'ang China." *Tamkang Review,* 4:2 (Oct. 1973), 101–19.

Kuraishi, Takeshirō. "On the Metamorphosis of the Story of the White Snake." *Sino-Indian Studies,* 5:3–4 (May 1957), 138–46.

Lau, Joseph S. M. "The Saint as Sinner: Paradox of Love and Virtue in 'The Predestined Couple.' " *Tamkang Review,* 1:1 (Apr. 1970), 183–91.

Liu, Chün-jo. "Syllabicity and Cadence in Two Early *Hua-pen:* An Exercise in Style Study." In *Papers of the C.I.C. Far Eastern Language Institute.* Vol. IV, 1968–1970. Joseph K. Yamagiwa Memorial Issue, edited by Richard B. Mather. Ann Arbor: Panel on Far Eastern Language Institute of the Committee on Institutional Cooperation, 1973, pp. 63–101.

Liu, James J. Y. *The Chinese Knight-Errant.* Chicago: University of Chicago Press, 1967.

Liu, Wu-chi. *Su Man-shu.* New York: Twayne Publishers, 1972.

Lu Hsün (pseud. of Chou Tso-jen). *A Brief History of Chinese Fiction.* Translated by Yang Hsien-yi and Gladys Yang. Peking: Foreign Languages Press, 1954.

Ma, Y. W. "Prose Writings of Han Yü and *Ch'uan-ch'i* Literature." *Journal of Oriental Studies,* 7:2 (July 1969), 195–223.

——— "Themes and Characterization in the *Lung-t'u kung-an.*" *T'oung Pao,* 59:1–5 (1973), 179–202.

—— "The Knight-Errant in *Hua-pen* Stories." *T'oung Pao*, 61:4–5 (1975), 266–300.

—— "The Textual Tradition of Ming *Kung-an* Fiction: A Study of the *Lung-t'u kung-an.*" *Harvard Journal of Asiatic Studies*, 35 (1975), 190–220.

—— "Facts and Fantasy in T'ang Tales." In *Critical Persuasion: Essays on Chinese Literature*, edited by Joseph S. M. Lau and Leo O. Lee to be published by Indiana University Press.

Mather, Richard B. "The *Shih-shuo hsin-yü* and Its Place in Chinese Literature." In *Papers of the C.I.C. Far Eastern Language Institute*. Vol. IV, 1968–1970, pp. 39–47.

—— "Introduction." In *Shih-shuo Hsin-yü: A New Account of Tales of the World*. Minneapolis: University of Minnesota Press, 1976, pp. xiii–xxx.

Nienhauser, William H., Jr. "A Structural Reading of the *Chuan* in the *Wen-yüan ying-hua.*" *Journal of Asian Studies*, 36:3 (May 1977), 443–56.

Průšek, Jaroslav. "Researches into the Beginnings of the Chinese Popular Novels." *Archiv Orientalní*, 11:1 (June 1939), 91–132; 23 (1955), 620–62. Reprint in Jaroslav Průšek, *Chinese History and Literature: Collection of Studies*. Dordrecht, Holland: D. Reidel Publishing Company, 1970, pp. 228–302, 561–67.

—— "The Creative Methods of Chinese Mediaeval Storyteller." In *Charisteria Orientalia praecipque ad Persiam pertinentia*, edited by Felix Tauser. Praha: Nakladatelství Československé akademie věd, 1956, pp. 253–73. Reprint in *Chinese History and Literature*, pp. 366–84, 572.

—— "*Liao-chai chih-i* by P'u Sung-ling: An Inquiry into the Circumstances under which the Collection Arose." In *Studia Serica, Bernhard Karlgren Dedicata*, edited by Egerod Søren. Copenhagen: Munksgaard, 1959, pp. 128–46. Reprint in *Chinese History and Literature*, pp. 92–108, 550.

—— "The Realistic and Lyric Elements in the Chinese Mediaeval Story." *Archiv Orientalni*, 32:1 (1964), 4–15. Reprint in *Chinese History and Literature*, pp. 385–95, 572.

—— *The Origins and the Authors of the Hua-pen*. Prague: Publishing House of the Czechoslovak Academy of Sciences, 1967.

—— "The Beginnings of the Popular Chinese Literature Urban Centres: The Cradle of Popular Fiction." *Archiv Orientalní*, 36 (1968), 67–121. Reprint in *Chinese History and Literature*, pp. 396–448, 573–75, and under a slightly different title in *Studies in Chinese Literary Genres*, pp. 259–98.

—— "Boccacio and his Chinese Contemporaries." *New Orient*, 1968, no. 2 (Apr. 1968), 45–48; 1968, no. 3 (June 1968), 65–68. Reprint in *Chinese History and Literature*, pp. 449–66, 576.

Schurmann, H. F. "On Social Themes in Sung Tales." *Harvard Journal of Asiatic Studies*, 20:1–2 (June 1957), 239–61.

Tschen, Yinkoh (Ch'en Yin-k'o). "Han Yü and the T'ang Novel." Translated by James R. Ware. *Harvard Journal of Asiatic Studies*, 1 (1936), 39–43.

Wivell, Charles J. "The Chinese Oral and Pseudo-Oral Narrative Traditions." *Transactions of the International Conference of Orientalists in Japan*, 16 (1971), 53–65.

—— "The Term 'Hua-pen.'" In *Transition and Permanence: Chinese History and Culture—A Festschrift in Honor of Dr. Hsiao Kung-ch'üan*, edited by David Buxbaum and Frederick W. Mote. Hong Kong: Cathay Press, 1972, pp. 295–306.

Yang, Wei-chen. "About *Shih-shuo hsin-yü.*" *Journal of Oriental Studies*, 2:2 (July 1955), 309–15.

Yen, Yüan-shu. "Biography of the White Serpent: A Keatsian Interpretation." *Tamking Review*, 1:2 (Oct. 1970), 227–43.

Yoshikawa, Kojiro. "The *Shih-shuo hsin-yü* and Six Dynasties Prose Style." Translated by Glen W. Baxter. *Harvard Journal of Asiatic Studies*, 18:1–2 (June 1956), 124–41. Reprint in *Studies in Chinese Literature*, edited by John L. Bishop. Cambridge, Mass.: Harvard University Press, 1965, pp. 166–41.

NOTES ON THE EDITORS

Y. W. Ma did graduate work at Yale University (Ph.D., 1971) after receiving his B.A. (First Class Honors) in Chinese literature and history from the University of Hong Kong in 1965. In 1970 he joined the faculty of the University of Hawaii, where he is at present Professor of Chinese Literature. He was Visiting Assistant Professor at Stanford University in 1976 and a recipient of two National Endowment for the Humanities grants in 1976-1979 for the preparation of a comprehensive annotated bibliography of modern studies of traditional Chinese fiction. In the spring term of 1977, he taught a course in comparative fiction at the National Taiwan University. Since he published his first learned article in the *Continent Magazine* during his freshman year, his writings have appeared in such journals as *Harvard Journal of Asiatic Studies, The Journal of Asian Studies, Tsing Hua Journal of Chinese Studies, Bibliography Quarterly, Modern Language Journal, T'oung Pao*, and several memorial volumes. Professor Ma's broad interests are reflected in the diversity of his publications, which range from Confucius as a literary critic to the development of the late Ch'ing navy, from historical geography to Nestorian Christianity. In recent years, however, his main interest has been concentrated on the study of traditional Chinese fiction. He has published widely in America, Europe, Hong Kong, Taiwan and the People's Republic of China.

Joseph S. M. Lau received his B.A. in English from National Taiwan University in 1960 and Ph.D. in Comparative Literature from Indiana University in 1966. He taught Chinese and Comparative Literature at the University of Hawaii and the University of Wisconsin, Madison, and taught English at Chung Chi College, the Chinese University of Hong Kong, in 1968. He was Senior Lecturer of English at the University of Singapore from 1971 to 1972. His English publications include *Ts'ao Yu: the Reluctant Disciple of Chekhov and O'Neill* (Hong Kong University Press, 1970) and *Modern Chinese Stories and Novellas: 1919-1949* (Columbia University Press, 1981). Dr. Lau has also translated into Chinese Bernard Malamud's *The Magic Barrel* (1970) and *The Assistant* (1971), as well as C. T. Hsia's *A History of Modern Chinese Fiction* (1978). He is recipient of grants from the American Council of Learned Societies (1975-76), Social Science Research Council (1979-80) and the Rockefeller Foundation (1981-82). He is at present Professor of Chinese and Chairman of the Department of East Asian Languages and Literature at the University of Wisconsin, Madison, and is a co-editor of the Chinese Translation Series for Indiana University Press. He is the editor of *Chinese Stories from Taiwan: 1960-1970* (Columbia University Press, 1976) and *The Unbroken Chain: An Anthology of Taiwan Fiction Since 1926* (Indiana University Press, 1983).

NOTES ON THE TRANSLATORS

Eugene Eoyang studied at Harvard (B.A., 1959), Columbia (M.A., 1960), and Indiana University (Ph.D., 1971), where he is now Associate Professor of Comparative Literature and Associate Dean of Research and Graduate Development, College of Arts and Sciences. From 1960 he worked as an editor for six years with the Anchor Books division of Doubleday. He spent the 1974–1975 academic year at Princeton as an Alfred Hodder Fellow. He has published in *Literature East and West, The Journal of Asian Studies, Paideuma, Yearbook of Comparative and General Literature,* and *Archiv Orientalni,* and contributed to *Sunflower Splendor: Three Thousand Years of Chinese Poetry,* edited by Wu-chi Liu and Irving Lo (Indiana University Press and Doubleday-Anchor, 1975), and *Chinese Narrative: Critical and Theoretical Essays,* edited by Andrew H. Plaks (Princeton University Press, 1977).

Donald E. Gjertson received his M.A. and Ph.D. (1975) from Stanford University, after periods of study and research in Taiwan and Japan. He is presently Assistant Professor of Chinese at the University of Massachusetts, Amherst.

Dell R. Hales received his M.A. (1966) and Ph.D. (1969) from Indiana University. His educational background includes two years of study aboard (Taiwan and Japan), as well as several years of teaching at Michigan State University and the University of Oregon.

George A. Hayden received his B.A. from Pomona College and his M.A. and Ph.D. from Stanford University. He currently teaches Chinese language and literature at the University of Southern California. His publications include "The Courtroom Plays of the Yüan and Early Ming Periods," *Harvard Journal of Asiatic Studies,* 34 (1974), and "The Legend of Judge Pao," in *Studia Asiatica* (see "Suggested Reading" above).

James R. Hightower, Professor of Chinese Language and Literature at Harvard University, is a graduate of University of Colorado (1936), with M.A. (1940) and Ph.D. (1946) from Harvard. He is a Fellow of the American Academy of Arts and Sciences and has held visiting appointments at the universities of Oxford, Hamburg, and British Columbia. He is the author of *Topics in Chinese Literature* (Harvard University Press, 1950; rev. ed., 1953), *Han Shih Wai Chuan: Han Ying's Illustrations of the Didactic Application of the Classic of Songs* (Harvard University Press, 1952), *The Poetry of T'ao Ch'ien* (Oxford University Press, 1970), and a number of learned articles in *Harvard Journal of Asiatic Studies* and other learned periodicals.

Richard M. W. Ho received his B.A. (1969) and M. Phil. (1972) from the University of Hong Kong and his Ph.D. (1975) from the University of London. He was Assistant Professor of Chinese at the University of Wisconsin, Madison, from 1974 to 1976. Dr. Ho has for the past several years interested himself in Chinese poetry and is preparing for publication of two monographs: one on the miscellaneous forms in Chinese poetry and the other on the poetry of Ch'en Tzu-ang.

C. T. Hsia, Professor of Chinese at Columbia University, did his undergraduate work in China and received his Ph.D. in English at Yale University (1951). A prolific author both in Chinese and in English, he is best known in the West for his two major studies: *A History of Modern Chinese Fiction* (Yale University Press, 1961; 2d ed., 1971) and *The Classic Chinese Novel: A Critical Introduction* (Columbia University Press, 1968). Among his numerous English articles, the following two have exercised considerable influence on the younger scholars and critics of Chinese fiction: (1) " 'To What Fyn Lyve I Thus?'—Society and Self in the Chinese Short Story" (1962); and (2) "Obsession with China: The Moral Burden of Modern Chinese Literature" (1967). Professor Hsia's writings in Chinese can be found in *Ai-ch'ing, she-hui, hsiao-shuo* (Love, Society, and the Novel, 1970), *Wen-hsüeh te ch'ien-t'u* (The Future of Literature, 1974, and *Jen-te wen-hsüeh* (Humane Literature, 1977). The Chinese translation of his *A History of Modern Chinese Fiction,* edited and translated by Joseph S. M. Lau, was published by Hong Kong's Union Press (1978).

Dennis T. Hu graduated from Case Institute of Technology majoring in mathematics and, continuing at Cornell in computer science, earned his M.S. in 1972. He received his Ph.D. in Chinese Linguistics and Literature from the University of Wisconsin, Madison, in 1977 and is at present Lecturer in Chinese at the University of Washington, Seattle. His translations have appeared in Joseph S. M. Lau, ed., *Chinese Stories from Taiwan: 1960–1970* (Columbia University Press, 1976).

William L. Jenny took his B.A. (1968) and M.A. (1971) in Chinese language and literature at Indiana University. He has taught at United College, Hong Kong, and is presently teaching at National Central University, Taiwan.

Dale Johnson (Ph.D., University of Michigan, 1968), a Foreign Area Fellow (1964–1967), teaches Chinese at Oberlin College and directs the East Asian program there. He recently spent a year at Kyoto University's Research Institute for Humanistic Studies researching Yüan drama. His publications include "The Prosody of Yüan Drama," *T'oung Pao,* 56 (1970), and "Yüan Dramas: New Notes to Old Texts," *Monumenta Serica,* 30 (1972–1973).

Morgan T. Jones is currently a graduate student in Chinese at the University of California at Berkeley. Previously he did graduate work at the University of Hawaii and the University of California at Los Angeles, as well as in Taiwan and Hong Kong.

Jeanne Kelly received her B.A. in Russian at Indiana University in 1969 and her M.A. in Chinese from the University of Wisconsin, Madison, in 1977. Her complete translation of Ch'ien Chung-shu's major novel *Wei-ch'eng* (Fortress Besieged) will be published by Indiana University Press.

Paul W. Kroll is Assistant Professor of Chinese at the University of Virginia. He received his Ph.D. from the University of Michigan in 1976. His primary field of interest is pre-Sung classical poetry, especially that of the early T'ang. He is currently preparing a book-length critical study of Meng Hao-jan's poetry for publication in the Twayne World Authors Series.

John Kwan-Terry studied English at the University of Hong Kong and Cambridge University, where he took his Ph.D. in 1969. Currently a Senior Lecturer in English at the University of Singapore, he taught previously at the Chinese University of Hong kong. He has published articles and reviews on Hopkins, Pound, Mallarmé, Camus, American studies, and modern Chinese literature.

Peter Li teaches Chinese language and literature at Livingston College, Rutgers University. His special interests are literary-biographical studies of modern Chinese writers, translation, and structural study of traditional Chinese fiction. He received his B.A. from the University of Washington and Ph.D. from the University of Chicago. His publications include *Tseng P'u (1872–1935):*

The Literary Journey of a Chinese Writer (Twayne, forthcoming), and "The Dramatic Structure of *Nieh-hai hua*," in *The Late Qing Novel*, edited by Milena Dolezelova (Toronto University Press, forthcoming). He is also the co-editor of *Classical Chinese Fiction: A Guide to Its Study and Appreciation* (Boston: G. K. Hall, 1978).

Rachel L. Liang is presently a humanities reference librarian at Hamilton Library, University of Hawaii. She received her B.A. in English literature from National Taiwan University and her M.L.S. from the University of Hawaii and is pursuing her second master's degree in Chinese literature.

Lorraine S. Y. Lieu studied Chinese literature at the University of Wisconsin after graduating from the University of Hawaii in 1975. She is now residing in Ikeja, Nigeria.

Amy Ling received her B.A. from Queens College of the City University of New York and M.A. in English and American literature from the University of California at Davis. She has taught at Cheng-kung University in Taiwan, City College and Brooklyn College of CUNY, and is currently teaching at Rutgers University. She has published articles on the Czech poet Miroslav Holub and Henry James.

Liu Wu-chi, Professor Emeritus of Chinese Language and Literature at Indiana University, graduated from Tsing Hua University, Peking, China, and received his Ph.D. in English literature from Yale University. He has taught in a number of Chinese and American universities, including Pittsburgh and Yale. He is the author of numerous articles and books on Chinese philosophy and literature, including *An Introduction to Chinese Literature* (Indiana University Press, 1966) and *Su Man-shu* (Twayne, 1972), and the co-editor of *Sunflower Splendor: Three Thousand Years of Chinese Poetry* (Indiana University Press and Doubleday, 1975) and *Readings in Contemporary Chinese Literature* (Far Eastern Publications, Yale University, 1967–1968).

Conrad Lung comes from Hong Kong and received his B.A. from Columbia University. He is presently a doctoral candidate in Chinese literature at Yale University, doing his dissertation on early *p'ing-hua* novels.

Tai-loi Ma received his B.A. from the University of Hong Kong and M.A. from the University of Chicago, where he is at present a doctoral candidate in Chinese history. He has published in *Tsing Hua Journal of Chinese Studies, Continent Magazine, Journal of the Institute of Chinese Studies of the Chinese University of Hong Kong, Oriens Extremus, T'oung Pao,* and other learned periodicals. He has been on the staff of the Far Eastern Library of the University of Chicago since 1972.

Russell E. McLeod has a B.A. and M.A. in Chinese from the University of Hawaii, where he is now Assistant Professor of Chinese Literature. He received his doctorate from Stanford in 1973, with a thesis on the T'ang poet Meng Chiao (751–814).

Robert L. Miller received his M.A. in Chinese philosophy from the University of Hawaii and has studied Chinese language and philosophy in Taiwan and Hong Kong.

William H. Nienhauser, Jr. was educated at the University of Bonn and Indiana University (Ph.D., 1972) and teaches at the University of Wisconsin. His field of interest is T'ang literature and he was an Alexander von Humboldt Fellow at the University of Hamburg in the 1975–1976 academic year. He was the co-author of *Liu Tsung-yüan* (Twayne, 1973) and the editor of *Critical Essays on Chinese Literature* (Chinese University of Hong Kong Press, 1976).

Timothy A. Ross studied in Taipei in 1964–1965 and since then has taught in the History Division of Arkansas State University. He received his doctorate in Far Eastern history from the University of Iowa in 1972. He is the author of *Chiang Kuei* in the Twayne World Authors Series and the translator of *The Whirlwind,* a novel by Chiang Kuei.

594

Peter Rushton received his B.A. from the University of Wisconsin and M.A. from Stanford University. His article on the poetry of Hsi K'ang is forthcoming in the *Journal of the American Oriental Society*. He spent two years (1974–1976) in Taiwan reading Ming and Ch'ing fiction for a proposed doctoral study of the narrative form of the *Chin P'ing Mei*.

Hsing-hua Tseng received her B.A. from National Taiwan University and M.A. in Linguistics from Indiana University. In Taiwan she taught for five years and had several short stories published. In the U.S. she taught at Indiana University, George Washington University, at the Far Eastern language summer institutes at several midwestern universities, at Middlebury College Chinese School, and is presently at Rutgers University.

Pao-chien Tseng received his B.A. from National Taiwan University and M.A. in Linguistics from Indiana University. In Taiwan he worked as a translator. In the U.S. he taught at Far Eastern language institutes at Minnesota and Michigan, at Middlebury College Chinese School, at George Washington University, and at the State University of New York at Buffalo. He is presently teaching at the City College of New York.

Earl Wieman obtained his B.A. in General Studies from the University of Maryland and studied Chinese at the University of Hawaii, where he was awarded an M.A. in 1972. He is now Special Correspondent to Hong Kong's *Orientations, Insight,* and *Modern Asia* magazines.   nd

Timothy C. Wong received his B.A. in Political Science from Saint Mary's College, California, in 1963, his M.A. in Asian studies from the University of Hawaii in 1968, and his Ph.D. in Chinese literature from Stanford University in 1975. Currently he is Assistant Professor of Chinese at Arizona State University and is completing a book on the eighteenth-century Chinese novel *Ju-lin wai-shih* and its author Wu Ching-tzu.

Diana Yu was born in Kwangsi, China, and educated in Hong Kong. She has worked as a teacher and as Managing Editor of *Renditions,* an English periodical devoted to translations from the Chinese. At present she teaches translation in the Department of Chinese at the University of Hong Kong.

Susan Arnold Zonana received her B.A. from Barnard College in 1968 and her M.A. in Chinese Literature from Columbia University in 1970. She has recently contributed a review of Eileen Chang's novel, *The Rouge of the North* to *Literature East and West*. She currently resides in Santa Barbara, California.

CHRONOLOGICAL ORDER
OF THE SELECTIONS

In order to supplement the thematic arrangement and the generic and bibliographical information in this anthology, the sixty-one selections are listed here in chronological sequence. The order and time divisions can only be approximate. For, in view of the textual, dating, and authorship problems involved, no arrangement can be free of uncertainty and controversy. Our main concern is only to place these stories in a sequential line for convenience of reference; we do not presume to solve their dating problems in a book of this nature. For this reason, we do not feel it necessary to mention the sources and philological methods with which we have prepared the present arrangement. What needs to be said is that whenever a reliable date of composition for a certain story is unavailable (as is usually the case), we have had to rely on other available data, such as the dates of the author, internal evidence, the date of the earliest extant version, and the date of the publication of the collection in which the story was first included. Stories of approximately identical composition dates in the same collection are arranged according to their order in the table of contents of that collection, such as the stories in the *Liao-chai chih-i.* The dating and authorship problems of a number of these selections have been carefully studied by modern scholars (most notably by Patrick Hanan in his *The Chinese Short Story*). Their findings have helped the Editors a great deal in preparing this chronological list. The readers are urged to use the Biobibliographical Notes along with this list for other pertinent information, such as the date of the collection in which a certain story is included.

CHRONOLOGICAL ORDER OF THE SELECTIONS

INDEX TO FOOTNOTES

This index does not cover all the footnotes. The main purpose is to help the reader to locate the footnotes that appear in the other selections. The footnotes are arranged on the basis of first appearance. Some terms have to be annotated more than once because different information is required in different contexts. Two figures are given in every entry; the first figure refers to the page number, the second to the number of the footnote.